Football Outsiders Almanac 2013

THE ESSENTIAL GUIDE TO THE 2013 NFL AND COLLEGE FOOTBALL SEASONS

Edited by Aaron Schatz

With Andy Benoit, Bill Connelly, Doug Farrar, Brian Fremeau, Tom Gower,

Matt Hinton, Sean McCormick, Rivers McCown, Brian McIntyre, Chase Stuart,

Mike Tanier, Danny Tuccitto, Vince Verhei, and Robert Weintraub

Copyright 2013 Football Outsiders, Inc.

ISBN-10: 1491008024

ISBN-13: 978-1491008027

Table of Contents

Introduction

Ten years.

That's how long Football Outsiders has been producing advanced analysis of the National Football League. It started in December 2002 when I was just a fan curious about whether "establishing the run" meant anything. By the spring, I had created some weird new metrics and written a few articles to circulate among friends. On July 30, 2003, we launched FootballOutsiders.com with the Extra Points blog and a grand total of three writers: myself, doing stat analysis, and Al Bogdan and Ian Dembsky, writing the fantasy football column "Scramble for the Ball." Within a few months, we had added our first outside writers, i.e., guys I didn't go to college with. By the start of the 2004 season, this was my full-time job.

Now it's 2013, and our goofy little website is about to celebrate its tenth anniversary. We've written nine books. We now cover both the NFL and college football. Our work appears regularly at the largest sports website on the Internet, ESPN.com. Other writers who got their start at Football Outsiders appear around the Web, from SI.com to Pro Football Talk to Grantland.

Meanwhile, the idea of advanced statistical analysis in football continues its march into the mainstream, as well as its march into front offices around the league. There are a number of people and websites doing analysis, both play-by-play breakdown similar to what we do with DVOA and the creation of additional stats off tape, similar to what we do with our game charting project. If you go to pro-football-reference.com, all the basic stats from ten years ago are joined by in-depth lists of starting lineups throughout NFL history, defensive stats like tackles and passes defensed where available, and even expected points per play analysis.

At this year's NFL Combine, "analytics" was one of the hot buzzwords, second only to "read option." The new team president of the Buffalo Bills talked about using analytics. So did the general managers in Atlanta and Chicago. Jacksonville and Cleveland now have full-time analytics guys. A number of salary-cap analysts around the league are using advanced statistics, from San Francisco to Detroit to Philadelphia to teams that we don't even know about.

We're proud to play our part in the spread of advanced metrics around the football world, but of course that's not all that we're about. As we remind people each year, Football Outsiders is not founded on the idea that statistics are all-encompassing or can tell us everything about football. There's a lot more to our analysis than numbers, and you're going to find a lot of scouting knowledge in this book as well. There's a rumor that stat analysts don't watch game tape. In reality, stat analysts watch more tape than most beat writers or national Internet columnists, and *a lot* more tape than the average fan. And the writers in this book who are film mavens rather than stat analysts—Doug Farrar and Andy Benoit, to give two examples—watch even more tape than that. We take everything we learn off the tape, synthesize it with the statistics, and deliver it to you. Occasionally, there are also jokes.

At its heart, the football analytics revolution is about learning more about the intricacies of the game instead of just accepting the boilerplate storylines produced by color commentators, lazy beat reporters, and crotchety old players from the past. It's about not accepting the idea that some guy "just wins." It's about understanding that the "skill players" aren't the only guys on the team with skills. It's about gaining insight into the complexity behind the modern offense, and that you don't just shove the ball into the line hoping to gain yardage. It's about understanding the dramatic way that strength of schedule affects the way we see a team's performance, especially at the college level. It's about figuring out which player skills translate from college to the pros, and which skills just produce meaningless scoutspeak. And it's about accepting that the pass dominates the run in the National Football League, and that it's been that way for 30 years.

Everybody who writes about football uses both statistics (whether they be basic yardage totals or more advanced stats like ours) and scouting (whether scouting reports by professionals or just their own eyes). The same goes for us, except that the statistics portion of our analysis is far more accurate than what you normally see from football coverage. Those numbers are based on two ideas:

1) Conventional football statistics are heavily dependent on context. If you want to see which teams are good and which are bad, which strategies work and which do not, you first need to filter out that context. Down and distance, field position, the current score, time left on the clock, the quality of the opponent—all of these elements influence the objective of the play and/or its outcome. Yet, the official NFL stats add together all yardage gained by a specific team or player without considering the impact of that particular yardage on wins and losses.

A close football game can turn on a single bounce of the ball. In a season of only 16 games, those effects can have a huge impact on a team's win-loss record, thus obscuring the team's true talent level. If we can filter out these bits of luck and random chance, we can figure out which teams are really more likely to play better for the rest of the season, or even in the following season.

2) On any one play, the majority of the important action is not tracked by the conventional NFL play-by-play. That's why we started the Football Outsiders game charting project in 2005. A cadre of football-obsessed volunteers watches every single game and adds new detail to our record of each play. We know how many pass rushers teams send on each pass, how often teams go three-wide or use two tight ends, how often teams use a play-fake or a zone blitz, and which defensive backs are in coverage, even when they don't get a tackle in the standard play-by-play.

There's also a third important precept that governs the work we do at Football Outsiders, although it's more about how to interpret numbers and not the numbers themselves. **A player's production in one year does not necessarily equal his production the next year.** This also applies to teams, of course. Even when stats are accurate, they're often extremely variable from year to year and subject to heavy forces of regression to the mean. Field-goal percentage, red-zone performance, third-down performance on defense, interceptions and fumble recoveries—these are but a few examples. In addition, the age curves for football players are much steeper than in other sports. Old players break down faster, and young players often improve faster. A number of football analysts concentrate on looking at what players did last year. We'll talk about that as well, but we're more interested in what players are going to do *this* year. Which performances from a year ago are flukes, and which ones represent long-term improvement or decline? What will one more year of experience do to this player's production? And how will a player's role change this year, and what does it mean for the team?

As with past books, *Football Outsiders Almanac 2013* starts off with "Pregame Show" (reviewing the most important research we've done in past books) and "Statistical Toolbox" (explaining all our stats). Once again, we preserve the ridiculousness of the football season for posterity with another version of "The Year in Quotes" and we introduce you to some of the more promising (and lesser-known) young bench players with our seventh annual list of Top 25 Prospects chosen in the third round or later.

Each NFL team gets a full chapter covering what happened in 2012 and our projections for the upcoming season. Are there reasons to believe that the team was actually better or worse than its record last year? What did the team do in the offseason, and what does that mean for the team's chances to win in 2013? Each chapter also includes all kinds of advanced statistics covering 2012 performance and strategic tendencies, plus detailed commentary on each of the major units of the team: offensive line, defensive front seven, defensive secondary, special teams, and coaching staff.

"Skill players" (by which we mean "players who get counted in fantasy football") get their own section in the back of the book. We list the major players at each position alphabetically, along with commentary and a 2013 KUBIAK projection that will help you win your fantasy football league. We also have the most accurate projections anywhere for two fantasy football positions that people wrongly consider impossible to predict: kickers and team defense.

Next comes our preview of the college football season. We preview every team from the six BCS conferences as well as the top independents and mid-majors. Just like with our NFL coverage, the goal of our college previews is to focus as much as possible on "why" and "how," not just "which team is better." We're not just here to rank the Football Bowl Subdivision teams from 1 to 125. We break things down to offense and defense, pass and run, and clutch situations compared to all plays.

We hope our book helps you raise your level of football expertise, win arguments with your friends, and win your fantasy football league. We hope you enjoy reading our book as much as we enjoy writing it every year.

Aaron Schatz
Framingham, MA
July 14, 2013

P.S. Don't forget to visit FootballOutsiders.com every day for fresh coverage of the NFL and college football, plus the most intelligent football discussion threads on the Internet.

Pregame Show 2013

It has now been ten years since we launched Football Outsiders. In that time, we've done a lot of primary research on the National Football League, and we reference that research in many of the articles and comments in *Football Outsiders Almanac 2013*. New readers may come across an offhand comment in a team chapter about, for example, the idea that fumble recovery is not a skill, and wonder what in the heck we are talking about. We can't repeat all our research in every new edition of *Football Outsiders Almanac*, so we start each year with a basic look at some of the most important precepts that have emerged from Football Outsiders research. You will see these issues come up again and again throughout the book.

You can also find this introduction online at http://www.footballoutsiders.com/info/FO-basics, along with links to the original research in the cases in which that research appeared online instead of (or as well as) in print.

Our various methods for projecting NFL success for college prospects are not listed below, but are referenced at times during the book. Those methods are detailed in an essay on page 434.

You run when you win, not win when you run.

If we could only share one piece of anti-conventional wisdom with you before you read the rest of our book, this would be it. The first article ever written for Football Outsiders was devoted to debunking the myth of "establishing the run." There is no correlation whatsoever between giving your running backs a lot of carries early in the game and winning the game. Just running the ball is not going to help a team score; it has to run successfully.

There are two reasons why nearly every beat writer and television analyst still repeats the tired old school mantra that "establishing the run" is the secret to winning football games. The first problem is confusing cause and effect. There are exceptions, but for the most part, winning teams have a lot of carries because their running backs are running out the clock at the end of wins, not because they are running wild early in games.

The second problem is history. Most of the current crop of NFL analysts came of age or actually played the game during the 1970s. They believe that the run-heavy game of that decade is how football is meant to be, and today's pass-first game is an aberration. As we addressed in an essay in *Pro Football Prospectus 2006* on the history of NFL stats, it was actually the game of the 1970s that was the aberration. The seventies were far more slanted towards the run than any era since the arrival of Paul Brown, Otto Graham, and the Cleveland Browns in 1946. Optimal strategies from 1974 are not optimal strategies for 2013.

A sister statement to "you have to establish the run" is "team X is 5-1 when running back John Doe runs for at least 100 yards." Unless John Doe is possessed by otherworldly spirits the way Adrian Peterson was a year ago, the team isn't winning because of his 100-yard games. He's putting up 100-yard games because his team is winning.

A great defense against the run is nothing without a good pass defense.

This is a corollary to the absurdity of "establish the run." With rare exceptions, teams win or lose with the passing game more than the running game—and by stopping the passing game more than the running game. Ron Jaworski puts it best: "The pass gives you the lead, and the run solidifies it." The reason why teams need a strong run defense in the playoffs is not to shut the run down early; it's to keep the other team from icing the clock if they get a lead. You can't mount a comeback if you can't stop the run.

Note that "good pass defense" may mean "good pass rush" rather than "good defensive backs."

Running on third-and-short is more likely to convert than passing on third-and-short.

On average, passing will always gain more yardage than running, with one very important exception: when a team is just one or two yards away from a new set of downs or the goal line. On third-and-1, a run will convert for a new set of downs 36 percent more often than a pass. Expand that to all third or fourth downs with 1 or 2 yards to go, and the run is successful 40 percent more often. With these percentages, the possibility of a long gain with a pass is not worth the tradeoff of an incomplete that kills a drive.

This is one reason why teams have to be able to both run and pass. The offense also has to keep some semblance of balance so they can use their play-action fakes, and so the defense doesn't just run their nickel and dime packages all game. Balance also means that teams do need to pass occasionally in short-yardage situations; they just need to do it less than they do now. Teams pass roughly 60 percent of the time on third-and-2 even though runs in that situation convert 20 percent more often than passes. They pass 68 percent of the time on fourth-and-2 even though runs in that situation convert twice as often as passes.

Standard team rankings based on total yardage are inherently flawed.

Check out the schedule page on NFL.com, and you will find that each game is listed with league rankings based on total yardage. That is still how the NFL "officially" ranks teams, but these rankings rarely match up with common sense. That is because total team yardage may be the most context-dependent number in football.

It starts with the basic concept that rate stats are generally more valuable than cumulative stats. Yards per carry says more about a running back's quality than total yardage, completion percentage says more than just a quarterback's total number of completions. The same thing is true for teams; in fact, it is even more important because of the way football strategy influences the number of runs and passes in the game plan. Poor teams will give up fewer passing yards and more rushing yards because opponents will stop passing once they have a late-game lead and will run out the clock instead. For winning teams, the opposite is true. For example, which team had a better pass defense last year: Washington or Kansas City? The answer is obviously Washington, yet according to the official NFL rankings, Kansas City (3,533 yards allowed on 464 passes, 8.0 yards per pass) was a better pass defense than Washington (4,511 yards allowed on 636 passes, 7.4 yards per pass).

Total yardage rankings are also skewed because some teams play at a faster pace than other teams. In 2010, for example, Tampa Bay (5,362) had roughly the same number of yards as the Washington Redskins (5,392). However, the Bucs were the superior offense and much more efficient; they gained those yards on only 163 drives while the Redskins needed 200 drives.

A team will score more when playing a bad defense, and will give up more points when playing a good offense.

This sounds absurdly basic, but when people consider team and player stats without looking at strength of schedule, they are ignoring this. In 2004, Carson Palmer and Byron Leftwich had very similar numbers, but Palmer faced a much tougher schedule than Leftwich did. Palmer was better that year, and better in the long run. A similar comparison can be made between Russell Wilson and Robert Griffin III, although the gap is not as large. Last year, Seattle played the fifth hardest schedule of opposing pass defenses in the league, according to our DVOA ratings. All four NFC West teams (including the Seahawks themselves) finished in the top 10 for pass defense DVOA. Seattle also had to play Chicago (first), Green Bay (seventh), and the Jets (tenth). On the other hand, Washington played the fourth easiest schedule of opposing pass defenses, including seven games against teams in the bottom ten (Minnesota, Tampa Bay, New Orleans, and then Dallas and Philadelphia twice each) and only one game against a team in the top eight (St. Louis). This is a big reason why Wilson comes out with a higher passing DVOA rating than Griffin, even though Griffin had slightly better standard stats.

If their overall yards per carry are equal, a running back who consistently gains yardage on every play is more valuable than a boom-and-bust running back who is frequently stuffed at the line but occasionally breaks a long highlight-worthy run.

Our brethren at Baseball Prospectus believe that the most precious commodity in baseball is outs. Teams only get 27 of them per game, and you can't afford to give one up for very little return. So imagine if there was a new rule in baseball that gave a team a way to earn another three outs in the middle of the inning. That would be pretty useful, right?

That's the way football works. You may start a drive 80 yards away from scoring, but as long as you can earn 10 yards in four chances, you get another four chances. Long gains have plenty of value, but if those long gains are mixed with a lot of short gains, you are going to put the quarterback in a lot of difficult third-and-long situations. That means more punts and more giving the ball back to the other team rather than moving the chains and giving the offense four more plays to work with.

The running back who gains consistent yardage is also going to do a lot more for you late in the game, when the goal of running the ball is not just to gain yardage but to eat clock time. If you are a Titans fan watching your team with a late lead, you don't want to see three straight Chris Johnson stuffs at the line followed by a punt. You want to see a game-icing first down.

A common historical misconception is that our preference for consistent running backs means that "Football Outsiders believes that Barry Sanders was overrated." Sanders wasn't just any boom-and-bust running back, though; he was the greatest boom-and-bust runner of all time, with bigger booms and fewer busts. Sanders ranked second in DYAR three times (1994, 1996, and 1997), although his first two seasons have still not been broken down for DVOA/DYAR.

Rushing is more dependent on the offensive line than people realize, but pass protection is more dependent on the quarterback himself than people realize.

Some readers complain that this idea contradicts the previous one. Aren't those consistent running backs just the product of good offensive lines? The truth is somewhere in between. There are certainly good running backs who suffer because their offensive lines cannot create consistent holes, but most boom-and-bust running backs contribute to their own problems by hesitating behind the line whenever the hole is unclear, looking for the home run instead of charging forward for the four-yard gain that keeps the offense moving.

As for pass protection, some quarterbacks have better instincts for the rush than others, and are thus better at getting out of trouble by moving around in the pocket or throwing the ball away. Others will hesitate, hold onto the ball too long, and lose yardage over and over.

Note that "moving around in the pocket" does not necessarily mean "scrambling." In fact, a scrambling quarterback will often take more sacks than a pocket quarterback, because while he's running around trying to make something happen, a defensive lineman will catch up with him.

Shotgun formations are generally more efficient than formations with the quarterback under center.

Over the past five seasons, offenses have averaged 6.0 yards per play from shotgun (or pistol), but just 5.1 yards per play with the quarterback under center. This wide split exists even if you analyze the data to try to weed out biases like teams using shotgun more often on third-and-long, or against prevent defenses in the fourth quarter. Shotgun offense is more efficient if you only look at the first half, on every down, and even if you only look at running back carries rather than passes and scrambles.

Clearly, NFL teams have figured the importance of the shotgun out for themselves. In 2001, NFL teams only used shotgun on 14 percent of plays. Five years later, in 2006, that had increased slightly, to 20 percent of plays. Last year, shotgun was used on a record-setting 47.5 percent of plays (including the pistol, but not counting the Wildcat or other direct snaps to non-quarterbacks). Before 2007, no team had ever used shotgun on more than half its offensive plays. In 2011, six different teams used shotgun more than 50 percent of the time. Last year, that doubled yet again, with a dozen teams using shotgun on over half their plays, led by Detroit at 71 percent. It is likely that if teams continue to increase their usage of the shotgun (and now, its offshoot the pistol), defenses will adapt and the benefit of the formation will become less pronounced. But it certainly isn't happening yet; the difference between success on shotgun and non-shotgun plays in the last two seasons was bigger than it was the previous three.

A running back with 370 or more carries during the regular season will usually suffer either a major injury or a loss of effectiveness the following year, unless he is named Eric Dickerson.

Terrell Davis, Jamal Anderson, and Edgerrin James all blew out their knees. Larry Johnson broke his foot. Earl Campbell and Eddie George went from legendary powerhouses to plodding, replacement-level players. Shaun Alexander broke his foot *and* became a plodding, replacement-level player. This is what happens when a running back is overworked to the point of having at least 370 carries during the regular season.

The "Curse of 370" was expanded in our book *Pro Football Prospectus 2005*, and now includes seasons with 390 or more carries in the regular season and postseason combined. Research also shows that receptions don't cause a problem, only workload on the ground.

Plenty of running backs get injured without hitting 370 carries in a season, but there is a clear difference. On average, running backs with 300 to 369 carries and no postseason appearance will see their total rushing yardage decline by 15 percent the following year and their yards per carry decline by two percent. The average running back with 370 or more regular-season carries, or 390 including the postseason, will see their rushing yardage decline by 35 percent, and their yards per carry decline by eight percent. However, the Curse of 370 is not a hard and fast line where running backs suddenly become injury risks. It is more of a concept where 370 carries is roughly the point at which additional carries start to become more and more of a problem.

It's worth noting that the return to the committee backfields that dominated the '60s and '70s may mean an end to the Curse of 370. No running back has gone over 370 carries since Michael Turner in 2008.

Wide receivers must be judged on both complete and incomplete passes.

In 2011, for example, Dwayne Bowe had 1,188 receiving yards, while Marques Colston was close behind with 1,169 yards. Both players ran routes of roughly the same average length. But there was a huge difference between them: Bowe caught 57 percent of passes, while Colston had a catch rate of 75 percent. Some work has been done on splitting responsibility for incomplete passes between quarterbacks and receivers, but not enough that we can incorporate this into our advanced stats at this time. We know that wide receiver catch rates are almost as consistent from year to year as quarterback completion percentages, but it is also important to look at catch rate in the context of the types of routes each receiver runs. Three

years ago, we expanded on this idea with a new plus-minus metric, which is explained in the introduction to the chapter on wide receivers and tight ends.

The total quality of an NFL team is four parts offense, three parts defense, and one part special teams.

There are three units on a football team, but they are not of equal importance. For a long time, the saying from Football Outsiders was that the total quality of an NFL team is three parts offense, three parts defense, and one part special teams. Further recent research suggests that offense is even more important than we originally believed. Recent recent work by Chase Stuart, Neil Paine, and Brian Burke suggests a split between offense and defense of roughly 58-42, without considering special teams. Our research suggests that special teams contributes about 13 percent to total performance; if you measure the remaining 87 percent with a 58-42 ratio, you get roughly 4:3:1. When we compare the range of offense, defense, and special teams DVOA ratings, we get the same results, with the best and worst offenses roughly 30 percent stronger than the best and worst defenses, and roughly four times stronger than the best and worst special teams.

Offense is more consistent from year to year than defense, and offensive performance is easier to project than defensive performance. Special teams is less consistent than either.

Nobody in the NFL understood this concept better than former Indianapolis Colts general manager Bill Polian. Both the Super Bowl champion Colts and the four-time AFC champion Buffalo Bills of the early 1990s were built around the idea that if you put together an offense that can dominate the league year after year, eventually you will luck into a year where good health and a few smart decisions will give you a defense good enough to win a championship. (As the Colts learned in 2006, you don't even need a year, just four weeks.) Even the New England Patriots, who are led by a defense-first head coach in Bill Belichick, have been more consistent on offense than on defense since they began their run of success in 2001.

Field-goal percentage is almost entirely random from season to season, while kickoff distance is one of the most consistent statistics in football.

This theory, which originally appeared in the *New York Times* in October 2006, is one of our most controversial, but it is hard to argue against the evidence. Measuring every kicker from 1999 to 2006 who had at least ten field goal attempts in each of two consecutive years, the year-to-year correlation coefficient for field-goal percentage was an insignificant .05. Mike Vanderjagt didn't miss a single field goal in 2003, but his percentage was a below-average 74 percent the year before and 80 percent the year after. Adam Vinatieri has long been considered the best kicker in the game. But even he had never enjoyed two straight seasons with accuracy better than the NFL average of 85 percent until 2010 and 2011, and then last year his field-goal percentage was back below 80 percent.

On the other hand, the year-to-year correlation coefficient for kickoff distance, over the same period as our measurement of field-goal percentage and with the same minimum of ten kicks per year, is .61. The same players consistently lead the league in kickoff distance. In recent years, that group includes Olindo Mare, Stephen Gostkowski, Robbie Gould, Billy Cundiff, and Pat McAfee.

Teams with more offensive penalties generally lose more games, but there is no correlation between defensive penalties and losses.

Specific defensive penalties of course lose games; we've all sworn at the television when the cornerback on our favorite team gets flagged for a 50-yard pass interference penalty. Yet overall, there is no correlation between losses and the total of defensive penalties or even the total yardage on defensive penalties. One reason is that defensive penalties often represent *good* play, not bad. Cornerbacks who play tight coverage may be just on the edge of a penalty on most plays, only occasionally earning a flag. Defensive ends who get a good jump on rushing the passer will gladly trade an encroachment penalty or two for ten snaps where they get off the blocks a split-second before the linemen trying to block them.

In addition, offensive penalties have a higher correlation from year to year than defensive penalties. The penalty that correlates highest with losses is the false start, and the penalty that teams will have called most consistently from year to year is also the false start.

Recovery of a fumble, despite being the product of hard work, is almost entirely random.

Stripping the ball is a skill. Holding onto the ball is a skill. Pouncing on the ball as it is bouncing all over the place is not a skill. There is no correlation whatsoever between the percentage of fumbles recovered by a team in one year and the percentage they recover in the next year. The odds of recovery are based solely on the type of play involved, not the teams or any of their players.

Fans like to insist that specific coaches can teach their teams to recover more fumbles by swarming to the ball. Chicago's Lovie Smith, in particular, is supposed to have this ability. However, in Smith's first three seasons as head coach of the Bears, their rate of fumble recovery on defense went from a league-best 76 percent in 2004 to a league-worst 33 percent in 2005, then back to 67 percent in 2006.

Fumble recovery is equally erratic on offense. In 2010, the Houston Texans recovered nine of 15 fumbles on offense. In 2011, they recovered only seven of 18 fumbles. Last year, they recovered five and lost five.

Fumble recovery is a major reason why the general public overestimates or underestimates certain teams. Fumbles are huge, turning-point plays that dramatically impact wins and losses in the past, while fumble recovery percentage says absolutely nothing about a team's chances of winning games in the future. With this in mind, Football Outsiders stats treat all fumbles as equal, penalizing them based on the likelihood of each type of fumble (run, pass, sack, etc.) being recovered by the defense.

Other plays that qualify as "non-predictive events" include two-point conversions, blocked kicks, and touchdowns during turnover returns. These plays are not "lucky," per se, but they have no value whatsoever for predicting future performance.

Field position is fluid.

As discussed in the Statistical Toolbox, every yard line on the field has a value based on how likely a team is to score from that location on the field as opposed to from a yard further back. The change in value from one yard to the next is the same whether the team has the ball or not. The goal of a defense is not just to prevent scoring, but to hold the opposition so that the offense can get the ball back in the best possible field position. A bad offense will score as many points as a good offense if it starts each drive five yards closer to the goal line.

A corollary to this precept: the most underrated aspect of an NFL team's performance is the field position gained or lost on kickoffs and punts. This is part of why players like Devin Hester and Patrick Peterson can have such an impact on the game, even when they aren't taking a kickoff or punt all the way back for a touchdown.

The red zone is the most important place on the field to play well, but performance in the red zone from year to year is much less consistent than overall performance.

Although play in the red zone has a disproportionately high importance to the outcome of games relative to plays on the rest of the field, NFL teams do not exhibit a level of performance in the red zone that is consistently better or worse than their performance elsewhere, year after year. The simplest explanation why is a small(er) sample size and the inherent variance of football, with contributing factors like injuries and changes in personnel.

Defenses which are strong on first and second down, but weak on third down, will tend to improve the following year. Defenses which are weak on first and second down, but strong on third down, will tend to decline the following year. This trend also applied to offenses through 2005, but may or may not still apply today.

We discovered this when creating our first team projection system in 2004. It said that the lowly San Diego Chargers would have of the best offenses in the league, which seemed a little ridiculous. But looking closer, our projection system treated the previous year's performance on different downs as different variables, and the 2003 Chargers were actually good on first and second down, but terrible on third.

Teams get fewer opportunities on third down, so third-down performance is more volatile—but it's also is a bigger part of a team's overall performance than first or second down, because the result is usually either very good (four more downs) or very bad (losing the ball to the other team with a punt). Over time, a team will play as well in those situations as it does in other situations, which will bring the overall offense or defense in line with the offense and defense on first and second down.

This trend is even stronger between seasons. Struggles on third down are a pretty obvious problem, and teams will generally target their off-season moves at improving their third-down performance ... which often leads to an improvement in third-down performance.

However, we have discovered something surprising over the past few years: The third-down rebound effect seems to have disappeared on offense, as we explained in the Philadelphia chapter of *Football Outsiders Almanac 2010*. We don't know yet if this change is temporary or permanent, and there is no such change on defense.

Injuries regress to the mean on the seasonal level, and teams that avoid injuries in a given season tend to win more games.

There are no doubt teams with streaks of good or bad health over multiple years. However, teams who were especially healthy or especially unhealthy, as measured by our Adjusted Games Lost (AGL) metric, almost always head towards league average in the subsequent season. Furthermore, injury—or the absence thereof—has a huge correlation with wins, and a significant impact on a team's success. There's no doubt that a few high-profile teams have resisted this trend in recent years. The Patriots seem to overcome injuries every year, and a number of recent Super Bowl champions such as the 2010 Packers and 2011 Giants have overcome a number of injuries to win the championship. Nonetheless, the overall rule still applies. Last year, the three teams that finished 1-2-3 in AGL were San Francisco, Minnesota, and Seattle, all playoff teams. On the other hand, only three of the top 12 teams in AGL made the playoffs (Washington 28th, Indianapolis 30th, and Green Bay 32nd).

In general, teams with a high number of injuries are a good bet to improve the following season. This year, that list would include Jacksonville, Pittsburgh, and the entire NFC East except for Philadelphia. However, while injury totals tend to regress towards the mean, there's also no doubt that certain teams have a record of staying healthier than others. We need to do more research on this issue, but teams with a consistent record of poor health include Indianapolis, New England, and St. Louis (although last year was an exception for the Rams), while teams with a consistent record of good health include Tennessee, Chicago, and San Francisco (particularly on defense).

By and large, a team built on depth is better than a team built on stars and scrubs.

Connected to the previous statement, because teams need to go into the season expecting that they will suffer an average number of injuries no matter how healthy they were the previous year. For a long time, the Redskins would go into every season with a number of stars, and generally end up 5-11 because they had no depth. (At this point, Dallas may be replacing Washington in this hole.) You cannot concentrate your salaries on a handful of star players because there is no

such thing as avoiding injuries in the NFL. The game is too fast and the players too strong to build a team based around the idea that "if we can avoid all injuries this year, we'll win."

Running backs usually decline after age 28, tight ends after age 29, wide receivers after age 30, and quarterbacks after age 32.

This research was originally done by Doug Drinen (editor of pro-football-reference.com) in 2000. In recent years, a few players have had huge seasons above these general age limits (most notably Tony Gonzalez), but the peak ages Drinen found a few years ago still apply to the majority of players.

As for "non-skill players," research we did in 2007 for *ESPN the Magazine* suggested that defensive ends and defensive backs generally begin to decline after age 29, linebackers and offensive linemen after age 30, and defensive tackles after age 31. However, because we still have so few statistics to use to study linemen and defensive players, this research should not be considered definitive.

The strongest indicator of how a college football team will perform in the upcoming season is their performance in recent seasons.

It may seem strange because graduation enforces constant player turnover, but college football teams are actually much more consistent from year to year than NFL teams. Thanks in large part to consistency in recruiting, teams can be expected to play within a reasonable range of their baseline program expectations each season. Our Program F/+ ratings, which represent a rolling five-year period of play-by-play and drive efficiency data, have an extremely strong (.76) correlation with the next year's F/+ rating.

Championship teams are generally defined by their ability to dominate inferior opponents, not their ability to win close games.

Football games are often decided by just one or two plays: a missed field goal, a bouncing fumble, the subjective spot of an official on fourth-and-1. One missed assignment by a cornerback or one slightly askew pass that bounces off a receiver's hands and into those of a defensive back five yards away and the game could be over. In a blowout, however, one lucky bounce isn't going to change things. Championship teams—in both professional and college football—typically beat their good opponents convincingly and destroy the cupcakes on the schedule.

Aaron Schatz

Statistical Toolbox

After ten years of Football Outsiders, some of our readers are as comfortable with DVOA and ALY as they are with touchdowns and tackles. Yet to most fans, including our newer readers, it still looks like a lot of alphabet soup. That's what this chapter is for. The next few pages define and explain all of all the unique NFL statistics you'll find in this book: how we calculate them, what the numbers mean, and what they tell us about why teams win or lose football games. We'll go through the information in each of the tables that appear in each team chapter, pointing out whether those stats come from advanced mathematical manipulation of the standard play-by-play or simple counting of what see on television with the Football Outsiders game charting project. This chapter covers NFL statistics only. College metrics such as Adjusted POE and F/+ are explained in the introduction to the college football section on page 364.

We've done our best to present these numbers in a way that makes them easy to understand. This explanation is long, so feel free to read some of it, flip around the rest of the book, and then come back. It will still be here.

Defense-Adjusted Value Over Average (DVOA)

One running back runs for three yards. Another running back runs for three yards. Which is the better run?

This sounds like a stupid question, but it isn't. In fact, this question is at the heart of nearly all of the analysis in this book.

Several factors can differentiate one three-yard run from another. What is the down and distance? Is it third-and-2, or second-and-15? Where on the field is the ball? Does the player get only three yards because he hits the goal line and scores? Is the player's team up by two touchdowns in the fourth quarter and thus running out the clock, or down by two touchdowns and thus facing a defense that is playing purely against the pass? Is the running back playing against the porous defense of the Raiders, or the stalwart defense of the Bears?

Conventional NFL statistics value plays based solely on their net yardage. The NFL determines the best players by adding up all their yards no matter what situations they came in or how many plays it took to get them. Now, why would they do that? Football has one objective—to get to the end zone—and two ways to achieve that, by gaining yards and achieving first downs. These two goals need to be balanced to determine a player's value or a team's performance. All the yards in the world won't help a team win if they all come in six-yard chunks on third-and-10.

The popularity of fantasy football only exacerbates the problem. Fans have gotten used to judging players based on how much they help fantasy teams win and lose, not how much they help *real* teams win and lose. Typical fantasy scoring further skews things by counting the yard between the one and the goal line as 61 times more important than all the other yards on the field (each yard worth 0.1 points, a touchdown worth 6.0). Let's say Larry Fitzgerald catches a pass on third-and-15 and goes 50 yards but gets tackled two yards from the goal line, and then Rashard Mendenhall takes the ball on first-and-goal from the two-yard line and plunges in for the score. Has Mendenhall done something special? Not really. When an offense gets the ball on first-and-goal at the two-yard line, they are going to score a touchdown five out of six times. Mendenhall is getting credit for the work done by the passing game.

Doing a better job of distributing credit for scoring points and winning games is the goal of **DVOA**, or Defense-adjusted Value Over Average. DVOA breaks down every single play of the NFL season, assigning each play a value based on both total yards and yards towards a first down, based on work done by Pete Palmer, Bob Carroll, and John Thorn in their seminal book, *The Hidden Game of Football*. On first down, a play is considered a success if it gains 45 percent of needed yards; on second down, a play needs to gain 60 percent of needed yards; on third or fourth down, only gaining a new first down is considered success.

We then expand upon that basic idea with a more complicated system of "success points," improved over the past four years with a lot of mathematics and a bit of trial and error. A successful play is worth one point, an unsuccessful play zero points, with fractional points in between (for example, eight yards on third-and-10 is worth 0.54 "success points"). Extra points are awarded for big plays, gradually increasing to three points for 10 yards (assuming those yards result in a first down), four points for 20 yards, and five points for 40 yards or more. Losing three or more yards is -1 point. Interceptions average -6 points, with an adjustment for the length of the pass and the location of the interception (since an interception tipped at the line is more likely to produce a long return than an interception on a 40-yard pass). A fumble is worth anywhere from -1.7 to -4.0 points depending on how often a fumble in that situation is lost to the defense—no matter who actually recovers the fumble. Red zone plays get a bonus: 20 percent for team offense, five percent for team defense, and 10 percent for individual players. There is a bonus given for a touchdown that acknowledges that the goal line is significantly more difficult to cross than the previous 99 yards (although this bonus is nowhere near as large as the one used in fantasy football).

(Our system is a bit more complex than the one in *Hidden Game* thanks to our subsequent research, which added larger penalty for turnovers, the fractional points, and a slightly higher baseline for success on first down. The reason why all fumbles are counted, no matter whether they are recovered by the offense or defense, is explained in the essay "Pregame Show.")

Every single play run in the NFL gets a "success value" based on this system, and then that number gets compared to the average success values of plays in similar situations for all players, adjusted for a number of variables. These include down and distance, field location, time remaining in game, and the team's lead or deficit in the game score. Teams are always compared to the overall offensive average, as the team made its own choice whether to pass or rush. When it comes to individual players, however, rushing plays are compared to other rushing plays, passing plays to other passing plays, tight ends to tight ends, wideouts to wideouts, and so on.

Going back to our example of the three-yard rush, if Player A gains three yards under a set of circumstances in which the average NFL running back gains only one yard, then Player A has a certain amount of value above others at his position. Likewise, if Player B gains three yards on a play on which, under similar circumstances, an average NFL back gains four yards, that Player B has negative value relative to others at his position. Once we make all our adjustments, we can evaluate the difference between this player's rate of success and the expected success rate of an average running back in the same situation (or between the opposing defense and the average defense in the same situation, etc.). Add up every play by a certain team or player, divide by the total of the various baselines for success in all those situations, and you get VOA, or Value Over Average.

Of course, the biggest variable in football is the fact that each team plays a different schedule against teams of disparate quality. By adjusting each play based on the opposing defense's average success in stopping that type of play over the course of a season, we get DVOA, or Defense-adjusted Value Over Average. Rushing and passing plays are adjusted based on down and location on the field; passing plays are also adjusted based on how the defense performs against passes to running backs, tight ends, or wide receivers. Defenses are adjusted based on the average success of the *offenses* they are facing. (Yes, technically the defensive stats are actually "offense-adjusted." If it seems weird, think of the "D" in "DVOA" as standing for "opponent-Dependent" or something.)

The biggest advantage of DVOA is the ability to break teams and players down to find strengths and weaknesses in a variety of situations. In the aggregate, DVOA may not be quite as accurate as some of the other, similar "power ratings" formulas based on comparing drives rather than individual plays, but, unlike those other ratings, DVOA can be separated not only by player, but also by down, or by week, or by distance needed for a first down. This can give us a better idea of not just which team is better, but why, and what a team has to do in order to improve itself in the future. You will find DVOA used in this book in a lot of different ways—because it takes every single play into account, it can be used to measure a player or a team's performance in any situation. All Pittsburgh third downs can be compared to how an average team does on third down. Kevin Kolb and John Skelton can each be compared to how an average quarterback performs in the red zone, or with a lead, or in the second half of the game.

Since it compares each play only to plays with similar circumstances, it gives a more accurate picture of how much better a team really is compared to the league as a whole. The list of top DVOA offenses on third down, for example, is more ac-

curate than the conventional NFL conversion statistic because it takes into account that converting third-and-long is more difficult than converting third-and-short, and that a turnover is worse than an incomplete pass because it eliminates the opportunity to move the other team back with a punt on fourth down.

One of the hardest parts of understanding a new statistic is interpreting its scale, or what numbers represent good performance or bad performance. We've made that easy with DVOA. For each season, ratings are normalized so that 0% represents league average. A positive DVOA represents a situation that favors the offense, while a negative DVOA represents a situation that favors the defense. This is why the best offenses have positive DVOA ratings (last year, New England led the league at 30.8%) and the best defenses have negative DVOA ratings (with Chicago on top at -26.7%).

In general, the scale of offensive ratings is slightly wider than the scale of defensive ratings, although the standard deviation of defenses has been particularly low for the last two seasons. In most years, the best and worst offenses tend to rate around +/- 30%, while the best and worst defenses tend to rate around +/- 25%. For starting players, the scale tends to reach roughly +/-40% for passing and receiving, and +/- 30% for rushing. As you might imagine, some players with fewer attempts will surpass both extremes.

Team DVOA totals combine offense and defense by subtracting the latter from the former because the better defenses will have negative DVOA ratings. (Special teams performance is also added, as described later in this essay.) Certain plays are counted in DVOA for offense and not for defense, leading to separate baselines on each side of the ball. In addition, although the league ratings for offense and defense are always 0%, the league averages for passing and rushing separately are *not* 0%. Because passing is more efficient than rushing, the average for team passing is almost always positive and the average for team rushing is almost always negative. However, ratings for individual players only compare passes to other passes and runs to other runs, so the league average for individual passing is 0%, as are the league averages for rushing and the three separate league averages for receiving by wide receivers, tight ends, and running backs.

Some other important notes about DVOA:

• Only four penalties are included in DVOA. Two penalties count as pass plays on both sides of the ball: intentional grounding and defensive pass interference. The other two penalties are included for offense only: false starts and delay of game. Because the inclusion of these penalties means a group of negative plays that don't count as either passes or runs, the league averages for pass offense and run offense are higher than the league averages for pass defense and run defense.

• Aborted snaps and incomplete backwards lateral passes are only penalized on offense, not rewarded on defense.

• Adjustments for playing from behind or with a lead in the fourth quarter are different for offense and defense, as are adjustments for the final two minutes of the first half when the offense is not near field-goal range.

• Offense gets a slight penalty and defense gets a slight bonus for games indoors.

Table 1. Correlation of Various Stats to Wins, 2000-2011

Stat	Offense	Defense	Total
Points Scored/Allowed	.744	-.678	.917
DVOA	.696	-.496	.856
Yards Gained/Allowed	.560	-.421	.694
Yards Gained/Allowed per Play	.540	-.363	.728

Table 2. Correlation of Various Stats to Wins Following Year, 2000-2011

Stat	Correlation	Stat	Correlation
DVOA	.374	Yards per Play Differential	.313
Point Differential	.329	Wins	.290
Pythagorean Wins	.324	Yardage Differential	.286

How well does DVOA work? Using correlation coefficients, we can show that only actual points scored are better than DVOA at indicating how many games a team has won (Table 1) and DVOA does a better job of predicting wins in the coming season than either wins or points scored in the previous season (Table 2).

(Correlation coefficient is a statistical tool that measures how two variables are related by using a number between 1 and -1. The closer to -1 or 1, the stronger the relationship, but the closer to 0, the weaker the relationship.)

Special Teams

The problem with a system based on measuring both yardage and yardage towards a first down is what to do with plays that don't have the possibility of a first down. Special teams are an important part of football and we needed a way to add that performance to the team DVOA rankings. Our special teams metric includes five separate measurements: field goals and extra points, net punting, punt returns, net kickoffs, and kick returns.

The foundation of most of these special teams ratings is the concept that each yard line has a different value based on the likelihood of scoring from that position on the field. In *Hidden Game*, the authors suggested that the each additional yard for the offense had equal value, with a team's own goal line being worth -2 points, the 50-yard line 2 points, and the opposing goal line 6 points. (-2 points is not only the value of a safety, but also reflects the fact that when a team is backed up in its own territory, it is likely that its drive will stall, forcing a punt that will give the ball to the other team in good field position. Thus, the negative point value reflects the fact that the defense is more likely to score next.) Our studies have updated this concept to reflect the actual likelihood that the offense or defense will have the next score from a given position on the field based on actual results from the past few seasons. The line that represents the value of field position is not straight, but curved, with the value of each yard increasing as teams approach either goal line.

Our special teams ratings compare each kick or punt to league average based on the point value of the position of the kick, catch, and return. We've determined a league average for how far a kick goes based on the line of scrimmage for each kick (almost always the 35-yard line for kickoffs, variable for punts) and a league average for how far a return goes based on both the yard line where the ball is caught and the distance that it traveled in the air.

The kicking or punting team is rated based on net points compared to average, taking into account both the kick and the return if there is one. Because the average return is always positive, punts that are not returnable (touchbacks, out of bounds, fair catches, and punts downed by the coverage unit) will rate higher than punts of the same distance which are returnable. (This is also true of touchbacks on kickoffs.) There are also separate individual ratings for kickers and punters that are based on distance and whether the kick is returnable, assuming an average return in order to judge the kicker separate from the coverage.

For the return team, the rating is based on how many points the return is worth compared to average, based on the location of the catch and the distance the ball traveled in the air. Return teams are not judged on the distance of kicks, nor are they judged on kicks that cannot be returned. As explained below, blocked kicks are so rare as to be statistically insignificant as predictors for future performance and are thus ignored. For the kicking team they simply count as missed field goals, for the defense they are gathered with their opponents' other missed field goals in Hidden value (also explained below).

Field goal kicking is measured differently. Measuring kickers by field goal percentage is a bit absurd, as it assumes that all field goals are of equal difficulty. In our metric, each field goal is compared to the average number of points scored on all field goal attempts from that distance over the past 16 years. The value of a field goal increases as distance from the goal line increases. Kickoffs, punts, and field goals are then adjusted based on weather and altitude. It will surprise no one to learn that it is easier to kick the ball in Denver or a dome than it is to kick the ball in Buffalo in December. Because we do not yet have enough data to tailor our adjustments specifically to each stadium, each one is assigned to one of four categories: Cold, Warm, Dome, and Denver. There is also an additional adjustment dropping the value of field goals in Florida (because the warm temperatures allow the ball to carry better) and raising the value of punts in San Francisco (because of those infamous winds).

The baselines for special teams are adjusted in each year for rule changes such as the introduction of the special-teams-use-only "k-ball" in 1999 as well as the move of the kickoff line from the 35 to the 30 in 1994 and then back to the 35 in 2011. Baselines have also been adjusted each year to make up for the gradual improvement of kickers over the last two decades.

Once we've totaled how many points above or below average can be attributed to special teams, we translate those points into DVOA so the ratings can be added to offense and defense to get total team DVOA.

There are three aspects of special teams that have an impact on wins and losses, but don't show up in the standard special teams rating because a team has little or no influence on them. The first is the length of kickoffs by the opposing team, with an asterisk. Obviously, there are no defenders standing on the 35-yard line, ready to block a kickoff after the whistle blows. However, over the past few years, some teams have deliberately kicked short in order to avoid certain top return men, such as Devin Hester and Josh Cribbs. The special teams formula now includes adjustments to give teams extra credit for field position on kick returns if kickers are deliberately trying to avoid a return.

The other two items that special teams have little control over are field goals against your team, and punt distance against your team. Research shows no indication that teams can influence the accuracy or strength of field-goal kickers and punters, except for blocks. As mentioned above, although blocked field goals and punts are definitely skillful plays, they are so rare that they have no correlation to how well teams have played in the past or will play in the future, thus they are included here as if they were any other missed field goal or botched punt, giving the defense no additional credit for their efforts. The value of these three elements is listed separately as "Hidden" value.

Special teams ratings also do not include two-point conversions or onside kick attempts, both of which, like blocks, are so infrequent as to be statistically insignificant in judging future performance.

Defense-Adjusted Yards Above Replacement (DYAR)

DVOA is a good stat, but of course it is not a perfect one. One problem is that DVOA, by virtue of being a percentage or rate statistic, doesn't take into account the cumulative value of having a player producing at a league-average level over the course of an above-average number of plays. By definition, an average level of performance is better than that provided by half of the league and the ability to maintain that level of performance while carrying a heavy workload is very valuable indeed. In addition, a player who is involved in a high number of plays can draw the defense's attention away from other parts of the offense, and, if that player is a running back, he can take time off the clock with repeated runs.

Let's say you have a running back who carries the ball 300 times in a season. What would happen if you were to remove this player from his team's offense? What would happen to those 300 plays? Those plays don't disappear with the player, though some might be lost to the defense because of the associated loss of first downs. Rather those plays would have to be distributed among the remaining players in the offense, with the bulk of them being given to a replacement running back. This is where we arrive at the concept of replacement level, borrowed from our partners at Baseball Prospectus. When a player is removed from an offense, he is usually not replaced by a player of similar ability. Nearly every starting player in the NFL is a starter because he is better than the alterna-

tive. Those 300 plays will typically be given to a significantly worse player, someone who is the backup because he doesn't have as much experience and/or talent. A player's true value can then be measured by the level of performance he provides above that replacement level baseline, totaled over all of his run or pass attempts.

Of course, the *real* replacement player is different for each team in the NFL. Last year, the second-string running back for the New York Jets (Bilal Powell) had a higher DVOA than the original starter (Shonn Greene). Sometimes a player like Ryan Grant or Danny Woodhead will be cut by one team and turn into a star for another. On other teams, the drop from the starter to the backup can be even greater than the general drop to replacement level. The 2011 Indianapolis Colts will now be the hallmark example of this until the end of time. The choice to start an inferior player or to employ a sub-replacement level backup, however, falls to the team, not the starter being evaluated. Thus we generalize replacement level for the league as a whole as the ultimate goal is to evaluate players independent of the quality of their teammates.

Our estimates of replacement level are computed differently for each position. For quarterbacks, we analyzed situations where two or more quarterbacks had played meaningful snaps for a team in the same season, then compared the overall DVOA of the original starters to the overall DVOA of the replacements. We did not include situations where the backup was actually a top prospect waiting his turn on the bench, since a first-round pick is by no means a "replacement-level" player.

At other positions, there is no easy way to separate players into "starters" and "replacements," since unlike at quarterback, being the starter doesn't make you the only guy who gets in the game. Instead, we used a simpler method, ranking players at each position in each season by attempts. The players who made up the final 10 percent of passes or runs were split out as "replacement players" and then compared to the players making up the other 90 percent of plays at that position. This took care of the fact that not every non-starter at running back or wide receiver is a freely available talent. (Think of Jonathan Stewart or Randall Cobb, for example.)

As noted earlier, the challenge of any new stat is to present it on a scale that's meaningful to those attempting to use it. Saying that Tony Romo's passes were worth 91 success value points over replacement in 2012 has very little value without a context to tell us if 91 is good total or a bad one. Therefore, we translate these success values into a number called "Defense-adjusted Yards Above Replacement," or DYAR. Thus, Romo was seventh among quarterbacks with 1,156 passing DYAR. It is our estimate that a generic replacement-level quarterback, throwing in the same situations as Romo, would have been worth 1,156 fewer yards. Note that this doesn't mean the replacement level quarterback would have gained exactly 1,156 fewer yards. First downs, touchdowns, and turnovers all have an estimated yardage value in this system, so what we are saying is that a generic replacement-level quarterback would have fewer yards and touchdowns (and more turnovers) that would total up to be equivalent to the value of 1,156 yards.

Problems with DVOA and DYAR

Football is a game in which nearly every action requires the work of two or more teammates—in fact, usually 11 teammates all working in unison. Unfortunately, when it comes to individual player ratings, we are still far from the point at which we can determine the value of a player independent from the performance of his teammates. That means that when we say, "In 2012, Matt Forte had a DVOA of 3.1%," what we are really saying is "In 2012, Matt Forte, playing in Mike Tice's offensive system with the Chicago offensive line blocking for him and Jay Cutler selling the fake when necessary, had a DVOA of 3.1%." (Or in the case of the Bears, perhaps this should read "not blocking for him.")

DVOA is limited by what's included in the official NFL play-by-play or tracked by the Football Outsiders game charting project (introduced below). Because we need to have the entire play-by-play of a season in order to compute DVOA and DYAR, these metrics are not yet ready to compare players of today to players throughout the league's history. As of this writing, we have processed 22 seasons, 1991 through 2012, and we add seasons at a rate of roughly two per year (the most recent season, plus one season back into history.) We'll be finishing both 1989 and 1990 in the next few weeks after releasing this book.

Pythagorean Projection

The Pythagorean projection is an approximation of each team's wins based solely on their points scored and allowed. This basic concept was introduced by baseball analyst Bill James, who discovered that the record of a baseball team could be very closely approximated by taking the square of team runs scored and dividing it by the sum of the squares of team runs scored and allowed. Statistician Daryl Morey, now general manager of the Houston Rockets, later extended this theorem to professional football, refining the exponent to 2.37 rather than 2.

The problem with that exponent is the same problem we've had with DVOA in recent years: the changing offensive levels in the NFL. 2.37 worked great based on the league 20 years ago, but in the current NFL it ends up slightly underprojecting teams that play high-scoring games. The most accurate method is actually to adjust the exponent based on the scoring environment of each individual team. Saints games have a lot of points. Jaguars games feature fewer points.

This became known as Pythagenport when Clay Davenport of Baseball Prospectus started doing it with baseball teams. In the middle of the 2011 season, we switched our measurement of Pythagorean wins to a Pythagenport-style equation, modified for the NFL[1]. The improvement is slight, but noticeable due to the high-scoring teams that have dominated the last few years.

For a long time, Pythagorean projections did a remarkable job of predicting Super Bowl champions. From 1984 through 2004, 10 of 21 Super Bowls were won by the team that led the NFL in Pythagorean wins. Seven other Super Bowls during that time were won by the team that finished second. Super Bowl champions that led the league in Pythagorean wins but not actual wins include the 2004 Patriots, 2000 Ravens, 1999 Rams, and 1997 Broncos.

As noted in the Introduction, Super Bowl champions have been much less predictable over the last few seasons. As of 2004, the 1980 Oakland Raiders held the mark for the fewest Pythagorean wins by a Super Bowl champion, 9.7. In the past seven seasons, four different teams have won the Super Bowl with a lower Pythagorean win total: the 2006 Colts (9.6), the 2012 Ravens (9.4), the 2007 Giants (8.6), and the 2011 Giants (7.9), the first team in the 90-year history of the National Football League to ever be outscored during the regular season and still go on to win the championship.

Despite these recent trends, Pythagoras is still a useful metric, particularly as a predictor of year-to-year improvement. Teams that win a minimum of one full game more than their Pythagorean projection tend to regress the following year; teams that win a minimum of one full game less than their Pythagorean projection tend to improve the following year, particularly if they were at or above .500 despite their underachieving. For 2012, the team that clearly stands out in this fashion is Seattle, which slipped into the playoffs at 11-5 but had 12.5 Pythagorean wins. Detroit is also notable for having 6.4 Pythagorean wins, far surpassing their 4-12 record on the field. On the other hand, Indianapolis had the second largest gap between actual wins (11) and Pythagorean projection (7.2) in NFL history, trailing only the 1992 Colts who went 9-7 despite being outscored 302-216.

Adjusted Line Yards

One of the most difficult goals of statistical analysis in football is isolating the degree to which each of the 22 men on the field is responsible for the result of a given play. Nowhere is this as significant as in the running game, in which one player runs while up to nine other players—including not just linemen but also wideouts and tight ends—block in different directions. None of the statistics we use for measuring rushing—yards, touchdowns, yards per carry—differentiate between the contribution of the running back and the contribution of the offensive line. Neither do our advanced metrics DVOA and DYAR.

We do, however, have enough play-by-play data amassed that we can try to separate the effect that the running back has on a particular play from the effects of the offensive line (and other offensive blockers) and the opposing defense. A team might have two running backs in its stable: RB A, who averages 3.0 yards per carry, and RB B, who averages 3.5 yards per carry. Who is the better back? Imagine that RB A doesn't just average 3.0 yards per carry, but gets exactly 3 yards on

---

[1] The equation, for those curious, is 1.5 x log ((PF+PA)/G).

every single carry, while RB B has a highly variable yardage output: sometimes 5 yards, sometimes -2 yards, sometimes 20 yards. The difference in variability between the runners can be exploited not only to determine the difference between the runners, but the effect the offensive line has on every running play.

At some point in every long running play, the running back passes all of his offensive line blocks as well as additional blocking backs or receivers. From there on, the rest of the play is dependent on the runner's own speed and elusiveness and the speed and tackling ability of the opposing defense. If Frank Gore breaks through the line for 50 yards, avoiding tacklers all the way to the goal line, his offensive line has done a great job—but they aren't responsible for the majority of the yards gained. The trick is figuring out exactly how much they *are* responsible for.

For each running back carry, we calculated the probability that the back involved would run for the specific yardage on that play based on that back's average yardage per carry and the variability of their yardage from play to play. We also calculated the probability that the offense would get the yardage based on the team's rushing average and variability using all backs *other* than the one involved in the given play, and the probability that the defense would give up the specific amount of yardage based on its average rushing yards allowed per carry and variability.

A regression analysis breaks the value for rushing yardage into the following categories: losses, 0-to-4 yards, 5-to-10 yards, and 11-plus yards. In general, the offensive line is 20 percent more responsible for lost yardage than it is for positive gains up to four yards, but 50 percent less responsible for additional yardage gained between five and ten yards, and not at all responsible for additional yardage past ten yards.

By applying those percentages to every running back carry, we were able to create **Adjusted Line Yards**, a statistic that measured offensive line performance. (We don't include carries by receivers, which are usually based on deception rather than straight blocking, or carries by quarterbacks, although we may need to reconsider that given the recent use of the read option in the NFL.) Those numbers are then adjusted based on down, distance, situation, opponent, and whether or not a team is in the shotgun. (Because defenses are generally playing pass when the quarterback is in shotgun, the average running back carry from shotgun last year gained 4.79 yards, compared to just 4.14 yards on other carries—and most years the difference is even greater than that.) The adjusted numbers are then normalized so that the league average for Adjusted Line Yards per carry is the same as the league average for RB yards per carry (in 2012, 4.25 yards).

The NFL distinguishes between runs made to seven different locations on the line: left/right end, left/right tackle, left/right guard, and middle. Further research showed no statistically significant difference between how well a team performed on runs listed as having gone up the middle or past a guard, so we separated runs into just five different directions (left/right end, left/right tackle, and middle). Note that there may not be a statistically significant difference between right tackle and middle/guard either, but pending further research (and for the sake of symmetry) we still list runs behind the right tackle

separately. These splits allow us to evaluate subsections of a team's offensive line, but not necessarily individual linemen, as we can't account for blocking assignments or guards who pull towards the opposite side of the line after the snap.

Success Rate

Success rate is a statistic for running backs that measures how consistently they achieve the yardage necessary for a play to be deemed successful. Some running backs will mix a few long runs with a lot of failed runs of one or two yards, while others with similar yards-per-carry averages will consistently gain five yards on first down, or as many yards as necessary on third down. This statistic helps us differentiate between the two.

Since Success Rate compares rush attempts to other rush attempts, without consideration of passing, the standard for success on first down is slightly lower than those described above for DVOA. In addition, the standard for success changes slightly in the fourth quarter when running backs are used to run out the clock. A team with the lead is satisfied with a shorter run as long as it stays in bounds. Conversely, for a team down by a couple of touchdowns in the fourth quarter, four yards on first down isn't going to be a big help.

The formula for Success Rate is as follows:

• A successful play must gain 40 percent of needed yards on first down, 60 percent of needed yards on second down, and 100 percent of needed yards on third or fourth down.
• If the offense is behind by more than a touchdown in the fourth quarter, the benchmarks switch to 50 percent, 65 percent, and 100 percent.
• If the offense is ahead by any amount in the fourth quarter, the benchmarks switch to 30 percent, 50 percent, and 100 percent.

The league-average Success Rate in 2012 was 47.2 percent. Success Rate is not adjusted based on defenses faced, and is not calculated for quarterbacks and wide receivers who occasionally carry the ball.

Similarity Scores

Similarity scores were first introduced by Bill James to compare baseball players to other baseball players from the past. It was only natural that the idea would spread to other sports as statistical analysis spread to other sports. NBA analyst John Hollinger has created his own version to compare basketball players, and we have created our own version to compare football players.

Similarity scores have a lot of uses, and we aren't the only football analysts who use them. Doug Drinen of the website Footballguys.com has his own system that is specific to comparing fantasy football performances. The major goal of our similarity scores is to compare career progressions to try to determine when players have a higher chance of a breakout, a decline, or—due to age or usage—an injury (much like Baseball Prospectus's PECOTA player projection system). Therefore we not only compare numbers such as attempts, yards, and touchdowns, but also age and experience. We often are looking not for players who had similar seasons, but for players who had similar two- or three-year spans in their careers.

Similarity scores have some important weaknesses. The database for player comparison begins in 1978, the year the 16-game season began and passing rules were liberalized (a reasonable starting point to measure the "modern" NFL), thus the method only compares standard statistics such as yards and attempts, which are of course subject to all kinds of biases from strength of schedule to quality of receiver corps. For our comparisons, we project full-season statistics for the strike years of 1982 and 1987, although we cannot correct for players who crossed the 1987 picket line to play more than 12 games.

In addition to our similarity scores for skill players, we also have a similarity score system for defensive players based on FO's advanced statistics going back to 1997. It measures things like average distance on run tackles or pass tackles, as well as Stops and Defeats. It does not account for game-charting stats like hurries or Success Rate in coverage.

If you are interested in the specific computations behind our similarity scores system, we have listed the standards for each skill position online at http://www.footballoutsiders.com/stats/similarity. (The defensive system is not yet listed.) In addition, as part of our online premium package, all player pages for current players—both offensive and defensive—list the top ten similar players over one-, two-, and three-year spans.

KUBIAK Projection System

Most "skill position" players whom we expect to play a role this season receive a projection of their standard 2013 NFL statistics using the KUBIAK projection system. KUBIAK takes into account a number of different factors including expected role, performance over the past two seasons, age, height, weight, historical comparables, and projected team performance on offense and defense. When we named our system KUBIAK, it was a play on the PECOTA system used by our partners at Baseball Prospectus—if they were going to name their system after a long-time eighties backup, we would name our system after a long-time eighties backup. Little did we know that Gary Kubiak would finally get a head coaching job the very next season. After some debate, we decided to keep the name, although discussing projections for Houston players can be a bit awkward.

To clear up a common misconception among our readers, KUBIAK projects individual player performances only, not teams.

2013 Win Projection System

In this book, each of the 32 NFL teams receives a **2013 Mean Projection** at the beginning of its chapter. These projections stem from three equations that forecast 2013 DVOA for offense, defense, and special teams based on a number of different factors, including the previous two years of DVOA in various situations, improvement in the second half of 2012, recent draft history, coaching experience, injury history, specific coaching styles, and the combined tenure of the offensive line.

These three equations produce precise numbers representing the most likely outcome, but also produce a range of possibilities, used to determine the probability of each possible offensive, defensive, and special teams DVOA for each team. This is particularly important when projecting football teams, because with only 16 games in a season, a team's performance may vary wildly from its actual talent level due to a couple of random bounces of the ball or badly timed injuries. In addition, the economic structure of the NFL allows teams to make sudden jumps or drops in overall ability more often than in other sports.

To create our simulation, we used the range of DVOA possibilities to produce 1,000 different simulated seasons with 32 sets of DVOA ratings. We then plugged those season-long DVOA ratings into the same equation we use during the season to determine each team's likely remaining wins for our Playoff Odds Report. The simulation takes each season game-by-game, determining the home or road team's chance of winning each game based on the DVOA ratings of each team as well as home-field advantage, warm-weather or dome-stadium teams playing in the cold after November 1, and several other variables that can affect the outcome of each game. Then a random number between 0 and 100 determines whether the home or road team has won that game. Further tweaks adjust the simulation further to produce results closer to the historic distribution of wins in the NFL. While 8-8 is still more likely than any other record, historically more NFL teams end up with records between 2-14 and 4-12 or between 12-4 and 14-2 than you would otherwise expect from a normal distribution. We ran 1,000 simulations with each of the 1,000 sets of DVOA ratings, creating a million different simulations. The simulation was programmed by Mike Harris.

Football Outsiders Game Charting Project

Each of the formulas listed above relies primarily on the play-by-play data published by the NFL. When we began to analyze the NFL, this was all that we had to work with. Just as a television broadcast has a color commentator who gives more detail to the facts related by the play-by-play announcer, so too do we need some color commentary to provide contextual information that breathes life into these plain lines of numbers and text. The Football Outsiders Game Charting Project is our attempt to provide color for the simple play-by-play.

Providing color to 512 hours of football is a daunting task. To put it into perspective, there were more than 54,000 lines of play-by-play information in the 2012 NFL season and our goal is to add several layers of detail to nearly all of them. We recruited more than 50 volunteers to collectively chart each week's NFL games, and we've charted data on nearly every play since 2005. Through trial-and-error, we have gradually narrowed our focus to charting things both traceable and definitive. Charting a game, and rewinding to make sure mistakes are minimized, can take two to three hours. More than a couple of these per week can be hazardous to one's marriage. Our goal was to provide comprehensive information while understanding that our charters were doing this on a volunteer basis.

This past season brought two huge changes to the Football Outsiders Game Charting Project. First, the NFL finally made coaches' film available publicly through their NFL Game Rewind project. That tape includes a sideline and end zone perspectives for each play, and shows all 22 players at all times, making it easier to see the cause-and-effect of certain actions taken on the field. The availability of coaches' film helped make our charting more accurate than ever before, although it is still imperfect. You often cannot tell which players did their jobs particularly well or made mistakes without knowing the play call and each player's assignment, particularly when it comes to zone coverage or pass rushers who reach the quarterback without being blocked. Therefore, the goal of Football Outsiders game charting is *not* to "grade" players, but rather to attempt to mark specific events: a pass pressure, a blown block, a dropped interception, and so on.

There are lots of things we would like to do with all-22 film that we simply haven't been able to do yet, such as charting coverage by cornerbacks when they aren't the target of a given pass, or even when pass pressure prevents the pass from getting into the air. Unfortunately, we are still limited by how much time our volunteers can give to the project, and the fact that our financial resources do not match those of our competitors.

The second major change for the game charting project in 2012 was an agreement to link our project up with the game charting done by the ESPN Stats & Information for internal ESPN use. ESPN charts games live on Sundays and our agreement allowed us to get access to their data immediately rather than waiting two to three weeks for our game charters to complete each game. In return, we provided suggestions to correct mistakes in the data—the more eyes we have on data like this, the more accurate it will be—and supplied ESPN with some of our older charting data, which will allow them to produce their new Total QBR metric for the 2006 and 2007 seasons. All data that comes from the ESPN Stats & Information is designated as such in the description of game charting that follows.

We emphasize that all data from the charting project is unofficial. Other sources for football statistics may keep their own measurements of yards after catch or how teams perform against the blitz. Our data will not necessarily match theirs. However, any other group that is publicly tracking this data is also working off the same footage, and thus will run into the same issues of difficulty.

The Football Outsiders game charting project tracks the following information:

Formation/Personnel

For each play, we have the number of running backs, wide receivers, and tight ends on the field courtesy of ESPN Stats & Information. Players were marked based on their designation on the roster, not based on where they lined up on the field. Obviously, this could be difficult with some hybrid players or players changing positions in 2012, but we did our best to keep things as consistent as possible.[2]

Football Outsiders charters then added to ESPN's data by marking the names of players who were lined up in unexpected positions. This included marking tight ends or wide receivers in the backfield, and running backs or tight ends who were lined up either wide or in the slot (often referred to as "flexing" a tight end). Football Outsiders charters also marked when a fullback or tight end was actually a sixth (or sometimes even seventh) offensive lineman, and they marked the backfield formation as empty back, single back, I formation, offset I, split backs, full house, or "other." These notations of backfield formation were recorded directly before the snap and do not account for positions before pre-snap motion.

Beginning with 2011, we also asked game charters to mark defensive formations by listing the number of linemen, linebackers, and defensive backs. There will be mistakes—a box safety may occasionally be confused for a linebacker, for example—but for the most part this data should be accurate. For the most part, we distinguished defensive ends from outside linebackers based on whether the player lined up with his hand on the ground before the snap. We did make an exception when defensive tackles stood up in an "everybody stand up to confuse the quarterback" style formation like Pittsburgh's "11 Angry Men." Players not on the screen were always assumed to be defensive backs.

Rushers and Blockers

ESPN Stats & Information provided us with two data points regarding the pass rush: the number of pass rushers on a given play, and the number defensive backs blitzing on a given play. Football Outsiders charters then added a count of blockers, although this has proved to be an art as much as a science. Offenses base their blocking schemes on how many rushers they expect. A running back or tight end's assignment may depend on how many pass-rushers cross the line at the snap. Therefore, an offensive player was deemed to be a blocker if he engaged in an actual block, or there was some hesitation before running a route. A running back who immediately heads out into the flat is not a blocker, but one who waits to verify that the blocking scheme is working and then goes out to the flat would, in fact, be considered a blocker.

Defensive back blitzes are new to our charting this year, and replace our previous attempts to count zone blitzes.

Pass Play Details

ESPN Stats & Information recorded the following data for all pass plays:

---

[2] The players who were the biggest issues: H-backs James Casey, Charles Clay, Dorin Dickerson, and Rhett Ellison were considered tight ends. Evan Rodriguez was considered a fullback. Return specialists and gadget players Stefan Logan and Darius Reynaud were listed as running backs, while Dexter McCluster was listed as a wide receiver.

• Did the play begin with a play-action fake, including read-option fakes that developed into pass plays instead of being handed to a running back. Football Outsiders charters also added notation of fake end-arounds and flea flickers.

   • Was the quarterback in or out of the pocket.
   • Was the quarterback hurried in making his pass.
   • Was this a screen pass.

Football Outsiders charters then added to the ESPN data by identifying the defender who caused the pass pressure. Charters were allowed to list two names if necessary, and could also attribute a hurry to "overall pressure." No defender was given a hurry and a sack on the same play, but defenders were given hurries if they helped force a quarterback into a sack that was finished by another player. Football Outsiders charters also identified which defender(s) caused the pass pressure which forced a quarterback to scramble for yardage. If the quarterback wasn't under pressure but ran anyway, the play could be marked either as "coverage scramble" (if the quarterback ran because there were no open receivers) or "hole opens up" (if the quarterback ran because he knew he could gain significant yardage).

For the most part, Football Outsiders defaulted to ESPN's opinion on whether a play counted as pass pressure or not. The exception was for plays where the quarterback ran around solely because nobody was open; even if the quarterback eventually threw a pass, we changed these plays to "coverage scramble" and did not count them when counting up performance under pressure.

Some places in this book, we divide pass yardage into two numbers: distance in the air and yards after catch. This information is tracked by the NFL, but it can be hard to find and the official scorers often make errors, so we corrected the original data based on input from our charters as well as ESPN Stats & Information. Distance in the air is based on the distance from the line of scrimmage to the place where the receiver either caught or was supposed to catch the pass. We do not count how far the quarterback was behind the line or horizontal yardage if the quarterback threw across the field. All touchdowns are counted to the goal line, so that distance in the air added to yards after catch always equals the official yardage total kept by the league.

Incomplete Passes

Quarterbacks are evaluated based on their ability to complete passes. However, not all incompletes should have the same weight. Throwing a ball away to avoid a sack is actually a valuable incomplete, and a receiver dropping an otherwise quality pass is hardly a reflection on the quarterback.

This year, our evaluation of incomplete passes began with ESPN Stats & Information, which marked passes as Overthrown, Underthrown, Thrown Away, Batted Down at the Line, Defensed, or Dropped. Our charters then made changes to reflect a couple of additional categories we have kept in past years for Football Outsiders: Hit in Motion (indicating the quarterback was hit as his arm was coming forward to make a pass), Caught out of Bounds, and Hail Mary.

Our count of passes defensed will be different from the un-

official totals kept by the league, as well as the totals kept by ESPN Stats & Information, for reasons explained below in the section on Defensive Secondary tables.

ESPN Stats & Information also marked when a defender dropped an interception, and Football Outsiders then added the name of the defender responsible. When a play is close, we tend to err on the side of not marking a dropped interception, as we don't want to blame a defender who, for example, jumps high for a ball and has it tip off his fingers. This year for the first time, we also counted a few "defensed" interceptions, when a quarterback threw a pass that would have been picked off if not for the receiver playing defense on the ball. These passes counted as dropped interceptions for quarterbacks but not for the defensive players.

Defenders

The NFL play-by-play lists tackles and, occasionally, tipped balls, but it does not definitively list the defender on the play. Charters were asked to determine which defender was primarily responsible for covering either the receiver at the time of the throw or the location to which the pass was thrown, regardless of whether the pass was complete or not.

Every defense in the league plays zone coverage at times, some more than others, which leaves us with the question of how to handle plays without a clear man assigned to that receiver. We gave charters three alternatives:

• We asked charters to mark passes that found the holes in zone coverage as Hole in Zone, rather than straining to assign that pass to an individual defender. We asked the charter to also note the player who appeared to be responsible for that zone, and these defenders are assigned half credit for those passes. Some holes were so large that no defender could be listed along with the Hole in Zone designation.
• Charters were free to list two defenders instead of one. This could be used for actual double coverage, or for zone coverage in which the receiver was right between two close defenders rather than sitting in a gaping hole. When two defenders are listed, ratings assign each with half credit.
• Screen passes and dumpoffs are marked as Uncovered unless a defender (normally a linebacker) is obviously shadowing that specific receiver on the other side of the line of scrimmage.

Since we began the charting project in 2005, nothing has changed our analysis more than this information on pass coverage. However, even now with the ability to view all-22 film, it can be difficult to identify the responsible defender except when there is strict man-to-man coverage. We continue to hone our craft and do our best.

Additional Details from ESPN Stats & Information

All draw plays were marked, whether by halfbacks or quarterbacks. Option runs and zone reads were also marked.

ESPN tracked when the formation was pistol as opposed to shotgun; the official play-by-play simply marks these plays all as shotgun.

ESPN also marks the number of defenders in the box for each snap, and tags each play as either "loaded" or "not loaded." A loaded box is when the defense has more players in the box than the offense has available blockers for running plays. Finally, ESPN marks yards after contact for each play.

Additional Details from Football Outsiders Charters

Football Outsiders game charters marked each quarterback sack with one of the following terms: Blown Block, Coverage Sack, QB Fault, or Blitz/Overall Pressure. Blown Blocks were listed with the name of a specific offensive player who allowed the defender to come through. (Some blown block sacks are listed with two blockers, who each get a half-sack. There are also a handful of rare three-man blown blocks.) Coverage Sack denotes when the quarterback has plenty of time to throw but cannot find an open receiver. QB Fault represents "self sacks" listed without a defender, such as when the quarterback drops back, only to find the ball slip out of his hands with no pass-rusher touching him.

Our charters track "broken tackles" on all runs or pass plays. We define a "broken tackle" as one of two events: Either the ballcarrier escapes from the grasp of the defender, or the defender is in good position for a tackle but the ballcarrier jukes him out of his shoes. If the ballcarrier sped by a slow defender who dived and missed, that did not count as a broken tackle. If the defender couldn't bring the ballcarrier down but slowed him and still had his hand on him when another player made a tackle, this did not count as a broken tackle. It was possible to mark multiple broken tackles on the same play. Occasionally, the same defender would get a broken tackle, then recover, run upfield, and get a tackle on the same play, but we went through after the season to make sure no charter marked a broken tackle for contact that the league determined was an actual tackle. Broken tackles are not marked for special teams.

Beginning in 2010, we tracked which defensive players drew the most offensive holding calls; the list of defenders for 2012 can be found in the appendix.

An additional column called Extra Comment allowed the charters to add any description they wanted to the play. These comments might be good blitz pickup by a running back, a missed tackle, a great hit, a description of a pass route, an angry tirade about the poor camera angles of network broadcasts, or a number of other possibilities.

Finally, we asked the game charters to mark when a mistake was made in the official play-by-play. These mistakes include missing quarterback hits, incorrect names on tackles or penalties, missing direction on runs or passes, or the absence of the "scramble" designation when a quarterback ran on a play that began as a pass. Thanks to the diligence of our volunteer game charters and a friendly contact at the league office, the NFL corrected more than 300 mistakes in the official play-by-play based on the data collected by our game charters.

Sack Timing Project

Separate from the regular game charting project is J.J. Cooper's sack timing project, which began as a series of columns for AOL Fanhouse in 2009-2010 and continued with Football Outsiders in 2011. Cooper has timed every sack in the NFL from the time of the snap to the time of initial contact on the sack. The median sack time is roughly 2.8 seconds. The proj-

ect also assigns blame for blown blocks that lead to sacks or designates a sack as "QB/Play Call," roughly akin to when the regular game charting project designates a sack as "Rusher Untouched" or "QB Fault." We used this data to clean up some mistakes in our original game charting of sacks.

Acknowledgements

None of this would have been possible without the time spent by all the volunteer game charters. There are some specific acknowledgements at the end of the book, but we want to give a general thank you here to everyone who has helped collect data over the last few seasons. Without your unpaid time, the task of gathering all this information would have been too time-consuming to yield anything useful. If you are interested in participating in next year's charting project, please e-mail your contact information to info@footballoutsiders.com with the subject "Game Charting Project." Please make sure to mention where you live, what team you follow, and whether or not you have the Sunday Ticket package.

Our thanks to lots of people at ESPN Stats & Information for helping us coordinate our sharing of data, particularly Edmundo Macedo, Allison Loucks, and Henry Gargiulo.

How to Read the Team Summary Box

Here is a rundown of all the tables and stats that appear in the 32 team chapters. Each team chapter begins with a box in the upper-right hand corner that gives a summary of our statistics for that team, as follows:

2012 Record gives each team's actual win-loss record. **Pythagorean Wins** gives the approximate number of wins expected last year based on this team's raw totals of points scored and allowed, along with their NFL rank. **Snap-Weighted Age** gives the average age of the team in 2012, weighted based on how many snaps each player was on the field and ranked from oldest (Atlanta, first at 28.1) to youngest (Seattle, 32nd at 25.8). **Average Opponent** gives a ranking of last year's schedule strength based on the average DVOA of all 16 opponents faced during the regular season. Teams are ranked from the hardest schedule (Arizona) to the easiest (Indianapolis).

2013 Mean Projection gives the average number of wins for this team based on the 2013 Win Projection System described earlier in this chapter. Please note that we do not expect any teams to win the exact number of games in their mean projection. First of all, no team can win 0.8 of a game. Second, because these projections represent a whole range of possible values, the averages naturally tend to drift towards 8-8. (This is even stronger than usual in 2013.) If every team were to hit its mean projection, the worst team in the league would finish 5-10-1 and the best team 10-5-1. Obviously, we're not expecting a season where no team goes 4-12 or 12-4. For a better way to look at the projections, we offer **Postseason Odds**, which give each team's chance of making the postseason based on our simulation, and **Super Bowl Appearance** odds, which give each team's chance of representing its conference in Super Bowl XLVIII in beautiful downtown East Rutherford. The average team will make the playoffs in 37.5 percent of simulations, and the Super Bowl in 6.3 percent of simulations.

Projected Average Opponent gives the team's strength of schedule for 2013; like the listing for last year's schedule strength in the first column of the box, this number is based not on last year's record but on the mean projected DVOA for each opponent. A positive schedule is harder, a negative schedule easier. Teams are ranked from the hardest projected schedule (Minnesota, first) to the easiest (Indianapolis, 32nd). This strength of schedule projection does not take into account which games are home and which are away, or the timing of the bye week.

The final column of the box gives the team's chances of finishing in four different basic categories of success:

- On the Clock (0-4 wins; NFL average 11%)
- Mediocrity (5-7 wins; NFL average 33%)
- Playoff Contender (8-10 wins; NFL average 38%)
- Super Bowl Contender (11-plus wins; NFL average 19%)

The percentage given for each category is dependent not only on how good we project the team to be in 2013, but the level of variation possible in that projection, and the expected performance of the teams on the schedule.

You'll also find a table with the team's 2013 schedule placed within each chapter, along with a graph showing each team's 2012 week-to-week performance by single-game DVOA. The second, dotted line on the graph represents a five-week moving average of each team's performance, in order to show a longer-term view of when they were improving and declining. After the essays come statistical tables and comments related to that team and its specific units.

Weekly Performance

The first table gives a quick look at the team's week-to-week performance in 2011. (Table 1). This includes the playoffs for those teams that made the postseason, with the four weeks of playoffs numbered 18 (wild card) through 21 (Super Bowl). All other tables in the team chapters represent regular-season performance only unless otherwise noted.

Looking at the first week for the Atlanta Falcons in 2012, the first five columns are fairly obvious: the Falcons opened the season with a 40-24 win in Kansas City. **YDF** and **YDA** are net yards on offense and net yards against the defense. These numbers do not include penalty yardage or special teams yardage. **TO** represents the turnover margin. Unlike other parts of the book in which we consider all fumbles as equal, this only represents actual turnovers: fumbles lost and interceptions. So, for example, the Falcons had two more turnovers than Tampa Bay when they played in Week 12, but forced one more turnover than Tampa Bay in the Week 16 rematch.

Finally, you'll see DVOA ratings for this game: Total **DVOA** first, then offense (**Off**), defense (**Def**), and special teams (**ST**). Note that these are DVOA ratings, adjusted for

Table 1: 2012 Falcons Stats by Week

Wk	vs.	W-L	PF	PA	YDF	YDA	TO	Total	Off	Def	ST
1	at KC	W	40	24	376	393	3	26%	35%	22%	13%
2	DEN	W	27	21	275	336	4	39%	5%	-30%	4%
3	at SD	W	27	3	384	280	3	59%	31%	-30%	-2%
4	CAR	W	30	28	426	404	0	-8%	4%	15%	3%
5	at WAS	W	24	17	421	316	0	47%	12%	-37%	-2%
6	OAK	W	23	20	286	474	0	-48%	-40%	10%	2%
7	BYE										
8	at PHI	W	30	17	392	270	0	6%	14%	8%	-1%
9	DAL	W	19	13	453	377	0	-38%	8%	28%	-18%
10	at NO	L	27	31	454	440	0	-26%	-1%	26%	1%
11	ARI	W	23	19	354	178	-5	-23%	-47%	-20%	4%
12	at TB	W	24	23	424	326	-2	-9%	23%	19%	-13%
13	NO	W	23	13	283	436	4	42%	-11%	-46%	7%
14	at CAR	L	20	30	362	475	-1	6%	33%	29%	2%
15	NYG	W	34	0	394	256	3	79%	20%	-57%	2%
16	at DET	W	31	18	344	522	3	28%	26%	8%	10%
17	TB	L	17	22	278	366	1	-20%	-6%	3%	-10%
18	BYE										
19	SEA	W	30	28	417	491	0	3%	25%	24%	2%
20	SF	L	24	28	477	373	-1	9%	42%	29%	-5%

opponent, so a loss to a good team will often be listed with a higher rating than a close win over a bad team.

Trends and Splits

Next to the week-to-week performance is a table giving DVOA for different portions of a team's performance, on both offense and defense. Each split is listed with the team's rank among the 32 NFL teams. These numbers represent regular season performance only.

Total DVOA gives total offensive, and defensive DVOA in all situations. **Unadjusted VOA** represents the breakdown of play-by-play considering situation but not opponent. A team whose offensive DVOA is higher than its offensive VOA played a harder-than-average schedule of opposing defenses; a team with a lower defensive DVOA than defensive VOA player a harder-than-average schedule of opposing offenses.

Weighted Trend lowers the importance of earlier games to give a better idea of how the team was playing at the end of the regular season. The final four weeks of the season are full strength; moving backwards through the season, each week is given less and less weight until the first three weeks of the season, which are not included at all. **Variance** is the same as noted above, with a higher percentage representing less consistency. This is true for both offense and defense: Baltimore, for example, was very consistent on defense (1.8% variance, second) but one of the league's *least* consistent offenses (10.9% variance, which ranked 30th). **Average Opponent** is that the same thing that appears in the box to open each chapter, except split in half: the average DVOA of all opposing defenses (for offense) or the average DVOA of all opposing offenses (for defense).

Passing and **Rushing** are fairly self-explanatory. Note that rushing DVOA includes all rushes, not just those by running backs, including quarterback scrambles that may have began as pass plays.

The next three lines split out DVOA on **First Down, Second Down**, and **Third Down**. Third Down here includes fourth downs on which a team runs a regular offensive play instead of punting or attempting a field goal. **First Half** and **Second Half** represent the first two quarters and last two quarters (plus overtime), not the first eight and last eight games of the regular season. Next comes DVOA in the **Red Zone**, which is any offensive play starting from the defense's 20-yard line through the goal line. The final split is **Late and Close**, which includes any play in the second half or overtime when the teams are within eight points of each other in either direction. (Eight points, of course, is the biggest deficit that can be made up with a single score, a touchdown and two-point conversion.)

Five-Year Performance

This table gives each team's performance over the past five seasons (Table 2). It includes win-loss record, Pythagorean Wins, **Estimated Wins**, points scored and allowed, and turnover margin. Estimated wins are based on a formula that estimates how many games a team would have been expected to win based on 2012 performance in specific situations, normalized to eliminate luck (fumble recoveries, opponents' missed field goals, etc.) and assuming average schedule strength. The formula emphasizes consistency and overall DVOA as well as DVOA in a few specifically important situations. The next columns of this table give total DVOA along with DVOA for offense, defense, and special teams, and the rank for each among that season's 32 NFL teams.

The next four columns give the Adjusted Games Lost for starters on both offense and defense, along with rank. (Our total for starters here includes players who take over as starters due to another injury, such as Dannell Ellerbe or D.J. Smith last year, as well as important situational players who may not necessarily start, such as pass-rush specialists and slot receivers.) Adjusted Games Lost was introduced in *Pro Football Prospectus 2008*; it gives a weighted estimate of the probability that players would miss games based on how they are listed on the injury report. Unlike a count of "starter games missed," this accounts for the fact that a player listed as questionable who does in fact play is not playing at 100 percent capability. Teams are ranked from the fewest injuries (2012: Houston on offense, San Francisco on defense) to the most (2012: Philadelphia on offense, Green Bay on defense).

Individual Offensive Statistics

Each team chapter contains a table giving passing and receiving numbers for any player who either threw five passes or was thrown five passes, along with rushing numbers for any players who carried the ball at least five times. These numbers also appear in the player comments at the end of the book (except for wide receiver rushing attempts). By putting them together in the team chapters we hope we make it easier to compare the performances of different players on the same team.

Players who are no longer on the team are marked with an asterisk. New players who were on a different team in 2012 are in italics. Changes should be accurate at least July 1. Rookies are not included.

All players are listed with DYAR and DVOA. Passing statistics (Table 3, next page) then list total pass plays (**Plays**), net yardage (**NtYds**), and net yards per pass (**Avg**). These numbers include not just passes (and the positive yardage from them) but aborted snaps and sacks (and the negative yardage from them). Then comes average yards after catch (**YAC**), as determined by the game charting project. This average is based on charted receptions, not total pass attempts. The final three numbers are completion percentage (**C%**), passing touchdowns (**TD**), and interceptions (**Int**).

It is important to note that the tables in the team chapters contain Football Outsiders stats, while the tables in the player comments later in the book contain official NFL totals, at least when it comes to standard numbers like receptions and yardage. This results in a number of differences between the two:

• Team chapter tables list aborted snaps as passes, not runs, although aborted handoffs are still listed as runs. Net yardage for quarterbacks in the team chapter tables includes the lost yardage from aborted snaps, sacks, and intentional grounding penalties. For official NFL stats, all aborted snaps are listed as runs.

• Football Outsiders stats omit kneeldowns from run totals and clock-stopping spikes from pass totals.

• In the Football Outsiders stats, we have changed a number of lateral passes to count as passes rather than runs, un-

Table 2: Minnesota Vikings' Five-Year Performance

Year	W-L	Pyth W	Est W	PF	PA	TO	Total	Rk	Off	Rk	Def	Rk	ST	Rk	Off AGL	Rk	Def AGL	Rk	Off Age	Rk	Def Age	Rk	ST Age	Rk
2008	10-6	9.3	7.1	379	333	-6	1.5%	19	-9.9%	25	-19.3%	4	-7.9%	32	10.0	4	24.0	18	28.4	5	27.7	9	26.7	14
2009	12-4	11.8	10.4	470	312	+6	18.5%	7	12.9%	8	-1.0%	15	4.7%	3	9.4	7	13.1	4	28.3	3	27.5	8	26.9	8
2010	6-10	6.0	6.5	281	348	-11	-13.9%	25	-15.1%	27	-2.5%	12	-1.4%	19	35.7	25	19.7	14	28.5	5	28.3	4	27.4	2
2011	3-13	5.3	4.6	340	449	-3	-22.2%	29	-10.2%	24	8.0%	23	-4.1%	27	20.5	9	28.3	19	27.7	10	27.3	14	26.4	15
2012	10-6	8.8	8.8	379	348	-1	2.0%	14	0.3%	15	3.1%	21	4.7%	5	10.4	3	18.5	8	25.5	31	27.2	12	25.5	28

Table 3: Houston Texans Passing

Player	DYAR	DVOA	Plays	NtYds	Avg	YAC	C%	TD	Int
M.Schaub	697	7.5%	572	3811	6.7	5.0	64.3%	22	12
T.J.Yates	-85	-128.3%	11	34	3.1	7.3	40.0%	0	1

Table 4: Arizona Cardinals Rushing

Player	DYAR	DVOA	Plays	Yds	Avg	TD	Fum	Suc
L.Stephens-Howling*	-63	-22.9%	110	356	3.2	4	0	34%
B.Wells*	-48	-21.6%	88	234	2.7	5	1	34%
W.Powell	21	0.1%	60	217	3.6	0	0	40%
R.Williams	-85	-45.5%	58	167	2.9	0	2	34%
K.Kolb*	49	80.7%	12	103	8.6	1	0	-
R.Mendenhall	-62	-38.5%	51	182	3.6	0	3	43%

Table 5: Denver Broncos Receiving

Player	DYAR	DVOA	Plays	Ctch	Yds	Y/C	YAC	TD	C%
D.Thomas	354	21.4%	141	94	1430	15.2	5.7	10	67%
E.Decker	392	27.2%	123	85	1071	12.6	3.1	13	69%
B.Stokley*	204	37.4%	59	45	544	12.1	3.3	5	76%
M.Willis*	-44	-42.6%	22	10	90	9.0	2.8	0	45%
W.Welker	251	6.1%	175	118	1354	11.5	5.8	6	67%
J.Tamme	18	-5.8%	84	52	555	10.7	3.8	2	62%
J.Dreessen	13	-1.2%	58	41	356	8.7	3.4	5	71%
V.Green	14	22.7%	6	5	63	12.6	12.4	0	83%
W.McGahee*	44	7.2%	33	26	221	8.5	9.0	0	79%
K.Moreno	58	25.3%	26	21	167	8.0	6.0	0	81%
L.Ball	5	-5.6%	12	8	58	7.3	5.1	1	67%
R.Hillman	-2	-17.0%	12	10	62	6.2	6.9	0	83%

der the theory that a pass play is still a pass play, even if the receiver is standing five inches behind the quarterback. This results in some small differences in totals. For example, Russell Wilson and Golden Tate are each listed with an additional 21 yards due to two Week 9 screen passes that were scored by the league as laterals.

• Players who played for multiple teams in 2012 are only listed in team chapters with stats from that specific team; combined stats are listed in the player comments section.

Rushing statistics (Table 4) start with DYAR and DVOA, then list rushing plays and net yards along with average yards per carry and rushing touchdowns. The final two columns are fumbles (**Fum**)—both those lost to the defense and those recovered by the offense—and Success Rate (**Suc**), explained earlier in this chapter. Fumbles listed in the rushing table include all quarterback fumbles on sacks and aborted snaps, as well as running back fumbles on receptions, but not wide receiver fumbles.

Receiving statistics (Table 5) start with DYAR and DVOA and then list the number of passes thrown to this receiver (**Plays**), the number of passes caught (**Catch**) and the total receiving yards (**Yds**). Yards per catch (**Y/C**) includes total yardage per reception, based on standard play-by-play, while yards after catch (**YAC**) is based on information from our game charting project. Finally we list total receiving touchdowns, and catch percentage (**C%**), which is the percentage of passes intended for this receiver which were caught. Wide receivers, tight ends, and running backs are separated on the table by horizontal lines.

Performance Based on Personnel

These tables provide a look at performance in 2012 based on personnel packages, as defined above in the section on marking formation/personnel as part of the Football Outsiders game charting project. There are four different tables, representing:

• Offense based on personnel
• Offense based on opponent's defensive personnel
• Defense based on personnel
• Defense based on opponent's offensive personnel

Most of these tables feature the top five personnel groupings for each team. Occasionally, we will list the personnel group which ranks sixth if the sixth group is either particularly interesting or nearly as common as the fifth group. Each personnel group is listed with its frequency among 2012 plays, yards per play, and DVOA. Offensive personnel are also listed with how often the team in question called a running play instead of a pass play from given personnel. (Quarterback scrambles are included as pass plays, not runs.)

Offensive personnel are given in the standard two-digit format where the first digit is running backs and the second digit is tight ends. You can figure out wide receivers by subtracting that total from five, with a couple of exceptions. Plays with six or seven offensive linemen will have a three-digit listing such as "611" or "622." Any play with a direct snap to a non-quarterback, or with a specific running quarterback taking the snap instead of the regular quarterback, was counted as "Wildcat." No team ends up with Wildcat listed among its top five offensive personnel groups.

When defensive players come in to play offense, defensive backs are counted as wide receivers, linebackers as tight ends, and defensive linemen as offensive linemen, even if they are blocking fullbacks, with the exception of San Francisco's Will Tukuafu (who actually switched to No. 48 during the season because he was playing fullback so often).

When defensive personnel groups are listed in a number format such as "4-3-4," the first number is defensive linemen, the second number is linebackers, and the third number is defensive backs. Except for 4-4-3 and 3-5-3, all personnel groups with fewer than four defensive backs are combined and listed as "Goal Line." On the suggestion of some of our friends on coaching staffs and in front offices, we've grouped personnel groups with five defensive backs into two groups this year: "Nickel Odd" (1-5-5, 3-3-5, and the occasional 5-1-5) or "Nickel Even" (4-2-5 or 2-4-5). The 2-4-5 and 4-2-5 in particular are essentially the same, with the two outside linebackers in 2-4-5 usually rushing the passer. All personnel groups with at least six defensive backs are grouped together under the heading "Dime+."

11, or three-wide personnel, was by far the most common grouping in the NFL last year, used on 46 percent of plays, followed by the standard two-tight end set 12 personnel (22 percent of plays) and the more traditional 21 personnel (15 percent). The most common defensive setup was Nickel Even (36 percent), followed by 4-3-4 (27 percent) and 3-4-4 (17 percent), Dime (8.9 percent), and Nickel Odd (8.6 percent).

Strategic Tendencies

The Strategic Tendencies table (Table 6) presents a mix of information garnered from both the standard play by play and the Football Outsiders game charting project. It gives you an idea of what kind of plays teams run in what situations and with what personnel. Each category is given a league-wide **Rank** from most often (1) to least often (32) except as noted below. The sample table shown here lists the NFL average in each category for 2012.

The first column of strategic tendencies lists how often teams ran in different situations. These ratios are based on the type of play, not the actual result, so quarterback scrambles count as "passes" while quarterback sneaks, draws and option plays count as "runs."

Runs, first half and **Runs, first down** should be self evident. **Runs, second-and-long** is the percentage of runs on second down with seven or more yards to go, giving you an idea of how teams follow up a failed first down. **Runs, power situations** is the percentage of runs on third or fourth down with 1 or 2 yards to go, or at the goal line with 1 or 2 yards to go. **Runs, behind 2H** tells you how often teams ran when they were behind in the second half, generally a passing situation. **Pass, ahead 2H** tells you how often teams passed when they had the lead in the second half, generally a running situation.

In each case, you can determine the percentage of plays that were passes by subtracting the run percentage from 100 (the reverse being true for "Pass, ahead 2H," of course).

The second column gives information about offensive formations and personnel, as tracked by ESPN Stats & Information.

The first two entries detail formation, i.e. where players were lined up on the field. **Form: Single Back** lists how often the team lined up with only one player in the backfield, and **Form: Empty Back** lists how often the team lined up with no players in the backfield.

The next three entries are based on personnel, no matter where players were lined up in the formation. **Pers: 3+ WR** marks how often the team plays with three or more wide receivers. **Pers: 4+ WR** marks how often the team plays with four or more wide receivers. (Although announcers will often refer to a play as "five-wide," formations with five wide receivers are actually quite uncommon.) **Pers: 2+ TE/6+ OL**

marks how often the team plays with either more than one tight end or more than five offensive linemen. Finally, we give the percentage of plays where a team used **Shotgun or Pistol** in 2012. This does not count "Wildcat" or direct snap plays involving a non-quarterback.

The third column shows how the defensive **Pass Rush** worked in 2012.

Rush 3/Rush 4/Rush 5/Rush 6+: The percentage of pass plays (including quarterback scrambles) on which our game charters recorded this team rushing the passer with three or fewer defenders, four defenders, five defenders, and six or more defenders. These percentages do not include goal-line plays on the one- or two-yard line.

Sacks by LB/Sacks by DB: The percentage of this team's sacks that came from linebackers and defensive backs. To figure out the percentage of sacks from defensive linemen, simply subtract the sum of these numbers from 100 percent.

The fourth column has more data on the use of defensive backs.

4 DB/5DB/6+ DB: The percentage of plays where this defense lined up with four, five, and six or more defensive backs.

CB by Sides: One of the most important lessons from game charting is that each team's best cornerback does not necessarily match up against the opponent's best receiver. Most cornerbacks play a particular side of the field and in fact cover a wider range of receivers than we assumed before we saw the charting data. This metric looks at which teams prefer to leave their starting cornerbacks on specific sides of the field. It replaces a metric from previous books called "CB1 on WR1," which looked at the same question but through the lens of how often the top cornerback covered the opponent's top receiver.

To figure CB by Sides, we took the top two cornerbacks from each team and looked at the percentage of passes where that cornerback was in coverage on the left or right side of the field, ignoring passes marked as "middle." For each of the two cornerbacks, we took the higher number, right or left, and then we averaged the two cornerbacks to get the final CB by Sides rating. Teams which prefer to leave their cornerbacks in the same place, such as Seattle, Atlanta, and Cincinnati, will have high ratings. Teams that do more to move their best cornerback around to cover the opponent's top targets, such as Arizona, Denver, and Houston, will have low ratings.

DB Blitz: A new item for this year's book, we have data on how often the defense used at least one defensive back in the pass rush courtesy of ESPN Stats & Information.

Hole in Zone: The percentage of passes where this defense was listed with "Hole in Zone" in the column for pass coverage. Obviously, it can be hard to determine whether a defense is trying to play a man or zone coverage, so these numbers are

Table 6: League Average Strategic Tendencies

Run/Pass	Rk	Formation	Rk	Pass Rush	Rk	Secondary	Rk	Strategy	Rk
Runs, first half	43%	6	Form: Single Back	47%	31	Rush 3	4.8%	21	4 DB	41%	23	Play action	35%	3
Runs, first down	54%	6	Form: Empty Back	2%	30	Rush 4	73.9%	7	5 DB	55%	2	Avg Box (Off)	6.67	3
Runs, second-long	45%	3	Pers: 3+ WR	39%	29	Rush 5	17.0%	23	6+ DB	3%	21	Avg Box (Def)	6.32	23
Runs, power sit.	42%	28	Pers: 4+ WR	0%	30	Rush 6+	4.3%	28	CB by Sides	81%	9	Offensive Pace	29.72	12
Runs, behind 2H	24%	28	Pers: 2+ TE/6+ OL	36%	10	Sacks by LB	13.6%	23	DB Blitz	5%	29	Defensive Pace	30.19	18
Pass, ahead 2H	43%	22	Shotgun/Pistol	35%	29	Sacks by DB	5.7%	15	Hole in Zone	13%	2	Go for it on 4th	0.75	27

imperfect, but we think they provide a general idea of whether a team's defense is more man- or zone-based.

Finally, in the final column, we have some elements of game strategy.

Play action: The percentage of pass plays (including quarterback scrambles) which began with a play-action fake to the running back. This percentage does not include fake end-arounds unless there was also a fake handoff. It does include flea flickers.

Average Box: Another item added to our charting this year courtesy of ESPN Stats & Information is the number of defenders in the box before the snap. We list the average box faced by each team's offense and the average box used by this team's defense.

Offensive Pace: Situation-neutral pace represents the seconds of game clock per offensive play, with the following restrictions: no drives are included if they start in the fourth quarter or final five minutes of the first half, and drives are only included if the score is within six points or less. Teams are ranked from quickest pace (New England, 24.5 seconds) to slowest pace (San Francisco, 33.2 seconds).

Defensive Pace: Situation-neutral pace based on seconds of game clock per defensive play. This is a representation of how a defense was approached by its opponents, not the strategy of the defense itself (an issue discussed in the Indianapolis chapter of *PFP 2006*). Teams are ranked from quickest pace (Houston, 28.5 seconds) to slowest pace (St. Louis, 32.4 seconds).

Go for it on fourth: This is the aggressiveness index (AI) introduced by Jim Armstrong in *Pro Football Prospectus 2006*, which measures how often a team goes for a first down in various fourth down situations compared to the league average. A coach over 1.00 is more aggressive, and one below 1.00 is less aggressive. Coaches are ranked from most aggressive to least aggressive. Contrary to popular wisdom, coaches on the whole have actually been less aggressive in recent seasons than they were five or six years ago. We recently re-did the Aggressiveness Index numbers to account for recent changes in the baseline, and even after making changes, the AI for the league in 2012 was still below 1.00.

Following each strategic tendencies table, you'll find a series of comments highlighting interesting data from that team's charting numbers. This includes DVOA ratings split for things like different formations, draw plays, or play-action passing. Please note that all DVOA ratings given in these comments are standard DVOA with no adjustments for the specific situation being analyzed, and the average DVOA for a specific situation will not necessarily be 0%. For example, the average offensive DVOA on play-action passes in 2012 was 21.9%. The average offensive DVOA when the quarterback was hurried was -90.9%; if we remove sacks, scrambles, and intentional grounding and only look at actual passes, the average offensive DVOA was -30.4%.

Previous books included an item in the Strategic Tendencies table called "max protect." Although we have not included it in the table this year, we do discuss it in some of the Strategic Tendencies comments. Max protect is defined as all passing plays where blockers outnumber pass rushers by at least two, with a minimum of seven blockers.

How to Read the Offensive Line Tables

This year's book includes expanded offensive line tables (Table 7) featuring individual statistics for the first time. For years, our game charters have marked blown blocks not just on sack but also on hurries, hits, and runs stuffed at the line. Unfortunately, in past years charters were so inconsistent about their frequency of marking blown blocks (except on sacks) that we couldn't really trust the numbers enough to present them to readers with any kind of confidence. This year, after the 2012 season ended, we went back and dedicated time to checking plays with possible blown blocks in order to create more consistency between charters. The result is much more useful numbers for individual linemen.

However, while we have blown blocks to mark bad plays, we still don't have a metric that consistently marks good plays, so blown blocks should not be taken as the end all and be all of judging individual linemen. It's simply one measurement that goes into the conversation.

All offensive linemen who had at least 100 snaps in 2012 (not including special teams) are listed in the offensive line tables along with the position they played most often and their **Age** as of the 2013 season, listed simply as the difference between birth year and 2013. Players born in January and December of the same year will have the same listed age.

Then we list games, games started, snaps, and offensive

Table 7: Seattle Seahawks Offensive Line

Player	Pos	Age	GS	Snaps	Pen	Sk	Pass	Run	Player	Pos	Age	GS	Snaps	Pen	Sk	Pass	Run
Breno Giacomini	RT	28	16/16	1006	13	4	25	8	John Moffitt	LG	27	8/6	403	4	0	6	5.5
Paul McQuistan	RG	30	16/16	992	8	1.5	13.5	11	James Carpenter	LG	24	7/7	344	1	2	2	2.5
Max Unger	C	27	16/16	977	2	0.5	6.5	3	J.R. Sweezy	G	24	13/3	295	4	0	5	1
Russell Okung	LT	26	15/15	911	11	2.5	8.5	4	Frank Omiyale*	G/T	31	16/1	114	1	0	1	0

Year	Yards	ALY	Rk	Power	Rk	Stuff	Rk	2nd Lev	Rk	Open Field	Rk	Sacks	ASR	Rk	Short	Long	F-Start	Cont.
2010	3.90	3.67	28	48%	29	26%	32	1.06	21	0.84	11	35	6.2%	14	15	14	21	21
2011	4.12	4.01	19	73%	2	18%	10	1.11	26	0.72	24	50	8.3%	24	19	18	35	27
2012	4.83	4.42	4	70%	4	15%	1	1.42	2	0.94	8	33	7.2%	20	9	19	23	23
2012 ALY by direction:		Left End 4.47 (6)			Left Tackle 4.96 (4)			Mid/Guard 3.91 (21)			Right Tackle 4.85 (1)			Right End 4.07 (16)				

penalties (**Pen**) for each lineman. Finally, there are three numbers for blown blocks in 2012.

- Blown blocks leading directly to sacks
- All blown blocks on pass plays, not only including those that lead to sacks but also those that lead to hurries, hits, or offensive holding penalties
- All blown blocks on run plays; generally this means plays where the running back is tackled for a loss or no gain, but it also includes a handful of plays where the running back would have been tackled for a loss if not for a broken tackle, as well as offensive holding penalties on running plays

Players are given half a blown block when two offensive players are listed with blown blocks on the same play; there are also a few plays where we assigned one-third of a blown block to three different players.

As with all player tables in the team chapters, players who are no longer on the team have an asterisk and those new to the team in 2013 are in italics. For offensive line and defensive player tables, players who spent time with multiple teams in 2012 are listed with the team where they ended the season.

The second offensive line table lists the last three years of our various line stats.

The first column gives standard yards per carry by each team's running backs (**Yards**). The next two columns give Adjusted Line Yards (**ALY**) followed by rank among the 32 teams.

Power gives the percentage of runs in "power situations" that achieved a first down or touchdown. Those situations include any third or fourth down with 1 or 2 yards to go, and any runs in goal-to-go situations from the two-yard line or closer. Unlike the other rushing numbers on the Offensive Line table, Power includes quarterbacks.

Stuff gives the percentage of runs that are stuffed for zero or negative gain. Since being stuffed is bad, teams are ranked from stuffed least often (1) to most often (32).

Second Level (**2nd Lev**) Yards and **Open Field** Yards represent yardage where the running back has the most power over the amount of the gain. Second Level Yards represent the number of yards per carry that come 5 to 10 yards past the line of scrimmage. Open Field Yards represent the number of yards per carry that come 11 or more yards past the line of scrimmage. A team with a low ranking in Adjusted Line Yards but a high ranking in Open Field Yards is heavily dependent on its running back breaking long runs to make the running game work, and therefore tends to have a less consistent running attack. Second Level Yards fall somewhere in between.

The next five columns give information about pass protection. That starts with total sacks, followed by Adjusted Sack Rate (**ASR**) and its rank among the 32 teams. Some teams allow a lot of sacks because they throw a lot of passes; Adjusted Sack Rate accounts for this by dividing sacks and intentional grounding by total pass plays. It is also adjusted for situation (sacks are much more common on third down, particularly third-and-long) and opponent, all of which makes it a better measurement than raw sack totals. Remember that quarterbacks share responsibility for sacks, and two different quarterbacks behind the same line can have very different Adjusted

Sack Rates. We also give two specific totals that come from J.J. Cooper's sack-timing project. **Short Sacks** are the total of sacks that took shorter than 2.5 seconds; **Long Sacks** are the total of sacks that took longer than 3.0 seconds.

F-Start gives the number of false starts, which is the offensive penalty which best correlates to both wins and wins the following season. This total includes false starts by players other than offensive linemen, but it does not include false starts on special teams. False starts in 2012 had a smaller range than usual, from nine (Atlanta) to 26 (Dallas and Washington), with the NFL average at 17.6. Finally, Continuity Score (**Cont.**) tells you how much continuity each offensive line had from game-to-game in that season. It was introduced in the Cleveland chapter of *Pro Football Prospectus 2007*. Continuity score starts with 48 and then subtracts:

- The number of players over five who started at least one game on the offensive line;
- The number of times the team started at least one different lineman compared to the game before; and
- The difference between 16 and that team's longest streak where the same line started consecutive games.

The perfect Continuity Score is 48, achieved last year by the Jets, Vikings, and 49ers.. The lowest Continuity Score belonged to San Diego and Indianapolis at 22. The NFL average was 32.5.

Finally, underneath the table in italics we give 2012 Adjusted Line Yards in each of the five directions with rank among the 32 teams. Note that the league average is usually higher on the left than the right, although last year the highest average was on runs around right end. Specifically in 2012, the league average was 3.95 on left end runs, 4.00 on left tackle runs, 4.05 on runs up the middle, 3.99 on right tackle runs, and 4.12 on right end runs.

How to Read the Defensive Front Seven Tables

Defensive players make plays. Plays aren't just tackles—interceptions and pass deflections change the course of the game, and so does the act of forcing a fumble or beating the offensive players to a fumbled ball. While some plays stop a team on third down and force a punt, others merely stop a receiver after he's caught a 30-yard pass. We still cannot measure each player's opportunities to make a tackle. We can measure opportunities in pass coverage, however, thanks to the Football Outsiders game charting project.

Defensive Linemen

Defensive linemen are listed in the team chapters (Table 8, next page) if they made at least 15 plays during the 2012 season. Players are listed with the following numbers:

Age, position (**Pos**) and the number of defensive **Snaps** played in 2012.

Plays (**Plays**): The total defensive plays including tackles, pass deflections, interceptions, fumbles forced, and fumble recoveries. This number comes from the official NFL game-books and therefore does not include plays on which the player is listed by the Football Outsiders game charting project as in coverage, but does not appear in the standard play-by-play. Special teams tackles are also not included.

Percentage of Team Plays (**TmPct**): The percentage of total team plays involving this defender. The sum of the percentages of team plays for all defenders on a given team will exceed 100 percent, primarily due to shared tackles. This number is adjusted based on games played, so an injured player may be fifth on his team in plays but third in **TmPct**.

Stops (**Stop**): The total number of plays which prevent a "success" by the offense (45 percent of needed yards on first down, 60 percent on second down, 100 percent on third or fourth down).

Defeats (**Dfts**): The total number of plays which stop the offense from gaining first down yardage on third or fourth down, stop the offense behind the line of scrimmage, or result in a fumble (regardless of which team recovers) or interception.

Broken Tackles (**BTkl**): The number of broken tackles recorded by our game charters.

The next five columns represent runs only, starting with the number of plays each player made on Runs. Stop Rate (**St%**) gives the percentage of these run Plays which were Stops. Average Yards (**AvYd**) gives the average number of yards gained by the runner when this player is credited with making the play.

Finally, we have pass rush numbers, starting with standard NFL **Sack** totals.

Hit: To qualify as a quarterback hit, the defender must knock the quarterback to the ground in the act of throwing or after the pass is thrown. We have listed hits on all plays, including those cancelled by penalties. (After all, many of the hardest hits come on plays cancelled because the hit itself draws a roughing the passer penalty.) Because official scorers are not entirely consistent, hits are adjusted slightly based on the home team of each game.

Hurries (**Hur**): The number of quarterback hurries recorded by the Football Outsiders game charting project. This includes both hurries on standard plays and hurries that force an offensive holding penalty that cancels the play and costs the offense yardage.

Tips: The number of plays where this player batted the ball down at the line of scrimmage or tipped it in the air, usually to force an incomplete pass. Occasionally tips lead to interceptions, and even more rarely they fall into the hands of offensive receivers. Some plays counted as tips by Football Outsiders were not counted as passes defensed by the NFL.

Defensive linemen are ranked by percentage of team plays, Run Stop Rate, and average yards per run tackle. The lowest number of average yards earns the top rank (negative numbers indicate the average play ending behind the line of scrimmage). Defensive ends are ranked if they made 24 or more plays during 2012. There are 71 defensive ends who qualified. Defensive tackles are ranked if they made 20 or more plays during 2012, with 69 players ranked.

Linebackers

Linebackers are listed in team chapters if they made at least 15 plays during the season. Most of the stats for linebackers are the same as those for defensive linemen, except that the sections for pass rush and run tackles are reversed.[3] Linebackers are ranked in percentage of team plays, and also in Stop Rate and average yards for running plays specifically. Linebackers are ranked in these standard stats if they have a

Table 8: Cincinnati Benglas Defensive Front Seven

Defensive Line	Age	Pos	Snaps	Plays	TmPct	Rk	Stop	Dfts	BTkl	Runs	St%	Rk	RuYd	Rk	Sack	Hit	Hur	Tips
					Overall						vs. Run				Pass Rush			
Michael Johnson	26	DE	852	53	6.3%	22	40	20	1	30	73%	45	2.5	42	12.5	8	10	2
Geno Atkins	25	DT	785	55	6.6%	7	49	30	1	35	86%	5	1.5	14	13	8	30	2
Domata Peko	29	DT	649	56	6.7%	5	42	9	1	47	72%	43	2.2	29	2	3	6	2
Robert Geathers	30	DE	646	30	3.6%	62	24	11	2	23	74%	42	1.7	12	3	3	10.5	0
Carlos Dunlap	24	DE	586	42	5.7%	30	35	21	3	25	80%	18	1.6	10	5.5	7	13	3
Wallace Gilberry	29	DE	308	24	3.3%	68	17	8	0	14	71%	49	2.7	50	6.5	5	7	0
Pat Sims*	28	DT	181	18	4.3%	--	10	3	1	16	56%	--	2.3	--	0	0	1	0

Linebackers	Age	Pos	Snaps	Plays	TmPct	Rk	Stop	Dfts	BTkl	Sack	Hit	Hur	Tips	Runs	St%	Rk	Yds	Rk	Tgts	Suc%	Rk	AdjYd	Rk	PD
					Overall					Pass Rush				vs. Run					vs. Pass					
Rey Maualuga	26	MLB	1022	126	15.1%	23	62	10	6	1	3	4	0	65	57%	95	4.6	104	59	53%	30	7.0	47	5
Vontaze Burfict	23	OLB	885	129	15.4%	20	58	18	8	1	2	2.5	1	72	54%	101	3.5	58	40	41%	64	6.9	45	1
Manny Lawson*	29	OLB	353	38	4.5%	108	16	5	3	2	0	2	0	19	47%	106	4.6	105	17	42%	63	8.7	70	0
James Harrison	35	OLB	811	69	11.3%	58	53	13	4	6	7	12	0	51	82%	9	2.2	17	13	36%	--	7.6	--	0

Year	Yards	ALY	Rk	Power	Rk	Stuff	Rk	2nd Level	Rk	Open Field	Rk	Sacks	ASR	Rk	Short	Long
2010	4.53	4.19	19	73%	32	18%	22	1.17	21	1.05	30	27	5.3%	30	6	13
2011	4.09	3.78	5	66%	23	20%	17	1.03	4	0.88	21	45	7.3%	10	15	20
2012	4.05	4.04	16	82%	32	18%	21	1.19	17	0.48	6	51	8.7%	2	13	22
2012 ALY by direction:		Left End 3.87 (13)			Left Tackle 3.3 (5)			Mid/Guard 4.23 (20)			Right Tackle 4.35 (27)				Right End 3.56 (10)	

[3] To be honest, this is a vestigial remnant of how we built these tables in previous books. By the time we realized things should be switched to look just like the defensive line, the book was mostly laid out. We'll take care of that next year.

minimum of 45 plays or 10 games started. Outside, inside (3-4), and middle (4-3) linebackers are all ranked together, with 110 players ranked in total.

The final six columns in the linebacker stats come from the Football Outsiders game charting project.

Targets (**Tgts**): The number of pass players on which our game charters listed this player in coverage.

Success Rate (**Suc%**): The percentage plays of targeting this player on which the offense did not have a successful play. This means not only incomplete passes and interceptions, but also short completions which do not meet our baselines for success (45 percent of needed yards on first down, 60 percent on second down, 100 percent on third or fourth down). Success Rate is adjusted for the quality of the receiver covered.

Adjusted Yards per Pass (**AdjYd**): The average number of yards gained on plays on which this defender was the listed target, adjusted for the quality of the receiver covered.

Passes Defensed (**PD**): Football Outsiders' count of passes defensed. Unlike the official NFL count of passes defensed, this does not include passes batted down or tipped at the line.

These stats, including other differences between the NFL's count of passes defensed and our own, are explained in more detail in the section on secondary tables. Plays listed with two defenders or as "Hole in Zone" with this defender as the closest player count only for half credit in computing both Success Rate and Average Yards per Pass. Seventy-six linebackers are ranked in the charting stats, with a minimum of 16 charted passes. As a result of the different thresholds, some linebackers are ranked in standard stats but not charting stats, or vice versa.

Further Details

Just as in the offensive tables, players who are no longer on the team are marked with asterisks, and players who were on other teams last year are in italics. Other than the game charting statistics for linebackers, defensive front seven player statistics are not adjusted for opponent.

Numbers for defensive linemen and linebackers unfortunately do not reflect all of the opportunities a player had to make a play, but they do show us which players were most active on the field. A large number of plays could mean a strong defensive performance, or it could mean that the linebacker

in question plays behind a poor part of the line. In general, defensive numbers should be taken as information that tells us what happened on the field in 2012, but not as a strict, unassailable judgment of which players are better than others—particularly when the difference between two players is small (for example, players ranked 20th and 30th) instead of large (players ranked 20th and 70th).

After the individual statistics for linemen and linebackers, the Defensive Front Seven section contains a table that looks exactly like the table in the Offensive Line section. The difference is that the numbers here are for all opposing running backs against this team's defensive front. As we're on the opposite side of the ball, teams are now ranked in the opposite order, so the number one defensive front seven is the one that allows the fewest Adjusted Line Yards, the lowest percentage in Power situations, and has the highest Adjusted Sack Rate. Directions for Adjusted Line Yards are given from the offense's perspective, so runs to left end and left tackle are aimed at the right defensive end and (assuming the tight end is on the other side) weakside linebacker.

How to Read the Secondary Tables

The first few columns in the secondary tables (Table 9) are based on standard play-by-play, not game charting, with the exception of Broken Tackles. Age, Total Plays, Percentage of Team Plays, Stops, and Defeats are computed the same way they are for other defensive players, so that the secondary can be compared to the defensive line and linebackers. That means that Total Plays here includes passes defensed, sacks, tackles after receptions, tipped passes, and interceptions, but not pass plays on which this player was in coverage but was not given a tackle or passed defense by the NFL's official scorer.

The middle five columns address each defensive back's role in stopping the run. Average Yardage and Stop Rate for running plays is computed in the same manner as for defensive linemen and linebackers.

The third section of statistics represents data from the game charting project. In all game charting coverage stats, passes

Table 9: Dallas Cowboys Defensive Secondary

Secondary	Age	Pos	Snaps	Plays	Overall TmPct	Rk	Stop	Dfts	BTkl	vs. Run Runs	St%	Rk	Yds	Rk	vs. Pass Tgts	Tgt%	Rk	Dist	Suc%	Rk	APaYd	Rk	PD	Int
Brandon Carr	27	CB	1008	63	8.0%	56	22	10	5	8	38%	53	9.0	71	78	20.1%	25	12.9	56%	22	7.6	45	10	3
Gerald Sensabaugh*	30	FS	949	57	7.7%	53	10	5	4	19	26%	60	14.1	73	22	6.0%	48	10.9	39%	73	9.3	65	3	0
Morris Claiborne	23	CB	875	63	8.5%	44	18	10	4	11	18%	79	7.8	61	59	16.2%	53	13.4	41%	83	7.9	54	9	1
Danny McCray	25	SS	637	66	8.9%	47	20	7	9	28	43%	20	8.4	56	34	9.2%	13	11.4	45%	66	9.1	61	3	1
Mike Jenkins*	28	CB	357	17	2.7%	--	8	2	4	4	50%	--	11.5	--	22	6.8%	--	9.9	53%	--	6.8	--	3	0
Sterling Moore	24	CB	327	24	3.7%	--	10	4	1	3	33%	--	10.0	--	23	6.3%	--	14.8	43%	--	15.4	--	1	0
Orlando Scandrick	26	CB	326	25	4.6%	--	12	6	2	4	50%	--	5.5	--	28	10.5%	--	11.9	68%	--	5.2	--	4	0
Eric Frampton*	29	FS	194	20	3.1%	--	7	1	1	9	44%	--	8.6	--	3	1.0%	--	14.7	100%	--	0.0	--	2	0

Year	Pass D Rank	vs. #1 WR	Rk	vs. #2 WR	Rk	vs. Other WR	Rk	vs. TE	Rk	vs. RB	Rk
2010	28	44.1%	32	15.5%	26	2.9%	20	-11.9%	4	-11.2%	6
2011	22	14.0%	19	53.3%	31	-26.9%	6	19.1%	21	-3.6%	15
2012	25	-7.0%	12	11.5%	29	19.5%	28	28.9%	32	3.5%	18

where two defenders are listed and those listed as "Hole in Zone" with this player as the closest zone defender count for half credit. We do not count pass plays on which this player was in coverage, but the incomplete was listed as Thrown Away, Batted Down, or Hit in Motion. Hail Mary passes are also not included.

Targets (**Tgts**): The number of pass plays on which our game charters listed this player in coverage.

Target Percentage (**Tgt%**): The number of plays on which this player was targeted divided by the total number of charted passes against his defense, not including plays listed as Uncovered. Like Percentage of Team Plays, this metric is adjusted based on number of games played.

Distance (**Dist**): The average distance in the air beyond the line of scrimmage of all passes targeted at this defender. It does not include yards after catch, and is useful for seeing which defenders were covering receivers deeper or shorter.

Success Rate (**Suc%**): The percentage plays of targeting this player on which the offense did not have a successful play. This means not only incomplete passes and interceptions, but also short completions which do not meet our baselines for success (45 percent of needed yards on first down, 60 percent on second down, 100 percent on third or fourth down). Defensive pass interference is counted as a failure for the defensive player similar to a completion of equal yardage (and a new first down).

Adjusted Yards per Pass (**AdjYd**): The average number of yards gained on plays on which this defender was the listed target, adjusted for the quality of the receiver covered.

Passes Defensed (**PD**): This is our count of passes defensed, and will differ from the total found in NFL gamebooks. Our count includes:

- All passes listed by our charters as Defensed.
- All interceptions, or tipped passes leading to interceptions.
- Any pass on which the defender is given a pass defensed by the official scorer, and our game charter marked either Miscommunication or Caught Out of Bounds.

Our count of passes defensed does not include passes marked as defensed in the official gamebooks but listed by our charters as Overthrown, Underthrown, or Thrown Away. It also does not include passes tipped in the act of rushing the passer (which are listed in the defensive line and linebackers tables as **Tips**). In addition, this year, we did a lot of work with both the NFL head office and the folks from ESPN Stats & Information to get the most accurate numbers possible for both drops and passes defensed. Official scorers and game charters will sometimes disagree on a drop vs. a pass defensed, or even an overthrown/underthrown ball vs. a pass defensed, and there are a number of passes where the league marked the official stats in one way and ESPN marked their stats the other way. We reviewed all these passes and on each one chose to either

go with the NFL's decision or ESPN Stats & Information's decision, so for 2012 we no longer have passes where we were unsure whether to give a pass defensed (as given by the NFL) or a drop (as given by charters). Each pass is marked as one or the other.

Interceptions (**Int**) represent the standard NFL interception total.

Cornerbacks need 40 charted passes or eight games started to be ranked in the defensive stats, with 87 cornerbacks ranked in total. Safeties need 16 charted passes or eight games started to be ranked in the defensive stats, with 75 safeties ranked in total. (We made an exception and did not rank Louis Delmas of Detroit, who had just eight targets in eight games started and would have topped the coverage rankings based on a tiny sample size.) Strong and free safeties are ranked together.

Just like the front seven, the secondary has a table of team statistics following the individual numbers. This table gives DVOA figured against different types of receivers. Each offense's wide receivers have had one receiver designated as number one, and another as number two. (Occasionally this is difficult, due to injury or an amorphous wide receiver corps like last year's Rams, but it's usually pretty obvious.) The other receivers form a third category, with tight ends and running backs as fourth and fifth categories. The defense is then judged on the performance of each receiver based on the standard DVOA method, with each rating adjusted based on strength of schedule. (Opponents with Roddy White and Calvin Johnson as top receivers, for example, are tougher than an opponent with Justin Blackmon as its number one receiver.) **Pass D Rank** is the total ranking of the pass defense, as seen before in the Trends and Splits table, and combines all five categories plus sacks and passes with no intended target.

The "defense vs. types of receivers" table should be used to analyze the defense as a whole rather than individual players. The ratings against types of receivers are generally based on defensive schemes, not specific cornerbacks, and the ratings against tight ends and running backs are in large part due to the performance of linebackers.

How to Read the Special Teams Tables

The special teams tables list the last three years of kick, punt, and return numbers for each team.

The first two columns list total special teams DVOA and rank among the 32 teams (Table 10). The next two columns list the value in actual points of field goals and extra points (**FG/XP**) when compared to how a league average kicker would do from the same distances, adjusted for weather and altitude, and rank among the 32 teams. Next, we list the estimated value in actual

Table 10: Philadelphia Eagles Special Teams

Year	DVOA	Rank	FG/XP	Rank	Net Kick	Rank	Kick Ret	Rank	Net Punt	Rank	Punt Ret	Rank	Hidden	Rank
2010	2.3%	12	3.7	9	8.2	7	-9.9	29	8.6	8	1.1	15	-5.1	20
2011	0.0%	17	3.9	9	7.5	5	-3.5	23	0.1	16	-7.9	27	1.7	14
2012	-2.2%	23	0.9	17	3.3	10	-0.5	18	-18.2	32	3.3	8	-9.1	29

points of field position over or under the league average based on net kickoffs (**Net Kick**), and rank that value among the 32 teams. That is followed by the estimated point values of field position for kick returns (**Kick Ret**), net punting (**Net Punt**), and punt returns (**Punt Ret**) and their respective ranks.

The final two columns represent the value of "**Hidden**" special teams, plays which throughout the past decade have usually been based on the performance of opponents without this team being able to control the outcome. We combine the opposing team's value on field goals, kickoff distance, and punt distance, adjusted for weather and altitude, and then switch the sign to represent that good special teams by the opponent will cost the listed team points, and bad special teams will effectively hand them points. We have to give the qualifier of "usually" because, as explained above, certain returners such as Devin Hester will affect opposing special teams strategy, and a handful of the missed field goals are blocked. Nonetheless, the "hidden" value is still "hidden" for most teams, and they are ranked from the most hidden value gained (Tampa Bay, 28.5 points) to the most value lost (Baltimore, -21.7 points). The best and worst individual values for kickers, punters, and returners are listed in the statistical appendix at the end of the book.

Administrative Minutia

Receiving statistics include all passes intended for the receiver in question, including those that are incomplete or intercepted. The word passes refers to both complete and incomplete pass attempts. When rating receivers, interceptions are treated as incomplete passes with no penalty.

For the computation of DVOA and DYAR, passing statistics include sacks as well as fumbles on aborted snaps. We do not include kneeldown plays or spikes for the purpose of stopping the clock. Some interceptions which we have determined to be "Hail Mary" plays that end the first half or game are counted as regular incomplete passes, not turnovers.

All statistics generated by ESPN Stats & Information or the Football Outsiders game charting project may be different from totals compiled by other sources.

Unless we say otherwise, when we refer to third-down performance in this book we are referring to a combination of third down and the handful of rushing and passing plays that take place on fourth down (primarily fourth-and-1).

Aaron Schatz

The Year In Quotes

THE DEVIL WENT DOWN TO BALTIMORE, HE WAS LOOKING FOR A LINEBACKER

"That's the trick of the devil. The trick of the devil is to kill, steal and destroy. That's what he comes to do. He comes to distract you from everything you're trying to do."

—**Ray Lewis**, on PED allegations (Deadspin)

"As a kid and young adult you make mistakes and I have made some. I have tried to do good, but sometimes the devil wins."

—**Rolando McClain**, right after signing on with Baltimore, but before retiring (Madison Weekly News)

EH, WHAT INCENTIVE DOES DELANEY HAVE TO LIE BESIDES COUNTLESS DOLLAR BILLS, SLUSH FUNDS, AND PROTECTING AN INSTITUTION THAT GETS TO KEEP NEARLY ALL OF ITS PROFITS?

"...it has been my longstanding belief that The Big Ten's schools would forgo the revenues in those circumstances and instead take steps to downsize the scope, breadth and activity of their athletic programs. Several alternatives to a 'pay for play' model exist, such as the Division III model, which does not offer any athletics-based grants-in-aid, and, among others, a need-based financial model. These alternatives would, in my view, be more consistent with The Big Ten's philosophy that the educational and lifetime economic benefits associated with a university education are the appropriate quid pro quo for its student athletes."

—Big Ten commissioner **Jim Delaney**, on the conference possibly moving down to Division III if college athletes are paid (Sports Illustrated)

WE WILL USE THESE FINES TO CREATE NEW STUDIES, WHICH YOU'LL NEVER SEE, WHICH WE'LL USE TO CREATE MORE RULES, TO CREATE MORE FINES, TO...

"Absolutely not. It's about protecting the players. I've been on the Committee for 20 years and it's never been a discussion in our room of, 'Well we're worried about a litigation about this or a litigation about a knee injury.' We're worried about player safety and I think one of the great things about the league is it's been a focus of ours for a long time and there's such a long process that goes into it."

—Falcons president **Rich McKay**, on the new rule preventing running backs from leading with their helmets (Pro Football Talk)

EVERYONE KNOWS 21ST CENTURY COLLEGES WERE BASICALLY EXPENSIVE DAYCARE CENTERS

"Unbelievable. This is what I get paid to do. Seriously. Create nap time. It's pathetic."

—Northwestern head coach **Pat Fitzgerald**, on his team lobbying for a nap before the game starts (Chicago Tribune)

THE YEAR IN TELLING QUOTES ABOUT REPLACEMENT OFFICIALS

"No timeout will be charged to Arizona."

—NFL replacement official **Craig Ochoa**, live from the Atlanta-Baltimore preseason game (Deadspin)

"It seems as if, after every call, all 35 refs come sprinting in to discuss the merits of Kafka's Metamorphosis as it relates to the economy of Bangladesh, and just when you think they've finally figured it out, they reconvene for Round 2. Then Round 3. I saw a baby born in the stadium reach full walking status during one ref conference, and at the end of it, when they finally announced something, no one had any idea whether it was even the right decision or not. We didn't care at that point; we just wanted to move on to the next play so we could finish the game before the Mayan apocalypse. I am slightly curious how the TV networks are going to handle eight-hour games."

—Raiders punter **Chris Kluwe**, on the replacement refs (Deadspin)

"Are they going to be Tom Brady? No. But they can be a Matt Hasselbeck."

—NFL vice president **Ray Anderson**, on replacement officials (CBS Sports)

"That is the beauty of sports and the beauty of officiating, that there are controversial calls and people see them differently. I understand that. That is the beauty of sports."

—NFL commissioner **Roger Goodell**, on Golden Tate's Hail Mary "catch" (Shutdown Corner)

I GUESS JOE WASN'T REALLY PAYING ATTENTION TO FOOTBALL IN 2000

"If you tell Ray you hear he's not playing any more, he'd freaking kill you."

—Ravens quarterback **Joe Flacco**, on Ray Lewis (said before Lewis tore his triceps in the middle of the season) (Ed Werder, ESPN)

THE FOCUS GROUP CONFERENCE OF AMERICA

"We have no plans to change the name. We are looking at pretty much everything, because the conference is reinvented. We're reinventing it. Obviously it's going to be a bigger conference, it's going to be a more national conference in scope."

—Big East commissioner **Mike Aresco**, on the future of his conference's name (Dr. Saturday)

"We worked with our institutions, sports marketing experts, media partners, and also solicited opinions and reactions from collegiate sports fans to create a compelling list of names. Versions that included the word 'American' led every list. American Athletic Conference represents a strong, durable and aspirational name for our reinvented Conference."

—American Athletic Conference commissioner **Mike Aresco**, on the name change (College Football Talk)

TOM BRADY SCHOOL FOR QUARTERBACKS WHO CAN'T READ GOOD AND WANT TO MAKE OTHER GOOD THROWS TOO

"He's such a good-looking guy. Obviously, he gets banged up, and he's probably the toughest metrosexual I've ever come across."

—Patriots wideout **Wes Welker**, on Tom Brady (Boston Herald)

STILL SLIGHTLY LESS CREEPY THAN BRENT MUSBURGER...

"Aye @_KatherineWebb hit me (240) 464-4150 when game over, lets go to wing stop then King of diamond."

—Cardinals defensive lineman **Darnell Dockett**, hitting on Alabama quarterback A.J. McCarron's girlfriend during the National Championship Game (SB Nation)

"If I really wanted to get his girl there's a bunch of different ways I'd have went about it. And I would have got her if I really wanted her. But I don't think she's my type. I'm not into the thinner girls and the modelling thing like that. I like hood chicks. I like girls with a couple stab wounds, bullet holes, been knocked up a few times. ... I like girls who you know have bad credit when they're 21."

—**Dockett**, on his Twitter "flirting" with Katherine Webb (Sports Radio Interviews)

WHEN YOU'RE READY TO QUIT PLAYING FOOTBALL, THE *FO* OFFICE IS HERE TO MAKE YOU FEEL BETTER ABOUT YOUR PHYSIQUE

"That dude, I was just watching him run at minicamp, and that dude has got muscles on top of muscles, and he eats like two quarts of Cold Stone a day. I have one bite of pizza and I put 13 pounds on. It's just ridiculous. This guy's got two percent body fat, shredded. I'm leaving my shirt on at the pool. It sucks."

—Vikings defensive end **Jared Allen**, on the enviable body of teammate Adrian Peterson (Pro Football Talk)

OH, NO! WE SUCK AGAIN!

"It was frustrating. You always think what could I have done better? Maybe I could've drank more water during the week. I should've known better. I knew it was going to be a hard-fought game. I needed to be hydrated. I totally blame myself."

—LSU linebacker **Kevin Minter**, on how humidity played a role in LSU's defeat at Florida (Shreveport Times)

WHEN EMPLOYED BY TOM COUGHLIN, ONE FUMBLE CAN BE A LIFE-CHANGING EVENT

"I'm like birth control. You have to believe in me. Like birth control, 99.9 percent of the time I'm going to come through for you."

—Giants running back **David Wilson** (Newsday)

SANS BITCH, AS THE FRENCH IN FRANCE SAY

"I want to stress ... that nothing about what I have learned has shaken my faith in Manti Te'o one iota ... The single most trusting human being I've ever met will never be able to trust in the same way for the rest of his life."

—Notre Dame athletic director **Jack Swarbick**, on the Manti Te'o saga (Pro Football Talk)

JOE FLACCO ACTUALLY DOES THINK WHITEWASHING IS POWERFUL FUN

"Joe is dull. As dull as he is portrayed in the media, he's that dull. He is dull."

—Joe Flacco's dad, **Steve Flacco**, on his son (New York Times)

"Just gonna look at it I guess."

—**Flacco**, on the money in his giant new contract (Will Brinson, CBS Sports)

I'M SURE THERE IS SOME WAY THAT NCAA RULES DISAGREE WITH THIS ASSERTION

"You can't get more possession than shoving it down your pants."

—Pullman police commander **Chris Tennant**, on redshirt freshman Washington State football player Drew Loftus attempting to steal tequila bottles by hiding them in the waistband of his pants (Deadspin)

SO THAT'S WHY REGGIE BUSH LEFT MIAMI

"That's you guys, how much you love [him]. Everybody loves him, but the same people go with the Kardashians. I don't know what they did, either."

—Dolphins receiver **Brian Hartline**, on Tim Tebow (South Florida Sun-Sentinel)

GET OVER TO KOHLINGEN AND BUY SOME REVIVIFY

"I think it's mixed. I think some it's stellar. I think Gino [Simone], Gino's a guy elected team captain this week. Came from not playing hardly at all to elected team captain. A lot of it is just he's kind of accelerated his focus and effort. Some of them have been great and some of them have been very poor. Some of them have had kind of this zombie-like, go through the motions, everything is like how it's always been, that's how it'll always be. Some of them quite honestly have an empty corpse quality. That's not pleasant to say or pleasant to think about, but that's a fact. That's why it's been necessary for us to have the youth moment that we've had."

—Washington State head coach **Mike Leach**, on his seniors being leaders (The Spokesman Review)

"Our five couldn't whip their two. Sometimes they only brought two. Our five couldn't whip their two. Which means, if five of our guys went in an alley and got in a fight with two of theirs, we would have gotten massacred. That's just ridiculously inexcusable. It was one of the most heartless efforts up front I've seen, and our defensive line wasn't any better."

—Washington State head coach **Mike Leach**, on the performance of his offensive line against Utah (Scout.com)

YES, IF ONLY NORV HAD THAT SEVENTH SEASON, THINGS WOULD HAVE TURNED AROUND

"Norv never really got a fair shake. I hope the next guy gets a fair shake."

—Chargers quarterback **Philip Rivers**, on recently fired Norv Turner (SI.com)

NO FRIENDS, HE'S TALKING ABOUT HIMSELF! BUT THANKS FOR LOOKING!

"I'll start with the football game. First of all, it wasn't very pretty to watch. It wasn't pretty to sit on the sideline and watch as a player, it sucks I can't do anything about it. Do I feel that we, at times, gave up out there? Absolutely. As a leader it sucks to see people not do their jobs and to see things go wrong, there has been a lot of things go that way. As a leader, at this point you have to look forward. There has been a lot of people jump off of the bandwagon and it is my job to keep everyone in this organization and this team in that locker room together. I am going to make sure of it going forward. We've got a big game against Rutgers next week. I am going to do everything in my power to be a part of it and be the starting quarterback when we run out onto the field. And most importantly, get a win. You have to start with one before you can get the rest of them. I give you my word, I am going to do the best I can to make that happen."

—Arkansas quarterback **Tyler Wilson**, on his team's "performance" against Alabama (College Football Talk)

"Smile! Smile! OK? Dang, you guys all right? If not, I'm not talking!"

—Ex-Arkansas interim head coach **John L. Smith**, during his press conference (College Football Talk)

GENE, WHAT WOULD YOU SAY ... YOU DO HERE?

"We've got to become a more talented team. It does start with talent. We can be a more talented team. You're always looking to add."

—Jaguars then-general manager **Gene Smith**, on his roster (AP)

CHARLIE WEIS IS GOING TO START KICKING AIR LIKE THIS, AND IF ANY PART OF YOU SHOULD FILL THAT AIR, IT'S YOUR FAULT

"I just simply advised him that if he did ask questions, he should be prepared for any kind of tone in his answer."

—Kansas director of football communications **Katy Longeran**, to a student reporter who wrote unflattering things about Charlie Weis (Daily Kansan)

EXCUSE ME STEWARDESS, I SPEAK JIVE

"Just gobble, gobble, gobble turkey from jive turkey gobblers ... that paints a pretty good picture. He's a very confident guy."

—49ers head coach **Jim Harbaugh**, on questions about Alex Smith's confidence (SB Nation)

JASON CAMPBELL'S AUBURN SQUAD WILL BE UP FIRST, RIGHT?

"I think we will get people saying 'hey the BCS was pretty good.' I think you will be surprised by how many people down the road will say that."

—BCS Executive Director **Bill Hancock**, on comparisons between the future four-team playoff and the BCS (Sports Radio Interviews)

DON'T GIVE SUH A TARGET

"I don't know too much about Adderall. I know guys, it is such a competitive league, guys try anything just to get that edge. I'm fortunate enough to be blessed with size and some smarts to give me my edge. But some guys, they'll do whatever they can to get an edge. I've heard of some crazy stories. I've heard (of) guys using like Viagra, seriously. Because the blood is supposedly thin, some crazy stuff. So, you know, it's kind of scary with some of these chemicals that are in some of these things so you have to be careful."

—Bears receiver **Brandon Marshall**, on the recent uptick in Adderall suspensions (Kissing Suzy Kolber)

CHAIRMAN BRINGS THE ROOM TO ORDER FOR PROPOSED NCAA REGULATION 11000839-B, THE REGULATION OF ROCKET POPSICLES

"I don't want to give out average Popsicles. We give out them bomb Popsicles. You know, the ones as a kid you love to have? These things are the mac daddy of Popsicles. We're giving out BCS-level, playoff-bound rocket Popsicles. And if they come out with a better one, we're going to get a better Popsicle. But the rockets are pretty good."

—Arizona head coach **Rich Rodriguez**, on post-practice popsicles (USA Today)

MARK RICHT HAS LOST CONTROL OF HIS HIP

"I was trying to show her what a good swinger I was. I was swinging really high on a big heavy swing set with those big heavy chains. Sometimes if you go super high, on the way back you get a little bit of that lag. You've got those big S-hooks on top, and you're swinging, and I swung enough to where the one on the left came out. So it comes out, but I didn't know. I'm still on the swing. So when I come back down, the chain on [on the right] stayed taut and the other one just goes. I turned sideways and the first thing that hits the ground is my left hip. Just smashed it. It was traumatic. I mean, when I hit I was like, 'I think I broke it.' I couldn't hardly breathe. Sometimes with an injury like that you get a full-body sweat and a little nauseous. But the pain kind of went away and I went about my business, until about a year and a half ago."

—Georgia head coach **Mark Richt**, revealing the back story behind a recent P90X injury leading him to hip-replacement surgery (Atlanta Journal-Constitution)

WILD HORSES COULDN'T KEEP ME AWAY ... INVISIBLE ROBOTS!?

"No. They're still using human beings."

—Vikings defensive end **Jared Allen**, on if teams are blocking him differently this year (Pro Football Talk)

HAVE YOU EVER BEEN TO A TURKISH PRISON?

"Did you come away with any more clarity on the receiving corps?"

"Did you?"

"No."

"OK. Next question."

...

"Coach does your offense need to be more effective against Ohio State next week?"

"Yes. Next question."

...

"I'm just loving all these questions 'cause they're great ones."

—Michigan State head coach **Mark Dantonio**, blowing up his press conference (SB Nation)

GOSH, IF ONLY THE NATIONAL MEDIA GAVE THE COWBOYS ANY LOVE

"It is a reminder that I've been here when it was gloryhole days and I've been here when it wasn't. And so having said that, I want me some gloryhole."

—Cowboys owner **Jerry Jones**, on the glory of the past (YouTube)

EXCEPT DURING THE CRUSADES

"Ricky, never bet against the Catholics."

—ESPN personality **Lee Corso**, explaining his Notre Dame win prediction (Awful Announcing)

SOUNDS LIKE A NEW SLOGAN FOR THE *FO* BANNER

"Stats are for girls."

—Giants receiver **Hakeem Nicks**, on his poor receiving statistics this season (Tom Rock, Newsday)

NEVER TELL ME THE ODDS

"We're going to compete for it, and that's still our goal ... So it doesn't change anything for us."

—North Carolina head coach **Larry Fedora**, on attempting to win the Coastal Division of the ACC despite being banned from doing so (News Observer)

YOU KEEP USING THAT WORD, I DON'T THINK IT MEANS WHAT YOU THINK IT MEANS

"I'm literally not a drinker."
—Jaguars receiver **Justin Blackmon**, on his relationship with alcohol, following his DUI arrest (Pro Football Talk)

WELL, AT LEAST *SOMEBODY* WAS WATCHING AUBURN THIS YEAR

"We always do what's in the best interest of our team. We have a curfew check and we have to employ people to help us with some of the kids off campus. Other than that I'm not going into any details of any of that."
—Auburn head coach **Gene Chizik**, on a report that Auburn has a private security firm enforcing curfew for its football players (Montgomery Advertiser)

WE'RE *REALLY* NOT SELLING JEANS HERE

"All of a sudden we're Moneyballing offensive linemen. The world I live in isn't a fantasy world. Those are big boys in there putting their head into another human being 75 times a game"
—Jets offensive line coach **Dave DeGuglielmo**, on statistical evaluations of his line (Fifth Down)

DON'T MIND WILL, HE'S JUST EOS'ING

"We say at our house when Will is jumping up and down and acting crazy on the sidelines, the boys and I say that he is having an EO—an emotional outburst. The boys will come home and say, 'Daddy, you had some major EOs on the sideline.'"
—Carol Muschamp, Wife of Florida head coach **Will Muschamp**, on his sideline demeanor (Gator Zone)

MAYBE NEW ENGLAND REALLY SHOULD JUST TRY TO RUN UP THE SCORE ON TEAMS

"It really [ticked] me off. It was disrespectful to us to run the same play over and over and be successful."
—Dolphins defensive lineman **Tony McDaniel**, on the Patriots running the same play over and over again in the fourth quarter (Palm Beach Post)

NOW PICTURING: BARKEVIOUS MINGO AS BANE

"(Mingo needs to) re-gear his eating apparatus,"
—LSU head coach **Les Miles**, on star defender Barkevious Mingo's weight loss (And The Valley Shook)

WHEN WILL THEY GET RID OF THE REPLACEMENT COMMISSIONER'S OFFICE?

"The Commissioner says he is disappointed in me. The truth is, I'm disappointed in him. His positions on player health and safety since a 2009 congressional hearing on concussions have been inconsistent at best. He failed to acknowledge a link between concussions & post-career brain disease, pushed for an 18-game regular season, committed to a full season of Thursday night games, has continually challenged players' rights to file workers compensation claims for on-the-job injuries, and he employed incompetent replacement officials for the start of the 2012 season. His actions or lack thereof are by the league's own definition, 'conduct detrimental.'"
—Browns linebacker **Scott Fujita**, on the NFL's continued pursuit of Saints bounty violations (Scott Fujita, Twitter)

I'D LEVEL HIM UP IN THE PYRAMID UNTIL HE'S A METALLIC CYBORG DOG

"Do you want to be a show dog or a hunting dog? [The Heisman] has nothing to do with our season. If he would win it, that would be wonderful. That's all great. But that's not for him to decide. For him to decide is what kind of teammate he's going to be. What kind of leader he's going to be and how he's going to go each week. If you want to parade him around and do all that, [fine]. I'd rather have a hunting dog."
—Florida State head coach **Jimbo Fisher**, on sudden Heisman buzz for quarterback E.J. Manuel (Orlando Sentinel)

YOUR NEUTRALNESS, IT'S A BEIGE ALERT!

"I don't know exactly how it feels, yet. I don't know quite how to feel right how. I've asked several people, some of our players. And I think they feel like I do. Don't know quite how to feel right now."
—49ers head coach **Jim Harbaugh**, after the Rams and 49ers tied (CSN Bay Area)

I WAS WORKING MY WAY UP TO LAFAYETTE

"I tell recruits and their parents when I meet with them that my two goals in college were to play football and to drink every beer in Muncie, Indiana."
—Michigan head coach **Brady Hoke**, on coaching's role in making his life a better place (Grantland)

QUOTE OF THE YEAR

"I was trying not to squeeze myself in front of women out there. I wanted to pull my pants down and run inside, but I couldn't do that. When those ants get close to those testicles, there ain't no laughing about that."
—Cowboys fullback **Lawrence Vickers**, on a poorly-timed training camp fire ant attack (Dallas Morning News)

Arizona Cardinals

2012 Record: 5-11	**Total DVOA:** -16.3% (26th)	**2013 Mean Projection:** 6.5 wins	**On the Clock (0-4):** 24%
Pythagorean Wins: 4.8 (27th)	**Offense:** -30.9% (32nd)	**Postseason Odds:** 11.8%	**Mediocrity (5-7):** 44%
Snap-Weighted Age: 27.2 (14th)	**Defense:** -13.5% (6th)	**Super Bowl Odds:** 0.6%	**Playoff Contender (8-10):** 28%
Average Opponent: 10.8% (1st)	**Special Teams:** 1.1% (11th)	**Proj. Avg. Opponent:** 0.5% (19th)	**Super Bowl Contender (11+):** 5%

2012: Come for the worst run-blocking line of the last 20 years. Stay for the parade of miserable quarterbacks.

2013: No longer the runt of the NFL's worst division; instead, Cardinals are now the runt of one of the NFL's best divisions. Is this progress?

"You gotta laugh to keep from crying."

When a team's most recognizable star makes a declaration like the one Larry Fitzgerald made after the Cardinals fell to the Jets in early December, it's a good sign the season has not gone well. That was the Cardinals' eighth straight loss, and it wasn't even the season's nadir. No, the Cardinals would reach that the following week when they went into Seattle and got keelhauled 58-0 by a Seahawks team the Cardinals had actually defeated in the season opener.

The game that spurred Fitzgerald's declaration of hopelessness was actually much closer, but since "much closer" involved the Cardinals losing 7-6, the proximate cause of Fitzgerald's despair was probably the play of quarterback Ryan Lindley. The sixth-round rookie was the third of four players who started under center for the Cardinals in 2012, and against the Jets he completed only 10 of 31 passes for 72 yards. This was one of the five games last season where Arizona had a passing DVOA of -75.0% or worse. It was not all Lindley's fault, either, as both Kevin Kolb and John Skelton also had starts that qualified. (Brian Hoyer, the fourth quarterback, only started one game.) All five games were losses.

And so, for the fourth straight year, the Cardinals essay in *Football Outsiders Almanac* will chronicle the team's never-ending search for a future at quarterback in the post-Kurt Warner era. Matt Leinart didn't even make it past the first Warner-less training camp. Derek Anderson came next, followed by Max Hall and Skelton. Kevin Kolb arrived from Philadelphia in 2011 with an immediate designation as the savior and a $63 million contract to convince the doubters. Kolb lasted a mere 14 starts over two seasons thanks to toe, rib, and head injuries, and ranked in the 30s in passing DVOA. The Cardinals released him this offseason rather than pay him his scheduled $11 million salary for 2013. Skelton drew more starts as a backup, Lindley in 2012 reprised Skelton's old role as the low-round rookie pressed into action, and Hoyer arrived off waivers late in the season. Like Kolb, Skelton and Hoyer will be playing elsewhere in 2013. Lindley is somehow still here, but that can't possibly last long.

The new answer at quarterback is Carson Palmer. Less than a season and a half ago, the Raiders sent two high draft picks to the Bengals for him. The Cardinals got him and his eight-figure salary for a 43-slot downgrade in the 2013 draft and a conditional seventh-round pick in 2014 if he starts at least 13

games. Compared to what the Raiders paid or Kolb's price of a second-round pick and a player, it's a veritable bargain. Of course, Palmer will be 33 when the season begins compared to Kolb's 27, so the reduced price makes some sense. It also means he is "just" the present at quarterback instead of the future. New head coach Bruce Arians will take it, though.

This offseason, the Cardinals finally gave up on Ken Whisenhunt's inability to translate his reputation as an offensive guru into on-field production without Warner. They handed their head coaching job to Arians, who filled in admirably for Chuck Pagano in Indianapolis last season. However, if we don't consider that an official head coaching position, then Arians is the ultra-rare coach to ascend to his first NFL head coaching position at age 60 or above. The recent history of such coaches is short and entirely lamentable (Table 1). Six other men since 1970 became an NFL head coach for the first time at age 60 or older, and not one of them ever finished with a record above 6-10.

Table 1: First-Time NFL Head Coaches Age 60 or Older, 1970-Present

Coach	Age	Year	Team	Career W-L
Ernie Hefferle	60	1975	NO*	1-7
Bud Wilkinson	62	1978	STLC	9-20
Rod Rust	62	1990	NE	1-15
Dick MacPherson	60	1991	NE	8-24
Dick LeBeau	63	2000	CIN*	12-33
Emmitt Thomas	64	2007	ATL*	1-2
Bruce Arians	60	2012	ARI	?

*Hired as interim head coach

With Palmer now around to (hopefully) stabilize the quarterback position, Arians and his offensive coordinator Harold Goodwin can turn to their other major responsibility: fixing the atrocious Arizona offensive line. The passing game, as bad as it was, was actually better than Kansas City's, but the run game ranked dead last in DVOA and looked even worse than it was against the formidable slate of run defenses the Cardinals faced in their division.

Our numbers place most of the blame for the dreadful ground game on the offensive line. The Cardinals finished with 2.93 Adjusted Line Yards, the worst figure in the 18 years

2013 Cardinals Schedule

Week	Opp.	Week	Opp.	Week	Opp.
1	at STL	7	SEA (Thu.)	13	at PHI
2	DET	8	ATL	14	STL
3	AT NO	9	BYE	15	at TEN
4	at TB	10	HOU	16	at SEA
5	CAR	11	at JAC	17	SF
6	at SF	12	IND		

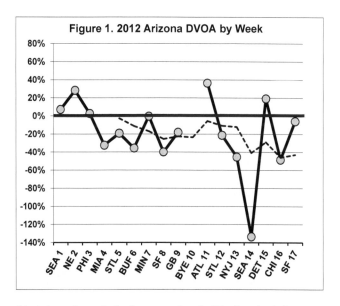

Figure 1. 2012 Arizona DVOA by Week

for which we are able to calculate the statistic (Table 2). Like most such teams, the Cardinals are relying on a mix of different offensive linemen and a new running back to improve the picture for the next season.

How are the Cardinals going to fix things? First, they get back left tackle Levi Brown, who missed the entire 2012 season with a triceps injury. As ineffective as he has been since the Cardinals selected him fifth overall in 2007, D'Anthony Batiste was clearly worse. The veteran backup had not started a game since playing guard for the Falcons in 2007, and it showed in his play. Second, the Cardinals used the seventh overall pick on North Carolina guard Jonathan Cooper. Cooper will be the highest-drafted rookie to start at guard since second overall pick Leonard Davis played there for the 2001 Cardinals. Unlike Davis, Cooper's future is on the interior rather than at tackle. He is fantastically mobile and athletic for a 300-pound man and a near-ideal fit for the zone principles Arians will be adding to the run game. The Cardinals will also get better overall performance from the line as long as right tackle Bobby Massie carries over the improvement he showed in the second half of last season, instead of reverting to his abysmal play from the first half of the year.

Like the other teams listed in Table 2, the Cardinals also turned over much of their running back corps. The two top runners are gone, as LaRod Stephens-Howling signed elsewhere in free agency and Beanie Wells was cut. The new starter will be former Steelers first-round pick Rashard Mendenhall, reunited

with Arians from their days together in Pittsburgh. Arians was effusive in his praise for the free-agent acquisition, declaring "He took me personally to a Super Bowl." Our numbers, however, indicate the Ben Roethlisberger-led passing game and the defense may have had more to do with it than Mendenhall. Mendenhall also had a worse 2012 DVOA than either Stephens-Howling or Wells. While his career numbers suggest he is unlikely to fumble every 17 carries again, he has never ranked in the top 20 in the league in DVOA. A savior, he will almost certainly not be. An improvement? That's a possibility, but not a certainty. If Mendenhall falters, the disappointing Ryan Williams will get yet another chance to stay healthy and actually live up to his second-round potential.

How Arians, Palmer, Mendenhall, and the new offensive linemen mesh with the existing personnel is an open question. Arians as a coordinator has shown a willingness to adapt his schemes to his personnel. Last year's Colts threw the ball a lot, but in Pittsburgh he managed some of the run-heavier teams of the past decade. The closest thing to a constant has been an inclination toward a vertical passing game. Palmer still has

Table 2: Fewest Offensive Adjusted Line Yards, 1995-2012

Team	Year	ALY	Run DVOA	Lead Back	ALY Y+1	Run DVOA Y+1	Lead Back Y+1
ARI	2012	2.93	-22.1%	L.Stephens-Howling	??	??	R.Mendenhall
HOU	2002	3.04	-27.4%	J.Wells	3.61	-8.0%	D.Davis
CLE	2001	3.17	-10.7%	J.Jackson	3.83	-6.4%	W.Green
DET	1999	3.18	-13.6%	G.Hill	4.11	0.2%	J.Stewart
NO	1998	3.25	-22.9%	L.Smith	3.42	-17.4%	R.Williams
OAK*	1997	3.27	-10.6%	N.Kaufman	3.66	-13.1%	N.Kaufman
ARI	2005	3.28	-29.1%	M.Shipp	4.01	-13.0%	E.James
ARI	1997	3.30	-14.4%	L.McElroy	3.76	-8.3%	A.Murrell
ARI	1999	3.33	-11.1%	A.Murrell	3.57	-14.4%	M.Pittman
CLE	1999	3.34	2.5%	T.Kirby	3.53	-12.6%	T.Prentice
CIN	2008	3.35	-14.7%	C.Benson	3.96	-1.7%	C.Benson
TEN	2012	3.35	-14.0%	C.Johnson	??	??	C.Johnson
MIA	2004	3.35	-14.5%	S.Morris	4.13	1.0%	R.Brown
AVG (non-2012 teams)		**3.26**	**-15.1%**		**3.78**	**-8.5%**	

*The 1997 Raiders were a particularly interesting example of how offensive line and running backs can diverge; they also averaged 1.50 Open Field Yards per Carry, tied for the sixth highest figure since 1995.

enough arm to run a competitive offense, but throwing the ball down the field requires protection. Arians won't be able to rely on the quarterback's mobility and ability to avoid sacks the way he did with Ben Roethlisberger and Andrew Luck. Additionally, in Fitzgerald, 2012 first-round pick Michael Floyd, and Andre Roberts, the Cardinals do not have a true vertical threat at wide receiver. Arians told the press this offseason that wide receiver is "not the position [he's] worried about." But like Whisenhunt over the past couple seasons, he will likely find himself forced into a short-to-intermediate quick passing game.

Another problem for Arians is that his arrival forced a move that will likely downgrade the defense. Before the losing streak and offensive ineptitude that drove Fitzgerald to despair, the Cardinals started the season 4-0, including an upset of the Patriots in New England. The key to the hot start was very strong defensive play, particularly the play of a pass defense that would be the Cardinals' strongest unit over the course of the season. A great deal of this success was due to the creative ways defensive coordinator Ray Horton was able to create pressure.

Horton's excellence—notwithstanding the excrescence on the other side of the ball—led him to expect the head coaching job when Whisenhunt was sent packing. He was reportedly quite angry when new general manager Steve Keim hired Arians. As Arians wanted his own defensive coordinator anyway, the Cardinals and Horton quickly found a meeting of the minds, and Horton was released from the rest of his contract.

Surprisingly, most of the secondary that was so effective in 2012 joins Horton, Whisenhunt, former general manager Rod Graves, and all those non-Lindley quarterbacks in plying their trade elsewhere in 2013. Nickel corner Greg Toler left in free agency. The Cardinals released starting corner William Gay and both starting safeties, Kerry Rhodes and Adrian Wilson. Only Patrick Peterson returns.

Individually, the moves mostly made sense. Wilson, a longtime Football Outsiders binky, turns 34 in October and isn't nearly the player he was earlier in his career. Rhodes turns 31 in August and had yet to find another team as of late June. Gay was not that effective, and Toler is a fine nickelback who drew a starter's salary from the Colts. However, the replacements—mostly free-agent signings—don't seem any better than the players Arizona got rid of. Jerraud Powers follows Arians over from Indianapolis to complete the pseudo-trade

for Toler and likely starts on the outside. He may be challenged by Chargers refugee Antoine Cason, who has ideal size to play on the outside but whose struggles in off and zone coverage may indicate he's a better slot option. Javier Arenas, acquired in a trade from Kansas City, fits the more traditional slot corner prototype. Our game charting statistics rate none of these players' 2012 performances particularly highly, and Cason's potential as a slot cornerback is based on trait prototyping rather than successful experience there.

The situation at safety is even more questionable. To start at strong safety, the Cardinals added Yeremiah Bell in free agency. The pro he brings is experience with new defensive coordinator Todd Bowles from their time in Miami. On the downside, he is even older than Wilson. The likely starter at free safety is Rashad Johnson, who started nine games for an injured Rhodes in 2011 but was primarily a special teams player last year. Behind him is third-round pick Tyrann Mathieu, a dynamic playmaker at LSU who is undersized, moving from his college position of cornerback, and did not play in 2012 thanks to drug problems.

Even when personnel and schemes are stable, defenses tend to be more inconsistent than offenses. Particularly given the age of the safeties, there is no guarantee the Cardinals would have had a very good pass defense once again had they kept the same personnel intact. Still, it certainly doesn't seem like the Cardinals have improved their defensive personnel, which makes it even more likely that this unit will not be able to repeat its excellent 2012 season.

Our projection for the Cardinals is not a particularly optimistic one. The offense has a long way to go to reach average, let alone good. The defense was below average in 2010 and 2011, and the general expectation of regression towards the mean is further strengthened by the departure of Horton. Their once-sleepy division now features two of the top teams in the NFL, plus a team in St. Louis that could fairly be regarded as similar but is clearly more talented. A playoff berth is unlikely, but at least Cardinals fans should be able to thank heaven for small favors—like potentially league-average quarterback play, no nine-game losing streaks, and not going 0-for-15 on third down in one game.

Tom Gower

2012 Cardinals Stats by Week

Wk	vs.	W-L	PF	PA	YDF	YDA	TO	Total	Off	Def	ST
1	SEA	W	20	16	253	254	0	7%	-21%	-43%	-15%
2	at NE	W	20	18	242	387	-1	28%	-9%	-29%	8%
3	PHI	W	27	6	292	307	3	3%	-20%	-12%	11%
4	MIA	W	24	21	297	480	2	-32%	-45%	-8%	5%
5	at STL	L	3	17	282	242	0	-19%	-25%	-7%	-2%
6	BUF	L	16	19	332	306	0	-36%	-40%	-1%	2%
7	at MIN	L	14	21	356	209	0	0%	-16%	-28%	-13%
8	SF	L	3	24	265	317	-1	-40%	-15%	14%	-11%
9	at GB	L	17	31	340	384	-1	-18%	-2%	-7%	-23%
10	BYE										
11	at ATL	L	19	23	178	354	5	36%	-42%	-67%	12%
12	STL	L	17	31	375	367	-3	-21%	-19%	10%	8%
13	at NYJ	L	6	7	137	289	3	-46%	-69%	-15%	8%
14	at SEA	L	0	58	154	493	-7	-134%	-95%	31%	-8%
15	DET	W	38	10	196	312	3	19%	-40%	-40%	19%
16	CHI	L	13	28	248	297	-2	-49%	-46%	16%	14%
17	at SF	L	13	27	262	407	-2	-6%	-9%	0%	3%

Trends and Splits

	Offense	Rank	Defense	Rank
Total DVOA	-30.9%	32	-13.5%	6
Unadjusted VOA	-37.5%	32	-7.7%	7
Weighted Trend	-36.0%	32	-10.0%	6
Variance	5.9%	14	6.3%	20
Average Opponent	-5.4%	4	4.7%	1
Passing	-30.2%	31	-21.3%	2
Rushing	-22.1%	32	-5.6%	16
First Down	-27.6%	32	-10.1%	5
Second Down	-21.8%	28	-13.0%	6
Third Down	-50.9%	32	-21.4%	3
First Half	-24.6%	32	-12.9%	4
Second Half	-38.1%	32	-14.0%	5
Red Zone	-39.2%	30	-16.6%	7
Late and Close	-60.4%	32	-14.9%	6

Five-Year Performance

Year	W-L	Pyth W	Est W	PF	PA	TO	Total	Rk	Off	Rk	Def	Rk	ST	Rk	Off AGL	Rk	Def AGL	Rk	Off Age	Rk	Def Age	Rk	ST Age	Rk
2008	9-7	8.0	7.2	427	426	0	-5.0%	21	4.6%	15	5.1%	21	-4.6%	28	23.5	14	14.3	8	26.9	25	27.5	14	27.0	8
2009	10-6	9.4	10.4	381	325	-7	11.2%	12	6.8%	13	-2.8%	11	1.7%	10	13.6	10	10.5	3	27.6	11	28.0	5	27.2	3
2010	5-11	4.3	3.1	289	434	-5	-37.1%	32	-35.6%	31	5.6%	25	4.2%	9	26.8	17	11.4	8	26.7	23	28.0	8	26.8	11
2011	8-8	6.9	4.9	312	348	-13	-19.7%	28	-18.4%	28	2.4%	20	1.2%	11	46.3	28	40.5	25	27.0	17	27.5	11	27.0	2
2012	5-11	4.8	4.8	250	357	-1	-16.3%	26	-30.9%	32	-13.5%	6	1.1%	11	50.3	28	22.0	12	26.7	18	27.6	8	27.1	4

2012 Performance Based on Most Common Personnel Groups

ARI Offense					ARI Offense vs. Opponents				ARI Defense				ARI Defense vs. Opponents			
Pers	Freq	Yds	DVOA	Run%	Pers	Freq	Yds	DVOA	Pers	Freq	Yds	DVOA	Pers	Freq	Yds	DVOA
11	44%	4.1	-37.9%	16%	Nickel Even	41%	4.2	-32.4%	3-4-4	50%	5.2	-18.8%	11	39%	5.3	-16.9%
12	20%	4.2	-11.9%	51%	4-3-4	30%	4.2	-23.5%	Nickel Even	42%	5.5	-7.0%	12	24%	4.9	-27.8%
21	13%	4.4	-28.6%	66%	Dime+	13%	4.5	-23.9%	Nickel Odd	4%	5.3	-58.5%	21	14%	6.2	-11.0%
10	11%	4.4	-14.0%	5%	3-4-4	7%	4.1	-13.3%	Dime+	2%	6.2	4.0%	22	9%	4.9	-6.5%
22	5%	2.3	-45.0%	86%	Nickel Odd	7%	4.4	-13.0%	4-4-3	1%	7.7	8.7%	13	3%	3.2	-26.8%
													20	3%	8.1	24.1%

Strategic Tendencies

Run/Pass		Rk	Formation		Rk	Pass Rush		Rk	Secondary		Rk	Strategy		Rk
Runs, first half	37%	20	Form: Single Back	70%	10	Rush 3	3.4%	28	4 DB	50%	5	Play action	13%	31
Runs, first down	47%	23	Form: Empty Back	6%	12	Rush 4	53.8%	26	5 DB	46%	18	Avg Box (Off)	6.16	28
Runs, second-long	26%	27	Pers: 3+ WR	60%	6	Rush 5	31.2%	5	6+ DB	2%	26	Avg Box (Def)	6.64	1
Runs, power sit.	49%	23	Pers: 4+ WR	14%	2	Rush 6+	11.6%	7	CB by Sides	60%	29	Offensive Pace	30.11	14
Runs, behind 2H	17%	32	Pers: 2+ TE/6+ OL	27%	22	Sacks by LB	61.5%	8	DB Blitz	15%	12	Defensive Pace	29.70	9
Pass, ahead 2H	44%	21	Shotgun/Pistol	56%	8	Sacks by DB	12.8%	4	Hole in Zone	3%	32	Go for it on 4th	1.14	6

Did you think protecting the lousy Arizona quarterbacks was going to help things? Not last year, not with that offensive line. The Cardinals had a league-worst -73.9% DVOA and 4.4 yards per play when using "max protect." ☜ The Cardinals were also terrible on screens. On running back screens, they had a league-worst average of 2.5 yards and -68.3% DVOA. They weren't the league's worst team on wide receiver screens, but still were below average with just 4.2 yards per pass and -7.1% DVOA. ☜ Despite the excellent sophomore season from Patrick Peterson, Cardinals opponents threw a league-leading 31 percent of passes to their No. 1 receivers. ☜ For the third straight season, the Cardinals defense just got destroyed by draw plays. Since 2010 they've allowed a combined 7.1 yards per carry and 64.4% DVOA on 60 running back draws. ☜ Arizona had the league's best defensive DVOA against passes in the red zone, but ranked 29th in defensive DVOA against runs in the red zone.

Passing

Player	DYAR	DVOA	Plays	NtYds	Avg	YAC	C%	TD	Int
J.Skelton	-324	-35.0%	216	1034	4.8	4.9	54.5%	2	8
K.Kolb*	-154	-23.1%	210	1008	4.8	4.4	59.6%	8	3
R.Lindley	-482	-55.8%	184	646	3.5	2.9	52.0%	0	7
B.Hoyer*	-60	-26.5%	57	300	5.3	3.1	56.6%	1	2
C.Palmer	*340*	*-2.2%*	*592*	*3820*	*6.5*	*5.7*	*61.7%*	*22*	*14*

Rushing

Player	DYAR	DVOA	Plays	Yds	Avg	TD	Fum	Suc
L.Stephens-Howling*	-63	-22.9%	110	356	3.2	4	0	34%
B.Wells*	-48	-21.6%	88	234	2.7	5	1	34%
W.Powell	21	0.1%	60	217	3.6	0	0	40%
R.Williams	-85	-45.5%	58	167	2.9	0	2	34%
K.Kolb*	49	80.7%	12	103	8.6	1	0	-
R.Mendenhall	*-62*	*-38.5%*	*51*	*182*	*3.6*	*0*	*3*	*43%*

Receiving

Player	DYAR	DVOA	Plays	Ctch	Yds	Y/C	YAC	TD	C%
L.Fitzgerald	-218	-23.8%	156	71	798	11.2	3.8	4	46%
A.Roberts	12	-6.5%	114	64	764	11.9	3.5	5	56%
M.Floyd	-3	-10.3%	86	45	562	12.5	3.5	2	52%
E.Doucet*	-144	-38.8%	53	28	207	7.4	2.9	0	53%
R.Housler	-60	-17.1%	68	45	417	9.3	4.0	0	66%
J.King	-47	-28.6%	29	17	129	7.6	3.6	0	59%
T.Heap	-3	-8.3%	13	8	94	11.8	4.6	0	62%
L.Stephens-Howling*	-48	-46.0%	30	17	106	6.2	7.9	0	57%
W.Powell	-6	-19.3%	25	19	132	6.9	4.3	0	76%
R.Williams	0	-14.1%	10	7	44	6.3	5.0	0	70%
A.Sherman	-2	-19.4%	8	5	39	7.8	8.2	0	63%
R.Mendenhall	*24*	*22.7%*	*11*	*9*	*62*	*6.9*	*10.9*	*1*	*82%*

Offensive Line

Player	Pos	Age	GS	Snaps	Pen	Sk	Pass	Run	Player	Pos	Age	GS	Snaps	Pen	Sk	Pass	Run
Daryn Colledge	LG	32	16/16	1051	7	4.5	13	5.5	Nate Potter	OT	25	8/6	428	1	7	14	0
Bobby Massie	RT	24	16/16	1051	5	11.5	27	3.5	Rich Ohrnberger*	G	27	13/4	286	4	1.5	3.5	2.5
Adam Snyder*	RG	31	14/14	865	2	2.5	10.5	7	Pat McQuistan*	OT	30	6/3	140	0	1	2	1
Lyle Sendlein	C	29	11/11	755	1	3.5	6.5	5	*Chilo Rachal*	*G*	*27*	*9/8*	*512*	*8*	*1*	*8.5*	*7.5*
D'Anthony Batiste*	LT	32	15/10	625	7	8	25.5	5									

Year	Yards	ALY	Rk	Power	Rk	Stuff	Rk	2nd Lev	Rk	Open Field	Rk	Sacks	ASR	Rk	Short	Long	F-Start	Cont.
2010	4.31	3.84	21	74%	5	21%	22	1.20	11	1.00	7	50	8.4%	27	24	13	14	39
2011	4.12	4.07	15	63%	16	20%	18	1.07	27	0.74	21	54	9.0%	27	21	22	16	31
2012	3.26	2.93	32	48%	31	27%	32	0.85	32	0.66	20	58	8.1%	26	25	16	17	31
2012 ALY by direction:		*Left End 3.35 (24)*			*Left Tackle 2.62 (32)*			*Mid/Guard 2.68 (32)*			*Right Tackle 3.29 (31)*				*Right End 3.9 (17)*		

Here's what Ken Whisenhunt said about replacement left tackle D'Anthony Batiste after Levi Brown tore his triceps in the preseason: "We felt very strongly about D'Anthony because of his work in the offseason and what he did last year." To our great disappointment, Whisenhunt was not asked for an updated opinion after getting fired; odds are he felt just as strongly, albeit in the opposite direction. Because Batiste only started 10 games, his numbers in the table above don't quite do his ineptitude justice. Prorated to 16 starts, he would have just missed the triple crown of suck, finishing second in all three blown block categories to San Diego's Mike Harris. But it wasn't just Batiste: If we prorate center Lyle Sendlein and right guard Adam Snyder to 16 starts as well, all five linemen finished no better than seventh-worst among starters at their respective positions in terms of blown blocks on passing plays. Even Nate Potter, who took over after Batiste's mercy-benching, prorates nearly as bad over a full season. That's right; Arizona had not one, but two, of the worst left tackles in the league last year.

After enduring an eyeball torture even Anthony Burgess would have deemed in bad taste, Cardinals fans deserve a restorative dénouement, so there's this: Although Bobbie Massie finished his rookie season with the second-most blown pass blocks among right tackles, 23.5 of the 27 came before Arizona's Week 10 bye.

So with Jonathan Cooper in town, Brown healthy, and Massie improving, the Cardinals' line should be much improved this season, right? Not so fast. With images of Batiste and Potter stuck in our heads, it's easy to forget that Brown was arguably the worst left tackle in football the *prior* two seasons. "We have an elite player that was out and once we put that elite left tackle in, everything is better," Arians told reporters in June. Perhaps Arians is the latest elite spin doctor to join the NFC West—or perhaps, after coaching the Colts and Steelers over the last couple years, he's simply forgotten what elite line play looks like. Or, for that matter, league-average line play.

Defensive Front Seven

Defensive Line	Age	Pos	Snaps	Plays	Overall TmPct	Rk	Stop	Dfts	BTkl	Runs	vs. Run St%	Rk	RuYd	Rk	Pass Rush Sack	Hit	Hur	Tips
Darnell Dockett	32	DE	792	37	4.8%	44	32	12	4	30	83%	11	2.3	31	1.5	7	10	3
Calais Campbell	27	DE	753	67	10.0%	2	53	18	4	52	77%	27	2.6	43	6.5	7	18.5	7
Dan Williams	26	DT	420	45	5.8%	13	35	9	0	43	79%	25	2.3	39	0	2	3	1
Matt Shaughnessy	*27*	*DE*	*668*	*31*	*4.0%*	*56*	*26*	*12*	*0*	*24*	*88%*	*3*	*0.3*	*2*	*3.5*	*5*	*5*	*0*
Frostee Rucker	*30*	*DE*	*593*	*49*	*5.6%*	*34*	*38*	*7*	*1*	*40*	*78%*	*24*	*2.8*	*55*	*4*	*2*	*8*	*1*

Linebackers	Age	Pos	Snaps	Plays	Overall TmPct	Rk	Stop	Dfts	BTkl	Pass Rush Sack	Hit	Hur	Tips	vs. Run Runs	St%	Rk	Yds	Rk	vs. Pass Tgts	Suc%	Rk	AdjYd	Rk	PD
Daryl Washington	25	ILB	1057	138	16.8%	13	74	28	11	9	5	8	1	93	57%	94	4.1	91	32	47%	50	7.4	56	3
Paris Lenon*	36	ILB	1013	106	12.9%	42	56	14	8	2	4	8.5	2	83	54%	100	4.9	108	18	34%	72	13.3	76	1
Sam Acho	25	OLB	995	48	5.8%	98	41	14	0	4	8	13	0	27	93%	2	1.1	3	14	68%	--	4.2	--	2
O'Brien Schofield	26	OLB	490	33	7.1%	81	22	8	2	4	5	9	0	26	65%	56	3.2	48	8	72%	--	2.9	--	0
Quentin Groves*	29	OLB	466	41	5.0%	--	31	14	3	4	4	9	0	30	73%	--	3.8	--	7	61%	--	4.1	--	0
Karlos Dansby	32	ILB	1099	143	17.2%	11	81	24	7	1	2	3.5	2	88	65%	61	3.2	47	56	57%	19	6.7	32	7
Jasper Brinkley	28	ILB	847	102	11.8%	53	51	14	11	0	3	2	0	64	66%	53	3.8	80	40	47%	53	6.1	21	5
Lorenzo Alexander	30	OLB	294	25	3.1%	--	13	7	0	2.5	9	11	0	7	71%	--	4.4	--	9	37%	--	7.8	--	0

Year	Yards	ALY	Rk	Power	Rk	Stuff	Rk	2nd Level	Rk	Open Field	Rk	Sacks	ASR	Rk	Short	Long
2010	4.60	4.28	23	63%	17	20%	15	1.32	29	1.01	28	33	6.0%	19	14	9
2011	4.23	4.11	19	71%	27	20%	13	1.27	23	0.69	10	42	6.4%	22	12	15
2012	4.58	4.49	32	55%	7	17%	25	1.31	28	0.80	17	38	7.2%	7	11	15
2012 ALY by direction:		Left End 3.92 (16)			Left Tackle 5.09 (31)			Mid/Guard 4.47 (30)			Right Tackle 4.21 (21)			Right End 4.3 (18)		

This unit had one of the weirder stat profiles in the league last season. Usually, pressure comes from the outside linebackers in a 3-4, but Arizona's sack leaders were inside linebacker Daryl Washington and defensive end Calais Campbell. In the running game, 3-4 defensive linemen are typically grunts who funnel glory toward inside linebackers, yet the opposite occurred with Arizona: Campbell, Darnell Dockett, and Dan Williams were more active in the play-making department than otherwise expected, while Washington and Paris Lenon ranked among the worst Stop Rates at their position. Much of this can be attributed to former defensive coordinator Ray Horton, who dialed up blitzes from unlikely places and built a collective unit that was better than the sum of its individual talents. That's not to say that the players were enjoying themselves, however. "Personally, I had nothing against Ray," Dockett told the press after Horton's departure, "but I hated that scheme. I really hated it." Still an excellent penetrator with great versatility, Dockett nonetheless had only five sacks in two seasons under Horton after a combined 25 sacks in the previous four seasons.

Perhaps Dockett will get more personal satisfaction from the hybrid front installed by new defensive coordinator Todd Bowles. The new scheme helps explain why the Cardinals replaced Lenon with Jasper Brinkley, who started in Minnesota's 4-3 defense last year. Washington will miss (at least) the first four games because of suspension—and possibly more, since he followed up a positive drug test with a domestic abuse arrest—so Arizona brought back Miami cap casualty Karlos Dansby, who has experience in both types of alignments. On the outside, fourth-round pick Alex Okafor (Texas) and free-agent additions Lorenzo Alexander (ex-Redskins) and Matt Shaughnessy (ex-Raiders) join Sam Acho and O'Brien Schofield. Just don't expect too much from the new additions. Alexander is a career special teamer, Shaughnessy is making a transition from playing with his hand in the dirt to standing up, and Okafor had the second-worst SackSEER rating among 2013 combine invitees.

Defensive Secondary

Secondary	Age	Pos	Snaps	Plays	Overall TmPct	Rk	Stop	Dfts	BTkl	vs. Run Runs	St%	Rk	Yds	Rk	vs. Pass Tgts	Tgt%	Rk	Dist	Suc%	Rk	APaYd	Rk	PD	Int
Patrick Peterson	23	CB	1040	71	8.6%	40	32	16	7	16	38%	53	10.1	77	92	22.9%	5	14.2	59%	11	6.6	21	15	7
Kerry Rhodes*	31	FS	1010	78	10.1%	35	31	17	6	36	36%	42	9.8	63	33	8.7%	18	10.4	57%	28	5.7	13	10	4
William Gay*	28	CB	1003	63	7.7%	60	19	13	8	21	33%	60	5.9	38	79	19.6%	28	12.3	50%	51	8.0	56	5	2
Adrian Wilson*	34	SS	846	59	7.7%	54	23	7	3	31	32%	49	6.9	35	20	5.3%	59	14.5	76%	4	5.3	10	4	1
Greg Toler*	28	CB	301	35	6.2%	76	14	8	0	8	25%	73	5.8	33	40	14.5%	65	15.7	66%	2	6.2	9	9	2
Jamell Fleming	24	CB	270	23	3.0%	--	3	3	2	2	0%	--	5.5	--	30	8.0%	--	10.3	44%	--	8.9	--	1	0
Rashad Johnson	27	FS	161	15	1.9%	--	4	4	1	4	0%	--	12.8	--	8	2.0%	--	10.4	31%	--	8.7	--	2	2
Yeremiah Bell	35	SS	1058	90	11.6%	25	26	8	4	45	38%	36	8.2	54	29	7.1%	31	14.0	48%	62	8.8	57	2	0
Antoine Cason	27	CB	1023	83	10.4%	16	24	8	4	14	57%	18	4.1	10	97	22.3%	7	11.4	40%	84	7.3	35	11	2
Javier Arenas	26	CB	709	69	8.8%	37	25	12	3	19	37%	56	9.4	73	55	14.4%	66	11.4	51%	45	7.7	48	9	0
Jerraud Powers	26	CB	505	48	12.1%	5	21	9	3	8	75%	5	8.4	67	57	25.3%	2	11.8	47%	67	8.0	55	8	1

Year	Pass D Rank	vs. #1 WR	Rk	vs. #2 WR	Rk	vs. Other WR	Rk	vs. TE	Rk	vs. RB	Rk
2010	22	25.0%	28	10.3%	21	-9.3%	12	-6.4%	7	-6.9%	8
2011	14	10.7%	17	4.4%	16	6.0%	24	9.6%	17	-26.8%	2
2012	2	-7.4%	11	-18.2%	4	-46.0%	1	-2.5%	15	-52.4%	1

Regular readers should be familiar with our mantra about cornerback prospects: Even the best of them take a year or two to show their true value. Patrick Peterson is no exception. As a rookie, he was arguably Arizona's worst cornerback; last year, he was their best. Sure, Greg Toler may have ranked higher according to Adjusted Success Rate, but Peterson's value was spread out across over twice as many targets, and he was often relied on to cover the opponent's top wideout without safety help. It's a good thing he reached lockdown status because what just last year was an impressive cornerback group has since been reduced to Patrick Peterson and the Pips. Jerraud Powers will replace William Gay in the starting lineup, but he missed half of last season with turf toe, and was mediocre at best when healthy. Arizona also signed San Diego's Antoine Cason, co-star of the 2012 short film *Ray Rice Converts 4th-and-29*. After one viewing, Chargers defensive coordinator John Pagano panned the lackluster effort, saying, "I think more or less he thought that the guy was going to be down, and you don't ever want to assume in this business." The Cardinals will also start two new safeties, Rashard Johnson and Yeremiah Bell. Of course, Johnson is a career backup, and Bell was already on the decline when Bowles coached him in the 2011 Dolphins secondary. He hasn't ranked among the top 32 safeties in Run Stop Rate or Adjusted Success Rate since 2010. The Cardinals also plan on converting third-round pick Tyrann Mathieu (Louisiana State) to free safety. However, the avatar of carefree weasels—not to mention sportswriting clichés like "talented but troubled"—is slated to spend most of his rookie season on special teams.

Special Teams

Year	DVOA	Rank	FG/XP	Rank	Net Kick	Rank	Kick Ret	Rank	Net Punt	Rank	Punt Ret	Rank	Hidden	Rank
2010	4.2%	9	9.1	2	7.3	8	13.8	4	0.7	17	-11.5	32	9.0	3
2011	1.2%	11	-5.2	24	-0.7	20	-3.5	24	-4.7	22	20.0	1	14.7	2
2012	1.1%	11	4.4	10	-6.7	27	-2.5	20	19.7	1	-9.3	31	14.4	2

With a pathetic offense in need of better field position last season, the Cardinals desperately called on the special teams cavalry to bring help. Instead, Peterson sure picked a fine time to impersonate General Custer on punt returns. After leading the NFL with 21.0 expected points added in 2011, he finished dead last with minus-8.8 points in 2012. There were minor setbacks along the way (e.g., fair-catching a punt at the 3-yard line in Week 4), but Little Big Horn came in Arizona's Week 14 game against the Seahawks, when Peterson's two fumbled punts contributed to a 58-0 slaughter. Of course, as his downfall demonstrates, special teams are even less predictable than the Indian Wars, so December 9, 2012, probably wasn't Peterson's last stand. Nevertheless, Arizona traded for Javier Arenas and drafted Tyrann Mathieu, both of whom may end up returning punts in addition to splitting kickoff return duties with William Powell.

Despite Peterson's worst efforts, the overall unit ended up with an above-average DVOA thanks to punter Dave Zastudil and kicker Jay Feely. At the very least, Zastudil's 112 punts last year (two shy of an NFL record shared by Bob Parsons of the 1981 Bears and Chad Stanley of the 2002 Texans) mean his leg has the stamina and synchronization for a job with the Rockettes should things not work out with the Cardinals. After finishing third among punters in estimated points of field position added via the boot (+13.6 gross, +19.7 net), his dancing career will have to wait. Feely's accuracy returned to pre-2011 levels, although his leg strength continued its decline to Gary Anderson levels, and he had negative gross kickoff value for the first time since 2008. Meanwhile, 2012 saw the Cardinals once again demonstrate their uncanny ability to turn Ray Finkles into Lois Einhorns. Arizona's opponents over the past three seasons made only 74.6 percent of their field goals (100 of 134) when the league average in that span was 80.0 percent. Calais Campbell alone does not account for this.

Coaching Staff

Bruce Arians has taken quite the circuitous route to his first NFL head coaching job. His only prior head coaching experience came 30 years ago with Temple, where a 21-45 record didn't exactly pad his résumé. It took 23 years of coaching before Arians earned his first NFL coordinator job (Cleveland), while his second (Pittsburgh) was as much a promotion out of necessity as anything else. His most-recent stint in Indianapolis only came about because the Steelers forced Arians into "retirement" after the 2011 season. Sixteen months, one #chuckstrong playoff run, and an unprecedented Coach of the Year award later, the man who just two years ago seemed destined to be an assistant for the rest of his career now has the full-time head coaching job that eluded him for three decades.

Another coach who knows plenty about being unable to break the chalkboard ceiling—in Pittsburgh and Indianapolis, no less—is living legend Tom Moore, whom Arians hired as an offensive consultant and assistant head coach. Everyone knows about Moore's influence on a young Peyton Manning, but he also guided below-average quarterbacks like Mark Malone and Scott Mitchell to the best seasons of their underwhelming careers. Between Moore and Arians, Carson Palmer and an as-of-yet-unnamed quarterback of the future won't have poor coaching to blame if they don't succeed.

The rest of Arians' initial staff looks to have resulted from a two-question interview process: "Have I coached with you before? Are you experienced?" Jobs went to those answering, "Yes" and "No," respectively. Harold Goodwin, brother of 49ers center Jonathan Goodwin, assisted Arians in Pittsburgh and Indianapolis, but has never been an offensive coordinator, and boasts only one season as a senior position coach. Todd Bowles played for Arians at Temple and worked with him in Cleveland, but 10 games in Philadelphia last year is the totality of his defensive coordinator experience. (Eagles fans will tell you it was quite an experience!) Amos Jones arrives in Arizona after six seasons in Pittsburgh, only one of which (2012) was spent as special teams coordinator. No word yet on whether Jones plans on using assistant strength and conditioning coach Pete Alosi (Sal's brother) in punt coverage.

Atlanta Falcons

2012 Record: 13-3	Total DVOA: 9.1% (10th)	2013 Mean Projection: 7.6 wins	On the Clock (0-4): 12%
Pythagorean Wins: 11.2 (5th)	Offense: 6.1% (12th)	Postseason Odds: 26.0%	Mediocrity (5-7): 36%
Snap-Weighted Age: 28.1 (1st)	Defense: -2.9% (12th)	Super Bowl Odds: 2.8%	Playoff Contender (8-10): 40%
Average Opponent: -4.3% (27th)	Special Teams: 0.1% (16th)	Proj. Avg. Opponent: 6.3% (1st)	Super Bowl Contender (11+): 12%

2012: At long last, a postseason win (just barely).

2013: Just because Delta has hourly flights to New York, Falcons fans shouldn't book tickets for February just yet.

As the founder of Home Depot, Arthur Blank is quite familiar with windows. As the owner of the Atlanta Falcons, Blank is quite familiar with windows of opportunity. It is the decided feeling in Atlanta that one may soon slam shut, and therefore the 2013 season is all about reaching the Super Bowl after coming up a few yards short in last year's NFC Championship game. This all-in sentiment was only enhanced when the Falcons managed to talk Tony Gonzalez out of starting his Canton Clock and getting back on to the field for one more go around this season, which this time is (almost?) assuredly his last. He wouldn't return unless he felt he could play his last game for the Lombardi Trophy, right?

Unfortunately for Artie B. and his loyal coterie of Falcons fans, our projections are not nearly so optimistic.

We don't forecast the Falcons to be one of the top Super Bowl contenders of 2013 because when you look at the numbers underlying their 13-3 record, the Falcons really shouldn't have been one of the top Super Bowl contenders of 2012 either. The 2012 Falcons resembled the 2010 Falcons, who were also 13-3 and clearly not the best team in the NFC despite finishing as the number-one seed. Except that by our numbers, the Falcons have actually declined since 2010.

Atlanta's DVOA peaked at seventh in 2010, then fell to eighth in 2011 and tenth last year. Locals took it as disrespect when the national media refused to give the Falcons their due even as they were coasting to home-field advantage in the playoffs, but the vaguely phrased distrust coming from the football commentariat simply reflected the numbers. The Falcons outperformed their Pythagorean record by nearly two full games and their Estimated Wins by nearly four. They benefited from the 27th toughest schedule in the league, particularly blessed by problems throughout their division. The implosion in New Orleans, Josh Freeman's inconsistency, and Ron Rivera's "coaching" all redounded in Atlanta's favor. Outside their division, the Falcons played five of the seven teams that finished last season 5-11 or worse.

The Falcons weren't just beating bad teams. They were *barely* beating bad teams. Seven wins in 2012 came by a touchdown or less, including a three-pointer over Oakland, a four-pointer over Arizona, and a six-pointer over Dallas, all of which came down to the final plays of the game. They won a game with Matt Ryan throwing five interceptions and no touchdowns, only the second time that's happened in modern

NFL history. (Bart Starr won a game in similarly repugnant fashion way back in 1967.) The Falcons only played two playoff teams during the regular season. They won both games, but it sure helped that Peyton Manning was still figuring out how to work with his new Denver teammates in Week 2 and Robert Griffin got knocked out of the game with an injury in Week 5.

That cushy schedule figures to toughen considerably in 2013. We project Atlanta's slate to be the hardest in the NFL. That starts with their division, where Sean Payton is back, the Buccaneers have added two Pro-Bowl level defensive backs, and the Panthers are straight-out too talented to suffer another losing record unless Rivera really is one of the worst head coaches in NFL history (note: possible). The schedule rotation and last year's first-place finish will have the Falcons playing New England, Green Bay, Seattle and San Francisco. (Schedule quirk alert: Oddly, despite the league loading up December with divisional games, the Falcons don't play an NFC South opponent between their Thanksgiving game against New Orleans and the season finale against Carolina 38 days later.)

The Falcons are also likely to see their luck regress when it comes to the bouncing ball. Last year's defense recovered 11 of 16 fumbles. The offense lost only four fumbles, tied with Houston for fewest in the NFL, and that number seems certain to rise in 2013. The Falcons only had nine fumbles on offense, so this isn't an issue of getting lucky with fumble recovery rate; the issue here is that it is really hard for any offense to go through a season with only nine fumbles.

Perhaps swept up in the news that Gonzalez was indeed returning, the Falcons' draft followed a win-now mindset. General manager Thomas Dimitroff traded up with St. Louis to select cornerback Desmond Trufant out of Washington, hoping to strike gold just as he did by moving up for Julio Jones in 2011. The team clearly fell hard for Trufant, and he may well prove to be starting material as early as this season. But the front office sees the roster as being only a couple of specific players away from a championship team, when in reality there are multiple holes in the hull. Furthermore, as we pointed out at length in the Dallas chapter of *Football Outsiders Almanac 2012*, even the most talented rookie cornerbacks usually struggle, with first-rounders averaging an Adjusted Success Rate under 50 percent since 2005.

In particular, those weaknesses are on the defensive side

2013 Falcons Schedule

Week	Opp.	Week	Opp.	Week	Opp.
1	at NO	7	TB	13	vs. BUF (Tor.)
2	STL	8	at ARI	14	at GB
3	at MIA	9	at CAR	15	WAS
4	NE	10	SEA	16	at SF (Mon.)
5	NYJ (Mon.)	11	at TB	17	CAR
6	BYE	12	NO (Thu.)		

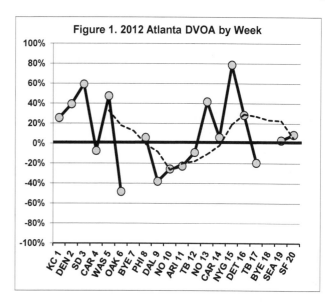

Figure 1. 2012 Atlanta DVOA by Week

of the ball. Our projections have the Falcons around the bottom third of the NFL in defensive DVOA. The unit let go both its top pass rusher (John Abraham) and a starting corner (Dunta Robinson) from a passing defense that was a relative strength—the pass defense DVOA was 11th in the league, compared to 20th for the run defense. The Falcons would say that this is a case of addition by subtraction, with Trufant and Osi Umenyiora being an upgrade over Robinson and Abraham. More likely it's a wash at best.

Much of Atlanta's success last year was thanks to the coaching wizardry of new defensive coordinator Mike Nolan. His schemes included playing more nickel defense than any team in the NFL, and heavy pre-snap movement that confused opponents, especially early in the season. Nolan's trickeration was perhaps most evident in the Broncos game, when Falcons defenders repeatedly wandered around while Manning attempted to identify the coverage, only to sprint to specific spots at the snap. Three first-quarter interceptions resulted in a 20-0 lead, and the Falcons went on to hand Denver one of its three losses.

Unfortunately, Falcons opponents began to figure out the defensive scheme as the year went along. Including the postseason, six of Atlanta's seven worst defensive games by DVOA came after Week 8. Teams learned to take advantage of the weak tackling of the Falcons' defensive backs (only Philadelphia had a higher percentage of blown tackles). Teams also attacked Nolan's schemes with shotgun formations. No team saw more shotgun as a percentage of opposing formations, and Atlanta had trouble stopping it (12.1% DVOA against shotgun formations). By contrast, when quarterbacks were under center, the Falcons were very effective—third in the league in DVOA against non-shotgun sets.

Still, Nolan was a breath of fresh air on a team used to the high-volume, blue-streaked micromanagement of previous coordinator Brian VanGorder, who was so mean apparently even the space between "Van" and "Gorder" couldn't stand being around him. Atlanta defenders spoke routinely of being screamed at for lining up inches away from VanGorder's preferred spot, and how Nolan's "milling cow" defense, and generally positive demeanor, was like being let out of prison.

Nolan was one of a matched set of new coordinators in Atlanta last year. Offensive coordinator Dirk Koetter certainly got the nicer set of trains to play with, starting with the guy under center wearing No. 2. In fact, the best way for the Falcons to get through that proverbial window of opportunity might be to have Ryan whip passes at it until the damn thing shatters.

After being pounded in 2011 (he took 68 hits by our counting, most in the NFL), Matty Ice made a dedicated effort to get stronger in the offseason. The result was a better ability to stand up to what was a similar beating in 2012 (he was hit 61 times, fourth-most in the league). Meanwhile, reports from his receivers indicated that he was throwing the ball harder, and squeezing the ball in to more remote areas on the field. Ryan set career highs in yards, touchdown passes, completion percentage, and DYAR, though of course the weak schedule helped play into that somewhat.

Perhaps no throw was more indicative of Ryan's power and overall mindset than the heave from his end zone he completed to Roddy White for 59 yards against the Panthers, with Falcons trailing by one with a minute left. The play set up the winning field goal. Onlookers screamed "miracle!" but really it was a blend of confidence, power, and moxie, all of which were on display throughout 2012.

We all spend plenty of time celebrating Ryan and his superlative receivers, but don't forget that a great offense also requires great blocking, and the Falcons will enter this season without two long-time offensive linemen. Center Todd McClure retired after 13 solid seasons, while right tackle Tyson Clabo, among the better players at his position in the NFL, and certainly one of the nastiest, was let go in a salary cap move. Despite the fact that Ryan was hit by pass rushers roughly as often as he was in 2011, the percentage of total plays Ryan faced pressure in the pocket actually dropped from 22 percent in 2011 to 16 percent last year. His DVOA was basically the same under pressure in both seasons—he didn't suddenly turn Roethlisberger on us—so give the line kudos for keeping him cleaner and some of the credit for Ryan's transcendent season. Whether those numbers hold up without McClure and Clabo is reason for concern.

Clabo in particular was one of the league's better run blockers, but his loss could be counteracted by a running back switch. Out goes Michael Turner, whose tires were so bald no amount of Rogaine could return him to efficiency. In his place comes Steven Jackson, which furthers the Super Bowl or Bust vibe around Flowery Branch. Jackson is an interesting case—on the one hand, running backs on the wrong side of thirty (Jackson hits the magic birthday on July 29) are usually best handled with those glove arms scientists use while standing on the other side of shatterproof glass. Mileage has to be a concern; over the last eight seasons, Jackson has averaged 283 carries and seemingly six groin pulls per year.

But Jackson actually had his best season in years in 2012, ranking tenth in DYAR. Contrary to his public image, Jackson has missed only two full games in the last four seasons. He broke tackles at roughly the same rate as Turner did (neither approached backup Jacquizz Rodgers in that category). And his receiving numbers, usually an early indicator of running-back decline, remain strong. Koetter, who never met a screen pass he didn't like, must be salivating at the idea of a lead running back who can actually catch the ball.

Jackson played in exactly two postseason games with St. Louis, both coming in his rookie season of 2004. Jackson had all of 19 carries in the two games, one of which ironically was a 47-17 thumping at the hands of his new team. That same year the Rams were on *Monday Night Football* three times; in the ensuing eight seasons Jackson's team only appeared on *MNF* four times. One can practically feel Jackson's desire to prove himself on the big stage bursting out of his sculpted physique.

"I'm here to go out on top," Jackson said on his first day as a Falcon, and indeed, his acquisition recalls the 2003-04 Lakers bringing in Karl Malone and Gary Payton in order to reward them for their brilliant careers with a title run. We all remember how that turned out, and besides, Ryan and Julio ain't quite Kobe and Shaq (presumably Jackson won't hit on Jones' girl, a la the Mailman and Vanessa Bryant). It's also possible the franchise just wanted to team Steven Jackson with Samuel L. Jackson, who memorably voices the "Rise Up!!!" videos that play on the Georgia Dome Jumbotron before games.

The Falcons Way™ is reflective of the Belichickian beginnings of Dimitroff and the low-key demand for disciplined football by Smith. While he hardly ever gets thrown in to discussions of the league's best coaches, Smith has been top-shelf quality since taking the helm. Two statistics (other than his 56-24 record) that best define his five seasons thus far: Smith is 11-0 against first-year head coaches—in 2013 he'll face Doug Marrone and Bruce Arians, who technically is a rookie head coach—and his teams annually are at the bottom of the league in penalties (Table 1).

The most unusual aspect of the "Victory or Death" attitude is that it is completely out of step for how the franchise has acted since its Phoenix-like rebirth in 2008. In almost every aspect, the Falcons are a rock solid franchise, with five straight winning seasons, a new stadium on the way, and an owner-GM-head coach-quarterback masthead that can stand with any in the league. But apparently, "steady as she goes" isn't a good enough ethos anymore, having been replaced by "shoot for the moon." Alas, our numbers and a cursory glance at the defensive roster indicate that, in this case, Apollo 13 is a more likely result than landing the Eagle. It's hard to argue the Falcons would have been better served by fully choking away the Seahawks game in the divisional playoffs, instead of pulling it out with a last-second field goal. But that long-lusted for playoff win, and the oh-so-close loss to the Niners the following Sunday, seems to have deluded the team with false hope. The entire "5 yards from the Super Bowl" mantra that has erupted in Flowery Branch is a meaningless construct that has somehow convinced the brain trust to go for the gusto in full defiance of the laws of regression and providence.

Ironically, the best bet for the Falcons in 2013 to defy regression and actually win it all might be to undergo a personality transplant and concentrate on simply outgunning opponents. The new paradigm in the league holds that defense does not necessarily win championships—the Ravens were just 19th in defensive DVOA last season, recent champs like the Giants and Saints won with middling units, and the Patriots annually compete for the title despite their opponents marching up and down the field each week.

Given the personnel on hand, and mental images of White and Jones hauling in bomb after bomb, one would think the Birds ripped off big chunks through the air last season. Actually, as Bill Barnwell pointed out over at Grantland, the Falcons gained 20 yards or more via the pass just 7.4 percent of the time when the game was within 14 points, a bottom-third ranking. Only 17 percent of Ryan's passes went deep (16 or more yards through the air), which ranked 30th in the league.

That fits in with the close-to-the-vest, low-risk style the team prizes, which is why Atlanta isn't a must watch on Sunday Ticket despite the great skill players. Compared to the Saints and Packers, to give just two examples, the Falcons are too often boring. But for their championship dreams to come true, it may be time to ditch the bland effectiveness and go the Full Namath. Let Matty Ice heave it and heave it and heave it some more, and just maybe Atlanta can make its defensive weakness immaterial.

Otherwise, the Falcons might find that window of opportunity slamming shut right on its metaphorical breast, scattering feathers all across the Georgia landscape.

Table 1. Falcons Accepted Penalties in the Mike Smith Era, 2008-2012

Year	Penalties	Rank
2008	72	3rd
2009	75	3rd
2010	58	1st
2011	96	10th*
2012	60	1st

Conspiracy theories over those flag-happy refs in 2011 still abound in Atlanta...

Robert Weintraub

2012 Falcons Stats by Week

Wk	vs.	W-L	PF	PA	YDF	YDA	TO	Total	Off	Def	ST
1	at KC	W	40	24	376	393	3	26%	35%	22%	13%
2	DEN	W	27	21	275	336	4	39%	5%	-30%	4%
3	at SD	W	27	3	384	280	3	59%	31%	-30%	-2%
4	Car	W	30	28	426	404	0	-8%	4%	15%	3%
5	at WAS	W	24	17	421	316	0	47%	12%	-37%	-2%
6	OAK	W	23	20	286	474	0	-48%	-40%	10%	2%
7	BYE										
8	at PHI	W	30	17	392	270	0	6%	14%	8%	-1%
9	DAL	W	19	13	453	377	0	-38%	8%	28%	-18%
10	at NO	L	27	31	454	440	0	-26%	-1%	26%	1%
11	ARI	W	23	19	354	178	-5	-23%	-47%	-20%	4%
12	at TB	W	24	23	424	326	-2	-9%	23%	19%	-13%
13	NO	W	23	13	283	436	4	42%	-11%	-46%	7%
14	at CAR	L	20	30	362	475	-1	6%	33%	29%	2%
15	NYG	W	34	0	394	256	3	79%	20%	-57%	2%
16	at DET	W	31	18	344	522	3	28%	26%	8%	10%
17	TB	L	17	22	278	366	1	-20%	-6%	3%	-10%
18	BYE										
19	SEA	W	30	28	417	491	0	3%	25%	24%	2%
20	SF	L	24	28	477	373	-1	9%	42%	29%	-5%

Trends and Splits

	Offense	Rank	Defense	Rank
Total DVOA	6.1%	12	-2.9%	12
Unadjusted VOA	9.0%	9	-3.8%	11
Weighted Trend	2.5%	12	-0.8%	14
Variance	5.7%	13	8.2%	30
Average Opponent	3.5%	32	1.4%	10
Passing	23.6%	10	-2.4%	11
Rushing	-17.2%	30	-3.6%	20
First Down	1.6%	15	-7.8%	8
Second Down	15.1%	6	4.5%	20
Third Down	0.1%	17	-5.1%	13
First Half	6.5%	12	2.2%	20
Second Half	5.6%	11	-7.8%	8
Red Zone	-1.5%	17	-5.1%	10
Late and Close	1.5%	13	-8.8%	13

Five-Year Performance

Year	W-L	Pyth W	Est W	PF	PA	TO	Total	Rk	Off	Rk	Def	Rk	ST	Rk	Off AGL	Rk	Def AGL	Rk	Off Age	Rk	Def Age	Rk	ST Age	Rk
2008	11-5	9.8	8.4	391	325	-3	4.7%	16	8.5%	9	7.5%	25	3.8%	7	15.5	11	13.3	7	27.0	22	27.2	19	26.2	24
2009	9-7	9.1	7.9	363	325	+3	0.5%	18	5.9%	14	4.1%	22	-1.3%	22	15.9	12	21.8	14	28.0	8	26.4	26	26.9	10
2010	13-3	11.4	11.3	414	288	+14	16.3%	7	8.0%	9	-2.1%	14	6.3%	3	5.2	1	10.9	6	28.6	4	26.6	19	27.1	6
2011	10-6	9.4	10.2	402	350	+8	13.9%	8	6.1%	11	-9.1%	8	-1.3%	22	22.2	13	26.4	16	28.0	4	26.7	20	26.4	12
2012	13-3	11.2	9.1	419	299	+13	9.1%	10	6.1%	12	-2.9%	12	0.1%	16	17.3	7	35.6	21	28.6	1	28.0	3	26.5	9

2012 Performance Based on Most Common Personnel Groups

ATL Offense					ATL Offense vs. Opponents				ATL Defense					ATL Defense vs. Opponents			
Pers	Freq	Yds	DVOA	Run%	Pers	Freq	Yds	DVOA	Pers	Freq	Yds	DVOA		Pers	Freq	Yds	DVOA
11	50%	6.3	18.6%	19%	Nickel Even	38%	6.1	13.4%	Nickel Even	53%	6.4	4.3%		11	51%	6.8	12.4%
21	20%	6.3	6.0%	50%	4-3-4	23%	5.9	3.5%	4-3-4	27%	5.2	-18.2%		12	17%	5.4	-16.8%
12	13%	5.8	16.4%	32%	3-4-4	19%	5.3	-12.2%	Nickel Odd	8%	6.2	-8.7%		21	17%	5.7	-9.6%
22	4%	4.0	-49.3%	73%	Dime+	11%	6.4	18.4%	Dime+	5%	7.3	43.3%		22	4%	2.9	-40.5%
20	3%	6.7	8.8%	31%	Nickel Odd	8%	6.3	35.6%	3-4-4	5%	4.5	-16.2%		20	3%	5.3	-28.6%

Strategic Tendencies

Run/Pass		Rk	Formation		Rk	Pass Rush		Rk	Secondary		Rk	Strategy		Rk
Runs, first half	33%	30	Form: Single Back	63%	19	Rush 3	11.9%	4	4 DB	32%	31	Play action	17%	23
Runs, first down	45%	26	Form: Empty Back	5%	18	Rush 4	60.2%	19	5 DB	61%	1	Avg Box (Off)	6.36	17
Runs, second-long	23%	28	Pers: 3+ WR	54%	14	Rush 5	21.5%	15	6+ DB	5%	16	Avg Box (Def)	6.27	25
Runs, power sit.	48%	25	Pers: 4+ WR	1%	22	Rush 6+	6.5%	18	CB by Sides	96%	2	Offensive Pace	29.91	13
Runs, behind 2H	19%	31	Pers: 2+ TE/6+ OL	27%	24	Sacks by LB	17.2%	19	DB Blitz	13%	15	Defensive Pace	31.03	28
Pass, ahead 2H	52%	9	Shotgun/Pistol	39%	25	Sacks by DB	12.1%	5	Hole in Zone	5%	29	Go for it on 4th	0.62	32

Is Mike Smith scarred by some of the failure of his past fourth-and-1 decisions? After ranking in the top ten every year of his head coaching career, Smith was the least aggressive coach in the league in 2012. ☞ The Falcons dramatically cut their use of the running game; their percentage of runs dropped from 45 percent to 33 percent in the first half and from 56 percent to 45 percent on first down. Their offensive pace sped up from 27th in the league to 13th. ☞ What happened to the Falcons on draw plays? In 2011, the Falcons had 52.8% DVOA and 8.5 yards per carry on draws. So in 2012, they decided to run the play more often—54 running-back draws, second in the league behind the Giants—only to see their performance plummet to -46.2% DVOA and just 2.7 yards per carry on draws. ☞ Matt Ryan took 61 quarterback hits, more than anyone other than Andrew Luck. ☞ Mike Nolan really changed the way the Falcons brought their pass rush. They increased about 50 percent in both rushing three and blitzing five or more.

Passing

Player	DYAR	DVOA	Plays	NtYds	Avg	YAC	C%	TD	Int
M.Ryan	1196	16.5%	644	4502	7.0	4.9	68.6%	32	14

Rushing

Player	DYAR	DVOA	Plays	Yds	Avg	TD	Fum	Suc
M.Turner*	-79	-16.6%	222	801	3.6	11	3	43%
J.Rodgers	-9	-10.9%	94	368	3.9	1	0	38%
M.Ryan	54	39.7%	22	152	6.9	1	0	-
J.Jones	16	11.7%	6	30	5.0	0	0	-
S.Jackson	147	5.3%	257	1042	4.1	4	0	47%

Receiving

Player	DYAR	DVOA	Plays	Ctch	Yds	Y/C	YAC	TD	C%
R.White	360	16.3%	143	92	1351	14.7	3.5	7	64%
J.Jones	340	16.0%	129	79	1198	15.2	5.9	10	61%
H.Douglas	-6	-16.6%	59	38	395	10.4	4.0	1	64%
DJ.Davis	8	-0.5%	6	4	40	10.0	5.8	1	67%
T.Gonzalez	286	20.6%	124	93	930	10.0	2.7	8	75%
M.Palmer	-2	-4.1%	6	6	22	3.7	2.8	1	100%
J.Rodgers	135	26.1%	59	53	402	7.6	8.2	1	90%
J.Snelling	10	-8.8%	35	31	203	6.5	6.9	1	89%
M.Turner*	-33	-33.6%	30	19	128	6.7	7.6	1	63%
L.Polite	-25	-82.3%	7	1	8	8.0	10.0	0	14%
S.Jackson	72	11.7%	53	38	321	8.4	7.4	0	72%

Offensive Line

Player	Pos	Age	GS	Snaps	Pen	Sk	Pass	Run	Player	Pos	Age	GS	Snaps	Pen	Sk	Pass	Run
Sam Baker	LT	28	16/16	1058	1	3	20.5	3.5	Peter Konz	RG	24	16/10	674	0	2	8.5	7.5
Justin Blalock	LG	30	16/16	1058	2	1	6	7.5	Garrett Reynolds	OT	26	7/6	392	2	0	2	0
Tyson Clabo*	RT	32	16/16	1048	5	4.5	15.5	2.5	Mike Johnson	G	26	16/1	105	0	1	1	0
Todd McClure*	C	36	16/16	1044	4	4.5	11	4.5									

Year	Yards	ALY	Rk	Power	Rk	Stuff	Rk	2nd Lev	Rk	Open Field	Rk	Sacks	ASR	Rk	Short	Long	F-Start	Cont.
2010	3.97	4.19	8	68%	9	19%	15	1.03	28	0.71	16	22	4.1%	3	9	8	8	48
2011	4.21	3.83	27	59%	22	25%	31	1.16	17	1.05	6	26	5.1%	7	13	9	13	34
2012	3.69	3.87	24	39%	32	23%	27	1.03	26	0.66	21	28	5.1%	8	9	9	9	40
2012 ALY by direction:		Left End 3.21 (27)			Left Tackle 4.81 (6)			Mid/Guard 3.73 (25)			Right Tackle 4.31 (9)				Right End 3.82 (20)			

The name Lamar Holmes may not mean much to Atlanta fans at the moment, but the 2012 third-round choice out of Southern Mississippi is squarely in the spotlight as the new right tackle. The untested Holmes (a mere seven snaps last year) steps in for salary-cap casualty Tyson Clabo, who was reliable and possessed a mean streak four lanes wide. It's a potential trouble spot for an otherwise potent offensive unit. Holmes is a "double-wide load," in Thomas Dimitroff's description, and he has the long arms and toughness required of a pro tackle. But a broken foot suffered last year in training camp set him back, and he comes in to this season raw as sushi.

Also leaving the line is longtime center Todd McClure, who retired. His replacement, Peter Konz, an alum of Big Ugly U (Wisconsin), started ten games at right guard a year ago and displayed quick feet and smarts. Konz is significantly bigger than McClure, but whether that proves boon or difficulty remains to be seen. Sam Baker's worth is likewise questionable, even though he was a priority offseason re-signing. The left tackle has had an injury-prone and at times ineffective career thus far, but showed some improvement in 2012. Still, only five left tackles had more blown blocks on passing plays than Baker, so he still has a ways to go. The guard combo of Garrett Reynolds and Justin Blalock looks solid, but the depth behind them is worrying. The team is still waiting for 2010 picks Mike Johnson and Joe Hawley to develop.

Defensive Front Seven

Defensive Line	Age	Pos	Snaps	Plays	TmPct	Rk	Stop	Dfts	BTkl	Runs	St%	Rk	RuYd	Rk	Sack	Hit	Hur	Tips
Jonathan Babineaux	32	DT	840	34	4.2%	33	29	16	5	23	87%	3	1.3	9	3.5	2	12.5	3
John Abraham*	35	DE	731	43	5.3%	37	38	22	5	20	85%	5	1.2	6	10	9	19.5	7
Kroy Biermann	28	DE	681	46	5.7%	31	33	12	4	34	76%	30	2.3	26	4	9	19.5	0
Vance Walker*	26	DT	530	32	4.0%	37	26	7	1	27	81%	19	1.9	23	3	2	7	0
Corey Peters	25	DT	433	16	3.2%	--	11	3	1	14	71%	--	2.7	--	0	0	3.5	1
Osi Umenyiora	33	DE	635	44	5.3%	38	31	14	3	26	77%	27	2.6	43	6	7	18.5	1

Linebackers	Age	Pos	Snaps	Plays	TmPct	Rk	Stop	Dfts	BTkl	Sack	Hit	Hur	Tips	Runs	St%	Rk	Yds	Rk	Tgts	Suc%	Rk	AdjYd	Rk	PD
Stephen Nicholas	30	OLB	873	99	12.3%	49	54	10	8	2	3	5	0	61	64%	64	3.1	43	41	51%	33	7.5	58	4
Sean Weatherspoon	26	OLB	828	99	15.1%	21	49	18	9	3	4	14	1	53	55%	99	4.1	95	37	59%	16	7.0	49	3
Akeem Dent	26	MLB	497	64	8.0%	75	35	8	5	0	2	2	0	46	63%	67	3.6	66	16	43%	61	6.9	44	2

Year	Yards	ALY	Rk	Power	Rk	Stuff	Rk	2nd Level	Rk	Open Field	Rk	Sacks	ASR	Rk	Short	Long
2010	4.28	3.83	13	64%	19	22%	5	1.19	22	0.92	22	31	5.8%	23	12	11
2011	4.10	3.72	3	63%	17	23%	2	1.19	17	0.81	20	33	6.0%	24	11	15
2012	4.47	3.81	8	65%	21	20%	11	1.18	14	1.11	29	29	5.8%	26	10	15
2012 ALY by direction:			Left End 3.39 (7)			Left Tackle 3.4 (7)			Mid/Guard 4.15 (18)			Right Tackle 3.69 (11)			Right End 3.6 (11)	

Osi Umenyiora is two years younger than the end he replaces in Atlanta, John Abraham, but he played 100 fewer snaps and recorded four fewer sacks than Abraham in 2012. Nevertheless, the Falcons cut the NFL's active sack leader loose in favor of Osi, who makes the Atlanta area his offseason home. Umenyiora's production could make or break his new team's season—minus Abraham, only 10.5 sacks return along the defensive line. No team had a higher percentage of what we charted as "coverage sacks," meaning regular push just wasn't forthcoming, even with Abraham in there. Rumors persist that another veteran pass rusher, perhaps Abraham himself, will be brought in before the season.

Opposite end Kroy Biermann is a versatile piece who often drops back in coverage, but hardly strikes fear in opposing linemen. As usual, he was around the quarterback plenty—equaling Abraham in hits and hurries—without bringing him down. Jonathan Babineaux continues to be a stalwart at one defensive tackle, but it's time for Peria Jerry to show some hint, any hint, of the talent that made him a first-round pick in 2009. Jerry blew out a knee before his rookie year, opening the door for Corey Peters to take his spot. Last preseason, a foot injury to Peters allowed Jerry to take over, until he too suffered leg injuries in midseason, at which point Peters returned as starter. Having both players healthy enough for a decent competition for the starting job in camp would be a refreshing change.

The linebacking trio returns intact despite much consternation about their play, especially in the playoffs, when Seattle and San Francisco treated Stephen Nicholas, Akeem Dent, and Sean Weatherspoon as turnstiles. Dent looked flat out lost at times last year, his first stepping in at Mike linebacker for Curtis Lofton. Improvement is a must. Outside, the rep is that Spoon Man is a boom or bust playmaker while Nicholas is a mediocre Steady Eddie, but our stats rate them essentially equal, and both could stand to clean up the broken tackles. Another thing they have in common: Both Weatherspoon and Nicholas missed OTAs due to surgeries, the former on his knee and the latter for a sports hernia.

Defensive Secondary

Secondary	Age	Pos	Snaps	Plays	TmPct	Rk	Stop	Dfts	BTkl	Runs	St%	Rk	Yds	Rk	Tgts	Tgt%	Rk	Dist	Suc%	Rk	APaYd	Rk	PD	Int
Thomas DeCoud	28	FS	1020	85	10.6%	34	28	17	13	38	39%	31	8.1	52	32	7.4%	28	13.2	48%	60	7.7	43	8	6
Dunta Robinson*	31	CB	930	88	10.9%	11	42	17	8	28	61%	12	5.7	32	83	19.4%	29	13.6	50%	56	8.0	57	8	1
Asante Samuel	32	CB	812	53	7.0%	66	28	12	11	5	40%	47	6.0	40	71	17.7%	44	13.8	61%	9	7.3	37	14	5
William Moore	28	SS	758	84	13.9%	7	33	15	6	45	36%	43	6.7	32	37	11.5%	5	12.1	58%	26	8.7	56	10	4
Robert McClain	25	CB	603	66	8.7%	38	29	11	7	12	42%	42	10.6	81	56	14.1%	69	9.5	64%	3	4.4	1	9	1
Chris Hope*	33	SS	258	16	2.0%	--	4	0	4	9	22%	--	7.2	--	6	1.4%	--	9.8	32%	--	7.9	--	0	0
Dominique Franks	25	CB	203	16	2.0%	--	5	1	2	6	0%	--	10.5	--	6	1.4%	--	10.7	52%	--	6.5	--	2	0
Chris Owens*	27	CB	168	21	3.2%	--	6	3	0	4	25%	--	4.0	--	27	7.7%	--	11.7	55%	--	4.8	--	4	0

Year	Pass D Rank	vs. #1 WR	Rk	vs. #2 WR	Rk	vs. Other WR	Rk	vs. TE	Rk	vs. RB	Rk
2010	10	7.4%	22	-11.3%	6	-6.9%	13	2.1%	13	3.1%	16
2011	10	30.9%	30	-5.6%	12	-32.1%	2	-16.9%	1	-13.2%	7
2012	11	-15.2%	7	-28.5%	1	-3.0%	13	3.0%	21	-3.0%	14

The cornerback position is in transition mode after Dunta Robinson, Chris Owens, and Brent Grimes (who missed most of 2012 with a knee injury) were let go. The Falcons then spent their top two draft picks on corners. Desmond Trufant fits the Atlanta profile—small (6-foot-0, 184 pounds), speedy, excellent press corner skills, iffy tackler. Practically raised to be an NFL corner (his two brothers, Marcus and Isaiah, both play the position in the league), he should start right away, rookie growing pains be damned. If anything, second-rounder Robert Alford out of Southeast Louisiana is even smaller (5-foot-10), faster, and stickier in coverage than Trufant, and even less reliable a tackler. Once he gets over the learning curve, he should take over for Asante Samuel, who was stolen from Philly for a seventh-round pick but is 32 and standing on the precipice of his decline phase.

Atlanta's success in stopping opposing No. 2 receivers was in large part thanks to Samuel's play, but give credit as well to nickelback Robert McClain. Only two corners had a higher Adjusted Success Rate, and he averaged the fewest yards per pass allowed of any qualifying cornerback. However, before they go agitating for McClain to move into the starting lineup, Falcons fans need to ask themselves how "real" those stats are. McClain was a seventh-round pick of the Panthers in 2010 and was cut by both Carolina and Jacksonville before Atlanta picked him up last offseason. His 2012 charting stats are very similar to the 2011 charting stats for Brice McCain of the Texans, who was stellar as a nickelback but struggled mightily when injuries forced him to play outside last season. Given the small sample size, there's a reasonable possibility that McClain's 2012 season was fluky, and an even more likely possibility that his skills in the slot wouldn't necessarily translate in a starting role. The Falcons clearly understand this; otherwise, they would not have used two high picks on cornerbacks.

Atlanta's safety combo of William Moore and Thomas DeCoud both hit the Pro Bowl (after the 49ers duo dropped out to play in a better Bowl), but only Moore is elite. Still, safety is the lone defensive position where the Falcons look settled.

Special Teams

Year	DVOA	Rank	FG/XP	Rank	Net Kick	Rank	Kick Ret	Rank	Net Punt	Rank	Punt Ret	Rank	Hidden	Rank
2010	6.3%	2	4.2	8	13.6	2	8.7	8	0.0	19	5.1	7	-9.8	28
2011	-1.3%	22	4.0	8	-8.0	29	-1.9	21	-1.4	17	0.9	14	-10.7	29
2012	0.1%	16	-2.3	20	4.7	7	0.8	13	1.1	14	-3.7	21	-0.6	19

A thoroughly mediocre unit, save perhaps for kicker Matt Bryant. Certainly Falcons fans feel that his iffy stats were offset by hitting three game-winning field goals, including the biggest kick in recent Falcons history, the game-winner against Seattle that gave the Birds their desperately needed playoff win. Matt Bosher is a mid-pack punter and kickoff specialist, the coverage units were decent if unspectacular, and Dominique Franks underwhelmed as a punt returner. Along with the solid Jacquizz Rodgers on kick returns, all *dramatis personae* figure to return to their jobs in 2013. For a franchise that once offered returners like Prime Time and White Shoes, the lack of excitement in the third phase is sad, but that's life.

Coaching Staff

Mike Smith has established an identity for the Falcons in his five seasons at the helm: tough, few mistakes, and purposefully dull. Last season brought a little-remarked upon but extraordinary piece of change, however. Coming off three playoff berths in four years, and unprecedented overall success for the historically downtrodden franchise, Smith nevertheless willfully changed both coordinators in an effort to improve. Offensive coordinator Mike Mularkey was encouraged to seek other jobs, and he found a promotion in Jacksonville, but he wasn't coming back anyway. Defensive coordinator Brian VanGorder resigned under pressure and was replaced by Mike Nolan.

Many coaches would balk at being asked to make such critical alterations to his staff, and interpret the suggestion as a power play aimed at his eventual firing. Smith didn't remotely handle it that way. He embraced the changes at the top of his flow chart, at least publicly, and relished the opportunity to get better, rather than find the personal slight. It was an egoless move by a humble coach, and it paid off. His profile deserves to be higher, though alas his name probably dooms him to a certain permanent anonymity.

Perhaps the most important coach on Smith's staff this season is offensive line coach Pat Hill. After a decade and a half spent building the Fresno State program, Hill returned to the NFL for the first time since he coached for the 1996 Ravens. (He was one of the only holdovers from Bill Belichick's Cleveland staff.) Hill admitted he leaned heavily on veterans like McClure and Clabo for guidance last season. Now the old pros are gone, and Hill is in the spotlight, having to mold an effective unit with fresh clay like Holmes, Konz and Johnson. Hill reportedly had the chance to return to college football by joining the USC staff, but elected to stay in Atlanta and ensure the offensive line doesn't derail the Falcons' high-powered attack. The job he does will be an important piece of Atlanta's 2013 season.

Baltimore Ravens

2012 Record: 10-6	**Total DVOA:** 9.8% (8th)	**2013 Mean Projection:** 9.6 wins	**On the Clock (0-4):** 3%
Pythagorean Wins: 9.4 (11th)	**Offense:** 3.0% (13th)	**Postseason Odds:** 64.2%	**Mediocrity (5-7):** 16%
Snap-Weighted Age: 27.4 (6th)	**Defense:** 2.2% (19th)	**Super Bowl Odds:** 14.4%	**Playoff Contender (8-10):** 46%
Average Opponent: -1.0% (16th)	**Special Teams:** 9.0% (1st)	**Proj. Avg. Opponent:** 1.7% (7th)	**Super Bowl Contender (11+):** 36%

2012: Baltimore closes out the Ray Lewis era as the latest team to follow a mediocre regular season with a surprising Super Bowl run.

2013: The post-Lewis Ravens need to figure out their identity, but that's easier to do when Ozzie Newsome and John Harbaugh are in charge.

The last time the Ravens won a Super Bowl, they changed quarterbacks. This time, they changed everything but the quarterback. They have changed their identity as deftly as a mobster scheduled to testify. They have gone from a defense-oriented team to … say, what *have* they become?

Ray Lewis was synonymous with Ravens football since before the phrase "Ravens football" existed. Lewis is a broadcaster now. Ed Reed was Robin to Lewis' Batman for 11 years. Reed plays for the Houston Texans now. Paul Kruger erupted on the scene as the latest in a long line of scary Ravens edge rushers, part of a tradition that dates back from Terrell Suggs to Adalius Thomas and Peter Boulware. Kruger plays for the Browns now. Dannell Ellerbe emerged from the bench to become a major contributor down the stretch and in the playoffs, the kind of player the Ravens effectively flanked Lewis with for over a decade. He's with the Dolphins now.

There were other losses. Bernard Pollard, Reed's fiery enforcer at strong safety? He's now in Tennessee. Cary Williams, last year's often-picked-upon interception leader? In Philadelphia, skipping practices for weddings and dance recitals. On offense, Anquan Boldin was the stabilizing veteran of the skill position players, the receiver Joe Flacco looked for when the team needed tough yards, right through third-and-1 in the fourth quarter of the Super Bowl. Boldin is in San Francisco. Matt Birk started 70 straight Ravens games at center, from 2009 through the Super Bowl. He's now retired. Brandon Ayanbadejo is thought of as a quasi-political figure because of his pro-marriage equality stance, but he was an important special-teamer and the first linebacker off the bench for five years. He's gone too.

The Ravens lost all of these players not from their usual dominant defense, but from a unit suffering its worst season since 1996, the year the franchise arrived from Cleveland and drafted a kid named Ray Lewis. The Ravens finished 19th in DVOA last year, their first finish outside the NFL's top six since 1998, due to the combination of an aging core and a rash of injuries. There was a midseason period, just after they lost Lewis and young shutdown corner Lardarius Webb, where their defense was downright awful (DVOA ratings of 30.6% and 28.4% against the Cowboys and Texans in Weeks 6 and 7). After the bye week, things got better. The Ravens had 7.5% defensive DVOA through Week 7 but improved to -2.5% DVOA in Weeks 9-to-17. By the playoffs, they were back to the Ravens as we know them, with -17.5% DVOA during the postseason.

But now the Ravens as we know them are gone for good. Those Ravens were Ray Lewis and his corps of scary defenders, the guys who constantly overcame a mediocre offense to produce 13-10 victories. Several important members of that defense are still around, including Haloti Ngata and the rapidly fading Suggs. The Ravens will also get Webb back from last year's ACL injury, and they can pair him with late-blooming cornerback Corey Graham. But the losses were huge, and they go well beyond the Lewis "heart and soul" bit.

Table 1 shows the percent of significant defensive plays the Ravens lost to free agency or retirement this season. Any way you slice it, more than half of the Ravens defensive production is gone: not just the raw tackles that defenses accumulate just by showing up, but the sacks, interceptions, Defeats, and other things that make a defense special.

Table 1: Defensive Plays Lost

Type of Play	Percent lost
Stops	53.4%
Defeat	55.8%
Sacks	52.7%
Interceptions	76.9%
Total Defensive Plays	59.3%

These Stops and Defeats just don't vanish, of course. A great deal of slack will be picked up by newcomers, and the Ravens did cobble together some quality reinforcements. Elvis Dumervil, Captain Faxtastic himself, is somewhere between an heir apparent for Suggs and a replacement for Kruger. He's a great player, and his arrival put the brakes on a Chicken Little offseason. Michael Huff is a capable veteran safety who can do a passable imitation of the late-career Ed Reed when not out of position at cornerback (like he was for the 2012 Raiders). The draft brought Matt Elam at safety and some interesting raw recruits; Arthur Brown could grow into a solid coverage linebacker, but he is no replacement for Ray Lewis. Even the God of Hellfire is no replacement for Ray Lewis.

Mix Elvis, Huff, Elam, and Brown with Ngata, Webb, Suggs, and Graham, and you have a fine defense. But it's likely to be fine, not great. It's not clear how much defensive pro-

2013 Ravens Schedule

Week	Opp.	Week	Opp.	Week	Opp.
1	at DEN (Thu.)	7	at PIT	13	PIT (Thu.)
2	CLE	8	BYE	14	MIN
3	HOU	9	at CLE	15	at DET (Mon.)
4	at BUF	10	CIN	16	NE
5	at MIA	11	at CHI	17	at CIN
6	GB	12	NYJ		

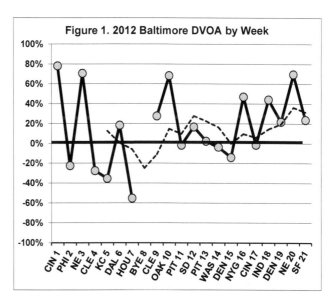

Figure 1. 2012 Baltimore DVOA by Week

duction the Ravens lost in the offseason, but the only reasonable answer is "some." The changes may not be immediately reflected in Baltimore's regular-season record, because 2012 already showed us what to expect from a Ravens team without a stifling defense. Even so, the dramatic turnover in personnel means we can't expect the rebound we normally would anticipate from a team that dropped from first in defensive DVOA one year to 19th the next.

So if the Ravens can no longer claim to be a Dominating Defense team, what kind of team are they? The fact that the Ravens won the Super Bowl last year despite their worst defensive season in memory reminds us that there is more to football, even Ravens football, than defense. Special teams played a major role in last season's championship, from Justin Tucker's kickoff prowess to Jacoby Jones' kick return heroics. John Harbaugh cut his teeth as a special teams coach, of course, but special teams excellence is volatile, and it is silly to suggest that a championship defense can be built on the kicking game. The Ravens offense, meanwhile, enjoyed its fourth straight year of being squarely above average. Poetic simplicity would suggest that the 2012 season represented a neat transition, with the champion linebacker stepping back so the new champion quarterback could step forward.

To claim that the Ravens are now Joe Flacco's team, however, is to retroactively apply his playoff success to an inconsistent, frustrating regular season. The Ravens offense went into a funk in Week 5 and didn't climb all the way out of it until Week 16, one game after coordinator Cam Cameron was fired. Flacco and the offense got out of their own way once Jim Caldwell began calling the plays, and Flacco's 11-touchdown, zero-interception postseason roll was an emphatic statement after a full calendar year of "justify your existence or leave town" speculation.

Flacco is now the face of the franchise and one of the veteran leaders, but if you called him a potential centerpiece of the organization as recently as early December you would have earned some ironic chuckles. The statement *"This is Joe Flacco's team"* rings hollow, something said to be arch and provocative or just provide a hook for an article. He's a good quarterback who got a little better in January and a lot richer in March, but he is not the beating heart of the franchise.

The "Flacco's Team" identity would fit better if Boldin were still around. The Ravens replaced Boldin with nobody. Torrey Smith and Jacoby Jones are penciled in as the starting receivers. Smith played great football early in the season and at the

end, but endured a punishing midseason funk, much like the offense around him. Jones is Jones: a postseason hero one year removed from misadventure in Houston, the kind of player the Raiders would have signed to a crazy contract during Al Davis' muddled years. Behind Smith and Jones are a cabal of interesting prospects like Tommy Streeter, Tandon Doss, and Deonte Thompson. A rebuilding team would be thrilled with such a crop of speedy unknowns. A defending champion striving to rebrand itself as a passing juggernaut needs veterans or high draft picks in the third-through-fifth receiver slots.

The Ravens' offense, like their defense, promises/threatens to be fine-just-fine. Ray Rice, now supported by postseason star Bernard Pierce, will provide plenty of rushing and receiving production. Gino Gradkowski should be an adequate replacement for Birk, so the line will be stable. Dennis Pitta and Ed Dickson give Caldwell a versatile tight end tandem for his no-huddle looks. But here we are, searching for identity but typing about the likes of Ed Dickson and Gino Gradkowski. We are looking for the kernel of the new Ravens in all the wrong places.

So again, who are these Ravens? DVOA projections tell us what common sense suggested: they are unlikely to return to the Super Bowl. The Ravens were improbable champions in 2012, after all, and even the most optimistic observer must consider their offseason transactions a net minus. On the other hand, the offensive improvement made during the postseason does mean something. A year ago, curious about our mediocre forecast for the 2012 Giants, Jason Lisk of TheBigLead.com did some research showing that teams which go on surprising playoff runs tend to carry over that improvement into the next season, particularly on offense[1]. There is plenty of ancillary evidence to suggest the Ravens will follow this trend, from the coordinator change to adjustments on the offensive line to Bernard Pierce's emergence as a Ray Rice counterpunch. Jack the offense up a little, downgrade the defense a bit, and you have a Ravens team that is in familiar territory. The Ravens always appear to be undermanned, especially on offense, until they are suddenly 12-4 and coming within a dropped pass of

---

[3] For some further Football Outsiders research on this, watch this video: http://www.youtube.com/watch?v=kMNBXsj3Pm0

the Super Bowl, or surging through a playoff hot streak with the help of a mixed-up Broncos defensive back. The Ravens are slightly down, but not out, not when they have Flacco, Rice, Ngata, Dumervil, John Harbaugh, and a developmental pipeline with the potential to turn Streeter, Elam, Gradkowski, Courtney Upshaw, or whoever into the next generation of Ravens playoff building blocks.

That last bit—the ability to develop, reload, and remain close to contention—reveals whose team the Ravens are, and whose team they always have been, even when Lewis was squirrel dancing atop opponents' backs. This is Ozzie Newsome's team. He drafted Lewis. He built the 2000 champions. He spent a decade cobbling together offenses to support the dominating defense. Brian Billick's hand-picked quarterback selections would blow up in his face, but Newsome provided good running backs and capable offensive lines so the team could go 10-6 under Kyle Boller and Anthony Wright. Harbaugh provides Newsome with the ultimate extension of his own personality as head coach: a program builder with an eye on both sides of the ball, a long-range planner with the flexibility to adapt on the fly.

Without Lewis in the spotlight, the 2013 Ravens are a Newsome team built on Newsome principles: lots of developmental players and no glaring weaknesses (in the leaner years, the only Achilles heel was usually the quarterback). This is a team built the old fashioned way. The 2012 Ravens were the same way, once you looked past the legends. Ellerbe and Kruger did not start the season as superstars, or even starters: they were slow-burn prospects who grew into their roles as the season progressed. Graham was a Bears special-teamer acquired by Newsome to be a nickelback. Not even Newsome expected him to emerge as a top-tier starter, but only Newsome saw more than just a kick gunner. The Ravens built their Super

Bowl run out of these players, as well as rookies (Pierce, Justin Tucker, Kelechi Osemele) and reclamation projects (Jones, Bryant McKinnie, Ma'ake Kemoeatu). The last few seasons of Ravens football have been a master feat of roster creation, facilitated by Harbaugh and his staff, who made sure every replacement part knows where he is supposed to fit.

The Newsome Ravens of 2013 are a little like the Steelers of 2013. Both teams have an organizational structure in place that staves off total collapse indefinitely. Newsome does things differently than the Steelers. He is more likely to make a big free agent move, is not as tied to one scheme, and is more likely to endure a 5-11 shake-up season when things go wrong. But both franchises have learned how to hover around .500 while rebuilding, a trick that requires stability from the front office down through the coaching staff, so that the about-to-blossom draft pick from two years ago doesn't discover that the system has been completely changed and his coaches want to start fresh with new guys. The Ravens and Steelers seem eternally locked together because they have been doing things similarly since the start of this millennium.

This looks like a year in which the Ravens will be slightly down and the Steelers will be somewhat sideways, with the Bengals interloping. That's what 2012 looked like in July as well: the top of the AFC North is always a close call. Even if the Ravens are shoved down toward .500 by competition and attrition, they will not be down for long. Newsome cannot *will* his team better, like Lewis allegedly could, but he has spent all of Ravens history *working* them better. They can rebuild their nucleus, because their general manager, not the Hall of Fame linebacker or the quarterback, is the one who supplies the team's DNA.

Mike Tanier

2012 Ravens Stats by Week

Wk	vs.	W-L	PF	PA	YDF	YDA	TO	Total	Off	Def	ST
1	CIN	W	44	13	430	322	2	78%	60%	-14%	4%
2	at PHI	L	23	24	325	486	2	-23%	-31%	10%	18%
3	NE	W	31	30	503	396	-1	71%	63%	-9%	-1%
4	CLE	W	23	16	438	357	1	-28%	-10%	5%	-13%
5	at KC	W	9	6	298	338	2	-36%	-35%	-4%	-4%
6	DAL	W	31	29	316	481	1	18%	24%	31%	25%
7	at HOU	L	13	43	176	420	-2	-55%	-48%	28%	21%
8	BYE										
9	at CLE	W	25	15	282	290	2	28%	17%	-13%	-2%
10	OAK	W	55	20	419	422	2	68%	31%	3%	40%
11	at PIT	W	13	10	200	309	3	-2%	-29%	-4%	24%
12	at SD	W	16	13	443	280	0	17%	4%	-6%	7%
13	PIT	L	20	23	288	366	1	2%	-7%	-3%	7%
14	at WAS	L	28	31	359	423	-1	-4%	3%	8%	1%
15	DEN	L	17	34	278	350	-2	-14%	-25%	6%	17%
16	NYG	W	33	14	533	186	0	47%	30%	-13%	4%
17	at CIN	L	17	23	352	189	-1	-2%	-6%	-7%	-3%
18	IND	W	24	9	439	419	0	44%	24%	-11%	9%
19	at DEN	W	38	35	479	398	2	22%	35%	-30%	-43%
20	at NE	W	28	13	356	428	3	70%	45%	-31%	-5%
21	at SF	W	34	31	367	468	1	24%	27%	11%	8%

Trends and Splits

	Offense	Rank	Defense	Rank
Total DVOA	3.0%	13	2.2%	19
Unadjusted VOA	4.1%	13	0.4%	17
Weighted Trend	-0.2%	16	3.0%	22
Variance	10.9%	30	1.8%	2
Average Opponent	1.0%	18	-0.6%	16
Passing	9.6%	15	3.5%	13
Rushing	7.5%	7	0.9%	25
First Down	2.1%	14	-0.4%	17
Second Down	7.4%	12	16.6%	29
Third Down	-2.0%	19	-14.6%	6
First Half	6.9%	11	2.7%	21
Second Half	-1.0%	13	1.8%	15
Red Zone	-6.1%	19	-10.4%	8
Late and Close	-11.7%	22	-4.6%	17

Five-Year Performance

Year	W-L	Pyth W	Est W	PF	PA	TO	Total	Rk	Off	Rk	Def	Rk	ST	Rk	Off AGL	Rk	Def AGL	Rk	Off Age	Rk	Def Age	Rk	ST Age	Rk
2008	11-5	12.0	11.7	385	244	+13	27.6%	2	-0.3%	19	-27.8%	2	0.1%	16	23.4	13	53.9	31	26.4	29	28.4	2	26.7	13
2009	9-7	11.6	12.0	391	261	+10	29.1%	1	12.8%	9	-14.2%	4	2.2%	8	8.4	5	22.2	15	26.7	26	28.0	4	25.9	24
2010	12-4	10.6	12.1	357	270	+7	21.7%	5	5.4%	12	-10.3%	6	6.0%	4	23.8	15	27.1	19	27.9	9	28.2	6	25.8	23
2011	12-4	11.2	10.6	378	266	+2	14.5%	7	2.9%	13	-17.1%	1	-5.6%	30	8.0	1	10.9	4	27.8	9	28.2	3	26.6	6
2012	10-6	9.4	9.2	398	344	+9	9.8%	8	3.0%	13	2.2%	19	9.0%	1	8.1	2	46.4	25	27.3	10	27.7	7	26.9	7

2012 Performance Based on Most Common Personnel Groups

BAL Offense					BAL Offense vs. Opponents				BAL Defense				BAL Defense vs. Opponents			
Pers	Freq	Yds	DVOA	Run%	Pers	Freq	Yds	DVOA	Pers	Freq	Yds	DVOA	Pers	Freq	Yds	DVOA
11	43%	5.7	5.1%	19%	4-3-4	29%	5.2	11.8%	3-4-4	43%	5.6	14.7%	11	46%	4.9	-6.7%
21	34%	5.8	14.0%	60%	Nickel Even	27%	6.5	12.5%	Nickel Even	26%	5.6	6.2%	12	30%	5.9	14.3%
12	15%	5.8	15.1%	45%	3-4-4	22%	5.4	-2.0%	Nickel Odd	20%	4.8	-13.7%	21	14%	6.0	11.3%
22	4%	3.2	-35.8%	76%	Nickel Odd	13%	6.2	33.2%	4-3-4	6%	4.3	-47.8%	22	4%	5.1	21.3%
20	1%	9.9	86.0%	47%	Dime+	4%	1.6	-78.7%	Dime+	3%	3.2	-85.6%	13	3%	3.0	-44.6%
622	1%	-0.3	-12.6%	83%					4-4-3	2%	2.7	23.5%				

Strategic Tendencies

Run/Pass		Rk	Formation		Rk	Pass Rush		Rk	Secondary		Rk	Strategy		Rk
Runs, first half	41%	9	Form: Single Back	52%	29	Rush 3	8.2%	10	4 DB	49%	6	Play action	24%	10
Runs, first down	49%	20	Form: Empty Back	5%	19	Rush 4	60.9%	17	5 DB	46%	19	Avg Box (Off)	6.47	9
Runs, second-long	39%	5	Pers: 3+ WR	45%	26	Rush 5	22.4%	13	6+ DB	3%	22	Avg Box (Def)	6.51	5
Runs, power sit.	67%	6	Pers: 4+ WR	1%	23	Rush 6+	8.5%	8	CB by Sides	90%	7	Offensive Pace	27.54	3
Runs, behind 2H	28%	18	Pers: 2+ TE/6+ OL	21%	29	Sacks by LB	54.1%	10	DB Blitz	15%	9	Defensive Pace	30.39	20
Pass, ahead 2H	53%	6	Shotgun/Pistol	41%	23	Sacks by DB	13.5%	2	Hole in Zone	12%	5	Go for it on 4th	0.98	15

Only Oakland used traditional 21 personnel more often than Baltimore. ☞ Calling Vonta Leach's reputation: for the second straight year, Baltimore's DVOA running with two backs wasn't really any different than it was running with one back. In fact, this year it was actually slightly lower (5.5% DVOA with 4.6 yards/carry with two backs, 8.7% DVOA with 4.4 yards/carry with one back). ☞ Baltimore's use of 3-plus wide receivers went up from 28 percent in 2011 to 45 percent in 2012, and their use of multiple tight ends dropped from 37 percent to 21 percent. ☞ We mention this every year, but it's worth mentioning every year because it never changes: Baltimore is consistently one of the rare offenses that is more productive when it *doesn't* use play action. The average team gains 1.5 more yards with 12 more percentage points of DVOA with play action. The Ravens gained just 0.6 more yards with play action and had 4.5% DVOA as opposed to 13.9% DVOA without a play fake. ☞ Baltimore also struggled with play action on the other side of the ball. The Ravens had the league's biggest gap in both yards and DVOA between passes with play action (37.0% DVOA, 8.7 yards per pass) and passes without play action (-5.2% DVOA, 5.6 yards per pass). Unlike on the offense, this has not been a long-term trend over multiple years. ☞ Baltimore was dramatically better against shotgun formations than against standard formations with the QB under center.

DVOA Shotgun	Rank	Yds Shotgun	Rank	DVOA Not Shotgun	Rank	Yds Not Shotgun	Rank	Dif DVOA	Rank	Dif Yds	Rank
-9.1%	6	5.2	2	8.7%	29	5.3	25	-17.8%	1	-0.1	1

Passing

Player	DYAR	DVOA	Plays	NtYds	Avg	YAC	C%	TD	Int
J.Flacco	358	-1.3%	566	3589	6.3	4.9	59.7%	22	10
T.Taylor	-34	-28.3%	32	149	4.7	4.7	58.6%	0	1

Rushing

Player	DYAR	DVOA	Plays	Yds	Avg	TD	Fum	Suc
R.Rice	205	11.5%	257	1143	4.4	9	1	44%
B.Pierce	54	4.1%	108	532	4.9	1	0	47%
J.Flacco	-32	-35.1%	18	30	1.7	3	3	-
A.Allen	9	4.4%	16	61	3.8	1	0	50%
T.Taylor	18	13.8%	11	76	6.9	1	0	-
V.Leach*	21	37.0%	9	32	3.6	1	0	89%

Receiving

Player	DYAR	DVOA	Plays	Ctch	Yds	Y/C	YAC	TD	C%
A.Boldin*	122	3.4%	112	65	921	14.2	3.6	4	58%
T.Smith	143	0.7%	110	49	855	17.4	4.6	8	45%
J.Jones	37	0.4%	55	30	406	13.5	2.8	1	55%
T.Doss	20	5.3%	17	7	123	17.6	7.4	1	41%
D.Reed	21	40.7%	6	5	66	13.2	4.6	0	83%
D.Thompson	13	-0.6%	6	5	51	10.2	4.6	0	83%
D.Pitta	51	4.3%	94	61	669	11.0	4.1	7	65%
E.Dickson	2	-5.8%	33	21	234	11.1	4.0	0	64%
R.Rice	10	-11.7%	83	61	478	7.8	7.7	1	73%
V.Leach*	36	11.6%	24	21	143	6.8	6.3	0	88%
B.Pierce	10	1.8%	11	7	47	6.7	6.1	0	64%

Offensive Line

Player	Pos	Age	GS	Snaps	Pen	Sk	Pass	Run	Player	Pos	Age	GS	Snaps	Pen	Sk	Pass	Run
Michael Oher	LT	27	16/16	1058	9	8	25.5	5	Bobbie Williams*	G	37	12/6	355	4	4.5	7	5
Matt Birk*	C	37	16/16	1017	2	3.5	14	3	Ramon Harewood	LG	26	6/5	341	0	1	6	4
Kelechi Osemele	RT	24	16/16	1017	7	7	21.5	5	Bryant McKinnie	LT	34	16/0	128	1	1	2.5	0
Marshal Yanda	RG	29	14/14	912	6	0	7.5	1	A.Q. Shipley	C	27	14/5	465	0	0	2	1
Jah Reid	LG	24	9/7	568	4	2	5	1									

Year	Yards	ALY	Rk	Power	Rk	Stuff	Rk	2nd Lev	Rk	Open Field	Rk	Sacks	ASR	Rk	Short	Long	F-Start	Cont.
2010	3.88	4.19	9	55%	24	15%	6	0.97	29	0.46	27	40	7.9%	25	8	27	25	38
2011	4.47	4.25	7	63%	15	18%	11	1.05	30	1.06	5	33	5.9%	12	4	19	23	36
2012	4.53	4.33	6	64%	14	16%	4	1.22	14	0.87	11	38	6.1%	13	9	13	23	30

2012 ALY by direction: Left End 3.69 (18) | Left Tackle 4.12 (14) | Mid/Guard 4.48 (5) | Right Tackle 4.03 (13) | Right End 5.16 (5)

Four-fifths of the Ravens' playoff line is back this season, and Joe Flacco is happy about it. "I think every year we've been here, we've juggled the offensive line around a pretty good amount," he told the *Baltimore Sun* in May. "So, I think the fact that we have a pretty good feel about who is going to be up there is definitely good for me, and the fact that they played so well together last year at the end of the season is definitely a big confidence booster."

The Ravens certainly juggled their offensive line a pretty good amount before the playoffs last year. Michael Oher moved from left to right tackle, rookie Kelechi Osemele moved from right tackle to left guard, and Bryant McKinnie moved from skid row to left tackle. It was a "where has this been all year" transformation. Both Oher and Osemele were overextended at their former positions, and a revolving cast of Bobbie Williams-type journeymen manned left guard before K.O. moved over. McKinnie is a jumbo-sized Dickens character, alternately respected and ridiculed, prosperous and penniless, so his solid play through the Super Bowl and lucrative new two-year contract are just the latest chapters in his neo-Victorian saga. Oher is a natural fit at right tackle, and K.O. could become another great guard in a league that is becoming flooded with them.

Marshall Yanda is already a great guard. The one sack he allowed last year was negated by defensive encroachment, and the one tackle for a loss he surrendered on a running play was also nullified because his defender jumped. To beat Yanda, you essentially have to cheat. 2012 fourth-round pick Gino Gradkowski of the Fightin' Gradkowski Brothers is the favorite to replace Matt Birk at center. Gradkowski and Flacco form an all-Delaware center-quarterback exchange, which is weird. The Ravens traded for journeyman A.Q. Shipley, who has had stints in Pittsburgh, Philadelphia, and Indianapolis, to push Gradkwoski.

Defensive Front Seven

Defensive Line	Age	Pos	Snaps	Plays	TmPct	Rk	Stop	Dfts	BTkl	Runs	St%	Rk	RuYd	Rk	Sack	Hit	Hur	Tips
Haloti Ngata	29	DE	819	52	6.7%	16	36	12	2	43	65%	67	3.0	61	5	9	13	1
Arthur Jones	27	DT	528	47	5.3%	21	31	8	2	41	61%	67	3.3	64	4.5	9	7	0
Ma'ake Kemoeatu*	34	DT	432	31	3.7%	44	20	5	2	28	61%	68	3.1	62	1	1	2	2
Pernell McPhee	24	DE	422	21	3.2%	--	18	5	1	19	84%	--	2.2	--	1.5	6	5.5	0
Terrence Cody	25	DT	362	26	3.1%	59	18	2	1	25	68%	57	2.6	52	0	1	3	1
Elvis Dumervil	29	DE	921	54	6.8%	12	41	19	3	35	66%	63	2.9	59	11	12	23	0
Marcus Spears	30	DE	388	26	3.5%	63	22	7	0	24	83%	11	1.8	15	1	0	2.5	1
Chris Canty	31	DT	297	26	5.6%	16	21	5	1	22	82%	16	2.5	45	3	3	5	0

Linebackers	Age	Pos	Snaps	Plays	Overall TmPct	Rk	Stop	Dfts	BTkl	Pass Rush Sack	Hit	Hur	Tips	vs. Run Runs	St%	Rk	Yds	Rk	vs. Pass Tgts	Suc%	Rk	AdjYd	Rk	PD
Paul Kruger*	27	OLB	789	46	5.6%	103	40	22	6	9	6	21	4	23	83%	8	1.7	5	7	51%	--	5.9	--	3
Courtney Upshaw	24	OLB	745	56	6.3%	91	43	13	5	1.5	2	8	1	51	76%	15	2.0	12	8	45%	--	7.2	--	0
Jameel McClain	28	ILB	737	82	11.4%	55	37	5	7	0	1	5	0	55	51%	104	5.4	110	22	47%	51	7.8	62	2
Dannell Ellerbe*	28	ILB	651	90	12.6%	48	56	21	8	4.5	3	8.5	0	51	73%	24	3.4	55	32	56%	20	5.3	17	1
Ray Lewis*	38	ILB	441	58	17.5%	8	26	3	1	1	2	1	0	42	45%	109	4.8	107	13	54%	--	6.7	--	1
Albert McClellan	27	OLB	426	44	5.7%	100	30	7	6	1	1	5.5	0	27	74%	18	4.3	96	9	55%	--	4.8	--	2
Terrell Suggs	31	OLB	407	25	5.7%	102	16	6	0	2	3	6	4	17	59%	87	3.5	57	2	71%	--	1.3	--	0
Josh Bynes	24	ILB	211	32	5.8%	--	15	4	2	0	1	2	0	24	50%	--	3.5	--	7	48%	--	10.4	--	1
Brendon Ayanbadejo*	37	ILB	170	31	3.5%	--	16	7	2	1	1	2	0	18	50%	--	4.0	--	7	82%	--	1.6	--	1

Year	Yards	ALY	Rk	Power	Rk	Stuff	Rk	2nd Level	Rk	Open Field	Rk	Sacks	ASR	Rk	Short	Long
2010	3.84	3.81	12	67%	24	19%	17	1.04	8	0.56	10	27	5.5%	27	9	12
2011	3.55	3.96	12	66%	22	17%	25	0.92	2	0.33	2	48	8.4%	2	14	18
2012	4.10	4.33	28	76%	29	14%	32	1.16	11	0.42	3	37	6.9%	10	11	14
2012 ALY by direction:			Left End 3.94 (18)			Left Tackle 4.35 (24)			Mid/Guard 4.41 (29)			Right Tackle 4.42 (29)			Right End 4.16 (16)	

The Known Commodities: Haloti Ngata spent the second half of the Super Bowl in the locker room with a sprained knee. He admitted in June that he was out of shape because he could not run while rehabbing the injury, but players who admit (without prompting) to being out of shape are usually capable of getting back into shape. Ngata remains an excellent 3-4 lineman. Newcomers Marcus Spears and Chris Canty add some veteran bulwarking to cover all of the free-agent losses. Elvis Dumervil is an exceptional upfield pass rusher who struggles with both the run and the fax machine. Jameel McClain has started beside Ray Lewis for three years and is smart and steady, if unspectacular. McClain missed the end of last season with a spinal cord contusion and was a limited participant in OTAs, but the Ravens expect him at full speed for training camp. Pernell McPhee and Albert McClellan are solid role players off the bench.

The Unknown Commodities: it's strange to talk about the Ravens' front seven and need to use the phrase "unknown commodities." Terrell Suggs is just two years removed from a Defensive Player of the Year award, but he is 30 years old and coming of an Achilles-plagued year. If Suggs bounces back to something resembling his 2011 form, he and Dumervil will be excellent pass-rush bookends. Second-round pick Arthur Brown was a fast and heady Cover-2 type at Kansas State and should compete for the starting job beside McClain on the inside, although he underwent sports hernia surgery at the end of May and could miss the start of camp.

A pair of former Alabama players have failed to live up to Crimson Tide expectations. Jim Harbaugh singled out Courtney Upshaw for being out of shape in training camp; Upshaw admitted that he let his conditioning lapse while dealing with some personal issues. Unlike Haloti Ngata, Upshaw was not rehabbing his knee, and he is not Haloti Ngata. Dumervil's arrival makes Upshaw less important, but the Ravens need him as both a situational pass rusher and Suggs insurance. At defensive tackle, Terrence Cody lost his starting job to Ma'ake Kemoeatu (who wasn't re-signed) and was relegated to 350-pound blocking-sled duties. He's penciled in as a starter this year, but will split time with both Arthur Jones and third-round rookie Brandon Williams. Williams is the highest draft pick in the history of Division II Missouri Southern State and earned rave reviews for his strength in minicamp.

Defensive Secondary

Secondary	Age	Pos	Snaps	Plays	Overall TmPct	Rk	Stop	Dfts	BTkl	vs. Run Runs	St%	Rk	Yds	Rk	vs. Pass Tgts	Tgt%	Rk	Dist	Suc%	Rk	APaYd	Rk	PD	Int
Cary Williams*	29	CB	1079	91	10.3%	17	29	10	2	12	42%	42	7.3	52	93	21.0%	15	13.5	44%	79	8.0	58	17	4
Ed Reed*	35	FS	1046	73	8.3%	49	29	14	15	23	26%	61	7.5	42	38	8.5%	20	14.6	54%	35	8.7	55	13	4
Bernard Pollard*	29	SS	895	103	14.4%	4	34	14	6	52	35%	44	5.6	13	24	6.7%	36	9.9	49%	53	7.3	36	3	1
Corey Graham	28	CB	573	62	7.0%	65	23	8	3	27	30%	69	7.3	53	43	9.6%	86	12.9	62%	6	5.6	4	8	2
Jimmy Smith	25	CB	463	34	5.6%	--	11	5	4	6	17%	--	7.2	--	38	12.5%	--	13.2	48%	--	8.2	--	2	0
Lardarius Webb	28	CB	376	31	9.4%	--	18	6	7	12	75%	--	3.5	--	22	13.0%	--	12.1	76%	--	3.7	--	5	1
James Ihedigbo	30	FS	289	19	2.2%	--	9	4	2	11	36%	--	7.6	--	6	1.4%	--	15.1	49%	--	4.1	--	1	0
Chykie Brown	27	CB	244	18	2.0%	--	10	6	1	1	100%	--	-2.0	--	23	5.2%	--	15.5	51%	--	9.1	--	4	0
Michael Huff	30	CB	945	68	8.7%	39	34	11	3	23	52%	24	6.0	39	73	19.2%	34	12.7	56%	21	8.2	64	10	2

Year	Pass D Rank	vs. #1 WR	Rk	vs. #2 WR	Rk	vs. Other WR	Rk	vs. TE	Rk	vs. RB	Rk
2010	6	-12.1%	8	5.2%	17	-29.6%	2	-14.0%	2	0.5%	12
2011	1	-4.5%	9	-4.2%	13	-28.8%	3	-0.4%	7	-18.0%	3
2012	13	6.4%	20	21.0%	30	-16.0%	6	-6.8%	9	-20.8%	7

We would do the Known-Unknown routine with this unit if we could find any real "knowns." Lardarius Webb has torn both ACLs in the past three years. He participated in individual drills during minicamp and is expected to be ready for training camp. Webb was excellent for the first six weeks of 2012, and he returned quickly from his 2009 injury; still, it's optimistic to expect him to return to immediate Pro Bowl-caliber form.

Before he signed with Baltimore last offseason, Chicago used Corey Graham almost exclusively on special teams. He had just 87 defensive snaps in 2011 and two in 2010. When Webb's injury forced him into the Ravens lineup, Graham was shockingly good, finishing in the top ten in both cornerback charting metrics. Webb and Graham could be the Ravens' best cornerback tandem since Chris McAlister and Duane Starks were in their primes, or they could be an injury case and a glorified nickel corner coming off a career year. Jimmy Smith, a tape-measure-and-stopwatch Hall of Famer, is still lurking on the depth chart and could challenge Graham. Smith took up boxing to shed weight in the offseason; at 6-foot-2 and now 200 pounds, he could be a big-receiver matchup solution if he avoids the lingering injuries and mental mistakes that plagued him in his first two seasons.

Rookie safety Matt Elam, chosen out of Florida with the final pick of the first round, combines Bernard Pollard's near-reckless hitting style with some of Ed Reed's range as a centerfielder. Of course, he lacks the 265 games of NFL experience Reed and Pollard shared, but the Ravens need him to make an immediate impact. Michael Huff moved from safety to cornerback in an attempt to rescue the Raiders secondary last year. The results were not pretty, but at safety Huff has speed, range, and some blitz capability. Huff is not Ed Reed 2008, but he can be just as good or better than Ed Reed 2012. James Ihedigbo, a special teams ace who turns 30 in December, is the only backup safety with any real experience.

Special Teams

Year	DVOA	Rank	FG/XP	Rank	Net Kick	Rank	Kick Ret	Rank	Net Punt	Rank	Punt Ret	Rank	Hidden	Rank
2010	6.0%	4	4.3	7	13.5	3	0.8	15	17.4	1	-5.7	26	-16.1	31
2011	-5.6%	30	-5.3	25	-7.4	28	-5.9	29	-7.7	27	-1.6	19	-8.2	25
2012	9.0%	1	9.4	3	12.4	3	13.3	3	7.4	10	2.5	9	-21.7	32

Justin Tucker joined Greg "The Leg" Zuerlein and Blair "The Project" Walsh in one of the best years ever for rookie kickers. In fact, once we adjust for the fact that Zuerlein and Walsh spent most of their rookie seasons indoors, Tucker comes out as the cream of the crop. Tucker led all kickers in gross kickoff value, and was third in field-goal value behind Walsh and Sebastian Janikowski. His booming kickoffs had a major impact on many close games. He nailed four touchbacks and just one returnable kick in the 31-30 victory over the Patriots in Week 3. He drilled five touchbacks while allowing just one 14-yard return in the 31-29 win against the Cowboys in Week 6. He was a perfect five-for-five on touchbacks to keep the Colts at bay in the Wild Card game. Then he played the Broncos and all hell broke loose, but he rebounded for four Super Bowl touchbacks, as well as two short-but-clutch field goals. Long segment short: awesome young kicker.

David Reed ceded kickoff return duties to Jacoby Jones but could earn them back, with Jones getting the nod when heroics are needed. Jones is likely to hold onto his punt return duties despite an increased role in the offense. Sam Koch, last seen running backwards for a clock-eating safety in the Super Bowl, is a trick-play threat as a punter and holder. Like Tucker, he gets good hang time but goes into a funk the moment he sees Trindon Holliday.

One note of optimism: the Ravens' special teams should look better next season as their "hidden" special teams value regresses towards the mean. During the regular season, Baltimore opponents only missed two field goals, none under 45 yards, and their punts were worth 8.2 estimated points worth of field position above average before the Ravens even had a chance to make returns.

Coaching Staff

Jim Caldwell did not have time to make major changes when he took over as offensive coordinator last December. He said during OTAs that he has a more thorough overhaul planned this season. Caldwell was predictably vague, but he specified yards per rush, first- and second-down efficiency, and passing-game efficiency as points of emphasis. That about covers everything, right? Caldwell also mentioned spreading the ball to more receivers and increasing the offensive tempo, which was usually fast under Cam Cameron (the Ravens were third in situation-neutral offensive pace) but sometimes suffered Keith Moon's Drugs Just Kicked In sputters.

Juan Castillo and Steve Spagnuolo, who served alongside John Harbaugh on Andy Reid's staff in Philly, have joined the Ravens as assistants in the hope of helping the team while reviving their careers. Castillo is back on the offensive side of the ball after a disastrous year-and-a-half as the Eagles defensive coordinator. Officially, Castillo is listed as the running game coordinator, but he appears to be acting as Bryant McKinnie's personal motivator. Castillo's fatherly, firm-but-upbeat routine is more effective when he is a positional assistant than when he is trying to put a game plan together. Spags followed up a poor showing as the Rams head coach with a weak effort trying to bail the Spygate boat in New Orleans. He's a "senior defensive assistant," which may be a nice way of saying "qualified friend of Super Bowl winning head coach who was unemployed in early May," but Spags is not that long removed from his Super Bowl success with the Giants. With so many young players and new faces to integrate on defense, Harbaugh and coordinator Dean Pees can use another set of eyes and ideas.

Buffalo Bills

2012 Record: 6-10	Total DVOA: -12.1% (23rd)	2013 Mean Projection: 6.9 wins	On the Clock (0-4): 18%
Pythagorean Wins: 5.7 (25th)	Offense: -4.2% (20th)	Postseason Odds: 21.7%	Mediocrity (5-7): 41%
Snap-Weighted Age: 26.5 (20th)	Defense: 10.6% (27th)	Super Bowl Odds: 1.3%	Playoff Contender (8-10): 33%
Average Opponent: -3.3% (23rd)	Special Teams: 2.7% (9th)	Proj. Avg. Opponent: 1.7% (8th)	Super Bowl Contender (11+): 7%

2012: We asked the Bills to not make us look like idiots, and they made us look like idiots.

2013: I don't need to walk around in circles, walk around in circles, walk around in circles, walk around in…

In *Football Outsiders Almanac 2011*, we started our Buffalo chapter with the sentence, "Every Bills season is very much like every other, and every Bills preview is the same."

Last year was supposed to be different. Last year, we thought the Bills were finally going to break out of their cycle of mediocrity. Last year, the Bills actually seemed like they had built something. The Bills somehow roped in the top free agent available, defensive end Mario Williams, and then for good measure they added another player with double-digit sacks, Mark Anderson. Those two pass rushers were going to bookend veteran Kyle Williams and 2011 third-overall pick Marcell Dareus, the two defensive tackles who were the top two players on the roster. If the Bills fielded a great pass rush, and young players like Kelvin Sheppard and Aaron Williams could take another step forward in their development, and Jairus Byrd continued to play at a Pro Bowl level, this was going to be one of the top defenses in the league. We projected the Bills with one of the league's easiest schedules, so as long as the special teams could rebound a bit and the offense could be average, the Bills were finally in line to compete for a wild card spot.

No, no, no. Almost none of it happened. The special teams did rebound, but the offense was a bit worse than mediocre, and the schedule ended up much harder than expected when teams in the NFC West and AFC South made unexpected improvements. The big-name, big-money defensive line ended up finishing 23rd in Adjusted Sack Rate and 24th in Adjusted Line Yards. When the line buckled, the whole defense buckled, and the Bills ended up finishing 27th with their worst defensive DVOA since 2001. It didn't help that most of the young talent did not continue its development. Cornerback Stephon Gilmore acquitted himself well as a rookie, but the Bills have traded away Sheppard and are moving Williams to safety. Byrd played well, but spent the last few weeks of the season jousting with the front office about his contract; the team stuck the franchise tag on him in the offseason, and he plans to hold out of training camp this year.

And so now we return to the hamster wheel. If this chapter seems like a collage made out of older Buffalo Bills chapters, it's because the Bills' plan to improve in 2013 and beyond seems like a Frankenstein's monster built out of past Bills' plans for improvement. The Bills hope that a new coaching staff with new philosophies will get them back on track, be-cause the Bills always seem to hope that a new coaching staff with new philosophies will get them back on track. This team gets rebooted more often than the DC Universe.

In *Pro Football Prospectus 2006*, the Bills chapter discussed how Steve Fairchild was going to revolutionize the Bills' offense by bringing in the system that Mike Martz turned into the Greatest Show on Turf. In *Football Outsiders Almanac 2009*, the Bills chapter talked about how Turk Schonert was going to bring back the K-gun offense with Trent Edwards as the starting quarterback. (*Trent Edwards!*) And it was only three years ago, in *Football Outsiders Almanac 2010*, the Bills chapter reviewed the decision to hire a coach (Chan Gailey) who promised to bring offensive innovation from the college game and a defensive coordinator (George Edwards) who wanted to transform the defense with an aggressive 3-4 scheme.

For 2013, the Bills have hired a coach who promises to bring offensive innovation from the college game and a defensive coordinator who wants to transform the defense with an aggressive 3-4 scheme.

At least this time the Bills are bringing in some younger coaching talent instead of an older coach nobody else wanted. Doug Marrone was only 25-25 in four years at Syracuse, but the Orange have not exactly been the easiest program to win with. They were 10-37 in the four years before he arrived. Going 8-5 with bowl victories in two of the past three years was considered by most college football fans to be a reasonably impressive accomplishment. Marrone also has a connection to one of the best offenses of the past few seasons—in fact, one of the best in NFL history—as he was offensive coordinator for the Saints from 2006 to 2008, the first three years of Sean Payton and Drew Brees.

Perhaps the most promising part of Marrone's offensive philosophy is that he doesn't seem wedded to a single strategy. A number of Buffalo's recent attempts to be innovative ran into problems because the talent on the roster didn't fit the goals of the coaches (once again: *K-gun offense led by Trent Edwards*). But at Syracuse, Marrone showed that he's willing to tailor the offense around his best personnel. In 2010, when his best player was running back Delone Carter, quarterback Ryan Nassib was just a sophomore, and the center couldn't execute a shotgun snap, the Orange employed a standard, pro-style running game. In 2012, with better depth at receiver and

2013 Bills Schedule

Week	Opp.	Week	Opp.	Week	Opp.
1	NE	7	at MIA	13	vs. ATL (Tor.)
2	CAR	8	at NO	14	at TB
3	at NYJ	9	KC	15	at JAC
4	BAL	10	at PIT	16	MIA
5	at CLE (Thu.)	11	NYJ	17	at NE
6	CIN	12	BYE		

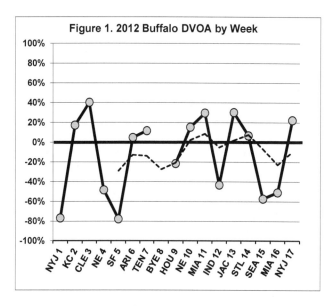

Figure 1. 2012 Buffalo DVOA by Week

Nassib now fully matured, the Orange ran a high-flying no-huddle attack.

Once he arrived in Buffalo, Marrone got to handpick his quarterback of the future, cutting Ryan Fitzpatrick and using the 16th overall pick of the draft to make E.J. Manuel the first quarterback off the board. It was a surprising pick to many, although by the end of the draft process, most outside draft experts had moved Manuel up and made him the second or third quarterback on their boards.

What makes Manuel the right pick for Marrone? He doesn't have a rocket arm, and he doesn't scare defenses by running all over the field. But he's intelligent and he can do a lot of different things well, which means he provides flexibility with upside.

Manuel was the second-fastest quarterback at the Combine, running the 40 in 4.65 seconds, and out of this year's quarterbacks he's the one who best fits a decision to use the read option. But that's not all he is. Jimbo Fisher's offense at Florida State used both the I formation and a traditional shotgun to go along with the read-option plays. Marrone got to work with Brees the last time in the NFL, and he wants a quarterback like Brees who can run a fast-paced offense and has strong fundamentals as a passer but also the ability to improvise. There aren't really holes in Manuel's game, things he just plain cannot do. If he's not yet ready to step into an NFL starting lineup, it's because of elements in his game that grade out at C instead of B, or B instead of A.

That being said, Manuel isn't the kind of slam-dunk superstar prospect that Andrew Luck and Robert Griffin were a year ago. (He might be a surprise superstar like Russell Wilson, but we don't know yet; that's why it is called a surprise.) It's very unlikely that Manuel will walk right into the starting lineup and lead the Bills to the playoffs. He's not even likely to walk right into the starting lineup and lead his team to a 7-9 record like Ryan Tannehill did. As a prospect, Manuel has a lot more in common with Colin Kaepernick. Not Colin Kaepernick, the quarterback who took his team to the Super Bowl this year. Manuel has more in common with Colin Kaepernick, the quarterback who was drafted at the top of the second round and sat on the bench for most of his rookie season. When Jim Harbaugh looked at Kaepernick at Nevada, he saw a quarterback with a lot of tools and the intangibles that suggested he could develop them. Marrone sees the same thing in Manuel, but development often takes time. That's fine; that's why they signed Kevin Kolb, and they're happy to let him take some lumps until they feel Manuel is ready for prime time.

Marrone spent the draft accumulating young offensive tal-

ent to put around Manuel, and those players join some promising young offensive talents who were here already. The Bills have taken three wide receivers in the first three rounds of the last two drafts, plus left tackle Cordy Glenn. Superstar running back C.J. Spiller, who led the league in rushing DVOA a year ago, is still just 26 years old. His ability to move between wide receiver positions and the backfield gives Marrone formation flexibility to help him run a no-huddle offense. Third-round pick Marquise Goodwin is a 5-foot-9 speed sprite who comes out of Texas with very little experience but could learn to play a Randall Cobb/Percy Harvin role. However, if Marrone wants to use as many different formations and personnel groups as he did in New Orleans, he'll need to find a newfangled tight end or two. Current starter Scott Chandler is an in-line tight end first and foremost; you might flex him out a bit, but he's not scaring anyone by going out wide past the numbers. And backup Lee Smith is essentially an offensive tackle.

Versatility and flexibility are also going to be the buzzwords for Mike Pettine's defense. As the former defensive coordinator of the Jets, Pettine comes from the Rex Ryan school of "move everyone around and bring crazy pressure." Bring out seven or eight defensive backs to stop Tom Brady? Sure, let's try it. Five linebackers? We'll try that sometimes. Five linebackers all blitzing? Sure, why the heck not?

The base will be a 3-4, two-gap system, but there will also be plenty of four-man lines playing a one-gap style, especially on passing downs. However, there are questions about whether the Bills' defenders are going to be able to do all the different things that Pettine wants them to do. Marcell Dareus should be flexible moving between 3-technique and 5-technique positions, but he needs to avoid being pushed around on running plays as often as he was a year ago. Mario Williams did play a year of outside linebacker after Houston hired Wade Phillips, and they even liked to drop him into coverage when he was a defensive end in their 4-3, but he was never particularly good at it. Mark Anderson is penciled in as the starting strongside linebacker, but he offers no versatility whatsoever: he's a pass rusher, pure and simple. Second-round linebacker Kiko Alonso has an outstanding mix of speed and power, and also excels in coverage, so he will immediately be a three-down linebacker as a rookie. Still, he's a rookie, and the Bills will need to be patient and live through rookie mistakes. The other three-down linebacker, Nigel Bradham, might continue to have growing pains as well.

There's also the question of whether the secondary is going to be good enough for Pettine to bring constant pressure. Stephon Gilmore is a promising talent and he's only going to get better after experiencing the ups and downs that are typical of highly-drafted cornerbacks, but he's not Darrelle Revis and he's probably never going to be Darrelle Revis. Leodis McKelvin is penciled in on the other side, but there's a reason the previous administration benched him. And the front office needs to work things out with Byrd if the Bills want to make any kind of wild card run in 2013.

Pettine at least seems to understand that you have to walk before you can learn to run. "The phrase comes to mind, 'jack of all trades, master of none,'" he said in an interview with WGR's John Murphy this offseason. "You don't want to start to push a guy towards learning a second position until he's mastered his original. But at the same time, the strength of the system is its versatility, that we can have a guy on a certain play play the role of a safety, then he's a corner the next play, then he's a linebacker the next play. Or guys at end can play outside linebacker, play off the ball linebacker. So that's the challenge of it, to make sure they've mastered their first position before we start to give them jobs that other positions might do."

The coaching changes the Bills have made this offseason bring with them a lot of hope for the future. But that was also true of the coaching changes the Bills made in past offseasons. The real cause for optimism in Buffalo is that the team also made major changes to the front office. Russ Brandon has served as director of non-football operations and then CEO since 2006. He's well respected as a member of a number of the league's business committees. Now he'll run the show in

Buffalo, both the football and business sides. Owner Ralph Wilson, with his health declining, named Brandon team president and handed him the keys to the franchise on January 1. Right from his initial press conferences after taking over, Brandon was expressing his interest in bringing analytics to the Bills' front office, a turn of events that obviously warmed the hearts of the Football Outsiders staff.

The front office mindset moved even further forward when 73-year-old Buddy Nix decided to step down as general manager. The Bills promoted his assistant, 40-year-old Doug Whaley, who comes with a great resume. As a former college player who started out on Wall Street before giving up the stock broker career track to get back into football, we imagine Whaley is as comfortable with analytics as Brandon is. And Whaley spent 11 years as Pittsburgh Steelers pro scouting coordinator before jumping to the Bills, which means he has been trained in the ways of one of the NFL's finest-run organizations and one of its smartest general managers, Kevin Colbert.

We would really like to stop writing these repetitive chapters about the Bills running in circles, almost as much as the Bills themselves would like to stop running in circles. (Cue Chris Berman: "Nobody runs in circles around their own wagons like the Buffalo Bills.") To do that, the Bills' ownership and executives will need to show some patience. Brandon plans to hire a full-time analytics guy, and they will need a year or two to both spread general analytics concepts around the organization and to find specific ideas that will improve the Bills. Marrone and Whaley need a couple years to develop their quarterback and assemble talent that fits their vision of the team. Getting away from the constant changes in philosophy and finding some kind of organizational consistency will help this team in the long run, even though it means waiting through Year 14 without a playoff appearance. And probably Year 15, and maybe Year 16, and...

Aaron Schatz

2012 Bills Stats by Week

Wk	vs.	W-L	PF	PA	YDF	YDA	TO	Total	Off	Def	ST
1	at NYJ	L	28	48	390	384	-3	-77%	-22%	37%	-18%
2	KC	W	35	17	379	422	3	17%	20%	23%	20%
3	at CLE	W	24	14	344	240	1	40%	13%	-22%	6%
4	NE	L	28	52	438	580	-4	-48%	-24%	28%	4%
5	at SF	L	3	45	204	621	-1	-78%	-20%	73%	16%
6	at ARI	W	19	16	306	332	0	5%	14%	3%	-6%
7	TEN	L	34	35	382	390	-2	12%	21%	35%	25%
8	BYE										
9	at HOU	L	9	21	304	374	-1	-22%	8%	25%	-5%
10	at NE	L	31	37	481	347	-3	15%	16%	2%	1%
11	MIA	W	19	14	281	184	3	30%	-15%	-41%	4%
12	at IND	L	13	20	304	312	1	-43%	-41%	-12%	-14%
13	JAC	W	34	18	344	236	0	30%	4%	-16%	10%
14	STL	L	12	15	281	285	-1	7%	-19%	-24%	1%
15	SEA	L	17	50	333	466	-3	-57%	-16%	43%	1%
16	at MIA	L	10	24	381	301	-4	-51%	-32%	14%	-5%
17	NYJ	W	28	9	334	332	1	22%	22%	2%	2%

Trends and Splits

	Offense	Rank	Defense	Rank
Total DVOA	-4.2%	20	10.6%	27
Unadjusted VOA	-6.1%	20	9.6%	26
Weighted Trend	-5.3%	18	2.9%	21
Variance	4.5%	7	8.8%	31
Average Opponent	-1.4%	10	-4.9%	30
Passing	-2.1%	24	13.1%	22
Rushing	5.3%	9	7.9%	31
First Down	-16.1%	28	-0.7%	16
Second Down	0.6%	17	7.3%	22
Third Down	14.3%	9	40.8%	32
First Half	5.7%	14	5.2%	25
Second Half	-14.4%	25	16.0%	28
Red Zone	-7.0%	20	36.0%	31
Late and Close	-6.9%	18	7.0%	27

Five-Year Performance

Year	W-L	Pyth W	Est W	PF	PA	TO	Total	Rk	Off	Rk	Def	Rk	ST	Rk	Off AGL	Rk	Def AGL	Rk	Off Age	Rk	Def Age	Rk	ST Age	Rk
2008	7-9	7.8	6.7	336	342	-8	-8.4%	23	-9.8%	24	5.8%	23	7.1%	1	13.3	8	34.9	25	26.5	28	26.6	25	26.7	16
2009	6-10	5.9	6.6	258	326	+3	-10.4%	24	-20.7%	29	-9.2%	8	1.1%	13	60.7	32	62.1	32	26.9	21	27.5	9	26.9	11
2010	4-12	4.3	5.5	283	425	-17	-21.3%	29	-14.5%	26	6.8%	28	-0.1%	17	10.4	5	31.2	22	26.4	27	27.5	13	27.1	8
2011	6-10	6.4	7.1	372	434	+1	-9.7%	23	0.3%	16	8.3%	24	-1.7%	24	33.8	20	37.1	21	26.3	27	27.4	12	26.7	5
2012	6-10	5.7	6.5	344	435	-13	-12.1%	23	-4.2%	20	10.6%	27	2.7%	9	51.5	29	28.2	16	26.2	25	26.7	18	26.5	10

2012 Performance Based on Most Common Personnel Groups

BUF Offense					BUF Offense vs. Opponents				BUF Defense					BUF Defense vs. Opponents			
Pers	Freq	Yds	DVOA	Run%	Pers	Freq	Yds	DVOA	Pers	Freq	Yds	DVOA		Pers	Freq	Yds	DVOA
11	72%	5.9	1.1%	35%	Nickel Even	45%	5.0	6.3%	4-3-4	40%	6.5	0.0%		11	44%	6.2	9.1%
12	10%	6.2	-0.7%	50%	Nickel Odd	17%	6.4	16.7%	Nickel Even	33%	6.8	35.2%		12	23%	5.9	15.2%
22	5%	4.3	-12.3%	71%	Dime+	14%	6.6	-3.8%	Nickel Odd	11%	4.8	-30.1%		21	15%	5.0	-5.9%
21	3%	4.1	-5.9%	43%	4-3-4	13%	4.7	-16.6%	Dime+	10%	5.7	-20.7%		22	6%	5.4	11.5%
20	3%	6.0	1.7%	59%	3-4-4	9%	5.0	-4.9%	3-4-4	4%	3.6	-29.9%		10	3%	4.9	18.7%

Strategic Tendencies

Run/Pass		Rk	Formation		Rk	Pass Rush		Rk	Secondary		Rk	Strategy		Rk
Runs, first half	40%	10	Form: Single Back	66%	17	Rush 3	6.7%	17	4 DB	44%	17	Play action	19%	17
Runs, first down	51%	12	Form: Empty Back	17%	1	Rush 4	76.4%	2	5 DB	44%	21	Avg Box (Off)	6.00	32
Runs, second-long	31%	16	Pers: 3+ WR	80%	1	Rush 5	13.5%	31	6+ DB	10%	10	Avg Box (Def)	6.30	24
Runs, power sit.	50%	22	Pers: 4+ WR	3%	10	Rush 6+	3.4%	30	CB by Sides	73%	17	Offensive Pace	32.19	29
Runs, behind 2H	32%	10	Pers: 2+ TE/6+ OL	16%	31	Sacks by LB	11.1%	27	DB Blitz	6%	26	Defensive Pace	29.55	8
Pass, ahead 2H	41%	24	Shotgun/Pistol	63%	4	Sacks by DB	0.0%	28	Hole in Zone	8%	18	Go for it on 4th	0.78	24

The development of Scott Chandler has definitely changed the Bills offense, which had at least one tight end in the formation on 95 percent of plays. That figure was just 75 percent in 2010 and 70 percent in 2011. The Bills also used a single personnel group more than any other team, using 11 personnel on 72 percent of plays. ⊜ Buffalo led the league with 24 plays that were direct snaps to a non-quarterback. (They were listing Brad Smith as a quarterback on their roster for a while, but let's get real here.) The Bills gained an average of 5.5 yards on these plays with 9.2% DVOA. ⊜ Even though the Bills went empty backfield more than any other team, they weren't particularly good at it. They had more yards per pass than average (6.8 vs. NFL average of 6.1) but a lower DVOA (-4.0% vs. an NFL average of 9.3%). ⊜ The Bills ran 49 running back draws, third in the league, and were excellent on these plays with 7.4 yards per carry and 48.5% DVOA. They also led the league with 46 running back screens, although they were only slightly above average on these plays (6.2 yards per pass, 18.8% DVOA). ⊜ While most defenses are far better on pass plays without play action, the Bills had the league's biggest gap in favor of their defense against play action, with -11.2% DVOA against play action (third in the NFL) but 23.6% DVOA against other pass plays (29th). This may be a fluke, as their splits against play action were the exact opposite the year before. ⊜ Buffalo allowed 0.6 yards per play and -109.6% DVOA when we marked them bringing pass pressure, and 7.8 yards per play with 45.8% DVOA without pressure. That's the biggest gap in the league in yardage and the second-biggest gap in DVOA (behind Cleveland).

Passing

Player	DYAR	DVOA	Plays	NtYds	Avg	YAC	C%	TD	Int
R.Fitzpatrick*	120	-7.6%	533	3235	6.1	5.9	60.8%	24	16
K.Kolb	-154	-23.1%	210	1008	4.8	4.4	59.6%	8	3

Rushing

Player	DYAR	DVOA	Plays	Yds	Avg	TD	Fum	Suc
C.J.Spiller	301	27.6%	207	1249	6.0	6	2	55%
F.Jackson	-27	-14.3%	115	438	3.8	3	4	47%
T.Choice	23	3.2%	47	193	4.1	1	0	43%
R.Fitzpatrick*	22	0.5%	38	205	5.4	1	0	-
B.Smith	41	66.2%	14	101	7.2	1	1	64%
J.White*	1	-6.7%	8	34	4.3	0	0	50%
K.Kolb	49	80.7%	12	103	8.6	1	0	-

Receiving

Player	DYAR	DVOA	Plays	Ctch	Yds	Y/C	YAC	TD	C%
S.Johnson	67	-4.7%	148	79	1046	13.2	4.6	6	53%
D.Jones*	30	-6.0%	66	41	443	10.8	4.4	4	62%
T.J.Graham	-57	-20.6%	58	31	322	10.4	5.8	1	53%
B.Smith	12	2.9%	23	14	152	10.9	3.1	2	61%
R.Martin*	12	19.0%	6	4	41	10.3	2.5	0	67%
S.Chandler	52	1.2%	74	43	571	13.3	4.4	6	58%
D.Dickerson	-17	-12.4%	15	9	117	13.0	7.2	0	60%
C.J.Spiller	91	16.3%	57	43	459	10.7	11.8	2	75%
F.Jackson	13	-8.4%	42	34	219	6.4	6.5	1	81%
T.Choice	-45	-101.9%	9	4	9	2.3	5.8	0	44%

Offensive Line

Player	Pos	Age	GS	Snaps	Pen	Sk	Pass	Run	Player	Pos	Age	GS	Snaps	Pen	Sk	Pass	Run
Andy Levitre*	LG	27	16/16	1007	5	1.5	1.5	7.5	Erik Pears	RT	31	7/7	378	5	3	12	1
Eric Wood	C	27	14/14	868	2	1.5	4.5	2	Sam Young	OT	26	12/4	332	1	1	5	1
Cordy Glenn	LT	24	13/13	799	9	7.5	19.5	1	Chad Rinehart*	G	28	7/2	164	0	1	3	0
Kraig Urbik	RG	28	13/13	779	2	2.5	8	3.5	David Snow	C	24	5/2	133	0	0	1	1
Chris Hairston	RT	24	12/8	564	5	2	7.5	6.5	Doug Legursky	C/G	27	16/3	409	2	2.5	11	0

Year	Yards	ALY	Rk	Power	Rk	Stuff	Rk	2nd Lev	Rk	Open Field	Rk	Sacks	ASR	Rk	Short	Long	F-Start	Cont.
2010	4.05	3.85	20	65%	11	20%	21	1.10	19	0.66	19	34	6.5%	17	12	15	20	26
2011	5.04	4.18	12	67%	7	18%	14	1.25	9	1.29	2	23	3.8%	1	8	10	9	25
2012	5.15	4.25	7	57%	26	17%	8	1.42	3	1.14	4	30	5.5%	10	11	13	22	27
2012 ALY by direction:			Left End 3.04 (29)			Left Tackle 4.12 (13)			Mid/Guard 4.38 (6)			Right Tackle 3.76 (21)			Right End 6.37 (1)			

Here's yet another place where the Bills have a new philosophy. In 2011, Buddy Nix was quoted in the papers as being excited about the Bills' "bigger and better offensive line." Now, two years later, Doug Marrone has had the linemen trying to lose weight all offseason in preparation for more no-huddle offense and a running game primarily built around zone blocking.

Cordy Glenn, for example, came into the league at 345 pounds; the Bills now want him to get down to 325 or so. Many teams projected Glenn as a guard in the NFL, but the Bills were happy to grab him in the second round of last year's draft and install him immediately as their franchise left tackle. He acquitted himself well as a rookie, particularly in run blocking. The right tackle position will see a camp battle between older veteran Erik Pears and third-year tackle Chris Hairston, who split the starts last season. Although Pears has a reputation as a mediocre run blocker, it's worth noting that our charters only marked him with one specific blown run block, and the Bills' Adjusted Line Yards dropped from 4.43 to 4.11 after he went on injured reserve with a hip injury and Hairston took over as the starter. 2012 fifth-round pick Zebrie Sanders provides depth after missing his rookie season due to surgeries to replace the labrums on both of his hips.

The Bills had a very solid interior line, but all three starters were set to be free agents in either 2013 or 2014. The Bills have one staying, one going, and one left to be decided. Right guard Kraig Urbik signed a four-year, $15 million extension last season, but the Bills were unable to re-sign left guard Andy Levitre, who signed with Tennessee. Next up for negotiation is center Eric Wood; escalators in his rookie deal boosted his salary from $925,000 to $2.3 million this year, and he's set to hit the open market in 2014. Meanwhile, a number of refugees from other teams will compete to replace Levitre. The favorite for the job is Sam Young, a 2010 Dallas sixth-rounder now in his third year with Buffalo. Other possibilities are Colin Brown, signed off the Baltimore practice squad in 2010; Chris Scott, signed off the Tennessee practice squad in 2012; and former Steelers backup Doug Legursky, signed in June.

Defensive Front Seven

Defensive Line	Age	Pos	Snaps	Plays	Overall TmPct	Rk	Stop	Dfts	BTkl	Runs	vs. Run St%	Rk	RuYd	Rk	Pass Rush Sack	Hit	Hur	Tips
Mario Williams	28	DE	928	49	6.0%	25	42	18	3	31	87%	4	1.4	8	10.5	6	18	3
Kyle Williams	30	DT	792	48	5.9%	12	38	21	3	37	76%	33	0.9	2	5	7	24	2
Marcell Dareus	24	DT	786	45	5.5%	18	35	8	0	29	72%	42	3.0	61	5.5	3	9	1
Kyle Moore*	27	DE	490	23	3.8%	--	15	4	1	19	63%	--	3.9	--	3	6	13.5	0
Alex Carrington	26	DT	343	21	2.6%	67	19	11	0	15	87%	4	1.4	11	2	2	7.5	3
Spencer Johnson*	32	DT	264	21	2.9%	62	15	4	1	17	65%	63	2.6	50	2	0	1	2
Shawne Merriman*	29	DE	206	17	3.3%	--	13	4	0	14	71%	--	2.5	--	1	2	2	1
Alan Branch	29	DT	560	30	4.0%	38	20	6	2	26	62%	66	3.7	68	1	5	9	2

Linebackers	Age	Pos	Snaps	Plays	Overall TmPct	Rk	Stop	Dfts	BTkl	Pass Rush Sack	Hit	Hur	Tips	Runs	vs. Run St%	Rk	Yds	Rk	Tgts	vs. Pass Suc%	Rk	AdjYd	Rk	PD
Nick Barnett*	32	OLB	998	112	13.8%	36	62	24	6	2	1	2	0	76	59%	84	3.4	56	34	36%	69	8.5	69	1
Bryan Scott	32	OLB	590	71	8.7%	67	36	14	1	0	1	1.5	0	35	63%	69	4.6	103	43	51%	39	7.2	51	8
Kelvin Sheppard*	25	MLB	504	78	9.6%	65	46	6	1	2	2	2	0	60	60%	77	4.1	93	13	60%	--	5.7	--	1
Nigel Bradham	24	OLB	394	48	5.9%	96	30	4	3	0	0	0	1	36	64%	65	4.1	90	18	65%	7	3.8	3	0
Arthur Moats	24	OLB	121	18	2.5%	--	10	2	0	0	0	1	0	16	63%	--	3.7	--	4	73%	--	5.6	--	0
Jerry Hughes	25	OLB	596	35	4.4%	--	23	13	1	4	6	15	1	22	68%	--	2.5	--	4	39%	--	12.3	--	0
Manny Lawson	29	OLB	353	38	4.5%	108	16	5	3	2	0	2	0	19	47%	106	4.6	105	17	42%	63	8.7	70	0

Year	Yards	ALY	Rk	Power	Rk	Stuff	Rk	2nd Level	Rk	Open Field	Rk	Sacks	ASR	Rk	Short	Long
2010	4.73	4.88	32	65%	21	12%	32	1.32	31	0.71	13	27	5.7%	24	8	9
2011	4.79	4.46	28	62%	14	15%	32	1.30	26	1.02	24	29	5.9%	26	7	16
2012	4.77	4.30	24	68%	25	18%	17	1.40	32	1.05	28	36	6.0%	23	8	17
2012 ALY by direction:			Left End 5.35 (32)			Left Tackle 4.15 (17)			Mid/Guard 4.36 (28)			Right Tackle 3.6 (5)			Right End 4.07 (14)

Fans in Buffalo seem to have the same feelings that were so prevalent among Texans fans: Sometimes, it just doesn't seem like Mario Williams is living up to his reputation. But our game charters were often adding extra comments about things Williams did that did not show up on the stat sheet, whether it was attracting a double team, forcing a tight end to chip before going on a route, or getting initial pressure that ended up in a sack credited to someone else. ("Shawne Merriman should send chocolates or something to Mario for having his last career sack gift wrapped like that.") In fact, Williams is really the only sure thing in the Bills' pass rush. Mark Anderson missed most of last season with a knee injury that required two surgeries, and wasn't yet at 100 percent during OTAs. His backup is Jerry Hughes, who was traded to Buffalo because he was such a disappointment in Indianapolis. Defensive tackles Marcel Dareus and Kyle Williams were much better as pass rushers than they were against the run last season—Williams and Geno Atkins were the only defensive tackles with more than 20 hurries—but their roles may change depending on how much two-gap this defense ends up playing. The Bills signed Manny Lawson to fill the weakside role most recently played on the Jets by Bryan Thomas, but that's less of a pass rush role than the other linebacker spot, and Lawson had just 3.5 sacks, four hits, and six hurries over his past two seasons with Cincinnati.

The inside linebacker positions are filled by talented youngsters with a lot of upside. Kiko Alonso, chosen out of Oregon in the second round, comes off as the prototype for a 3-4 linebacker in his scouting reports. He has strength, speed, and a high motor. He can blitz the A gap or drop into coverage equally well. The negatives with Alonso are more about instincts and off-field issues. He sometimes takes himself out of plays by guessing wrong, and he didn't get on the field much in his first two seasons because of alcohol issues and a torn ACL. The list of strengths on NFL.com's draft report reads like Alonso is the stud savior of the Bills defense … until you get to the part listing Ben Leber as the most comparable player. A nice starting linebacker, but not really the stud savior of anyone's defense. Alonso will start next to 2012 fourth-round pick Nigel Bradham, who moved into the starting lineup in Week 6 and showed improved play over the last few games of the season. Bradham is yet another young NFL player with a freakish combination of size and speed. Second-rate instincts and awareness were the knocks on him coming out of Florida State, but he didn't look much different from your average rookie in that regard, and he was very good in pass coverage. Arthur Moats, the fourth-year player Bradham replaced in the starting lineup, is the main backup on the inside.

Defensive Secondary

| Secondary | Age | Pos | Snaps | Plays | Overall | | | | | vs. Run | | | | | vs. Pass | | | | | | | | | |
					TmPct	Rk	Stop	Dfts	BTkl	Runs	St%	Rk	Yds	Rk	Tgts	Tgt%	Rk	Dist	Suc%	Rk	APaYd	Rk	PD	Int
Stephon Gilmore	23	CB	1055	77	9.5%	23	29	7	2	22	23%	77	7.5	58	88	20.1%	24	14.4	52%	44	8.3	67	13	1
Jairus Byrd	27	FS	1021	82	10.1%	36	37	20	2	37	46%	13	7.3	39	21	4.8%	64	14.3	50%	50	7.7	42	6	5
George Wilson*	32	SS	895	102	12.5%	15	34	9	4	64	34%	45	7.6	43	21	4.7%	66	13.9	70%	5	4.7	7	4	0
Aaron Williams	24	CB	547	39	7.0%	67	14	4	0	11	9%	83	13.4	85	43	14.3%	67	16.6	51%	49	8.4	70	6	0
Justin Rogers	25	CB	537	41	5.0%	81	15	9	3	10	50%	26	9.6	75	51	11.7%	81	9.5	47%	66	7.4	40	5	1
Leodis McKelvin	28	CB	347	23	3.5%	--	7	3	1	7	29%	--	10.6	--	27	7.6%	--	14.8	51%	--	8.3	--	3	1
Da'Norris Searcy	25	SS	272	36	4.7%	--	17	7	0	25	60%	--	5.7	--	4	0.9%	--	14.7	26%	--	12.6	--	1	0
Ron Brooks	25	CB	162	17	3.7%	--	6	1	0	4	25%	--	9.5	--	27	11.0%	--	13.9	47%	--	6.8	--	4	0

Year	Pass D Rank	vs. #1 WR	Rk	vs. #2 WR	Rk	vs. Other WR	Rk	vs. TE	Rk	vs. RB	Rk
2010	25	32.3%	31	9.9%	20	-43.5%	1	13.2%	23	-8.7%	7
2011	25	16.5%	22	33.3%	29	-41.0%	1	20.6%	23	5.1%	21
2012	22	20.7%	26	-2.7%	15	24.2%	29	-24.5%	2	20.1%	26

Whither Jarius Byrd? The Bills slapped the franchise tag on their star free safety, but as of press time Byrd had not signed the tender, and he was absent from all offseason activities. If Byrd holds out, the backup plan at free safety is former cornerback Aaron Williams. Mike Pettine believes that Williams' combination of size and range makes him a better fit for safety in his defense. "If you can have a safety that has corner skills, that to me is ideal," Pettine told reporters this offseason. "I would sacrifice the ability to be a 'box player,' a thicker guy and a thumper type: I'd sacrifice that for the cover skills any day." Of course, that statement makes you wonder why the Bills drafted not one but two box safeties in this year's draft: Duke Williams out of Nevada in the fourth round and Jonathan Meeks out of Clemson in the fifth. They'll spend their rookie year backing up Da'Norris Searcy, who finally gets his chance to move into the starting lineup after George Wilson signed with Tennessee.

Rookie cornerback Stephon Gilmore was last year's one constant at cornerback, and he should continue to improve with experience. One good sign is that Gilmore's Adjusted Success Rate went from 48 percent before Buffalo's bye week to 50 percent after, while his Adjusted Yards per Pass dropped from 9.3 to 8.0. After Gilmore, the cornerback position offers a lot of bodies but not a lot of certainty. With Williams now at safety, veteran Leodis McKelvin is penciled in to start, but he hasn't played much the last couple of years thanks to a front-row seat in Chan Gailey's doghouse. McKelvin has never lived up to his first-round draft position and has a habit of getting burned deep. Justin Rogers was the main nickelback a year ago and will battle Ron Brooks for that position in 2013. However, since both Rogers and Brooks are much better inside than outside, the main backup to Gilmore and McKelvin is Crezdon Butler, who is now on his fourth team (including two stints with Arizona) in four years.

Special Teams

Year	DVOA	Rank	FG/XP	Rank	Net Kick	Rank	Kick Ret	Rank	Net Punt	Rank	Punt Ret	Rank	Hidden	Rank
2010	-0.1%	17	-0.5	18	3.4	10	-4.5	21	-0.4	21	1.6	14	0.2	14
2011	-1.7%	24	-7.1	28	4.6	7	-0.1	17	-10.6	29	4.7	6	-11.5	30
2012	2.7%	9	1.1	15	-5.1	26	13.3	2	-12.3	26	16.2	2	4.0	6

Buffalo's strong special teams in 2012 were built on a superlative return game. McKelvin led the league with 18.0 estimated points worth of punt returns, including two touchdowns. Other than fair catches, McKelvin didn't have a single punt return where he was caught behind the 20. On kick returns, McKelvin was worth 3.8 points and Brad Smith 7.3 points, each on 18 returns. When it comes to the kicking specialists, the Bills are finally bringing in some new blood. They cut Brian Moorman after he scuffled early and turned the punter job over to Shawn Powell, who was above-average on gross punt value (+2.6 points) but was betrayed by poor punt coverage. The next veteran to go will likely be Rian Lindell, who has had huge problems with kickoff distance over the last couple of years even after adjusting for the difficult weather conditions in Buffalo. The Bills used a sixth-round pick on Dustin Hopkins of Florida State, a big-legged kicker who has good range on long field goals and had touchbacks on nearly 40 percent of his college kickoffs.

Coaching Staff

Marrone brought along seven different Syracuse assistants. The most important is his Syracuse offensive coordinator, Nathaniel Hackett, who is the son of former Chiefs and Jets offensive coordinator Paul Hackett. Hackett's father was a disciple of the West Coast offense who worked for Bill Walsh in the mid-'80s. Marrone's NFL experience also has its basis in the West Coast offense—the Saints offense moves things around much more than the classic West Coast system, and uses vertical routes a lot more often, but Sean Payton's first job came working for Jon Gruden when he was Eagles offensive coordinator in the late '90s. If you've ever watched one of Gruden's QB Camp specials on ESPN, you know what E.J. Manuel is now in for: lots and lots and lots of verbiage.

Special teams coordinator Danny Crossman has also run special teams for the Panthers and Lions. His Panthers units showed the inconsistency typical of special teams, with DVOA rankings ranging from fifth to 30th during his five years in charge. In recent years, his units have struggled, as the Lions finished 29th and 30th in our special teams ratings the last two years.

Carolina Panthers

2012 Record: 7-9	Total DVOA: 5.5% (13th)	2013 Mean Projection: 9.5 wins	On the Clock (0-4): 3%
Pythagorean Wins: 7.8 (18th)	Offense: 7.2% (10th)	Postseason Odds: 58.4%	Mediocrity (5-7): 17%
Snap-Weighted Age: 26.3 (22nd)	Defense: -3.1% (11th)	Super Bowl Odds: 11.1%	Playoff Contender (8-10): 46%
Average Opponent: 0.8% (13th)	Special Teams: -4.8% (29th)	Proj. Avg. Opponent: 1.7% (9th)	Super Bowl Contender (11+): 34%

2012: Dang, we almost won. Dang, we almost won. Dang, we almost won…

2013: How much can a bad head coach screw up good talent?

Every year, there's a surprise team in our projections, a dark horse that we expect will rise from a losing record to a Super Bowl contender. This year, that team is the Carolina Panthers.

There's a lot to like about the talent on this squad. Cam Newton is a superstar quarterback going into his third season, and his continued development should vault the offense forward several notches. The defense features a potentially dominant front seven, led by another young blossoming star in Luke Kuechly, which should cover up for some question marks in the secondary. They finished the year on a four-game winning streak, which inspired hope for the following season.

For all those positive signs, though, there is one big weakness that can't be ignored, and for that reason we're subjectively skeptical of our objective optimism. It's not the lack of depth at receiver that has us worried, nor the shaky status of the secondary, though those are certainly viable concerns. In fact, it's not a player that has us worried at all. It's the head coach. Through two seasons, Ron Rivera has done little to show that he's capable of managing an NFL team on Sundays, and that will likely be the reason Carolina comes up short again this year.

Rivera played nine seasons for the Chicago Bears in the 1980s and '90s, including three seasons as a starter. He was an NFL assistant coach every season from 1997 to 2010, including stints as defensive coordinator for Chicago (2004-06) and San Diego (2008-10). The Carolina Panthers hired him as head coach following their disastrous 2-14 campaign in 2010. Since then, Rivera and the Panthers have gone 13-19. That's not horrible, especially considering the state of the team when Rivera took over. Yet closer examination suggests that the Panthers have the talent to win even more games, and Rivera and his staff are holding the team back. That's not just our opinion, either. Unfortunately for Rivera, it may be the opinion of the man who signs his paychecks.

In fact, Rivera has been fighting to keep his head above water since his first day on the job. ESPN's Chris Mortensen has reported that Panthers owner Jerry Richardson disapproved of the hire, and had to be talked into the move by then-general manager Marty Hurney. It didn't help Rivera's case when the Panthers lost eight of their first ten games in 2011, but with first-overall draft pick Cam Newton putting up stellar fantasy numbers, at least the team's fans had something to cheer for.

Then they won four of their next five games, a strong finish that seemed to justify Hurney's decision and raised expectations for the following season.

Those expectations were dashed when the Panthers opened 2012 by going 1-5. The fifth loss in that stretch, a 14-19 fall-from-ahead defeat at home against the Cowboys, led to Hurney's dismissal after a decade with the team. Three weeks later, special teams coach Brian Murphy was fired. (Not that it did any good—in the next game, Carolina fumbled a punt, missed a field-goal attempt, and lost four yards on a fake punt gone wrong.) With heads rolling in Charlotte, Rivera seemed destined for the chopping block, but he survived to finish the year. That was his first escape of the season, but it wouldn't be his last.

Hurney's firing failed to motivate the club, which proceeded to lose three out of the next four games. Once the Panthers sunk to 2-8, however, they rallied just like the year before: they won five of their last six games, including each of their last four. Consensus opinion said this was all too little, too late for Rivera, and Michael Lombardi of NFL Network (he had not yet left for the Browns) reported that the Panthers would make a change. Nevertheless, as one coach after another was fired on Black Monday, Rivera somehow lived to see another day. That four-game win streak to end the year had earned Rivera one more season in charge. Not all his coaches were retained, however. Running backs coach John Settle, receivers coach Fred Graves, and linebackers coach Warren Belin were shown the door, decisions that Rivera insists were his and his alone. Whether that's true or the firings were ordered from upon high, the sense of urgency is clear: It's win or bust for Rivera this season, and he'd better win right away.

As noted, Carolina's total number of losses the last two years isn't particularly galling. It's the style of those losses that has raised the temperature of Rivera's seat. Fifteen times in two seasons the Panthers have blown a lead and lost, tied with Jacksonville for most in the league, and they're the only team with at least seven blown-lead losses in both years. Remember that Rivera learned coaching strategy in part from Norv Turner, who has had his own troubles protecting leads. Five times in his career, Turner finished .500 or worse in games in which his teams led at some point, and in his last year in San Diego, the Chargers amassed another six blown-lead losses.

That's nothing, though, compared to Carolina's record in

2013 Panthers Schedule

Week	Opp.	Week	Opp.	Week	Opp.
1	SEA	7	STL	13	TB
2	at BUF	8	at TB (Thu.)	14	at NO
3	NYG	9	ATL	15	NYJ
4	BYE	10	at SF	16	NO
5	at ARI	11	NE (Mon.)	17	at ATL
6	at MIN	12	at MIA		

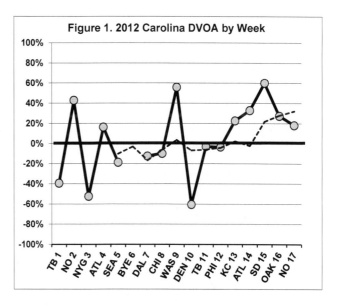

Figure 1. 2012 Carolina DVOA by Week

close games. In contests decided by eight points or less, the Panthers are 6-13. Five teams have won fewer close games in that span, but the Panthers lead the league in close losses, and have the worst percentage (.316) in tight games.

Is that all Rivera's fault? For all the advanced statistical studies we've completed, it's still impossible to separate the performance of a coach from that of his players. After all, in games decided by more than eight points, Rivera's Panthers are 7-6. Those successes speak more to what Rivera is able to do developing players in practice, either during training camp or between games in the season. The close games reflect Rivera's weaknesses as a gameday coach.

We don't have space to list all of Rivera's bad calls, lest the Createspace people reject the book for being too long *again* this year, but here's a sample of some of his notable gaffes from 2012 alone:

Week 4 at Atlanta: The most famous of Rivera's bad decisions. Leading 28-27 with a about a minute to go and facing a fourth-and-1 at the Atlanta 45, Rivera elected to punt rather than try for a first down. The Panthers punted despite the presence of Cam Newton, possibly the best short-yardage rushing quarterback in NFL history, as well as DeAngelo Williams, Jonathan Stewart, and short-yardage specialist Mike Tolbert. By the end of the year, the Panthers had the NFL's best rushing success rate in Power situations. Carolina already had 199 rushing yards at that point in the game, so it's not as if they had trouble rushing against the Falcons defense. Brad Nortman pinned Atlanta on its own 1-yard line with 50 seconds left and no timeouts, so Rivera's decision to punt worked out as well as possible. It didn't matter. The Falcons' first play was a 59-yard pass to Roddy White, moving well past where they would have had the ball had Carolina failed on fourth down, and they eventually kicked a game-winning field goal with ten seconds to spare.

Even before that, though, Rivera's coaching was questionable. After Atlanta scored a second-quarter touchdown to go ahead 17-14, Carolina got the ball at its own 20-yard line with 1:49 to go and all three timeouts left. They then ran a series of short passes and runs, wasting valuable time, and eventually went into halftime with a timeout in their pocket without even crossing midfield. When Carolina should have shown urgency, they played as if they were killing a lead.

Week 5 vs. Seattle: The Panthers had a fourth-and-goal at the 1-yard line down 16-10 in the fourth quarter. We've already discussed how effective Carolina was in short-yardage rushing, but here they opted for a rollout pass, even though Newton has been a lousy red-zone passer so far in his career,

ranking 25th in DVOA each of the last two years (minimum 20 red-zone passes per season). Newton had Ben Hartsock open in the end zone, but underthrew him by 5 yards, and the ball bounced harmlessly to the turf. That's a failure by Rivera to recognize his own team's strengths and weaknesses.

Week 8 at Chicago: Carolina led 13-7 with three seconds left in the first half and the ball at the Chicago 33-yard line. Justin Medlock had already kicked two field goals on the day, and he would kick three more in the second half, including shots from 43 and 45 yards. Rather than attempt a 50-yard field goal, however, Rivera called for Newton to throw a Hail Mary pass, which sailed over everyone's heads. Rivera said after the game that he didn't regret his decision, that he didn't want a missed kick in swirling winds to hurt Medlock's confidence. Which begs the question: If a missed kick from 50 yards in windy conditions is all it takes to shake your kicker's confidence, then why is he your kicker? By the way, after the Chicago game, Medlock missed every kick he attempted the rest of the season, and he was cut three weeks later. That probably didn't help his confidence either.

Later in that same game, the Bears got the ball on their own 22, trailing 22-20 with 2:20 to play, plenty of time to drive and kick a winning field goal. Carolina moved to a soft zone coverage, giving up easy short completions. Jay Cutler proceeded to complete 6-of-7 passes on the drive for 52 yards, with no completion longer than 12 yards. The Bears only had one third down on the drive. With 18 seconds left, Matt Forte ran for three yards, the Bears leisurely called their last timeout, and Robbie Gould kicked a 41-yard field goal to win. "They threw the same pass play I think all the way down the field," Panthers safety Charles Godfrey said after the game. "That was a great play for that coverage and they just ran that play all the way down the field. And the coverage we were in, we just stayed in that coverage." This was not the only time in 2012 a Panthers player would publicly take a shot at his coaches or teammates.

Switch those three games and Carolina finishes 10-6 and contends for the playoffs, and nobody out there is wondering about Rivera's job security. That's assuming, however, that the rest of Carolina's results remain unchanged, but there's reason to believe that the Panthers would have played differently under different circumstances. For two years in a row now, the Panthers have been knocked out of playoff contention before Thanksgiving. Once they are eliminated, and the pressure is off, they seem to magically improve. This isn't just about their win-loss record. DVOA shows that once nothing is on the line, the Panthers have played much better in nearly all phases of the game (Table 1).

Table 1: Late Bloomers: Carolina's strong finishes

Weeks	W-L	Off	Rk	Def	Rk	ST	Rk	Tot	Rk
2011 Weeks 1-11	2-8	10.4%	7	17.8%	32	-9.0%	31	-16.4%	26
2011 Weeks 12-17	4-2	31.9%	5	12.5%	26	-2.3%	28	17.1%	9
2012 Weeks 1-11	2-8	-5.2%	20	-7.1%	8	-9.0%	30	-7.1%	20
2012 Weeks 12-17	5-1	26.1%	2	4.3%	24	2.3%	12	24.1%	6

So Carolina's coach makes so many mistakes that he constantly turns winnable games into losses, and his players are at their worst when there's something to play for. Given all that, why are we predicting the Panthers to take a leap forward this year? Quite simple, really: Their talent level may be high enough to overcome the burden of Rivera's coaching.

For starters, there's the front seven, which should be the best in the division. Rookie defensive tackles Star Lotulelei (14th overall) and Kawann Short (44th) join Dwan Edwards, who set career highs in Stops, Defeats, Stop Rate, and sacks in 2012. Playing behind that trio will be second-year linebacker Luke Kuechly, who made most all-rookie teams last year. Few teams in the league will be this stout up the middle.

On the outside, Charles Johnson and Greg Hardy were one of four duos in the league to each collect 11 sacks last year. Hardy, the marketing whiz of the group, has already dubbed the defensive line as "MonStrz, Inc.," which should be just original enough to avoid harassing phone calls from scary Disney lawyers. Hardy has renamed each member of the unit as a mythological beast, starring himself as "Da Kraken." (Does that mean Matt Ryan is Andromeda?)

As for the offense, casual fans and fantasy owners may be surprised to learn that Newton's passing DVOA improved ever so slightly in his second season, from 0.8% to 2.0%. That's really stagnation more than improvement, but it still defies the popular opinion that Newton suffered a sophomore slump, and it also suggests that Newton will follow the typical quarterback's career path and take another step forward in his third year.

The problem there is that computer projections, by their nature, treat football players as mathematical abstracts, not human beings with emotions, and Newton may be the most emotional player in the league. The volatile young quarterback wears his heart on his sleeve, and while he's known for celebrating big wins and touchdowns, he's equally well known for sulking on the sidelines and in press conferences when the Panthers lose. Some of this (not all) is overblown by the 24-hour sports news cycle, and the idea that Newton is the only player in Carolina who matters. It's a lot easier to make fun of Newton for doing a press conference with his eyes closed than is to break down statistical or mechanical flaws in his game. Instead, we're left discussing whether or not Newton is too sad after a loss, as if indifference would be a better reaction.

If Newton's emotions did get the better of him on the field, it would show up in his numbers somewhere, wouldn't it? His passing numbers in a variety of quote-unquote clutch situations paint a murky picture. We discussed his red-zone struggles earlier, and his passing DVOA on third downs was -9.2%, significantly lower than his overall average. However, in late and close situations (second half or overtime, score within a touchdown), his passing DVOA soared to 26.8%.

Still, Newton must learn to keep his emotions in check. New offensive coordinator Mike Shula acknowledged in May that the most important part of his job isn't fixing Newton's throwing motion or designing protection schemes. Shula's first job this year is to manage Newton's psyche. The rest, to some degree, will take care of itself.

It won't be an easy task. Newton's reputation for moody behavior is no secret, and his own teammates have grown tired of the act. After throwing his third interception of the game in Week 3 against the Giants, Newton retreated alone to the bench, hung a towel over his head, and stared at the ground. Veteran wideout and team captain Steve Smith confronted Newton, and later told the media he had shared what he called "unchoice words" with the passer and told him to stand on the sideline with the rest of the team. It's somewhat ironic to see Smith taking a leadership role. This is the same guy who not once, but twice, injured his own teammates in fights during practice. His maturation shows that it's still possible for Newton to grow up.

Smith's comments on Newton were followed by Godfrey's veiled shot at the play-calling in the Bears game, which were in turn followed by Charles Johnson publicly calling out his teammates via Twitter after Carolina blew an 11-point fourth-quarter lead in an overtime loss to Tampa Bay. Johnson said he was "embarrassed" by the last drive of the game, and that teammates who didn't study or work hard had been "exposed." (Johnson had left the game in the second quarter with a concussion.)

Rivera refused to punish or chastise any of these players for airing their dirty laundry, only saying meekly that he wished the remarks had been kept in-house. None of the comments by themselves seem terribly harmful, and even when taken as a group, they would be nothing but talk radio fodder in most cities, forgotten by kickoff on Sunday. Not on this team, though, and particularly not for this coach. Rivera lost the benefit of the doubt long ago, and when players verbally attack each other or the staff in the press, it's just another sign of a system in desperate need of repair.

Honestly, a lot of the trends that suggest a turnaround in 2013 could easily be interpreted as Rivera's weaknesses. Our projection system sees a team that went 0-7 in games decided by less than a touchdown and expects that record to regress to the mean. Our look at those close losses shows there's plenty of reason to think otherwise. Similarly, the Panthers' improvement throughout the year seems like a sign of further improvement in 2013. But as we've discussed, what looks like improvement might really be an uninspired team playing up to its talent level only after the games have lost all meaning.

For his part, Rivera feels like he's a better coach now than when he was hired. "Without a doubt in my mind," he told Scott Fowler of the *Charlotte Observer*. "I think the biggest thing is management, more than anything else. ... I'll put myself up against anybody with X's and O's. I feel very confident about that.

"But I've had to learn a lot about management. When you're managing 26 people and five coaches (as a defensive coordinator) and now you're managing 61 people and 17 coaches, it's a little bit different."

Something else different in Carolina is Dave Gettleman, the new general manager in town, hired shortly after the 2012 season ended. Panthers owner Jerry Richardson did not consult Rivera before hiring Gettleman. In fact, the coach and GM did not even meet until after Gettleman was hired. And Gettleman is the man who will make the ultimate judgment on Rivera's career.

So that's where Rivera sits now, on the hottest seat in the league, his shortcomings laid bare for all to see, his future tied to a shoegazer at quarterback, his fate decided by a general manager who owes him no loyalty and an owner who never wanted him in the first place. One thing's for sure: Ron Rivera will not coach this team to a 2-8 start again. If the losses start to pile up, Rivera will be fired long before then.

Vince Verhei

2012 Panthers Stats by Week

Wk	vs.	W-L	PF	PA	YDF	YDA	TO	Total	Off	Def	ST
1	at TB	L	10	16	301	258	-2	-39%	-29%	8%	-2%
2	NO	W	35	27	463	486	1	43%	44%	1%	0%
3	NYG	L	7	36	327	405	-5	-52%	-27%	16%	-9%
4	at ATL	L	28	30	404	426	0	16%	18%	1%	-1%
5	SEA	L	12	16	190	310	1	-19%	-49%	-36%	-6%
6	BYE										
7	DAL	L	14	19	328	312	-1	-13%	-16%	-9%	-6%
8	at CHI	L	22	23	416	210	1	-10%	-12%	-13%	-12%
9	at WAS	W	21	13	330	337	0	56%	34%	-24%	-3%
10	DEN	L	14	36	250	360	0	-61%	-41%	-18%	-38%
11	TB	L	21	27	331	403	2	-3%	7%	-4%	-14%
12	at PHI	W	30	22	398	311	3	-4%	39%	35%	-8%
13	at KC	L	21	27	385	355	0	23%	43%	24%	3%
14	ATL	W	30	20	475	362	1	33%	44%	15%	4%
15	at SD	W	31	7	372	164	1	60%	25%	-35%	1%
16	OAK	W	17	6	271	189	-1	27%	-18%	-46%	0%
17	at NO	W	44	38	530	441	0	18%	19%	14%	13%

Trends and Splits

	Offense	Rank	Defense	Rank
Total DVOA	7.2%	10	-3.1%	11
Unadjusted VOA	9.0%	10	-0.6%	16
Weighted Trend	12.0%	8	-3.9%	12
Variance	10.5%	28	5.3%	17
Average Opponent	1.3%	19	2.9%	7
Passing	17.3%	12	0.8%	12
Rushing	6.0%	8	-8.4%	11
First Down	14.4%	7	8.9%	26
Second Down	-6.3%	21	-9.5%	7
Third Down	13.6%	10	-16.6%	5
First Half	16.2%	7	-3.7%	13
Second Half	-2.8%	15	-2.7%	11
Red Zone	15.4%	8	1.4%	15
Late and Close	-5.6%	17	-9.7%	11

Five-Year Performance

Year	W-L	Pyth W	Est W	PF	PA	TO	Total	Rk	Off	Rk	Def	Rk	ST	Rk	Off AGL	Rk	Def AGL	Rk	Off Age	Rk	Def Age	Rk	ST Age	Rk
2008	12-4	10.2	10.3	414	329	+6	18.0%	6	12.9%	6	-2.4%	13	2.7%	10	14.4	9	5.6	4	27.5	16	26.3	27	27.1	5
2009	8-8	8.2	8.3	315	308	+6	7.1%	15	-2.0%	20	-12.8%	6	-3.7%	29	28.9	20	39.8	25	27.4	14	26.1	28	25.9	25
2010	2-14	2.4	2.2	196	408	-8	-36.2%	31	-35.8%	32	-1.1%	16	-1.5%	22	39.8	27	35.2	24	25.7	30	25.4	32	25.0	32
2011	6-10	7.4	6.9	406	429	+1	-4.1%	20	18.2%	4	15.8%	32	-6.5%	32	47.6	29	61.5	32	27.2	15	25.3	32	26.0	25
2012	7-9	7.8	8.8	357	363	+1	5.5%	13	7.2%	10	-3.1%	11	-4.8%	29	23.1	10	53.0	27	27.1	15	25.7	28	26.0	19

2012 Performance Based on Most Common Personnel Groups

CAR Offense					CAR Offense vs. Opponents				CAR Defense					CAR Defense vs. Opponents			
Pers	Freq	Yds	DVOA	Run%	Pers	Freq	Yds	DVOA	Pers	Freq	Yds	DVOA		Pers	Freq	Yds	DVOA
11	57%	6.4	12.4%	32%	Nickel Even	41%	6.5	17.1%	Nickel Even	49%	5.6	-3.4%		11	48%	5.8	0.2%
12	20%	4.9	-10.3%	49%	4-3-4	27%	5.4	1.7%	4-3-4	42%	5.2	-4.3%		21	21%	5.1	-8.1%
21	13%	6.5	32.3%	50%	3-4-4	14%	5.5	-0.5%	3-4-4	4%	5.6	2.3%		12	15%	5.1	-4.7%
22	4%	5.4	-8.0%	75%	Nickel Odd	10%	5.4	-1.2%	Nickel Odd	3%	7.7	11.9%		22	8%	5.8	7.2%
622	1%	1.5	67.3%	92%	Dime+	6%	7.9	47.1%	Goal Line	1%	0.8	5.1%		20	1%	4.8	30.6%

Strategic Tendencies

Run/Pass		Rk	Formation		Rk	Pass Rush		Rk	Secondary		Rk	Strategy		Rk
Runs, first half	38%	17	Form: Single Back	69%	13	Rush 3	4.7%	22	4 DB	46%	13	Play action	33%	4
Runs, first down	49%	19	Form: Empty Back	3%	27	Rush 4	75.6%	4	5 DB	52%	6	Avg Box (Off)	6.39	14
Runs, second-long	34%	9	Pers: 3+ WR	58%	9	Rush 5	16.0%	25	6+ DB	1%	31	Avg Box (Def)	6.33	22
Runs, power sit.	80%	1	Pers: 4+ WR	1%	24	Rush 6+	3.7%	29	CB by Sides	77%	14	Offensive Pace	31.12	21
Runs, behind 2H	35%	4	Pers: 2+ TE/6+ OL	28%	21	Sacks by LB	2.6%	32	DB Blitz	8%	23	Defensive Pace	31.90	31
Pass, ahead 2H	41%	25	Shotgun/Pistol	68%	2	Sacks by DB	0.0%	28	Hole in Zone	12%	4	Go for it on 4th	0.90	17

Note to Carolina: Stop big blitzing with six or more pass rushers. You allowed 8.4 yards per play on a big blitz, compared to just 6.2 yards per play otherwise. At least that's not as bad as the year before, when the Panthers allowed a ridiculous 12.2 yards per play when big-blitzing. ☞ Despite the great seasons from Carolina linebackers like Luke Kuechly and Thomas Davis, Panthers opponents threw 26 percent of passes to running backs, the highest rate in the league. ☞ Carolina used the pistol roughly twice per game, but they'll likely use it more often in 2013. The Panthers averaged 9.0 yards per play from pistol with 67.7% DVOA. That breaks down to 12.7 yards per play on passes and 7.4 yards per play on runs (including option keepers for Cam Newton). ☞ Carolina's opponents blitzed Cam Newton with at least one defensive back on 14.8 percent of pass plays, second behind Philadelphia, even though Newton averaged 7.9 yards on these plays, fifth in the NFL. ☞ The Panthers gained a league-leading 10.3 yards per pass on running back screens, with 63.9% DVOA (third).

Passing

Player	DYAR	DVOA	Plays	NtYds	Avg	YAC	C%	TD	Int
C.Newton	422	2.0%	521	3621	7.0	6.1	58.1%	19	12

Rushing

Player	DYAR	DVOA	Plays	Yds	Avg	TD	Fum	Suc
D.Williams	14	-6.7%	174	741	4.3	5	2	48%
C.Newton	149	11.3%	114	746	6.5	8	3	–
J.Stewart	-36	-18.4%	93	340	3.7	1	1	42%
M.Tolbert	103	25.8%	54	183	3.4	7	0	65%

Receiving

Player	DYAR	DVOA	Plays	Ctch	Yds	Y/C	YAC	TD	C%
S.Smith	171	4.0%	138	73	1174	16.1	3.7	4	53%
B.LaFell	106	2.8%	76	44	677	15.4	7.1	4	58%
L.Murphy*	-118	-37.2%	62	26	339	13.0	2.6	1	42%
A.Edwards	23	25.5%	9	5	121	24.2	14.4	0	56%
D.Hixon	177	23.6%	59	39	567	14.5	3.6	2	66%
G.Olsen	157	13.6%	104	69	843	12.2	3.5	5	66%
G.Barnidge	42	96.5%	6	6	78	13.0	7.2	1	100%
M.Tolbert	48	7.7%	39	27	268	9.9	10.2	0	69%
J.Stewart	34	15.0%	23	17	157	9.2	10.5	1	74%
D.Williams	60	38.9%	20	13	187	14.4	16.4	2	65%

Offensive Line

Player	Pos	Age	GS	Snaps	Pen	Sk	Pass	Run	Player	Pos	Age	GS	Snaps	Pen	Sk	Pass	Run
Jordan Gross	LT	33	16/16	1024	3	5.5	19.5	3	Garry Williams	RG	27	16/9	606	1	1	7	1
Byron Bell	RT	25	15/15	943	5	2.5	20.5	2	Jeff Byers	C	28	14/7	471	4	2	10.5	1
Amini Silatolu	LG	25	15/15	882	10	4	17.5	7	Ryan Kalil	C	28	5/5	286	1	0	2	1
Geoff Hangartner	C	31	12/12	755	3	0	6	7	Thomas Austin	G	27	4/1	125	0	0.5	0.5	2

Year	Yards	ALY	Rk	Power	Rk	Stuff	Rk	2nd Lev	Rk	Open Field	Rk	Sacks	ASR	Rk	Short	Long	F-Start	Cont.
2010	4.29	3.74	27	62%	14	21%	23	1.22	9	0.99	9	50	9.9%	31	23	9	22	36
2011	5.30	4.32	5	71%	4	17%	6	1.38	5	1.40	1	35	7.2%	21	8	24	14	32
2012	3.88	3.49	30	75%	1	23%	26	1.08	22	0.72	19	36	7.6%	21	2	21	17	25
2012 ALY by direction:		Left End 3.57 (22)			Left Tackle 2.87 (29)			Mid/Guard 3.57 (29)			Right Tackle 3.67 (24)				Right End 3.71 (23)			

The Panthers made two personnel changes on the offensive line in 2012, though only one of them was planned. At center, starter Ryan Kalil was lost for the season with a Lisfranc injury in October. At left guard, the Panthers swapped out an aging Travelle Wharton for second-round rookie Amini Silatolu. Combining runs and passes, Silatolu led all left guards with 24.5 blown blocks despite missing the week 17 game against New Orleans. Our charters also noted several occasions when confusion between Silatolu and left tackle Jordan Gross allowed free rushers to come through unblocked. The good news is that Silatolu clearly improved with experience. In Weeks 1-9, Carolina had 3.04 ALY, and Silatolu had 18.5 blown blocks. From Week 10 on, that ALY climbed to 3.91, and Silatolu only blew six blocks. As for center, the Panthers replaced Kalil by sliding Geoff Hangartner over to the middle, but that left them with no good option at right guard, forcing them to rotate undrafted bench players Jeff Byers and Garry Williams.

All five starters return in 2013, so we should expect the line to play like it did in 2011, right? Well, not necessarily. At 32, Gross has noticeably declined from his Pro Bowl peak. Right tackle Byron Bell has fared well for an undrafted player and secured a starting position, but on his best day he's just average. Both players were among the top 20 tackles in blown pass blocks, though neither made the top 40 in blown run blocks. Gross and Hangartner are both in their thirties, and Kalil's foot injury kept him out of OTAs, although he was expected to be back for training camp. Fourth-round rookie Edmund Kugbila out of Division II Valdosta State, a punishing run-blocker, could challenge Hangartner for a starting role, which would let the veteran return to a utility backup role.

Cam Newton and his receivers also have a big impact on Carolina's pass blocking numbers. Forty-three percent of the Panthers' sacks were "long" sacks. No other team was higher than 40 percent.

Defensive Front Seven

Defensive Line	Age	Pos	Snaps	Plays	TmPct	Overall Rk	Stop	Dfts	BTkl	Runs	vs. Run St%	Rk	RuYd	Rk	Pass Rush Sack	Hit	Hur	Tips
Charles Johnson	27	DE	833	45	5.4%	36	34	18	3	25	64%	68	2.7	51	12.5	6	26.5	2
Greg Hardy	25	DE	748	60	7.7%	8	49	23	1	41	80%	17	2.7	48	11	9	19	1
Dwan Edwards	32	DT	703	52	7.1%	3	44	14	1	37	84%	14	2.5	47	6	3	6	1
Frank Alexander	24	DE	552	21	2.5%	--	19	8	0	11	82%	--	1.5	--	2.5	5	12	3

Linebackers	Age	Pos	Snaps	Plays	TmPct	Overall Rk	Stop	Dfts	BTkl	Sack	Pass Rush Hit	Hur	Tips	Runs	vs. Run St%	Rk	Yds	Rk	Tgts	vs. Pass Suc%	Rk	AdjYd	Rk	PD
Luke Kuechly	22	MLB	921	171	20.4%	1	96	27	8	1	0	0	0	93	67%	44	3.2	49	45	59%	14	6.9	40	7
Thomas Davis	30	OLB	778	104	13.3%	39	61	23	7	0	1	2	0	46	57%	96	4.4	101	44	65%	6	3.7	2	3
James Anderson*	30	OLB	521	74	11.8%	52	39	7	4	0	0	0.5	0	49	65%	58	2.9	31	24	44%	58	6.8	36	1
Jon Beason	28	MLB	262	30	14.4%	--	15	4	3	0	1	0.5	0	17	65%	--	3.9	--	15	44%	--	10.9	--	3
Chase Blackburn	30	MLB	783	99	12.8%	44	59	15	6	3	4	3.5	1	72	65%	59	3.7	71	23	37%	68	10.8	74	4

Year	Yards	ALY	Rk	Power	Rk	Stuff	Rk	2nd Level	Rk	Open Field	Rk	Sacks	ASR	Rk	Short	Long
2010	4.02	3.77	10	62%	14	22%	6	1.15	18	0.87	20	31	6.2%	18	9	14
2011	5.00	4.68	32	64%	18	17%	23	1.47	31	1.08	26	31	6.7%	16	4	13
2012	4.45	4.30	23	66%	23	16%	29	1.23	24	0.88	22	39	7.8%	5	9	20

2012 ALY by direction:	Left End 4.38 (24)	Left Tackle 4.32 (23)	Mid/Guard 4.29 (25)	Right Tackle 3.77 (14)	Right End 4.66 (24)

Defensive tackle Ron Edwards started 11 games in 2012 before his season ended with an elbow injury. The Panthers finished out the season with some bottom-of-the-roster filler, then doubled up on the position in the draft, taking Utah's Star Lotulelei in the first round and Purdue's Kawann Short in the second. Lotulelei, former defensive lineman of the year in the Pac-12, might have been a top-five pick if a pre-draft physical test hadn't revealed a heart condition. Further testing found nothing wrong with Lotulelei's heart, and he should be a (ahem) star for Carolina, a one-gap or two-gap player who will start next to Dwan Edwards from day one. Edwards, signed just a week before the season after Buffalo cut him in camp, was one of the most active tackles in the league last year. Just ask the Bucs—in two games against Tampa Bay, Edwards collected 11 tackles, two sacks and a pass defensed. He signed a one-year contract to stay with the team this year, so Short will spend at least one season as rotational depth before entering the starting lineup. Meanwhile, Charles Johnson and Greg Hardy were both in the top 15 in sacks and top 35 in hurries. This should be one of the league's elite lines.

Speaking of elite lines, take a gander at Luke Kuechly's stat line as a rookie. Our individual defensive numbers go back to 1996, and in that time the only other rookie to lead the NFL in percentage of his team's plays was Patrick Willis with the 49ers in 2007. On the strong side, Thomas Davis often plays more like an old-school "monster" defensive back than a linebacker. That partly explains his lousy run defense numbers and stellar pass coverage stats. He managed to play 15 games last year after tearing his ACL three times in three years, but that's still three more torn ACLs than you would like from a 30-year-old linebacker. Speaking of linebackers who can't stay healthy, three-time Pro Bowler Jon Beason missed 12 games last year and 15 games the year before with Achilles tendon and knee injuries. Rivera said that Beason had passed his physical before minicamp, "so I'm assuming he is 100 percent." He added that Beason had flashed energy and quickness, whatever that's worth when nobody is wearing pads.

With those injury histories, the depth provided by Chase Blackburn, Jordan Senn, and fifth-round rookie A.J. Klein could prove critical. Last year was the first time Blackburn started more than eight games in a season, but he failed to rank among the top 50 linebackers in Defeats or any of our run defense or pass coverage metrics. The Panthers signed him away from the Giants by offering him two years and a $200,000 signing bonus instead of a one-year veteran minimum deal. He's strictly a backup player, but he's versatile enough to play inside or outside. Senn has started seven games in his five-year career, all in 2011, but we list him with only one broken tackle that season. Klein started at all three linebacker positions at Iowa State, and was named co-Big 12 defensive player of the year in 2011. He's noted for quick reactions and pass coverage ability, though he lacks the elite athleticism and straight-line speed to be a good pass rusher. In Carolina, that hardly matters.

Defensive Secondary

Secondary	Age	Pos	Snaps	Overall						vs. Run					vs. Pass									
				Plays	TmPct	Rk	Stop	Dfts	BTkl	Runs	St%	Rk	Yds	Rk	Tgts	Tgt%	Rk	Dist	Suc%	Rk	APaYd	Rk	PD	Int
Charles Godfrey	28	SS	985	76	9.9%	38	29	10	6	37	54%	8	6.4	25	23	5.4%	57	10.2	53%	42	6.4	17	5	2
Captain Munnerlyn	25	CB	915	68	8.2%	54	29	17	7	18	44%	39	6.8	47	62	13.9%	71	9.1	56%	23	5.4	2	11	2
Josh Norman	26	CB	769	78	9.4%	29	22	10	7	20	35%	58	7.5	56	79	17.8%	42	12.0	42%	80	8.3	69	9	1
Haruki Nakamura	27	FS	591	49	7.2%	57	9	4	5	26	15%	73	11.9	71	11	3.1%	73	26.4	69%	10	9.8	71	4	2
Josh Thomas	24	CB	517	35	4.2%	85	18	10	0	3	100%	1	-1.3	1	54	12.1%	79	11.5	52%	40	7.3	36	6	0
Chris Gamble*	30	CB	280	17	8.2%	--	6	1	1	6	33%	--	10.8	--	14	12.7%	--	7.0	51%	--	4.8	--	2	0
Sherrod Martin*	29	FS	272	23	3.7%	--	9	3	2	7	43%	--	6.3	--	9	2.6%	--	14.7	40%	--	7.4	--	2	0
James Dockery	25	CB	158	18	4.9%	--	4	3	0	3	33%	--	6.7	--	16	8.0%	--	14.8	31%	--	9.3	--	1	0
D.J. Moore	26	CB	363	36	5.4%	--	15	6	3	7	43%	--	7.0	--	31	8.1%	--	10.0	46%	--	8.9	--	5	2
Mike Mitchell	26	SS	329	31	4.0%	--	14	7	1	20	55%	--	4.9	--	8	2.0%	--	5.0	47%	--	4.0	--	0	0
Drayton Florence	33	CB	301	26	6.6%	--	13	7	7	8	38%	--	9.0	--	29	14.0%	--	13.7	57%	--	8.9	--	7	1

Year	Pass D Rank	vs. #1 WR	Rk	vs. #2 WR	Rk	vs. Other WR	Rk	vs. TE	Rk	vs. RB	Rk
2010	8	-8.4%	10	-27.4%	1	8.6%	24	35.1%	32	-17.5%	3
2011	29	26.5%	27	12.7%	22	-21.7%	8	40.2%	32	20.8%	27
2012	12	-4.9%	15	10.1%	26	-1.9%	15	-0.1%	19	-6.9%	13

Before the draft, our own Andy Benoit dubbed this "the worst secondary in football." Since the Panthers selected no defensive backs on draft day, it's safe to say the gap between them and the rest of the league has grown since then.

Chris Gamble's release and subsequent retirement leaves Captain Munnerlyn and Josh Norman as the incumbent starters at corner. In his four NFL seasons, Munnerlyn has now ranked 11th, third, 79th, and second in Adjusted Yards Allowed per target, an average ranking of 24 with a standard deviation of 37. That's a nerdy way of saying he has been very good except for one puke-tacular year. Speaking of puke-tacular, Josh Norman played like the fifth-round rookie he was last year, finally benched in December for waiver pickups Josh Thomas and James Dockery. Theoretically, Drayton Florence could contend for Norman's spot, but Florence doesn't have a particularly strong track record himself. Last year's 8.9 Adjusted Yards per Pass would have ranked in the 70s among cornerbacks if he had seen enough targets to qualify for the leaderboards, and that would have been his fourth season ranked 65th or worse.

Safeties Haruki Nakamura and Charles Godfrey lined up about as far away from the line of scrimmage as possible in 2012. The strategy served to take away the home-run ball. Only 16 percent of opponents' passes traveled more than 15 yards past the line of scrimmage, the lowest rate in the league. Opponents were forced to go to slants, curls, and flat routes, where the short defenders (most often Norman, Munnerlyn, or Thomas Davis) limited them to 4.0 YAC per reception, better than any defense except Chicago.

The strategy also kept Nakamura and Godfrey off the stat sheet. As a group, Panthers safeties made less than 20 percent of the team's plays, the lowest rate in the league. Nakamura is the bigger problem, a long-time special teamer who didn't start a single game in four seasons with Baltimore before the Panthers let him start 13 a year ago. One alternative is former Raiders safety Mike Mitchell, the notorious second-round draft pick with the seventh-round grade. But after only nine starts in four seasons in Oakland (which has hardly been a powerhouse in that time), it's hard to see Mitchell starting in Carolina either. A dark horse might be undrafted rookie Robert Lester out of Alabama, who has strong instincts and leadership experience with a championship team. Some draftniks saw Lester as a first- or second-round pick going into his senior year, but his stock fell due to inconsistency and worries about his 4.66-second forty at the combine. Of course, that's .03 seconds slower than Kenny Vaccaro and .01 seconds faster than Jonathan Cyprien, so was it really worth worrying about?

Special Teams

Year	DVOA	Rank	FG/XP	Rank	Net Kick	Rank	Kick Ret	Rank	Net Punt	Rank	Punt Ret	Rank	Hidden	Rank
2010	-1.5%	20	6.4	6	6.3	9	-9.5	28	-9.0	28	-1.7	18	-5.3	21
2011	-6.5%	32	-7.6	31	-0.8	21	2.2	10	-19.6	32	-6.7	24	6.7	8
2012	-4.8%	29	-6.3	30	4.6	8	-6.9	29	-13.4	28	-1.9	17	-15.5	31

Exhibit No. 2,491 for why you never draft a punter: Ignoring coverage, sixth-round rookie Brad Nortman was last in the league in gross punting value. Justin Medlock, kicking in the NFL for the first time since 2007, made each of his first seven field-goal attempts, but was cut in mid-November after missing three in a row. Despite playing just 10 games, Medlock's gross kickoff value (discounting coverage) was the third-worst in the league. Graham Gano was a big improvement there (fourth in the league in value in six games), and he made 9-of-11 field-goal tries. However, that success doesn't match Gano's past performance: he was close to average on kickoffs in 2010 and 2011 with Washington, and the Redskins ranked 32nd and 30th in field-goal value those years.

Joe Adams and Captain Munnerlyn split punt return duties last year, while kickoffs were primarily handled by Armanti Edwards, Kealoha Pilares, and Adams. None of them were above average. Free-agent addition Ted Ginn, Jr., was good at punt returns in 2010 and 2011, but just average for San Francisco last year. Sixth-round rookie Kenjon Barner scored on punt and kickoff returns in his Oregon career, and in 2009 was third in the country in punt return average. Any of these players could end up returning kicks for Carolina this year. Journeymen Jason Phillips and Colin Jones tied for the team lead with 12 special teams tackles, tied for 20th in the NFL.

Coaching Staff

Rob Chudzinski, offensive coordinator for Ron Rivera's first two seasons in Carolina, moved on to become the head coach in Cleveland, so Rivera promoted quarterbacks coach Mike Shula to fill that spot. Shula joined Carolina's staff when Rivera was hired in 2011, so he deserves some credit for Cam Newton's success, but otherwise Shula's resume isn't exactly golden. In stints as offensive coordinator or quarterbacks coach in Tampa Bay, Miami, and Jacksonville, he failed to develop Trent Dilfer, Jay Fiedler, or David Garrard into anything more than average quarterbacks. In between, he managed to go 26-23 as head coach for the Alabama Crimson Tide, a school that has won three national championships in six years since Shula was canned. The four NFL head coaches who have hired Shula (Tony Dungy, Dave Wannstedt, Jack Del Rio, and Rivera) are all defensive types, three of them former NFL players, each hoping Shula could turn the offense around. It hasn't really happened yet. Replacing Shula at quarterbacks coach is Ken Dorsey, who twice finished in the top five in Heisman Trophy voting for the Miami Hurricanes before spending five years playing for the 49ers and Browns. He has since worked as an instructor for IMG Passing Academy and as a scout for Carolina. Another notable name working his way up the Panthers coaching staff is Ricky Proehl, who once caught a game-tying touchdown pass for the Panthers in the Super Bowl. He takes over as wide receivers coach after serving as an assistant to the same position in 2012, and an offensive consultant in 2011. Sean McDermott returns for his third season at defensive coordinator after two years in the same position in Philadelphia. Three of his prior teams finished 11th or better in DVOA (the exception being his first Carolina team, which was last).

Chicago Bears

2012 Record: 10-6	**Total DVOA:** 20.5% (6th)	**2013 Mean Projection:** 8.1 wins	**On the Clock (0-4):** 8%
Pythagorean Wins: 10.8 (6th)	**Offense:** -10.9% (26th)	**Postseason Odds:** 33.5%	**Mediocrity (5-7):** 32%
Snap-Weighted Age: 27.4 (5th)	**Defense:** -26.7% (1st)	**Super Bowl Odds:** 3.2%	**Playoff Contender (8-10):** 44%
Average Opponent: 2.7% (8th)	**Special Teams:** 4.7% (6th)	**Proj. Avg. Opponent:** 1.6% (11th)	**Super Bowl Contender (11+):** 16%

2012: And all the rain falls down, amen, on the works of last year's man.

2013: Darlin' don't you go and Cutler hair, do you think it's gonna make him change?

It's hard not to admire the ruthlessness and conviction that Chicago general manager Phil Emery has shown in his first couple of years on the job. The Bears have proven under his watch that they are willing to attack their needs early and that they won't let sentimentality keep them from making sound football decisions. Nowhere was this more evident than at the end of the 2012 season, when a pair of long-time organizational leaders—head coach Lovie Smith and future Hall of Fame linebacker Brian Urlacher—were quickly dismissed. They were summarily replaced by a coach and a pair of middle linebackers without an iota of the prestige Urlacher and Smith had.

Urlacher—who may manage the rare feat of simultaneously being one of the 10 best middle linebackers of all-time and the fourth-best Bears middle linebacker of all-time—stood his ground on his contract demands. Emery put forth an offer that he felt was fair, reportedly worth $2.5 million for one season, and didn't budge. Urlacher found the rest of the NFL just as stoic about overpaying for the name attached to his 35-year-old body, eventually retiring. A smooth general manager lets a process like that play out, shrugs his shoulders, and moves on. Emery not only did that, but also signed D.J. Williams away from the Broncos and drafted Jon Bostic out of Florida in the second round, giving his team multiple options to fill the spot Urlacher vacated before he had even made up his mind to retire.

Keep in mind that these were not your standard "old-washed-up coach and player meet chopping block" moves. The Bears finished with one of the best defensive seasons of the DVOA era (1991-2012). They had the No. 1 pass defense, they had the No. 1 rush defense, and their -26.8% defensive rating was the sixth-best score that we have recorded thus far (Table 1).

The defense faded down the stretch—Chicago's five worst single-game defensive DVOA ratings all came after Week 11—but typically, a season like this is rewarded with handshakes and a swift promise to maintain the work done on that side of the ball (or at least to maintain it within the confines of the salary cap). Instead, Emery is pulling double-duty by trying to keep the defense as similar to last season's as possible while simultaneously replacing the coach who built it and the linebacker who defined it.

Statistically, Lovie Smith was a coach of extremes. The Bears defense finished as a top-10 DVOA unit in eight of his nine seasons (Table 2). Outside of the Ravens and Steelers, teams are killing themselves to keep streaks like that going after four seasons. Until last season, for example, the Bengals had not fielded a top-10 DVOA defense over the course of the entire DVOA era (i.e., since 1991). Bears special teams, led by Dave Toub, have finished in the top six in special teams DVOA for seven consecutive seasons. This wasn't just cherry-picking a threshold, either: the Bears defense finished first or second in DVOA three times, and Chicago special teams, buoyed by Devin Hester, finished first four separate times.

But Lovie's legacy in Chicago is ultimately defined by his inability to generate an offense worthy of his defense. It didn't matter if the play-calling was in the hands of Terry Shea, Ron Turner, Mike Martz, or Mike Tice. It didn't matter if the signal-caller was considered a franchise quarterback on arrival like Jay

Table 1: Best Defensive DVOA, 1991-2012

Year	Team	DVOA
1991	PHI	-42.4%
2002	TB	-31.8%
2008	PIT	-29.0%
2004	BUF	-28.5%
2008	BAL	-27.8%
2012	**CHI**	**-26.8%**
2009	NYJ	-25.5%
2000	TEN	-25.0%
2003	BAL	-25.0%
1991	NO	-24.5%
2000	BAL	-23.8%
1995	SF	-23.7%

Note: The top of this table is not a misprint. The 1991 Eagles defense really was that much better than any defense over the past 20 years.

Table 2: All Defense, No Offense

Most top-10 Defensive DVOA finishes, 2004-2012		Most bottom-10 Offensive DVOA finishes, 2004-2012	
BAL	8	SF	7
PIT	8	**CHI**	**7**
CHI	**8**	CLE	7
MIA	4	DET	6
TB	4	OAK	6
WAS	4	STL	5
DEN	4	BUF	5
NYJ	4	MIN	5

2013 Bears Schedule

Week	Opp.	Week	Opp.	Week	Opp.
1	CIN	7	at WAS	13	at MIN
2	MIN	8	BYE	14	DAL (Mon.)
3	at PIT	9	at GB (Mon.)	15	at CLE
4	at DET	10	DET	16	at PHI
5	NO	11	BAL	17	GB
6	NYG (Thu.)	12	at STL		

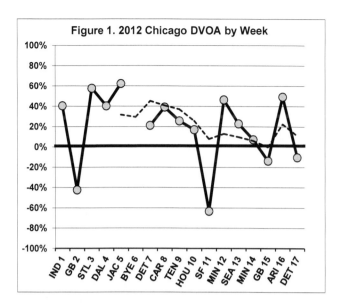

Figure 1. 2012 Chicago DVOA by Week

Cutler, or if he was a rookie forced to play too soon like Kyle Orton. It didn't matter if the Bears tried to fix the offense with high draft picks like Cedric Benson, or big free-agent signings like Muhsin Muhammad. The Bears finished in the bottom 12 in offensive DVOA in every season under Smith, and finished 26th or worse in seven of nine seasons, including the last four in a row. Chicago made it to the Super Bowl once, with the defense and special teams dragging Rex Grossman behind them as a frustrated parent pulls a crying toddler in a wagon. Then Peyton Manning embarrassed them on a rainy night in Miami, and the Bears have spent the last seven years trying in vain to create an offense that even slightly resembles the one that beat them. They still haven't come close.

Perhaps there was a way for the Bears to mesh Smith's brilliant defensive schemes with competent offense. Perhaps a coordinator that they passed on at one point would have been able to work with Cutler and generate an offense that was empirically better than, say, Matt Cassel's 2009 Chiefs. But the important thing is that the Bears can't spend any more time waiting to find out. Great defense and special teams be damned, if Smith had input on the fifth offensive coordinator that was going to join his staff, the evidence suggests he would have flubbed it.

Emery made the only move a team with actual championship aspirations could: he got rid of good enough. Defensive coordinator Mel Tucker, brought in from the Jaguars over the offseason, will oversee the exact kind of unit Tucker desires: one where the players are good enough to make the scheme work. Tucker runs mostly passive Cover-2 and zone schemes that relied on his front four to generate pass pressure, which worked well in 2011 when the Jaguars finished fifth in defensive DVOA. Last season's Jaguars pass rush was so bereft of talent that rookie Shea McClellin, who played just 35 percent

Table 3: Top 10 Receivers in Percentage of Team's Targets, 1991-2012

Name	Year	Team	Targets	Yards	Pct
Brandon Marshall	2012	CHI	195	1,506	40.2%
Sterling Sharpe	1993	GB	188	1,274	35.6%
Marvin Harrison	1999	IND	193	1,663	35.3%
Marvin Harrison	2002	IND	205	1,722	34.7%
Rob Moore	1997	ARI	208	1,584	34.6%
Roddy White	2008	ATL	148	1,383	34.1%
Herman Moore	1995	DET	206	1,686	34.0%
Andre Johnson	2006	HOU	164	1,155	34.0%
Rod Smith	2001	DEN	171	1,343	33.5%
Steve Smith	2005	CAR	150	1,563	33.4%

of the snaps as Chicago's fourth defensive end, would have been the best pass-rusher on Jacksonville's roster. Tucker will be tasked with keeping the defense good enough to possibly send aging star linebacker Lance Briggs out with the title Urlacher didn't get; compared to the project assigned to new head coach Marc Trestman, that should be child's play.

Trestman, who spent the last five years coaching the Montreal Alouettes of the CFL and is best known for his work as an offensive coordinator with the early-2000s Raiders, is tasked with creating an offense that best suits quarterback Jay Cutler's talents. While it's hard to pinpoint exactly what schemes and ideas he'll be bringing over the border (no rouges—if the NFL had rouges, Lovie and Toub would have attempted at least five a game), some ideas can be gleaned by the new hires and signings the Bears made this offseason.

The biggest problem that the Bears offense faced last season was a lack of receiving talent. Brandon Marshall was targeted on 40.5 percent of Bears passes last season, the highest percentage of a team's passes being thrown to one receiver we have recorded since 1991 (Table 3). Marshall's obvious talents played a large part in the number of targets headed his way, but the rest of his receiving corps was so shallow that Cutler's best percentage play often was to just loft it in Marshall's general direction. Alshon Jeffrey wasn't able to separate from press coverage consistently and lost time to injury. Earl Bennett is a fourth receiver in a good offense. Devin Hester and Eric Weems, special teamers masquerading as actual receivers, saw the field on 35 percent and 12 percent of Chicago's offensive snaps, respectively. The only thing the receivers had going for them last season was that they weren't the tight ends.

The signing of Martellus Bennett theoretically fixes a huge hole for the Bears. After one year with Martz, the Bears jettisoned Greg Olsen to Carolina for a third-round pick. That was an idea with some merit, given Martz's disdain for the tight end as a non-blocker. But with Martz lasting only two seasons, Tice was left with a cadre of irrelevant tight ends and *still* ran multiple tight-end sets 43 percent of the time, an increase of 16 percent over the year before. Imagine how much 12 personnel the Bears would have used if Kellen Davis or Matt Spaeth could actually catch a football.

In fairness to Tice, a lot of the theory of using those sets last season was to help with the dismal offensive line that has been the source of 60 percent of all radio griping in Chicago since Olin Kreutz retired. Despite spending a first-round pick on Gabe Carimi, the Bears have been looking at Roberto Garza and a floating opera of characters who could never prove they belonged on an NFL field for the entirety of Tice's employment. Some of that was Tice's fault—nobody should be trying to willingly convince his general manager that he can make a passable left tackle out of J'Marcus Webb—but the lack of investment at the position was a source of much consternation. Yes, the Bears used first-round picks on Carimi and Chris Williams, but otherwise they haven't invested anything higher than a seventh-round pick on an offensive lineman since they spent a fourth-rounder on Josh Beekman in the 2007 draft.

Enter Jermon Bushrod, the rare Pro Bowl tackle who did just as little as Vince Young did to earn his spot on the team. Bushrod does not change the dynamic of this Bears offense, but he should be more credible at left tackle than his predecessor. Joining him from New Orleans is new offensive coordinator Aaron Kromer, who coached the Saints offensive line before becoming interim coach for a few games last season. That could be a sign that the Bears are interested in producing the same sort of blocking scheme that New Orleans uses with Drew Brees: an "inside-out" emphasis that tries to divert rushers to the outside and allows the quarterback to step up into a clean pocket.

While those changes make schematic sense, each move comes with more than a little risk. Bennett flourished with the Giants when given a starting opportunity, but this is the same player who never had a positive DVOA before last season. The speed and size have always been there for Bennett to be a threat, and he oozes potential based on them. He also managed just a 61 percent catch rate last year and had eight drops, which tied him with Brandon Pettigrew and Brent Celek for the second-most among tight ends behind Jimmy Graham. But the real problem is not that the Bears brought in Bennett. It's that they need Bennett to be a reliable underneath receiver immediately. Other than spending a seventh-round pick on wideout Marquess Wilson, Bennett is the only new face in the Bears passing game. It is reasonable to expect improvement

from Jeffrey, and Bennett should be a fine secondary target. But things get thin awfully fast beyond those three, and neither Jeffrey nor Bennett has shown enough to convince anyone they are sure-fire second bananas at this point.

Bushrod has a strong reputation, but you may be surprised to learn just how poorly he showed in our charting project last season. He allowed 21.5 pass pressures on blown blocks, blew seven run blocks, and allowed three sacks. Players that were near his overall total of 31.5 blown blocks tended to be guys like Austin Howard and Marshall Newhouse, not Pro Bowlers who received giant contracts to save an offensive line. We didn't track blown running blocks in previous seasons, but Bushrod allowed two sacks in 2011 and we noted him with 13 additional pass pressures on blown blocks. It's probably fair to expect Bushrod to play closer to his 2011 form, but it's also fair to wonder how that will translate when Brees becomes Cutler.

It's been hard to separate Cutler from his offensive line since he's been in Chicago, because it's a ready-made excuse when a quarterback gets sacked as often as he has. Cutler does have decent feet and good pocket movement to buy time, but he has tended to overuse it and (obviously, as you can tell by the stats above) not trust his secondary receivers unless he was sure they were open. Perhaps stepping up like Brees will make him more comfortable. The only sure thing at this point seems to be that Trestman, a devotee of rational analysis, will be willing to mold his scheme to the player rather than vice versa.

How the passing game works out will answer a lot of questions for Emery going forward. It's not imperative that the Bears show instant results, but there should be marked improvement by the end of this season with Trestman tinkering with the X's and O's. "Very impressed," quarterbacks coach Matt Cavanaugh said when asked about Cutler in OTA's. "He's borderline football brilliant. I think he gets it. I think he knows the game. I think he knows offensive schemes. I think he knows defenses."

It doesn't take much digging to see how Cutler's general manager feels about borderline. If Cutler doesn't take appreciable steps towards actual brilliance this year, Chicago could spend next spring looking for a quarterback who can provide it.

Rivers McCown

2012 Bears Stats by Week

Wk	vs.	W-L	PF	PA	YDF	YDA	TO	Total	Off	Def	ST
1	IND	W	41	21	428	356	4	40%	25%	-15%	10%
2	at GB	L	10	23	168	321	-2	-42%	-70%	-20%	8%
3	STL	W	23	6	274	160	1	58%	-17%	-64%	10%
4	at DAL	W	34	18	360	430	4	40%	9%	-25%	6%
5	at JAC	W	41	3	501	189	2	62%	5%	-63%	-5%
6	BYE										
7	DET	W	13	7	296	340	4	21%	-25%	-40%	6%
8	CAR	W	23	22	210	416	-1	39%	-17%	-43%	13%
9	at TEN	W	51	20	365	339	4	26%	-6%	-23%	9%
10	HOU	L	6	13	249	215	-2	17%	-42%	-56%	4%
11	at SF	L	7	32	143	353	-2	-63%	-57%	2%	-5%
12	MIN	W	28	10	296	258	1	46%	15%	-27%	5%
13	SEA	L	17	23	365	459	1	23%	24%	4%	3%
14	at MIN	L	14	21	438	248	-1	7%	-9%	-11%	6%
15	GB	L	13	21	190	391	1	-14%	-41%	-8%	20%
16	at ARI	W	28	13	297	248	2	49%	16%	-42%	-9%
17	at DET	W	26	24	389	327	4	-10%	-10%	-5%	-5%

Trends and Splits

	Offense	Rank	Defense	Rank
Total DVOA	-10.9%	26	-26.7%	1
Unadjusted VOA	-10.1%	25	-23.6%	1
Weighted Trend	-10.6%	24	-22.7%	1
Variance	7.8%	23	4.8%	14
Average Opponent	-1.4%	9	2.2%	9
Passing	-5.5%	25	-29.0%	1
Rushing	-4.1%	17	-23.1%	1
First Down	-11.6%	25	-16.9%	2
Second Down	-3.9%	20	-42.8%	1
Third Down	-20.2%	26	-21.3%	4
First Half	-16.2%	27	-27.0%	1
Second Half	-5.5%	20	-26.4%	1
Red Zone	-2.7%	18	-24.2%	4
Late and Close	-4.7%	16	-37.1%	1

Five-Year Performance

Year	W-L	Pyth W	Est W	PF	PA	TO	Total	Rk	Off	Rk	Def	Rk	ST	Rk	Off AGL	Rk	Def AGL	Rk	Off Age	Rk	Def Age	Rk	ST Age	Rk
2008	9-7	8.7	9.0	375	350	+5	5.6%	15	-9.0%	22	-9.8%	7	4.7%	5	14.4	10	19.3	15	28.1	8	27.1	21	26.0	28
2009	7-9	6.7	6.1	327	375	-6	-18.1%	25	-19.7%	28	3.0%	21	4.7%	4	8.2	4	42.7	26	26.9	20	27.0	20	26.8	12
2010	11-5	9.5	8.3	334	286	+4	2.4%	14	-15.8%	28	-10.9%	4	7.4%	1	6.8	3	5.5	2	27.1	21	28.3	5	27.6	1
2011	8-8	8.3	7.3	353	341	+2	1.3%	15	-21.4%	30	-14.2%	4	8.5%	1	42.2	24	12.4	6	26.9	18	28.0	4	26.5	9
2012	10-6	10.8	11.0	375	277	+20	20.5%	6	-10.9%	26	-26.7%	1	4.7%	6	17.6	8	13.6	4	27.2	12	27.9	4	26.9	6

2012 Performance Based on Most Common Personnel Groups

CHI Offense					CHI Offense vs. Opponents				CHI Defense				CHI Defense vs. Opponents			
Pers	Freq	Yds	DVOA	Run%	Pers	Freq	Yds	DVOA	Pers	Freq	Yds	DVOA	Pers	Freq	Yds	DVOA
1.1	42%	5.3	-9.2%	19%	4-3-4	34%	5.3	-1.5%	Nickel Even	52%	4.9	-33.6%	1.1	45%	5.0	-32.4%
1.2	34%	5.6	5.6%	53%	Nickel Even	32%	5.5	6.0%	4-3-4	46%	5.1	-21.5%	1.2	25%	4.7	-22.8%
2.1	11%	5.7	-4.2%	56%	3-4-4	21%	5.6	-2.0%	Nickel Odd	1%	4.6	-15.9%	2.1	11%	6.5	-1.7%
1.3	5%	3.5	-32.0%	82%	Dime+	7%	3.8	-104.3%					2.2	7%	4.4	-10.4%
2.2	4%	3.8	-5.4%	79%	Nickel Odd	3%	4.1	-30.0%					61.1	2%	4.9	-13.9%

Strategic Tendencies

Run/Pass		Rk	Formation		Rk	Pass Rush		Rk	Secondary		Rk	Strategy		Rk
Runs, first half	41%	8	Form: Single Back	68%	14	Rush 3	2.1%	31	4 DB	46%	11	Play action	17%	27
Runs, first down	56%	4	Form: Empty Back	6%	14	Rush 4	74.3%	6	5 DB	53%	5	Avg Box (Off)	6.50	5
Runs, second-long	32%	15	Pers: 3+ WR	43%	27	Rush 5	15.2%	27	6+ DB	0%	32	Avg Box (Def)	6.51	6
Runs, power sit.	70%	3	Pers: 4+ WR	0%	29	Rush 6+	8.4%	9	CB by Sides	65%	27	Offensive Pace	31.26	22
Runs, behind 2H	32%	8	Pers: 2+ TE/6+ OL	46%	7	Sacks by LB	7.3%	29	DB Blitz	9%	19	Defensive Pace	30.56	23
Pass, ahead 2H	46%	17	Shotgun/Pistol	34%	30	Sacks by DB	0.0%	28	Hole in Zone	11%	10	Go for it on 4th	1.01	12

With Mike Martz gone, the Bears went from using shotgun 15 percent of the time to using it 34 percent of the time… but in the modern NFL, that still ranked just 30th. You have to figure Marc Trestman is *really* going to change things there. ☙ With a star like Matt Forte in the backfield, perhaps the Bears should consider trying to fool their opponents a bit more often with a play fake. First down stands out in particular; even though the Bears ranked fourth with 56 percent runs on first down, they only play-faked on 22 percent of their passes on first down, 29th in the league. ☙ Chicago's Adjusted Sack Rate on offense got significantly better with each successive down: 12.2 percent (32nd) on first downs, 7.2 percent (20th) on second downs, and 4.7 percent (10th) on third downs. ☙ Once again, the Bears were very straight-ahead on defense, using either a 4-3 or an even nickel defense on all but 16 plays during the 2012 season. ☙ Chicago allowed just 3.8 average yards after catch, best in the league. That included just 6.3 average yards after catch on passes caught behind the line of scrimmage, best in the league by almost a yard. ☙ Chicago was tied with Kansas City for the fewest penalties by opponents, 92. And somehow the Bears only got the opposing pass rush to jump twice in the entire season: two offsides, no encroachments, and no neutral zone infractions.

Passing

Player	DYAR	DVOA	Plays	NtYds	Avg	YAC	C%	TD	Int
J.Cutler	-81	-13.8%	474	2787	5.9	4.5	58.9%	19	14
J.Campbell*	-129	-50.2%	57	216	3.8	2.4	62.7%	2	2

Rushing

Player	DYAR	DVOA	Plays	Yds	Avg	TD	Fum	Suc
M.Forte	109	3.1%	248	1095	4.4	6	2	44%
M.Bush	67	4.5%	114	411	3.6	5	1	50%
K.Bell*	-42	-42.7%	29	76	2.6	0	0	31%
A.Allen	7	-2.3%	27	124	4.6	1	0	48%
J.Cutler	114	96.2%	24	248	10.3	0	0	-

Receiving

Player	DYAR	DVOA	Plays	Ctch	Yds	Y/C	YAC	TD	C%
B.Marshall	267	0.0%	195	119	1506	12.7	2.9	11	61%
E.Bennett	60	0.3%	49	29	375	12.9	6.4	2	59%
A.Jeffery	97	6.7%	48	24	367	15.3	2.7	3	50%
D.Hester	-37	-28.8%	40	23	242	10.5	4.5	1	58%
K.Adams	-12	-30.2%	8	4	40	10.0	1.3	0	50%
D.Aromashodu	39	3.5%	22	11	182	16.5	3.5	0	50%
K.Davis*	-72	-26.0%	44	19	229	12.1	3.7	2	43%
M.Spaeth*	-14	-33.7%	10	6	28	4.7	2.3	1	60%
M.Bennett	85	4.6%	90	55	626	11.4	3.6	5	61%
S.Maneri	-29	-42.5%	12	5	51	10.2	6.0	0	42%
M.Forte	40	-1.1%	60	44	340	7.7	6.7	1	73%
M.Bush	23	24.9%	11	9	83	9.2	9.3	0	82%
E.Rodriguez*	-7	-27.6%	8	4	21	5.3	4.8	0	50%

Offensive Line

Player	Pos	Age	GS	Snaps	Pen	Sk	Pass	Run	Player	Pos	Age	GS	Snaps	Pen	Sk	Pass	Run
Roberto Garza	C	34	16/16	1045	4	1	5	5	Jonathan Scott	RT	30	12/7	333	1	1.5	9.5	1
J'Marcus Webb	LT	25	16/16	1045	9	5	18	2.5	James Brown	LG	25	5/3	215	2	2.5	4.5	3
Gabe Carimi*	G/T	25	16/14	914	10	4.5	16.5	2	Edwin Williams	G	27	6/2	151	0	0	0	1
Lance Louis*	RG	28	11/11	692	2	2	4	2.5	Jermon Bushrod	LT	29	16/16	1104	6	3	21.5	7
Chilo Rachal*	LG	27	9/8	512	8	1	8.5	7.5	Matt Slauson	LG	27	16/16	820	3	1.3	2.8	3
Chris Spencer*	G	31	10/5	345	1	2	6.5	3	Eben Britton	G/T	26	11/5	267	2	2	8	0

Year	Yards	ALY	Rk	Power	Rk	Stuff	Rk	2nd Lev	Rk	Open Field	Rk	Sacks	ASR	Rk	Short	Long	F-Start	Cont.
2010	3.79	3.64	29	44%	32	25%	30	1.06	22	0.80	13	56	10.4%	32	20	26	23	34
2011	4.39	3.92	24	61%	20	24%	30	1.24	11	1.03	8	49	9.8%	31	23	14	27	31
2012	4.08	4.05	16	57%	25	21%	25	1.12	19	0.73	18	44	8.0%	24	9	22	24	30

2012 ALY by direction:	Left End 3.63 (21)	Left Tackle 4.12 (12)	Mid/Guard 3.9 (23)	Right Tackle 3.68 (23)	Right End 5.39 (4)

What can we say about this unit's 2012 performance that hasn't already been said about Afghanistan? It wasn't as consistently bad as it was in 2011, but it still looked bombed out and depleted. The nadir of the season was an 11-blown-block de-pantsing at the hands of San Francisco, which included six sacks, two hurries, and three stuffed runs.

Most of the biggest offenders have been sent packing or given less responsibility, in stark contrast to recent Bears history. Chilo Rachal, who we marked with an astonishing 16 blown blocks in just over 500 snaps, essentially quit on the team following the San Francisco game, then was placed on the reserve list and let go. Former Left Tackle of the Future Gabe Carimi (not to be confused with Former Left Tackle of the Future Chris Williams, who was finally let go in the middle of the 2012 season) has been traded to Tampa Bay for a late-round pick. Backup Plan When We Discover Our Left Tackles of the Future Suck J'Marcus Webb will be moved over to right tackle after the Bears finally spent big on Jermon Bushrod in an attempt to fix the position. Webb's slow feet will play better at right tackle, and while he doesn't use his hands very well, he can be a plus in the running game. Center Roberto Garza is the one stable part of this line. He'll have first-round rookie Kyle Long on one side with free-agent signee Matt Slauson (ex-Jets) getting the first crack at the other guard spot over James Brown. Garza has lost a step and can't be relied on to pull, but has the typically ascribed center traits of veteran experience and know-how, as well as the ability to look pretty fat in Jay Cutler's jersey for commercials. Long is the kind of prospect that normally terrifies us: overaged and inexperienced. He'll be 25 by the end of the season and comes out of Oregon with only four career starts. If he can learn quickly at the NFL level and hold his blocks longer, he does have the athleticism and quick feet to potentially play tackle down the line. The flip side to his inexperience is his bloodline. You may have heard of his family members, Howie and Chris—we think they're lumberjacks or something. Slauson is a technically-sound drive blocker who seals defensive linemen off with angles very effectively. This sounds like a nice asset to have around, but the Jets let him walk because, like Garza, he's also a bit of a plodder.

How comfortable was Cutler behind last year's line? Well, he had a DVOA of -1.7% on plays where he was marked "in the pocket," and a DVOA of 46.8% on plays where he was marked "out of the pocket." That's the biggest DVOA gap for any quarterback with at least 300 pass attempts, and the kind of numbers that will make coaches start thinking about screen passes to quarterbacks out of the Wildcat. The Bears went "max protect" on 16.3 percent of all passes last year, second behind Washington. ("Max protect" is defined as using at least seven blockers with at least two more blockers than pass rushers.)

Defensive Front Seven

Defensive Line	Age	Pos	Snaps	Plays	Overall TmPct	Rk	Stop	Dfts	BTkl	Runs	vs. Run St%	Rk	RuYd	Rk	Pass Rush Sack	Hit	Hur	Tips
Julius Peppers	33	DE	785	39	4.7%	47	32	20	0	21	76%	32	2.4	34	11.5	6	14.5	2
Israel Idonije*	33	DE	711	47	5.7%	32	40	19	2	36	81%	16	2.2	22	7.5	2	19	0
Henry Melton	27	DT	607	43	6.0%	11	33	16	1	36	72%	44	2.3	36	6	3	9.5	0
Stephen Paea	25	DT	595	25	3.2%	58	20	8	0	18	83%	15	1.9	22	2.5	3	9	1
Corey Wootton	26	DE	572	28	3.4%	67	22	11	0	18	67%	61	3.2	64	7	4	14	2
Kyle Moore	27	DE	490	23	3.8%	--	15	4	1	19	63%	--	3.9	--	3	6	13.5	0

Linebackers	Age	Pos	Snaps	Plays	Overall TmPct	Rk	Stop	Dfts	BTkl	Pass Rush Sack	Hit	Hur	Tips	Runs	vs. Run St%	Rk	Yds	Rk	vs. Pass Tgts	Suc%	Rk	AdjYd	Rk	PD
Lance Briggs	33	OLB	1007	114	13.9%	34	66	25	6	1.5	0	7.5	1	60	67%	44	3.9	85	41	56%	21	4.8	13	8
Brian Urlacher*	35	MLB	715	74	12.0%	51	48	20	8	0	0	2.5	3	38	76%	16	1.9	10	30	62%	9	4.9	15	4
Nick Roach*	28	OLB	697	69	8.4%	72	34	12	7	1.5	0	2	0	42	55%	98	4.0	88	28	66%	5	3.7	1	1
Geno Hayes*	26	OLB	138	16	2.1%	--	9	4	3	0	0	0	0	4	75%	--	0.8	--	10	57%	--	6.5	--	2
James Anderson	30	OLB	521	74	11.8%	52	39	7	4	0	0	0.5	0	49	65%	58	2.9	31	24	44%	58	6.8	36	1
D.J. Williams	31	OLB	129	15	4.3%	--	9	3	0	0	0	0	0	7	71%	--	1.9	--	6	98%	--	1.6	--	1

Year	Yards	ALY	Rk	Power	Rk	Stuff	Rk	2nd Level	Rk	Open Field	Rk	Sacks	ASR	Rk	Short	Long
2010	3.95	3.54	2	72%	31	25%	1	1.16	20	0.80	18	34	6.0%	20	9	12
2011	4.13	3.29	1	65%	20	26%	1	1.18	16	1.07	25	33	5.2%	29	7	12
2012	4.11	3.52	3	60%	14	24%	5	1.20	19	0.92	24	41	6.4%	15	6	13

2012 ALY by direction:	Left End 3.56 (10)	Left Tackle 4.55 (27)	Mid/Guard 3.75 (8)	Right Tackle 3.55 (4)	Right End 1.82 (1)

Say what you will about Lovie Smith's last stand, but his defense buoyed the Bears' playoff chances in 2012, and it's in a good position to continue that in 2013. The Bears had long been a team that ran a very standard defense, rushing the front four without many blitzes. But last year, they added a new wrinkle by turning superstar end Julius Peppers into a bit of a joker, moving him around the formations and trying to exploit mismatches. Much like everything else the Bears tried, it was very effective. Henry Melton, brought back on the franchise tag, is a three-technique with a ton of get-off who spends entire games in the backfield. Between Peppers, Melton, and Israel Idonije, the Bears were spoiled with pass-rushing options before we even get to 2012 first-rounder Shea McClellin or the unheralded Corey Wootton. Wootton's numbers may have been a bit inflated by the competition he faced. Two of the blown blocks leading to his pressures were by tight ends, and other than Matt Kalil, his sack and blown-block pressure list is populated by the likes of Jeff Linkenbach, Cameron Bradfield, and other devotees of the Guy Whimper school of blocking. Still, it was quite a leap for an end who hadn't even started a game before the 2012 season, and with McClellin also lurking, you can see why the Bears would think that Idonije was expendable.

Finding a weakness in Chicago's top-ranked run defense is an exercise in nit-picking. The team did its worst work against 21 personnel, but most of the problem there was the uninstinctual play of Nick Roach, probably the only starting 2012 Bears defender who could be declared "just a guy." Stephen Paea has been a durable and stout—if not exactly Wilfork-esque—nose tackle since being selected in the second round of the 2011 draft, and he gets a little more pass pressure than you'd expect a man of his size to create. Lance Briggs combines 32-year-old instincts with 22-year-old movement, and has been the leading cause of your favorite NFC North team's screen being blown up in the backfield since 2003.

The big change here, of course, is the departure of Brian Urlacher. Though Urlacher missed the last few games of 2012 with a hamstring strain and had certainly slowed down, he was far from a husk of himself last year (unlike, say, certain other future Hall of Fame linebackers who may have played in the Super Bowl). Emery refused to pay Urlacher for the past, and instead the Bears will have an interesting camp battle to replace Urlacher and the departed Roach, featuring a pair of touted rookies and a pair of veterans coming off down seasons. D.J. Williams lost most of last year to suspension for failing a drug test, then lost his starting spot to Jack Del Rio's love of Keith Brooking. He'll duel with second-round rookie Jon Bostic (Florida), who is seen by scouts as more of a thumping Mike linebacker than Urlacher, for the job inside. Most draftniks had Khaseem Greene going in the second round after a sensational season at Rutgers; his fall to the fourth round is even more surprising when you realize the Patriots somehow passed on him five times. Greene will try to wrestle the strongside job away from former Panthers linebacker James Anderson, an offseason signing who combined for 53 Defeats in 2010 and 2011 before seeing his playing time drop in 2012.

Defensive Secondary

Secondary	Age	Pos	Snaps	Plays	TmPct	Rk	Stop	Dfts	BTkl	Runs	St%	Rk	Yds	Rk	Tgts	Tgt%	Rk	Dist	Suc%	Rk	APaYd	Rk	PD	Int
Major Wright	25	SS	1028	79	9.6%	42	30	14	7	42	43%	20	5.9	18	27	5.6%	53	12.8	52%	43	6.8	24	7	4
Charles Tillman	32	CB	921	103	12.5%	4	42	17	5	22	41%	46	9.3	72	95	20.2%	22	9.9	49%	58	5.9	7	17	3
Tim Jennings	30	CB	885	81	11.2%	10	40	20	4	12	58%	16	7.4	54	99	24.1%	3	11.9	56%	24	7.2	32	21	9
Chris Conte	24	FS	856	75	9.7%	40	20	10	8	28	25%	62	10.3	66	32	7.3%	29	13.5	50%	51	7.6	39	8	2
Kelvin Hayden	30	CB	460	40	4.9%	82	15	8	4	10	50%	26	5.8	35	43	9.0%	87	10.4	47%	64	8.3	66	4	1
D.J. Moore*	26	CB	363	36	5.4%	--	15	6	3	7	43%	--	7.0	--	31	8.1%	--	10.0	46%	--	8.9	--	5	2
Tom Zbikowski	28	FS	681	41	7.5%	56	15	4	6	16	31%	52	10.8	67	21	6.7%	37	11.8	65%	14	5.4	11	4	1

Year	Pass D Rank	vs. #1 WR	Rk	vs. #2 WR	Rk	vs. Other WR	Rk	vs. TE	Rk	vs. RB	Rk
2010	5	-1.8%	15	16.6%	28	-22.1%	6	-0.9%	11	-17.6%	2
2011	7	-9.1%	6	-18.9%	4	-26.7%	7	0.9%	8	-5.5%	13
2012	1	-31.0%	2	-5.2%	11	-30.2%	3	-24.7%	1	-27.2%	3

Charles Tillman led the NFL in forced fumbles and had one of the more unique seasons in our database last season. He didn't have an incredibly successful year by our charting statistics, but he still allowed an average of just 5.9 Adjusted Yards per Pass despite playing outside most of the time. Opposing quarterbacks attempted only 20 deep passes against Tillman in 2012—a number straight out of a nickelback's stat line—and completed just seven of them. (However, eight of them were marked as under or over-thrown, so it's not like Tillman was cutting off every deep ball with pure speed or anything.) Tim Jennings, his running mate, took a more common approach to his statistically successful season: a high success rate, but more big plays allowed. Neither Kelvin Hayden nor D.J. Moore, who essentially split time at nickelback, flashed in a positive way.

Major Wright and Chris Conte form one of the better young safety combos in the game, though neither of them is especially dynamic in the flow of this defense. Wright, as the more instinctual of the two, tends to be in the box more and draws more man coverage assignments. Conte is a bit iffy as a tackler (eight blown tackles in 56 attempts), but provides adequate deep range and takes smart drops. Both of them improved on their positioning. Tillman told ESPN Chicago in late October that the pair "have done a phenomenal job of not giving up the big plays and letting guys get behind them like they did last year," which wasn't anywhere near as passive-aggressive as it sounds. The main young depth here comes in the form of 2012 third-rounder Brandon Hardin, who missed his rookie year with a neck injury. Craig Steltz assumed most of the snaps at free safety during Conte's one-game absence and also got some work in dime packages—that should be his ceiling.

It's only fear-mongering at this point, but it should be pointed out that the Bears are the only NFL team to have their projected top three cornerbacks all be older than 30. (The Bengals are closest, but Leon Hall is 29 and Dre Kirkpatrick could crack their lineup this year.) With Moore allowed to leave in free agency, and only 2012 sixth-rounder Isaiah Frey on the roster as "young depth," this is a position that could collapse quickly in the near future.

Special Teams

Year	DVOA	Rank	FG/XP	Rank	Net Kick	Rank	Kick Ret	Rank	Net Punt	Rank	Punt Ret	Rank	Hidden	Rank
2010	7.4%	1	0.6	16	-4.0	24	14.6	3	-0.2	20	26.0	1	4.7	6
2011	8.5%	1	7.5	3	0.4	18	4.4	5	19.7	1	10.5	2	-5.1	23
2012	4.7%	6	-4.4	24	13.0	2	0.5	14	18.8	2	-4.4	23	2.0	13

Is this the end of the Devin Hester punt return superstar era? Outside of 2009, when he was made a de facto No. 1 receiver and missed time with a calf injury, the Bears had finished in the top five in punt return value every year since they drafted Hester. That plummeted to 20th in 2012, and at 30, Hester's explosion and tackle-breaking ability may not be coming back. Hester dealt with a quad injury and a concussion in 2012, offering hope that a healthy Hester could rebound, but his similar contemporary Dante Hall hung up his cleats after his age-30 season. Hester contemplated retirement as well during an emotional reaction to Lovie Smith's ouster, but ultimately chose to return for at least one more season.

Even if Hester is merely a shell of himself, this should still be a strong unit. Since poaching Adam Podlesh from the Jaguars before the 2011 season, the Bears have finished first and second in net punt value, and main gunners Eric Weems and Zack Bowman combined for a 94 percent stop rate on 17 special teams tackles. Robbie Gould is reliable enough that we all have to avoid noting that he is "good as," because it's been done. He did have a couple of unexpected misses this year, and Olindo Mare was brought in after Gould blew out a tendon in his left leg near the end of the season, but nothing during OTAs indicated Gould was in danger of losing his job.

Coaching Staff

A cross-section of the traits most often ascribed to new Bears coach Marc Trestman would definitely include the words "detail-oriented" and "hard-working." A cross-section of the traits we would ascribe to Trestman for the purposes of humor include "thick-rimmed glasses" (coaching in the CFL gives him the indie cred to pull off the hipster look), "rouges" (screw your two-point conversion chart!), and "quarterback whisperer" (a subset of a coaching archetype that has spawned terrific head coaches such as Norv Turner and Jason Garrett). In reality, Trestman was likely hired for his intellectual curiosity, as he was dubbed "Coach Cerebral" by former North Carolina State head coach Chuck Amato. Phil Emery needed a head coach who would take his input and analysis to heart, and when that coach did not seem to be on the radar in the States, he went north and did not give a damn about the reaction. Offensive coordinator Bountygate Kromer (his legal name) has already admitted that he won't call the plays, but his experience coordinating a top-flight offense in recent NFL years should be a boon to Trestman.

The Bears stuck with simplicity in hiring former Jaguars defensive coordinator Mel Tucker. Tucker runs one of the most player-oriented vanilla schemes in the league, and that bit him in 2012 when the Jaguars trotted out a bunch of players who did not belong in the NFL. What lengths will Tucker go to in the name of continuing what this defense has done? Word out of minicamp was that the Bears kept the exact same verbiage they used last season.

Long-time special teams coordinator Dave Toub joined pal Andy Reid in Kansas City this year after the Smith crew broke up. He'll be replaced by Joe DeCamillis, who is probably best-known for suffering fractured vertebrae when the Cowboys practice facility collapsed in a 2009 wind storm. If DeCamillis is smart, he won't try to change much.

Cincinnati Bengals

2012 Record: 10-6	Total DVOA: 6.1% (12th)	2013 Mean Projection: 8.9 wins	On the Clock (0-4): 4%
Pythagorean Wins: 9.9 (10th)	Offense: -1.8% (17th)	Postseason Odds: 51.5%	Mediocrity (5-7): 23%
Snap-Weighted Age: 26.1 (28th)	Defense: -3.8% (10th)	Super Bowl Odds: 7.5%	Playoff Contender (8-10): 48%
Average Opponent: -5.7% (29th)	Special Teams: 4.1% (7th)	Proj. Avg. Opponent: 0.6% (17th)	Super Bowl Contender (11+): 26%

2012: The most anonymous two-time playoff squad in recent memory.

2013: A subtle approach to team building leads to subtle improvements, not spectacular ones.

The Bengals took a step forward in 2012. Or perhaps the little gather-step you have to take before making a great leap. Or maybe they plateaued. Or even took a teensy-weensy step backward. It's all a matter of interpretation.

Even the stats are not 100 percent certain. The Bengals inched forward in DVOA from 0.1% to 6.1%, but that modest jump is within system tolerances. An early iteration of our 2013 projections had them holding precisely at 6.1% for 2013, which is spooky. Our projection also has them veering back toward .500 slightly, in acknowledgment of a tough division and the fact that they outplayed their Pythagorean projection slightly last year. So there is something in the numbers for nearly every argument.

What's certain is that the Bengals made the playoffs in back-to-back seasons for the first time since 1981-82. They made the playoffs for the third time in four years, which has never happened in team history. Plateau, gather-step, or what-have-you, the Bengals have distanced themselves from the Bungles and shed their reputation as a shoestring operation with a knack for botching the draft and larding the roster with unrepentant troublemakers. The front office may still be teeming with members of the Brown-Blackburn clan, but executive vice president Katie Blackburn is a better administrator than father Mike Brown, Duke Tobin has run several productive drafts, and infrastructure and scouting budgets are finally close to league standards. The Bengals finally have the "organization" part of their organization down pat.

Yet they lost to the Texans in the playoffs for the second time in two years. They passed the too-old-to-rock-'n'-roll Steelers in the standings, and finally won a pair of late-season games against the Steelers and Ravens (the latter after playoffs were slotted and starters began resting), but it was easy to perceive them as the third-best team in their division. They finished 12th in DVOA, which screams "final team to make the playoffs." (The Vikings and Colts were below them, but you get the idea.) The Bengals were in a much better rut than they occupied for most of franchise history, but as the Texans shut them down in a 19-13 playoff victory, it still looked like a rut.

The 2012 season felt like an opportunity squandered. The Steelers and Ravens were vulnerable, lumbering old heavyweights. The Bengals, sleek and young, raced out to a 3-1 start, then suddenly got the vapors. They played poorly in losses to the Dolphins and Browns and not well enough in losses to the Steelers and Broncos. They rebounded, but the Bengals proved that they were a notch below where they needed to be. At times—like in a frustrating, mistake-and-penalty filled loss to the Cowboys, or in the playoff loss—it looked like they knew it, too.

At the same time, the Bengals consolidated many gains. A young defensive line came of age. Andy Dalton and A.J. Green did not advance considerably, but they spent another year growing up together. The rookie class brought a pair of promising-if-oft-injured receivers, a starting guard in Kevin Zeitler, and linebacker Vontae Burfict, the kind of troubled soul who would have become a headache in years past but became a playmaker in a tighter organization. And that's before you get to the defensive players who barely saw action. More on them later.

And so it goes: the Bengals took one step up and one step back, their net progress lost in the rounded decimals. Tellingly, the team did not panic after a second straight Wild Card loss. There were no major overhauls or "one player away histrionics." Remember that the Bengals became the T. Ocho show after a 10-6 season just four years ago. This time, they stayed the course and drafted judiciously. Having conquered front office professionalism, the Bengals are taking a whack at careful player development.

The Bengals biggest offensive problem last season was their lack of quality weapons to complement A.J. Green. Jermaine Graham and BenJarvus Green-Ellis are capable players, but defensive coordinators do not stay up late game-planning for them. The second receiving spot was a revolving door of injured youngsters. The slot was manned by Andrew Hawkins, an occasionally-dangerous former walk-on. The bench was full of replacement value.

Opponents had multiple ways to stop the Bengals. They could double Green all game and dare Green-Ellis and the others to beat them, or they could give Green his due and clamp down on everything else. Both strategies had their merits. The Browns allowed Green to catch seven passes for 135 yards and two touchdowns, but also intercepted two Dalton passes to Green, plus a third in the flat to Brandon Tate, in a 34-24 win. The Steelers held Green to one catch for eight yards on six targets, and Dalton threw for just 105 yards in a 24-17 loss. The Texans did a little of both in the playoffs. Dal-

2013 Bengals Schedule

Week	Opp.	Week	Opp.	Week	Opp.
1	at CHI	7	at DET	13	at SD
2	PIT (Mon.)	8	NY	14	IND
3	GB	9	at MIA (Thu.)	15	at PIT
4	at CLE	10	at BAL	16	MIN
5	NE	11	CLE	17	BAL
6	at BUF	12	BYE		

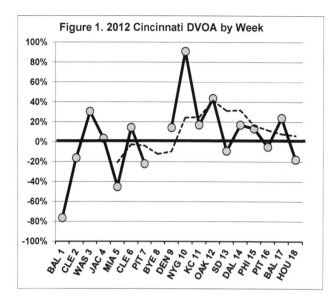

Figure 1. 2012 Cincinnati DVOA by Week

ton compounded the problem by being erratic on deep passes for long stretches: he was 0-for-14 on passes over 25 yards in air length in the final four games. Green made life harder by concentration-dropping passes at critical times: an apparent touchdown against the Cowboys, for example. An offense built exclusively around these two talents is not going to crack the 10-6 mark.

Rookie tight end Tyler Eifert's arrival changes the complexion of the Bengals offense. He joins Gresham to give the Bengals a Patriots-style tight end tandem. Both can stretch the seam or line up as wide receivers; Eifert has leaping capability that makes him look like the tight end version of Green at times. Second-round pick Giovanni Bernard, an all-purpose back from North Carolina, adds another dimension that the Bengals lacked last season: a true backfield receiving threat. Actually, it feels like the Bengals have lacked that direction since James Brooks left. Only twice since 2002 has a Bengals running back caught at least 40 passes in a season. Last year, all the Bengals backs combined for just 344 receiving yards on 43 catches. Bernard, meanwhile, caught 47 passes for 490 yards in just ten games for the Tar Heels.

Eifert and Bernard make the Bengals much more difficult to scheme against. Once Green lifts the safety lid off the coverage, two matchup-headache tight ends will be working the middle, and Bernard has the hands and moves to exploit all the open space underneath. The Bengals hope patience provides the final puzzle piece, a true No. 2 receiver. Mohamed Sanu and Marvin Jones both flashed potential between injuries and mistakes as rookies; the shifty Hawkins proved effective when not getting force-fed screen passes. The Bengals added Arkansas burner Cobi Hamilton late in the draft, and someone is going to emerge as a credible complement for Green, a job made far easier by the presence of two all-purpose tight ends.

On defense, the Bengals have displayed a similar mix of awareness of their own weaknesses and patience with players in their system. The strength of last year's defense was a young, multi-dimensional pass rush that finished second in the NFL in Adjusted Sack Rate. The weaknesses were more subtle: a terrible short yardage defense (dead last in Power Success, allowing first downs or touchdowns on 82 percent of short-yardage runs), and an aging secondary that got more mileage from Terence Newman and Pacman Jones than anyone could have expected.

The Bengals are counting on several "redshirts" from last year's draft class to improve those weaknesses. Brandon Thompson and Devon Still, second- and third-round picks who rarely played last year, are still in the team's plans at defensive tackle. Both left college as well-regarded talents, and neither got the full "doghouse" treatment: the Bengals finally reached the point in 2012 when they did not have to rush unprepared players onto the field, so they didn't. Cornerback Dre Kirkpatrick, last year's first-round pick, battled knee injuries all season and appeared in just five games. Kirkpatrick is expected back and will get a chance to win a starting job opposite Leon Hall. Newman and Jones remain on the roster as insurance.

With redshirts expected to play larger roles, the Bengals worked this offseason to maximize their defensive strengths instead of covering weaknesses. James Harrison is no longer a Pro Bowler, but he adds menace as a pass rusher for a team that already boasts Michael Johnson, Geno Atkins, Carlos Dunlap, and others. Margus Hunt, one of the many technically raw, athletically stellar International pass rushers in this year's class, adds yet another likely sack producer. Neither Harrison nor Hunt has to be a 60-snap contributor: Marvin Lewis and Mike Zimmer have the ingredients for all sorts of pass rush packages. And the Bengals secondary does not have to be outstanding if quarterbacks only have three-fourths of a second to get rid of the football.

The offensive and defensive changes, and the way the organization went about them, give the Bengals something they have needed for a long time: an identity. That veers awful close to sportswriter babble, but there is something to it. When a team defines its strengths, it helps set expectations and focus coaching and scouting. The Ravens and Steelers spent a decade honing (and slowly adjusting) their identities, and that contributed to their success. Now the Bengals have an identity, and not as the Bungles or hapless problem children or T. Ocho's rumpus room. On offense, they are Green-as-Randy Moss with a two-headed tight end monster behind him. On defense, they are sack-happy marauders. Off the field, they are a team that builds through the draft and promotes from within. The third element of the identity is as important as the first two.

Having an identity does not automatically make the Bengals a great team. The projection system is skeptical of sudden, major improvements coming from a group of sophomore defenders who barely made the field last year. It is also not too sanguine about a rookie tight end and change-up back suddenly moving the needle on offense. Nothing on Dalton's resume suggests a sudden quantum leap forward: he can run the system, but he does not elevate it. The Bengals have taken the subtle approach to roster developments, and subtlety often produces subtle results. Eifert's contribution is likely to be significant, but contributions by Kirkpatrick, Still, Thompson, Sanu, Jones, and even Bernard are unlikely to leap off the spreadsheet. They could be pebbles that contribute to an avalanche. They could just as well be pebbles that simply raise the water level a few imperceptible inches.

The good news is that while improvement may be hard to see, steep decline is even harder to imagine. The Bengals roster is now too talented and professional for a sudden 4-12 circus flop. The team is deep in serviceable players at every position, and the front office is now nimble enough to keep the shelves stocked. The Bengals are not yet great, but they are demonstrating a sustained ability to not be terrible, which is a new development for the franchise.

Meanwhile, the Ravens and Steelers are rebuilding on the fly. This season is another great opportunity to seize a division in transition, then take a crack at the aging conference superpowers. Next season may find the Bengals in the same position. Stay within sight of the summit long enough, and the mountain might wear down enough to meet you halfway.

Mike Tanier

2012 Bengals Stats by Week

Wk	vs.	W-L	PF	PA	YDF	YDA	TO	Total	Off	Def	ST
1	at BAL	L	13	44	322	430	-2	-77%	-17%	59%	-1%
2	CLE	W	34	27	375	439	0	-16%	18%	52%	18%
3	at WAS	W	38	31	478	381	-1	31%	40%	8%	-2%
4	at JAC	W	27	10	382	212	0	3%	-14%	-8%	10%
5	MIA	L	13	17	298	279	-1	-45%	-38%	4%	-3%
6	at CLE	L	24	34	438	328	-3	14%	7%	-7%	0%
7	PIT	L	17	24	185	431	1	-22%	-9%	19%	6%
8	BYE										
9	DEN	L	23	31	366	359	1	14%	29%	0%	-15%
10	NYG	W	31	13	275	318	3	91%	36%	-45%	9%
11	at KC	W	28	6	409	284	1	17%	9%	-3%	5%
12	OAK	W	34	10	415	218	2	44%	19%	-26%	-1%
13	at SD	W	20	13	339	297	-1	-9%	-14%	-2%	3%
14	DAL	L	19	20	336	288	0	17%	-7%	-13%	10%
15	at PHI	W	34	13	249	219	3	13%	-26%	-37%	3%
16	at PIT	W	13	10	267	280	0	-5%	-44%	-34%	5%
17	BAL	W	23	17	189	352	1	24%	-11%	-17%	18%
18	at HOU	L	13	19	198	420	0	-18%	-21%	3%	6%

Trends and Splits

	Offense	Rank	Defense	Rank
Total DVOA	-1.8%	17	-3.8%	10
Unadjusted VOA	2.2%	16	-7.5%	8
Weighted Trend	-2.9%	17	-16.3%	3
Variance	6.4%	18	8.2%	29
Average Opponent	3.2%	30	-3.6%	27
Passing	5.0%	19	-5.6%	9
Rushing	-1.4%	14	-1.4%	23
First Down	-3.5%	19	-3.7%	12
Second Down	4.9%	14	-1.0%	16
Third Down	-9.1%	21	-8.3%	8
First Half	7.4%	10	-9.8%	7
Second Half	-12.5%	24	2.1%	18
Red Zone	7.2%	10	8.4%	24
Late and Close	-13.3%	24	-4.0%	19

Five-Year Performance

Year	W-L	Pyth W	Est W	PF	PA	TO	Total	Rk	Off	Rk	Def	Rk	ST	Rk	Off AGL	Rk	Def AGL	Rk	Off Age	Rk	Def Age	Rk	ST Age	Rk
2008	4-11-1	3.3	4.6	204	364	-2	-20.7%	27	-18.3%	28	-0.3%	15	-2.8%	26	59.8	31	48.3	30	27.9	11	25.6	31	26.2	25
2009	10-6	8.4	8.0	305	291	0	-0.1%	19	-0.9%	19	-2.0%	13	-1.3%	21	34.1	24	36.5	24	28.0	6	25.9	29	25.9	26
2010	4-12	6.0	6.6	322	395	-8	-3.4%	19	1.7%	17	1.5%	17	-3.5%	28	14.9	7	47.5	30	28.9	1	26.4	22	26.0	21
2011	9-7	8.6	8.5	344	323	0	0.10%	17	-1.4%	17	0.80%	17	2.3%	7	25.2	15	26.5	17	26.5	24	27.4	13	26.4	13
2012	10-6	9.9	8.7	391	320	+4	6.1%	12	-1.8%	17	-3.8%	10	4.1%	7	37.0	21	22.2	13	25.1	32	27.3	11	26.0	17

2012 Performance Based on Most Common Personnel Groups

CIN Offense					CIN Offense vs. Opponents				CIN Defense					CIN Defense vs. Opponents			
Pers	Freq	Yds	DVOA	Run%	Pers	Freq	Yds	DVOA	Pers	Freq	Yds	DVOA		Pers	Freq	Yds	DVOA
11	52%	5.6	4.6%	26%	Nickel Even	31%	6.2	25.0%	Nickel Even	51%	5.5	-2.8%		11	52%	5.9	2.7%
12	20%	4.4	-2.9%	54%	4-3-4	23%	5.3	9.7%	4-3-4	44%	4.6	-5.6%		12	19%	4.6	-13.6%
21	14%	5.8	-3.4%	63%	3-4-4	21%	4.9	-14.5%	Nickel Odd	2%	6.0	-35.4%		21	17%	4.2	-15.9%
01	6%	6.1	7.2%	8%	Nickel Odd	15%	5.1	-17.1%	Dime+	1%	3.9	-19.5%		22	3%	3.1	-14.8%
22	2%	4.8	-35.5%	74%	Dime+	8%	4.9	-37.8%	Goal Line	1%	1.1	31.4%		10	3%	5.5	17.2%

Strategic Tendencies

Run/Pass		Rk	Formation		Rk	Pass Rush		Rk	Secondary		Rk	Strategy		Rk
Runs, first half	39%	14	Form: Single Back	68%	16	Rush 3	2.3%	30	4 DB	44%	19	Play action	17%	25
Runs, first down	52%	9	Form: Empty Back	10%	5	Rush 4	72.8%	9	5 DB	54%	4	Avg Box (Off)	6.35	19
Runs, second-long	20%	32	Pers: 3+ WR	59%	8	Rush 5	18.6%	21	6+ DB	1%	29	Avg Box (Def)	6.34	20
Runs, power sit.	68%	5	Pers: 4+ WR	7%	7	Rush 6+	6.3%	19	CB by Sides	94%	5	Offensive Pace	28.82	7
Runs, behind 2H	31%	12	Pers: 2+ TE/6+ OL	27%	23	Sacks by LB	11.8%	26	DB Blitz	13%	13	Defensive Pace	29.76	12
Pass, ahead 2H	54%	3	Shotgun/Pistol	46%	17	Sacks by DB	3.9%	19	Hole in Zone	6%	26	Go for it on 4th	1.31	4

As in 2011, the Bengals used a lot of six-lineman sets (4.5 percent of plays, seventh in the NFL) and weren't very good with them (-10.6% DVOA and just 2.2 yards per play). ⬤ The Bengals defense killed both running back screens (3.4 yards per play, -40.1% DVOA) and draws (3.5 yards per carry, -41.2% DVOA). However, they were susceptible to shotgun runs that we didn't mark as draws, allowing 5.7 yards per carry and 8.8% DVOA (25th in the NFL). ⬤ Bengals opponents only threw 18 percent of passes to their No. 1 receivers, the lowest rate in the league. ⬤ The Bengals didn't blitz much compared to most teams—25 percent of passes, compared to an NFL average of 30 percent—but they were very successful when they did blitz: 6.2 yards per pass with three or four pass rushers, but 5.8 yards per pass with five pass rushers and 4.4 yards per pass with six or more.

Passing

Player	DYAR	DVOA	Plays	NtYds	Avg	YAC	C%	TD	Int
A.Dalton	194	-5.9%	571	3422	6.0	5.0	62.8%	27	15
B.Gradkowski*	-3	-14.9%	12	60	5.0	1.0	45.5%	0	0

Rushing

Player	DYAR	DVOA	Plays	Yds	Avg	TD	Fum	Suc
B.Green-Ellis	6	-8.1%	278	1094	3.9	6	3	48%
C.Peerman	56	26.6%	36	258	7.2	1	0	53%
B.Leonard*	-4	-11.1%	33	106	3.2	0	0	42%
A.Dalton	53	18.9%	29	137	4.7	4	0	-
B.Scott	-3	-15.6%	8	35	4.4	0	0	38%
A.Hawkins	23	56.7%	6	30	5.0	0	0	-
M.Sanu	4	-27.0%	5	15	3.0	0	0	-

Receiving

Player	DYAR	DVOA	Plays	Ctch	Yds	Y/C	YAC	TD	C%
A.J.Green	205	4.1%	164	97	1350	13.9	3.9	11	59%
A.Hawkins	13	-9.2%	80	51	533	10.5	6.7	4	64%
A.Binns*	-7	-20.8%	29	18	211	11.7	4.8	1	62%
M.Jones	36	-2.1%	32	18	201	11.2	1.9	1	56%
M.Sanu	42	13.8%	25	16	154	9.6	4.4	4	64%
B.Tate	18	-6.2%	25	13	211	16.2	4.9	1	52%
R.Whalen	-18	-15.1%	12	7	53	7.6	2.0	0	58%
J.Gresham	24	3.2%	94	64	737	11.5	6.5	5	68%
O.Charles	24	28.1%	10	8	101	12.6	6.0	0	80%
A.Smith	-76	-72.6%	18	13	47	3.6	2.8	0	72%
B.Green-Ellis	-39	-36.9%	29	22	104	4.7	4.1	0	76%
B.Leonard*	-23	-41.3%	15	11	67	6.1	7.1	0	73%
C.Peerman	50	81.1%	9	9	85	9.4	8.2	0	100%

Offensive Line

Player	Pos	Age	GS	Snaps	Pen	Sk	Pass	Run	Player	Pos	Age	GS	Snaps	Pen	Sk	Pass	Run
Clint Boling	LG	24	16/16	1053	1	5.5	12	1.5	Jeff Faine	C	32	8/7	455	3	0	6.3	2
Kevin Zeitler	RG	23	16/16	1048	2	4.5	10.8	2	Trevor Robinson	C/G	23	13/7	451	1	1	4.5	2.5
Andre Smith	RT	26	16/16	1045	5	4	13.3	1	Kyle Cook	C	30	4/2	155	1	0	0	1
Andrew Whitworth	LT	32	16/16	992	9	3	12	3	Dennis Roland	OT	30	16/2	103	3	0	2	2

Year	Yards	ALY	Rk	Power	Rk	Stuff	Rk	2nd Lev	Rk	Open Field	Rk	Sacks	ASR	Rk	Short	Long	F-Start	Cont.
2010	3.76	4.04	18	51%	28	23%	27	1.15	15	0.38	31	28	5.1%	7	14	6	21	29
2011	3.81	3.99	20	56%	25	22%	27	1.12	23	0.51	28	25	4.5%	4	10	11	25	32
2012	4.17	4.15	11	69%	5	17%	9	0.91	31	0.90	10	46	8.3%	28	9	26	16	35

2012 ALY by direction:	Left End 2.5 (31)	Left Tackle 3.58 (24)	Mid/Guard 4.59 (4)	Right Tackle 4.12 (12)	Right End 3.86 (19)

Andre Smith finally fulfilled his potential, with a breakthrough year where game charters marked him with a blown block only once every 73.1 snaps (best among right tackles). But can the Bengals keep Smith's head on straight when it isn't a contract year? He signed a new three-year, $18-million contract over draft weekend, then celebrated by missing several weeks of OTAs. The Smith contract was a source of high drama in the Bengals front office, with Katie Blackburn hurriedly finalizing the negotiations after the first round of the draft so the team could erase right tackle from its list of needs. Smith missed the voluntary workouts for the usual "personal reasons," and Marvin Lewis did not sound too irritated about it, but Smith has a long history of going off the reservation and coming back looking like a food truck.

Left tackle Andrew Whitworth shed 20 pounds before the 2012 season but needed time to adjust to the new weight, committing four holds in the first half of the season and surrendering sacks against the Browns and Redskins. He settled down and blocked well in the second half of the season, and although he had a knee scoped in February, he is expected to be a full participant in camp. Right guard Kevin Zeitler got pushed around in his first few games as a rookie but improved quickly. He is effective both as a drive blocker and on the move. Travelle Wharton tore his ACL in the first preseason game last season and was replaced by Clint Boling; the pair will battle for the starting job at left guard. Wharton is more powerful. Boling is a "play within himself" type (i.e., not that talented). Veteran Kyle Cook, who missed most of last season with foot and ankle injuries, will battle second-year man Trevor Robinson for the center position.

Defensive Front Seven

Defensive Line	Age	Pos	Snaps	Plays	TmPct	Overall Rk	Stop	Dfts	BTkl	Runs	St%	vs. Run Rk	RuYd	Rk	Sack	Pass Rush Hit	Hur	Tips
Michael Johnson	26	DE	852	53	6.3%	22	40	20	1	30	73%	45	2.5	42	12.5	8	10	2
Geno Atkins	25	DT	785	55	6.6%	7	49	30	1	35	86%	5	1.5	14	13	8	30	2
Domata Peko	29	DT	649	56	6.7%	5	42	9	1	47	72%	43	2.2	29	2	3	6	2
Robert Geathers	30	DE	646	30	3.6%	62	24	11	2	23	74%	42	1.7	12	3	3	10.5	0
Carlos Dunlap	24	DE	586	42	5.7%	30	35	21	3	25	80%	18	1.6	10	5.5	7	13	3
Wallace Gilberry	29	DE	308	24	3.3%	68	17	8	0	14	71%	49	2.7	50	6.5	5	7	0
Pat Sims*	28	DT	181	18	4.3%	--	10	3	1	16	56%	--	2.3	--	0	0	1	0

Linebackers	Age	Pos	Snaps	Plays	TmPct	Overall Rk	Stop	Dfts	BTkl	Sack	Hit	Pass Rush Hur	Tips	Runs	St%	vs. Run Rk	Yds	Rk	Tgts	Suc%	vs. Pass Rk	AdjYd	Rk	PD
Rey Maualuga	26	MLB	1022	126	15.1%	23	62	10	6	1	3	4	0	65	57%	95	4.6	104	59	53%	30	7.0	47	5
Vontaze Burfict	23	OLB	885	129	15.4%	20	58	18	8	1	2	2.5	1	72	54%	101	3.5	58	40	41%	64	6.9	45	1
Manny Lawson*	29	OLB	353	38	4.5%	108	16	5	3	2	0	2	0	19	47%	106	4.6	105	17	42%	63	8.7	70	0
James Harrison	35	OLB	811	69	11.3%	58	53	13	4	6	7	12	0	51	82%	9	2.2	17	13	36%	--	7.6	--	0

Year	Yards	ALY	Rk	Power	Rk	Stuff	Rk	2nd Level	Rk	Open Field	Rk	Sacks	ASR	Rk	Short	Long
2010	4.53	4.19	19	73%	32	18%	22	1.17	21	1.05	30	27	5.3%	30	6	13
2011	4.09	3.78	5	66%	23	20%	17	1.03	4	0.88	21	45	7.3%	10	15	20
2012	4.05	4.04	16	82%	32	18%	21	1.19	17	0.48	6	51	8.7%	2	13	22
2012 ALY by direction:		Left End 3.87 (13)			Left Tackle 3.3 (5)			Mid/Guard 4.23 (20)			Right Tackle 4.35 (27)			Right End 3.56 (10)		

The Bengals led the NFL in with 137 Pass Defeats last year, one more than the Texans, and their defensive line was a major reason. One of the best front fours in the NFL is now also arguably the deepest. Starters Geno Atkins, Domata Peko, Michael Johnson, and Robert Geathers are all back, as is designated pass rusher Carlos Dunlap. Devon Still and Brandon Thompson, rock-solid prospects on the interior who saw minimal playing time, are also back, and both are still a part of the team's long-term plans. To this group we can also add second-round pick Margus Hunt (SMU), part of the new wave of European pass rushers. As you might expect from an Estonian shot-putter who learned about football by playing Madden, Hunt is a little on the raw side. Mike Zimmer said during minicamp that Hunt has the football IQ of a 12-year-old, and Zimmer has dealt with Adam Jones for the last three years. Hunt is also a little on the freakishly strong side, and if he can learn to use his height to an advantage (as opposed to having a high center of gravity become a disadvantage), he can be the kind of shot-blocking pass rusher Watt-envying teams crave. Hunt is in a great learning environment: Geathers is a great mentor and technician, Johnson knows what it is like to be a little too tall for his position, and Hunt will face limited snaps and zero double teams.

The Bengals whiffed on many Vontaze Burfict-types over the last decade, so they were due to hit a hanging curve ball—a curve ball with terrible workout numbers, failed drug tests, and poisonous buzz—out of the ballpark. Burfict moved from middle linebacker to the weak side to cover an injury to Thomas Howard, and immediately made a case for himself as a high-motor fly-around defender. Tackle totals aside, he still has much to learn. Rey Maualuga is back at middle linebacker after a poor 2012 season, but Burfict may get the opportunity to challenge him. Fast, hungry Emmanuel Lamur, like Burfict an undrafted 2012 rookie, would then take Burfict's place on the weak side.

James Harrison and Aaron Maybin replace Manny Lawson on the strong side, where the Bengals prefer to use more of a 3-4-type outside linebacker. Harrison you know about: he still has enough in the tank to be menacing in small doses. Maybin appeared to get his career in order with six sacks for the Jets in 2011 but was ineffective before getting waived last year. Behind this front four, Cloris Leachman would be able to get a handful of cleanup sacks, so Harrison or Maybin could stage a mini-comeback.

Defensive Secondary

Secondary	Age	Pos	Snaps	Plays	Overall TmPct	Rk	Stop	Dfts	BTkl	Runs	vs. Run St%	Rk	Yds	Rk	Tgts	Tgt%	Rk	Dist	vs. Pass Suc%	Rk	APaYd	Rk	PD	Int
Reggie Nelson	30	FS	889	91	12.4%	17	39	18	4	39	46%	12	6.3	24	26	6.8%	35	15.3	63%	16	7.8	45	9	3
Leon Hall	29	CB	882	49	6.7%	69	27	14	3	11	55%	22	5.8	36	56	14.9%	62	13.2	57%	19	7.6	44	11	2
Terence Newman	35	CB	864	84	10.7%	14	33	14	2	19	42%	41	5.6	28	78	19.3%	31	11.5	53%	34	6.5	18	11	2
Chris Crocker*	33	SS	598	46	6.8%	62	10	6	5	19	16%	72	7.6	46	20	5.6%	54	11.5	59%	24	9.4	67	5	3
Adam Jones	30	CB	595	46	5.5%	79	23	14	5	5	40%	47	7.2	50	58	13.5%	75	10.8	58%	14	6.5	19	10	0
Nate Clements*	34	SS	585	56	7.1%	58	17	10	4	20	40%	29	7.6	45	32	7.8%	22	12.5	42%	67	7.3	37	4	1
Taylor Mays	25	FS	244	17	2.0%	--	5	1	0	10	30%	--	8.6	--	5	1.2%	--	16.6	41%	--	10.5	--	0	0
Jeromy Miles	26	SS	121	15	1.8%	--	4	0	2	8	25%	--	7.6	--	3	0.7%	--	11.7	30%	--	13.7	--	0	0

Year	Pass D Rank	vs. #1 WR	Rk	vs. #2 WR	Rk	vs. Other WR	Rk	vs. TE	Rk	vs. RB	Rk
2010	14	0.5%	17	-1.7%	14	-5.6%	14	2.8%	14	-25.0%	1
2011	18	14.9%	21	31.9%	28	-5.6%	15	11.4%	19	-11.8%	10
2012	9	-12.3%	9	7.3%	22	9.5%	24	-3.9%	12	-8.4%	10

The Bengals got an amazing rebound season from 34-year-old Terence Newman and a very good one from Adam "no longer Pac-man" Jones. Newman's efforts were even more remarkable because he was matched up against top receivers almost as often as Cincinnati's No. 1 cornerback, Leon Hall; Marv Lewis and Mike Zimmer like to align their cornerbacks by the side of the field, not the coverage assignment. (The Bengals were fifth in "CB by sides.") Much of Newman's renaissance can be chalked up to a savvy veteran making the most of a nasty pass rush: Bengals cornerbacks only had to sustain coverage for so long last year.

The pass rush is still there, but Newman is now 35, so the Bengals are hoping Dre Kirkpatrick rebounds from an injury-plagued rookie year to supplant Newman. Unfortunately, Kirkpatrick's knee is still an issue. "I don't want to rate [the health of my knee]," Kirkpatrick told the *Dayton Daily News* in late May "I know when the time is right, I'll be ready." Kirkpatrick was a central-casting, outstanding Alabama defensive prospect before the injuries. Jones, still blessedly agile and no longer quite as much of a flighty goof-off, fits well in slot coverage.

Taylor Mays is expected to replace Nate Clements and Chris Crocker at strong safety. He earned the starting job in preseason last year, then lost it when Lewis and Zimmer opted for the more reliable Crocker. Crocker later suffered a quad injury, and Clements slid over from cornerback to take the job. Mays is a big-hitting speedster who is still making rookie mistakes four years into his career. Don't be surprised if Mays loses the starting job again, this time to third-round pick Shaun Williams, a hard working in-the-box safety from Cincinnati's AAA affiliate in Georgia. Crocker has a habit of lingering on the waiver wire until the Bengals need him again, so he may return to prevent a crisis. Reggie Nelson is reliable and effective at free safety.

Special Teams

Year	DVOA	Rank	FG/XP	Rank	Net Kick	Rank	Kick Ret	Rank	Net Punt	Rank	Punt Ret	Rank	Hidden	Rank
2010	-3.5%	28	-7.4	31	-11.2	29	-3.5	19	8.7	6	-4.3	24	-3.8	18
2011	2.3%	7	3.3	11	10.0	2	-7.5	31	0.7	15	4.8	5	4.8	10
2012	4.1%	7	5.9	8	-1.8	22	-6.3	26	18.0	3	4.9	7	4.2	5

The Bengals get a subtle-but-significant boost from the punting game. Kevin Huber has developed into one of the league's best punters: very consistent, with excellent hang time. Dan Skuta (10 special teams stops and 19 tackles) and Jeremy Miles (eight stops and 13 tackles) led reliable coverage units, but Skuta signed with San Francisco in free agency. Adam Jones remains daring and elusive as a punt returner, if a little reckless. Brandon Tate replaces him when the Bengals want to be conservative.

The kicking game is not as strong. Tate had a great year returning kicks for the Patriots back in 2010 but has been lousy in Cincinnati, worth a combined -9.9 estimated points of field position over the last two seasons. Mike Nugent is strictly a short-game kicker on field goals. His touchback percentage was low (32.3 percent, ranked 31st in the NFL), and he kicks his share of line drives. Josh Brown replaced the injured Nugent late in the season, but Brown was not retained, and Nugent signed a two-year contract in March.

Coaching Staff

Coordinators Jay Gruden and Mike Zimmer are often mentioned as potential head coaching candidates. Zimmer, in particular, has spent a lot of time on the interview trail in the past two years. Both could use a signature season to vault from "guy we talk to when Chip Kelly turns off his cellphone" to short-listers. Zimmer must emerge from Marvin Lewis' shadow: building on last year's 50-sack defensive performance can achieve that. Gruden must emerge from his brother's shadow: turning the new two-tight end offense into something that out-Patriots the Patriots can achieve that. Getting the Bengals past the one-and-done playoff stage will help both coordinators.

Marvin Lewis is the longest-tenured head coach in Bengals history and the second-longest tenured active coach, behind Bill

Belichick. The inmates no longer run the asylum, as they did three years ago, and Lewis deserves much of the credit for rebuilding the team culture. (Adding buffer levels between the players and Mike Brown, who was brutal as a hands-on administrator, also helped). Lewis is still just under .500 for his career and 0-4 in playoff games. At some point, even the most process-oriented analysts have to stop focusing on discipline and development and demand some real results.

Meanwhile, for your SAT prep courses, remember that *Hue Jackson : Lewis :: Josh McDaniels : Belichick.* Lewis knows how to keep Jackson from turning from Dr. Strangelove into Colonel Guano, as he did during his brief, strange dictatorship in Oakland. Jackson is now Cincinnati's running backs coach, replacing Jim Anderson, who retired after last season and earned a Lifetime Achievement Award from the Fritz Pollard Alliance, a coaching-leadership diversity group. While Jackson has big shoes to fill, the Bengals needed some fresh ideas in the backfield after getting little from their running backs last year, particularly in the passing game.

Cleveland Browns

2012 Record: 5-11	Total DVOA: -13.5% (24th)	2013 Mean Projection: 6.7 wins	On the Clock (0-4): 20%
Pythagorean Wins: 6.1 (24th)	Offense: -15.2% (27th)	Postseason Odds: 17.6%	Mediocrity (5-7): 43%
Snap-Weighted Age: 25.8 (31st)	Defense: 4.5% (22th)	Super Bowl Odds: 0.9%	Playoff Contender (8-10): 31%
Average Opponent: -2.5% (20th)	Special Teams: 6.1% (2nd)	Proj. Avg. Opponent: 1.0% (15th)	Super Bowl Contender (11+): 6%

2012: What a man gotta do to make a half million without the FBI catchin' feelings?

2013: What a man gotta do is find a new quarterback. Yes, another one.

If an NFL team were the subject of a classical Greek tragedy, the seeds of the team's downfall would be present from the moment of a new king's (owner's) coronation. The very traits that won the crown are the ones that doom the kingdom, and triumph only presages tragedy.

If an NFL team were run by the typical talk-radio caller, it would change both the general manager and the head coach every two years or so. The roster would be a jumble of last year's failed projects and next year's fleeting hopes. There would always be two quarterbacks: the young prospect who cannot quite put it together, and the stubbly veteran who proves irresistible after some fluky relief appearances. The team would forever pursue whims, never building anything with the potential to last.

If Euripides collaborated with Sid the Squid from Shaker Heights to create a football team, that team would be the Cleveland Browns.

In the annals of statistics-oriented football preview essays, the phrase "FBI raid" rarely came up before this year, even in Browns previews. Carmen Policy kept some edgy company, but he was never the subject of an FBI raid. Eric Mangini treated fringe players like the serfs in a Tolstoy novel, but he was never the subject of an FBI raid. Phil Savage got into e-mail flame wars with random fans, but he was never the subject of an FBI raid. Art Modell engaged in all manner of creative accounting, some of it actionable, but ... you get the idea. Jimmy Haslam dug yet another new sub-basement of despair in 2013 when the FBI raided the headquarters of his Pilot Flying J truck-stop enterprise seeking evidence of fraud in mid-April, just six months after Haslam became majority owner of the Browns.

Six months. Call him *Jimmy of the 180 Days*. The Haslam Browns could not even make it to their first draft before something horrible happened. Granted, Pilot Flying J is on a whole different page of the financial ledger than the Browns; it's not like the FBI confiscated Jim Brown's jersey or discovered that Brandon Weeden was a Latvernian spy. Still, try to get enthusiastic about a new regime when the commander-in-chief is issuing statements about "cooperating in every way with authorities" instead of shaking hands with Barkevious Mingo. Just try. We double-Dawgpound dare you.

We barely know this Jimmy of 180 Days. We first saw him peering down from the owner's box like angry Caesar while Pat Shurmur coached his way into a paper bag and suffocated himself against the Colts last October. The Browns punted from the Colts' 41-yard line on fourth-and-1, trailing by four, with 6:38 to play in what became a 17-13 loss. Haslam showed restraint by not demoting Sherman to diesel jockey immediately. Haslam then began a long, complicated, tortuous regime change that was only slightly longer, more complicated, and more tortuous than the other three regime changes of the last Browns decade.

Joe Banner came aboard as CEO. Mike Holmgren hung around to finish the 2012 season, though he had been receding by increments since his 2009 arrival. Alec Scheiner, formerly a Cowboys executive, became team president. Mike Lombardi arrived in January with a title that was quickly changed. Shurmur never had a chance, of course. Rob Chudzinski became the new Browns head coach. This brief summary makes everything sound much tidier than it was; for a more realistic view, read this paragraph slowly over the course of three months. There was lots of overlap, a side foray into Chip Kelly pursuit, and much confusion about who calls which shot in the Haslam-Banner-Lombardi-Chud power structure.

The confusion has not been 100 percent cleared up. When Ray Farmer came aboard as assistant general manager, with Lombardi earning a promotion to general manager, Banner tried to explain the personnel process to Vic Carucci at ESPN Radio. "Some of that is to be worked out. Ray will work under Mike (Lombardi) so Mike will be his boss. The scouts in both the pro area and college area will probably both report through Ray to Mike. Ray will be on the road scouting college players, probably even more so than Mike, although our philosophy is to have them both on the road. I think the strategic decisions we will make as we go into free agency, we'll make draft decisions, Ray will be an integral part of those discussions with myself, Mike (Lombardi), coach (Rob Chudzinski), and Jimmy (Haslam)."

Got all that? Lombardi was formerly Director of Player Personnel, for all of about seven weeks, but Farmer could not make a lateral move from the Chiefs organization, so the Browns needed to create something with "general manager" in the title without making Farmer the actual general manager. Banner also made it clear that Chud answers directly to him, not Lombardi, Scheiner, or anyone else. You can picture the flowchart now, up on the wall in some FBI office, with Frankie Five Angels in there somewhere.

2013 Browns Schedule

Week	Opp.	Week	Opp.	Week	Opp.
1	MIA	7	at GB	13	JAC
2	at BAL	8	at KC	14	at NE
3	at MIN	9	BAL	15	CHI
4	CIN	10	BYE	16	at NYJ
5	BUF (Thu.)	11	at CIN	17	at PIT
6	DET	12	PIT		

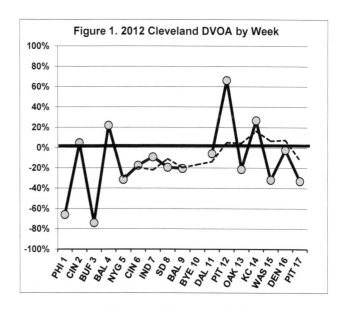

Figure 1. 2012 Cleveland DVOA by Week

To sort out the principal characters … Joe Banner was Andy Reid's cap guru and bad cop in Philadelphia. He excels at salary cap healthcare management, and he saved Reid from some of the coach's squishier instincts during the Eagles' glory years. He was the guy who applied the quick axe to veterans about to fade, as well as the gatekeeper who finally decided which younger players got lucrative extensions. Think of Banner as a George Martin who needs either a Lennon or McCartney to do what he does best.

Lombardi was … a competitor of ours? A television personality? Sort of both, though before his work at National Football Post and on the NFL Network he was a longtime scout and personnel executive with Browns and Raiders tenures. He oversaw the Browns scouting department as the Marty Schottenheimer era faded and the team sputtered to irrelevance and ended up becoming the Ravens. He was with the Raiders from 1998 through 2007: five good years followed by five putrid ones and a woeful aftermath, exactly the opposite of the timeline a scout wants to achieve. Also, National Football Post never lived up to expectations. (Kidding! It's a great site!)

Chudzinski became a hot head-coaching prospect when he designed a brilliant offense around Cam Newton, an offense since eclipsed by the contraptions assembled by the Redskins, Seahawks, and 49ers. Farmer was one of the men behind Scott Pioli's curtain in Kansas City. Scheiner has an analytics background, which means we love him and Cleveland reporters are obligated to mention *Moneyball* every time they type his name. Jim Brown is listed as a "special advisor." Haslam runs truck stops and cooperates fully with the FBI. Also, Norv Turner, because why not.

That's a lot of cooks, and some of them know their way around a kitchen. Banner and Chud have done some impressive things. Defensive coordinator Ray Horton was also a hot coaching commodity and could be the key hire of the busy offseason. Scheiner brought analytics guy Ken Kovash with him from Dallas, and together they might keep the team from drafting injured running backs and 28-year-olds in future first rounds. The challenge is seeing how they all fit, and what they will do with a roster that is not as barren as the team's record and recent upheavals would have you believe.

The Browns fielded one of the youngest lineups in the NFL last year, despite the fact that their rookie quarterback was a year older than Jimi Hendrix was when he died. Their leading rusher was 22 years old, their top two receivers 23 and 21. Their best pass-rusher and top cornerback were both 23, as were the rookie starters at right tackle, linebacker, and defensive tackle. Three other regular starters were 25. Only four starters were over 29 years old by the end of last season. One of them, not to belabor the point, was the rookie quarterback.

The young Browns are not quite the nucleus of a great team, but they are a start. Some of them, like receiver Josh Gordon, leap off the tape at you, though Gordon followed the big boss' lead and got into legal trouble before fans could get too excited. Cornerback Joe Haden is on the verge of Pro Bowl status. Some of the youngsters were playing because the Browns were bad and their front office was a flock of lame ducks, but the core of Gordon, Haden, Trent Richardson, Joe Thomas, Phil Taylor, Jabaar Sheard, and a few others should stick. Banner and Friends added significant talent in the offseason, though the acquisitions did not quite mesh with the needs, as will happen when a team's command structure is not quite intact.

Paul Kruger and Barkevious Mingo were the team's top two offseason acquisitions. They do roughly the same thing, and it also happens to be the thing that Sheard does relatively well: rush the quarterback from the edge. A team can never have too much pass rush, and Horton can get three top pass rushers onto the field at the same time in creative ways. Still, the Browns are dangerously weak around Haden in the secondary, depth-thin everywhere, and painted into a corner at quarterback. The binge shopping at edge rusher may have been a gambit to play to Horton's strengths, though the pessimist imagines college and pro scouting departments addressing the same need and ignoring each other's memos.

The acquisition of Davone Bess for during the draft was another questionable move. Bess is a "consummate pro" type on a receiving corps led by the troubled Gordon (not yet suspended at the time of trade) and stone-handed (but otherwise gifted) Greg Little. On the other hand, acquiring Bess cost Cleveland a fifth-round pick (along with moving a few other picks around). The Browns needed sure hands and proper routes, but this draft class was flooded with possession slot receivers. The Browns were in no position to toss around draft picks—even fifth-round picks—for a veteran who will likely be on the decline by the time this team is ready to be competitive.

The front office questions have to be asked because the Browns have spent a decade bouncing from Policy to Butch Davis to Mangini-Savage to Holmgren and never quite settling anywhere. When rumors of a Banner-Lombardi power struggle erupted in May, it was one more reason to be nervous that history is repeating itself, again, already.It's easy to categorize the 2013 Browns as a young team growing up together, and if Weeden was the typical 23-year-old second-year quarterback, that would be accurate. But Weeden is like the career minor leaguer who hit 30 homers in AAA ball at age 27 and ended up as a bad team's cleanup hitter. The Browns (Banner, reportedly) hedged with Jason Campbell and Brian Hoyer instead of replacing Weeden, so a team with a solid offensive line and exciting youth at the skill positions will go through a typically dreary Browns-style quarterback competition. The team is likely to look a lot like the 2012 Cardinals: a Horton front sev-

en clobbering everything in sight, one fine young cornerback playing Little Dutch Boy to any passes that leak through, and a quarterback situation based on wishful thinking.

Beyond 2013, we have to figure out if this is Halsam's team, Banner's, or someone else's; if Haslam is a robber baron or if Banner becomes Nixon without Reid; if Lombardi, Scheiner, or Farmer get a word in edgewise; if Chud has more to offer than some two-tight end read-option concepts; and on and on. If history is any indication, most of the principle characters will be gone by the time we sort them out, and the tragedy will continue.

Mike Tanier

2012 Browns Stats by Week

Wk	vs.	W-L	PF	PA	YDF	YDA	TO	Total	Off	Def	ST
1	PHI	L	16	17	210	456	1	-66%	-94%	-18%	11%
2	at CIN	L	27	34	439	375	0	5%	48%	28%	-15%
3	BUF	L	14	24	240	344	-1	-74%	-49%	14%	-11%
4	at BAL	L	16	23	357	438	-1	22%	5%	-4%	13%
5	at NYG	L	27	41	375	502	-1	-32%	-2%	51%	21%
6	CIN	W	34	24	328	438	3	-18%	-14%	15%	11%
7	at IND	L	13	17	319	321	1	-9%	1%	5%	-5%
8	SD	W	7	6	250	265	1	-20%	-25%	-5%	0%
9	BAL	L	15	25	290	282	-2	-21%	-23%	7%	9%
10	BYE										
11	at DAL	L	20	23	311	320	0	-6%	-20%	-12%	2%
12	PIT	W	20	14	238	242	7	66%	-25%	-79%	13%
13	at OAK	W	20	17	475	429	-1	-22%	20%	32%	-10%
14	KC	W	30	7	352	310	1	27%	-20%	-9%	37%
15	WAS	L	21	38	291	430	-1	-32%	-35%	1%	4%
16	at DEN	L	12	34	233	457	0	-2%	-6%	12%	15%
17	at PIT	L	10	24	320	212	-4	-33%	-19%	17%	3%

Trends and Splits

	Offense	Rank	Defense	Rank
Total DVOA	-15.2%	27	4.5%	22
Unadjusted VOA	-10.9%	26	3.0%	19
Weighted Trend	-13.9%	27	0.9%	19
Variance	9.5%	25	8.0%	27
Average Opponent	3.0%	29	-0.7%	17
Passing	-9.3%	27	11.8%	20
Rushing	-10.3%	25	-4.7%	18
First Down	-5.1%	20	0.1%	18
Second Down	-20.8%	27	16.0%	28
Third Down	-25.6%	27	-5.6%	10
First Half	-8.9%	23	10.4%	28
Second Half	-21.7%	29	-1.2%	14
Red Zone	-18.6%	27	21.6%	30
Late and Close	-30.7%	29	-11.5%	7

Five-Year Performance

Year	W-L	Pyth W	Est W	PF	PA	TO	Total	Rk	Off	Rk	Def	Rk	ST	Rk	Off AGL	Rk	Def AGL	Rk	Off Age	Rk	Def Age	Rk	ST Age	Rk
2008	4-12	4.4	5.7	232	350	+5	-20.3%	26	-21.3%	29	3.9%	20	4.9%	4	43.3	26	31.3	23	27.0	24	26.6	24	26.8	10
2009	5-11	4.3	4.8	245	375	-12	-23.1%	16	-16.4%	24	16.4%	30	9.7%	1	37.4	25	43.3	27	27.3	15	27.5	10	26.6	17
2010	5-11	6.1	6.7	271	332	-1	-4.0%	20	-5.0%	22	1.7%	18	2.7%	10	42.7	31	52.0	32	27.7	13	27.7	9	27.4	3
2011	4-12	5.0	5.5	218	307	+1	-14.2%	25	-11.2%	25	4.2%	22	1.3%	10	45.5	27	26.3	15	26.1	29	26.6	24	26.1	23
2012	5-11	6.1	6.2	302	368	+3	-13.5%	24	-15.2%	27	4.5%	22	6.1%	2	26.4	13	57.0	29	25.7	30	26.1	26	25.2	30

2012 Performance Based on Most Common Personnel Groups

CLE Offense				CLE Offense vs. Opponents				CLE Defense				CLE Defense vs. Opponents			
Pers	Freq	Yds	DVOA	Run%	Pers	Freq	Yds	DVOA	Pers	Freq	Yds	DVOA	Pers	Freq	Yds	DVOA
11	39%	5.1	-21.7%	24%	3-4-4	29%	5.1	-6.1%	Nickel Even	48%	6.2	12.2%	11	52%	6.1	11.4%
12	35%	5.3	6.2%	46%	Nickel Even	28%	5.5	-5.0%	4-3-4	42%	4.9	-7.1%	21	16%	5.3	-4.1%
21	7%	5.8	-1.2%	49%	4-3-4	23%	5.0	-10.0%	Dime+	5%	5.2	2.4%	12	15%	5.4	1.7%
13	5%	3.3	-53.9%	60%	Nickel Odd	9%	5.8	16.2%	Nickel Odd	3%	4.9	19.7%	22	8%	3.8	-11.3%
10	4%	7.9	32.5%	19%	Dime+	9%	4.0	-73.1%	3-4-4	1%	4.8	20.0%				
20	4%	3.7	-22.3%	19%												

Strategic Tendencies

Run/Pass		Rk	Formation		Rk	Pass Rush		Rk	Secondary		Rk	Strategy		Rk
Runs, first half	42%	7	Form: Single Back	69%	11	Rush 3	4.3%	24	4 DB	43%	20	Play action	25%	9
Runs, first down	46%	24	Form: Empty Back	3%	26	Rush 4	69.1%	10	5 DB	51%	10	Avg Box (Off)	6.48	7
Runs, second-long	35%	8	Pers: 3+ WR	49%	20	Rush 5	22.2%	14	6+ DB	5%	17	Avg Box (Def)	6.25	26
Runs, power sit.	48%	26	Pers: 4+ WR	5%	9	Rush 6+	4.4%	27	CB by Sides	80%	11	Offensive Pace	28.26	5
Runs, behind 2H	24%	27	Pers: 2+ TE/6+ OL	44%	8	Sacks by LB	23.0%	16	DB Blitz	9%	21	Defensive Pace	30.60	24
Pass, ahead 2H	50%	12	Shotgun/Pistol	30%	31	Sacks by DB	9.5%	10	Hole in Zone	9%	16	Go for it on 4th	1.04	9

Brandon Weeden led the league with 24 passes tipped or batted down at the line, five more than any other quarterback. ☞ Despite the presence of Trent Richardson to scare defenses, the Browns had the league's worst gap between DVOA using play action (-25.7%) and DVOA without play action (0.0%). ☞ The Browns were surprisingly good when they blitzed a defensive back, allowing just 2.7 yards per pass. But they needed to sneak that defensive back in with a standard pass rush. When they big-blitzed with six or more guys, they allowed 8.0 yards per pass and only pressured the quarterback on 11 percent of plays. (The league average on big blitzes was 31 percent.) ☞ Browns opponents only dropped 16 passes, or 2.8 percent of all passes; both figures were the lowest in the NFL. ☞ The Browns had the league's best defense against running back draws, allowing -48.5% DVOA and 2.5 yards per carry (although there was a small sample size, just 19 plays).

Passing

Player	DYAR	DVOA	Plays	NtYds	Avg	YAC	C%	TD	Int
B.Weeden	-291	-19.4%	546	3185	5.8	6.0	57.8%	14	17
T.Lewis	42	6.5%	35	190	5.4	2.8	68.8%	1	1
C.McCoy*	10	-2.7%	21	54	2.6	2.7	52.9%	1	0
J.Campbell	-129	-50.2%	57	216	3.8	2.4	62.7%	2	2
B.Hoyer	-60	-26.5%	57	300	5.3	3.1	56.6%	1	2

Receiving

Player	DYAR	DVOA	Plays	Ctch	Yds	Y/C	YAC	TD	C%
J.Gordon	64	-3.6%	95	50	797	15.9	5.9	5	53%
G.Little	45	-7.7%	93	54	639	11.8	3.4	4	58%
T.Benjamin	33	-1.5%	37	18	298	16.6	3.6	2	49%
M.Massaquoi*	-2	-13.4%	33	17	254	14.9	6.1	0	52%
J.Norwood	9	-19.9%	19	13	137	10.5	4.6	0	68%
J.Cooper	-3	-18.3%	18	8	102	12.8	6.0	0	44%
J.Cribbs*	-10	-28.8%	12	7	63	9.0	6.0	0	58%
D.Bess	71	-3.7%	105	61	783	12.8	4.1	1	58%
B.Watson*	-37	-12.8%	81	49	505	10.3	4.4	3	60%
J.Cameron	-28	-13.5%	40	20	226	11.3	5.4	1	50%
A.Smith*	-76	-72.6%	18	13	47	3.6	2.8	0	72%
K.Davis	-72	-26.0%	44	19	229	12.1	3.7	2	43%
T.Richardson	73	4.4%	70	51	367	7.2	8.6	1	73%
C.Ogbonnaya	23	-1.9%	32	24	187	7.8	8.7	0	75%

Rushing

Player	DYAR	DVOA	Plays	Yds	Avg	TD	Fum	Suc
T.Richardson	-51	-13.3%	267	954	3.6	11	3	43%
M.Hardesty	-39	-23.5%	65	271	4.2	1	2	45%
B.Weeden	24	8.0%	21	116	5.5	0	0	-
B.Jackson	15	36.1%	8	54	6.8	0	0	50%
C.Ogbonnaya	-5	-23.2%	8	30	3.8	0	0	50%
J.Cribbs*	-1	-14.1%	6	32	5.3	0	1	50%
T.Benjamin	31	65.4%	6	66	11.0	0	0	-
D.Lewis	29	45.5%	13	69	5.3	1	0	54%

Offensive Line

Player	Pos	Age	GS	Snaps	Pen	Sk	Pass	Run	Player	Pos	Age	GS	Snaps	Pen	Sk	Pass	Run
Shawn Lauvao	RG	26	16/16	1031	8	2	17.5	3	Joe Thomas	LT	29	16/16	1031	8	3	8	6
Alex Mack	C	28	16/16	1031	9	2.5	5.5	6	John Greco	LG	28	14/10	691	6	2	4.5	0
Mitchell Schwartz	RT	24	16/16	1031	5	4.5	14.5	3	Jason Pinkston	LG	26	6/6	332	0	0	3	3

Year	Yards	ALY	Rk	Power	Rk	Stuff	Rk	2nd Lev	Rk	Open Field	Rk	Sacks	ASR	Rk	Short	Long	F-Start	Cont.
2010	3.95	4.04	17	74%	4	14%	4	0.93	30	0.55	24	36	7.6%	23	10	17	12	31
2011	3.60	3.94	23	66%	9	16%	2	0.85	32	0.41	31	39	6.4%	15	11	22	19	39
2012	3.79	4.03	20	53%	29	19%	16	1.08	23	0.40	31	36	6.0%	12	15	25	40
2012 ALY by direction:		Left End 3.66 (19)			Left Tackle 3.77 (23)			Mid/Guard 4.06 (16)			Right Tackle 4.16 (11)				Right End 5.86 (3)			

Factor in all of the rookies manning the Browns' skill positions and Pat Shurmur's connect-the-dots offense, and the Browns line's middle-of-the-pack results in most of our metrics start to look pretty good. Blockers can only do so much while Brandon Weeden is simultaneously taking rookie lumps and washing that gray right out of his hair, Trent Richardson is battling injuries while getting fed to the defensive line, and the head coach is getting the punter ready on second down.

Joe Thomas is a steady Pro Bowler on the left side, and led all left tackles with one blown block every 73.6 snaps. Mitchell Schwartz earned a starting job as a rookie and looks like a fixture. Alex Mack was a Pro Bowl center in 2010 and could have been one last year if anyone was paying attention to the Browns. Mack has not missed a start in four seasons; Thomas has not missed a start in six. Thomas, Schwartz, and Mack give the Browns an intriguing mix of talent, youth, and experience: they have 176 starts under their belt, but none is older than the second-year quarterback.

Jason Pinkston missed most of last year with a blood clot in his lung. Pinkston is back from the frightening ailment and was playing with the first team in minicamp. John Greco played very well in Pinkston's absence and will get a chance to compete with Shawn Lauvao, the weak link of the line, on the right side. Veteran Oniel Cousins backs up Thomas. Pinkston could be asked to slide to tackle in a pinch.

Defensive Front Seven

Defensive Line	Age	Pos	Snaps	Plays	Overall TmPct	Rk	Stop	Dfts	BTkl	vs. Run Runs	St%	Rk	RuYd	Rk	Pass Rush Sack	Hit	Hur	Tips
Jabaal Sheard	24	DE	985	58	6.6%	18	51	17	1	42	83%	11	2.2	24	7	4	16	4
Billy Winn	24	DT	701	29	3.3%	55	23	9	1	20	80%	22	1.6	18	1	4	9	2
Ahtyba Rubin	27	DT	670	45	6.3%	8	33	12	2	39	69%	55	2.9	60	2	3	11	1
Frostee Rucker*	30	DE	593	49	5.6%	34	38	7	1	40	78%	24	2.8	55	4	2	8	1
Juqua Parker*	35	DE	528	23	2.6%	--	18	14	1	15	67%	--	1.9	--	6	6	15	0
John Hughes	25	DT	513	35	4.0%	36	25	6	1	28	68%	58	2.3	37	3	0	6.5	1
Ishmaa'ily Kitchen	25	DT	208	17	2.1%	--	11	1	1	13	77%	--	3.8	--	0	1	3	0
Desmond Bryant	28	DT	631	37	4.8%	28	32	14	3	30	90%	2	1.4	10	4	11	12.5	0

Linebackers	Age	Pos	Snaps	Plays	Overall TmPct	Rk	Stop	Dfts	BTkl	Pass Rush Sack	Hit	Hur	Tips	vs. Run Runs	St%	Rk	Yds	Rk	vs. Pass Tgts	Suc%	Rk	AdjYd	Rk	PD
D'Qwell Jackson	30	MLB	1119	127	14.5%	31	74	20	7	3.5	1	1	0	70	69%	36	3.5	59	45	59%	15	4.8	12	8
Craig Robertson	25	OLB	610	86	9.8%	63	40	17	10	1	2	2	0	33	58%	91	4.1	94	45	48%	48	8.0	66	3
Kaluka Maiava*	26	OLB	486	50	5.7%	101	31	5	4	2	1	1	0	32	63%	71	3.9	82	11	72%	--	2.9	--	3
James-Michael Johnson	24	OLB	288	32	5.8%	99	22	4	0	0	0	1	0	25	80%	10	2.2	18	8	37%	--	5.2	--	1
L.J. Fort	23	OLB	97	16	1.8%	--	7	2	1	1	1	0	1	9	33%	--	8.7	--	3	55%	--	3.1	--	2
Paul Kruger	27	OLB	789	46	5.6%	103	40	22	6	9	6	21	4	23	83%	8	1.7	5	7	51%	--	5.9	--	3
Quentin Groves	29	OLB	466	41	5.0%	--	31	14	3	4	4	9	0	30	73%	--	3.8	--	7	61%	--	4.1	--	0

Year	Yards	ALY	Rk	Power	Rk	Stuff	Rk	2nd Level	Rk	Open Field	Rk	Sacks	ASR	Rk	Short	Long
2010	4.18	4.68	31	68%	28	14%	31	1.00	4	0.44	4	29	5.9%	21	3	19
2011	4.55	4.60	31	65%	21	16%	26	1.24	20	0.78	17	32	5.8%	27	12	15
2012	4.36	4.31	25	77%	30	15%	31	1.20	20	0.68	14	38	6.3%	18	7	21
2012 ALY by direction:	Left End 4.57 (26)			Left Tackle 4.4 (26)			Mid/Guard 4.13 (15)			Right Tackle 4.15 (18)			Right End 6.23 (32)			

Terry Pluto of the *Cleveland Plain Dealer* provided an outstanding roundup of the Browns front seven at the conclusion of June minicamp. Pluto sees Paul Kruger and Jabaal Sheard starting the season at the two outside linebacker positions, with rookie Barkevious Mingo coming off the bench. Coordinator Ray Horton is innovative with his pass-rush packages, however, and Sheard or Kruger will likely move to the defensive line to accommodate Mingo on passing downs. There will be a lot of shifting, so no matter who ends up where, Horton will get his best pass rushers onto the field in passing situations.

Mingo lit up our SackSEER projection system with a rating of 94.6 percent and a projection of 34.5 sacks in his first five seasons. He draws comparisons to Jevon Kearse with his lanky frame, and runs like a 250-pound strong safety in the open field. Horton, whose scheme accommodates talented square pegs, may be the ideal coordinator for him, and playing behind Kruger and Sheard will help Mingo develop. The Browns should have a nasty pass rush, which will be a very big important improvement over last year. Our charting lists Cleveland bringing pass pressure on only 16.7 percent of pass plays (31st in the NFL), and the Browns had the largest gap in the league between DVOA allowed with pressure (-124.4%, 1.2 yards per play) and DVOA allowed without pressure (37.9%, 7.4 yards per play).

D'Qwell Jackson remains both a fine all-purpose defender and the heart of the Browns defense. Horton loves him and is building around him. Craig Robinson, who spent most of his time in the nickel package last year, is now the starter beside Jackson. Depth behind Jackson and Robinson is a major issue, with undrafted 2012 free agents L.J. Fort and Tank Carder (undrafted, then waived by the Bills) as the top backups.

Phil Taylor will play nose tackle after missing most of 2012 with a torn pectoral muscle. Taylor was dominating at times as a rookie in 2011 but will need to be spelled. Ahtyba Rubin, who slimmed down to 300 pounds in the offseason to move from tackle to end in Horton's scheme, may move inside to give Taylor breathers, with Billy Winn or John Hughes (who saw significant action in 2012 as rookies and survived) coming off the bench. Rubin had the worst yard-per-run figures of any defensive tackle in the league in both 2010 and 2011; he was slightly better while battling calf injuries last year, but his role is hardly guaranteed. Desmond Bryant, more of a penetrator than the typical 3-4 end, arrives from Oakland to round out the defensive line. He may play the Darnell Dockett role in Horton's system.

Defensive Secondary

Secondary	Age	Pos	Overall							vs. Run					vs. Pass									
			Snaps	Plays	TmPct	Rk	Stop	Dfts	BTkl	Runs	St%	Rk	Yds	Rk	Tgts	Tgt%	Rk	Dist	Suc%	Rk	APaYd	Rk	PD	Int
T.J. Ward	27	SS	980	72	9.4%	44	36	12	2	48	56%	6	5.9	21	22	5.0%	61	14.4	62%	18	4.7	6	5	1
Sheldon Brown*	34	CB	878	73	8.9%	34	28	13	2	15	47%	36	3.8	7	91	19.3%	32	13.7	49%	59	7.4	41	13	3
Joe Haden	24	CB	773	62	10.3%	18	29	10	4	12	42%	42	5.6	29	60	17.5%	45	13.6	53%	37	7.6	46	12	3
Buster Skrine	24	CB	722	83	9.5%	22	30	16	7	17	47%	35	5.3	23	84	16.7%	49	12.8	42%	81	9.1	75	10	0
Usama Young*	28	FS	666	58	8.1%	51	18	7	2	26	27%	59	9.2	59	16	3.9%	69	18.2	45%	65	12.0	75	5	3
Dimitri Patterson	31	CB	490	38	7.7%	59	15	8	2	5	40%	47	4.6	13	55	19.1%	35	10.0	48%	63	6.3	11	2	0
Tashaun Gipson	23	FS	367	30	5.5%	--	9	3	1	21	33%	--	6.9	--	5	1.6%	--	18.4	48%	--	9.6	--	1	1
Eric Hagg*	24	FS	351	23	3.5%	74	9	3	2	7	43%	20	9.7	62	20	5.3%	58	8.1	55%	34	7.1	33	1	0
Chris Owens	27	CB	168	21	3.2%	--	6	3	0	4	25%	--	4.0	--	27	7.7%	--	11.7	55%	--	4.8	--	4	0

Year	Pass D Rank	vs. #1 WR	Rk	vs. #2 WR	Rk	vs. Other WR	Rk	vs. TE	Rk	vs. RB	Rk
2010	16	12.1%	25	6.7%	18	5.3%	21	-0.8%	12	1.4%	14
2011	17	1.1%	14	20.9%	26	-19.7%	9	22.1%	25	13.8%	25
2012	20	-2.9%	17	9.3%	24	10.3%	25	0.7%	20	-2.2%	15

Joe Haden missed four games for a PED suspension and another with an oblique injury. In between, Haden's charting numbers were unimpressive, but Haden drew a lot of No. 1 receivers as the Browns tried to hide Sheldon Brown (now departed) and Buster Skrine, both of whom got targeted hard. Haden still has Pro Bowl potential, and Ray Horton will likely keep him on one side of the field: Horton's Cardinals cornerbacks lined up by sides 90 percent of the time (seventh in the NFL), even though one was Patrick Peterson and the other was clearly not. Skrine, a tiny defender with poor tackling skills, was still taking first-team reps in OTAs but is best suited for the slot. Journeyman Chris Owens also saw some first-team reps in the offseason, but when trying to replace a bad tackler, it is best not to rely on a bit player you just signed away from the Falcons. Third-round pick Leon McFadden is quick, smooth, and polished and should be able to win a starting job. McFadden was a three-year starter at San Diego State and should easily adapt to an NFL defense, though he lacks the size-speed profile to be a No. 1 cornerback.

T.J. Ward is a classic in-the-box strong safety, and Horton likes classic in-the-box safeties. "What I see in T.J. is a player that's dynamic in the run game; a player that's going to get better because he will hit. He will hit you," Horton said in January. Free safety is a trouble spot, with undrafted 2012 rookies Tashaun Gipson and Johnson Bademosi battling for the role. Sixth-round pick Jamoris Slaughter may also be in the mix, but Slaughter is more of a strong safety or Horton mix-and-match player. Slaughter played everywhere from nickel linebacker to cornerback for Notre Dame, but in the NFL he lacks the size for the former and the speed for the latter.

Special Teams

Year	DVOA	Rank	FG/XP	Rank	Net Kick	Rank	Kick Ret	Rank	Net Punt	Rank	Punt Ret	Rank	Hidden	Rank
2010	2.7%	10	-1.1	21	12.5	4	-7.3	24	11.8	3	-2.1	19	2.2	10
2011	1.3%	10	5.0	6	-1.0	23	4.8	4	-2.3	19	-0.1	17	1.2	15
2012	6.1%	2	8.2	4	9.2	4	0.1	16	1.6	13	11.7	3	-4.8	24

Josh Cribbs and Phil Dawson, two players synonymous with the Browns special teams for years, are gone. Both will be missed. Cribbs remained effective on kick and punt returns, as a gunner, and as an offensive gadget player. Dawson, the Browns kicker since 1999, was reliable from short range and knew how to cope with a stiff wind off Lake Erie, although he wasn't particularly strong on kickoffs. (Cleveland's excellent ratings in net kickoff value two of the last three years were the product of great coverage teams, not lots of Dawson touchbacks.) That said, one of the Browns' fundamental problems of the last decade was that their special teams ace and kicker were two of their most recognizable players. There is some value in a clean break.

On the other hand, a clean break shouldn't be an opportunity to bring in replacement-level replacements. The favorite to replace Dawson is Shayne Graham, now on his sixth team in four seasons. He was 4-of-9 on 50-plus-yard field goals for the Texans last year; the Texans may have been a little too optimistic about the deep leg he once possessed, as Graham was just 2-of-5 from 50-plus yards in the previous five years. The current alternative is Brandon Bogotay, who was Georgia's kickoff specialist while Blair Walsh handled field goals for the Bulldogs in 2011. Walsh went on to an outstanding rookie season for the Vikings, while Bogotay attended kicking camps to improve his precision. Even if Bogotay can't beat out Graham for the full-time kicker job, he could stick as a kickoff specialist, as Graham had a league-low minus-11.3 estimated points worth of field position in gross kickoff value a year ago.

The punt and kickoff return depth charts at Ourlads.com were blank in mid-June. That never happens. Maybe they had Cribbs hard-wired into their programs, Y2K style. Travis Benjamin is likely to get first crack at both chores. Benjamin averaged 49.7 yards per punt return in 2012. Extrapolate that over a full season, and the Browns win the Super Bowl. But seriously, he had returns of 16, 40, and 93 yards, plus a fair catch. When a player's shortest return is 16 yards, most coaches would give him more than four opportunities, even with Cribbs around … but, well, Shurmur. Davone Bess also has return experience.

Punter Reggie Hodges never came completely back from his 2011 Achilles injury and had a poor 2012 season. He is an unsigned free agent. T.J. Conley, the Jets regular punter in 2011, is the favorite to replace Hodges. Spencer Lanning, a veteran of the Bears and Jaguars practice squads, is also in the mix.

Coaching Staff

It's time once again to pull out the old saw about Norv Turner being a great offensive coordinator but terrible head coach and see if it cuts any wood. Turner has been an offensive coordinator for four seasons in the 19 years since his Cowboys days: 2001 (Chargers), 2002-2003 (Dolphins), and 2006 (49ers). Those four offenses ranked 17th, 11th, 17th, and 23rd in DVOA. Some of them showed improvement under Turner, but improvement is a relative thing: the 49ers went from 32nd to 23rd on his watch, but of course it would have required expansion for them to drop in the rankings .

Turner's talents are: a) improving the technique and fundamentals of young quarterbacks; b) developing the technique and fundamentals of young receivers; and c) game-planning to let talent be talent, so Troy-Emmitt-Michael or Rivers-LaDainian-Gates triplets can do their stuff without a lot of gadgets or flummery. The Browns, it cannot be stressed enough, do not have a young quarterback. But Josh Gordon, Greg Little, and the other Browns receivers could benefit greatly from Turner's detail-oriented coaching. Turner's game plans may look vanilla when Emmitt-types are not spicing them up, but there is some talent here, and Turner Vanilla will taste palatable after two seasons of Shurmur Spackle. Rob Chudzinski has some offensive ideas that weren't buried in an early-'90s time capsule, so Team NorvChud could be greater than the sum of its parts.

Ray Horton developed an excellent defense for the Cardinals, a scheme that mixed vintage Steelers principles with new ideas about packages and shifting fronts. He has been considered a head coaching candidate in recent years, and if his defense attracts the right kind of attention this year, he will be a short-lister. The Browns may have set themselves up with a one-year rental, but Horton is a heck of a rental.

Dallas Cowboys

2012 Record: 8-8	**Total DVOA:** -0.4% (17th)	**2013 Mean Projection:** 6.9 wins	**On the Clock (0-4):** 19%
Pythagorean Wins: 7.4 (19th)	**Offense:** 6.1% (11th)	**Postseason Odds:** 16.2%	**Mediocrity (5-7):** 41%
Snap-Weighted Age: 26.7 (16th)	**Defense:** 6.7% (23rd)	**Super Bowl Odds:** 1.0%	**Playoff Contender (8-10):** 33%
Average Opponent: 4.0% (7th)	**Special Teams:** 0.2% (15th)	**Proj. Avg. Opponent:** 0.4% (20th)	**Super Bowl Contender (11+):** 8%

2012: Jerry Jones' flash-and-dash franchise once again personifies organizational mediocrity.

2013: You can't coat a stale cracker in Swiss chocolate and call it a delicacy.

For the second straight season, the Dallas Cowboys faced a de facto playoff game in the final week of the regular season, and for the second straight season, the Cowboys lost. They finished the 2011 season with a 31-14 loss to the Super Bowl champion New York Giants, and left the 2012 season dejected after a 28-18 loss to the Washington Redskins.

Last year's Week 17 flop was particularly frustrating, as the most talented Cowboys failed in the national spotlight. Quarterback Tony Romo threw three interceptions. Dez Bryant was held to just four catches by DeAngelo Hall, who for the previous 16 weeks was one of the league's worst starting corners. Primary pass-rusher DeMarcus Ware was completely befuddled by Robert Griffin III's backfield action. It didn't help that the Cowboys had lost nearly half their starting defense to injury, and the backups got sliced and diced by Alfred Morris for 200 yards and three touchdowns.

With all the surface talent the Cowboys possess, this team always *seems* to be just a few smart moves away from real postseason contention. Look closer, however, and it appears that a number of bad decisions have left Jerry Jones in line for a long win drought that resembles the dreaded Dave Campo era, and for much the same reason: A lack of legitimate and experienced talent in the front office, and a subsequent bleeding of talent on the field. Just a few years removed from fielding one of the best rosters in the NFL, Dallas appears to be very much on the decline, and it's pretty easy to connect the dots when asking why.

"When Dallas enters the draft next year, they will need to avoid trades, and stay away from the so-called playmakers. What this team needs is a couple of big uglies, some powerhouses who will see the door to the postseason and knock it down."

That's how Vince Verhei ended the Cowboys team chapter in *Football Outsiders Almanac 2012*. And after finishing 8-8 for the second straight year with an offense full of empty calories and a defense full of holes, the Cowboys took Mr. Verhei's advice in the 2013 draft ... to a point. Jerry Jones and his son Stephen, who now carries the all-encompassing title of "Chief Operating Officer, Executive Vice President, and Director of Player Personnel," recognized the need for a big ugly, and made a big, ugly trade to get one. Positioned with

the 18th overall pick in the first round of the draft, Jones and Jones decided to trade down and acquire the San Francisco 49ers' 31st overall pick, plus a third-round pick for good measure. With that 31st overall pick, Dallas selected Wisconsin center Travis Frederick, the eighth-ranked offensive lineman on NFLDraftScout.com's Big Board, and a second- to third-round prospect in the minds of most in the know.

The resulting apoplectic response to the pick wasn't a specific indictment of Frederick's football skills; he was a four-year starter in a program long known for providing the NFL with technically sound offensive linemen. The response to the pick was based more on Dallas' over-inflated concept of positional value, especially in their agreement to receiving just a third-round pick in exchange for dropping 13 spots in the first round. Frederick, for his part, was refreshingly honest about his new status. "I thought I was a second-round offensive lineman," he told Dallas radio station 105.3 The Fan. "I thought somewhere in the second round would be more of a fit for me. I truly didn't expect this."

Stephen Jones later said that the Cowboys had LSU safety Eric Reid ranked as the second safety on their board behind Texas safety Kenny Vaccaro (who the Saints took with the 15th pick), but Jones thought there was more value in trading down and getting that extra selection. Never mind that the 49ers (a team with a few good ideas these days when it comes to player personnel) took Reid with the pick formerly owned by Dallas, and that according to the traditional trade value chart, the Cowboys should have received a second-round pick instead. There's also the small matter that the Cowboys likely could have nabbed Frederick in the second round if they really wanted to.

Jones the Younger, as is his wont, disagreed with the negative Nellies—especially when it came to the value chart.

"Not accurate," he told the media. "We actually did better than the chart."

Jerry Jones then said that "it's a mistake to think that transactions go by any trade chart ... We invented trade charts; invented them in the NFL."

The problem is not that Jerry Jones is taking credit as owner for something that specific people working for the franchise created. The problem is that, most likely, Jones has convinced himself that he was behind the creation of the chart, and as such, he's got it aced.

58

2013 Cowboys Schedule

Week	Opp.	Week	Opp.	Week	Opp.
1	NYG	7	at PHI	13	OAK (Thu.)
2	at KC	8	at DET	14	at CHI (Mon.)
3	STL	9	MIN	15	GB
4	at SD	10	at NO	16	at WAS
5	DEN	11	BYE	17	PHI
6	WAS	12	at NYG		

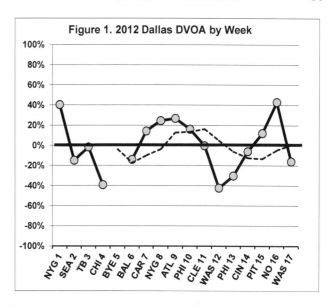

Figure 1. 2012 Dallas DVOA by Week

The point here isn't to pick on Travis Frederick, who very well could develop into a starting center with a 10-year career. The Frederick trade is just a symptom of the larger problem, a disconnect between cost and value that has plagued the Cowboys franchise in recent years, especially when it comes to the draft.

"Business is a contact sport. If you're not moving forward, you'll get run over."—Jerry Jones, 1989

Dallas has tried to address its offensive line issues in bits and bobs over the last few years, and things are a bit better in certain directions. Also, to be fair, Dallas' protection and running game issues aren't entirely the fault of those aforementioned big uglies. In 2012, the Cowboys ranked in the middle of the pack with 21 blown blocks leading to sacks. There were 11 takedowns attributed to coverage sacks, seventh in the league, which would infer that Romo doesn't always get rid of the ball quickly enough and fails to make optimal decisions at times. Anyone with a cursory view of the Cowboys over the last few years could tell you that. Left tackle Tyron Smith, playing his first full season in that prime spot after spending his rookie year on the right side, allowed just two sacks and 10 pass pressures in 15 games. And Frederick, though a reach pick, will improve things in the middle.

However, even when the Joneses target specific team needs that should contribute to team success, the results tend to fall short. They spent heavy to improve a horrid secondary before the 2012 season, signing free agent Brandon Carr and selecting LSU cornerback Morris Claiborne with the sixth overall pick. But the defense actually dropped in efficiency against the pass, falling from 20th to 25th in pass defense DVOA. In particular, a collection of embarrassments against mobile quarterbacks (starting and ending with Robert Griffin III) revealed that the Cowboys' safety situation was still tenuous at best.

Then, there's the situation at running back, which has been iffy for a while now. This franchise, long known for a dominant rushing attack, has not finished anywhere hear the top 10 in rushing DVOA since 2009, and optimal solutions don't seem to be on the horizon. DeMarco Murray was penciled in as the new lead back in his second NFL season, but he missed six games due to injuries and saw his yards per carry drop from 5.5 in his rookie campaign to 4.1 in 2012. Felix Jones, the former first-round pick who has never lived up to expectations, ranked 26th in DYAR and 25th in DVOA as the backup and signed a one-year deal with the Philadelphia Eagles after his Cowboys contract ran out.

And on the subject of Felix Jones, cue the front office dys-function again. Jones and cornerback Mike Jenkins were left to test the free-agent waters, never having lived up to their high-pick potential. Jerry Jones validated those flawed decisions by moving the goalposts and insisting that the Cowboys did indeed get the proper value out of the players.

"We got starting time out of both of them," Jones said of the two players in April. "That's not enough, but those guys aren't NFL busts. We were proud to have [Felix Jones] with that No. 1 pick, and as late as last year I was proud to have that No. 1 in Jenkins. But it is five years down the road now."

So, a running back taken with the 22nd overall pick in 2008 who rushed for 2,728 yards and 11 touchdowns in 23 starts over five years is a relative success. As is Jenkins (selected 25th overall in that same draft), who had just a single interception in his last 38 games, whose decline outlined the need for Carr and Claiborne in the first place, and who was relegated to a situational role when all was said and done. OK, then. Those numbers would certainly make Jones and Jenkins quality late-round picks. As mid-round picks, they would have qualified as the kind of initially promising yet ultimately disappointing players that pepper the draft record of every team. As two first-round picks who should have been entering their primes last season, they present a real problem.

The 2008 draft isn't the only one that's biting the Cowboys organization. There are no players left on the roster from the 2009 draft, known primarily for the trade that sent Dallas' first-round pick to Detroit for Roy Williams. In fact, only three players from that draft—linebackers Jason Williams and Victor Butler, and tight end John Phillips—are even in the league anymore. The 2010 draft netted Dez Bryant and Sean Lee, but nothing else of note. Smith, Murray, and the underrated (and still improving) Bruce Carter came out of the 2011 draft, which makes that one a relative win for the Joneses. It's too early to judge the 2012 draft after one year, but the results appear to be entirely dependent on Claiborne's development; he was their only pick in the top 80, and only three of the six players chosen after Claiborne saw the field as rookies.

Generally speaking, when personnel executives strike out this wildly, they're asked to seek alternate employment after a time ... unless, of course, they own the team.

"There's no way that I would be involved here and not be the final decision-maker on something as important as players, and that is a key area. That's never been anybody's misunderstanding. It's been a debated thing, but it's just not going to happen."—Jerry Jones, November, 2012

The Cowboys' inability to re-stock their roster through the draft is the fatal flaw that will show itself more and more over time. Two 8-8 seasons in a row, and a series of internal issues that point to coaching and personnel mistakes, leave the franchise in a state of flux that no amount of talent at certain skill positions can solve, and no amount of deck chair re-shuffling will repair. Not that the Joneses didn't try.

Jerry Jones fired defensive coordinator Rob Ryan in January, insisting that Ryan was throwing too many schemes on the field, and repeatedly insisting that there was a need to "skinny it down." To commandeer Dallas' new defensive diet plan, the Joneses hired 73-year-old Monte Kiffin, the pioneer of the under front and Tampa-2 defenses, but a man who hasn't coached in the NFL since 2008. Kiffin was last seen coaching the defense for his son, Lane, at Tennessee and USC, but he resigned in December of 2012. Later, Lane Kiffin (an epic jerk under the best of circumstances) threw his old man under the bus by insisting that if USC quarterback Matt Barkley had the benefit of the defenses that Matt Leinart and Carson Palmer did, Barkley would have won the Heisman Trophy.

Ouch. In Dallas, Kiffin will be taking personnel that spent the last several seasons in a 3-4 schemes with defensive backs playing predominantly man coverage, and moving those players to his preferred four-man fronts with zone coverages. There will be multiplicity, but generally speaking, when you go out of your way to simplify a scheme, and you don't add talent, and you're switching people around, bad things happen. Ware, who has been an elite "endbacker" since the Cowboys picked him in 2005, will now join Spencer as the lightest tandem of 4-3 defensive ends in the NFL. Then there's the question of whether this team can possibly find two safeties who can play Kiffin's defense competently. Safeties in the Tampa-2 system are often asked to be rangy, multi-faceted, and relatively interchangeable. Dallas' clump of safeties include two "maybes" coming off injuries (Barry Church and Matt Johnson), a veteran free-agent acquisition who has started a grand total of nine games total since 2007 (Will Allen), and a third-round rookie (J.J. Wilcox).

That's not to say there aren't some places where Kiffin's strategies won't mesh with the talent on the Dallas roster. Lee and Carter, along with free-agent signing Justin Durant, should fit very well as Tampa-2 linebackers. And Claiborne, like most highly-regarded cornerback prospects, should improve significantly between his first and second professional seasons. He need look no further than his old LSU teammate Patrick Peterson, who ranked 68th in Adjusted Success Rate against the pass in 2011, then jumped up to 11th in 2012 while establishing himself as one of the few legitimate week-to-week boundary shutdown cornerbacks in the game. Claiborne may not have Peterson's specific downfield abilities, but he followed his predecessor as the NCAA's Thorpe Award winner, and he has the ability to play press and off coverage at a level that over time should make him a perfect asset in Kiffin's defensive scheme.

KIffin isn't the only one with potential problems. Jerry Jones has insisted that head coach Jason Garrett isn't coaching for his job in 2013, but he's also given new offensive coordinator Bill Callahan, formerly the team's offensive line coach, a larger role in play-calling. Callahan hasn't been in charge of an NFL playbook since he took over for Jon Gruden in Oakland. That went so well, ex-Raiders receivers Jerry Rice and Tim Brown recently accused Callahan of "sabotaging" Oakland's efforts in Super Bowl XXXVII.

Then, there's the matter of Romo, who Jerry Jones wants to see take a greater responsibility overall, commensurate with the new six-year, $108 million contract extension Romo signed in March. That deal, which gives Romo $55 million guaranteed, has Jones insisting that his quarterback align himself with the very best. Jones referred to "Peyton Manning-type time on the job," and said that "If Tony, for instance, would be here Monday through Saturday … from seven in the morning to six o'clock at night all over this place then that's better than the way it's been. We'll have more success, and Jason believes that. It's certainly at quarterback but he believes it at the other positions."

Jones, of course, then insisted that Romo was ready to help with the game planning. Along with goodness knows how many others.

"The swagger had never left, even if their record no longer justified the confident arrogance that defined Dallas the team and Dallas the people. In fans' minds, Deion was still intercepting passes, Troy, Roger and Dandy Don were passing with pinpoint accuracy to Michael and Drew and Bullet Bob; and Emmitt and Dorsett were forever running free."—Joe Nick Patoski, "The Dallas Cowboys: The Outrageous History of the Biggest, Loudest, Most Hated, Best Loved Football Team in America"

The ghosts of seasons and glories past—that's what this franchise is left with now, and into the near future. Our projection for the 2013 Cowboys speaks to things that go beyond the vagaries of any one season. Romo will most likely alternate as he does between epic splash plays and weirdness in the pocket. The defense will rush the passer and fall flat in coverage—especially if Kiffin leads with a Cover-2/Tampa-2 set of schemes that the rest of the NFL figured out to perfection half a decade ago. These days, even teams that subscribe to the old school in this regard have to run a lot more nickel and dime sets to counteract more expansive offensive formations. Jason Garrett will continue to experience his own set of data dumps in critical situations, and that will continue to be less his fault than the fault of the front office which put him in a position several feet over his own head.

And that front office, led as it is in ways that will both define and succeed Jerry Jones, will continue to make choices that lurch the team forward on the surface, and kill it with gut shots behind the scenes.

Doug Farrar

2012 Cowboys Stats by Week

Wk	vs.	W-L	PF	PA	YDF	YDA	TO	Total	Off	Def	ST
1	at NYG	W	24	17	433	269	0	40%	29%	-14%	-2%
2	at SEA	L	7	27	296	315	-2	-15%	11%	-2%	-27%
3	TB	W	16	10	297	166	-1	-2%	-61%	-50%	10%
4	CHI	L	18	34	430	360	-4	-39%	-8%	33%	1%
5	BYE										
6	at BAL	L	29	31	481	316	-1	-14%	39%	34%	-20%
7	at CAR	W	19	14	312	328	1	14%	2%	-8%	5%
8	NYG	L	24	29	434	293	-4	24%	-7%	-35%	-4%
9	at ATL	L	13	19	377	453	0	27%	42%	15%	-1%
10	at PHI	W	38	23	294	369	2	16%	4%	12%	24%
11	CLE	W	23	20	320	311	0	0%	-12%	-4%	8%
12	WAS	L	31	38	458	437	-2	-42%	-20%	26%	3%
13	PHI	W	38	33	417	423	1	-30%	35%	46%	-20%
14	at CIN	W	20	10	288	336	0	6%	5%	9%	-2%
15	PIT	W	27	24	415	388	1	12%	24%	16%	5%
16	NO	L	31	34	446	562	-1	43%	38%	6%	11%
17	at WAS	L	18	28	296	361	-3	-16%	-3%	26%	13%

Trends and Splits

	Offense	Rank	Defense	Rank
Total DVOA	6.1%	11	6.7%	23
Unadjusted VOA	3.5%	14	8.7%	25
Weighted Trend	9.6%	10	12.6%	30
Variance	7.3%	20	6.4%	21
Average Opponent	-0.3%	13	3.1%	5
Passing	25.5%	7	16.2%	25
Rushing	-9.2%	24	-4.1%	19
First Down	8.7%	8	11.4%	28
Second Down	2.0%	15	-2.7%	13
Third Down	8.1%	14	12.1%	26
First Half	-5.2%	20	4.9%	24
Second Half	16.0%	6	8.6%	24
Red Zone	-16.0%	23	8.2%	23
Late and Close	10.4%	8	3.2%	23

Five-Year Performance

Year	W-L	Pyth W	Est W	PF	PA	TO	Total	Rk	Off	Rk	Def	Rk	ST	Rk	Off AGL	Rk	Def AGL	Rk	Off Age	Rk	Def Age	Rk	ST Age	Rk
2008	9-7	7.9	8.1	362	365	-11	2.5%	18	1.8%	17	-4.2%	9	-3.6%	27	24.2	17	29.1	19	28.8	3	27.5	12	25.8	29
2009	11-5	11.3	11.9	361	250	+2	25.5%	5	21.7%	3	-2.9%	10	1.0%	14	14.5	11	7.7	2	28.5	2	27.1	18	25.7	27
2010	6-10	7.0	6.8	394	436	0	-10.5%	23	-4.7%	21	6.3%	27	0.6%	15	20.7	12	11.1	7	28.7	2	27.4	15	25.6	27
2011	8-8	8.6	8.4	369	347	+4	3.5%	14	5.9%	12	0.4%	16	-2.1%	25	43.5	25	19.0	11	26.6	22	28.2	2	26.0	27
2012	8-8	7.4	7.9	376	400	-13	-0.4%	17	6.1%	11	6.7%	23	0.2%	15	29.0	17	57.5	30	27.2	11	26.7	19	25.6	26

2012 Performance Based on Most Common Personnel Groups

DAL Offense					DAL Offense vs. Opponents				DAL Defense					DAL Defense vs. Opponents			
Pers	Freq	Yds	DVOA	Run%	Pers	Freq	Yds	DVOA	Pers	Freq	Yds	DVOA		Pers	Freq	Yds	DVOA
11	53%	6.3	22.3%	15%	Nickel Even	43%	6.2	18.8%	3-4-4	45%	5.6	-3.1%		11	47%	6.1	9.4%
12	18%	6.0	6.2%	35%	4-3-4	27%	5.7	4.1%	Nickel Even	22%	6.4	12.9%		12	20%	5.8	5.8%
21	12%	6.7	23.9%	54%	3-4-4	15%	5.9	14.9%	Dime+	16%	6.0	11.3%		21	18%	6.5	20.9%
22	7%	3.7	-22.1%	77%	Dime+	8%	6.3	30.8%	Nickel Odd	12%	6.2	16.7%		22	4%	4.1	-24.1%
13	3%	4.2	7.0%	70%	Nickel Odd	4%	6.5	26.2%	4-3-4	1%	3.6	-29.5%		611	3%	4.5	-20.5%
01	3%	6.0	-13.1%	0%					Goal Line	1%	1.1	26.3%					

Strategic Tendencies

Run/Pass		Rk	Formation		Rk	Pass Rush		Rk	Secondary		Rk	Strategy		Rk
Runs, first half	35%	26	Form: Single Back	71%	7	Rush 3	15.7%	2	4 DB	47%	9	Play action	11%	32
Runs, first down	39%	32	Form: Empty Back	4%	22	Rush 4	60.5%	18	5 DB	34%	30	Avg Box (Off)	6.32	20
Runs, second-long	23%	29	Pers: 3+ WR	56%	11	Rush 5	19.0%	20	6+ DB	17%	7	Avg Box (Def)	6.40	13
Runs, power sit.	55%	17	Pers: 4+ WR	3%	11	Rush 6+	4.8%	24	CB by Sides	69%	22	Offensive Pace	31.72	25
Runs, behind 2H	24%	25	Pers: 2+ TE/6+ OL	32%	14	Sacks by LB	77.9%	1	DB Blitz	6%	27	Defensive Pace	30.53	22
Pass, ahead 2H	53%	7	Shotgun/Pistol	53%	10	Sacks by DB	0.0%	28	Hole in Zone	11%	11	Go for it on 4th	0.69	29

Can someone explain to us why Jason Garrett doesn't like to use play action? The Cowboys were dead last in using play action after ranking 30th in 2011, even though they are pretty good at it. Romo last year had 2.1 more yards per play and 30.0% higher DVOA with play action. That's not a one-year fluke; in 2011, the Cowboys had 18.2% higher DVOA with play action. (The average NFL team has about 10% better DVOA with play action.) ☞ Roster changes meant big formation changes for the Cowboys. Their use of single-back sets increased from 51 percent of plays in 2010 and 52 percent in 2011 to 68 percent of plays last year. They also saw usage of three-wide sets go way up (from 37 percent to 56 percent) and usage of two-tight end sets go way down (from 53 percent to 32 percent). ☞ Dallas went max protect on only 7.2 percent of pass plays, 30th in the NFL. ☞ The Cowboys didn't blitz a defensive back much, which is good because they allowed 10.3 yards per play (31st in the league) when doing so.

Passing

Player	DYAR	DVOA	Plays	NtYds	Avg	YAC	C%	TD	Int
T.Romo	1156	14.8%	683	4635	6.8	4.6	66.1%	28	19
K.Orton	95	110.7%	10	89	8.9	2.7	90.0%	1	0

Rushing

Player	DYAR	DVOA	Plays	Yds	Avg	TD	Fum	Suc
D.Murray	72	1.7%	162	662	4.1	4	3	54%
F.Jones*	11	-6.1%	111	408	3.7	3	1	49%
P.Tanner	-53	-58.2%	24	57	2.4	0	0	38%
L.Dunbar	-5	-13.9%	21	75	3.6	0	0	52%
T.Romo	-2	-14.9%	14	63	4.5	1	1	-

Receiving

Player	DYAR	DVOA	Plays	Ctch	Yds	Y/C	YAC	TD	C%
D.Bryant	392	18.3%	138	92	1382	15.0	4.9	12	67%
M.Austin	184	3.3%	119	66	943	14.3	4.4	6	55%
K.Ogletree*	92	4.5%	55	32	436	13.6	2.6	4	58%
D.Harris	39	-1.2%	31	17	222	13.1	6.5	1	55%
C.Beasley	-4	-17.4%	24	15	128	8.5	3.9	0	63%
J.Witten	192	10.0%	149	111	1039	9.4	2.8	3	74%
J.Hanna	6	-1.5%	11	8	86	10.8	6.3	0	73%
J.Phillips*	11	2.0%	10	8	55	6.9	0.8	1	80%
D.Rosario	-6	-18.3%	18	10	101	10.1	4.3	3	56%
D.Murray	60	10.4%	42	35	251	7.2	6.9	0	83%
F.Jones*	109	45.1%	36	25	262	10.5	9.0	2	69%
L.Vickers	51	40.7%	15	13	104	8.0	6.8	0	87%
L.Dunbar	-20	-41.4%	12	6	33	5.5	4.0	0	50%

Offensive Line

Player	Pos	Age	GS	Snaps	Pen	Sk	Pass	Run	Player	Pos	Age	GS	Snaps	Pen	Sk	Pass	Run
Mackenzy Bernadeau	RG	27	16/16	1100	3	5	14.5	4	Ryan Cook	C	30	13/11	813	3	1	4	4
Nate Livings	LG	31	16/16	1093	6	4	18	4.5	Jermey Parnell	OT	27	16/1	260	2	2	6	0
Doug Free	RT	29	16/16	1019	15	4	27.5	3	Derrick Dockery*	G	33	15/2	174	1	0.5	3.5	0
Tyron Smith	LT	23	15/15	949	10	2	10	6	Phil Costa	G	26	3/3	120	0	0	0	0

Year	Yards	ALY	Rk	Power	Rk	Stuff	Rk	2nd Lev	Rk	Open Field	Rk	Sacks	ASR	Rk	Short	Long	F-Start	Cont.
2010	3.87	4.14	12	54%	26	18%	13	1.10	20	0.49	26	31	5.8%	11	13	8	27	34
2011	4.63	4.26	6	57%	23	19%	16	1.31	8	0.97	9	39	6.1%	13	10	19	23	36
2012	3.78	3.92	22	63%	15	19%	12	1.04	25	0.52	26	36	5.8%	11	11	14	26	28

2012 ALY by direction:	Left End 4.4 (8)	Left Tackle 4.59 (9)	Mid/Guard 4.03 (17)	Right Tackle 3.25 (32)	Right End 3.3 (28)

Despite the criticism for the Travis Frederick pick, you have to give the Cowboys credit for at least trying to address obvious issues on a line that had been by turns ignored and badly stocked for years. Frederick will compete with Ryan Cook for the starting center position, though he certainly has the advantage to start. Dallas' right side is still an issue, with Mackenzy Bernadeau spackling his way through a heavy-rep season at right guard, and Doug Free—once the team's ostensible best hope at the tackle position—playing his way down to a $3.5 million pay cut just to hold his job after the Cowboys showed an interest in free agents Tyson Clabo and Eric Winston. Given the team's need to re-structure several contracts to stay on the right side of the salary cap, that may have been posturing, but the point is the same—Free hasn't lived up to the four-year, $32 million deal he agreed to in 2011, and he may face the same competition from Jeremy Parnell that he did down the stretch last season. Although he allowed only four sacks, Free allowed so many hurries and drew so many holding calls that our game charters marked only Anthony Castanzo of the Colts with more blown blocks on passing plays than Free's 27.5.

Nate Livings struggled through a subpar season and led left guards with 18 blown blocks on pass plays. So it was fortunate for Tony Romo's blind side that Tyron Smith, selected in the first round of the 2011 draft and moved from the right to the left side for 2012, proved to be a real find with great potential at that all-important position. Line coach Bill Callahan said that he's never had anyone with Smith's athletic potential, and the third-year man wants to bulk up to 315 pounds to accentuate his positive traits and eliminate a few lapses in his game. "I just want to be a better run-blocker and be stronger and more physical," Smith told the Dallas Morning News in May. "There were times last year where I felt like I was too fast and I was a little off-balanced. I just basically want to add a little weight and stay there, be fast and strong at the same time." That Smith did what he did despite a nightmarish family financial situation that forced him to file protective orders against his own parents speaks well of his determination and concentration. He's also trying to get his linemates into karate, and why not? With this group, every little bit helps.

Defensive Front Seven

Defensive Line	Age	Pos	Snaps	Plays	TmPct	Rk	Stop	Dfts	BTkl	Runs	St%	Rk	RuYd	Rk	Sack	Hit	Hur	Tips
					Overall						vs. Run				Pass Rush			
Jason Hatcher	31	DE	756	52	6.6%	19	39	9	1	43	74%	39	2.3	27	4	11	20.5	1
Marcus Spears*	30	DE	388	26	3.5%	63	22	7	0	24	83%	11	1.8	15	1	0	2.5	1
Sean Lissemore	26	DT	311	35	7.1%	4	21	3	0	32	63%	65	3.8	69	1	1	5	0
Josh Brent	25	DT	309	23	3.9%	42	16	4	0	20	65%	62	2.6	48	1.5	3	4.5	0
Tyrone Crawford	24	DT	295	19	2.4%	--	8	0	0	18	44%	--	2.9	--	0	4	1	0
Jay Ratliff	32	DT	260	16	5.4%	--	10	3	0	14	64%	--	2.7	--	0	6	9	0
Kenyon Coleman*	34	DE	163	15	4.3%	--	13	3	0	15	87%	--	2.3	--	0	0	0.5	0

Linebackers	Age	Pos	Snaps	Plays	TmPct	Rk	Stop	Dfts	BTkl	Sack	Hit	Hur	Tips	Runs	St%	Rk	Yds	Rk	Tgts	Suc%	Rk	AdjYd	Rk	PD
					Overall					Pass Rush				vs. Run					vs. Pass				
DeMarcus Ware	31	OLB	864	56	7.1%	82	46	23	7	11.5	11	22	0	36	83%	7	1.8	7	7	32%	--	8.0	--	0
Anthony Spencer	29	OLB	842	99	14.3%	32	76	27	4	11	5	12	1	65	85%	5	2.4	23	17	61%	11	3.9	5	3
Bruce Carter	25	ILB	605	72	13.3%	40	34	14	0	0	2	1	0	39	59%	66	3.6	69	29	55%	22	5.3	16	2
Ernie Sims	29	OLB	364	42	8.5%	--	18	2	5	1	2	3	0	29	45%	--	5.6	--	12	53%	--	2.8	--	1
Dan Connor*	28	ILB	340	54	7.8%	76	32	7	4	0	0	1	0	39	67%	44	3.3	50	12	43%	--	6.3	--	1
Sean Lee	27	ILB	314	60	20.3%	2	35	10	1	0	1	3	0	38	66%	52	4.1	89	13	44%	--	4.5	--	2
Victor Butler*	26	OLB	290	26	3.3%	--	17	8	1	3	2	4	3	18	61%	--	3.1	--	3	25%	--	7.6	--	0
Alex Albright	26	OLB	179	18	2.6%	--	10	2	0	0	0	1	0	13	69%	--	4.2	--	5	59%	--	3.2	--	0
Justin Durant	28	OLB	849	103	13.1%	41	57	22	7	0.5	1	1.5	1	57	70%	34	2.8	29	40	50%	41	6.8	34	1

Year	Yards	ALY	Rk	Power	Rk	Stuff	Rk	2nd Level	Rk	Open Field	Rk	Sacks	ASR	Rk	Short	Long
2010	4.40	4.27	22	70%	29	14%	29	1.10	14	0.87	19	35	6.9%	11	14	14
2011	4.03	3.92	10	57%	10	22%	9	1.13	11	0.66	9	42	7.6%	6	14	18
2012	4.37	4.14	19	65%	20	16%	28	1.13	8	0.83	18	34	6.9%	9	10	16

2012 ALY by direction:	Left End 4.36 (23)	Left Tackle 3.69 (10)	Mid/Guard 4.29 (26)	Right Tackle 4.57 (31)	Right End 3.25 (6)

The stats for DeMarcus Ware and Anthony Spencer correctly reflect what the tape showed in 2012—if you were watching All-22 cutups, squinted your eyes until you couldn't make out the jersey numbers for Dallas' endbackers, and Ware and Spencer switched sides, it would be hard to tell most of the time. That's obviously a tremendous compliment to Spencer, and it's one he's earned. Not only does he have a full palette of pass-rush moves and impressive functional strength when dealing with blockers, but he covers screens with impressive lateral agility. He also called the defenses after Sean Lee and Bruce Carter were lost for the season with injuries. The Cowboys franchised Spencer for the second straight season, and though Jerry Jones hinted at the scouting combine that Spencer doesn't have the optimal size to play end for Monte Kiffin, it would be goofy even for this franchise to jettison a player just as he's so obviously hitting his stride. As for Ware, elbow and shoulder injuries limited his effectiveness late in the season, but he's still everything you'd want from a franchise pass-rusher when healthy.

In Kiffin's base four-man fronts, it's possible that Jay Ratliff could be the one-technique tackle, shading between the center and guard. Former Cowboys scouting director Larry Lacewell told ESPN Dallas in January that such a role for the 300-pound Ratliff would be similar to the one La'Roi Glover played for Mike Zimmer's Cowboys defense from 2002 through 2005. As for tackle Jason Hatcher, expect him to play three-tech, where he can use the athleticism that allowed him to amass as many quarterback hits as Ware and more quarterback hurries than anyone but Ware, on the Cowboys' 2012 roster, even while playing 3-4 end.

The Cowboys' linebackers actually look to be a pretty nice fit for what Kiffin has historically done. And in Sean Lee—at least, in a healthy Sean Lee—Kiffin will benefit from the best range linebacker in football. Lee tackles with authority and reads plays at the line with exceptional ability, but what sets him apart is his ability to cover ground and break angles as well as any player at his position. Lee is perfectly suited to play the Mike role in a Tampa-2, precisely because there isn't an in-cut or slant or skinny post he can't defend. As Lacewell said, Lee will be "absolutely great. He's already great, but when you become a Mike [in a 4-3], that means you're a whole-field player. In the 3-4, you're a half-the-field player a lot of times. It's just going to add to his greatness." Of course, Lee's greatness is contingent on his ability to actually get on the field—he missed the last 10 games of the 2012 season with a severe case of turf toe. Ernie Sims and Dan Connor tried to simulate Lee's overall excellence in the interim, but that's a tall order.

Bruce Carter, who will play the weak side in Kiffin's base defense, is that rarest of all NFL entities—an underrated Dallas Cowboys player. Carter proved to have a much-needed acumen against the pass—especially after Lee was lost for the season. Though his sack and hurry numbers don't indicate it, Carter also helped the front seven with his ability to come up to the line and provide additional pressure in blitz packages. Not that we're comparing Carter to Derrick Brooks, but as Brooks defined the WILL position for Kiffin with the Buccaneers for so many years, Carter can for him now. Like Lee, Carter needs to find ways to stay on the field—he missed the last six games of the regular season with a dislocated elbow. The Cowboys signed Justin Durant, the former Lions and Jaguars linebacker, to a two-year deal in hope that he can fill out the third spot in that starting trio.

Defensive Secondary

Secondary	Age	Pos	Snaps	Plays	Overall TmPct	Rk	Stop	Dfts	BTkl	vs. Run Runs	St%	Rk	Yds	Rk	vs. Pass Tgts	Tgt%	Rk	Dist	Suc%	Rk	APaYd	Rk	PD	Int
Brandon Carr	27	CB	1008	63	8.0%	56	22	10	5	8	38%	53	9.0	71	78	20.1%	25	12.9	56%	22	7.6	45	10	3
Gerald Sensabaugh*	30	FS	949	57	7.7%	53	10	5	4	19	26%	60	14.1	73	22	6.0%	48	10.9	39%	73	9.3	65	3	0
Morris Claiborne	23	CB	875	63	8.5%	44	18	10	4	11	18%	79	7.8	61	59	16.2%	53	13.4	41%	83	7.9	54	9	1
Danny McCray	25	SS	637	66	8.9%	47	20	7	9	28	43%	20	8.4	56	34	9.2%	13	11.4	45%	66	9.1	61	3	1
Mike Jenkins*	28	CB	357	17	2.7%	--	8	2	4	4	50%	--	11.5	--	22	6.8%	--	9.9	53%	--	6.8	--	3	0
Sterling Moore	24	CB	327	24	3.7%	--	10	4	1	3	33%	--	10.0	--	23	6.3%	--	14.8	43%	--	15.4	--	1	0
Orlando Scandrick	26	CB	326	25	4.6%	--	12	6	2	4	50%	--	5.5	--	28	10.5%	--	11.9	68%	--	5.2	--	4	0
Eric Frampton*	29	FS	194	20	3.1%	--	7	1	1	9	44%	--	8.6	--	3	1.0%	--	14.7	100%	--	0.0	--	2	0

Year	Pass D Rank	vs. #1 WR	Rk	vs. #2 WR	Rk	vs. Other WR	Rk	vs. TE	Rk	vs. RB	Rk
2010	28	44.1%	32	15.5%	26	2.9%	20	-11.9%	4	-11.2%	6
2011	22	14.0%	19	53.3%	31	-26.9%	6	19.1%	21	-3.6%	15
2012	25	-7.0%	12	11.5%	29	19.5%	28	28.9%	32	3.5%	18

The Cowboys understood the need to upgrade their secondary after a 2011 season that saw them finish 20th in pass defense DVOA, and they certainly put money towards that need by signing free agent Brandon Carr and selecting Morris Claiborne with the sixth overall pick. The result? Dallas' pass defense was even worse in 2012, as Rob Ryan's multiple-front schemes frequently left the Cowboys' back four on islands they were not equipped to defend.

It's a bit of a myth that Kiffin's schemes will have Dallas' cornerbacks playing off-coverage most of the time. The Tampa-2 is based on the ability of outside pass defenders to press receivers into disadvantageous situations, and Carr seemed to like the overall look. "It allows the corners to be aggressive at the line of scrimmage, every play challenging receivers," Carr said in May. "It allows us to go out there and dictate the flow of the game." That concept should also benefit second-year cornerback Morris Claiborne, who excelled in press concepts at LSU. Carr held up decently in Rob Ryan's defense, through far below what was expected. Part of the issue was that he didn't benefit from a great bookend like Brandon Flowers in Kansas City. In fact, Claiborne underperformed even given the rookie curve we detailed in last year's book. Rookie cornerbacks drafted in the first round from 2005 to 2011 averaged a 49 percent Success Rate and 7.9 Adjusted Yards per Pass; Claiborne matched the 7.9 yards but had a 41 percent Success Rate. Depth is good here; Orlando Scandrick has always performed well in sub-packages, and fourth-round pick B.W. Webb (William and Mary) could excel in nickel and dime situations. Webb was a standout facing strong competition at the Senior Bowl, and his 5-foot-10, 184-pound frame and solid inside speed project well for sub packages. Mike Jenkins, having been demoted right off the currency sheet (even Rob Ryan doesn't play half-dollar defenses), left for Oakland this offseason.

Even if Dallas' cornerbacks improve under Kiffin—and there are strong reasons for optimism, starting simply with Claiborne developing with more experience—the secondary will still be an overall problem, because the safety position is a gaping hole and the team's weakest position overall. Sensabaugh had his second straight subpar season against the pass—he ranked 77th (dead last) in Adjusted Success Rate in 2011. Even though they had given him a new five-year, $22.5 million contract a year before, Dallas released Sensabaugh in March as part of the post-Romo extension salary-cap purge, and he retired from the NFL two months later. Danny McCray was a special-teams ace thrown into the starting lineup because of injuries, and he wasn't much better. It got so bad, the Cowboys were forced to move Carr to a deep safety position against teams that took more shots downfield.

Barry Church and Matt Johnson are the most likely starters for 2013. Church's best asset is his range, but he's also a strong hitter who played a bit of linebacker in his first two seasons. He won last year's starting strong safety job in training camp, but a torn Achilles ended his season in late September. Johnson, a fourth-round pick out of Eastern Washington, couldn't stay healthy during his rookie year and says that lifting too much weight was a root cause of his hamstring injuries. For depth, the Cowboys will have third-round rookie J.J. Wilcox and veteran Will Allen, signed to a one-year, veteran-expendable contract. Wilcox is a great athlete but also a project, a former receiver who played safety for just one season at FCS-level Georgia Southern. Allen played in Kiffin's Tampa Bay secondary from 2004 through 2008, then for the Pittsburgh Steelers over the last three seasons. It's nice that Kiffin is familiar with Allen, but until he started seven games last year for the injured Troy Polamalu, Allen had only started two games total from 2007 through 2011, and he hasn't intercepted a pass since 2005. Whether any of these guys can play at the level demanded in a Tampa-2 system remains to be seen, and don't be surprised if you see the same downfield burns from Dallas all over again.

Special Teams

Year	DVOA	Rank	FG/XP	Rank	Net Kick	Rank	Kick Ret	Rank	Net Punt	Rank	Punt Ret	Rank	Hidden	Rank
2010	0.6%	15	-5.5	29	1.2	15	-14.6	31	6.3	10	15.3	2	-14.6	30
2011	-2.1%	25	1.6	13	1.6	14	1.2	14	-5.0	23	-9.7	30	3.6	11
2012	0.2%	15	7.8	5	-3.1	24	-10.9	32	-1.4	17	8.4	4	2.5	10

The circumstances regarding the hire of new special teams coach Rich Bisaccia were pretty strange—we'll get to that in a moment—but the guy knows that he's doing. Bisaccia replaces Joe DeCamillis, who was "allowed to leave" and join the Chicago Bears. In his fourth season with the Cowboys, DeCamillis found himself under fire for a few marquee embarrassments in the 2012 season; for example, in Week 2, Dallas spotted the Seahawks an early 10 points with a fumbled Felix Jones kick return and a blocked Chris Jones punt returned for a touchdown.

Kicker Dan Bailey missed just two field goal tries in 31 attempts during his second season, and both of those misses were from more than 50 yards out. His kickoffs were still below average, but improved from 2011. The Cowboys' punting situation was more muddled. Dallas signed veteran Brian Moorman to challenge Chris Jones in September, but both players were decidedly average. Jones will compete with undrafted Spencer Benson out of Clemson for this year's job.

Receiver Dwayne Harris was worth 12.0 estimated points on punt returns, second only behind Buffalo's Leodis McKelvin. However, he wasn't very good on kick returns, and neither was the player likely to share that job with him in 2013, Lance Dunbar. On coverage teams, the Cowboys had two players—safety Eric Frampton and linebacker Alex Albright—finish in the top 10 in Return Stops, our stat which credits players for making tackles that stop opponents from making return gains that match or exceed the NFL's average.

Coaching Staff

The best head coaches are able to take their personnel and maximize their people in key situations. Cowboys head coach Jason Garrett exposed his own inability to do this with late-game mental meltdowns that probably cost his team a division title, and play-calling issues that had Jerry Jones calling on everyone from line coach/offensive coordinator Bill Callahan to Tony Romo to Skip Bayless to help out with the schemes. (Note: We're kidding about Bayless. We think.) Callahan has said he's willing to do whatever needs to be done to improve the team, though he'll have his hands full once again with the Cowboys' front five. Things should interesting on defense, where Monte Kiffin will team with new defensive line coach Rod Marinelli to take a old-school Tampa Bay approach to a defense that appeared confused and out of place under Rob Ryan.

One doesn't usually find controversy in the hire of special teams coaches, but hey—we're talking about the Cowboys here. Three weeks after he accepted the position of assistant head coach and special teams coordinator at Auburn, Rich Bisaccia bailed on the Tigers when Jason Garrett asked him to coach Dallas' special teams instead. "A little embarrassed about how it happened, having to go through Auburn and only spending 22 days there," Bisaccia said in February. "That's not really my style. I've actually been really proud of the long stays I've had at some particular places, but for it to work out like this and to have an opportunity like this, I just feel certainly blessed in one way and certainly fortunate." Bisaccia was the special teams coach for the San Diego Chargers in 2011 and 2012, where he turned one of the worst units in recent NFL history into a relative strength. He previously worked with Kiffin and Marinelli in Tampa Bay from 2002 through 2008.

Denver Broncos

2012 Record: 13-3   **Total DVOA:** 36.5% (2nd)   **2013 Mean Projection:** 10.3 wins   **On the Clock (0-4):** 1%

Pythagorean Wins: 12.5 (2nd)   **Offense:** 22.1% (2nd)   **Postseason Odds:** 82.7%   **Mediocrity (5-7):** 8%

Snap-Weighted Age: 27.4 (7th)   **Defense:** -13.8% (5th)   **Super Bowl Odds:** 23.2%   **Playoff Contender (8-10):** 38%

Average Opponent: -6.8% (31st)   **Special Teams:** 0.6% (13th)   **Proj. Avg. Opponent:** -4.5% (29th)   **Super Bowl Contender (11+):** 52%

2012: John Elway's $18 million gamble pays off.

2013: Likely defensive regression makes Denver *a* top Super Bowl contender rather than *the* top Super Bowl contender.

Last year, Broncos Executive Vice President of Football Operations John Elway made an $18 million bet that Peyton Manning would regain his form despite four neck operations. The bet paid off. The version of Manning that Denver got was very similar to the version that Indianapolis had long enjoyed.

Unfortunately, the similarities between Denver Manning and Indianapolis Manning included the type of disappointing playoff exit that, about a decade ago, had fairly or unfairly defined Manning's career. It's a little surprising that John Fox's reputation has not taken more of a hit for the ridiculously cautious—if not outright stupid—decision he made to take a knee at the end of regulation in the Divisional Round loss to Baltimore. The reason you pay $18 million for a quarterback is so you don't have to even think about settling for overtime when your offense has first-and-10 on the 20 with 31 seconds and two timeouts still remaining. (At *home*, no less!)

Disappointing as the early playoff exit was for Manning and the Broncos, many still viewed their 2012 campaign as a wild success. Thirty-six years of age and four neck surgeries did not wind up significantly weakening the future Hall of Fame quarterback. Manning's arm strength noticeably improved as the season wore on—his average pass distance went from 8.1 yards in the first half of the season to 8.8 yards in the second half—and he finished just 12 votes shy of collecting a record fifth MVP trophy.

Elway made a more substantial bet on Manning this past offseason, picking up an option on the contract that guarantees the quarterback $40 million over the next two years. This bet hardly feels like a gamble, though. For one, the Broncos have insurance in the event of Manning re-injuring his neck. Secondly, it's crystal clear that Manning is still a top-five (if not top-two or -three) NFL quarterback.

With Manning now much less of a risk than he was a year ago, it's no surprise that our projections call for the Broncos to easily win the so-so AFC West. Yet they are also projected to take a slight step back in 2013. This may seem counterintuitive. After all, Manning has now had a full year to regain his football physique and integrate himself (plus his system) with the rest of the organization. What's more, the Broncos offense, which finished second in DVOA last season, is even more talented this time around. They've added Wes Welker to a receiving corps that last year had the most prolific pair of wideouts in the NFL (Eric Decker and Demaryius Thomas combined for a DYAR of 782; next highest was New Orleans' Marques Colston and Lance Moore with 698). Weaving Welker, the league's preeminent slot weapon, into the system shouldn't be hard; last year, the Broncos lined up with three wideouts 64.4 of the time, which was second in the NFL behind only the Buffalo Bills (73.7 percent).

In addition to the most dangerous wide receiver trio in the NFL, the Broncos with Jacob Tamme and Joel Dreessen also have a potent two-tight end section in their playbook. Statistically, neither Tamme nor Dreessen was particularly impressive last year (both had negative DVOA ratings). But what the stats can't show is how their position flexibility (and literal flexibility when it comes to route running and on-the-move run-blocking) lends a valuable dimension of versatility to Denver's offense. Defenses must make the tough decision about whether they should play nickel against Denver's two-tight end personnel or go with their base defense. If they go base, they become very predictable, especially given that they must respond to the quick tempo of Denver's hurry-up.

Manning's brilliance in conducting the passing attack (particularly in the pre-snap phase) has a trickle-down effect that dramatically aids Denver's run game. Whichever running back is in Denver's backfield is often facing simple seven-man boxes. This year, the Broncos appear set to go with second-round rookie Montee Ball, who has the quickness to the hole and ability to change directions required by this offensive scheme. Behind him will be second-year scatback Ronnie Hillman, with Knowshon Moreno (just a guy) providing depth.

Manning and these backs will be working behind a front line that was very good in 2012 and figures to be even better with mobile free agent pickup Louis Vasquez taking over for underrated veteran right guard Chris Kuper (who now gives the line some much-needed depth).

So yes, one of the best offenses in football has somehow improved. Conventional wisdom would say that the team as a whole should thus improve. But football teams do not thrive with offense alone. The Broncos' big 2012 season was powered just as much by dramatic improvement on defense, and that improvement will be much more difficult to carry over into 2013.

The din of the Manning buzz kept a lot of people from fully appreciating the fact that Denver ranked fifth in pass defense DVOA and fourth in run defense DVOA last season. Just like in Carolina, John Fox and Jack Del Rio worked well

2013 Broncos Schedule

Week	Opp.	Week	Opp.	Week	Opp.
1	BAL (Thu.)	7	at IND	13	at KC
2	at NYG	8	WAS	14	TEN
3	OAK (Mon.)	9	BYE	15	SD (Thu.)
4	PHI	10	at SD	16	at HOU
5	at DAL	11	KC	17	at OAK
6	JAC	12	at NE		

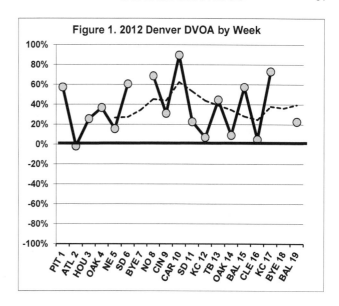

Figure 1. 2012 Denver DVOA by Week

together as head coach and defensive coordinator. They ran a fundamentally firm 4-3 base scheme, but the real magic was in the sub packages that housed their bevy of disguises and tricks. They did a fantastic job capitalizing on the rarer-than-rare talents of Von Miller. The second-year superstar posted 18.5 sacks mostly by coming off the edge, but he also brought tremendous value as a hybrid inside blitzer and quarterback spy. (Seven-and-a-half of Miller's sacks came from an unconventional rush: either three rushers or some form of blitz.)

It helped that Denver had mid- and back-level defenders who could play man coverage. Cornerback Champ Bailey was a true No. 1 cover artist, handling opponents' top receivers week in and week out with minimal safety help. No. 2 corner Chris Harris was solid on the outside and sensational when sliding into the slot. Undersized nickelback Tony Carter also proved to be an impressively athletic man-to-man defender. What set Denver's scheme apart was they also had reliable man defenders up the middle in versatile safety Mike Adams and fluid linebacker Wesley Woodyard. This allowed the Broncos to conventionally cover most tight ends (i.e., quarterbacks' safety outlets) one-on-one, which allowed for more aggression in disguises and blitzes.

Good as this defense was in 2012, the laws of statistical regression suggest that a decline in 2013 is inevitable. This starts with a general rule about defensive regression: defenses that play much better on third down than on first or second down tend to decline the following season. The 2012 Denver Broncos were sixth in defensive DVOA on first down,

18th on second down, and first on third down with a fabulous -47.8% DVOA. How fabulous? On third downs, the Broncos had the second-best defensive DVOA in our entire database, surpassed only by the 1991 Saints (-48.7%). Their third-down pass defense DVOA (-66.8%) was the best since the 2001 Browns (-69.2%).

As you might expect, teams with extremely strong defenses on third down see a lot of regression towards the mean the following season (Table 1). Prior to last year's Broncos, 25 teams had third-down defensive DVOA of -30% or lower. These teams saw their overall defensive DVOA rise by an average of 9.4% the following season. Only two of the 25 teams improved on defense the following season, the 2001-02 Buccaneers and the 1992-93 Chiefs.

The third-down regression effect means that Denver's defense would have a very hard time equaling last season even if it brought back all the same personnel. Of course, we know that the Broncos won't have all the same personnel. Some players will get injured, some players will be older, and some players are gone for good. These are all additional reasons to expect decline.

Injury: The Broncos' defense was particularly healthy in 2012, finishing 11th in Adjusted Games Lost after finishing 28th and 24th the previous two seasons. Most of those Adjusted Games Lost came from defensive tackle Ty Warren and cornerback Tracy Porter, who were easily replaced in the lineup and won't be back with the team this season. The odds suggest there will be more injuries in 2013, and more meaningful ones.

Age: Champ Bailey had a phenomenal season last year. However, he's also going to be 35 years old this year, and his game-charting numbers had been declining steadily over the past few seasons before rebounding in 2012. (Until last season, Bailey's Adjusted Success Rate had dropped every year except 2009.) Common sense says you should expect decline from any 35-year-old football player, but what about cornerbacks specifically? What can we learn now that Football Outsiders has eight years of game charting data on pass coverage?

Table 1. Best Third-Down Defensive DVOA, 1991-2012

Team	Year	3rd Down Def DVOA	All Downs Def DVOA	All Downs Def DVOA Y+1	Change
NO	1991	-48.7%	-24.5%	-18.3%	+6.2%
DEN	**2012**	**-47.8%**	**-13.8%**	--	--
BAL	2003	-46.7%	-25.0%	-19.9%	+5.1%
PHI	1991	-46.3%	-42.4%	-18.1%	+24.2%
CLE	2001	-41.6%	-13.1%	-5.1%	+8.0%
PHI	2002	-41.1%	-11.2%	3.0%	+14.2%
SF	1995	-39.5%	-23.7%	-15.8%	+7.9%
DEN	1999	-38.7%	-6.9%	-1.1%	+5.8%
PIT	2008	-38.5%	-29.0%	-4.6%	+24.4%
JAC	2006	-36.7%	-16.1%	-2.5%	+13.6%
GB	2006	-36.2%	-5.3%	-1.2%	+4.1%
TB	2001	-35.6%	-15.4%	-31.8%	-16.3%
AVERAGE		**-41.5%**	**-18.9%**	**-10.5%**	**+8.8%**

Well, the numbers don't suggest that a 35-year-old cornerback will decline significantly, and they don't suggest that he will play as well as the year before. What they suggest is that he won't play much at all. In eight years, only five cornerbacks played enough at age 35 to qualify for our cornerback rankings (40 charted targets or eight games started): Nick Harper and Al Harris in 2009, Ronde Barber in 2010, Charles Woodson in 2011, and Antoine Winfield in 2012. These cornerbacks are outliers when it comes to the aging process, and obviously so is Bailey.

What's evident on film is that while Bailey is still an excellent corner, he's not quite the athlete he once was. Yes, overall he has still been performing at a high level. But at some point, his natural decline will drop him below the "high level" threshold. For discussion's sake, let's say that 2013 is the season when Bailey fulfills this inevitable prophecy and really declines. That would significantly alter Denver's defense, as they'd have to start giving more help to Bailey's side, either with a safety over the top or with linebackers buzzing underneath. That would take away from the resources that make up many of Fox's and Del Rio's disguises and blitzes. Another way to think of it: at the end of the day, football is a numbers game. The more help a cornerback needs, the less advantaged a defense becomes numbers-wise. Currently, Denver's scheme relies fairly heavily on the advantages Bailey creates.

The signing of veteran cornerback Dominique Rodgers-Cromartie could simply be a case of Elway jumping at the opportunity to sign a talented player for a relatively low price. However, considering they already had solid second and third corners in Harris and Carter, the signing of Rodgers-Cromartie could also be a hedge in the event that Bailey suddenly shows significant decline. (In that event, Bailey would likely move to safety.) Despite the inconsistency he has shown in his career so far, Rodgers-Cromartie profiles better than either Harris or Carter as the kind of No. 1 corner who could allow the Broncos to continue playing a similar defense. The coaching staff now has a year to use him and evaluate him. That should give them a sense of the possible alternative next offseason, when

the Broncos have to decide if it makes sense to let a 36-year-old Bailey take up $9 million on the team's 2014 salary cap.

Departure: One thing the development of our annual team projection system has shown is that, in general, no single move has a greater impact on a defense than adding or removing a top pass-rusher. The contract timing snafu which caused the Broncos to lose Elvis Dumervil was a significant mistake that sent 25 sacks and hurries per year out the door.

It's possible that the loss of Dumervil will be offset by the natural progression of second-year defensive lineman Derek Wolfe, the addition of first-round rookie Sylvester Williams, and the signing of Shaun Phillips away from the division-rival Chargers. Of those three, Phillips is likely to have the most dramatic immediate impact. He quietly had 9.5 sacks last season in San Diego. Phillips, with his long arms and willowy athleticism, is best suited to be a No. 2 edge rusher, operating on the weak side. That's exactly what he'll do in Denver's base defense.

The greater concern with this defense is at middle linebacker, where either Joe Mays or Nate Irving will replace reliable veteran Keith Brooking in the base 4-3. Brooking had one of his most valuable seasons in years, partly because the scheme and linebackers/safeties around him kept him from getting caught in a lot of coverage situations. Mays and Irving both move well enough, but neither has the pre-snap recognition and awareness that Brooking offered. That's critical given what this scheme demands from its middle linebacker.

Nevertheless, let's not get carried away with pessimism about the 2013 Denver Broncos and their defense. Even if the issues above lead to decline, it's still unlikely that this defense will suddenly become worse than average. The offense should be one of the four or five best in the league, and our mediocre projection for the rest of the AFC West suggests that Denver will once again have one of the league's easiest schedules. The forecast for defensive regression means the path to the Super Bowl will not be easy. But really, what Super Bowl path ever is?

Andy Benoit

2012 Broncos Stats by Week

Wk	vs.	W-L	PF	PA	YDF	YDA	TO	Total	Off	Def	ST
1	PIT	W	31	19	334	284	0	57%	45%	-17%	-5%
2	at ATL	L	21	27	336	275	-4	-2%	-13%	-4%	7%
3	HOU	L	25	31	375	436	1	26%	28%	6%	3%
4	OAK	W	37	6	503	237	-1	37%	20%	-20%	-3%
5	at NE	L	21	31	394	444	-2	16%	18%	1%	-1%
6	at SD	W	35	24	365	307	3	61%	39%	-30%	-8%
7	BYE										
8	NO	W	34	14	530	252	0	69%	38%	-35%	-4%
9	at CIN	W	31	23	359	366	-1	31%	28%	15%	17%
10	at CAR	W	36	14	360	250	0	90%	15%	-51%	23%
11	SD	W	30	23	386	277	1	23%	1%	-35%	-13%
12	at KC	W	17	9	368	264	0	7%	12%	-3%	-7%
13	TB	W	31	23	333	306	0	45%	27%	-9%	9%
14	at OAK	W	26	13	428	324	1	9%	15%	13%	7%
15	at BAL	W	34	17	350	278	2	57%	31%	-36%	-10%
16	CLE	W	34	12	457	233	0	5%	22%	11%	-6%
17	KC	W	38	3	488	119	-1	73%	39%	-32%	2%
18	BYE										
19	BAL	L	35	38	398	479	-2	23%	-7%	13%	42%

Trends and Splits

	Offense	Rank	Defense	Rank
Total DVOA	22.1%	2	-13.8%	5
Unadjusted VOA	22.5%	2	-14.0%	3
Weighted Trend	23.3%	3	-17.4%	2
Variance	2.3%	2	4.2%	10
Average Opponent	3.4%	31	-3.2%	26
Passing	49.7%	2	-10.5%	5
Rushing	-2.8%	15	-18.1%	4
First Down	19.4%	5	-9.8%	6
Second Down	22.1%	4	2.2%	18
Third Down	28.1%	3	-47.8%	1
First Half	18.1%	6	-6.2%	10
Second Half	26.2%	3	-21.6%	2
Red Zone	24.1%	6	5.6%	19
Late and Close	46.8%	1	-28.5%	2

Five-Year Performance

Year	W-L	Pyth W	Est W	PF	PA	TO	Total	Rk	Off	Rk	Def	Rk	ST	Rk	Off AGL	Rk	Def AGL	Rk	Off Age	Rk	Def Age	Rk	ST Age	Rk
2008	8-8	6.1	6.3	370	448	-17	-8.5%	24	19.2%	1	20.7%	31	-7.0%	31	45.3	28	30.1	22	26.8	27	27.9	6	26.5	18
2009	8-8	8.1	9.2	326	324	+7	10.6%	13	1.3%	18	-9.8%	7	-0.4%	18	16.5	13	3.3	1	27.7	10	29.1	2	26.4	19
2010	4-12	4.9	5.3	344	471	-9	-17.1%	26	2.1%	15	16.6%	30	-2.6%	27	11.0	6	40.8	28	26.6	24	28.9	2	25.6	28
2011	8-8	5.8	7.0	309	390	+1	-11.8%	24	-9.9%	23	1.6%	18	-0.2%	18	15.0	5	40.4	24	25.6	32	27.5	10	25.9	28
2012	13-3	12.5	14.7	481	289	-1	36.5%	2	22.1%	2	-13.8%	5	0.6%	13	27.8	15	21.4	11	28.3	5	27.0	15	25.9	21

2012 Performance Based on Most Common Personnel Groups

DEN Offense					DEN Offense vs. Opponents				DEN Defense					DEN Defense vs. Opponents			
Pers	Freq	Yds	DVOA	Run%	Pers	Freq	Yds	DVOA	Pers	Freq	Yds	DVOA	Pers	Freq	Yds	DVOA
11	64%	6.4	30.2%	35%	Nickel Even	49%	6.3	24.2%	Nickel Odd	39%	5.0	-9.4%	11	54%	4.7	-11.7%
12	28%	6.3	32.6%	56%	Dime+	14%	6.2	46.1%	4-3-4	33%	4.4	-12.7%	12	24%	5.3	-11.9%
02	2%	4.3	-41.7%	0%	Nickel Odd	14%	6.8	38.0%	Nickel Even	13%	4.3	-15.4%	21	16%	3.8	-28.7%
13	2%	4.0	-47.2%	82%	3-4-4	13%	5.7	20.4%	Dime+	10%	4.0	-62.2%	22	2%	4.1	-0.7%
22	1%	2.1	-17.3%	82%	4-3-4	9%	5.1	1.3%	3-4-4	4%	7.2	12.5%	13	1%	4.6	-5.3%

Strategic Tendencies

Run/Pass		Rk	Formation		Rk	Pass Rush		Rk	Secondary		Rk	Strategy		Rk
Runs, first half	38%	16	Form: Single Back	91%	1	Rush 3	5.1%	20	4 DB	37%	28	Play action	29%	5
Runs, first down	53%	8	Form: Empty Back	4%	25	Rush 4	63.1%	16	5 DB	52%	6	Avg Box (Off)	6.18	27
Runs, second-long	31%	17	Pers: 3+ WR	67%	4	Rush 5	25.1%	10	6+ DB	10%	11	Avg Box (Def)	6.25	27
Runs, power sit.	52%	19	Pers: 4+ WR	0%	26	Rush 6+	6.7%	17	CB by Sides	54%	31	Offensive Pace	27.45	2
Runs, behind 2H	26%	24	Pers: 2+ TE/6+ OL	34%	12	Sacks by LB	51.0%	11	DB Blitz	16%	8	Defensive Pace	29.43	5
Pass, ahead 2H	45%	19	Shotgun/Pistol	57%	6	Sacks by DB	8.7%	11	Hole in Zone	6%	27	Go for it on 4th	0.66	30

"Don't blitz Peyton Manning," right? That's not actually the strategy that Denver opponents used a year ago. Denver opponents blitzed on 32 percent of passes, which is above the NFL average of 30 percent, and big-blitzed on 9.6 percent of passes compared to an NFL average of 7.6 percent. And Manning actually struggled against the big blitzes, with just 5.3 yards per pass, although he was just fine against five-man blitzes. ☞ Peyton Manning runs an excellent play-fake, and he really likes to use it. In fact, the Broncos actually play-faked more often during 2012 than they did during 2011, even though Tim Tebow was their starting quarterback for half of 2011. ☞ Only 6.9 percent of carries by Broncos running backs came with two backs in the formation, which is good because they were horrible running the ball with two backs in the game: just -35.8% DVOA and 1.3 yards per carry. ☞ Could it be that Manning has trouble getting yardage when he dumps the ball off? Denver had -11.9% DVOA on passes thrown behind the line of scrimmage (26th in the NFL) but 82.4% DVOA on passes thrown beyond the line of scrimmage (fourth). ☞ Denver only recovered three of 15 fumbles on offense. ☞ The Broncos' defense more than doubled its Adjusted Sack Rate on third down, from 6.3 percent on first and second downs to 13.8 percent on third downs.

Passing

Player	DYAR	DVOA	Plays	NtYds	Avg	YAC	C%	TD	Int
P.Manning	1805	32.8%	602	4526	7.5	4.7	69.0%	37	11

Rushing

Player	DYAR	DVOA	Plays	Yds	Avg	TD	Fum	Suc
W.McGahee*	49	-2.1%	167	727	4.4	4	5	58%
K.Moreno	56	1.1%	138	525	3.8	4	1	56%
R.Hillman	-24	-15.7%	85	330	3.9	1	2	51%
L.Ball	-1	-9.2%	41	160	3.9	1	0	39%
J.Hester	21	27.4%	17	81	4.8	2	0	41%
P.Manning	2	-5.4%	6	27	4.5	0	0	-

Receiving

Player	DYAR	DVOA	Plays	Ctch	Yds	Y/C	YAC	TD	C%
D.Thomas	354	21.4%	141	94	1430	15.2	5.7	10	67%
E.Decker	392	27.2%	123	85	1071	12.6	3.1	13	69%
B.Stokley*	204	37.4%	59	45	544	12.1	3.3	5	76%
M.Willis*	-44	-42.6%	22	10	90	9.0	2.8	0	45%
W.Welker	251	6.1%	175	118	1354	11.5	5.8	6	67%
J.Tamme	18	-5.8%	84	52	555	10.7	3.8	2	62%
J.Dreessen	13	-1.2%	58	41	356	8.7	3.4	5	71%
V.Green	14	22.7%	6	5	63	12.6	12.4	0	83%
W.McGahee*	44	7.2%	33	26	221	8.5	9.0	0	79%
K.Moreno	58	25.3%	26	21	167	8.0	6.0	0	81%
L.Ball	5	-5.6%	12	8	58	7.3	5.1	1	67%
R.Hillman	-2	-17.0%	12	10	62	6.2	6.9	0	83%

Offensive Line

Player	Pos	Age	GS	Snaps	Pen	Sk	Pass	Run	Player	Pos	Age	GS	Snaps	Pen	Sk	Pass	Run
Zane Beadles	LG	27	16/16	1145	4	1	11.5	10	Manny Ramirez	RG	30	15/11	831	6	5.5	9.5	5
Orlando Franklin	RT	26	16/16	1135	9	1.5	13.5	5	Chris Kuper	RG	31	7/5	311	1	0	3	2.5
Ryan Clady	LT	27	16/16	1115	8	1	13	4	J.D. Walton	C	26	4/4	248	1	0	0	0
Dan Koppen*	C	34	15/12	890	1	1	2	5.5	Louis Vasquez	RG	26	16/16	1017	0	0.5	6	3

Year	Yards	ALY	Rk	Power	Rk	Stuff	Rk	2nd Lev	Rk	Open Field	Rk	Sacks	ASR	Rk	Short	Long	F-Start	Cont.
2010	3.62	3.60	30	52%	27	23%	25	1.12	16	0.45	28	40	6.4%	16	10	20	17	32
2011	4.67	4.19	11	56%	26	17%	9	1.31	7	0.94	10	42	9.5%	29	9	25	7	48
2012	4.07	4.13	12	67%	9	20%	20	1.19	16	0.53	25	21	4.2%	2	10	5	12	29
2012 ALY by direction:		Left End 3.37 (23)			Left Tackle 3.96 (18)			Mid/Guard 4.24 (10)			Right Tackle 3.75 (22)				Right End 5.07 (6)			

Not to take anything away from what's become a very good offensive line in Denver, but playing with Peyton Manning makes life a lot easier for a linemen. Manning's brilliant pre-snap diagnostic abilities make defenses inherently hesitant. Consequently, there are fewer eight-man boxes for this line to run-block against and fewer blitzes to react to in pass protection. Manning also has a sixth sense when it comes to compensating for weaknesses in protection. This is why someone like right tackle Orlando Franklin, who has great size but not the quickest feet you'll ever see, can survive in one-on-one pass protection so much of the time. Manning excels at setting protection slides, moving within the pocket, and regulating his sixth blocker (which is generally his running back). He also knows how to get the ball out quickly. Last season the Broncos only had 13 blown blocks that directly resulted in a sack, the third-lowest figure in the NFL, and 5.5 of those blocks came from perpetually overmatched backup guard Manny Ramirez.

While Manning occasionally goes out of his way to help Franklin, he rarely has to think twice about his protection on the left side. Sixth-year pro Ryan Clady was the best all-around left tackle in football last season. With almost no chip-block help all season, Clady had just one blown block resulting in a sack, proving that the supposed struggles he had in 2011 were more a product of blocking for the scattershot Tim Tebow. Impressive as Clady was in protection, he may have been even better in the ground game, where his athleticism both in the box and extended short-area space was a major plus in Denver's frequent runs from shotgun.

Inside, the Broncos were solid and will likely be better in 2013, signing free-agent Louis Vasquez away from San Diego to replace underrated but injury-prone veteran Chris Kuper at right guard. On the left side, Zane Beadles is a stellar run-blocker who, like Kuper, has a good feel for executing double teams. Between them was supposed to be J.D. Walton, but he's once again sidelined with ankle problems, so the Broncos brought back serviceable veteran Dan Koppen. The alternative option at center would be last year's fourth-round pick Philip Blake or the porous Ramirez.

Defensive Front Seven

Defensive Line	Age	Pos	Snaps	Plays	Overall TmPct	Rk	Stop	Dfts	BTkl	Runs	vs. Run St%	Rk	RuYd	Rk	Pass Rush Sack	Hit	Hur	Tips
Elvis Dumervil*	29	DE	921	54	6.8%	12	41	19	3	35	66%	63	2.9	59	11	12	23	0
Derek Wolfe	23	DE	901	40	5.0%	43	29	11	0	29	66%	65	2.2	25	6	3	8.5	2
Justin Bannan*	34	DT	523	46	5.8%	14	35	3	1	39	72%	47	2.7	54	0	0	3.5	4
Kevin Vickerson	30	DT	482	41	5.2%	23	31	10	0	34	74%	37	1.9	24	2	3	4.5	1
Mitch Unrein	26	DT	387	20	2.5%	68	17	0	1	20	85%	7	2.3	38	0	3	4	0
Terrance Knighton	27	DT	657	33	3.7%	45	29	11	2	28	86%	5	1.5	16	2	6	4.5	1

Linebackers	Age	Pos	Snaps	Plays	Overall TmPct	Rk	Stop	Dfts	BTkl	Pass Rush Sack	Hit	Hur	Tips	Runs	vs. Run St%	Rk	Yds	Rk	Tgts	vs. Pass Suc%	Rk	AdjYd	Rk	PD
Von Miller	24	OLB	960	69	8.7%	68	58	39	3	18.5	12	41	0	38	87%	4	0.4	1	13	43%	--	8.0	--	2
Wesley Woodyard	27	OLB	875	119	16.0%	19	72	25	3	5.5	3	6	0	64	69%	35	3.5	62	44	67%	3	4.5	9	5
Keith Brooking*	38	MLB	452	53	6.7%	86	25	1	1	1	0	1	0	39	56%	97	4.3	98	13	72%	--	2.9	--	0
Joe Mays	28	MLB	291	19	6.4%	--	11	2	5	0.5	1	0	0	10	80%	--	2.9	--	10	37%	--	6.8	--	0
Danny Trevathan	23	OLB	239	32	4.0%	--	16	5	0	1	0	0	0	14	57%	--	3.3	--	16	71%	2	4.7	11	2
D.J. Williams*	31	OLB	129	15	4.3%	--	9	3	0	0	0	0	0	7	71%	--	1.9	--	6	98%	--	1.6	--	1
Shaun Phillips	32	OLB	839	50	6.3%	93	33	22	5	10	5	14	3	26	58%	90	3.7	74	7	72%	--	6.2	--	1

Year	Yards	ALY	Rk	Power	Rk	Stuff	Rk	2nd Level	Rk	Open Field	Rk	Sacks	ASR	Rk	Short	Long
2010	4.52	4.40	29	57%	9	15%	27	1.11	16	0.99	26	23	4.6%	32	6	15
2011	4.26	3.88	9	60%	12	22%	8	1.28	24	0.78	18	41	7.8%	5	18	14
2012	3.69	3.91	14	52%	6	18%	18	1.02	3	0.35	1	52	8.7%	1	19	18
2012 ALY by direction:		Left End 4.7 (27)			Left Tackle 4.35 (25)			Mid/Guard 3.73 (6)			Right Tackle 3.62 (6)			Right End 3.53 (9)		

Because of the drastic schematic differences between Denver's base defense and its sub packages, it's almost like this team has two front sevens: the run-stopping one and the pass-stopping one.

Against the run, Broncos coaches emphasize the importance of being destructive with just seven box defenders. In fact, Broncos defensive linemen and linebackers are taught not to differentiate their technical approach even when there is an eighth man in the box. Having an active defensive line is critical, as evidenced by the fact that John Elway made it a priority to restock the defensive tackle position this past offseason. Last season's rotation of Justin Bannan, Kevin Vickerson and Mitch Unrein did a tremendous job using strong lateral movement and gap-clogging techniques to prevent blockers from reaching the second level. Their destructiveness made for one of the most immovable front fours in football—at least in the middle and on the offense's right side. Adjusted Line Yards on runs to the left were noticeably worse, which may suggest that Elvis Dumervil's lack of size was indeed an issue at times in play-side run defense.

This offseason, Vickerson, a talented but mercurial veteran with great initial get-off, was re-signed (two years, $5 million). So was Unrein, an exclusive rights free agent. The aging Bannan was allowed to walk, and the Broncos signed Terrance "Pot Roast" Knighton, a potentially destructive force, away from the Jaguars. He was likely to battle the up-and-coming Unrein for a starting spot, but both became destined for backup duties after Elway drafted North Carolina's Sylvester Williams in the first round. Williams intrigued scouts with his strong lower body and penetrating burst.

The upgrades inside mean that last season's second-round pick, Derek Wolfe, will likely play a full-time defensive end role in the base defense. Wolfe plays with terrific tenacity and movement skills. He's perfect for strongside duties, which means veteran free-agent pickup Shaun Phillips can operate as a space-oriented chase defender on the weak side. Also in the mix for playing time is the quietly effective and athletic Robert Ayers, an example of how a first-rounder who doesn't live up to his draft status can still develop into a useful player. Further depth is provided by 2012 fifth-rounder Malik Jackson (at 284 pounds, he moves between tackle and end) and 2013 fifth-rounder Quanterus Smith (a smaller pass-rush specialist out of Western Kentucky).

The only linebacker spot that's set is the Sam, where Von Miller has evolved into an outstanding playside run-stopper. His dominating performance was somewhat overshadowed by J.J. Watt having one of the four or five best defensive seasons of all-time, but Miller's total of 39 Defeats tied Ray Lewis' 2003 season for the sixth-highest total since 1996. (The full list of best seasons can be found in the Houston chapter.) Miller's greatest value is in Denver's nickel/dime package, where he headlines many of Denver's complex amoeba sub-package pass rushes. Miller is much more than just a devastating edge rusher. Last season he was used extensively as an inside blitzing joker and quarterback spy.

Veteran Keith Brooking, who stabilized this defense after taking over for Joe Mays at Mike last season, was not re-signed. Presumably, the Broncos would love for athletic third-year pro Nate Irving to fill the void. A safer option, however, might be Wesley Woodyard, a smooth space-oriented veteran who may lack ideal strength to play the run in traffic but has the awareness that Fox and Del Rio demand in the middle. If Woodyard started in the middle, then last year's intriguing sixth-round pick, Danny Trevathan, would get a chance to replace departed veteran D.J. Williams on the weak side. Then again, playing Woodyard slightly out of position may not be worthwhile; he's much better when he can play to his strengths, and his strength is operating in space. In fact, in nickel, one key reason the Broncos can afford to be creative and diverse with Miller in their pass rush designs because Woodyard is such a heady, fluid pass defender. That stabilizes the intermediate areas that are usually the most vulnerable when the defense blitzes.

Defensive Secondary

Secondary	Age	Pos	Snaps	Plays	Overall TmPct	Rk	Stop	Dfts	BTkl	vs. Run Runs	St%	Rk	Yds	Rk	vs. Pass Tgts	Tgt%	Rk	Dist	Suc%	Rk	APaYd	Rk	PD	Int
Rahim Moore	23	FS	1042	77	9.7%	41	24	8	7	32	31%	52	7.6	44	28	6.3%	42	12.2	41%	69	8.3	49	3	1
Champ Bailey	35	CB	1011	74	9.3%	30	31	11	2	17	59%	15	3.3	6	71	16.2%	54	13.7	59%	13	6.6	20	5	2
Mike Adams	32	FS	980	90	11.3%	28	34	11	2	38	45%	16	6.4	27	45	10.3%	10	11.3	49%	55	6.9	29	8	0
Chris Harris	24	CB	902	70	9.4%	27	38	20	4	23	52%	24	5.6	27	62	15.2%	61	9.9	54%	31	6.4	15	7	3
Tony Carter	27	CB	496	35	4.7%	83	16	9	4	2	0%	84	7.5	57	58	14.1%	68	15.4	63%	4	6.7	24	9	2
Tracy Porter*	27	CB	301	27	9.1%	--	14	7	4	9	56%	--	4.6	--	34	20.5%	--	14.5	44%	--	10.8	--	6	1
Jim Leonhard*	31	SS	260	17	2.1%	--	8	5	1	8	50%	--	7.6	--	8	1.8%	--	14.9	42%	--	8.3	--	2	2
Quentin Jammer	34	CB	992	73	9.2%	31	27	15	4	12	58%	16	6.7	46	95	21.9%	9	15.5	49%	61	8.1	61	8	3
D. Rodgers-Cromartie	27	CB	992	67	8.5%	46	27	11	12	11	27%	71	8.4	66	79	20.7%	19	14.5	48%	62	8.0	60	16	3

Year	Pass D Rank	vs. #1 WR	Rk	vs. #2 WR	Rk	vs. Other WR	Rk	vs. TE	Rk	vs. RB	Rk
2010	31	7.1%	21	16.1%	27	28.9%	32	13.5%	24	8.8%	21
2011	24	21.7%	23	-1.2%	14	2.5%	22	6.1%	14	26.3%	30
2012	5	-12.5%	8	-20.3%	3	-18.1%	4	6.9%	24	-7.7%	11

Another reason the Broncos can get maximum value out of Miller's brilliance is they have a strong collection of versatile defensive backs. In fact, although 12-time Pro-Bowler Champ Bailey is clearly still the secondary's best player, veteran safety Mike Adams is arguably the secondary's most *important* player. Adams can line up in the box and either blitz, disguise and execute a zone coverage or, most often, defend a tight end man-to-man. He lends a lot of deception to Denver's scheme. Backup Quinton Carter can also do some of these things, though the third-year pro is better suited to play back in coverage. So is Rahim Moore, a hard hitter with solid speed and one giant playoff mistake to atone for. The Broncos also signed former Chargers cornerback Quentin Jammer and moved him to safety, where they hope he can push all of these guys for playing time. Versatile as Denver's safeties can be, none of them are flawless natural starters. The diversification of their usage is not always a method of disguising coverage; it's sometimes a means for hiding these players' weaknesses. Nevertheless, it's a real luxury to have as much freedom in the use of safeties as Fox and Del Rio have.

This style of play requires cornerbacks who can hold up in solo coverage (which often means man-to-man), and the Broncos have them. Bailey reversed a recent slide in his charting stats, showing why he remains one of the preeminent corners in the NFL. Last season he regularly shadowed the opposing No. 1 receiver, playing without significant help a lot of the time. (Bailey was covering the No. 1 receiver 65 percent of the time our charters marked him in coverage, tied with Ike Taylor for fifth in the league.) Youngsters Chris Harris and Tony Carter also were excellent last season. Harris has emerged as one of the best pure slot man-defenders in the league, while John Fox has said that Carter is as good a pure cover corner as he's seen. (Of course, this begs the question of why Carter was once cut by Denver, then cut by New England, and only played three games for Fox and the Broncos when he returned to the team in 2011.) Given the quality they already had at the position, the free-agent signing of Dominique Rodgers-Cromartie was a bit curious. Perhaps adding the extremely gifted but up-and-down sixth-year corner is a hedge against the possibility of the 35-year-old Bailey suddenly succumbing to Father Time. Or, maybe signing a potential true No. 1 corner for just $10 million over two years ($5 million guaranteed) was simply too good of a deal for Elway to pass up. With Rodgers-Cromartie on board, plus 2012 fourth-rounder Omar Bolden (Arizona State) and 2013 third-rounder Kayvon Webster (South Florida), the Broncos have a lot of long-term options at cornerback.

Special Teams

Year	DVOA	Rank	FG/XP	Rank	Net Kick	Rank	Kick Ret	Rank	Net Punt	Rank	Punt Ret	Rank	Hidden	Rank
2010	-2.6%	27	2.4	11	-4.5	26	2.9	14	-13.0	29	-0.6	16	-17.6	32
2011	-0.2%	18	-6.4	27	1.8	13	0.6	16	-5.3	24	8.2	4	4.8	9
2012	0.6%	13	-4.7	26	-1.6	20	0.9	12	13.2	5	-4.6	24	-0.1	18

Trindon Holliday might be the new Devin Hester, or he might just be another return man to flash with a few spectacular plays in a limited timeframe, only to spend the rest of his career bouncing around the league average with hot and cold streaks. He had an electrifying kick return *and* punt return for a touchdown in the Divisional Round game against Baltimore. He also had two touchdown returns in the regular season, plus three touchdown returns for the Texans in the preseason. On the other hand, Holliday was so bad for Houston once the regular season began that they cut him after Week 5. Holliday's returns for Houston were worth a combined minus-7.4 estimated points worth of field position compared to average. His returns for Denver were worth 6.4 estimated points during the regular season and 12.8 estimated points in that single playoff game.

The good news for Denver is that a Peyton Manning team is the perfect place for an inconsistent but sometimes spectacular return specialist. Manning is so steady that the Broncos get away with focusing less on establishing field position in the return game and more on making game-breaking plays. As long as Holliday doesn't fumble—which was a big problem for him last season, as he had six fumbles including four muffed punts—the Broncos should have no hesitation about letting him cut loose.

We've written for years about how playing eight games at mile-high elevation does wonders for a kicker and punter's bottom line. As former FO writer Bill Barnwell has written at Grantland, the Broncos failed to consider this when they signed Matt Prater to a four-year, $13 million deal last offseason. Just as in the year before signing his new deal, Prater missed six field goals last season, though that was on 32 attempts (versus 25). Things were better on punts, where Britton Colquitt and a good coverage team helped lead Denver to the fifth-best punt unit in the league.

Coaching Staff

John Fox's hands are mainly on the defense, which he runs alongside coordinator Jack Del Rio. The two worked together in Carolina and have a great feel for featuring their stars and diversifying game plans each week. Offensively, coordinator Mike McCoy is now the head man in San Diego; quarterbacks coach Adam Gase has taken his place. Gase has a good working relationship with Peyton Manning, which is all that matters. With Gase likely focusing almost solely on the game-planning side of things with Manning, the Broncos brought in Greg Knapp to oversee the quarterback position. He'll presumably work closest with Brock Osweiler. Also still on staff is well-respected running backs coach Eric Studesville, who served as interim head coach at the end of the Josh McDaniels debacle in 2010.

Detroit Lions

2012 Record: 4-12

Pythagorean Wins: 6.4 (23rd)

Snap-Weighted Age: 27.5 (4th)

Average Opponent: 4.1% (6th)

Total DVOA: 0.1% (16th)

Offense: 12.3% (8th)

Defense: 7.1% (24th)

Special Teams: -5.1% (30th)

2013 Mean Projection: 7.4 wins

Postseason Odds: 23.5%

Super Bowl Odds: 1.9%

Proj. Avg. Opponent: 2.4% (6th)

On the Clock (0-4): 15%

Mediocrity (5-7): 37%

Playoff Contender (8-10): 38%

Super Bowl Contender (11+): 11%

2012: The young ones wait in the fields, hoping that their Detroit will heal.

2013: Wait 'til I get my money right… then you can't tell me nothing right.

This chapter could easily start with an essay about how the Detroit Lions need to grow up, both on and off the field. We could start with a thorough discussion of franchise quarterback Matthew Stafford's throwing mechanics and how the wrong NFC North quarterback got the "DON'T CAAAAAARE" meme attached to him. Continue to the troubling number of game-management situations that Jim Schwartz bungled last year; challenging a play that was already getting reviewed to ensure a Houston Texans touchdown may have made him the only coach to join the Ron Rivera stratosphere of ineptitude. Raise the temperature a bit by bringing up the latest police blotter—for which the team has held no one but Aaron Berry accountable—and declare Detroit the official sponsor of Pro Football Talk's "Days Without an Arrest" counter. Then we would come in on a gentle descent with the predilection defensive tackles Nick Fairley and Ndamukong Suh have for committing unnecessary penalties and taking "That's my purse! I don't know you!" nut shots at opposing quarterbacks.

We're not going to write that essay. For one thing, we figure that essay will get written a lot this offseason. But, more importantly, there's no empirical evidence that those issues explain why the Lions crashed and burned last season. Stafford, for example, had a highly successful year. 1,148 DYAR (seventh among all quarterbacks) and an 11.9% DVOA (12th) were not transcendent totals, but these numbers were respectable given the fact that every non-Calvin Johnson receiver got hurt, played poorly, or went AWOL. Schwartz has made some highly divisive coaching decisions that have probably hurt the team, but viewed through the perspective of pure game theory, there isn't a single coach who is perfect in this area in any season. Putting Jim Harbaugh or Bill Belichick in charge of the Lions wasn't going to change the fundamental flaws

this team had last season, though it may have won a game or two on craftier decision-making. Off-field and penalty issues do matter, to an extent, but defensive penalties don't actually correlate with playing bad defense. Moreover, after the Matt Millen Era, we're guessing most Detroit fans do not care how saintly their team is off the field if they aren't winning on it.

In actuality, the root problem for the Lions is that they are one of the last victims of the winner's curse in the NFL Draft. To cut through an economic theory succinctly in plain English: the top ten picks in the NFL Draft used to get exorbitant salaries that were in line with the best players at their positions despite the rookies not having proven their worth yet. The fact that these contracts were so out of line made them very hard to re-negotiate and effectively locked teams into paying franchise money for players who may or may not have been saviors—or taking enormous cap hits to get rid of them. After the NFL's lockout in 2011, enormous rookie contracts were lost in a concession by the NFLPA, and a slotting system was instituted that gave players more reasonable (well, reasonable to the owners, anyway) salaries.

From 2007 to 2010, the last four years of inflated deals for top-10 picks, five teams had a top-10 pick three or more times. From 2010 to 2012, those five teams combined to go 90-149-1. The teams notched two playoff appearances—both quick first-round eliminations—and four seasons with a DVOA above 0.0%. Three of those four above-average DVOA seasons were between 0.0% and 1.1%.

The Calvin Johnson selection was the one Millen pick that proved that some sure things are so sure that even the worst general managers can't screw them up. Martin Mayhew followed that up with two other successful picks, setting the tone for the Lions to do the best job of the group (Table 1). They

Table 1: The Winner's Curse and the Cream of the Crap

Team	Top-10 picks, 2007-2010	Players	W-L 2010-2012	2013 Mean Win Projection	"Dead Money" 2013
OAK	4	JaMarcus Russell*, Darren McFadden, Darrius Heyward-Bey**, Rolando McClain**	20-28	6.4	$49.64** million
DET	3	Calvin Johnson, Matthew Stafford, Ndamukong Suh	20-28	7.4	$7.56 million
KC	3	Glenn Dorsey**, Tyson Jackson, Eric Berry	19-29	6.6	$13.85** million
STL	3	Chris Long, Sam Bradford, Jason Smith**	16-31-1	5.8	$10.4** million
JAC	3	Derrick Harvey*, Eugene Monroe, Tyson Alualu	15-33	6.1	$25.6 million

*No longer with team. ** No longer with team and counting as "Dead Money" under the salary cap this season.

Week	Opp.	Week	Opp.	Week	Opp.
			2013 Lions Schedule		
1	MIN	7	CIN	13	GB
2	at ARI	8	DAL	14	at PHI
3	at WAS	9	BYE	15	BAL (Mon.)
4	CHI	10	at CHI	16	NYG
5	at GB	11	at PIT	17	at MIN
6	at CLE	12	TB		

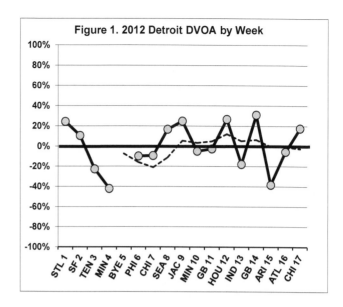

Figure 1. 2012 Detroit DVOA by Week

had the best DVOA season (2011) and one of the winning records. They nailed all three of their top-ten picks. They have managed the cap as best as they possibly could to avoid dead money. And they are the only one of these five teams whose 2013 mean projection is better than 7-9.

But things get a little murkier when you realize that for Detroit, "top-10 picks" here actually means "top 2." Johnson, Stafford, and Suh each received a top-of-the-line rookie contract. Those contracts were also negotiated against a salary cap that was continuing to rise, rather than the reduced (and now stagnant) cap introduced under threat of lockout. Most of the other players on this list that have stunk—your Tyson Jacksons and Jason Smiths—have either been released, traded, or re-structured their contracts under the threat of release. But the Lions are "stuck" with three star players with three megastar contracts and zero leverage. They've already re-structured Stafford and Suh twice, with each separate fix converting base salaries into signing bonuses. That process provides short-term cap relief in exchange for ballooning their cap numbers in later years. After getting Calvin Johnson to sign his monster eight-year, $132 million deal in the 2012 offseason, they've already begun the same process with him, re-structuring his base salary into a signing bonus this offseason in order to help pay for Reggie Bush, Glover Quin, and Jason Jones.

Eventually, there comes a time when there's no can left to kick down the road. Stafford's $20.8 million cap hit this season was going to be second only to Eli Manning's before it was lowered to roughly $17.8 million by his three-year extension as we headed to press. In 2013, Suh's cap hit is scheduled to be $21.4 million. The Lions can keep borrowing cap space from Johnson's extension with the base salary-to-signing bonus conversion trick for a while, but eventually his cap numbers will be just as untenable. If Detroit's stars were drafted

under the current NFL Draft system, their low salaries today would be an asset for the Lions in negotiations, as Detroit could give them long-term deals with large up-front bonuses that effectively spread the cap costs of the contract around. Instead, since they are working from humongous deals with gigantic cap hits, the Lions are effectively trying to play a game of Cap Hit Minesweeper with no safety net. The franchise tag that normally helps teams out in negotiations will be of no use to them in a new contract for Suh because he is already well above the franchise salary line. Rather than getting the average salary of the 10 best players at their position, he'd get 120 percent of last year's salary. That means franchising Suh in 2015 would conceivably result in a $25.65 million cap hit.

Unless the new NFL TV money raises the salary cap or they cut bait on Suh, the Lions are going to be carrying nearly 50 percent of their cap on three players for the foreseeable future. This isn't quite a 2000s Redskins situation, where the stars that eat up the money are aging and prone to collapse at any moment. It would be hard to find two more talented building blocks in the pass-happy NFL than Stafford and Johnson. But the fact that so much salary cap space is tied up in them effectively means that the Lions can't afford to rush out and fix every leaking position in free agency. More than any other team, Detroit has needed its recent cost-controlled draft picks to pan out. So far, that hasn't happened. (Table 2)

Despite slow starts to their careers due to injuries and depth

Table 2: Lions Draft Picks, 2009-2012, Rounds 1 to 3, Exempting Top Picks

Year	Round/Pick	Name	Position	Starts	Notes
2009	1 (20)	Brandon Pettigrew	TE	54	Versatile tight end, but most drop-prone receiver of the last three seasons.
2009	2 (33)	Louis Delmas	S	48	Borderline Pro Bowler on talent. Missed 13 games over past two seasons.
2009	3 (76)	DeAndre Levy	LB	49	Adequate starting linebacker.
2009	3 (82)	Derrick Williams	WR	1	Receiver with straight-line speed and that was it.
2010	1 (30)	Jahvid Best	RB	15	Career ruined by concussions.
2010	3 (66)	Amari Spievey	CB/S	26	Couldn't hack it as corner, concussion problems put career in jeopardy.
2011	2 (44)	Titus Young	WR	17	Off the reservation.
2011	2 (57)	Mikel LeShoure	RB	13	Injury-prone power back with no second gear.
2012	2 (54)	Ryan Broyles	WR	3	Back-to-back ACL tears, but still promise if he can stay healthy.
2012	3 (85)	Bill Bentley	CB	3	Four games last year before shoulder surgeries sent him to IR.

in front of them, Riley Reiff and Fairley look like they have the talent to be long-term fixtures at their positions who can supplement the very expensive core of this team. The problem Detroit has had is finding supplementary talent later in the first round and, especially, on what is now Day 2 of the draft. Of the players in Table 2, only DeAndre Levy and Brandon Pettigrew are guaranteed starting jobs in 2013—with ten premium picks, Detroit has drafted more players that have been released (Derrick Williams and Titus Young) or effectively retired (Jahvid Best) than actual starters. This isn't to say that the Lions have necessarily drafted poorly—only Williams was a complete zero in the NFL—but they have continually wound up with injury-prone players that have missed games. Some of that is chance, but Best had a long concussion history in college and Ryan Broyles tore his ACL in his senior year at Oklahoma. Calculated risks have played a part too.

The Lions front office has done an excellent job of taking creative fliers on younger free agents and finding players with some upside left to tap. Chris Houston, acquired from Atlanta for sixth- and seventh-round picks, is perhaps the best example of this, as he has blossomed into a quality cornerback under Schwartz's watch. Starting left guard Rob Sims, who came in a deal involving a trade of lower-round picks and a toss-in player, is another who matches this pattern. Cornerback Eric Wright rode his second chance in Detroit to an obscene contract with Tampa Bay. Stephen Tulloch is a quality linebacker that the Lions originally signed to a one-year deal after he overstayed his welcome on the open market. The signings of Bush, Quin, and Jones all fit this pattern—Quin more than the others because his experience as a corner makes him more versatile than the average safety.

The problem is that as long as Detroit is saddled up with the Stafford, Johnson, and Suh contracts, it takes a best-case scenario for their roster to contend. They've got the stars and they've proven they can field a cost-effective supporting cast, but when you get as little as they have out of three straight drafts, it leaves you praying that a lot of longshots come through. You have to hope that a camp battle between two players with a combined five NFL starts will somehow reveal a starting right tackle who can keep Stafford from being hassled. You have to hope that Jones, Israel Idonije, and Willie Young can find enough pass pressure to make losing Cliff Avril in free agency a non-factor. You have to hope that Louis Delmas, a Pro-Bowl level player at his best, can get and stay healthy. You have to hope that the pair of special teamers battling for the third linebacker spot can maintain gap discipline and hold the fort. You have to hope that between 2013 second-rounder Darius Slay and 2012 third rounder Bill Bentley, you can find better cornerback play opposite Houston. And you have to hope that Broyles can stay healthy enough to give them a second quality receiver next to Johnson.

We're predicting Detroit to be just about the same team this year as they were last year. Before you go running for the suicide booths, keep in mind that our advanced metrics rated them as a much better team than their 4-12 record would indicate. They ranked 16th in DVOA, with 7.6 estimated wins and 6.4 Pythagorean wins. But if they want to be better than that, if they want to overcome one of the league's tougher projected schedules and actually compete for a playoff spot, they will have to fix a lot of the issues mentioned in the previous paragraph. And that's hoping for a lot of hopes to become reality.

And so, the winner's curse will continue to take its toll. Until those cap hits can be reined in or their drafts improve significantly, Detroit's playoff chances will be tied not to Johnson or Stafford, and not even to Bush or Quin, but to replacement-level players such as Corey Hilliard and Ashlee Palmer.

Rivers McCown

2012 Lions Stats by Week

Wk	vs.	W-L	PF	PA	YDF	YDA	TO	Total	Off	Def	ST
1	STL	W	27	23	429	250	-3	24%	6%	-12%	7%
2	at SF	L	19	27	296	349	0	11%	17%	15%	8%
3	at TEN	L	41	44	583	437	1	-23%	42%	27%	-38%
4	MIN	L	13	20	341	227	-1	-42%	-10%	-4%	-37%
5	BYE										
6	at PHI	W	26	23	449	357	2	-10%	-5%	6%	1%
7	at CHI	L	7	13	340	296	-4	-10%	-5%	-4%	-8%
8	SEA	W	28	24	415	369	1	17%	34%	16%	-2%
9	at JAC	W	31	14	434	279	2	25%	52%	23%	-5%
10	at MIN	L	24	34	368	403	-2	-5%	2%	11%	4%
11	GB	L	20	24	362	314	-3	-3%	-24%	-16%	5%
12	HOU	L	31	34	525	501	0	27%	38%	6%	-5%
13	IND	L	33	35	451	459	2	-18%	-12%	12%	6%
14	at GB	L	20	27	386	288	-1	31%	26%	-10%	-5%
15	at ARI	L	10	38	312	196	-3	-38%	-20%	9%	-9%
16	ATL	L	18	31	522	344	-3	-6%	26%	27%	-5%
17	CHI	L	24	26	327	389	-4	18%	23%	6%	1%

Trends and Splits

	Offense	Rank	Defense	Rank
Total DVOA	12.3%	8	7.1%	24
Unadjusted VOA	5.8%	11	7.8%	24
Weighted Trend	10.4%	9	6.7%	24
Variance	5.5%	11	1.8%	1
Average Opponent	-5.5%	2	-1.8%	20
Passing	24.8%	8	12.0%	21
Rushing	0.3%	12	0.9%	26
First Down	5.3%	10	-6.9%	10
Second Down	17.9%	5	11.0%	24
Third Down	17.8%	7	30.7%	30
First Half	-3.7%	19	5.8%	26
Second Half	28.3%	2	8.2%	23
Red Zone	-0.2%	15	2.8%	17
Late and Close	9.9%	9	6.1%	26

Five-Year Performance

Year	W-L	Pyth W	Est W	PF	PA	TO	Total	Rk	Off	Rk	Def	Rk	ST	Rk	Off AGL	Rk	Def AGL	Rk	Off Age	Rk	Def Age	Rk	ST Age	Rk
2008	0-16	2.5	2.1	268	517	-9	-48.4%	32	-25.3%	30	24.3%	32	1.3%	15	44.3	27	60.7	32	27.8	13	27.7	11	27.0	6
2009	2-14	2.7	0.0	262	494	-18	-51.6%	32	-28.4%	31	17.9%	32	-5.3%	31	20.4	14	55.1	31	27.2	16	26.9	21	26.7	14
2010	6-10	7.8	7.5	362	369	+4	-1.1%	18	-0.8%	19	2.9%	22	2.6%	11	26.6	16	24.4	17	27.7	12	26.1	26	27.2	5
2011	10-6	10.1	9.4	474	387	+11	10.1%	11	7.1%	10	-8.1%	9	-5.1%	29	13.3	4	14.8	8	27.9	7	26.0	28	27.5	1
2012	4-12	6.4	7.6	372	437	-16	0.1%	16	12.3%	8	7.1%	24	-5.1%	30	23.2	11	58.3	31	28.3	4	26.7	17	27.8	1

2012 Performance Based on Most Common Personnel Groups

DET Offense					DET Offense vs. Opponents				DET Defense				DET Defense vs. Opponents			
Pers	Freq	Yds	DVOA	Run%	Pers	Freq	Yds	DVOA	Pers	Freq	Yds	DVOA	Pers	Freq	Yds	DVOA
11	39%	6.1	22.7%	31%	Nickel Even	57%	5.5	12.2%	4-3-4	46%	5.4	-3.4%	11	44%	6.0	19.3%
611	9%	5.1	-1.3%	61%	4-3-4	18%	5.7	2.1%	Nickel Even	43%	5.9	17.8%	12	21%	5.7	5.3%
02	3%	6.4	40.4%	3%	Dime+	12%	8.9	105.1%	Dime+	3%	7.6	-40.3%	21	15%	4.5	-19.1%
610	3%	5.4	2.7%	79%	3-4-4	7%	4.0	-9.6%	Nickel Odd	3%	8.8	66.3%	22	6%	6.8	29.0%
21	1%	3.3	-58.6%	56%	Nickel Odd	6%	4.8	-20.5%	Goal Line	2%	1.4	32.1%	10	4%	9.4	98.0%

Strategic Tendencies

Run/Pass		Rk	Formation		Rk	Pass Rush		Rk	Secondary		Rk	Strategy		Rk
Runs, first half	37%	21	Form: Single Back	80%	2	Rush 3	3.7%	26	4 DB	46%	12	Play action	16%	28
Runs, first down	44%	27	Form: Empty Back	14%	3	Rush 4	75.0%	5	5 DB	46%	20	Avg Box (Off)	6.01	31
Runs, second-long	22%	30	Pers: 3+ WR	47%	24	Rush 5	13.6%	30	6+ DB	3%	20	Avg Box (Def)	6.48	8
Runs, power sit.	40%	30	Pers: 4+ WR	1%	20	Rush 6+	7.7%	12	CB by Sides	76%	15	Offensive Pace	29.70	11
Runs, behind 2H	23%	29	Pers: 2+ TE/6+ OL	58%	2	Sacks by LB	3.0%	31	DB Blitz	10%	18	Defensive Pace	30.03	14
Pass, ahead 2H	55%	2	Shotgun/Pistol	71%	1	Sacks by DB	3.0%	23	Hole in Zone	12%	6	Go for it on 4th	0.65	31

Detroit had terrible fumble luck in 2012, recovering just four of 17 fumbles on offense and just five of 16 fumbles on defense. ⬤ Detroit's offense ranked just 19th in DVOA before halftime, but was second after halftime and first in the fourth quarter. ⬤ The Lions used a pistol formation roughly twice per game. It was *not* successful, with just 3.8 yards per play and -31.8% DVOA. ⬤ Only 6.2 percent of carries by Lions running backs came with two backs in the formation, which is good because they were horrible running the ball with two backs in the game: just -48.6% DVOA and 2.6 yards per carry. ⬤ The Lions pass rush gets anxious. Detroit led the league with 25 penalties for offsides, encroachment, or neutral zone infraction after finishing second with 24 such penalties in 2011. ⬤ Detroit's defense had -13.8% DVOA on passes thrown behind the line of scrimmage (seventh in the NFL) but 50.8% DVOA on passes thrown beyond the line of scrimmage (25th).

Passing

Player	DYAR	DVOA	Plays	NtYds	Avg	YAC	C%	TD	Int
M.Stafford	1160	12.2%	753	4766	6.3	4.7	60.2%	20	17
S.Hill	128	136.4%	12	172	14.3	4.7	83.3%	2	0

Rushing

Player	DYAR	DVOA	Plays	Yds	Avg	TD	Fum	Suc
M.Leshoure	63	-1.6%	215	798	3.7	9	3	47%
J.Bell	71	12.6%	82	414	5.0	3	1	54%
K.Smith*	6	-4.4%	37	134	3.6	1	0	41%
M.Stafford	23	0.9%	30	128	4.3	4	2	-
N.Burleson	29	48.0%	8	48	6.0	0	0	-
R.Bush	3	-8.3%	227	988	4.4	6	4	51%
M.Owens	41	14.5%	42	209	5.0	1	0	52%

Receiving

Player	DYAR	DVOA	Plays	Ctch	Yds	Y/C	YAC	TD	C%
C.Johnson	488	16.0%	203	122	1964	16.1	4.1	5	60%
T.Young*	50	2.3%	56	33	383	11.6	2.4	4	59%
N.Burleson	-24	-14.0%	43	27	240	8.9	3.1	2	63%
R.Broyles	140	38.7%	32	22	310	14.1	6.9	2	69%
K.Durham	6	-15.2%	21	8	125	15.6	3.1	1	38%
M.Thomas	-19	-44.1%	13	5	28	5.6	3.0	1	38%
B.Robiskie	35	47.8%	6	4	44	11.0	2.0	1	67%
M.Spurlock	45	6.8%	29	23	200	8.7	2.8	1	79%
M.Willis	-44	-42.6%	22	10	90	9.0	2.8	0	45%
B.Pettigrew	-123	-25.3%	102	59	570	9.7	4.0	3	58%
T.Scheffler	-33	-16.2%	85	42	504	12.0	2.8	1	49%
W.Heller*	27	3.8%	23	17	150	8.8	4.9	1	74%
J.Bell	193	32.8%	69	52	485	9.3	8.3	0	75%
M.Leshoure	10	-10.2%	48	34	217	6.4	6.8	0	71%
K.Smith*	27	17.0%	16	10	79	7.9	10.0	1	63%
S.Logan*	7	1.7%	7	6	28	4.7	4.3	0	86%
R.Bush	54	7.9%	51	35	292	8.3	7.8	2	69%
M.Owens	43	62.6%	10	8	113	14.1	12.8	0	80%

Offensive Line

Player	Pos	Age	GS	Snaps	Pen	Sk	Pass	Run	Player	Pos	Age	GS	Snaps	Pen	Sk	Pass	Run
Gosder Cherilus*	RT	29	16/16	1200	9	1.5	18.5	5	Jeff Backus*	LT	36	15/15	1065	6	1	19	7
Stephen Peterman*	RG	31	16/16	1200	4	6	20.5	2	Riley Reiff	OT	25	16/8	325	5	0.5	5.5	4.5
Dominic Raiola	C	35	16/16	1200	2	1.5	5	5	Jake Scott	G	32	7/7	461	7	1.5	7	1
Rob Sims	LG	30	16/16	1200	5	0.5	5.5	6.5	Leroy Harris	G	29	8/8	434	2	5	9	2

Year	Yards	ALY	Rk	Power	Rk	Stuff	Rk	2nd Lev	Rk	Open Field	Rk	Sacks	ASR	Rk	Short	Long	F-Start	Cont.
2010	3.46	3.35	32	56%	21	23%	28	1.04	26	0.43	30	27	4.3%	4	10	10	22	42
2011	4.22	3.70	31	52%	28	21%	24	1.13	21	0.89	14	36	5.8%	11	11	19	19	43
2012	4.01	4.05	15	56%	27	17%	5	1.10	20	0.49	27	29	3.7%	1	5	18	19	39
2012 ALY by direction:			Left End 3.01 (30)			Left Tackle 3.84 (22)			Mid/Guard 4.36 (7)			Right Tackle 3.57 (25)			Right End 5.01 (8)			

Losing three starters from last year's offensive line is rarely a good thing, but if it has to happen, you'd prefer it to be three starters who were fairly unimpressive. The Lions lucked out in that regard. Recent retiree Jeff Backus has been an institution in Detroit, blocking for everyone from Mike McMahon to Jon Kitna to Daunte Culpepper. That's probably not the eulogy anyone would want for his football career, but at least Backus saw out a six-year, $40 million deal with the Lions despite never being a difference maker. Mediocrity still made him markedly better than new Colts signing Gosder Cherilus, who up until last year made it a habit to get himself benched for poor play at least once a season. Cherilus and Backus both finished in the top 15 in blown blocks leading to sacks in 2011; though they allowed fewer sacks in 2012, they still allowed plenty of pressures. Luckily, Stephen Peterman was around to make them feel better about themselves with his six blown blocks leading to sacks (second among guards to Uche Nwaneri) and 20.5 total blown blocks on passes (second among guards to Mike McGlynn).

The returning starters are powerful drive-blocking guard Rob Sims and ancient center Dominic Raiola, who was drafted with Backus in 2001 and took a pay cut to stay on the roster. 2012 first-round tackle Riley Reiff will likely man the left side. Reiff spent most of last season as an overqualified fullback and sixth lineman, but despite the first-round status and obvious athleticism, there are questions about how well he'll stick at left tackle. He's got short arms and his punch was lacking at Iowa. At the other tackle spot, we've got a camp battle brewing between 2007 sixth-rounder Corey Hilliard (six career starts, all in 2011) and 2010 fourth-rounder Jason Fox (zero career starts, five career games played). If we had Camp Battle Similarity Scores, we're 99 percent sure the most similar recent camp battle it would spit out here would be Jason Hill versus Jarrett Dillard for the 2011 Jaguars No. 2 wideout job.

Third-round rookie Larry Warford (Kentucky) is the heavy favorite to take over Peterman's right guard spot. Warford is very powerful, but he has had issues keeping his weight down and isn't a guy you want to run any pulls behind. Titans retreads Leroy Harris and Jake Scott are the most notable backups inside. We use the word retread almost literally here, because we can't tell if the tread marks on the back of their jerseys came from defenders that bowled them over or Chris Johnson throwing them under the bus.

Defensive Front Seven

Defensive Line	Age	Pos	Snaps	Plays	Overall TmPct	Rk	Stop	Dfts	BTkl	Runs	vs. Run St%	Rk	RuYd	Rk	Pass Rush Sack	Hit	Hur	Tips
Ndamukong Suh	26	DT	878	34	4.3%	30	30	20	1	22	82%	16	1.1	4	8	22	27.5	2
Cliff Avril*	27	DE	684	35	4.5%	50	28	15	1	20	70%	52	1.7	11	9.5	7	13.5	1
Kyle Vanden Bosch	35	DE	641	35	4.5%	50	23	13	2	26	65%	66	2.7	47	3.5	10	9	0
Nick Fairley	25	DT	493	35	5.5%	19	29	16	2	24	79%	24	1.0	3	5.5	7	7.5	1
Sammie Lee Hill*	27	DT	402	18	2.4%	--	15	4	2	14	86%	--	1.4	--	0	1	7	2
Lawrence Jackson*	28	DE	384	19	2.6%	--	15	7	0	14	79%	--	1.4	--	2.5	2	7.5	0
Israel Idonije	33	DE	711	47	5.7%	32	40	19	2	36	81%	16	2.2	22	7.5	2	19	0
C.J. Mosley	30	DT	618	45	5.1%	26	32	6	0	38	74%	35	2.3	41	2.5	6	5	0

Linebackers	Age	Pos	Snaps	Plays	Overall TmPct	Rk	Stop	Dfts	BTkl	Pass Rush Sack	Hit	Hur	Tips	Runs	vs. Run St%	Rk	Yds	Rk	vs. Pass Tgts	Suc%	Rk	AdjYd	Rk	PD
Stephen Tulloch	28	MLB	1021	118	15.0%	24	68	21	9	0.5	6	7.5	0	68	57%	93	3.6	65	47	59%	17	4.7	10	4
Justin Durant*	28	OLB	849	103	13.1%	41	57	22	7	0.5	1	1.5	1	57	70%	34	2.8	29	40	50%	41	6.8	34	1
DeAndre Levy	26	OLB	697	84	12.2%	50	44	22	7	0	0	5	0	48	58%	88	3.1	40	25	51%	37	7.1	50	3

Year	Yards	ALY	Rk	Power	Rk	Stuff	Rk	2nd Level	Rk	Open Field	Rk	Sacks	ASR	Rk	Short	Long
2010	4.44	4.07	17	56%	7	20%	13	1.25	26	0.93	23	44	7.7%	6	14	19
2011	4.60	3.99	14	52%	5	21%	11	1.23	19	1.16	28	41	6.4%	21	16	16
2012	4.30	3.69	5	72%	28	26%	2	1.33	29	1.03	27	34	5.2%	29	5	20
2012 ALY by direction:			Left End 3.85 (12)			Left Tackle 2.9 (1)			Mid/Guard 3.53 (5)			Right Tackle 4.36 (28)			Right End 4.4 (19)

How did general manager Martin Mayhew rebuild the defensive end position after losing Cliff Avril, Kyle Vanden Bosch, and Lawrence Jackson this offseason? The answer is arms: specifically, long ones. "We talked about that with our coaching staff and spoke at length with some of our guys about those guys being able to make more plays," Mayhew said after defensive coordinator Gunther Cunningham commissioned a study that found correlations between arm length and sacks. SackSEER doesn't really incorporate those elements—unless you consider passes defensed a function of arm length—but it likes both of Detroit's rookie ends. Ezekiel Ansah finished with the second-highest SackSEER projection of the class, and though he's as raw as you would expect from someone who has only been playing football since 2010, players with his combination of speed and power don't come along very often. Ansah's high SackSEER projection is driven by his combine performance, which gives him a very high explosion index, and the fact that he had nine passes defensed in 2012, more than all of BYU's defensive backs except one. South Carolina end Devin Taylor, a fourth-round pick, had as many passes defensed as sacks and was one of SackSEER's lower-round sleepers. It's possible that his college sack rate was boosted because SEC offensive coordinators were so busy worrying about the teammate on the other side, Jadeveon something-or-other. Tackle-end swingman Jason Jones, who is gifted with a quick first step and could be an interesting projection as a Wide-9 rusher, will probably open the season as a starter. If Ansah needs more than a single camp to get ready, backup and lonely incumbent Willie Young has produced some very intriguing hurry rates in spite of his shorter arms and would finally get a shot to start outside. The Lions probably wish 2012 SackSEER sleeper Ronnell Lewis had kept sleeping through the offseason rather than drawing an arrest for disturbing the peace and public intoxication. The Lions also added Israel Idonije as we ran up against our publication deadline. It was a bit puzzling that he was still unsigned in the middle of June, as he can penetrate and hold his ground in the run game well, but we'll chalk it up to the bias against older players.

Detroit is blessed at defensive tackle. Among interior NFL defenders, only J.J. Watt is clearly more talented than Ndamukong Suh, who finished seventh in hurries and fourth in quarterback hits. This time last year, Nick Fairley had as many NFL arrests (two) as defensive tackles in front of him on the depth chart (the departed Sammie Lee Hill and Corey Williams). Fairley's predilection to getting nicked up and missing games is troublesome, but the talent clearly shone through as he started seven games in his second season. We do expect some regression in his sack total, as 5.5 sacks is a lot for a guy with just 7.5 hurries. C.J. Mosley is an effective backup who had some impressive games with the Jaguars.

We all know that the NFL Network's Top 100 Players list is a joke, but usually if you squint and accept that popularity and recent playoff success factor into it, you can see why a player makes the list. Neither of those things applied to this year's No. 63 player, linebacker Stephen Tulloch. Admittedly he has had better seasons than 2012, but last year he was dreadful in the run game—there were times where he would flat-out disappear at the goal line. The Lions desperately need him to turn back the clock, because the rest of this corps isn't any better. DeAndre Levy has nice instincts in zone coverage, but he's a step slower than you'd like a nickel linebacker to be and is only steady in the run game. The competition for the third linebacker spot appears to be between 2012 fifth-rounder Tahir Whitehead and veteran backup Ashlee Palmer, both of whom spent much more time playing on special teams than defense last year. "I had trouble with my alignments and stuff last year," said Whitehead. "This year, I just plan on learning the defense a lot more than I did last year." Perhaps by year three he'll have progressed to learning the whole thing.

Defensive Secondary

Secondary	Age	Pos	Snaps	Plays	Overall TmPct	Rk	Stop	Dfts	BTkl	vs. Run Runs	St%	Rk	Yds	Rk	vs. Pass Tgts	Tgt%	Rk	Dist	Suc%	Rk	APaYd	Rk	PD	Int
Chris Houston	29	CB	897	66	9.6%	21	32	13	3	9	78%	4	2.1	2	79	21.6%	10	14.8	54%	33	7.4	39	8	2
Jacob Lacey*	26	CB	573	39	7.2%	62	18	9	4	9	33%	60	7.4	55	35	12.3%	78	9.5	46%	73	9.8	84	4	1
Erik Coleman	31	SS	460	48	8.2%	50	16	3	4	25	32%	51	6.5	31	20	6.4%	41	17.0	49%	59	11.6	74	2	1
Louis Delmas	26	FS	434	40	10.2%	--	13	6	4	20	40%	--	5.2	--	8	3.9%	--	22.9	89%	--	0.7	--	2	1
Patrick Lee*	29	CB	428	35	4.8%	--	15	5	5	7	29%	--	8.0	--	21	5.2%	--	15.0	52%	--	7.5	--	4	1
Ron Bartell	31	CB	412	32	9.4%	--	10	5	1	8	38%	--	10.1	--	33	19.8%	--	16.8	43%	--	9.6	--	5	0
Ricardo Silva	25	SS	412	40	8.2%	--	10	3	3	19	21%	--	9.3	--	9	3.5%	--	13.8	71%	--	7.0	--	3	1
Jonte Green	24	CB	396	33	4.5%	--	13	7	2	8	25%	--	9.1	--	31	7.8%	--	11.3	36%	--	9.6	--	4	1
Don Carey	26	FS	357	32	7.2%	--	15	8	1	16	38%	--	5.3	--	15	6.2%	--	18.0	77%	--	4.6	--	5	2
Drayton Florence*	33	CB	301	26	6.6%	--	13	7	7	8	38%	--	9.0	--	29	14.0%	--	13.7	57%	--	8.9	--	7	1
Amari Spievey	25	SS	189	18	7.3%	--	5	1	0	11	36%	--	10.9	--	7	5.4%	--	7.0	63%	--	2.9	--	1	0
John Wendling	30	SS	167	19	2.4%	--	4	2	1	9	22%	--	8.2	--	3	0.6%	--	17.4	1%	--	20.1	--	0	0
Bill Bentley	24	CB	164	15	7.6%	--	3	1	3	3	33%	--	9.7	--	20	19.3%	--	10.6	27%	--	11.2	--	0	0
Glover Quin	27	SS	1027	97	12.2%	20	43	22	6	46	41%	25	6.5	29	60	12.4%	3	9.9	55%	32	5.5	12	12	2
Chris Hope	33	SS	258	16	2.0%	--	4	0	4	9	22%	--	7.2	--	6	1.4%	--	9.8	32%	--	7.9	--	0	0

Year	Pass D Rank	vs. #1 WR	Rk	vs. #2 WR	Rk	vs. Other WR	Rk	vs. TE	Rk	vs. RB	Rk
2010	19	15.4%	26	-23.4%	2	10.8%	25	23.6%	29	6.9%	20
2011	4	-18.3%	3	-18.5%	5	-4.8%	16	1.1%	9	-12.9%	8
2012	21	-5.1%	13	24.6%	31	2.0%	20	14.3%	26	-37.1%	2

"It's tough to play corner [in the NFL]," head coach Jim Schwartz told the team's official website. "I think it's probably the most difficult thing to do in all of sports." After dealing with four years of Lions cornerbacks, it's hard to fault Schwartz for that line of thinking. Chris Houston's game-charting statistics outstrip his public reputation, and it's not a one-year fluke; he was 18th in Adjusted Success Rate and 31st in Adjusted Yards per Pass in 2011. Although he's hardly an elite physical specimen, it was nice of Detroit to finally sink real money into keeping a cornerback. The other spots are less settled now that Jacob Lacey has been set adrift. 2013 second-round pick Darius Slay and 2012 third-round pick Bill Bentley figure to be involved prominently. Bentley is coming off surgeries on both shoulders, and Slay tore his meniscus in the pre-draft process, so Ronald Bartell will also have a shot to play as the in-house veteran depth. The ideal alignment probably sees Slay outside, Bentley inside, and both healthy. But as you can see by how many players we had to squeeze into the above table, nothing ideal ever happens to Detroit cornerbacks.

The Lions filled a long-time hole at safety by bringing Glover Quin over from the Houston Texans. Quin was the third-most targeted safety in the NFL last year. (Only Eric Berry and Devin McCourty—who had snaps as a cornerback too—were listed in coverage more often by our game charters.) Despite a mediocre Success Rate, Quin was very good near the line and finished 11th in Adjusted Yards per Pass among safeties; he had the lowest Adjusted Yards per Pass of any safety targeted on at least 10 percent of his defense's passes. The plan is for Quin to start next to the re-signed Louis Delmas, who spent last year hurt and clearly tried to play through it when he got back on the field. Knee tendonitis continued to keep him out through OTAs, so that plan may not come to fruition. 2010 third-rounder Amari Spievey is next man up, but has lost most of the last two seasons to concussions and is no safer bet than Delmas to return to the field. Fourth in the pecking order is Don Carey, a founding member of The Original AFC South Kings of Safety Comedy along with C.C. Brown, Aaron Francisco, and Michael Griffin. The Lions also signed veteran Chris Hope, who would have been a great answer for Detroit in 2008. It's not 2008.

Special Teams

Year	DVOA	Rank	FG/XP	Rank	Net Kick	Rank	Kick Ret	Rank	Net Punt	Rank	Punt Ret	Rank	Hidden	Rank
2010	2.6%	11	6.4	5	-1.4	18	10.9	7	-6.8	26	3.7	10	-13.3	29
2011	-5.1%	29	-2.5	21	-8.8	30	-0.6	18	-6.8	26	-7.1	26	-8.6	27
2012	-5.1%	30	4.5	9	-9.4	30	-4.8	24	-9.1	25	-6.9	29	0.2	16

Lions special teams were below average in every area except field goals and extra points, but that's OK because Jason Hanson is the modern-day Gary Anderson and will play until he's 59.

Wait, he won't? Uh-oh. Two kickers will compete for the right to replace Hanson. The first is David Akers, who has had a sparkling career but spent last year living through one of the worst field-goal kicking seasons in over 20 years of Football Outsiders stats. (The San Francisco chapter gives you the sad, sad details.) Akers will engage in a kicker battle royale with undrafted Norwegian Havard "Kickalicious" Rugland, who parlayed a YouTube video of trick shots and 60-yard field goals into a tryout with the Lions. Akers blames his poor season on inflammation from his double hernia surgery prior to camp in 2012, but if we're going to be treated to another comedy of missed kicks, sign us up for wanting them to come from someone named Kickalicious.

Return specialist Stefan Logan and punter Nick Harris were also let go after the season. The Lions spent a fifth-rounder on their likely new punter, Sam "A Pimp Named Sam Martin" Martin. Detroit will mine the bottom of their depth chart for this year's return men, probably coming up with some combination of Micheal Spurlock, Patrick Edwards, and Mike Thomas.

Coaching Staff

Most readers know that Jim Schwartz has been a supporter of Football Outsiders since the very beginning ten years ago. There's no question that the rebuilding project he had to take on was unprecedented in this day and age. But we have to be honest: Very few NFL head coaches have stayed employed following a .344 winning percentage over four seasons, and the ones who kept their jobs typically needed to make season five a winner to stay on board. Another possible alternative is to have a special Gary Kubiak mask made. And Coach, we're begging you, for the sake of our sanity and your continued NFL employment, please please *please* be more aggressive on fourth downs. If you're going to draft a guy like Larry Warford, pound the damn rock on fourth-and-1.

Defensive coordinator Gunther Cunningham is a deep well of excellent quotes and fits in well with Schwartz's general philosophy. The last two seasons represent the first time Scott Linehan has coordinated back-to-back top 10 DVOA offenses since the 2003-2004 Vikings, which is a kind way of saying that he has a lot of experience working with bad teams.

Green Bay Packers

2012 Record: 11-5	**Total DVOA:** 26.3% (5th)	**2013 Mean Projection:** 10.4 wins	**On the Clock (0-4):** 1%
Pythagorean Wins: 10.5 (7th)	**Offense:** 19.5% (3rd)	**Postseason Odds:** 77.4%	**Mediocrity (5-7):** 8%
Snap-Weighted Age: 26.2 (25th)	**Defense:** -7.0% (8th)	**Super Bowl Odds:** 20.7%	**Playoff Contender (8-10):** 39%
Average Opponent: 2.2% (9th)	**Special Teams:** -0.2% (18th)	**Proj. Avg. Opponent:** 0.6% (16th)	**Super Bowl Contender (11+):** 52%

2012: Leading the league in Adjusted Games Lost is no problem as long as none of those lost games belong to Aaron Rodgers.

2013: They're healthy, they're dangerous, and they're now aware that the read option exists.

"Everything is amazing and nobody is happy," begins a Louis C.K. monologue on the dangers of taking things for granted. The spiel ends with humanity whining about the mundane act of human flight, even though it only started to become possible within the last 100 years, but it also could apply to the media reality for a successful team that dares to not win a championship every other year. The Packers are not quite at the New England stage of the success cycle, where everything from an unexpected loss to an ill-timed nor'easter to signing Tim Tebow can signal the phrase "the day the dynasty ended." Instead offseason talking points for the Packers have been focused on either vague and circumstantial criticism or the dreadful performance that the defense displayed in a 45-31 thumping by the 49ers in the divisional round. The underlying premise, as always, is the cottage industry that says something is wrong with 31 of the 32 franchises by the time February rolls around. And whoever won the Super Bowl probably has some holes they could fill too.

Let's settle a little reality in to the proceedings. The Packers have finished in the top five in DVOA for four consecutive seasons. The list of teams that have done that in the DVOA era (1991-present) includes the dynasty Cowboys (1992-1996), the dynasty 49ers (1991-1998), another recent Packers squad that readers may be familiar with (1994-1997), and the current Patriots (2009-2012). That's it. Green Bay's expertly-managed front office just doled out reasonable long-term extensions to the team's two best players, Aaron Rodgers and Clay Matthews. The underlying waves of young talent that Ted Thompson and company bring in each offseason have allowed the team to replace Nick Collins with Morgan Burnett and Al Harris with Tramon Williams, and the development of Randall Cobb and Casey Hayward allowed the Packers to

replace Greg Jennings and Charles Woodson this offseason without any fuss at all. The Vikings aren't sure if Christian Ponder is an answer at quarterback, the Bears are trying to find the right selection of receivers around Brandon Marshall to make Jay Cutler successful, and the Lions are trying to rebuild an entire defense and offensive line on the fly. The Packers are dealing with problems like "Should we lock up B.J. Raji to a long-term deal? He's kind of up-and-down," "Nick Perry needs to heal up so we can have a second difference-making pass rusher," and "We sure hope that offensive line gels and stays healthy so Rodgers can be uber-productive instead of just excellent." It's good to be the king.

Speaking of staying healthy, a big reason that we are so high on Green Bay this season is that they were, by far, the most-injured team in our Adjusted Games Lost (AGL) database last year. They became only the sixth team ever to conjure up more than 100 AGL in a season (Table 1).

While there was no great upward trend in this specific sample of teams—something your author blames on small sample size theatre and Matt Millen—they all showed a marked improvement in health next season. The fact is, teams that tend to be that unhealthy tend to be really bad. They tend to bring in new coaches and front offices, and those new coaches and front offices usually gut the roster of injured players and succeed or fail on their own merits. That's not the case with the current Green Bay Packers, which is an incredible demonstration of how deep this team has been built. Going back to 2002, every other team that finished dead last in AGL posted a negative DVOA, and usually it wasn't even close to league-average (Table 2).

Injuries don't make for a sexy narrative, though. There's no humanity in them. They are often accused of being excuses rather than explanations. It's much easier to worry aloud if

Table 1: Teams with 100-plus AGL in a Season

Year	Team	DVOA	AGL	DVOA Y+1	AGL Y+1
2008	CIN	-20.7%	107.8	-0.1%	70.6
2008	DET	-48.4%	104.2	-51.6%	75.5
2009	BUF	-10.4%	122.8	-21.3%	47.7
2011	CAR	-4.1%	109.2	5.5%	76.1
2011	STL	-35.4%	110.0	1.1%	36.2
2012	GB	26.6%	108.1	??	??
Average		**-15.4%**	**110.6**	**-13.2%**	**61.2**

Table 2: Most-Injured Teams, Year by Year, 2002-2012

Year	Team	AGL	DVOA	Year	Team	AGL	DVOA
2002	CHI	67.7	-12.5%	2008	CIN	107.8	-20.7%
2003	OAK	91.5	-16.7%	2009	BUF	122.8	-10.4%
2004	TEN	88.4	-17.6%	2010	CLE	94.7	-4.0%
2005	NYJ	74.1	-20.9%	2011	STL	110.0	-35.4%
2006	CLE	98.0	-16.1%	2012	GB	108.1	26.6%
2007	STL	79.3	-35.5%				

2013 Packers Schedule

Week	Opp.	Week	Opp.	Week	Opp.
1	at SF	7	CLE	13	at DET (Thu.)
2	WAS	8	at MIN	14	ATL
3	at CIN	9	CHI (Mon.)	15	at DAL
4	BYE	10	PHI	16	PIT
5	DET	11	at NYG	17	at CHI
6	at BAL	12	MIN		

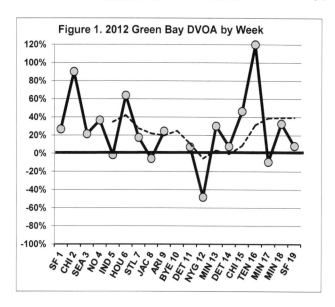

Figure 1. 2012 Green Bay DVOA by Week

Dom Capers' scheme is just poor at stopping the read option than to point out that Green Bay's linebacker corps was playing reserves and severely banged-up starters. With an AGL of 40.1, the Packers had more Adjusted Games Lost at linebacker than seven teams had on all units *combined*; postseason starters Brad Jones and Erik Walden were backups forced into the lineup due to injury, while Matthews was dealing with hamstring problems down the stretch. Capers hardly had all the answers in that game—in fact, recent reports noted that he barely prepared for the read option *at all*—but along with Dick LeBeau and Wade Phillips he's probably one of the three best defensive coordinators in the modern history of the NFL. He's successfully shifted his scheme from the grind-it-out '90s to the modern spread attacks of today; he probably knows a thing or two about making adjustments. "'Ugh … it won't…,'" Louis C.K. mimes a spoiled person with a smartphone that isn't automatically loading. *"Give it a second! It's going to space!"*

Another manufactured "problem" storyline for the Packers this offseason was a lack of toughness. "…Some people close to Mike McCarthy and Ted Thompson say the Green Bay Packers' football leaders have freely acknowledged the perception [that the team is soft and small] in private over the past three months, and now are bound and determined to do something about it," wrote the excellent Bob McGinn of the *Milwaukee Journal-Sentinel* in advance of the draft. McGinn went on to cite the signing of blocking tight end Matthew Mulligan and the re-instatement of the hulking Johnny Jolly as reasons the Packers are taking toughness seriously.

And maybe they are, to a certain point, paying more attention to getting bigger in situational packages in order to become a more diverse offense. But the identity of this team is locked in. To the extent that Rodgers, Cobb, Jordy Nelson, and Jermichael Finley combine for an aerial display that's inferred to be finesse, well, a lot of teams would kill to be that finesse. Matthews, Raji, Burnett, and Hayward are the leaders of a "soft" unit that finished with the second-lowest broken tackle rate in the NFL despite often playing with just two defensive linemen. How about other forms of toughness? Want to second-guess the Packers' mental toughness, as their defense finished eighth in DVOA in the face of all those injuries?

Look, there may be something to the combination of height-weight standards and injuries. The Tony Dungy Colts had a defense that tied higher AGLs to tinier players that fit their Cover-2 scheme, for instance. Every year from 2004 to 2010, the Colts had more Adjusted Games Lost on defense than on offense, and often the difference drastically favored the offense.

Green Bay finished 30th in AGL in 2010, to go along with last year's last-place finish. However, given that Thompson excels at finding talent on the fringes, it makes sense that a) some of that talent is going to have flaws that kept them from going high (for example, being undersized or injury-prone) and b) Thompson's ability to scrounge up good freely available talent minimizes the actual risk of bringing in players with injury concerns. That's the kind of player-acquisition style that can keep a team both infused with talent and constantly managing injuries, a tradeoff the Packers are more than willing to make.

The big change coming to Green Bay this year is an infusion of running back talent. The Packers gambled on another supposedly injury-prone player when Alabama running back Eddie Lacy, considered by many to be the only first-round talent at running back in the draft, fell to them at the bottom of the second round. Green Bay then doubled up at the position when they traded up to the fourth round and took UCLA's Johnathan Franklin, who our own Matt Waldman regarded as the third-best running back in the draft. In the three years since Ryan Grant lost the skills that made him effective, the Packers have had a very pedestrian running game with a lot of personnel turnover. The highest seasonal yardage total the Packers have had over the past three seasons was Brandon Jackson's 703 yards in 2010. Last season, Alex Green led the way with 464 yards on the ground, and Green Bay became an outpost for waiver-wire running backs like Johnny White and DuJuan Harris while Grant, Green, Cedric Benson, and James Starks all struggled with effectiveness and injury issues.

Chase Stuart, who is graciously writing a few chapters in our book this year, did a study about the fantasy football implications of drafting two backs on his own site, Football Perspective. He found that in past situations similar to this, where a team selected a back in the second or third round and another back within two rounds of the first one, there didn't tend to be much separation between the two for fantasy purposes. To look at what these selections meant for each team's rushing efficiency regardless of fantasy football numbers, we mixed Chase's study together with DVOA. How much empirical improvement can Green Bay expect to see out of their running back duo? (Table 3)

Table 3: Teams Adding Two Backs In Same Draft, 1992-2013

Year	Team	Rush DVOA Y-1	Players Added	Rush DVOA Y	Rush DVOA Y+1
1992	PHI	-23.0% (27)	Siran Stacy (2), Tony Brooks (4)	16.5% (5)	3.1% (14)
1994	GB	-1.2% (21)	LeShon Johnson (3), Dorsey Levens (5)	-4.4% (15)	-3.3% (19)
1995	GB	-4.4% (15)	William Henderson (3), Travis Jervey (5)	-3.3% (19)	6.9% (11)
1995	SD	1.9% (7)	Terrell Fletcher (2), Aaron Hayden (4)	5.3% (9)	-16.1% (27)
1996	MIA	-1.8% (16)	Karim Abdul-Jabbar (3), Jerris McPhail (5)*	-5.9% (19)	-5.6% (20)
1996	CAR	-14.3% (26)	Winslow Oliver (3), Marquette Smith (5)	-7.8% (20)	6.8% (12)
1999	NYG	7.0% (9)	Joe Montgomery (2), Sean Bennett (4)	-13.1% (26)	-3.2% (24)
2008	SD	5.0% (11)	Jacob Hester (3), Marcus Thomas (5)	-1.0% (19)	-13.3% (31)
2011	NE	24.2% (2)	Shane Vereen (2), Stevan Ridley (3)	12.6% (4)	11.9% (4)
2013	GB	-0.8% (13)	Eddie Lacy (2), Johnathan Franklin (4)	?	?
AVERAGE		**-0.1%**		**0.0%**	**-1.4%**

- The Dolphins also drafted fullback Stanley Pritchett in the fourth round, but we didn't include any combinations that relied on pure blocking fullbacks on this list. Sorry, Rob Konrad.

The only thing that is notable here is how different and unique each situation was; it's almost not surprising that the scores added up to be so incredibly average. The 1991 Eagles had a very similar statistical profile to the Packers of 2013—but then they named Randall Cunningham their starting quarterback and acquired Herschel Walker, so neither of the picks mattered. Carolina was an expansion team with no real running back situation to speak of. San Diego's 2008 appearance on the list was about trying to milk the last marrow of the LaDainian Tomlinson era. The 2011 Patriots had received stellar contributions from Danny Woodhead and BenJarvus Green-Ellis, but had no established franchise back.

The two most similar situations to the current Packers were the 1994-95 Packers and the 1996 Dolphins. Each team had an established franchise quarterback and a dearth of talent at running back, though they were both not legitimate contenders yet, like the present-day Packers are. The Dolphins entrusted the main role to Karim Abdul-Jabbar, and while he was a great goal-line pounder, nobody would ever mistake him for a franchise back. Eventually, the mid-'90s Packers dynasty found a stable of productive backs they could rely on. Edgar Bennett morphed from a third-down back and receiving threat out of the backfield to a more reliable speed runner, Dorsey Levens was better between the tackles, and after a breakout 1996 season where he finished sixth in DVOA among qualifying backs, settled in as a solid committee back. William Henderson played fullback, but was a receiving threat in his own right.

In our current version of Green Bay, Thompson is helped by the fact that running backs are not as highly thought of as they used to be. Nobody would call any of the 1990s players listed in Table 3 a top-three back in their class. Those great backs used to go in the first 20 picks, not the second round. Lacy has an injury history worthy of note. He also has a rare combination of speed, size, and football instincts that make him a difference-maker when he is on his game. He's the kind of back who could have teams that passed on him shaking their heads for years to come. And if he doesn't pan out, Franklin is a more-than-capable prospect in his own right.

With these selections, the running back situation in Green Bay is a microcosm of the team as a whole. They are supremely talented. There is risk, but it is covered with good depth. It is a series of gambles constructed on a sharply-considered strategy and game plan.

Thirty-one of 32 teams do not win a championship every year, but only a select few are perennial contenders. The Packers are working on a current run that rivals just about any stretch of success in the modern era, and our forecast system gives them the best chance to represent the NFC in Super Bowl XLVIII. "Everybody on every plane should just constantly be going *Oh my god! Wow!* You're sitting in a chair in the sky!" Packers fans, you are sitting in a chair in the sky right now.

Rivers McCown

2012 Packers Stats by Week

Wk	vs.	W-L	PF	PA	YDF	YDA	TO	Total	Off	Def	ST
1	SF	L	22	30	324	377	-1	27%	19%	10%	18%
2	CHI	W	23	10	321	168	2	90%	32%	-57%	1%
3	at SEA	L	12	14	268	238	0	22%	7%	-16%	-2%
4	NO	W	28	27	421	474	-2	37%	41%	6%	1%
5	at IND	L	27	30	356	464	0	-2%	6%	-2%	-10%
6	at HOU	W	42	24	427	321	3	64%	55%	-23%	-14%
7	at STL	W	30	20	402	354	1	18%	29%	15%	4%
8	JAC	W	24	15	238	341	0	-6%	-18%	-10%	3%
9	ARI	W	31	17	384	340	1	24%	24%	13%	13%
10	BYE										
11	at DET	W	24	20	314	362	3	7%	-13%	-36%	-15%
12	at NYG	L	10	38	317	390	-2	-48%	-28%	23%	2%
13	MIN	W	23	14	435	359	1	30%	36%	3%	-3%
14	DET	W	27	20	288	386	1	8%	4%	3%	7%
15	at CHI	W	21	13	391	190	-1	46%	35%	-37%	-26%
16	TEN	W	55	7	460	180	2	122%	52%	-55%	15%
17	at MIN	L	34	37	405	444	-1	-10%	11%	22%	2%
18	MIN	W	24	10	326	324	3	33%	18%	-16%	-2%
19	at SF	L	31	45	352	579	-1	8%	44%	34%	-2%

Trends and Splits

	Offense	Rank	Defense	Rank
Total DVOA	19.5%	3	-7.0%	8
Unadjusted VOA	15.1%	4	-4.6%	10
Weighted Trend	19.0%	4	-6.4%	11
Variance	6.0%	15	6.7%	23
Average Opponent	-3.1%	7	-0.9%	18
Passing	40.7%	3	-7.4%	7
Rushing	-0.7%	13	-6.4%	14
First Down	5.2%	11	-15.7%	3
Second Down	26.4%	1	-3.5%	12
Third Down	36.6%	2	3.8%	21
First Half	20.5%	4	-5.1%	12
Second Half	18.6%	5	-9.1%	6
Red Zone	42.5%	2	-0.8%	14
Late and Close	14.9%	6	-17.0%	4

Five-Year Performance

Year	W-L	Pyth W	Est W	PF	PA	TO	Total	Rk	Off	Rk	Def	Rk	ST	Rk	Off AGL	Rk	Def AGL	Rk	Off Age	Rk	Def Age	Rk	ST Age	Rk
2008	6-10	9.0	8.6	419	380	+7	9.2%	11	7.3%	11	-2.5%	12	-0.5%	19	12.5	6	37.2	26	27.0	23	27.2	20	25.0	32
2009	11-5	12.0	11.0	461	297	+24	29.1%	2	18.8%	5	-17.7%	2	-7.5%	32	22.4	15	25.3	16	27.1	18	27.4	14	25.3	31
2010	10-6	12.1	10.9	388	240	+10	23.0%	4	11.5%	7	-13.9%	2	-2.4%	26	40.4	28	45.9	29	27.2	19	26.5	21	25.8	26
2011	15-1	12.2	13.3	560	359	+24	27.0%	1	33.8%	1	8.6%	25	1.8%	8	21.3	11	37.5	22	26.3	26	26.7	23	25.1	32
2012	11-5	10.5	11.8	433	336	+7	26.3%	5	19.5%	3	-7.0%	8	-0.2%	18	38.7	23	62.8	32	26.9	16	25.8	27	24.9	32

2012 Performance Based on Most Common Personnel Groups

GB Offense					GB Offense vs. Opponents				GB Defense				GB Defense vs. Opponents			
Pers	Freq	Yds	DVOA	Run%	Pers	Freq	Yds	DVOA	Pers	Freq	Yds	DVOA	Pers	Freq	Yds	DVOA
11	54%	6.4	35.5%	27%	Nickel Even	54%	6.3	26.7%	Nickel Even	36%	4.7	-14.5%	11	43%	5.7	1.9%
12	14%	5.1	7.0%	54%	4-3-4	23%	4.4	-0.9%	Dime+	31%	5.9	5.0%	12	23%	4.6	-19.4%
01	8%	6.3	50.6%	6%	Dime+	13%	7.0	67.9%	3-4-4	29%	6.0	-8.9%	21	16%	5.4	-21.0%
21	7%	5.2	24.6%	52%	3-4-4	5%	5.9	25.0%	4-4-3	3%	3.2	-20.1%	22	5%	8.0	25.0%
22	7%	3.4	-22.0%	83%	Nickel Odd	3%	3.9	-7.7%	Nickel Odd	1%	6.1	20.2%	10	3%	3.0	-22.9%

Strategic Tendencies

Run/Pass		Rk	Formation		Rk	Pass Rush		Rk	Secondary		Rk	Strategy		Rk
Runs, first half	33%	31	Form: Single Back	70%	9	Rush 3	10.4%	6	4 DB	29%	32	Play action	19%	18
Runs, first down	50%	17	Form: Empty Back	7%	10	Rush 4	50.3%	31	5 DB	37%	28	Avg Box (Off)	6.26	23
Runs, second-long	28%	23	Pers: 3+ WR	68%	2	Rush 5	34.7%	1	6+ DB	31%	3	Avg Box (Def)	6.13	30
Runs, power sit.	42%	29	Pers: 4+ WR	10%	4	Rush 6+	4.7%	26	CB by Sides	69%	23	Offensive Pace	28.69	6
Runs, behind 2H	31%	11	Pers: 2+ TE/6+ OL	28%	20	Sacks by LB	63.0%	7	DB Blitz	18%	4	Defensive Pace	30.18	17
Pass, ahead 2H	53%	5	Shotgun/Pistol	60%	5	Sacks by DB	12.0%	6	Hole in Zone	9%	14	Go for it on 4th	1.14	7

Message to offensive coordinators around the NFC North: Green Bay opponents threw only 10 percent of passes behind the line of scrimmage (fewest in the league) even though the Packers allowed an average of 10.4 YAC on these passes (29th) with 14.2% DVOA (22nd). ☞ With some injuries among the linebackers and two good rookie defensive backs, the Packers ended up using six defensive backs almost as often as they used five. The Packers got about 300 more snaps out of defensive backs compared with 2011, and 270 fewer snaps out of linebackers. ☞ The Packers rushed five more than any other team for the second straight year. ☞ Green Bay benefited from a league-high 152 opponent penalties. ☞ The Packers dropped 6.8 percent of passes, second in the league behind only Jacksonville.

Passing

Player	DYAR	DVOA	Plays	NtYds	Avg	YAC	C%	TD	Int
A.Rodgers	1395	23.4%	602	4016	6.7	5.5	67.7%	39	8

Rushing

Player	DYAR	DVOA	Plays	Yds	Avg	TD	Fum	Suc
A.Green	-44	-16.8%	133	451	3.4	0	0	42%
J.Starks	13	-4.3%	71	255	3.6	1	1	51%
C.Benson*	7	-6.1%	71	248	3.5	1	1	52%
A.Rodgers	94	30.6%	41	276	6.7	2	0	-
D.Harris	50	31.1%	34	157	4.6	2	0	41%
R.Grant*	17	4.1%	31	127	4.1	2	1	45%
J.Kuhn	1	-7.9%	23	63	2.7	1	0	39%
R.Cobb	98	142.5%	10	132	13.2	0	0	-

Receiving

Player	DYAR	DVOA	Plays	Ctch	Yds	Y/C	YAC	TD	C%
R.Cobb	357	24.1%	104	80	954	11.9	5.7	8	77%
J.Jones	318	22.6%	98	64	784	12.3	3.6	14	65%
J.Nelson	292	30.8%	73	49	745	15.2	5.1	7	67%
G.Jennings*	37	-5.2%	62	36	366	10.2	4.6	4	58%
D.Driver	21	-0.5%	13	8	77	9.6	1.5	2	62%
J.Boykin	-8	-25.6%	6	5	27	5.4	1.2	0	83%
J.Finley	95	7.0%	87	61	667	10.9	4.8	2	70%
D.Williams	-25	-40.8%	15	7	57	8.1	5.7	0	47%
T.Crabtree*	82	76.8%	12	8	203	25.4	18.1	3	67%
M.Mulligan	*24*	*19.6%*	*12*	*8*	*84*	*10.5*	*4.4*	*1*	*67%*
A.Green	-20	-25.6%	31	20	140	7.0	9.1	0	65%
J.Kuhn	60	47.8%	18	15	148	9.9	8.5	0	83%
C.Benson*	45	37.8%	15	14	97	6.9	7.1	0	93%
J.Starks	-4	-24.9%	6	4	31	7.8	10.5	0	67%

Offensive Line

Player	Pos	Age	GS	Snaps	Pen	Sk	Pass	Run	Player	Pos	Age	GS	Snaps	Pen	Sk	Pass	Run
Marshall Newhouse	LT	25	16/16	1102	5	9.5	22	1.5	Bryan Bulaga	RT	24	9/9	579	5	4	13	2
Josh Sitton	RG	27	16/16	1102	6	3	11	3	Evan Dietrich-Smith	G	27	16/6	459	5	2	6	2
T.J. Lang	LG	26	15/15	999	6	8.5	15	4.5	Don Barclay	RT	24	16/4	320	5	2.5	10.5	1
Jeff Saturday*	C	38	14/14	959	1	2.5	7.5	7									

Year	Yards	ALY	Rk	Power	Rk	Stuff	Rk	2nd Lev	Rk	Open Field	Rk	Sacks	ASR	Rk	Short	Long	F-Start	Cont.
2010	3.52	3.82	23	55%	25	18%	12	0.88	31	0.44	29	38	7.2%	21	10	15	20	42
2011	4.06	4.05	17	61%	21	21%	25	1.15	18	0.63	26	41	7.4%	23	13	19	28	30
2012	3.58	3.86	25	68%	7	19%	13	0.97	29	0.28	32	51	8.6%	31	9	29	13	35
2012 ALY by direction:		Left End 3.66 (20)			Left Tackle 2.68 (30)			Mid/Guard 4.21 (12)			Right Tackle 3.53 (26)				Right End 4.33 (14)			

If one is looking for reasons for cynicism in Green Bay, this is the place to begin. Only the Jaguars and Cardinals had more sacks directly caused by blown blocks, but the only real change made to this season's line is the retirement of "Pro Bowl" center Jeff Saturday.

Marshall Newhouse finished behind only Bobby Massie in blown blocks that led to sacks, and had the 10th-most blown blocks in the league on passing plays. Newhouse just doesn't have the feet to protect the outside edge without overcommitting, and this makes him very vulnerable to quick inside counters. Green Bay's decision to place Bryan Bulaga at left tackle and move Newhouse to the right side should pay dividends for Newhouse, as his foot speed won't be as much of an issue there. Six of Bulaga's blown blocks came in the Week 3 disaster in Seattle, which was a bit of a fluke, and if anyone on this team has the skill set to play left tackle, it's him. Newhouse's current challengers for the right tackle spot include 2011 first-rounder Derek Sherrod, who has yet to set foot on the field since breaking his tibia at the end of his rookie season, and second-year undrafted free agent Don Barclay. Fourth-rounder David Bakhtiari, who follows in Nate Solder's footsteps as a fluid tackle from a morbid Colorado program, could be an option later in the season, particularly if the alternative is Aaron Rodgers drunk-dialing Chad Clifton.

Inside, Josh Sitton—the only Packers lineman worthy of praise last season—will join Bulaga in moving to the left to protect Rodgers' blind side. T.J. Lang has limitations in pass protection, but with fourth-round pick J.C. Tretter fracturing his fibula and tearing ankle ligaments in OTAs, Lang has no real job competition at right guard unless one of the tackles moves inside. Center Evan Dietrich-Smith, best known for being "that guy Ndamukong Suh stomped on," cannot help but be better than Saturday was last season.

Defensive Front Seven

Defensive Line	Age	Pos	Snaps	Plays	Overall TmPct	Rk	Stop	Dfts	BTkl	Runs	vs. Run St%	Rk	RuYd	Rk	Pass Rush Sack	Hit	Hur	Tips
B.J. Raji	27	DT	644	28	3.9%	40	24	3	1	26	85%	9	2.2	27	0	1	9	2
Ryan Pickett	34	DE	570	52	6.4%	21	39	6	0	49	76%	36	2.0	16	0	2	2	1
C.J. Wilson	26	DE	274	25	4.5%	52	17	3	1	21	62%	70	3.5	69	2.5	1	2	1

Linebackers	Age	Pos	Snaps	Plays	TmPct	Rk	Stop	Dfts	BTkl	Sack	Hit	Hur	Tips	Runs	St%	Rk	Yds	Rk	Tgts	Suc%	Rk	AdjYd	Rk	PD
Erik Walden*	28	OLB	763	50	6.5%	88	40	13	1	3	11	11.5	0	35	77%	13	2.9	30	11	78%	--	1.7	--	5
A.J. Hawk	29	ILB	734	120	14.7%	28	70	15	2	3	2	2.5	1	90	66%	54	3.7	78	23	38%	66	6.9	41	0
Clay Matthews	27	OLB	727	46	7.5%	79	36	22	1	13	14	20	2	22	73%	22	3.1	45	2	100%	--	1.0	--	0
Brad Jones	27	ILB	673	81	9.9%	62	43	17	7	2	1	4.5	0	50	60%	77	3.5	61	22	43%	60	6.8	38	4
Dezman Moses	24	OLB	437	26	3.2%	--	20	8	1	4	4	5.5	2	15	87%	--	2.4	--	4	18%	--	14.4	--	0
D.J. Smith*	24	ILB	369	43	14.0%	--	21	8	1	2	1	6	1	23	52%	--	3.7	--	17	23%	75	9.2	72	3
Nick Perry	23	OLB	200	19	6.2%	--	8	3	0	2	0	5	1	14	36%	--	4.7	--	4	5%	--	12.2	--	0

Year	Yards	ALY	Rk	Power	Rk	Stuff	Rk	2nd Level	Rk	Open Field	Rk	Sacks	ASR	Rk	Short	Long
2010	4.02	4.26	21	46%	2	18%	21	1.11	15	0.44	5	47	8.1%	4	15	24
2011	4.49	4.50	29	67%	24	16%	30	1.30	27	0.70	12	29	4.8%	32	6	16
2012	4.40	4.25	22	51%	4	17%	24	1.17	12	0.80	16	47	8.0%	4	12	23
2012 ALY by direction:		Left End 4.71 (28)			Left Tackle 4.13 (16)			Mid/Guard 3.95 (12)			Right Tackle 4.47 (30)			Right End 4.59 (22)		

Ted Thompson spent a first-round pick on Datone Jones in an attempt to help settle a position that has been in flux since the Packers let Cullen Jenkins walk. Jones had five sacks and 19.5 tackles for loss for UCLA last season, and his hand techniques are very advanced for someone without any NFL seasoning. The bet here is that he'll be in the starting lineup for the opener, and he should be a nice pass-rushing fit in the Packers' 2-4-5 fronts. Ryan Pickett, the ageless immovable object, will continue to clog up the middle of the defense. For the second straight season, there were times where the effort didn't match the reputation with B.J. Raji, and he goes into training camp in a walk year without an extension. For a man who puts the planet in Planet Theory, he was pretty ordinary last season. C.J. Wilson provides depth as a run-stopper, and will keep the seat warm for 2012 second-rounder Jerel Worthy while Worthy recovers from a torn ACL suffered in Week 17. Johnny Jolly, returning from a three-year controlled substance suspension, is the wild card on the line.

There are good pass-rushing outside linebackers, and then there is Clay Matthews. He doesn't have the quickest get-off, and he isn't as physically intimidating as a DeMarcus Ware, but nobody gets off blocks better than Matthews. Finding pass rush on the opposite side of the line has been a real chore for Dom Capers and company. 2012 first-rounder Nick Perry will be given every chance to remedy that. SackSEER projected Perry to be the best pass-rusher in the 2012 Draft, and he flashed evidence of his skills in the 200-snap sample we saw before injuring his wrist and heading to IR. 2010 second-round defensive end Mike Neal was getting work as an outside linebacker at OTAs, which probably says more about the lack of depth Green Bay has at the position than any untapped potential that Neal has. Dezman Moses is the top returning backup after Frank Zombo and Erik Walden walked.

Descriptions used for A.J. Hawk in the past three editions of *Football Outsiders Almanac* include "disappointing," "highly-ordinary," and "not what you'd expect a No. 5 overall pick to be." Hawk has restructured his contract twice in the past three seasons, and is a liability in coverage, but it's 2013 and he's still hanging on as a starter. He's the odds-on favorite to survive the Tralfamadorian Occupation of Earth in 2039, and he'll probably do it because one of his bunker-mates tears an ACL. Brad Jones has a clear path to the starting spot opposite Hawk following the release of Desmond Bishop. Jones actually began his career as an outside linebacker, but has shown solid cover skills on the inside and earned a three-year contract this offseason. Bishop was a better blitzer, and was much better in 2011 than Jones was in 2012, but the torn hamstring that sidelined him for the entire 2012 season and limited him in OTAs convinced the Packers it was time to pull the plug. Depth at the position is a problem; the top backups are 2012 fifth-round pick Terrell Manning, who played zero defensive snaps last season, and third-year undrafted free agent Jamari Lattimore, who played seven.

Defensive Secondary

Secondary	Age	Pos	Snaps	Plays	TmPct	Rk	Stop	Dfts	BTkl	Runs	St%	Rk	Yds	Rk	Tgts	Tgt%	Rk	Dist	Suc%	Rk	APaYd	Rk	PD	Int
Morgan Burnett	24	FS	1088	126	15.4%	2	47	15	6	57	47%	11	5.8	16	41	8.6%	19	13.4	51%	47	9.3	66	6	2
Tramon Williams	30	CB	1073	77	9.4%	25	25	8	8	16	31%	66	10.5	80	93	19.7%	26	11.9	52%	42	6.6	23	12	2
Casey Hayward	24	CB	683	68	8.3%	52	40	25	3	16	50%	26	3.8	8	65	13.8%	72	11.0	67%	1	5.6	5	19	6
Sam Shields	26	CB	586	36	7.1%	64	18	9	3	10	40%	47	8.0	62	45	15.3%	60	15.9	57%	18	9.2	76	11	3
Jerron McMillian	24	FS	586	31	3.8%	73	13	8	1	10	40%	29	4.3	4	32	6.8%	32	11.8	48%	61	9.8	70	6	1
M.D. Jennings	25	SS	562	47	5.8%	67	10	4	2	18	22%	67	12.8	72	10	2.0%	74	11.6	69%	8	3.8	4	2	1
Charles Woodson*	37	SS	467	43	12.0%	21	20	8	2	16	50%	9	3.9	2	24	11.4%	6	11.9	65%	13	6.6	20	5	1
Davon House	24	CB	310	29	6.3%	74	8	3	2	3	0%	84	8.0	62	43	16.3%	52	11.9	50%	50	7.8	50	6	0

Year	Pass D Rank	vs. #1 WR	Rk	vs. #2 WR	Rk	vs. Other WR	Rk	vs. TE	Rk	vs. RB	Rk
2010	1	-23.5%	3	-18.5%	5	-24.6%	4	12.8%	22	-15.7%	5
2011	23	14.1%	20	-16.2%	7	-28.2%	4	23.2%	26	1.4%	18
2012	7	16.3%	24	-25.1%	2	-31.6%	2	-11.6%	6	22.8%	27

A very auspicious debut season for Casey Hayward has the Packers back at their usual surplus of solid defensive backs. Hayward wasn't Charles Woodson in his prime, but flashes of it were there, and he could start outside and shift inside on passing downs if he can avoid the Devin McCourty sophomore slump. Tramon Williams admitted that he never felt healthy last season, and he seemed to be more willing to cede ground underneath than he has in past years, which is a real disappointment to those of us who loved the "Admiral Armbar" nickname. Outside in the nickel is Sam Shields, who rebounded from a somewhat disappointing 2011 season in our metrics, or Davon House, who is more promising than your average dime corner. House has a real future in this league as a physical outside corner if he can actually put together a healthy season.

Nick Collins is never coming back, but the Green Bay secondary is just fine in the hands of Morgan Burnett. Burnett played every single snap, missed just six tackles, and showed stellar range. The three-safety look was common in Green Bay, and Jerron McMillian and M.D. Jennings showed enough for Ted Thompson to give them another year without competition—not counting their competition with each other for playing time in standard personnel groupings, of course. Jennings is better in coverage, while McMillian is more of a box safety. Neither of them are big fans of replacement referees.

Special Teams

Year	DVOA	Rank	FG/XP	Rank	Net Kick	Rank	Kick Ret	Rank	Net Punt	Rank	Punt Ret	Rank	Hidden	Rank
2010	-2.4%	26	-0.1	17	-7.0	27	-6.1	23	3.5	15	-2.4	20	-5.7	22
2011	1.8%	8	3.0	12	1.4	15	3.1	8	-2.2	18	3.8	9	-2.8	18
2012	-0.2%	18	-11.8	31	-1.5	18	0.0	17	9.7	7	2.5	10	3.4	8

If there is one thing that is profoundly confusing about the Packers, it's the fact that Mason Crosby is still on the roster. Only an even worse implosion by David Akers kept Crosby from finishing last in placekicking value. Crosby has never been particularly good at kickoffs, his career field-goal percentage is hovering at 76.8 percent, and he's at 42 percent on attempts of 50 yards or longer. Giorgio Tavecchio, a Cal product who was in San Francisco's camp a year ago, will push Crosby for the job during the preseason.

The other drama at the moment is what to do with the returner job. Randall Cobb has clearly outgrown it, and performed worse last season as his responsibilities on offense grew. Mike McCarthy has noted that Cobb is still an option if the Packers don't feel they have a capable alternative in-house, but between DuJuan Harris and Jeremy Ross, they can probably find someone to be better than a distracted Cobb.

Coaching Staff

Other than the typical complaints that every coach gets about particular goofs in game management or challenges, what can anyone really hold against Mike McCarthy? He's got a .661 win percentage over seven years in Green Bay and has built a deep and talented coaching staff. The San Francisco playoff loss aside, Dom Capers is one of the best defensive coordinators in the NFL. Defensive line coach Mike Trgovac was a solid defensive coordinator in Carolina and gets the most out of his unit, but the skill position coach with the most helium at this point is wide receivers coach Edgar Bennett. Bennett has also worked in the front office and as a running backs coach, and Green Bay has put out some pretty good receivers over the past couple of years, if you hadn't noticed.

Houston Texans

2012 Record: 12-4	**Total DVOA:** 6.7% (11th)	**2013 Mean Projection:** 9.3 wins	**On the Clock (0-4):** 3%
Pythagorean Wins: 10.2 (8th)	**Offense:** 0.1% (16th)	**Postseason Odds:** 67.0%	**Mediocrity (5-7):** 18%
Snap-Weighted Age: 27.2 (11th)	**Defense:** -14.2% (4th)	**Super Bowl Odds:** 11.5%	**Playoff Contender (8-10):** 48%
Average Opponent: -4.0% (26th)	**Special Teams:** -7.7% (32nd)	**Proj. Avg. Opponent:** -4.9% (30th)	**Super Bowl Contender (11+):** 32%

2012: How can the best season in franchise history feel so unsatisfying?

2013: They'll sleepwalk into the playoffs in unimpressive fashion, then hope to catch whatever recent magic animated the Giants and Ravens.

In some ways, 2012 was the best season in Houston Texans history. They finished with a 12-4 record, two more wins than in any of the franchise's previous ten seasons. They had the best defensive DVOA in franchise history, even improving off 2011's historic turnaround season, thanks in large part to J.J. Watt having one of the greatest seasons by a defensive player in NFL history. They blew out the eventual Super Bowl champion Ravens by 30, harassing Joe Flacco into a miserable performance. They won the AFC South and hosted a playoff game, which they won. Yes, it was a very good year for the Texans.

At the same time, it was a deeply disappointing season for the Texans. Winning the AFC South was nothing new; they did that in 2011. Winning a home playoff game was also a repeat experience, and 2011's triumph came in a blowout, not a 19-13 squeaker. In 2011, Houston's season ended in a close loss that was somewhat excused considering their top two quarterbacks were out for the season with injuries; in 2012, Matt Schaub was on the field but the Texans were blown out and trailed by four scores in the fourth quarter. The Texans also limped to the finish line in 2012, losing three of their last four regular season games, all to eventual playoff teams and all by double digits, costing themselves not just a bye but also home-field advantage that seemed like a lock when they were 11-1. In short, the Texans measured themselves up against the NFL's best and were found wanting. That 2012 could still be regarded as perhaps the best season in team history looks more like a sad joke than a testament to the success of a long franchise-building period.

The 2013 Texans will look a lot like the 2012 Texans. Matt Schaub will be under center. Arian Foster will be running outside zone. Duane Brown, Wade Smith, and Chris Myers will be blocking for him. Andre Johnson and Owen Daniels will be catching many of the passes Schaub throws. Gary Kubiak will be directing the offense, with assistance from Rick Dennison. Wade Phillips will be coordinating the defense. Antonio Smith and J.J. Watt will be playing defensive end, Brooks Reed linebacker. Johnathan Joseph and Kareem Jackson will be the starting cornerbacks. Do the Texans have anything to look forward to other than more of the same?

On offense, the three biggest names are Schaub, Foster and Johnson. After handing out extensions last offseason to Schaub and Foster, the Texans are financially committed to all three players. All are past the typical ascent stage of a player's career. Foster is at his peak and should expect to remain there, but Schaub turned 32 in June; quarterbacks typically decline after age 32. Johnson turns 32 in July; wide receivers typically decline after age 30. Even Daniels is 30, turning 31 in November; tight ends typically decline after age 29. Considering the offensive DVOA has declined the past two seasons, from second in 2010 to ninth to 16th, this aging does not seem like good news.

The good news, such as it is, is that bad offensive line play drove a lot of the offensive decline, not problems with the core "skill position" players. The problem was predictable and unsurprising. Predictable, because the Texans lost both right guard Mike Brisiel and Eric Winston and hoped to find a starter from a collection of backups and mostly untouted young players. Unsurprising, because the Texans' outside zone scheme benefits from very precise timing by the offensive line. That timing takes experience to develop, experience right tackle Derek Newton and a right guard rotation of Antoine Caldwell, Ben Jones, and Brandon Brooks did not have.

The offensive line difficulties meant the Texans underwent a remarkable change in the literal direction of the run game. For each of the previous six seasons Gary Kubiak had been head coach, the Texans had more runs marked right tackle and right end than they had marked left tackle and left end, by an average of 25 percent. In 2012, the Texans ran left 31 percent more often than they ran right. Translating these directional statistics into how playcalling changed is hard; a called outside zone run to the right side may be listed in the play by play as anywhere from right end to left guard depending on where the back finds the lane and what the official scorer had for lunch. Suffice it to say that Arian Foster found it harder than in previous seasons to run play-side when the Texans called outside zone right, and the Texans ran outside zone right less frequently than they had in previous seasons. The pin-and-pull outside run, a staple behind Winston, virtually disappeared from the playbook. The Texans use play-action off the outside zone to set up their trademark bootleg pass, and their DVOA off play-action slipped from 46.0% to 21.8%, which was below league average. Poor play by Matt Schaub late in the season (-13.1% passing DVOA, essentially replacement level, in the last five games of the regular season) and lack of a secondary receiver also contributed to the decline in the

2013 Texans Schedule

Week	Opp.	Week	Opp.	Week	Opp.
1	at SD (Mon.)	7	at KC	13	NE
2	TEN	8	BYE	14	at JAC (Thu.)
3	at BAL	9	IND	15	at IND
4	SEA	10	at ARI	16	DEN
5	at SF	11	OAK	17	at TEN
6	STL	12	JAC		

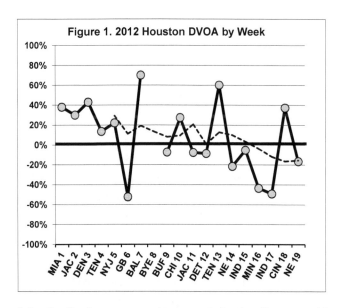

Figure 1. 2012 Houston DVOA by Week

pass game.

Will things be better in 2013? There's a case for optimism at right guard, as Brooks flashed dominant strength at times late in the season and dropped 25 pounds from a frame that had 25 pounds to lose. If the reduced weight translates to better quickness, which it should, he could become a very good starter quickly. Right tackle is a much bigger question mark. Newton was slow to recover from offseason knee surgery, gaining too much weight in the process. The Texans selected Brennan Williams out of North Carolina in the third round, but he was injured early in minicamp. Ryan Harris also returns, but veterans who aren't good enough tend not to immediately become good enough. The Texans should be closer to their traditional run game in 2013, but it will probably be once again on Arian Foster to use his superb vision to make more yards on his own than he had to in 2010 or 2011. To take some of the workload off Johnson, the Texans used their first-round pick on Clemson wideout DeAndre Hopkins. Rookie receivers are always an uncertain proposition, but last season the Texans got so little from rookies DeVier Posey and Keshawn Martin and the now-departed Kevin Walter that Hopkins is almost guaranteed to be an upgrade.

Defensively, the story of the Texans is the story of J.J. Watt. The second-year defensive end, who played defensive tackle in sub packages, had a truly remarkable season. The numbers are staggering. Start with what he did to opposing passers. He earned the nickname J.J. "Swatt" by batting down a remarkable 18 passes. That was more than twice as many as any other defensive lineman (Corey Liuget was second with eight). He had 20.5 sacks, the most by a 3-4 end in the 31 years the NFL has officially been keeping track of sacks. Watt was a factor in 9.2 percent of pass plays against the Texans. No other defensive lineman in the league was involved in more than 5.5 percent.

He may have been even better against the run than he was against the pass, registering an almost-perfect 98 percent Stop rate on 58 total plays. Tired of running at him and having him soak up or split a double team to make a play in the backfield, teams tried running away from him. Plenty of times, that did not help at all as his specialty became wrapping up ball-carriers from behind with backside penetration. He was a factor in 15.7 percent of all runs against the Texans, a figure exceeded only by Justin Smith's 16.0 percent among all defensive linemen.

Add all those numbers up, and you get 97 total plays, 23 more than any other defensive lineman. He was involved in 12.2 percent of all plays against the Texans. Calais Campbell

of the Cardinals was second among defensive linemen with 10.0 percent. He finished with 56 total Defeats. In the 17 years for which we have individual defensive player statistics, the second-best total by a defensive lineman was 37 by Robert Porcher, a 4-3 defensive end, in 1997. The second-best total by any player was 45 by Ray Lewis in 1999 (Table 1). When Wade Phillips declared Watt had the best season by a defensive lineman in NFL history, he might have been right.

Table 1: Most Defeats, 1996-2012

Year	Player	Team	Position	Defeats
2012	J.J. Watt	HOU	3-4 DE	56
1999	Ray Lewis	BAL	4-3 MLB	45
1999	Derrick Brooks	TB	4-3 OLB	42
1998	Ed McDaniel	MIN	4-3 MLB	40
1998	Zach Thomas	MIA	4-3 MLB	40
2003	Ray Lewis	BAL	3-4 ILB	39
2012	Von Miller	DEN	4-3 OLB	39
2006	London Fletcher	BUF	4-3 MLB	38
2001	Jamir Miller	CLE	4-3 OLB	38
2002	Brian Urlacher	CHI	4-3 MLB	38
2004	Marcus Washington	WAS	4-3 OLB	38
2006	Lance Briggs	CHI	4-3 OLB	37
2000	Derrick Brooks	TB	4-3 OLB	37
2009	Brian Cushing	HOU	4-3 OLB	37
1998	Ray Lewis	BAL	4-3 MLB	37
1997	Robert Porcher	DET	4-3 DE	37

What can Watt possibly do for an encore? It's hard to say, but probably not quite as much. Watt's dominance helped inspire all three divisional foes to make significant investments on the right side of their offensive lines: Jacksonville and Tennessee through the draft, and Indianapolis through free agency. Of Watt's 20.5 sacks, 9.5 came in the six divisional games. His pace of 11.5 sacks in the other 10 games still gives him a projection of 18.5 sacks even without feasting on Guy Whimper, Leroy Harris, and Jeff Linkenbach, but the rest of the teams on the Houston schedule will also be concentrating on countering him. Watt had a season-low one solo tackle in the playoff loss to the Patriots. He still penetrated well, but New England running backs were taking wider initial steps to make it harder for Watt to make plays from the backside.

Beyond the personnel and schematic adjustments by opponents, it's hard to forecast what Watt can do in 2013 because Watt is such a unique player historically. Table 2 shows a complete list of players who had at least 15.0 sacks in one of their first three professional seasons, along with their position and their sack total the next season.

Table 2: Players with 15 or More Sacks During First Three Seasons, 1982-2012

Player	Position	Sacks	Year	Next Year Sacks
Bruce Smith	3-4 DE	15.0	1986	12.0
Reggie White	4-3 DE	18.0	1986	21.0
Derrick Thomas	3-4 OLB	20.0	1990	13.5
Dwight Freeney	4-3 DE	16.0	2004	11.0
Shawne Merriman	3-4 OLB	17.0	2006	12.5
Jason Pierre-Paul	4-3 DE	16.5	2011	6.5
Von Miller	4-3 OLB	18.5	2012	?
Aldon Smith	3-4 OLB	19.5	2012	?
J.J. Watt	3-4 DE	20.5	2012	?

That is precisely one player in 31 years who had at least 70 percent of Watt's production at the same position and a similar age. While we lack numbers like Defeats for Smith's early career, we know he had 63 tackles compared to Watt's 81 on a team that went 6-10, not 12-4. His 12.0 sacks the next season came in the strike season, when he played in 12 games. By and large, the table suggests that Watt will likely see some regression in his sack numbers, though double-digits seems to be a reasonable expectation.

One thing that would help Watt's production is better play around him. While the Texans posted the best defensive DVOA in team history, they were too often exposed in key moments, particularly by teams that spread them out and exploited their dime package. That was particularly true after the loss of Brian Cushing to a knee injury in Week 5. Aaron Rodgers shredded them for six touchdown passes, and Tom Brady played well against them twice. The Patriots' offensive pace bothered the Texans, catching them shifting as the ball was snapped multiple times—including in the playoff game, even though the Texans had a week to prepare for what they had already seen a few weeks earlier. The Texans' defense may have been good, but they did not seem resilient.

Owner Bob McNair concurred, noting a need for Kubiak to improve the team's mental toughness. That need drove the Texans' most interesting free agency decision. They allowed free safety Glover Quin, just 27 years old and the only decent safety the franchise has ever developed, to depart for the Lions in free agency. In his place, they signed future Hall of Famer Ed Reed. Reed may turn 35 in September, but he could provide championship experience, leadership, and that proverbial mental toughness when he steps on the field. Precisely when he actually will step on the field is currently an open question, as he spent OTAs rehabbing a hip injury apparently more severe than the Texans' doctors deemed it when they originally examined him. The Texans would surely like to have him sooner, but the time Houston really needs Reed to show that he is more than just an old safety who misses too many tackles (a league-worst among defensive backs 18 in 2012) is in December and January, not September.

Whatever their other faults, we project the Texans as clearly the best team in the AFC South, likely to win the division by a couple games. But that's not their goal at this point. Their goal is the Lombardi Trophy, and more often than not, the team that's won that lately is the team that played well in the postseason, no matter how they got there. If veterans like Schaub, Johnson, and Reed can stay fresh and play their best come January and February, a little bit of aging or questionable health during the regular season won't matter to Texans fans. The window is closing here, but there's still time to leap through that shrinking space before it slams shut.

Tom Gower

2012 Texans Stats by Week

Wk	vs.	W-L	PF	PA	YDF	YDA	TO	Total	Off	Def	ST
1	MIA	W	30	10	337	275	4	38%	11%	-59%	-32%
2	at JAC	W	27	7	411	117	1	30%	19%	-17%	-6%
3	at DEN	W	31	25	436	375	-1	43%	27%	-23%	-7%
4	TEN	W	38	14	297	325	3	14%	14%	4%	4%
5	at NYJ	W	23	17	378	286	1	22%	17%	-27%	-22%
6	GB	L	24	42	321	427	-3	-52%	-33%	20%	0%
7	BAL	W	43	13	420	176	2	70%	24%	-57%	-11%
8	BYE										
9	BUF	W	21	9	374	304	1	-7%	10%	9%	-9%
10	at CHI	W	13	6	215	249	2	27%	-21%	-53%	-5%
11	JAC	W	43	37	653	458	-2	-8%	9%	15%	-2%
12	at DET	W	34	31	501	525	0	-9%	2%	6%	-5%
13	at TEN	W	24	10	331	354	6	60%	-3%	-50%	13%
14	at NE	L	14	42	323	419	0	-22%	-19%	0%	-3%
15	IND	W	29	17	417	272	1	-5%	3%	-6%	-14%
16	MIN	L	6	23	187	345	-1	-44%	-58%	-10%	4%
17	at IND	L	16	28	352	265	-2	-49%	-20%	2%	-28%
18	CIN	W	19	13	420	198	0	37%	10%	-26%	1%
19	at NE	L	28	41	425	457	-1	-17%	-8%	30%	22%

Trends and Splits

	Offense	Rank	Defense	Rank
Total DVOA	0.1%	16	-14.2%	4
Unadjusted VOA	4.4%	12	-16.0%	2
Weighted Trend	-7.6%	20	-10.1%	5
Variance	5.3%	9	7.1%	25
Average Opponent	2.4%	24	-2.5%	23
Passing	11.0%	14	-12.4%	4
Rushing	-3.6%	16	-16.8%	5
First Down	-0.9%	16	-7.3%	9
Second Down	8.6%	11	-28.8%	2
Third Down	-12.3%	23	-5.1%	12
First Half	6.1%	13	-19.3%	2
Second Half	-6.0%	21	-8.9%	7
Red Zone	-0.6%	16	-24.9%	3
Late and Close	-10.8%	21	-16.4%	5

Five-Year Performance

Year	W-L	Pyth W	Est W	PF	PA	TO	Total	Rk	Off	Rk	Def	Rk	ST	Rk	Off AGL	Rk	Def AGL	Rk	Off Age	Rk	Def Age	Rk	ST Age	Rk
2008	8-8	7.3	6.4	366	394	-10	-7.4%	22	6.2%	13	13.5%	29	-0.1%	17	20.3	12	22.7	17	26.3	31	26.2	28	27.1	4
2009	9-7	9.5	10.0	388	333	-1	9.7%	14	9.9%	10	2.5%	20	2.4%	7	39.9	28	17.5	7	26.4	28	25.3	32	26.9	7
2010	6-10	7.1	7.9	390	427	0	2.5%	13	21.7%	2	17.5%	31	-1.7%	23	31.0	20	24.2	16	27.4	15	25.5	30	26.2	15
2011	10-6	10.9	10.0	381	278	+7	18.6%	5	8.4%	9	-9.5%	6	0.7%	13	31.3	17	18.9	10	28.1	2	25.7	29	26.1	24
2012	12-4	10.2	8.3	416	331	+12	6.7%	11	0.1%	16	-14.2%	4	-7.7%	32	6.7	1	30.6	19	28.1	6	26.5	22	26.4	11

2012 Performance Based on Most Common Personnel Groups

HOU Offense					HOU Offense vs. Opponents				HOU Defense				HOU Defense vs. Opponents			
Pers	Freq	Yds	DVOA	Run%	Pers	Freq	Yds	DVOA	Pers	Freq	Yds	DVOA	Pers	Freq	Yds	DVOA
12	61%	6.1	14.9%	48%	4-3-4	51%	5.5	10.5%	3-4-4	46%	5.0	-18.5%	11	48%	6.3	-1.6%
11	21%	5.4	-27.5%	27%	Nickel Even	20%	6.2	-2.9%	Dime+	36%	6.1	-5.3%	12	29%	4.1	-28.4%
13	8%	3.7	-21.6%	60%	3-4-4	18%	6.4	14.9%	Nickel Even	6%	4.4	-24.3%	21	9%	5.1	-4.2%
21	4%	4.1	-13.1%	84%	Dime+	5%	5.5	-49.4%	Nickel Odd	6%	5.7	-3.9%	22	4%	5.0	-20.9%
01	1%	13.0	92.2%	0%	Nickel Odd	3%	4.6	-29.9%	3-5-3	3%	2.6	-42.7%	10	2%	1.3	-76.0%
02	1%	4.1	10.4%	0%					4-3-4	2%	4.3	-3.1%				

Strategic Tendencies

Run/Pass		Rk	Formation		Rk	Pass Rush		Rk	Secondary		Rk	Strategy		Rk
Runs, first half	40%	13	Form: Single Back	58%	26	Rush 3	2.5%	29	4 DB	48%	8	Play action	25%	8
Runs, first down	52%	11	Form: Empty Back	8%	9	Rush 4	49.9%	32	5 DB	12%	32	Avg Box (Off)	6.70	2
Runs, second-long	35%	7	Pers: 3+ WR	24%	31	Rush 5	29.8%	6	6+ DB	36%	2	Avg Box (Def)	6.38	15
Runs, power sit.	67%	6	Pers: 4+ WR	2%	15	Rush 6+	17.8%	14	CB by Sides	52%	32	Offensive Pace	30.52	16
Runs, behind 2H	34%	6	Pers: 2+ TE/6+ OL	73%	1	Sacks by LB	29.5%	14	DB Blitz	13%	14	Defensive Pace	28.49	1
Pass, ahead 2H	36%	30	Shotgun/Pistol	22%	32	Sacks by DB	5.7%	15	Hole in Zone	7%	24	Go for it on 4th	0.86	20

Houston was the only team to use 12 personnel on more than half their plays… unless you want to consider James Casey a fullback instead of a tight end, in which case they were the only team to use 21 personnel on more than half their plays. ☞ Houston opponents may want to consider big-blitzing Matt Schaub more often. Last year, Schaub only faced six or more pass rushers on a league-low 4.5 percent of pass plays, but the Texans gained only 5.3 yards per pass on these plays. In 2011, it was also rare for opponents to big-blitz Schaub, while he had only 5.0 yards per pass. ☞ In a related stat, Houston opponents only blitzed a defensive back on 7.4 percent of passes, the lowest rate in the league. ☞ Only Tennessee was less likely to use "max protect" blocking. ☞ The Texans were actually the worst rushing team in the league when they were spread out with three or more wide receivers: just 4.1 yards per carry with -45.0% DVOA. ☞ This was the second straight season the Texans used a nickel defense less than any other team. Their standard defense against multiple-receiver sets is generally dime. ☞ Houston benefitted from a league-high 40 passes (7.7 percent of all passes) dropped by their opponents.

Passing

Player	DYAR	DVOA	Plays	NtYds	Avg	YAC	C%	TD	Int
M.Schaub	697	7.5%	572	3811	6.7	5.0	64.3%	22	12
T.J.Yates	-85	-128.3%	11	34	3.1	7.3	40.0%	0	1

Rushing

Player	DYAR	DVOA	Plays	Yds	Avg	TD	Fum	Suc
A.Foster	105	-1.6%	351	1422	4.1	15	3	47%
B.Tate	18	-2.2%	65	279	4.3	2	1	49%
J.Forsett*	53	13.2%	63	374	5.9	1	0	48%
G.Jones	-4	-19.4%	5	8	1.6	0	0	60%

Receiving

Player	DYAR	DVOA	Plays	Ctch	Yds	Y/C	YAC	TD	C%
A.Johnson	461	19.5%	163	112	1598	14.3	4.9	4	69%
K.Walter*	78	2.3%	68	41	518	12.6	2.3	2	60%
K.Martin	-92	-47.2%	28	10	85	8.5	3.7	1	36%
D.Posey	-23	-36.4%	14	6	87	14.5	4.8	0	43%
L.Jean	43	33.5%	12	6	151	25.2	13.8	1	50%
O.Daniels	33	0.6%	104	62	716	11.5	5.0	6	60%
J.Casey*	58	13.1%	44	34	330	9.7	6.2	3	77%
G.Graham	36	6.8%	40	28	263	9.4	4.1	3	70%
A.Foster	-43	-28.0%	58	40	217	5.4	6.9	2	69%
B.Tate	-9	-27.7%	11	11	49	4.5	3.6	0	100%
G.Jones	12	1.3%	14	11	64	5.8	4.5	0	79%

Offensive Line

Player	Pos	Age	GS	Snaps	Pen	Sk	Pass	Run	Player	Pos	Age	GS	Snaps	Pen	Sk	Pass	Run
Chris Myers	C	32	16/16	1128	4	0	4.5	8	Ben Jones	RG	24	16/10	690	3	4	6	5.5
Wade Smith	LG	32	16/16	1114	2	2	6	9.5	Ryan Harris	OT	28	16/2	411	1	2	7	1
Duane Brown	LT	28	16/16	1109	6	3	14.5	7	Antoine Caldwell*	RG	27	11/6	346	1	1	6	5.5
Derek Newton	RT	26	14/14	756	7	4	10	8.5	Brandon Brooks	G	24	6/0	110	1	1	1	0

Year	Yards	ALY	Rk	Power	Rk	Stuff	Rk	2nd Lev	Rk	Open Field	Rk	Sacks	ASR	Rk	Short	Long	F-Start	Cont.
2010	5.12	4.52	4	66%	10	16%	9	1.42	1	1.32	2	32	5.9%	12	14	13	12	31
2011	4.66	4.37	4	64%	14	18%	12	1.43	4	0.93	11	33	7.3%	22	15	15	15	43
2012	4.34	4.17	9	61%	18	20%	23	1.26	10	0.85	12	28	5.3%	9	14	7	18	33
2012 ALY by direction:		Left End 4.74 (2)			Left Tackle 3.16 (28)			Mid/Guard 4.1 (13)			Right Tackle 4.84 (2)				Right End 4.29 (15)			

Duane Brown drew plaudits from many sources as perhaps the league's best left tackle in 2012. Our numbers were more equivocal, as he registered similar blown block totals to those he had put up in previous seasons. But he was never beat cleanly until Dwight Freeney did so for a sack in Week 15. His Pro Bowl trip was a deserved one, as his excellent mobility was a big reason the Texans ran so well around left end. Center Chris Myers, like Brown, is very mobile and earned a deserved trip to the Pro Bowl. He still struggles with bigger defensive tackles, particularly 3-4 nose tackles. Turning 32 in September, he may be nearing the point in his career at which he's a year-to-year proposition, but the Texans will happily trot him out there again in 2013 even if he doesn't merit another trip to Hawaii.

Joining Myers and Brown in the Pro Bowl was the man who played between them, left guard Wade Smith. It's hard to make a case Smith's trip was based on anything other than reputation, even taking into account that his struggles against Geno Atkins and particularly Vince Wilfork in the postseason came after the voting booths had closed. As those names indicate, he struggled against the better defensive tackles he faced; he also had more difficulty than in previous seasons getting off double teams and picking up linebackers in open space. He's not yet at the point where the Texans need to replace him, but 2013 is the final year of his contract and likely his last in battle red, liberty white, and steel blue.

The primary interior backup is Ben Jones, who as a rookie played right guard like a player who played only center in college. An understanding of assignments and the weaknesses of the players competing with him account for his playing time in 2012, while his lack of timing and strength account for his backup status in 2013. The loser of the Newton-Brennan Williams battle for right tackle provides depth, as does sixth-round pick David Quessenberry (San Jose State).

Defensive Front Seven

Defensive Line	Age	Pos	Snaps	Plays	TmPct	Rk	Stop	Dfts	BTkl	Runs	St%	Rk	RuYd	Rk	Sack	Hit	Hur	Tips
					Overall						vs. Run				Pass Rush			
J.J. Watt	24	DE	936	97	12.2%	1	95	56	3	58	98%	1	-0.2	1	20.5	25	29.5	18
Antonio Smith	32	DE	797	33	4.2%	55	27	13	0	21	71%	49	3.0	62	7	11	17	2
Earl Mitchell	26	DT	397	33	4.2%	35	22	4	3	25	72%	46	2.2	28	0	1	2	2
Shaun Cody*	30	DT	257	19	2.9%	--	16	1	0	16	88%	--	2.9	--	0	0	0	2
Jared Crick	24	DE	216	24	3.2%	69	18	3	1	21	76%	32	3.2	66	0	1	0.5	2

Linebackers	Age	Pos	Snaps	Plays	TmPct	Rk	Stop	Dfts	BTkl	Sack	Hit	Hur	Tips	Runs	St%	Rk	Yds	Rk	Tgts	Suc%	Rk	AdjYd	Rk	PD
					Overall					Pass Rush				vs. Run					vs. Pass					
Connor Barwin*	27	OLB	998	48	6.1%	95	36	17	3	3	14	16.5	5	28	64%	63	2.5	24	8	84%	--	2.0	--	0
Bradie James*	32	ILB	638	79	10.6%	61	42	5	1	0.5	2	5.5	--	58	53%	102	4.0	87	23	55%	24	3.9	4	2
Brooks Reed	26	OLB	582	29	4.9%	106	20	10	2	2.5	4	10	2	20	65%	60	2.3	20	7	55%	--	4.8	--	0
Whitney Mercilus	23	OLB	500	19	2.4%	--	15	10	0	6	1	9	1	9	89%	--	1.1	--	0	--	--	--	--	0
Tim Dobbins	31	ILB	389	39	5.6%	--	28	7	5	0	3	0	0	24	67%	--	4.0	--	19	64%	8	5.7	20	2
Darryl Sharpton	25	ILB	280	28	8.1%	--	16	2	1	0	2	0.5	0	16	81%	--	3.4	--	12	39%	--	6.1	--	1
Brian Cushing	26	ILB	246	32	12.9%	--	21	8	4	0	2	2	0	22	68%	--	4.1	--	8	70%	--	6.0	--	2

Year	Yards	ALY	Rk	Power	Rk	Stuff	Rk	2nd Level	Rk	Open Field	Rk	Sacks	ASR	Rk	Short	Long
2010	4.14	4.28	24	62%	15	19%	19	1.32	30	0.53	9	30	6.3%	17	15	9
2011	4.04	3.85	7	67%	25	20%	15	1.07	8	0.75	14	44	8.4%	3	14	18
2012	3.93	3.62	4	59%	11	25%	4	1.22	23	0.67	12	44	7.3%	6	11	15
2012 ALY by direction:		Left End 1.57 (1)			Left Tackle 3.8 (12)			Mid/Guard 3.83 (9)			Right Tackle 3.63 (7)				Right End 2.85 (3)	

Antonio Smith, bookend to J.J. Watt, looks like a really good player at times. He has very good pass-rush numbers for a 3-4 end who, like Watt, plays tackle in sub packages. He's very good on stunts and twists, which the Texans tend to use to great effect. Yet at the end of the day he only made 21 plays against the run on almost 800 total snaps, and that's more than the 16 he made in 2011. Backup Jared Crick was much more active against the run, though he's not nearly the pass rusher Smith is. Nose tackle

Earl Mitchell gave the middle of the Bears line fits in Week 10, but who didn't? Most of the time, he was more hit or miss, one play penetrating to help disrupt a run, then the next getting reach-blocked and pushed aside to create a hole. He should see a few more snaps with Shaun Cody's departure, though not too many more as he won't play in dime.

Inside linebacker was a strength for Houston just a couple of seasons ago, but the trade of DeMeco Ryans and an injury that cost Brian Cushing most of last season left the position as a weakness. Bradie James, Tim Dobbins, Daryl Sharpton, and Barrett Ruud were all tried at inside linebacker, with at best moderate success. The Texans had problems in base personnel, as the linebackers were too slow to fill the hole before it was blocked. Sharpton has struggled with injuries, and when he's on the field he's been inconsistent. Neither James, Dobbins, nor Ruud moved well enough to be a successful dime linebacker. With Cushing still recovering, the Texans took a look at Brooks Reed on the inside in May. If Whitney Mercilus can set the edge in the run game instead of just rushing the passer, and rookies Sam Montgomery (LSU) and Trevardo Williams (Connecticut) progress quickly, Reed's switch may be permanent.

Defensive Secondary

					Overall						vs. Run						vs. Pass							
Secondary	Age	Pos	Snaps	Plays	TmPct	Rk	Stop	Dfts	BTkl	Runs	St%	Rk	Yds	Rk	Tgts	Tgt%	Rk	Dist	Suc%	Rk	APaYd	Rk	PD	Int
Danieal Manning	31	FS	1047	85	10.7%	33	28	14	5	37	30%	54	7.8	50	32	6.6%	39	13.7	49%	57	11.4	73	7	2
Glover Quin*	27	SS	1027	97	12.2%	20	43	22	6	46	41%	25	6.5	29	60	12.4%	3	9.9	55%	32	5.5	12	12	2
Kareem Jackson	25	CB	1010	70	8.8%	35	25	11	4	15	20%	78	8.9	70	86	18.0%	41	13.5	59%	12	7.1	29	19	4
Johnathan Joseph	29	CB	826	67	9.7%	20	23	12	5	12	17%	80	11.2	82	88	21.0%	14	12.8	53%	39	7.7	47	10	2
Brice McCain	27	CB	450	27	4.5%	84	13	6	4	1	0%	84	10.0	76	49	13.6%	74	9.6	51%	48	9.6	79	6	1
Quintin Demps*	28	FS	347	32	5.4%	69	12	7	3	5	20%	69	11.4	69	20	5.6%	55	12.3	70%	6	7.5	38	5	0
Brandon Harris	25	CB	176	15	3.8%	--	7	2	2	4	50%	--	5.8	--	19	7.9%	--	15.2	59%	--	12.9	--	4	0
Ed Reed	35	FS	1046	73	8.3%	49	29	14	15	23	26%	61	7.5	42	38	8.5%	20	14.6	54%	35	8.7	55	13	4

Year	Pass D Rank	vs. #1 WR	Rk	vs. #2 WR	Rk	vs. Other WR	Rk	vs. TE	Rk	vs. RB	Rk
2010	32	16.0%	27	28.1%	29	0.9%	19	26.3%	30	33.8%	32
2011	9	24.0%	24	-15.9%	8	-14.7%	13	5.1%	12	-12.5%	9
2012	4	-26.7%	4	11.3%	28	1.8%	19	-12.2%	4	-23.1%	5

The arrival of Johnathan Joseph in 2011 had a transformative effect on the Texans' pass defense. Then an in-season groin injury and two sports hernias had a transformative effect on Joseph's play in 2012. A year after locking down everyone except Anquan Boldin and Steve Smith, he was decidedly mortal at times. The Texans played him in more off coverage to disguise his difficulties running deep, which then opened up comebacks and slants in front of him. Some teams, like the Packers, still found success attacking him deep anyway. Joseph's injury struggles were not as big an issue as they would have been in 2011, though, due to the remarkable growth in Kareem Jackson's game. While he still lacks ideal deep speed, meaning he also has to play off coverage more often than the Texans might like, he's vastly improved from the player who allowed 11.5 Adjusted Yards per Pass as a rookie in 2010.Nickelback Brice McCain was fifth in Adjusted Success Rate in 2011, but followed that up with a very inconsistent season. He struggled when injuries forced him to cover better receivers. Taller receivers were an issue, although he also got killed by Randall Cobb in Week 6. Perhaps the strangest aspect of McCain's 2012 numbers is that he was much worse against passes in the middle of the field, even though his skill set fits the slot so much better than playing outside. McCain allowed 5.7 Adjusted Yards per Pass with 63 percent Adjusted Success Rate on passes marked left or right, but 15.8 Adjusted Yards per Pass with 33 percent Success Rate on passes in the middle of the field. (It would be 11.9 Adjusted Yards per Pass if we removed one huge 81-yard touchdown by Justin Blackmon, but that's still an ugly number.) 2011 second-rounder Brandon Harris wasn't ready for his close-up when McCain went down in Week 13, and depth behind him is even worse.

If and when Ed Reed misses time, Danieal Manning will step back into the high safety role he generally played in 2012, while second-round pick D.J. Swearinger (South Carolina) will fill Glover Quin's role as the extra man in the box. Swearinger should be able to replicate Quin's physical play as an undersized linebacker in dime personnel, but will need to show he can be as effective a run blitzer and in coverage against tight ends. Quin's previous experience at cornerback helped him out there, and Swearinger will probably be a downgrade. If Reed misses an extended period of time, the Texans will need Shiloh Keo to look more like a safety and less like a solid special-teams player forced into duty beyond his ability.

Special Teams

Year	DVOA	Rank	FG/XP	Rank	Net Kick	Rank	Kick Ret	Rank	Net Punt	Rank	Punt Ret	Rank	Hidden	Rank
2010	-1.7%	23	9.2	1	1.6	13	-10.0	30	-4.5	25	-4.9	25	2.2	11
2011	0.7%	13	-3.6	22	3.7	10	-1.9	20	0.9	14	4.6	7	-3.2	20
2012	-7.7%	32	-5.8	29	-25.9	32	-6.9	28	-1.2	16	1.4	13	5.7	4

The Texans doubly deserved their ranking as the league's worst kickoff unit in 2012. Shayne Graham's "veteran savvy" was just declining leg strength, and he finished last in the league with an estimated minus-11.3 points of gross kick value, well past Rian Lindell's next-to-last minus-6.3 points. Normally short kicks tend to produce returns of more moderate length, but the Texans lapped the field by allowing 20.8 points of return value, much worse than second-place Oakland's 12.4 points.[1] Graham also struggled on long field goals, making just 11 of 18 from 40 yards and beyond, though Gary Kubiak deserves some of the blame for having him attempt so many long field goals in the first place. 2012 fifth-round pick Randy Bullock, who spent his rookie season on injured reserve, will probably replace Graham, although Kubiak has made some comments suggesting that he may not be fully confident in Bullock.

The Texans were only a little below average when it came to covering punts. They let punter Donnie Jones depart in free agency after a solid season and replaced him with longtime Raiders punter Shane Lechler. Long known for his booming kicks, Lechler's performance slipped to below average in gross punt value in 2012. There's a chance that's due to age-related decline, as he turns 37 in August, though reviews from OTAs were positive.

Texans fans were enraged when Trindon Holliday seemingly turned into Devin Hester Jr. for the Denver Broncos, but his release by Houston wasn't ridiculous because he was so awful for the Texans: minus-7.4 points worth of estimated field position on his returns through five weeks. Keshawn Martin took over both duties after his departure and was below average on kickoffs and above average on punts. He'll probably face competition from two rookies, wideout Alan Bonner and running back Dennis Johnson. Danieal Manning is an excellent kickoff returner, but has been deemed too valuable to do that in the regular season.

Coaching Staff

It's a popular thing to claim the Texans need to "open up" or otherwise "diversify" their offense after their playoff failures the past two seasons. Yet detailed reviews of the team's play show a scheme that stresses defenses and punishes indiscipline, often with big plays. Gary Kubiak handles more of the pass game and Rick Dennison more of the run game, and both do an excellent job of getting the most out of the talent they have. It will be up to well-regarded offensive line coach John Benton to help get the right side of the line in better shape this season.

Between Brice McCain and Kareem Jackson, defensive backs coach Vance Joseph has produced a breakthrough player each of his first two years with the team. Given the depth questions at both corner and safety, the Texans will be looking to him to work his magic again. Defensive line coach Bill Kollar deserves credit for J.J. Watt's development as a pass rusher.

---

[1] In case you are wondering why gross kick value (for Graham, -11.3) minus return value allowed (-20.8) does not equal net kickoff value (-25.3), it has to do with the way each element of the kicking game is compared to a league average. The average length of a return based on the length of the kickoff isn't a linear function; neither is the average length of a return based on where the return begins. Therefore the value of the two legs of a kickoff return added together won't necessarily equal the value of the function that measures the average endpoint of an entire kickoff play based solely on the starting point of that kickoff play (which is usually, but of course not always, the 35).

Indianapolis Colts

2012 Record: 11-5	Total DVOA: -16.0% (25th)	2013 Mean Projection: 7.6 wins	On the Clock (0-4): 12%
Pythagorean Wins: 7.2 (20th)	Offense: -2.9% (18th)	Postseason Odds: 32.9%	Mediocrity (5-7): 37%
Snap-Weighted Age: 26.1 (29th)	Defense: 14.0% (31st)	Super Bowl Odds: 2.3%	Playoff Contender (8-10): 40%
Average Opponent: -7.4% (32nd)	Special Teams: 0.9% (12th)	Proj. Avg. Opponent: -6.0% (32)	Super Bowl Contender (11+): 11%

2012: An improbable playoff season, driven by a lot of luck and a lot of Luck.

2013: They won't win as many close games, but they should be a better team facing another weak schedule.

Expectations for the 2012 Indianapolis Colts were justifiably low. The franchise was coming off a 2-14 season that prompted owner Jim Irsay to sweep the deck. He replaced general manager Bill Polian with Ryan Grigson, and Grigson in turn replaced head coach Jim Caldwell with Chuck Pagano. The new regime quickly decided to move on from Peyton Manning, their future Hall of Fame quarterback who had missed the entire 2011 season after undergoing multiple neck surgeries, and focused instead on rebuilding around Stanford quarterback Andrew Luck, who they would add with the No. 1 overall pick in the 2012 NFL Draft.

The clean break the Colts made with their past also included dramatic changes in the organizational philosophy on the field. Gone was the Tom Moore-Peyton Manning offense built around a limited number of plays run from multiple formations. First-year offensive coordinator Bruce Arians implemented an aggressive, downfield passing attack, although his new system didn't exactly mesh with the West Coast offense that Luck had run to great success at Stanford. On the defensive side, former Ravens defensive coordinator Pagano moved the team from Tony Dungy's classic 4-3, Cover-2 scheme to a "hybrid" 3-4 system that would have Pro Bowl defensive ends Dwight Freeney and Robert Mathis moving to outside linebacker.

New systems require new players with different skill sets, and so the Colts cut numerous veterans and went into the 2012 season carrying $40 million in dead money on their salary cap. They filled the holes by promoting backups and signing a couple of low-cost free agents who had played for Pagano in Baltimore. The turnover was particularly severe on the offensive side of the ball; the original starting lineup featured just two holdovers from the previous season, one of whom (Anthony Castonzo) was only in his second NFL campaign.

This much rebuilding all at once does not generally lead to the postseason, and so the Colts went into the season with no expectations. When ESPN.com and NFL.com ran their season predictions, not one personality at either network had the Colts in the playoffs. In *Football Outsiders Almanac 2012*, the Colts' mean win projection was for six wins with projected postseason odds of 9.3 percent.

The beginning of the 2012 season validated the lack of faith in the Colts. They were blown out by Chicago in Week 1, gave away a 14-point fourth-quarter lead before rallying to beat Minnesota in Week 2, and then lost at home to Jacksonville in Week 3. During the Colts' bye week came the devastating news that head coach Pagano had been diagnosed with leukemia. In the first game after the bye week, with Arians serving as interim head coach, the Colts shocked the football world when they rallied from a 21-3 halftime deficit and beat the Green Bay Packers 30-27. The game-winning score came via a four-yard pass from Luck to long-time Colts veteran Reggie Wayne, whose decision to re-sign with the Colts was largely due to his history with Pagano, who had recruited Wayne to the University of Miami.

Starting with that game against the Packers, the "#chuckstrong" Colts would win 10 of their final 13 games—eight of them by a touchdown or less—to finish with 11 wins and a berth in the AFC playoffs. It was a storybook season, as Luck set the NFL single-season rookie records for passing attempts and passing yardage, and the Colts rallied behind their head coach with dramatic win after dramatic win.

Of course, storybook seasons are not always what they seem on the surface. On a play-by-play basis, the Colts weren't even close to postseason quality. Over the course of the season, they were outscored by 30 points and had a turnover margin of minus-12. Even in the midst of #chuckstrong, they somehow allowed Mark Sanchez and the New York Jets to reach the end zone five times in a 35-9 loss. (We repeat: *Mark Sanchez and the New York Jets.*) Another key part of the Colts' successful season was their relatively soft schedule, the easiest in the league with an average opponent DVOA of -7.4%. No team has the luxury of picking and choosing its own schedule, but in retrospect their storybook season was clearly built on narrow wins over teams well out of playoff contention. The Colts posted a negative single-game DVOA in eight of their final 13 games, including a -48.5% DVOA in an overtime win over the Tennessee Titans. Based on the Colts' DVOA both overall and in specific situations, our estimated wins metric projected the Colts to win just 6.2 games; that's the largest gap between wins and estimated wins in the history of DVOA (Table 1). Despite their 11-5 record and playoff appearance, the Colts were still a work in progress and needed to address certain key positions in the offseason to be considered playoff contenders in 2013.

The first major change was the departure of Arians, who left for the head coaching position with the Arizona Cardinals.

2013 Colts Schedule

Week	Opp.	Week	Opp.	Week	Opp.
1	OAK	7	DEN	13	TEN
2	MIA	8	BYE	14	at CIN
3	at SF	9	at HOU	15	HOU
4	at JAC	10	STL	16	at KC
5	SEA	11	at TEN (Thu.)	17	JAC
6	at SD (Mon.)	12	at ARI		

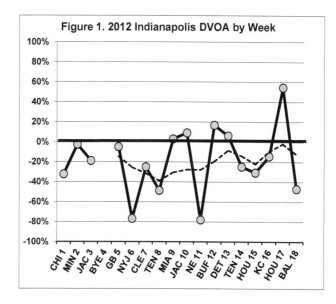

Figure 1. 2012 Indianapolis DVOA by Week

For most quarterbacks entering their second NFL season, losing the offensive coordinator would mean having to learn new offensive language for the second time in as many years. Fortunately for Luck, the "new" offense he will have to learn in the NFL is the same system he ran to perfection in college, as Pagano hired Stanford offensive coordinator Pep Hamilton to replace Arians. If the buzzword among newly hired defensive coordinators is "aggressive," the offensive equivalent is "balance," which was used quite frequently by Hamilton during the implementation of the system during OTAs. Hamilton has some credibility in this regard, as Stanford ran the ball well over 50 percent of the time during his two seasons as the play-caller. Hamilton also believes in balance in ball distribution: Stanford got 38 percent of its receptions from wide receivers, 28 percent from running backs, and 33 percent from tight ends (including current Colts starter Coby Fleener). Even with Hamilton bringing a West Coast-influenced scheme from Stanford, however, the Colts plan to continue to have vertical elements in their passing game. Wayne and the tight ends—Fleener and Dwayne Allen—are ideal short-to-intermediate targets, while free-agent addition Darrius Heyward-Bey and 2012 third-round pick T.Y. Hilton will be sent deep to gain big chunks of yardage on shot plays.

Luck didn't just attempt more passes (627) than any rookie quarterback in NFL history; he also led the league with 83 quarterback hits (20 more than any other quarterback) and 122

knockdowns (29 more than any other quarterback). Luck was an "ironman" in 2012, one of only two quarterbacks to play in 100 percent of his team's snaps (Philip Rivers was the other), and there is no reason to continually expose the most important player on the roster to that much abuse. A more balanced approach on offense should help limit Luck's exposure to contact. Grigson also dedicated much of his second offseason to protecting Luck by improving the personnel both in front of him and behind him.

"We don't need him running for his life. We need him to feel as comfortable as possible," Grigson said about Luck at the conclusion of the offseason program. Grigson doled out $49 million in contracts to improve the offensive line: $35 million to right tackle Gosder Cherilus and $14 million to left guard Donald Thomas. Then he invested two mid-round picks on guard Hugh Thornton and center Khaled Holmes. The Colts offensive line used six different starting configurations last year, and the offseason maneuvers should improve both the starting five and the depth of that unit. In early June, running back Ahmad Bradshaw, whose pass blocking is regarded as superb, was signed to a $2 million deal—an impressive dollar amount at a time when most remaining free agents are signing for merely the opportunity to attend training camp and score some free Nike workout gear.

The Colts operated a 4-3 defense for a very long time before the arrivals of Grigson and Pagano, and there are only so many roster moves a team can make in one offseason, so the Colts ran what was essentially a "hybrid" 3-4 defense last season. More of the same is expected in 2013, though more 3-4 players were added this offseason. Versatile defensive lineman Ricky Jean-Francois, who played for defensive coordinator Greg Manusky with the San Francisco 49ers, signed a $22 million contract and is projected to start at the three-technique. Another free-agent addition who played for Manusky in San Francisco, Aubrayo Franklin, adds a sturdy, veteran presence for recent draft picks Josh Chapman (2012) and Montori Hughes (2013) to learn from. Former Packers outside linebacker Erik Walden's experience in a 3-4 system earned him a contract worth an eye-popping $16 million from the Colts. The Colts hope that he and strong safety LaRon

Table 1. Biggest Gap Between Wins and DVOA Estimated Wins, 1991-2012

Team	Year	W-L	Estim. Wins	Dif	DVOA	Rk	W-L Y+1	DVOA Y+1	Rk Y+1
IND	2012	11-5	6.2	-4.8	-16.0%	25	--	--	--
DEN	1991	12-4	8.0	-4.0	3.5%	12	8-8	-14.9%	22
ATL	2012	13-3	9.1	-3.9	9.1%	10	--	--	--
STL	2003	12-4	8.2	-3.8	1.3%	14	8-8	-27.2%	31
OAK	1998	8-8	4.2	-3.8	-18.3%	27	8-8	21.2%	3
HOU	2012	12-4	8.3	-3.7	6.7%	11	--	--	--
SEA	2006	9-7	5.4	-3.6	-13.0%	24	10-6	14.7%	9
IND	1999	13-3	9.5	-3.5	4.0%	17	13-3	19.9%	7
IND	1992	9-7	5.5	-3.5	-27.2%	27	4-12	-37.2%	28
CHI	2001	13-3	9.6	-3.4	15.8%	8	4-12	-12.5%	26
CAR	2003	11-5	7.7	-3.3	0.6%	16	7-9	1.3%	14
MIN	1996	9-7	5.7	-3.3	-14.5%	24	9-7	-4.6%	19
ATL	2004	11-5	7.7	-3.3	-4.8%	17	8-8	-5.8%	19
AVERAGE*		**10.6**	**7.2**		**-5.3%**		**7.9**	**-4.5%**	

*Average does not include 2012 teams

Landry, who is built more like a linebacker, can improve a group that ranked 32nd in run defense DVOA last season.

The Colts' transition to a 3-4 system remains a work in progress, however, and the best example of that is first-round pick Bjoern Werner. The German-born Werner played defensive end at Florida State, but at 6-foot-3 and 266 pounds, will be an outside linebacker in the Colts' base defense. How quickly Werner actually contributes on early downs will depend on how quickly he acclimates to his new position and learns to function in space. Reports out of the OTAs were positively glowing—they rarely are otherwise—but the real tests will come when contact increases in training camp and the preseason. At the very least, the Colts hope that Werner can play defensive end in a four-man nickel front to add some teeth to a pass rush whose only veteran pass-rush presence is now Mathis, who had eight sacks (his lowest total since 2007) in 12 games. Werner had 23.5 sacks in college, including 13 in 2012, and has a five-year SackSEER projection of 28.5 sacks. The Colts got to opposing quarterbacks just 32 times last season, so they're banking on Werner to create pressure on opponents. Better cornerback play from Vontae Davis (who improved significantly in the final few weeks of last season) and free-agent Gregory Toler should also give the pass rush more time to work.

The Colts hope that all these offseason moves will help them take the next step and become Super Bowl contenders in 2013. Given that the Colts' magical #chuckstrong playoff run was built on remarkable amounts of serendipity, most readers are probably expecting us to counter that expectation with a 6-10 projection and a long screed about regression towards the mean. But the most realistic forecast for the Colts' 2013 season is actually somewhere between the two. The defense should be better, and it's reasonable to expect Luck to make continued improvement in his second season. The team's development on the field will almost certainly be countered by less good fortune, especially when it comes to winning those close games. But the Colts are still gifted by good fortune when it comes to the strength of their opponents. We are projecting the Colts to play the weakest schedule in the NFL for the second straight season. The AFC South is not very strong and the AFC West, apart from Denver, is filled with mediocrity.

The 2012 Colts were a rare example of a team that made the playoffs while going through a rebuilding process. If the defense makes progress, and the Colts can take some pressure off Luck with a better offensive line and an improved running game, the 2013 Colts could be an even rarer beast: a team that makes the playoffs *twice* while going through a rebuilding process.

Brian McIntyre

2012 Colts Stats by Week

Wk	vs.	W-L	PF	PA	YDF	YDA	TO	Total	Off	Def	ST
1	at CHI	L	21	41	356	428	-4	-32%	12%	32%	-12%
2	MIN	W	23	20	278	327	1	-3%	1%	7%	4%
3	JAC	L	17	22	437	333	1	-19%	3%	18%	-4%
4	BYE										
5	GB	W	30	27	464	356	0	-5%	-2%	-3%	-7%
6	at NYJ	L	9	35	298	351	-4	-77%	-33%	51%	7%
7	CLE	W	17	13	321	319	-1	-25%	2%	28%	1%
8	at TEN	W	19	13	457	339	-1	-49%	13%	47%	-14%
9	MIA	W	23	20	516	365	0	3%	29%	19%	-7%
10	at JAC	W	27	10	359	337	1	9%	5%	6%	11%
11	at NE	L	24	59	448	446	-4	-78%	-12%	32%	-35%
12	BUF	W	20	13	312	304	-1	17%	-29%	-27%	18%
13	at DET	W	35	33	459	451	-2	6%	-1%	1%	8%
14	TEN	W	27	23	269	356	0	-25%	-44%	-9%	10%
15	at HOU	L	17	29	272	417	-1	-31%	4%	22%	-13%
16	at KC	W	20	13	288	507	3	-15%	4%	16%	23%
17	HOU	W	28	16	265	352	2	55%	-22%	-10%	24%
18	at BAL	L	9	24	419	439	0	-47%	-13%	30%	-4%

Trends and Splits

	Offense	Rank	Defense	Rank
Total DVOA	-2.9%	18	14.0%	31
Unadjusted VOA	0.8%	17	12.0%	30
Weighted Trend	-5.8%	19	11.5%	29
Variance	3.9%	4	4.5%	13
Average Opponent	0.7%	17	-6.2%	32
Passing	2.3%	21	18.0%	27
Rushing	-4.3%	18	9.1%	32
First Down	-14.9%	27	6.5%	25
Second Down	-0.6%	18	22.9%	32
Third Down	18.7%	6	15.3%	27
First Half	0.7%	16	15.0%	31
Second Half	-6.7%	22	13.0%	26
Red Zone	3.0%	13	5.1%	18
Late and Close	-3.6%	15	2.1%	22

Five-Year Performance

Year	W-L	Pyth W	Est W	PF	PA	TO	Total	Rk	Off	Rk	Def	Rk	ST	Rk	Off AGL	Rk	Def AGL	Rk	Off Age	Rk	Def Age	Rk	ST Age	Rk
2008	12-4	10.2	10.4	377	298	+9	15.0%	8	14.2%	5	-3.1%	11	-2.3%	24	31.8	21	39.6	27	27.8	12	25.7	30	25.6	30
2009	14-2	10.9	11.1	416	307	+2	16.5%	8	16.8%	6	-0.8%	16	-1.1%	19	30.1	21	51.9	30	27.8	9	25.7	30	25.2	32
2010	10-6	9.2	8.2	435	388	-4	1.3%	16	13.1%	6	5.5%	24	-6.3%	31	42.5	30	48.1	31	28.0	8	26.4	23	25.4	31
2011	2-14	3.2	3.0	243	430	-12	-32.8%	31	-17.2%	27	9.3%	26	-6.2%	31	37.5	22	47.2	28	27.9	8	26.0	27	25.4	30
2012	11-5	7.2	6.2	357	387	-12	-16.0%	25	-2.9%	18	14.0%	31	0.9%	12	44.4	24	43.1	24	25.9	28	26.6	20	25.2	31

2012 Performance Based on Most Common Personnel Groups

IND Offense					IND Offense vs. Opponents				IND Defense				IND Defense vs. Opponents			
Pers	Freq	Yds	DVOA	Run%	Pers	Freq	Yds	DVOA	Pers	Freq	Yds	DVOA	Pers	Freq	Yds	DVOA
1.1	50%	5.9	10.2%	28%	Nickel Even	36%	5.6	7.5%	3-4-4	39%	6.3	17.9%	1.1	34%	6.3	18.6%
1.2	22%	5.1	-5.2%	48%	4-3-4	25%	5.1	-11.4%	Nickel Even	25%	6.4	31.8%	1.2	32%	6.3	4.6%
0.1	7%	5.5	-44.6%	3%	Dime+	19%	6.2	-2.7%	4-3-4	18%	6.4	-1.0%	2.1	16%	7.3	37.2%
1.0	6%	6.8	52.4%	10%	3-4-4	11%	4.2	-17.8%	Nickel Odd	12%	4.5	-28.7%	2.2	5%	3.2	-16.4%
1.3	4%	2.4	-55.2%	76%	Nickel Odd	8%	7.3	23.1%	Dime+	4%	8.8	79.0%	1.0	4%	6.3	21.8%
61.2	4%	5.8	8.2%	85%												

Strategic Tendencies

Run/Pass		Rk	Formation		Rk	Pass Rush		Rk	Secondary		Rk	Strategy		Rk
Runs, first half	33%	32	Form: Single Back	76%	4	Rush 3	6.8%	16	4 DB	57%	2	Play action	18%	21
Runs, first down	43%	28	Form: Empty Back	14%	2	Rush 4	54.0%	25	5 DB	37%	26	Avg Box (Off)	6.24	24
Runs, second-long	29%	21	Pers: 3+ WR	65%	5	Rush 5	27.5%	8	6+ DB	4%	19	Avg Box (Def)	6.53	3
Runs, power sit.	51%	20	Pers: 4+ WR	14%	1	Rush 6+	11.7%	6	CB by Sides	69%	24	Offensive Pace	29.47	10
Runs, behind 2H	28%	16	Pers: 2+ TE/6+ OL	34%	13	Sacks by LB	67.7%	5	DB Blitz	8%	22	Defensive Pace	29.10	3
Pass, ahead 2H	48%	14	Shotgun/Pistol	45%	18	Sacks by DB	16.1%	1	Hole in Zone	5%	30	Go for it on 4th	0.78	25

New philosophies on both offense and defense brought dramatic changes to the Colts' strategic tendencies. The Colts went from 31st to second in using empty back formations, and from 29th to first in using four-wide receiver formations. Their run-pass ratio in the first half of games dropped from 46 percent runs (ninth in 2011) to 33 percent (dead last in 2012). On defense, the old Colts rushed four a league-leading 82 percent of the time in 2011; the new Colts rushed four just 54 percent of the time in 2012. The Colts had five sacks by defensive backs last season; they had only one half-sack by a defensive back in the previous four seasons *combined* (Antoine Bethea in 2010). ☞ Indianapolis gained a league-leading 1,208 yards thanks to opponent penalties; they were second in total opponent penalties with 150, two behind Green Bay. ☞ The Colts' offense really worked when they protected Andrew Luck. They used "max protect" on 12.2 percent of passes and had 47.2% DVOA on those passes. Only Seattle and Denver had better DVOA when using max protect. ☞ Surprisingly, given the way they are building their offense around last year's two rookie tight ends, the Colts didn't use a single tight end on 7.3 percent of plays (sixth in the NFL) and had 6.8 yards per pass and 51.0% DVOA on these plays. ☞ The Colts only threw a league-low 8.1 percent of passes to running backs.

Passing

Player	DYAR	DVOA	Plays	NtYds	Avg	YAC	C%	TD	Int
A.Luck	257	-5.1%	662	4089	6.2	4.9	55.0%	23	17
M.Hasselbeck	-6	-11.5%	236	1268	5.4	4.1	62.4%	7	5

Rushing

Player	DYAR	DVOA	Plays	Yds	Avg	TD	Fum	Suc
V.Ballard	10	-7.4%	211	814	3.9	2	3	48%
D.Brown	-5	-9.8%	108	417	3.9	1	0	44%
A.Luck	123	41.0%	42	270	6.4	5	0	-
D.Carter	55	24.7%	32	122	3.8	3	0	63%
M.Moore	-34	-68.4%	13	20	1.5	0	1	31%
T.Y.Hilton	9	-1.2%	5	29	5.8	0	0	-
A.Bradshaw	230	15.8%	221	1015	4.6	6	3	52%
S.Havili	8	24.2%	6	22	3.7	1	0	50%

Receiving

Player	DYAR	DVOA	Plays	Ctch	Yds	Y/C	YAC	TD	C%
R.Wayne	73	-6.8%	196	107	1350	12.6	3.4	5	55%
D.Avery*	-75	-19.1%	125	60	781	13.0	3.5	3	48%
T.Y.Hilton	151	10.7%	90	50	861	17.2	7.7	7	56%
L.Brazill	5	-6.6%	24	11	186	16.9	6.5	1	46%
K.Adams*	-20	-51.5%	8	2	26	13.0	2.5	0	25%
D.Heyward-Bey	31	-5.3%	80	41	606	14.8	5.6	5	51%
D.Allen	67	14.9%	66	45	521	11.6	5.4	3	68%
C.Fleener	-2	-3.6%	48	26	281	10.8	4.0	2	54%
V.Ballard	38	10.7%	27	17	152	8.9	6.9	1	63%
D.Brown	11	0.9%	13	9	93	10.3	11.0	0	69%
M.Moore	44	83.4%	8	6	77	12.8	7.3	1	75%
A.Bradshaw	35	8.5%	31	23	245	10.7	11.9	0	74%
S.Havili	-12	-33.3%	12	7	43	6.1	4.4	0	58%

Offensive Line

Player	Pos	Age	GS	Snaps	Pen	Sk	Pass	Run	Player	Pos	Age	GS	Snaps	Pen	Sk	Pass	Run
Anthony Castonzo	LT	25	16/16	1169	5	8.5	28.5	7.5	Joe Reitz	LG	28	9/8	474	2	0	9.5	2
Mike McGlynn	RG	28	16/16	1167	1	3.5	21	9.5	A.Q. Shipley*	C	27	14/5	465	0	0	2	1
Winston Justice*	RT	29	12/12	778	7	4	15.5	2	Seth Olsen*	G	28	5/4	283	2	1	5	4
Jeffrey Linkenbach	LG	26	16/8	771	2	3.5	15	3.5	Gosder Cherilus	RT	29	16/16	1200	9	1.5	18.5	5
Samson Satele	C	29	11/11	631	3	3	7	2	Donald Thomas	G	28	16/7	606	3	2	9	4.5

Year	Yards	ALY	Rk	Power	Rk	Stuff	Rk	2nd Lev	Rk	Open Field	Rk	Sacks	ASR	Rk	Short	Long	F-Start	Cont.
2010	3.91	3.82	22	56%	22	20%	20	1.04	24	0.64	21	16	2.8%	1	12	1	20	29
2011	4.12	3.91	25	50%	30	20%	17	1.13	20	0.72	23	35	6.9%	18	17	8	19	22
2012	3.78	3.76	26	72%	2	25%	30	1.23	13	0.48	28	41	6.8%	17	8	17	10	22

2012 ALY by direction:	Left End 4.11 (16)	Left Tackle 4.07 (16)	Mid/Guard 3.54 (30)	Right Tackle 4 (14)	Right End 3.42 (27)

The Colts invested the No. 1 overall pick on Andrew Luck; now they need to figure out how to protect him. The Colts only finished in the middle of the pack in Adjusted Sack Rate in part because of Luck's ability to get rid of the ball or scramble under pressure, but the pressure and blown block numbers for the Colts were horrific. Luck took 83 quarterback hits where he was knocked to the ground after a pass, 22 more than any other quarterback. He was under pressure on 26.3 percent of pass plays, fourth in the league.

Left tackle Anthony Castonzo had the dubious honor of leading all NFL offensive linemen with 36 blown blocks. This is a worrying sign about Castonzo's development; it's one thing for a first-round pick to have an awful year as a rookie, but by year two he should be improving. Closely behind Castonzo was right guard Mike McGlynn, who our game charters had leading all NFL guards with 30.5 blown blocks. That includes 9.5 blown blocks on running plays, which may partially explain the Colts ranking 30th in both Adjusted Line Yards on mid/guard runs and Stuffs. Castonzo and McGlynn were the mainstays on the line, while center Samson Satele and right tackle Winston Justice missed a handful of games apiece and veterans Jeff Linkenbach and Joe Reitz split duties at left guard.

A terrible 2012 performance means change is coming for 2013. In the first three days of free agency, Colts GM Ryan Grigson properly guessed the rock lyrics to open Jim Irsay's checkbook, which he used to sign guard Donald Thomas to a four-year, $14 million contract. That's a surprising investment in a player who was a part-timer with the New England Patriots last season and who hasn't been a regular starter since 2009. A bigger investment was made in former Detroit right tackle Gosder Cherilus: a five-year, $35 million contract that included $16.5 million in guaranteed money. The Colts continued to bolster their offensive line depth in the middle rounds of the draft, snagging Hugh Thornton out of Illinois in the third round and Khaled Holmes out of USC in the fourth. Holmes can play center or guard; he battled injuries at USC and will need to improve his pass-blocking to earn a starting job at the next level. Thornton played left tackle for the Illini last season, and while he has the athleticism, feet and arm length to play on the right side, he is projected to move to guard in the NFL. The Colts do not *need* either to start right away, but Thornton could push for the starting right guard job in training camp. The Colts continued to bolster their tackle depth after the draft, signing Boston College (where else) left tackle Emmett Cleary to a deal that included a $20,000 signing bonus, the second-largest signing bonus received by a 2013 undrafted free agent. Ben Ijalana, a 2011 second-round pick out of Villanova who has played just 36 NFL snaps due to knee injuries, will also vie for a roster spot during the preseason.

Given the overall poor performance of this line, the Colts' 72 percent success rate in short-yardage situations seems a bit absurd. The best explanation there revolves around other players: backup running back Delone Carter was particularly strong getting those tough yards, and the Colts got very good blocking when Dwayne Allen lined up at fullback.

Defensive Front Seven

Defensive Line	Age	Pos	Snaps	Plays	TmPct	Rk	Stop	Dfts	BTkl	Runs	St%	Rk	RuYd	Rk	Sack	Hit	Hur	Tips
					Overall						vs. Run					Pass Rush		
Cory Redding	33	DE	584	40	5.7%	29	31	9	2	29	83%	14	1.7	13	2	2	7.5	5
Antonio Johnson*	29	DT	450	25	3.6%	48	19	3	3	23	78%	27	2.3	33	0	2	3	0
Fili Moala	28	DT	311	15	3.8%	--	13	3	1	13	85%	--	1.2	--	0	3	4	1
Drake Nevis	24	DT	260	15	3.4%	--	13	2	0	12	92%	--	2.3	--	1	1	1	0
Lawrence Guy	23	DE	184	17	3.8%	--	12	1	0	16	69%	--	3.3	--	1	1	1	0
Ricky Jean-Francois	27	DT	286	22	2.8%	64	17	5	0	20	75%	34	2.1	26	2	0	0	0
Aubrayo Franklin	33	DT	280	20	3.3%	54	17	1	3	20	85%	7	2.3	31	0	0	3	0

Linebackers	Age	Pos	Snaps	Plays	TmPct	Rk	Stop	Dfts	BTkl	Sack	Hit	Hur	Tips	Runs	St%	Rk	Yds	Rk	Tgts	Suc%	Rk	AdjYd	Rk	PD
					Overall					Pass Rush				vs. Run					vs. Pass					
Jerrell Freeman	27	OLB	1041	148	18.6%	7	77	26	7	2	0	0.5	1	97	60%	79	4.5	102	30	49%	46	7.9	63	2
Dwight Freeney*	25	OLB	699	13	1.9%	110	74	28	0	5	8	18	1	6	67%	44	1.8	8	1	98%	--	1.0	--	3
Robert Mathis	32	OLB	624	35	5.9%	97	27	16	5	8	6	8.5	1	20	80%	10	1.9	11	7	60%	--	6.8	--	1
Jerry Hughes*	25	OLB	596	35	4.4%	--	23	13	1	4	6	15	1	22	68%	--	2.5	--	4	39%	--	12.3	--	0
Moise Fokou*	28	ILB	379	40	5.0%	--	23	10	2	1	4	3.5	0	18	56%	--	3.1	--	18	49%	47	6.5	30	1
Kavell Conner	26	ILB	324	56	8.7%	69	38	6	4	1	2	3	0	46	67%	43	2.1	14	14	48%	--	7.8	--	4
Pat Angerer	26	ILB	299	29	5.3%	--	17	3	2	0	2	1	0	19	68%	--	3.5	--	10	47%	--	9.4	--	1
Erik Walden	28	OLB	763	50	6.5%	88	40	13	1	3	11	11.5	0	35	77%	13	2.9	30	11	78%	--	1.7	--	5
Kelvin Sheppard	25	ILB	504	78	9.6%	65	46	6	1	2	2	2	0	60	60%	77	4.1	93	13	60%	--	5.7	--	1

Year	Yards	ALY	Rk	Power	Rk	Stuff	Rk	2nd Level	Rk	Open Field	Rk	Sacks	ASR	Rk	Short	Long
2010	4.58	4.40	28	57%	8	17%	24	1.28	27	0.89	21	30	5.6%	25	17	7
2011	4.36	4.41	27	65%	19	17%	24	1.27	22	0.70	11	29	6.8%	15	12	12
2012	5.10	4.32	27	64%	19	16%	30	1.15	10	1.49	32	32	5.8%	27	14	9

2012 ALY by direction:	Left End 4.24 (21)	Left Tackle 3.91 (13)	Mid/Guard 4.31 (27)	Right Tackle 4.27 (24)	Right End 5.21 (29)

Chuck Pagano's 3-4 scheme meant significant changes to the Colts' front seven. Dwight Freeney was slow to adjust to the transition from defensive end to outside linebacker, posting five sacks as he battled a lingering high ankle sprain. The all-time franchise leader in sacks was not re-signed and is now playing for Pagano's brother in San Diego. Robert Mathis fared better in his first season at linebacker, picking up a team-high eight sacks and his first career interception. He'll move into Freeney's "rush" outside linebacker position this year, and goes from playing mostly on the left side to mostly on the right. The Colts took a two-pronged approach to replacing Freeney. For the short-term, they signed Erik Walden away from Green Bay with a four-year, $16 million contract (with $8 million guaranteed). Walden had a 78 percent Adjusted Success Rate in pass coverage and is good against the run. (OK, not the read option. Let's say *most* runs,) However, the contract seems a bit exorbitant for a journeyman who is now on his fifth team and has never posted more than three sacks in a season. The long-term replacement is first-round pick Bjoern Werner, a German-born pass rusher who had 23.5 sacks during his 41-game career at Florida State. Werner has a SackSEER projection of 28.5 sacks over his first five seasons, which ranked third among edge rushers in the 2013 draft. The arrivals of Werner and Walden effectively pushed 2010 first-rounder Jerry Hughes off the roster. In April, the Colts dealt the disappointing Hughes to Buffalo for Kelvin Sheppard, who could push Pat Angerer for one of the two starting jobs at inside linebacker. The other will continue to be manned by Jerrell Freeman, a former CFL All-Star who led the Colts in defensive Plays.

Up front, the Colts got a solid season from free-agent addition Cory Redding, who knew Pagano's system from Baltimore and was solid against the run while recording a pair of sacks and 7.5 hurries. Redding returns at defensive end, but will have new linemates. The Colts are high on 2012 fifth-round pick Josh Chapman, a 6-foot-1, 316-pounder from Alabama who missed most of his rookie season with a knee injury. The Colts also signed veteran nose tackle Aubrayo Franklin and used a fifth-round pick on Montori Hughes (Tennessee-Martin), a 6-foot-4, 340-pound behemoth who moves like a linebacker. They get Brandon McKinney, a potential starter at nose tackle last season, back from a torn ACL. And they added versatile former 49ers lineman Ricky Jean-Francois. Jean-Francois can play all three spots on the line and while he was not working with the No. 1 unit during the OTAs, he is expected to start somewhere on the line this season. The new additions mean that recent high draft picks Fili Moala and Drake Nevis will have to earn their roster spots this season.

Defensive Secondary

Secondary	Age	Pos	Snaps	Plays	TmPct	Rk	Stop	Dfts	BTkl	Runs	St%	Rk	Yds	Rk	Tgts	Tgt%	Rk	Dist	Suc%	Rk	APaYd	Rk	PD	Int
Antoine Bethea	29	FS	1049	107	13.4%	9	35	15	7	57	33%	46	10.2	65	27	6.1%	47	10.1	54%	37	6.7	23	2	0
Cassius Vaughn	26	CB	818	75	9.4%	26	23	7	4	11	27%	71	14.4	86	106	23.7%	4	10.4	44%	78	7.9	52	8	1
Tom Zbikowski*	28	SS	681	41	7.5%	56	15	4	6	16	31%	52	10.8	67	21	6.7%	37	11.8	65%	14	5.4	11	4	1
Vontae Davis	25	CB	590	58	11.7%	8	27	11	2	13	62%	11	4.2	11	54	19.4%	30	14.5	41%	82	9.9	85	7	3
Jerraud Powers*	26	CB	505	48	12.1%	5	21	9	3	8	75%	5	8.4	67	57	25.3%	2	11.8	47%	67	8.0	55	8	1
Darius Buttler	27	CB	370	35	6.4%	72	16	9	6	4	100%	1	2.5	3	41	13.4%	76	11.7	54%	29	6.8	26	8	4
Joe Lefeged	25	SS	343	20	2.5%	--	8	2	1	13	62%	--	5.9	--	3	0.6%	--	11.6	42%	--	19.5	--	0	0
Josh Gordy	26	CB	210	15	2.0%	--	4	3	0	2	0%	--	8.0	--	25	5.9%	--	9.3	46%	--	8.9	--	0	0
Greg Toler	28	CB	301	35	6.2%	76	14	8	0	8	25%	73	5.8	33	40	14.5%	65	15.7	66%	2	6.2	9	9	2
LaRon Landry	29	SS	1019	106	13.6%	8	41	11	9	60	42%	23	5.9	20	42	10.4%	9	14.6	55%	33	7.6	41	6	2

Year	Pass D Rank	vs. #1 WR	Rk	vs. #2 WR	Rk	vs. Other WR	Rk	vs. TE	Rk	vs. RB	Rk
2010	26	-9.0%	9	-6.0%	10	-2.9%	17	28.8%	31	18.8%	28
2011	28	26.2%	26	25.3%	27	33.7%	32	19.6%	22	-2.5%	17
2012	27	11.0%	22	3.0%	17	28.5%	31	22.2%	30	-22.3%	6

Desperately in need of a No. 1 cornerback, the Colts dealt their 2013 second-round pick to Miami two weeks before the season began for veteran Vontae Davis. Davis struggled with injuries for the first half of the season, which led to him ranking towards the bottom of the league among cornerbacks in Adjusted Yards per Pass and Adjusted Success Rate. The good news for the Colts is that Davis was much improved when he returned to the lineup late in the season. In his first five games, he allowed 10.9 Adjusted Yards per Pass with an abominable 22 percent Adjusted Success Rate. After he returned to the lineup in Week 13, his Adjusted Yards per Pass dropped to 9.2 and his Adjusted Success Rate rose to 53 percent. Davis was just one of the many Colts cornerbacks to be plagued by injuries in 2012. Jerraud Powers once again failed to make it through a full season as a toe injury landed him on injured reserve in Week 11. The Colts essentially "traded" him to Arizona in free agency; Powers signed with Arizona one day after the Colts signed former Arizona cornerback Greg Toler. Toler will fit right in to this unit because he has only played 301 snaps over the last two seasons due to, yes, injuries. The Colts are banking on him staying healthy as the starter opposite Davis, and we wish them good luck with that. Returning in a nickel role is Cassius Vaughn, who was the only Colts cornerback to play in more than 60 percent of the defensive snaps in 2012. Darius Butler did not join the Colts until Week 4, but ended up with a handful of starts and led the team with four interceptions, two of which he returned for touchdowns. Butler looked like a complete bust after the Patriots took him in the second round of the 2009 draft, but he operates well in the slot and could push Vaughn for the nickelback role.

Antoine Bethea has been a steady performer at free safety, although he hasn't had an interception since he picked off the now-retired David Garrard in 2010. The Colts signed strong safety LaRon Landry away from the Jets in free agency, which rendered veteran Tom Zbikowski expendable. Landry brings impressive physical attributes to the Colts secondary and will be expected to be a game-changer both against the run and pass. Unfortunately, he also has a miserable history of injuries, and missed most of the 2010 and 2011 seasons with Achilles and groin injuries. The Colts certainly hope they can keep Landry healthy so that he can help solve their problem with tackling running backs in the open field; the Colts allowed 1.49 Open Field Yards per carry last season, narrowly surpassing the 2008 Detroit Lions to set a new record for the worst figure in our defensive line data (since 1995).

Special Teams

Year	DVOA	Rank	FG/XP	Rank	Net Kick	Rank	Kick Ret	Rank	Net Punt	Rank	Punt Ret	Rank	Hidden	Rank
2010	-6.3%	31	6.9	4	-3.4	23	-17.6	32	-8.1	27	-9.5	30	-4.2	19
2011	-6.2%	31	-0.1	16	-2.8	25	-9.1	32	-10.9	30	-8.3	28	-5.8	24
2012	0.9%	12	-3.1	22	4.4	9	0.1	15	-2.4	19	5.3	6	1.4	14

With a new front-office regime and a wave of young talent at the bottom of the roster, the Colts had above-average special teams for the first time since 2004 and only the second time since 1996. The improvement was largely due to improvement in kickoffs and the return game. Punter and kickoff specialist Pat McAfee finished second in the NFL with 5.8 estimated points of gross kickoff value. He also had his best year so far with a 40.3-yard net average on punts, though poor coverage led to a negative net punt value for the Colts as a team. The Colts felt McAfee was valuable enough to use the franchise tag on him this offseason. 40-year-old kicker Adam Vinatieri was 26-of-33 on field goal attempts, with three of his misses coming from beyond 50 yards but three others coming in the 30-to-39 yard range.

Rookie wide receiver T.Y. Hilton injected life into the Colts' punt return game, averaging 11.5 yards per return with a 75-yard touchdown. He was one of many kick returners the Colts tried, who as a group averaged just 18.7 yards on 33 returns through Week 14. Then the Colts signed free agent running back Deji Karim, who would average 36.4 yards on nine returns, including a 101-yard touchdown in the season-ending win over Houston. On just those nine returns, Karim was fifth in the league with 8.5 estimated points worth of field position. Small sample size? The Colts front office seemed to think so, because they chose not to tender Karim as a restricted free agent, and he's now with the Texans. Hilton could take on both kickoff and punt returns this year, or the kickoff job might go to seventh-round running back Kerwynn Williams, who averaged 25.2 yards with one touchdown during his career at Utah State.

Coaching Staff

For keeping the ship afloat and helping to guide the Colts to a 9-3 record that allowed them to qualify for the playoffs, offensive coordinator/interim head coach Bruce Arians was named the AP NFL Coach of the Year, receiving 36.5 of 50 votes. Second on the balloting was Chuck Pagano with 5.5 votes. Arians, who was not credited with any coaching "wins" as the interim head coach, was a hot commodity on the head coaching market and will now lead the Arizona Cardinals. Arians' departure did not lead to a mass exodus of Colts assistants to the desert, though offensive line coach Harold Goodwin was named the Cardinals' offensive coordinator. To replace Arians as offensive coordinator, the Colts hired Pep Hamilton, who was Andrew Luck's quarterbacks coach and offensive coordinator at Stanford. Assistant offensive line coach Jeff Gilbert was promoted to replace Goodwin. Despite last year's improvement on special teams, the Colts and special teams coach Marwan Maalouf "mutually agreed" to part ways in January. Former St. Louis Rams and Kansas City Chiefs special teams coach Tom McMahon was hired to replace Maalouf, who accepted an assistant special teams position with the Miami Dolphins.

Jacksonville Jaguars

2012 Record: 2-14	Total DVOA: -33.0% (31st)	2013 Mean Projection: 6.1 wins	On the Clock (0-4): 28%
Pythagorean Wins: 3.3 (31st)	Offense: -18.4% (28th)	Postseason Odds: 13.9%	Mediocrity (5-7): 46%
Snap-Weighted Age: 26.6 (18th)	Defense: 11.7% (28th)	Super Bowl Odds: 0.4%	Playoff Contender (8-10): 22%
Average Opponent: -3.3% (24th)	Special Teams: -3.0% (25th)	Proj. Avg. Opponent: -5.1% (31st)	Super Bowl Contender (11+): 4%

2012: The worst season in Jaguars history finally shuts the door on the Gene Smith era.

2013: A journey of a thousand miles begins with a single draft.

Once upon a time, the Jacksonville Jaguars were one of the top teams in the NFL. The last time they made the playoffs, in 2007, they finished third in DVOA (24.1%). They haven't had a positive DVOA since.

From there, the Jaguars posted DVOA ratings of -1.1% (2008), -9.3% (2009) and -9.0% (2010) before careening towards the bottom of the league. In the last two years, they've had -17.4% DVOA and -33.0% DVOA, and their 2-14 record in 2012 was the worst in franchise history. A lot of the Jaguars' on-field failure can be laid at the feet of Gene Smith, a longtime scout and personnel executive with the Jaguars who was promoted to general manager between the 2008 and 2009 seasons. Fourteen of the 26 players Smith drafted during his tenure as general manager were no longer with the team at the conclusion of the 2013 offseason program. "The "dirty dozen" players that remain include quarterback Blaine Gabbert, wide receiver Justin Blackmon and punter Bryan Anger. Those are selections that may have, at some point in the last two seasons, caused Smith to pull a Gob Bluth from *Arrested Development* and mutter to himself "I've made a huge mistake.""

Gabbert, the tenth overall pick in 2011, had -1,009 DYAR in his rookie season, the second-lowest mark of the DVOA era behind David Carr with the expansion Houston Texans in 2002. Last year, Gabbert had -269 DYAR in a little over half a season that would be shortened by injuries, and he is entering a "make or break" season in 2013. While hindsight is and will always be 20/20, Smith chose Gabbert ahead of Christian Ponder, Andy Dalton, and Colin Kaepernick, each of whom have already led their teams to the playoffs (Dalton twice). The following year, Smith used a third-round pick on Anger, who came off the board five spots ahead of Seattle Seahawks quarterback Russell Wilson.

The desire to give Gabbert a receiver to develop with may have spurred Smith to trade up two spots in the 2012 draft to pick Blackmon, who posted huge numbers at Oklahoma State but had off-field issues and lacked top-end speed. Before Blackmon had even signed his first NFL contract, he was arrested in Oklahoma on DUI charges, and he has since followed that up with a four-game suspension to start the 2013 season for violating the league's substance abuse policy. One of the two picks that the Jaguars dealt to the Tampa Bay Buccaneers to move up and select Blackmon was in the fourth round, the No. 101 overall pick that could have been used on Michigan State's Kirk Cousins, who posted a positive DYAR (58) in limited duty as the No. 2 behind Robert Griffin III.

Of course, there are no guarantees that Ponder, Dalton, Kaepernick or Wilson would have developed the way that they have, or as quickly as they have, had they been drafted by Jacksonville instead. But even with the rookie compensation system reigning in the contracts of Top-10 picks, swinging and missing on a quarterback with that valuable of a draft choice is still cause for a team to part ways with a general manager.

Owner Shahid Khan's search to replace Smith began with, and ultimately finished with, David Caldwell. Caldwell had spent the previous five seasons with the Atlanta Falcons, first as director of scouting before he was promoted to director of player personnel. Caldwell worked previously as a scout for the Indianapolis Colts during their reign as one of the most successful franchises of the 2000s and was a hot commodity on the GM market this offseason. According to Peter King of *Sports Illustrated*, Caldwell turned down an offer from the New York Jets that included a $1 million housing allowance to accept the job in Jacksonville.

If Caldwell's first major decision as the general manager of the Jaguars is any indication, he's not going to let familiarity get in the way of finding the right fit. Most new general managers are going to want one of "their guys" as head coach, but incumbent Jaguars head coach Mike Mularkey was one of Caldwell's guys; the two worked together in Atlanta for four years. Caldwell decided this guy who was one of his guys wasn't actually his guy, letting him go after just one year with the Jaguars. Almost immediately, 49ers offensive coordinator Greg Roman, Caldwell's former teammate at John Carroll University, was rumored to be the favorite for the position, with other candidates including Falcons defensive coordinator Mike Nolan and Falcons special teams coordinator Keith Armstrong. None of them got the job either. Instead, Caldwell settled on Gus Bradley, to whom he had no previous connection other than watching Bradley make impressive second-half adjustments as Seattle's defensive coordinator during the Falcons' 30-28 divisional playoff win over the Seahawks. A quarter of NFL teams hired new coaches in the offseason and Bradley was the only defensive-minded coach to land one of the top jobs.

Caldwell and Bradley both come from successful programs, but it may take a while to clean up the mess they inherited.

2013 Jaguars Schedule

Week	Opp.	Week	Opp.	Week	Opp.
1	KC	7	SD	13	at CLE
2	at OAK	8	vs. SF (U.K.)	14	HOU (Thu.)
3	at SEA	9	BYE	15	BUF
4	IND	10	at TEN	16	TEN
5	at STL	11	ARI	17	at IND
6	at DEN	12	at HOU		

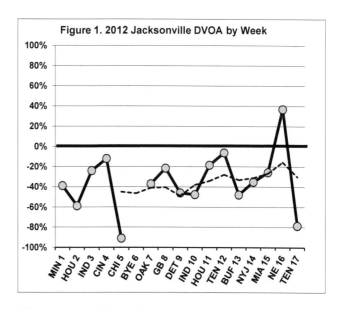

Figure 1. 2012 Jacksonville DVOA by Week

Draft mistakes were not Smith's only missteps; perhaps out of desperation to save his job, Smith spent a lot of Shahid Khan's money in 2012 free agency, and he didn't spend it well. The most glaring example of that was deciding that one decent season from Laurent Robinson as the third receiver in Dallas somehow warranted a five-year, $32.5 million contract that included $13.6 million in guaranteed money. For more than $9.1 million in cash, Robinson logged 264 snaps ($34,470 per play) during a concussion-filled 2012 season and was cut. Defensive end Jeremy Mincey was re-signed; the $9 million the Jaguars gave him in the first year of the new contract got them just three sacks. Cornerback Aaron Ross earned $2.6 million in cash, was allowed to leave training camp to watch his wife compete in the London Olympics, had zero interceptions and, following his release this offseason, went on the NFL Network and referred to his one season in Jacksonville as a "vacation."

Khan took responsibility for the free-agent spending in 2012, stating that the franchise had overestimated the talent level it possessed and how close the team actually was to competing. Khan cautioned fans to not be "delusional" about the roster. "The delusional part came from the amount of money they spent in free agency last year thinking they may be one or two pieces away and then to come back and have the end result be a 2-14 season," Caldwell said at the 2013 scouting combine. "There is a good core of players here that we feel good about it. We have our work cut out for us. We're going to have a very young team this season and it's going to be built through the draft and through college free agency."

So far, Caldwell has remained true to that vision. The Jaguars were mostly spectators in free agency, and the Jaguars sunk towards the bottom of the league in terms of cash spending in 2013. The largest free-agent contract belonged to defensive tackle Roy Miller, who pried $4.4 million over two seasons out of Caldwell. Caldwell was also fairly quiet during the 2013 NFL draft, staying put in most rounds except for one trade that added a seventh-round pick (cornerback Demetrius McCray) when the Eagles wanted to move up to take Matt Barkley. The draft also served as an example of how the Jaguars are incorporating advanced analytics, spearheaded by Tony Khan, Shad Khan's son and the team's senior vice president of football technology and analytics. Khan's group, which also includes Daniel Adler and Mike Stoeber, discovered that Gabbert was in the upper third of quarterbacks statistically when given at least 2.6 seconds to throw. That data helped Caldwell decide that offensive tackle was the right way to go with the No. 2 overall pick, which was used on Texas A&M's Luke Joeckel; he's slated to open at right tackle

while veteran (and 2014 free agent) Eugene Monroe continues to start at left tackle.

Who Joeckel and Monroe will be protecting will not be determined until training camp. Gabbert and Henne headline the competition, but Caldwell alluded to a much deeper competition upon the conclusion of the team's offseason program. Fortunately for Jaguars fans, that competition won't include Tim Tebow, a Jacksonville-area native; allegedly, one stipulation of Caldwell accepting the Jaguars' job is that he wouldn't sign or trade for Tebow. However, the Jaguars did bring in Mike Kafka, the former Eagles backup whom the Patriots cut when they decided to bring the Tebow circus to town. The Jaguars also spent $12,500 in guaranteed money on undrafted Arizona quarterback Matt Scott, an intriguing run-pass threat who was regarded as a mid-round prospect until questions about his size and durability caused him to slide completely out of the draft. Rounding out the competition is undrafted rookie Jordan Rodgers out of Vanderbilt. He takes over the all-important role of "Jordan who is the less-talented younger brother of a current NFL starting quarterback" from recent Jaguars third-stringer Jordan Palmer.

Whichever quarterback emerges in the starting role will not have the benefit of playing with a deep supporting cast. We project the Jaguars to be the league's worst offense in 2013. Running back Maurice Jones-Drew, the Jaguars' all-time leader in rushing touchdowns, missed the final 10 games of the regular season with a Lisfranc foot injury before undergoing surgery in December. Why the team and Jones-Drew waited so long to have that procedure is unclear, but the 28-year-old spent the offseason rehabbing the injury and was unable to participate in OTAs or minicamp. There is no guarantee Jones-Drew will be ready for training camp, and the Jaguars have very little depth behind him; Justin Forsett (53 DYAR in 63 runs as the No. 3 back with Houston last season) is the top backup entering camp. First-year offensive coordinator Jedd Fisch also plans to get the ball into the hands of former Michigan quarterback-turned- running back Denard Robinson about 10 to 15 times per game. However, it's unclear in what capacity those touches will come, and when was the last time that a rookie gimmick player undergoing a position change actually got ten touches a game? Jacksonville's receiving corps is fairly thin, as well, especially considering Blackmon's four-game suspension. Cecil Shorts is coming off a breakout season (154 DYAR, seven touchdowns) in 2012, but the main receivers after him are injury-prone slot receiver Jordan Shipley, replacement-level Cleveland refugee Mohamed Massaquoi, and fourth-round rookie Ace Sanders.

There is more hope for the defense. Bradley was instrumental in the Seahawks' growth into one of the NFL's most physical defenses. Though he was originally a protégé of Monte Kiffin, whose Tampa-2 is similar to the defense the Jaguars have run in recent seasons, Bradley plans to use a defense much closer to the Pete Carroll-influenced Seattle defense that mixes 3-4 and 4-3 principles. The clearest changes will take place on the outside of the defensive line. The Jaguars will now utilize the "Leo," a hybrid defensive end/outside linebacker position that is responsible for setting the edge against the run, creating a pass rush, and occasionally dropping into coverage. With such diverse responsibilities, "Leo" players tend to be undersized, weighing in the 245- to 265-pound range. They line up in a one- or two-point stance very wide on the weak side of the defense. Opposite the "Leo" will be a larger (290-plus pounds) strongside defensive end who will be responsible for two gaps and whose primary responsibility will be stopping the run.

When Bradley and Carroll arrived in Seattle, the Seahawks had to look outside the organization and think outside the box to fill those roles, trading for Chris Clemons to play the "Leo" and moving Red Bryant, an oft-injured defensive tackle, to defensive end. Those moves paid off as Clemons became a 10-sack per year player and Bryant emerged as a run-stopping force. The Jaguars have a natural fit at strongside defensive end in 295-pound Tyson Alualu, the 2010 first-round pick who played a similar position at Cal. Alulalu also has the versatility to slide inside and rush the passer from the defensive tackle position in nickel and dime packages. Jason Babin accumulated 36 sacks and two Pro Bowl appearances playing defensive end in a "Wide 9" front with the 2010 Tennessee Titans and 2011-12 Philadelphia Eagles, which makes him the likely starter at the "Leo." Over the long term, the Jaguars would

like to see 2012 second-round pick Andre Branch develop into that role. Branch had a SackSEER projection of 19.5 sacks over his first five seasons, but just one in limited action as a rookie. This year, he'll see more playing time as a second "Leo" in nickel packages.

Another big change on defense will come in the secondary, which will go from a simple zone scheme to one that will utilize more man-to-man press coverage and Cover-3 looks. How quickly the Jaguars are able to employ those principles hinges largely on them finding cornerbacks with the length and strength to play that style of defense. Even the Seahawks, who had been collecting cornerbacks to fit their press-man system for the previous three offseasons, used Cover-2 about 25 percent of the time during the 2012 season. The Jaguars devoted most of their draft resources to the secondary, using five of their eight picks on defensive backs. Second-round strong safety Jonathan Cyprien is slated to start, as is third-round cornerback Dwayne Gratz. It's no coincidence that the three cornerbacks taken by Jacksonville (Gratz and two seventh-rounders, Demetrius McCray and Jeremy Harris) are either over six feet tall or are strong enough to press opposing receivers at the line. Once the flurry of transactions begins in late August, it would not be a surprise to see the Jaguars claim former Seahawks, particularly those who play in the back seven. They already got a head start in the offseason by signing veteran cornerback Marcus Trufant.

Over the last few seasons, it has not been easy to be a Jaguars fan. The team has been mocked for the tarps covering sections of the upper deck at EverBank Field and lower bowls that were "less than capacity." They've had to deal with the annual rumors of the team relocating to Los Angeles and, during this past offseason became the team most likely to move to London, England. Things are looking up for this franchise, but it will take a miraculous turnaround or calamitous collapses by the Texans or Colts for the Jaguars to contend in the AFC South this season. It's going to take at least two or three seasons, but Khan hired the right man in Caldwell, who in turn hired the right man in Bradley, to steer the ship towards contention.

Brian McIntyre

2012 Jaguars Stats by Week

Wk	vs.	W-L	PF	PA	YDF	YDA	TO	Total	Off	Def	ST
1	at MIN	L	23	26	355	389	0	-39%	-6%	18%	-15%
2	HOU	L	7	27	117	411	-1	-59%	-37%	25%	2%
3	at IND	W	22	17	333	437	1	-24%	-10%	15%	1%
4	CIN	L	10	27	212	382	0	-12%	-9%	1%	-2%
5	CHI	L	3	41	189	501	-2	-91%	-53%	45%	7%
6	BYE										
7	at OAK	L	23	26	209	351	2	-37%	-48%	1%	12%
8	at GB	L	15	24	341	238	0	-22%	-14%	-25%	-32%
9	DET	L	14	31	279	434	-2	-46%	-15%	39%	9%
10	IND	L	10	27	337	359	-1	-48%	-29%	16%	-3%
11	at HOU	L	37	43	458	653	2	-19%	9%	18%	-10%
12	TEN	W	24	19	321	360	1	-6%	-2%	16%	12%
13	at BUF	L	18	34	236	344	0	-48%	-44%	6%	1%
14	NYJ	L	10	17	291	270	0	-35%	-29%	6%	0%
15	at MIA	L	3	24	299	389	1	-26%	-5%	34%	13%
16	NE	L	16	23	436	349	-1	37%	4%	-31%	2%
17	at TEN	L	20	38	375	221	-3	-79%	-37%	-3%	-44%

Trends and Splits

	Offense	Rank	Defense	Rank
Total DVOA	-18.4%	28	11.7%	28
Unadjusted VOA	-17.1%	28	10.4%	27
Weighted Trend	-18.1%	28	8.2%	26
Variance	3.8%	3	4.2%	9
Average Opponent	0.4%	16	-2.4%	22
Passing	-14.3%	28	22.0%	29
Rushing	-15.1%	27	2.1%	27
First Down	-10.8%	23	12.5%	29
Second Down	-18.0%	25	12.3%	26
Third Down	-32.4%	31	9.1%	25
First Half	-7.5%	22	3.9%	22
Second Half	-29.7%	30	18.9%	32
Red Zone	-18.2%	25	2.7%	16
Late and Close	-38.0%	30	5.0%	25

Five-Year Performance

Year	W-L	Pyth W	Est W	PF	PA	TO	Total	Rk	Off	Rk	Def	Rk	ST	Rk	Off AGL	Rk	Def AGL	Rk	Off Age	Rk	Def Age	Rk	ST Age	Rk
2008	5-11	6.1	8.5	302	367	-7	-1.1%	20	6.0%	14	6.3%	24	-0.8%	21	48.8	29	15.4	11	27.0	21	27.2	18	26.3	23
2009	7-9	5.5	7.0	290	380	+2	-9.3%	23	3.8%	17	11.3%	28	-1.8%	25	4.5	2	43.5	28	26.9	22	25.5	31	25.5	29
2010	8-8	6.3	6.5	353	419	-15	-9.0%	22	3.9%	14	17.7%	32	4.8%	7	19.7	9	17.8	11	27.2	20	25.8	29	26.0	22
2011	5-11	5.3	5.5	243	329	+5	-17.4%	27	-26.5%	31	-11.3%	5	-2.2%	26	20.5	10	52.8	29	26.2	28	26.9	18	26.5	8
2012	2-14	3.3	2.7	255	444	-3	-33.0%	31	-18.4%	28	11.7%	28	-3.0%	25	63.7	30	36.2	22	26.5	20	27.0	14	25.8	23

2012 Performance Based on Most Common Personnel Groups

JAC Offense					JAC Offense vs. Opponents				JAC Defense				JAC Defense vs. Opponents			
Pers	Freq	Yds	DVOA	Run%	Pers	Freq	Yds	DVOA	Pers	Freq	Yds	DVOA	Pers	Freq	Yds	DVOA
11	45%	5.7	-12.7%	22%	Nickel Even	35%	5.1	-15.4%	4-3-4	55%	5.3	12.3%	11	35%	6.2	5.0%
21	16%	4.9	-12.3%	47%	4-3-4	23%	4.2	-18.9%	Nickel Even	36%	6.3	6.6%	12	32%	6.0	22.4%
12	12%	4.2	-18.0%	46%	Dime+	15%	6.5	13.9%	Dime+	6%	8.9	63.3%	21	15%	5.9	10.7%
10	12%	5.1	-3.7%	2%	3-4-4	15%	5.4	-6.1%	Goal Line	1%	0.7	-22.9%	13	4%	4.3	-2.0%
22	5%	3.2	-24.5%	83%	Nickel Odd	9%	3.7	-50.9%	4-4-3	1%	0.8	19.8%	22	4%	3.1	9.0%
									Nickel Odd	1%	3.3	-54.2%	01	3%	7.5	14.8%

Strategic Tendencies

Run/Pass		Rk	Formation		Rk	Pass Rush		Rk	Secondary		Rk	Strategy		Rk
Runs, first half	39%	15	Form: Single Back	68%	15	Rush 3	3.7%	26	4 DB	55%	3	Play action	15%	30
Runs, first down	43%	29	Form: Empty Back	5%	21	Rush 4	76.1%	3	5 DB	37%	27	Avg Box (Off)	6.15	30
Runs, second-long	26%	26	Pers: 3+ WR	60%	7	Rush 5	14.4%	29	6+ DB	6%	14	Avg Box (Def)	6.52	4
Runs, power sit.	55%	16	Pers: 4+ WR	12%	3	Rush 6+	5.8%	21	CB by Sides	70%	20	Offensive Pace	30.69	18
Runs, behind 2H	24%	26	Pers: 2+ TE/6+ OL	23%	26	Sacks by LB	13.5%	24	DB Blitz	7%	24	Defensive Pace	29.22	4
Pass, ahead 2H	54%	4	Shotgun/Pistol	48%	13	Sacks by DB	5.4%	17	Hole in Zone	10%	13	Go for it on 4th	1.61	1

The Jaguars ran 15.1 percent of plays without a tight end, the highest rate in the league. However, even though the Jaguars used 10 personnel more than any other team, they only handed the ball off twice. They might want to consider doing that a bit more often so that "Marcedes Lewis left the field" doesn't automatically mean "pass play." ⊜ The Jaguars had a league-worst 3.1 yards per play and -71.3% DVOA with an empty backfield. ⊜ As bad as the Jaguars' quarterbacks were, they certainly weren't helped by the receivers. The Jaguars led the league in both dropped passes (44) and percent of dropped passes (7.9 percent). No other team dropped more than 7.0 percent of passes. ⊜ Mike Mularkey's status as the most aggressive coach in the league on fourth downs could be the effect of Jacksonville's new front-office analytics department. Or it could just be the head coach of last-place team throwing caution into the wind because why the hell not. Hopefully new head coach Gus Bradley learned something working under Pete Carroll, whose 1.33 career AI ranks 13th among all coaches since 1991 with a minimum of three seasons.

Passing

Player	DYAR	DVOA	Plays	NtYds	Avg	YAC	C%	TD	Int
C.Henne	-286	-24.6%	334	1912	5.7	5.1	54.4%	11	10
B.Gabbert	-268	-25.3%	301	1491	5.0	4.3	58.3%	9	6

Rushing

Player	DYAR	DVOA	Plays	Yds	Avg	TD	Fum	Suc
R.Jennings*	-97	-31.8%	101	285	2.8	2	3	38%
M.Jones-Drew	27	-0.9%	86	414	4.8	1	1	48%
M.Owens*	41	14.5%	42	209	5.0	1	0	52%
J.Parmele*	-7	-12.8%	40	143	3.6	0	0	33%
R.Murphy	14	5.7%	23	92	4.0	0	0	48%
K.Toston*	-5	-15.7%	17	74	4.4	0	0	53%
B.Gabbert	5	-6.8%	15	58	3.9	0	0	-
C.Henne	-17	-33.3%	15	67	4.5	1	1	-
G.Jones*	-4	-19.4%	5	8	1.6	0	0	60%
J.Forsett	53	13.2%	63	374	5.9	1	0	48%

Receiving

Player	DYAR	DVOA	Plays	Ctch	Yds	Y/C	YAC	TD	C%
J.Blackmon	-4	-15.0%	132	64	865	13.5	4.4	5	48%
C.Shorts	138	5.2%	105	55	979	17.8	6.5	7	52%
L.Robinson*	-25	-32.1%	43	24	252	10.5	2.3	0	56%
J.Shipley	-42	-19.0%	39	23	244	10.6	1.8	1	59%
K.Elliott	-95	-47.7%	31	10	108	10.8	2.7	0	32%
M.Thomas*	-97	-63.6%	27	13	80	6.2	0.9	0	48%
M.Spurlock*	21	-10.8%	19	14	121	8.6	1.6	1	74%
T.Clemons	-48	-60.6%	11	3	41	13.7	0.7	0	27%
M.Massaquoi	-2	-13.4%	33	17	254	14.9	6.1	0	52%
M.Lewis	21	0.0%	77	52	540	10.4	4.7	4	68%
Z.Potter	-24	-74.1%	6	2	6	3.0	2.0	0	33%
R.Jennings*	-11	-22.6%	26	19	130	6.8	8.2	0	73%
M.Jones-Drew	18	5.8%	18	14	86	6.1	5.1	1	78%
G.Jones*	12	1.3%	14	11	64	5.8	4.5	0	79%
M.Owens*	43	62.6%	10	8	113	14.1	12.8	0	80%
J.Parmele*	7	-1.7%	9	7	60	8.6	7.7	0	78%

Offensive Line

Player	Pos	Age	GS	Snaps	Pen	Sk	Pass	Run	Player	Pos	Age	GS	Snaps	Pen	Sk	Pass	Run
Brad Meester	C	36	16/16	1061	3	2	4.5	5	Guy Whimper*	OT	30	16/6	382	4	5.5	16.3	4
Eugene Monroe	LT	26	16/16	1061	6	4	14.3	5	Eben Britton*	LG	26	11/5	267	2	2	8	0
Uche Nwaneri	RG	29	15/15	925	3	6.8	8.8	3	Austin Pasztor	G	23	3/3	215	2	1	3.5	1
Cameron Bradfield	RT	26	14/12	749	6	4.5	15	1	Steve Vallos*	OT	30	4/1	124	1	0	1	0
Michael Brewster	C/LG	24	12/7	548	4	1.5	6.5	2									

Year	Yards	ALY	Rk	Power	Rk	Stuff	Rk	2nd Lev	Rk	Open Field	Rk	Sacks	ASR	Rk	Short	Long	F-Start	Cont.
2010	4.62	4.63	2	63%	13	13%	3	1.35	2	0.70	18	38	7.7%	24	11	14	13	30
2011	4.28	4.14	13	64%	13	17%	8	1.19	16	0.76	20	44	8.9%	26	12	19	10	31
2012	3.89	4.05	17	61%	20	19%	15	1.01	28	0.58	23	50	7.8%	22	17	13	16	25

2012 ALY by direction: Left End 4.27 (13) — Left Tackle 5.32 (1) — Mid/Guard 3.9 (22) — Right Tackle 4.45 (7) — Right End 3.72 (22)

According to our game charters, 90 percent of the 50 sacks that the Jaguars allowed in 2012 were the result of either "blown blocks" or "rusher untouched/overall pressure." Only Arizona had more sacks allowed by blown blocks, and only the Jets and Eagles had more marked as rusher untouched or overall pressure. So it came as no surprise when the Jaguars used the second overall pick on Texas A&M left tackle Luke Joeckel. Joeckel will begin his NFL career at right tackle, though a move to the left side in the future is a possibility. The left tackle spot has been and continues to be occupied by Eugene Monroe, a 2009 first-round pick out of Virginia who has started 58 of 61 games over the last four seasons and is entering the final year of his rookie contract. Monroe is a solid but not spectacular left tackle and there could be a scenario within the next two years where he and Joeckel switch sides. At the very least, the selection of Joeckel gives the Jaguars security at the tackle position and a whole lot of leverage over Monroe in contract talks. The addition of Joeckel moves the inconsistent Cameron Bradfield back to a reserve role.

On the interior, the Jaguars re-signed veteran center Brad Meester, who logged 100 percent of the Jaguars' snaps in 2012 but often looked like the 36-year-old center that he is, particularly when run blocking. Michael Brewster, an undrafted rookie from Ohio State, started seven games at guard last season and could push Meester for the starting center position. Will Rackley, who allowed 6.5 sacks as a "green as grass" rookie from Lehigh in 2011, will likely start at left guard after missing all of last season with ankle injury. Veteran right guard Uche Nwaneri is coming off a rough season, which could be partially explained by a right knee injury he sustained in the first half of Week 1. Nwaneri had that knee scoped in January and should be back in time for training camp. Brewster, Austin Pasztor, and Jason Spitz give the Jaguars reasonable depth, but this is still a unit that Caldwell will likely address in the 2014 draft.

Defensive Front Seven

Defensive Line	Age	Pos	Snaps	Plays	TmPct	Rk	Stop	Dfts	BTkl	Runs	St%	Rk	RuYd	Rk	Sack	Hit	Hur	Tips
Jeremy Mincey	30	DE	954	46	5.2%	41	32	13	2	36	64%	69	2.5	38	3	13	22.5	4
Tyson Alualu	26	DT	834	46	5.2%	22	33	7	0	40	70%	54	2.4	43	3.5	1	8	1
Terrance Knighton*	27	DT	657	33	3.7%	45	29	11	2	28	86%	5	1.5	16	2	6	4.5	1
Jason Babin	33	DE	654	36	4.6%	49	28	14	5	23	70%	54	4.6	71	7	14	24	0
C.J. Mosley*	30	DT	618	45	5.1%	26	32	6	0	38	74%	35	2.3	41	2.5	6	5	0
Austen Lane*	26	DE	373	31	5.1%	42	23	4	0	27	74%	41	2.0	19	2	7	7	0
George Selvie*	26	DE	237	15	3.0%	--	13	4	0	14	86%	--	0.7	--	1	3	4	0
Sen'Derrick Marks	26	DT	678	43	5.6%	17	34	12	1	30	80%	22	1.5	15	1.5	4	4	4
Kyle Love	27	DT	543	24	3.0%	61	17	4	1	21	71%	48	2.0	25	1.5	0	7	0
Roy Miller	26	DT	494	25	3.3%	57	18	7	0	19	79%	26	1.2	5	0	1	3	1
Brandon Deaderick	26	DE	374	18	2.5%	--	14	5	0	15	80%	--	2.9	--	1	0	4	1

Linebackers	Age	Pos	Snaps	Plays	TmPct	Rk	Stop	Dfts	BTkl	Sack	Hit	Hur	Tips	Runs	St%	Rk	Yds	Rk	Tgts	Suc%	Rk	AdjYd	Rk	PD
Paul Posluszny	29	MLB	1127	146	16.5%	14	69	19	7	2	3	6.5	0	95	46%	107	4.9	109	40	50%	40	6.8	37	6
Russell Allen	27	OLB	1000	134	15.1%	22	69	25	9	0.5	4	7	0	82	65%	62	3.1	38	42	41%	65	6.4	28	5
Julian Stanford	23	OLB	351	17	1.9%	--	8	2	0	0	0	0	0	11	64%	--	2.1	--	5	57%	--	4.2	--	0
Kyle Bosworth*	27	OLB	250	27	3.0%	--	15	5	3	0	1	0	0	18	67%	--	3.5	--	14	34%	--	6.5	--	1
Geno Hayes	26	OLB	138	16	2.1%	--	9	4	3	0	0	0	0	4	75%	--	0.8	--	10	57%	--	6.5	--	2

Year	Yards	ALY	Rk	Power	Rk	Stuff	Rk	2nd Level	Rk	Open Field	Rk	Sacks	ASR	Rk	Short	Long
2010	4.76	3.89	15	68%	26	23%	3	1.22	24	1.43	32	26	5.8%	22	10	11
2011	3.94	3.82	6	68%	26	21%	10	1.03	3	0.77	16	31	7.2%	13	13	12
2012	4.16	4.31	26	69%	26	18%	20	1.14	9	0.67	10	20	4.0%	32	6	10

2012 ALY by direction: Left End 4.11 (19) — Left Tackle 4.15 (18) — Mid/Guard 4.27 (24) — Right Tackle 4.9 (32) — Right End 4.55 (21)

Bradley was a linebackers coach under Monte Kiffin with the Tampa Bay Buccaneers before he became defensive coordinator in Seattle in 2009, and he was actively involved in the Seahawks' front seven's transformation from soft-as-Charmin to physically dominant. So this is expected to be the area of the defense where Bradley has the most immediate impact. He has his work cut out for him, as he inherits a Jaguars defense that had fewer sacks (20) than J.J. Watt (20.5) and drew as many offensive holding calls as Von Miller did all by himself (nine).

Dramatic changes, both in terms of personnel and how they will be used, are taking place this offseason. Tyson Alualu, who led the Jaguars with 3.5 sacks last season, is moving to a run-stopping "5-technique" defensive end role. It's a role Alualu excelled in at Cal as well as the role that rejuvenated the career of Red Bryant with the Seahawks. Another player in the mix to start at that defensive end position is Jeremy Mincey, who was a disappointment with just three sacks last season; both Mincey and Alualu could move inside to rush the quarterback on obvious passing downs. The favorite to start at the "Leo" position is Jason Babin, who was abruptly released by the Eagles two-thirds of the way through their miserable 2012 campaign and then claimed by the Jaguars, who hoped he could resurrect their pass rush. Alas, Babin had just 1.5 sacks and five hurries in his five games with Jacksonville, and he's coming off offseason groin surgery. Behind Babin at the "Leo" is 2012 second-round pick Andre Branch, who had just one sack before a groin injury ended his rookie season with three games remaining. (Apparently, while other teams worry about contagious MRSA infections in the locker room, the Jaguars have to worry about contagious groin injuries.)

Up the middle, the Jaguars let C.J. Mosley and Terence Knighton walk in free agency and replaced them with Roy Miller (ex-Tampa Bay) and Sen'Derrick Marks (ex-Tennessee), each of whom performed similarly to Knighton against the run last season. They will start next to each other in two-down roles, with Miller at nose tackle shaded off the center with two-gap responsibilities, and Marks as a penetrating three-technique tackle. With 2010 third-round pick D'Anthony Smith coming off yet another injury-marred season—Smith missed the 2010 and 2011 seasons with injuries and finished 2012 on IR due to a concussion—the Jaguars added much-needed depth to the interior defensive line by claiming former New England Patriots defensive linemen Brandon Deaderick and Kyle Love off waivers just days apart in May. There is disagreement as to why Love was cut by the Patriots. His agent claims that Love was released after refusing to sit out the 2013 season without pay following a Type-2 diabetes diagnosis. A number of Patriots beat reporters pointed instead to the fact that Love was benched after 11 starts due to declining play… ironically, in favor of his once and future teammate Deaderick. Both ex-Patriots possess the versatility to play multiple positions along the line, which will allow Bradley and defensive line coach Todd Wash to keep the defensive front fresh.

Middle linebacker Paul Posluszny returned from a torn labrum to start all 16 games, playing nearly 99 percent of snaps and leading the team in tackles. Unfortunately, those tackles occurred over a yard further down the field than they had the previous season (3.8 in 2012, 4.9 in 2013). A base salary increase from $2.95 million to $6.45 million and the hiring of a new coaching staff and front office would normally have a veteran linebacker on the hot seat, but the new regime is looking for Posluszny to take on a leadership role this season. Rangy veteran Russell Allen played well in his first full season in a starting role, finishing among the top 20 defenders with 25 Defeats. One veteran who was not brought back is Daryl Smith, who missed all but two games in 2012 with a groin injury and signed with the Baltimore Ravens late in the offseason. Free-agent signee Geno Hayes, who played for Jaguars defensive coordinator Bob Babich in Chicago last season, will compete for the weakside linebacker position with Julian Stanford, who played well as a core special-teamer and spot starter during his rookie season. Stanford gives Gus Bradley another former Seahawk to play with, with a twist; Jacksonville signed Stanford as an undrafted free agent out of Staten Island's famous football non-factory Wagner College, whose teams are called the Seahawks. 2012 fifth-round pick Brandon Marshall and a gaggle of street free agents will compete for one or two depth spots on the roster.

Defensive Secondary

Secondary	Age	Pos	Snaps	Plays	Overall TmPct	Rk	Stop	Dfts	BTkl	vs. Run Runs	St%	Rk	Yds	Rk	vs. Pass Tgts	Tgt%	Rk	Dist	Suc%	Rk	APaYd	Rk	PD	Int
Dawan Landry*	31	SS	1139	102	11.5%	26	33	9	6	62	39%	35	6.5	28	30	6.8%	33	10.2	51%	46	7.1	34	2	1
Derek Cox*	27	CB	765	71	10.7%	15	29	15	8	14	50%	26	5.2	22	83	25.5%	1	12.5	51%	46	8.0	59	11	4
Chris Prosinski	26	FS	675	54	6.1%	65	14	5	4	18	33%	46	7.2	38	22	5.1%	60	12.4	39%	74	9.1	60	3	1
Aaron Ross*	31	CB	673	49	6.3%	73	19	6	5	16	50%	26	4.7	14	49	13.1%	77	11.3	33%	86	9.7	82	3	0
Dwight Lowery	27	FS	545	35	7.0%	59	12	6	2	17	29%	55	9.5	61	19	7.8%	23	13.9	81%	2	3.2	2	3	1
Mike Harris	24	CB	530	52	6.3%	--	16	3	2	19	32%	--	4.8	--	32	7.9%	--	9.9	50%	--	5.5	--	5	1
Rashean Mathis*	33	CB	473	25	3.8%	87	9	2	3	2	100%	1	6.0	40	45	13.7%	73	13.8	38%	85	11.2	87	5	0
William Middleton*	37	CB	195	19	3.4%	--	6	2	0	9	22%	--	8.9	--	14	5.2%	--	16.4	64%	--	7.3	--	1	0
Marcus Trufant	33	CB	352	36	6.4%	--	16	8	2	3	100%	--	4.7	--	34	10.0%	--	6.9	62%	--	6.3	--	3	0

Year	Pass D Rank	vs. #1 WR	Rk	vs. #2 WR	Rk	vs. Other WR	Rk	vs. TE	Rk	vs. RB	Rk
2010	30	28.8%	29	8.7%	19	26.3%	30	9.3%	17	5.8%	18
2011	6	-14.4%	4	14.2%	24	2.9%	23	18.5%	20	-38.8%	1
2012	29	16.8%	25	4.9%	18	36.6%	32	-1.5%	18	1.7%	17

For the second consecutive season, injuries were a major issue in the Jaguars' secondary. Starting cornerbacks Derek Cox and Rashean Mathis played less than 70 percent of defensive snaps while free safety Dwight Lowery, a solid acquisition in 2011, played less than half the snaps as he battled ankle and foot injuries. These injuries combined with an ineffectual pass rush as the Jaguars' pass defense DVOA plummeted in 2012. Perhaps the biggest disappointment might have been Cox, who missed 10 games in 2011 and needed to stay healthy and show that he could handle opposing No. 1 receivers in order get an extension from the Jaguars. Cox covered opposing No. 1 receivers on 69 percent of the passes where he was marked in coverage, tied with Antonio Cromartie for the highest rate in the league, and the Jaguars ranked 25th against opposing No. 1 receivers, so the new front office and coaching staff had no qualms in letting the injury-prone Cox leave via free agency. Cox isn't alone, however; three-quarters of the secondary that began the 2012 regular season—Cox, Mathis and strong safety Dawan Landry—will play elsewhere in 2013. So will nickel cornerback Aaron Ross, cut after just one season of a misguided three-year, $9.75 million contract.

All told, 11 of the 16 defensive backs the Jaguars had on their roster during OTAs were not on the team last season, and nearly half of the new faces arrived via the draft. The big name in that group is second-round safety Johnathan Cyprien out of Florida International, who has the size (6-foot, 217 pounds) to be used as an "in-the-box" defender against the run and is equally adept in pass coverage. Cyprien should have little trouble beating out 2011 fourth-round pick Chris Prosinski for the starting role next to Lowery, whose leadership, performance (when healthy), and communication skills kept him safe from the offseason purge. Another rookie with a chance to start right away is Dwayne Gratz, a third-round pick out of Connecticut with the strength and speed to play press coverage at the NFL level. The Jaguars invested a sixth-round pick in free safety prospect Josh Evans and added a pair of tall cornerbacks in the seventh round: Demetrius McCray (6-foot-1), who played for first-year Jaguars defensive backs coach Dwayne Walker at Appalachian State, and Jeremy Harris (6-foot-2) out of New Mexico State. Bradley had considerable success with tall corners in Seattle, so those particular selections at corner were not a surprise. The Jaguars were also thrifty shoppers in free agency, adding the versatile Alan Ball and scooping up former Seahawks veteran Marcus Trufant. If Trufant can stay healthy, and can beat out holdover Mike Harris, he could play a nickel role this season. The 6-foot-2, 197-pound Ball has the length to play press man coverage, but had a minimal role in the Houston Texans' defense last season and has never been a full-time starter at cornerback in the NFL.

Special Teams

Year	DVOA	Rank	FG/XP	Rank	Net Kick	Rank	Kick Ret	Rank	Net Punt	Rank	Punt Ret	Rank	Hidden	Rank
2010	4.8%	7	1.9	13	12.2	5	-1.8	16	8.6	7	3.0	13	-1.8	17
2011	-2.2%	26	5.4	5	3.0	11	-5.3	28	-3.8	21	-10.5	31	15.6	1
2012	-3.0%	25	1.9	13	-3.6	25	-3.8	23	-3.2	21	-5.9	28	1.0	15

Former GM Gene Smith invested considerable resources in the Jaguars' special teams units. Smith used a third-round pick in the 2012 NFL draft on punter Bryan Anger and referred to the rookie punter as a "starter," which spoke volumes about the expectations for the Jaguars' offense last season. Smith also used the franchise tag on kicker Josh Scobee, who would sign a four-year, $13.8 million contract before training camp. In return for these investments, the Jaguars had a bottom-10 special teams unit for the second straight season.

To be fair, the problem wasn't Scobee or Anger. Scobee had another solid season on field goals, converting 25 of 28 attempts. However, the flip side of Mike Mularkey's league-leading Aggressiveness Index is that Scobee didn't get much opportunity to use his strong leg; he finished just 13th in our field-goal values because he had only four attempts longer than 45 yards. Anger's 47.8-yard gross average was among the highest in the league, but the Jaguars coverage units allowed two punt return touchdowns and a league-high 495 return yards.

The Jaguars had six players return punts and nine players return kicks in 2012. That communal approach was necessary due in large part to injuries, and it resulted in the team having an ineffective return game for the second consecutive season. Three rookies could be leaned on to improve the Jaguars' return game. Fourth-round wide receiver Ace Sanders averaged 11.2 yards per punt return with three touchdowns during his career at South Carolina, and was fourth in the nation with a 15.3-yard average in 2012. Sanders could also factor on kicks along with fifth-round running back Denard Robinson, who has speed to burn but is new to the return game, and undrafted rookie receiver Tobias Palmer, who averaged 25.5 yards with two touchdowns on 44 kick returns last season for North Carolina State.

Coaching Staff

Few head coaches can survive a 2-14 season *and* a change at general manager, and Mike Mularkey was no exception. Mularkey knew the writing was on the wall when Gene Smith was fired and replaced by David Caldwell. So did his assistants, who received permission from the team to hunt for jobs elsewhere even before Caldwell made things official by firing Mularkey on January 10. One week later, Caldwell hired Seattle defensive coordinator Gus Bradley, who had also drawn interest for the Philadelphia Eagles' head coaching vacancy. Jedd Fisch, who coached with Bradley in Seattle under Pete Carroll, was hired as offensive coordinator, a role he's performed in stints with the University of Minnesota (2009) and University of Miami (2011-12). Former Chicago Bears defensive coordinator Bob Babich was hired to coordinate the Jaguars' defense, though Bradley is expected to have a large role when it comes to devising game plans and play-calling on the that side of the ball.

Kansas City Chiefs

2012 Record: 2-14	Total DVOA: -40.1% (32nd)	2013 Mean Projection: 6.6 wins	On the Clock (0-4): 22%
Pythagorean Wins: 2.5 (32nd)	Offense: -25.1% (31st)	Postseason Odds: 16.8%	Mediocrity (5-7): 43%
Snap-Weighted Age: 26.2 (27th)	Defense: 13.0% (30th)	Super Bowl Odds: 0.7%	Playoff Contender (8-10): 29%
Average Opponent: -1.5% (18th)	Special Teams: -2.0% (22nd)	Proj. Avg. Opponent: -4.1% (26th)	Super Bowl Contender (11+): 6%

2012: The Chiefs somehow have three times as many Pro Bowlers as they have wins.

2013: Guaranteed to be much better, but not guaranteed to be in the playoff hunt.

There are a thousand different clichés about turnovers in football, all of which say the same thing: winning the turnover battle strongly correlates with winning games. In 2012, the Kansas City Chiefs proved every one of these clichés true. Despite a roster that ostensibly had .500-level talent, the Chiefs had a league-worst turnover differential of minus-24 en route to a 2-14 record and the worst DVOA in the league.

When a team loses 14 games despite the presence of five Pro Bowlers (with a sixth player chosen as an injury replacement), you can pretty much guarantee the leadership will be overhauled. The Chiefs fired both controversial general manager Scott Pioli and head coach Romeo Crennel. Perhaps remembering the disastrous ending to the short-lived Todd Haley era, team owner Clark Hunt sought a stable, proven veteran coach to come in and run the show. He lured in the freshly fired Andy Reid with a five-year contract, forever cementing the longtime Eagles coach's lovable nickname, "Big Red."

Eight days after Reid's hiring was announced, Hunt named Packers Director of Football Operations John Dorsey as his new general manager. To the surprise of many, Dorsey, not Reid, will have final say on personnel (although Dorsey may have to run some of his decisions by Hunt).

Though Reid and Dorsey joined a franchise that was bad enough to earn the first overall pick in the 2013 draft, they may not spend much time languishing near the bottom of the standings. There are strong positive indicators suggesting that Kansas City can quickly turn things around. Superstars like Tamba Hali and Jamaal Charles give Reid and Dorsey a strong framework for their rebuilding project. The Chiefs were weakest in 2012 at quarterback, the position where a personnel change can bring the most improvement for the team overall. And most importantly, turnover differential may be the NFL statistic affected strongest by regression towards the mean.

The Chiefs' turnover margin of minus-24 wasn't just tied for the worst in the league (ironically, with Reid's Philadelphia Eagles). It was also the worst turnover margin in the league since 2005. Since 1991, only 16 teams have put up a turnover margin of minus-20 or worse, and only the 2000 San Diego Chargers had a turnover margin worse than last year's Chiefs. These same teams averaged a turnover differential of just minus-2.4 the following season (Table 1).

The year-to-year inconsistency of turnovers is something we've written a lot about at Football Outsiders, both when it comes to the highly variable (interceptions, fumbles forced) and the completely arbitrary (fumble recoveries). Interceptions, for example, are notoriously hard to forecast from year to year, because there's so much random chance and statistical noise involved. Based on our adjusted interceptions metric (described further in the introduction to the quarterback player comments on page 232), the Chiefs were the only team in the league to have more interceptions caused by receivers dropping or deflecting an easy catch (four) than would-be interceptions dropped by defenders (two). Still, that's nothing compared to poor fumble recovery luck, which just destroyed the Chiefs last year. Kansas City recovered only six of 21 fumbles on offense and just three out of 14 fumbles on defense.

Turnover regression may have an even stronger than usual effect on the Chiefs because a disproportionate number of Kansas City's turnovers were extra costly. Thirteen of their turnovers occurred inside their own 30-yard-line. To compare, the Jets, who were second in the AFC in total turnovers, had only four offensive turnovers inside their own 30-yard-line. The Colts, which led all AFC playoff teams in total turnovers with 20, lost the ball just twice inside their own 30-yard-line. Consequently, the Chiefs were constantly playing from be-

Table 1. Turnover Differential -20 or Worse, 1991-2012

Year	Team	W-L	DVOA	TO Dif	W-L Y+1	DVOA Y+1	TO Dif Y+1
1991	LARM	3-13	-10.7%	-21	6-10	-12.3%	-4
1991	TB	3-13	-38.1%	-20	5-11	-23.3%	+4
1994	CIN	3-13	-25.7%	-23	7-9	-7.0%	-8
1996	NYJ	1-15	-30.9%	-20	9-7	2.6%	+3
1997	ARI	4-12	-21.2%	-22	9-7	-17.1%	+3
1997	BUF	6-10	-14.9%	-20	10-6	19.2%	+11
1997	NO	6-10	-27.6%	-24	6-10	-16.0%	-1
1998	SD	5-11	-14.5%	-24	8-8	-9.4%	-8
2000	ARI	3-13	-38.7%	-24	7-9	-13.6%	-3
2000	SD	1-15	-23.7%	-28	5-11	6.9%	+2
2001	MIN	5-11	-27.4%	-21	6-10	-19.6%	-18
2005	GB	4-12	-11.4%	-24	8-8	-4.3%	0
2005	NO	3-13	-22.8%	-24	10-6	6.4%	-4
2006	OAK	2-14	-32.9%	-23	4-12	-29.2%	-11
2012	KC	2-14	-40.1%	-24	--	--	--
2012	PHI	4-12	-22.4%	-24	--	--	--
AVERAGE		3.4	-25.2%	-22.9	7.1	-8.3%	-2.4

2013 Chiefs Schedule

Week	Opp.	Week	Opp.	Week	Opp.
1	at JAC	7	HOU	13	DEN
2	DAL	8	CLE	14	at WAS
3	at PHI (Thu.)	9	at BUF	15	at OAK
4	NYG	10	BYE	16	IND
5	at TEN	11	at DEN	17	at SD
6	OAK	12	SD		

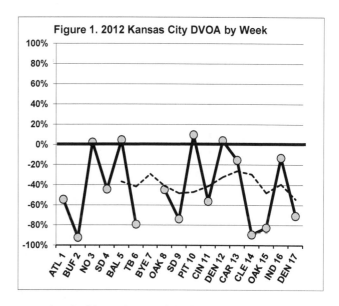

Figure 1. 2012 Kansas City DVOA by Week

hind; in fact, they did not have a lead at any point in a game until the first quarter of what would turn out to be a Week 10 loss against Pittsburgh. No team is built to play this way, but especially not this one, and so the disaster snowballed. The Chiefs flip-flopped between two subpar quarterbacks, Matt Cassel and Brady Quinn, who combined for -796 DYAR. Kansas City's offensive line and running backs were charged with 27 blown blocks, the fifth-highest total in the NFL. Only one player with at least 10 pass targets, tight end Tony Moeaki, had a receiving DVOA above 0%. Burdened with a heavier share of the load, the Chiefs defense cracked, allowing 36 passing plays of 25 yards or more. The Chiefs were sixth in the league despite facing a league-low 464 pass attempts. That rate of giving up at least 25 yards on 7.8 percent of passes was the highest rate since 2009 and the seventh highest rate since 2000 (Table 2).

Even after considering all the regression trends, there's one more reason to believe that the Chiefs will have a better turnover ratio in 2013: Alex Smith. The Chiefs traded the 34th overall pick and a conditional 2014 pick to San Francisco for the ninth-year veteran, which is probably too steep a price for someone with conspicuous limitations as a pocket passer. But the most common praise of Smith is he does not turn the ball over. In his 21 starts over the last two years in San Francisco, Smith had just 10 interceptions and four lost fumbles.

For Smith to protect the ball for Kansas City as well as he did for San Francisco, the Kansas City coaches will need to manage him as well as the San Francisco coaches did. A big

reason that Smith rarely turned the ball over the last two years is that Jim Harbaugh and Greg Roman were smart enough to hide his weaknesses. The Niners had a run-oriented offense. Most of their passing game was comprised of defined reads and took place out of base personnel, which meant Smith was facing more vanilla defenses. When they took a downfield shot, it was usually off play-action on first down. If Smith were asked to make more full-field progression reads in obvious passing situations, the way many NFL quarterbacks are, his turnover numbers would almost certainly have been higher. (For two strong examples, if you have NFL Game Rewind, check out two interceptions that Smith threw to Antrel Rolle in the third quarter of the Week 6 game against the Giants last year. The first comes on third-and-6 with 10:17 left, the second on third-and-16 with 7:56 left.)

Ball security will be as important as ever because this Chiefs offense is no more equipped to play from behind than last year's offense was. Dwayne Bowe is still the top receiver. He's an admirable possession target and someone who must be double-teamed here and there, but he does not have threatening breakaway speed. Neither does No. 2 wideout Jon Baldwin. In fact, Baldwin has looked downright sluggish most of the time since entering the league as a first-round pick three years ago. When a good athlete plays slow, it usually means he's not mentally comfortable. Baldwin has flashed scintillating play-on-ball prowess (i.e. the ability to attack the ball and make a tough catch when it's a 50/50 ball in the air) but he remains disconcertingly raw.

What speed the Chiefs do have at wide receiver comes with caveats. The newly-signed Donnie Avery is a burner. However, he has trouble staying healthy and struggles with drops. Last year's fourth-round pick, Devon Wylie, shows intrigue as a Lance Moore-type intermediate target with some quickness. However, he played just 77 offensive snaps in 2012 and will likely still be a project in 2013. So will utility weapon Dexter McCluster, who at this point has been a project longer than Alan Parsons.

Given Smith's skill set, as well as the question marks the team has at receiver, Andy Reid would be wise to put Smith in a run-first system. It's simple logic: Kansas City's best player is Jamaal Charles. He has otherworldly lateral quickness and breakaway speed. The two-time Pro Bowler has averaged at

Table 2. Defenses Allowing Gains of 25-plus Yards on Highest Rate of Passes, 2000-2012

Year	Team	>25 Yd Passes	All Passes	Rate	Def DVOA	Def DVOA +1	Dif
2004	KC	44	522	8.4%	16.0%	-2.9%	-18.8%
2008	JAC	39	465	8.4%	6.3%	11.3%	+4.9%
2009	OAK	35	438	8.0%	7.9%	-2.3%	-10.2%
2009	MIA	39	489	8.0%	1.5%	-4.8%	-6.3%
2001	NO	36	452	8.0%	3.0%	1.7%	-1.4%
2003	OAK	37	467	7.9%	9.5%	11.5%	+2.0%
2008	STL	35	444	7.9%	18.3%	17.2%	-1.1%
2012	KC	36	464	7.8%	13.0%	--	--
2010	JAC	38	506	7.5%	17.7%	-11.3%	-29.0%
2012	NYG	40	534	7.5%	1.5%	--	--
2008	DET	33	443	7.4%	24.3%	17.9%	-6.4%
2002	MIN	40	542	7.4%	14.5%	6.9%	-7.6%
2011	NE	45	619	7.3%	13.2%	1.4%	-11.9%
AVERAGE					11.3%	4.2%	-7.8%

least 5.3 yards per carry in each of his five NFL seasons, and his current 5.8 career yards per carry is an all-time record. As he has shown the last few years, Charles is perfectly built for running behind a zone-blocking offensive line. Reid, whose system has a lot of West Coast principles, should keep a lot of the zone-blocking tactics around, which is good for a Chiefs front five that is well-sized and, as a unit, surprisingly athletic.

Of course, Reid's modus operandi has never been to run the ball. Over the last four years, Reid's Eagles ranked third overall, passing the ball 62.3 percent of the time (including scrambles). The rest of the league during that time passed the ball 60.0 percent of the time. A 55-year-old man entering his 15th season as a head coach is unlikely to suddenly change his style. Even last season, when the Eagles offensive line was a mess and Philly's best weapon was running back LeSean McCoy, Reid had his quarterbacks drop back 740 times. Twenty-four of those plays resulted in a turnover and 44 of them resulted in a sack. Granted, some of these negative numbers were a product of Michael Vick's iffy fundamentals and decision-making, two areas where Smith is a sounder quarterback than Vick. But that's not to say Smith is cerebral. Smith may be smart off the field—he famously graduated from Utah in three years—but his football IQ and poise is much closer to Vick's than to, say, Peyton Manning's.

Of course, the difference between Smith and Vick is that Smith will likely do what's asked of him instead of straining to make a spectacular play. With Smith at the helm, the Chiefs can get away with throwing frequently as long as they, like the Niners, ask Smith to make mostly just defined reads and throws. Simple, short throws are common in Reid's quasi-West Coast-style system anyway. Plus, despite the questions at wide receiver, the Chiefs have the personnel to make it work. Charles would make a terrifying weapon as a pass-catcher in the flats. (Granted, he'll have to polish his receiving skills this summer.) Assuming he avoids the ankle problems that have plagued him, third-round rookie running back Knile Davis poses some intrigue in this department as well. Scouts like his breakaway speed and the improvements he made as a pass-blocker in college.

There's also talent here at tight end. The fact that Kansas City signed veteran Anthony Fasano and drafted the raw-but-athletic Travis Kelce in the third round suggests they're looking to use more of the two-tight end base package designs that are all the rage in today's NFL. Kelce will likely spend most of this season learning the ropes while Fasano gets the majority of the snaps along with incumbent starter Moeaki. The Chiefs hope that Moeaki can fully regain his pre-2011 knee injury form, when he was a multidimensional chess piece who could serve as both a run-blocker and a pass-catching weapon at the short and intermediate levels.

Encouraging as some of the signs are for Kansas City's offense, improvements on just that side of the ball won't be enough to bounce this team back in 2013. The defense must also play up to its abilities more consistently. It's a talented young group that features the AFC's most fluid and dynamic inside linebacker in Derrick Johnson, athletic bookend edge-rushers in Tamba Hali and Justin Houston, an upper-echelon boundary press-corner in Brandon Flowers, a rising young safety in Eric Berry, and an encouraging nose tackle with potential in 2012 first-round pick Dontari Poe.

Yet, despite all this talent, the Chiefs last year gave up too many big plays (all those deep completions noted earlier) and made too few of their own (just seven interceptions). It's on new defensive coordinator Bob Sutton to help change this. Sutton had been with the New York Jets since 2000, primarily working with linebackers. During his tenure there, he was on a Herm Edwards staff that ran a 4-3 Tampa-2 scheme, an Eric Mangini staff that went with a more traditional two-gap 3-4 scheme, and a Rex Ryan staff that used a lot of one-gap concepts in its attacking 3-4.

It's difficult to forecast whether Sutton will be conservative or aggressive in his scheme. Last season, this group was much more comfortable playing man than playing zone. However, the lower-end defensive backs could not always hold up in man, which led to a lot of big plays given up. Improved depth in 2013 should make it easier to play man coverage. With Flowers and Sean Smith, the Chiefs have outside cornerbacks they can trust one-on-one, and Dunta Robinson improves slot coverage when opponents spread things out. That allows them to be more aggressive with their blitzes, including the safety blitzes that Sutton is quite familiar with from his days in New York. The versatility, explosiveness and strength of Berry would be great in a blitzing role, and Berry already was tied for sixth among defensive backs with 5.5 hurries last season.

What's more, Kansas City's front seven is built for winning one-gap battles. Poe is a sensational athlete who is more suited to play in attack mode, rather than a more technique-oriented two-gap react mode. Defensive end Tyson Jackson is worth giving more one-gap assignments to since it's been apparent over the years that the former No. 3 overall pick is very average as a two-gap controller. Jackson is not a pure three-technique type, but he has a build and athleticism more fit for penetrating than simply fighting to hold ground. It's known that newly-signed end Mike DeVito can thrive in an attack scheme because he did with the Jets. Furthermore, being attack-oriented would make it harder for opponents to combat Kansas City's athletic linebackers.

All these positives are balanced by some of the typical concerns for a group that was so prone to allowing big plays the previous year. The front-seven depth is subpar. The safeties can be mistake-prone which, coupled with the question marks at No. 2 inside linebacker, could make for a defense that's susceptible up the middle. Issues with depth and concentrated weaknesses can make a defense ripe for exploitable mismatches.

If the Chiefs defense can come together under the right scheme, it could potentially be a top-10 unit. This, coupled with even an average offense, would put the Chiefs in position to drastically outperform their projections for 2013. But without additional improvement on both sides of the ball, simply improving the turnover differential won't be enough to catapult the Chiefs into playoff contention. If you turn back to Table 1 and look at the other teams since 1991 with a turnover differential of minus-20 or worse, you will notice that most of these teams still had below-average DVOA the following season, with the average team gaining 3.7 wins. That average gain would put the Chiefs at 6-10, which happens to be just about where our mean projection puts them for 2013.

Andy Benoit

2012 Chiefs Stats by Week

Wk	vs.	W-L	PF	PA	YDF	YDA	TO	Total	Off	Def	ST
1	ATL	L	24	40	393	376	-3	-55%	4%	41%	x
2	at BUF	L	17	35	422	379	-3	-92%	-35%	39%	x
3	at NO	W	27	24	510	288	-2	2%	-25%	-23%	x
4	SD	L	20	37	349	293	-5	-44%	-37%	15%	x
5	BAL	L	6	9	338	298	-2	5%	-30%	-23%	x
6	at TB	L	10	38	260	463	0	-79%	-37%	43%	x
7	BYE										x
8	OAK	L	16	26	299	344	-3	-45%	-44%	8%	x
9	at SD	L	13	31	289	339	-2	-74%	-25%	41%	x
10	at PIT	L	13	16	290	249	0	10%	-6%	-23%	x
11	CIN	L	6	28	284	409	-1	-56%	-34%	24%	x
12	DEN	L	9	17	264	368	0	4%	-10%	-7%	x
13	CAR	W	27	21	355	385	0	-15%	22%	46%	x
14	at CLE	L	7	30	310	352	-1	-89%	-39%	7%	x
15	at OAK	L	0	15	119	385	0	-83%	-95%	3%	x
16	IND	L	13	20	507	288	-3	-13%	-19%	-11%	x
17	at DEN	L	3	38	119	488	1	-71%	-35%	38%	x

Trends and Splits

	Offense	Rank	Defense	Rank
Total DVOA	-25.1%	31	13.0%	30
Unadjusted VOA	-26.2%	31	14.9%	31
Weighted Trend	-25.1%	31	12.6%	31
Variance	6.4%	19	6.6%	22
Average Opponent	2.4%	23	0.4%	14
Passing	-35.0%	32	23.3%	31
Rushing	-7.0%	20	3.0%	28
First Down	-17.0%	29	-1.5%	15
Second Down	-31.0%	32	22.8%	31
Third Down	-31.6%	30	26.1%	29
First Half	-20.2%	29	10.6%	29
Second Half	-20.0%	31	15.7%	27
Red Zone	-65.5%	32	6.2%	20
Late and Close	-25.0%	27	9.7%	29

Five-Year Performance

Year	W-L	Pyth W	Est W	PF	PA	TO	Total	Rk	Off	Rk	Def	Rk	ST	Rk	Off AGL	Rk	Def AGL	Rk	Off Age	Rk	Def Age	Rk	ST Age	Rk
2008	2-14	4.2	3.5	291	440	+5	-29.4%	30	-9.2%	23	13.3%	28	-7.0%	30	30.4	20	16.9	13	26.9	26	25.0	32	25.5	31
2009	4-12	4.6	3.5	294	424	+1	-29.2%	28	-18.0%	25	9.2%	27	-2.1%	27	13.0	9	15.3	6	27.1	17	26.5	23	25.4	30
2010	10-6	9.1	8.3	366	326	+9	0.3%	17	4.4%	13	2.1%	20	-2.1%	24	5.8	2	4.2	1	27.9	10	25.9	28	25.8	24
2011	7-9	4.2	6.3	212	338	-2	-16.9%	26	-19.3%	29	-3.2%	13	-0.9%	19	43.8	26	21.7	13	28.0	5	26.3	25	26.1	22
2012	2-14	2.5	2.4	211	425	-24	-40.1%	32	-25.1%	31	13.0%	30	-2.0%	22	50.0	27	29.3	17	26.3	24	26.1	25	26.0	14

2012 Performance Based on Most Common Personnel Groups

KC Offense					KC Offense vs. Opponents					KC Defense					KC Defense vs. Opponents			
Pers	Freq	Yds	DVOA	Run%	Pers	Freq	Yds	DVOA		Pers	Freq	Yds	DVOA		Pers	Freq	Yds	DVOA
11	47%	5.3	-17.7%	24%	4-3-4	36%	4.9	-27.6%		3-4-4	46%	5.6	3.3%		11	47%	6.9	28.8%
12	25%	4.7	-26.7%	56%	Nickel Even	31%	5.4	-12.2%		Dime+	40%	6.6	29.8%		21	18%	6.2	-3.9%
21	22%	5.9	-10.3%	70%	3-4-4	19%	5.4	-17.3%		Nickel Even	8%	6.0	12.8%		12	18%	5.2	7.0%
22	3%	3.5	-40.3%	88%	Nickel Odd	10%	5.4	-18.3%		Nickel Odd	5%	7.5	40.8%		22	5%	4.6	0.6%
611	1%	4.3	-15.9%	67%	Dime+	4%	4.8	-51.8%		Goal Line	1%	0.2	-82.1%		13	4%	3.9	0.7%

Strategic Tendencies

Run/Pass		Rk	Formation		Rk	Pass Rush		Rk	Secondary		Rk	Strategy		Rk
Runs, first half	50%	1	Form: Single Back	73%	6	Rush 3	16.8%	1	4 DB	46%	10	Play action	20%	15
Runs, first down	58%	2	Form: Empty Back	1%	32	Rush 4	59.0%	21	5 DB	12%	31	Avg Box (Off)	6.43	13
Runs, second-long	39%	6	Pers: 3+ WR	47%	22	Rush 5	18.5%	22	6+ DB	40%	1	Avg Box (Def)	6.40	14
Runs, power sit.	68%	4	Pers: 4+ WR	0%	30	Rush 6+	5.7%	22	CB by Sides	83%	8	Offensive Pace	31.57	24
Runs, behind 2H	38%	1	Pers: 2+TE/6+ OL	31%	15	Sacks by LB	77.8%	2	DB Blitz	9%	20	Defensive Pace	28.64	2
Pass, ahead 2H	34%	31	Shotgun/Pistol	38%	28	Sacks by DB	3.7%	20	Hole in Zone	8%	20	Go for it on 4th	0.85	21

New Chiefs head coach Andy Reid has gradually become more and more aggressive on fourth down, even as the league as a whole has become more conservative. With Philadelphia, Reid ranked 26th in Aggressiveness Index in 2009, then climbed to 24th in 2010, 11th in 2011, and eighth last year. ☙ The Chiefs doubled their use of empty-backfield formations compared to 2011. ☙ Kansas City's offense scored a touchdown on just 27 percent of red-zone chances. Every other team was at 40 percent or above. ☙ Kansas City was one of three teams that pressured the quarterback less than 15 percent of the time with a standard four-man pass rush. ☙ Kansas City was tied with Chicago for the fewest penalties by opponents, 92.

Passing

Player	DYAR	DVOA	Plays	NtYds	Avg	YAC	C%	TD	Int
M.Cassel*	-353	-30.4%	291	1668	5.7	4.9	59.9%	6	11
B.Quinn*	-440	-43.8%	219	1018	4.6	4.3	57.1%	2	7
A.Smith	418	14.8%	243	1610	6.6	5.1	70.3%	13	5

Rushing

Player	DYAR	DVOA	Plays	Yds	Avg	TD	Fum	Suc
J.Charles	109	1.4%	284	1518	5.3	5	5	46%
P.Hillis*	-71	-27.5%	85	310	3.6	1	2	40%
S.Draughn	34	5.8%	59	240	4.1	2	1	47%
M.Cassel*	35	17.8%	22	148	6.7	1	1	-
B.Quinn*	-4	-17.5%	15	69	4.6	0	0	-
D.McCluster	42	38.7%	12	70	5.8	0	0	-
C.Gray	20	58.0%	7	44	6.3	0	0	71%
N.Eachus	4	6.9%	5	18	3.6	0	0	60%
A.Smith	36	26.0%	21	142	6.8	0	0	-

Receiving

Player	DYAR	DVOA	Plays	Ctch	Yds	Y/C	YAC	TD	C%
D.Bowe	60	-4.1%	114	59	801	13.6	4.0	3	52%
D.McCluster	-34	-21.1%	76	52	452	8.7	3.9	1	68%
J.Baldwin	-24	-22.9%	47	20	325	16.3	5.5	1	43%
J.Newsome	-21	-23.5%	16	5	73	14.6	3.8	0	31%
S.Breaston	-18	-27.7%	15	7	74	10.6	0.9	0	47%
T.Copper	4	-12.4%	12	8	79	9.9	2.0	0	67%
D.Wylie	-27	-43.8%	12	6	53	8.8	1.8	0	50%
D.Avery	-75	-19.1%	125	60	781	13.0	3.5	3	48%
T.Moeaki	49	7.1%	56	33	453	13.7	3.8	1	59%
S.Maneri*	-29	-42.5%	12	5	51	10.2	6.0	0	42%
A.Fasano	-44	-19.4%	69	41	332	8.1	2.2	5	59%
J.Charles	0	-13.8%	49	36	236	6.6	7.3	1	73%
S.Draughn	-13	-23.3%	30	24	158	6.6	6.0	0	80%
P.Hillis*	-10	-29.1%	13	10	62	6.2	7.4	0	77%

Offensive Line

Player	Pos	Age	GS	Snaps	Pen	Sk	Pass	Run	Player	Pos	Age	GS	Snaps	Pen	Sk	Pass	Run
Eric Winston*	RT	30	16/16	1052	10	2.5	17	6.5	Donald Stephenson	OT	25	16/7	363	5	5	11	3
Jon Asamoah	RG	25	15/15	990	3	2.5	9.5	6.5	Rodney Hudson	C	24	3/3	183	0	0	0	1
Ryan Lilja*	C	32	15/15	990	2	2.5	7.5	5	Russ Hochstein*	C/G	36	11/1	116	1	0	3	1
Jeff Allen	LG	23	16/13	815	5	3	11.5	9	Geoff Schwartz	G	27	13/0	157	0	0	3	0
Branden Albert	LT	29	13/11	705	5	1	7	5									

Year	Yards	ALY	Rk	Power	Rk	Stuff	Rk	2nd Lev	Rk	Open Field	Rk	Sacks	ASR	Rk	Short	Long	F-Start	Cont.
2010	4.82	4.44	5	57%	20	15%	5	1.35	3	1.00	8	32	6.8%	18	6	19	17	32
2011	3.89	3.81	28	62%	18	20%	21	1.11	25	0.55	27	34	7.1%	19	6	20	26	39
2012	4.84	4.04	19	59%	23	20%	19	1.33	8	1.25	2	40	8.2%	27	10	20	20	30
2012 ALY by direction:			Left End 4.35 (10)			Left Tackle 2.63 (31)			Mid/Guard 4.07 (14)				Right Tackle 3.91 (16)				Right End 5.05 (7)	

Kansas City's offensive line was a little better last season than its numbers suggest. There were too many individual breakdowns, likely due to youth and players changing positions, but technique-wise, players showed gradual improvements in the second half of the season. Collectively, this well-sized group played with good cohesiveness and athleticism. Nevertheless, changes were made this offseason because while Andy Reid's system has a lot of on-the-move blocking concepts, it's not as heavy on the zone-blocking as that of previous coordinator Brian Daboll.

Reid and new general manager John Dorsey chose to keep the interior of the line intact, while the outside was overhauled. The selection of Eric Fisher No. 1 overall was simply a case of choosing the best player available in a draft with no superstars. It's not like offensive tackle had been a glaring weak spot on this team; Branden Albert was at worst an average NFL left tackle, and probably better than that. The Chiefs tried to trade him but his contract demands scared teams away, so he'll play out his one-year, $9.8 million franchise tender at right tackle. Albert should thrive on the right side, but when he hits the open market, he'll have to hope that a strong 2013 can offset the salary-shrinking stigma of being moved from left to right. With Albert sticking around, Donald Stephenson will be pushed to backup duties. That's too bad; the 2012 third-round pick was able to hold his own for stretches last year and deserves a chance to keep developing. Stephenson does show a concerning tendency to bend at the waist, particularly as a pass-blocker when it gets late in the down. Still, his decently quick feet and steady improvements lend reason for optimism, and he still figures to be the long-term right tackle when Albert leaves after this season.

The hope is that Stephenson's fellow 2012 rookie, Jeff Allen, can be the long-term solution at left guard. The second-rounder from Illinois is fairly comfortable playing on the move, but his lack of power at short angles in a phone booth is an issue that defenses can easy exploit. At right guard, Jon Asamoah is a noticeably better run-blocker now than he was as a young first-time starter in 2011. Can he continue to progress without a savvy veteran (and former guard) like Ryan Lilja starting next to him at center? The man now at center is Rodney Hudson, a 2011 second-round pick who is coming off a season-ending ankle injury suffered late last September.

Defensive Front Seven

Defensive Line	Age	Pos	Snaps	Plays	TmPct	Overall Rk	Stop	Dfts	BTkl	Runs	vs. Run St%	Rk	RuYd	Rk	Pass Rush Sack	Hit	Hur	Tips
Dontari Poe	23	DT	743	42	5.4%	20	36	8	2	38	84%	10	2.3	34	0	3	4	3
Tyson Jackson	27	DE	596	46	6.3%	23	38	9	1	40	80%	18	3.0	60	3	1	2	3
Ropati Pitoitua*	28	DE	494	50	6.8%	13	37	8	3	45	76%	35	2.7	52	2	2	0	1
Mike DeVito	29	DE	629	52	6.7%	17	37	6	2	48	73%	46	2.4	29	1	0	3	0
Austen Lane	26	DE	373	31	5.1%	42	23	4	0	27	74%	41	2.0	19	2	7	7	0

Linebackers	Age	Pos	Snaps	Plays	TmPct	Overall Rk	Stop	Dfts	BTkl	Sack	Hit	Pass Rush Hur	Tips	Runs	vs. Run St%	Rk	Yds	Rk	Tgts	vs. Pass Suc%	Rk	AdjYd	Rk	PD
Justin Houston	24	OLB	993	72	9.2%	66	48	17	1	10	10	22.5	3	44	68%	38	3.5	60	19	49%	44	7.6	60	2
Derrick Johnson	31	ILB	963	127	16.2%	16	80	26	7	2	4	2.5	0	89	73%	19	2.6	25	30	51%	38	7.7	61	3
Tamba Hali	30	OLB	919	52	7.1%	83	30	14	3	9	7	15.5	2	30	53%	103	4.4	100	3	35%	--	6.5	--	0
Jovan Belcher*	26	ILB	332	37	6.9%	84	22	2	0	0	0	1	0	26	77%	14	3.0	35	9	11%	--	14.8	--	0
Akeem Jordan	28	ILB	330	33	4.8%	--	16	5	2	0	0	0	0	29	52%	--	3.8	--	5	40%	--	7.1	--	0

Year	Yards	ALY	Rk	Power	Rk	Stuff	Rk	2nd Level	Rk	Open Field	Rk	Sacks	ASR	Rk	Short	Long
2010	4.34	4.29	25	66%	22	14%	28	1.12	17	0.67	12	39	6.5%	12	11	18
2011	4.13	4.31	24	55%	9	16%	29	1.06	7	0.57	7	29	6.3%	23	12	11
2012	4.48	4.18	20	52%	5	18%	23	1.17	13	0.99	25	27	6.5%	14	4	17

2012 ALY by direction:	Left End 3.92 (17)	Left Tackle 5.4 (32)	Mid/Guard 4.24 (22)	Right Tackle 4.23 (22)	Right End 3.09 (5)

Andy Reid has traditionally hired defensive coordinators who run a 4-3 scheme, but he was wise enough to recognize that the fairly well-constructed defense he's inheriting here is best suited for a 3-4. The new Chiefs defensive coordinator is former Jets linebackers coach Bob Sutton, who presumably will have a variegated, attacking scheme like the one he learned while working for Rex Ryan. Last season, the Chiefs sent six or more rushers just 27 times during the year, which was sixth-lowest in the league. With Sutton, expect that number to go up.

Despite Kansas City's deplorable win-loss record, linebacker Derrick Johnson had an excellent season. His key-and-diagnose prowess, coupled with fluid speed and athleticism, made him a devastating run-defender—not just out of Kansas City's base front, but also in their frequently-used dime packages. Johnson afforded the Chiefs the uncommon and significant luxury of being able to play the run with just one linebacker on the field. He led the AFC with 65 Run Stops, and his 80 total Stops were fifth in the NFL. Of course, playing the run and stopping the run are two different things. Despite Johnson's excellence, the Chiefs had a 12.4% run defense DVOA when opponents had three or more wide receivers in the game (last in the NFL) and allowed 5.41 yards per carry (30th). Those numbers are a great example of football as a team sport; Johnson and safety Eric Berry played the run well, but if an offense could get those guys blocked, the rest of the defensive backs on the field were awful at stopping running backs. That's part of the reason that Kansas City's dime defensive unit faced 122 rushing attempts on the season, not including scrambles, while the other 31 teams only faced a combined 245 carries when playing dime.

The other superstar in Kansas City's front seven is Tamba Hali. He may not match the dramatic sack totals of other leading edge-rushers, but in terms of sheer disruption, he's as impactful as any defensive attacker in football. He profits from natural leverage and a relentless motor in both run and pass defense. With players like Hali, it's important to have pass rushers opposite them who can consistently beat one-on-one blocking. Justin Houston is gradually emerging as one of those guys. He has the athleticism to dip and skim the corner against most right tackles. His only consistent issues have been when he's caught in space as a pass defender (which is something that can be minimized, as it's usually a function of the offense out-scheming the defense on a given play).

The major concern with this front seven is that the depth outside is comprised only of fringe veterans Frank Zombo and Edgar Jones. Inside, the Chiefs must settle on a second starting linebacker, though whoever wins the job will likely play less than half the snaps in 2013. Between the selection of Alabama's Nico Johnson in the fourth round and the signing of athletic veteran backups/fringe starters Akeem Jordan and Zac Diles, the second inside linebacker position figures to be adequately filled. The Chiefs hope the addition of ex-Jet Mike DeVito and the natural development of 2012 first-round pick Dontari Poe will give them a more destructive front line and make things easier on the linebackers.

Defensive Secondary

Secondary	Age	Pos	Snaps	Plays	Overall					vs. Run					vs. Pass									
					TmPct	Rk	Stop	Dfts	BTkl	Runs	St%	Rk	Yds	Rk	Tgts	Tgt%	Rk	Dist	Suc%	Rk	APaYd	Rk	PD	Int
Eric Berry	25	SS	993	96	12.2%	19	58	26	5	56	64%	2	3.4	1	51	13.5%	1	10.7	54%	38	8.2	48	11	1
Brandon Flowers	27	CB	864	60	8.2%	53	26	11	6	10	30%	68	7.8	60	74	20.9%	17	12.9	62%	5	5.7	6	11	3
Javier Arenas*	26	CB	709	69	8.8%	37	25	12	3	19	37%	56	9.4	73	55	14.4%	66	11.4	51%	45	7.7	48	9	0
Kenrick Lewis	25	FS	551	27	6.1%	64	2	0	7	13	0%	75	18.3	75	9	4.2%	68	18.8	49%	58	9.6	68	1	0
Abram Elam*	32	FS	451	37	6.3%	--	7	2	1	19	16%	--	10.8	--	10	3.5%	--	11.6	44%	--	10.7	--	2	0
Stanford Routt*	30	CB	406	25	5.7%	--	7	4	3	3	33%	--	13.7	--	39	18.1%	--	13.6	49%	--	9.6	--	4	2
Jalil Brown	26	CB	363	22	3.0%	--	7	6	2	6	33%	--	15.2	--	31	8.7%	--	13.7	53%	--	8.2	--	2	0
Travis Daniels*	31	CB	284	17	2.3%	--	4	3	1	5	20%	--	11.2	--	10	2.7%	--	8.5	41%	--	10.1	--	0	0
Tysyn Hartman	24	FS	237	25	4.6%	--	7	3	2	16	19%	--	9.2	--	9	3.5%	--	5.8	55%	--	5.7	--	2	0
Sean Smith	26	CB	1044	70	8.4%	49	22	12	3	13	31%	67	13.2	84	110	21.3%	12	11.5	49%	60	7.2	31	9	2
Dunta Robinson	31	CB	930	88	10.9%	11	42	17	8	28	61%	12	5.7	32	83	19.4%	29	13.6	50%	56	8.0	57	8	1
Quintin Demps	28	FS	347	32	5.4%	69	12	7	3	5	20%	69	11.4	69	20	5.6%	55	12.3	70%	6	7.5	38	5	0

Year	Pass D Rank	vs. #1 WR	Rk	vs. #2 WR	Rk	vs. Other WR	Rk	vs. TE	Rk	vs. RB	Rk
2010	18	-12.4%	7	11.2%	22	-3.3%	16	11.3%	20	16.1%	26
2011	13	-22.9%	2	6.8%	19	-27.2%	5	6.5%	16	34.5%	31
2012	31	22.1%	28	7.0%	21	2.8%	22	-4.0%	11	33.4%	32

The new front office understands that if Sutton is to have a successful attack-oriented scheme like the one he learned under Rex Ryan, the Chiefs need corners who can win in man coverage. They already have an outstanding press-boundary corner in Brandon Flowers, who had his best season by our metrics. The physical sixth-year pro plays with good technique and has a natural understanding for angles and positioning in downfield coverage. To play opposite him, the Chiefs brought in lanky ex-Dolphin Sean Smith. He's gifted enough to stifle most No. 2 receivers, but he must improve in off-coverage when isolated on the outside. The Chiefs also signed Dunta Robinson after he was cut by Atlanta. Many observers expected Robinson to move to safety, where he would replace Kenrick Lewis. His improved physicality as a tackler in recent years, coupled with the fact that he's clearly most comfortable in off-coverage, suggests that he would be a good fit at this position. However, the trade of Javier Arenas likely changed that, unless the Chiefs want to test their luck by playing Jalil Brown in the slot. They drafted Sanders Commings out of Georgia in the fifth round, though he figures to be strictly an outside player (NFL.com compares him, style-wise, to Brandon Browner).

Rounding out the secondary is Eric Berry. Last year he bounced back from his 2011 ACL injury well enough to lead all AFC safeties with 26 Defeats and earn Pro Bowl honors. However, to say the former first-round pick had a great year would be inaccurate. Too often Berry got abused in coverage, particularly when playing man-to-man against a quality tight end. Sutton could ostensibly make Berry a LaRon Landry-type blitzer and rover, but it would be better if Berry could just improve his pass defense. He's versatile enough to become a genuine difference-maker.

Special Teams

Year	DVOA	Rank	FG/XP	Rank	Net Kick	Rank	Kick Ret	Rank	Net Punt	Rank	Punt Ret	Rank	Hidden	Rank
2010	-2.1%	24	-2.8	28	-2.3	21	-9.1	27	-1.5	23	5.3	6	-1.3	15
2011	-0.9%	19	-2.3	20	-1.0	22	-6.6	30	3.2	12	2.1	12	-15.4	32
2012	-2.0%	22	-2.2	19	-1.5	19	-9.8	31	8.8	8	-5.4	26	2.4	12

Kansas City's special teams have been generally mediocre the last couple seasons except for punter Dustin Colquitt. Colquitt got a much-deserved Pro Bowl selection, as our metrics say his gross punt value was worth 14.9 points over average. Colquitt had 10 punts that went 60 yards or more, and he was one of two punters to land more than half his punts inside the 20 (Andy Lee was the other). Unfortunately, the Chiefs' coverage teams weren't as good as their punter, so the team couldn't even finish in the top five for net punt value. The return jobs are up in the air with Arenas gone. Dexter McCluster has done the job in the past, of course, and both running back Shaun Draughn and wide receiver Devon Wylie got some work on kickoffs last year. Ryan Succop, a former Mr. Irrelevant, will continue to be the Chiefs' kicker and will continue to be irrelevant.

Coaching Staff

The question with Andy Reid is whether he can find it within himself to run a balanced offense. He never could quite commit to the ground game in Philadelphia; a failure to commit here would be a failure to fully utilize Jamaal Charles, clearly Kansas City's best weapon. Perhaps Reid can compromise with himself by designing a high volume of short passes for Charles. To help run his offense (and, who knows, maybe one day call plays), Reid brought over with him former Eagles quarterbacks coach Doug Pederson as the new offensive coordinator. The longtime backup quarterback has been on Reid's staff since 2009. Defensively, Sutton was a good hire in terms of scheme fitting personnel. Sutton will work with a few of Romeo Crennel's defensive assistants who were retained, including respected linebackers coach Gary Gibbs and secondary coach Emmitt Thomas.

Miami Dolphins

2012 Record: 7-9	Total DVOA: -7.2% (21st)	2013 Mean Projection: 6.1 wins	On the Clock (0-4): 27%
Pythagorean Wins: 7.1 (21st)	Offense: -8.4% (22nd)	Postseason Odds: 13.0%	Mediocrity (5-7): 45%
Snap-Weighted Age: 26.2 (26th)	Defense: -0.8%(14th)	Super Bowl Odds: 0.6%	Playoff Contender (8-10): 23%
Average Opponent: -1.9% (19th)	Special Teams: 0.4% (14th)	Proj. Avg. Opponent: 3.4% (3rd)	Super Bowl Contender (11+): 4%

2012: The papers don't want to know whose shirts you wear.

2013: Holes on the offensive and defensive lines will not be filled by wide receiver Mike Wallace.

Forty years ago, Arizona State University social psychology professor Robert Cialdini and his colleagues conducted a seminal series of experiments on a phenomenon called "basking in reflected glory (BIRGing)," or the tendency to publicly associate oneself with the success of others. In line with expectations (and common sense), they found that football fans wear apparel and use the word "we" to describe game results more often after their favorite teams win. You probably recognize this by its more colloquial name, "jumping on the bandwagon."

BIRGing exists across sports and continents, but image-conscious South Florida has taken it to new heights. In a region prided on its beautiful people, fancy cars, and sprawling waterfront estates, "glory" means more than just winning. Unless a local team wins *championships*, residents prefer a more heliocentric form of basking. It's easy to forget now but, when LeBron James took his talents to South Beach, the Miami Heat had just seen attendance drop 10 percent from its high in 2005-2006 despite finishing above .500 three of the previous four years. In baseball, given Marlins fans' open rebellion against unscrupulous owners since Wayne Huizenga's 1997 fire sale, it's easy to forget that attendance spiked 36 percent in their 2003 championship season; so much for conscientious objection. Meanwhile, the Florida Panthers averaged 40 sellouts in the two seasons after their 1996 Stanley Cup Finals run; they've averaged less than five sellouts over the past 13 years despite six above-.500 finishes.

As South Florida's longest-standing professional sports franchise, the Dolphins have been immune to this BIRG-dependent fandom. For the better part of four decades, a walk around Miami would find just as many people wearing Dolphins apparel, and just as many using "we" instead of "they" as their pronoun of choice, regardless of whether the team won or lost. (Cubs fans, of course have been doing this for the better part of 10 decades.)

Increasingly, however, patience is growing thin, and the fan base is shifting toward the opposite mode: cutting off reflected failure (CORFing). There's a lot more "they" than "we" being uttered in Miami these days, and those who still show up to games are more frequently wearing the opponents' apparel. A stadium that was 90 percent full as recently as 2010 had one of four seats empty in 2012. If not for the team buying thousands of its own tickets, seven of eight games would have

been blacked out locally. Perhaps the most poignant example of growing dissociation was the Dolphins' December home game against Jacksonville. During a halftime ceremony honoring the 40th anniversary of Miami's perfect season, there were nearly as many surviving members of the 1972 team on hand as there were fans to salute them. This prompted Bob Griese to tell *South Florida Sun Sentinel*'s Craig Davis, "I came in '67, the second year of the franchise, and the stadium wasn't full. In '70, when [Don] Shula came and we started winning, I think we sold more season tickets than any team in the NFL."

The difference between then and now is the absence of expansion team-driven hope. Instead of seeing Joe Robbie and Don Shula building a franchise, fans have watched a steady flow of NFL incompetents tearing a franchise down. In four years, starting in 2001, Rick Spielman (somehow employed in Minnesota) and Dave Wannstedt (now operating an animatronic parrot in Tampa) undid much of the successful-in-comparison Jimmy Johnson era. Only nine of the duo's 27 draft picks from 2001 to 2004 performed above historical expectation, and that group made only three Pro Bowls combined. When he wasn't busy making bad picks, Spielman was making bad trades, the most infamous of which involved A.J. Feeley and Marty Booker.

Then Nick Saban came to town, and blazed a trail not seen in the southeast since General Sherman's March to the Sea. His legacy of scorched Miami earth includes signing Daunte Culpepper over Drew Brees in free agency, drafting as poorly as the previous regime, and setting an example for Bobby Petrino. Perhaps worst of all, he saddled the organization with general manager Randy Mueller, whose first two moves after Saban left were to hire Cam Cameron as head coach and to select Ted Ginn ninth overall in the 2007 NFL draft.

You might be wondering why we're rehashing seemingly ancient history. It's to set up the following anecdote, which further illustrates our larger theme: Dolphins fans have become so used to these sorts of failures that they just don't care anymore about the franchise that put South Florida on the sports map.

One day after no one showed up to commemorate the '72 Dolphins, Saban appeared on Dan LeBatard's local sports radio show to discuss Alabama's upcoming national championship game at Sun Life Stadium. Mind you, LeBatard is the

2013 Dolphins Schedule

Week	Opp.	Week	Opp.	Week	Opp.
1	at CLE	7	BUF	13	at NYJ
2	at IND	8	at NE	14	at PIT
3	ATL	9	CIN (Thu.)	15	NE
4	at NO (Mon.)	10	at TB (Mon.)	16	at BUF
5	BAL	11	SD	17	NYJ
6	BYE	12	CAR		

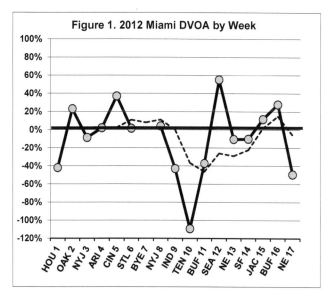

Figure 1. 2012 Miami DVOA by Week

man who wrote a July 2008 column for the *Miami Herald* subtitled, "Saban Left Dolphins a Loser, Weasel." In the body of the piece were additional epithets like "gasbag," "complete and utter amateur," "quitter," "fraud," and our personal favorite, "infomercial sermonizer." And yet, not even LeBatard—now the national spokesman for South Florida sports fans—could conjure up enough give-a-damn to call out his one-time archenemy. Radio is a (dying) business, so no one should have expected him to call Saban a gasbag on air (maybe "infomercial sermonizer," though), but what transpired was a 20-minute Alphonse-and-Gaston routine: "After you, Daniel… No, you first, my dear Nicholas."

The Dolphins' gradually increasing irrelevance, already enough to make Dan LeBatard CORF, continued into the new year. Channeling his inner Jeffrey Loria, owner Stephen Ross stated publicly that Miami's bids to host a Super Bowl in 2016 or 2017 hinged on public financing of stadium renovations, going so far as to intimate selling or moving the team if the money didn't materialize. In May, the Florida House of Representatives politely said "thanks, but no thanks," not bothering to take up the funding legislation. Even if they had passed the bill, voters were already 57 percent opposed to the Miami-Dade referendum that would have resulted.

The Dolphins' on-field outlook isn't much better. In *Football Outsiders Almanac 2012*, Mike Tanier detailed general manager Jeff Ireland's status as a modern-day Matt Millen. This offseason's questionable decisions made him look more like David Bowie's "Major Tom," because his spaceship clearly does not know which way to go. Ireland made a half-hearted attempt to re-sign franchise left tackle Jake Long, first by low-balling an offer during the season, then by putting him in medical-evaluation purgatory after the season despite Dr. James Andrews declaring him healthy. It's true that Long has underperformed his lofty standards the past two seasons, mainly due to an increasing number of bumps and bruises. However, considering that Ireland (along with Bill Parcells) anointed Long the cornerstone of the franchise in 2008, and Long really made the grade, you would think some benefit of the doubt was in order. This wasn't a JaMarcus Russell situation, so we're perplexed as to why Ireland proceeded as if he didn't think a healthy Long could rebound in 2013.

With Long gone, Ireland next applied his eccentric brand of decision-making to the question of how Miami would replace him. For a month preceding the draft, Adam Schefter—and therefore most of Twitter—monitored rumors of a potential trade for disgruntled Kansas City left tackle Branden Albert. It made perfect sense, but didn't happen. On draft day, Ireland

traded up to the No. 3 pick, presumably to select Oklahoma left tackle Lane Johnson. It made perfect sense, but didn't happen. As was the case with last offseason, Miami seemed to once again settle for the third- or fourth-best option. (This time, his name was Tyson Clabo, and while he's still a good player, he doesn't actually play the position in question.)

In another verse of Ireland's "Replace Oddity," the stars at cornerback look very different today. As recently as August 2012, Sean Smith and Vontae Davis formed a promising young tandem; less than a year later, neither remains with the team. Richard Marshall was supposed to fill the hole created when Ireland traded Davis last year, but he missed 12 games. Brent Grimes takes over for Smith, but he was injured for most of 2012 as well. If healthy, Marshall and Grimes are adequate replacements, but the larger point still holds: Ireland seems to be the rare general manager who gives up on young, above average players he drafted. While the fan base is distancing itself from team failures, Ireland is distancing himself from his own (sporadic) successes.

But if there was one offseason move that saw Ireland floating in a most peculiar way, it was signing free agent wide receiver Mike Wallace for $60 million over five years, with $30 million guaranteed. It's the mother of all boom-bust acquisitions, and yet Ireland chose to buy high. Make no mistake; Wallace's disastrous 2012 season was an aberration given his talent level, so he's due for a bounce back. A context-free look at history agrees: Our similarity scores for wide receivers show that the 10 players most similar to Wallace over a three-year span improved from an average of 63 catches for 897 yards and 5.4 touchdowns in their down year to an average of 74 catches for 1,106 yards and 8.2 touchdowns the following year (Table 1). Six of these players made the Pro Bowl.

Unfortunately, if there is one underlying theme to everything we've learned over the past 10 years, it's that football performance depends on context, and wide receiver may be the most context-dependent position on the field. Therefore, we can't ignore that all 10 of the wideouts most comparable to Wallace bounced back with the same team they had played on the year before. We also can't ignore that Wallace will be catching passes from Ryan Tannehill rather than Ben Roethlisberger.

Table 1. Most Similar Wide Receivers to Mike Wallace 2010-2012

Player	Years	Team	3Y SIM	Year One					Year Two					Year Three					Year Four			
				Rec	Yd	TD	Avg	SIM	Rec	Yd	TD	Avg	SIM	Rec	Yd	TD	Avg	SIM	Rec	Yd	TD	Avg
Mike Wallace	10-12	PIT	--	60	1,257	10	21.0	--	72	1,193	8	16.6	--	64	836	8	13.1	--	?	?	?	?
Gary Clark	86-88	WAS	848	74	1,265	7	17.1	835	75	1,421	9	19.0	807	59	892	7	15.1	877	79	1,229	9	15.6
Ernest Givins	87-89	HOIL	839	71	1,244	8	17.6	870	60	976	5	16.3	786	55	794	3	14.4	854	72	979	9	13.6
Plaxico Burress	01-03	PIT	839	66	1,008	6	15.3	735	78	1,325	7	17.0	875	60	860	4	14.3	883	35	698	5	19.9
Terrell Owens	97-99	SF	834	60	936	8	15.6	739	67	1,097	14	16.4	855	60	754	4	12.6	879	97	1,451	13	15.0
Sterling Sharpe	89-91	GB	828	90	1,423	12	15.8	734	67	1,105	6	16.5	899	69	961	4	13.9	849	108	1,461	13	13.5
Keyshawn Johnson	98-00	NYJ/TB	819	83	1,131	10	13.6	725	89	1,170	8	13.1	834	71	874	8	12.3	867	106	1,266	1	11.9
Mike Quick	84-86	PHI	817	61	1,052	9	17.2	756	73	1,247	11	17.1	888	60	939	9	15.7	818	61	1,053	15	17.2
Steve Largent	78-80	SEA	812	71	1,168	8	16.5	826	66	1,237	9	18.7	879	66	1,064	6	16.1	776	75	1,224	9	16.3
Peerless Price	01-03	BUF/ATL	808	55	895	7	16.3	682	94	1,252	9	13.3	804	64	838	3	13.1	894	45	575	3	12.8
Cris Collinsworth	82-84	CIN	799	87	1,244	2	14.3	719	66	1,130	5	17.1	842	64	989	6	15.5	824	65	1,125	5	17.3
AVERAGE				72	1,137	8	15.9		73	1,196	8	16.5		63	897	5	14.3		74	1,106	8	15.3

Note: 1982 and 1987 stats prorated for strike; average does not include Wallace.

Miami's 2013 offseason did nothing to reverse the team's decade-long retreat from regional consciousness, and may have actually accelerated it. Judging from the current conventional wisdom, though, our opinion seems to be in the minority. At press time, Las Vegas has Miami's over-under at 7.5 wins, which means the betting public foresees an improvement on last year's 6-10 record. What's more, bets are currently favoring the over (-145) to the under (+125). (Note: We bring this up for narrative purposes only.)

So why does our projection model disagree? To begin with, lack of continuity along the offensive line is typically a bad omen. Ireland's tackle fiasco means Jonathan Martin is moving to the left side, while Clabo is assuming Martin's former position. At guard, incumbents Richie Incognito and John Jerry will have a hard time keeping their jobs ahead of third-rounder Dallas Thomas and free-agent signee Lance Louis. All told, there's

a better than 50-50 chance that the only constant up front is center Mike Pouncey. That much turnover does Wallace (and Tannehill) no favors in the deep passing game.

For the sake of argument, let's assume Wallace manages to uphold his end of the bargain and has another 1,200-yard season. Even then, recent history suggests that signing a No. 1 receiver—even one who has a productive season—doesn't do much to improve a team's overall pass offense. Just last season, Tampa Bay only improved six spots in pass offense DVOA despite Vincent Jackson's individual exploits. Terrell Owens had 72 catches for 983 yards and nine touchdowns with Cincinnati in 2010, but the Bengals pass offense only improved four spots. In 2009, T.J. Houshmandzadeh had an Owens-like stat line after signing with Seattle, but the Seahawks finished 25th for a second consecutive season.

These are not isolated occurrences. Eighteen times be-

Table 2. Star Wide Receivers Changing Teams, 2000-2012

Team	Year	Receiver	RecYd Prev 2 Years	RecYd This Year	Pass DVOA Prev Year	Rk	Pass DVOA This Year	Rk	DVOA Dif	Rk Dif
CHI	2005	Muhsin Muhammad	2,242	750	-50.6%	32	-21.2%	28	29.5%	+4
NYJ	2010	Santonio Holmes	2,069	746	-21.4%	28	6.5%	19	27.9%	+9
CHI	2012	Brandon Marshall	2,228	1,508	-21.9%	30	-5.5%	25	16.4%	+5
PHI	2004	Terrell Owens	2,402	1,200	19.3%	11	28.9%	10	9.6%	+1
WAS	2003	Laveranues Coles	2,132	1,204	-7.5%	26	1.3%	19	8.8%	+7
MIA	2010	Brandon Marshall	2,385	1,014	8.5%	18	15.9%	16	7.4%	+2
TB	2000	Keyshawn Johnson	2,301	874	3.6%	21	9.9%	14	6.3%	+7
BAL	2010	Anquan Boldin	2,062	837	21.9%	11	26.3%	8	4.4%	+3
TB	2002	Keenan McCardell	2,317	670	8.8%	12	11.5%	13	2.7%	-1
BAL	2005	Derrick Mason	2,471	1,073	-3.6%	22	-1.1%	22	2.5%	0
OAK	2005	Randy Moss	2,399	1,005	8.6%	16	10.7%	16	2.2%	0
NE	2012	Brandon Lloyd	2,414	911	55.3%	2	53.9%	1	-1.4%	+1
SD	2003	David Boston	2,110	880	4.5%	20	-1.9%	22	-6.4%	-2
BUF	2009	Terrell Owens	2,407	829	-13.2%	27	-21.1%	27	-7.8%	0
SEA	2009	T.J. Houshmandzadeh	2,047	911	-8.5%	25	-18.7%	25	-10.2%	0
NYJ	2009	Braylon Edwards	2,162	541	0.8%	21	-21.4%	28	-22.2%	-7
ATL	2003	Peerless Price	2,147	838	8.2%	17	-20.0%	29	-28.2%	-12
NYJ	2005	Laveranues Coles	2,154	845	33.7%	8	-23.2%	31	-56.9%	-23
AVERAGE					2.6%	19.3	1.7%	19.6	-0.9%	-0.3

Includes all receivers changing teams after two years with more than 2,000 yards combined.

tween 2000 and 2012, a wide receiver with over 2,000 yards combined in the previous two seasons switched teams in the offseason. On average, those teams went from a passing DVOA of 2.6% which ranked 19th in the league to a passing DVOA of 1.7% that ranked 20th (Table 2). Only three of these teams—the 2005 Bears with Muhsin Muhammad, the 2010 Jets with Santonio Holmes, and the 2012 Bears with Brandon Marshall—improved their passing DVOA by more than 10 percentage points, but those happen to be the only three teams in the study group that had passing DVOA below -20% the prior year. This track record of free-agent signings suggests that an improved Miami win total this season will depend on Tannehill, not Wallace, and we just don't foresee enough growth in Tannehill's second year.

The stars also have to align on defense. Miami fell from seventh to 19th in Adjusted Sack Rate last season, so it's important for Dion Jordan to prove that his potential was worth the third overall pick. (We're not holding our collective breath.) According to SackSEER, Jordan wasn't even among the top three pass rushers in this year's draft, let alone the top three players. For a comparison, in 2011, Denver took SackSEER's No. 1 prospect, Von Miller, second overall, and San Francisco took No. 2 prospect Aldon Smith seventh overall. In both 2011 and 2012, the fifth-best prospect according to SackSEER (i.e., Jordan's ranking) didn't come off the board until the mid-teens. And according to our model of draft efficiency, Jordan would have to match the production of some-

one like Justin Tuck to meet expectations. That's asking a lot, especially from a rookie. Meanwhile, Grimes and Marshall have to avoid consecutive injury-plagued seasons because human torch Nolan Carroll and rookie Jamar Taylor comprise the cornerback depth behind them. There's also the issue of expecting a unit with five new starters to coalesce in the midst of a defensive scheme change.

Other concerns include a schedule we project to be the third-toughest in the league (up from 19th in 2012), as well as a likely drop in team health (Miami finished last season seventh in Adjusted Games Lost).

Admittedly, we are not painting a pretty picture of Miami's immediate past, present, and future. Is it possible for us to inject some optimism into a fan base no longer capable of producing it naturally? Think about our Dolphins projection this way: If it turns out to underestimate them, that still is unlikely to lead to a playoff appearance. It probably means another finish approaching .500, which would be a win for the soul-crushing status quo. No, what Miami needs in the long run is for our model to be right. That would end the Ireland era, and Ross would be inclined to either sell the team or realize he needs to do the exact opposite of what he's done to date (a la Arthur Blank or John York ca. 2008.) As an added bonus, a total Dolphins collapse would allow South Floridians to start basking in the Heat's reflected glory before Christmas.

Danny Tuccitto

2012 Dolphins Stats by Week

Wk	vs.	W-L	PF	PA	YDF	YDA	TO	Total	Off	Def	ST
1	at HOU	L	10	30	275	337	-4	-42%	-61%	11%	29%
2	OAK	W	35	13	452	396	1	23%	30%	8%	1%
3	NYJ	L	20	23	381	388	0	-9%	3%	-12%	-24%
4	at ARI	L	21	24	480	297	-2	2%	-3%	-6%	-1%
5	at CIN	W	17	13	279	298	1	37%	9%	-36%	-8%
6	STL	W	17	14	192	462	1	2%	2%	21%	20%
7	BYE										
8	at NYJ	W	30	9	236	363	1	4%	-15%	1%	20%
9	at IND	L	20	23	365	516	0	-43%	-13%	26%	-5%
10	TEN	L	3	37	255	293	-4	-109%	-82%	25%	-2%
11	at BUF	L	14	19	184	281	-3	-37%	-55%	-18%	0%
12	SEA	W	24	21	435	312	-1	55%	71%	-5%	-21%
13	NE	L	16	23	277	321	0	-11%	-28%	-23%	-5%
14	at SF	L	13	27	227	321	-1	-10%	-8%	5%	3%
15	JAC	W	24	3	389	299	-1	12%	16%	9%	6%
16	BUF	W	24	10	301	381	4	28%	2%	-24%	2%
17	at NE	L	0	28	256	443	-2	-49%	-33%	9%	-7%

Trends and Splits

	Offense	Rank	Defense	Rank
Total DVOA	-8.4%	22	-0.8%	14
Unadjusted VOA	-6.8%	21	-1.2%	15
Weighted Trend	-11.4%	25	0.4%	17
Variance	13.6%	32	3.3%	6
Average Opponent	-0.5%	12	-2.6%	24
Passing	-1.8%	23	8.4%	17
Rushing	-8.4%	23	-13.3%	8
First Down	-2.9%	18	-1.5%	14
Second Down	-9.6%	23	-1.5%	14
Third Down	-16.7%	25	1.6%	18
First Half	-13.4%	25	2.0%	19
Second Half	-3.4%	17	-3.4%	10
Red Zone	-8.2%	21	-38.2%	1
Late and Close	6.8%	11	-8.6%	14

Five-Year Performance

Year	W-L	Pyth W	Est W	PF	PA	TO	Total	Rk	Off	Rk	Def	Rk	ST	Rk	Off AGL	Rk	Def AGL	Rk	Off Age	Rk	Def Age	Rk	ST Age	Rk
2008	11-5	8.8	8.5	345	317	+17	6.2%	14	12.0%	8	-0.1%	16	-5.9%	29	24.1	16	1.6	1	26.2	32	28.3	3	26.1	27
2009	7-9	7.2	8.4	360	390	-8	4.4%	16	4.1%	16	1.5%	18	1.8%	9	26.9	18	21.2	13	26.2	30	27.5	11	26.1	23
2010	7-9	6.2	8.5	273	333	-12	1.8%	15	0.7%	18	-4.8%	9	-3.7%	29	27.1	19	24.0	15	26.5	26	26.3	24	25.8	25
2011	6-10	8.5	7.7	329	313	-6	-1.3%	18	-7.5%	20	-3.7%	12	2.5%	6	22.1	12	9.6	3	26.6	21	27.7	6	26.3	16
2012	7-9	7.1	7.6	288	317	-10	-7.2%	21	-8.4%	22	-0.8%	14	0.4%	14	19.7	9	18.0	7	25.7	29	26.8	16	25.7	25

2012 Performance Based on Most Common Personnel Groups

MIA Offense Pers	Freq	Yds	DVOA	Run%	MIA Offense vs. Opponents Pers	Freq	Yds	DVOA	MIA Defense Pers	Freq	Yds	DVOA	MIA Defense vs. Opponents Pers	Freq	Yds	DVOA
11	45%	5.5	-8.9%	19%	4-3-4	33%	5.3	1.1%	4-3-4	42%	5.6	0.8%	11	41%	5.5	-5.6%
21	26%	6.0	-0.5%	65%	Nickel Even	29%	5.6	-2.0%	Nickel Even	31%	5.5	1.6%	12	26%	5.7	2.8%
12	21%	5.3	-0.1%	51%	3-4-4	17%	5.7	-12.2%	Nickel Odd	21%	5.4	-7.0%	21	10%	6.1	11.6%
22	5%	2.9	-41.3%	82%	Nickel Odd	12%	3.8	-41.2%	Dime+	3%	7.2	37.9%	22	5%	6.9	16.5%
10	1%	4.9	-10.2%	0%	Dime+	7%	7.6	12.7%	Goal Line	1%	0.1	-76.2%	10	4%	5.6	31.0%

Strategic Tendencies

Run/Pass		Rk	Formation		Rk	Pass Rush		Rk	Secondary		Rk	Strategy		Rk
Runs, first half	44%	5	Form: Single Back	51%	30	Rush 3	7.2%	13	4 DB	43%	21	Play action	16%	29
Runs, first down	63%	7	Form: Empty Back	8%	8	Rush 4	53.5%	28	5 DB	52%	9	Avg Box (Off)	6.35	18
Runs, second-long	30%	20	Pers: 3+ WR	46%	25	Rush 5	32.1%	4	6+ DB	3%	25	Avg Box (Def)	6.38	16
Runs, power sit.	57%	13	Pers: 4+ WR	1%	17	Rush 6+	7.2%	15	CB by Sides	71%	19	Offensive Pace	29.23	9
Runs, behind 2H	29%	15	Pers: 2+ TE/6+ OL	28%	19	Sacks by LB	16.7%	20	DB Blitz	18%	2	Defensive Pace	29.76	11
Pass, ahead 2H	51%	11	Shotgun/Pistol	48%	14	Sacks by DB	11.9%	7	Hole in Zone	12%	3	Go for it on 4th	0.88	18

In 2011, the Dolphins used single-back formations on 75 percent of plays, fifth in the NFL. Last year that dropped to just 51 percent of plays. However, use of empty-backfield formations improved significantly. ☞ When Miami went "max protect," they averaged a league-high 9.8 yards per play with 43.3% DVOA (fifth in the league). ☞ The Dolphins had the league's worst offense running the ball on second-and-long, with 3.5 yards per carry and -52.8% DVOA. ☞ Miami had the league's third-biggest gap between performance with play action (46.6% DVOA, 9.0 yards per pass) and performance without (-10.4% DVOA, 5.7 yards per pass). ☞ The Dolphins' surprisingly strong run defense was particularly strengthened by success against runs from shotgun: -32.1% DVOA and 3.8 yards per carry allowed were both second behind only New England.

Passing

Player	DYAR	DVOA	Plays	NtYds	Avg	YAC	C%	TD	Int
R.Tannehill	39	-9.9%	517	3069	5.9	4.4	58.5%	12	13
M.Moore	40	15.5%	21	122	5.8	2.5	57.9%	1	0

Receiving

Player	DYAR	DVOA	Plays	Ctch	Yds	Y/C	YAC	TD	C%
B.Hartline	158	0.6%	131	74	1083	14.6	3.2	1	56%
D.Bess*	71	-3.7%	105	61	783	12.8	4.1	1	58%
R.Matthews	20	-1.4%	20	11	151	13.7	2.7	0	55%
A.Binns	-19	-14.1%	11	6	67	11.2	4.3	0	55%
M.Moore*	20	18.2%	11	6	116	19.3	3.8	1	55%
J.Gaffney	-2	-16.8%	10	4	68	17.0	2.8	0	40%
A.Armstrong	-36	-65.6%	9	3	12	4.0	1.0	0	33%
M.Wallace	-19	-17.4%	119	64	833	13.0	4.2	8	54%
B.Gibson	214	23.3%	82	51	691	13.5	2.2	5	62%
A.Fasano*	-44	-19.4%	69	41	332	8.1	2.2	5	59%
C.Clay	-19	-16.0%	33	18	212	11.8	4.5	2	55%
D.Keller	76	26.4%	36	28	317	11.3	3.3	2	78%
R.Bush*	54	7.9%	51	35	292	8.3	7.8	2	69%
D.Thomas	14	0.8%	22	15	156	10.4	9.6	0	68%
J.Lane	12	1.0%	12	11	79	7.2	5.4	1	92%
L.Miller	6	-2.0%	9	6	45	7.5	6.7	0	67%
E.Rodriguez	-7	-27.6%	8	4	21	5.3	4.8	0	50%

Rushing

Player	DYAR	DVOA	Plays	Yds	Avg	TD	Fum	Suc
R.Bush*	3	-8.3%	227	988	4.4	6	4	51%
D.Thomas	-9	-10.8%	91	326	3.6	4	3	51%
L.Miller	35	7.5%	51	250	4.9	1	0	55%
R.Tannehill	2	-11.0%	33	226	6.8	2	4	-
J.Lane	-31	-46.8%	13	18	1.4	2	1	46%

Offensive Line

Player	Pos	Age	GS	Snaps	Pen	Sk	Pass	Run	Player	Pos	Age	GS	Snaps	Pen	Sk	Pass	Run
John Jerry	RG	27	16/16	1033	3	2.8	5.3	5.5	Jake Long*	LT	28	12/12	729	8	4	14	2
Jonathan Martin	RT	24	16/16	1031	5	6.7	22.2	2	Nate Garner	OT	28	16/4	326	3	2.5	6.5	0
Mike Pouncey	C	24	16/16	1031	4	1.2	3.7	1.5	Tyson Clabo	RT	32	16/16	1048	5	4.5	15.5	2.5
Richie Incognito	LG	30	16/16	1026	6	3.5	8.5	11	Lance Louis	G	28	11/11	692	2	2	4	2.5

Year	Yards	ALY	Rk	Power	Rk	Stuff	Rk	2nd Lev	Rk	Open Field	Rk	Sacks	ASR	Rk	Short	Long	F-Start	Cont.
2010	3.78	4.07	16	83%	1	16%	7	0.86	32	0.38	32	38	6.3%	15	18	9	18	24
2011	4.28	4.05	16	46%	32	18%	13	1.14	19	0.82	17	52	9.6%	30	22	20	13	29
2012	4.15	3.93	21	63%	17	18%	11	1.14	17	0.76	17	37	6.8%	18	14	14	14	42

2012 ALY by direction: Left End 4.46 (7) — Left Tackle 4.22 (11) — Mid/Guard 3.94 (20) — Right Tackle 3.3 (29) — Right End 3.9 (18)

Despite his underwhelming charting stats last season, perhaps we should cut Jonathan Martin some slack. Recent history says expectations for a rookie right tackle are pretty low: Over the past 10 years, only 27 started 12 or more games, and none earned Pro Bowl or All-Pro honors. Two of the past three years, a rookie right tackle gave up the most blown block sacks in the NFL (Anthony Davis in 2010, and Bobby Massie in 2012).

Furthermore, if a team thinks their rookie is good enough to switch sides the following season, right tackle past doesn't seem to be left tackle prologue. Tyron Smith, Nate Solder, and J'Marcus Webb improved from 19 combined blown-block sacks allowed in Year 1 to 10.5 in Year 2. Prior to that, Jammal Brown was first-team All-Pro as a second-year left tackle after playing right tackle as a rookie. Two players often compared to Martin heading into the 2012 draft, Jordan Gross and Michael Roos, have amassed three Pro Bowls and two All-Pro selections since moving to the left side after their rookie years. Unlike those players, however, Martin actually spent some time at left tackle last season, the results of which don't inspire much confidence in the transition: Martin's 14.8 blown blocks in pass protection over 12 games at right tackle prorate to 19.7 for a full season; his 7.4 blown blocks in four games replacing Jake Long prorate to 29.6.

Of course, with Martin's move, someone has to play right tackle, and—thankfully for Dolphins fans—it's not going to be Nate Garner or Will Yeatman. Tyson Clabo may not have been who Miamians wanted (i.e., Branden Albert), but he has only allowed 14.5 blown block sacks the past four seasons, and his 2012 total comes with the important caveat that Atlanta was the most pass-happy offense in the NFL.

The interior line conjures childhood memories of watching Sesame Street, and playing along with "one of these things is not like the others." While center Mike Pouncey and right guard John Jerry do their jobs play in and play out, left guard Richie Incognito constantly misses blocks, sometimes laughably so. Particularly ominous for Martin's transition is that many of Incognito's mistakes come on plays requiring collaboration with his neighbors (i.e., protecting against stunts and clearing holes on stretch plays). Given Incognitio's liabilities both on the field and on the balance sheet ($5.4 million cap hit in 2013), it wouldn't surprise us if third-round pick Dallas Thomas (Tennessee) is the Week 1 starter.

Defensive Front Seven

Defensive Line	Age	Pos	Snaps	Plays	Overall TmPct	Rk	Stop	Dfts	BTkl	Runs	vs. Run St%	Rk	RuYd	Rk	Pass Rush Sack	Hit	Hur	Tips
Jared Odrick	26	DE	925	36	4.3%	53	31	17	2	25	84%	8	1.5	9	5	9	13.5	2
Cameron Wake	31	DE	913	54	6.5%	20	42	27	3	32	69%	57	2.8	53	15	17	27.5	0
Randy Starks	30	DT	809	30	3.6%	46	24	10	4	22	73%	39	1.6	19	4.5	4	13.5	2
Paul Soliai	30	DT	619	30	3.6%	46	30	13	1	24	100%	1	0.5	1	1.5	3	4	1
Olivier Vernon	23	DE	432	23	2.8%	--	16	10	0	13	62%	--	4.4	--	3.5	5	8	0
Vaughn Martin	*27*	*DE*	*460*	*19*	*3.2%*	*--*	*13*	*4*	*1*	*16*	*69%*	*--*	*1.8*	*--*	*1*	*1*	*4*	*0*

Linebackers	Age	Pos	Snaps	Plays	Overall TmPct	Rk	Stop	Dfts	BTkl	Pass Rush Sack	Hit	Hur	Tips	Runs	vs. Run St%	Rk	Yds	Rk	Tgts	vs. Pass Suc%	Rk	AdjYd	Rk	PD
Karlos Dansby*	32	MLB	1099	143	17.2%	11	81	24	7	1	2	3.5	2	88	65%	61	3.2	47	56	57%	19	6.7	32	7
Kevin Burnett*	31	OLB	1071	113	13.6%	38	62	11	5	2.5	2	8	0	67	61%	76	3.7	76	40	49%	43	8.4	68	5
Koa Misi	26	OLB	550	62	8.5%	71	37	13	5	3.5	1	3	1	37	59%	82	3.7	77	20	52%	32	7.0	48	0
Philip Wheeler	*29*	*OLB*	*1015*	*116*	*14.9%*	*26*	*63*	*18*	*8*	*3.5*	*9*	*14*	*1*	*51*	*63%*	*70*	*3.8*	*81*	*42*	*46%*	*55*	*9.1*	*71*	*4*
Dannell Ellerbe	*28*	*MLB*	*651*	*90*	*12.6%*	*48*	*56*	*21*	*8*	*4.5*	*3*	*8.5*	*0*	*51*	*73%*	*24*	*3.4*	*55*	*32*	*56%*	*20*	*5.3*	*17*	*1*

Year	Yards	ALY	Rk	Power	Rk	Stuff	Rk	2nd Level	Rk	Open Field	Rk	Sacks	ASR	Rk	Short	Long
2010	3.56	3.76	9	61%	12	23%	4	1.03	5	0.41	2	39	7.1%	9	9	16
2011	3.79	3.96	13	73%	29	20%	14	1.15	14	0.38	3	41	7.6%	7	15	22
2012	3.88	3.85	11	64%	18	21%	10	1.04	5	0.63	9	42	6.3%	19	15	14
2012 ALY by direction:		Left End 4.13 (20)			Left Tackle 3.02 (3)			Mid/Guard 4.14 (16)			Right Tackle 3.68 (9)			Right End 3.28 (7)		

Someone in the Dolphins' front office—presumably not Jeff Ireland—must have figured out that a strong pass rush can mask weaknesses in coverage more than vice versa, especially in Tom Brady's division. We'll get to the secondary shortly, but the first half of the equation is personified by third overall pick Dion Jordan (Oregon), who likely will start opposite Cameron Wake from jump street; if not, even Johnny Depp can't save this team. Jordan finished among the top performers at his position in three of four drills that matter for our SackSEER projection system (40-yard dash, broad jump, and three-cone), but his 14.5 sacks and two passes defensed in 39 games at Oregon ranked near the bottom of the 2013 class. Provided that Jordan's Superman combine performance trumps his Bizarro college stats with respect to our projection, Miami could have one of the most productive pass rushes in the NFL over the next few seasons. Wake made his first All-Pro team in 2012, an accolade long since overdue, as he's actually been the best pass rusher in the league since 2010 according to our charting stats. His 104.5 hurries and 91 quarterback knockdowns (sacks plus hits) were both tops in the NFL over the past three seasons, and he was one of only four players with at least 20 hurries and 20 knockdowns each year over that span. (The others were Jared Allen, Jason Babin, and DeMarcus Ware.) 2012 third-rounder Olivier Vernon, a situational pass rusher during his rookie season, was sneaky good: As a reserve, his stats don't jump of the page, but his play-making ability in 2012 jumped off the screen for anyone who bothered to watch.

Supplementing that trio are holdovers Randy Starks and Jared Odrick. As part of the latter's move inside to make room for Jordan, he will be subbing in for run stopper extraordinaire Paul Soliai on passing downs. In two full seasons at defensive end, Odrick amassed 24 hurries and 25 knockdowns while posting a similar Run Stop Rate as Soliai. Meanwhile, despite doing the grunt work of a 4-3 defensive tackle and 3-4 defensive end since 2010, Starks has been a surprisingly effective pass rusher, totaling 41.5 hurries and 26 knockdowns.

The Dolphins' offseason focus on pass rush also manifested itself at linebacker, where Dannell Ellerbe and Philip Wheeler are bigger threats to quarterback safety than their predecessors, Karlos Dansby and Kevin Burnett. Whereas the skill sets of Dansby and Burnett were better suited to coverage on passing downs, Ellerbe and Wheeler add a blitz arrow to defensive co-ordinator Kevin Coyle's quiver. As a bonus, the newcomers are also significantly younger and just as good against the run. At the third linebacker spot, though, Koa Misi will reprise his role as the guy who doesn't do anything to distinguish himself on standard downs, then leaves the field on nickel downs.

Defensive Secondary

Secondary	Age	Pos	Snaps	Plays	Overall TmPct	Rk	Stop	Dfts	BTkl	vs. Run Runs	St%	Rk	Yds	Rk	vs. Pass Tgts	Tgt%	Rk	Dist	Suc%	Rk	APaYd	Rk	PD	Int
Reshad Jones	25	FS	1114	103	12.4%	18	36	19	7	44	36%	40	6.4	26	30	5.8%	51	12.3	69%	7	6.4	16	9	4
Chris Clemons	28	FS	1094	98	11.8%	23	34	11	6	48	46%	14	5.8	17	25	4.9%	63	10.8	69%	9	7.9	47	3	2
Sean Smith*	26	CB	1044	70	8.4%	49	22	12	3	13	31%	67	13.2	84	110	21.3%	12	11.5	49%	60	7.2	31	9	2
Nolan Carroll	26	CB	641	52	7.2%	63	14	5	6	6	33%	60	5.2	19	73	16.2%	55	12.5	44%	77	8.1	63	8	0
Jimmy Wilson	24	FS	588	38	4.9%	71	17	10	2	10	60%	3	4.9	8	46	9.6%	12	9.9	51%	45	6.9	27	3	0
Richard Marshall	29	CB	237	23	11.1%	--	11	2	1	3	100%	--	2.7	--	23	17.9%	--	15.1	39%	--	10.7	--	4	1
R.J. Stanford	25	CB	143	15	1.8%	--	5	3	3	4	75%	--	1.3	--	14	3.1%	--	13.1	15%	--	12.7	--	0	0

Year	Pass D Rank	vs. #1 WR	Rk	vs. #2 WR	Rk	vs. Other WR	Rk	vs. TE	Rk	vs. RB	Rk
2010	23	11.2%	24	-7.2%	8	11.2%	26	20.6%	28	9.0%	22
2011	12	2.0%	15	0.5%	15	13.7%	29	1.7%	10	-13.9%	6
2012	17	5.2%	19	10.0%	25	-2.4%	14	-3.4%	13	22.9%	28

Miami's offseason moves at cornerback complemented those in their front seven. The theory goes that better pass rushers means less blitzing, which in turn allows defensive coordinator Kevin Coyle to fully implement his zone coverage scheme. In 2012, he tried a more gradual transition, but it ended up being a disaster. Players often looked unsure of their assignments, which resulted in receivers getting covered by air an inordinate amount of the time: We charted "Hole in Zone" as the primary defender on 5.9 percent of passes, the second-highest rate in the league. In addition, no cornerback reached 50 percent in Success Rate while Reshad Jones and Chris Clemons both finished in the top 20 among safeties, which is what happens when you ask man-to-man corners Sean Smith and Nolan Carroll to start playing Cover-3 and inverted Cover-2.

In that context, it's less surprising that the Dolphins jettisoned Smith (like Vontae Davis before him), demoted Carroll to the end of the bench, and will enter 2013 with three zone corners at the top of their depth chart. Miami's marquee free agent signing was Brent Grimes, who made a Pro Bowl in Atlanta's zone scheme. Our charting stats for 2011 had Grimes second in the NFL at 5.0 Adjusted Yards per Pass and third with 66 percent Adjusted Success Rate. That's somewhat affected by playing a lot of zone coverage, but still seriously impressive. Starting across from Grimes will be Richard Marshall, who missed most of his first season in Miami with a back injury, but played a similar coverage scheme in Carolina most of his career. And in the second round of April's draft, Miami selected Jamar Taylor, who excelled in zone and off-man coverage at Boise State. Of course, Grimes and Marshall are both coming off serious injuries and Taylor is, after all, just a rookie. So although their skill sets may match the scheme better than their predecessors', it doesn't necessarily follow that their performance will be any better.

Special Teams

Year	DVOA	Rank	FG/XP	Rank	Net Kick	Rank	Kick Ret	Rank	Net Punt	Rank	Punt Ret	Rank	Hidden	Rank
2010	-3.7%	29	-2.0	24	-7.7	28	-3.6	20	-4.1	24	-1.0	17	-9.5	25
2011	2.5%	6	-0.4	18	2.5	12	1.3	13	8.7	9	0.7	15	11.5	4
2012	0.4%	14	-4.9	27	0.5	16	7.4	6	-2.8	20	2.0	12	3.7	7

If NFL teams have little patience for injury-prone position players, then they have practically none for injury-prone kickers. The past two seasons, Dan Carpenter's uncooperative groin has forced him to miss four games. Not wanting a repeat of 2012, when desperation required signing former Chargers castoff Nate Kaeding for the final two weeks, Miami selected Caleb Sturgis out of Florida in the fifth round of April's draft. Even when healthy, Carpenter has been mediocre over the past three seasons, both in terms of field goals and kickoff distance. And with both Justin Tucker and Blair Walsh showing that a team can win with a rookie kicker, only Jim Joyce would consider Carpenter's job safe. Unlike Carpenter, punter Brandon Fields and return man Marcus Thigpen have earned the right to keep their jobs this season. The Dolphins' below-average net punt values in 2010 and 2012 are more of a reflection on their coverage unit than on Fields. Both seasons, he was above average on in gross punt value, and he finished third in that stat two years ago. Meanwhile, Thigpen was one of only two players last season (along with Buffalo's Leodis McKelvin) who finished among the top 10 in return points added on both kickoff returns and punt returns.

Coaching Staff

Miami's offensive coaching staff might be described as an NFL experiment. Is it effective to have an offensive-minded head coach who cedes control of said unit to a coordinator? Is it effective to have an offensive coordinator who was your young quarterback's college coach? The situation is so rare, and the NFL is such a copycat league, that the Dolphins' success (or lack thereof) over the next few seasons is pivotal for more than just the individuals and fanbase involved. If Ryan Tannehill becomes an elite quarterback, franchises will be more open-minded about making a Sherman-esque hire. If Miami enjoys success overall as a team, franchises will give the "head coach as macromanager" concept—once the league standard—another look. If neither of these things happens, it might be a generation before we see it again. No pressure, guys.

Defensive coordinator Kevin Coyle will be under pressure of a different kind in 2013. After muddling through last season with personnel that didn't suit his scheme, Miami's offseason moves have put that excuse to bed. With zone cornerbacks and productive pass rushers in tow, Coyle's job security after this year depends on the Dolphins defense ranking higher than 19th in Adjusted Sack Rate and not having "Hole in Zone" play as prominent a role in coverage.

Minnesota Vikings

2012 Record: 10-6	Total DVOA: 2.0% (14th)	2013 Mean Projection: 5.5 wins	On the Clock (0-4): 37%
Pythagorean Wins: 8.8 (13th)	Offense: 0.3% (15th)	Postseason Odds: 5.6%	Mediocrity (5-7): 45%
Snap-Weighted Age: 26.3 (23rd)	Defense: 3.1% (21st)	Super Bowl Odds: 0.2%	Playoff Contender (8-10): 15%
Average Opponent: 4.9% (5th)	Special Teams: 4.7% (5th)	Proj. Avg. Opponent: 6.0% (2nd)	Super Bowl Contender (11+): 3%

2012: Nine yards what?

2013: If your championship hopes depend on the running back repeating one of the four or five greatest seasons in the history of the position, you have a problem.

The 2012 Minnesota Vikings were an unfinished rebuilding project that hopped on Adrian Peterson's back and rode him to the last NFC playoff spot. Finishing the season with four straight wins, including impressive victories over the playoff-bound Texans and Packers, was enough for Minnesota to top the Bears on a tiebreaker. General manager Rick Spielman was officially handed the reins to the franchise before the 2012 season after six years as director of player personnel, and thus far he has done a stellar job of adding young pieces to rejuvenate the aging remnants of the Brett Favre Vikings. His first draft with final say found a pair of immediate first-round contributors in left tackle Matt Kalil and safety Harrison Smith. New kicker Blair Walsh, selected in the sixth round, rejuvenated a special teams unit that had been horrid for years. Spielman also found a number of contributing parts with upside in cornerback Josh Robinson, wideout Jarius Wright (who was the best Minnesota receiver by the end of the season), and fullback Rhett Ellison. As far as 2012 draft classes go, it wasn't Colts-good, but it was close.

For his next trick, Spielman will need to learn a very important skill in the general manager's tool kit: when to admit that you've made a mistake.

Minnesota doubled down on quarterback Christian Ponder this offseason after some better results during the December stretch that got them into the playoffs. Because Ponder's triceps swelled up and he couldn't play in the NFC Wild Card game against Green Bay, we were denied a public forum to see how much improvement Ponder could show when the stakes were at their highest. So instead of finding a reasonable second option that could push Ponder, the Vikings brought in Matt Cassel to replace backup "quarterback" Joe Webb and made sure to underline to the press in no uncertain terms that he was not competing for the starting job. Percy Harvin wore out his welcome by complaining about Ponder behind the scenes yet again, so the Vikings jettisoned Harvin, sending him to Seattle for a first-rounder and two other picks. To replace him, they signed ex-Packers downfield threat Greg Jennings in free agency; unlike Harvin, Jennings flatters Ponder with glowing compliments every time he talks to the press. Finally, they traded up to get a third first-round pick from the Patriots, and spent it on Tennessee wideout Cordarrelle Patterson, a physical marvel who has Harvin-esque qualities in the open field.

The crew Minnesota had at receiver after Harvin was placed on IR and before Wright's emergence could hold back any young quarterback. If it's possible to be a blocking specialist as a wide receiver, Michael Jenkins achieved it; Kim Kardashian has separated from a football player more recently than Jenkins has. Jerome Simpson is the football equivalent of a baseball tools bust: all the physicality in the world but no starting-quality skills to go with it. Stephen Burton and Devin Aromashadu were never meant to be more than filler and never were. While Minnesota lost its best receiver this offseason, Jennings and Patterson are a combination with the potential to elevate a passing game that was too reliant on Harvin.

But Minnesota's passing-game problems were not just about the passengers, they were about the driver. It doesn't take a lot of digging to figure out Ponder's main issue as a quarterback: an inability to consistently connect on deep passes. At Florida State, Ponder could neatly be divided into two different prospects. There's the junior who was averaging 8.2 yards per attempt before he separated his throwing shoulder on a vicious hit by Clemson's DeAndre McDaniel, and there's the senior who averaged 6.8 yards per attempt and struggled through constant nagging injuries. While draftniks disagreed on the extent of Ponder's arm-strength problem, all of them agreed that it would be an issue. Doug Farrar, writing on Yahoo!, called his deep ball "evident but not consistent," and noted that Ponder could "leave his receivers hanging" in an offense that required a lot of vertical routes. ESPN's Todd McShay said that Ponder "has average to adequate arm strength … and his accuracy as he throws down the field starts to tail off." Mel Kiper, the grand poobah of draft analysts, compared Ponder to a "poor man's Chad Pennington," and that was *before* the regression in his senior season. Our own Matt Waldman, in his *Rookie Scouting Portfolio 2011*, summed up the debate well: "The question most will have with Ponder is: will he be the player who looked like a borderline franchise QB in 2009, or the weaker-armed player who was inconsistent and rusty in 2010?"

Ponder's NFL play has resembled the senior season vintage. We marked the Vikings with 22 completions and five pass interference penalties on Ponder's 77 passes that travelled 15 or more yards past the line of scrimmage ("deep" passes, from here on). That's good for a DVOA of 10.7%, which sounds nice until you realize that the average DVOA on deep passes

2013 Vikings Schedule

Week	Opp.	Week	Opp.	Week	Opp.
1	at DET	7	at NYG (Mon.)	13	CHI
2	at CHI	8	GB	14	at BAL
3	CLE	9	at DAL	15	PHI
4	vs. PIT (U.K.)	10	WAS (Thu.)	16	at CIN
5	BYE	11	at SEA	17	DET
6	CAR	12	at GB		

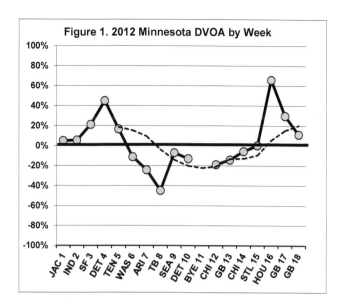

Figure 1. 2012 Minnesota DVOA by Week

fluctuates somewhere between 45% and 65% on a seasonal basis. We have pass distance data for the past eight years. In that time Ponder was one of just 41 quarterbacks to post a DVOA below 20% on deep passes in more than 50 attempts. The list of signal-callers to do that in the first three years of their career (Table 1) is one that shows just how hard it is to be a great passer without being able to attack downfield.

Let's hunt some of the outliers from the list. Stafford's season was more of an outgrowth of the fact that he wasn't ready to contribute at all as a rookie. His -36.6% DVOA was second-worst in the league in 2009, ahead of only JaMarcus Russell. Even Daunte Culpepper had a -19.7% DVOA as Stafford's backup, and he was five seasons removed from being a relevant NFL quarterback at that point. Plus, Stafford was regarded as having elite arm strength coming out of Georgia—the floor of his throwing power was top five in the NFL. He's not a real match for Ponder. That Ryan season was an extremely odd year. In 2008, Ryan had a 126.8% DVOA on 89 deep balls, and in 2010, a 57.9% DVOA on 112 deep balls. While Ryan doesn't have a cannon, he had much more down-field success than Ponder has had so far. (Ponder had a 33.5% DVOA on 55 deep passes in 2011. Better than last season, but still a far cry from 2011's average deep-ball DVOA of 61.5%.)

The only other names on that list that have starting jobs

Table 1: Quarterbacks With DVOA Below 20% On Deep Passes In One Of Their First Three Seasons (min. 50 deep attempts), 2006-2012

Name	Year	Team	DYAR	DVOA	Deep Attempts	Career Year
Chad Henne	2009	MIA	144	17.6%	81	2
Christian Ponder	2012	MIN	108	10.7%	77	2
Cleo Lemon	2007	MIA	65	7.9%	58	3
Sam Bradford	2010	STL	77	7.6%	71	1
Matt Ryan	2009	ATL	58	0.2%	83	2
Josh Freeman	2011	TB	55	0.0%	73	3
Bruce Gradkowski	2006	TB	20	-5.2%	54	1
Brandon Weeden	2012	CLE	27	-6.3%	87	1
Blaine Gabbert	2011	JAC	22	-6.4%	74	1
Kellen Clemens	2007	NYJ	-14	-16.3%	50	2
Vince Young	2007	TEN	-86	-28.8%	76	2
Andrew Walter	2006	OAK	-68	-29.6%	68	1
Josh Freeman	2009	TB	-83	-33.3%	59	1
Matthew Stafford	2009	DET	-137	-43.6%	71	1
Jamarcus Russell	2009	OAK	-189	-58.6%	67	3
Tarvaris Jackson	2007	MIN	-184	-65.3%	52	2

today are Weeden, Gabbert, Freeman, and Bradford. Weeden and Gabbert are on uncertain ground with new regimes and will be lucky to finish out the year as starters, while Freeman and Bradford have shown some signs of life but have combined for one season of above-average DVOA in seven tries.

Next we'll bring up Ponder's similarity scores (Table 2) and look at the modern players that show up—because while they are statistically similar, Ponder has as much in common with Troy Aikman as Joe Buck has with Kanye West. Aikman and John Elway generated slash line statistics that are similar to Ponder's 2012 season, but they did that in an era of low completion percentages and simpler "pro-style" offenses. They didn't have Adrian Peterson behind them for the sake of distraction, either. (Elway had Sammy Winder, while Aikman had a rookie Emmitt Smith; both backs averaged less than four yards per carry.) Among the modern comparisons, you'll again find Freeman, plus Colt McCoy and Mark Sanchez. You will also find that a player like Ponder is not very easy to generate a similar player to, mostly because his yards per attempt are so low.

This isn't to say that Ponder is incapable of improving on last season's performance. It's feasible that new receiving talent and some riskier route combinations from offensive coordinator Bill Musgrave could lead him to be better on downfield passes than he was last season. The problem is that we're starting from such a low baseline that the upper ceiling of his improvements leads him to become ... well, someone like Josh Freeman. Tampa Bay, by the way, has so much faith in Freeman that they selected Mike Glennon in the third round of this year's draft.

Ultimately, this is still a passing league. Teams that have quarterbacks who can't transcend the talent of their surrounding pieces have two options: they can try their hand at a new quarterback, or they can build a better box. Minnesota's problem isn't just that they aren't trying a new quarterback, it's that it would be hard to build a better box than what they had last season, when Peterson went on a rampage and left defenses quivering in his wake throughout the second half of the year. Ponder's numbers aren't solely the product of his talent and his receivers. Minnesota faced the third-highest number of average players in the box. Minnesota had a 12.9% DVOA on play-action passes—12.3% higher than their DVOA on regular pass-

Table 2: Similar Players To Christian Ponder Through Two Seasons (Second Season Listed)

Name	Team	Year	Pass	PaTD	INT	Runs	Cmp%	Yd/Att	Yd/Rec	Age	SIM	SIM Y-1	2Y SIM
Christian Ponder	MIN	2012	483	18	12	60	62.1%	6.08	9.78	24	1000	1000	1000
Jeff George	IND	1991	485	10	12	16	60.2%	6.00	9.97	24	844	801	829
Troy Aikman	DAL	1990	399	11	18	40	56.6%	6.46	11.41	24	659	817	704
Colt McCoy	CLE	2011	463	14	11	61	57.2%	5.90	10.31	25	726	574	667
Josh Freeman	TB	2010	474	25	6	68	61.4%	7.28	11.86	22	591	888	665
J.P. Losman	BUF	2006	429	19	14	38	62.5%	7.11	11.38	25	707	587	662
John Elway	DEN	1984	380	18	15	56	56.3%	6.84	12.14	24	608	796	660
Mark Sanchez	NYJ	2010	507	17	13	30	54.8%	6.49	11.84	24	686	611	659
Byron Leftwich	JAC	2004	441	15	10	39	60.5%	6.67	11.01	24	781	498	656
Jake Plummer	ARI	2000	475	13	21	37	56.8%	6.20	10.91	26	684	596	652

es—even though they ran the third-most play-action fakes in the league. Play-action passes as a whole were 12.1% more effective than regular passes last year, so it might sound like there wasn't much of a Peterson effect there, but most play-action passes around the rest of the NFL did not involve Ponder short-arming a ball in the general direction of Jerome Simpson; most of them involved at least one offensive player who was competent. Despite the effect Peterson had on opposing defenses, Ponder had a below average DVOA. Without Peterson around, it likely would have been below replacement level.

And what happens if Peterson is merely extremely good next year? After last season, it is hard to believe that Peterson can't do anything he wants. He could delete these next two paragraphs from the book before it comes out and it wouldn't even crack the ten most ridiculous things he's done in the last calendar year. But, statistically speaking, seasons like the one Peterson just had tend to be prone to regression.

Table 3 shows the 13 most similar seasons to Adrian Peterson's 2012. Let's ignore Terrell Davis' 1999 season that was lost to injury, as well as Marshawn Lynch's 2013 season that hasn't happened yet. For the other ten seasons on the list, the year after offers a reality check for would-be fantasy owners and for the Vikings as well. These eight running backs saw an average decline of 490 yards, 2.2 touchdowns, and 0.8 yards per carry.

Minnesota's projection is not pretty this season, but seen through what we knew about this team after the 2011 season, it makes a lot of sense. We start with a team that finished with 2.0% DVOA and just 8.8 Pythagorean wins. We're projecting regression for their special teams unit because Harvin's electric returns are gone and no statistical system will ever project a kicker to go a perfect 10-of-10 on 50-yard field goals. The defense stays virtually the same. The offense slides a bit because no team can bank on a season like the one Peterson just pulled off happening again. Add the hardest projected schedule in the league, and the Vikings are looking up at a lot of teams in the projected win column.

In a feature piece with NFL.com's Albert Breer, Spielman did the only thing a general manager in his situation can do: offered cheap hope that Ponder can continue to improve. Spielman pointed to Ponder's improved play in the last month of the season and offered that he gives "[Ponder] just as much credit for getting us in the playoffs as Adrian."

It's our guess that one of those guys will be taking a lot of credit for the Vikings struggles this season. It probably won't be Peterson.

Rivers McCown

Table 3: Most Similar Seasons To Adrian Peterson 2012

Name	Year	Team	Rush	RuYd	RuTD	Yds/Car	SIM	Runs +1	RuYd +1	RuTD +1	Yd/Car +1
Adrian Peterson	2012	MIN	348	2097	12	6.03	1000	?	?	?	?
Barry Sanders	1997	DET	335	2053	11	6.13	806	343	1491	4	4.35
Barry Sanders	1994	DET	331	1883	7	5.69	774	314	1500	11	4.78
Ahman Green	2003	GB	355	1883	15	5.30	769	259	1163	7	4.49
Eric Dickerson	1984	LARM	379	2105	14	5.55	744	292	1234	12	4.23
Chris Johnson	2009	TEN	358	2006	14	5.60	733	316	1364	11	4.32
Jamal Lewis	2003	BAL	387	2066	14	5.34	710	235	1006	7	4.28
Shaun Alexander	2004	SEA	353	1696	16	4.80	681	370	1880	27	5.08
Marshawn Lynch	2012	SEA	315	1590	11	5.05	680	?	?	?	?
Terrell Davis	1998	DEN	392	2008	21	5.12	667	67	211	2	3.15
Tiki Barber	2005	NYG	357	1860	9	5.21	663	327	1662	5	5.08
Eric Dickerson	1986	LARM	404	1821	11	4.51	641	377	1717	8	4.55
Earl Campbell	1980	HOIL	373	1934	13	5.18	637	361	1376	10	3.81
Eric Dickerson*	1987	2TM	377	1717	8	4.55	636	388	1659	14	4.28
Average			**362**	**1909**	**12.5**	**5.29**		**304**	**1355**	**9.8**	**4.36**

* Numbers prorated for 1987 strike season.

2012 Vikings Stats by Week

Wk	vs.	W-L	PF	PA	YDF	YDA	TO	Total	Off	Def	ST
1	JAC	W	26	23	389	355	0	5%	4%	17%	18%
2	at IND	L	20	23	327	278	-1	5%	2%	1%	5%
3	SF	W	24	13	344	280	1	21%	8%	-31%	-18%
4	at DET	W	20	13	227	341	1	45%	-10%	-17%	38%
5	TEN	W	30	7	433	267	0	17%	8%	-16%	-7%
6	at WAS	L	26	38	421	361	-2	-11%	-14%	9%	11%
7	ARI	W	21	14	209	356	0	-24%	-14%	16%	5%
8	TB	L	17	36	369	416	-3	-45%	-34%	16%	4%
9	at SEA	L	20	30	287	385	-2	-7%	8%	18%	3%
10	DET	W	34	24	403	368	2	-13%	-2%	8%	-4%
11	BYE										
12	at CHI	L	10	28	258	296	-1	-19%	0%	11%	-8%
13	at GB	L	14	23	359	435	-1	-14%	6%	16%	-5%
14	CHI	W	21	14	248	438	1	-6%	6%	10%	-2%
15	at STL	W	36	22	322	432	2	0%	-1%	21%	23%
16	at HOU	W	23	6	345	187	1	66%	8%	-54%	5%
17	GB	W	37	34	444	405	1	30%	26%	4%	8%
18	at GB	L	10	24	324	326	-3	11%	-3%	-8%	7%

Trends and Splits

	Offense	Rank	Defense	Rank
Total DVOA	0.3%	15	3.1%	21
Unadjusted VOA	-3.4%	19	3.0%	20
Weighted Trend	0.8%	14	6.3%	23
Variance	1.8%	1	4.3%	12
Average Opponent	-5.1%	5	1.0%	12
Passing	0.3%	22	15.1%	24
Rushing	7.8%	6	-14.0%	7
First Down	-9.3%	22	10.4%	27
Second Down	12.3%	8	-0.8%	17
Third Down	0.2%	16	-4.5%	14
First Half	2.8%	15	-5.2%	11
Second Half	-2.3%	14	11.2%	25
Red Zone	-15.3%	22	14.4%	28
Late and Close	5.7%	12	-0.4%	21

Five-Year Performance

Year	W-L	Pyth W	Est W	PF	PA	TO	Total	Rk	Off	Rk	Def	Rk	ST	Rk	Off AGL	Rk	Def AGL	Rk	Off Age	Rk	Def Age	Rk	ST Age	Rk
2008	10-6	9.3	7.1	379	333	-6	1.5%	19	-9.9%	25	-19.3%	4	-7.9%	32	10.0	4	24.0	18	28.4	5	27.7	9	26.7	14
2009	12-4	11.8	10.4	470	312	+6	18.5%	7	12.9%	8	-1.0%	15	4.7%	3	9.4	7	13.1	4	28.3	3	27.5	8	26.9	8
2010	6-10	6.0	6.5	281	348	-11	-13.9%	25	-15.1%	27	-2.5%	12	-1.4%	19	35.7	25	19.7	14	28.5	5	28.3	4	27.4	2
2011	3-13	5.3	4.6	340	449	-3	-22.2%	29	-10.2%	24	8.0%	23	-4.1%	27	20.5	9	28.3	19	27.7	10	27.3	14	26.4	15
2012	10-6	8.8	8.8	379	348	-1	2.0%	14	0.3%	15	3.1%	21	4.7%	5	10.4	3	18.5	8	25.5	31	27.2	12	25.5	28

2012 Performance Based on Most Common Personnel Groups

MIN Offense					MIN Offense vs. Opponents				MIN Defense				MIN Defense vs. Opponents			
Pers	Freq	Yds	DVOA	Run%	Pers	Freq	Yds	DVOA	Pers	Freq	Yds	DVOA	Pers	Freq	Yds	DVOA
11	39%	5.3	0.6%	18%	4-3-4	32%	6.0	4.8%	Nickel Even	54%	6.2	16.9%	11	48%	6.1	15.0%
21	25%	6.0	-6.4%	65%	Nickel Even	25%	5.1	-2.9%	4-3-4	40%	4.6	-12.9%	12	22%	4.6	-16.4%
12	19%	5.1	10.3%	41%	3-4-4	25%	5.5	-2.5%	Dime+	3%	3.1	-16.6%	21	13%	4.8	-4.1%
22	14%	6.4	22.8%	77%	Dime+	8%	8.2	56.6%	Goal Line	1%	0.4	17.9%	22	5%	2.7	-32.5%
13	2%	8.5	25.0%	50%	Nickel Odd	6%	4.4	-1.6%	Nickel Odd	1%	6.2	-5.0%	10	4%	5.4	2.1%

Strategic Tendencies

Run/Pass		Rk	Formation		Rk	Pass Rush		Rk	Secondary		Rk	Strategy		Rk
Runs, first half	43%	6	Form: Single Back	47%	31	Rush 3	4.8%	21	4 DB	41%	23	Play action	35%	3
Runs, first down	54%	6	Form: Empty Back	2%	30	Rush 4	73.9%	7	5 DB	55%	2	Avg Box (Off)	6.67	3
Runs, second-long	45%	3	Pers: 3+ WR	39%	29	Rush 5	17.0%	23	6+ DB	3%	21	Avg Box (Def)	6.32	23
Runs, power sit.	42%	28	Pers: 4+ WR	0%	30	Rush 6+	4.3%	28	CB by Sides	81%	9	Offensive Pace	29.72	12
Runs, behind 2H	24%	28	Pers: 2+ TE/6+ OL	36%	10	Sacks by LB	13.6%	23	DB Blitz	5%	29	Defensive Pace	30.19	18
Pass, ahead 2H	43%	22	Shotgun/Pistol	35%	29	Sacks by DB	5.7%	15	Hole in Zone	13%	2	Go for it on 4th	0.75	27

As you might expect given the strength of Adrian Peterson, Minnesota's most efficient personnel groupings were the ones that were most run-oriented. But whether it was a fluke or something real in his game, Christian Ponder played really well when opponents used six defensive backs. These plays primarily came against Tampa Bay, Green Bay, and Houston. Even in the Week 13 loss to Green Bay where the Vikings scored just 14 points, Ponder threw four of his five double-digit completions against dime but both of his interceptions against other defensive personnel. ◉ Minnesota showed a very strange trend for an offense based around the running back: when the Vikings were losing or tied, they had the seventh-best offensive DVOA in the NFL, but when they were winning, their offensive DVOA dropped to 25th. ◉ The Vikings ranked third in use of max protect blocking, 15.8 percent of all passes. ◉ The Minnesota defense got successively worse with each quarter, ranking sixth in DVOA in the first quarter, 15th in the second quarter, 23rd in the third quarter, and 27th in the fourth quarter. ◉ Minnesota recovered 13 out of 18 fumbles on defense. ◉ Although the Vikings didn't blitz with a defensive back very often, they were pretty good when they did, allowing just 5.6 yards per pass.

Passing

Player	DYAR	DVOA	Plays	NtYds	Avg	YAC	C%	TD	Int
C.Ponder	173	-6.1%	516	2747	5.3	5.3	62.2%	18	12
M.Cassel	-353	-30.4%	291	1668	5.7	4.9	59.9%	6	11

Rushing

Player	DYAR	DVOA	Plays	Yds	Avg	TD	Fum	Suc
A.Peterson	458	24.9%	348	2097	6.0	12	3	49%
T.Gerhart	-34	-26.0%	50	169	3.4	1	2	44%
C.Ponder	36	4.2%	44	271	6.2	2	2	-
P.Harvin*	20	-21.6%	21	105	5.0	1	2	-
M.Cassel	35	17.8%	22	148	6.7	1	1	-

Receiving

Player	DYAR	DVOA	Plays	Ctch	Yds	Y/C	YAC	TD	C%
P.Harvin*	194	4.6%	86	63	670	10.6	8.5	3	73%
M.Jenkins*	37	-13.2%	72	40	449	11.2	3.2	2	56%
J.Simpson	-37	-24.5%	51	26	274	10.5	2.2	0	51%
J.Wright	68	4.4%	36	22	310	14.1	5.0	2	61%
D.Aromashodu*	39	3.5%	22	11	182	16.5	3.5	0	50%
S.Burton	-33	-49.6%	11	5	35	7.0	4.2	1	45%
G.Jennings	37	-5.2%	62	36	366	10.2	4.6	4	58%
K.Rudolph	64	-3.4%	94	53	493	9.3	5.2	9	56%
J.Carlson	-38	-49.6%	14	8	43	5.4	2.3	0	57%
R.Ellison	-2	-8.7%	9	7	65	9.3	9.4	0	78%
A.Peterson	-3	-14.9%	51	40	217	5.4	4.7	1	78%
T.Gerhart	55	25.0%	27	20	155	7.8	7.3	0	74%

Offensive Line

Player	Pos	Age	GS	Snaps	Pen	Sk	Pass	Run	Player	Pos	Age	GS	Snaps	Pen	Sk	Pass	Run
Matt Kalil	LT	24	16/16	1035	6	2.5	13	7.5	Brandon Fusco	RG	24	16/16	882	0	1.5	18	4
Phil Loadholt	RT	27	16/16	1035	11	3.8	16.3	6	Geoff Schwartz*	RG	27	13/0	157	0	0	3	0
John Sullivan	C	28	16/16	1034	2	1	3.5	9	Seth Olsen	G	28	5/4	283	2	1	5	4
Charlie Johnson	LG	29	16/16	1032	6	2	14.5	7.5									

Year	Yards	ALY	Rk	Power	Rk	Stuff	Rk	2nd Lev	Rk	Open Field	Rk	Sacks	ASR	Rk	Short	Long	F-Start	Cont.
2010	4.33	4.15	11	70%	6	19%	18	1.25	8	0.82	12	36	6.8%	20	8	18	27	30
2011	4.72	4.05	18	73%	1	23%	28	1.43	3	1.15	3	49	9.8%	32	13	24	18	33
2012	5.67	4.17	10	53%	30	24%	29	1.41	4	2.08	1	32	6.5%	16	7	15	14	48
2012 ALY by direction:		Left End 4.25 (15)			Left Tackle 4.63 (8)			Mid/Guard 3.98 (19)			Right Tackle 4.64 (5)				Right End 4.36 (13)			

Our game charting project does not agree with conventional wisdom in the case of John Sullivan's run blocking: he led all centers in blown blocks on runs. The majority of whiffs came on zone-blocking plays asking him to move laterally at the snap. However, he played much better down the stretch, and his pass blocking was excellent all year. Microfracture surgery—even a supposedly minor version of it—isn't an injury to shrug off, but both the team and Sullivan believe that he'll be 100 percent for training camp.

The Vikings dropped from first to 30th in converting short-yardage Power runs, but these stats had less to do with Sullivan and more to do with the weak links on the Minnesota line: guards Brandon Fusco and Charlie Johnson. Fusco finished among the top five guards in blown blocks leading to pass pressures—the lasting image of his season is Minnesota puzzlingly asking him to block Ndamukong Suh one-on-one. Christian Ponder would have been dead by October if Fusco regularly played anyone with Suh's talent. The thought with Johnson was that after years of being a Peyton Manning-approved left tackle, he would thrive with a move inside to guard. Not so much! Our charters noted that he was especially slow picking up stunts and games, which isn't surprising given how much he struggled with speed at tackle. Minnesota sunk a pair of late-round picks into improving the guard play with Jeff Baca (sixth round, UCLA) and Travis Bond (seventh round, North Carolina). The lack of established depth behind Minnesota's starters led Bond to play some tackle at OTAs as well.

Outside the Vikings have a pair of textbook tackles in 2012 first-rounder Matt Kalil and newly-rich Phil Loadholt. Like Sullivan, Kalil's run blocking improved as the season went on—only one of his blown run blocks came after Week 8. Kalil's pass protection was upper-echelon from the first snap, though he did have some problems with extra rushers coming off the edge. Even after pneumonia cost him 20 pounds in December, he was shutting out opponents regularly. According to our own Ben Muth, Loadholt has "Fred Flintstone feet" that hurt him in pass blocking and playside run blocking. However, he's also one of the NFL's best backside blockers on the inside zone. Calls to the Minnesota public relations department inquiring about Loadholt's love of bronto burgers and ribs were not returned.

Defensive Front Seven

Defensive Line	Age	Pos	Snaps	Plays	Overall TmPct	Rk	Stop	Dfts	BTkl	vs. Run Runs	St%	Rk	RuYd	Rk	Pass Rush Sack	Hit	Hur	Tips
Jared Allen	31	DE	1048	49	5.6%	33	43	25	1	32	84%	7	2.5	41	12	12	27	3
Brian Robison	30	DE	856	44	5.4%	35	35	13	0	26	69%	56	2.9	58	8.5	7	19.5	6
Kevin Williams	33	DT	807	37	4.3%	31	27	8	6	24	71%	51	2.3	40	2	5	16.5	7
Everson Griffen	26	DE	605	25	2.9%	71	20	14	1	11	73%	47	2.5	36	8	13	15	1
Letroy Guion	26	DT	489	32	3.9%	39	22	4	1	23	78%	27	3.3	65	2	0	2	1
Christian Ballard	24	DT	379	15	1.7%	--	13	3	2	13	92%	--	0.6	--	1	4	6.5	0
Fred Evans	30	DT	336	25	2.9%	63	22	7	1	19	84%	10	1.3	6	2	1	4	2
Lawrence Jackson	28	DE	384	19	2.6%	--	15	7	0	14	79%	--	1.4	--	2.5	2	7.5	0

Linebackers	Age	Pos	Snaps	Plays	Overall TmPct	Rk	Stop	Dfts	BTkl	Pass Rush Sack	Hit	Hur	Tips	vs. Run Runs	St%	Rk	Yds	Rk	vs. Pass Tgts	Suc%	Rk	AdjYd	Rk	PD
Chad Greenway	30	OLB	1123	152	17.5%	9	76	25	8	3	2	8	0	84	58%	88	3.5	64	40	32%	73	7.4	53	5
Jasper Brinkley*	28	MLB	847	102	11.8%	53	51	14	11	0	3	2	0	64	66%	53	3.8	80	40	47%	53	6.1	21	5
Erin Henderson	27	OLB	677	83	10.9%	60	50	16	2	3	2	2	1	51	71%	32	2.9	33	30	54%	28	6.8	35	2

Year	Yards	ALY	Rk	Power	Rk	Stuff	Rk	2nd Level	Rk	Open Field	Rk	Sacks	ASR	Rk	Short	Long
2010	3.80	3.64	6	66%	23	22%	8	1.05	9	0.71	14	31	5.6%	26	13	11
2011	3.91	3.85	8	62%	16	22%	7	1.26	21	0.51	5	50	8.7%	1	20	21
2012	3.75	3.87	12	59%	12	24%	6	1.11	7	0.46	4	44	6.4%	16	9	21
2012 ALY by direction:		Left End 4.9 (29)			Left Tackle 4.18 (19)			Mid/Guard 3.43 (3)			Right Tackle 3.68 (10)			Right End 4.42 (20)		

Minnesota's defensive line manages to be both stacked and unsettled because three of the four starters and top backup end Everson Griffen are scheduled to be free agents after the season. Griffen, who mostly played as a "joker" pass rusher, sits atop our Top 25 Prospects list this year (page 436) because his production has finally matched his physical skill set. He'll probably cut into Brian Robison's playing time in 2013, and he's the most likely one of the ends to draw a contract extension before the season. Robison has picked up right where Ray Edwards left off after Edwards left in free agency, averaging 20 hurries a year. It is worth noting that most of them were against mediocre-at-best right tackles who Robison can bend the edge against, but you tend to draw those matchups when you play across from Jared Allen. Allen has shown no statistical signs of slowing down. General manager Rick Spielman has responded with no offer of an extension or re-structure, making the six-year, $72 million deal Allen signed before 2008 one of the rare NFL contracts that will actually be seen to completion. "We haven't talked one iota. It is what it is," Allen told the *Minneapolis Star-Tribune*. You can tell Allen isn't thrilled: His usual quote-sheet contribution is good for a belly laugh.

On the inside, a re-structure that actually did occur will leave Kevin Williams as a free agent after the season. It's hard to believe it's already been 10 years since the Vikings allowed two teams to pick ahead of them by letting the clock elapse in the 2003 draft, but at least missing out on Jordan Gross and Byron Leftwich didn't haunt them forever. Williams isn't as dynamic of a force as he used to be, but he still bats down more balls than anyone not named J.J. Watt and his on-field intelligence masks a lot of the physical decline. His long-term replacement will be first-round pick Sharrif Floyd, a draftnik favorite who was expected by many to be a top-five pick. His fall to 23rd overall isn't too hard to understand: he lacks elite explosiveness or physical gifts, he didn't show top-tier production at Florida, and he was best-utilized in the 4-3 under tackle role that a lot of teams don't carry anymore. That doesn't mean Minnesota shouldn't be thrilled to pick him up, because he is an excellent prospect. Fred Evans and Letroy Guion, both good scheme fits, will battle for the starting nose tackle job. Both have shown the ability to physically overwhelm smaller guards at times.

Strongside linebacker Chad Greenway is a heady defender who covers a lot of ground and is often asked to defend the best offensive threat among the tight ends and running backs. He also had an offseason knee scope and has been in the bottom 75 of Run Stop Rate for linebackers three of the past four seasons. Erin Henderson played middle linebacker for most of OTAs after Jasper Brinkley was let go, but he'll return to the weak side after the Vikings picked up Packers castoff Desmond Bishop late in the offseason. Bishop is coming off a year lost to a torn hamstring, but had a pair of stellar seasons inside the Packers 3-4 prior to that. If he's fully healthy, Bishop will probably play on nickel downs, where he has historically been solid rushing the passer and in coverage. Henderson was fairly reliable in the nickel last year, but lacks the pedigree that Bishop has. Should Bishop wind up not being ready for the start of the season—he hasn't participated in any offseason activities so far—the most likely scenario has Henderson inside and 2013 fourth-round pick Gerald Hodges (Penn State) outside. Inside linebacker Audie Cole, a 2012 seventh-rounder, is the other healthy in-house depth. 2013 seventh-rounder Michael Mauti (also out of Penn State) would have gone much higher in the draft and been a real threat to start, but he's still recovering from the torn ACL that cut his senior season short.

Defensive Secondary

Secondary	Age	Pos	Snaps	Plays	Overall TmPct	Rk	Stop	Dfts	BTkl	vs. Run Runs	St%	Rk	Yds	Rk	vs. Pass Tgts	Tgt%	Rk	Dist	Suc%	Rk	APaYd	Rk	PD	Int
Harrison Smith	24	FS	1037	108	12.4%	16	43	16	11	44	50%	9	5.8	15	34	7.1%	30	15.2	56%	31	6.9	28	8	3
Antoine Winfield*	36	CB	1026	114	13.1%	1	58	20	5	42	64%	7	2.9	4	69	14.7%	63	9.0	50%	54	5.9	8	11	3
Jamarca Sanford	28	SS	786	66	7.6%	55	24	8	7	29	41%	24	7.3	40	21	4.4%	67	16.3	63%	17	9.1	63	4	0
Josh Robinson	22	CB	636	56	6.5%	71	15	4	6	5	60%	13	5.2	20	69	14.6%	64	10.9	45%	74	6.8	27	2	2
Chris Cook	26	CB	611	41	7.6%	61	15	7	2	8	25%	73	10.3	78	54	18.2%	38	11.2	52%	43	7.0	28	5	0
A.J. Jefferson	25	CB	581	41	5.0%	80	8	4	5	5	40%	47	6.0	40	48	10.8%	85	13.1	33%	87	10.0	86	4	0
Mistral Raymond	25	FS	377	17	3.1%	--	3	1	1	6	33%	--	7.8	--	14	4.6%	--	15.9	46%	--	7.4	--	1	0
Jacob Lacey	26	CB	573	39	7.2%	62	18	9	4	9	33%	60	7.4	55	35	12.3%	78	9.5	46%	73	9.8	84	4	1

Year	Pass D Rank	vs. #1 WR	Rk	vs. #2 WR	Rk	vs. Other WR	Rk	vs. TE	Rk	vs. RB	Rk
2010	20	-1.2%	16	14.5%	25	14.0%	27	-6.0%	8	-16.7%	4
2011	32	30.4%	28	41.1%	30	33.6%	31	21.5%	24	15.5%	26
2012	24	3.9%	18	38.6%	32	-8.7%	9	4.6%	22	18.4%	25

Antoine Winfield's defection to Seattle hurts, especially after the Vikings offered more guaranteed money on a restructure. Winfield was getting long in the tooth, and once the base level of his speed gives way, his career will be over quickly. But he was stellar against both the run and the pass last season, and Josh Robinson, his likely replacement in the slot on nickel downs, has never played inside. Not even at Central Florida. "Not very high since I didn't really learn nickel last year. This is all new to me," Robinson rated his confidence level at OTAs. It doesn't take any mind-reading to deduce that he's not happy about the switch. But Robinson was a necessary sacrifice after the Vikings drafted first-rounder Xavier Rhodes to pair with Chris Cook on the outside. Cook had allowed just five completions of 15 yards or longer before breaking his arm in Week 8. His instincts took a big step forward and he spent this offseason begging coaches to let him shadow No. 1 receivers. Rhodes, a press-man specialist out of Florida State, may not be ready to play optimal off coverage right away, and could also rack up the penalties as he's a bit grabby. He's also not A.J. Jefferson, so, by default, he'll probably be an improvement on what Minnesota had outside when Cook got injured. Jacob Lacey, a veteran Cover-2 speed bump, will be waiting in the wings should injuries strike.

Harrison Smith was considered a bit of a reach by some as a first-round pick, but he acquitted himself nicely in his rookie season. Smith had good instincts and ball skills right away, but gradually improved his positioning and technique as the season wore on. By the end of the year, he was being trusted to handle receivers tight to the line in Cover-0 situations. Jamarca Sanford saw the majority of the snaps as the deep safety. He's got more range and less tackling ability than backup Mistral Raymond. Between "mist," and hints of "crystal" and "mystic," Raymond's first name is our best chance to make a *Final Fantasy* reference in this year's book. We won't force it—the Mist Dragon protects the inhabitants of its village fiercely.

Special Teams

Year	DVOA	Rank	FG/XP	Rank	Net Kick	Rank	Kick Ret	Rank	Net Punt	Rank	Punt Ret	Rank	Hidden	Rank
2010	-1.4%	19	2.0	12	-15.7	31	4.3	11	6.2	11	-3.7	22	1.8	12
2011	-4.1%	27	-9.1	32	-13.2	31	11.7	1	-6.7	25	-3.0	20	-11.5	31
2012	4.7%	5	9.5	2	2.5	11	7.9	5	4.0	12	-0.1	16	-3.4	23

Replacing Ryan Longwell with rookie Blair Walsh was a move that turned this entire unit around. The Vikings had finished second-to-last on kickoff value two seasons in a row, and dead last on field goal and extra point value in 2011. Walsh upped those figures to 11th and first, respectively, and was a perfect 10-for-10 on attempts of 50 yards or longer. He wasn't quite as good in our numbers as Ravens kicker Justin Tucker, because his kickoffs weren't as powerful and he didn't have to kick outside half the time, but he was a big reason the unit jumped from 27th to fifth. It also helped that the Vikings had strong coverage teams, allowing below-average return value on both kickoffs and punts.

More turnover struck this year as the Vikings released outspoken Deadspin author Chris Kluwe, and traded outspoken anti-Ponder advocate and awesome kick returner Percy Harvin to the Seahawks. Kluwe will be replaced by fifth-round UCLA punter Jeff Locke, who wants you to know that he is a treasure hun—dammit, we already used up the *Final Fantasy* reference. Marcus Sherels was the definition of average on punt returns last year—he was worth -0.1 points of value—and Cordarrelle Patterson will probably get a chance to unseat him on both kick and punt returns.

Coaching Staff

Leslie Frazier, like mentor Tony Dungy, is a soft-spoken Cover-2 advocate who would prefer to keep the plays in front of his unit. Alan Williams, who was with the Colts at the same time Frazier was, coordinates the defense and preaches the merits of aggressive play and playmaking. Statistically speaking, the team actually rushed the basic four about five percent more than they did under previous coordinator Fred Pagac. Offensive coordinator Bill Musgrave is not a sexy head-coaching candidate, but he's quietly done a lot of impressive work playing to the strengths of the few pieces he's had to work with in Minnesota. The narrative is how Ponder will work with his fancy new toys, but the better question might be how Musgrave manipulates the offense to work with them. Linebackers coach Mike Singletary is the biggest name on the staff that isn't a coordinator. You remember his coaching tenure, right? He hasn't sent anyone to the locker room yet on this stop, though there's still time.

New England Patriots

2012 Record: 12-4	**Total DVOA:** 34.9% (3rd)	**2013 Mean Projection:** 10.6 wins	**On the Clock (0-4):** 1%
Pythagorean Wins: 12.7 (1st)	**Offense:** 30.8% (1st)	**Postseason Odds:** 81.1%	**Mediocrity (5-7):** 6%
Snap-Weighted Age: 26.7 (17th)	**Defense:** 1.4% (15th)	**Super Bowl Odds:** 25.4%	**Playoff Contender (8-10):** 39%
Average Opponent: -2.9% (21st)	**Special Teams:** 5.5% (4th)	**Proj. Avg. Opponent:** 1.3% (14th)	**Super Bowl Contender (11+):** 54%

2012: Another year, another strong Patriots team that doesn't quite finish the job.

2013: Got a haircut, got a silver tooth, gonna get myself arrested.

Everyone reading this book knows about the turnover that hit the New England Patriots offense this past offseason. A long, drawn out negotiation process between the Patriots and leading receiver Wes Welker finally broke down in mid-March, and Welker signed a two-year, $12 million contract with the rival Denver Broncos. That was followed by running back Danny Woodhead, a frequent receiver out of the backfield, signing with San Diego. A couple weeks later came the reports about a stubborn infection in the surgically repaired left arm of star tight end Rob Gronkowski. A surgery in May to address this infection was the fourth Gronkowski has undergone since breaking the arm against Indianapolis in Week 10 of last season. Gronkowski also had back surgery in May; the back troubles he has dealt with since his days at the University of Arizona were the reason he fell to the Patriots in the second round of the 2010 draft. He'll start camp on the PUP list and is likely to miss at least the first couple weeks of the upcoming season.

Then, of course, the biggest drama of the NFL offseason, the murder allegations and then arrest of the second man who powered the Patriots' two-tight end offense, Aaron Hernandez. The Patriots cut Hernandez immediately upon his arrest, with owner Robert Kraft sucking up a huge 2014 salary cap penalty to just get this schmuck off his roster as soon as possible.

Many column inches worth of ink have already been spilled on Hernandez's troubled personality, questions about his gang ties, and the possibility of additional murders in his past. (I guess the first time he remembered to take the used shell casings *out of his car*.) There have been declarations that this represents the final end of the Patriots dynasty, which oddly has ended roughly 4,682 different times over the past eight years despite a lack of Super Bowl titles since 2004. Writers across the country and personalities across the Boston radio dial have asked what this means for "The Patriots Way," the mythological organizational philosophy the Patriots use to fill their roster with nothing but hard-working, high-character guys—except for the players with troubled pasts who come to the Patriots to be personally rehabilitated by all those hard-working, high-character guys.

This being *Football Outsiders Almanac 2013*, however, the Patriots Way we're concerned with is primarily the Patriots' way of gaining yardage and scoring touchdowns. It's a statistic that's been talked about all across the Internets: With the release of Hernandez, the Patriots have lost four of last year's top five receivers, making up 66 percent of their receiving yards. If Gronkowski were to have further complications and not play this year, that would be 83 percent of their receiving yards.

With all that offensive production gone, it's natural to expect the 2013 Patriots to fall short of their established scoring levels, which are somewhere between historic and ludicrous. And yet, if you look up at the top of this chapter, you'll see that we give the Patriots both the highest mean win projection and the best odds to make the Super Bowl. (They are narrowly behind Denver in overall playoff odds.)

This doesn't mean that the offensive turnover doesn't matter. Our current projections account for the loss of Hernandez and assume that Gronkowski will miss half the year (or, at least, be at full strength for just half the year). When we did early projections in May before changing these variables, the Patriots had a mean projection of 11.5 wins, more than a win more than any other team. Their odds put them slightly ahead of the rest of the AFC because, before this summer, their odds put them far ahead of the rest of the AFC.

No matter how much the offensive personnel may change, it's hard to doubt the Patriots as long as Bill Belichick and Tom Brady are still in town. The Patriots now have ten straight years of double-digit wins. They have ranked first in offensive DVOA in four of the last six seasons; the exceptions were 2008, when Brady was injured, and 2011, when they finished third behind Green Bay and New Orleans but still had one of the ten best offensive DVOAs of all-time. The NFL projection system is less dependent on long-term success than our college projection system, and there's no equivalent to "Program FEI." But there's no getting around the fact that New England's run of consistent success also makes them a more dependable bet to be successful again in 2013.

Both historical numbers and specific numbers from last year's Patriots further support the idea that the New England offense is more likely to decline slightly than to collapse altogether. After the news came out about Hernandez as a murder suspect, Jason Lisk of The Big Lead put together an article looking at other great quarterbacks who turned over more than 50 percent of the previous year's receiving yards.[1] The quar-

---

[1] http://bit.ly/19W1wcU

2013 Patriots Schedule

Week	Opp.	Week	Opp.	Week	Opp.
1	at BUF	7	at NYJ	13	at HOU
2	NYJ (Thu.)	8	MIA	14	CLE
3	TB	9	PIT	15	at MIA
4	at ATL	10	BYE	16	at BAL
5	at CIN	11	at CAR (Mon.)	17	BUF
6	NO	12	DEN		

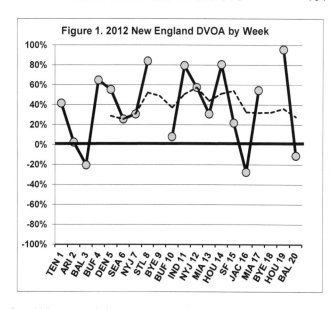

Figure 1. 2012 New England DVOA by Week

terback he listed with the most turnover was Boomer Esiason with the 1995 Jets, who lost 66 percent of his receiving yards and had a dismal season. But does the Boomer Esiason of the mid-'90s even qualify as a great quarterback? Esaison had just 5.8 yards per attempt after he lost Rob Moore and Art Monk in 1995, but he had only gained 6.3 yards per attempt the year before, and between 1990 and his retirement in 1998 he only made the Pro Bowl once.

The rest of the quarterbacks on Lisk's list declined slightly or not at all. Take Brett Favre, for example, who appeared on the list twice. In 1995, Favre lost 55 percent of its receiving yards from the year before. Mostly, that meant the end of Sterling Sharpe's stellar career due to a neck injury; the previous year he had caught 94 passes for 1,119 yards and 18 touchdowns (second in NFL history at the time). Favre also lost starting tight end Ed West and starting halfback Reggie Cobb. Without those receivers, Favre still won the MVP, guided the Packers to the NFC Championship game, and had the second-highest DYAR total of his career.

Then in 2002, Favre lost 63 percent of his receiving yards from the year before, including his top three wideouts: Bill Schroeder, Antonio Freeman, and Corey Bradford. Though Favre's advanced numbers were not as good as previous seasons (it was the first year since 1993 where he didn't rank in the DYAR top ten), the Packers still went 12-4 and won their division.

Dan Marino in 1993 was the only other quarterback listed to lose 60 percent of his receiving yards from the year before. Marino was injured after five games so we can't tell you what he would have done over the course of the entire season. But in those five games, Marino led the Dolphins to a 4-1 record and had 29.8% passing DVOA, his best season in the '90s.

Brady himself is fourth and fifth on Lisk's list, for 2007 and 2006 respectively. We all know what he did in 2007. Even in 2006, with Reche Caldwell and Jabar Gaffney as his best receivers, Brady took the Patriots to the AFC Championship game and finished fifth in the NFL in passing DYAR.

The point here is not that losing all your receivers in the offseason doesn't matter, but rather that a great quarterback can usually overcome significant turnover in his receiving corps with the help of some good roster management by the front office. The Patriots were not prepared for the loss of Hernandez or Gronkowski, but they were certainly prepared to go without Welker, Lloyd, and Woodhead. They made no real attempt to re-sign either Lloyd (who is still a free agent) or Woodhead, and they felt so comfortable with Danny Amendola as the replacement for Welker that they of-

fered him a much better contract than Welker got from Denver (five years, $31 million with $10 million guaranteed). Mike Reiss of ESPN Boston reported that the Patriots didn't sign Amendola after Welker turned them down; the deal with Amendola was done before Welker had decided to leave for Denver. The Patriots preferred Amendola in part because he's four years younger than Welker, and they believe he can be as good as Welker once he receives the "Tom Brady bump." Amendola's injury history is certainly a worry, although it is worth noting that his injuries have been severe and dramatic—a dislocated elbow in 2011, a broken clavicle in 2012—rather than the kind of nagging hamstring or back problems that tend to lead to missed games year after year. The Patriots have to hope that these injuries were just a case of bad luck and not a sign that Amendola's body can't hold up to the speed and force of the NFL game.

The loss of Hernandez is a bigger deal than the loss of Welker, because the Patriots were completely unprepared for it. Yet it may not be as big a deal as most people think. Hernandez missed six games last year with various injuries, plus most of a seventh. (He started the Week 2 loss to Arizona but left with an injury after just eight minutes.) How much did the loss of Hernandez hurt the Pats? Surprisingly, it didn't. The Patriots actually had more offensive production without Hernandez than they did with him, no matter whether you measure by points scored, yards per play, or DVOA (Table 1).

A seven-game sample is certainly not definitive proof that Hernandez didn't mean much to the Patriots offense. There's no doubt that he provided significant flexibility that allowed the Patriots to go no huddle and still constantly change their formations despite keeping the same personnel on the field. He was a talented receiver who created huge mismatch problems for opposing defenses. But we've seen what the Patriots look like without Hernandez, and it was far from a disaster.

The biggest change for the Patriots' offense when Hernandez was out was the switch from a predominantly two-tight end offense to a predominantly three-receiver offense. That makes sense considering that Hernandez lined up either in the slot or out wide on more than half his snaps last season. When Hernandez was healthy, the Pats used 12 personnel on

51 percent of plays and 11 personnel on 38 percent of plays. In the seven games without Hernandez, that ratio more than reversed, with New England using 12 personnel on just 26 percent of plays and 11 personnel on 67 percent of plays.

Some of Hernandez's snaps went to backup tight ends Daniel Fells and Michael Hoomanawanui, but the reason the Patriots' usage of 11 personnel shot up so much is that so many of Hernandez's snaps went to slot receiver Julian Edelman. The top three Patriots receivers (Welker, Lloyd, and Deion Branch) saw roughly the same number of snaps whether Hernandez was healthy or not, but Edelman's offensive snaps went from 23 per game with Hernandez healthy to 41 per game when he was out.

The plan to replace Hernandez in 2013 will likely be similar. The decision in early 2012 to grab Jake Ballard when the Giants tried to pass him through waivers and then wait out his ACL recovery now looks brilliant. But while Ballard had good receiving numbers with the Giants, he's not going to be moving all around the formation like Hernandez. He's more of an in-line tight end. Fells and Hoomanawanui aren't moving all around either; they're H-back move types. The Patriots will use more formations with running backs lining up wide, particularly Shane Vereen, but for the most part the replacement for Hernandez will be a slot receiver: probably Edelman, but maybe a veteran pick-up like Michael Jenkins or Donald Jones. The Patriots also have two talented rookies, Aaron Dobson and Josh Boyce, but they're more outside receivers who will serve to replace Lloyd and Branch.

However, there's one thing that all the players mentioned in the previous column have in common. Some combination of these players can probably replace Hernandez. No combination of these players can replace Gronkowski. When healthy, Gronkowski is the best tight end in the game and probably one of the five best tight ends of all-time. There are other tight ends in today's NFL who are game-breaking receivers, but none of them come close to Gronkowski as a blocker (except perhaps for Jason Witten, but he's inferior to Gronkowski in both areas). Unlike with Hernandez, the numbers clearly show that the Patriots offense struggles without Gronkowski (Table 2). These numbers are regular season only; the Patriots were also without Gronkowski when the Ravens completely shut them down in the second half of the AFC Championship game.

Yet even if the Patriots have to go the whole year without Gronkowski, they still have a very good chance to make the postseason thanks to an improving defense. It often seems like the Patriots are now entirely powered by offense, with one of the most porous defenses in the league. That was true in 2011, when the Patriots finished 30th in defensive DVOA and 31st in yards allowed. However, last season the Patriots improved to 15th in defensive DVOA. They were still just 25th in yards allowed, but their defense was better in advanced metrics for a

number of reasons. The Patriots are the only team that consistently plays better defense in the red zone than it does overall, year after year. They ranked second in the league with 41 takeaways, and although they are unlikely to get a league-leading 36 fumbles from opposing offenses again, they didn't have an abnormal fumble recovery rate (56 percent) or a striking number of "lucky" interceptions.

There are also good reasons to expect further improvement from this defense in 2013, starting with youth. Last year, the Patriots were the fourth youngest defense according to snap-weighted age. They have taken a lot of defensive players high in the last few drafts, and while not all of those picks have hit—their record for drafting cornerbacks is atrocious—they've built a deep base of young talent that will continue its development this season. The Patriots will also get a full season out of the cornerbacks who improved their pass defense significantly in the second half of last year. New England moved rookie Alfonzo Dennard into the starting lineup in Week 7, moving cornerback Devin McCourty over to free safety. Then they acquired Aqib Talib in a trade with Tampa Bay, and installed him as the left cornerback in Week 11 with Dennard becoming the permanent starter on the right side. That moved Kyle Arrington to the slot, where he's a much better fit. The numbers show the improvement as the secondary changed during the season:

• Weeks 1-6 (McCourty and Arrington starting): 23.9% pass defense DVOA
• Weeks 7-10 (Dennard and Arrington starting, McCourty moves to safety): 8.6% pass defense DVOA
• Weeks 11-15 (Dennard and Talib starting, Arrington moves to nickel): 4.5% pass defense DVOA
• Weeks 16-17 (Dennard and Talib injured, Arrington and McCourty start at cornerback again): 13.9% pass defense DVOA

Talib came back for the Divisional round playoff game against Houston, but when he left the AFC Championship game with a thigh injury in the first quarter, the dominoes fell. Arrington moved back outside, Marquise Cole had to come in at nickelback, and all of a sudden the Patriots couldn't cover Anquan Boldin. The more Talib and Dennard can stay on the field together this year, the better the Patriots defense will be, and the easier it will be to overcome the loss of Hernandez and any games missed by Gronkowski.

Of course, the Patriots only have Talib and Dennard because of the same willingness to take chances on troubled players that opened the door for the Hernandez nightmare. The Bucs dumped Talib because of his attitude, and he discovered a soft free-agent market this offseason because of past legal problems. Dennard was a steal in the seventh round, but he fell that far because he was facing charges of punching a police officer,

Table 1. Patriots Offense with and without Aaron Hernandez in 2012

Weeks	DVOA	Pts/G	Yd/Play
with Hernandez (1, 6-7, 12-17)	24.2%	31.7	5.69
without Hernandez (2-5, 8-11)	39.4%	38.9	6.10

Table 2. Patriots Offense with and without Rob Gronkowski in 2012

Weeks	DVOA	Pts/G	Yd/Play
with Gronkowski (1-11, 17)	34.7%	35.1	5.93
without Gronkowski (12-16)	22.3%	34.2	5.74

and even though he was convicted, the Patriots were fortunate when he was sentenced to just 30 days in jail plus two years of probation.[2] Once again, the "Patriots Way" is about winning football games, not providing a shining beacon for the community, and the locker room in Foxborough isn't made up of Tom Brady and 52 Tedy Bruschis.

Actually, the quintessential Patriots may not be Brady and (the now-retired) Bruschi but guys like Matt Slater and Nate Ebner who demonstrate the commitment this franchise has made to the third phase of the game. Thanks in part to draft picks specifically on guys who will mostly be kick gunners and jacks-of-all-trades, the Patriots enjoy excellent and abnormally consistent special teams. The Patriots have had above average special teams for 17 straight seasons: that's not just the entire Bill Belichick era, but also the entire Pete Carroll era. They've ranked in the top eight of special teams DVOA in six of the last seven years, and they've added Leon Washington, one of the most consistently productive kickoff returners in NFL history. Special teams are the biggest difference between the Patriots and the team with the second highest mean projection for 2013, the Green Bay Packers.

The Patriots certainly go into this season with more question marks than any season since 2006, but it's hard to see this team missing the playoffs despite the turnover on offense. The offense will still be good, the defense is likely to get better, and the special teams should once again be excellent. As an added bonus, the Patriots play in the easier conference with very little competition within their division. In 42 percent of our season simulations, New England was the only team in the AFC East to finish with a winning record. They could drop to 11-5 or 10-6 and still make the playoffs easily, which gives Tom Brady an entire season to get used to his new receivers and Rob Gronkowski an entire season to get healthy. The Hernandez fiasco is an embarrassment for the organization, but this team still has to be considered one of the top two or three contenders to win Super Bowl XLVIII.

Aaron Schatz

2012 Patriots Stats by Week

Wk	vs.	W-L	PF	PA	YDF	YDA	TO	Total	Off	Def	ST
1	at TEN	W	34	13	390	284	2	42%	40%	-3%	-2%
2	ARI	L	18	20	387	242	1	3%	22%	6%	-13%
3	at BAL	L	30	31	396	503	1	-21%	24%	53%	8%
4	at BUF	W	52	28	580	438	4	65%	54%	-20%	-9%
5	DEN	W	31	21	444	394	2	55%	42%	-9%	4%
6	at SEA	L	23	24	475	368	0	26%	15%	-4%	7%
7	NYJ	W	29	26	381	403	1	31%	22%	12%	21%
8	at STL	W	45	7	473	326	2	84%	66%	-16%	2%
9	BYE										
10	BUF	W	37	31	347	481	3	8%	22%	26%	13%
11	IND	W	59	24	446	448	4	80%	51%	5%	34%
12	at NYJ	W	49	19	475	405	4	58%	51%	0%	7%
13	at MIA	W	23	16	321	277	0	31%	11%	-24%	-4%
14	HOU	W	42	14	419	323	0	81%	51%	-21%	9%
15	SF	L	34	41	520	388	-2	22%	23%	-2%	-3%
16	at JAC	W	23	16	349	436	1	-28%	-15%	19%	6%
17	MIA	W	28	0	443	256	2	55%	32%	-14%	8%
18	BYE										
19	HOU	W	41	28	457	425	1	96%	95%	-10%	-10%
20	BAL	L	13	28	428	356	-3	-11%	2%	24%	10%

Trends and Splits

	Offense	Rank	Defense	Rank
Total DVOA	30.8%	1	1.4%	15
Unadjusted VOA	29.3%	1	-3.7%	12
Weighted Trend	28.4%	2	-0.8%	15
Variance	4.1%	6	4.0%	8
Average Opponent	-2.1%	8	-5.2%	31
Passing	53.9%	1	14.0%	23
Rushing	11.9%	4	-16.0%	6
First Down	24.8%	2	17.7%	31
Second Down	24.7%	2	-19.7%	3
Third Down	55.3%	1	1.7%	19
First Half	31.4%	1	0.7%	18
Second Half	30.2%	1	2.1%	17
Red Zone	34.6%	3	-6.8%	9
Late and Close	25.7%	4	-10.9%	9

Five-Year Performance

Year	W-L	Pyth W	Est W	PF	PA	TO	Total	Rk	Off	Rk	Def	Rk	ST	Rk	Off AGL	Rk	Def AGL	Rk	Off Age	Rk	Def Age	Rk	ST Age	Rk
2008	11-5	10.7	10.4	410	309	+1	13.1%	9	12.5%	7	3.6%	17	4.2%	6	38.6	25	39.9	28	28.4	4	27.7	10	27.1	2
2009	10-6	11.7	11.2	427	285	+6	28.8%	4	26.4%	1	-1.1%	14	1.3%	12	27.1	19	19.1	10	29.4	1	27.0	19	26.2	22
2010	14-2	12.6	14.6	518	313	+28	44.6%	1	42.2%	1	2.3%	21	4.7%	8	32.9	23	39.5	27	28.3	6	25.5	31	26.2	18
2011	13-3	11.9	12.2	513	342	+17	22.8%	3	31.9%	3	13.2%	30	4.1%	5	40.0	23	57.5	31	28.5	1	26.7	22	26.1	21
2012	12-4	12.7	13.4	557	331	+25	34.9%	3	30.8%	1	1.4%	15	5.5%	4	46.7	25	28.0	15	27.9	7	25.6	29	26.2	12

---

[2] In fact, Dennard was stupid enough to get arrested for drunk driving right before publication, which either will lead the Patriots to cut him or will bring him a long suspension courtesy of Roger Goodell. If bad things happen in threes, the Patriots better assign 24-hour security to watch over Talib and make sure he doesn't do anything foolish.

2012 Performance Based on Most Common Personnel Groups

NE Offense					NE Offense vs. Opponents				NE Defense				NE Defense vs. Opponents			
Pers	Freq	Yds	DVOA	Run%	Pers	Freq	Yds	DVOA	Pers	Freq	Yds	DVOA	Pers	Freq	Yds	DVOA
11	50%	6.2	42.8%	30%	Nickel Even	52%	6.2	38.8%	Nickel Even	26%	6.5	16.8%	11	52%	6.0	2.6%
12	40%	6.0	28.1%	54%	Nickel Odd	20%	5.4	21.5%	Nickel Odd	25%	5.6	-3.4%	12	19%	6.5	18.0%
13	4%	6.4	27.8%	58%	4-3-4	12%	5.9	16.7%	4-3-4	25%	6.0	6.2%	21	12%	5.8	-4.3%
613	1%	0.1	1.0%	54%	3-4-4	9%	5.8	27.6%	3-4-4	15%	5.8	-8.6%	22	4%	5.2	-20.7%
02	1%	4.5	47.4%	8%	Dime+	4%	8.6	114.2%	Dime+	7%	6.4	-33.0%	13	2%	4.0	-4.3%
22	1%	1.3	-52.6%	90%					Goal Line	2%	-0.5	-63.2%	20	2%	6.4	-60.7%

Strategic Tendencies

Run/Pass		Rk	Formation		Rk	Pass Rush		Rk	Secondary		Rk	Strategy		Rk
Runs, first half	40%	12	Form: Single Back	77%	3	Rush 3	6.9%	15	4 DB	40%	24	Play action	24%	12
Runs, first down	48%	21	Form: Empty Back	14%	4	Rush 4	68.8%	11	5 DB	51%	12	Avg Box (Off)	6.15	29
Runs, second-long	33%	12	Pers: 3+ WR	52%	15	Rush 5	19.1%	19	6+ DB	7%	13	Avg Box (Def)	6.08	31
Runs, power sit.	67%	6	Pers: 4+ WR	0%	27	Rush 6+	5.3%	23	CB by Sides	74%	16	Offensive Pace	24.53	1
Runs, behind 2H	26%	22	Pers: 2+ TE/6+ OL	49%	4	Sacks by LB	21.6%	18	DB Blitz	4%	31	Defensive Pace	29.72	10
Pass, ahead 2H	49%	13	Shotgun/Pistol	48%	15	Sacks by DB	2.7%	24	Hole in Zone	10%	12	Go for it on 4th	0.81	22

The Patriots only went three-and-out on 12.2 percent of drives, the third-lowest rate since 1997. (Surprisingly, the lowest rate belongs to the 2010 Jaguars, followed less surprisingly by the 2001 Rams.) ☞ Injuries significantly cut the Patriots' use of two-tight end sets, dropping from a league-leading 74 percent of plays in 2011 to just 49 percent last year. ☞ New England had 45 wide receiver/tight end screens, third in the NFL, with 8.2 yards per pass (sixth) and 73.2% DVOA (best in the league). ☞ The Patriots ran only 10 running back draws with a dismal -20.6% DVOA and 1.9 yards per carry. ☞ The Patriots led the league with 59 defensive penalties. ☞ New England's use of a three-man rush dropped almost in half compared to 2011. ☞ The Patriots allowed a league-best 3.6 yards per carry and -42.4% DVOA when opponents ran out of the shotgun or pistol. ☞ Bill Belichick, one of the most aggressive coaches of the past 20 years, was shockingly conservative on fourth down last season. Belichick ranked in the top six for Aggressiveness Index every year from 2004 to 2010 before dropping to 11th in 2011 and then 23rd last year. It was only the third season out of 18 career years where Belichick has ranked in the bottom half of the league in AI; the others were 1994 and 2003.

Passing

Player	DYAR	DVOA	Plays	NtYds	Avg	YAC	C%	TD	Int
T.Brady	2035	35.1%	662	4623	7.0	5.5	63.5%	34	8
T.Tebow	-9	-24.2%	10	32	3.2	4.2	75.0%	0	0

Rushing

Player	DYAR	DVOA	Plays	Yds	Avg	TD	Fum	Suc
S.Ridley	192	6.1%	290	1266	4.4	12	4	55%
D.Woodhead*	101	22.4%	76	301	4.0	4	0	55%
S.Vereen	47	9.6%	62	251	4.0	3	0	52%
B.Bolden	53	12.8%	56	274	4.9	2	0	54%
T.Brady	56	40.3%	13	41	3.2	4	0	-
L.Blount	-2	-9.5%	41	151	3.7	2	0	37%
T.Tebow	-26	-26.1%	33	106	3.2	0	0	-
L.Washington	-1	-9.9%	23	83	3.6	1	0	22%

Receiving

Player	DYAR	DVOA	Plays	Ctch	Yds	Y/C	YAC	TD	C%
W.Welker*	251	6.1%	175	118	1354	11.5	5.8	6	67%
B.Lloyd*	130	1.8%	130	74	911	12.3	2.3	4	57%
J.Edelman	65	10.3%	32	21	235	11.2	6.7	3	66%
D.Branch*	-20	-14.3%	29	16	145	9.1	2.8	0	55%
D.Amendola	80	-7.6%	101	63	679	10.8	3.8	3	62%
M.Jenkins	37	-13.2%	72	40	449	11.2	3.2	2	56%
D.Jones	30	-6.0%	66	41	443	10.8	4.4	4	62%
L.Hawkins	-21	-35.1%	11	5	62	12.4	1.4	0	45%
A.Hernandez	35	1.6%	83	51	483	9.5	4.4	5	61%
R.Gronkowski	279	41.2%	80	55	790	14.4	5.5	11	69%
D.Fells	10	16.8%	9	4	85	21.3	6.5	0	44%
M.Hoomanawanui	31	63.8%	7	5	109	21.8	9.6	0	71%
D.Woodhead*	149	35.9%	55	40	446	11.2	9.3	3	73%
S.Ridley	-19	-38.4%	14	6	51	8.5	7.8	0	43%
S.Vereen	64	69.6%	13	8	149	18.6	17.5	1	62%
L.Washington	-1	-16.4%	8	4	31	7.8	5.8	0	50%

Offensive Line

Player	Pos	Age	GS	Snaps	Pen	Sk	Pass	Run	Player	Pos	Age	GS	Snaps	Pen	Sk	Pass	Run
Nate Solder	LT	25	16/16	1234	5	3.5	20	4	Donald Thomas*	G	28	16/7	606	3	2	9	4.5
Ryan Wendell	C	27	16/16	1231	2	2.5	8.5	5	Nick McDonald	G	26	12/1	246	0	0.5	1.5	1
Sebastian Vollmer	RT	29	15/15	1096	5	5	16	6	Marcus Cannon	OT	25	16/1	175	0	0	0	0
Dan Connolly	RG	31	14/14	890	1	2.5	9	4	Tyronne Green	G	27	13/13	733	3	1	4	5.5
Logan Mankins	LG	31	10/10	744	3	0.5	3.5	3.5									

Year	Yards	ALY	Rk	Power	Rk	Stuff	Rk	2nd Lev	Rk	Open Field	Rk	Sacks	ASR	Rk	Short	Long	F-Start	Cont.
2010	4.54	4.82	1	68%	8	12%	2	1.30	6	0.56	22	25	4.9%	6	12	8	13	34
2011	4.17	4.53	2	61%	19	17%	7	1.22	14	0.45	30	32	5.4%	9	13	15	17	24
2012	4.32	4.45	3	66%	13	18%	10	1.33	9	0.63	22	27	4.5%	5	9	8	13	23
2012 ALY by direction:		Left End 4.32 (12)			Left Tackle 4.73 (7)			Mid/Guard 4.62 (3)			Right Tackle 4.6 (6)			Right End 3 (29)				

Over the past couple of seasons, plenty of column inches have been written about the prospective holes in the Patriots' offensive line, but in the end those holes were either filled easily or never opened up in the first place. 2011 first-rounder Nate Solder easily slid into the left tackle position when Matt Light retired, and should continue to improve in his second year as a full-time starter, although he may be too tall to ever be a great run blocker. When Brian Waters never showed up for training camp, the Patriots moved Dan Connolly over to right guard and gave the center spot to Ryan Wendell, who was finally ready for prime time after developing on the roster for four years. He's agile with a knack for dissecting the defense, the kind of solid and cost-effective contributor you need to put in between your stars. This offseason's big question was whether Sebastian Vollmer, one of the best right tackles in the league, would get poached in free agency. Surprisingly—especially to Vollmer and his agent—the market for right tackles proved to be non-existent, and Vollmer returned to the Patriots on a four-year deal packed with incentives and bonuses. (It has only $8.25 million guaranteed, but could be worth up to $27 million.)

The question going forward is whether the Pats' best linemen can stay healthy. Pro Bowl left guard Logan Mankins has struggled with injuries over the last two seasons; he played through a partially torn ACL during the 2011 playoffs, then missed six games with ankle and calf injuries last year. Vollmer has back issues and had offseason knee surgery. The Patriots surprised many by not choosing a single offensive lineman in this year's draft, instead bringing in two veterans with starting experience: former Atlanta tackle Will Svitek and former San Diego guard Tyronne Green. The first lineman off the bench, however, will probably be Marcus Cannon, the TCU product who fell to the fifth round in the 2011 draft due to cancer which is now in remission. Cannon has mostly played tackle but can also play guard and may even challenge Connolly for his starting spot.

Defensive Front Seven

Defensive Line	Age	Pos	Snaps	Plays	TmPct	Rk	Stop	Dfts	BTkl	Runs	St%	Rk	RuYd	Rk	Sack	Hit	Hur	Tips
					Overall						vs. Run				Pass Rush			
Rob Ninkovich	29	DE	906	58	7.2%	11	46	22	4	43	79%	20	2.4	30	8	5	14.5	0
Vince Wilfork	32	DT	888	54	6.7%	6	46	18	2	43	81%	20	1.3	8	3	2	9.5	4
Chandler Jones	23	DE	729	48	6.8%	15	34	14	2	35	66%	63	2.5	37	6	7	25.5	3
Kyle Love*	27	DT	543	24	3.0%	61	17	4	1	21	71%	48	2.0	25	1.5	0	7	0
Jermaine Cunningham	25	DE	439	24	3.9%	58	19	8	0	17	76%	30	3.2	65	2.5	5	10	0
Brandon Deaderick*	26	DE	374	18	2.5%	--	14	5	0	15	80%	--	2.9	--	1	0	4	1
Tommy Kelly	33	DT	756	47	6.0%	10	36	10	1	39	77%	30	2.8	55	1	4	4	3

Linebackers	Age	Pos	Snaps	Plays	TmPct	Rk	Stop	Dfts	BTkl	Sack	Hit	Hur	Tips	Runs	St%	Rk	Yds	Rk	Tgts	Suc%	Rk	AdjYd	Rk	PD
					Overall					Pass Rush				vs. Run					vs. Pass					
Jerod Mayo	27	OLB	1047	151	18.6%	6	79	22	2	3	5	6	0	97	60%	79	3.9	83	46	42%	62	7.4	55	3
Brandon Spikes	26	ILB	721	98	12.9%	43	53	17	3	1	6	5	0	58	66%	55	2.6	26	36	47%	52	6.9	43	6
Dont'a Hightower	23	OLB	568	61	8.6%	70	32	12	3	4	6	5	0	32	50%	105	3.7	73	29	54%	27	6.9	42	3

Year	Yards	ALY	Rk	Power	Rk	Stuff	Rk	2nd Level	Rk	Open Field	Rk	Sacks	ASR	Rk	Short	Long
2010	4.10	4.25	20	71%	30	14%	30	1.06	11	0.52	8	36	6.3%	15	6	23
2011	4.48	4.51	30	58%	11	16%	27	1.28	25	0.66	8	40	6.5%	19	9	23
2012	3.97	3.83	10	50%	2	19%	13	1.29	27	0.49	7	37	6.0%	24	4	20
2012 ALY by direction:		Left End 5.28 (31)			Left Tackle 3.29 (4)			Mid/Guard 3.52 (4)			Right Tackle 4.16 (19)			Right End 5.4 (30)	

Although pass rusher Chandler Jones was the most visible addition to the Patriots' front seven last year, the real improvement came in run defense. Vince Wilfork is still one of the top two or three defensive tackles in the league, and while middle linebacker Brandon Spikes is subpar in pass coverage, he's excellent at stopping the run. The Patriots were much stronger against inside runs than outside runs, in part because they want their outside linebackers to read and react rather than aggressively attacking the line of scrimmage. That leads to fewer mistakes, but also plenty of runs that gain an extra yard or two.

Defensive tackles Kyle Love and Brandon Deaderick also contributed to the strong run defense, but the Patriots cut both veterans in an effort to get stronger pass rushers into that position. New starter Tommy Kelly was a hard-working tackle whose steady play in Oakland was overshadowed by a gargantuan and ridiculous contract. Now he gets to be a hard-working but aging tackle whose contract matches his actual production. Although Kelly's pass-rush numbers weren't too impressive in 2012, he's still just two years removed from a season with 7.5 sacks, six hurries, and 11 quarterback hits. Depth will be provided by Armond Armstead, a former starter at USC who went to the CFL after medical problems kept NFL teams from taking him in the 2012 draft. He ended his rookie year as a CFL all-star, and six sacks is a lot when only four players in the league have more than seven.

The Patriots' other strategy for improving the pass rush is to completely saturate the roster with defensive ends in the hope that somebody other than the two starters can emerge. Built from shredded scouting reports fished out of a dumpster in Piscataway, this depth chart has *everything*: a rising young stud (Chandler Jones), a steady but unspectacular veteran (Rob Ninkovich), a highly-drafted bust facing his last chance (Jermaine Cunningham), a guy the team claims is a linebacker (second-round pick Jamie Collins, a SackSEER favorite), a late draft pick from when the team was just throwing anything at the wall to see what would stick (Michael Buchanan), a free agent coming off a year lost to injury (Marcus Benard), a guy from last year's draft everybody has forgotten about (Jake Bequette), a CFL refugee (Jason Vega), and, of course, an undrafted guy from Rutgers (Justin Francis). The bouncer's a bulldog who looks like Wilford Brimley, and the password is "Kyle Love has diabetes."

Defensive Secondary

Secondary	Age	Pos	Snaps	Plays	Overall TmPct	Rk	Stop	Dfts	BTkl	vs. Run Runs	St%	Rk	Yds	Rk	Tgts	vs. Pass Tgt%	Rk	Dist	Suc%	Rk	APaYd	Rk	PD	Int
Devin McCourty	26	FS	1073	91	11.2%	29	30	18	7	29	28%	58	8.9	58	62	12.6%	2	14.6	54%	36	7.8	44	13	5
Kyle Arrington	27	CB	824	74	9.1%	32	26	12	5	15	47%	36	8.5	68	69	14.0%	70	12.9	46%	69	9.8	83	11	0
Steve Gregory	30	SS	733	42	6.9%	60	10	4	5	12	25%	62	7.2	37	22	5.8%	50	18.2	54%	39	6.8	26	5	3
Alfonzo Dennard	24	CB	583	43	8.5%	45	16	9	3	12	33%	60	8.7	69	51	16.6%	50	14.5	55%	25	7.5	43	9	3
Aqib Talib	27	CB	574	50	9.9%	19	18	10	5	6	33%	60	7.2	49	62	20.6%	21	14.1	46%	71	9.5	78	11	2
Patrick Chung*	26	SS	531	48	7.9%	52	11	4	3	18	22%	67	7.8	48	23	6.1%	46	12.7	61%	19	6.9	30	5	2
Tavon Wilson	23	FS	465	42	5.2%	70	23	10	1	12	67%	1	4.9	9	33	6.6%	38	13.6	51%	48	8.5	53	6	4
Adrian Wilson	34	SS	846	59	7.7%	54	23	7	3	31	32%	49	6.9	35	20	5.3%	59	14.5	76%	4	5.3	10	4	1

Year	Pass D Rank	vs. #1 WR	Rk	vs. #2 WR	Rk	vs. Other WR	Rk	vs. TE	Rk	vs. RB	Rk
2010	15	7.9%	23	-5.9%	11	-23.3%	5	11.9%	21	23.0%	30
2011	27	45.4%	32	7.0%	20	6.5%	25	25.8%	29	-14.7%	5
2012	23	-5.0%	14	-16.4%	6	27.3%	30	21.3%	29	14.8%	23

Aqib Talib's 2012 season is an example of the limitations of game charting statistics, even after the public has gained access to all-22 film. As noted earlier in the chapter, the Patriots' pass defense took a step forward with Talib's arrival and struggled when he got hurt in the AFC Championship game. Yet our game charting stats for Talib came out awful, even after we went back and double-checked every pass. The numbers above reflect his entire season; although he allowed fewer Adjusted Yards per Pass in just his games with the Patriots (8.9), he also had a lower Adjusted Success Rate (41 percent). Those don't sound like the numbers of a player who represented a big improvement, but that's exactly what Talib was. We honestly don't know the reason for the disconnect here between individual and team stats, although one possibility is that Talib's influence was felt more in the passes that were not thrown to receivers he was covering, rather than the passes that were.

Re-signing Talib was a big step towards carrying last year's second-half improvement into 2013, but the outlook for this unit got a lot cloudier right before our publication deadline with the DUI arrest of the player who along with Talib was most responsible for that improvement: right cornerback Alfonzo Dennard. The worst possible thing for the Patriots' secondary would be for the loss of Dennard (either through release or an NFL suspension) to force Kyle Arrington into a role as an outside cornerback. Last year, Arrington allowed 11.1 Adjusted Yards per Pass with 38 percent Adjusted Success Rate as a starter on the outside, and those numbers would be worse without two reasonable games Arrington played as a starter in the final two weeks of the regular season. In Weeks 11 through 15, however, Arrington played in the slot and allowed 6.8 Adjusted Yards per Pass with 65 percent Adjusted Success Rate. The Patriots will be better off with a scenario where either Ras-I Dowling is healthy enough to play more than two games in Dennard's place or third-round pick Logan Ryan (Rutgers) can adapt quickly enough to the NFL to be at least a passable starter on the outside. The first is nigh-improbable; the second is at least a reasonable possibility, as Ryan was lauded at Rutgers for his discipline in coverage and ability to recognize pass plays. Every NFL defense has defensive keys that depend on the offensive motion and formation, but the Patriots change their coverage based on reading the offense even more than usual.

The Patriots are also better off if they don't have to move Devin McCourty back to cornerback, because he's been superlative when he can play at free safety and diagnose plays without worrying about tracking a specific receiver. The Patriots brought in Adrian Wilson with the hope that he can provide a Rodney Harrison-like injection of physical veteran play, but at age 34 he's no longer the Pro-Bowl caliber star he was when we put him on the cover of our book in 2007. The Pats will rotate him with Steve Gregory and Tavon Wilson to keep him fresh. Nobody's quite sure what the Patriots will do with mystery man Duron Harmon, who represents both their obsession with Rutgers players and their total disregard for scouting conventional wisdom. Harmon was only the third player since 2000 to be chosen in the first three rounds despite being projected as an undrafted free agent by NFLDraftScout.com. The jury's still out on Cincinnati's second-year defensive tackle John Hughes, but the Patriots hope Harmon lives up to his draft position at least as well as Derek Cox did for the Jacksonville Jaguars.

Special Teams

Year	DVOA	Rank	FG/XP	Rank	Net Kick	Rank	Kick Ret	Rank	Net Punt	Rank	Punt Ret	Rank	Hidden	Rank
2010	4.7%	8	1.2	15	-4.1	25	11.4	6	7.3	9	7.7	3	7.6	4
2011	4.1%	5	1.2	14	8.3	3	-3.7	25	15.2	2	-0.3	18	0.0	16
2012	5.5%	4	-1.8	18	15.0	1	2.2	11	6.2	11	5.9	5	0.0	17

As noted earlier in the chapter, New England's consistently valuable special teams have generally been built on coverage and return teams, not kicking specialists. Matthew Slater, for example, has taken the special teams spot on the AFC for two straight seasons. Last year all 16 of his special teams tackles qualified as Stops, meaning that the return ended up with below-average value by our metrics. Yet as good as the Patriots have been on special teams in recent years, there are three reasons to believe they will be even better in 2013. The first two reasons are likely rebound seasons from kicker Stephen Gostkowski and punter Zoltan Mesko. Gostkowski had some badly-timed missed field goals last season, starting with the 42-yarder that would have beaten Arizona in Week 2. Strong coverage made the Patriots the league's best team on net kickoff value, but Gostkowski had his worst year for gross kickoff value. (Of course, Gostkowski's worst year is still above average.) Mesko also declined a bit after a very strong 2011. The third reason for the Pats to improve is that they will likely turn over the majority of returns to free-agent signing Leon Washington. Washington is one of the most consistently good kickoff return men in NFL history, and ranked third in the NFL with 9.5 estimated points worth of field position above average last year. He's never been quite as good on punts, but that's fine because he can share those duties with Julian Edelman, who has been worth a combined 16.0 points more than the average punt returner over the past three seasons.

Coaching Staff

Like a lot of other elements of the New England organization, the coaching staff demonstrates an astonishing level of stability. Bill Belichick, of course, is now the longest-serving head coach in the league, entering his 14th season with the team. Every defensive coach has been with the team since at least 2009. Linebackers coach Pepper Johnson arrived with Belichick in 2000, running backs coach Ivan Fears has been in Foxborough since 1999, and assistant head coach Dante Scarnecchia has been with the Pats for 29 years. Even the recent arrivals have past connections with the Patriots organization. Josh McDaniels played the part of prodigal son/offensive coordinator and had no problems running the tight end-focused offense that the Patriots had switched to while he was elsewhere. This year, McDaniels will be able to bounce ideas off of Brian Daboll; the former Patriots assistant (2000-2006) who was offensive coordinator for Kansas City last year (and Miami and Cleveland during the three years before that) has been brought back to the Patriots in a nebulous "offensive consultant" role.

New Orleans Saints

2012 Record: 7-9	**Total DVOA:** -5.2% (19th)	**2013 Mean Projection:** 8.5 wins	**On the Clock (0-4):** 6%
Pythagorean Wins: 8.2 (15th)	**Offense:** 11.9% (9th)	**Postseason Odds:** 38.9%	**Mediocrity (5-7):** 27%
Snap-Weighted Age: 27.2 (9th)	**Defense:** 14.8% (32nd)	**Super Bowl Odds:** 5.0%	**Playoff Contender (8-10):** 47%
Average Opponent: 2.0% (12th)	**Special Teams:** -2.3% (24th)	**Proj. Avg. Opponent:** 2.9% (5th)	**Super Bowl Contender (11+):** 21%

2012: *HMS Bountygate* shipwrecks the Saints

2013: Under Capt. Payton, a return to playoff waters is likely.

Not since General Douglas MacArthur waded ashore at Leyte Gulf in October 1944 has a return been so breathlessly awaited by a citizenry. After a year in exile thanks to his role in the epic boondoggle known as Bountygate, New Orleans head coach Sean Payton is back in charge for 2013, ready to lead his team back from the depths of a 7-9 season played in his absence. No word as yet on whether he plans to affect a corncob pipe on Sundays.

Payton, of course, was banished for the season, the bold-faced punishment amid a huge and unprecedented smackdown administered by Roger Goodell. The Saints didn't fare nearly as well under interim coaches Vitt and Aaron Kromer, the offensive line coach who helmed the team to a 2-4 record over the first six games while Vitt himself was suspended. They plummeted from second to 19th in total DVOA. The downtrodden defense, coached by emergency replacement Steve Spagnuolo, finished dead last in DVOA, giving up an NFL-record 7,042 yards as well as 454 points, more than any team except Tennessee. The Saints did eventually recover from a dismal 0-4 start to finish 7-9, but they were never in the playoff hunt.

Payton gained even higher stature in his absence; the team's collapse offered him leverage that Payton parlayed into a new five-year contract that pays him more than any coach in the NFL—indeed, at approximately $8 million per year, he's the highest paid coach in any of the major pro sports. Not a bad payoff for spending a full season without a challenge flag, so to speak.

Mission No. 1 upon his return is fixing the defense, which has never been Payton's area of expertise. There is some good news regarding that beleaguered unit. As worst defenses go, New Orleans was pretty good. The Saints' 14.8% defensive DVOA was the best of any last-place defense since the 1995 expansion Jaguars (Table 1). Given the fact that defensive regression towards the mean is stronger from season to season than offensive regression, improvement is almost mandatory. The 21 previous teams that finished dead last in our defensive rankings improved the following season by an average of -10.6% DVOA. Only the 1998 Bengals and 2008 Lions got worse on defense by more than a tenth of a percentage point.

On the other hand, with rare exceptions, the improvement of godawful defenses tends to stop somewhere around "still pretty bad." The 2006 Redskins (Department of Irony: their

defensive coordinator that year was Gregg Williams) were crushed by injuries, and set a record for fewest takeaways in a season, with but 12. Health and turnover regression helped propel them back to strength in 2007. The 2010 Jags imported a raft of free agents and made a quantum leap up the charts in 2011 (before giving back almost all their gains a year ago). But for the most part, quick turnarounds are rare. Indeed, both the Cardinals at the beginning of the millennium and the Lions at the end of its first decade remained the NFL's worst defense for three straight seasons.

Payton's first step to avoid that fate was the most obvious one, completely changing the direction of the defense by pink-slipping Spagnuolo and replacing him with the hirsute Rob Ryan, late of Dallas. Despite his poor record as head coach in St. Louis, Spagnuolo had a good rep around the league, mainly as a result of his Giants defense that shocked the 2007

Table 1. Worst Defenses in NFL by DVOA 1991-2012, with Performance in Following Season

Year	Team	DVOA	Rk	DVOA Y+1	Rk Y+1
1991	MIA	14.5%	28	-0.3%	14
1992	ATL	21.3%	28	11.9%	25
1993	LARM	18.9%	28	5.1%	20
1994	TB	14.0%	28	4.9%	18
1995	JAC	13.3%	30	5.3%	21
1996	ATL	21.6%	30	4.0%	22
1997	CIN	17.8%	30	19.4%	30
1998	CIN	19.4%	30	16.6%	29
1999	CLE	22.2%	31	9.8%	25
2000	MIN	26.0%	31	18.1%	30
2001	ARI	19.4%	31	18.2%	32
2002	ARI	18.2%	32	18.3%	32
2003	ARI	18.3%	32	-2.5%	15
2004	MIN	21.6%	32	3.8%	23
2005	HOU	20.1%	32	13.7%	31
2006	WAS	15.0%	32	-7.9%	7
2007	DET	15.2%	32	24.3%	32
2008	DET	24.3%	32	17.9%	32
2009	DET	17.9%	32	2.9%	22
2010	JAC	17.7%	32	-11.3%	5
2011	CAR	15.8%	32	-3.1%	
2012	NO	14.8%	32	??	??

2013 Saints Schedule					
Week	Opp.	Week	Opp.	Week	Opp.
1	ATL	7	BYE	13	at SEA (Mon.)
2	at TB	8	BUF	14	CAR
3	ARI	9	at NYJ	15	at STL
4	MIA (Mon.)	10	DAL	16	at CAR
5	at CHI	11	SF	17	TB
6	at NE	12	at ATL (Thu.)		

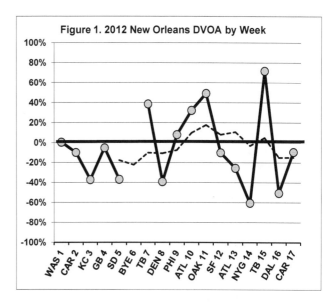

Figure 1. 2012 New Orleans DVOA by Week

Patriots machine in Super Bowl XLII. Clearly, the Saints roster didn't particularly suit his system, which abandoned Williams' "blitz 'em early and often" tactics for a defense that depended on pressure from the front four.

Then again, we're not certain the defensive roster of the 2012 Saints would fit any system—not well, anyway. For all the attention and resultant grief given the coach when results are poor, at a certain point the players have to perform. The Saints finished 29th in our count of broken tackles. They were 31st in Adjusted Line Yards, Second-Level Yards, *and* Open-Field Yards, a trifecta that points an accusatory finger of blame at every defensive position group. They were also 28th in Adjusted Sack Rate and dead last in defending opposing No. 1 receivers, an indictment mainly of overmatched top corner Patrick Robinson. Defenders were consistently blown off the line, out of position, or taking poor angles on ballcarriers.

But you won't find much accountability from the Saints defenders. Several ripped Spags after his firing and subsequent hiring as a defensive assistant by Baltimore, a squad that linebacker Scott Shanle (since released) said on Twitter was a "good team 4 him 2 learn defense." Another defender crushed Spags anonymously to the *New Orleans Times-Picayune*, saying, "He does have that good-guy persona, but he is a control freak and treats people like crap." The player went on to say, "To give up what we gave up can't be all talent. Look at where his units (have) been ranked before. I think one top 10? Players have no say in anything...It was (a) complete opposite from before where it was a simple D that players had lot of control and say. We couldn't suggest (expletive)...Nothing ever changed. It was his way only. Don't even get me started on lack (of) ability to adjust during games. Bad, bad, bad."

C'mon, dude, don't sugarcoat it. Tell us how you really feel.

Ryan doesn't have quite that same "my way or the highway" rep among former players, or at least it hasn't come out in public. Regardless, the players aren't likely to be doing much "suggesting" in 2013 as they shift to a 3-4 defensive scheme. While some front-seven holdovers may thrive in the new setup, particularly ends Cameron Jordan and Akiem Hicks, many others will doubtless struggle or become obsolete as they adjust to the formation. Ryan, who coaches as though auditioning for a reality show at all times, rarely hesitates to let the world know that the fault lies not in our stars but in one of his players who screwed up. Defensive coordinator in general isn't a job for the meek and retiring type, and many good ones (Mike Zimmer leaps to mind, as does Rob's brother Rex) seem to carry around a cursing dictionary in order to vary their high-volume verbal whippings. But Saints players who have

toiled under Williams, Spagnuolo, and now Ryan in a span of three seasons deserve not only sympathy but a bonus. Some sort of pay-for-performance scheme, perhaps?

Some blame for the defensive debacle, and the overall lack of high-impact players outside of the Saints' reliable passing attack, belongs to the scouting and personnel departments. Loomis oversees that area, and of course he was absent during the first half of the season, when some roster course-correction might have helped. Indeed, you can argue that last season was as much about the net effect of recent misfires at the top of the draft as it was about doling out cash for kill shots. Since the Saints picked Reggie Bush with the second pick of the 2006 draft, their first-rounders have been generally unimpressive. Bush (2006), Robert Meachem (2007), and Sedrick Ellis (2008) are no longer on the roster. The picks since 2009 range from decent (Cameron Jordan, Malcolm Jenkins until last season) to disappointing (Patrick Robinson, Mark Ingram). Of these seven players, only Bush in 2008 and Jenkins in 2010 sniffed the All-Pro team. By contrast, during a similar stretch of years before 2006, the Saints drafted the likes of Jammal Brown, Will Smith, Deuce McAllister, Ricky Williams, and Kyle Turley in the first round.

Jenkins and Robinson were particular culprits in the defensive collapse of 2012, so it was no surprise when the Saints took a defensive back with their top choice this April: Kenny Vaccaro, a highly-regarded safety out of Texas. How impactful he can be as a rookie remains to be seen, but certainly the Saints can't afford him to miss outright. This team needs quality young stars, especially given the age that is creeping into the team's lifeblood: the passing game.

Remember the thought process when Payton was first suspended, which held that Drew Brees would keep the offense going even without his mentor around to guide the game plan? That mostly held true, on the surface at least. The Saints scored 28.8 points per game, second in the NFL. Brees topped the league in touchdown passes and passing yards for the second straight year. In October, he broke Johnny Unitas' seemingly unbreakable record for consecutive games with a touchdown pass, eventually extending the streak to 54 games before the Falcons ended it late in the season.

But it sure felt different, and here is where advanced metrics earn their paycheck by revealing just how much the offense suffered without Payton. The Saints' offensive DVOA suffered a significant fall, from 33.0% to 11.9%. Brees personally dropped from 38.3% to 19.9% in passing DVOA, and from second in the league to ninth in ESPN's Total QBR. Brees clearly forced matters at times, a trait that spoke to his overall frustration with the team's play and perhaps the lack of confidence in his defense. He threw 19 interceptions, which tied Tony Romo for the most in the league. Seven of those were charted as coming on deep throws, speaking to his more reckless, Favre-ian approach in 2012.

Of course, there was plenty of payoff to the aggressive style—New Orleans led the league with 77 passing gains of 20 yards or more. Yet there was a reason Brees' press conferences were littered with references to "climbing the mountain" all year. He played less like Sir Edmund Hillary and more like Sisyphus, forever pushing the boulder to the summit only to have it roll back down the hill, as the opposition went 80 yards in five plays to push its lead back to double digits. On that level, Brees can be forgiven a few "screw it, we can't stop them anyway, I have to score every time out" throws.

Brees will be 35 by the time the playoffs roll around, and both of his top receivers, Marques Colston and Lance Moore, as well as the multi-dimensional Darren Sproles, turn 30 this year. There's no reason to expect significant declines from any of them in 2013, especially Brees, but given the outsized importance of the offense in New Orleans, the team can only regain its Super Bowl contending form if they all party like it's 2011 again. And that's asking a lot without getting help from younger players. Tight end Jimmy Graham is the most likely bounce-back player under 30. A wrist injury caused his numbers to fall off considerably, but if he's 2011 Graham again, that could make up for any fall off from the aging weapons.

Equally important is a return to the high-quality running game usually seen in the Superdome. After sterling numbers in 2011 (18.5% DVOA, good for second in the league), the rushing attack wasn't nearly as effective last year (1.7% DVOA, 11th). Much was made of the Saints 671/370 pass/run split, with the assumption being that Payton's absence led the team to rely too heavily on Brees as a crutch. But the previous two seasons weren't much different—662/431and 661/380—

and the Saints have been near the bottom of the league in first-half runs (i.e., when the score doesn't heavily tilt the splits in one direction or the other) for years. They ranked 30th or lower in four of the last five years, the exception being when they ranked 23rd in 2009. The Saints pass to set up the run, as we always advise. Last year's futility stemmed not from a lack of commitment, just a lack of execution.

A glut at running back prevented any one of the quartet of ballcarriers—Mark Ingram, Pierre Thomas, Darren Sproles, and Chris Ivory—from establishing himself on the ground. In 2010, the Saints saw a potential championship run derailed by a historic run of injuries in the backfield. Last season, the problem was the exact opposite: they had four backs who mostly stayed healthy, meaning a quality player like Ivory was often inactive or simply didn't play. The rest had to divvy up a limited workload, since Brees was chucking it so often. Ivory has been traded to the Jets, and the fervent hope is that Ingram justifies his first-round selection and takes over as the primary hoss. (Ingram was working with the second team during OTAs, but it's hard to tell if that represents a demotion or a motivation attempt by the coaching staff.) No matter how the carries are split between the running backs, improvement along the offensive line is mandatory: the Saints fell from first to 18th in Adjusted Line Yards, and guard Carl Nicks still isn't coming back from Tampa Bay.

While we expect the Saints to return to playoff contention, if not quite top-seed form, the truth is it's difficult to gauge the impact of Payton's return on the psyche of the team. Being a metrics-based organization, we won't even try. What we can point to as a reason to temper expectations is the increased difficulty of the NFC South, where the Saints will face Atlanta's high-flying receivers, the rebuilt secondary of the Bucs, and a likely-to-rebound Cam Newton. Those six divisional games are the spine of the fifth-hardest schedule in the NFL. The switch to a new defense, poor special teams, and uncertainty at left tackle also are factors that could prevent Payton's return from being as triumphant as that of "Dugout Doug."

Nevertheless, we feel fairly confident in saying the Saints would rather attack the 2013 season with Payton than without him.

Robert Weintraub

2012 Saints Stats by Week

Wk	vs.	W-L	PF	PA	YDF	YDA	TO	Total	Off	Def	ST
1	WAS	L	32	40	358	459	-3	0%	3%	11%	9%
2	at CAR	L	27	35	486	463	-1	-10%	29%	43%	4%
3	KC	L	24	27	288	510	2	-37%	-24%	8%	-6%
4	at GB	L	27	28	474	421	2	-5%	32%	33%	-5%
5	SD	W	31	24	404	427	1	-37%	-7%	29%	-2%
6	BYE										
7	at TB	W	35	28	458	513	-1	39%	52%	19%	5%
8	at DEN	L	14	34	252	530	0	-39%	-13%	31%	5%
9	PHI	W	28	13	371	447	0	8%	18%	1%	-9%
10	ATL	W	31	27	440	454	0	32%	35%	5%	3%
11	at OAK	W	38	17	380	404	2	49%	31%	-3%	16%
12	SF	L	21	31	290	375	0	-10%	-10%	11%	10%
13	at ATL	L	13	23	436	283	-4	-26%	-33%	-1%	6%
14	al NYG	L	27	52	487	394	-2	-61%	7%	20%	-48%
15	TB	W	41	0	447	386	5	72%	40%	-26%	6%
16	at DAL	W	34	31	562	446	1	-51%	6%	42%	-15%
17	CAR	L	38	44	441	530	0	-9%	32%	25%	-17%

Trends and Splits

	Offense	Rank	Defense	Rank
Total DVOA	11.9%	9	14.8%	32
Unadjusted VOA	12.9%	8	15.2%	32
Weighted Trend	13.2%	6	11.0%	28
Variance	6.2%	17	3.3%	5
Average Opponent	0.3%	14	4.0%	3
Passing	24.7%	9	20.8%	28
Rushing	1.6%	11	7.1%	30
First Down	14.5%	6	25.9%	32
Second Down	8.9%	10	6.0%	21
Third Down	11.8%	12	4.6%	22
First Half	21.4%	3	13.1%	30
Second Half	2.0%	12	16.4%	30
Red Zone	56.5%	1	-3.2%	13
Late and Close	-19.8%	25	10.5%	30

Five-Year Performance

Year	W-L	Pyth W	Est W	PF	PA	TO	Total	Rk	Off	Rk	Def	Rk	ST	Rk	Off AGL	Rk	Def AGL	Rk	Off Age	Rk	Def Age	Rk	ST Age	Rk
2008	8-8	9.7	9.1	463	393	-4	7.6%	13	16.3%	4	7.8%	26	-0.9%	22	24.0	15	33.4	24	27.2	19	27.5	13	26.5	20
2009	13-3	11.8	11.2	510	341	+11	21.3%	6	24.3%	2	-0.4%	17	-3.4%	28	45.6	30	32.9	21	27.5	12	27.7	6	27.4	2
2010	11-5	9.3	9.2	384	307	-6	9.2%	10	6.4%	11	-4.3%	10	-1.5%	21	19.8	10	25.2	18	28.2	7	27.6	12	27.0	10
2011	13-3	12.4	12.0	547	339	-3	23.8%	2	33.0%	2	10.2%	28	1.0%	12	17.4	7	7.2	1	27.7	11	26.9	19	26.2	18
2012	7-9	8.2	6.4	461	454	+2	-5.2%	19	11.9%	9	14.8%	32	-2.3%	24	11.5	4	23.6	14	28.3	3	26.6	21	25.9	22

2012 Performance Based on Most Common Personnel Groups

NO Offense					NO Offense vs. Opponents				NO Defense				NO Defense vs. Opponents			
Pers	Freq	Yds	DVOA	Run%	Pers	Freq	Yds	DVOA	Pers	Freq	Yds	DVOA	Pers	Freq	Yds	DVOA
11	47%	6.6	27.5%	13%	Nickel Even	39%	6.7	28.1%	4-3-4	38%	7.3	23.6%	11	49%	6.3	11.7%
21	20%	6.5	22.1%	40%	4-3-4	22%	5.7	-2.5%	Nickel Even	38%	6.3	12.2%	12	19%	7.6	27.0%
12	10%	5.3	-7.2%	42%	Dime+	15%	8.3	66.7%	Dime+	18%	6.4	11.2%	21	16%	7.7	19.5%
611	6%	5.6	-18.6%	56%	3-4-4	15%	5.1	-5.2%	Goal Line	2%	0.2	-24.6%	22	8%	6.4	18.2%
22	4%	7.0	20.5%	67%	Nickel Odd	7%	4.3	-29.7%	Nickel Odd	2%	10.8	31.1%	622	1%	0.3	-51.1%
620	4%	4.7	-11.2%	75%												
621	4%	4.4	10.2%	83%												

Strategic Tendencies

Run/Pass		Rk	Formation		Rk	Pass Rush		Rk	Secondary		Rk	Strategy		Rk
Runs, first half	34%	29	Form: Single Back	60%	22	Rush 3	4.5%	23	4 DB	39%	26	Play action	20%	16
Runs, first down	51%	13	Form: Empty Back	10%	6	Rush 4	66.6%	13	5 DB	40%	24	Avg Box (Off)	6.20	26
Runs, second-long	21%	31	Pers: 3+ WR	50%	17	Rush 5	17.0%	24	6+ DB	18%	5	Avg Box (Def)	6.37	17
Runs, power sit.	34%	31	Pers: 4+ WR	0%	30	Rush 6+	11.9%	5	CB by Sides	72%	18	Offensive Pace	27.82	4
Runs, behind 2H	22%	30	Pers: 2+ TE/6+ OL	30%	17	Sacks by LB	8.3%	28	DB Blitz	15%	11	Defensive Pace	29.97	13
Pass, ahead 2H	52%	10	Shotgun/Pistol	52%	11	Sacks by DB	3.3%	21	Hole in Zone	9%	15	Go for it on 4th	0.79	23

The Saints had excellent fumble luck in 2012, recovering eight of 12 fumbles on offense and 10 of 14 fumbles on defense. ☞ The switch from Gregg Williams to Steve Spagnuolo was very apparent in the pass rush, as the Saints big-blitzed with six or more guys less than half as often as they did in 2011 but went from dead last to 13th in frequency of sending the standard four. Things are going to change again this season, in particular because nobody likes to send a three-man pass rush with maximum coverage as often as Rob Ryan does. ☞ The Saints' defensive problems weren't just about big plays downfield. They allowed a league-high 10.9 average yards after catch on passes caught behind the line of scrimmage. League average was 8.9 and no other defense was above 10.4. ☞ The Saints ran out of 11 personnel less than any team in the league, only 13 percent of the time. ☞ The Saints were the only team to use play action more often on second down (27 percent) than on first down (26 percent). ☞ Interim coaches Joe Vitt and Aaron Kromer were far less aggressive on third downs than Sean Payton normally is.

Passing

Player	DYAR	DVOA	Plays	NtYds	Avg	YAC	C%	TD	Int
D.Brees	1441	19.8%	693	4914	7.1	5.1	63.7%	43	18

Receiving

Player	DYAR	DVOA	Plays	Ctch	Yds	Y/C	YAC	TD	C%
M.Colston	327	19.7%	130	83	1154	13.9	3.5	10	64%
L.Moore	356	31.2%	104	65	1041	16.0	2.2	6	63%
D.Henderson*	-65	-26.0%	47	22	316	14.4	3.6	1	47%
J.Morgan	135	65.0%	21	10	379	37.9	8.7	3	48%
J.Graham	105	2.7%	135	85	982	11.6	3.6	9	63%
D.Thomas*	37	18.0%	17	11	86	7.8	3.9	4	65%
B.Watson	-37	-12.8%	81	49	505	10.3	4.4	3	60%
D.Sproles	214	21.5%	104	75	667	8.9	8.9	7	72%
P.Thomas	99	18.7%	53	39	354	9.1	9.3	1	74%
J.Collins	10	-3.2%	16	14	70	5.0	3.9	2	88%
M.Ingram	-21	-45.4%	10	6	29	4.8	5.3	0	60%
T.Cadet	8	4.9%	8	5	44	8.8	10.8	0	63%

Rushing

Player	DYAR	DVOA	Plays	Yds	Avg	TD	Fum	Suc
M.Ingram	62	0.8%	156	602	3.9	5	0	49%
P.Thomas	97	15.1%	105	473	4.5	1	0	53%
D.Sproles	34	10.9%	48	244	5.1	1	0	44%
C.Ivory*	33	12.5%	40	217	5.4	2	0	48%

Offensive Line

Player	Pos	Age	GS	Snaps	Pen	Sk	Pass	Run	Player	Pos	Age	GS	Snaps	Pen	Sk	Pass	Run
Brian de la Puente	C	28	16/16	1108	3	1	7	2	Will Robinson*	OT	29	6/1	178	0	2.5	3.5	1
Ben Grubbs	LG	29	16/16	1108	2	3	8.5	6	Eric Olsen	C	25	16/4	174	2	0	2	0
Jahri Evans	RG	30	16/16	1106	5	0	7.5	4.5	Charles Brown	OT	26	10/3	120	1	0	0	0
Jermon Bushrod*	LT	29	16/16	1104	6	3	21.5	7	Jason Smith	OT	27	16/0	256	2	1	1	1
Zach Strief	RT	30	12/12	787	6	6	18	1									

Year	Yards	ALY	Rk	Power	Rk	Stuff	Rk	2nd Lev	Rk	Open Field	Rk	Sacks	ASR	Rk	Short	Long	F-Start	Cont.
2010	4.23	4.42	6	68%	7	19%	17	1.21	10	0.71	17	26	4.7%	5	12	9	14	48
2011	5.02	4.95	1	65%	12	15%	1	1.50	1	0.91	13	24	4.5%	3	10	9	16	34
2012	4.40	4.04	18	71%	3	19%	14	1.25	12	0.90	9	26	4.9%	7	12	7	22	32
2012 ALY by direction:			Left End 4.71 (3)			Left Tackle 3.52 (25)			Mid/Guard 4.07 (15)				Right Tackle 3.97 (15)				Right End 3.5 (26)	

Sean Payton was quoted during the offseason as saying the left tackle position "keeps him up at night." He should have plenty of company wandering around Bourbon Street circa 4 a.m. With Jermon Bushrod off to Chicago, fourth-year lineman Charles "Don't Call Me Charlie" Brown gets the first crack at protecting Drew Brees' blind side. Brown impressed in limited action last year—we didn't chart him for a single blown block in 120 snaps—but it's not a good sign when a second-round pick only plays 529 snaps through his first three seasons. Still, even though Brown's skills are still a bit raw, he's twice-cooked bacon compared to third-round pick Terron Armstead, a physical marvel out of Arkansas Pine-Bluff. If that tiny Ozark town sounds familiar to Crescent City swells, it's because Saints Hall of Famer Willie Roaf called Pine Bluff home. Armstead had the fastest forty time of any lineman at the combine, and out-vertical leaped Saints fifth-rounder Kenny Stills, a wide receiver. Zach Strief is likely to start at right tackle while Armstead adjusts to the pro game.

Our game charters were potent in their criticisms of left guard Ben Grubbs, with comments such as "it was because Grubbs was shoved back into the runner that the tackler could get to him in the backfield" and "appears that Grubbs was too slow out of his stance to reach the second-level defender who made the tackle." But his blown block numbers were hardly in Nate Livings territory, or even that much higher than those of All-Pro right guard Jahri Evans. The trouble for Grubbs was that he was replacing the league's best guard, Carl Nicks, who had left for a big free-agent payday in Tampa. The Grubbs/Evans combo, along with center Brian de la Puente, forms a solid interior core that is important when the short quarterback they protect steps up to throw.

Defensive Front Seven

Defensive Line	Age	Pos	Snaps	Plays	Overall TmPct	Rk	Stop	Dfts	BTkl	Runs	vs. Run St%	Rk	RuYd	Rk	Pass Rush Sack	Hit	Hur	Tips
Cameron Jordan	24	DE	1038	70	8.0%	7	52	17	4	55	75%	38	2.8	55	8	5	16.5	3
Will Smith	32	DE	986	59	6.8%	14	42	18	4	46	74%	42	2.3	28	6	15	15	2
Sedrick Ellis*	28	DT	709	37	4.2%	32	25	5	1	35	66%	60	3.4	66	0	5	7	2
Tom Johnson	29	DT	418	28	3.4%	51	19	5	1	22	73%	39	2.3	35	2	4	5.5	0
Akiem Hicks	24	DT	371	21	2.8%	65	16	4	0	19	74%	35	2.4	42	0	4	5.5	1
Brodrick Bunkley	30	DT	367	25	3.1%	60	21	5	3	19	84%	10	2.5	46	2.5	0	3	2
Junior Galette	25	DE	299	18	2.8%	--	13	9	0	12	67%	--	4.3	--	5	5	12	0
Martez Wilson	25	DE	271	15	1.7%	--	9	9	2	6	33%	--	12.5	--	3	3	7	0
Kenyon Coleman	34	DE	163	15	4.3%	--	13	3	0	15	87%	--	2.3	--	0	0	0.5	0

Linebackers	Age	Pos	Snaps	Plays	Overall TmPct	Rk	Stop	Dfts	BTkl	Pass Rush Sack	Hit	Hur	Tips	vs. Run Runs	St%	Rk	Yds	Rk	vs. Pass Tgts	Suc%	Rk	AdjYd	Rk	PD
Curtis Lofton	27	MLB	1121	129	14.8%	27	75	26	10	1	1	4.5	1	76	72%	25	3.4	51	41	53%	29	6.4	26	4
Jonathan Vilma	31	OLB	406	38	6.3%	92	27	9	5	1	1	4	1	28	71%	29	2.3	22	13	55%	--	6.6	--	1
David Hawthorne	28	OLB	321	39	6.5%	89	22	5	2	0	0	2	0	28	68%	41	3.5	63	9	29%	--	8.1	--	0
Jonathan Casillas*	26	OLB	249	27	3.5%	--	17	6	1	0	0	0	0	16	69%	--	3.4	--	10	63%	--	7.3	--	0
Scott Shanle*	34	OLB	220	21	5.5%	--	8	2	1	0.5	0	0	0	10	30%	--	7.2	--	8	13%	--	10.7	--	1
Victor Butler	26	OLB	290	26	3.3%	--	17	8	1	3	2	4	3	18	61%	--	3.1	--	3	25%	--	7.6	--	0

Year	Yards	ALY	Rk	Power	Rk	Stuff	Rk	2nd Level	Rk	Open Field	Rk	Sacks	ASR	Rk	Short	Long
2010	4.01	4.00	16	40%	1	21%	12	1.06	12	0.79	17	33	6.3%	16	17	9
2011	5.20	4.13	21	73%	30	18%	20	1.42	30	1.45	32	33	6.0%	25	13	16
2012	5.29	4.47	31	60%	15	18%	19	1.38	31	1.48	31	30	5.5%	28	6	18
2012 ALY by direction:		Left End 5.06 (30)			Left Tackle 4.62 (28)			Mid/Guard 4.24 (21)			Right Tackle 3.38 (2)			Right End 5.14 (28)		

Often a transition to a 3-4 defense spells trouble for incumbent linemen, but Cameron Jordan actually projects to be as good if not better as a five-technique end. Jordan was a stout run-stopper at Cal, and his play in that area, while closer to solid than to spectacular, was nevertheless one of the few highlights on that side of the ball in 2012. He also led the team with eight sacks. At the other end spot, the Saints will likely use a platoon of promising sophomore Akiem Hicks and former Cowboys vet Kenyon Coleman. Hicks has the size (6-foot-5, 318 pounds) to play nose, and may well get time there, but his agility could make him even more valuable at end. The Saints drafted Jonathan Jenkins out of Georgia to man the nose position, and it's his job to lose. Jenkins ballooned to nearly 375 pounds late in the season, and it cost him during the SEC Championship game, when he ran out of petrol and Alabama put him on roller skates. He reported to minicamp at 346 pounds, and should be a reliable space-eater if, ironically, he takes up just a little less space as a pro.

The linebackers are in flux. Moving to play 3-4 linebacker at age 32 isn't likely to come easily to Will Smith; if he can't grasp the subtleties, a player to watch is Junior Galette, who had five sacks and 17 hits/hurries in just 299 snaps and flipped between end and linebacker in college. A vet of Ryan's system, Victor Butler, was brought in from Dallas to play outside. Buried behind DeMarcus Ware and Anthony Spencer, Butler played sparingly, but managed three sacks in 290 snaps, more than the entire 2012 Saints linebacker corps combined. Butler told NOLA.com that he expects the Saints to have the No. 1 defense in the NFL, so clearly Ryan's bombast has rubbed off on him, if nothing else.

Curtis Lofton will man one inside post. In his first season with the Saints he was third among 4-3 Mike linebackers in Defeats, but had the most blown tackles as well. Early reports from Louisiana have David Hawthorne moving inside with Jonathan Vilma backing him up, in a bid for more athleticism at the spot, but Vilma is still sturdy against the run and will press for snaps. Vilma struggled playing in Eric Mangini's 3-4 system in New York, but Ryan's system tends to keep the weak inside linebacker mostly in space, with under principles that prevent one-on-one tangles with guards. That suits the speedy if undersized Vilma. The team also likes Chris Chamberlain, but after tearing his ACL in preseason last year, he has ground to make up.

To bolster depth New Orleans went hard at the position in the undrafted free agent pool, and two signees have the potential to stick. Chase Thomas was a hybrid end/linebacker at Stanford, and he led the Pac-12 in tackles for loss in 2011. Last season's TFL leader in the ACC was Kevin Reddick of North Carolina, and he will be competing for an inside linebacker job in Saints camp.

Defensive Secondary

Secondary	Age	Pos	Snaps	Plays	Overall TmPct	Rk	Stop	Dfts	BTkl	vs. Run Runs	St%	Rk	Yds	Rk	vs. Pass Tgts	Tgt%	Rk	Dist	Suc%	Rk	APaYd	Rk	PD	Int
Roman Harper	31	SS	1097	126	14.4%	3	42	18	7	58	36%	41	8.4	57	53	11.2%	7	7.8	41%	70	9.2	64	9	2
Patrick Robinson	26	CB	1092	82	9.4%	28	35	10	9	16	63%	9	6.6	44	100	20.9%	16	15.2	53%	36	8.9	72	16	3
Malcolm Jenkins	26	FS	873	100	14.1%	6	30	7	12	49	41%	27	9.9	64	35	9.1%	14	10.2	53%	41	6.4	18	5	1
Jabari Greer	31	CB	818	65	8.5%	43	28	16	8	12	42%	42	5.8	33	64	15.4%	58	13.7	54%	30	8.3	68	13	3
Corey White	23	CB	517	31	5.7%	--	11	5	8	6	50%	--	5.5	--	33	11.1%	--	12.2	45%	--	8.4	--	3	1
Isa Abdul-Quddus	24	FS	473	46	5.6%	68	13	5	6	12	25%	62	7.8	49	16	3.5%	72	20.2	83%	1	2.6	1	8	2
Elbert Mack*	27	CB	253	18	4.7%	--	12	7	2	3	0%	--	10.0	--	30	14.4%	--	8.0	68%	--	5.2	--	6	1
Johnny Patrick*	25	CB	215	23	2.8%	--	4	1	2	3	33%	--	5.7	--	35	7.7%	--	12.7	39%	--	8.4	--	2	0
Keenan Lewis	27	CB	919	90	12.0%	7	41	15	9	21	57%	18	3.2	5	102	22.7%	6	14.2	54%	32	6.3	13	20	0
Jim Leonhard	31	SS	260	17	2.1%	--	8	5	1	8	50%	--	7.6	--	8	1.8%	--	14.9	42%	--	8.3	--	2	2

Year	Pass D Rank	vs. #1 WR	Rk	vs. #2 WR	Rk	vs. Other WR	Rk	vs. TE	Rk	vs. RB	Rk
2010	9	2.3%	18	1.8%	16	-14.7%	7	19.4%	27	14.3%	24
2011	26	12.8%	18	-6.6%	11	9.3%	27	9.8%	18	21.5%	28
2012	28	38.3%	32	8.5%	23	-4.1%	12	-7.4%	8	17.5%	24

Patrick Robinson's epic fail against Dez Bryant in late December encapsulated the Saints' defensive struggles quite nicely. Dez torched Robinson to the tune of nine receptions for 224 yards and a pair of 58-yard touchdowns. Robinson was an easy target for Saints fans, but most of his struggles were a result of too much time in the deep end. The average pass with Robinson in coverage went 15.2 yards through the air, eighth among 87 qualifying cornerbacks. Our charting also shows that Robinson drew the enemy's top wideout on 53 percent of his targets, which made him look a little worse than he was. He allowed 9.6 yards per pass before adjusting for the receivers he was covering, 8.9 yards per pass after. On the other hand, only two corners in the league allowed more yards after the catch, so Robinson-rippers have some basis for their hatred.

Keenan Lewis was brought in as a free agent import from Pittsburgh, presumably to replace Robinson, though Robinson could still earn a starting role over Jabari Greer—the two should battle throughout the summer. Lewis was one of only three cornerbacks targeted by enemy passers more often than Robinson, although Lewis was up against the opposition's No. 1 receiver on just 29 percent of charted targets. The two cornerbacks had similar Adjusted Success Rates, but Lewis was far superior when it came to Adjusted Yards per Pass. Lewis is a New Orleans native, and was pushed to sign with the Saints by his mother. No word yet on whether Muriel Lewis will be cooking up jambalaya for the team after every victory.

Saints safeties struggled all season, so the team spent its top draft choice on Kenny Vaccaro, the latest product from the Austin Finishing School for Safeties (recent grads include Michael Huff, Earl Thomas, and Michael Griffin). Vaccaro's physical gifts are evident, but his versatility may be most prized. Vaccaro played both safety spots in college, along with linebacker, and he should push both incumbents, Roman Harper and Malcolm Jenkins. Ryan could use the strong and rangy Vaccaro as a hybrid player, especially against the run, before permanently settling on a spot for him.

Special Teams

Year	DVOA	Rank	FG/XP	Rank	Net Kick	Rank	Kick Ret	Rank	Net Punt	Rank	Punt Ret	Rank	Hidden	Rank
2010	-1.5%	21	-6.1	30	1.4	14	-3.3	17	4.1	14	-3.9	23	-9.6	27
2011	1.0%	12	-4.1	23	-6.2	26	1.9	11	10.2	6	3.0	11	2.3	12
2012	-2.3%	24	-4.1	23	-7.3	28	-6.2	25	8.6	9	-2.5	18	14.2	3

A strong season in this phase of the game might have alleviated a bit of the Saints' pain, but alas, the team was poor almost across the board. Only punter Thomas Morstead had a solid season. Though he was only average on kickoffs, he finished second behind Kansas City's Dustin Colquitt in gross punt value. Otherwise, *blecch*. And the Saints benefitted from "hidden" special teams more than all but two other teams, or else matters might have been worse.

The Saints started to phase Darren Sproles out of return duty, and it took the edge off his effectiveness. He fell from decent to poor numbers on both punt and kickoff returns, especially the latter, where rookie Travaris Cadet handled the majority of returns. Sproles will be 30 by the time you read this, and it seems likely his best return days came when fewer candles were on his birthday cake. As for Cadet, his defining moment came against Atlanta, when he fielded a kickoff deep in the end zone and sprinted out, only to discover his foot was ruled to have been across the back line, causing an automatic touchback. Going for a 110-yard touchdown was how Cadet approached the game. He was a classic example of a reserve player whose lone opportunity to shine came on kick returns, and he was too aggressive for his own good. Twenty-two of his 28 returns started in the end zone, including one that was eight yards deep, five that were six yards deep, and five that were five yards deep. If it weren't for a 75-yard return against the Raiders, his numbers would have been much worse. "It's hard (to take a knee)," Cadet admitted to CBSSports.com. Perhaps the Saints should send him to a seminary in the offseason instead of OTAs.

Coaching Staff

Rob Ryan wasn't unemployed for only "five minutes," as he boasted upon being let go by Dallas, but he found a new gig quickly enough. Ryan brings to his new team the high energy of a Justin Bieber concert and the personal hygiene and fashion sense of Nick Nolte's homeless character from *Down and Out in Beverly Hills*. While his getting punted from JerryWorld was viewed as a "we need a fall guy, let's can the werewolf with the big mouth" sorta deal, in truth the Cowboys fell from 16th to 23rd in defensive DVOA last year. Injuries certainly played a role in that, but the Ryans tend to write checks with their mouths that their advanced metrics can't cash, and Rob hasn't even matched his brother or his father in building defenses. Meanwhile, the roster has a couple of decent 3-4 fits but overall the change in philosophy figures to take at least a season to sink in. At least in New Orleans he'll have nowhere to go but up, and the offense should paper over most failures, as usual.

Offensive line (and interim to the interim head) coach Aaron Kromer left to join old mentor Marc Trestman's staff in Chicago. Replacing him to supervise the big uglies is Bret Ingalls, who moves over from coaching the running backs. When Ingalls was offensive coordinator at San Diego State in 1993, his senior superstar Marshall Faulk had a rising young talent as his position coach: Sean Payton. Ingalls' replacement in the backfield is Dan Rousher; he comes over from Michigan State, where he helped mold Le'Veon Bell.

New York Giants

2012 Record: 9-7	Total DVOA: 13.4% (7th)	2013 Mean Projection: 8.3 wins	On the Clock (0-4): 7%
Pythagorean Wins: 10.2 (9th)	Offense: 12.8% (7th)	Postseason Odds: 34.6%	Mediocrity (5-7): 30%
Snap-Weighted Age: 27.3 (8th)	Defense: 1.5% (16th)	Super Bowl Odds: 3.8%	Playoff Contender (8-10): 45%
Average Opponent: 2.1% (10th)	Special Teams: 2.0% (10th)	Proj. Avg. Opponent: 1.7% (10th)	Super Bowl Contender (11+): 18%

2012: Defending champion Giants look to improve upon 9-7 regular season.

2013: Disappointing Giants look to improve upon 9-7 regular season.

"What's wrong with the Giants?" is a tempting question to ask after New York followed up a Super Bowl championship by missing the postseason in 2012. But that's only one narrative. The Giants finished with a 9-7 record for the second year in a row, and in many ways were a better team in 2012 than they were the year before. New York scored 35 more points and allowed 56 fewer points than they did in 2011. Football Outsiders' advanced statistics tell a similar story, as the Giants improved from 12th to seventh in total DVOA.

Since 2006, the Giants have gone 42-14 in the first eight games of the season, which averages to a 6-2 start through the halfway mark. But on the back eight, Tom Coughlin's team has a 24-32 record, and rough second halves have kept New York out of the playoffs in three of the last four years. If not for one poor pass from Tony Romo to Miles Austin, New York's second-half woes might have kept the team home in January for four straight seasons, and Coughlin would probably be out of a job. But by winning Super Bowls XLII and XLVI, the Giants have avoided the media criticism and the "choker" label that would befit a team that struggles down the stretch.

But it's not all the Giants' fault, as Howard Katz and his team of schedule makers on Park Avenue have back-loaded the Giants schedule nearly every year. Since 2006, the Giants' average first-half opponent has had a .446 winning percentage while the average second-half opponent has had a .573 winning percentage. That's roughly equivalent to facing the same opponent each week, but playing them at home in the first half of the year and on the road in the second half. If you're having a sense of déjà vu, don't worry about seeing a doctor:

we hit on this point last year, and the year before, and... well, just take a look at Table 1, which shows the Giants' average strength of schedule in the first half and second half of each of the last seven seasons.

Last year produced the latest data point in a long trend, as the Giants started 6-2 but finished 9-7 after second-half losses to Pittsburgh, Cincinnati, Washington, Atlanta, and Baltimore. But the team can't just blame the schedule. For the umpteenth straight season, the Giants' performance dipped significantly in November and December, even after adjusting for the tougher schedule, and once again the biggest culprit was the pass defense (Table 2). Until Coughlin shows the ability to reverse this trend, questions will persist about the Giants second-half struggles. Once again this year, the schedule isn't going to help things: Our average projection for New York's first eight opponents is a -2.4% DVOA, while the teams in the back half average 4.7% DVOA. Although the Giants to get to play five of their last eight games at home, the second-half opponents include Green Bay, Seattle, and Washington twice—with Robert Griffin likely to be more healthy than he will be in September.

But the 2013 Giants have bigger issues to worry about than just their schedule. In particular, New York needs rebound seasons from two of its bigger stars from two years ago. In 2011, Victor Cruz and Jason Pierre-Paul had breakout seasons, propelling the Giants to the Super Bowl. Last year, each player regressed, and getting them back on track is one of the big goals for the team in 2013. Two years ago, Cruz ranked third in both receiving yards and DYAR among wide receivers. But last year, with Mario Manningham in San Francisco and Hakeem Nicks banged up, Cruz fell to just 26th in DYAR. The NFL's latest soup spokesman actually caught four more passes in 2012, but his average yards per reception dropped from 18.7 in 2011 to 12.7 last year.

Cruz ranked second in the NFL (behind Calvin Johnson) with nine receptions of more than 40 yards in 2011. That level of production was unsustainable, and he came back to earth in a big way with just three catches of more than 40 yards last season. As a slot receiver, Cruz works best when there are other threats that can attract the attention of opposing defenses. Domenik Hixon graded out very well in our system in 2012 (with 177 DYAR, he actually ranked ahead of Cruz) but the passing attack wasn't the same without a healthy Hakeem

Table 1. Giants' Strength of Schedule, 2006-2012

Year	1H SOS	1H Rk	2H SOS	2H Rk
2006	.484	21	.555	5
2007	.445	29	.586	3
2008	.395	32	.609	1
2009	.477	20	.594	2
2010	.422	29	.484	20
2011	.430	28	.609	2
2012	.473	22	.570	5
Average	**.446**	**26**	**.573**	**5**
2013*	.488	24	.543	3

*based on 2013 mean projections

145

2013 Giants Schedule

Week	Opp.	Week	Opp.	Week	Opp.
1	at DAL	7	MIN (Mon.)	13	at WAS
2	DEN	8	at PHI	14	at SD
3	at CAR	9	BYE	15	SEA
4	at KC	10	OAK	16	at DET
5	PHI	11	GB	17	WAS
6	at CHI (Thu.)	12	DAL		

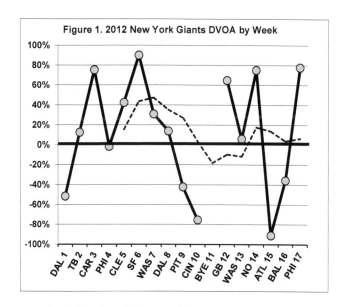

Figure 1. 2012 New York Giants DVOA by Week

Nicks, who was hampered with foot and knee injuries for most of last season. On the surface, replacing tight end Martellus Bennett (14th in DYAR, 21st in DVOA in 2012) with former Raider Brandon Myers (sixth in DYAR, 14th in DVOA) could be viewed as an upgrade to the offense. However, Bennett is the more well-rounded player and—at least compared to Myers—has a longer track record. Regardless of who plays tight end, what Cruz really needs is a healthy Hakeem Nicks. In 2011, Cruz ranked second in the league in average yards after the catch (7.2), but his 3.8 average YAC in 2012 ranked 54th among players with at least 50 targets.

As for the team's best defensive player, the concerns are more severe. Jason Pierre-Paul picked up 16.5 sacks and earned first-team All-Pro honors in 2011, just his second season in the league. He joined Shawne Merriman as the only players since the sack became an official statistic in 1982 to record a 16-sack season before turning 23 years old. But in 2012, Pierre-Paul had just 6.5 sacks, and was shut out in New York's final seven games.

Since 1982, only six players under the age of 25 had 12 or more sacks in a season and then had a drop-off of at least eight sacks in the following year (while playing in at least 12 games). Not one of those sack artists recorded double-digit sacks two years after his big sack season (Table 3).

If we increase the sample size by removing the age limit, we find precedent to give Giants fans hope that Pierre-Paul will return to form in 2013. John Abraham's sack totals went from 16.5 to 5.5 and back to 13 from 2008 to 2010. Julius Peppers had a similar dip with just 2.5 sacks in 2007 despite putting up double-digit sacks every other season between 2004 and 2009. However, both Abraham and Peppers had a much stronger track record than Pierre-Paul currently has. A better reason for optimism comes from looking at the Football Outsiders game charting. In 2011, Pierre-Paul was responsible for 25

quarterback hurries. We've got him down for 24.5 hurries in 2012, which means he was just a half-second away from getting a sack on a number of other pass plays. In general, defensive ends will record roughly 2.5 hurries for every sack, which suggests that Pierre-Paul was a bit "lucky" when it came to recording sacks in 2011 and quite a bit "unlucky" a year later. Given how sacks are notoriously inconsistent from year to year, it's tempting to project Pierre-Paul for double-digit sacks again in 2013. Unfortunately, New York's top defensive player will remain a wild card: he underwent surgery to repair a herniated disc in his lower back in early June, which could hamper his production or even keep him out of the lineup early in the season.

Putting Pierre-Paul aside, the Giants still enter the season with questions about their pass rush for the first time in years. In 2010, the Giants ranked 7th with a 7.6 percent Adjusted Sack Rate, and nearly matched that in 2011 (7.3 percent). But in 2012, the defending champs dropped to 22nd with an unimpressive 6.0 percent Adjusted Sack Rate. The blame doesn't fall solely on Pierre-Paul, either. Justin Tuck's sack total dropped from 11.5 to 5.0 to 4.0 over the last three years, and Osi Umenyiora went from 11.5 to 9.0 to 6.0. With Umenyiora now in Atlanta, the Giants will need more than just rebound years from Tuck and Pierre-Paul. For the Giants to regain their reputation as one of the top pass-rushing teams in the NFL, another player (perhaps rookie Damontre Moore or veteran defensive tackle Cullen Jenkins) will have to emerge for the Giants.

Table 2. Big Blue's Second-Half Stumbles, 2006-2012

Year	Offensive DVOA					Defensive DVOA (All Plays)					Defensive DVOA (Passes Only)				
	Wk 1-9	Rk	Wk 10-17	Rk	Dif	Wk 1-9	Rk	Wk 10-17	Rk	Dif	Wk 1-9	Rk	Wk 10-17	Rk	Dif
2006	15.9%	5	7.5%	14	-8.4%	-12.3%	5	7.7%	25	20.0%	-12.1%	4	15.8%	26	27.9%
2007	7.2%	11	-9.0%	21	-16.2%	-1.0%	13	-6.6%	10	-5.6%	2.7%	12	-1.1%	15	-3.8%
2008	19.2%	2	18.7%	5	-0.5%	-12.9%	7	1.6%	14	14.5%	-19.5%	4	13.9%	23	33.4%
2009	6.2%	14	12.3%	9	6.2%	-8.1%	8	13.2%	28	21.3%	-11.6%	7	25.3%	26	36.9%
2010	12.9%	7	1.4%	14	-11.5%	-24.0%	1	-0.5%	15	23.5%	-29.9%	1	-4.5%	10	25.4%
2011	20.7%	6	10.0%	13	-10.7%	-1.3%	9	15.8%	26	17.1%	1.6%	8	25.5%	25	24.0%
2012	15.4%	6	9.3%	9	-6.0%	-6.1%	8	11.5%	30	17.6%	-8.0%	5	26.9%	31	34.9%
Average	13.9%	7	7.2%	12	-6.7%	-9.4%	7	6.1%	21	15.5%	-11.0%	6	14.5%	22	25.5%

At the height of their pass rushing powers, the Giants would place four defensive ends on the field, with Mathias Kiwanuka and Umenyiora joining Tuck and Pierre-Paul to give opposing offenses headaches. But Kiwanuka struggled to get to the quarterback in 2012, and although the Giants plan on moving him back from linebacker to full-time defensive end, it's hard to expect a career revival now that he's 30 years old. New York might have found the answer to their problems when 2012 consensus All-American Damontre Moore fell to them in the third round. The Texas A&M defensive end recorded 21.0 tackles for loss and 12.5 sacks as a junior last year, but fell in the draft due to off-the-field issues and a miserable combine (lowlighted by a 4.95 40-yard dash and an anemic 12 reps on the bench press). Our SackSEER system rates him as a good-but-not great prospect, with an 80.1 percent SackSEER rating and a projection of 23.5 sacks over five years. At 250 pounds, Moore will need to bulk up to play defensive end in the NFL, but if any team has earned the benefit of the doubt when drafting pass rushers, it's the Giants. At a minimum, expect him see time in obvious pass-rushing situations, similar to how New York used Pierre-Paul during his rookie year.

Even when Pierre-Paul and the pass rush were dominant in 2012, the Giants were never a complete defense. New York's run defense wasn't a strength in recent years, but the bottom fell out last season. For the first time since 1995, the Giants ranked in the bottom quarter of the league in both rushing yards allowed and yards per carry allowed. Much of the problem came right up the gut: we ranked the Giants dead last in Adjusted Line Yards against runs up the middle or behind either guard.

Middle linebacker Chase Blackburn (and Giants fans) found out the hard way that toughness, intelligence, and hustle aren't enough to shut down opposing running games. Blackburn always had physical limitations, and they were unfortunately on display for much of 2012. But he wasn't the only one responsible for teams gashing New York up the middle: Chris Canty and Rocky Bernard both struggled as the other defensive tackle next to Linval Joseph.

But the outlook is brighter this year. Veteran Shaun Rogers missed all of 2012 with a blood clot in his calf, and the de-

Table 3. Dude ,Where's My Sacks?

Player	Year	Team	Age	Sacks	Sacks Y+1	Change	Sacks Y+2
Keith Willis	1983	PIT	24	14	5	-9	5.5
Mike Merriweather	1984	PIT	24	15	4	-11	6
Sean Jones	1986	LARD	24	15.5	6	-9.5	7.5
Bryan Cox	1992	MIA	24	14	5	-9	3
Eric Hicks	2000	KC	24	14	3.5	-10.5	9
Jason Pierre-Paul	2011	NYG	22	16.5	6.5	-10	??

fensive tackle would provide a boost to the run defense if he can return to form. The Giants also overhauled the linebacker position, and former Cowboy Dan Connor will take over Blackburn's spot in the middle of the defense. Keith Rivers should see a bigger role this season and will start on the strong side, giving New York—on paper, at least—a much better unit against the run in 2013.

Building a winning team starts with the quarterback and the head coach, and with Eli Manning and Tom Coughlin, the Giants are the envy of a lot of teams. But in an ultra-competitive NFC, the Giants can't expect to turn the switch on in late December and win another Super Bowl—especially if they have to turn that switch on because they turned it off on November 1. The Giants ranked second in points per offensive drive in 2012, and the offense will remain dynamic as long as Manning, Cruz and Nicks are healthy. The real question marks are on defense. We don't know how quickly Pierre-Paul will recover from back surgery, while Justin Tuck has not been consistently the same consistent force since he began dealing with neck problems in 2011. Considering the revolving door at linebacker and the annual question marks in the secondary, New York needs big years out of Pierre-Paul and Tuck to turn around a defense that ranked 31st in yards allowed in 2012. In a division headlined by RG3, Tony Romo, and now the arrival of Chip Kelly's dynamic offense, getting All-Pro caliber seasons out of Tuck and Pierre-Paul could be the keys to reclaiming the NFC East.

Chase Stuart

2012 Giants Stats by Week

Wk	vs.	W-L	PF	PA	YDF	YDA	TO	Total	Off	Def	ST
1	DAL	L	17	24	269	433	0	-52%	-7%	42%	-2%
2	TB	W	41	34	604	307	-1	13%	7%	-5%	1%
3	at CAR	W	36	7	405	327	5	75%	44%	-18%	13%
4	at PHI	L	17	19	366	422	-1	-2%	7%	17%	9%
5	CLE	W	41	27	502	375	1	42%	68%	10%	-16%
6	at SF	W	26	3	342	314	3	90%	36%	-54%	1%
7	WAS	W	27	23	393	480	2	31%	10%	-14%	7%
8	at DAL	W	29	24	293	434	4	14%	-26%	-24%	16%
9	PIT	L	20	24	182	349	1	-42%	-18%	3%	-22%
10	at CIN	L	13	31	318	275	-3	-75%	-41%	29%	-6%
11	BYE										
12	GB	W	38	10	390	317	2	65%	32%	-33%	0%
13	at WAS	L	16	17	390	370	1	6%	28%	19%	-4%
14	NO	W	52	27	394	487	2	75%	29%	-3%	43%
15	at ATL	L	0	34	256	394	-3	-91%	-42%	39%	-10%
16	at BAL	L	14	33	186	533	0	-36%	-11%	25%	1%
17	PHI	W	42	7	397	317	1	78%	75%	-2%	1%

Trends and Splits

	Offense	Rank	Defense	Rank
Total DVOA	12.8%	7	1.5%	16
Unadjusted VOA	13.9%	6	3.0%	21
Weighted Trend	8.7%	11	1.8%	20
Variance	12.4%	31	7.0%	24
Average Opponent	1.6%	22	4.1%	2
Passing	22.9%	11	5.7%	16
Rushing	9.2%	5	-3.3%	21
First Down	6.3%	9	-6.7%	11
Second Down	23.1%	3	12.9%	27
Third Down	10.0%	13	-2.3%	17
First Half	16.1%	8	0.4%	16
Second Half	8.7%	10	2.5%	19
Red Zone	18.2%	7	-24.0%	5
Late and Close	14.2%	7	4.2%	24

Five-Year Performance

Year	W-L	Pyth W	Est W	PF	PA	TO	Total	Rk	Off	Rk	Def	Rk	ST	Rk	Off AGL	Rk	Def AGL	Rk	Off Age	Rk	Def Age	Rk	ST Age	Rk
2008	12-4	11.5	11.5	427	294	+9	26.0%	3	18.9%	2	-5.1%	8	1.9%	11	6.2	1	29.6	20	27.7	14	26.2	29	27.1	3
2009	8-8	7.4	8.4	402	427	-7	4.2%	17	8.7%	12	2.4%	19	-2.0%	26	8.5	6	47.2	29	26.9	23	26.7	22	26.4	20
2010	10-6	10.1	10.4	394	347	-3	13.0%	9	7.5%	10	-11.2%	3	-5.8%	30	39.7	26	18.4	13	27.3	18	27.2	16	26.0	20
2011	9-7	7.8	9.1	394	400	+7	8.5%	12	10.5%	7	2.4%	19	0.3%	15	25.2	14	53.1	30	27.4	13	27.6	8	26.1	20
2012	9-7	10.2	9.5	429	344	+14	13.4%	7	12.8%	7	1.5%	16	2.0%	10	26.1	12	56.6	28	27.8	8	27.2	13	26.2	13

2012 Performance Based on Most Common Personnel Groups

NYG Offense					NYG Offense vs. Opponents				NYG Defense				NYG Defense vs. Opponents			
Pers	Freq	Yds	DVOA	Run%	Pers	Freq	Yds	DVOA	Pers	Freq	Yds	DVOA	Pers	Freq	Yds	DVOA
11	46%	6.7	30.1%	23%	Nickel Even	36%	6.5	27.4%	Nickel Even	49%	6.4	5.4%	11	44%	6.6	5.8%
21	29%	6.2	13.0%	53%	3-4-4	25%	5.2	-3.0%	4-3-4	41%	6.2	0.0%	21	20%	7.9	36.6%
12	10%	4.8	-22.5%	46%	4-3-4	24%	6.3	23.5%	4-4-3	3%	6.4	9.3%	12	17%	5.1	-11.9%
22	7%	5.4	24.4%	90%	Dime+	7%	6.7	-9.8%	Dime+	3%	5.1	-42.0%	22	9%	5.0	-26.7%
10	2%	5.8	-80.8%	0%	Nickel Odd	6%	7.8	24.6%	Nickel Odd	2%	7.3	91.0%	20	3%	5.9	9.6%

Strategic Tendencies

Run/Pass		Rk	Formation		Rk	Pass Rush		Rk	Secondary		Rk	Strategy		Rk
Runs, first half	37%	23	Form: Single Back	60%	23	Rush 3	5.7%	19	4 DB	41%	22	Play action	17%	26
Runs, first down	48%	22	Form: Empty Back	2%	31	Rush 4	68.0%	12	5 DB	51%	11	Avg Box (Off)	6.45	11
Runs, second-long	34%	10	Pers: 3+ WR	50%	19	Rush 5	20.1%	16	6+ DB	3%	24	Avg Box (Def)	6.44	10
Runs, power sit.	60%	10	Pers: 4+ WR	2%	12	Rush 6+	6.3%	20	CB by Sides	70%	21	Offensive Pace	30.79	19
Runs, behind 2H	32%	9	Pers: 2+ TE/6+ OL	22%	28	Sacks by LB	22.7%	17	DB Blitz	7%	25	Defensive Pace	30.13	16
Pass, ahead 2H	45%	18	Shotgun/Pistol	48%	16	Sacks by DB	0.0%	28	Hole in Zone	7%	22	Go for it on 4th	0.77	26

The Giants were much better when they were winning than when they were not. With a lead, the Giants had the best offensive DVOA in the league and ranked eighth on defense. When losing or tied, the Giants ranked 15th on offense and dead last on defense. The Giants defense had a similar split in 2011, although the offense did not. Eli Manning has just destroyed big blitzes over the last two seasons: 12.0 yards per pass in 2012 and 12.3 yards per pass in 2011. Ahmad Bradshaw faced a loaded box on just 2.7 percent of his carries, the lowest percentage for any running back with at least 100 carries. Expect more of the same for Big Blue this year: in 2012, only two of David Wilson's 71 carries came with a loaded box. The Giants ran a league-leading 57 running back draws; they were above average on these plays with 5.8 yards per carry and 16.4% DVOA compared to a league average of 5.0 yards per carry and -3.5% DVOA. New York's defense only forced a three-and-out on 13.5 percent of drives, the third-lowest rate since 1997. (The lowest rates belonged to the 2005 Bengals and the 2004 Colts.)

Passing

Player	DYAR	DVOA	Plays	NtYds	Avg	YAC	C%	TD	Int
E.Manning	753	9.0%	555	3785	6.8	4.3	60.1%	26	15

Rushing

Player	DYAR	DVOA	Plays	Yds	Avg	TD	Fum	Suc
A.Bradshaw*	230	15.8%	221	1015	4.6	6	3	52%
A.Brown	185	45.6%	73	385	5.3	8	0	63%
D.Wilson	30	1.5%	71	359	5.1	4	1	39%
E.Manning	-15	-40.5%	10	41	4.1	0	1	-
K.Lumpkin*	-34	-80.7%	9	39	4.3	0	1	33%
D.Scott	-7	-32.9%	6	9	1.5	0	0	50%
H.Hynoski	-1	-18.3%	5	20	4.0	0	0	40%

Receiving

Player	DYAR	DVOA	Plays	Ctch	Yds	Y/C	YAC	TD	C%
V.Cruz	165	1.2%	143	86	1092	12.7	3.8	10	60%
H.Nicks	67	-5.9%	100	53	692	13.1	3.7	3	53%
D.Hixon*	177	23.6%	59	39	567	14.5	3.6	2	66%
R.Randle	96	16.3%	32	19	298	15.7	3.8	3	59%
R.Barden	68	22.3%	21	14	220	15.7	3.4	0	67%
L.Murphy	-118	-37.2%	62	26	339	13.0	2.6	1	42%
K.Adams	-20	-51.5%	8	2	26	13.0	2.5	0	25%
M.Bennett*	85	4.6%	90	55	626	11.4	3.6	5	61%
B.Pascoe	-7	-24.4%	9	4	35	8.8	4.5	1	44%
B.Myers	112	10.7%	105	79	806	10.2	3.6	4	75%
A.Bradshaw*	35	8.5%	31	23	245	10.7	11.9	0	74%
A.Brown	-3	-17.3%	17	12	86	7.2	6.1	0	71%
H.Hynoski	-14	-26.9%	15	11	50	4.5	4.0	1	73%
D.Wilson	-2	-17.4%	9	4	34	8.5	3.5	1	44%

Offensive Line

Player	Pos	Age	GS	Snaps	Pen	Sk	Pass	Run	Player	Pos	Age	GS	Snaps	Pen	Sk	Pass	Run
Kevin Boothe	LG	30	16/16	1010	0	1.5	9	5	Chris Snee	RG	31	16/16	950	4	2.3	9.3	2
David Baas	C	32	16/16	1001	2	1	7	4	Sean Locklear*	OT	32	12/10	645	5	0	10.5	1
William Beatty	LT	28	16/15	951	10	4	14.5	4.5	David Diehl	RT	33	13/9	479	1	3.3	12.3	1

Year	Yards	ALY	Rk	Power	Rk	Stuff	Rk	2nd Lev	Rk	Open Field	Rk	Sacks	ASR	Rk	Short	Long	F-Start	Cont.
2010	4.83	4.22	7	59%	18	19%	16	1.31	4	1.25	3	16	3.3%	2	9	2	16	23
2011	3.77	3.81	29	53%	27	19%	15	1.05	29	0.49	29	28	5.0%	6	11	10	16	26
2012	4.75	4.47	2	67%	8	19%	18	1.38	7	0.96	7	20	4.4%	3	1	11	13	33
2012 ALY by direction:		Left End 4.54 (4)			Left Tackle 4.07 (15)			Mid/Guard 4.76 (1)			Right Tackle 3.78 (20)				Right End 4.49 (12)			

After the running game made a big rebound last year, this line's performance in 2011 definitely looks like an outlier. It helped to have more continuity than in years past; four of the five starters played in all 16 games. The interior is where the Giants' line really shines, as you can tell by New York's league-leading average of Adjusted Line Yards up the middle. Meanwhile, left tackle William Beatty finally had a full healthy season, and it earned him a new five-year, $38.75 million deal with $19 million in guarantees.

Nevertheless, while the rest of the line was quite solid, there was a big hole at right tackle where playing time was split between declining veterans David Diehl and Sean Locklear. While Diehl is still around to provide depth, the Giants have slotted first-round pick Justin Pugh as their 2013 starter. The Syracuse product is well-regarded for his technique, agility, and footwork, but some scouts worry about his small arms (31.5 inches) and struggles with bull rushers.

The Giants have ranked in the top six in Adjusted Sack Rate in each of the last three years, and a lot of that is Eli Manning making the line look good by getting rid of the ball when necessary. But it isn't all Manning; last year, the Giants' offensive linemen didn't allow a single sack that came in less than 2.5 seconds. The only "short sack" allowed by the Giants came when Carolina's Frank Alexander ran over running back Andre Brown.

Defensive Front Seven

Defensive Line	Age	Pos	Snaps	Plays	TmPct	Rk	Stop	Dfts	BTkl	Runs	St%	Rk	RuYd	Rk	Sack	Hit	Hur	Tips
							Overall						vs. Run			Pass Rush		
Jason Pierre-Paul	24	DE	873	71	8.6%	6	56	23	4	53	77%	25	2.5	40	6.5	3	24.5	4
Linval Joseph	25	DT	692	59	7.2%	2	43	7	1	54	72%	44	2.8	56	4	4	8	0
Justin Tuck	30	DE	645	46	6.0%	27	31	8	3	35	60%	71	3.1	63	4	5	10.5	1
Osi Umenyiora*	33	DE	635	44	5.3%	38	31	14	3	26	77%	27	2.6	43	6	7	18.5	1
Rocky Bernard*	34	DT	385	30	4.9%	27	21	3	1	27	70%	53	2.9	58	1	0	2	0
Chris Canty*	31	DT	297	26	5.6%	16	21	5	1	22	82%	16	2.5	45	3	3	5	0
Cullen Jenkins	32	DT	626	26	3.3%	56	20	11	3	17	71%	52	2.6	50	4	5	19	1

Linebackers	Age	Pos	Snaps	Plays	TmPct	Rk	Stop	Dfts	BTkl	Sack	Hit	Hur	Tips	Runs	St%	Rk	Yds	Rk	Tgts	Suc%	Rk	AdjYd	Rk	PD
							Overall				Pass Rush				vs. Run					vs. Pass				
Michael Boley	31	OLB	839	95	11.5%	54	51	14	2	0.5	1	2	0	50	66%	50	3.6	67	46	51%	35	6.9	39	4
Chase Blackburn*	30	MLB	783	99	12.8%	44	59	15	6	3	4	3.5	1	72	65%	59	3.7	71	23	37%	68	10.8	74	4
Mathias Kiwanuka	30	OLB	525	31	3.8%	--	16	9	2	3	2	10	0	24	50%	--	4.3	--	4	2%	--	12.0	--	0
Jacquian Williams	24	OLB	286	28	5.4%	--	11	3	0	1	0	4	0	11	36%	--	4.0	--	12	49%	--	5.9	--	0
Keith Rivers	27	OLB	234	39	6.9%	--	16	3	2	0	2	3	0	27	52%	--	4.5	--	12	27%	--	7.8	--	1
Mark Herzlich	26	MLB	175	20	2.4%	--	7	0	1	0	0	1	0	11	55%	--	5.1	--	7	33%	--	6.0	--	0
Spencer Paysinger	25	OLB	134	18	2.2%	--	8	1	1	0	0	0	0	8	75%	--	3.3	--	8	27%	--	8.2	--	0
Dan Connor	28	MLB	340	54	7.8%	76	32	7	4	0	0	1	0	39	67%	44	3.3	50	12	43%	--	6.3	--	1
Kyle Bosworth	27	OLB	250	27	3.0%	--	15	5	3	0	1	0	0	18	67%	--	3.5	--	14	34%	--	6.5	--	1

Year	Yards	ALY	Rk	Power	Rk	Stuff	Rk	2nd Level	Rk	Open Field	Rk	Sacks	ASR	Rk	Short	Long
2010	3.96	3.78	11	65%	20	19%	20	1.03	6	0.75	15	46	7.6%	7	14	16
2011	4.49	4.12	20	61%	13	21%	12	1.14	13	1.01	23	48	7.3%	11	8	23
2012	4.65	4.42	30	48%	1	19%	15	1.26	25	0.87	21	33	6.0%	22	9	15
2012 ALY by direction:		Left End 4.49 (25)			Left Tackle 4.69 (30)			Mid/Guard 4.55 (32)			Right Tackle 3.98 (15)				Right End 4.13 (15)	

One aspect New York missed from its front seven last year was the strip-sack turnover. From 2009 to 2011, the Giants recovered 18 strip-sack fumbles, but that number dropped to just two in 2012. A once dominant and deep defensive line is suddenly surrounded by some question marks. With Osi Umenyiora now in Atlanta and Jason Pierre-Paul coming off back surgery, the Giants are moving Mathias Kiwanuka back to defensive end. A promising and versatile young player a half-decade ago, it now seems that Kiwanuka is destined to plug whatever hole the team has on defense. Depending on JPP's health, the Giants may end up relying more on Kiwanuka or rookie Damontre Moore opposite Justin Tuck. The team is much more settled on the inside: Linval Joseph won't steal the spotlight from Pierre-Paul or Tuck, but he has become one of the more dependable defensive tackles in the NFL.

Despite the defense's struggles up the middle generally, the Giants ranked No.1 last year against Power runs, and Joseph's presence on the inside is one of the big reasons for the team's success in short-yardage situations. Free-agent signing Cullen Jenkins replaces Chris Canty in the other defensive tackle spot, although he's more valuable as a pass rusher than he is against the run.

The Giants still use their Big Nickel formation (a 4-2-5 set with three safeties on the field), but not quite as much as in seasons past. They went from using a conventional 4-3 on 28 percent of snaps in 2011 to 41 percent in 2012. Despite relying more on linebackers—a trend that should continue with safety Kenny Phillips now in Philadelphia—no team has ignored that position at the top of the draft like the Giants. Big Blue hasn't chosen a linebacker in the first round of the draft since taking Carl Banks third overall in 1984. Since 1987, 204 linebackers have been selected in the first two rounds of NFL drafts. Only two of those players were drafted by the Giants, and neither player panned out: New York used second-round selections on Kanavis McGhee (Colorado) in 1991 and Clint Sintim (Virginia) in 2009.

Keith Rivers, Dan Connor, and Jacquian Williams could walk down Broadway unnoticed, but they'll need to improve on the inconsistent performances delivered by Michael Boley, Chase Blackburn, and Mathias Kiwanuka last year. The Giants allowed more than 190 rushing yards in four games, and no performance was more embarrassing than the 248 rushing yards allowed to Robert Griffin III, Alfred Morris, and the Washington Redskins. New York ranked 30th in Adjusted Line Yards, and blame falls equally on a below-average group of linebackers and an underachieving defensive line. The Giants have little choice but to hope that their high-priced line returns to form, but it was odd that management continued to avoid the linebacker position in the draft.

Defensive Secondary

Secondary	Age	Pos	Snaps	Plays	Overall TmPct	Rk	Stop	Dfts	BTkl	Runs	vs. Run St%	Rk	Yds	Rk	Tgts	vs. Pass Tgt%	Rk	Dist	Suc%	Rk	APaYd	Rk	PD	Int
Corey Webster	31	CB	1016	69	8.4%	50	21	6	5	8	25%	73	5.5	24	91	21.1%	13	15.3	47%	68	9.1	73	11	4
Antrel Rolle	31	FS	1015	97	11.8%	24	33	18	10	48	33%	46	7.9	51	47	11.0%	8	9.7	60%	22	5.7	14	4	2
Stevie Brown	26	FS	829	77	9.3%	45	23	16	4	30	20%	69	11.3	68	27	6.2%	44	14.2	59%	23	6.7	22	10	8
Prince Amukamara	24	CB	728	59	8.8%	36	18	8	5	16	38%	53	5.5	24	67	19.3%	33	12.7	53%	35	6.7	25	6	1
Jayron Hosley	23	CB	452	39	6.3%	--	18	10	2	14	50%	--	10.8	--	29	9.0%	--	14.8	36%	--	10.0	--	3	1
Kenny Phillips*	27	SS	293	27	7.5%	--	11	2	0	13	54%	--	4.7	--	5	2.7%	--	16.9	98%	--	-0.3	--	2	0
Will Hill	23	FS	213	29	4.7%	--	12	9	0	10	60%	--	5.8	--	14	4.4%	--	6.4	39%	--	7.1	--	1	0
Aaron Ross	31	CB	673	49	6.3%	73	19	6	5	16	50%	26	4.7	14	49	13.1%	77	11.3	33%	86	9.7	82	3	0
Ryan Mundy	28	SS	284	26	3.5%	--	5	3	4	9	11%	--	7.9	--	12	2.6%	--	7.6	32%	--	7.5	--	2	0

Year	Pass D Rank	vs. #1 WR	Rk	vs. #2 WR	Rk	vs. Other WR	Rk	vs. TE	Rk	vs. RB	Rk
2010	3	-25.4%	2	-10.1%	7	26.8%	31	-13.0%	3	-0.9%	11
2011	19	0.6%	13	5.7%	17	18.2%	30	5.1%	13	9.0%	23
2012	16	11.9%	23	-4.0%	13	18.2%	26	-20.2%	3	-7.6%	12

Injuries in the secondary have been responsible for some of the problems in coverage over the last two years. Terrell Thomas missed all of 2011 with a torn ACL in his right knee; he re-aggravated the injury last summer, requiring another surgery in September, causing him to miss his second straight season. With three surgeries on his right ACL (including the one he had in college), he's aiming to become 2013's version of Thomas Davis, the Carolina Panthers linebacker who recovered from three such surgeries but played well in 15 games last year. The Giants resigned him to the veteran minimum contract, and are also considering moving him to safety. He's a great story if he hits, but when it comes to the Giants' secondary, "best-case scenarios" tend to land on the cutting room floor.

Prince Amukamara, the Giants first-round pick in 2011, missed nine games due to a broken left foot in his rookie year and three games last year with ankle and hamstring injuries. New York hopes he'll spend less time on ice this year (I'll be here all week, folks) and turn into a capable starting cornerback. The team's top cover corner, Corey Webster, has been the one mainstay in the secondary, but his play slipped last year. Webster dropped from 36th to 38th in Adjusted Success Rate; it was the first time since 2006 that he ranked in the bottom half of the league for that metric. It's difficult to find an explanation for Webster's decline: he was simply beat, beat deep, and beat often. Some of his struggle came because he was covering the opponent's No. 1 wide receiver on 60 percent of the targets he faced last year, ninth among qualifying cornerbacks. However, the Giants tended to use him to cover the opposition's top receiver in past years as well, so that's not really a change. Webster particularly struggled in games against the Cowboys and Ravens. Dez Bryant gained 140 yards on 14 targets in two games when Webster was assigned to him, while Torrey Smith burned Webster for 88 yards and a touchdown on eight targets.

One bright spot in the defensive backfield was the emergence of safety Stevie Brown (eight interceptions and a league-leading 307 interception return yards in 2012). The other starting safety, Antrel Rolle, is your typical Giants defender. He's versatile and athletic but prone to mistakes. He racked up 10 broken tackles for the second year in a row, but is one of the league's better safeties in pass coverage and is often asked to cover slot receivers. When Rolle wasn't moved over to nickelback, that job went to Jayron Hosley, who struggled as a rookie and may lose some snaps to veteran Aaron Ross. Ross returns after a year in Jacksonville, where the only notable thing he did was miss part of training camp to watch his wife, Sanya Richards-Ross, pick up a pair of gold medals in track and field at the London Olympics. After re-signing with the Giants, Ross labeled his year in Jacksonville as a "paid vacation." In an unrelated note, Mike Mularkey remains unemployed.

Special Teams

Year	DVOA	Rank	FG/XP	Rank	Net Kick	Rank	Kick Ret	Rank	Net Punt	Rank	Punt Ret	Rank	Hidden	Rank
2010	-5.8%	30	-0.7	19	3.4	11	-7.9	25	-15.6	30	-8.2	29	1.5	13
2011	0.3%	15	-1.7	19	4.2	8	-3.4	22	10.9	5	-8.4	29	-3.8	21
2012	2.0%	10	-3.0	21	1.5	13	14.6	1	0.9	15	-4.0	22	-3.1	22

"Kicker Lawrence Tynes is boring and inoffensive, like a grilled cheese sandwich." That's what we wrote in this section last year, after the Giants ranked 22nd, 19th, and 19th in field goal kicking value in 2009, 2010, and 2011. Last year, the team ranked 21st. Don't say we never got one right. Since the Giants replaced Matt Dodge with Steve Weatherford, the punting game has thankfully been uneventful: DeSean Jackson's game-winner in 2010 was the last punt return touchdown Big Blue has allowed. Weatherford slightly regressed from the great years he had in 2010 and 2011, but he remains an above-average punter.

New York finally became exciting in one area, kickoff returns, ranking first in the league after three poor seasons. David Wilson was electric in that role last year, but the Giants may use Jerrel Jernigan or Andre Brown more on returns this year as Wilson shoulders a larger load on offense. In the last 25 years, only Fred Jackson in 2009 recorded 200 carries and 30 kickoff returns in the same season. Rueben Randle was nothing special as the punt returner during his rookie season, but he'll probably handle those duties again in 2013.

Coaching Staff

Tom Coughlin turns 67 in August, making him one of the oldest coaches in history. The only men to coach at age sixty-seven: George Halas, Paul Brown, Marv Levy, Ted Marchibroda, Dick Vermeil, and Joe Gibbs. And only Halas, Levy, and Vermeil were still head coaches at 68. On average, head coaches in 2013 will be 52 years old; the next oldest coaches after Coughlin are Pete Carroll (62) and a trio of 61-year-old coaches (Bruce Arians, Bill Belichick, and Mike Shanahan). While being at an advanced age isn't necessarily a negative—Vermeil went 13-3 when he was 67, Levy made a Super Bowl at 68, and Halas fielded one of his best teams in '63 when he was 68—don't expect that to prevent the New York media from finding the next reason to start the "Fire Coughlin" chants if New York struggles this year.

Kevin Gilbride remains one of the game's best offensive coordinators. The Giants have gained 6,000 yards of offense only twice in their history: 2010 and 2011. And while New York failed to hit that mark in 2012, that was because New York had the second fewest number of drives in the league. The Giants averaged 37.4 yards per drive last year, more than any other season under Gilbride.

New York Jets

2012 Record: 6-10	Total DVOA: -18.0% (27th)	2013 Mean Projection: 7.5 wins	On the Clock (0-4): 12%
Pythagorean Wins: 5.3 (26th)	Offense: -20.7% (30th)	Postseason Odds: 29.5%	Mediocrity (5-7): 37%
Snap-Weighted Age: 27.2 (13th)	Defense: -4.2% (9th)	Super Bowl Odds: 2.3%	Playoff Contender (8-10): 39%
Average Opponent: 0.2% (14th)	Special Teams: -1.5% (21st)	Proj. Avg. Opponent: 1.6% (12th)	Super Bowl Contender (11+): 11%

2012: Rex Ryan and Mark Sanchez face make-or-break season.

2013: Wait, what? Rex Ryan and Mark Sanchez are still here?

No NFL team starts with a clean slate, but more than most, the 2013 Jets carry with them the ghosts of their predecessors. From 2009 to 2012, the Jets were defined by four men: general manager Mike Tannenbaum, head coach Rex Ryan, quarterback Mark Sanchez, and cornerback Darrelle Revis. And in case you just woke up from an eight-month nap, the half of that quartet *not* involved in foot fetish videos or the Buttfumble are the ones who are gone.

New York made the AFC Championship Game in 2009 thanks to a dominant defense created by Ryan and centered around Revis. History repeated itself a year later, when New York once again fell just one game short of reaching the Super Bowl. Things fell apart in 2011 before the wheels came completely off last season. Both years, the biggest culprit was the quarterback. Two years ago, Mark Sanchez finished second in the league with 26 turnovers (just one behind Josh Freeman), causing a Jets team that was playoff caliber everywhere but quarterback to finish 8-8.

Ryan blamed Sanchez's struggles on offensive coordinator Brian Schottenheimer, so Ryan replaced Schottenheimer with former Miami head coach Tony Sparano. The result? Sanchez again committed 26 turnovers, this time leading the league, and did it on fewer plays to boot. Sanchez also set career lows in both traditional statistics (yards per attempt, sack rate, touchdown rate) and our advanced stats (DVOA and DYAR). A disastrous 6-10 season that felt more like 6-100 resulted in significant changes throughout the organization.

Tannenbaum is now gone, a casualty of back-to-back disappointing seasons. So too are Sparano, Mike Westhoff (special teams), Mike Smith (outside linebackers), Bill Hughan (strength and conditions), Matt Cavanaugh (quarterbacks), Dave DeGuglielmo (offensive line), Mike Pettinte (defensive coordinator), Jim O'Neil (defensive backs), and Bob Sutton (linebackers). The Black Death resulted in a few more evacuations than the 2012 Jets, but it's close. When the music stopped, Rex Ryan was left sitting in the only chair.

Owner Woody Johnson embarked on a 19-day search for a new general manager, with the one requirement being that Ryan must be retained. Johnson eventually landed on John Idzik, who spent the past six seasons as the Seahawks' vice president of football administration. It only took a few hours for Idzik to be flung into the Revis Situation™, which eventually ended with the All-Pro cornerback traded to Tampa Bay.

Idzik also inherited a salary cap nightmare, and the solution involved massive bloodletting. Gone are long-tenured Jets like Brandon Moore, Bart Scott, Bryan Thomas, Eric Smith, Dustin Keller, Shonn Greene, Mike DeVito, and Sione Pouha.

Incredibly, Mark Sanchez returns as the likely starting quarterback. We're long past the point where we need to convince folks focused on playoff wins that Sanchez is a below-average quarterback. But to put in perspective how incredible it is that Sanchez may start in 2013, consider that only five quarterbacks in NFL history have met the following criteria in four straight seasons:

- Finished below league average in completion percentage.
- Finished below league average in yards per attempt.
- Thrown at least 300 passes for the same team each year.

One of them, of course, is Mark Sanchez. The other four were also high first-round picks.

The first was Trent Dilfer, who like Sanchez saw some success opposite excellent defenses. Dilfer's streak ran from 1995, his second season in the league, until 1998. In 1999, Dilfer's completion percentage soared to above league average, but a benching and a season-ending injury limited him to just 10 starts. The next season, of course, he joined the Ravens and won a Super Bowl.

The second quarterback was Donovan McNabb (2000-2003), but he's a poor comparison. McNabb was an excellent runner early in his career, and he was outstanding at avoiding interceptions, a label never applied to Sanchez. The third was Joey Harrington (2002-2005), who was a much more similar player. The main difference between Sanchez and Harrington is that the Lions gave him no help—Detroit ranked 19th or worse in defensive DVOA each of those seasons—so Harrington limped to an 18-37 record. After four years, even Detroit had seen enough, and Harrington had a fifth straight year of below-average play as quarterback of the Dolphins in 2006.

The fourth comparison is, presumably, the only reason Johnson and Ryan continue to believe in the Sanchize. New York fans criticized Eli Manning early in his career about as much as they do Sanchez now. If you include his 197-attempt rookie season, Manning finished below league average in both completion percentage and yards per attempt in each of his first five seasons.

2013 Jets Schedule

Week	Opp.	Week	Opp.	Week	Opp.
1	TB	7	NE	13	MIA
2	at NE (Thu.)	8	at CIN	14	OAK
3	BUF	9	NO	15	at CAR
4	at TEN	10	BYE	16	CLE
5	at ATL (Mon.)	11	at BUF	17	at MIA
6	PIT	12	at BAL		

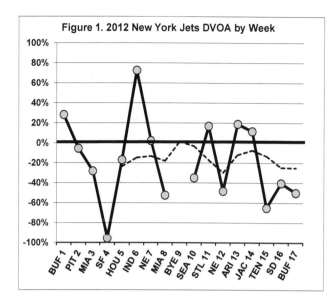

Figure 1. 2012 New York Jets DVOA by Week

Still, there's a pretty big difference between Manning and Sanchez. Manning won his first Super Bowl in 2007, his third season as a full-time starter, and he was trending upward by 2008. Although Manning was still (barely) below average in completion percentage and yards per attempt that season, it also was the year he made his first Pro Bowl, and Manning posted impressive rate numbers with respect to both sacks and interceptions. It takes the greenest of glasses to project a similar career arc for Sanchez. And with a $13.1M cap number in 2014, Sanchez will be out of New York after the season unless he turns into Eli Manning overnight. Sanchez' bloated salary is the only reason he's on the 2013 roster, as releasing him would have counted for more against the cap than keeping him.

That said, even though Sanchez won't ever live up to his first-round status, it's also unlikely he will play so poorly for the second year in a row. The Jets ranked 30th in pass DVOA, and Sanchez ranked dead last in DYAR. Even for Sanchez, throwing five more interceptions than touchdowns is uncharacteristic; he threw 43 touchdowns against 31 interceptions in 2010 and 2011. And if nothing else, new offensive coordinator Marty Mornhinweg represents a major upgrade in the area of "not being Tony Sparano."

The Jets also selected Geno Smith with the 39th pick in the draft, so the team finally has a backup who is neither in his 40s (Mark Brunell) nor has a completion percentage in the 40s. Smith fell in the draft because of his inconsistent play at West Virginia. At his best, he was video game good, as evidenced by his stat line against Baylor: 45-of-51 for 656 yards and eight touchdowns. But Smith slumped in the second half of his senior season, and his flaws were exposed as the team finished 2-5 down the stretch.

Smith doesn't possess top-end arm strength. His high completion percentage (71.2 percent last season) was a function of a very passer-friendly offense, and he needs to improve on both his pre- and post-snap reads. But he's an athletic quarterback with a good arm who can make the big play, even if he's streaky and prone to mistakes. If he hits, he's Tony Romo. If he misses, well, the Jets already have one Mark Sanchez on the roster. And while some folks will fawn over last year's college stats (42 touchdowns, just six interceptions, and 8.1 yards per attempt), remember that his head coach was Dana Holgorsen, the same man responsible for Brandon Weeden's outstanding numbers at Oklahoma State in 2010.

But the Jets are hoping that they won't be forced to rely on the passing game for big plays in 2013. New York had just four runs of over 20 yards last season, tied for the second low-

est mark in the league (the Colts had just two). Shonn Greene was responsible for only two of those runs (Tim Tebow and Joe McKnight had the others), but the plodding back is now in Tennessee. The Jets added Chris Ivory (New Orleans) and Mike Goodson (Oakland) to replace Greene, and both players are upgrades in the excitement department.

As an undrafted rookie in 2010, Ivory excelled for the Saints in a part-time role: He finished in the top ten in both DVOA and DYAR and ranked first in Success Rate. But when the Saints added Darren Sproles and Mark Ingram in 2011, Ivory's playing time decreased even as his production stayed strong. With Ivory, there are two big questions: can he stay healthy, and can he be as successful against defenses not focused on stopping Drew Brees? At his best, Ivory is a powerful runner with more agility than Greene, making him a good under-the-radar addition for a cap-strapped team.

Ivory doesn't need to be a 300-carry back, either. Assuming Goodson makes the team (he was arrested in May on drug possession and weapon charges), he gives the Jets the explosive back New York was looking for when they drafted Joe McKnight. On just 35 carries last year with the Raiders, Goodson had three runs of over 20 yards. Goodson caught every pass thrown to him last year, and had the most receptions (16) of any player with a 100 percent catch rate. He should have a bigger role in New York, and could be a fantasy sleeper.

Of course, Goodson has long been one of the NFL's great teases. He has started only three games in his career, all of which came in November 2010 with the Panthers. In those games, Goodson totaled 400 yards from scrimmage, and twice rushed for 100 yards. But like Ivory, he has struggled to stay healthy, with an added side of fumbling problems.

With Marty Mornhinweg and his West Coast Offense now in New York, that could mean good things for Goodson. Regardless of system, expecting consistent production from either Santonio Holmes or Kellen Winslow, Jr., is foolhardy, so the Jets may wind up throwing a bunch of short passes to the running backs. Over the last three seasons, LeSean McCoy has caught 180 passes in just 42 games while playing under Mornhinweg. Last year, Greene led all Jets backs with 19 catches, but a healthy Goodson—who is a better receiver than Ivory—

could easily double that number. The offense won't be great, but fewer turnovers from the quarterback and more big plays from the running backs could go a long way towards making this unit respectable. The Jets' average rank in offensive DVOA for the first three years of Ryan and Sanchez was 19th. That's not above average, but it's also a long way from ranking 30th.

If you're still wondering why Rex Ryan was brought back, it's because Woody Johnson knows Ryan can coach a defense. Even without Revis, the Jets defense still ranked ninth in DVOA, and the future is bright for 2013. The most successful 3-4 defenses have at least one dominant edge rusher at linebacker, and that's been the Achilles heel for the Jets defense since even before Ryan's arrival. For years, Bryan Thomas and Calvin Pace graded out as "barely satisfactory" in those roles, but they have been the ex-girlfriend the team clings to the morning after their one-night stands (Vernon Gholston, Jason Taylor, Aaron Maybin, Jamaal Westerman). This year, it's former defensive end Quinton Coples making the position switch, although he's a curious fit as an edge rusher (as we detail later in this chapter). In any event, Coples is much more athletic and a more disruptive force than Bryan Thomas, and the former first-round pick will play with his hand in the dirt more often than the typical outside linebacker. Pace and former San Diego Charger Antwan Barnes will share the other spot, but neither are long-term solutions. The Jets will be in the market for a 3-4 outside linebacker again next year in what is starting to look like a football production of Goldilocks: Aaron Maybin was too light, Coples is too heavy, but next year, the Jets hope to find a pass rusher that's just right.

With Revis gone, the best player on the defense is now Muhammad Wilkerson, who has become one of the best five-technique linemen in the league after just two seasons. (He and Calais Campbell get to fight for J.J. Watt's scraps, and then everyone else has to fight for *their* scraps.) The other defensive end spot will be manned by rookie Sheldon Richardson, the player the Jets selected with the pick they got from Tampa Bay for Revis. Draftniks considered the Missouri product one of the most versatile defensive linemen in the draft—the Tigers even used him as a spy against Heisman Trophy winner Johnny Manziel—but Richardson is probably best suited as a one-gap player in a four-man front. The Jets use both three- and four-man fronts, and Richardson's versatility should suit the scheme well. When the Jets make Coples the fourth down lineman, Richardson will shift to the three-technique, where his pass-rushing skill set will be on full display.

The only question mark on the line is at nose tackle. With Sione Pouha hampered by injuries most of 2012, the Jets rush defense regressed. After allowing 130-plus rushing yards just nine times from 2009 to 2011, New York let opponents hit that mark in eight different games last year. Curiously, the team ignored this position on draft day; as talented as Richardson is, drafting Star Lotulelei and keeping Quinton Coples at end would have been made a lot more sense in terms of need. But the Jets have to trust Rex Ryan when it comes to the front seven—if not, where else can they trust him? As it stands, the Jets appear to be banking on some combination of Kenrick Ellis, Antonio Garay, and Damon Harrison to hold down the middle of the defense.

Even in a post-Revis world, the cornerback position remains one of the strengths of the team. After drafting Dee Milliner (Alabama) with the ninth overall pick, the Jets' top three cornerbacks will have first-round pedigrees for the fourth year in a row. For you trivia buffs out there, the Jets and Bengals were the only teams to field three former first-round picks at cornerback each of the last three years, and both teams will make it four straight in 2013. The real concern in the secondary is at safety. Dawan Landry, last seen being mediocre in Jacksonville, will be the strong safety, and that's *not* the problem spot. Josh Bush and Antonio Allen, each low on both pedigree and production, will battle to start at free safety. Considering the struggles of inside linebacker David Harris in pass coverage, the Jets could again be very vulnerable against the tight end this year. New York ranked 27th in DVOA against tight ends in 2011, and were much improved last year (14th) largely due to the presence of safeties LaRon Landry and Yeremiah Bell, who are now in Indianapolis and Arizona, respectively. At least the Jets can take solace in seeing their biggest rival having a bit of trouble at the tight end position these days.

For years, the Jets spent the offseason trying to plug leaks as part of a Super Bowl push. With a new general manager who was given a long leash and a lot of bad contracts, this offseason wasn't about maximizing the team's chances in 2013 but getting the team on the right long-term track. It may take some time, but the outlook on offense is promising for 2014 if Smith can match his potential. For this year, the goal is more modest: simply holding onto the ball. The Jets have 71 turnovers the last two years, a number only eclipsed by the Eagles (with 75). Yet despite the focus on the future, this season is not necessarily a total write-off. With a younger, faster, and potentially better defense (remember, they didn't have Revis for 14 games last year), a playoff push is not out of the question if the offense can improve from embarrassing to mediocre.

Chase Stuart

2012 Jets Stats by Week

Wk	vs.	W-L	PF	PA	YDF	YDA	TO	Total	Off	Def	ST
1	BUF	W	48	28	384	390	3	28%	1%	-6%	22%
2	at PIT	L	10	27	219	331	-1	-6%	19%	21%	-4%
3	at MIA	W	23	20	388	381	0	-28%	-33%	4%	9%
4	SF	L	0	34	145	381	-4	-96%	-71%	17%	-8%
5	HOU	L	17	23	286	378	-1	-17%	-38%	7%	28%
6	IND	W	35	9	351	298	4	73%	29%	-31%	13%
7	at NE	L	26	29	403	381	-1	2%	-6%	-14%	-5%
8	MIA	L	9	30	363	236	-1	-52%	-31%	-10%	-31%
9	BYE										
10	at SEA	L	7	28	185	363	-1	-35%	-41%	-10%	-4%
11	at STL	W	27	13	289	281	3	17%	1%	-32%	-15%
12	NE	L	19	49	405	475	-4	-48%	-13%	26%	-10%
13	ARI	W	7	6	289	137	-3	19%	-18%	-43%	-6%
14	at JAC	W	17	10	270	291	0	12%	-12%	-15%	8%
15	at TEN	L	10	14	253	294	-5	-65%	-70%	0%	4%
16	SD	L	17	27	225	223	-2	-40%	-22%	7%	-12%
17	BUF	L	9	28	332	334	-1	-50%	-30%	7%	-13%

Trends and Splits

	Offense	Rank	Defense	Rank
Total DVOA	-20.7%	30	-4.2%	9
Unadjusted VOA	-19.9%	29	-6.0%	9
Weighted Trend	-21.6%	30	-8.9%	10
Variance	7.5%	21	3.8%	7
Average Opponent	-0.7%	11	-1.2%	19
Passing	-25.3%	30	-2.6%	10
Rushing	-8.2%	21	-5.8%	15
First Down	-13.4%	26	-3.3%	13
Second Down	-24.1%	31	-14.1%	5
Third Down	-29.0%	29	8.0%	24
First Half	-23.2%	31	-7.3%	9
Second Half	-17.9%	27	-1.4%	13
Red Zone	-28.8%	29	7.3%	22
Late and Close	-22.7%	26	-9.4%	12

Five-Year Performance

Year	W-L	Pyth W	Est W	PF	PA	TO	Total	Rk	Off	Rk	Def	Rk	ST	Rk	Off AGL	Rk	Def AGL	Rk	Off Age	Rk	Def Age	Rk	ST Age	Rk
2008	9-7	9.3	8.7	405	356	-1	4.0%	17	0.0%	18	-0.8%	14	3.2%	8	7.3	2	10.5	5	29.1	2	27.4	15	26.7	15
2009	9-7	11.4	9.2	342	236	+1	25.8%	9	-12.5%	22	-25.5%	1	2.8%	6	4.1	1	21.0	12	28.1	4	27.6	7	27.0	5
2010	11-5	9.8	10.1	367	304	+9	18.7%	6	2.1%	16	-10.9%	5	5.8%	5	8.9	4	33.0	23	27.6	14	28.1	7	26.5	13
2011	8-8	8.4	8.4	377	363	-3	13.5%	10	-8.3%	21	-16.1%	2	5.6%	4	9.2	2	21.2	12	27.6	12	27.5	9	26.2	17
2012	6-10	5.3	5.6	281	375	-14	-18.0%	27	-20.7%	30	-4.2%	9	-1.5%	21	37.7	22	41.0	23	26.6	19	28.1	2	26.0	16

2012 Performance Based on Most Common Personnel Groups

NYJ Offense					NYJ Offense vs. Opponents				NYJ Defense				NYJ Defense vs. Opponents			
Pers	Freq	Yds	DVOA	Run%	Pers	Freq	Yds	DVOA	Pers	Freq	Yds	DVOA	Pers	Freq	Yds	DVOA
1.1	34%	4.8	-28.4%	15%	4-3-4	37%	4.8	-21.9%	3-4-4	25%	4.6	-14.0%	1.1	37%	5.4	-5.1%
1.2	21%	4.8	-25.8%	44%	Nickel Even	25%	4.8	-15.5%	Nickel Even	23%	5.7	-14.0%	1.2	31%	5.7	5.2%
2.1	13%	5.4	-11.0%	60%	3-4-4	22%	5.4	3.9%	Dime+	17%	5.6	8.7%	2.1	11%	4.5	-21.6%
2.2	8%	4.0	-20.6%	87%	Nickel Odd	9%	3.5	-44.0%	Nickel Odd	16%	6.3	18.0%	2.2	6%	3.2	-26.2%
61.2	5%	3.5	-23.0%	90%	Dime+	4%	5.6	-51.9%	4-3-4	14%	4.7	-7.5%	1.0	5%	7.8	37.6%
													1.3	4%	4.5	-17.9%

Strategic Tendencies

Run/Pass		Rk	Formation		Rk	Pass Rush		Rk	Secondary		Rk	Strategy		Rk
Runs, first half	46%	3	Form: Single Back	57%	27	Rush 3	9.0%	9	4 DB	40%	25	Play action	17%	24
Runs, first down	62%	1	Form: Empty Back	7%	11	Rush 4	56.7%	24	5 DB	39%	25	Avg Box (Off)	6.59	4
Runs, second-long	29%	22	Pers: 3+ WR	40%	28	Rush 5	26.9%	9	6+ DB	17%	6	Avg Box (Def)	6.41	12
Runs, power sit.	57%	12	Pers: 4+ WR	2%	13	Rush 6+	7.3%	14	CB by Sides	59%	30	Offensive Pace	30.43	15
Runs, behind 2H	33%	7	Pers: 2+ TE/6+ OL	47%	5	Sacks by LB	48.3%	12	DB Blitz	22%	1	Defensive Pace	30.45	21
Pass, ahead 2H	24%	32	Shotgun/Pistol	39%	26	Sacks by DB	10.0%	8	Hole in Zone	6%	25	Go for it on 4th	1.42	3

The Jets' offense was so bad that they somehow managed a horrible -41.7% DVOA when using play action. The league average with play action was 21.9% DVOA. Nine of Sanchez's 18 interceptions came off play action. Perhaps that's why the run-first Jets were actually below average on frequency using play action, especially on second downs, where they used it on just 14 percent of pass plays (31st in the NFL). ☞ Gang Green recovered 11 of 14 fumbles on defense. ☞ The Jets had the smallest gap in the league between DVOA when bringing pass pressure (-56.4% DVOA, 3.1 yards per play) and DVOA without pressure (13.4% DVOA, 6.6 yards per play). Does this signal the quality of the Jets' cornerbacks, or the impotence of their pass rush? ☞ The Jets blitzed a defensive back on 21.8 percent of pass plays; no other defense was above 18.5 percent. ☞ In 2011, the Jets used quarter personnel (seven or more defensive backs) on 11 percent of plays, five times as much any other defense. Last season they were more in line with the rest of the NFL; they still led the league, but with only 3.7 percent of snaps.

Passing

Player	DYAR	DVOA	Plays	NtYds	Avg	YAC	C%	TD	Int
M.Sanchez	-593	-29.4%	487	2676	5.5	4.0	54.6%	13	18
G.McElroy	-82	-44.6%	42	146	3.5	6.5	61.3%	1	1
T.Tebow*	-9	-24.2%	10	32	3.2	4.2	75.0%	0	0

Rushing

Player	DYAR	DVOA	Plays	Yds	Avg	TD	Fum	Suc
S.Greene*	49	-4.5%	275	1044	3.8	9	4	52%
B.Powell	63	5.6%	110	437	4.0	4	0	50%
T.Tebow*	-26	-26.1%	33	106	3.2	0	0	-
J.McKnight	12	1.7%	30	182	6.1	0	1	47%
M.Sanchez	-67	-85.4%	15	30	2.0	0	3	-
G.McElroy	2	-4.7%	6	32	5.3	0	0	-
J.Kerley	-6	-63.6%	5	6	1.2	0	0	-
C.Ivory	33	12.5%	40	217	5.4	2	0	48%
M.Goodson	37	24.8%	33	219	6.6	0	0	48%

Receiving

Player	DYAR	DVOA	Plays	Ctch	Yds	Y/C	YAC	TD	C%
J.Kerley	14	-8.1%	97	57	832	14.6	5.3	2	59%
S.Hill	-19	-15.4%	47	21	252	12.0	1.5	3	45%
C.Schilens*	20	-5.6%	41	28	294	10.5	1.9	2	68%
S.Holmes	-3	-2.8%	41	20	272	13.6	5.2	1	49%
B.Edwards*	-3	-1.4%	18	10	125	12.5	2.4	0	56%
C.Gates	-26	-16.1%	35	16	224	14.0	1.3	0	46%
M.Gilyard*	-27	-80.0%	5	2	15	7.5	5.5	0	40%
B.Obomanu	-20	-37.0%	9	4	58	14.5	5.3	0	44%
J.Cumberland	-12	-8.5%	53	29	359	12.4	3.9	3	55%
D.Keller*	76	26.4%	36	28	317	11.3	3.3	2	78%
K.Reuland	-15	-10.7%	16	11	83	7.5	4.5	0	69%
B.Powell	-22	-24.7%	36	17	140	8.2	7.1	0	47%
S.Greene*	-47	-41.4%	31	19	151	7.9	6.9	0	61%
L.Hilliard	-17	-46.9%	9	4	23	5.8	3.6	0	44%
M.Goodson	83	70.1%	18	18	197	10.9	12.9	1	100%

Offensive Line

Player	Pos	Age	GS	Snaps	Pen	Sk	Pass	Run	Player	Pos	Age	GS	Snaps	Pen	Sk	Pass	Run
D'Brickashaw Ferguson	LT	30	16/16	1073	2	2.3	12.8	2	Vladimir Ducasse	OT	26	16/0	273	1	0.5	2.5	2
Austin Howard	RT	26	16/16	1072	4	9	22	2	Jason Smith*	OT	27	16/0	256	2	1	1	1
Nick Mangold	C	29	16/16	1065	2	2.3	6.8	1.5	Willie Colon	LG	30	11/11	713	12	4	6	9
Brandon Moore*	RG	33	16/16	1062	4	2.5	11.5	4	Stephen Peterman	RG	31	16/16	1200	4	6	20.5	2
Matt Slauson*	LG	27	16/16	820	3	1.3	2.8	3									

Year	Yards	ALY	Rk	Power	Rk	Stuff	Rk	2nd Lev	Rk	Open Field	Rk	Sacks	ASR	Rk	Short	Long	F-Start	Cont.
2010	4.48	4.56	3	76%	2	12%	1	1.15	14	0.56	23	28	5.4%	8	9	15	19	43
2011	3.87	4.23	8	66%	10	16%	4	1.06	28	0.32	32	40	6.7%	17	16	19	26	41
2012	4.00	4.38	5	67%	10	16%	2	1.06	24	0.45	29	47	8.6%	30	16	19	16	48
2012 ALY by direction:			Left End 4.27 (14)			Left Tackle 4.06 (17)			Mid/Guard 4.27 (9)				Right Tackle 4.82 (3)			Right End 5.92 (2)		

No matter how bad the rest of the offense has been over the past few years, the Jets' line has given the quarterback time to throw and made nice big holes for the running backs. It's not their fault that neither the quarterback nor the running backs have been able to do much with that blocking. Unfortunately, after another solid year—four-fifths of a strong year, at least—free agency is forcing change and a loss of continuity that could neutralize the only strength of New York's offense. Left tackle D'Brickashaw Ferguson, center Nick Mangold, and right guard Brandon Moore had played together every year since 2006; left guard Matt Slauson joined them in 2010. Moore and Slauson are now gone after the Jets decided their prices were too high in free agency, but instead of replacing them with young and developing talent, the Jets replaced them with two fellow veterans. New left guard Colon was good for the Steelers last season, but he's three years older than the man he replaces and missed nearly all of 2010 and 2011 with injuries. New right guard Peterman had pretty much run out of gas in Detroit; last year, our game charters recorded him with more blown blocks on pass plays than any guard except Mike McGlynn of the Colts (of course, the Lions did set a new record for pass attempts). Fortunately, knowing these veterans may not have much time left, the Jets used two mid-round picks on developmental linemen. Both third-rounder Brian Winters (Kent State) and fifth-rounder Obay Aboushi (Virginia) played left tackle in college but will move to right tackle or guard in the pros, and both will need a lot of technique work to learn how to pass-block in the NFL.

The three linemen carried over from last season include not just the two building blocks Ferguson and Mangold but also the weak link, right tackle Austin Howard. Howard was at least better than the man he replaced at the start of last year, Wayne Hunter, but this may be one of the great examples of "damning with faint praise" in the history of human existence. Howard was good on runs, but he finished among the top ten tackles in the league for blown blocks on pass plays, and our charters blamed more sacks directly on Howard than on the rest of the Jets' starters put together.

Defensive Front Seven

Defensive Line	Age	Pos	Snaps	Plays	TmPct	Overall Rk	Stop	Dfts	BTkl	Runs	vs. Run St%	Rk	RuYd	Rk	Pass Rush Sack	Hit	Hur	Tips
Muhammad Wilkerson	24	DE	910	74	9.5%	4	60	17	3	60	82%	15	2.0	18	5	10	19	4
Mike DeVito*	29	DE	629	52	6.7%	17	37	6	2	48	73%	46	2.4	29	1	0	3	0
Quinton Coples	23	DE	503	31	4.0%	57	25	17	1	22	77%	26	2.4	33	5.5	8	7	2
Sione Pouha*	34	DT	305	30	5.1%	24	22	3	1	28	71%	48	2.9	59	1	0	0	1
Kenrick Ellis	26	DT	233	17	2.9%	--	15	4	0	16	94%	--	1.7	--	0	0	1	0
Antonio Garay	34	DT	148	16	4.0%	--	11	2	0	15	67%	--	2.9	--	1	1	1.5	0

Linebackers	Age	Pos	Snaps	Plays	TmPct	Overall Rk	Stop	Dfts	BTkl	Pass Rush Sack	Hit	Hur	Tips	Runs	vs. Run St%	Rk	Yds	Rk	Tgts	vs. Pass Suc%	Rk	AdjYd	Rk	PD
David Harris	29	ILB	1062	126	16.2%	17	68	16	7	3	3	6	0	85	62%	72	3.7	75	32	44%	59	6.2	22	2
Calvin Pace	33	OLB	1005	56	7.2%	80	35	12	5	3	5	22	1	41	66%	51	3.1	39	18	47%	49	5.3	18	1
Bart Scott*	33	OLB	574	61	8.4%	73	44	15	5	2.5	2	5.5	0	50	72%	27	2.1	13	17	35%	71	12.1	75	1
Garrett McIntyre	29	OLB	407	28	3.6%	--	20	8	2	3.5	2	5	1	21	71%	--	2.2	--	2	50%	--	7.2	--	0
Bryan Thomas*	34	OLB	373	25	4.3%	109	17	9	0	2.5	2	5.5	1	19	68%	37	1.2	4	3	34%	--	2.4	--	0
Demario Davis	24	ILB	308	27	3.5%	--	13	2	2	0	0	6	0	19	63%	--	3.2	--	7	21%	--	8.0	--	0

Year	Yards	ALY	Rk	Power	Rk	Stuff	Rk	2nd Level	Rk	Open Field	Rk	Sacks	ASR	Rk	Short	Long
2010	3.47	3.64	5	67%	25	19%	16	0.88	3	0.42	3	40	7.0%	10	18	16
2011	3.86	3.65	2	45%	2	22%	6	1.04	6	0.72	13	35	7.3%	12	6	23
2012	4.33	4.09	18	56%	8	16%	27	1.10	6	0.89	23	30	6.2%	20	9	19

| 2012 ALY by direction: | Left End 3.59 (11) | Left Tackle 4.21 (21) | Mid/Guard 4.16 (19) | Right Tackle 4.29 (25) | Right End 3.64 (12) |

Last season brought a decline in nearly all of our front seven metrics, so the buzzwords for the Jets front seven this offseason are "change" and "flexibility." However, it's hard to see how much more flexible the Jets can be. The Jets were one of just three defenses that we marked down playing both 3-4 and 4-3 at least 10 percent of the time, and in sub packages they alternated between odd and even looks.

With the linebackers aging, the star of the Jets' front seven is now defensive end Muhammad Wilkerson. Wilkerson was excellent against the run, and though he couldn't match J.J. Watt's ridiculous season, he still produced far more pass pressure than you usually see from a five-tech end. The new starter opposite Wilkerson will be first-round pick Sheldon Richardson, who should kick inside to tackle when the Jets use a four-man front. Richardson has a freakish combination of size and athleticism, and in his senior season at Missouri he led all SEC interior linemen with 75 tackles and added on 10.5 tackles for loss and 4.5 sacks. He also has experience as a stand-up rusher and dropping into short zone coverage. Again, the buzzword is "flexibility."

Richardson's arrival moves last year's first-round pick, Quinton Coples, from defensive end to outside linebacker when the Jets are using three-man fronts. That would get all the Jets' best players on the field, but it may not be the best use of Coples' talents. Coples is listed at 285 pounds; last year, no outside linebacker had a listed weight above 270 (although Mario Williams will be a linebacker again this year at 290). Coples had an underwhelming SackSEER rating of 25.4 percent, mainly because of poor performance at the Combine in the drills which make up our "Explosion Index," including the 40-yard dash, broad jump, and vertical jump. In college, his best year rushing the passer came as a defensive tackle, not a defensive end. His skill set calls for overwhelming blockers with strength, not dominating them with speed and movement, and the lack of a first-step burst will hurt him more as a linebacker than it would with his hand on the ground. Calvin Pace will be back at the other outside linebacker spot; he was cut in February to make salary cap space, then re-signed to a much cheaper one-year, $1 million contract. Pace may not have recorded many sacks last year, but our pass pressure numbers show he still spent a lot of time harassing opposing quarterbacks. Both Pace and Coples will spend plenty of time with a hand on the ground in passing situations. They're backed up by free-agent signing Antwan Barnes, who, after an 11-sack season in 2011, had only five hurries and three sacks on fewer than 200 snaps for San Diego last year. On the inside, David Harris continues to decline as he nears age 30 and is far from the run-stopping machine he once was, but he's still a respectable starter. Demario Davis is the kind of aggressive, hard-working player that Rex Ryan loves. As a rookie, he played over Bart Scott in sub packages and showed up with some big plays on film. It's important that he plays well as he moves into the starting lineup this year, because the backup inside linebackers are special teams-only roster fodder like Josh Mauga and Nick Bellore. On passing downs when the Jets field only one inside linebacker, Harris will likely take a backseat to the more athletic Davis.

The Jets cut veteran Sione Pouha and look ready to hand the nose tackle position to 2011 third-round pick Kenrick Ellis. However, Ellis hasn't developed much in his first two seasons and there are signs the Jets are a bit lukewarm on his talents. He didn't get on the field much last year despite Pouha struggling with back problems, and he'll get competition for the nose tackle role from ex-Chargers veteran Antonio Garay. A sleeper to watch here is Damon "Big Snacks" Harrison, a second-year development project from NAIA-level William Penn. He was one of the team's stars in the 2012 preseason, played the run well as a rookie, and looked good this summer in OTAs.

Defensive Secondary

Secondary	Age	Pos	Snaps	Plays	TmPct	Rk	Stop	Dfts	BTkl	Runs	St%	Rk	Yds	Rk	Tgts	Tgt%	Rk	Dist	Suc%	Rk	APaYd	Rk	PD	Int
											vs. Run					vs. Pass								
Yeremiah Bell*	35	SS	1058	90	11.6%	25	26	8	4	45	38%	36	8.2	54	29	7.1%	31	14.0	48%	62	8.8	57	2	0
Antonio Cromartie	29	CB	1035	48	6.2%	77	24	10	3	9	56%	20	9.6	74	84	20.8%	18	15.2	60%	10	6.2	10	14	3
LaRon Landry*	29	FS	1019	106	13.6%	8	41	11	9	60	42%	23	5.9	20	42	10.4%	9	14.6	55%	33	7.6	41	6	2
Kyle Wilson	26	CB	947	52	6.7%	70	20	7	5	14	64%	7	6.6	45	74	18.2%	39	15.6	52%	41	7.2	34	4	1
Ellis Lankster	26	CB	326	35	4.8%	--	15	10	7	7	0%	--	8.3	--	37	9.8%	--	11.7	61%	--	5.4	--	6	2
Eric Smith*	30	FS	321	19	3.3%	75	7	4	1	7	29%	56	5.9	18	17	5.4%	56	9.3	61%	20	8.4	51	4	1
Darrelle Revis*	28	CB	91	15	15.4%	--	6	3	1	6	17%	--	9.3	--	9	16.8%	--	8.1	74%	--	3.4	--	2	1
Dawan Landry	31	SS	1139	102	11.5%	26	33	9	6	62	39%	35	6.5	28	30	6.8%	33	10.2	51%	46	7.1	34	2	1

Year	Pass D Rank	vs. #1 WR	Rk	vs. #2 WR	Rk	vs. Other WR	Rk	vs. TE	Rk	vs. RB	Rk
2010	7	-7.5%	12	12.2%	23	-9.6%	11	-3.4%	9	-6.0%	9
2011	2	-32.5%	1	-25.1%	2	-3.1%	18	23.3%	27	-14.7%	4
2012	10	-19.4%	5	-4.9%	12	-0.9%	16	-3.1%	14	4.1%	19

Football Outsiders has now been keeping cornerback charting stats since 2005, and one of the shocking issues is just how inconsistent they tend to be from year to year. We don't know yet if this is an issue with how we track coverage, a sample-size problem, or something endemic to the cornerback position. However, we do know that only two cornerbacks have finished in the top ten for Adjusted Yards per Pass twice in the past three years, and one of them plays for the Jets. Notice we didn't say *played* for the Jets, because the cornerback in question is Antonio Cromartie, not Darrelle Revis.[1] In fact, Cromartie has had two-and-a-half stellar years out of the last three, since he improved significantly in the second half of 2011. When Cromartie was this good in 2010, we thought it might be a byproduct of the way Darrelle Revis forced quarterbacks to play against the Jets' secondary. Now that he's played this well with Revis battling injuries (second half of 2011) or gone altogether (second half of 2012), I think we can safely say that Cromartie is really quite good on his own. Kyle Wilson improved in his third season and moved into the starting lineup when Revis went down, but he'll have to hold off stud rookie Dee Milliner to hold onto that spot. Milliner is a big, physical, and intelligent, with press coverage experience and strong play-recognition skills. There are some worries about his injury history (which includes a torn labrum, a rod in his tibia, and hernia surgery) and the fact that Nick Saban doesn't teach his cornerbacks at Alabama to backpedal. At safety, the Jets swapped out LeRon Landry for his brother Dawan in free agency; Dawan is the older and less talented brother, but he's also the healthier one. Two low-round 2012 picks, Josh Bush and Antonio Allen, will battle in camp for the other safety spot.

Special Teams

Year	DVOA	Rank	FG/XP	Rank	Net Kick	Rank	Kick Ret	Rank	Net Punt	Rank	Punt Ret	Rank	Hidden	Rank
2010	5.8%	5	-2.2	25	-0.1	17	19.4	1	14.8	2	-3.2	21	5.9	5
2011	5.6%	4	-0.1	15	11.2	1	10.8	2	13.2	3	-7.0	25	-8.3	26
2012	-1.5%	21	-5.0	28	-0.2	17	4.4	8	-7.9	24	1.3	14	-6.7	26

The great Mike Westhoff Era sputtered out to an ignominious end, as the Jets finished 21st in our special teams values after ranking in the top ten in nine of the previous ten seasons. Nick Folk had three field goals blocked and missed three others; he also ranked in the bottom six in gross kickoff value for the third straight season. If ever there was a chance for a team to spend a late pick on a kicker without anyone laughing at them, this would have been it, but instead the only camp competition for Folk will be ex-Nebraska walk-on Brett Maher. At least Maher has some promise on kickoffs, with nearly 60 percent touchbacks in his senior year. Robert Malone is nothing special as a punter and will also get camp competition, from Boston College grad Ryan Quigley. Returns are in better hands with Joe McKnight on kickoffs and Jeremy Kerley on punts. Coverage teams are led by linebacker Nick Bellore and cornerback Ellis Lankster and should rebound after a down year.

Coaching Staff

Offensive coordinator Marty Mornhinweg got a lot of the credit when Michael Vick finally calmed down a bit and reached his potential as quarterback of the 2010 Eagles. The Jets want him to instill that same improvement in discipline and consistency as he tries to mold Geno Smith into an NFL quarterback. Hopefully, Mornhinweg can avoid indoctrinating Smith with whatever mistaken lesson made Vick revert to his old bad habits and inconsistent ways in 2011, *Flowers for Algernon*-style. It will be interesting to see how Mornhinweg merges his pass-first mentality with Ryan's desire for "ground and pound," but the Mornhinweg passing game is not going to just be a bunch of little crossing patterns. Despite his West Coast offense reputation,

---

[1] OK, it's a bit of a trick, because obviously Revis didn't have enough pass targets to even be ranked in 2012. In case you are wondering, the other cornerback to appear in the top ten twice is Antoine Winfield.

Mornhinweg's Eagles teams often were close to the top of the league in big downfield passing plays. The Jets players seem very happy with Mornhinweg. "Marty's like a Cadillac," Jeremy Kerley told *Newsday* during the June minicamp. "He's laid back. He's cool. He gives us leeway to be ourselves." Well, if there's anything that's been missing from the Jets locker room the last few years, it's enough leeway for players to be themselves.

With Mike Pettine leaving town, the Jets gave the title of defensive coordinator to former defensive backs coach Dennis Thurman, although Ryan himself will take over defensive play-calling duties in 2013. The Jets also promoted their new special teams coordinator from within, tapping Mike Westhoff's assistant Ben Kotwica. Kotwica has an interesting background: he was a three-year starter at Army and defensive captain of the 1996 team that won 10 games, the most in Army history. After graduation, he flew helicopters in the early years of Operation Desert Storm and was a high school coach before he was brought to the Jets by his Army head coach, and former Jets defensive coordinator, Bob Sutton.

Oakland Raiders

2012 Record: 4-12	Total DVOA: -27.8% (29th)	2013 Mean Projection: 6.4 wins	On the Clock (0-4): 24%
Pythagorean Wins: 4.1 (29th)	Offense: -9.5% (23rd)	Postseason Odds: 15.0%	Mediocrity (5-7): 44%
Snap-Weighted Age: 27.2 (10th)	Defense: 12.5% (29th)	Super Bowl Odds: 0.6%	Playoff Contender (8-10): 27%
Average Opponent: -3.8% (25th)	Special Teams: -5.8% (31st)	Proj. Avg. Opponent: -3.2% (25th)	Super Bowl Contender (11+): 5%

2012: Oakland's salary cap mess finally forces a reckoning.

2013: Fables of the reconstruction.

It is hard to envision any reconstruction project more substantial than the one Reggie McKenzie inherited upon taking over as the Raiders general manager in 2012. McKenzie still has not even really reached the building phase of this reconstruction project—his first two offseasons have been spent doing demolition work. There were an ungodly number of Al Davis mistakes that McKenzie has had to fix.

McKenzie got his feet wet last offseason releasing four would-be starters: tight end Kevin Boss, cornerback Stanford Routt, defensive tackle John Henderson, and defensive end Kamerion Wimbley. He also did not re-sign running back Michael Bush, quarterback Jason Campbell, center Samson Satele, wide receiver Chaz Schilens, defensive end Trevor Scott, or cornerback Lito Sheppard.

After spending the 2012 season evaluating the roster (and, likely, confirming what he probably assumed from the get-go, which was that this collection of players did not work), McKenzie brought out the bulldozers this past spring. He chose to not re-sign 12 regular contributors whose contracts were up: guard Cooper Carlisle; defensive ends Desmond Bryant and Matt Shaughnessy; linebackers Omar Gaither and Phillip Wheeler; running back Mike Goodson; safeties Matt Giordano and Mike Mitchell; wide receiver Derek Hagan; punter Shane Lechler; tight end Brandon Myers; and cornerback Shawntae Spencer.

Six more major contributors were either released or traded. That so many of them were former high draft choices and/or carried big salaries speaks to the overwhelming ineptitude with which this organization had previously been managed. Take a look at the list in all its glory:

- Wide receiver Darrius Heyward-Bey: drafted seventh overall in 2009; scheduled salary for 2013 was $8.0 million.
- Defensive back Michael Huff: drafted seventh overall in 2006; scheduled salary: $8 million.
- Linebacker Rolando McClain: drafted eighth overall in 2010; scheduled salary: $4.1 million (release caused a cap hit of $7.3 million).
- Defensive tackle Tommy Kelly: scheduled salary: $6.3 million.
- Defensive tackle Richard Seymour: scheduled salary: $13.7 million.
- Quarterback Carson Palmer: traded along with a seventh-round pick (219th overall) to Arizona in exchange for Arizona's sixth-round pick (176th overall) and a conditional 2014 draft choice. Was originally acquired in a 2011 trade with the Bengals in exchange for the Raiders' 2012 first-rounder and their 2013 second-rounder. Scheduled salary for 2013 had been $13 million.

With all of these moves (plus a few from previous years), the Raiders have a mind-boggling $49 million in dead money eating up their cap this season. That's barely one bad contract less than the entire payroll of their Coliseum co-tenants, the Athletics ($60.3 million). With 38 percent of the team's cap space dedicated to players who are no longer around, McKenzie had roughly $78 million with which to fill out a 53-man roster. Most NFL teams are spending over $120 million on their 2013 rosters.

McKenzie did not necessarily *have* to make so many cap-eating moves in 2013, but given how much the roster demolition efforts were delaying the rebuilding efforts, he chose to take his medicine and get past mistakes out of Oakland's present. Why keep a few expensive veterans around another year or two if all they're going to do is give you a better chance at getting a 2014 first-round pick in the low teens instead of the single digits? This isn't to say that McKenzie is tanking this season. He probably isn't even thinking about his team's youth movement this way. But that doesn't mean this is not what's essentially going on.

McKenzie is taking the realistic, smart approach of getting his team a clean slate as soon as possible. This in mind, any suggestion that head coach Dennis Allen's job could be on the line in 2013 must be presumed as patently false. Unless McKenzie is as flaky and impatient as the last Raiders boss, Allen should be able to coach this season knowing full well that he's not being evaluated completely on the bottom line that is wins and losses. Next year, this will change, as the Raiders are expected to have nearly $70 million in cap space. But that's a story for another day and another book, called *Football Outsiders Almanac 2014.*

Smart as McKenzie's "clean slate ASAP" approach might be, it has created an awkward "one foot in, one foot out" scenario for the Raiders in 2013. Being a disciple of Packers general manager Ted Thompson, McKenzie believes in building through the draft. However, thanks to the Palmer

2013 Raiders Schedule

Week	Opp.	Week	Opp.	Week	Opp.
1	at IND	7	BYE	13	at DAL (Thu.)
2	JAC	8	PIT	14	at NYJ
3	at DEN (Mon.)	9	PHI	15	KC
4	WAS	10	at NYG	16	at SD
5	SD	11	at HOU	17	DEN
6	at KC	12	TEN		

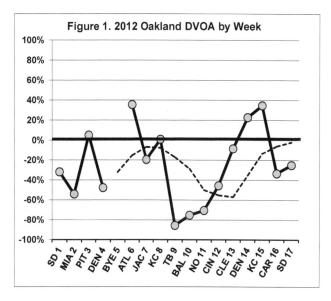

Figure 1. 2012 Oakland DVOA by Week

trade and some 2011 draft-day dealing, plus the previous year's third-round selection of Terrell Pryor in the supplemental draft, McKenzie last year did not even have a pick until late in the third round (he took offensive lineman Tony Bergstrom 95th overall). Consequently, the Raiders had fewer developmental projects to lean on heading into this season, and an inordinate number of their roster spots had to be filled with veteran free agents.

With limited cap space, it was impossible for McKenzie to make splashes with bank-breaking free-agent acquisitions. To his credit, he still managed to bring in a respectable haul of immediate contributors:

- Defensive tackle Pat Sims (one year, $1.5 million).
- Defensive tackle Vance Walker (one year, $2 million).
- Defensive end Jason Hunter (one year, $715,000).
- Linebacker Kevin Burnett (two years, $5.25 million).
- Linebacker Nick Roach (four years, $13 million).
- Linebacker Kaluka Maiava (three years, $6 million).
- Cornerback Mike Jenkins (one year, $1.5 million).
- Quarterback Matt Flynn (acquired via trade from Seattle, he cost a fifth-round pick in 2014 plus a conditional pick in 2015; he also was signed to a new two-year contract worth $11.5 million, $6.5 million of which is guaranteed).

The Flynn trade is the move that most stands out. It's the embodiment of the Raiders' one foot in/one foot out approach to 2013. They presumably see Flynn as a wild card, with this season being a trial period to determine whether he is worth building around. It can be surmised that they're skeptical of the 28-year-old's chances, as teams these days don't sign their long-term quarterbacks to short-term contracts. Locking Flynn up for two years (instead of one) was clever. If he is playing really well come midseason, McKenzie won't have to hastily decide whether the performance is sustainable or not. (The Buffalo Bills' mistaken contract extension for Ryan Fitzpatrick taught everyone this lesson in 2011.) If Flynn is not playing well, McKenzie won't have any trouble getting rid of him after the season—or doing what Seattle did last year and just making him a moderately expensive backup.

The other free-agent signings noted above also illustrate McKenzie's approach to 2013. Essentially, all of the veterans who were brought in are here to ensure that the Raiders' rebuilding defense does not completely embarrass itself in 2013. None are viewed as long-term building blocks, which is why, with the exception of the linebackers, all of the pickups are on one-year contracts.

One reason the linebackers were signed to longer deals might be because in Dennis Allen's defensive scheme, the linebacker position has mostly assignment-based responsibilities. The scheme does not demand stars at that position, it just demands reliability. The Raiders just need guys who can get to the simple spots that they're told to get to, so that's not where McKenzie is likely to use Oakland's salary cap space or top draft picks in 2014. Where Allen's scheme does become more dependent on high-level play is in the secondary.

This in mind, it's no surprise that McKenzie made it a priority to keep safety Tyvon Branch on the roster. Instead of releasing the gifted but expensive hard-hitter after a disappointing 2012 season, McKenzie restructured Branch's contract, creating $5 million in cap space. McKenzie also signed versatile veteran Charles Woodson, who can still play either safety or nickelback. And he spent his first ever first-round draft pick as a GM at cornerback: Houston's D.J. Hayden. Many believe Hayden was the best pure cover artist in this year's draft. McKenzie wanted him at No. 3 overall but was able to trade down and get him at No. 12. (That trade brought about an additional early second-round pick, which was used on Florida State offensive tackle Menelik Watson.)

All told, the Raiders defense will go into 2013 with nine new starters. But while the defense that ranked 29th in DVOA last year is essentially no more, the offense that ranked 23rd is still mostly the same. Or, if anything, it's worse. Yes, there is a new quarterback in Flynn, but he's less physically gifted than Palmer and will be plagued by the same surrounding issues.

To start with, Oakland's front line is, at best, resoundingly average. That will be a problem given that quarterbacks like Flynn, who lack dynamic athleticism or raw arm strength, are more dependent on their protection.

A bigger problem is Flynn's receiving corps. It's headlined by Jacoby Ford and Denarius Moore. Ford showed scintillating playmaker potential as a rookie in 2010, but he missed all of last season with a Lisfranc injury—the same injury that caused him to miss eight games in 2011. Moore flashed rare speed and separation instincts against man coverage as a rookie in 2011, but he did not quite take the forward steps that many were expecting in his sophomore 2012 season.

Recent history says it's unlikely that Ford and Moore will both emerge as major weapons in 2013. Even if they do, depth at wide receiver is still a concern. Rod Streater has good open-field speed and surprised people with his intermediate-level receiving at times last year. That said, he's not physically imposing enough to consistently create matchup problems. Juron Criner flashed intrigue a time or two as a fifth-round rookie last year, but it's concerning that he only saw 164 offensive snaps in 12 active games with a depleted receiving corps. At tight end, the Raiders are downright laughable: 2011 sixth-rounder Richard Gordon and 2011 seventh-rounder David Ausberry have just 12 NFL catches in their first two seasons. The other options are a pair of 2013 sixth-rounders, Nick Kasa and Mychal Rivera. Each of the last two seasons, running backs have accounted for 22 percent of Oakland's passing yards (which is among the highest figures in the league). That number could increase in 2013. Marcel Reece is the offense's most versatile weapon, and Darren McFadden, when healthy, is its most explosive. Of course, banking on McFadden to stay healthy is the very definition of a "bad plan." And it's not like a healthy McFad-den is a miracle worker anyway. He has very limited lateral agility and hip swivel. Being limited to only downhill running was a big reason why last season he finished dead last among running backs with -155 rushing DYAR.

Of course, last season McFadden was playing behind a zone-blocking line, which his running style simply does not fit. This year, the Raiders will be back in a man-blocking scheme under Greg Olson. The former Lions/Rams/Bucs offensive coordinator is stepping in for Greg Knapp, who was fired after one season. By making this change, McKenzie and Dennis Allen tacitly admitted that they made a mistake with the direction they took the offense in their first year together. They thought they wanted one thing and after seeing it play out (or not play out) with Knapp, they changed their mind.

It's too bad given that a lot of young Raiders players will now have to learn yet another new system. Then again, given what's happened to the defense, it's likely that McKenzie will wind up overhauling the offensive side of the ball next offseason anyway.

Andy Benoit

2012 Raiders Stats by Week

Wk	vs.	W-L	PF	PA	YDF	YDA	TO	Total	Off	Def	ST
1	SD	L	13	35	396	452	-1	-32%	6%	2%	-36%
2	at MIA	L	34	31	321	433	1	-54%	-3%	43%	-9%
3	PIT	W	6	37	237	503	1	5%	19%	23%	8%
4	at DEN	L	20	23	474	286	0	-48%	-23%	19%	-6%
5	BYE										
6	at ATL	L	26	23	351	209	-2	35%	2%	-33%	1%
7	JAC	W	26	16	344	299	3	-20%	-29%	-20%	-11%
8	at KC	W	32	42	424	515	-2	1%	-6%	-4%	3%
9	TB	L	20	55	422	419	-2	-86%	-15%	64%	-6%
10	at BAL	L	17	38	404	380	-2	-75%	-21%	26%	-29%
11	NO	L	10	34	218	415	-2	-71%	-29%	30%	-11%
12	at CIN	L	17	20	429	475	1	-46%	-31%	24%	9%
13	CLE	L	13	26	324	428	-1	-8%	24%	35%	3%
14	DEN	L	15	0	385	119	0	23%	21%	0%	2%
15	KC	W	6	17	189	271	1	35%	-19%	-44%	9%
16	at CAR	L	21	24	265	210	-1	-34%	-49%	-12%	4%
17	at SD	L						-25%	9%	9%	-25%

Trends and Splits

	Offense	Rank	Defense	Rank
Total DVOA	-9.5%	23	12.5%	29
Unadjusted VOA	-7.2%	23	10.7%	28
Weighted Trend	-12.9%	26	9.0%	27
Variance	4.6%	8	8.1%	28
Average Opponent	1.6%	20	-2.8%	25
Passing	4.2%	20	22.6%	30
Rushing	-17.1%	29	0.8%	24
First Down	-17.3%	30	2.8%	20
Second Down	-7.6%	22	9.2%	23
Third Down	3.2%	15	36.1%	31
First Half	-15.0%	26	9.5%	27
Second Half	-4.4%	18	16.0%	29
Red Zone	-18.4%	26	11.1%	26
Late and Close	-10.5%	20	16.3%	32

Five-Year Performance

Year	W-L	Pyth W	Est W	PF	PA	TO	Total	Rk	Off	Rk	Def	Rk	ST	Rk	Off AGL	Rk	Def AGL	Rk	Off Age	Rk	Def Age	Rk	ST Age	Rk
2008	5-11	4.5	5.7	263	388	+1	-23.2%	29	-16.1%	31	3.7%	19	6.5%	2	35.8	23	18.4	14	27.0	20	27.0	23	26.8	11
2009	5-11	2.9	3.9	197	379	-13	-34.0%	30	-25.8%	30	7.9%	24	-0.3%	17	32.4	23	18.9	8	26.4	29	27.3	16	27.0	6
2010	8-8	9.0	7.1	410	371	-2	-4.1%	21	-8.3%	23	-2.3%	13	1.8%	13	15.1	8	15.4	10	26.6	25	26.2	25	27.1	7
2011	8-8	6.1	7.3	359	433	-4	-8.0%	22	2.6%	14	9.6%	27	-1.0%	20	36.7	21	41.4	26	26.8	19	27.1	16	26.8	4
2012	4-12	4.1	3.7	290	443	-7	-27.8%	29	-9.5%	23	12.5%	29	-5.8%	31	31.8	19	35.0	20	27.1	13	27.5	9	26.6	8

2012 Performance Based on Most Common Personnel Groups

OAK Offense					OAK Offense vs. Opponents					OAK Defense					OAK Defense vs. Opponents			
Pers	Freq	Yds	DVOA	Run%	Pers	Freq	Yds	DVOA		Pers	Freq	Yds	DVOA		Pers	Freq	Yds	DVOA
1.1	45%	6.1	13.4%	23%	Nickel Even	29%	5.4	-17.9%		Nickel Even	44%	6.4	19.5%		1.1	49%	6.2	14.0%
2.1	38%	5.2	-16.1%	42%	4-3-4	29%	5.2	-14.8%		4-3-4	44%	5.7	9.2%		2.1	19%	6.5	25.1%
1.2	6%	3.8	-34.0%	47%	3-4-4	22%	5.0	-7.1%		Dime+	5%	3.7	-45.6%		1.2	18%	5.8	22.9%
2.2	5%	4.4	3.7%	57%	Dime+	11%	6.8	45.2%		Nickel Odd	4%	8.0	42.9%		2.2	6%	4.4	-16.4%
61.1	2%	3.6	-32.9%	71%	Nickel Odd	9%	7.3	56.0%		5-3-3	2%	2.6	9.8%		1.3	2%	3.6	4.2%

Strategic Tendencies

Run/Pass		Rk	Formation		Rk	Pass Rush		Rk	Secondary		Rk	Strategy		Rk
Runs, first half	37%	22	Form: Single Back	63%	20	Rush 3	7.1%	14	4 DB	44%	15	Play action	20%	14
Runs, first down	42%	30	Form: Empty Back	5%	20	Rush 4	53.5%	27	5 DB	48%	15	Avg Box (Off)	6.37	15
Runs, second-long	33%	11	Pers: 3+ WR	48%	21	Rush 5	23.9%	12	6+ DB	5%	18	Avg Box (Def)	6.34	21
Runs, power sit.	51%	21	Pers: 4+ WR	1%	16	Rush 6+	15.5%	2	CB by Sides	77%	12	Offensive Pace	30.57	17
Runs, behind 2H	26%	21	Pers: 2+ TE/6+ OL	15%	32	Sacks by LB	24.0%	15	DB Blitz	17%	5	Defensive Pace	30.66	25
Pass, ahead 2H	37%	29	Shotgun/Pistol	38%	27	Sacks by DB	4.0%	18	Hole in Zone	11%	9	Go for it on 4th	1.57	2

Assuming we count Houston's James Casey as a tight end, Oakland used "conventional" 21 personnel more than any other offense and the league, and even that was just 38 percent of the time. This is what happens when your best offensive weapon is a fullback. ☞ In a dramatic change on defense, the Raiders went from using dime personnel on 32 percent of snaps in 2011 to just five percent of snaps in 2012. ☞ Oakland was one of three teams that pressured the quarterback less than 15 percent of the time with a standard four-man pass rush. ☞ The Raiders finished 10th in the NFL with 123 penalties, including declined and offsetting. It was the first year since 2006 that the Raiders didn't finish first or second in penalties, and represents a drop of 3.6 penalties per game compared to 2011 when they set an NFL record with 181 penalties.

Passing

Player	DYAR	DVOA	Plays	NtYds	Avg	YAC	C%	TD	Int
C.Palmer*	340	-2.2%	592	3820	6.5	5.7	61.7%	22	14
M.Leinart*	-77	-51.2%	34	106	3.1	2.5	48.5%	0	1
T.Pryor	4	-9.1%	31	155	5.0	2.1	48.4%	2	1
M.Flynn	27	64.3%	9	68	7.6	8.2	55.6%	0	0

Rushing

Player	DYAR	DVOA	Plays	Yds	Avg	TD	Fum	Suc
D.McFadden	-153	-26.7%	214	716	3.3	2	1	36%
M.Reece	4	-6.9%	59	264	4.5	0	1	54%
M.Goodson*	37	24.8%	33	219	6.6	0	0	48%
J.Stewart	0	-8.3%	25	101	4.0	0	0	32%
C.Palmer	23	17.1%	11	40	3.6	1	0	-
T.Pryor	22	23.2%	10	51	5.1	1	0	-
T.Jones	4	4.1%	6	21	3.5	0	0	33%
R.Jennings	-97	-31.8%	101	285	2.8	2	3	38%
J.Cribbs	-1	-14.1%	6	32	5.3	0	1	50%

Receiving

Player	DYAR	DVOA	Plays	Ctch	Yds	Y/C	YAC	TD	C%
D.Moore	-33	-12.4%	114	51	741	14.5	5.0	7	45%
D.Heyward-Bey*	31	-5.3%	80	41	606	14.8	5.6	5	51%
R.Streater	43	-1.9%	75	39	584	15.0	3.6	3	52%
D.Hagan*	32	-1.9%	36	20	259	13.0	3.4	0	56%
J.Criner	-52	-36.1%	33	16	151	9.4	5.0	1	48%
J.Cribbs	-10	-28.8%	12	7	63	9.0	6.0	0	58%
B.Myers*	112	10.7%	105	79	806	10.2	3.6	4	75%
D.Ausberry	-6	-8.8%	12	7	92	13.1	6.1	0	58%
R.Gordon	-25	-48.5%	7	2	9	4.5	3.0	1	29%
M.Reece	90	7.6%	73	52	497	9.6	6.3	1	71%
D.McFadden	-82	-36.7%	64	44	259	5.9	6.2	1	69%
M.Goodson*	83	70.1%	18	18	197	10.9	12.9	1	100%
J.Stewart	11	23.7%	8	8	62	7.8	9.6	0	100%
R.Jennings	-11	-22.6%	26	19	130	6.8	8.2	0	73%

Offensive Line

Player	Pos	Age	GS	Snaps	Pen	Sk	Pass	Run	Player	Pos	Age	GS	Snaps	Pen	Sk	Pass	Run
Jared Veldheer	LT	26	16/16	1078	6	3	17.5	4	Khalif Barnes	RT	31	9/9	557	5	4	13	3
Cooper Carlisle*	LG	36	16/16	1076	5	0	10.5	5	Willie Smith	RT	27	9/7	505	3	4.5	16.5	4
Stefen Wisniewski	C	24	15/15	1007	5	0	4	5	Alex Parsons	C	26	16/1	120	0	1	3	2
Mike Brisiel	RG	30	15/15	962	10	2	13	3	Tony Bergstrom	OT	27	9/1	110	2	1.5	3.5	2

Year	Yards	ALY	Rk	Power	Rk	Stuff	Rk	2nd Lev	Rk	Open Field	Rk	Sacks	ASR	Rk	Short	Long	F-Start	Cont.
2010	4.60	4.11	15	61%	15	16%	8	1.10	18	1.15	6	44	8.3%	26	14	21	29	33
2011	4.52	4.13	14	67%	8	16%	3	1.12	24	1.05	7	25	5.0%	5	10	8	18	37
2012	3.90	3.52	29	55%	28	21%	24	1.10	21	0.78	15	27	4.4%	4	10	7	16	32

2012 ALY by direction:	Left End 2.16 (32)	Left Tackle 4.42 (10)	Mid/Guard 3.58 (28)	Right Tackle 3.82 (19)	Right End 3.71 (24)

Much was made last year about this line's struggles in Greg Knapp's zone-blocking system. In all likelihood, though, this is a line that could struggle in any system. It's not an embarrassingly awful unit, but its individual parts are iffy. The pass blocking has been better than the run blocking over the last couple seasons, which is surprising given how they've had to make such a concerted effort hiding weaknesses in certain spots (namely right tackle). However, keep in mind, a league-high 38.8 percent of Oakland's passes last season came out of two-back personnel, which means the offensive line is often getting extra help in protection.

Because Reggie McKenzie can't overhaul his entire personnel on *both* sides of the ball, the Raiders are settling for an overhaul of just the scheme up front offensively. New coordinator Greg Olson is installing predominantly man-blocking concepts. How will his personnel respond?

At left tackle, Jared Veldheer has developed well enough after entering the league as a fourth-round pick from tiny Hillsdale four years ago, but he's not a dominant enough force to survive against upper-level talent one-on-one for long durations. New left guard Tony Bergstrom was an over-aged third-round pick last year. He played right tackle at Utah and was not able to pick up a new position quickly enough to beat out veteran Cooper Carlisle last season. The quick-footed Bergstrom was initially described as a good fit for a zone scheme, but can he succeed in a man scheme? Even if he struggles, he'll likely keep a starting job, as Oakland's depth at guard consists only of undrafted youngsters.

Center Stefen Wisniewski entered the league to much acclaim because of his bloodlines, but through two full NFL seasons he's been nothing special, perhaps due in part to frequently changing positions and schemes. The good news is he does not make a ton of outlandishly bad plays, as evidenced by his low total of blown blocks from last year's game charting. Right guard Mike Brisiel was a good zone-blocker for Houston a couple years ago, but at this point he's just a guy. He probably would not have been signed last season if the Raiders had planned on featuring man blocking. Right tackle Khalif Barnes is a little less mistake-prone than he was earlier in his career, but he's still better fit for coming off the bench as an extra tackle or move-blocker in six-man lines (a la Riley Reiff last year in Detroit). Don't be at all surprised if the Raiders actualize this in 2013 and start rookie Menelik Watson at right tackle. The second-round pick from Florida State has just 19 college football games under his belt—with seven of them coming at Saddleback Junior College—but he's a very talented athlete. He has the movement skills to thrive in the NFL, it's just a matter of whether he can hone his technique.

Defensive Front Seven

Defensive Line	Age	Pos	Snaps	Plays	Overall TmPct	Rk	Stop	Dfts	BTkl	Runs	vs. Run St%	Rk	RuYd	Rk	Pass Rush Sack	Hit	Hur	Tips
Lamarr Houston	26	DE	856	71	9.1%	5	53	17	3	54	76%	34	2.2	23	4	9	21	2
Tommy Kelly*	33	DT	756	47	6.0%	10	36	10	1	39	77%	30	2.8	55	1	4	4	3
Matt Shaughnessy*	27	DE	668	31	4.0%	56	26	12	0	24	88%	3	0.3	2	3.5	5	5	0
Desmond Bryant*	28	DT	631	37	4.8%	28	32	14	3	30	90%	2	1.4	10	4	11	12.5	0
Richard Seymour*	34	DT	348	17	4.4%	--	14	7	1	10	90%	--	0.9	--	3	3	4.5	2
Andre Carter	34	DE	315	19	3.3%	--	14	7	1	11	73%	--	2.0	--	2.5	5	4	0
Vance Walker	26	DT	530	32	4.0%	37	26	7	1	27	81%	19	1.9	23	3	2	7	0
Pat Sims	28	DT	181	18	4.3%	--	10	3	1	16	56%	--	2.3	--	0	0	1	0

Linebackers	Age	Pos	Snaps	Plays	Overall TmPct	Rk	Stop	Dfts	BTkl	Pass Rush Sack	Hit	Hur	Tips	Runs	vs. Run St%	Rk	Yds	Rk	Tgts	vs. Pass Suc%	Rk	AdjYd	Rk	PD
Philip Wheeler*	29	OLB	1015	116	14.9%	26	63	18	8	3.5	9	14	1	51	63%	70	3.8	81	42	46%	55	9.1	71	4
Miles Burris	25	OLB	867	99	12.7%	46	63	16	8	1.5	6	9.5	0	59	76%	17	2.7	27	30	26%	74	7.5	59	3
Rolando McClain*	24	MLB	496	61	11.4%	56	38	9	5	1	1	1	0	45	67%	44	2.9	32	17	74%	1	6.2	23	2
Kevin Burnett	31	OLB	1071	113	13.6%	38	62	11	5	2.5	2	8	0	67	61%	76	3.7	76	40	49%	43	8.4	68	5
Nick Roach	28	OLB	697	69	8.4%	72	34	12	7	1.5	0	2	0	42	55%	98	4.0	88	28	66%	5	3.7	1	1
Kaluka Maiava	26	OLB	486	50	5.7%	101	31	5	4	2	1	1	0	32	63%	71	3.9	82	11	72%	--	2.9	--	3

Year	Yards	ALY	Rk	Power	Rk	Stuff	Rk	2nd Level	Rk	Open Field	Rk	Sacks	ASR	Rk	Short	Long
2010	4.38	3.63	4	62%	13	24%	2	1.09	13	1.17	31	47	9.5%	1	15	18
2011	4.87	4.04	18	72%	28	19%	18	1.33	28	1.28	30	39	6.4%	20	12	18
2012	4.27	3.80	6	58%	9	22%	9	1.01	2	1.18	30	25	4.9%	30	8	11
2012 ALY by direction:		Left End 2.73 (4)			Left Tackle 4.32 (22)			Mid/Guard 4.06 (13)			Right Tackle 3.5 (3)			Right End 2.15 (2)		

Evaluating the 2012 Raiders front seven is a waste of time, as every starter from that group save for end Lamarr Houston has been replaced. Dennis Allen and coordinator Jason Tarver are eager to install more hybrid fronts and complex disguises and attacks in 2013, as they now, presumably, have more of the types of players that they want.

The most important changes are at linebacker, where just getting rid of the pathetic Rolando McClain will make everything easier on the entire defense. McClain had already been benched at midseason for Omar Gaither, a player the Raiders didn't even bother re-signing, and Oakland fans will need to look elsewhere for their recommended weekly allowance of bad angles, missed assignments, and frustratingly squandered potential. (Don't get carried away by the good pass coverage numbers listed above, a product of small sample size.)

Of course, while addition by subtraction is nice, addition by addition would be better. The Raiders have not really found a true middle linebacker to replace McClain. Kevin Burnett is best suited for an outside slot in a 4-3 or the weak inside slot in a 3-4. Kaluka Maiava is a classic strongside linebacker (and a very underrated one, by the way). Nick Roach was at his best playing the outside in Chicago, where he could rely more on his run-and-chase skills. He performed very poorly last season when filling in for an injured Brian Urlacher at the Mike position. Top backup Miles Burris is more familiar with the scheme having been a starter here last year, but he doesn't have the instincts to be first-stringer in the middle. Third-round pick Sio Moore (Connecticut), who was coached by the Raiders in the Senior Bowl, projects as a nickel linebacker who can maybe play the weak side in a base 4-3.

Up front, the Raiders are less talented than they were a year ago, but most of the downgrades will prove worthwhile given the enormous cap savings that came with them. As it stands, there really isn't a viable starter opposite Houston. Andre Carter can still get around the edge, but only in spot duty. Jason Hunter's production has never quite matched his athleticism. Jack Crawford is inexperienced, having only played 49 snaps as a fifth-round rookie last season. Inside, Vance Walker and Pat Sims were both good signings, as each flashed last season as gap-shooting rotational players. Both have enough strength to occasionally clog multiple gaps, though will that strength show in the fourth quarter given that both are likely to play more snaps than they've been accustomed to in the past?

Defensive Secondary

Secondary	Age	Pos	Snaps	Plays	Overall TmPct	Rk	Stop	Dfts	BTkl	Runs	vs. Run St%	Rk	Yds	Rk	Tgts	Tgt%	Rk	Dist	vs. Pass Suc%	Rk	APaYd	Rk	PD	Int
Michael Huff*	30	CB	945	68	8.7%	39	34	11	3	23	52%	24	6.0	39	73	19.2%	34	12.7	56%	21	8.2	64	10	2
Tyvon Branch	27	SS	835	97	14.2%	5	30	8	9	46	39%	33	6.0	22	28	8.2%	21	10.5	45%	64	7.0	31	2	1
Matt Giordano*	31	FS	802	52	6.7%	63	11	6	7	16	13%	74	15.2	74	25	6.6%	40	16.6	49%	56	8.9	58	5	2
Joselio Hanson	32	CB	553	65	8.4%	51	28	15	2	15	60%	13	5.7	31	46	11.9%	80	10.1	45%	75	9.2	77	3	2
Brandian Ross	24	CB	331	17	2.4%	--	7	3	0	4	75%	--	5.8	--	14	3.7%	--	10.4	56%	--	5.8	--	0	0
Mike Mitchell*	26	SS	329	31	4.0%	--	14	7	1	20	55%	--	4.9	--	8	2.0%	--	5.0	47%	--	4.0	--	0	0
Phillip Adams	25	CB	175	17	2.3%	--	9	6	1	3	33%	--	7.7	--	13	3.5%	--	13.4	75%	--	7.3	--	5	2
Usama Young	28	FS	666	58	8.1%	51	18	7	2	26	27%	59	9.2	59	16	3.9%	69	18.2	45%	65	12.0	75	5	3
Charles Woodson	37	SS	467	43	12.0%	21	20	8	2	16	50%	9	3.9	2	24	11.4%	6	11.9	65%	13	6.6	20	5	1
Mike Jenkins	28	CB	357	17	2.7%	--	8	2	4	4	50%	--	11.5	--	22	6.8%	--	9.9	53%	--	6.8	--	3	0
Tracy Porter	27	CB	301	27	9.1%	--	14	7	4	9	56%	--	4.6	--	34	20.5%	--	14.5	44%	--	10.8	--	6	1

Year	Pass D Rank	vs. #1 WR	Rk	vs. #2 WR	Rk	vs. Other WR	Rk	vs. TE	Rk	vs. RB	Rk
2010	17	5.0%	20	-3.6%	13	-4.9%	15	14.4%	25	1.0%	13
2011	21	-1.1%	11	20.8%	25	-1.7%	19	-2.3%	5	-2.9%	16
2012	30	25.9%	30	5.0%	19	-13.4%	7	15.3%	28	11.0%	21

After trying but ultimately failing to survive with callow fringe players and veteran castoffs at corner last year, the Raiders invested at the position a little more aggressively during the offseason. They spent a first-round pick on D.J. Hayden, whom a few highly respected analysts thought was the best corner in the 2013 draft. The University of Houston graduate has a very fluid backpedal and ball skills. Last year he also had a freak sternum injury that ruptured the main blood vessel to his heart, but the Raiders have faith in the doctors who have pronounced Hayden medically cleared.

The Raiders also signed veterans Mike Jenkins and Tracy Porter, two once-rising pros who have both struggled with injuries and consistency in recent years. Hedging against the strong possibility of one of these players failing to get back on track, the Raiders also re-signed Joselio Hanson and brought in Charles Woodson. Hanson was arguably the only reliable defensive back in last year's secondary (though his charting numbers weren't great). He has an excellent feel for blitzing out of the slot, which is a featured element of Allen's scheme. Same goes for Woodson, who remained unsigned for several months but, if healthy, still has star-level gas left in his tank. Woodson is versatile enough to start at safety, but his main value will likely be as a utility box weapon in Oakland's sub packages.

At safety, Usama Young and Tyvon Branch must be interchangeable in their free and strong positions in order to thrive in this scheme. Young is generally a centerfielder who will have to hold up in the box. Branch is a downhill box player who must get more comfortable and alert against the pass in deep space.

Special Teams

Year	DVOA	Rank	FG/XP	Rank	Net Kick	Rank	Kick Ret	Rank	Net Punt	Rank	Punt Ret	Rank	Hidden	Rank
2010	1.8%	13	3.5	10	0.8	16	5.0	10	9.9	4	-10.2	31	16.2	1
2011	-1.0%	20	16.6	1	-14.0	32	4.0	7	-8.3	28	-3.1	21	9.2	5
2012	-5.8%	31	11.8	1	-12.1	31	-2.8	21	-15.3	31	-10.4	32	-7.4	27

The idea that a special teams unit featuring Sebastian Janikowski ranked 31st in the league seems ridiculous, but there's only so much the guy can do on his own. Seabass still has one of the biggest legs in the game, which is why Dennis Allen was comfortable asking him to attempt a field goal from 50-plus yards nine times in 2012. Janikowski rewarded Allen's faith six of those times, and those three misses from long distance were his only misses on the season. Janikowski's leg strength has never translated to stellar kickoff distance, but he was still above average in 2012. The problem was the coverage team, which allowed an estimated 12.4 points worth of field position more than average on kick returns.

Punter Shane Lechler had a wonderful 13-year run in Oakland, but his performance collapsed in 2012 and the Raiders felt it was time to cut bait. Vikings refugee Chris Kluwe will compete for the job with 24-year-old UDFA Marquette King from Division II HBCU Fort Valley State. Most of the return duties will be handled by free-agent signing Joshua Cribbs, who in Cleveland was above-average on both kick and punt returns every year except for a subpar 2010. Cribbs has outstanding speed and strength in the open field and, as a bonus, also contributes to coverage teams. If the Raiders want to spread things around, they could use Jacoby Ford, who took four kickoffs back for touchdowns in his first two seasons, or cornerback Phillip Adams, who handled punts last season but was not particularly explosive with just 5.6 yards per return.

Coaching Staff

Some are speculating that Allen could be out of a job if the Raiders don't show improvement in 2013. Such is the treatment for anyone who gets a head coaching job in his late 30s after just one year of experience as a coordinator (2011 in Denver). If there is a "make or break" year for Allen, it will likely be 2014, given that it's patently unfair to expect any coach to produce more than five or six wins with this current cap-strapped Raiders' roster.

Allen's expertise is in defense, which means offensive coordinator Greg Olson can expect quite a bit of autonomy. Olson, who works closely with quarterbacks, has been a coordinator every year since 2004 (save for last season, where he was the assistant head coach in Jacksonville). His previous stops were Detroit, St. Louis and Tampa Bay. He'll have some familiar names at assistant spots to bounce ideas off of, as Tony Sparano is his offensive line coach and Al Saunders is on the staff as a senior consultant.

Philadelphia Eagles

2012 Record: 4-12	**Total DVOA:** -22.4% (28th)	**2013 Mean Projection:** 7.8 wins	On the Clock (0-4): 10%
Pythagorean Wins: 3.9 (30th)	**Offense:** -10.8% (25th)	**Postseason Odds:** 26.1%	Mediocrity (5-7): 35%
Snap-Weighted Age: 26.5 (19th)	**Defense:** 9.4% (26th)	**Super Bowl Odds:** 1.9%	Playoff Contender (8-10): 42%
Average Opponent: 2.0% (11th)	**Special Teams:** -2.2% (23rd)	**Proj. Avg. Opponent:** 0.4% (21st)	Super Bowl Contender (11+): 13%

2012: After 14 years, WIP's "Fire Andy" campaign finally reaches fruition.

2013: In a division filled with star quarterbacks, the Eagles fight back with a ground attack.

For the last 14 years, Andy Reid was the head coach and identity of the Philadelphia Eagles. Before the team fired him at the end of last season, he had been the NFL's longest-tenured head coach. And for good reason: Philadelphia won 130 games in 14 seasons under Reid, the sixth highest mark in the league. The five teams with more wins—the Patriots, Colts, Steelers, Packers, and Ravens—won nine Super Bowls during that period. Despite Reid's success, many will remember him as the offensive genius with an overly aggressive mentality who failed to win it all.

Which is ironic, since that is one way to describe new head coach Chip Kelly's tenure with Oregon. Kelly went 46-7 in Eugene, and his teams were famous for stepping on the accelerator and ending games early. Nine times last season, Oregon scored more points in the first half than their opponents scored all game. In eight of 13 games, the Ducks went on at least one stretch in which they scored 28 or more unanswered points.

It may surprise some NFL fans to learn that Kelly's scorched-earth attack was a run-oriented offense. From 2009 to 2012, Oregon was one of just four teams at the FBS level to rush for 15,000 yards, and the Ducks led the nation with 6.0 yards per carry. The other three schools were Georgia Tech and Air Force, who each run a triple-option, extremely run-heavy offense, and Nevada, where Chris Ault's pistol formation, two years of Colin Kaepernick, and an inferior conference helped the Wolfpack dominate teams on the ground. Kelly's offenses weren't only great on the ground—Oregon finished first in total offense among BCS programs from 2009 to 2012—but the Ducks' success always fed off the running attack setting the tone.

That might be very good news for LeSean McCoy, who was one of the most disappointing players in the NFL in 2012 (although if we grade him on an Eagles curve, he gets "meets expectations" in our yearly review). In 2011, "Shady" led the NFL in rushing DYAR, more than 100 ahead of any other running back; his 20 total touchdowns and 17 rushing touchdowns each led the league, too, and McCoy averaged an electric 4.8 yards per carry. But last season, he dropped to 35th in DYAR among running backs with 100 carries. His yards per carry dropped to a more modest 4.2, but what caused fantasy owners to pull out their hair was seeing his rushing touchdowns drop from 17 to two.

McCoy's 2012 season was one of the worst follow-up sea-

sons by a DYAR rushing champion. Table 1 lists each player's rushing DYAR in the season where he led the league, along with his DYAR and DYAR ranks in the following two years. The final row shows the average DYAR for each player and his median rank. The last three DYAR champions had miserable follow-up seasons, although that doesn't mean we expect Adrian Peterson to suffer the same fate. As for McCoy, his minus-34 DYAR ranks as the worst follow-up performance by any of these DYAR champs.

McCoy shouldn't shoulder all the blame, as injuries turned the Philadelphia offensive line from a strength into a weakness. All-Pro left tackle Jason Peters did not play a snap after tearing his Achilles in the offseason, while right tackle Todd Herremans missed the final half of the year with an ankle injury. The inside of the line wasn't much better: center Jason

Table 1. Rushing DYAR Leaders, 1991-2011

Running Back	Team	Year	DYAR	Yr N+1 DYAR	Yr N+1 Rk	Yr N+2 DYAR	Yr N+2 Rk
LeSean McCoy	PHI	2011	304	-34	35	--	--
Jamaal Charles	KC	2010	382	2	DNQ	109	12
Chris Johnson	TEN	2009	328	18	30	-67	49
DeAngelo Williams	CAR	2008	350	172	8	-16	DNQ
Brian Westbrook	PHI	2007	339	130	11	36	DNQ
LaDainian Tomlinson	SD	2006	460	285	2	56	22
Larry Johnson	KC	2005	488	236	8	-38	42
Curtis Martin	NYJ	2004	398	-17	38	Retired	Retired
Priest Holmes	KC	2003	485	248	4	79	19
Priest Holmes	KC	2002	497	485	1	248	4
Priest Holmes	KC	2001	426	497	1	485	1
Marshall Faulk	STL	2000	501	347	2	143	7
Stephen Davis	WAS	1999	526	175	10	117	12
Terrell Davis	DEN	1998	602	-1	DNQ	19	DNQ
Terrell Davis	DEN	1997	526	602	1	-1	DNQ
Jerome Bettis	PIT	1996	384	280	4	46	26
Emmitt Smith	DAL	1995	505	142	14	84	17
Emmitt Smith	DAL	1994	461	505	1	142	14
Emmitt Smith	DAL	1993	377	461	1	505	1
Emmitt Smith	DAL	1992	416	377	1	461	1
Thurman Thomas	BUF	1991	306	275	4	79	20
Average/Median	--	--	**431**	**247**	**4**	**131**	**19.5**

*DNQ: Fewer than 100 carries in the given season.

2013 Eagles Schedule

Week	Opp.	Week	Opp.	Week	Opp.
1	at WAS (Mon.)	7	DAL	13	ARI
2	SD	8	NYG	14	DET
3	KC (Thu.)	9	at OAK	15	at MIN
4	at DEN	10	at GB	16	CHI
5	at NYG	11	WAS	17	at DAL
6	at TB	12	BYE		

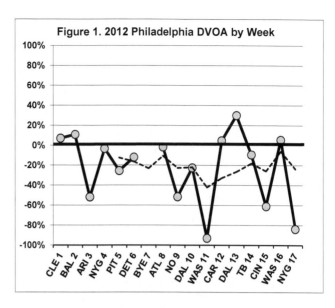

Figure 1. 2012 Philadelphia DVOA by Week

Kelce only lasted two games before tearing ligaments in his knee, and right guard Danny Watkins was either injured or benched for much of the season. McCoy missed four games with a concussion as well. The good news is that Philadelphia revamped the offensive line in the offseason and McCoy has shown no lingering effects from the concussion. Peters, Herremans, and Kelce are back, left guard Evan Mathis is coming off a strong season, and the Eagles selected Oklahoma tackle Lane Johnson with the fourth pick in the draft. That gives the Eagles one of the most athletic offensive lines in the NFL, which should make their new head coach very happy.

Kelly has been tight-lipped about the type of offense he and offensive coordinator Pat Shurmur plan to run this year, but the Eagles may have tipped their hand with some of their personnel moves. On the first day of free agency, Philadelphia signed Houston's James Casey, the sort of versatile player Kelly loves. A former baseball star, Casey played a little quarterback in college, but made his mark at Rice by catching 111 passes in 2008. The Texans lined him up at tight end, fullback, and wide receiver, and we expect Kelly to do the same.

Philadelphia then used its second-round pick to draft Stanford tight end Zach Ertz, who led all FBS tight ends with 69 receptions and 898 receiving yards last year. Ertz caught 11 passes for 106 yards and the touchdown that forced overtime in Stanford's upset victory over Kelly's Ducks last year, but Kelly ensured that he won't have to watch Ertz beat him again anytime soon. Brent Celek and Clay Harbor return as well, giving the team great depth at tight end.

While we've seen the Patriots use their two-tight end offense to obliterate teams through the air, expect Kelly to load the field with tight ends and try to overpower teams. When defenses have three or four linebackers on the field, Philadelphia can line Celek, Casey, and/or Ertz in the slot and create a mismatch. And if defenses try to counter that by sending in their nickel or dime units, Philadelphia can stay in the same personnel and overpower teams on the ground.

Only nine teams in NFL history have had three tight ends finish with over 250 receiving yards in the same season. James Casey was on the last two, the 2011 and 2012 Texans. He teamed with Owen Daniels and either Joel Dreessen (2011) or Garrett Graham (2012) to help an offense that relied on a run-based attack (necessitating the presence of multiple tight ends) and had little to complement Andre Johnson in the passing game.

According to our game charters, 19 of Casey's 34 receptions in 2012 came via the play-action pass, and you can expect that to be a big staple of Kelly's attack in 2013. Another Houston

team, the 1980 Oilers, used a tight-end heavy offense that was otherwise centered around Hall of Fame running back Earl Campbell. That season, Mike Barber (59-712-5) and Dave Casper (34-526-3) led the team in receiving yards, while Rich Caster added 341 yards and three touchdowns on 31 catches. No one knows what Kelly is thinking, but the evidence suggests a similar run-heavy attack that places two or three tight ends on the field to provide for maximum flexibility.

Oregon ranked 11th nationally in run/pass ratio in 2012, and none of the ten teams ahead of the Ducks came within 10 points per game of Oregon. Oregon ran on 65 percent of plays, nearly 10 percent more than any of the other teams that finished in the FBS top ten for points per game. (Baylor was second at 56 percent.) We also know that Chip Kelly likes to get more than one running back involved: In both 2011 and 2012, two different Oregon running backs rushed for over 700 yards. That's good news for the 2013 Eagles, as few NFL teams can boast a depth chart at running back like Philadelphia. When McCoy was out last year, rookie Bryce Brown flashed his star potential, rushing for 347 yards in his first two NFL starts. Felix Jones (career 4.8 yards per carry for the Cowboys) and Chris Polk (fourth among all college backs in yards from scrimmage 2010-2011) will be competing for the No. 3 role.

It's difficult to commit to the run when trailing, so it's fair to wonder how much success can be expected from a team that finished 4-12 a year ago. But many of the team's struggles were self-inflicted last year. Philadelphia led the NFL with a mind-boggling 37 fumbles in 2012, four more than second-place Pittsburgh. Nineteen of Philadelphia's fumbles came from the quarterbacks (11 for Michael Vick, eight for Nick Foles), which is hard to do without either Daunte Culpepper or Kerry Collins on your team. That doesn't include one fumbled snap charged to Dallas Reynolds, either. LeSean McCoy and Bryce Brown each fumbled four times, and Damaris Johnson added two more on punt returns. Philadelphia also fumbled twice on kickoff returns, which still leaves one each for DeSean Jackson, Jeremy Maclin, Celek, Harbor, and Jason Avant. Incredibly, ten percent of Eagles drives last year ended in a lost fumble, the highest mark in the league.

But if you're a regular reader of Football Outsiders—or if you've already read this year's Kansas City chapter—you know that last year's turnover problems don't mean much for this year. The 2012 Eagles were the 45th team since 1990 to fumble 35 times or more in a season. The first 44 teams, on average, fumbled 37.7 times, but that number dropped to 28.1 in the following season. Some regression towards the mean should be expected, and an improved offensive line should cut down on the quarterback sack/fumbles, too. And while the Eagles often looked more like a traveling comedy act than a football team, they also experienced their share of bad luck. Philadelphia lost 22 fumbles, another number that is prime for some regression. Thirty-one other teams since 1990 have lost 20-plus fumbles in a season, although the Eagles are the first team since the 2007 Ravens to join the list. On average, that group lost 21.3 fumbles, but only 14.7 fumbles the following season.

As bad as the situation was on offense, the team was even worse at recovering opponent's fumbles. The Eagles recovered just five of the 21 fumbles they forced last year. All told, of the 58 fumbles in Eagles games in 2012, the team recovered just 34.5 percent of them, the fourth lowest mark in the league (behind Kansas City, Detroit, and Buffalo).

But the defense had more problems than just failing to fall on the ball. The Eagles ranked third in defensive DVOA in 2008 and 2009, and then finished 11th the next two years. Last season, the team dropped to 26th, and Kelly is moving the team to a 3-4 defense in hopes of reversing that trend. The run defense has declined over the last five years, but the real issue in Philadelphia is the pass defense. Philadelphia ranked 15th in yards allowed last year, and actually gained more yards than they allowed. That's an argument to ignore looking at total yards, not to say that the Eagles defense was better than you might think. Last year, the Eagles finished 32nd in pass defense DVOA.

Thanks to their 37 turnovers, the Eagles defense faced the worst average starting field position in 2012. On average, offenses started drives at the 32-yard line, which naturally lowers the amount of yards a team can gain. Another reason to ignore the team's rank in yards allowed: teams passed so efficiently and effectively against Philadelphia—the Eagles allowed 33 passing touchdowns last year, the most in the league—that by the fourth quarter, offenses stopped trying to gain yards. The Eagles faced only 485 pass attempts last season, the second lowest number in the league.

The pass rush wasn't great, but Trent Cole, Brandon Gra-ham, and Fletcher Cox were effective at times in getting to the quarterback. Fortunately, all three return and the team bolstered the pass rush by signing Connor Barwin from Houston. And while the scheme shift may be what dominates the WIP airwaves this summer, the more important changes occurred in the defensive backfield.

There wasn't a worse starting secondary in the NFL last year than Dominique Rodgers-Cromartie, Nnamdi Asomugha, Nate Allen, and Kurt Coleman. The Eagles became just the fifth team in NFL history to allow more than 30 passing touchdowns while forcing fewer than 10 interceptions. Despite facing the second fewest number of pass attempts, Philadelphia allowed 25 pass plays of 30 yards or longer, tied for the third most in the league. Among cornerbacks with 40 charted passes or eight starts, Rodgers-Cromartie (62nd) and Asomugha (65th) both ranked in the bottom of the league in Adjusted Success Rate. Both safeties struggled in pass coverage, and tackling was a huge problem for the secondary, too. Rodgers-Cromartie, Allen, and Coleman (along with linebacker Mychal Kendricks) ranked in the top ten in missed tackles in 2012.

The Eagles will have four new starters in the secondary this year, starting with two free-agent cornerbacks: Cary Williams (ex-Ravens) and Bradley Fletcher (ex-Rams). It appears that the Eagles are banking on someone else's trash turning into their treasure. Williams ranked 79th in Adjusted Success Rate in 2012, while Fletcher was inconsistent as the nickelback in St. Louis. At safety, both of last year's starters are still on the team, but they've fallen to the second spot on the depth chart. That's because the Eagles signed Kenny Phillips and Patrick Chung, two hard-hitting safeties who are both upgrades and injury risks. Phillips had issues with both knees with the Giants (he had microfacture surgery on the left in 2009, and missed much of last year with an MCL injury in his right knee) and was in and out of the lineup in OTAs. Chung missed time with foot and knee injuries in 2010 and 2011 before losing four games to a shoulder injury last year in New England.

On paper, the Eagles have the talent for a rebound season. Kelly brings an up-tempo offense and a sense of hope to a team that fell on hard times in 2012. Better health and fewer turnovers are almost assured. Nonetheless, a competitive division in the tougher conference will make it hard for the Eagles to make the playoffs in 2013.

Chase Stuart

2012 Eagles Stats by Week

Wk	vs.	W-L	PF	PA	YDF	YDA	TO	Total	Off	Def	ST
1	at CLE	W	17	16	456	210	-1	7%	-37%	-61%	-16%
2	BAL	W	24	23	486	325	-2	11%	-2%	-26%	-13%
3	at ARI	L	6	27	307	292	-3	-52%	-14%	32%	-6%
4	NYG	W	19	17	422	366	1	-3%	13%	3%	-13%
5	at PIT	L	14	16	246	343	-2	-26%	-10%	16%	0%
6	DET	L	23	26	357	449	-2	-12%	-17%	-1%	4%
7	BYE										
8	ATL	L	17	30	270	392	0	-2%	12%	21%	7%
9	at NO	L	13	28	447	371	0	-52%	-29%	21%	-1%
10	DAL	L	23	38	369	294	-2	-23%	-2%	5%	-16%
11	at WAS	L	6	31	257	361	-3	-93%	-95%	6%	8%
12	CAR	L	22	30	311	398	-3	5%	21%	30%	13%
13	at DAL	L	33	38	423	417	-1	30%	43%	41%	28%
14	at TB	W	23	21	367	314	-1	-10%	11%	10%	-11%
15	CIN	L	13	34	219	249	-3	-61%	-56%	-11%	-16%
16	WAS	L	20	27	411	313	-1	6%	9%	7%	3%
17	NYG	L	7	42	317	397	-1	-84%	-14%	64%	-6%

Trends and Splits

	Offense	Rank	Defense	Rank
Total DVOA	-10.8%	25	9.4%	26
Unadjusted VOA	-11.6%	27	11.9%	29
Weighted Trend	-10.3%	22	17.1%	32
Variance	10.9%	29	8.0%	26
Average Opponent	1.6%	21	3.6%	4
Passing	-6.8%	26	24.1%	32
Rushing	-8.3%	22	-5.4%	17
First Down	-10.8%	24	2.2%	19
Second Down	-24.1%	30	11.1%	25
Third Down	11.8%	11	20.7%	28
First Half	-17.9%	28	15.5%	32
Second Half	-3.3%	16	2.9%	20
Red Zone	-48.3%	31	12.7%	27
Late and Close	-7.7%	19	8.3%	28

Five-Year Performance

Year	W-L	Pyth W	Est W	PF	PA	TO	Total	Rk	Off	Rk	Def	Rk	ST	Rk	Off AGL	Rk	Def AGL	Rk	Off Age	Rk	Def Age	Rk	ST Age	Rk
2008	9-6-1	11.4	11.6	416	289	+3	31.8%	1	6.5%	12	-23.6%	3	1.7%	13	35.5	22	3.5	2	28.3	7	27.3	17	26.6	17
2009	11-5	10.4	11.2	429	337	+15	28.8%	3	9.7%	11	-14.3%	3	4.8%	2	37.4	26	31.5	20	26.0	32	27.4	15	26.9	9
2010	10-6	9.5	11.9	439	377	+9	23.2%	5	17.3%	3	-3.6%	11	2.3%	12	41.4	29	28.7	21	25.6	32	26.6	18	26.2	16
2011	8-8	9.8	9.0	396	328	-14	13.5%	9	9.8%	8	-3.7%	11	0.0%	17	10.5	3	11.4	5	26.7	20	26.9	17	25.7	29
2012	4-12	3.9	4.5	280	444	-24	-22.4%	28	-10.8%	25	9.4%	26	-2.2%	23	65.2	32	8.1	2	26.8	17	26.5	23	25.6	27

2012 Performance Based on Most Common Personnel Groups

PHI Offense					PHI Offense vs. Opponents					PHI Defense					PHI Defense vs. Opponents			
Pers	Freq	Yds	DVOA	Run%	Pers	Freq	Yds	DVOA		Pers	Freq	Yds	DVOA		Pers	Freq	Yds	DVOA
11	50%	5.7	5.6%	33%	Nickel Even	51%	5.5	4.0%		Nickel Even	47%	6.1	14.9%		11	42%	5.8	12.2%
12	17%	5.4	-14.0%	37%	4-3-4	18%	4.9	-24.5%		4-3-4	46%	5.6	7.6%		21	20%	6.4	21.6%
21	15%	4.7	-19.6%	41%	3-4-4	13%	5.0	-0.3%		Dime+	2%	4.4	4.9%		12	19%	5.6	0.5%
10	8%	6.7	34.0%	13%	Dime+	10%	5.4	-4.8%		5-2-4	2%	3.0	-26.2%		22	7%	3.6	-21.9%
20	5%	2.5	-45.2%	26%	Nickel Odd	7%	6.0	-36.4%		Goal Line	1%	1.8	15.4%		10	2%	6.6	17.5%

Strategic Tendencies

Run/Pass		Rk	Formation		Rk	Pass Rush		Rk	Secondary		Rk	Strategy		Rk
Runs, first half	35%	27	Form: Single Back	75%	5	Rush 3	0.8%	32	4 DB	48%	7	Play action	26%	7
Runs, first down	40%	31	Form: Empty Back	5%	17	Rush 4	77.8%	1	5 DB	47%	16	Avg Box (Off)	6.21	25
Runs, second-long	30%	19	Pers: 3+ WR	67%	3	Rush 5	13.1%	32	6+ DB	2%	27	Avg Box (Def)	6.49	7
Runs, power sit.	45%	27	Pers: 4+ WR	9%	5	Rush 6+	8.2%	10	CB by Sides	66%	26	Offensive Pace	29.23	8
Runs, behind 2H	30%	13	Pers: 2+ TE/6+ OL	20%	30	Sacks by LB	6.3%	30	DB Blitz	5%	30	Defensive Pace	30.34	19
Pass, ahead 2H	63%	1	Shotgun/Pistol	57%	7	Sacks by DB	3.2%	22	Hole in Zone	3%	31	Go for it on 4th	1.06	8

The Eagles' defensive line was still bringing it, despite the rest of the problems on the team. They pressured the quarterback 27 percent of the time with a four-man pass rush, the highest rate in the league. Overall, the Eagles pressured the quarterback 25.3 percent of the time, second in the league behind Denver. ☞ The Eagles moved their cornerbacks around much more than they did in 2011, dropping from 95 percent (third) to 66 percent (26th) in "CB by Sides." ☞ Philadelphia opponents blitzed a defensive back on a league-high 15.6 percent of passes. ☞ If you like running back screens, Philadelphia was the team to watch. The Eagles were third in the league in running back screens, and second in running back screens by opponents. On both offense and defense, Philadelphia was roughly average in DVOA but gained/allowed a yard per play less than average.

Passing

Player	DYAR	DVOA	Plays	NtYds	Avg	YAC	C%	TD	Int
M.Vick	-78	-14.4%	380	2173	5.7	4.9	58.6%	12	10
N.Foles	-166	-20.4%	286	1550	5.4	5.2	61.8%	6	5

Rushing

Player	DYAR	DVOA	Plays	Yds	Avg	TD	Fum	Suc
L.McCoy	-34	-12.6%	199	834	4.2	2	4	48%
B.Brown	29	-2.2%	115	564	4.9	4	4	39%
M.Vick	3	-11.1%	52	329	6.3	1	4	--
D.Lewis*	29	45.5%	13	69	5.3	1	0	54%
N.Foles	11	11.7%	9	38	4.2	1	1	--
S.Havili*	8	24.2%	6	22	3.7	1	0	50%
F.Jones	11	-6.1%	111	408	3.7	3	1	49%

Receiving

Player	DYAR	DVOA	Plays	Ctch	Yds	Y/C	YAC	TD	C%
J.Maclin	132	-6.5%	121	68	856	12.6	3.8	7	56%
D.Jackson	42	-10.6%	88	45	700	15.6	5.1	2	51%
J.Avant	137	6.8%	77	54	635	11.8	2.7	0	70%
R.Cooper	-15	-22.8%	48	23	248	10.8	4.0	3	48%
D.Johnson	69	5.8%	31	19	256	13.5	5.3	0	61%
A.Benn	-8	-38.6%	6	4	26	6.5	5.8	0	67%
B.Celek	23	-12.8%	87	57	684	12.0	5.4	1	66%
C.Harbor	-66	-37.2%	39	25	186	7.4	2.8	2	64%
J.Casey	58	13.1%	44	34	330	9.7	6.2	3	77%
L.McCoy	90	9.2%	68	55	378	6.9	8.9	3	81%
B.Brown	-26	-38.9%	19	13	56	4.3	7.0	0	68%
S.Havili*	-12	-33.3%	12	7	43	6.1	4.4	0	58%
F.Jones	109	45.1%	36	25	262	10.5	9.0	2	69%

Offensive Line

Player	Pos	Age	GS	Snaps	Pen	Sk	Pass	Run	Player	Pos	Age	GS	Snaps	Pen	Sk	Pass	Run
Evan Mathis	LG	32	16/16	1123	4	1	10.5	5	Jake Scott*	RG	32	7/7	461	7	1.5	7	1
Dallas Reynolds	C	29	16/14	990	1	1.5	11.5	6.5	Danny Watkins	RG	29	11/6	448	2	1	9	1.5
King Dunlap*	LT	28	14/12	817	8	6.5	20.5	5	Demetrius Bell*	LT	29	9/5	446	9	2.5	20	2.5
Dennis Kelly	G/T	23	13/10	684	2	5	23	8	Jason Kelce	C	26	2/2	136	1	0	2	1
Todd Herremans	RT	31	8/8	529	3	3	11.5	4.5									

Year	Yards	ALY	Rk	Power	Rk	Stuff	Rk	2nd Lev	Rk	Open Field	Rk	Sacks	ASR	Rk	Short	Long	F-Start	Cont.
2010	4.96	4.17	10	76%	3	17%	10	1.25	7	1.35	1	49	8.4%	28	13	28	16	21
2011	4.54	3.89	26	67%	6	25%	32	1.43	2	1.10	4	32	5.8%	10	7	20	21	31
2012	4.47	3.56	28	69%	6	26%	31	1.39	6	1.06	6	48	8.1%	25	17	19	15	31
2012 ALY by direction:		Left End 3.34 (25)			Left Tackle 3.41 (27)			Mid/Guard 3.59 (27)			Right Tackle 3.89 (17)				Right End 3.67 (25)			

The Eagles have an offensive line that would be the envy of many playoff teams. Philadelphia upgrades both tackle spots by inserting Jason Peters and Lane Johnson into the lineup in 2013. Peters made five straight Pro Bowls from 2007 to 2011, but missed the entire 2012 season after two Achilles surgeries. If you are wondering how much the Eagles struggled to replace him, note that neither of last year's left tackles are still on the roster. The right side will be manned by Johnson, the fourth overall draft pick out of Oklahoma. Some in the scouting community have called Johnson the most athletically gifted offensive linemen prospect in years. He played quarterback in junior college and was a tight end early in his Sooners career. Johnson's broad jump (9 feet, 10 inches) ranks first among offensive linemen since 2006, and his 4.72 second 40-yard dash was just 0.01 off the high-water mark (set by Terron Armstead this year).

Left guard Evan Mathis was an unheralded journeyman who played for three teams in six years before coming to the Eagles in 2011. Since then, he has put together back-to-back Pro Bowl-caliber years, even if he remains mostly anonymous to the football world (Mathis has never actually made a Pro Bowl). Todd Herremans played well at right tackle the last two years after starting at left guard from 2006 to 2010. Now, with Johnson on the right edge and Mathis at Herremans' old spot, the team is moving him to right guard. Look for him to have a strong year inside: he has proven he can excel both at guard and on the right side of the line, and he will be one of the more athletic interior linemen in the NFL. Center Jason Kelce is another player who has excellent measurables for his position; he missed nearly all of 2012 with a torn MCL in his right knee, but that shouldn't slow him down this year.

Defensive Front Seven

Defensive Line	Age	Pos	Snaps	Plays	Overall TmPct	Rk	Stop	Dfts	BTkl	vs. Run Runs	St%	Rk	RuYd	Rk	Pass Rush Sack	Hit	Hur	Tips
Trent Cole	31	DE	735	41	5.2%	40	29	9	0	33	70%	53	3.3	67	3.5	6	19	1
Cullen Jenkins*	32	DT	626	26	3.3%	56	20	11	3	17	71%	52	2.6	50	4	5	19	1
Fletcher Cox	23	DT	509	42	5.7%	15	34	17	1	30	73%	38	2.6	49	5	4	8	1
Derek Landri*	30	DT	483	21	2.7%	66	13	6	3	15	67%	59	2.5	44	0	2	7.5	1
Brandon Graham	25	DE	421	37	4.7%	48	31	11	2	25	84%	8	1.8	14	5.5	6	26	1
Cedric Thornton	25	DT	395	27	3.4%	52	20	4	1	25	76%	32	3.3	63	1	2	1.5	1
Darryl Tapp*	29	DE	247	16	2.5%	--	13	3	1	12	92%	--	1.2	--	0.5	1	2.5	0
Isaac Sopoaga	32	DT	333	26	3.5%	49	18	5	0	22	77%	29	1.9	21	1	0	1	0

Linebackers	Age	Pos	Snaps	Plays	Overall TmPct	Rk	Stop	Dfts	BTkl	Pass Rush Sack	Hit	Hur	Tips	vs. Run Runs	St%	Rk	Yds	Rk	vs. Pass Tgts	Suc%	Rk	AdjYd	Rk	PD
DeMeco Ryans	29	MLB	1041	116	14.7%	29	66	30	7	1	1	3	0	82	60%	81	3.7	72	31	49%	42	8.4	67	3
Mychal Kendricks	23	OLB	926	84	11.3%	57	50	17	11	1	0	1.5	0	45	62%	73	4.1	92	46	57%	18	4.8	14	6
Akeem Jordan*	28	OLB	330	33	4.8%	--	16	5	2	0	0	0	0	29	52%	--	3.8	--	5	40%	--	7.1	--	0
Jamar Chaney	27	MLB	230	21	3.0%	--	14	1	2	0	0	0	0	17	76%	--	3.5	--	8	35%	--	8.1	--	1
Connor Barwin	27	OLB	998	48	6.1%	95	36	17	3	3	14	16.5	5	28	64%	63	2.5	24	8	84%	--	2.0	--	0

Year	Yards	ALY	Rk	Power	Rk	Stuff	Rk	2nd Level	Rk	Open Field	Rk	Sacks	ASR	Rk	Short	Long
2010	4.03	3.71	8	63%	16	22%	9	1.20	23	0.76	16	39	7.7%	5	15	11
2011	4.53	4.02	16	47%	3	23%	3	1.35	29	0.98	22	50	8.3%	4	22	18
2012	4.06	3.82	9	60%	16	22%	8	1.26	26	0.67	13	30	6.5%	12	7	11

2012 ALY by direction:	Left End 3.41 (8)	Left Tackle 3.49 (9)	Mid/Guard 3.93 (11)	Right Tackle 3.7 (12)	Right End 4.19 (17)

Brandon Graham had a breakout season as a part-time player last year, not that anyone outside of Philadelphia noticed. His 26 hurries ranked 10th in the league, but Graham was on the field for only 421 snaps, far fewer than the rest of the pass rushers in the top ten. Graham easily averaged the most hurries per snap last year, and Seattle's Bruce Irvin was the only other player with 15-plus hurries on fewer than 500 snaps. Graham will play as a 3-4 outside linebacker this year, and has the potential for double-digit sacks. But he'll have to do that as a situational player, because Trent Cole and Connor Barwin seem likely to start ahead of him. Barwin recorded 11.5 sacks in 2011, and while his sack total dropped to just three last year, some of that might have been bad luck: he ranked in the top 10 with 14 quarterback hits. Cole also had a down year: after producing 55 sacks in the prior five years, he dropped to just three sacks in 2012. But with the way the secondary and the offense played last year, we can't fault Cole too much. If the Eagles offense can get the team a lead, the defense has the players to attack the quarterback.

At linebacker, DeMeco Ryans is a top player against the run but is a liability in coverage. He led all inside linebackers with 30 Defeats last year, but he also allowed 8.1 yards per pass in coverage. The scheme change may have Ryans experiencing an unfortunate sense of déjà vu, and not just because he'll be playing alongside Barwin again. Ryans was a very good middle linebacker from 2006 to 2009 before missing most of 2010 with a torn Achilles. When he returned in 2011, the Texans had switched to a 3-4 defense, and Ryans was an overpaid, two-down linebacker that season. That prompted the trade to Philadelphia, yet after one season, Ryans is back in the 3-4 scheme. But in reality, Ryans' limitations may be better hid in a 3-4, where he'll have less ground to cover. The truth is he's much better against the run than the pass regardless of formation. The other inside linebacker is Mychal Kendricks, who was the team's second-round draft pick a year ago; with a 4.47 forty, he brings a lot of speed to the Eagles defense. Unfortunately, that didn't translate into production in 2012, as he was overmatched for most of the season. At OTAs, Kendricks acknowledged that his rookie year was a serious disappointment, but a return to 3-4 inside linebacker (the position he played in college) should help accelerate his maturation. His agility and lateral quickness will keep him on the field over Ryans in sub packages.

The bigger questions in the front seven are along the defensive line. In any 3-4 defense, the nose tackle is one of the key players and one of the hardest spots to fill. Isaac Sopoaga was brought in from San Francisco to man that spot in 2013, but he's not a long-term answer. The 330-pound veteran has experience at the position but turns 32 in September. He had become a part-time player with the 49ers and expecting much more from him in 2013 may be unrealistic. Last year's first-round pick Fletcher Cox will be making a position switch after a strong rookie season at defensive tackle. The former Mississippi State star recorded 17 Defeats, fifth among defensive tackles behind only Geno Atkins, Kyle Williams, Ndamukong Suh, and Vince Wilfork. That's great company, but Cox now will be positioned as a 3-4 defensive end. He has the size to play the position, and has some experience as a 3-4 end from college, but his athleticism may be wasted if the Eagles ask him to just eat up blockers. Cedric Thornton and Vinny Curry will share the other 3-4 end spot, but neither is a proven player at this level. Curry is the upside pick: he recorded 11 sacks his senior year of college, and bulked up to 280 pounds this offseason as he prepares for the more physical role of a 3-4 end.

Defensive Secondary

Secondary	Age	Pos	Snaps	Plays	Overall TmPct	Rk	Stop	Dfts	BTkl	vs. Run Runs	St%	Rk	Yds	Rk	vs. Pass Tgts	Tgt%	Rk	Dist	Suc%	Rk	APaYd	Rk	PD	Int
D. Rodgers-Cromartie*	27	CB	992	67	8.5%	46	27	11	12	11	27%	71	8.4	66	79	20.7%	19	14.5	48%	62	8.0	60	16	3
Nnamdi Asomugha*	32	CB	983	67	8.5%	46	29	13	8	26	38%	52	7.2	51	63	16.4%	51	13.7	47%	65	9.7	80	12	1
Kurt Coleman	25	SS	878	92	13.3%	10	27	8	11	53	38%	37	7.3	41	25	7.5%	27	12.9	53%	40	8.3	50	4	2
Nate Allen	26	FS	845	73	9.9%	39	24	4	12	32	44%	18	6.8	34	43	12.0%	4	12.5	58%	27	6.3	15	4	0
Brandon Boykin	23	CB	505	33	4.2%	86	12	5	7	3	0%	84	8.3	65	43	11.3%	82	11.2	58%	15	6.5	17	4	0
Colt Anderson	28	SS	291	28	4.1%	--	11	2	7	20	40%	--	7.9	--	13	3.9%	--	15.5	45%	--	6.5	--	3	1
Cary Williams	29	CB	1079	91	10.3%	17	29	10	2	12	42%	42	7.3	52	93	21.0%	15	13.5	44%	79	8.0	58	17	4
Patrick Chung	26	SS	531	48	7.9%	52	11	4	3	18	22%	67	7.8	48	23	6.1%	46	12.7	61%	19	6.9	30	5	2
Bradley Fletcher	27	CB	364	30	3.5%	--	13	8	3	2	0%	--	17.5	--	29	6.9%	--	9.4	53%	--	5.9	--	8	1
Kenny Phillips	27	SS	293	27	7.5%	--	11	2	0	13	54%	--	4.7	--	5	2.7%	--	16.9	98%	--	-0.3	--	2	0

Year	Pass D Rank	vs. #1 WR	Rk	vs. #2 WR	Rk	vs. Other WR	Rk	vs. TE	Rk	vs. RB	Rk
2010	11	-8.0%	11	-19.3%	4	-12.6%	9	10.9%	19	27.7%	31
2011	11	-0.5%	12	7.9%	21	-15.2%	12	-8.2%	3	22.5%	29
2012	32	35.5%	31	11.1%	27	19.2%	27	-2.5%	16	11.0%	22

Cary Williams was a 16-game starter for the Ravens the last two years, but he may add more in veteran leadership than pure ability. Williams will never be confused for a shutdown corner: he recorded 46 tackles on passes where he was in coverage, nine more than any other player in the league. The silver lining of that stat for Eagles fans is that at least Williams *can* tackle; among defensive backs with at least 50 tackles, only Carlos Rogers and Tarell Brown of the 49ers had a lower broken tackle rate. Bradley Fletcher is similar to Williams: a physical player, a sure tackler, and nothing special as a pure cover corner. He missed 2011 with a torn ACL, and wasn't the same player in 2012 that he was prior to the injury. He was limited to spot duty as a nickelback, and seemed to land in Jeff Fisher's doghouse by the end of the year.

Patrick Chung may be new to Philadelphia, but he'll recognize at least one familiar face in training camp: Chip Kelly was the offensive coordinator at Oregon during Chung's junior and senior years. At his best, Chung is an athletic strong safety capable of making big plays, but he's a question mark in coverage and has struggled with injuries most of his career. Chung plays bigger than his size, but a reckless attitude on a 5-foot-11, 212-pound frame is a recipe for missed games. Like Fletcher, Chung seemed to fall out of favor with his coaches, and the Patriots made no attempt to resign him. Kenny Phillips was part of the Giants' Big Nickel package that helped them win Super Bowl XLVI; when healthy, few safeties can match his combination of size, coverage skills, and athleticism. Unfortunately, knee injuries have taken a toll on Phillips, and it's telling that he accepted a contract with no guaranteed money. While both Chung and Phillips have played well, it is a bit surprising that Philadelphia didn't add a centerfielder type to help revitalize a terrible pass defense. Nate Allen finished first among safeties in Success Rate in 2011, but he sank to the bottom with the rest of the secondary in 2012. He's well-suited as a third safety, and given the injury history of the other starters, he'll likely be on the field often in 2013.

Special Teams

Year	DVOA	Rank	FG/XP	Rank	Net Kick	Rank	Kick Ret	Rank	Net Punt	Rank	Punt Ret	Rank	Hidden	Rank
2010	2.3%	12	3.7	9	8.2	7	-9.9	29	8.6	8	1.1	15	-5.1	20
2011	0.0%	17	3.9	9	7.5	5	-3.5	23	0.1	16	-7.9	27	1.7	14
2012	-2.2%	23	0.9	17	3.3	10	-0.5	18	-18.2	32	3.3	8	-9.1	29

From Week 2 through Week 12, Alex Henery didn't miss a field goal, part of an overall strong sophomore season with the Eagles. He doesn't have top-end power, but he has been a reliable kicker in two seasons in Philadelphia. While Henery was generally good, he did have some odd misses. Excluding blocks, only 11 extra points or field goals from inside of 31 yards were missed league-wide last year, and Henery was responsible for three of them. But the real disaster was at punter, where both Chas Henry and Mat McBriar were disappointments. In the offseason, the team signed Donnie Jones, a reliable veteran who should provide an instant upgrade. Playing for Houston last season, 28 of Jones' punts were downed inside the 20, versus just 12 for Henry and McBriar.

DeSean Jackson returned four punts for touchdowns from 2008 to 2010, but punt-return duties are now handled by Damaris Johnson. As a rookie in 2012, Johnson returned a punt 98 yards for a score, the longest in the league, but he must get his fumbling problems under control. Another second-year player, Brandon Boykin, is the primary kickoff returner. Boykin returned four kickoffs for touchdowns in three years at Georgia, and had a 92-yard punt return for a score in the 2012 Outback Bowl. Boykin's longest return last year was just 44 yards, but he has the potential to turn into an above-average special teams player.

Coaching Staff

Oregon ran a play every 20.7 seconds last year, the seventh quickest pace in major college football. Keep in mind that the run-heavy attack (which kept the clock running) and the number of blowouts (which caused the Ducks to run out the clock in the second half) impacts that number, so Oregon's reputation as a high-octane, up-tempo attack is well-deserved. Transitioning to that pace may not be that hard for the Eagles, however, as the team ranked eighth in situation-neutral pace and fourth in total pace last season.

Let's be blunt: Offensive coordinator Pat Shurmur was a strange hire. He had modest success in that role with the Rams in 2009 and 2010, which earned him the head coaching job in Cleveland. But Shurmur was a disaster as head coach, and his conservative style of coaching didn't suit a Browns team that was often less talented than their opponents. Shurmur was with the Eagles for the first decade of Reid's tenure, mostly as quarterbacks coach, but it's unclear how his West Coast offense roots will meld with Kelly's vision for the Eagles.

Billy Davis was the Cardinals' defensive coordinator in 2009 and 2010, and coached the linebackers in Cleveland under Shurmur the past two seasons. When the Cardinals fired Davis, critics said his play-calling had been too predictable; that position was vindicated as the Cardinals defense was much better the past two seasons. Davis was a ball boy for the Eagles during the Dick Vermeil era, but has a much more daunting task this time around.

Pittsburgh Steelers

2012 Record: 8-8	Total DVOA: -1.2% (18th)	2013 Mean Projection: 8.7 wins	On the Clock (0-4): 5%
Pythagorean Wins: 8.7 (14th)	Offense: -4.0% (19th)	Postseason Odds: 47.1%	Mediocrity (5-7): 25%
Snap-Weighted Age: 27.6 (3rd)	Defense: -2.9% (13th)	Super Bowl Odds: 6.2%	Playoff Contender (8-10): 47%
Average Opponent: -5.2% (28th)	Special Teams: -0.1% (17th)	Proj. Avg. Opponent: -0.3% (22nd)	Super Bowl Contender (11+): 23%

2012: Don't take that third step, 'cause that's just a sad lovers' waltz.

2013: In Steelers We Trust, although this is looking like a two-year rebuild.

The Steelers have been playing playoff hopscotch for 12 years. They reached the postseason in 2001 and 2002, then fell to a 6-10 record in 2003. They returned to the playoffs in 2004 and 2005, but missed with an 8-8 record in 2006. Back to the postseason went the Steelers in 2007 and 2008, but 9-7 wasn't good enough in 2009. Two 12-4 records and playoff appearances followed, but the Steelers slipped back to .500 last year. Pittsburgh fans didn't like those down years, but it's hard to complain when the last three measures of this postseason waltz included trips to the Super Bowl.

If this were a toddler education cartoon, like *Team Umizoomi*, we would rigidly adhere to the pattern and predict two fresh seasons of Steelers greatness. Life is more complicated than Nick Jr., however, and we do too much math around here to fall into the trap of thinking such a pattern will repeat until infinity.

Still, the Steelers are not quite like other teams, who might change coaches and philosophies three or four times in a 12-year stretch. The Steelers operate on a geological timeframe, by NFL standards. Studying a 12-year cycle can provide some clues about how the Steelers stayed great for so long, and how they so often managed to quickly rebound from seasons like 2012.

The hopscotch pattern is a little harder to see if you analyze the last 12 seasons using DVOA (Table 1). The downturns in 2003 and 2012 are easy to spot; the ones in 2006 and 2009

Table 1: Pittsburgh Steelers DVOA Ranks, 2001-2012

Year	W-L	Total Rank	Off. Rank	Def. Rank	ST Rank	Sched. Rank
2001	13-3	7	4	9	26	31
2002	10-5-1	13	12	9	28	16
2003	6-10	19	19	15	3	15
2004	15-1	1	8	3	10	7
2005	11-5	4	8	3	10	17
2006	8-8	10	9	9	30	12
2007	10-6	6	9	3	21	22
2008	12-4	4	21	1	23	3
2009	9-7	10	7	9	30	26
2010	12-4	2	5	1	16	9
2011	12-4	4	6	7	9	28
2012	8-8	18	19	13	17	28

(.500 or better seasons, mind you) don't leap off the chart. Both of those teams were just typical Steelers teams offensively and defensively—maybe not quite as strong as usual, but definitely in the same ballpark. Instead, the 2006 and 2009 Steelers were essentially victims of special teams volatility, kept out of the playoffs by a play here and a play there in the kicking game. The 2009 Steelers, for example, allowed four kickoff return touchdowns, two of which directly impacted close losses to the Bengals and Chiefs.

The 2012 Steelers, however, weren't a kickoff return or two away from greatness. As in 2003, last year's team came in a clear notch below the team's established offensive and defensive performance levels. Steelers fans know that the 2003 team rebounded with a 15-1 season in 2004 and a championship in 2005. Sudden turnarounds are possible, which of course does not mean they are inevitable.

Look carefully at the last column of Table 1, and you can see one of the two by-products of the hopscotch pattern that has worked in the Steelers' favor for 12 years. The not-so-great seasons give the Steelers a relative schedule break every third year. An easy schedule in 2004 helped the team go 15-1 with a rookie quarterback. The Steelers gained little-to-no edge in 2007, but a break in the brutality was a big deal in 2010, when a slight flick of the difficulty switch helped them match the Ravens' 12-4 record despite a four-game Ben Roethlisberger suspension. A little of what we see in the Steelers' three-step waltz is a perennially good team bobbing up and down with its schedule: the tough competition hammers them when anything goes wrong, then the resulting opportunity to face second- and third-place opponents instead of the Patriots or a Peyton Manning team can make a modest improvement the following year look more extreme.

Our projections say the Steelers' schedule this year is neither particularly easy nor particularly difficult. Their average opponent has a mean projection of 0.4% DVOA, which gives them edge over the Bengals (1.3%) and the Ravens (2.1%). The schedule will have an impact on the won-loss column, though it will not be extreme enough to vault the Steelers back into contention by itself.

There is another advantage of having a down season every three years: it gives the Steelers a chance to draft a better player than the ones typically waiting for them at the very end of the first round. The Steelers drafted Ben Roethlisberger

2013 Steelers Schedule

Week	Opp.	Week	Opp.	Week	Opp.
1	TEN	7	BAL	13	at BAL (Thu.)
2	at CIN (Mon.)	8	at OAK	14	MIA
3	CHI	9	at NE	15	CIN
4	vs. MIN (U.K.)	10	BUF	16	at GB
5	BYE	11	DET	17	at CLE
6	at NYJ	12	at CLE		

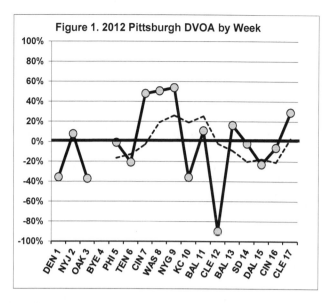

Figure 1. 2012 Pittsburgh DVOA by Week

11th overall in 2004, after a poor season. In 2007, they selected Lawrence Timmons 15th overall. Maurkice Pouncey arrived in 2010 with the 18th overall pick. In other seasons, while the Steelers have acquired productive first-rounders like Heath Miller and Ziggy Hood, they have picked 30th, 31st, and 32nd, as well as 23rd, 24th, and 25th. The Steelers are rarely in position to draft a blue-chip rookie, which is a major drawback for a team that is economically limited in free agency. They solved that problem in 2003 by trading up from 27th to 16th for Troy Polamalu, but trading out of the late 20s or early 30s every year is not a sustainable draft strategy. The Steelers need to slide into the middle of the first round every once and a while to get a franchise quarterback, an All-Pro center, or a rook for their blitzing chessboard.

It's important to note that the Steelers generally have productive drafts, and except for the first-round picks, the Roethlisberger-Pouncey-Timmons classes were not unusually deep by Pittsburgh standards. Timmons arrived with LaMarr Woodley; Pouncey with Antonio Brown and Emmanuel Sanders; Big Ben with Max Starks. It is not unusual for a Steelers draft class to bring two quality starters, plus a useful sub or two. The Steelers always draft well, or more precisely, they draft adequately but develop talent exceptionally well. Still, those high first-round picks bring premium talent, the kind that cannot be manufactured from raw materials in the Steelers' fast-receiver or outside-pass rusher factories.

This year's "skills you cannot teach" prospect is Jarvis Jones, who arrives from Georgia with solid sack production, great edge quickness, and plenty of questions from both our statistical and scouting departments. SackSEER hates Jones: his 4.88-second Pro Day forty was brutal (as were his broad jump and vertical leap, SackSEER's two "explosiveness" measurables), and at 245 pounds Jones needs all the burst he can muster. The list of edge rushers drafted since 1998 who were under 250 pounds with 4.8-plus forties is a who's who of nobodies, plus one *Real House Husband of Atlanta*: Kroy Biermann, Casey Daley, Bryant McNeal, and Chita Ozougwu. Reality television jokes aside, Biermann has developed into a fine player, but not one who would have been worth a first-round pick. Furthermore, when we are done fretting about Jones' workout numbers, we can worry about his scouting tape. Jones was a one-trick pony outside rusher for the Bulldogs, and he earned many of his sacks when coaches stunted and schemed to get him a free shot at the quarterback.

The Jones assessment pits our admittedly-limited metrics and diligent-but-part-time scouts against a franchise whose track record for finding and developing excellent linebackers

dates back to our days of watching *Mister Rogers' Neighborhood*. There is no reason both of us have to be wrong: the Steelers have taken their time developing pass-rush projects in the past (see James Harrison) and could extend Jones' window of production past what SackSEER is designed to see (the first five seasons). Still, if we are looking for rookies who can provide an immediate jolt, we should look past Jones. There, we will find one of the most interesting Steelers drafts of the 21st century, and potentially the deepest.

Second-round pick Le'Veon Bell is precisely what we imagine when we think of the quintessential Steelers running back. He is big, yet nimble, with a deft spin move. The Steelers chose him over Eddie Lacy, another spin-tastic big man with a higher rating on most draft boards. The difference between them was not that great on the scouting tape, once you adjusted your eyes to the fact that Lacy was running behind an NFL-quality offensive line at Alabama. Third-round pick Markus Wheaton, like Bell, is a Steelers casting call special, only this time at wide receiver: a smallish burner who can pop the lid off the coverage, then juke around in all the space he created. Bell and Wheaton replace departed free agents Rashard Mendenhall and Mike Wallace; Bell is a probable upgrade over the injured-disgruntled Mendenhall, while Wheaton must grow into Wallace's shoes. The fourth round brought quarterback Landry Jones, less an heir apparent to Big Ben than recognition that the team cannot slap a helmet on a glorified offensive coordinator and expect to win games during Roethlisberger's frequent absences.

This draft class, while brimming with potential, is not the immediate spark plug the Steelers appear to need. It's instructive to look back at 2004 once again. Roethlisberger provided an upgrade over Tommy Maddox, even as a rookie, but DVOA reminds us that defense was a major part of the Steelers problem in 2003. That year's defense, like last year's, was getting old fast. The 2003 Steelers got last-legs seasons from players like Jason Gildon, Kimo van Oelhoffen, Dewayne Washington, and Brent Alexander. Their defensive improvement in 2004 was the result of Polamalu, Joey Porter, and others coming of age, not the sudden arrival of rookies. That is the Steelers way: there is a pipeline, and the next batch of players comes of age just as the last crop grows old or expensive.

If you want to stretch the 2003-04 and 2012-13 comparison even further—and it is admittedly well past recommended tolerances all ready—we can compare the arrivals of Landry Jones and Bruce Gradkowski to the replacement of Maddox with Roethlisberger. The old Steelers replaced a broken-down journeyman with an exceptional rookie who later became a franchise quarterback. The new Steelers replaced three-to-four games of rickety Byron Leftwich and Charlie Batch with a fiery pepperpot and a red-chip prospect with plenty of college starting experience. Throw in Bell to help a running game that was embarrassing last year, and the Steelers could get an offensive improvement close to what they experienced in 2004. But who steps up on defense, where the problems of age were even more acute last year than they were a decade ago? Besides Jarvis Jones, the likely step-up candidates include Hood, Jason Worilds, Steve McLendon, and Cameron Heyward. There's no Polamalu in the bunch, and the most interesting prospect in the secondary, Keenan Lewis, bolted for the Saints.

Patterns aside, the Steelers simply got old last year. Their lineup was old, and their bench was scary old at some positions: not just the Sunshine Boys at quarterback, but Jerricho Cotchery and Plaxico Burress rounding out the wide receiver depth chart with Will Allen coming off the bench at safety. Such "deep age" suggests that the Steelers are finally in need of a two-year rebuild, especially with Wallace gone and tight end Heath Miller's season in doubt due to an ACL injury. The 12-year high-wire act may finally be losing its balance.

Or it may not. It's a remarkably close call. The Steelers remain on the fringe of the playoff picture by our projections, even as they replace big pieces like Wallace and milk extra years out of 30-something defenders. The Steelers could squeak back into the playoffs and keep the pattern alive. If they don't, they should be fully loaded for 2014: this year's rookies; whatever stars emerge from the Worlds brigade; a gelled line of Pouncey, David DeCastro, and maybe Mike Adams; plus whoever they get in the 2014 draft. Projecting the Steelers for the 2013 playoffs is tricky. Projecting them for the 2014 playoffs, barring the wreck of the good ship Roethlisberger, is downright easy.

But that's just history talking. We now have DVOA dating back to 1991. The Steelers defense has never ranked below 15th in the NFL. The offense has never ranked below 21st. The Steelers have weak years about one-third of the time, but they refuse to have a true train wreck of a season. There's a chance we will find one once DVOA gets back to 1988, when the Steelers went 5-11 with an offense led by Bubby Brister, running back Warren Williams, and receivers Louis Lipps (good) and Weegie Thompson (weegie), or in 1986, when Mark Malone led some limping last-gasp Steel Curtain hangers-on. If the Steelers didn't post truly bad DVOA numbers in those years, then we will have to work our way back to the Nixon administration to find one, a quest that will take the rest of our careers.

If that is not extended excellence, it is certainly uncannily extended competence. It's a testament to a philosophy and a system of top-down football management, a coaching, scouting, and development model that has stood the test of time. The Steelers model is more powerful than any quirky statistical pattern. The Steelers don't have to be great exactly two years out of three. They just have to keep doing things the Steelers way, and they will succeed often enough.

Mike Tanier

2012 Steelers Stats by Week

Wk	vs.	W-L	PF	PA	YDF	YDA	TO	Total	Off	Def	ST
1	at DEN	L	19	31	284	334	0	-36%	-10%	22%	-4%
2	NYJ	W	27	10	331	219	1	8%	24%	26%	10%
3	at OAK	L	31	34	433	321	-1	-37%	320%	29%	-11%
4	BYE										
5	PHI	W	16	14	343	246	2	-1%	-2%	0%	2%
6	at TEN	L	23	26	412	359	0	-21%	-1%	1%	-19%
7	at CIN	W	24	17	431	185	-1	48%	26%	-13%	9%
8	WAS	W	27	12	355	255	0	51%	36%	-13%	2%
9	at NYG	W	24	20	349	182	-1	54%	5%	-25%	24%
10	KC	W	16	13	249	290	0	-36%	-39%	2%	4%
11	BAL	L	10	13	309	200	-3	11%	-1%	-36%	-24%
12	at CLE	L	14	20	242	238	-7	-90%	-100%	-18%	-8%
13	at BAL	W	23	20	366	288	-1	16%	-5%	-13%	8%
14	SD	L	24	34	340	294	-2	-2%	-7%	3%	9%
15	at DAL	L	24	27	388	415	-1	-23%	4%	22%	-5%
16	CIN	L	10	13	280	267	0	-6%	-40%	-37%	-3%
17	CLE	W	24	10	212	320	4	29%	19%	-4%	7%

Trends and Splits

	Offense	Rank	Defense	Rank
Total DVOA	-4.0%	19	-2.9%	13
Unadjusted VOA	-1.8%	18	-8.0%	6
Weighted Trend	-8.9%	21	-9.3%	9
Variance	10.4%	27	4.3%	11
Average Opponent	2.6%	27	-4.3%	29
Passing	12.3%	13	5.3%	15
Rushing	-18.1%	31	-13.3%	9
First Down	-8.2%	21	5.2%	24
Second Down	-13.3%	24	-9.3%	9
Third Down	17.4%	8	-8.3%	9
First Half	-0.7%	17	-7.4%	8
Second Half	-7.5%	23	2.0%	16
Red Zone	12.7%	9	10.5%	25
Late and Close	-12.2%	23	-6.1%	16

Five-Year Performance

Year	W-L	Pyth W	Est W	PF	PA	TO	Total	Rk	Off	Rk	Def	Rk	ST	Rk	Off AGL	Rk	Def AGL	Rk	Off Age	Rk	Def Age	Rk	ST Age	Rk
2008	12-4	11.8	11.3	347	223	+4	26.0%	4	-1.5%	21	-29.0%	1	-1.5%	23	37.6	24	16.5	12	26.4	30	28.8	1	26.4	21
2009	9-7	9.2	10.0	368	324	-3	14.2%	10	14.4%	7	-4.6%	9	-4.8%	30	23.9	16	29.2	17	27.0	19	29.4	1	26.6	16
2010	12-4	12.1	12.1	375	232	+17	35.4%	2	14.3%	5	-20.7%	1	0.4%	16	32.0	22	17.9	12	27.0	22	29.2	1	26.7	12
2011	12-4	11.1	11.3	325	227	-13	22.6%	4	11.4%	6	-9.4%	7	1.7%	9	33.2	19	27.3	18	26.4	25	29.1	1	26.2	19
2012	8-8	8.7	7.4	336	314	-10	-1.2%	18	-4.0%	19	-2.9%	13	-0.1%	17	64.3	31	19.1	9	26.5	21	29.2	1	25.9	20

2012 Performance Based on Most Common Personnel Groups

PIT Offense					PIT Offense vs. Opponents				PIT Defense				PIT Defense vs. Opponents			
Pers	Freq	Yds	DVOA	Run%	Pers	Freq	Yds	DVOA	Pers	Freq	Yds	DVOA	Pers	Freq	Yds	DVOA
11	51%	5.8	0.7%	29%	Nickel Even	34%	5.5	-1.8%	3 4 4	61%	5.2	-3.0%	11	32%	4 4	-10.1%
21	19%	4.9	-10.7%	52%	4-3-4	23%	5.0	-19.4%	Nickel Even	28%	4.2	-2.9%	12	26%	5.9	13.4%
12	13%	5.8	5.9%	25%	3-4-4	20%	5.4	-2.9%	Nickel Odd	5%	6.1	3.3%	21	24%	5.4	0.8%
22	10%	4.6	-24.1%	70%	Nickel Odd	11%	5.8	24.8%	Dime+	2%	4.3	-53.2%	13	5%	4.3	8.1%
13	3%	4.0	22.4%	77%	Dime+	10%	5.8	2.8%	4-3-4	2%	4.3	-10.5%	22	4%	2.0	-40.3%

Strategic Tendencies

Run/Pass		Rk	Formation		Rk	Pass Rush		Rk	Secondary		Rk	Strategy		Rk
Runs, first half	36%	25	Form: Single Back	69%	12	Rush 3	7.5%	12	4 DB	63%	1	Play action	18%	22
Runs, first down	51%	15	Form: Empty Back	6%	15	Rush 4	52.3%	30	5 DB	34%	29	Avg Box (Off)	6.47	8
Runs, second-long	28%	24	Pers: 3+ WR	54%	13	Rush 5	32.7%	2	6+ DB	2%	28	Avg Box (Def)	6.56	2
Runs, power sit.	56%	15	Pers: 4+ WR	1%	19	Rush 6+	7.5%	13	CB by Sides	64%	28	Offensive Pace	31.89	27
Runs, behind 2H	35%	3	Pers: 2+ TE/6+ OL	28%	18	Sacks by LB	67.6%	6	DB Blitz	12%	16	Defensive Pace	29.44	6
Pass, ahead 2H	53%	8	Shotgun/Pistol	44%	20	Sacks by DB	2.7%	24	Hole in Zone	6%	28	Go for it on 4th	1.02	11

Pittsburgh changed up its formation habits on both sides of the ball in 2012. On offense, the use of empty-back sets went from 14 percent (third) in 2011 to 5.6 percent (15th) in 2012. On defense, the Steelers went from 16 percent dime and 25 percent nickel in 2011 to 2.2 percent dime and 34 percent nickel in 2012. ☞ Pittsburgh opponents may want to consider trying more draw plays. Although the Steelers have faced a league-low 25 draws over the past two seasons, they've allowed a combined 7.8 yards per carry and 63.6% DVOA on those plays. In fact, all runs from shotgun were a problem for Pittsburgh last year, draw or otherwise, as they allowed a league-worst 36.8% DVOA on shotgun runs. ☞ Steelers opponents only threw 11 percent of passes to running backs, the lowest figure in the league.

Passing

Player	DYAR	DVOA	Plays	NtYds	Avg	YAC	C%	TD	Int
B.Roethlisberger	761	13.2%	473	3068	6.5	5.2	64.3%	25	8
C.Batch*	-8	-13.0%	74	469	6.3	5.8	64.8%	1	4
B.Leftwich*	-12	-14.5%	56	248	4.4	4.6	47.2%	0	1
B.Gradkowski	-3	-14.9%	12	60	5.0	1.0	45.5%	0	0

Rushing

Player	DYAR	DVOA	Plays	Yds	Avg	TD	Fum	Suc
J.Dwyer	-60	-18.0%	156	623	4.0	2	2	44%
I.Redman	-31	-15.0%	110	410	3.7	2	2	43%
R.Mendenhall*	-62	-38.5%	51	182	3.6	0	3	43%
C.Rainey*	26	16.0%	26	102	3.9	2	0	50%
B.Batch	-21	-28.7%	25	49	2.0	1	0	28%
B.Roethlisberger	5	-6.2%	17	98	5.8	0	1	-
A.Brown	10	-7.7%	6	20	3.3	0	0	-
M.Wallace*	-8	-75.1%	5	7	1.4	0	0	-
L.Stephens-Howling	-63	-22.9%	110	356	3.2	4	0	34%

Receiving

Player	DYAR	DVOA	Plays	Ctch	Yds	Y/C	YAC	TD	C%
M.Wallace*	-19	-17.4%	119	64	833	13.0	4.2	8	54%
A.Brown	88	-1.9%	106	67	790	11.8	5.3	4	63%
E.Sanders	124	9.5%	74	44	624	14.2	4.8	1	59%
J.Cotchery	35	2.8%	27	17	205	12.1	2.5	0	63%
P.Burress	32	28.7%	7	3	42	14.0	1.3	1	43%
H.Miller	165	21.0%	101	71	816	11.5	4.8	8	70%
D.Paulson	-39	-65.2%	11	7	51	7.3	4.1	0	64%
M.Spaeth	-14	-33.7%	10	6	28	4.7	2.3	1	60%
W.Johnson	43	14.3%	26	15	137	9.1	5.2	1	58%
J.Dwyer	8	-8.2%	25	18	106	5.9	5.8	0	72%
I.Redman	75	36.1%	23	19	247	13.0	10.6	0	83%
C.Rainey*	-102	-97.5%	22	14	60	4.3	5.8	0	64%
R.Mendenhall*	24	22.7%	11	9	62	6.9	10.9	1	82%
L.Stephens-Howling	-48	-46.0%	30	17	106	6.2	7.9	0	57%

Offensive Line

Player	Pos	Age	GS	Snaps	Pen	Sk	Pass	Run	Player	Pos	Age	GS	Snaps	Pen	Sk	Pass	Run
Max Starks*	LT	31	16/16	1065	3	3	16.5	2.5	Doug Legursky*	C/G	27	16/3	409	2	2.5	11	0
Ramon Foster	RG	27	16/16	1010	3	2	7	8	Kelvin Beachum	RT	24	7/5	307	2	0.5	8.5	1
Maurkice Pouncey	C	24	15/15	929	2	4	11	6	Marcus Gilbert	RT	25	5/5	241	2	0	6	1.5
Willie Colon*	LG	30	11/11	713	12	4	6	9	David DeCastro	RG	23	4/3	134	0	3.5	4.5	2
Mike Adams	OT	23	10/6	488	3	6	13	2	Guy Whimper	OT	30	16/6	382	4	5.5	16.3	4

Year	Yards	ALY	Rk	Power	Rk	Stuff	Rk	2nd Lev	Rk	Open Field	Rk	Sacks	ASR	Rk	Short	Long	F-Start	Cont.
2010	3.93	3.87	19	64%	12	21%	24	1.04	23	0.73	15	43	8.6%	29	9	26	14	31
2011	4.49	4.44	3	57%	24	21%	23	1.32	6	0.82	16	42	7.2%	20	17	19	18	22
2012	3.71	3.72	27	61%	19	19%	17	0.95	30	0.54	24	37	6.3%	15	12	18	13	26
2012 ALY by direction:			Left End 4.51 (5)			Left Tackle 4.87 (5)			Mid/Guard 3.44 (31)			Right Tackle 4.17 (10)				Right End 4.89 (9)		

New offensive line coach Jack Bicknell Jr. is helping Todd Haley install an outside zone-blocking scheme. The scheme has to help a running game that finished 31st in the NFL in runs up the middle last year, while running up the middle a league-high 75 percent of the time. Despite the "outside" in the name, outside zone runs often bounce inside once the defense has been stretched laterally. The new system earned rave reviews in minicamp, as new systems often do in minicamp. What's not clear is how suited the Steelers' linemen are to a scheme that emphasizes quickness and technique over size and force. Maurkice Pouncey, who was slowed by injuries last year but still played at a high level, should be fine. Right guard David DeCastro missed most of his rookie season with a dislocated kneecap and got beaten up by Marcus Spears and Geno Atkins in late-season action against the Cowboys and Bengals, but he is still a fine prospect and good system fit who should settle down. At left guard will be Ramon Foster, who signed a three-year contract after testing the free-agent waters and finding them frigid. He looked terrible when trying to block on the move last season and is an odd fit for a zone-blocking scheme.

Marcus Gilbert started six games at right tackle before suffering a knee injury. Technically, he allowed no sacks, but Ben Roethlisberger made him look good several times by side-stepping the defender Gilbert set free. This year, he's expected to slide over to left tackle. Mike Adams, a hulking square peg for a zone-blocking system, is expected to start on the right side despite suffering a stab wound while stopping a carjacking in early June. Like DeCastro, he earned a late-season cup of coffee in 2012 but got pushed around.

Pittsburgh's top backups will be Guy Whimper and Kelvin Beachum, who fit the small-quick zone-blocker profile but don't have the talent for full-time starting duty. Guy Whimper, famous in Jacksonville for the "Whimper Waggle" play that had him catching a short pass as a sixth offensive lineman, will be the first tackle off the bench. Whimper has the best hands of any offensive tackle in the NFL, which says volumes about his blocking skills. 2012 seventh-round pick Beachum played left tackle at SMU, was drafted as a guard, then saw injuries force him into the lineup at right tackle.

Defensive Front Seven

Defensive Line	Age	Pos	Overall Snaps	Plays	TmPct	Rk	Stop	Dfts	BTkl	vs. Run Runs	St%	Rk	RuYd	Rk	Pass Rush Sack	Hit	Hur	Tips
Brett Keisel	35	DE	858	47	6.2%	24	35	10	5	39	72%	48	2.7	49	4.5	4	11.5	1
Ziggy Hood	26	DE	806	45	6.0%	26	32	9	0	38	66%	62	3.5	70	3	1	5	3
Casey Hampton*	36	DT	495	26	3.5%	50	22	8	2	25	84%	13	1.4	11	0	1	1.5	0
Cameron Heyward	24	DE	263	20	2.7%	--	14	3	0	15	73%	--	2.7	--	1.5	1	2	0

Linebackers	Age	Pos	Overall Snaps	Plays	TmPct	Rk	Stop	Dfts	BTkl	Pass Rush Sack	Hit	Hur	Tips	vs. Run Runs	St%	Rk	Yds	Rk	vs. Pass Tgts	Suc%	Rk	AdjYd	Rk	PD
Lawrence Timmons	27	ILB	982	110	14.6%	30	69	26	7	6	12	19.5	0	62	73%	23	2.3	21	38	54%	26	6.5	29	3
Larry Foote	33	ILB	967	113	15.0%	25	65	14	8	4	4	7	0	69	68%	39	3.1	46	32	36%	70	7.9	65	3
James Harrison*	35	OLB	811	69	11.3%	58	53	13	4	6	7	12	0	51	82%	9	2.2	17	13	36%	--	7.6	--	0
LaMarr Woodley	29	OLB	621	39	6.4%	90	26	10	2	4	6	10	0	25	72%	27	2.2	18	11	41%	--	9.5	--	1
Jason Worilds	25	OLB	422	24	3.2%	--	18	7	0	5	5	3.5	0	14	71%	--	2.9	--	6	41%	--	4.8	--	0

Year	Yards	ALY	Rk	Power	Rk	Stuff	Rk	2nd Level	Rk	Open Field	Rk	Sacks	ASR	Rk	Short	Long
2010	3.07	3.46	1	59%	10	21%	10	0.85	2	0.17	1	48	8.3%	3	16	16
2011	3.91	4.00	15	62%	15	18%	22	1.04	5	0.55	6	35	6.8%	14	16	14
2012	3.78	3.89	13	66%	22	19%	14	1.03	4	0.47	5	37	6.7%	11	11	15
2012 ALY by direction:			Left End 2.52 (3)			Left Tackle 4.19 (20)			Mid/Guard 3.73 (7)			Right Tackle 4.09 (17)			Right End 4.85 (25)

Steve McClendon is the most important player in Pittsburgh that no one is talking about. McClendon spent the first two seasons of his career behind both Casey Hampton and Chris Hoke at nose tackle, then spent last season behind Hampton. He has recorded just 17 solo tackles and three sacks in his career, but the Steelers thought highly enough of McClendon to sign him to a three-year, $7.5 million contract in the offseason and hand him an uncontested starting job. The Steelers are patient talent developers on defense, of course, so they know what they have in McClendon even if we don't.

Veteran journeyman Al Woods took minicamp reps as the backup nose tackle; Woods is a thick, traditional 3-4 lineman (though he played end at other stops), while McClendon is smaller than the Steelers prototype. Second-year tackle Alameda Ta'amu received probation for a DUI bust in the offseason, then tweeted a picture of his buddy holding a bottle of whiskey while he drove. Worst of all, it was rock gut. Ta'amu remains in the team's plans, theoretically.

Jason Worilds takes over for James Harrison after three seasons as a package defender. Worilds was a second-round pick in 2010; it is easy to imagine Jarvis Jones taking a similar career path, if slightly accelerated. Jones could not crack the first team in minicamp, with Worilds and a reinvigorated LaMarr Woodley ahead of him. An anonymous teammate ripped Woodley's conditioning habits early in the offseason, and Woodley took the criticism (and/or Jones' arrival) in stride, restructuring his contract and working hard in OTAs. Lawrence Timmons remains an excellent all-purpose weapon on the inside. Larry Foote, who signed a three-year contract in the offseason, had a fine season as the stay-at-home inside linebacker. Foote turned 33 years old in June, so the final two years of that three-year deal may just be creative accounting.

Defensive end Brett Keisel, now 35, joins Foote as the holdover old-timers on the front seven. Cameron Heyward should finally start to push Keisel aside after two seasons as a wave defender. Some commentators have looked at Ziggy Hood's raw stats and criticized him as "one of the least productive players at his position" because, you know, it makes a lot of sense to compare a Steelers 3-4 defensive end with someone like Trent Cole, because their roles are so totally the same. Hood's issue is a lack of consistency, not a lack of statistics.

Defensive Secondary

Secondary	Age	Pos	Snaps	Plays	Overall TmPct	Rk	Stop	Dfts	BTkl	vs. Run Runs	St%	Rk	Yds	Rk	vs. Pass Tgts	Tgt%	Rk	Dist	Suc%	Rk	APaYd	Rk	PD	Int
Keenan Lewis*	27	CB	919	90	12.0%	7	41	15	9	21	57%	18	3.2	5	102	22.7%	6	14.2	54%	32	6.3	13	20	0
Ryan Clark	34	FS	882	109	15.4%	1	45	16	8	64	45%	15	4.8	7	26	6.2%	43	13.6	67%	12	5.3	9	6	2
Ike Taylor	33	CB	646	45	8.0%	57	20	9	3	11	36%	57	3.9	9	72	21.5%	11	15.1	56%	20	6.4	16	13	1
Cortez Allen	25	CB	542	57	8.1%	55	27	16	4	9	56%	20	6.9	48	65	15.4%	59	11.4	55%	26	6.3	12	10	2
Will Allen	31	FS	422	33	4.4%	--	8	4	3	16	25%	--	6.9	--	14	3.0%	--	12.1	52%	--	5.9	--	2	0
Troy Polamalu	32	SS	386	37	11.2%	--	12	2	2	17	41%	--	6.5	--	11	5.4%	--	16.8	77%	--	3.4	--	3	1
Ryan Mundy*	28	SS	284	26	3.5%	--	5	3	4	9	11%	--	7.9	--	12	2.6%	--	7.6	32%	--	7.5	--	2	0
William Gay	28	CB	1003	63	7.7%	60	19	13	8	21	33%	60	5.9	38	79	19.6%	28	12.3	50%	51	8.0	56	5	2

Year	Pass D Rank	vs. #1 WR	Rk	vs. #2 WR	Rk	vs. Other WR	Rk	vs. TE	Rk	vs. RB	Rk
2010	2	-18.5%	4	-23.3%	3	0.2%	18	-9.7%	5	2.0%	15
2011	3	-5.5%	8	-9.9%	10	-0.8%	20	-6.9%	4	-5.1%	14
2012	15	-30.1%	3	-1.8%	16	0.5%	17	23.4%	31	4.5%	20

Ike Taylor started the season miserably, allowing four touchdowns and incurring seven holding/interference penalties in the first six weeks. Taylor then settled down and was playing excellent football before a hairline fracture of the right ankle shelved him late in the season. In Weeks 1 to 6, Taylor was targeted 45 times, allowing 8.6 Adjusted Yards per Pass and a 42 percent Adjusted Success Rate. From Week 7 until his Week 13 injury, he was targeted just 28 times, allowing 3.2 Adjusted Yards per Pass and a remarkable 81 percent Adjusted Success Rate . Now 33 but well-versed in the Steelers' zone coverage schemes, Taylor sometimes takes unnecessary flak because he is assigned so much three-deep coverage. Many of the 10-yard passes he allows are a residue of the scheme's design. That said, age + an autumn slump + a December injury = several reasons for pessimism.

Ryan Clark is another geezer with mounting medical problems: Clark suffered two concussions last season, and sickle-cell anemia remains a problem that affects more than the ability to play in Denver. Rookie Shamarko Thomas is an unguided missile who flies around and hits everything in sight but whiffs or injures himself too often. Pencil Thomas into Clark's role in 2014. Troy Polamalu is now 32 and played through calf injuries last season, but remains an All-Pro when he is at full speed. The *Pittsburgh Tribune-Review* reported that Polamalu reported to minicamp in the best shape since his USC days. Baseball fans know that "best shape of his life" reports are just "say something nice about slumping veteran" reports, so take that report for what it is worth. That's right folks: we're a baseball publication now.

Cortez Allen replaces Keenan Lewis in the starting lineup. The Steelers plan to move Allen into the slot and use William Gay on the outside in nickel packages. Tight end coverage was a real problem for the Steelers last year; at 6-foot-1, Allen has the size to compete with the tight ends the Steelers will see in the slot when they face opponents like the Patriots, Ravens and Bengals. The smaller Gay returns from a season in exile in Arizona. Like Taylor, he is well-versed in Dom Capers' "keep the play in front of you" secondary tactics.

Special Teams

Year	DVOA	Rank	FG/XP	Rank	Net Kick	Rank	Kick Ret	Rank	Net Punt	Rank	Punt Ret	Rank	Hidden	Rank
2010	0.4%	16	-1.9	23	-2.1	20	3.8	13	8.7	5	-6.3	28	-6.3	23
2011	1.7%	9	-7.3	29	8.0	4	-1.1	19	4.5	10	4.6	8	-9.0	28
2012	-0.1%	17	6.8	6	-1.8	21	5.6	7	-6.3	23	-4.8	25	-9.4	30

The Steelers are looking for someone to supplant Antonio Brown as the primary punt returner. Brown averaged just 6.8 yards per return and had a catastrophic game in the Cowboys loss, muffing one punt and fumbling while returning another. Brown is also the No. 1 receiver, too valuable on offense to have to double as a return man. Undrafted rookie Reggie Dunn has blazing speed and returned five kickoffs over 100 yards to set an NCAA career record at Utah, but he did not return punts in college and had trouble fielding them in minicamp. Sixth-round pick Justin Brown returned punts for Oklahoma and should also get a look. LaRod Stephens-Howling will replace the departed Chris Rainey as the kickoff returner. Stephens-Howling scored three kickoff return touchdowns in 2009 and 2010. He has tailed off, but he is still productive and dependable, with excellent ball security. Dunn will also get a look as a kickoff returner.

Brian Moorman was signed to compete with Drew Butler for the punting job; most observers felt Moorman was well ahead of Butler in minicamp. Moorman, a reliable leg for over a decade, slumped at the start of the 2012 season; the Bills pushed the panic button and released him, and he finished the year punting well for the Cowboys. Shaun Suisham has found a home in Pittsburgh after years as a AAA kicker who bounced between the Redskins and Cowboys. Suisham is entering his fourth year with the Steelers; he is adequate on kickoffs and reliable on short-to-midrange field goals.

Coaching Staff

Mike Tomlin mishandled his running back situation horribly last year, benching backs after every fumble. After he fumbled against the Raiders in Week 3, Jonathan Dwyer learned that he lost his starting job by reading the team bulletin board. In the Week 12 Browns loss, Tomlin benched Rashard Mendenhall, then Dwyer, and then Redman for fumbling, leaving Chris Rainey to handle every-down duties before Mendenhall was given a second chance. (He fumbled again.) Tomlin is generally popular with players, and his tough-guy temperament usually works, but pitching a hissy fit after every fumble had the opposite effect: Mendenhall mutinied, Dwyer and Redman played below their abilities, and Rainey and Baron Batch got carries they did not earn. Tomlin needs to revisit his attitude on fumbles: it has gone beyond tough to become stubborn and spiteful.

Todd Haley is an odd duck, of course. There was a lot of "Haley and Roethlisberger are quarreling" speculation during last season. Everyone denied everything, but come on. None of the problems spilled beyond the kind of thing that happens in any office after the top salesman enters the regional manager's office and slams the door, however, and any potential Haley-Roethlisberger feud belonged near the bottom of the list of Steelers problems. Haley's game plans still cause some head scratching: the "keep running up the gut until it never works" tactics were counterproductive, and some of the running back juggling was his idea. Haley faces a new set of challenges this year, from implementing the outside zone scheme to building a passing game without Mike Wallace and, for at least the start of the season, an injured Heath Miller. A productive season can silence much of the *"Haley is a crazy person who hates his quarterback"* speculation.

St. Louis Rams

2012 Record: 7-8-1	Total DVOA: 1.5% (15th)	2013 Mean Projection: 5.8 wins	On the Clock (0-4): 33%
Pythagorean Wins: 6.6 (22nd)	Offense: -4.2% (21st)	Postseason Odds: 6.1%	Mediocrity (5-7): 46%
Snap-Weighted Age: 26.2 (24th)	Defense: -9.1% (7th)	Super Bowl Odds: 0.2%	Playoff Contender (8-10): 17%
Average Opponent: 9.6% (2nd)	Special Teams: -3.4% (26th)	Proj. Avg. Opponent: 1.4% (13th)	Super Bowl Contender (11+): 3%

2012: Significant improvement on both sides of the ball puts St. Louis back in contention.

2013: Many observers see another step forward, but we see a consolidation year to sort through the young talent.

It has been ten years now since the St. Louis Rams last had a winning record. Back in 2003, Mike Martz was their coach, Marc Bulger their quarterback, Marshall Faulk their top runner, Torry Holt the No. 1 receiver. Then the curtain fell on the Greatest Show on Turf. The team got older and declined, then was effectively euthanized by Billy Devaney, the general manager who led the team to a league-worst 12-52 record from 2008 to 2011.

In that light, it's hard to view 2012 as anything but a major success. The Rams' DVOA climbed above zero for the first time since that 2003 campaign. They came within one victory of a winning season, and it's not just because they feasted on an easy schedule. They went 3-4-1 against teams that made the postseason, including a 2-1-1 record against Seattle and San Francisco, the new powers of the NFC West.

In a pass-happy league, the Rams have begun to construct a team the right way. They've built one of the league's best young front sevens, one capable of forcing opposing quarterbacks into third-and-long, then forcing them into the turf. On offense, they've gone all-in with franchise passer Sam Bradford and have drafted numerous receivers in an effort to surround him with as much young talent as possible. It's a solid theory of roster management.

In many ways, the Rams are still being punished for the sins of Devaney, who has since admitted that his game plan in St. Louis was, quote, "let's blow the whole damn thing up." That mission was certainly accomplished. Obviously, the second part of Devaney's plan was to rebuild, but that proved easier said than done. Devaney's poor drafts left Bradford bereft of weapons, an unarmed cowboy in a league full of gunslingers. The newly hired duo of GM Les Snead and coach Jeff Fisher did their best to fix the situation, but early returns on their first draft are decidedly mixed. All told, the Rams drafted 21 offensive players between 2008 and 2012, nine of them in the first three rounds. Only four of those players (Bradford, offensive tackle Rodger Saffold, tight end Lance Kendricks, and wideout Chris Givens) were starting for St. Louis last year.

Snead and Fisher could see this was not working, and so they decided to blow the whole damn thing up again—although given the sorry nature of the Rams' roster, that was a pretty passive decision. Steven Jackson, the franchise's all-time leading rusher, opted out of his contract after the season. Danny Amendola, who led the team with 63 catches last year despite missing five games, also hit free agency, as did second-leading receiver Brandon Gibson. The Rams made little effort to sign any of these players, allowing them to leave for Atlanta, New England, and Miami respectively.

With their 2012 leaders gone, the Rams were left with holes at both running back and wide receiver. They attempted to fill both holes at once in the draft, trading up eight spots to select West Virginia's Tavon Austin. (Austin, by the way, was 12 years old the last time the Rams had a winning record.) The former Mountaineer played runner, receiver, and returner in college, with cartoonish success. He finished his NCAA career with 3,413 yards receiving and 1,031 rushing (at 9.5 yards per carry!), plus five touchdowns on punt and kickoff returns. At 5-foot-8 and 181 pounds, he'll probably spend most of his time on offense in the slot, but the Rams will do anything they can to get him the ball, including putting him out wide or in the backfield. He should contend for the Rookie of the Year award—but he's still a rookie, with no NFL experience.

Which means he'll fit in well in St. Louis. Going into training camp, the Rams' running backs, as a group, have only 529 career rushing yards, and their wideouts have only 1,371 career receiving yards. Those figures would be among the five lowest at either position in the DVOA era, dating back to 1991 (Tables 1 and 2). The league has expanded four times since then, and each of those expansion teams managed to field more experience at both running back and wide receiver than the 2013 St. Louis Rams (assuming Snead doesn't go out and sign Terrell Owens or something).

Is experience necessary at these positions to win? At running back, at least, the results are mixed. Forty-two teams since 1991 have entered a season with fewer than 2,000 career rushing yards on their running back depth chart. (Remarkably, the Cardinals have pulled this off seven times, including three years in a row at the turn of the century.) Those teams went a combined 328-344 (a .488 winning percentage), with an average offensive DVOA of -1.9%. Their average rushing offense DVOA was also -1.9%. Ironically, those teams that added a high-profile rookie runner to these shallow talent pools usually fared worse than those that didn't. Teams whose leading rusher was a first- or second-round rookie had an average rushing DVOA of -5.6%. Those same teams had a passing DVOA 14.2%, but that's because in many cases they were quarterbacked by Tom Brady or Peyton Manning or Philip

2013 Rams Schedule

Week	Opp.	Week	Opp.	Week	Opp.
1	ARI	7	at CAR	13	at SF
2	at ATL	8	SEA (Mon.)	14	at ARI
3	at DAL	9	TEN	15	NO
4	SF (Thu.)	10	at IND	16	TB
5	JAC	11	BYE	17	at SEA
6	at HOU	12	CHI		

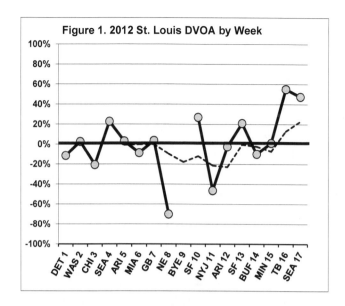

Figure 1. 2012 St. Louis DVOA by Week

Rivers, not so much because of anything their rookie runners did. All told, eight of these teams finished with an offensive DVOA of 10.0% or higher, while 11 finished at -10.0% or worse. It looks like inexperience at running back is usually a weakness, but a minor one that can be overcome by a great quarterback. Thirteen of those teams were led by a rookie rusher, and seven of those rookies went over a thousand yards.

What about receivers? There were 31 teams since 1991 whose wideouts entered the season with fewer than 3,000 combined receiving yards. Those teams went just 210-286 (a .423 win-loss rate), with an average offensive DVOA of -8.2%. Only one of those teams had an offensive DVOA higher than 10.0%: the 1996 Kansas City Chiefs. Running backs Kimble Anders, Marcus Allen, and Todd McNair were first, third, and fifth on that team in receptions. Meanwhile, 13 of those teams finished with a DVOA worse than -10.0%. Most disturbing for the Rams, even on these teams with so few proven commodities at wide receiver, only seven rookies were

able to break through and lead their squads in receiving yards. That list includes Marvin Harrison, Anquan Boldin, Andre Johnson, and A.J. Green, so even in these dire circumstances it usually takes a special rookie to lead a team. On the other hand, those teams that were led by rookies had an average offensive DVOA of just -11.3%, and only one (the 2010 Tampa Bay Buccaneers, whose leading receiver was tight end Kellen Winslow) was above zero.

As it turns out, when your top wide receiver is a rookie, it's usually a bad thing. Since 1991, 35 rookies have led their team's wideouts in receiving yards, with a cumulative re-

Table 1: Most Inexperienced Teams at Running Back, 1991-2012

Year	Team	Total Career Rush Yds, RBs	W-L	Off. DVOA	Rushing DVOA	Lead rusher (Experience, Draft Round)	Yds
2001	CLE	147	7-9	-19.8%	-10.7%	James Jackson (Rookie, Rd 3)	554
1998	NE	234	9-7	-0.1%	-16.0%	Robert Edwards (Rookie, Rd 1)	1,115
2000	ARI	387	3-13	-19.6%	-14.4%	Michael Pittman (3rd Yr, Rd 4)	719
1993	ARI	545	7-9	4.1%	4.7%	Ronald Moore (Rookie, Rd 4)	1,018
1994	IND	717	8-8	-5.8%	-4.4%	Marshall Faulk (Rookie, Rd 1)	1,282
2007	GB	788	13-3	15.7%	4.3%	Ryan Grant (Rookie, undrafted)	956
2002	ARI	788	5-11	-12.3%	-0.6%	Marcel Shipp (2nd Yr, undrafted)	834
2003	WAS	986	5-11	-6.7%	1.2%	Trung Canidate (4th Yr, Rd 1)	600
1995	TB	1,011	7-9	-13.4%	8.3%	Errict Rhett (2nd Yr, Rd 2)	1207
2007	IND	1,081	13-3	22.2%	11.2%	Joseph Addai (2nd Yr, Rd 1)	1072

Table 2: Most Inexperienced Teams at Wide Receiver, 1991-2012

Year	Team	Total Career Rec Yds, WRs	W-L	Off. DVOA	Passing DVOA	Lead wideout (Experience, Draft Round)	Yds
2010	Buccaneers	944	10-6	8.0%	25.2%	Mike Williams (Rookie, Rd 4)	964
1992	Browns	1,348	7-9	-1.3%	14.5%	Michael Jackson (2nd Yr, Rd 6)	755
2003	Cardinals	1,358	4-12	-21.5%	-20.2%	Anquan Boldin (Rookie, Rd 2)	1,377
1995	Jets	1,360	3-13	-30.7%	-35.6%	Wayne Chrebet (Rookie, undrafted)	726
1992	Steelers	1,391	11-5	4.1%	12.4%	Jeff Graham (2nd Yr, Rd 2)	711
2001	Eagles	1,421	11-5	2.9%	6.7%	James Thrash (5th Yr, undrafted)	833
2004	Bears	1,468	5-11	-36.5%	-50.6%	David Terrell (4th Yr, Rd 1)	699
1995	Patriots	1,552	6-10	-9.3%	-8.2%	Vincent Brisby (3rd Yr, Rd 2)	974
2002	Ravens	1,765	7-9	-6.1%	0.7%	Travis Taylor (3rd Yr, Rd 1)	869
1999	Giants	1,894	7-9	-6.8%	8.2%	Amani Toomer 4th Yr, Rd 2)	1,183

cord of 250-308-2 (.488). Eight of those teams won at least 10 games, but twice that many lost at least 10. The average offensive DVOA was -7.1%, with 26 teams below zero, 16 below -10.0%, and six below -20.0%.

While no team since 1991 has been as inexperienced as these Rams at both running back and wide receiver, four squads did qualify at both positions in our sample groups: the 1991 Cardinals, 1993 Patriots, 2001 Browns, and 2002 Ravens. Those four teams went a combined 23-41 with an average offensive DVOA of -14.6%. None had a winning record or a positive offensive DVOA. Coincidentally, the 1993 Pats and 2001 Browns, like this year's Rams, were quarterbacked by former first-overall draft picks in Drew Bledsoe and Tim Couch, respectively.

So inexperience at wideout is likely to be the Rams' undoing in 2013, but what about Austin individually? What kind of numbers can we expect from such a unique player?

Before the Rams' 2003 collapse, the crew at STATS, Inc., invented a statistic they called the Marshall Faulk Number to measure a player's ability to accrue both rushing and receiving yardage. We're openly stealing their idea, but what the hell, they stole it from Bill James' "Power-Speed Number." A player's MFN could be found by calculating the harmonic mean of his rushing and receiving yardage totals. In layman's terms, to have a high Marshall Faulk Number, a player must score high numbers in both departments—a poor result in one category will drag down a high figure in the other. STATS, Inc., dubbed the result the Marshall Faulk Number for obvious reasons—Faulk posted MFNs over 1,000 in three different seasons, once with the Colts and twice with the Rams. Only three other players have ever gone over 1,000: Steven Jackson, Roger Craig, and LaDainian Tomlinson.

None of those men were rookies, though. It's hard to imagine Austin putting up an MFN that high. Realistic best-case scenario, he joins the list of the best freshman seasons (Table 3).

Can Austin crack that leaderboard? For better or worse, he'll probably be the Rams' top wideout this year. Since 1991, rookie No. 1 receivers have averaged 835 yards; since he'll spend some time in the backfield, let's be conservative and give Austin 800 receiving yards. His rushing numbers are much harder to predict. First of all, it's hard to establish a standard for wideout rushing numbers, because we have to figure out what to do with proto-Austins like Eric Metcalf who bounced back and forth between the two positions. But best as we can tell, since the 1970 merger, the record for must rushes by a player who was primarily a wide receiver in that particular season (and boy, doesn't that roll off the tongue?) is 55 by Cleveland's Josh Cribbs in 2009. Percy Harvin had 52 rushes for Minnesota in 2011. Nobody else has gone over 40, but four players (including Metcalf with Atlanta in 1995,

Table 3: Best Rookie Seasons, Marshall Faulk Number

Player	Year	Team	RuYd	RecYd	MFN
Edgerrin James	1999	IND	1553	586	851
Billy Sims	1980	DET	1303	621	841
Herschel Walker	1986	DAL	737	837	784
Charley Taylor	1964	WAS	755	814	783
Marshall Faulk	1994	IND	1282	522	742
Doug Martin	2012	TB	1454	472	713
Abner Haynes	1960	KC	875	576	695
Matt Forte	2008	CHI	1238	477	689
Eric Dickerson	1983	STL	1808	404	660
Reggie Bush	2006	NO	565	742	642

Cribbs in 2008, Brad Smith with the Jets in 2010, and Harvin last year) have gone over 20. Now, back to Austin. Let's say he gets 40 carries this season, and we'll generously assume a 5.0-yard average. (He ain't getting nine yards a pop in the pros.) That would be 200 yards rushing, and an MFN of 320. So the size of Austin's contribution likely won't be anything special, even if its shape is quite unique.

Before 2012, the Rams finished among the bottom three teams in offensive DVOA for five straight seasons. The dire situations at the so-called skill positions threaten a plummet back to the bottom of the offensive rankings. Meanwhile there's no guarantee that a defense that took great strides in 2012 will improve again. In fact, that improvement could be a bad omen, as teams that show dramatic improvement in one season often decline the next (Jim Harbaugh's 49ers excluded, apparently). Further, Tim Walton takes over as defensive coordinator, and while that seems like an automatic improvement over the vacancy the Rams had there last year, most teams struggle with first-year coordinators. Obviously, the Rams were an exception a year ago, but that doesn't mean they'll be an exception two straight years. And the secondary looks like a mess—as noted later in the chapter, St. Louis may have less experience at safety than they do at running back or wide receiver.

All told, the Rams have too much youth at too many positions to be a serious contender this year. Yet all hope is not lost. Remember those four other teams that were just as inexperienced at both running back and receiver? None of those teams made the playoffs that year, but three of them—Bledsoe's Patriots, Couch's Browns, and a Ravens team quarterbacked by first-round rookie Kyle Boller—made the playoffs one season later.

St. Louis fans have waited ten years to see a team with a winning record. They'll probably have to wait one more.

Vince Verhei

2012 Rams Stats by Week

Wk	vs.	W-L	PF	PA	YDF	YDA	TO	Total	Off	Def	ST
1	at DET	L	23	27	250	429	3	-12%	-23%	-12%	0%
2	WAS	W	31	28	452	373	-2	3%	-8%	-10%	1%
3	at CHI	L	6	23	160	274	-1	-21%	-37%	-15%	2%
4	SEA	W	19	13	286	319	2	23%	-13%	-28%	8%
5	ARI	W	17	3	242	282	0	3%	-5%	-2%	5%
6	at MIA	L	14	17	462	192	-1	-9%	25%	-5%	-38%
7	GB	L	20	30	354	402	-1	4%	10%	10%	3%
8	NE	L	7	45	326	473	-2	-70%	-36%	29%	-5%
9	BYE										
10	at SF	T	24	24	458	341	-1	27%	29%	-8%	-10%
11	NYJ	L	13	27	281	289	-3	-46%	-34%	15%	3%
12	at ARI	W	31	17	367	375	3	-3%	9%	-2%	-13%
13	SF	W	16	13	293	339	1	21%	-10%	-29%	3%
14	at BUF	W	15	12	285	281	1	-10%	-32%	-28%	-6%
15	MIN	L	22	36	432	322	-2	1%	5%	11%	-14%
16	at TB	W	28	13	285	429	3	55%	13%	-33%	9%
17	at SEA	L	13	20	331	362	-1	48%	32%	-17%	-1%

Trends and Splits

	Offense	Rank	Defense	Rank
Total DVOA	-4.2%	21	-9.1%	7
Unadjusted VOA	-7.1%	22	-3.3%	13
Weighted Trend	0.4%	15	-9.3%	8
Variance	5.5%	12	2.9%	4
Average Opponent	-6.0%	1	2.7%	8
Passing	7.4%	17	-6.2%	8
Rushing	-4.5%	19	-12.6%	10
First Down	4.3%	12	-15.0%	4
Second Down	0.8%	16	-9.5%	8
Third Down	-27.0%	28	3.6%	20
First Half	-3.7%	18	-11.0%	5
Second Half	-4.7%	19	-7.1%	9
Red Zone	-16.8%	24	-17.9%	6
Late and Close	-0.2%	14	-4.5%	18

Five-Year Performance

Year	W-L	Pyth W	Est W	PF	PA	TO	Total	Rk	Off	Rk	Def	Rk	ST	Rk	Off AGL	Rk	Def AGL	Rk	Off Age	Rk	Def Age	Rk	ST Age	Rk
2008	2-14	2.5	1.6	232	465	-5	-47.1%	31	-28.2%	32	18.3%	30	-0.6%	20	50.3	30	29.9	21	28.0	10	27.8	7	27.0	7
2009	1-15	1.6	0.9	175	436	-13	-45.1%	31	-29.5%	32	17.2%	31	1.7%	11	38.4	27	36.3	23	26.8	24	26.2	27	25.5	28
2010	7-9	6.8	5.4	289	328	+5	-19.4%	28	-18.1%	30	2.1%	19	0.8%	14	47.1	32	9.7	4	25.7	29	26.8	17	26.1	19
2011	2-14	2.3	2.2	193	407	-5	-35.4%	32	-27.2%	32	3.4%	21	-4.8%	28	66.6	32	43.5	27	27.1	16	27.6	7	26.4	11
2012	7-8-1	6.6	8.2	299	348	-1	1.5%	15	-4.2%	21	-9.1%	7	-3.4%	26	28.0	16	8.3	3	26.3	23	26.3	24	25.5	29

2012 Performance Based on Most Common Personnel Groups

SL Offense					SL Offense vs. Opponents				SL Defense				SL Defense vs. Opponents			
Pers	Freq	Yds	DVOA	Run%	Pers	Freq	Yds	DVOA	Pers	Freq	Yds	DVOA	Pers	Freq	Yds	DVOA
11	48%	5.6	8.4%	23%	Nickel Even	39%	5.8	16.4%	Nickel Even	44%	5.4	-5.3%	11	44%	5.4	-14.7%
12	26%	4.7	-19.0%	62%	4-3-4	24%	4.8	-16.2%	4-3-4	44%	5.0	-19.3%	12	20%	5.4	-3.9%
21	8%	6.0	0.0%	54%	3-4-4	21%	5.4	-3.5%	Nickel Odd	5%	7.6	31.9%	21	14%	5.4	-20.5%
10	7%	7.1	52.1%	3%	Dime+	8%	5.4	15.5%	5-3-3	3%	4.9	-18.3%	22	9%	4.4	-25.2%
13	4%	4.1	14.1%	61%	Nickel Odd	8%	5.7	-2.1%	Dime+	3%	8.1	-14.2%	10	3%	5.6	25.2%

Strategic Tendencies

Run/Pass		Rk	Formation		Rk	Pass Rush		Rk	Secondary		Rk	Strategy		Rk
Runs, first half	37%	19	Form: Single Back	71%	8	Rush 3	7.7%	11	4 DB	44%	18	Play action	22%	13
Runs, first down	52%	10	Form: Empty Back	5%	16	Rush 4	53.3%	29	5 DB	49%	13	Avg Box (Off)	6.31	22
Runs, second-long	26%	25	Pers: 3+ WR	57%	10	Rush 5	24.5%	11	6+ DB	3%	23	Avg Box (Def)	6.35	18
Runs, power sit.	33%	32	Pers: 4+ WR	8%	6	Rush 6+	14.4%	3	CB by Sides	81%	10	Offensive Pace	31.79	26
Runs, behind 2H	26%	23	Pers: 2+ TE/6+ OL	36%	11	Sacks by LB	13.7%	22	DB Blitz	16%	7	Defensive Pace	32.37	32
Pass, ahead 2H	39%	28	Shotgun/Pistol	41%	21	Sacks by DB	9.8%	9	Hole in Zone	17%	1	Go for it on 4th	1.25	5

The Rams led the NFL with 150 penalties, including declined and offsetting. This wasn't an issue of over-litigious referees, as Rams opponents had just 112 penalties. However, the Rams were just fourth with 978 penalty yards, primarily because they were only called for Defensive Pass Interference five times for just 43 yards. ☞ Sam Bradford had only 19 passes marked "deep middle" in the play-by-play, but the Rams were phenomenal on these passes: 14-of-19 with 23.6 yards per pass, three touchdowns, and no picks. Perhaps they signed Jared Cook with a dream of a million deep seam routes. ☞ Although it was only 19 plays, the Rams had a league-leading 8.8 yards per pass and 45.8% DVOA on wide receiver screens. ☞ The Rams had the worst starting field position in the league, starting the average drive with 76.3 yards to go for a touchdown. ☞ On defense, the Rams were really bad against play-action passes, with the second-biggest gap in the league behind Baltimore. They had 37.0% DVOA against play action, but -13.7% DVOA against other pass plays.

Passing

Player	DYAR	DVOA	Plays	NtYds	Avg	YAC	C%	TD	Int
S.Bradford	388	-0.8%	580	3457	6.0	4.7	60.4%	21	12

Rushing

Player	DYAR	DVOA	Plays	Yds	Avg	TD	Fum	Suc
S.Jackson*	147	5.3%	257	1042	4.1	4	0	47%
D.Richardson	40	1.7%	98	475	4.8	0	2	42%
S.Bradford	42	29.6%	21	140	6.7	1	1	-
I.Pead	23	49.9%	10	54	5.4	0	0	60%

Receiving

Player	DYAR	DVOA	Plays	Ctch	Yds	Y/C	YAC	TD	C%
D.Amendola*	80	-7.6%	101	63	679	10.8	3.8	3	62%
B.Gibson*	214	23.3%	82	51	691	13.5	2.2	5	62%
C.Givens	80	0.0%	80	42	698	16.6	6.6	3	53%
A.Pettis	35	0.6%	48	30	261	8.7	2.6	4	63%
B.Quick	-33	-25.0%	27	11	156	14.2	2.1	2	41%
S.Smith*	-8	-20.0%	25	14	131	9.4	2.8	0	56%
L.Kendricks	67	13.0%	64	42	519	12.4	5.4	4	66%
M.Mulligan*	24	19.6%	12	8	84	10.5	4.4	1	67%
M.McNeill	-17	-47.1%	7	4	31	7.8	3.8	0	57%
J.Cook	9	-3.7%	72	44	530	12.0	3.8	4	61%
S.Jackson*	72	11.7%	53	38	321	8.4	7.4	0	72%
D.Richardson	-65	-46.9%	36	24	163	6.8	7.6	0	67%

Offensive Line

Player	Pos	Age	GS	Snaps	Pen	Sk	Pass	Run	Player	Pos	Age	GS	Snaps	Pen	Sk	Pass	Run
Robert Turner*	C/LG	29	16/16	1042	8	1	5	10	Shelley Smith	G	26	11/6	343	6	1	9	1
Barry Richardson*	RT	27	16/16	1021	6	7.5	18.5	3	Wayne Hunter*	OT	32	14/4	334	3	2	8	0
Harvey Dahl	RG	32	14/14	913	3	2.5	14	2.5	Quinn Ojinnaka	OT	29	6/5	316	2	2	8	2
Rodger Saffold	LT	25	10/10	598	8	1.5	9	5	Joseph Barksdale	OT	24	6/2	118	1	2	2	0
Scott Wells	C	32	7/7	420	3	1.5	2.5	4	Jake Long	LT	28	12/12	729	8	4	14	2

Year	Yards	ALY	Rk	Power	Rk	Stuff	Rk	2nd Lev	Rk	Open Field	Rk	Sacks	ASR	Rk	Short	Long	F-Start	Cont.
2010	3.63	3.77	26	58%	19	19%	14	1.03	27	0.51	25	34	5.6%	10	12	14	27	37
2011	4.22	3.75	30	48%	31	20%	20	1.25	10	0.72	22	55	9.1%	28	19	19	29	27
2012	4.30	4.08	14	63%	16	20%	21	1.26	11	0.76	16	35	6.2%	14	8	12	22	26
2012 ALY by direction:		Left End 3.32 (26)			Left Tackle 5.04 (3)			Mid/Guard 4.23 (11)			Right Tackle 3.3 (30)				Right End 4.55 (11)			

For the second straight year, the Rams' offensive line has undergone a major overhaul. In fact, this unit has been particularly unstable for a while now. Three of last year's starters (Barry Richardson, Robert Turner, and Scott Wells) were in their first year with the team, Harvey Dahl was in his second, and Rodger Saffold his third. Now Richardson and Turner are gone (Turner joined the Titans, while Richardson remained unsigned as of press time), and the others are all coming back from injury.

The plan is for Jake Long (signed from Miami in free agency) to take the left tackle spot and slide Saffold over to the right side, in theory making the Rams better at two positions. A solid plan in theory, but flawed in execution. First of all, neither player was healthy last year. Long's season ended in December due to a triceps tear, and he has been slowed through the years by ankle and back problems. Saffold missed six games last year with an MCL sprain. Further, it appears Saffold isn't thrilled with the position switch. Shortly after the draft, Jeff Fisher admitted to Jim Thomas of the *St. Louis Dispatch* that Saffold had not been returning the team's calls, and in fact they didn't even know where he was. Saffold is entering the last year of his contract, and a move to the right side is likely to cost him money on his next free-agent deal.

On the inside, the Rams are sticking with Wells at center and Dahl at right guard. Wells had knee surgery in spring of 2012, then missed nine games with a foot injury, followed by another knee surgery in January. Dahl went on injured reserve in December with a torn biceps. The options at left guard are slim. Shelley Smith, a 2010 Houston draft pick whose first regular-season action came after the Rams signed him off the street in September, blew eight blocks in two weeks against the 49ers and Jets. Fifth-round rookie Rokevious Watkins hurt his ankle in Week 1 and missed the rest of the year, and he'll miss Week 1 this year due to a one-game suspension for substance abuse violations. The best choice might be fourth-round rookie Barrett Jones, who won the Rimington Trophy as the nation's best center at Alabama.

Defensive Front Seven

Defensive Line	Age	Pos	Snaps	Plays	TmPct	Overall Rk	Stop	Dfts	BTkl	Runs	vs. Run St%	Rk	RuYd	Rk	Pass Rush Sack	Hit	Hur	Tips
Chris Long	28	DE	875	32	3.7%	59	28	19	3	18	78%	23	1.3	7	11.5	7	33.5	0
Robert Quinn	23	DE	825	29	3.5%	64	23	13	1	16	69%	57	2.4	35	10.5	9	13	1
Kendall Langford	27	DT	747	29	3.4%	53	21	10	1	21	76%	31	1.5	13	2	3	11.5	2
Michael Brockers	23	DT	602	31	4.5%	29	24	12	3	22	82%	16	1.5	17	4	1	5	1
Eugene Sims	27	DE	396	20	2.9%	--	17	8	1	13	85%	--	3.0	--	3	2	5	2
William Hayes	28	DE	370	37	4.3%	54	30	16	1	26	77%	27	2.1	20	7	6	7.5	1
Jermelle Cudjo	27	DT	342	19	2.4%	--	14	4	1	18	72%	--	2.7	--	1	0	1	0

Linebackers	Age	Pos	Snaps	Plays	Overall TmPct	Rk	Stop	Dfts	BTkl	Pass Rush Sack	Hit	Hur	Tips	vs. Run Runs	St%	Rk	Yds	Rk	vs. Pass Tgts	Suc%	Rk	AdjYd	Rk	PD
James Laurinaitis	27	MLB	1075	146	17.0%	12	81	22	6	0.5	2	4	1	94	68%	40	3.4	54	37	45%	57	7.3	52	4
Jo-Lonn Dunbar	28	OLB	1059	118	13.8%	35	71	32	11	4.5	7	10.5	0	59	73%	21	2.2	15	48	51%	36	6.3	25	5
Rocky McIntosh*	31	OLB	447	40	4.7%	107	20	7	4	1	0	2	0	27	59%	83	3.1	41	10	50%	--	5.7	--	1

Year	Yards	ALY	Rk	Power	Rk	Stuff	Rk	2nd Level	Rk	Open Field	Rk	Sacks	ASR	Rk	Short	Long
2010	4.56	4.07	18	55%	6	21%	11	1.31	28	1.05	29	43	7.1%	8	20	11
2011	4.83	4.26	23	55%	8	18%	19	1.21	18	1.26	29	39	7.4%	9	17	16
2012	4.09	3.50	2	59%	13	25%	3	1.21	21	1.02	26	52	8.5%	3	18	24
2012 ALY by direction:		Left End 3.46 (9)			Left Tackle 3.72 (11)			Mid/Guard 2.94 (1)			Right Tackle 4.18 (20)			Right End 5.13 (27)		

While the offensive line remains in a state of flux, the front seven stands nearly unchanged. Six of the seven starters (plus the top reserve) return, and the only departure will be replaced by a first-round draft pick as Georgia's Alec Ogletree, takes over for Rocky McIntosh. Ogletree started his collegiate career as a safety, and at 242 pounds he could have trouble shedding bigger blockers, but he's a tremendous athlete who should make tons of plays in space. In early minicamps, the Rams had him lining up on the strong side of the formation, suggesting they value his coverage skills against tight ends so much that they will give up some strength at the point of attack. He was suspended for the first four games of 2012 due to team rules violations, so there are off-field concerns as well. Ogletree will line up next to James Laurinaitis (third in the league in Run Stops, fourth in total Stops) and Jo-Lonn Dunbar. In four years with the Saints, Dunbar never totaled more than nine Defeats in a season, but in his first year with the Rams he was very quietly fourth in the league in that category, including 17 Defeats on run plays. If he can repeat that performance, the Rams will have one of the best sets of linebackers in the league, but on paper it looks like a statistical fluke.

The Rams rebuilt their interior line before last season, drafting LSU's Michael Brockers in the first round and pairing him with Kendall Langford, who was a 3-4 end in Miami for years before joining St. Louis as a 4-3 tackle. The results were sensational—note the improvement in ALY and Stuff Rate. The success of the Rams' run stuffers allowed Chris Long and Robert Quinn (like Brockers, former first-round picks) to focus on pass rushing, which they did well enough for the Rams to rank third in Adjusted Sack Rate. Even when the Rams didn't get put the opposing quarterback down, they made his life miserable. They were third in the NFL in percentage of pass plays with pressure, and Long was second in hurries. The wild card in the group is William Hayes, who finished sixth among Rams linemen in snaps but somehow managed to lead them all in Plays, making one Play every 10.0 snaps. (Houston lineman J.J. Watt, in one of the great defensive seasons of all time, made one Play every 9.6 snaps.) Hayes won't produce like that every year, but the Rams were perfectly happy to sign their super-sub to a multi-year contract after the season.

Defensive Secondary

Secondary	Age	Pos	Snaps	Plays	Overall TmPct	Rk	Stop	Dfts	BTkl	vs. Run Runs	St%	Rk	Yds	Rk	vs. Pass Tgts	Tgt%	Rk	Dist	Suc%	Rk	APaYd	Rk	PD	Int
Craig Dahl*	28	SS	1035	73	8.5%	48	16	6	11	34	18%	71	11.7	70	15	3.6%	71	16.8	46%	63	10.4	72	2	1
Quintin Mikell*	33	FS	1021	94	11.0%	30	40	13	6	42	55%	7	4.7	6	31	7.5%	26	10.7	49%	54	7.6	40	0	0
Cortland Finnegan	29	CB	1003	108	12.6%	3	41	17	8	30	50%	26	5.2	20	73	17.7%	43	8.0	46%	72	6.6	22	8	3
Janoris Jenkins	25	CB	953	87	10.8%	12	30	15	10	20	35%	58	11.7	83	86	22.3%	8	12.5	50%	55	7.2	33	14	4
Bradley Fletcher*	27	CB	364	30	3.5%	--	13	8	3	2	0%	--	17.5	--	29	6.9%	--	9.4	53%	--	5.9	--	8	1
Trumaine Johnson	23	CB	353	37	4.3%	--	19	13	5	8	50%	--	3.3	--	34	8.3%	--	13.7	54%	--	8.6	--	8	2

Year	Pass D Rank	vs. #1 WR	Rk	vs. #2 WR	Rk	vs. Other WR	Rk	vs. TE	Rk	vs. RB	Rk
2010	21	-17.0%	5	28.6%	30	7.7%	23	10.0%	18	16.9%	27
2011	15	8.3%	16	6.1%	18	8.5%	26	-11.3%	2	6.9%	22
2012	8	-17.3%	6	-7.7%	9	5.3%	23	5.4%	23	26.6%	31

After the mess of 2011 saw St. Louis spend a good chunk of the year with fourth- and fifth-string corners in the starting lineup (with both players ranking in the 70s and 80s in our two pass coverage metrics), it was time to hit reset. Cortland Finnegan was brought over from Tennessee, and Janoris Jenkins was drafted out of North Alabama in the second round. Things improved radically, especially when it came to preventing (and making) big plays. Between interceptions and fumble returns, Jenkins scored four touchdowns, while allowing only five in coverage. He played much better after the Rams' Week 9 bye, giving up 8.5 Adjusted Yards per Pass up to that point but 4.8 Adjusted Yards per Pass in the second half of the year. After a horrible 2010 and a fantastic 2011, Finnegan's pass coverage numbers fell somewhere in the middle, close to where they have been for most of his career.

The Rams gave up a league-high 54 completions that our charters marked as "Hole in Zone." They were 25th in DVOA against play-action passes, and next-to-last on passes to the middle of the field. These are all signs of bad safety play. So are missed tackles and a general lack of playmaking ability. Rams safeties had only 19 Defeats all season, ranking as a group in the league's bottom five. This is why the Rams declined to bring back either of last season's starters, saying goodbye to both Quintin Mikell and Craig Dahl. On the downside, they did very little to find suitable replacements. They passed on safeties until the third round of the draft, when they grabbed T.J. McDonald (son of former Cardinals/49ers safety Tim) out of USC. McDonald projects as an in-the-box safety who hits like a missile, but lacks natural coverage skills.

McDonald may not have been a first-round pick, but at least he was drafted. That's not something you can say about any other St. Louis safety. No, really, six of the seven safeties on the Rams roster going into training camp went undrafted out of college. Three of them (Memphis' Cannon Smith, Texas Tech's Cody Davis, and Virginia's Rodney McLeod) are rookies. Two of them (Quinton Pointer and Matt Daniels) are second-year players with a combined 10 snaps on defense last year. That leaves Darian Stewart as the only safety in town with meaningful experience: 13 starts in 2011 which led to him leading the league with 19 broken tackles before he fell behind Dahl on the 2012 depth chart. Mikell remains unsigned and could return if he'll take a pay cut. One report said the Rams had even left his nameplate on his locker. Looks like somebody's still hoping for a deal.

Special Teams

Year	DVOA	Rank	FG/XP	Rank	Net Kick	Rank	Kick Ret	Rank	Net Punt	Rank	Punt Ret	Rank	Hidden	Rank
2010	0.8%	14	-2.3	27	2.4	12	-8.8	26	5.6	12	6.0	5	-9.6	26
2011	-4.8%	28	-6.1	26	-0.3	19	-4.4	26	-14.8	31	1.6	13	-4.1	22
2012	-3.4%	26	1.0	16	1.3	14	-8.4	30	-2.3	18	-8.2	30	-1.4	20

The Rams had some of the worst return numbers in the NFL in 2012, a big reason they drafted Tavon Austin in the first round. Jeff Fisher made it clear after the draft that the Rams would get Austin the ball "as often as we can," including on special teams. Austin led the Big East in punt return average in 2011, then finished third in the Big 12 in kickoff return average (including a pair of scores) the next season. Rookie Johnny Hekker was below average as a punter, but he was a terror on fakes, completing all three of his passes for 42 yards with every completion picking up a first down or touchdown. (As a quarterback at Bothell High School, Hekker twice played in the Washington state championship game.) Fellow rookie Greg Zuerlein had mediocre numbers kicking for points because of a few short misses, but his powerful leg changes the way the Rams can play offense. He attempted 13 field goals last year from 50 yards or more, hitting seven. Nobody else this century has tried more than ten in a season. Oddly, though, he was nothing special on kickoffs.

Coaching Staff

The first time the Rams win in 2013, Jeff Fisher will become the 19th coach in NFL history with 150 wins. That's the good news. The bad news is that if he finishes the year with a losing record, he'll have the worst win-loss record of those 19 coaches, and he'll join Bud Grant, Chuck Knox, Dan Reeves, and Marty Schottenheimer as the only members of that group without a championship. In short, Fisher could be the worst good coach we've ever seen. His resemblance to Schottenheimer may have helped him attract Brian Scottenheimer, who joined the Rams last season as offensive coordinator after six seasons with the Jets. From Chad Pennington to Brett Favre to Mark Sanchez to Sam Bradford, his teams have finished in the lower half of the league in passing DVOA for six straight years. The Rams hired Gregg Williams as defensive coordinator before the 2012 season, but when he was suspended for his role in the Saints' bounty scandal, they opted to leave the position vacant, and Fisher took a large role in running the defense himself. This year they've gone the more conventional route, hiring Tim Walton to fill the position. Walton had previously coached defensive backs for Fisher's protégé Jim Schwartz in Detroit. Assistant head coach Dave McGinnis will serve as Fisher's top flunky for the tenth straight season. Defensive line coach Mike Wauffle made a name for himself with the Giants, where he turned Osi Umenyiora and Justin Tuck into Super Bowl winners. He then had a successful two-year run in Oakland (first in Adjusted Sack Rate, fourth in Adjusted Line Yards in 2010) before working wonders with the Rams last year.

San Diego Chargers

2012 Record: 7-9	**Total DVOA:** -9.0% (22nd)	**2013 Mean Projection:** 7.5 wins	**On the Clock (0-4):** 13%
Pythagorean Wins: 8.0 (16th)	**Offense:** -10.0% (24th)	**Postseason Odds:** 28.8%	**Mediocrity (5-7):** 37%
Snap-Weighted Age: 28.0 (2nd)	**Defense:** 2.0% (18th)	**Super Bowl Odds:** 2.1%	**Playoff Contender (8-10):** 39%
Average Opponent: -6.6% (30th)	**Special Teams:** 3.0% (8th)	**Proj. Avg. Opponent:** -4.4% (27th)	**Super Bowl Contender (11+):** 11%

2012: With departure of A.J. Smith and Norv Turner, Chargers finally stop beating a dead horse to death.

2013: Can Mike McCoy fix Philip Rivers?

After the 2009 Chargers capped a 13-3 regular season with a one-and-done Divisional Round playoff loss to the Jets, Football America started speculating about whether the team had missed its Super Bowl window. Indeed they had, though unlike most Super Bowl windows, San Diego's did not slam shut. Instead, it closed gradually. The Chargers went 9-7 in 2010 but battled myriad injuries on offense that year. They went 8-8 in 2011 but still had a chunk of core players in their primes. After those core players went 7-9 in 2012, team president Dean Spanos finally decided to take the franchise in a different direction, firing general manager A.J. Smith and head coach Norv Turner.

When a Super Bowl window slams shut, it tends to lock—or even shatter. There's only one response to this: rebuild the team and get a new window. When a window closes gradually, things can be a bit ambiguous. Do you break the window and start over, or do you try to pry it back open, hoping it hasn't sealed shut?

For now, the Chargers appear to be trying to pry the window back open. The new men Spanos brought in to run the show are noticeably similar to their predecessors. General manager Tom Telesco, having come from Indianapolis, believes strongly in building through the draft—much like A.J. Smith. Both earned their opportunities with this franchise after serving as the long-time top assistants to widely respected GMs (Telesco to Bill Polian, Smith to the late John Butler). At head coach, Mike McCoy is an offensive authority, like Norv Turner.

The Chargers are hoping they can pry their window open by just changing leaders, not their foundational philosophies as a franchise. They have to take this approach because of quarterback Philip Rivers. The questions about Rivers mirror those about the team as a whole. Can his window be re-opened? Or is it just a matter of time before it locks or shatters?

At 31, Rivers is supposed to be dead-smack in his prime. But he has posted the worst seasons of his starting career each of the last two years. In 2011 his completion percentage dropped by 2.5 percent compared to his prior three-year average, including a 3.1 percent drop from 2010. He dropped from 8.7 to 7.9 yards per attempt, and set a career-high in interceptions. By both DVOA and DYAR, he had his worst season since 2007.

In 2012, things got even worse, as Rivers set career lows (as a starter) in nearly every statistic except interceptions. He dropped to 6.8 yards per attempt and had just 10.7 yards per completion after being at 12.6 or above for four straight seasons. By ESPN's Total QBR, he plunged from 62.7 to 40.6. He ranked just 22nd in both DVOA and DYAR, and his -7.3% DVOA represented the first time as a starter that he registered below average.

The film agrees with the numbers, as Rivers the last two years has been wildly inconsistent by "four-time Pro Bowler" standards. At times, he shows solid arm strength and his usual ability to make aggressive, anticipatory throws in the face of pressure. At other times, he's over-reactive to the prospect of pressure and reckless in his ball placement (particularly downfield and on the outside). That's when his lack of mobility—even functional pocket mobility—becomes a real issue. Last year, no quarterback had a bigger gap between DVOA without pass pressure (51.1%, eighth out of 39 qualifying quarterbacks) and DVOA with pass pressure (-160.1%, 37th).

It's likely no coincidence that Rivers' turbulent play has coincided with the decline of San Diego's offensive line. Injuries struck left tackle Marcus McNeill and left guard Kris Dielman in 2011, and when these injuries ultimately ended their careers, the franchise was totally unprepared. San Diego's front line last year was the worst in the NFL in adjusted sack rate. They had 31 blown blocks resulting in a sack, trailing only the Cardinals and Jaguars. Surprisingly, the Chargers had the league's ninth best success rate against six or more pass-rushers, but what the stats can't show is how disruptive the *prospect* of pressure was to the flow of this entire offense. It's not unfair to speculate that just the expectation of getting shoddy protection on most snaps contributed strongly to Rivers' uneven play.

Poor offensive line play certainly contributed to San Diego's ineptitude in the ground game. With the front five consistently unable to blow opponents off the ball, San Diego's four running backs—Ryan Mathews, Ronnie Brown, Jackie Battle and Curtis Brinkley—combined for -77 DYAR. Their average DVOA was -14.5%. To be fair, the offensive line was not solely responsible for the running backs' poor production. San Diego backs' second-level yardage ranked 27th, and their open-field yardage ranked 30th.

Telesco and McCoy are presumably using 2013 to determine whether they can build their program around Rivers or whether they'll have to shatter the team's window and bring in a differ-

2013 Chargers Schedule

Week	Opp.	Week	Opp.	Week	Opp.
1	HOU (Mon.)	7	at JAC	13	CIN
2	at PHI	8	BYE	14	NYG
3	at TEN	9	at WAS	15	at DEN (Thu.)
4	DAL	10	DEN	16	OAK
5	at OAK	11	at MIA	17	KC
6	IND (Mon.)	12	at KC		

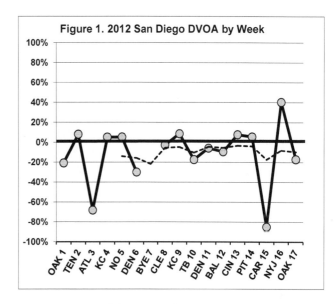

Figure 1. 2012 San Diego DVOA by Week

ent quarterback. Rivers' current contract is set to expire after the 2015 season, and he has cap numbers over $15 million each of the next two years. As respected *San Diego Union-Tribune* writer Kevin Acee pointed out, it "speaks volumes" that the new regime chose not to restructure Rivers' deal this past off-season when his cap number was $17.8 million.

Personnel-wise, the Chargers are no better up front or in the backfield this year than they were in 2012. The right side of the line has been revamped but not necessarily improved, with mauling rookie first-rounder D.J. Fluker stepping in at tackle and veteran Jeromey Clary sliding over to right guard (where he'll almost certainly be a downgrade from Louis Vasquez). The left side has also been revamped but not necessarily improved, as the lumbering Max Starks is projected to start at tackle and utility backup veteran Chad Rinehart is projected to play guard. Both would be mid-level backups on just about any other team.

In the backfield, the personnel is largely the same. Ryan Mathews returns as the lead back. Questions about his durability, awareness in pass protection, toughness on contact, and dependability in terms of ball security all remain. That should not be the case when a fluid, agile first-round talent is entering his fourth pro season. Ronnie Brown was also re-signed, and it would not be a surprise if this new regime, just like the old regime, winds up trusting him more than Mathews in crunch time. Brown is no longer explosive (he never particularly was, in fact), but he's very steady in protection and short-area receiving on passing downs.

The good news for Rivers is that the old adage about a run game being a quarterback's best friend is no longer true. And he's playing for a very smart coach who understands this. Mike McCoy drew praise as Denver's offensive coordinator when he humbly rewrote his playbook midway through 2011 to accommodate the change from Kyle Orton to Tim Tebow. He showed even more humility the next year when he altered his playbook again, adding chapters that were written by Peyton Manning.

This year, McCoy is crafting a spread-out, quick-passing system that fits perfectly with the way today's NFL has evolved. Instead of asking the immobile Rivers to drop back seven steps behind a porous offensive line, McCoy will ask him to rely more on his sharp pre-snap diagnostic skills and get the ball out on three- and five-step timing. McCoy has said he thinks Rivers can complete 70 percent of his passes in this system. That's pretty unlikely given that only three quarterbacks in NFL history have completed over 70 percent of their passes in a full season (Ken Anderson, Drew Brees and Steve Young), but at least this kind of system should help Rivers

rediscover some of the mechanical discipline that has leaked from his game over the past two years.

This system is significantly different from the one Rivers played in under Turner. In that system, the Chargers operated out a base two-back set roughly 25 times per game over the past four seasons. The Broncos, under McCoy during that same timeframe, used a two-back set an average of just 12 times per game (and that includes the half-season with Tebow).

Fewer backs in the backfield mean more spread and, generally, quicker post-snap play tempo. This makes sense; while San Diego does not have the personnel to rectify last year's offensive line and running game woes, they *do* have the personnel to make this new system work. Malcom Floyd is back at wide receiver, where he'll go back to playing the "X" spot (i.e. "split end," lining right up on the line of scrimmage with minimal pre-snap motion) after having to be miscast in a "Z" role last season thanks to the total face-plant by free-agent pickup Robert Meachem. Meachem is still on the roster, but only because it would have cost the Chargers more than $10 million to cut him. He'll get a chance to start fresh because of the new regime, but based on his work last season, he will likely wind up being a No. 5 receiver or healthy scratch most weeks.

Playing Meachem's Z-receiver (i.e., flanker) spot will be Danario Alexander, assuming the ex-Ram's creaky left knee holds up. Alexander was borderline sensational upon joining the Chargers last October. In Weeks 9-to-14 he averaged 92.5 receiving yards per game and scored five touchdowns. For the season, his 41.6% DVOA was the highest for any wideout with at least 25 targets. Rivers called him the most fluid route runner he's ever played with. The Chargers re-signed him to a one-year, $1.3 million "prove it" deal this past offseason.

Alexander and Floyd give the Chargers a pair of 6-foot-5, 215-plus-pound targets on the outside. Inside, the Chargers have Vincent Brown and Keenan Allen, two potentially excellent fits for this system if they can stay healthy. Brown was an intriguingly smooth all-around receiver before missing the 2012 season with a foot injury. He's expected to be fully healthy in 2013. Allen, a third-round rookie out of Cal, was projected by many as a first-round talent until teams were scared off by his knee issues in the pre-draft process. He has reminded some (reportedly including Telesco) of Reggie Wayne when he came out of Miami in 2001.

Also inside, of course, will be Antonio Gates. Yes, the sore-footed 33-year-old is clearly wearing down; he had just 62 DYAR in 2012, a 26 percent decrease from the previous low that he had from his rookie year. But just because Gates is no longer the dynamic super athlete of yesteryear doesn't mean he's a complete stiff. Many safeties still have trouble covering him one-on-one, and he should draw plenty of those favorable matchups, as the signing of Danny Woodhead suggests the Chargers will have plenty of packages involving a shift into an empty 3x2 set (something their offensive line woes did not allow them to do once in Turner's system last season). Woodhead is a very potent weapon when used for his quickness and lateral agility.

So the pieces are in place for San Diego's passing game to get back on track. But all the injury-prone receiving targets must stay healthy—and it's not a given they will. And the offensive line must prove it can at least not self-destruct in situations where three-step timing just isn't an option. And, most of all, the quarterback must regain the discipline and consistency that once made him a star.

If all these things can happen, the defense should be good enough to compete for at least a Wild Card. The Chargers are young and (somewhat quietly) talented up front, and most players return from a defense that improved last year from 29th to 18th in defensive DVOA. The main players who aren't returning are the cornerbacks, who were the weakest links in last year's defense. If new starting cornerbacks Derek Cox and Shareece Wright can do a better job than Quentin Jammer and Antoine Cason did last year, defensive coordinator John Pagano will be able to unleash a lot more of the creative aspects that are supposed to define his hybrid scheme. Losing Melvin Ingram to a torn ACL during OTAs will hurt, but free-agent addition Dwight Freeney still has enough in the tank to hold things over as a part-time starter.

Solid as this defense seems overall, it almost certainly won't be good enough to carry the Chargers to the postseason. This current teams' fate hinges on Rivers and the offense regaining their form. The pressure is on. Unless the Chargers can climb back into the playoffs, it won't be hard for Telesco to pull the trigger and rebuild the whole thing.

So even if the Chargers ride their defense, their offensive stars, and their seemingly favorable schedule to a playoff appearance, the real action will take place during the evaluation process. Telesco and McCoy will make final decisions on Rivers and Mathews while assembling the pieces of a working line. They must determine the new shape of a roster that still looks a lot like the old Smith-Turner roster. This season represents one last look at that Super Bowl window to determine what can be salvaged. It's best to proceed carefully with a construction project like this; too much random demolition can leave a team with nothing but shattered glass.

Andy Benoit

2012 Chargers Stats by Week

Wk	vs.	W-L	PF	PA	YDF	YDA	TO	Total	Off	Def	ST
1	at OAK	W	22	14	258	321	1	-21%	-21%	18%	18%
2	TEN	W	38	10	416	212	0	8%	11%	-4%	-7%
3	ATL	L	3	27	280	384	-3	-68%	-46%	19%	-3%
4	at KC	W	37	20	293	349	5	5%	-3%	-10%	-2%
5	at NO	L	24	31	427	404	-1	5%	5%	-7%	-7%
6	DEN	L	24	35	307	365	-3	-30%	-22%	13%	5%
7	BYE										
8	at CLE	L	6	7	265	250	-1	-3%	-15%	-5%	7%
9	KC	W	31	13	339	289	2	9%	10%	4%	3%
10	at TB	L	24	34	426	279	-2	-18%	21%	20%	-19%
11	at DEN	L	23	30	277	386	-1	-6%	-27%	-23%	-2%
12	BAL	L	13	16	280	443	0	-10%	-12%	-4%	-1%
13	CIN	L	13	20	297	339	1	8%	-3%	-16%	-5%
14	at PIT	W	34	24	294	340	2	6%	0%	13%	19%
15	CAR	L	7	31	164	372	-1	-85%	-70%	16%	1%
16	at NYJ	W	27	17	223	225	2	40%	8%	-9%	24%
17	OAK	W	24	21	210	265	1	-17%	-22%	13%	17%

Trends and Splits

	Offense	Rank	Defense	Rank
Total DVOA	-10.0%	24	2.0%	18
Unadjusted VOA	-8.9%	24	-1.5%	14
Weighted Trend	-10.5%	23	0.7%	18
Variance	5.4%	10	1.9%	3
Average Opponent	2.4%	25	-3.7%	28
Passing	7.4%	16	9.4%	18
Rushing	-16.5%	28	-7.9%	13
First Down	-2.2%	17	3.0%	21
Second Down	-18.8%	26	-1.2%	15
Third Down	-11.1%	22	5.0%	23
First Half	-5.7%	21	-3.6%	14
Second Half	-14.6%	26	7.9%	22
Red Zone	1.4%	14	48.7%	32
Late and Close	-26.9%	28	-10.2%	10

Five-Year Performance

Year	W-L	Pyth W	Est W	PF	PA	TO	Total	Rk	Off	Rk	Def	Rk	ST	Rk	Off AGL	Rk	Def AGL	Rk	Off Age	Rk	Def Age	Rk	ST Age	Rk
2008	8-8	10.3	10.3	439	347	+4	15.3%	7	18.8%	3	5.3%	22	1.8%	12	12.4	5	22.2	16	27.3	18	26.5	26	26.1	26
2009	13-3	11.3	10.4	454	320	+8	13.5%	11	19.7%	4	6.5%	23	0.2%	16	26.6	17	29.5	18	26.8	25	26.5	24	26.5	18
2010	9-7	11.0	9.4	441	322	-6	15.4%	8	15.5%	4	-10.0%	7	-10.2%	32	26.8	18	12.7	9	27.4	16	27.5	14	27.1	9
2011	8-8	8.7	7.4	406	377	-7	0.70%	16	13.0%	5	10.8%	29	-1.6%	23	32.6	18	40.0	23	28.0	6	28.0	5	26.4	10
2012	7-9	8.0	6.6	350	350	+2	-9.0%	22	-10.0%	24	2.0%	18	3.0%	8	30.2	18	19.3	10	28.4	2	27.8	6	27.1	2

2012 Performance Based on Most Common Personnel Groups

SD Offense					SD Offense vs. Opponents				SD Defense				SD Defense vs. Opponents			
Pers	Freq	Yds	DVOA	Run%	Pers	Freq	Yds	DVOA	Pers	Freq	Yds	DVOA	Pers	Freq	Yds	DVOA
11	35%	6.0	10.6%	15%	4-3-4	33%	4.1	-15.0%	3-4-4	43%	4.9	-6.9%	11	54%	6.0	13.4%
12	31%	4.9	1.7%	32%	Nickel Even	28%	5.6	9.3%	Nickel Odd	29%	6.1	19.1%	21	18%	4.9	1.4%
21	17%	4.2	-15.3%	57%	3-4-4	17%	4.3	-3.1%	Nickel Even	19%	5.4	-5.2%	12	16%	5.0	-6.5%
22	12%	3.9	-12.9%	90%	Dime+	12%	6.7	19.1%	Dime+	7%	6.5	23.3%	22	4%	3.2	-36.3%
13	2%	2.3	-69.2%	70%	Nickel Odd	9%	5.1	-5.0%	4-3-4	1%	2.0	-35.9%	01	1%	5.5	11.8%

Strategic Tendencies

Run/Pass		Rk	Formation		Rk	Pass Rush		Rk	Secondary		Rk	Strategy		Rk
Runs, first half	36%	24	Form: Single Back	63%	21	Rush 3	3.8%	25	4 DB	44%	16	Play action	18%	19
Runs, first down	49%	18	Form: Empty Back	3%	28	Rush 4	58.9%	22	5 DB	47%	17	Avg Box (Off)	6.36	16
Runs, second-long	30%	18	Pers: 3+ WR	36%	30	Rush 5	32.6%	3	6+ DB	7%	12	Avg Box (Def)	6.42	11
Runs, power sit.	56%	14	Pers: 4+ WR	0%	28	Rush 6+	4.7%	25	CB by Sides	96%	1	Offensive Pace	32.79	30
Runs, behind 2H	28%	17	Pers: 2+ TE/6+ OL	47%	6	Sacks by LB	55.3%	9	DB Blitz	15%	10	Defensive Pace	29.53	7
Pass, ahead 2H	46%	16	Shotgun/Pistol	55%	9	Sacks by DB	6.6%	14	Hole in Zone	11%	8	Go for it on 4th	1.03	10

How much will the departure of Norv Turner change the receiving totals of the San Diego running backs? Chargers backs had a league-leading 30 percent of all targets last year, the fifth straight year they ranked in the top three. ◎ Related: San Diego ran 39 running back screens, fifth in the league, but had just 4.0 yards per pass and -40.0% DVOA on these plays. ◎ The Chargers' offense dropped only 13 passes, or 2.7 percent of passes; both figures led the league. ◎ Although the Chargers ranked 28th overall in run offense DVOA, they were very good at running from shotgun formations, with 5.1 yards per carry (seventh in the NFL) and 13.1% DVOA (fifth). ◎ The Chargers' rate of blitzing (i.e., more than four pass rushers) jumped from 24.4 percent of pass plays in 2011 to 37.3 percent of pass plays last year. That was almost all five-man blitzes, but where the Chargers defense was surprisingly effective was with six or more pass rushers, allowing just 2.7 yards per pass.

Passing

Player	DYAR	DVOA	Plays	NtYds	Avg	YAC	C%	TD	Int
P.Rivers	138	-7.3%	576	3266	5.7	5.3	64.7%	26	14

Rushing

Player	DYAR	DVOA	Plays	Yds	Avg	TD	Fum	Suc
R.Mathews	6	-7.7%	184	707	3.8	1	2	47%
J.Battle*	-67	-23.8%	95	311	3.3	3	0	38%
R.Brown	31	10.2%	45	222	4.9	0	0	42%
C.Brinkley*	-48	-36.7%	39	115	2.9	0	1	41%
L.McClain	-24	-46.6%	14	42	3.0	0	0	36%
P.Rivers	-19	-46.5%	11	56	5.1	0	1	-
D.Woodhead	101	22.4%	76	301	4.0	4	0	55%

Receiving

Player	DYAR	DVOA	Plays	Ctch	Yds	Y/C	YAC	TD	C%
M.Floyd	281	36.0%	84	56	814	14.5	1.8	5	67%
D.Alexander	266	41.6%	62	37	658	17.8	7.6	7	60%
E.Royal	-56	-22.7%	44	23	234	10.2	3.9	1	52%
R.Meachem	-10	-12.3%	32	14	207	14.8	2.4	2	44%
M.Spurlock*	25	38.4%	10	9	79	8.8	4.8	0	90%
A.Gates	79	4.6%	80	49	538	11.0	2.7	7	61%
D.Rosario*	-6	-18.3%	18	10	101	10.1	4.3	3	56%
R.McMichael*	-49	-66.5%	13	9	51	5.7	6.0	0	69%
J.Phillips	11	2.0%	10	8	55	6.9	0.8	1	80%
R.Brown	79	12.2%	60	50	369	7.4	7.8	0	83%
R.Mathews	-5	-15.4%	57	39	252	6.5	8.8	0	68%
J.Battle*	63	60.4%	15	15	108	7.2	7.4	1	100%
C.Brinkley*	-2	-16.1%	15	12	77	6.4	8.6	0	80%
L.McClain	-10	-32.0%	10	8	29	3.6	4.5	0	80%
D.Woodhead	149	35.9%	55	40	446	11.2	9.3	3	73%

Offensive Line

Player	Pos	Age	GS	Snaps	Pen	Sk	Pass	Run	Player	Pos	Age	GS	Snaps	Pen	Sk	Pass	Run
Nick Hardwick	C	32	16/16	1017	4	0.5	5.5	3.5	Jared Gaither*	LT	27	4/4	243	4	3	8.5	1
Louis Vasquez*	RG	26	16/16	1017	0	0.5	6	3	Reggie Wells*	G	33	2/2	112	1	2	2	1
Jeromey Clary	RT	30	14/14	831	2	8.5	18.5	3	Max Starks	LT	31	16/16	1065	3	3	16.5	2.5
Tyronne Green*	LG	27	13/13	733	3	1	4	5.5	King Dunlap	LT	28	14/12	817	8	6.5	20.5	5
Michael Harris	LT	25	15/9	583	9	8.5	27	4.5	Rich Ohrnberger	G	27	13/4	286	4	1.5	3.5	2.5
Rex Hadnot*	C	31	16/3	290	0	2	2.5	1	Chad Rinehart	G	28	7/2	164	0	1	3	0
Kevin Haslam*	OT	27	5/3	277	2	3	7	0									

Year	Yards	ALY	Rk	Power	Rk	Stuff	Rk	2nd Lev	Rk	Open Field	Rk	Sacks	ASR	Rk	Short	Long	F-Start	Cont.
2010	4.18	4.12	14	61%	16	19%	19	1.11	17	0.78	14	38	6.8%	19	10	15	11	28
2011	4.42	4.21	9	69%	5	16%	5	1.23	13	0.85	15	30	5.4%	8	8	13	15	28
2012	3.71	3.91	23	60%	21	17%	6	1.01	27	0.41	30	49	8.9%	32	14	19	22	22
2012 ALY by direction:		Left End 3.99 (17)			Left Tackle 3.42 (26)			Mid/Guard 3.99 (18)			Right Tackle 4.81 (4)				Right End 2.59 (30)		

The Chargers were ill-prepared last season for turmoil along the left side of their offensive line. Guard Kris Dielman and tackle Marcus McNeill both retired prematurely due to health issues. Their replacements, Tyrone Green and Jared Gaither, had up-and-down seasons plagued by injuries. Both are gone now, though San Diego's problems on the left side will likely get worse before they get better. The current projected starters are guard Chad Rinehart and tackle Max Starks. Rinehart is a serviceable run-blocker but better suited for backup duties. He'll get a good crack at starting here because the next likely option for San Diego would be Rich Ohrnberger, a journeyman backup who has landed on injured reserve each of the past two seasons (head injury in New England in 2011, knee injury in Arizona in 2012). Starks almost found himself out of the league this past offseason, but the Chargers brought him in because they ostensibly could not stand the thought of their starting left tackle being King Dunlap, a lumbering, upright backup-caliber player who has never been able to consistently manage his technique.

At right guard will be former right tackle Jeromy Clary, replacing the more nimble Louis Vasquez. He'll play alongside center Nick Hardwick, a tenth-year veteran who is in mild decline but really understands the game. The only position up front that San Diego upgraded was the one that did not have a glaring weakness: right tackle. Clary was "just a guy" at this spot, but coaches at least knew what they were getting with him. The new coaching staff and front office, however, has no history with Clary, which is why they did not hesitate to draft Alabama' mauler D.J. Fluker.

Defensive Front Seven

Defensive Line	Age	Pos	Snaps	Plays	TmPct	Overall Rk	Stop	Dfts	BTkl	Runs	St%	vs. Run Rk	RuYd	Rk	Sack	Pass Rush Hit	Hur	Tips
Corey Liuget	23	DE	718	60	7.5%	9	47	17	1	39	74%	40	2.1	21	7	4	10	8
Kendall Reyes	24	DE	532	29	3.6%	61	25	8	0	20	85%	5	2.4	31	5.5	5	10.5	1
Vaughn Martin*	27	DE	460	19	3.2%	--	13	4	1	16	69%	--	1.8	--	1	1	4	0
Cam Thomas	27	DT	400	20	2.5%	69	12	3	0	20	60%	69	2.3	31	0	1	7.5	0
Aubrayo Franklin*	33	DT	280	20	3.3%	54	17	1	3	20	85%	7	2.3	31	0	0	3	0
Antonio Garay*	34	DT	148	16	4.0%	--	11	2	0	15	67%	--	2.9	--	1	1	1.5	0

Linebackers	Age	Pos	Snaps	Plays	TmPct	Overall Rk	Stop	Dfts	BTkl	Sack	Pass Rush Hit	Hur	Tips	Runs	St%	vs. Run Rk	Yds	Rk	Tgts	vs. Pass Suc%	Rk	AdjYd	Rk	PD
Shaun Phillips*	32	OLB	839	50	6.3%	93	33	22	5	10	5	14	3	26	58%	90	3.7	74	7	72%	--	6.2	--	1
Donald Butler	25	ILB	714	82	13.7%	37	47	20	5	3	2	3	1	49	63%	66	3.0	34	24	61%	10	6.9	46	4
Takeo Spikes*	37	ILB	702	78	9.8%	64	43	8	2	0.5	4	2.5	0	60	62%	75	3.4	53	13	53%	--	5.7	--	1
Jarret Johnson	32	OLB	511	40	5.4%	104	29	6	4	1.5	2	2	0	26	85%	5	1.7	6	5	75%	--	2.7	--	0
Melvin Ingram	24	OLB	463	33	4.1%	--	23	9	6	1	3	18	3	20	65%	--	3.2	--	6	35%	--	11.5	--	1
Demorrio Williams*	33	ILB	354	47	6.7%	85	24	9	3	0	3	5	0	22	59%	85	4.4	99	15	50%	--	6.5	--	3
Bront Bird	24	ILB	111	17	6.4%	--	8	3	0	0	0	0	1	8	25%	--	5.1	--	9	75%	--	2.0	--	1
Dwight Freeney	25	ILB	699	138	1.9%	110	74	28	0	5	8	18	1	6	67%	44	1.8	8	1	98%	--	1.0	--	3
D.J. Smith	24	ILB	369	43	14.0%	--	21	8	1	2	1	6	1	23	52%	--	3.7	--	17	23%	75	9.2	72	3

Year	Yards	ALY	Rk	Power	Rk	Stuff	Rk	2nd Level	Rk	Open Field	Rk	Sacks	ASR	Rk	Short	Long
2010	3.74	3.86	14	50%	3	20%	14	1.06	10	0.46	6	47	9.0%	2	13	25
2011	4.38	4.32	25	75%	32	16%	28	1.12	10	0.79	19	32	6.5%	18	6	21
2012	3.81	3.80	7	59%	10	23%	7	1.18	15	0.54	8	38	7.0%	8	14	11
2012 ALY by direction:		Left End 3.36 (6)			Left Tackle 2.96 (2)			Mid/Guard 3.88 (10)			Right Tackle 3.76 (13)				Right End 5.44 (31)	

It was wise of McCoy to retain defensive coordinator John Pagano. Getting another year in a familiar system, this young and talented front seven could erupt in 2013. Or at least it was on track to erupt, prior to Melvin Ingram's ACL injury in May. On film, the first-rounder looked a lot more like the rookie who finished the year with an impressive 18 hurries than he did like the disappointment who had only one sack. Ingram played a variety of different sub-package positions, including standup outside linebacker, defensive end, defensive tackle and interior standup joker. He showed natural explosiveness, not just in his first step but in his all-around movement. He also played with great lateral athleticism and leverage, which made it very difficult for blockers to get clean angles on him. The Chargers mitigated the damage as much as possible with the signing of Dwight Freeney. The 33-year-old ex-Colt is not slowing down nearly as dramatically as his shrinking raw sack numbers suggest. Freeney still transitions from speed to power with great effectiveness. Yes, he's best suited for a 4-3, but that doesn't mean he can't play outside linebacker in a 3-4. And in the San Diego scheme, a lot of the assignments are similar to those of a 4-3 end. With Ingram out, San Diego's most impressive rising young player is defensive end Corey Liuget, who was taken in the first round a year before Ingram. Liuget has very good movement for his size, which shows in his disruptive run defense and opportunistic pass rushing. Opposite Liuget is 2012 second-rounder Kendall Reyes, a quick athlete with very good hand technique.

Fourth-year pro Donald Butler returns as one starting inside linebacker; when healthy, he has proven to be an increasingly fluid and instinctive hunter. And, of course, there is Manti Te'o, whom Telesco liked enough to trade up and draft early in the second round. With sturdy run-stuffing veteran Takeo Spikes gone, Te'o will start ahead of Jonas Mouton, a 2011 second-rounder who has seen minimal action due to injuries. Mouton, actually, might have trouble keeping his spot on the depth chart ahead of D.J. Smith, an athletic free agent pickup from Green Bay who, assuming his surgically repaired knee can hold up, is a very good inside blitzer.

While there's optimism for this front seven's immediate and long-term future, there are legitimate concerns about depth. Starting in the base 3-4 opposite Freeney is Jarret Johnson. He is a terrific edge-setter against the run, but as a pass-rusher he's someone whom offenses only respect, not fear. For some defenses, Johnson would come off the field on passing downs. But in San Diego, the only backup edge players are the unimaginative Larry English and sixth-round rookie Tourek Williams (Florida International). There's even more concern about the depth at nose tackle, as there doesn't appear to be anyone at all behind starter Cam Thomas (who has been a rotational player most of his career).

Defensive Secondary

				Overall						vs. Run						vs. Pass							
Secondary	Age	Pos	Snaps	Plays	TmPct	Rk	Stop	Dfts	BTkl	Runs	St%	Rk	Yds	Rk	Tgts	Tgt%	Rk	Dist	Suc%	Rk	APaYd	Rk	PD	Int
Eric Weddle	28	FS	1036	105	13.2%	11	49	14	6	49	59%	4	5.2	11	33	7.6%	25	10.8	64%	15	5.0	8	7	3
Antoine Cason*	27	CB	1023	83	10.4%	16	24	8	4	14	57%	18	4.1	10	97	22.3%	7	11.4	40%	84	7.3	35	11	2
Quentin Jammer*	34	CB	992	73	9.2%	31	27	15	4	12	58%	16	6.7	46	95	21.9%	9	15.5	49%	61	8.1	61	8	3
Marcus Gilchrist	25	CB	622	58	7.3%	--	22	10	3	15	47%	--	2.7	--	39	9.0%	--	9.3	40%	--	9.1	--	2	0
Atari Bigby*	32	SS	619	63	11.5%	27	16	3	7	30	23%	66	7.7	47	23	7.7%	24	7.7	41%	72	7.8	46	2	0
Corey Lynch*	28	FS	495	46	5.8%	66	18	11	6	23	39%	33	4.5	5	17	3.8%	70	15.8	67%	11	4.6	5	7	2
Derek Cox	27	CB	765	71	10.7%	15	29	15	8	14	50%	26	5.2	22	83	25.5%	1	12.5	51%	46	8.0	59	11	4
Johnny Patrick	25	CB	215	23	2.8%	--	4	1	2	3	33%	--	5.7	--	35	7.7%	--	12.7	39%	--	8.4	--	2	0

Year	Pass D Rank	vs. #1 WR	Rk	vs. #2 WR	Rk	vs. Other WR	Rk	vs. TE	Rk	vs. RB	Rk
2010	4	-35.5%	1	-4.5%	12	-26.9%	3	18.1%	26	15.4%	25
2011	31	32.5%	31	13.5%	23	2.1%	21	32.8%	31	-6.2%	11
2012	18	21.6%	27	-17.3%	5	-11.2%	8	-12.0%	5	23.4%	29

Last season, struggling cornerbacks Quintin Jammer and Antoine Cason had to be kept primarily in off coverage, which limited Pagano's play-calling options, including in third-and-long—the down his blitz-oriented system is built around. Both corners are gone now, though just like with the offensive line, there's no guarantee that the personnel changes will bring about improvement.

The first new starter is Derek Cox, signed in free agency after four wildly up and down seasons in Jacksonville. Cox is capable of thriving as an NFL corner, especially if he can play trail technique and rely on his natural movement skills. However, far too often he has gone through prolonged slumps and been abused. Most concerning is that the slumps seem to come about when he faces top-shelf competition. Calvin Johnson and Reggie Wayne both humiliated Cox last year. Having Cox as a No. 1 cornerback would be a stretch, but the Chargers don't really have a No. 1 cornerback, per se; last year they led the league in keeping their cornerbacks to specific sides instead of having them play against specific receivers.

Opposite Cox will be Shareece Wright, a third-year pro who has looked solid in man coverage but hasn't played enough to fully evaluate. (Remember, there's always a reason a player doesn't play, and the reason is almost always football-related.). With third-year corner Marcus Gilchrist moving to strong safety this season, the nickel corner will now be either Johnny Patrick, a 2011 third-rounder who was cut by the Saints after just two seasons, or fifth-round rookie Steve Williams out of Cal. At this point, neither is an option most teams would want. (It's possible the Chargers will wind up sliding Gilchrist into a slot corner role in sub packages and calling upon either Brandon Taylor or Darrell Stuckey to come in at safety.)

On the bright side, this very iffy secondary is at least stabilized somewhat by the presence of an upper-echelon safety. Eric Weddle is one of the league's best at diagnosing offensive designs and disguising his intentions. He's very effective in the box but also capable of impacting a game in deep, roving coverage.

Special Teams

Year	DVOA	Rank	FG/XP	Rank	Net Kick	Rank	Kick Ret	Rank	Net Punt	Rank	Punt Ret	Rank	Hidden	Rank
2010	-10.2%	32	1.5	14	-17.7	32	-3.5	18	-34.3	32	3.2	12	-7.8	24
2011	-1.6%	23	-0.4	17	-7.0	27	2.8	9	1.6	13	-5.0	22	-3.0	19
2012	3.0%	8	6.4	7	7.7	6	3.2	9	-4.9	22	2.4	11	2.8	9

Kicker Nick Novak was successful on 18 of his 20 field-goal attempts last season, with the only two misses coming from 50-plus yards out. He was solid but not spectacular on kickoffs, helped out by quality coverage teams. Lately, punter Mike Scifres has not quite been the marvelous ball-placement weapon that he was a few years ago; he's had negative net and gross punt value two of the past three seasons. San Diego's return game at this point is a big TBD. Richard Goodman and Eddie Royal are the leading candidates, but it's possible neither will end up making the final roster. In fact, the only player who returned kicks or punts for San Diego last year and is sure to be on the final roster this year is Weddle, and he's essentially a fair catch specialist.

Coaching Staff

By firing Norv Turner and hiring Mike McCoy, the Chargers are trading one passing game connoisseur for another, ostensibly with hopes that the latter will bring more motivational firepower to the table. While passionate locker room speeches can make for great television, the greatest motivator in pro football is coming up with game plans that give your players the best chance to succeed. McCoy exhibited an uncanny grasp of this in Denver. In 2011, he rewrote his playbook midseason to accommodate Tim Tebow, who took over for the more conventional Kyle Orton. In 2012, he rewrote his playbook again to integrate his system with what Peyton Manning wanted to run.

Upon arriving in San Diego, McCoy tabbed fired Cardinals head coach Ken Whisenhunt to coordinate the offense, and Whisenhunt will call the plays. In the past, he has run a system that puts a heavy burden on the quarterback to identify blitzes pre-snap and get rid of the ball quickly. Given San Diego's porous offensive line, expect him to put Philip Rivers in a lot of shotgun, quick-release designs. Defensively, John Pagano is getting another shot to run his hybrid 3-4 defense after poor cornerback play kept a ceiling on what the Chargers were able to do schematically last season.

San Francisco 49ers

2012 Record: 11-4-1	**Total DVOA:** 29.5% (4th)	**2013 Mean Projection:** 9.7 wins	**On the Clock (0-4):** 2%
Pythagorean Wins: 11.4 (4th)	**Offense:** 16.5% (5th)	**Postseason Odds:** 59.6%	**Mediocrity (5-7):** 14%
Snap-Weighted Age: 27.2 (12th)	**Defense:** -14.4% (3rd)	**Super Bowl Odds:** 11.1%	**Playoff Contender (8-10):** 47%
Average Opponent: 6.4% (3rd)	**Special Teams:** -1.5% (20th)	**Proj. Avg. Opponent:** 0.5% (18th)	**Super Bowl Contender (11+):** 37%

2012: 49ers to historical regression trends: drop dead.

2013: One season might be a fluke, but two seasons turn our numbers into believers.

At Football Outsiders, we have a saying about our mean win projections: "A few of them will look strange to you. A few of them look strange to *us*." Last season, far and away our strangest projection belonged to San Francisco, a team we said would drop from 13-3 to (approximately) 7-9. It was such an enigma that we spent the better part of the preseason painstakingly explaining why we did and (more often) did not agree with our own 49ers math. Factors like estimated win differential, record in close games, reliance on special teams, projected schedule strength, turnover rates, and the Plexiglass Principle all screamed, "San Francisco will regress in 2012!" Lo and behold, they hardly regressed at all from a win-loss perspective, and actually advanced farther in the playoffs.

So what happened? Mainly, last year's 49ers were a perfect example of the blind spots in most any football projection system. Without getting too technical, statistical models generally operate under two assumptions. First, it's assumed that a predictor (e.g., Pythagorean wins in Year N-1) affects the thing being predicted (e.g., total wins in Year N) *on average*. For instance, even though studies show that, on average, smokers are 15 to 30 times more likely to get lung cancer, an individual with super-immunity or impeccable genes may be able to puff away to their heart's content without ever contracting the disease. (If you're a smoker, we certainly don't suggest you bank on possessing these above-average traits.) Second, it's assumed that a prediction is based only on factors included in the model. Continuing our smoking analogy, there may be several unknown factors—say, whether or not a person was born on the planet Krypton—that decrease a smoker's lung cancer risk. (Note to smokers: You were not born on the planet Krypton.) Let's take each of these (ultimately faulty) assumptions one at a time.

Looking at the potential of the raw talent on the San Francisco roster rather than trends in the team's performance over the previous two or three years, it was clear going into 2012 that the 49ers were far from an average team. In the pre-Harbaugh years, Trent Baalke and Paraag Marathe had amassed one of the most talented rosters in the NFL; it just wasn't being utilized properly by the previous coaching regime. In 2010, San Francisco went 6-10 despite getting a combined 161 starts from the first-round picks on their roster, which was second-most in the NFL that year. (The Jets went 11-5 behind 186 starts from 15 former first-rounders.) That total also ranked 11th among all teams over a 20-year period from 1991 to 2010; eight of the top 10 finished over .500. Even more to the point, the 2011 49ers got 162 starts by former first-round picks, which was second-highest among the 81 Plexiglass Principle candidates since 1991 (*i.e.*, teams that improved by at least 20 percentage points of DVOA the previous season). Only the 2008 Baltimore Ravens had more (177), and they too avoided a bounce off the plexiglass a year later (29.1% DVOA in 2009). In other words, San Francisco's quantum leap to 13-3 in 2011 was due in no small part to the sudden eruption of dormant talent that had been on the roster all along.

It's important not to forget the specific ways in which Mike Singletary and company actively mismanaged the 2010 roster. Last season, Alex Smith may have been benched for wunderkind Colin Kaepernick, but Singletary benched him in 2010 for current Ohio State graduate student Troy Smith. As a rookie, All-Pro linebacker NaVorro Bowman played only 20 percent of San Francisco's defensive snaps as a backup to Takeo Spikes. Underrated strongside linebacker Ahmad Brooks was stuck behind mediocre-at-best Parys Haralson. Tarell Brown, arguably San Francisco's best cornerback last season, sat behind veteran Shawntae Spencer, who subsequently couldn't even hold a starting job in the Oakland Raiders' porous secondary. Left end Ray McDonald, who is now on the field more than 90 percent of the time, was also a backup. Under Singletary, the 49ers bench may have been more talented than the starting lineup.

After replacing Singletary and company with a coaching staff that better manages San Francisco's depth chart, Baalke then took a roster brimming with underutilized talent and made it even better. He got rid of dead weight like the currently unemployed quartet of Spikes, Spencer, fullback Moran Norris, and cornerback Nate Clements. Another player jettisoned by Baalke, 2010 starting right guard Chilo Rachal, is now a third-stringer on Arizona's laughable offensive line. Meanwhile, Baalke has added underrated young talents like cornerback Chris Culliver (third round), and running back Kendall Hunter (fourth round), while also acquiring buy-low free agents like center Jonathan Goodwin, strong safety Donte Whitner, and cornerback Carlos Rogers.

So given the level of talent in San Francisco, both on and off the field, it's clear that the 49ers were an outlier, and therefore shouldn't have been subject to an average regression to the

2013 49ers Schedule

Week	Opp.	Week	Opp.	Week	Opp.
1	GB	7	at TEN	13	STL
2	at SEA	8	vs. JAC (U.K.)	14	SEA
3	IND	9	BYE	15	at TB
4	at STL (Thu.)	10	CAR	16	ATL
5	HOU	11	at NO	17	at ARI
6	ARI	12	at WAS (Mon.)		

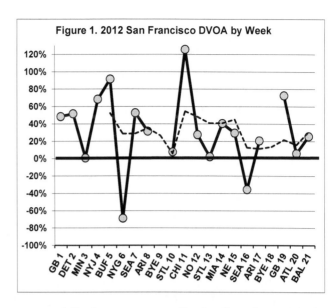

Figure 1. 2012 San Francisco DVOA by Week

mean. And again, this isn't hindsight: We implied as much before last season started.

Nevertheless, it's also the case that the 2012 49ers exhibited an incredible rare immunity to the Plexiglass Principle even though most of the factors that we expected to regress towards the mean actually did so.

Here's a taste of what we mean by that. In 2012, the 49ers improved by 11.3 percentage points of DVOA a year after improving by 29.8 percentage points. Going back to our group of Plexiglass Principle candidates, 78 of 81 saw their big improvement occur prior to 2011. Of those 78 teams, only 11 ended up improving by more than 10 percentage points the following year, which means the historical chances of San Francisco accomplishing the feat in 2012 were a mere one in seven.

And yet, the astonishing thing is that they beat those odds despite our projection model being incredibly accurate with regard to *why* they would regress. Our 2011 estimated wins metric suggested that the 49ers won approximately two more games than the stats otherwise suggested. A year later, two San Francisco wins turned into a loss and a tie. We said the 49ers wouldn't be as good in games decided by eight points or less, and they dropped from 7-2 to 2-1-1. Their schedule strength went from the easiest in the league in 2011 to the third-toughest in 2012. Their special teams ranked second-worst last season after ranking second-best the year before.

As predicted, the 2012 version of Alex Smith had a higher interception rate than the 2011 version. San Francisco's turnover differential did in fact nosedive from plus-28 to plus-nine. Their fumble recovery rate dropped from 65 percent in 2011 to 53 percent last season. Literally, the only regression-to-the-mean prediction that didn't come to fruition in 2012 was that the 49ers followed up an extremely healthy 2011 season (just 38.4 Adjusted Games Lost, eighth in the NFL) with even fewer injuries to critical players in 2012 (16.2 AGL, best in the NFL).

The second assumption that contributed to our projection going awry was that several characteristics of the 2012 49ers simply weren't (and couldn't be) accounted for in our model. Chief among these is the impact of strategic thinking. Above and beyond simply putting the right players on the field, Harbaugh and offensive coordinator Greg Roman are also superior tacticians compared to their predecessors. And yet, even though various media have detailed the duo's play-calling triumphs over the past two years, it's always after the secret's been revealed. In *Football Outsiders Almanac 2012*, we wrote about the various oddities they unleashed on the NFL in 2011: the fly sweep, the tight end-around, the mesmerizing

pre-snap shift, the seven-man offensive line, the nose tackle playing fullback, etc. But who saw any of that coming before the season? We even suggested in last year's book that the offense's poker-playing brain trust had an ace up their sleeve for 2012. Did we know it would be the ace of pistol diamonds? Of course not. As outsiders, we can provide charting data on a team's broad strategic tendencies after the fact, but tactics that win or lose specific games are unknowable beforehand. Usually, this issue washes out in our projections because the NFL is a copycat league; Harbaugh and Roman look more like the cats that eat our canary.

In addition, the mere existence of a coaching change seems to dampen the Plexiglass Principle, although we didn't discover that trend until after publishing our projections. When a team enjoys a massive DVOA improvement under an incumbent head coach, it declines by about 13 percentage points the following season. However, when improvement comes on the heels of a coaching change (a la the 2011 49ers), a plexiglass candidate can be expected to decline by about five percentage points of DVOA. That eight percentage point difference approaches statistical significance.

Those are factors for which we didn't account, what Donald Rumsfeld might call "known unknowns." The 49ers also benefitted from "unknown unknowns." We couldn't have known that Colin Kaepernick would supplant Alex Smith as the starting quarterback, which drastically changed San Francisco's offensive scheme, and in turn sent opposing defenses into a "this wasn't part of our film study" panic for the better part of four months. Of course, with the benefit of hindsight, the writing was squarely inscribed on the wall. Smith was a holdover from a previous regime, and Kaepernick was the new regime's selection at the top of the second round; the 2011 lockout was probably a major factor in handing Smith an uncontested starting job. And yet, despite Smith leading the 49ers to the NFC Championship game, San Francisco engaged in a brief flirtation with Peyton Manning two months later.

Our projection also couldn't have known that the 49ers would have the good fortune of facing the New York Jets without Darrelle Revis in Week 4 and a Bears team led by Jason Campbell instead of Jay Cutler in Week 11. And though we projected a Kevin Kolb-led Cardinals team to win 1.4 fewer games than San Francisco last season, the Keystone Kops rotating at quarterback after Kolb got hurt gave Arizona almost no shot of beating the 49ers in Weeks 8 and 17. Add these three or four lay-up victories to our forecast, and all of a sudden it looks much better.

Looking ahead to 2013, there's one glaring known unknown that could wreak havoc on this year's San Francisco projection. Michael Crabtree, who broke out as a bona fide No. 1 wide receiver after Kaepernick took the helm of the offense last season, is on the shelf after tearing his Achilles tendon in May. In 2012, Baltimore outside linebacker Terrell Suggs and Tampa Bay defensive end Da'Quan Bowers suffered the same injury (around the same time) as Crabtree, and both returned in Week 7. Denver wide receiver Demaryius Thomas was in Crabtree's boat in February 2011, and was back on the field by October of that year. Of course, none of the three were anywhere near full strength, and the lone wideout of the bunch said he didn't fully recover until the following summer.

That said, with or without Crabtree, San Francisco's offense has evolved to the point that one has to expect more passing this upcoming season. Kaepernick had as many attempts as Smith in 2012 despite two fewer starts. Furthermore, the team's off-season personnel changes included trading for a wide receiver who actually catches passes (i.e., Anquan Boldin) to replace a wide receiver who just runs decoy routes (i.e., Randy Moss). And in the second round of April's draft, the 49ers selected Vance McDonald (Rice) to replace Delanie Walker. Although Walker was as malleable as Play-Doh in the 49ers' offensive scheme, he had developed hands of stone when called upon to catch actual passes. Meanwhile, even with the potential likelihood of an abbreviated season from Crabtree, San Francisco is four-deep at receiver with A.J. Jenkins no doubt exceeding the 35 snaps he played in 2012 and Kyle Williams returning from last season's ACL tear.

Another indicator of the offense's likely evolution in 2013 regards the backfield. In Jimmy Raye's offense in 2010, Frank Gore played 88 percent of San Francisco's offensive snaps. Since Harbaugh and Greg Roman took over, however, Gore's had participation rates of 68 percent and 73 percent in 2011 and 2012, respectively. With Kendall Hunter's return from a torn Achilles tendon, and the emergence of LaMichael James towards the end of last season, we can expect to see even less of Gore in 2013, especially given James' potential as a Darren Sproles-type of player.

On defense, depth was the main concern heading into this offseason. Vic Fangio has substituted as infrequently as any defensive coordinator in the league over the past two years: In 2011, nine defenders played at least 90 percent of snaps when healthy; a total that increased to 10 last year when Aldon Smith began playing full time. While you can't blame Fangio for giving as much playing time to Pro Bowl-caliber starters as possible, that strategy had negative consequences for the defense's playoff run. When the Smiths (Justin and Aldon) got hurt at the end of last season—possibly a byproduct of inadequate rest in

its own right—San Francisco had no adequate replacements; the best backup, Ricky-Jean Francois, was stretched as a starter. The effects of fatigue and injuries show up in their weekly DVOA splits: From Weeks 1 to 14, San Francisco's defense DVOA was -16.4%; it was 3.7% over their final six games (including the playoffs). The most embarrassing performance during this stretch was their Week 17 home game against the Cardinals. Needing a win to secure a division title and first-round bye, the beleaguered defense could only muster 5.0% DVOA against an offense led by one of Arizona's Keystone Kops.

Baalke and company finally addressed the depth issue this offseason. In free agency, they added cornerback Nnamdi Asomugha, a much better fit for the 49ers' man-to-man proclivities than the Eagles' zone, as well as safety Craig Dahl. In the draft, San Francisco used their first-round pick on safety Eric Reid (Louisiana State), who will immediately replace free-agent loss Dashon Goldson at free safety. Combined with Dahl and second-year strong safety Trenton Robinson, the 49ers' depth chart is now four-deep at the position after being two-deep last year. In the second round, San Francisco took defensive end Tank Carradine (Florida State) as the heir apparent to Justin Smith, who will be a 34-year-old free agent after this season. Getting Carradine on the field in 2013 is a win-win situation: He gains valuable playing time while also keeping Smith fresh for the playoffs. Third-round pick Corey "Earl of" Lemonier (Auburn) can give either Aldon Smith or Ahmad Brooks a much-needed breather at outside linebacker.

Most of San Francisco's changes from 2012 to 2013 are positive signs for the future (i.e., more passing with Boldin, McDonald, and a full year of Kaepernick and James; more depth on defense; etc.), and we're sure as hell not going to make the same mistake twice. The collective Football Outsiders gut tells us that the 49ers will win 10 or more games for the third consecutive season. Thankfully, this time the projection model agrees.

The biggest factor in the projection is simply that San Francisco has averaged 24.3% DVOA over the course of two seasons, not just one; at this point, the Plexiglass Principle is moot. Elsewhere, unlike the 2011 49ers, last year's incarnation had a *positive* estimated win differential, which portends good things for 2013. Finally, their schedule looks to be slightly easier this season, dropping from third to 10th in difficulty. To be sure, with plenty of top-10 opponents according to our DVOA projections (Green Bay, Seattle, Washington, Carolina, Houston, and New Orleans), the path to a third straight NFC Championship game won't be easy. Nevertheless, given the historical trends working against San Francisco last year, it should be a lot easier this time around.

Our rosy outlook for Seattle in Russell Wilson's second year suggests that 10 wins may not be enough for San Francisco to win the NFC West. Nevertheless, even if they might not get the opportunity to send Candlestick Park out with an NFC Championship game, they still have good odds to open Levi's Stadium as the defending Super Bowl champions.

Danny Tuccitto

2012 49ers Stats by Week

Wk	vs.	W-L	PF	PA	YDF	YDA	TO	Total	Off	Def	ST
1	at GB	W	30	22	377	324	1	48%	38%	-11%	0%
2	DET	W	27	19	349	296	0	52%	44%	-14%	-6%
3	at MIN	L	13	24	280	344	-1	1%	-19%	-8%	12%
4	at NYJ	W	34	0	381	145	4	68%	21%	-60%	-13%
5	BUF	W	45	3	621	204	1	92%	69%	-33%	-10%
6	NYG	L	3	26	314	342	-3	-69%	-46%	4%	-19%
7	SEA	W	13	6	313	251	0	53%	-1%	-36%	18%
8	at ARI	W	24	3	317	265	1	32%	36%	13%	9%
9	BYE										
10	STL	T	24	24	341	458	1	8%	31%	22%	-1%
11	CHI	W	32	7	353	143	2	126%	54%	-61%	11%
12	at NO	W	31	21	375	290	0	28%	13%	-33%	-18%
13	at STL	L	13	16	339	293	-1	2%	-7%	-16%	-7%
14	MIA	W	27	13	321	227	1	41%	30%	-9%	2%
15	at NE	W	41	34	388	520	2	30%	-1%	-24%	6%
16	at SEA	L	13	42	313	346	-1	-36%	-23%	12%	-1%
17	ARI	W	27	13	407	262	2	21%	33%	5%	-7%
18	BYE										
19	GB	W	45	31	579	352	1	73%	66%	7%	13%
20	at ATL	W	28	24	373	477	1	6%	45%	34%	-5%
21	BAL	L	31	34	468	367	-1	26%	45%	3%	-16%

Trends and Splits

	Offense	Rank	Defense	Rank
Total DVOA	16.5%	5	-14.4%	3
Unadjusted VOA	14.1%	5	-11.5%	5
Weighted Trend	12.7%	7	-12.4%	4
Variance	9.5%	24	6.0%	18
Average Opponent	-4.7%	6	0.6%	13
Passing	32.2%	5	-10.4%	6
Rushing	12.7%	3	-19.7%	2
First Down	31.7%	1	-22.2%	1
Second Down	10.0%	9	-5.8%	11
Third Down	-5.9%	20	-13.8%	7
First Half	19.3%	5	-13.1%	3
Second Half	13.6%	8	-15.6%	4
Red Zone	7.1%	11	-4.1%	11
Late and Close	29.2%	2	-26.6%	3

Five-Year Performance

Year	W-L	Pyth W	Est W	PF	PA	TO	Total	Rk	Off	Rk	Def	Rk	ST	Rk	Off AGL	Rk	Def AGL	Rk	Off Age	Rk	Def Age	Rk	ST Age	Rk
2008	7-9	6.8	6.1	339	381	-17	-14.1%	25	-15.6%	27	3.6%	18	5.2%	3	24.9	18	5.4	3	27.3	17	27.7	8	27.0	9
2009	8-8	9.5	7.1	280	390	-8	-1.2%	20	-14.1%	23	-14.0%	5	-1.1%	20	9.5	8	34.1	22	26.6	27	27.4	12	26.7	13
2010	6-10	6.8	6.9	305	346	-1	-11.2%	24	-11.1%	24	-1.4%	15	-1.5%	20	20.7	11	6.8	3	25.8	28	27.6	11	25.6	29
2011	13-3	12.3	10.8	380	229	+2	18.6%	6	-3.9%	18	-14.6%	3	7.8%	2	29.6	16	8.8	2	26.5	23	26.7	21	26.6	7
2012	11-4-1	11.4	12.5	397	273	+9	29.5%	4	16.5%	5	-14.4%	3	-1.5%	20	11.7	5	4.5	1	27.1	14	27.3	10	26.9	5

2012 Performance Based on Most Common Personnel Groups

SF Offense					SF Offense vs. Opponents				SF Defense				SF Defense vs. Opponents			
Pers	Freq	Yds	DVOA	Run%	Pers	Freq	Yds	DVOA	Pers	Freq	Yds	DVOA	Pers	Freq	Yds	DVOA
22	24%	5.7	23.4%	68%	4-3-4	47%	6.6	30.6%	3-4-4	34%	4.6	-19.9%	11	47%	4.3	-22.5%
12	23%	7.1	41.1%	28%	Nickel Even	20%	5.3	-3.8%	Nickel Even	33%	4.8	-8.4%	12	19%	5.7	-12.0%
21	21%	6.6	31.5%	50%	3-4-4	19%	5.8	16.1%	Nickel Odd	21%	4.0	-37.7%	21	9%	4.4	-29.8%
11	20%	5.2	-12.5%	22%	Dime+	4%	7.3	76.4%	Dime+	11%	7.1	33.8%	22	6%	3.8	-36.0%
13	3%	5.4	-28.1%	54%	4-4-3	3%	6.3	25.3%	4-4-3	1%	-0.2	-40.1%	10	5%	6.0	34.8%
721	2%	4.1	25.5%	95%	Nickel Odd	3%	7.0	39.6%					01	5%	7.4	33.8%
622	2%	1.8	-11.2%	100%	5-3-3	2%	4.8	32.1%					621	2%	4.3	21.5%
					Goal Line	2%	0.3	-30.6%					13	2%	4.7	-8.6%

Strategic Tendencies

Run/Pass		Rk	Formation		Rk	Pass Rush		Rk	Secondary		Rk	Strategy		Rk
Runs, first half	40%	11	Form: Single Back	47%	32	Rush 3	9.9%	7	4 DB	34%	30	Play action	27%	6
Runs, first down	50%	16	Form: Empty Back	4%	24	Rush 4	73.2%	8	5 DB	54%	3	Avg Box (Off)	6.79	1
Runs, second-long	52%	1	Pers: 3+ WR	21%	32	Rush 5	14.6%	28	6+ DB	11%	8	Avg Box (Def)	5.97	32
Runs, power sit.	71%	2	Pers: 4+ WR	0%	25	Rush 6+	2.3%	32	CB by Sides	95%	4	Offensive Pace	33.17	32
Runs, behind 2H	29%	14	Pers: 2+ TE/6+ OL	57%	3	Sacks by LB	75.0%	4	DB Blitz	6%	28	Defensive Pace	31.51	30
Pass, ahead 2H	40%	26	Shotgun/Pistol	39%	24	Sacks by DB	2.6%	26	Hole in Zone	7%	23	Go for it on 4th	0.92	16

No coach switches up his personnel quite like Jim Harbaugh. Last year, the 49ers had four different personnel groups they used on at least 20 percent of plays. Washington was the only other team to even use three personnel groups on at least 20 percent of plays. Colin Kaepernick was blitzed on a league-leading 39.2 percent of pass plays, and it was successful, at least during the regular season, when he had 8.8 yards per play with four pass rushers but just 5.8 yards per play with five or more. The blitzing wasn't successful in the postseason, but nothing was: Kaepernick averaged 10.0 yards per play against four pass rushers *and* against blitzes. Before Kaepernick took over at midseason, Alex Smith was also heavily blitzed, with opponents sending five or more pass rushers 34.0 percent of the time. ☞ The 49ers gradually used more and more pistol formations as the year went on, but you may be surprised to learn that with Colin Kaepernick at quarterback, the 49ers were actually more efficient from other formations.

Weeks	Pistol Formation			Shotgun Formation			Quarterback Under Center		
	Pct of Plays	Yd/Play	DVOA	Pct of Plays	Yd/Play	DVOA	Pct of Plays	Yd/Play	DVOA
Weeks 1-10 (Alex Smith starter)	4.8%	7.2	62.2%	31.7%	5.6	-4.7%	63.5%	6.4	35.2%
Weeks 11-17 (Colin Kaepernick starter)	10.8%	5.8	6.2%	31.1%	6.8	29.4%	58.1%	5.5	12.6%
Playoffs (Colin Kaepernick starter)	49.2%	7.5	44.7%	31.6%	7.4	51.8%	19.3%	9.1	74.5%

74 percent of runs by 49ers running backs came with two backs in the formation, the highest rate in the league. Yet the 49ers were actually much better running the ball from single-back formations: 34.8% DVOA and 5.9 yards per carry compared to 0.4% DVOA and 4.3 yards per carry with two backs. ☞ Perhaps the 49ers should consider going empty backfield more often; they had a league-leading 9.2 yards per play and 74.1% DVOA without anyone in the backfield. ☞ The 49ers defense allowed 10.4 average YAC on passes caught behind the line of scrimmage (31st in the league, ahead of only New Orleans) but only 3.1 average YAC on passes caught beyond the line of scrimmage (second behind Carolina). ☞ For the second straight year, the 49ers sent fewer big blitzes than any other team. ☞ Is there something about the 49ers special teams that draws opponent penalties? The 49ers were tied for second with 25 opponent penalties on special teams after leading the league with 33 the year before.

Passing

Player	DYAR	DVOA	Plays	NtYds	Avg	YAC	C%	TD	Int
A.Smith*	418	14.8%	243	1610	6.6	5.1	70.3%	13	5
C.Kaepernick	555	25.8%	234	1687	7.2	5.2	62.7%	10	3
C.McCoy	10	-2.7%	21	54	2.6	2.7	52.9%	1	0

Rushing

Player	DYAR	DVOA	Plays	Yds	Avg	TD	Fum	Suc
F.Gore	268	17.4%	258	1213	4.7	8	3	48%
K.Hunter	109	29.1%	72	371	5.2	2	0	60%
C.Kaepernick	31	-1.5%	57	406	7.1	5	7	-
L.James	9	-0.2%	27	125	4.6	0	1	41%
A.Dixon	23	15.9%	21	78	3.7	2	0	67%
A.Smith*	36	26.0%	21	142	6.8	0	0	-
B.Miller	2	-0.9%	5	18	3.6	0	0	60%
B.Jacobs	-5	-35.1%	5	7	1.4	0	0	20%

Receiving

Player	DYAR	DVOA	Plays	Ctch	Yds	Y/C	YAC	TD	C%
M.Crabtree	334	21.9%	127	86	1113	12.9	6.5	9	68%
M.Manningham	36	-2.3%	57	42	451	10.7	4.1	1	74%
R.Moss*	66	6.8%	50	28	434	15.5	3.0	3	56%
K.Williams	32	2.6%	22	14	212	15.1	5.2	1	64%
A.Boldin	122	3.4%	112	65	921	14.2	3.6	4	58%
M.Moore	20	18.2%	11	6	116	19.3	3.8	1	55%
V.Davis	104	17.5%	61	41	548	13.4	4.1	5	67%
D.Walker*	32	-2.8%	39	21	345	16.4	2.7	3	54%
G.Celek	2	-15.7%	7	4	51	12.8	5.3	0	57%
F.Gore	50	13.1%	36	28	234	8.4	7.9	1	78%
B.Miller	23	17.7%	13	12	84	7.0	5.3	0	92%
K.Hunter	21	17.7%	12	9	60	6.7	6.3	0	75%

Offensive Line

Player	Pos	Age	GS	Snaps	Pen	Sk	Pass	Run	Player	Pos	Age	GS	Snaps	Pen	Sk	Pass	Run
Alex Boone	RG	26	16/16	1004	4	4	9	4	Joe Staley	LT	29	16/16	957	6	5.5	15	3.5
Anthony Davis	RT	24	16/16	1004	4	6	16.5	2	Leonard Davis*	G	35	16/0	128	2	2	2	1
Jonathan Goodwin	C	35	16/16	979	4	0	7	4.5	Adam Snyder	G	31	14/14	865	2	2.5	10.5	7
Mike Iupati	LG	26	16/16	979	8	1.5	7.5	9									

Year	Yards	ALY	Rk	Power	Rk	Stuff	Rk	2nd Lev	Rk	Open Field	Rk	Sacks	ASR	Rk	Short	Long	F-Start	Cont.
2010	4.05	4.14	13	56%	23	17%	11	1.04	25	0.65	20	44	8.9%	30	15	16	20	33
2011	4.17	3.96	21	51%	29	20%	22	1.12	22	0.92	12	44	8.4%	25	16	13	28	43
2012	4.74	4.50	1	66%	12	17%	7	1.49	1	0.79	14	41	8.5%	29	4	26	13	48
2012 ALY by direction:		Left End 5.12 (1)			Left Tackle 3.91 (20)			Mid/Guard 4.64 (2)			Right Tackle 4.36 (8)				Right End 3.79 (21)			

Like iron isotopes and the Cleaver family, San Francisco's offensive line is one of the most stable things known to mankind. They've finished tied for first in continuity score each of the past two seasons, and last year became just the ninth team since 2006 to have five offensive linemen each play at least 95 percent of snaps. A combined 2.1 AGL over the last two seasons clearly helps, but it's also the case that the unit's age (only Jonathan Goodwin is over 30) and talent level (three former first-round picks and a Super-Bowl winning center) mean no one's been on the brink of being benched.

Joe Staley is a left tackle straight out of *Back to the Future*. Despite their much-ballyhooed pistol gimmickry, San Francisco's base scheme is as close to a 1985 West Coast offense as there is in the league today. That makes Staley's athleticism on screens and outside runs more valuable than his prowess as a vaunted blind side protector, the latter of which may be extinct by the time the Cubs win it all in 2015. Last season's charting stats bear this out: both Staley and right tackle Anthony Davis ranked better in blown blocks on runs than in blown blocks leading to sacks. Nonetheless, the fact that the 49ers have finished 25th or lower in Adjusted Sack Rate for three straight seasons can't be blamed entirely on the tackles. Sacks are often more about the quarterback than the offensive line, and that's true of many of San Francisco's 41 sacks allowed. Only one came from an untouched rusher but 15.5 were the result of coverage.

San Francisco's interior linemen, on the other hand, were generally better at pass blocking than run blocking in 2012. Center Jonathan Goodwin was one of six starting centers to not allow a single blown-block sack last season, but was only middle-of-the-road as a run blocker. All-Pro left guard Mike Iupati also was stalwart in pass protection but made a surprising number of mistakes in the running game, particularly when compared to his 2011 performance. Right guard Alex Boone, a long-time tackle playing inside for the first time, arguably had a better season than Iupati, with his ability to block downfield playing a large role in San Francisco's No. 1 ranking in second-level yards.

Jim Harbaugh's 49ers rank near the top of the league in using six or more linemen in their formations; the team decided to bring back former starter Adam Snyder instead of re-signing last year's sixth man, Leonard Davis. Unlike Davis, Snyder can play both inside and outside, so he has the added value of being San Francisco's swing tackle. In his first and only season with the Cardinals, Snyder was arguably the best performer on the worst line in the league.

Defensive Front Seven

				Overall								vs. Run				Pass Rush			
Defensive Line	Age	Pos	Snaps	Plays	TmPct	Rk	Stop	Dfts	BTkl	Runs	St%	Rk	RuYd	Rk	Sack	Hit	Hur	Tips
Ray McDonald	29	DE	962	38	4.8%	46	30	8	1	32	78%	22	2.8	53	2.5	2	18	1
Justin Smith	34	DE	819	68	9.7%	3	52	15	0	61	75%	37	2.6	46	3	6	11	2
Isaac Sopoaga*	32	DT	333	26	3.5%	49	18	5	0	22	77%	29	1.9	21	1	0	1	0
Ricky Jean-Francois*	27	DT	286	22	2.8%	64	17	5	0	20	75%	34	2.1	26	2	0	0	0

				Overall						Pass Rush				vs. Run				vs. Pass			
Linebackers	Age	Pos	Snaps	Plays	TmPct	Rk	Stop	Dfts	BTkl	Sack	Hit	Hur	Tips	Runs	St%	Rk	Yds	Rk	Tgts	Suc%	Rk	AdjYd	Rk	PD
NaVorro Bowman	25	ILB	1003	149	18.7%	4	88	18	6	2	3	3	1	101	65%	57	3.1	44	54	60%	13	4.2	6	6
Aldon Smith	24	OLB	1003	65	8.1%	74	52	27	2	19.5	11	27	0	37	73%	20	3.1	36	11	44%	--	6.2	--	1
Patrick Willis	28	ILB	986	129	16.2%	18	73	24	2	0.5	2	9	1	71	62%	74	3.7	79	52	60%	12	4.3	8	8
Ahmad Brooks	29	OLB	976	53	6.6%	87	47	20	4	6.5	8	21	4	33	94%	1	1.8	9	12	51%	--	7.3	--	2

Year	Yards	ALY	Rk	Power	Rk	Stuff	Rk	2nd Level	Rk	Open Field	Rk	Sacks	ASR	Rk	Short	Long
2010	3.36	3.56	3	61%	11	19%	18	0.78	1	0.48	7	36	6.4%	14	14	14
2011	3.49	3.77	4	44%	1	15%	31	0.86	1	0.31	1	42	6.5%	17	15	17
2012	3.68	3.92	15	60%	17	19%	16	0.97	1	0.42	2	38	6.4%	17	16	10

2012 ALY by direction:	Left End 2.97 (5)	Left Tackle 4.04 (15)	Mid/Guard 4.13 (14)	Right Tackle 3.66 (8)	Right End 3.37 (8)

There are several ways to measure greatness. At least according to one of them, NFL fans are currently witnessing perhaps the greatest front seven of all time. In *Football Outsiders Almanac 2012*, we noted that the 2011 49ers joined select post-merger company with three first-team All-Pros in their defensive front seven. Well, by accomplishing the feat again in 2012 (this time with Aldon Smith instead of Justin Smith joining Patrick Willis and NaVorro Bowman), they're now in a party of one: No front seven has ever gone back-to-back with three All-Pros.

Willis and Bowman form the best inside linebacker duo of any base 3-4 defense, but their skill sets are such that the team could switch to 4-3 tomorrow and both would still rank among the best at their new positions. They're involved in a ton of plays all over the field, they don't miss tackles, they don't allow second-level running yards, and they're "lockdown linebackers" in coverage if such a thing exists. Last season, San Francisco finished seventh in pass defense DVOA against tight ends and eighth against running backs, rankings mostly due to Willis and Bowman: Of the 156 passes to opposing backs or tight ends with a San Francisco defender in primary coverage, Willis or Bowman was that defender 61 percent of the time; next-highest was Donte Whitner at just 10 percent.

For the second straight season, pass-rushing wunderkind Aldon Smith had 32 quarterback knockdowns (i.e., hits plus sacks), good for a top-four ranking both years. He also once again finished in the top 10 of quarterback hurries. However, with no sacks and only one knockdown in 11 halves of play after Justin Smith got hurt, some wonder how much of Aldon Smith's production depends on the elder Smith, his dancing partner in stunts and twists. Not to worry: The younger Smith had eight hurries over that same timeframe despite playing with a torn labrum that required offseason surgery. Of course, no one questioned his ability to harass opposing quarterbacks heading into 2012. No, the main concern with transitioning Smith from situational pass rusher to every-down outside linebacker was whether or not he would be a liability in weak-side run defense. After individually ranking 20th in run stop rate among all linebackers and helping the unit finish fifth in ALY on left-end runs, it's safe to say Smith has put those concerns to bed. Ahmad Brooks isn't as celebrated as San Francisco's three All-Pro linebackers, but 2012 saw him finally settle into the team's preferred strong-side role. He essentially matched his 2011 stats in terms of sacks, hits, and hurries, but added the elite run-stopping performance needed from a left outside linebacker.

With the free agent losses of nose tackle Isaac Sopoaga and versatile backup Ricky Jean-Francois, defensive line is a bit of a concern. Right defensive end Justin Smith may have made his fourth straight Pro Bowl last season, but he will be 34 years old in the first month of the 2013 season, he's played 87 percent of possible defensive snaps since his arrival in 2008, he's coming off his first injury absence in 11 years, and he's entering the final year of his contract. Given that the 49ers drafted Tank Carradine (Florida State) as Smith's heir apparent, it's clear those alarm bells were going off in Santa Clara this offseason. If Carradine does see significant snaps in 2013—he's coming off a torn ACL—it will probably be in relief of both Smith and left defensive end Ray McDonald, whose production declined slightly last season.

Ideally, San Francisco would redshirt Carradine this season, and instead rely on free-agent addition Glenn Dorsey as their replacement for Jean-Francois. However, at this point in his career, Dorsey is a bona fide draft bust, and, like Carradine, is coming off a season-ending injury. Furthermore, with Ian Williams (39 defensive snaps since signing as an undrafted free agent in 2011) currently the only true nose tackle on San Francisco's roster, Dorsey may be forced to start at a position he's never played. The 49ers line up without a nose tackle more than half the time, so the loss of Sopoaga won't be devastating overall. On base downs, though, the lack of an experienced anchor is an omen suggesting the 49ers' Adjusted Line Yards allowed could increase yet again next season.

Defensive Secondary

Secondary	Age	Pos	Snaps	Plays	Overall TmPct	Rk	Stop	Dfts	BTkl	vs. Run Runs	St%	Rk	Yds	Rk	vs. Pass Tgts	Tgt%	Rk	Dist	Suc%	Rk	APaYd	Rk	PD	Int
Carlos Rogers	32	CB	1036	62	7.8%	58	22	10	1	12	33%	60	5.1	18	80	17.2%	46	9.6	51%	47	6.3	14	5	1
Donte Whitner	28	SS	1035	86	10.8%	32	25	10	5	27	37%	39	8.2	55	32	6.8%	34	10.7	41%	68	7.1	35	4	1
Tarell Brown	28	CB	1030	69	8.6%	41	19	8	0	13	15%	81	10.4	79	94	20.2%	23	14.1	50%	52	7.9	53	13	2
Dashon Goldson*	29	FS	1026	79	9.9%	37	32	15	6	35	37%	38	6.5	30	29	6.1%	45	15.1	81%	3	3.3	3	13	3
Chris Culliver	25	CB	669	54	6.8%	68	21	9	4	4	50%	26	5.0	16	74	15.8%	57	14.2	55%	27	7.5	42	9	2
Perrish Cox	26	CB	160	15	1.9%	--	8	6	1	0	0%	--	0.0	--	12	2.6%	--	7.0	34%	--	8.9	--	1	0
Craig Dahl	28	SS	1035	73	8.5%	48	16	6	11	34	18%	71	11.7	70	15	3.6%	71	16.8	46%	63	10.4	72	2	1
Nnamdi Asomugha	32	CB	983	67	8.5%	46	29	13	8	26	38%	52	7.2	51	63	16.4%	51	13.7	47%	65	9.7	80	12	1

Year	Pass D Rank	vs. #1 WR	Rk	vs. #2 WR	Rk	vs. Other WR	Rk	vs. TE	Rk	vs. RB	Rk
2010	24	31.3%	30	33.3%	31	6.1%	22	-16.9%	1	-2.9%	10
2011	5	-5.7%	7	-17.8%	6	-3.9%	17	-1.1%	6	2.1%	19
2012	6	-10.3%	10	-16.2%	7	2.1%	21	-9.5%	7	-17.0%	8

Entering 2013, a few things are clear about San Francisco's secondary, and a few are anyone's guess at best. Let's start with the former. Given Carlos Rogers' advancing age (32 years old) and Tarell Brown's contract status (free agent after 2013), Chris Culliver is the 49ers' No. 1 cornerback of the future. Despite only entering the field on nickel downs (with Rogers moving to the slot), Culliver played 63 percent of the 49ers' defensive snaps, and finished 2012 as their highest-ranked corner in both run stop rate and coverage success rate; unlike Green Bay's young standout Casey Hayward, Culliver is both the team's best corner *and* works almost exclusively outside the numbers. Also clear is that 2012 sixth-rounder Trenton Robinson is the team's strong safety of the future. After a redshirt rookie season (zero defensive snaps), Robinson is poised to spell starter Donte Whitner from time to time if for no other reason than that Whitner will be a free agent at the end of the season, and, like those DISH commercial guys, San Francisco needs to see what they have in the hopper.

The unclear side of the ledger starts with replacing 2012 All-Pro free safety Dashon Goldson, who now resides in Tampa. San Francisco traded up to draft Eric Reid in the first round, but will the team that had the lowest rookie participation rate in the NFL last season (1.3 percent of snaps) take an unprecedented Harbaugh-era leap by starting the Louisiana State standout? (As a reminder, even Aldon Smith didn't start as a rookie.) Do they dare go into the season with newcomer Craig Dahl as the starter even though he's worse in coverage than a Wal-Mart umbrella in a hail storm?

The other unknown heading into 2013 is the role of Nnamdi Asomugha. At 32 years of age, he's on the downside of his NFL career. On the other hand, he was woefully misused in Philadelphia's zone pass defense after multiple All-Pro seasons playing man-to-man in Oakland. The vast majority of plays, San Francisco cornerbacks are asked to do the latter, so he's a perfect scheme fit—and a cheap one to boot. Asomugha's also more talented than the 49ers' dime cornerback in 2012, Perrish Cox. Nevertheless, given San Francisco's frequency of dime personnel in 2011 (10 percent) and 2012 (11 percent), are they really going to have his talent rot on the bench for 90 percent of 2013? Taking nickel snaps from Culliver is a non-starter, so, given the state of the 49ers' cornerbacks corps, either a) Asomugha does, in fact, have a better shot of hitting a gutshot straight at the Bay 101 Shootout, or b) he supplants Rogers or Brown as outside corners on base downs.

Special Teams

Year	DVOA	Rank	FG/XP	Rank	Net Kick	Rank	Kick Ret	Rank	Net Punt	Rank	Punt Ret	Rank	Hidden	Rank
2010	-1.5%	22	-1.3	22	-11.8	30	-5.0	22	4.9	13	5.1	8	-1.6	16
2011	7.8%	2	4.7	7	6.4	6	4.8	3	13.1	4	10.0	3	-2.6	17
2012	-1.5%	20	-17.8	32	-2.6	23	-0.6	19	13.4	4	0.3	15	-2.0	21

When space is limited in future Football Outsiders content, "2012 49ers" may become shorthand for "special teams (especially field-goal accuracy) is not consistent from year to year." Punter Andy Lee, awesome as ever, was the exception. But David Akers went from an All-Pro, record-setting season in 2011 to a liability in 2012 to a free-agent castoff in 2013. Perhaps we should cut him some slack given that he played through a double sports hernia all of last season, but his accuracy on field goals inside 40 yards dipped to 87 percent from a career average of 94percent. San Francisco replaced Akers with Phil Dawson, who has led Cleveland to a top-six ranking in expected points added from field goals the last two seasons. Of course, over the same time-frame, Dawson has produced much less value in kickoff distance (-3.1 expected points) than Akers (+3.2), so the move may be a wash. At the very least, kicking in Cleveland prepares Dawson for the schizophrenic winds at Candlestick this fall and winter.

Table 1. Worst FG/XP Values, 1991-2012

Year	Team	FG Pts+	Main Kicker(s)	Year	Team	FG Pts+	Main Kicker(s)
1999	CHI	-21.6	Chris Boniol, Jeff Jaeger	1999	MIN	-16.9	Gary Anderson
2003	JAC	-20.3	Seth Marler	2010	WAS	-16.6	Graham Gano
1993	NE	-19.5	Scott Sisson	1995	NO	-15.9	Doug Brien, Chip Lohmiller
2012	SF	-17.8	David Akers	1991	SF	-15.9	Mike Cofer
2003	SF	-17.5	Owen Pochman, Todd Peterson	1991	NYJ	-15.6	Pat Leahy

The 49ers also regressed to the mean on returns. Ted Ginn, another special teams player San Francisco allowed to walk this offseason, was the primary offender. On kickoff returns, Kyle Williams produced positive value (+3.0 expected points) while Ginn was nursing an ankle injury the first six weeks, as did LaMichael James (+2.3), who took over when Ginn was forced to focus on his wide receiver duties after Williams tore his ACL. In the interim, Ginn ranked 59th out of 68 in expected points (-3.0) among players with at least five kickoff returns; this after finishing fifth in 2011 (+4.6). Meanwhile on punt returns, he dropped from second in the league with +10.6 expected points in 2011 to just average in 2012. With Ginn having moved on to Carolina, Williams will return punts and James will return kickoffs in 2013.

Coaching Staff

For as much praise that Jim Harbaugh receives regarding his tactical prowess and ability to breathe new life into a languishing franchise, perhaps his biggest coaching accomplishment since joining the 49ers has been keeping the band together. Despite back-to-back championship game appearances, the rest of the NFL has yet to poach San Francisco's coordinators or position coaches. Offensive coordinator Greg Roman got a look-see from the Browns, Eagles, and Jaguars in their head-coach searches, but a promotion didn't materialize. It's likely that defensive coordinator Vic Fangio, offensive line coach Mike Solari, linebackers coach Jim Leavitt, and secondary coach Ed Donatell—each in their late 50s—are past their primes as head-coaching candidates, and won't be seeking lateral moves anytime soon. Meanwhile, John Morton (wide receivers, not to be confused with former Lions, Chiefs, and 49ers wide receiver Johnnie Morton) and Reggie Davis (tight ends) are still making their bones in the business. However, Geep Chryst (quarterbacks), Tom Rathman (running backs), and Jim Tomsula (defensive line) don't much seem to be interested in leaving San Francisco despite impressive track records.

As we and others have discussed ad nauseum, coaching is a big reason why the 49ers have seen so much success on the field over the past two years. And just like the consistency of double-digit wins bodes well for our projections, the continuity of a core staff entering its third season together insures against the likelihood that San Francisco's players underperform in 2013.

Seattle Seahawks

2012 Record: 11-5	**Total DVOA:** 38.7% (1st)	**2013 Mean Projection:** 10.3 wins	**On the Clock (0-4):** 1%
Pythagorean Wins: 12.5 (3rd)	**Offense:** 18.5% (4th)	**Postseason Odds:** 72.9%	**Mediocrity (5-7):** 8%
Snap-Weighted Age: 25.8 (32nd)	**Defense:** -14.5% (2nd)	**Super Bowl Odds:** 15.0%	**Playoff Contender (8-10):** 41%
Average Opponent: 5.1% (4th)	**Special Teams:** 5.7% (3rd)	**Proj. Avg. Opponent:** -2.9% (24th)	**Super Bowl Contender (11+):** 49%

2012: Unlike their quarterback's Lewin Career Forecast, Seattle's No. 1 finish in DVOA gets no asterisk.

2013: The Seahawks are set up better than most "surprise playoff teams" when it comes to resisting the Plexiglass Principle.

Fight On, for Puget Sound
Where skies are gray, the whole year 'round
Our software engineers
Look up to you
Fight on and win
For Puget Sound
Fight On
Paul Allen's proud
Fight On!

No, the Seattle Seahawks don't have a fight song. They don't even have a marching band. In many other ways, though, general manager John Schneider and head coach Pete Carroll have done their best to turn this club into a major league version of a college team.

The game-day aspects are obvious, as the team has built an A-plus home-field advantage, whipping the fanbase into a frenzy with corny-but-cool traditions like the ceremonial raising of the 12th Man flag. But the similarities go beyond pomp and circumstance. From on-field tactics to roster construction methodology, the Seahawks have done their best to mimic the college football dynasty Carroll built with the USC Trojans. We're not the first media observers to point this out, but the similarities grow stronger with each passing year. Seattle is not just one of the best teams in the league, but one of the most unique as well.

In nine seasons at USC, Carroll went 97-19 with seven bowl wins, including four Rose Bowls and one national championship. The Seahawks brought him back to the NFL in 2010, hiring Schneider away from the Packers (where he was Director of Football Operations under Ted Thompson) to be Carroll's front-office partner. Carroll and Schneider spent the next two years cleaning house, with steady improvements in DVOA but stagnation in the win-loss record. It all came together in 2012, though, as the Seahawks were able to complement their stout defense and punishing ground game with a quarterback who outplayed his diminutive stature. Russell Wilson, whose projection in the Lewin Career Forecast was so high we dubbed him "the Asterisk," slipped to Seattle in the third round. He surprised everyone, including Carroll and Schneider, by beating out free-agent signee Matt Flynn for the starting job. By midseason, the Seahawks began using a read-option offense designed to get the most out of Wilson's athleticism. By the end of the year, Wilson had set rookie records for DYAR in a game (twice, against Chicago and

then against Atlanta in the playoffs) and a season, tied Peyton Manning's rookie record with 26 touchdown passes, and twice led comebacks in playoff games on the road, even though his defense could not preserve the lead against Atlanta.

The results of 2012 speak to the upside of this college-style methodology. The Seahawks have one of the league's youngest rosters, and the same management that has turned this team around should keep it in contention for the foreseeable future, thanks in no small part to the franchise quarterback who fell into their lap last year. There are some ways Seattle would be well served to grow up a little, but the Seahawks will stick with their collegiate model. After all, while they may not have a marching band, they do have a drumline.

The collegiate theme in Seattle starts with the Xs and Os. Compared to the wide variety of offensive and defensive schemes seen in college football, NFL formations are fairly vanilla. Offenses will usually run from I-formations or three-receiver sets, maybe bringing in a second tight end. Defenses generally start with a clearly identifiable 4-3 or 3-4 set; when the opposition spreads the field with extra receivers, one or two linebackers will be replaced by a cornerback. There are exceptions, certainly, such as Rex Ryan's 7-DB blitz attacks, and Sean Payton's Saints could go an entire game without using the same formation on offense twice. And the plays that NFL teams run from these formations, on either side of the ball, are worlds more complex than anything seen in the NCAA. But for sheer formational weirdness, there's nothing in the NFL nearly as exotic as what you'll find in college football, home of Georgia Tech's flexbone, Oregon's fast-break spread option, Nevada's full-time pistol attack, Mike Leach's Air Raid, or Rich Rodriguez' 3-3-5 defense.

Pete Carroll employs some of the more unique defensive sets the NFL. The coach has termed it "a 4-3 scheme with 3-4 personnel." You could probably flip that terminology around and get something just as accurate, but the point is, Carroll's scheme takes players who would get lost in more mainstream formations and gives them a chance to shine. Red Bryant couldn't get on the field as a defensive tackle under Jim Mora, but Carroll moved him outside as a massive 5-technique defensive end and let him ruin the perimeter run games of the NFC West. The Eagles thought so little of Chris Clemons that they threw in a draft pick when they traded him to Seattle years ago (a deal that sent Darryl Tapp to Philadelphia), but he has taken over Seattle's hybrid end/linebacker Leo position and become one of the team's most criti-

2013 Seahawks Schedule

Week	Opp.	Week	Opp.	Week	Opp.
1	at CAR	7	at ARI (Thu.)	13	NO
2	SF	8	at STL (Mon.)	14	at SF
3	JAC	9	TB	15	at NYG
4	at HOU	10	at ATL	16	ARI
5	at IND	11	MIN	17	STL
6	TEN	12	BYE		

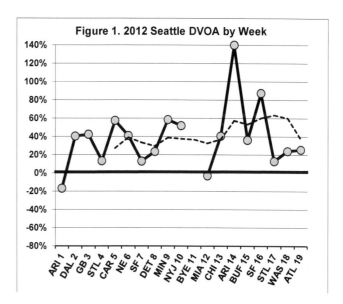

Figure 1. 2012 Seattle DVOA by Week

cal defenders. Brandon Browner, a CFL refugee, lacks the speed to be a star corner for most teams, but his immense size makes him a perfect fit for Carroll's press coverage concepts. Carroll's not the only coach with this kind of system—the Ravens just won a Super Bowl using some of these concepts, Clancy Pendergast used a similar defense to get Arizona to a Super Bowl, and Bill Belichick has been using hybrid 3-4/4-3 fronts for most of the past decade—but it's still a somewhat rare system, and it helps Carroll get the most of the pieces around him.

The Seahawks' offensive scheme is unusual as well. Offensive coordinator Darrell Bevell learned a version of the Bill Walsh offense under Mike Sherman in Green Bay, and in Seattle he has meshed those principles with the zone blocking concepts of offensive line coach Tom Cable. The midseason installation of the zone-read option added another wrinkle. The blend of all these styles left the Seahawks with a playbook that was one part Bill Walsh, one part Mike Shanahan, and one part Urban Meyer.

The Seahawks' acquisition of Percy Harvin makes their offense even more unusual. In a league where so many players are specialists—slot receivers or third-down backs or red-zone threats—Harvin may be the league's best example of an "athlete," the term that college recruiters use for prospects who can play multiple positions. Harvin isn't just another slants-and-flants wideout; he's a terror with the ball in his hands, ranking in the top 10 for total yards after catch despite missing half the season with an ankle injury. That will plug some of the holes in Seattle's offense. The 2012 Seahawks threw only 62 passes at or behind the line of scrimmage, one of the ten lowest totals in the league. You can bet that total will climb in 2013. Harvin can also play running back, and his cameos in the backfield will make the Seattle option running attack even more dangerous.

Acquiring Harvin for two picks (including a first-rounder) and a $67 million contract was a bold move, but the Seahawks regime has not hesitated to make bold moves. Or meek moves. Or run-of-the-mill moves. Schneider and Carroll are not afraid of roster turnover, and why would they be? While most NFL teams try to build stability long-term, NCAA teams know their best players will be gone in four years or less. Seattle has followed suit, turning over their roster like almost nobody else. Only nine players who were on the Seahawks roster last season (including just five

Table 1: Seahawks' Roster Turnover by Season

Season	Holdovers	New Players	Turnover%	Rk
2010	27	38	58%	1
2011	33	34	51%	1
2012	40	18	31%	27

starters) are holdovers from 2009, the year before Carroll and Schneider arrived. Only the Rams had fewer players left over from that season, and only four of those players will return in 2013: Defensive linemen Red Bryant and Brandon Mebane, offensive lineman Max Unger, and punter Jon Ryan.

However, while Carroll and Schneider have shown no qualms about shaking things up, they have not just been making moves for the sake of making moves. After two years of rabid overhaul, they have now found a crew they like, and they've been more willing to stand pat (Table 1).

Expect that turnover number to shrink even further in 2013. Only one of last year's starters has left the team (defensive tackle Alan Branch, who signed with Buffalo), with one other (linebacker Leroy Hill, another holdover from 2009) unsigned and unlikely to return. Harvin will get a starting receiver's spot, and the front seven has been boosted in both the draft and free agency. By and large, however, the Seahawks will go into 2013 with the same players in the same roles they had in 2012.

Beyond that, though, nothing is guaranteed, and further turnover is likely in the future. Carroll's mantra is "always compete," and he really means that for everyone on the roster. A lot of coaches would have given lip service to the idea of a third-round quarterback competing with a big-money free agent signee for a starting job, but how many really would have gambled on Russell Wilson over Matt Flynn?

With no veteran's job guaranteed, the Seahawks have readied themselves for the next wave of departures. While other teams tried to patch holes during the offseason, the Seahawks added to positions of strength. They traded for Harvin even though Sidney Rice and Golden Tate were both among the top 20 wideouts in DYAR. In the second round of the draft, they took running back Christine Michael out of Texas A&M, even though Marshawn Lynch was second in the league in rushing DYAR and already had a highly-regarded backup, second-year back Robert Turbin. Not until the third round did they address their Branch-sized hole at defensive tackle, grabbing Penn State's Jordan Hill.

Why did the Hawks ignore weaknesses to address positions that were already strengths? First, as the rest of the league is focusing more and more on the pass, Seattle remains devoted to the run. No team ran more or passed less than the Seahawks in

2012, and they'd like to keep it that way. Remember also that college teams must prepare to replace stars even before they burn brightest. Even if a junior quarterback is set to take over the team, it's time to find his replacement, because he'll be gone in two years or less. Carroll is used to carrying as many weapons as possible, knowing none of them will be around forever. Marshawn Lynch has been the offensive face of the Carroll era in Seattle, but he is also 27 years old, and due more than $5 million in salary in each of the next three seasons. With Michael in tow, the Seahawks can afford to cut ties with Lynch if he slips, rather than pay him premium money for the decline phase of his career. The philosophy isn't universal for every position—it's a safe bet that Seattle won't be drafting a quarterback early anytime soon—but it's a tactic that protects the Hawks from investing too heavily (financially and otherwise) in one player, giving them insurance when he leaves or breaks down.

All this emotion and enthusiasm has led to a lot of wins, but there are drawbacks to the amateurish atmosphere—specifically, amateurish (as in, unprofessional) behavior at critical moments. The Seahawks were flagged for 132 penalties last year, fourth in the NFL. Many of these penalties were avoidable fouls caused by antagonistic behavior. Led by the thuggish behavior of tackle Breno Giacomini, Seattle was called for personal fouls, unnecessary roughness, unsportsmanlike conduct, or taunting 18 times, second-most in football.

And then there's the big mouth on Richard Sherman. A lot of players in the NFL like to talk trash during games, but they know to stop when the clock hits zeroes. Not Sherman. The former fifth-rounder carries a permanent chip on his shoulder, and at least twice last year antagonized opponents after games, confronting Tom Brady in Week 6 and drawing punches from Redskins tackle Trent Williams after the Wild Card game. Keep in mind these were both Seahawks wins. Sherman later went on ESPN and got into a flame war with professional troll Skip Bayless, an embarrassing exchange for all parties involved. Former Seahawks coach Mike Holmgren has said that Sherman's behavior is bound to draw negative attention from officials. If Sherman's postgame antics continue, it seems inevitable that the league will step in and punish Sherman individually or the Seahawks as a team, but Carroll seems content to let Sherman flap his gums.

Late hits and postgame chatter may not lead directly to losses on the field, but defensive breakdowns in the fourth quarter do. And the Seahawks, despite ranking fourth in defensive DVOA including ninth in the fourth quarter, had some noticeable late-game disasters. Seattle gave up a league-high six go-ahead or game-tying touchdowns in the fourth quarter, blowing last-period leads in losses to Arizona, Miami, and Detroit. (They actually blew the lead twice against the Lions.) That doesn't count the blown lead against Green Bay that set up the notorious Fail Mary pass, or Chicago's last-minute field-goal drive to force overtime, or Atlanta's game-winning field-goal drive that ended Seattle's season. How could such a great defense come up short in so many critical situations? It could be a statistical fluke, a handful of bad plays that just happened to come up in the most inopportune times. In the context of this team, though, it looks like the negative aspects of amateurism—a literal lack of professionalism, a failure to complete the tasks at hand. Either way, Seattle can't afford a repeat performance if they hope to win the Super Bowl this year.

There's one final aspect of college life that permeates the Seahawks program, and it's a touchy one: the pervasive drug culture. Seattle will play the first four games of 2013 without Bruce Irvin, their 2012 first-round pick who led all rookies in sacks, after the defensive end was suspended for substance abuse. This is nothing new in Seattle. According to John McGrath of the *Tacoma News Tribune*, Irvin is the seventh Seahawks player to test positive since 2011. Six of those—practice-squad running back Vai Taua, guard John Moffitt, tackle Allen Barbre, safety Winston Guy, cornerback Brandon Browner, and Irvin—were suspended. Sherman, the seventh, had his suspension overturned on appeal due to a mishandled urine sample. He insists that he had taken nothing on the banned substances list.

The league does not reveal the specific results of drug tests, but most reports say the suspended Seahawks tested positive for Adderall, and Moffitt has admitted that he used the drug. Adderall, a psychostimulant prescribed for attention-deficit disorders, is reportedly used as a study aid in colleges. Some believe it could also mask the presence of other PEDs in the body. Sherman has said it is widely used in the NFL and should be removed from the banned substances list, but that's no excuse for so many test failures.

Carroll had kept his mouth shut on the subject for years. When Browner and Sherman were suspended, he said only that it was a "league issue," with no further reaction. After Irvin's suspension, though, Carroll could no longer get away with a "no comment," and finally addressed the issue at the team's May minicamp.

"It's a very important opportunity, in a sense, for us to try and figure it out and to help these guys so they can get what they deserve," Carroll said. "Unfortunately, you go wrong, you get popped—and that's how this thing works. And I'm really disappointed that we have to deal with anything like this. But there's going to be other issues, too, and we are going to have to deal with them."

That's not exactly a scathing condemnation of his players, but how much of this problem is Carroll's fault? Can the coach be fairly blamed for what his players are putting into their bodies? That's a complicated question and one we can't answer here. Nonetheless, this series of problems—the trash talk, the fouls, the late-game breakdowns, the drug use—points to a lack of institutional control. Those words may ring familiar to Carroll—the NCAA has used them in sanctioning USC for violations that occurred under his watch. Carroll takes pride in being a player's coach, but it may be in everyone's best interest to lay down the law once in a while.

The strengths of this Seattle team are obvious: A precocious, prodigious quarterback who doesn't realize he's too short and too inexperienced to play as well he has. A cadre of running threats capable grinding out tough yards against almost any opponent. An unorthodox defensive front tailored to create mismatches up and down the line. An oversized secondary waiting to knock opponents black and blue.

Their weaknesses are not so obvious, but it's often those subtle weaknesses that make the difference between a playoff exit and a champion.

Vince Verhei

2012 Seahawks Stats by Week

Wk	vs.	W-L	PF	PA	YDF	YDA	TO	Total	Off	Def	ST
1	at ARI	L	16	20	254	253	0	-17%	-26%	-3%	6%
2	DAL	W	27	7	315	296	2	40%	9%	-16%	16%
3	GB	W	14	12	238	268	0	42%	0%	-34%	9%
4	at STL	L	13	19	319	286	-2	13%	-12%	-19%	6%
5	CAR	W	16	12	310	190	-1	57%	-8%	-64%	2%
6	NE	W	24	23	368	475	0	41%	21%	-33%	-13%
7	at SF	L	6	13	251	313	0	13%	-2%	-30%	-16%
8	at DET	L	24	28	369	415	-1	23%	32%	9%	1%
9	MIN	W	30	20	385	287	2	58%	41%	-13%	4%
10	NYJ	W	28	7	363	185	1	52%	20%	-26%	6%
11	BYE										
12	at MIA	L	21	24	312	435	1	-3%	16%	53%	33%
13	at CHI	W	23	17	459	365	-1	41%	55%	24%	10%
14	ARI	W	58	0	493	154	7	141%	57%	-69%	16%
15	at BUF	W	50	17	466	333	3	36%	39%	0%	-3%
16	SF	W	42	13	346	313	1	87%	44%	-40%	4%
17	STL	W	20	13	362	331	1	13%	19%	16%	10%
18	at WAS	W	24	14	380	203	1	24%	-1%	-18%	7%
19	at ATL	L	28	30	491	417	0	26%	46%	19%	-1%

Trends and Splits

	Offense	Rank	Defense	Rank
Total DVOA	18.5%	4	-14.5%	2
Unadjusted VOA	13.6%	7	-11.7%	4
Weighted Trend	31.1%	1	-10.0%	7
Variance	6.0%	16	10.0%	32
Average Opponent	-5.4%	3	-0.3%	15
Passing	37.3%	4	-18.8%	3
Rushing	16.5%	1	-8.2%	12
First Down	19.9%	3	-9.7%	7
Second Down	13.5%	7	-14.3%	4
Third Down	23.9%	4	-25.1%	2
First Half	21.8%	2	-10.5%	6
Second Half	15.4%	7	-18.9%	3
Red Zone	28.6%	4	-32.1%	2
Late and Close	9.8%	10	-7.4%	15

Five-Year Performance

Year	W-L	Pyth W	Est W	PF	PA	TO	Total	Rk	Off	Rk	Def	Rk	ST	Rk	Off AGL	Rk	Def AGL	Rk	Off Age	Rk	Def Age	Rk	ST Age	Rk
2008	4-12	5.3	5.0	294	392	-7	-30.8%	29	-14.2%	26	11.3%	27	2.9%	9	66.3	32	12.7	6	28.1	9	27.0	22	26.5	19
2009	5-11	4.9	3.1	330	281	+9	-30.8%	29	-19.6%	27	12.0%	29	0.8%	15	44.3	29	30.9	19	27.5	13	27.2	17	27.1	4
2010	7-9	5.4	6.9	310	407	-9	-22.9%	30	-17.3%	29	12.0%	29	6.4%	2	34.3	24	27.2	20	27.8	11	27.6	10	26.4	14
2011	7-9	8.2	8.1	321	315	+8	-1.5%	19	-8.7%	22	-7.1%	10	0.2%	16	53.4	30	25.2	14	25.8	31	26.2	26	26.0	26
2012	11-5	12.5	13.0	412	245	+13	38.7%	1	18.5%	4	-14.5%	2	5.7%	3	14.8	6	15.0	6	25.9	27	25.6	31	26.0	18

2012 Performance Based on Most Common Personnel Groups

SEA Offense					SEA Offense vs. Opponents				SEA Defense				SEA Defense vs. Opponents			
Pers	Freq	Yds	DVOA	Run%	Pers	Freq	Yds	DVOA	Pers	Freq	Yds	DVOA	Pers	Freq	Yds	DVOA
11	36%	6.2	38.3%	35%	4-3-4	30%	6.0	14.9%	4-3-4	49%	5.2	-21.0%	11	44%	5.2	-12.3%
12	20%	6.2	18.5%	49%	Nickel Even	30%	6.0	43.0%	Nickel Even	38%	5.0	-15.6%	12	24%	5.3	-17.8%
21	18%	5.6	9.2%	66%	3-4-4	23%	5.4	9.2%	Dime+	6%	7.8	72.0%	21	13%	5.7	-4.7%
22	11%	5.9	24.6%	76%	Nickel Odd	9%	7.4	57.4%	Nickel Odd	4%	5.4	-4.2%	22	7%	4.3	-45.1%
01	3%	8.5	92.5%	3%	Dime+	7%	6.2	9.7%	3-4-4	3%	3.4	-35.3%	10	2%	6.9	32.5%
13	3%	4.6	25.8%	48%									13	2%	3.8	-39.7%

Strategic Tendencies

Run/Pass		Rk	Formation		Rk	Pass Rush		Rk	Secondary		Rk	Strategy		Rk
Runs, first half	46%	4	Form: Single Back	58%	25	Rush 3	12.7%	3	4 DB	51%	4	Play action	35%	2
Runs, first down	57%	3	Form: Empty Back	9%	7	Rush 4	63.9%	15	5 DB	41%	22	Avg Box (Off)	6.46	10
Runs, second-long	46%	2	Pers: 3+ WR	47%	23	Rush 5	20.0%	17	6+ DB	6%	15	Avg Box (Def)	6.35	19
Runs, power sit.	54%	18	Pers: 4+ WR	6%	8	Rush 6+	3.3%	31	CB by Sides	91%	6	Offensive Pace	33.00	31
Runs, behind 2H	36%	2	Pers: 2+ TE/6+ OL	37%	9	Sacks by LB	12.5%	25	DB Blitz	11%	17	Defensive Pace	31.13	29
Pass, ahead 2H	39%	27	Shotgun/Pistol	41%	22	Sacks by DB	8.3%	12	Hole in Zone	11%	7	Go for it on 4th	1.00	14

Were you worried about Russell Wilson's height? He had only seven passes tipped or batted down at the line, less than one-third as many as fellow rookie Brandon Weeden. ☞ The Seahawks' situation-neutral pace slowed down significantly with Wilson taking over at quarterback, dropping from 29.3 seconds in 2011 (sixth) to 33.0 seconds in 2012 (31st). ☞ The Seahawks ran 34 percent of the time with three or more receivers in the game, second behind only Buffalo, and were the most successful team in the league with 6.0 yards per carry and 39.6% DVOA. That included 44.1% DVOA on runs from shotgun, over twice as good as any other offense. ☞ Seattle led the league with 70 offensive penalties. ☞ The Seahawks didn't blitz as much as most teams but their blitzes definitely worked. They only sent five pass rushers on 20 percent of plays, but allowed just 5.1 yards per pass. They only sent six or more pass rushers on 3.3 percent of plays, but allowed just 3.1 yards per pass. ☞ Pete Carroll had a perfectly average Aggressiveness Index of 1.00 for the second straight season.

Passing

Player	DYAR	DVOA	Plays	NtYds	Avg	YAC	C%	TD	Int
R.Wilson	872	19.7%	432	2935	6.8	5.0	64.6%	26	9
M.Flynn*	27	64.3%	9	68	7.6	8.2	55.6%	0	0
B.Quinn	-440	-43.8%	219	1018	4.6	4.3	57.1%	2	7

Rushing

Player	DYAR	DVOA	Plays	Yds	Avg	TD	Fum	Suc
M.Lynch	361	19.2%	315	1592	5.1	11	4	50%
R.Wilson	147	22.3%	82	501	6.1	4	0	-
R.Turbin	11	-5.2%	80	354	4.4	0	0	46%
L.Washington*	-1	-9.9%	23	83	3.6	1	0	22%
M.Robinson	29	26.8%	12	49	4.1	0	0	83%
P.Harvin	20	-21.6%	21	105	5.0	1	2	-
B.Quinn	-4	-17.5%	15	69	4.6	0	0	-

Receiving

Player	DYAR	DVOA	Plays	Ctch	Yds	Y/C	YAC	TD	C%
S.Rice	283	29.7%	82	51	751	14.7	3.0	7	62%
G.Tate	245	31.6%	70	48	702	14.6	5.9	7	69%
D.Baldwin	45	0.0%	50	29	366	12.6	2.7	3	58%
B.Edwards*	-9	-29.9%	18	8	74	9.3	1.1	1	44%
B.Obomanu*	-20	-37.0%	9	4	58	14.5	5.3	0	44%
J.Kearse	-1	-22.9%	7	3	31	10.3	0.3	0	43%
C.Martin	14	-8.4%	6	4	42	10.5	3.0	0	67%
P.Harvin	194	4.6%	86	63	670	10.6	8.5	3	73%
Z.Miller	47	8.1%	53	38	396	10.4	3.4	3	72%
A.McCoy	90	35.5%	28	18	291	16.2	8.4	3	64%
M.Lynch	50	13.2%	30	23	199	8.7	8.8	1	77%
R.Turbin	48	21.2%	23	19	181	9.5	6.7	0	83%
M.Robinson	85	75.5%	15	13	126	9.7	8.8	2	87%
L.Washington*	-1	-16.4%	8	4	31	7.8	5.8	0	50%

Offensive Line

Player	Pos	Age	GS	Snaps	Pen	Sk	Pass	Run	Player	Pos	Age	GS	Snaps	Pen	Sk	Pass	Run
Breno Giacomini	RT	28	16/16	1006	13	4	25	8	John Moffitt	LG	27	8/6	403	4	0	6	5.5
Paul McQuistan	RG	30	16/16	992	8	1.5	13.5	11	James Carpenter	LG	24	7/7	344	1	2	2	2.5
Max Unger	C	27	16/16	977	2	0.5	6.5	3	J.R. Sweezy	G	24	13/3	295	4	0	5	1
Russell Okung	LT	26	15/15	911	11	2.5	8.5	4	Frank Omiyale*	G/T	31	16/1	114	1	0	1	0

Year	Yards	ALY	Rk	Power	Rk	Stuff	Rk	2nd Lev	Rk	Open Field	Rk	Sacks	ASR	Rk	Short	Long	F-Start	Cont.
2010	3.90	3.67	28	48%	29	26%	32	1.06	21	0.84	11	35	6.2%	14	15	14	21	21
2011	4.12	4.01	19	73%	2	18%	10	1.11	26	0.72	24	50	8.3%	24	19	18	35	27
2012	4.83	4.42	4	70%	4	15%	1	1.42	2	0.94	8	33	7.2%	20	9	19	23	23
2012 ALY by direction:		Left End 4.47 (6)			Left Tackle 4.96 (4)			Mid/Guard 3.91 (21)			Right Tackle 4.85 (1)			Right End 4.07 (16)				

The Seahawks put together an offensive line with two very good starters, two very bad ones, and a big question mark, and somehow made the whole thing work. Part of that is due to the success the running backs had in the read option, but they also fared well in more conventional running schemes. (Seattle backs averaged 6.6 yards per carry on plays our charters marked as options, 4.7 yards a pop on all other runs.)

Left tackle Russell Okung and center Max Unger made the Pro Bowl in their third and fourth seasons, respectively. Ankle and pectoral injuries knocked Okung out of the lineup for several games in his first two years, but last year he played 16 straight games (including the playoffs) after missing the Week 2 game against Dallas with a bruised knee. Not coincidentally, he had his best season as a pro, finally delivering on his first-round potential and becoming a worthy successor to Walter Jones. Unger has been solid but unspectacular since he was chosen in the second round of the 2009 draft (aside from 2010, when he missed most of the year with a toe injury). He enjoyed his best season in 2012, as teammates and opponents alike credited him for coordinating the line's efforts. He's a bit undersized, but makes for it leadership and technique.

Those are the good players. After that the drop off is pretty steep. Breno Giacomini was second in the NFL (and first among right tackles) in total blown blocks, and he was also called for 13 penalties. Of all players in the league, regardless of position, only Doug Free of Cowboys was flagged more often. Paul McQuistan flipped back and forth between left and right guard and had 11 blown blocks on runs, tied with Richie Incognito for the most in the league. Whichever guard spot wasn't being filled by McQuistan was filled by either James Carpenter or John Moffitt, two members of the 2011 draft class who have struggled to stay healthy, or rookie J.R. Sweezy, who played defensive end at North Carolina State before the Seahawks turned him into a guard. Former first-round pick Carpenter was a bust at tackle, but he played much better at guard last year. His ratio of blown blocks per snap was better than any other Seahawks lineman except Unger. The bad news is that he couldn't finish the season due to pain in his knee, the same knee injury that ended his rookie season prematurely.

It would seem there was plenty of room for improvement here, but unless Sweezy or Moffitt wins a starting job at guard, Seattle will use the same lineup in 2013. Those seven players will all be back, and though Seattle picked up 11 players in the draft, only three were offensive linemen, and all three came in the seventh round: Vanderbilt's Ryan Seymour, Northeast Oklahoma State's Michael Bowie, and New Hampshire's Jared Smith (who, like Sweezy, played on the defensive line in college).

Defensive Front Seven

Defensive Line	Age	Pos	Snaps	Plays	TmPct	Rk	Stop	Dfts	BTkl	Runs	St%	Rk	RuYd	Rk	Sack	Hit	Hur	Tips
				Overall							vs. Run				Pass Rush			
Chris Clemons	32	DE	868	44	5.8%	28	34	14	3	24	71%	51	2.8	57	11.5	13	31.5	4
Red Bryant	29	DE	625	28	3.7%	60	20	4	1	22	68%	59	2.5	38	0	0	6	3
Brandon Mebane	28	DT	623	59	7.8%	1	49	9	3	51	80%	21	1.7	20	3	3	6	3
Alan Branch*	29	DT	560	30	4.0%	38	20	6	2	26	62%	66	3.7	68	1	5	9	2
Bruce Irvin	23	DE	434	16	2.1%	--	11	9	1	6	33%	--	4.7	--	8	12	18.5	0
Clinton McDonald	26	DT	287	25	3.8%	43	16	4	0	23	65%	61	3.5	67	0	1	3.5	0
Michael Bennett*	28	DE	956	43	5.3%	39	35	23	1	23	78%	21	1.1	5	9	10	23.5	3
Cliff Avril	27	DE	684	35	4.5%	50	28	15	1	20	70%	52	1.7	11	9.5	7	13.5	1

Linebackers	Age	Pos	Snaps	Plays	TmPct	Rk	Stop	Dfts	BTkl	Sack	Hit	Hur	Tips	Runs	St%	Rk	Yds	Rk	Tgts	Suc%	Rk	AdjYd	Rk	PD
				Overall						Pass Rush				vs. Run					vs. Pass					
K.J. Wright	24	OLB	863	101	14.3%	33	50	18	6	1	2	4.5	0	42	71%	29	3.6	70	46	52%	31	6.4	27	4
Bobby Wagner	23	MLB	849	141	18.7%	3	72	23	4	2	5	5	0	94	57%	92	4.3	97	33	51%	34	6.2	24	4
Leroy Hill*	31	OLB	505	47	7.7%	78	27	5	0	1.5	1	1	0	33	67%	44	3.6	68	18	55%	23	7.4	54	0
Malcolm Smith	24	OLB	166	18	2.4%	--	13	2	1	0	0	3	0	10	90%	--	2.6	--	6	60%	--	3.4	--	1

Year	Yards	ALY	Rk	Power	Rk	Stuff	Rk	2nd Level	Rk	Open Field	Rk	Sacks	ASR	Rk	Short	Long
2010	4.34	4.29	26	68%	27	16%	26	1.04	7	0.93	24	36	5.3%	28	21	11
2011	3.79	3.95	11	49%	4	20%	16	1.11	9	0.49	4	33	5.5%	28	17	12
2012	4.44	4.22	21	50%	3	18%	22	1.22	22	0.86	20	36	6.1%	21	15	14
2012 ALY by direction:		Left End 3.89 (15)			Left Tackle 3.99 (14)			Mid/Guard 4.25 (23)			Right Tackle 4.24 (23)			Right End 4.63 (23)	

Seattle uses a heavy rotation along their defensive line. Although none of their starters missed a single game, only Chris Clemons was among the top 75 defensive linemen in snaps played last season. It's unfortunate, then, that the torn ACL and meniscus that ended Clemons' season in the Wild Card game against Washington have also put his 2013 season in jeopardy. Clemons has said that he'll be back for the season opener. Pete Carroll has been more reserved, saying Clemons might be healthy by then, but insisting the team would be patient with his return. Clemons has been remarkably consistent, with 11 sacks in 2010, 11 in 2011, and 11.5 last year, leading the team each season. The Seahawks added a pair of insurance options in free agency: Cliff Avril (29 sacks over the last three seasons in Detroit) and Michael Bennett (who led Tampa Bay with nine sacks last year). However, Bennett has his own injury issues; Seattle signed him despite the fact that he has a torn rotator cuff and is planning to play hurt before having surgery after the 2013 season.

Defensive tackle Alan Branch signed with Buffalo in free agency, the most significant player departure on the roster. The Seahawks filled those shoes twice over in the draft, taking Penn State's Jordan Hill in the third round, then trading up to select Alabama's Jesse Williams in the fifth. Williams is the more intriguing prospect here. Most expected him to go in the second round, but concerns about offseason knee surgery caused him to slide down the board. He claims his knee is 100 percent, and if so he could win a starting job.

Pro Bowl nose tackle Brandon Mebane returns for his seventh season in Seattle's starting lineup, as does mammoth strongside end Red Bryant, who's hoping to rebound from a poor 2012 caused by plantar fascia. Bruce Irvin, who led all rookies with eight sacks and did very little else, will miss the first four games of the season due to suspension for substance abuse. As a third-down specialist, he's quite good, but he may never be a full-time player. He started in place of Clemons in the playoff loss to Atlanta and played 46 snaps, but his sole appearance on the stat sheet was a tackle of Julio Jones on a short pass.

Bobby Wagner led all NFL defenders with a tackle or assist on 27.5 percent of running plays—NaVorro Bowman and Jerod Mayo ranked second and third—and was named to several all-rookie teams. Third-year man K.J. Wright, another Seattle late-round find, looks like a fixture on the outside. The other outside linebacker spot remains something of a mystery. Leroy Hill remained unsigned in mid-May and could always be brought back, if the Seahawks are willing to look past his age (he turns 31 in September) and long arrest record. More likely, 2011 seventh-rounder Malcolm Smith will get first crack at the job. John Schneider has talked about the possibility of moving Avril or Irvin (or both) to linebacker as well. In many of Seattle's fronts, the difference between end and linebacker is almost semantic anyway, depending mostly on whether or not the player has his hand on the turf.

Defensive Secondary

Secondary	Age	Pos	Snaps	Plays	TmPct	Rk	Stop	Dfts	BTkl	Runs	St%	Rk	Yds	Rk	Tgts	Tgt%	Rk	Dist	Suc%	Rk	APaYd	Rk	PD	Int
				Overall						vs. Run					vs. Pass								
Kam Chancellor	25	SS	976	97	12.8%	13	35	13	4	38	39%	31	5.6	12	40	8.9%	16	8.4	50%	49	6.4	19	2	0
Earl Thomas	24	FS	959	69	9.1%	46	29	13	12	27	44%	17	6.7	33	26	5.8%	49	8.4	60%	21	8.4	52	7	3
Richard Sherman	25	CB	949	87	11.5%	9	38	19	5	18	28%	70	7.8	59	88	19.7%	27	14.0	61%	8	7.1	30	22	8
Brandon Browner	29	CB	746	51	9.0%	33	15	7	2	9	11%	82	17.9	87	64	19.0%	36	13.6	61%	7	5.5	3	9	3
Marcus Trufant*	33	CB	352	36	6.4%	--	16	8	2	3	100%	--	4.7	--	34	10.0%	--	6.9	62%	--	6.3	--	3	0
Antoine Winfield	36	CB	1026	114	13.1%	1	58	20	5	42	64%	7	2.9	4	69	14.7%	63	9.0	50%	54	5.9	8	11	3

Year	Pass D Rank	vs. #1 WR	Rk	vs. #2 WR	Rk	vs. Other WR	Rk	vs. TE	Rk	vs. RB	Rk
2010	29	-3.0%	14	33.8%	32	20.9%	28	-2.8%	10	19.4%	29
2011	8	-3.3%	10	-44.1%	1	-17.8%	11	2.0%	11	35.2%	32
2012	3	-37.5%	1	-7.4%	10	-6.0%	10	-1.6%	17	-9.3%	9

Good luck finding a defensive backfield with an outlook as bright as this one. Richard Sherman ranked among the league leaders in both Adjusted Success Rate and Adjusted Trash Talk Rate. At 6-foot-4, Brandon Browner is a press-man specialist and a perfect fit for Seattle's system. Off coverage would expose his lack of pure speed, but he's a monster when he's allowed to jam receivers at the line of scrimmage. It's not a big enough difference to be considered a major statement, but Browner actually gave up fewer Adjusted Yards per Pass than Sherman, and even faced opponents' top receivers more often than Sherman did. Kam Chancellor is one of the biggest safeties in our database at 232 pounds, but he still has the speed to cover seams and deep-underneath zones. Earl Thomas is the centerfielder who can take away the deep ball and cover up a lot of his teammate's mistakes (even if he did rank in the top 10 in broken tackles). All four are liberated by the strengths of their teammates. The corners can take risks on short routes, knowing their safeties will bail them out. On running downs, either safety can fill the box, knowing the corners can survive on an island.

And then the secondary got better over the offseason. Antoine Winfield, the league's pre-eminent run-stopping corner, was signed to replace Marcus Trufant at nickelback. They also drafted for depth at the position by adding Tharold Simon from LSU. Simon is a 6-foot-2 fifth-rounder—just like Sherman. If he develops, he could replace Browner in a few years. Seattle also has Jeremy Lane, who played well at the end of the year (53 percent Adjusted Success Rate, 6.5 Adjusted Yards per Pass) while Browner served a suspension for PEDs. If there's a concern here, it's depth at safety. None of the Seahawks's backups at that position have significant NFL experience, and only one (2012 sixth-rounder Winston Guy) was even drafted.

Special Teams

Year	DVOA	Rank	FG/XP	Rank	Net Kick	Rank	Kick Ret	Rank	Net Punt	Rank	Punt Ret	Rank	Hidden	Rank
2010	6.4%	3	-2.3	26	11.6	6	18.3	2	-1.0	22	4.4	9	11.1	2
2011	0.2%	16	3.6	10	-2.0	24	1.9	12	-3.0	20	0.3	16	13.2	3
2012	5.7%	3	1.9	11	8.5	5	9.1	4	12.0	6	-3.0	19	-6.4	25

As soon as they acquired Percy Harvin, the Seahawks announced that he would be returning kicks as well as playing offense. They released Leon Washington shortly thereafter, cementing Harvin's special teams role. Harvin has returned at least one kickoff for a touchdown in each of his NFL seasons, he led the league in average return in 2011 and 2012, and he comes to Seattle averaging 27.9 yards per return, one of the top 10 rates in history. Advanced stats back that up—he was fourth in kickoff return value last season, and second the year before, though he was barely above average in 2010. However, he has never returned a punt in the NFL, and it's anyone's guess who'll be doing that for Seattle this season. Golden Tate did return 16 punts for a 12.6-yard average in 2010. Punter Jon Ryan and kicker Steven Hauschka have both been solidly above average if not world-beaters over the past few seasons. Excellent coverage teams are led by Heath Farwell, tied for the league lead with 10 Stops on kickoffs (i.e. tackles that stopped a kick return short of what our metrics consider an average length).

Coaching Staff

If you could play for any coach in the NFL, and the sole determining factor was how much fun you would have day in and day out, there's a good chance Pete Carroll would be your guy. He has fostered a loose, positive, summer-camp vibe that makes players enjoy coming to work, but at the same time his "always compete" mantra ensures accountability and doesn't let players get away with lackluster performance. Offensive coordinator Darrell Bevell and offensive line coach Tom Cable both joined the team in 2011, and it's been an ideal marriage of West Coast passing and zone blocking. They deserve extra credit for installing the read-option offense midseason. Bevell interviewed with the Bears and Cardinals in the offseason, and another good year in Seattle could earn him a head coaching job in 2014. With Gus Bradley now the head coach in Jacksonville, former Seahawks defensive line coach Dan Quinn returns as defensive coordinator after two years in that same position for the Florida Gators. He has worked with Carroll in Seattle before, and it should be a smooth transition.

Tampa Bay Buccaneers

2012 Record: 7-9	Total DVOA: -6.6% (20th)	2013 Mean Projection: 8.3 wins	On the Clock (0-4): 7%
Pythagorean Wins: 7.9 (17th)	Offense: 0.6% (14th)	Postseason Odds: 35.1%	Mediocrity (5-7): 29%
Snap-Weighted Age: 26.0 (30th)	Defense: 2.9% (20th)	Super Bowl Odds: 4.0%	Playoff Contender (8-10): 45%
Average Opponent: -1.1% (17th)	Special Teams: -4.3% (27th)	Proj. Avg. Opponent: 3.2% (4th)	Super Bowl Contender (11+): 18%

2012: With strong run defense and running game, Bucs were well-built to win the 1975 NFC Central.

2013: Maturity and all-star additions should improve pass defense, but can pass offense gain consistency?

While most NFL teams try to build a balanced defense, the 2012 Tampa Bay Buccaneers found themselves with a unit that had great strengths and great weaknesses. That's not unusual—there are unbalanced defenses across the league every year, including a surprising number of Super Bowl winners. There's a key difference, however, between the Bucs and those championship teams. While a number of squads have won titles by giving up bundles of rushing yards, they made up for it with suffocating pass defenses. Tampa Bay, on the other hand, sported an all-time great rushing defense, but was powerless to stop most of the quarterbacks they faced. It's a balancing act that must be corrected for 2013, because no defense so heavily slanted towards stopping the run has ever won a Super Bowl.

Stout run defense has certainly not been the norm in Tampa Bay, which ranked 28th or worse in run defense DVOA for each of the three prior seasons. Over that time, though, the Bucs were loading up on front-seven talent. In the first three rounds of the draft, Tampa Bay selected defensive tackle Gerald McCoy in 2010; linebacker Mason Foster and defensive linemen Adrian Clayborn and Da'Quan Bowers in 2011; and outside linebacker Lavonte David in 2012. They also added first-rounder Mark Barron in 2012: not technically a front seven player, but a key run defender as an in-the-box safety.

Tampa Bay also had a number of veterans on the roster who played key roles last year. Defensive ends Michael Bennett and Daniel Teo'Nesheim, bench players for most of their careers, stepped up big when injuries felled Clayborn and Bowers. Most importantly, Ronde Barber, long the NFL's pre-eminent run defender at cornerback, proved just as reliable after moving to safety.

Just as important as any player is the man pulling the strings, new head coach Greg Schiano. After a decade as a defensive assistant with the Bears, the Dolphins, and college powerhouse Penn State, Schiano was hired as head coach of the Rutgers Scarlet Knights in 2001. Schiano took over a team that had given up a Big East-worst 222.2 rushing yards per game the year before, at 4.3 yards per carry. They were actually even worse than that in Schiano's first season, but then showed steady improvement, peaking in 2006 when they ranked second with 101.0 rushing yards allowed per game, and led the conference with a 2.9-yard average.

Take that coach and put him in charge of these players, and you get sensational results. The Bucs had six players in the top 50 in the league in Rushing Defeats. Barber and Barron were second and third among safeties, and David led all outside linebackers. The team totals are even more stunning. After years of futility, the Bucs were third in the league in run defense DVOA, and first in Adjusted Line Yards and Stuff Rate. It's those latter two numbers where they really shine. Since 1995, only three defenses have had better ALY: the 2006 Williams Wall Vikings; the 1998 Chargers with Junior Seau and Rodney Harrison; and the Super Bowl champion 2000 Ravens with Ray Lewis at the peak of his power. None of those teams, however, could match the 2012 Buccaneers for Stuff Rate. For as long as we've been tracking teams, nobody has hit opposing runners in the backfield as often as Tampa Bay did last year, stopping running backs for no gain or a loss nearly one-third of the time (Table 1).

Table 1: Top Ten Run Defense Teams, 1995-2012

Adjusted Line Yards				Stuff Rate			
Rk	Team	Year	ALY	Rk	Team	Year	Stuff Rate
1	MIN	2006	2.75	1	TB	2012	32.8%
2	SD	1998	2.78	2	BAL	2000	31.1%
3	BAL	2000	2.82	3	MIN	2006	30.8%
4	TB	2012	2.96	4	SD	1998	30.2%
5	PIT	2001	3.07	5	TEN	2000	29.5%
6	BAL	1998	3.08	6	MIA	1998	29.1%
7	TEN	2000	3.08	7	OAK	1998	29.1%
8	BAL	1999	3.10	8	MIN	1995	28.3%
9	PIT	1997	3.12	9	BAL	1998	28.2%
10	NYG	2000	3.12	10	TEN	2001	27.9%

That's all well and good—very good, actually—but we're still left with a team that finished 7-9 and 20th in overall defensive DVOA. The problem, as Tampa Bay fans and practitioners of deductive reasoning can tell you, is that the pass defense was horrible. The pass rush, specifically, was abysmal without Clayborn (lost for most of the year with a torn ACL) and Bowers (who tore his Achilles in OTAs, missed the start of the season, and never played at 100 percent). Unable to pressure opposing quarterbacks, the Buccaneers could do nothing to cover for their faltering secondary. Desperate times

2013 Buccaneers Schedule

Week	Opp.	Week	Opp.	Week	Opp.
1	at NYJ	7	at ATL	13	at CAR
2	NO	8	CAR (Thu.)	14	BUF
3	at NE	9	at SEA	15	SF
4	ARI	10	MIA (Mon.)	16	at STL
5	BYE	11	ATL	17	at NO
6	PHI	12	at DET		

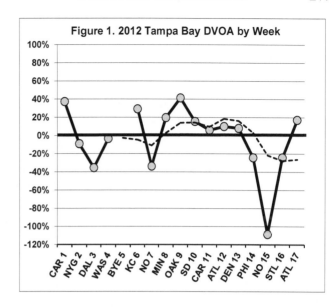

Figure 1. 2012 Tampa Bay DVOA by Week

call for desperate measures, and while Tampa Bay didn't blitz often, they went all-out when they did, sending six or more pass rushers (13.8 percent of passes) almost as often as they sent five (15.8 percent). The tactic didn't work—they gave up 10.0 yards per play on big blitzes, a few decimal points better than Detroit and Philadelphia, and worse than everybody else.

There's no question that personnel and injuries played a big part in that shoddy pass defense. However, part of the problem may be Schiano himself. Sander Philipse, one of the FO game charters who also writes for BucsNation.com, discovered a presentation Schiano gave on his defensive philosophy at the 2011 Nike Coach of the Year Clinic. The first building block of Schiano's game plan: Stop the run. Schiano emphasized his point by pointing out the win-loss records of teams that did or did not rush for 100 yards in a game. Schiano correctly noted that the team that rushes for more yards usually wins the game. In the process, though, Schiano failed to distinguish correlation from causation, and also showed that he is not a reader of Football Outsiders. It was the first research piece that launched our site ten years ago this summer, and we've written about it over and over since then: High rushing yardage totals come because winning teams run, not because running teams win. Most successful teams pass to build a lead, then pile up ground yards in the fourth quarter as they run out the clock.

If Schiano's focus on stopping the run is in any way hurting Tampa Bay's ability to stop the pass, then he's doing his team a disservice. Pass defense is simply more important than run defense. That is especially true in this, one of the most passer-friendly eras in league history, but it was also true in the 1990s, the 1980s, and even in the dead-ball 1970s. Frankly, teams with bad run defenses win Super Bowls all the time. Five teams this century have won the Super Bowl with a run defense that ranked 20th or worse in DVOA, including last year's Ravens. Four teams pulled it off in the 1990s. Our DVOA database only goes back to 1991, but two teams in the 1980s won championships despite ranking 20th or worse in yards allowed per rush, two more pulled it off in the 1970s, and the 1967 Green Bay Packers won Super Bowl II despite ranking 15th in a 16-team league. Meanwhile, only two teams have ever won the Super Bowl despite ranking 20th or worse in either pass defense DVOA or net yards allowed per passing play: the 1998 Denver Broncos and the 1976 Oakland Raiders.

The Bucs recognized that they needed to improve their pass defense in order get back to the playoffs. They signed All-Pro safety Dashon Goldson away from San Francisco, then made one of the biggest deals of the offseason, trading for

Jets cornerback Darrelle Revis. With Barron theoretically improving in his second season, Eric Wright returning to health, and second-round rookie Johnthan Banks around to provide a further influx of young talent, there's every reason to expect improvement in the secondary this fall. Really, there's no reason to expect otherwise. It's not like they can get much worse. The question is whether they can maintain their rock-solid run defense in the process.

From 1991 to 2011, 35 teams finished in the top ten in run defense DVOA, but the bottom ten in pass defense. Not surprisingly, 31 of those teams had a better pass defense DVOA the following season, and the average team improved by 14.1%. On the flip side, 25 teams declined in run defense, worse by an average of 4.1%. In overall DVOA, the average improvement was small, from 4.2% to 0.2%. Only eight teams made significant improvement of 10.0% or more, led by the Tennessee Titans, whose defense went from 4.2% in 1999 (in their Super Bowl year, oddly enough) to -25.0% the following season. The majority of these teams were more balanced the following season, but very few were actually better.

However, there's a difference between the average team where the run defense was far superior to the pass defense, and this Buccaneers team. The additions of Revis and Goldson should be a significant help. Healthy seasons from Bowers, Clayborn, and Eric Wright would also be a big plus. Perhaps more important, this defense was very, very young in 2012. Tampa Bay ranked 30th in snap-weighted age, and that's with 37-year-old Ronde Barber skewing the average—no other starter was older than 27. In 2013, the 29-year-old Goldson will probably be the oldest defensive starter (Adam Hayward, who could be the third linebacker, is a few months older). Three likely starters on the line—Bowers, Clayborn, and fourth-round rookie Akeem Spence—are all 25 or younger. Not a single projected starter is in the decline phase of his career, and most are on the upswing.

The Buccaneers are counting on another year of experience to solve their defensive balance problems, but that will still leave their offense out of alignment. In this case, though, it's not a matter of run vs. pass, it's a patter of explosiveness vs. security. Led by the feet of rookie running back Doug Martin, the arm of fourth-year quarterback Josh Freeman, and the downfield threat of veteran receiver Vincent Jackson, Tampa Bay had one of the most volatile offenses in the NFL in 2012. The run game ranked fifth in Open-Field Yards, and more than a quarter of their pass attempts traveled at least 15 yards past the line of scrimmage, a higher rate than any team except the Colts. Between ground and sky the Bucs ripped off 21 plays of 40 yards or more, four more than any other team and double the average squad.

Sometimes, though, while the Bucs were racking up chunks of yardage, they forgot to hang on to the ball. Actually, that's not fair to Martin. The Bucs had no trouble with ball security in the run game (as a team they fumbled only three times on running plays all year), but they did throw too many interceptions. That can't be blamed on any particular receiver, either. Jackson and Dallas Clark were the targets on five interceptions apiece, tied for the team lead, and hardly a surprise since they were first and third on the team in targets.

No, there is only one individual who can be blamed for those interceptions: Josh Freeman, the man who threw them. Only four quarterbacks threw more picks last year. The problem was nothing new for Freeman, who now has thrown 63 picks in his first four seasons. That's among the top ten such numbers in the DVOA era going back to 1991, even though it includes a fluky six-interception season in 2010. In his other three seasons, Freeman has finished fourth, second, and fifth in total interceptions.

Have other passers who threw so many interceptions been able to turn their careers around? Most names in the top ten, as you'd suspect, are ominous. Kerry Collins had a very long career which topped out at "slightly above average." Jake Plummer and Joey Harrington also make the list, as does Mark Sanchez, who entered the league with Freeman in 2009. On the other hand, Eli Manning, Carson Palmer, and Jay Cutler also threw many interceptions early in their careers, and they all turned out to be various levels of OK. And the leader of the pack, with 81 picks in his first four years, is Peyton Manning, who went on to become Peyton Manning, though it should be noted that even as a youngster he was doing so many good things it almost offset his interceptions.

There's certainly hope here that Freeman will be able to get his career on track, but he has a long way to go. Let's turn the reigns over to our game charters, who recorded the following observations from a handful of Freeman's errant passes:

• "Freeman misses a WIDE OPEN Vincent Jackson when the Redskins mess up coverage on the right side."
• "Williams is wiiiide open for a TD and Freeman just way overthrows him."
• "My god is this a terrible throw."

Freeman, like the Tampa Bay defense, is young and improving, and he deserves credit for his big plays as well as his mistakes. The unfortunate fact, however, is that Freeman could take a step forward in 2013 and still be the worst starting quarterback in the NFC South.

And in a nutshell, that explains the problem for the Bucs in 2013. In their division alone, they play two games each against Atlanta, the team with an NFC-best 56-24 record since 2008; Carolina, FO's pick for most improved team this season; and New Orleans, whose Hall of Fame quarterback is reuniting with his Super Bowl-winning head coach.

Tampa Bay isn't safe out of the division, either. If the NFC South isn't the best division in the league, then the NFC West is, and the Bucs have four games against that group, plus a road game against New England. That's why, for all of their improvement and untapped potential, we see the Buccaneers as a fringe playoff contender in 2013. They should be in the mix for a wild card spot well into December, but the best of times for this group are probably a year or two ahead.

Vince Verhei

2012 Buccaneers Stats by Week

Wk	vs.	W-L	PF	PA	YDF	YDA	TO	Total	Off	Def	ST
1	CAR	W	16	10	258	301	2	37%	12%	-27%	-2%
2	at NYG	L	34	41	307	604	1	-9%	0%	10%	1%
3	at BAL	L	10	16	166	297	1	-36%	-67%	-46%	-15%
4	WAS	L	22	24	373	474	-1	-3%	6%	18%	8%
5	BYE										
6	KC	W	38	10	463	260	0	29%	35%	-23%	-29%
7	NO	L	28	35	513	458	1	-34%	10%	28%	-16%
8	at MIN	W	36	17	416	369	3	20%	14%	-12%	-6%
9	at OAK	W	42	32	515	424	2	41%	43%	-5%	-7%
10	SD	W	34	24	279	426	2	16%	32%	18%	2%
11	at CAR	W	27	21	403	331	-2	6%	3%	2%	5%
12	ATL	L	23	24	326	424	2	10%	28%	12%	-6%
13	at DEN	L	23	31	306	333	0	8%	11%	-1%	-3%
14	PHI	L	21	23	314	367	1	-24%	-1%	20%	-4%
15	at NO	L	0	41	386	447	-5	-109%	-62%	46%	-1%
16	STL	L	13	28	429	285	-3	-24%	-27%	-2%	1%
17	at STL	W	22	17	366	278	-1	17%	6%	-8%	4%

Trends and Splits

	Offense	Rank	Defense	Rank
Total DVOA	0.6%	14	2.9%	20
Unadjusted VOA	3.4%	15	4.6%	22
Weighted Trend	2.3%	13	7.6%	25
Variance	9.6%	26	5.1%	15
Average Opponent	2.8%	28	3.0%	6
Passing	6.6%	18	16.9%	26
Rushing	2.7%	10	-19.6%	3
First Down	3.6%	13	14.1%	30
Second Down	-1.7%	19	-8.0%	10
Third Down	-1.8%	18	-2.7%	16
First Half	-9.3%	24	0.5%	17
Second Half	8.8%	9	5.6%	21
Red Zone	5.8%	12	7.0%	21
Late and Close	22.7%	5	-0.9%	20

Five-Year Performance

Year	W-L	Pyth W	Est W	PF	PA	TO	Total	Rk	Off	Rk	Def	Rk	ST	Rk	Off AGL	Rk	Def AGL	Rk	Off Age	Rk	Def Age	Rk	ST Age	Rk
2008	9-7	9.1	8.9	361	323	+4	9.7%	10	-0.5%	20	-10.7%	6	-0.5%	18	27.6	19	15.2	10	27.7	15	28.2	4	26.4	22
2009	3-13	3.7	4.8	244	400	-5	-23.8%	27	-19.3%	26	8.0%	25	3.5%	5	32.3	22	18.9	9	26.1	31	26.4	25	26.3	21
2010	10-6	8.7	8.4	341	318	+9	3.7%	12	8.0%	8	3.7%	23	-0.5%	18	22.9	14	37.9	25	25.6	31	25.9	27	25.4	30
2011	4-12	3.2	5.5	287	494	-16	-25.1%	30	-11.5%	26	14.2%	31	0.6%	14	17.1	6	34.3	20	26.0	30	25.6	31	25.3	31
2012	7-9	7.9	7.8	389	394	+3	-6.6%	20	0.6%	14	2.9%	20	-4.3%	27	26.7	14	30.1	18	26.4	22	25.6	30	25.7	24

2012 Performance Based on Most Common Personnel Groups

TB Offense					TB Offense vs. Opponents				TB Defense				TB Defense vs. Opponents			
Pers	Freq	Yds	DVOA	Run%	Pers	Freq	Yds	DVOA	Pers	Freq	Yds	DVOA	Pers	Freq	Yds	DVOA
11	47%	6.1	4.6%	21%	Nickel Even	32%	5.8	6.9%	Nickel Even	40%	6.3	21.8%	11	51%	6.5	17.2%
21	27%	5.9	2.4%	58%	4-3-4	31%	5.7	6.3%	4-3-4	35%	5.1	-15.0%	12	18%	5.9	0.7%
12	11%	6.2	4.3%	31%	3-4-4	15%	6.9	11.2%	Dime+	24%	7.3	3.2%	21	18%	6.0	-8.4%
22	9%	5.7	30.3%	76%	Dime+	9%	6.7	-14.9%	Nickel Odd	1%	5.9	-8.1%	22	4%	4.1	-10.6%
20	2%	4.0	-50.3%	52%	Nickel Odd	8%	5.2	1.5%					20	3%	6.7	-23.6%

Strategic Tendencies

Run/Pass		Rk	Formation		Rk	Pass Rush		Rk	Secondary		Rk	Strategy		Rk
Runs, first half	38%	18	Form: Single Back	57%	28	Rush 3	10.4%	5	4 DB	35%	29	Play action	24%	11
Runs, first down	51%	14	Form: Empty Back	2%	29	Rush 4	60.0%	20	5 DB	41%	23	Avg Box (Off)	6.43	12
Runs, second-long	32%	14	Pers: 3+ WR	51%	16	Rush 5	15.8%	26	6+ DB	24%	4	Avg Box (Def)	6.22	28
Runs, power sit.	58%	11	Pers: 4+ WR	1%	18	Rush 6+	13.8%	4	CB by Sides	77%	13	Offensive Pace	31.53	23
Runs, behind 2H	27%	20	Pers: 2+ TE/6+ OL	22%	27	Sacks by LB	14.8%	21	DB Blitz	18%	3	Defensive Pace	30.97	27
Pass, ahead 2H	42%	23	Shotgun/Pistol	45%	19	Sacks by DB	7.4%	13	Hole in Zone	8%	17	Go for it on 4th	0.74	28

Tampa Bay: The team where pass pressure matters less than you think. The Bucs had the league's second lowest gap between defensive DVOA with pass pressure (-55.7% DVOA, 3.5 yards per pass) and defensive DVOA without pass pressure (34.2% DVOA, 8.2 yards per pass). On the offensive side, Josh Freeman had a similarly small gap between performance under pressure (-57.5% DVOA, 3.3 yards per pass) and performance without pressure (29.2% DVOA, 7.8 yards per pass). Only Andrew Luck and Ben Roethlisberger had a smaller gap. 🏈 Tampa Bay recovered eight of 11 fumbles on offense. 🏈 Tampa Bay was one of three teams that pressured the quarterback less than 15 percent of the time with a standard four-man pass rush. 🏈 Tampa Bay's defense had -13.3% DVOA on passes thrown behind the line of scrimmage (ninth in the NFL) but 51.8% DVOA on passes thrown beyond the line of scrimmage (26th). 🏈 Opponents clearly wanted to take advantage of the Bucs' attempts to bring all-out pressure. The Bucs faced 36 draws (second in the NFL) and 33 running back screens (tied for third). They were average against screens, but actually quite good against draws, allowing just 3.3 yards per carry with -40.9% DVOA.

Passing

Player	DYAR	DVOA	Plays	NtYds	Avg	YAC	C%	TD	Int
J.Freeman	118	-8.0%	583	3897	6.7	5.4	55.1%	27	17
D.Orlovsky	5	0.4%	7	51	7.3	3.5	57.1%	0	0

Rushing

Player	DYAR	DVOA	Plays	Yds	Avg	TD	Fum	Suc
D.Martin	155	3.9%	319	1454	4.6	11	1	48%
L.Blount*	-2	-9.5%	41	151	3.7	2	0	37%
J.Freeman	26	3.7%	29	159	5.5	0	1	-
D.J.Ware*	16	28.2%	11	51	4.6	0	0	45%
B.Leonard	-4	-11.1%	33	106	3.2	0	0	42%

Receiving

Player	DYAR	DVOA	Plays	Ctch	Yds	Y/C	YAC	TD	C%
V.Jackson	224	10.5%	147	72	1384	19.2	5.0	8	49%
M.Williams	62	-1.4%	126	63	996	15.8	5.1	9	50%
T.Underwood	4	-7.0%	55	28	425	15.2	3.6	2	51%
A.Benn*	-8	-38.6%	6	4	26	6.5	5.8	0	67%
K.Ogletree	92	4.5%	55	32	436	13.6	2.6	4	58%
D.Hagan	32	-1.9%	36	20	259	13.0	3.4	0	56%
D.Clark*	-60	-14.5%	75	47	435	9.3	2.4	4	63%
L.Stocker	-28	-26.4%	28	16	165	10.3	5.5	1	57%
T.Crabtree	82	76.8%	12	8	203	25.4	18.1	3	67%
D.Martin	66	3.1%	70	49	472	9.6	8.9	1	70%
D.J.Ware*	-28	-42.7%	20	14	100	7.1	7.3	0	70%
E.Lorig	-6	-18.1%	19	12	83	6.9	6.9	1	63%
B.Leonard	-23	-41.3%	15	11	67	6.1	7.1	0	73%

Offensive Line

Player	Pos	Age	GS	Snaps	Pen	Sk	Pass	Run	Player	Pos	Age	GS	Snaps	Pen	Sk	Pass	Run
Donald Penn	LT	30	16/16	1047	4	2	12.5	3.5	Jamon Meredith	RG	27	14/12	795	4	1.5	8	2.5
Jeremy Zuttah	C/LG	27	16/16	1018	9	2	11.5	6	Carl Nicks	LG	30	7/7	442	1	1	4	4
Demar Dotson	RT	28	16/15	986	9	5.5	21.5	3	Gabe Carimi	G/T	25	16/14	914	10	4.5	16.5	2
Ted Larsen	C	26	16/13	843	6	0	3	2									

Year	Yards	ALY	Rk	Power	Rk	Stuff	Rk	2nd Lev	Rk	Open Field	Rk	Sacks	ASR	Rk	Short	Long	F-Start	Cont.
2010	4.43	3.78	25	60%	17	23%	26	1.18	13	1.21	5	30	6.1%	13	12	12	16	24
2011	4.32	3.96	22	65%	11	21%	26	1.23	12	0.79	19	32	6.2%	14	7	14	13	32
2012	4.50	4.09	13	60%	22	20%	22	1.19	15	1.09	5	26	4.8%	6	4	13	17	36
2012 ALY by direction:			Left End 4.33 (11)			Left Tackle 5.18 (2)			Mid/Guard 3.89 (24)			Right Tackle 3.87 (18)			Right End 2.23 (31)			

The Bucs had a solid plan for 2012: Sign All-Pro Carl Nicks away from the division-rival Saints, match him with Pro-Bowler Davin Joseph, and unleash the NFL's most imposing guard tandem for 16 games of mayhem. It never came to be, however. Joseph tore the patellar tendon in his knee during the preseason and was out for the year, while Nicks lasted only seven games before he was sidelined with a toe injury. Both players are expected to be ready for the start of training camp, but any setback could mean more time for Jamon Meredith and Ted Larsen. Larsen has been pressed into a starting role due to injuries in two of his three seasons, and in those years the Bucs have ranked 22nd and 24th in ALY on runs up the middle. In the year in between, they ranked tenth. Larsen is a quality depth player, but he's not the kind of guy you want to rely on for extended periods. Meredith, meanwhile, has been on five teams in the last three years. The other alternative is Gabe Carimi, acquired from Chicago in June. Like a lot of first-round busts at tackle, Carimi's future is likely as a mediocre guard.

Jeremy Zuttah finished with 17.5 blown blocks. That would have been second-most among centers (where Zuttah started seven games) but a little more than average among left guards (where he started nine times after Nicks went down). At right tackle, longtime starter Jeremy Trueblood was benched after Week 1, when Carolina's Charles Johnson burned him for two hurries and a sack. He was later placed on IR with a shoulder injury and signed with Washington in the offseason. Trueblood was replaced by Demar Dotson, who had started only two games before last season. Dotson finished in the top ten among right tackles for blown blocks, but the Bucs liked his potential so much they signed him to a four-year extension in the offseason. Donald Penn rounds out the Tampa Bay line; his individual numbers were fine for a starting left tackle, although our charters noticed several times that when he was beaten, he was made to look *very* bad.

We also counted Tampa Bay's backs with 11.5 blown blocks leading to sacks or hurries. Only two teams (Indianapolis and Philadelphia) had more. It's the second year in a row the Bucs' runners have struggled in pass protection.

Defensive Front Seven

Defensive Line	Age	Pos	Snaps	Plays	Overall TmPct	Rk	Stop	Dfts	BTkl	Runs	vs. Run St%	Rk	RuYd	Rk	Pass Rush Sack	Hit	Hur	Tips
Michael Bennett*	28	DE	956	43	5.3%	39	35	23	1	23	78%	21	1.1	5	9	10	23.5	3
Gerald McCoy	25	DT	938	32	3.9%	40	25	14	3	22	73%	39	1.3	7	5	10	18	2
Daniel Te'o-Nesheim	26	DE	732	39	4.8%	45	33	17	0	31	84%	10	1.1	4	4	4	10.5	0
Roy Miller*	26	DT	494	25	3.3%	57	18	7	0	19	79%	26	1.2	5	0	1	3	1
Gary Gibson	31	DT	280	18	2.2%	--	15	7	0	16	94%	--	0.3	--	0	1	2	0
Derek Landri	30	DT	483	21	2.7%	66	13	6	3	15	67%	59	2.5	44	0	2	7.5	1
George Selvie	26	DE	237	15	3.0%	--	13	4	0	14	86%	--	0.7	--	1	3	4	0

Linebackers	Age	Pos	Snaps	Plays	Overall TmPct	Rk	Stop	Dfts	BTkl	Pass Rush Sack	Hit	Hur	Tips	Runs	vs. Run St%	Rk	Yds	Rk	vs. Pass Tgts	Suc%	Rk	AdjYd	Rk	PD
Lavonte David	23	OLB	1059	143	17.5%	10	79	30	10	2	3	9.5	0	77	68%	42	3.4	52	47	45%	56	7.4	57	4
Mason Foster	24	MLB	739	103	12.6%	47	62	17	4	2	2	4	0	68	72%	26	2.8	28	15	34%	--	6.7	--	1
Quincy Black*	29	OLB	294	32	7.0%	--	11	5	3	0	0	0	0	14	50%	--	3.4	--	10	19%	--	12.6	--	0
Adam Hayward	29	OLB	149	20	2.4%	--	14	2	0	0	0	0	0	11	91%	--	1.5	--	6	35%	--	6.0	--	1
Jonathan Casillas	26	OLB	249	27	3.5%	--	17	6	1	0	0	0	0	16	69%	--	3.4	--	10	63%	--	7.3	--	0

Year	Yards	ALY	Rk	Power	Rk	Stuff	Rk	2nd Level	Rk	Open Field	Rk	Sacks	ASR	Rk	Short	Long
2010	4.92	4.56	30	55%	5	17%	23	1.49	32	1.01	27	26	4.8%	31	7	14
2011	5.16	4.37	26	74%	31	23%	4	1.61	32	1.37	31	23	5.2%	30	13	6
2012	3.58	2.96	1	71%	27	33%	1	1.19	18	0.74	15	27	4.9%	31	10	8
2012 ALY by direction:			Left End 2.35 (2)			Left Tackle 3.4 (8)			Mid/Guard 3.23 (2)			Right Tackle 1.88 (1)			Right End 2.92 (4)

If you have ever sacked a quarterback, anywhere, you should immediately send your resume to One Buccaneer Place, Tampa, Florida. The Bucs have a league-low 76 sacks over the last three seasons, and their leader in sacks last year (Michael Bennett) signed with the Seahawks, meaning nobody on the Tampa Bay roster finished in the top 50 in sacks last season. The starters at defensive end will most likely be Adrian Clayborn and Da'Quan Bowers, both drafted in the first two rounds in 2011. Clayborn had an impressive 7.5 sacks as a rookie, but his sophomore season ended with a knee injury in Week 3. Bowers, meanwhile, has only 4.5 sacks in his first two seasons. After tearing his Achilles tendon in May of 2012, he missed the season's first six games, and never re-entered the starting lineup. The Bucs did find two possible solutions in the draft, taking defensive end William Gholston (Michigan State) in the third round and end/linebacker hybrid Steven Means (Buffalo) in the fourth. Neither of these players had a season with more than 7.5 sacks in college, and our SackSEER system doesn't project either one with more than 10 sacks through their first five years. But Means, with a SackSEER rating of 83.1 percent, is a much more intriguing prospect than Gholston at 48.3 percent. Means is athletic with a strong pass-defensed rate in college; his projection is low because NFL Draft Scout listed him before the draft as a projected UDFA.

Gerald McCoy didn't make many plays himself, but his disruptive presence in the middle of the field created bountiful opportunities for his teammates. It's not clear who will be starting next to him after Roy Miller signed with Jacksonville in free agency. First in line will be high-motor rookie Akeem Spence, a fourth-rounder out of Illinois. Other candidates include Gary Gibson, a 31-year-old whose only prior starting experience came on a 2010 Rams team that finished 20th in rush defense DVOA; Derek Landri, who is now on his fourth team in five years; and all-name team candidate Lazarius "Pep" Levingston, a 2011 seventh-rounder who played in three games last year. Whoever wins the job, Schiano wants his starting nose tackle to attack at an angle, the "tilted nose" style made famous by Mean Joe Greene.

A replacement must also be found for outside linebacker Quincy Black, who was released following a career-threatening neck injury. Competing for that role will be veteran backups Jonathan Casillas, Adam Hayward, and Dekoda Watson—who have a combined 22 starts in 12 NFL seasons—plus youngster Najee Goode, a fifth-round draft pick out of West Virginia in 2012.

Defensive Secondary

Secondary	Age	Pos	Snaps	Plays	TmPct	Rk	Stop	Dfts	BTkl	Runs	St%	Rk	Yds	Rk	Tgts	Tgt%	Rk	Dist	Suc%	Rk	APaYd	Rk	PD	Int
Mark Barron	24	SS	1074	98	12.0%	22	31	14	11	46	41%	25	6.2	23	46	9.6%	11	15.5	41%	71	8.7	54	9	1
Ronde Barber*	38	FS	1071	105	12.9%	12	57	33	10	36	58%	5	5.7	14	42	8.9%	15	11.4	59%	25	7.0	32	11	4
E.J. Biggers*	26	CB	798	56	8.4%	48	24	9	3	11	45%	38	5.5	26	66	17.2%	47	15.0	54%	28	8.1	62	7	1
Leonard Johnson	23	CB	582	46	5.6%	78	23	11	4	8	63%	9	4.8	15	52	11.0%	84	12.7	58%	16	8.2	65	9	3
Eric Wright	28	CB	495	44	8.6%	42	17	9	4	9	44%	39	4.3	12	49	18.9%	37	13.6	50%	53	9.1	74	6	1
Ahmad Black	24	SS	417	37	4.5%	--	10	7	3	7	43%	--	11.7	--	15	3.2%	--	14.1	60%	--	4.6	--	5	2
Brandon McDonald*	28	CB	210	23	4.1%	--	9	3	1	3	33%	--	6.0	--	17	5.2%	--	11.5	33%	--	10.8	--	1	1
Dashon Goldson	29	FS	1026	79	9.9%	37	32	15	6	35	37%	38	6.5	30	29	6.1%	45	15.1	81%	3	3.3	3	13	3
Darrelle Revis	28	CB	91	15	15.4%	--	6	3	1	6	17%	--	9.3	--	9	16.8%	--	8.1	74%	--	3.4	--	2	1

Year	Pass D Rank	vs. #1 WR	Rk	vs. #2 WR	Rk	vs. Other WR	Rk	vs. TE	Rk	vs. RB	Rk
2010	13	-14.2%	6	0.7%	15	-12.0%	10	3.9%	16	12.3%	23
2011	30	-11.1%	5	56.6%	32	12.1%	28	6.4%	15	9.8%	24
2012	26	6.5%	21	6.7%	20	0.6%	18	12.8%	25	-1.5%	16

The Bucs had Aqib Talib and Eric Wright at cornerback for four games last season before Talib was suspended and later traded, and their pass defense DVOA for those four games was 7.8%. E.J. Biggers then stepped in for six more games (DVOA: 19.2%) until Wright's season ended due to Achilles and hamstring injuries. They finished out the string with Biggers on one side and Leonard Johnson on the other for the final six contests (DVOA: 20.4%). Talib and Biggers are now in New England and Washington, respectively, and Darrelle Revis is in Tampa Bay. Revis is the preeminent shutdown corner of this generation, and perhaps the NFL's best player from 2009-2011. Then a torn ACL ended his 2012 campaign after only two games. Adrian Peterson has redefined the limits (or lack thereof) of athletic achievement following ACL surgery, and our old friend Will Carroll, writing for Bleacher Report, believes that Revis' knee should be 100 percent by the time the season begins. However, Carroll also noted that due to backpedalling and rotating, cornerbacks put even more stress on their knees than running backs do. He also listed a number of NFL corners (Al Harris, Dominique Foxworth, and Terrell Thomas) who were unable to hold on to starting jobs after they tore their ACLs. Of course, Harris was 37 when he tore his ACL, but the fates of Foxworth and Thomas—both starters in their mid-20s in 2009 who then missed almost all of 2011 and 2012—are more troubling.

Mark Barron returns at strong safety, joined by free safety Dashon Goldson, formerly of San Francisco. Goldson is coming off an All-Pro season short of 30 years old, so there's not much concern there. It should be pointed out, though, that before 2012 his pass coverage numbers had never ranked in the top 30 at his position.

Special Teams

Year	DVOA	Rank	FG/XP	Rank	Net Kick	Rank	Kick Ret	Rank	Net Punt	Rank	Punt Ret	Rank	Hidden	Rank
2010	-0.5%	18	-0.7	20	-3.1	22	3.9	12	3.3	16	-5.9	27	3.1	8
2011	0.6%	14	7.5	4	1.1	17	0.7	15	4.5	11	-11.0	32	7.2	7
2012	-4.3%	27	1.9	12	1.7	12	-6.8	27	-15.1	30	-3.1	20	28.5	1

The most notable thing about the 2012 Buccaneers special teams has nothing to do with the performance of anyone on the actual Buccaneers roster. Horrible performance by opposing kickers and punters led Tampa Bay to accumulate the third highest total of "hidden" special teams points since 1991, behind only the 2007 Bears and the 1997 Bucs. Opponents were only 21-for-30 on field goals, including three misses from 31 yards or closer, and were worth minus-6.6 estimated points worth of field position in gross punt value.

The Bucs can't count on their opponents to play that badly in 2013, so their coverage teams and return men need to be better. Connor Barth is in the top ten for field-goal accuracy since 2010, only partly because he gets to kick in Florida, so he's not really part of the problem. Michael Koenen has been above average in kickoff value but below average in punting in each of the past three years. His weaknesses outweigh his strengths, but the only competition in camp will be Chas Henry, who was an even worse punter for Philadelphia and has never kicked off in the NFL. With Roscoe Parrish unsigned and Arrelious Benn in Philadelphia, the Bucs have lost both of their top returners from 2012, and there are no clear replacements in sight. Top candidates include undrafted free agent Matt Brown (83 kickoff returns at Temple, including two touchdowns) and track star Jeff Demps (21 kickoff returns for the Florida Gators with one touchdown, but never saw the field as a rookie with New England). Coach Greg Schiano has said that return ability will go a long way in deciding which wide receivers make the team. Or maybe they'll just fair-catch everything.

Coaching Staff

Let us recap the controversies surrounding Greg Schiano in his first 15 months as an NFL head coach. His authoritarian style upset veterans and effectively made Kellen Winslow quit the team. He ordered his defenders to attack on kneeldowns, infuriating Giants coach Tom Coughlin. Assistant coach Bryan Cox (no stranger to controversy himself) got into a sideline shoving match with linebacker Adam Hayward during a game against New Orleans. Anonymous players grumbled to Mike Florio about "sending coaches back to college." And then Roy Cummings of the *Tampa Tribune* said that players were illegally hitting during OTAs, and that the league was likely to investigate the team. Schiano replied by saying his drills were "99.9 percent" legal. In short, despite the good fortunes of Pete Carroll and Jim Harbaugh, it's clear that success at the collegiate level still does not guarantee achievement in the NFL.

Bill Sheridan has the title of defensive coordinator, but that's largely ceremonial; Butch Davis and Greg Schiano really run the show on that side of the ball. Davis is a source of controversy himself. His title with the Bucs is "Special Assistant to the Head Coach," because hiring him as a coach would void his contract with the University of North Carolina Tar Heels and cost him hundreds of thousands of dollars. He's not working at North Carolina, of course, due to multiple NCAA violations involving improper benefits from tutors and agents. Then, this July, multiple sources (including the *Miami Herald* and Fox Sports) reported that Davis would be the next coach at Florida International, only for Davis to pull out of the deal at the last minute. Instead, FIU hired Ron Turner—who had been Tampa Bay's quarterbacks coach. Turner would later say that Davis had been the one to suggest him to the FIU staff. The Bucs then replaced Turner with John McNulty, who had served in the same position for the Cardinals before being fired along with the rest of Ken Whisenhunt's staff. He also worked on Schiano's staff at Rutgers. In other words, it appears that the Special Assistant to the Head Coach facilitated Turner's exit to create a vacancy so they could hire Schiano's old buddy.

Speaking of coaches leaving jobs, offensive coordinator Mike Sullivan interviewed with the Bears for their head coaching vacancy after just one season at his position. He probably needs only one more good year to land a head job of his own.

Tennessee Titans

2012 Record: 6-10	Total DVOA: -29.4% (30th)	2013 Mean Projection: 6.4 wins	On the Clock (0-4): 24%
Pythagorean Wins: 4.6 (28th)	Offense: -20.5% (29th)	Postseason Odds: 17.2%	Mediocrity (5-7): 45%
Snap-Weighted Age: 26.4 (21st)	Defense: 7.5% (25th)	Super Bowl Odds: 0.6%	Playoff Contender (8-10): 27%
Average Opponent: -3.0% (22nd)	Special Teams: -1.4% (19th)	Proj. Avg. Opponent: -4.5% (28th)	Super Bowl Contender (11+): 5%

2012: Jake Locker, this is the broad side of a barn. Broad side of a barn, this is Jake Locker. Please become acquainted.

2013: The Titans try to return to their running-and-defense ways, which were already outdated a decade ago.

After a surprising 9-7 record in Mike Munchak's first season as head coach, the Tennessee Titans thought they were on the upswing. True, a difficult early schedule in 2012 would not help matters, but the defense seemed young and talented, and the pass rush couldn't possibly be worse. Jake Locker appeared ready to step into the starting lineup, bringing a stronger arm and better mobility to an offense that stagnated at times in 2011. It all looked reasonable on paper, though both conventional wisdom and our projections were a touch pessimistic.

It turns out that pessimism was well-founded. Even with a less moribund pass rush, the defense regressed. Locker was a downgrade from Matt Hasselbeck at quarterback. The Titans went 6-10, and our numbers indicate they were fortunate to do even that. Owner Bud Adams was not happy, firing team president Mike Reinfeldt and indicating a return to at least playoff contention was in order or more heads would roll after 2013. Munchak's fate depends on Locker, and Locker remains a work in progress as an NFL quarterback.

When the Titans selected Locker two years ago, we sounded a note of caution. Players who posted as poor a collegiate completion percentage as he did at Washington—53.9 percent over his four-year career, with a high of 58.2 percent as a junior—rarely turn into quality NFL passers. Locker's first year as an NFL starter did nothing to assuage our concerns, as the Titans fell from 15th to 29th in offensive DVOA.

That decline had nothing to do with inconsistent running back Chris Johnson; although he has had a below-average DVOA for three straight seasons, his performance actually improved a little bit in 2012. No, the real problem came in the passing game, as Locker struggled in nearly every area where Hasselbeck had been successful the year before.

Hasselbeck was among the league's most efficient third-down passers with a DVOA of 23.9%; Locker's was -38.2%. Hasselbeck had a 25.7% red-zone DVOA; Locker posted a red-zone DVOA of -46.8%. Hasselbeck posted an Adjusted Sack Rate of 3.7 percent; Locker's was 8.2 percent. Hasselbeck threw interceptions at a below-average rate; Locker at an above-average one. Even with the benefit of his mobility, Locker struggled to make positive plays on a consistent basis.

Locker's struggles on third downs and in the red zone proved the undoing of offensive coordinator Chris Palmer, who was fired after a Week 12 loss at Jacksonville that fea-tured one touchdown and five field-goal attempts. In some ways, Palmer's employment by the Titans was one of the odder mismatches in recent league history. For almost the entirety of Jeff Fisher's tenure, the Titans' offense was heavily devoted to the running game. Even when Steve McNair was at his peak and could have sustained a pass-heavier offense, Fisher was content to plunge Eddie George into the line for three yards per carry. Palmer's background was with the run-and-shoot, and his arrival gave the Titans one of the league's more pass-oriented schemes. We chronicled this transition in *Football Outsiders Almanac 2012*, noting the change from a team that ranked in the top ten in run-pass ratio and the bottom ten in how often they lined up with three or more wide receivers to one that ranked 30th in run-pass ratio and sixth in three or more wide receiver use. Perhaps no statistic exemplifies the Palmer-led change like the fact that when Hasselbeck posted his very good third-down numbers in 2011, the Titans threw the ball about 19 times as often as they ran it when it was third down with more than a yard to go.

Dowell Loggains, formerly the quarterbacks coach, was Palmer's interim replacement and was named the permanent offensive coordinator in the offseason. His ability to make changes during those final five games was limited, but comments from Loggains, Munchak, and general manager Ruston Webster this offseason, plus the team's moves, all make it clear the Titans will return to their run-based roots. As Loggains noted in an offseason media session, Munchak and Webster believe only three things can happen when you pass and two of them are bad. The Titans had a fairly successful offense at times under Loggains' mentor, the late Mike Heimerdinger. He'll have to show, though, the creativity in the run game that marked Heimerdinger's tenure if the Titans are to achieve the level of offensive success they need.

One thing that severely constrained the Titans' offense late in the season was a makeshift offensive line caused by a series of injuries. Starting center Eugene Amano was lost in training camp, right guard Leroy Harris in Week 8, and left guard Steve Hutchinson and right tackle David Stewart both in Week 13. All told, the Titans ranked second among all offensive lines by Adjusted Games Lost. In the final five games, with left tackle Michael Roos the only remaining member of the original offensive line, the Titans scored just 57 points on offense with a -40.5% DVOA.

217

2013 Titans Schedule

Week	Opp.	Week	Opp.	Week	Opp.
1	at PIT	7	SF	13	at IND
2	at HOU	8	BYE	14	at DEN
3	SD	9	at STL	15	ARI
4	NYJ	10	JAC	16	at JAC
5	KC	11	IND (Thu.)	17	HOU
6	at SEA	12	at OAK		

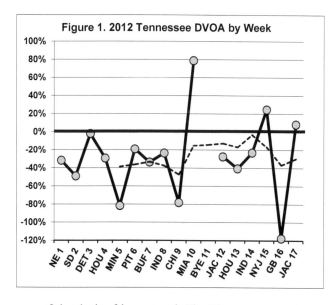

Figure 1. 2012 Tennessee DVOA by Week

You can't build an offense around the run without one of the league's top offensive lines, especially with a running back as inconsistent as Johnson. So the Titans went out and invested heavily in the position. They handed top free agent Andy Levitre $46 million over six years to fill the left guard spot. They had not spent a first- or second-round draft pick on an offensive lineman other than a left tackle in more than 20 years, but used the tenth overall pick on Alabama's Chance Warmack to fill the right guard spot. To expand their depth, the Titans signed interior linemen Rob Turner and Chris Spencer, who both started games in 2012, and drafted center Brian Schwenke in the fourth round.

It is difficult to say just how much difference even relatively acclaimed additions like Levitre and Warmack will make. Levitre is renowned primarily as a pass protector and is not a people-mover in the run game. As for Warmack, guards drafted in the first round generally turn into good players, but the Titans need him to be an impact starter in his first season, in part to handle Texans defensive end J.J. Watt. How will he transition from being part of a dominant team in college to one that struggles to win games in the NFL? Munchak, a renowned technician as a player who developed quality offensive linemen as a position coach before taking the head job, has indicated he will be taking a more hands-on role with the offensive linemen this year. The Titans' offensive line, however, has not had a regular starter with less than three years of NFL experience since tackles Stewart and Roos were in their third seasons in 2007. Some level of growing pains should be expected.

The best comparison for this year's Titans is probably the 2001 Arizona Cardinals, the only other team since 1999 to add two new starters at guard while returning both starting tackles and the starting center. Like the Titans, they added a left guard as a big-money free agent (Pete Kendall) and a right guard early in the draft (Leonard Davis, chosen second overall). The additions seemed to have only a modest impact, as the Cardinals went from 3.57 Adjusted Line Yards (3.52 between the tackles) to 3.67 Adjusted Line Yards (3.64 between the tackles). The Cardinals as a whole improved on offense, but the improvement came mostly from the passing game; lead back Michael Pittman's DVOA only improved from -11.4% to -8.7%, though backup Thomas Jones did do better in his second season.

To aid the running game, the Titans also handed running back Shonn Greene $10 million over three seasons. Greene, a between-the-tackle runner who lacks long speed, is nothing if not a stylistic complement to Chris Johnson. Greene ranked ninth in success rate, but posted a below-average DVOA be-

cause of that lack of long speed. The Titans are counting on him to improve their short yardage rushing game, noting his 12-for-12 performance on third-and-short in 2012. Over the course of his career, though, Greene has not outperformed the Jets' other running backs at converting third-and-short. If the Titans are a better short-yardage rushing team in 2013, Levitre and Warmack will likely deserve at least as much credit as Greene, if not more.

The third big-money free-agent addition on offense is tight end Delanie Walker, who received $17.6 million over four years. A movable chess piece for the 49ers behind Vernon Davis, he gives the Titans more versatility and much better blocking than the departed Jared Cook. The Titans also seem to be counting on him to be a significant target in the passing game, a questionable proposition considering his below-average hands. Walker has been in the NFL for seven seasons and has never even reached 30 catches in a season.

The Titans are counting on the more effective running game to aid the passing game, through the use of play-action passes. Our research has shown, though, that play action depends on the effectiveness of the play-faker much more than the efficiency of the running game. Proficient play-fakers, including both heralded quarterbacks like Peyton Manning and those less so like Kyle Orton, can be effective even with an ineffective run game. The Titans were one of the league's seven worst offenses when using play action in 2012, however, so using play action more frequently is unlikely to improve the passing efficiency much by itself.

As Munchak has noted several times, the Titans are also counting on the running game to improve the defense through the magic of "time of possession." After all, the offense tended to sputter out quickly, and the Titans' defense struggled badly in the second half, finishing 31st in DVOA. Does Munchak have the cause and effect correct here? We doubt it. After all, it was not just the second half where the Titans struggled on defense. They had the league's worst defense in the first quarter, finishing last in DVOA and giving up 49 more points in the quarter than any other team in the league. Starting the game by allowing 10 points is not recommended when trying to run a ball-control offense.

In addition, as we have chronicled since the early days of Football Outsiders, time of possession is associated with winning football games because teams that are already leading tend to run the ball more and face more passing attempts, giving them an edge in time of possession. The Titans' Week 10 victory against the Dolphins illustrates this well. Munchak praised his team for winning the time of possession battle in that game—but they only won that battle in the second half, which they entered with a 24-3 lead. If the Titans are going to have a better defense, they'll need to get there by playing better defense, not by some alchemical process involving the run game and time of possession.

With the biggest personnel additions coming on offense, the Titans' designated solution to getting better on defense is new senior defensive assistant Gregg Williams. After spending the 2012 season suspended by the league for his role in the Saints' bounty scandal, Williams returns to the city where he had success 13 years ago and will face a press corps that only occasionally breaks into the double digits. As far as unobtrusive returns go, he's in about the best situation he could be in. The Titans return incumbent defensive coordinator Jerry Gray, who served under Williams in Tennessee, Buffalo, and Washington. It is unclear, perhaps even to the Titans, precisely what relationship Williams and Gray will have during the season, but the best bet seems to be something like co-coordinators.

Beyond the bounty scandal, Williams brings with him a reputation for aggressiveness, physicality, and pressure. Despite his reputation, however, his teams do not accumulate nearly as many sacks or interceptions as you would think. His defenses ranked last in the league in interception rate three times between 2006 and 2011, and no defense of his has ranked in the top ten in Adjusted Sack Rate since the 2000 Titans. He's had some good defenses since then, notably in Washington, but his most effective stratagem has been rushing three and forcing teams to throw into tight windows against good zone coverage while his least effective has been the sort of press-man blitz the Titans seem to be implementing.

It's certainly not unheard of for a new defensive mind to take an already established roster and make it more effective. But most of these successful new coordinators, like Wade Phillips in Houston in 2011, typically see their hiring accompanied by a major influx of defensive talent—sometimes free agents, sometimes high draft picks, and sometimes important players returning from injury. The Titans were the fifth-healthiest defense in the league by Adjusted Games Lost, so getting players back from injury is not a reason to expect improvement. Between free agency and the draft, they added only two new projected starters, strong safety Bernard Pollard and defensive tackle Sammie Lee Hill. Pollard's Houston experience in 2010 shows his presence is no sure impediment to fielding a terrible defense, as he can be a liability in deep or man coverage, while Hill is being counted on for a much bigger role than the fourth defensive tackle he was in Detroit last year. Even with the additions of a mélange of other backups and mid- and late-round picks, this is not a sure-fire recipe for success.

Our research has found, though, that defense tends to be much more inconsistent from year to year than offense. Furthermore, the Titans fielded one of the league's youngest defensive squads for the second consecutive season. The Titans are hoping that Williams' schemes and fiery attitude and Pollard's much-needed leadership and similarly fiery attitude can help those young players make a leap forward.

The Titans' biggest defensive problem remains, though, that they lack premium players on defense, as paying cornerback Jason McCourty and free safety Michael Griffin last offseason failed to turn either one into an elite player. Of the defensive starters, it seems fair to describe only defensive end Derrick Morgan as a very good player who isn't stretched in his current role. The 2010 first-round pick had a break-through season as a pass rusher in 2012, but needs to convert more of his hurries into sacks. One or more of their passel of young players must make the same sort of career leap Morgan did in 2012 if that unlikely defensive improvement is to occur. Otherwise, the Titans are likely to end up with a 2013 record that resembles greatly their 2012 record, bringing with it adverse consequences for Mike Munchak, Jake Locker, and others.

Tom Gower

2012 Titans Stats by Week

Wk	vs.	W-L	PF	PA	YDF	YDA	TO	Total	Off	Def	ST
1	NE	L	13	34	284	390	-2	-32%	-16%	15%	-2%
2	at SD	L	10	38	212	416	0	-49%	-36%	21%	8%
3	DET	W	44	41	437	583	-1	-2%	3%	29%	24%
4	at HOU	L	14	38	325	297	-3	-29%	-5%	20%	-5%
5	at MIN	L	7	30	267	433	0	-8%	-73%	17%	8%
6	PIT	W	26	23	359	412	0	-19%	-12%	6%	-2%
7	at BUF	W	35	34	390	382	2	-34%	18%	24%	-27%
8	IND	L	13	19	339	457	1	-24%	1%	20%	-4%
9	CHI	L	20	51	339	365	-4	-78%	-17%	28%	-32%
10	at MIA	W	37	3	293	255	4	79%	18%	-48%	13%
11	BYE										
12	at JAC	L	19	24	360	321	-1	-28%	-12%	14%	-1%
13	HOU	L	10	24	354	331	-6	-41%	-45%	-7%	-2%
14	at IND	L	23	27	356	269	0	-23%	-48%	-26%	-2%
15	NYJ	W	14	10	294	253	5	25%	-2%	-36%	-9%
16	at GB	L	7	55	180	460	-2	-118%	-70%	36%	-12%
17	JAC	W	38	20	221	375	3	8%	-28%	-14%	-23%

Trends and Splits

	Offense	Rank	Defense	Rank
Total DVOA	-20.5%	29	7.5%	25
Unadjusted VOA	-20.2%	30	7.5%	23
Weighted Trend	-21.0%	29	-0.8%	16
Variance	7.7%	22	6.2%	19
Average Opponent	0.3%	15	-2.3%	21
Passing	-17.2%	29	10.7%	19
Rushing	-14.0%	26	3.8%	29
First Down	-22.6%	31	4.4%	23
Second Down	-23.2%	29	19.1%	30
Third Down	-12.4%	24	-5.3%	11
First Half	-20.4%	30	-1.5%	15
Second Half	-20.7%	28	16.7%	31
Red Zone	-28.0%	28	18.3%	29
Late and Close	-40.1%	31	11.2%	31

Five-Year Performance

Year	W-L	Pyth W	Est W	PF	PA	TO	Total	Rk	Off	Rk	Def	Rk	ST	Rk	Off AGL	Rk	Def AGL	Rk	Off Age	Rk	Def Age	Rk	ST Age	Rk
2008	13-3	12.1	11.8	375	234	+14	23.8%	5	4.0%	16	-18.6%	5	1.3%	14	9.0	3	14.4	9	28.3	6	27.3	16	26.8	12
2009	8-8	6.7	7.9	354	402	-4	-6.6%	21	4.2%	15	9.1%	26	-1.7%	24	7.4	3	14.9	5	28.1	5	27.4	13	26.6	15
2010	6-10	8.5	8.6	356	339	-4	6.6%	11	-4.5%	20	-5.8%	8	5.3%	6	21.0	13	10.6	5	27.4	17	26.5	20	26.2	17
2011	9-7	8.2	8.3	325	317	+1	6.6%	13	0.6%	15	0.3%	15	6.3%	3	20.0	8	17.7	9	28.1	3	25.7	30	26.4	14
2012	6-10	4.6	3.3	330	471	-4	-29.4%	30	-20.5%	29	7.5%	25	-1.4%	19	49.9	26	14.6	5	27.7	9	25.3	32	26.0	15

2012 Performance Based on Most Common Personnel Groups

TEN Offense					TEN Offense vs. Opponents				TEN Defense				TEN Defense vs. Opponents			
Pers	Freq	Yds	DVOA	Run%	Pers	Freq	Yds	DVOA	Pers	Freq	Yds	DVOA	Pers	Freq	Yds	DVOA
11	52%	5.6	-14.1%	15%	Nickel Even	33%	5.6	-12.7%	Nickel Even	48%	5.5	5.9%	11	47%	5.9	9.3%
21	20%	6.1	4.4%	57%	4-3-4	28%	5.2	-10.9%	4-3-4	39%	5.4	4.0%	12	26%	5.6	3.3%
12	18%	4.4	-28.0%	52%	3-4-4	19%	4.9	-17.6%	Dime+	11%	8.3	30.0%	21	8%	4.9	-23.4%
22	5%	2.8	-32.1%	89%	Dime+	14%	5.4	-35.5%	5-3-3	2%	0.2	1.7%	13	5%	5.2	16.8%
13	2%	3.8	-33.1%	59%	Nickel Odd	4%	7.6	29.1%	Nickel Odd	1%	3.7	-6.0%	22	4%	6.9	1.4%

Strategic Tendencies

Run/Pass		Rk	Formation		Rk	Pass Rush		Rk	Secondary		Rk	Strategy		Rk
Runs, first half	35%	28	Form: Single Back	63%	18	Rush 3	9.6%	8	4 DB	39%	27	Play action	18%	20
Runs, first down	46%	25	Form: Empty Back	6%	13	Rush 4	64.5%	14	5 DB	49%	14	Avg Box (Off)	6.31	21
Runs, second-long	33%	13	Pers: 3+ WR	54%	12	Rush 5	19.2%	18	6+ DB	11%	9	Avg Box (Def)	6.18	29
Runs, power sit.	49%	24	Pers: 4+ WR	1%	21	Rush 6+	6.7%	16	CB by Sides	95%	3	Offensive Pace	31.04	20
Runs, behind 2H	27%	19	Pers: 2+ TE/6+ OL	26%	25	Sacks by LB	32.1%	13	DB Blitz	4%	32	Defensive Pace	30.90	26
Pass, ahead 2H	47%	15	Shotgun/Pistol	51%	12	Sacks by DB	2.6%	27	Hole in Zone	7%	21	Go for it on 4th	0.88	19

Tennessee was last in the NFL with only 6.3 percent of pass plays qualifying as "max protect," defined as having seven or more blockers with at least two more blockers than pass rushers. ☞ Tennessee is one of two teams that never used more than five offensive linemen, even at the goal line. ☞ Titans opponents threw a league-high 26 percent of passes to their tight ends. ☞ The 2011 Titans' huge gap in run defense DVOA against one-back sets compared to two-back sets went away in 2012, but they still gave up 4.6 yards per carry against one-back sets compared to 3.9 yards per carry against two-back sets. (Leaguewide, running backs get about 4.25 yards per carry no matter how many backs are in the backfield.) ☞ Although the Titans brought fewer defensive back blitzes than any other team, those 20 plays at least hit home, bringing pressure on the quarterback a league-high 45 percent of the time.

Passing

Player	DYAR	DVOA	Plays	NtYds	Avg	YAC	C%	TD	Int
J.Locker	-265	-23.6%	341	2004	5.9	4.7	56.9%	10	10
M.Hasselbeck*	-6	-11.5%	236	1268	5.4	4.1	62.4%	7	5
R.Fitzpatrick	120	-7.6%	533	3235	6.1	5.9	60.8%	24	16

Rushing

Player	DYAR	DVOA	Plays	Yds	Avg	TD	Fum	Suc
C.Johnson	-30	-11.3%	275	1246	4.5	6	3	41%
J.Locker	54	20.4%	39	292	7.5	1	1	-
J.Harper*	-3	-12.0%	19	30	1.6	3	0	37%
D.Reynaud	-33	-68.2%	16	33	2.1	0	0	13%
M.Hasselbeck	9	24.9%	6	45	7.5	0	0	-
C.Mooney	2	2.5%	5	19	3.8	0	0	60%
S.Greene	49	-4.5%	275	1044	3.8	9	4	52%
J.Parmele*	-7	-12.8%	40	143	3.6	0	0	33%
R.Fitzpatrick	22	0.5%	38	205	5.4	1	0	-

Receiving

Player	DYAR	DVOA	Plays	Ctch	Yds	Y/C	YAC	TD	C%
K.Wright	15	-14.4%	104	64	627	9.8	4.9	4	62%
N.Washington	66	-3.2%	90	46	748	16.3	5.3	4	51%
K.Britt	-46	-23.7%	90	45	583	13.0	2.8	4	50%
D.Williams	32	-2.7%	45	30	324	10.8	2.5	0	67%
L.Hawkins*	-21	-35.1%	11	5	62	12.4	1.4	0	45%
M.Preston	5	2.2%	7	5	59	11.8	1.8	0	71%
K.Walter	78	2.3%	68	41	518	12.6	2.3	2	60%
J.Cook*	9	-3.7%	72	44	530	12.0	3.8	4	61%
C.Stevens	30	0.8%	33	23	278	12.1	5.7	1	70%
T.Thompson	-38	-53.3%	13	6	46	7.7	2.5	0	46%
D.Walker	32	-2.8%	39	21	345	16.4	2.7	3	54%
C.Johnson	-9	-17.6%	49	37	239	6.5	6.5	0	76%
D.Reynaud	-5	-24.0%	9	5	35	7.0	6.8	0	56%
Q.Johnson	-9	-30.6%	8	5	40	8.0	6.4	0	63%
S.Greene	-47	-41.4%	31	19	151	7.9	6.9	0	61%
J.Parmele	7	-1.7%	9	7	60	8.6	7.7	0	78%

Offensive Line

Player	Pos	Age	GS	Snaps	Pen	Sk	Pass	Run	Player	Pos	Age	GS	Snaps	Pen	Sk	Pass	Run
Fernando Velasco	C	28	16/16	997	4	0	5	3	Kevin Matthews	C	26	14/2	213	4	1	5.5	0
Michael Roos	LT	31	15/15	937	5	3	8.5	6	Kyle DeVan*	G/C	28	4/1	124	1	0	2	1
Steve Hutchinson*	LG	36	12/12	688	2	1.5	5.5	4	Byron Stingily	OT	25	5/2	114	0	0	1	1
David Stewart	RT	31	12/12	677	7	2	9	3	Robert Turner	C/G	29	16/16	1042	8	1	5	10
Deuce Lutui*	RG	30	8/8	501	4	3	10	6.5	Andy Levitre	LG	27	16/16	1007	5	1.5	1.5	7.5
Leroy Harris*	RG	29	8/8	434	2	5	9	2	Chris Spencer	G	31	10/5	345	1	2	6.5	3
Michael Otto	OT	30	6/3	267	1	2	4	2									

Year	Yards	ALY	Rk	Power	Rk	Stuff	Rk	2nd Lev	Rk	Open Field	Rk	Sacks	ASR	Rk	Short	Long	F-Start	Cont.
2010	4.36	3.47	31	46%	31	26%	31	1.20	12	1.25	4	27	5.6%	9	8	10	22	34
2011	3.78	3.39	32	72%	3	24%	29	1.03	31	0.81	18	24	4.2%	2	11	10	12	39
2012	4.21	3.35	31	67%	11	24%	28	1.13	18	1.19	3	39	7.1%	19	13	13	17	28
2012 ALY by direction:		Left End 3.13 (28)				Left Tackle 3.87 (21)				Mid/Guard 3.61 (26)				Right Tackle 3.49 (27)			Right End 0.37 (32)	

Survivor: Tennessee Titans Offensive Line concluded with left tackle Michael Roos the only man standing, though an appendectomy cost even him a game. He remained what he is, more or less, a left tackle who depends on preparation to compensate for a lack of elite athleticism and a consistent but never outstandingly effective run-blocker. While 8.5 blown blocks on pass plays may seem high, only Joe Thomas had fewer among left tackles who started at least 12 games. On the right side, David Stewart's broken leg should be healed by the time the regular season begins. The Titans' success running right has rarely matched his reputation as a mauler and he remains vulnerable to outside speed rushers, but he is still one of the league's better right tackles.

Steve Hutchinson played fairly well at times, but his advanced age was apparent from his lack of mobility, formerly an elite trait. 2012 was the third consecutive season he finished on injured reserve, and he retired rather than be released. Our charters registered his replacement Andy Levitre with just 1.5 blown blocks on pass plays, the fewest in the league by any regular starter at left guard. He has a tendency to lose leverage and get overwhelmed in the run game, though. The Titans' challenge will be to take advantage of his mobility and disguise his lack of power. Center Fernando Velasco will be involved in the latter effort, although he may be challenged for his job by fourth-round pick Brian Schwenke (California). Velasco played well enough after the loss of Eugene Amano in training camp but could have done more to help the guards. The combination of Leroy Harris and Deuce Lutui was as ineffective as any right guard in the league, though Lutui did liven things with at least one amusingly bad play per game. Just about anybody might be an upgrade, and first-round pick Chance Warmack is far from "just about anybody."

Defensive Front Seven

Defensive Line	Age	Pos	Snaps	Plays	TmPct	Rk	Stop	Dfts	BTkl	Runs	St%	Rk	RuYd	Rk	Sack	Hit	Hur	Tips
					Overall						vs. Run				Pass Rush			
Jurrell Casey	24	DT	780	54	6.1%	9	37	11	0	48	69%	56	2.7	53	3	4	4.5	0
Kamerion Wimbley	30	DE	910	30	3.4%	66	23	14	0	22	68%	59	3.4	68	6	4	14.5	0
Sen'Derrick Marks*	26	DT	678	43	5.6%	17	34	12	1	30	80%	22	1.5	15	1.5	4	4	4
Mike Martin	23	DT	428	37	4.2%	34	25	9	0	31	65%	64	2.8	57	3	4	8.5	0
Derrick Morgan	24	DE	914	64	7.3%	10	52	20	1	46	74%	42	2.6	45	6.5	17	28.5	4
Ropati Pitoitua	28	DE	494	50	6.8%	13	37	8	3	45	76%	35	2.7	52	2	2	0	1
Antonio Johnson*	29	DT	450	25	3.6%	48	19	3	3	23	78%	27	2.3	33	0	2	3	0
Sammie Lee Hill	27	DT	402	18	2.4%	--	15	4	2	14	86%	--	1.4	--	0	1	7	2

Linebackers	Age	Pos	Snaps	Plays	TmPct	Rk	Stop	Dfts	BTkl	Sack	Hit	Hur	Tips	Runs	St%	Rk	Yds	Rk	Tgts	Suc%	Rk	AdjYd	Rk	PD
					Overall					Pass Rush				vs. Run					vs. Pass					
Akeem Ayers	24	OLB	862	112	12.7%	45	65	16	9	6	5	8.5	2	63	71%	29	3.1	41	38	38%	67	7.9	64	7
Zach Brown	24	OLB	739	97	11.0%	59	60	19	2	5.5	3	4	0	51	71%	32	3.1	37	32	66%	4	5.5	19	6
Will Witherspoon*	33	OLB	388	47	6.1%	94	19	7	4	1	1	1	0	29	45%	110	3.9	84	21	22%	76	9.7	73	2
Colin McCarthy	25	MLB	385	39	10.1%	--	23	6	4	0	0	0	0	22	77%	--	4.1	--	13	35%	--	12.1	--	1
Tim Shaw	29	OLB	224	35	4.0%	--	15	2	1	0	0	0.5	0	25	56%	--	3.8	--	7	49%	--	7.6	--	0
Moise Fokou	28	MLB	379	40	5.0%	--	23	10	2	1	4	3.5	0	18	56%	--	3.1	--	18	49%	47	6.5	30	1

Year	Yards	ALY	Rk	Power	Rk	Stuff	Rk	2nd Level	Rk	Open Field	Rk	Sacks	ASR	Rk	Short	Long
2010	3.88	3.71	7	64%	18	22%	7	1.16	19	0.59	11	40	6.5%	13	22	11
2011	4.49	4.03	17	53%	6	22%	5	1.18	15	1.09	27	28	5.0%	31	13	12
2012	4.35	4.39	29	67%	24	20%	12	1.36	30	0.67	11	39	6.5%	13	16	9
2012 ALY by direction:		Left End 4.29 (22)				Left Tackle 4.67 (29)				Mid/Guard 4.5 (31)				Right Tackle 4.34 (26)		Right End 3.69 (13)

If there was a good play made by a Titans defensive lineman, chances were very good it came from either Derrick Morgan or Jurrell Casey. Morgan combined his normal stoutness against the run with much improved pass-rushing technique. Now he needs to show his disproportionate hurries-to-sacks ratio is not a result of a lack of quickness and closing burst. Casey showed a knack as an interior penetrator, though he was rarely the one who finished the plays he created.

The most consistent problem for the Titans on defense was the run defense when they were in their nickel package. (Tennessee ranked 30th with 9.3% run DVOA allowed when opponents had three or more wideouts on the field.) Teams would intentionally spread the Titans out and run right at them, often with a power back, and had success doing so. Kamerion Wimbley came with a hefty price tag in the offseason, but was too often overwhelmed against the run game in his first season as a full-time defensive end. Nor did he provide the pressure he did in Oakland as a hybrid player. The Titans are hoping better depth at defensive end, from fifth-round pick Lavar Edwards (LSU) and free-agent import Ropati Pitoitua (ex-Jets), can improve both his game and Morgan's. On the inside, the Titans added 340-pound Sammie Lee Hill to provide beef, but he needs to show he can maintain his effectiveness playing 50 snaps a game instead of the 25 he played for the Lions.

The Titans are hoping a high ankle sprain sustained in Week 1 was the main reason for Colin McCarthy's 2012 struggles. After a surprisingly effective rookie season, he alternated good plays as an attacking linebacker with getting blocked away from the play and getting beat in coverage by backs and tight ends. Both Akeem Ayers and Zach Brown combined flashes of talent with extreme inconsistency. Ayers is a prototype strongside linebacker who can defeat blocks and rush the passer, but struggles in space. Brown is a good complement, a prototype weakside player who struggles to defeat blocks but can chase all day and run with any non-wideout. Will Witherspoon was a sad example of what happens to space players when veteran savvy can no longer compensate for declining physical ability. Moise Fokou provides insurance against another McCarthy injury.

Defensive Secondary

Secondary	Age	Pos	Snaps	Plays	Overall TmPct	Rk	Stop	Dfts	BTkl	vs. Run Runs	St%	Rk	Yds	Rk	Tgts	Tgt%	Rk	vs. Pass Dist	Suc%	Rk	APaYd	Rk	PD	Int
Jason McCourty	26	CB	1125	106	12.0%	6	44	18	4	26	54%	23	5.7	30	91	20.6%	20	11.1	49%	57	7.8	51	16	4
Michael Griffin	28	FS	1114	83	9.4%	43	22	13	18	48	25%	62	9.3	60	21	4.8%	65	20.1	57%	29	9.0	59	4	4
Alterraun Verner	25	CB	1046	83	9.4%	24	36	18	10	26	50%	26	5.1	17	71	16.1%	56	10.7	53%	38	7.7	49	9	2
Jordan Babineaux*	31	SS	764	95	10.8%	31	37	14	7	47	40%	28	7.0	36	39	8.8%	17	9.4	56%	30	6.8	25	7	1
Ryan Mouton*	27	CB	386	45	6.3%	75	15	6	1	8	50%	26	6.4	43	40	11.0%	83	9.3	44%	76	7.3	38	2	0
Coty Sensabaugh	25	CB	310	28	3.2%	--	5	4	2	6	0%	--	9.8	--	30	6.8%	--	9.7	29%	--	9.7	--	2	0
Al Afalava	26	SS	234	16	2.4%	--	5	0	4	11	36%	--	5.7	--	6	1.8%	--	13.2	30%	--	10.1	--	1	1
Bernard Pollard	29	SS	895	103	14.4%	4	34	14	6	52	35%	44	5.6	13	24	6.7%	36	9.9	49%	53	7.3	36	3	1
George Wilson	32	SS	895	102	12.5%	15	34	9	4	64	34%	45	7.6	43	21	4.7%	66	13.9	70%	5	4.7	7	4	0

Year	Pass D Rank	vs. #1 WR	Rk	vs. #2 WR	Rk	vs. Other WR	Rk	vs. TE	Rk	vs. RB	Rk
2010	12	4.4%	19	-6.1%	9	-14.3%	8	3.2%	15	6.0%	19
2011	20	30.6%	29	-20.5%	3	-14.1%	14	29.6%	30	-6.2%	12
2012	19	24.3%	29	-13.5%	8	-5.4%	11	-5.5%	10	23.5%	30

If you like, you could see the 2012 Titans pass defense as an indictment of the (lack of) value of Cortland Finnegan. Despite losing the corner to a big money deal, the Titans posted a similar DVOA against the pass, with similar strengths (vs. No. 2 WR) and weaknesses (vs. No. 1 WR). On the other hand, handing Jason McCourty $40 million over five years did not prevent teams from throwing comebacks in front of him with regularity and success, and both he and Alterraun Verner posted worse charting numbers compared to 2011. The Titans also struggled to find an acceptable slot cornerback. Reggie Wayne and weakness in the run game sent Ryan Mouton to the bench at midseason, while even Chad Henne found success targeting Coty Sensabaugh, ill-matched in the slot due to lack of agility. The situation in 2013 is not clearly better. Verner, perhaps the best slot option, is not a fit for Gregg Williams' press schemes due to his lack of size and deep speed. Third-round pick Blidi Wreh-Wilson (Connecticut), like McCourty and Sensabaugh, is better suited as an outside corner due to questionable agility.

Like McCourty, Michael Griffin refuted the hypothesis that if you pay a player a lot of money, he'll become a better player. His 18 broken tackles led all safeties, giving statistical support to the sobriquet he's earned from Titans fans: Michael "Whiffin." He did show off ball skills in intercepting a couple passes. Yes, they were thrown by Mark Sanchez, but those still count, and he didn't do that off anybody the previous couple seasons. Jordan Babineaux was the kind of strong safety who was not very good in coverage and tackled neither well nor often; in other words, the sort of strong safety not long for the NFL. Bernard Pollard likely starts over George Wilson in his stead. He is definitely a hitter and is not a downgrade in coverage.

Special Teams

Year	DVOA	Rank	FG/XP	Rank	Net Kick	Rank	Kick Ret	Rank	Net Punt	Rank	Punt Ret	Rank	Hidden	Rank
2010	5.3%	6	9.0	3	-2.0	19	11.9	5	0.2	18	7.3	4	2.5	9
2011	6.3%	3	13.7	2	1.1	16	4.1	6	9.4	7	3.4	10	7.5	6
2012	-1.4%	19	-4.6	25	-9.1	29	2.3	10	-13.1	27	17.8	1	2.4	11

Rob Bironas proved he was human with the sort of inconsistent field-goal kicking season we had been waiting for his entire career. Previously a highly reliable distance kicker, he was below average from 40 yards and beyond. He also struggled with distance on kickoffs, at least until the Titans took the risk of having him kick more line drives. The Titans struggled enough covering regular kickoffs that they were willing to take the risk. The strategy worked out last year—Tennessee actually had above-average net kickoff value over the final nine weeks of the season—but in the long run tends to produce high-variance outcomes. In a make-or-break 2013, the Titans re-signed Bironas, hoping for a bounce-back season, rather than risk a kicking competition. Punter Brett Kern was about average when he got a punt off but remained more inconsistent than most punters, with the occasional shank among the boomers.

Darius Reynaud won the return job when Marc Mariani broke his leg in training camp. He was better than Mariani had been on punts and worse on kickoffs, leading the league with 18 kick returns that failed to make it back to the 20 yard line. If he can learn to accept more touchbacks, his superiority on punt returns makes him more valuable in today's NFL. That may decide this training camp's battle between the two return specialists for one roster spot.

Coaching Staff

Changes in the senior offensive and defensive assistants were accompanied by a shakeup in position coaches. Most of the changes brought familiar names, loud and energetic voices, or both. New quarterbacks coach Dave Ragone is a familiar name as the old wide receivers coach. New running backs coach Sylvester Croom seems loud and energetic. New linebackers coach Chet Parlavecchio is both, having served as special teams assistant last year and, more importantly, Mike Munchak's roommate at Penn State.

Munchak indicated this offseason he plans to spend more time with the offensive linemen, helping out position coach Bruce Matthews. It's perhaps a bit too easy to see this as a reflection on their playing careers, where Munchak was the consummate technician while Matthews was athletic enough not to need proper technique to play very effectively. The other key assistant is pass-rushing coach Keith Millard, who deserves credit for Morgan and Ayers' improvement in that regard.

Washington Redskins

2012 Record: 10-6	**Total DVOA:** 9.3% (9th)	**2013 Mean Projection:** 10.3 wins	**On the Clock (0-4):** 1%
Pythagorean Wins: 9.2 (12th)	**Offense:** 15.3% (6th)	**Postseason Odds:** 74.2%	**Mediocrity (5-7):** 8%
Snap-Weighted Age: 27.0 (15th)	**Defense:** 1.7% (17th)	**Super Bowl Odds:** 17.6%	**Playoff Contender (8-10):** 40%
Average Opponent: -0.7% (15th)	**Special Teams:** -4.3% (28th)	**Proj. Avg. Opponent:** -1.0% (23rd)	**Super Bowl Contender (11+):** 51%

2012: RG3 becomes the biggest Redskins icon since Gibbs, Riggo and the Hogs.

2013: This offense—and its quarterback—may have an expiration date. But it won't be 2013.

Safe to say, the Football Outsiders staff has been on the Washington Redskins' case regarding roster construction since FO was, itself, constructed. In *Pro Football Prospectus 2005*, Mike Tanier pointed out that "this franchise makes one bad decision after another, changing long-term strategies at the drop of a hat." In the 2006 *Prospectus*, Al Bogdan opined that "Washington treats its early draft picks like a few extra Euros an American discovers in his pocket before boarding his flight back home from Amsterdam." The 2007 *Prospectus* featured Aaron Schatz referring to a *Washington Post* series of articles that detailed "a season of infighting in the front office and on the field from a franchise that clearly had too many cooks stirring the pot." In 2008, Bill Barnwell recalled a near-trade with the Cincinnati Bengals that could have sent two first-round picks in exchange for Chad Johnson, and would have been an epic disaster even for this franchise.

In *Football Outsiders Almanac 2009*, yours humbly opined that "the Redskins' blueprint for success hasn't worked to date, and it's not one that's been effective through NFL history." (Book title concepts change more quickly and easily than do team dysfunctions, apparently). In 2010, Mr. Tanier was back in the saddle, calling owner Dan Snyder's team "the NFL's unrepentant junkies for over a decade." Tanier upped the ante in 2011, writing that "Snyder's management is a plague, and all the money in the world won't help the Redskins as long as he's making decisions." Last year, Mr. Schatz was back on the beat, re-re-re-re-re-reiterating that "the Redskins are going to have to figure out how to mine more talent with their lower-round picks, find diamonds in the rough among undrafted free agents, and stop paying for overrated players in free agency."

2012 was the season in which it all *finally* changed, because for the first time in the Snyder era, the Redskins actually did all of those things. Sixth-round rookie Alfred Morris finished second in the league in rushing yards behind only Adrian Peterson, as well as fifth in DYAR and eighth in DVOA. In his third season, undrafted tight end Logan Paulsen started ten games and finished fourth among tight ends in receiving DVOA. Several members of the Redskins' 2011 draft class also made significant contributions, especially outside linebacker Ryan Kerrigan.

The move to pay former Indianapolis Colts receiver Pierre Garcon to a five-year, $42.5 million contract with $20.5 million guaranteed smacked of old-school Redskins overcorrec-

tion, but for every one of those moves, there was another that made a lot of sense. After Mike Shanahan and general manager Bruce Allen traded their 2013 and 2014 first-round picks to the St. Louis Rams for the right to move up to the second overall slot and take Robert Griffin III, they went back to the well in the fourth round and picked up Michigan State quarterback Kirk Cousins, who proved to be efficient enough in spot duty when Griffin was hurt. For the first time in the Snyder era, the Redskins had the right plan, and they exploited it for all it was worth. And Griffin was the key, because he was exactly as valuable as the Redskins hoped he'd be.

Despite Washington's historically execrable judgment in such situations, the trade to acquire Griffin was less a Euro dump, and more a rare and worthy all-in push on a franchise-altering player. As was pointed out in last year's Redskins chapter, 17 different quarterbacks selected in the first 12 picks since 1993 have started at least eight games, and the average offensive DVOA improvement for those teams has been 6.5%. The Redskins far surpassed that average, climbing from -7.0% to 15.3% in overall offensive DVOA, and from -1.7% to 29.3% passing DVOA.

As good as Morris might be in a hypothetical vacuum, Griffin's effect on his teammates' rushing efficiency was similar to that which Cam Newton had on the Carolina Panthers in his rookie season. In 2012, Washington's rushing DVOA climbed from -5.0% to 16.3%. Washington's offensive line looked better than it was from a talent perspective (Trent Williams aside), because its zone-trained blockers aligned perfectly with Griffin's mesh-point, fake-heavy attack. Washington's play-action rate of 42 percent was the highest since our game charting project began in 2005. And not only did Washington use play action more often than any other team, they also were more successful than any other team, with the league's biggest difference in both yards per play (10.1 with play action, 5.5 without) and DVOA (66.7% with play action, 5.0% without).

There was no aspect of the Redskins' offense that Griffin did not affect in a monumentally positive sense. Griffin is not just another Velveeta spread-boosted quarterback better outside the pocket than in it—unlike Vince Young, Jake Locker, and (gasp) Tim Tebow, he is totally comfortable when asked to stand in the pocket, scan his reads, and fire the stick throw under pressure. His first regular-season touchdown pass, an 88-yarder to Garcon, was a 15-yard in-cut on which Griffin

2013 Redskins Schedule

Week	Opp.	Week	Opp.	Week	Opp.
1	PHI (Mon.)	7	CHI	13	NYG
2	at GB	8	at DEN	14	KC
3	DET	9	SD	15	at ATL
4	at OAK	10	at MIN (Thu.)	16	DAL
5	BYE	11	at PHI	17	at NYG
6	at DAL	12	SF (Mon.)		

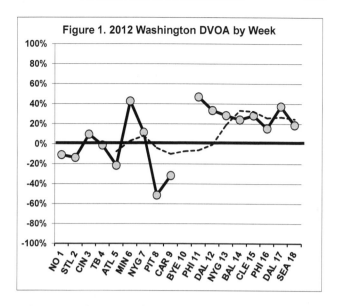

Figure 1. 2012 Washington DVOA by Week

sold boot action right to Morris, looked the defense off to his left, waited for Garcon to make his turn, and fired the ball with precision despite the fact that Saints safety Malcolm Jenkins was right in Griffin's face, preventing Griffin from even setting his feet before the throw. Garcon won a footrace downfield with cornerback Patrick Robinson, and the void created by Jenkins' blitz left it wide open—which Griffin clearly read on a dime. That was the indicator, and Griffin took it from there.

How comfortable is Griffin on traditional plays, taking a snap from center and scanning the field from the pocket? Believe it or not, Washington was most efficient going old school. When the quarterback was under center, Washington averaged 6.8 yards per play with 34.1% DVOA. From pistol, Washington averaged 6.4 yards per play with 21.7% DVOA. From shotgun, Washington averaged 5.7 yards per play with 7.5% DVOA. This is not a fluke; Griffin is a real-life, bona-fide pocket quarterback who just happens to have three extra gears on the ground. In fact, Griffin's 54.1% passing DVOA under center was the highest for any NFL quarterback in 2012 with more than 100 attempts.

Still, as great as Griffin was, he wasn't the true star of the Redskins offense. Mike and Kyle Shanahan were. After the Shanahans went full bore to acquire Griffin, they did the smartest thing they possibly could by welding the West Coast Offense/zone blocking/one-cut running style Mike Shanahan has used since the 1980s with specific shotgun and option ideas Griffin used at Baylor. In addition, they took the pistol formation concept to a new level in the NFL by using their tight ends in a dizzying array of sets, formations, motions, and blocking concepts. During the regular season, the Redskins used the pistol on 320 plays, over 100 plays more than every other team in the NFL combined. The scheme changes made by the Shanahans were just impressive as the changes that then-Denver Broncos offensive coordinator Mike McCoy

made to turn Tim Tebow into a quarterback-like substance in 2011. But since Griffin is about 10 levels up the food chain in an actual football sense, the results were that much more dynamic and transcendent.

It is worth noting that if we drop the minimum to 25 pass attempts, then the best DVOA under center last year belonged not to Griffin but to Cousins. Griffin's backup will get the majority of reps in training camp, and the Shanahans have already said that they'll put Cousins in more option packages. While he's more Matt Hasselbeck than anything close to Griffin, he can handle a minimized starting playbook when required.

Of course, the Redskins would rather not see Cousins on the field at all, but can Griffin play a full season without changing his style? Griffin's mobility leaves him open to injury risk, and that risk has obviously manifested itself in ways that should make the Redskins nervous[1]. He first hurt his right knee against the Baltimore Ravens on December 9, missed the following game against the Cleveland Browns, and then injured that same knee again in the wild-card playoff loss to the Seahawks. Dr. James Andrews repaired the lateral collateral and anterior cruciate ligaments in Griffin's knee on January 8, which was followed by a series of public disputes between Dr. Andrews and Mike Shanahan about whether Shanahan left Griffin in the game knowing full well that he was risking further injury. That little furor dissipated, but this is the same ACL that Griffin tore back at Baylor in 2009. Unless the Redskins intend to make Griffin a most-of-the-time pocket passer, the risks will continue, even and especially if Griffin

---

[1] Then again, what if Griffin isn't open to more injury risk than other quarterbacks? During the postseason, Omar Bashir and Chris Oates wrote an article for Slate.com suggesting that over the past 11 NFL seasons, mobile quarterbacks haven't actually suffered any more injuries than pocket quarterbacks (http://slate.me/XsL8XT). The problem with the study, however, is that a mobile quarterback in today's game plays differently than a mobile quarterback did just four or five years ago. Most of the mobile quarterbacks in the study were players such as Michael Vick and Vince Young whose runs were primarily scrambles when a pass play broke down. Current mobile quarterbacks such as Griffin and Colin Kaepernick are running much more often on planned options, a very different kind of play—and one which sometimes offers the possibility of being leveled by a deliberately unblocked defender. With this in mind, we believe a more accurate study to discern whether today's mobile quarterbacks have a higher level of injury risk would need to look at *college* quarterbacks over the past few years, not NFL quarterbacks. This would provide both a larger sample size and more examples of quarterbacks who put themselves in danger through option runs.

maintains the current timeline that will have him starting the team's regular-season opener in 2013.

According to Kyle Shanahan, there are no plans to change the system. "He stayed healthy last year running the zone read," Shanahan told the *Washington Post* in June. "So I feel pretty good about that. You really hope no one gets hurt. It's hard to control injuries. ... When you do the zone read, everyone [on the opposing defense] is accounted for. There's not many free hitters in it."

What we may be looking at here is a Michael Vick-style career arc, in which Griffin fails to log a full season of starts at any time in his career (Vick has done so just once, in 2006), but defines his offense when he's in there. The Redskins appear willing and able to make that trade-off, because the reward outweighs the risk. But if Griffin does miss serious time, the Shanahans may be forced—by their owner, by their own good sense, or by threats to their employment—to alter the paradigm. The good news is that Griffin, unlike Vick, has already proven able to operate in a more "conventional" style—although one could argue that in today's NFL, the option is the new convention.

So, for the first time in years—maybe since the salad days of John Riggins—the Redskins have a historically valuable and volatile asset around which they must build. In 2012, they did so with a group of receivers that failed to rank anywhere in the top 35 in DYAR. They did so with an offensive line that had a half-yard less in Adjusted Line Yards than the running backs had in yards per carry, which implies that the backs were doing the lion's share of the work. And they did so with a defense that ranked 14th in DVOA against the pass, and 22nd against the run. It's still possible for this franchise to put forth a sustained book of success even if Griffin misses more time or regresses, but some other folks will obviously have to step up.

In a positive sense, we can start with the front seven, which played well overall despite the Week 2 losses of outside linebacker Brian Orakpo and defensive end Adam Carriker. Nose tackle Barry Cofield had a career-best season, especially considering that he was taking on more than one blocker on most plays. He ranked first on the team in quarterback hits with 13, and second in quarterback hurries (behind Kerrigan) with 19. Kerrigan had a great second season, amassing 8.5 sacks and 27 hurries despite the fact that Orakpo's absence allowed opposing offenses to shift to his side. And inside linebacker London Fletcher proved once and for all that he has found a way to beat the hell out of the NFL's age curve. Fletcher's advanced metrics weren't what they had been in years past—he missed a team-high 11 tackles, and ranked 108th in the league in Stop Rate against the run. But he also led the Redskins with five interceptions, and his play-recognition skills often showed that he was the smartest guy on the field.

Of course, the downside to Fletcher's pass defense leadership is the fact that nobody in Washington's secondary presented a serious threat to it, or to many enemy receivers, for that matter. The Redskins re-signed starting cornerbacks DeAngelo Hall and Josh Wilson, but faced with a limited market in the 2013 offseason, Hall almost called it quits.

"I felt like I could do some things off the field that would have been just as lucrative as coming to play," Hall said in June, two months after agreeing to a one-year, $1.25 million contract with barely any guaranteed money. "So I really had to sit back and just examine the situation, see if I did feel like I could do it again. And I felt like I could. I felt like the coaches are going to do a good job of putting me in position to be successful, and that's all you can ask for."

Per our metrics, no other cornerback gave up more yards when targeted than Hall did, and for years he's been writing checks with his mouth that his butt can't cash. He was tasked with some safety roles in 2012, and the reads were an adjustment, but that sort of switch wasn't a problem for, say, Charles Woodson or Rod Woodson. Perhaps Hall should change his last name to "Woodson" and see if that helps. Wilson (not Woodson) was better than Hall, especially against No. 1 receivers, but the fact that Washington selected three defensive backs in the 2013 draft—cornerback David Amerson and safeties Phillip Thomas and Bacarri Rambo—wasn't a case of "best player available." If they are to take the proverbial next step, improvement in the secondary is a requirement.

This is the first of two seasons in which the Redskins will not have a first-round pick, and when you add the weird salary-cap penalties implemented by the league as a result of the team trying to dump a bunch of horribly-spent personnel dollars during the uncapped year of 2010, this is the second of two seasons in which the franchise will have to figure out how to keep that roster construction going when a total of $36 million in cap room is unavailable. That said, at least the team is on the right track; one can only imagine what horrific mistakes Vinny Cerrato would have made in these same circumstances.

Despite the question marks, we have the Redskins projected as NFC East favorites. Our forecast assumes that RG3 comes back at a reasonable level of health and durability. The defense is likely to improve a little bit with an infusion of new blood and the return of Orakpo. Given the instability around the rest of the NFC East, it's easy to see the ways in which Bruce Allen and the Shanahans will benefit from the more intelligent approach they've taken—even though it cost them some major draft collateral to get there.

The Redskins have reversed many of the trends that made them an unstable laughingstock for most of the past 15 years. They have a once-in-a-decade player at the game's most important position, and they've quietly filled in many other holes left by so much capricious thinking. That doesn't make them a paragon of franchise stability and forward motion, but the steps forward in such a short time should prove encouraging in the long term. At the very least, we can finally delete those "WTF" macros we've been using for every Redskins chapter since we started writing these books.

Doug Farrar

2012 Redskins Stats by Week

Wk	vs.	W-L	PF	PA	YDF	YDA	TO	Total	Off	Def	ST
1	at NO	W	40	32	459	358	3	-11%	16%	-4%	-30%
2	at STL	L	28	31	373	452	2	-14%	0%	3%	-11%
3	CIN	L	31	38	381	478	1	10%	41%	37%	6%
4	at TB	W	24	22	474	373	1	-1%	34%	4%	-31%
5	ATL	L	17	24	316	421	0	-22%	-14%	4%	-4%
6	MIN	W	38	26	361	421	2	43%	32%	-11%	-1%
7	at NYG	L	23	27	480	393	-2	12%	5%	-2%	4%
8	at PIT	L	12	27	255	355	0	-51%	-16%	34%	-2%
9	CAR	L	13	21	337	330	0	-32%	-7%	23%	-2%
10	BYE										
11	PHI	W	31	6	361	257	3	47%	-8%	-57%	-3%
12	at DAL	W	38	31	437	458	2	34%	25%	-8%	-70%
13	NYG	W	17	16	370	390	-1	29%	43%	18%	4%
14	BAL	W	31	20	423	359	1	24%	18%	5%	11%
15	at CLE	W	38	21	430	291	1	28%	10%	-17%	1%
16	at PHI	W	27	20	313	411	1	16%	26%	19%	8%
17	DAL	W	28	18	361	296	3	37%	39%	-19%	-20%
18	SEA	L	14	24	203	380	-1	19%	0%	-19%	-1%

Trends and Splits

	Offense	Rank	Defense	Rank
Total DVOA	15.3%	6	1.7%	17
Unadjusted VOA	19.9%	3	1.5%	18
Weighted Trend	16.1%	5	-2.0%	13
Variance	4.0%	5	5.2%	16
Average Opponent	2.5%	26	1.3%	11
Passing	29.1%	6	4.4%	14
Rushing	16.4%	2	-2.5%	22
First Down	19.6%	4	4.3%	22
Second Down	6.8%	13	2.2%	19
Third Down	19.5%	5	-4.2%	15
First Half	11.4%	9	4.9%	23
Second Half	18.7%	4	-1.6%	12
Red Zone	25.2%	5	-3.9%	12
Late and Close	26.7%	3	-11.0%	8

Five-Year Performance

Year	W-L	Pyth W	Est W	PF	PA	TO	Total	Rk	Off	Rk	Def	Rk	ST	Rk	Off AGL	Rk	Def AGL	Rk	Off Age	Rk	Def Age	Rk	ST Age	Rk
2008	8-8	7.0	9.1	265	296	0	9.1%	12	8.2%	10	-3.4%	10	-2.6%	25	12.6	7	42.5	29	29.6	1	28.1	5	27.9	1
2009	4-12	5.8	6.6	266	336	-11	-7.8%	22	-8.3%	21	-2.1%	12	-1.7%	23	55.0	31	20.2	11	28.0	7	28.0	3	27.7	1
2010	6-10	5.9	4.7	302	377	-4	-19.4%	28	-11.3%	25	5.8%	26	-2.3%	25	31.6	21	38.3	26	28.6	3	28.5	3	27.3	4
2011	5-11	5.7	6.3	288	367	-14	-7.0%	21	-7.0%	19	-1.2%	14	-1.2%	21	54.3	31	13.2	7	27.3	14	27.3	15	26.9	3
2012	10-6	9.2	9.8	436	388	+17	9.3%	9	15.3%	6	1.7%	17	-4.3%	28	34.8	20	48.8	26	26.1	26	27.8	5	27.1	3

2012 Performance Based on Most Common Personnel Groups

WAS Offense					WAS Offense vs. Opponents				WAS Defense				WAS Defense vs. Opponents			
Pers	Freq	Yds	DVOA	Run%	Pers	Freq	Yds	DVOA	Pers	Freq	Yds	DVOA	Pers	Freq	Yds	DVOA
11	46%	6.1	19.2%	29%	4-3-4	41%	6.5	26.7%	Nickel Even	42%	6.3	5.3%	11	52%	6.6	5.2%
21	22%	6.6	26.2%	68%	Nickel Even	37%	5.9	13.9%	3-4-4	42%	5.7	-9.2%	12	16%	4.9	-12.0%
12	20%	6.9	29.9%	60%	3-4-4	13%	6.3	14.3%	Nickel Odd	9%	7.2	24.8%	21	15%	6.3	-3.4%
22	7%	6.3	14.4%	70%	Dime+	4%	6.5	21.7%	4-3-4	3%	2.8	-35.4%	22	6%	3.6	-16.6%
02	2%	4.6	14.0%	12%	Nickel Odd	3%	7.4	22.9%	Dime+	1%	8.4	116.6%	10	3%	9.5	92.8%
01	2%	6.1	-55.9%	7%					Goal Line	1%	0.8	60.8%	20	2%	2.3	-74.2%

Strategic Tendencies

Run/Pass		Rk	Formation		Rk	Pass Rush		Rk	Secondary		Rk	Strategy		Rk
Runs, first half	48%	2	Form: Single Back	60%	24	Rush 3	6.1%	18	4 DB	45%	14	Play action	42%	1
Runs, first down	55%	5	Form: Empty Back	4%	23	Rush 4	56.9%	23	5 DB	52%	8	Avg Box (Off)	6.49	6
Runs, second-long	43%	4	Pers: 3+ WR	50%	18	Rush 5	29.2%	7	6+ DB	1%	30	Avg Box (Def)	6.44	9
Runs, power sit.	66%	9	Pers: 4+ WR	2%	14	Rush 6+	7.9%	11	CB by Sides	66%	25	Offensive Pace	31.96	28
Runs, behind 2H	34%	5	Pers: 2+ TE/6+ OL	30%	16	Sacks by LB	75.8%	3	DB Blitz	16%	6	Defensive Pace	30.05	15
Pass, ahead 2H	45%	20	Shotgun/Pistol	66%	3	Sacks by DB	12.9%	3	Hole in Zone	8%	19	Go for it on 4th	1.00	13

It will take more than one year to see if this is a consistent issue or just a one-year fluke, but the worst possible thing you could do last year was blitz Robert Griffin III. Griffin averaged 7.3 yards per play with three or four pass rushers, 9.0 yards per play with five pass rushers, and a mind-blowing 13.1 yards per play with six or more pass rushers. Those last two numbers were both league highs. Opponents apparently got the memo, because Griffin was blitzed on a league-low 20 percent of pass plays (15 percent with five rushers, 4.8 percent with six or more). ☻ Washington led the NFL with 17 percent of pass plays that qualified as "max protect," defined as having seven or more blockers with at least two more blockers than pass rushers. ☻ Washington is one of two teams that never used more than five offensive linemen, even at the goal line. ☻ Washington recovered 15 of 21 fumbles on offense. ☻ Washington opponents only threw 13 percent of passes to their No. 2 receivers, the lowest figure in the league. They balanced that by throwing 27 percent of passes to No. 1 receivers (fourth) and 25 percent of passes to tight ends (second).

Passing

Player	DYAR	DVOA	Plays	NtYds	Avg	YAC	C%	TD	Int
R.Griffin	727	16.6%	425	2961	7.0	5.6	66.6%	20	5
K.Cousins	59	6.4%	51	429	8.4	5.8	70.2%	4	3

Rushing

Player	DYAR	DVOA	Plays	Yds	Avg	TD	Fum	Suc
A.Morris	254	10.3%	335	1614	4.8	13	4	52%
R.Griffin	109	7.8%	110	816	7.4	7	7	-
E.Royster	32	23.6%	23	88	3.8	2	0	43%
D.Young	17	14.3%	14	60	4.3	0	0	57%
B.Banks*	22	27.2%	7	42	6.0	0	0	-

Receiving

Player	DYAR	DVOA	Plays	Ctch	Yds	Y/C	YAC	TD	C%
J.Morgan	17	-6.9%	74	48	510	10.6	4.9	2	65%
P.Garcon	131	8.2%	68	45	640	14.2	7.1	4	66%
S.Moss	98	11.6%	63	42	575	13.7	5.8	8	67%
L.Hankerson	129	11.6%	57	38	543	14.3	3.9	3	67%
A.Robinson	88	51.4%	19	11	237	21.5	5.6	3	58%
B.Banks*	-61	-91.0%	9	9	14	1.6	4.3	0	100%
D.Henderson	-65	-26.0%	47	22	316	14.4	3.6	1	47%
L.Paulsen	69	23.7%	36	25	308	12.3	4.4	1	69%
F.Davis	63	21.6%	32	24	325	13.5	5.5	0	75%
N.Paul	4	-3.9%	15	8	152	19.0	7.0	1	53%
E.Royster	-23	-34.2%	23	15	109	7.3	7.7	0	65%
A.Morris	-1	-14.6%	16	11	77	7.0	5.9	0	69%
D.Young	83	158.0%	9	8	109	13.6	9.6	2	89%
R.Helu	10	14.8%	7	7	45	6.4	6.7	0	100%

Offensive Line

Player	Pos	Age	GS	Snaps	Pen	Sk	Pass	Run	Player	Pos	Age	GS	Snaps	Pen	Sk	Pass	Run
Chris Chester	RG	30	16/16	1032	3	0	7	2	Trent Williams	LT	25	16/16	969	8	4	9.5	8
Will Montgomery	C	30	16/16	1026	2	0.5	3.5	2	Tyler Polumbus	RT	28	15/15	936	2	4.5	18.5	6
Kory Lichtensteiger	LG	28	16/16	1011	11	2	5.5	8	Jordan Black*	OT	33	14/0	106	1	2	5	1

Year	Yards	ALY	Rk	Power	Rk	Stuff	Rk	2nd Lev	Rk	Open Field	Rk	Sacks	ASR	Rk	Short	Long	F-Start	Cont.
2010	4.19	3.81	24	48%	30	25%	29	1.30	5	0.90	10	46	7.3%	22	18	14	22	22
2011	4.19	4.21	10	62%	17	20%	19	1.19	15	0.67	25	41	6.5%	16	13	15	11	23
2012	4.72	4.24	8	58%	24	16%	3	1.40	5	0.85	13	33	7.8%	23	9	18	26	43
2012 ALY by direction:			Left End 4.38 (9)			Left Tackle 3.95 (19)			Mid/Guard 4.31 (8)			Right Tackle 3.35 (28)				Right End 4.82 (10)		

As Redskins offensive line coach Chris Foerster told the *Washington Times* in June, 2012, "Continuity is great. Now, obviously, you want to be good." Very astute, coach. The Redskins did have the same starting five along its line for 15 of 16 regular season games in 2012, though it wasn't the front five Foerster may have wanted. Right tackle Jammal Brown suffered the most recent in a string of hip injuries in late July, and he was ruled out for the season in November after an extensive waiting game. That moved Tyler Polumbus from projected right guard to actual right tackle, where he was the weakest link in on the line.

Polumbus, who failed to catch on in Denver or Seattle, was even more overmatched than his numbers indicate, but the team didn't make any serious moves to replace him in the offseason—they brought in veterans Tony Pashos and Jeremy Trueblood to compete with Polumbus, which is roster spackle at best. (Brown is a free agent and will not return.) Left tackle Trent Williams, the only real "elite" talent on this line, had a lot to prove after missing the last four games of the 2011 season after failing multiple drug tests, and he responded with a quality season while playing through knee and thigh injuries. Washington's interior three didn't miss a regular-season start, and along with Lichtensteiger, center Will Montgomery and right guard Chris Chester took a new book of responsibilities in Mike and Kyle Shanahan's RG3-led offense and did their level best. Washington's 2012 line wasn't always dominant—far from it—but Foerster did a great job installing slide protections, and teaching his veterans to hit the second level with accuracy and authority. These things were doubly important when those same veterans were learning to block in training camp for read-option, zone-option, and pistol schemes they hadn't seen since their college days, if ever. As with Mike Shanahan's lines in Denver under Alex Gibbs, a clear focus on fundamentals allowed everyone but Williams to play over his head, and Williams was frequently dominant for long stretches of time in 2012. Only 50 percent of Washington sacks were blamed directly on blown blocks, the sixth best figure in the league.

When limited veterans are maximizing their abilities, there will obviously be worries about regression the following year. The Redskins didn't take any offensive linemen in this year's draft, but they do have some young depth thanks to players chosen a year ago. Third-round guard Josh LeRibeus (SMU) didn't see any action at all until November, when he made some time on special teams. However, LeRibeus replaced left guard Kory Lichtensteiger early in the wild-card loss to the Seahawks after Lichtensteiger sprained his ankle, and acquitted himself decently in that game. If there's an injury on the interior, LeRibeus is next man up; if the injury is to Montgomery, Chester would likely slide to center to make room.

Defensive Front Seven

Defensive Line	Age	Pos	Snaps	Plays	TmPct	Overall				vs. Run					Pass Rush			
						Rk	Stop	Dfts	BTkl	Runs	St%	Rk	RuYd	Rk	Sack	Hit	Hur	Tips
Stephen Bowen	29	DE	773	28	3.5%	65	25	6	1	18	89%	2	0.7	3	1	5	8.5	3
Barry Cofield	29	DT	716	41	5.1%	25	32	13	3	28	71%	48	2.2	30	2.5	13	19	2
Jarvis Jenkins	25	DE	541	25	3.1%	70	17	3	1	23	70%	54	2.0	16	0	3	6	0
Kedric Golston	30	DE	357	16	2.0%	--	10	5	0	14	57%	--	2.4	--	0	1	4	0
Chris Baker	26	DT	197	16	2.3%	--	13	1	0	15	80%	--	1.9	--	0	0	3	1
Darryl Tapp	29	DE	247	16	2.5%	--	13	3	1	12	92%	--	1.2	--	0.5	1	2.5	0

Linebackers	Age	Pos	Snaps	Plays	TmPct	Overall				Pass Rush				vs. Run					vs. Pass					
						Rk	Stop	Dfts	BTkl	Sack	Hit	Hur	Tips	Runs	St%	Rk	Yds	Rk	Tgts	Suc%	Rk	AdjYd	Rk	PD
Ryan Kerrigan	25	OLB	1061	62	7.7%	77	50	16	1	8.5	7	27	6	32	78%	12	2.2	16	16	55%	25	4.3	7	1
Perry Riley	25	ILB	1054	131	16.3%	15	72	16	5	3.5	1	5	1	73	63%	68	4.0	86	64	46%	54	6.6	31	3
London Fletcher	38	ILB	1005	150	18.6%	5	66	23	11	3	1	5	0	76	46%	108	4.7	106	67	49%	45	6.7	33	10
Rob Jackson	28	OLB	586	41	5.1%	105	35	20	6	4.5	1	1	3	23	87%	3	0.0	2	10	73%	--	2.7	--	5
Lorenzo Alexander*	30	OLB	294	25	3.1%	--	13	7	0	2.5	9	11	0	7	71%	--	4.4	--	9	37%	--	7.8	--	0

Year	Yards	ALY	Rk	Power	Rk	Stuff	Rk	2nd Level	Rk	Open Field	Rk	Sacks	ASR	Rk	Short	Long
2010	4.62	4.37	27	52%	4	17%	25	1.24	25	0.97	25	29	5.3%	29	8	14
2011	4.26	4.19	22	54%	7	18%	21	1.14	12	0.76	15	41	7.4%	8	14	18
2012	4.35	4.08	17	79%	31	17%	26	1.19	16	0.86	19	32	5.9%	25	9	11
2012 ALY by direction:	Left End 3.89 (14)			Left Tackle 3.33 (6)			Mid/Guard 4.14 (17)			Right Tackle 3.99 (16)			Right End 4.91 (26)			

Defensive coordinator Jim Haslett didn't see much of outside linebacker Brian Orakpo or defensive end Adam Carriker in 2012. Orakpo suffered a season-ending pectoral tear in Washington's Week 2 loss to the Rams, and Carriker was lost for the season with a torn quadriceps muscle in the same game. Rob Jackson was the main man in Orakpo's place, but one doesn't easily replace players of Orakpo's caliber, and it showed on the field and in the stat sheets—the Redskins suffered a precipitous drop in Adjusted Sack Rate with Orakpo out. 2011 second-round pick Jarvis Jenkins subbed for Carriker after missing his entire rookie season with a torn ACL, and though he didn't set the world afire, Jenkins started to pick it up late in the season. Orakpo has said that he wants 2013 to be the season in which he wins the Defensive Player of the Year award, and that's entirely possible as long as a) he's healthy and b) J.J. Watt is run over by a bus.

The good news for Washington's 2012 pass rush was the continued ascent of Ryan Kerrigan—Orakpo's ostensible bookend proved to be a very versatile player in his second NFL season. Kerrigan had a breakout season as the primary focus of every opposing offensive line. The secondary focus of every Redskins opposing offensive line might have been a bit less expected, but tackle Barry Cofield had his best NFL season to date, racking up outstanding pressure numbers at the nose in Washington's 5-2 fronts. Cofield has developed the ability to take on double teams with strength and power, but it's his knack for sifting through blocks that has allowed him to make more plays than the average bowling ball up the middle.

London Fletcher came into the NFL in 1998, the same year that Mike Shanahan won his second Super Bowl with John Elway. Fifteen years later, Fletcher has become Shanahan's veteran of primary importance, still playing at a high level at a position that generally spits its practitioners out much earlier. Fletcher has not missed a start since 2000, and not only has he now outlasted his more celebrated contemporary Ray Lewis, but his 2012 season may have been his best in some regards. His five interceptions led Washington's defense, and his two sacks of Tony Romo in the Redskins' Week 17 win over the Cowboys helped clinch the division title. Fletcher led the team with 11 broken tackles, but given how many tackles he makes, that number isn't too awful. Alongside Fletcher, third-year man Perry Riley proved to be an asset in his first season as a full-time starter. With Orakpo out, Haslett relied on his inside linebackers to bring more pressure up the middle. The numbers don't necessarily reflect it, but Fletcher and Riley were able to do so fairly consistently.

Defensive Secondary

Secondary	Age	Pos	Snaps	Plays	TmPct	Overall				vs. Run					vs. Pass									
						Rk	Stop	Dfts	BTkl	Runs	St%	Rk	Yds	Rk	Tgts	Tgt%	Rk	Dist	Suc%	Rk	APaYd	Rk	PD	Int
DeAngelo Hall	30	CB	1042	102	12.7%	2	44	19	7	26	65%	6	5.8	37	92	18.1%	40	11.9	46%	70	9.7	81	12	4
Josh Wilson	28	CB	1024	87	10.8%	13	34	18	5	20	25%	73	8.3	64	87	17.1%	48	12.2	57%	17	8.5	71	10	2
Madieu Williams*	32	FS	1022	103	12.8%	14	31	9	7	53	32%	50	8.1	53	29	5.6%	52	13.1	52%	44	9.1	62	6	1
DeJon Gomes	24	SS	385	36	4.8%	72	10	3	5	7	29%	56	5.1	10	24	5.0%	62	13.2	49%	52	9.6	69	4	1
Reed Doughty	31	SS	383	55	6.8%	61	19	6	4	37	43%	19	4.2	3	5	1.0%	75	6.6	21%	75	6.7	21	1	1
Cedric Griffin*	31	CB	350	38	8.4%	--	12	4	0	7	43%	--	3.9	--	32	11.9%	--	16.3	56%	--	6.9	--	4	0
Richard Crawford	23	CB	198	19	3.8%	--	6	5	2	4	0%	--	6.0	--	22	7.0%	--	13.2	58%	--	9.1	--	2	1
E.J. Biggers	26	CB	798	56	8.4%	48	24	9	3	11	45%	38	5.5	26	66	17.2%	47	15.0	54%	28	8.1	62	7	1

Year	Pass D Rank	vs. #1 WR	Rk	vs. #2 WR	Rk	vs. Other WR	Rk	vs. TE	Rk	vs. RB	Rk
2010	27	-5.6%	13	12.7%	24	21.7%	29	-9.7%	6	5.8%	17
2011	16	24.6%	25	-15.7%	9	-19.3%	10	23.7%	28	3.6%	20
2012	14	-3.1%	16	-3.3%	14	-17.5%	5	14.5%	27	-24.1%	4

Before the 2012 season, DeAngelo Hall estimated that the Redskins' plan to have him taking some reps at safety could lead to a Charles Woodson-style career rebirth in a more multiple role. And as it has generally been with Hall, the divide between fantasy and reality was severe. Hall led all NFL players with 869 passing yards allowed in coverage, and gave up the league's third-highest total of first downs and touchdowns with 41 (tied with Atlanta's Dunta Robinson and Baltimore's Cary Williams). To be fair, Hall was thrown into different situations in 2012, and not always to his benefit. Injuries to other players had him playing some deep safety, and the looks required from that position are often very different than what Hall was used to. Hall had to read more and freelance less in those instances, and his value to the back four was at times higher than what the stats might indicate. Still, Hall is far from the ideal Woodson-style hybrid defensive back. He struggles with more advanced coverage concepts, and he has historically lucked into many of his turnovers. Example: Hall's Week 12 pick of Eagles quarterback Nick Foles was a ball that was thrown to tight end Brent Celek up the seam, the great coverage was London Fletcher's, and Hall was there for the tip drill. On the plus side, Hall's coverage of Dez Bryant in Week 17 helped the Redskins wrap up the NFC East title. Hall signed a one-year, $1.25 million contract to stay in D.C., but with only $250,000 of that guaranteed, the reunion could be short lived. Hall may be a decent box safety and slot cornerback—he tackles pretty well (with his coverage skills, he's had a lot of practice), and a more forward role would offset his tendency to get torched deep.

So, you may ask, if Hall was playing under par, why did the Redskins rank 14th in the league in DVOA against No. 1 receivers? That was more about the efforts of Josh Wilson, currently the team's best cornerback (though we're talking about a low bar, to be sure). For the second straight season, Wilson was far better against premier targets than Hall—he gave up 9.0 Adjusted Yards per Pass and had a 53 percent Success Rate, as opposed to Hall's 11.6 AdjYd and 38 percent Success Rate. Wilson was also far better against No. 3 and 4 receivers, but Hall spent more time in the slot than any other Redskins defender in 2012. Like Hall, Wilson signed a one-year deal in the 2013 offseason, but his was for $3.3 million, and $1.3 million guaranteed. The Redskins selected North Carolina State's David Amerson in the second round, and Amerson may very well start outside alongside Wilson. Amerson had a solid season for North Carolina State in 2012, though he was primarily known for getting torched by Cordarrelle Patterson in the season opener against Tennessee, and it took him a while to get over that. He's a taller (6-foot-1) defender who sometimes struggles with double moves and boundary speed. If it takes Amerson some time to get acclimated, there's always E.J. Biggers (ex-Tampa Bay), who signed a one-year deal with the Redskins and could be a relative bargain in a spot role.

The Redskins' brain trust also selected two safeties in the draft—Fresno State's Phillip Thomas in the fourth round, and Georgia's Bacarri Rambo in the sixth. Thomas led the nation with eight interceptions in 2012, and he could easily fill the free safety slot formerly held by Madieu Williams. The Redskins signed Brandon Meriwether to a two-year contract in March of 2012, but knee injuries prevented him from playing in all but one game last season. The coaches like Meriweather's coverage and blitzing abilities, but he has no firm recovery timetable. Things are no more locked down at the strong safety position, where Rambo would seem to have as much of a shot as anyone. The overall coolness of Rambo's name? Well, that's a bit of a conceit—he changed it from Bacarri Fudge. "When people see the name 'Rambo' on the back of my jersey, they expect me to be a hard-nosed killer with a scarf around my head and paint under my eyes," he told the Associated Press in 2010. "If I was playing in the secondary and named Fudge, everybody would say I was soft. I went from being soft to being hard." The Redskins can only hope it remains so.

Special Teams

Year	DVOA	Rank	FG/XP	Rank	Net Kick	Rank	Kick Ret	Rank	Net Punt	Rank	Punt Ret	Rank	Hidden	Rank
2010	-2.3%	25	-16.6	32	17.0	1	6.9	9	-22.1	31	3.4	11	4.3	7
2011	-1.2%	21	-7.6	30	4.0	9	-5.1	27	8.8	8	-6.2	23	2.0	13
2012	-4.3%	28	1.2	14	0.6	15	-3.6	22	-13.8	29	-5.9	27	-9.0	28

Kai Forbath was yet another star in the Year of the Rookie Kicker. He didn't gain the same notoriety as Minnesota's Blair Walsh and St. Louis' Greg "The Leg" Zuerlein, but he did successfully convert his first 17 professional field-goal tries, which was good for an NFL record. Forbath wasn't making just junk-ball attempts, either—12 of those field goals came from 40 yards or more. Don't be fooled by the season total in the table above, which is dragged down by five weeks of Billy Cundiff; Forbath was worth 8.7 points above average on field goals. He was below average on kickoffs, however, just one reason why the Redskins came out among the league's worst special teams units. Other issues included punter Sav Rocca, who ranked 29th in net average and had two punts blocked, and the overall return units. Brandon Banks is gone after a poor year on both punt and kickoff returns. Expect Richard Crawford, who set up Forbath's overtime winner against the Ravens with a 64-yard punt return, to get more reps with Banks out of the picture. Niles Paul should see a similar uptick on kick returns. Linebacker Lorenzo Alexander led the NFL in special teams tackles in 2012 and brought some quarterback pressure in Orakpo's place, but he signed with the Cardinals in the offseason, with a possible every-down role as incentive.

Coaching Staff

As detailed earlier in this chapter Mike and Kyle Shanahan did an incredible job of adapting to a new quarterback and a decidedly new offense. But the head guys weren't the only ones impressing. Offensive line coach Chris Foerster took a group of physically limited blockers (Trent Williams aside) and coached them up in ways that brought to mind the work Alex Gibbs did with Mike Shanahan's Broncos back in the day. Running backs coach Bobby Turner has been a part of Shanahan's staffs since those Broncos days.

Jim Haslett finally had the right kind of personnel for his 3-4 switch, and having Orakpo and Carriker back will help the front seven a lot in 2013. Haslett deserves praise for filling Orakpo's and Kerrigan's roles with lesser players in effective ways. In particular, his directive to his outside linebackers to drop into coverage in specific situations led to the Redskins ranking fourth in the NFL in DVOA against running backs catching passes out of the backfield. The man with the most to deal with is defensive backs coach Raheem Morris, whose perpetually optimistic outlook will be tested by a secondary in which question marks abound, and sure things are few and far between.

Quarterbacks

On the following pages, we provide the last three years' statistics for the top two quarterbacks on each team's depth chart, as well as a number of other quarterbacks who played significant time in 2012.

Each quarterback gets a projection from our KUBIAK fantasy football projection system, based on a complicated regression analysis that takes into account numerous variables including projected role, performance over the past two years, performance on third down vs. all downs, experience of the projected offensive line, historical comparables, collegiate stats, height, age, and strength of schedule.

It is difficult to accurately project statistics for a 162-game baseball season, but it is exponentially more difficult to accurately project statistics for a 16-game football season because of the small size of the data samples involved. With that in mind, we ask that you consider the listed projections not as a prediction of exact numbers, but the mean of a range of possible performances. What's important is not so much the exact number of yards and touchdowns we project, but whether or not we're projecting a given player to improve or decline. Along those same lines, rookie projections will not be as accurate as veteran projections due to lack of data.

Our quarterback projections look a bit different than our projections for the other skill positions. At running back and wide receiver, second-stringers see plenty of action, but, at quarterback, either a player starts or he does not start. We recognize that, when a starting quarterback gets injured in Week 8, you don't want to grab your *Football Outsiders Almanac* to find out if his backup is any good only to find that we've projected that the guy will throw 12 passes this year. Therefore, each year we project all quarterbacks to start all 16 games. If Tom Brady goes down in November, you can look up Ryan Mallett, divide the stats by 16, and get an idea of what we think he will do in an average week. There are full-season projections for the top two quarterbacks on all 32 depth charts.

The first line of each quarterback table contains biographical data—the player's name, height, weight, college, draft position, birth date, and age. Height and weight are the best data we could find; weight, of course, can fluctuate during the offseason. **Age** is very simple: the number of years between the player's birth year and 2013, but birthdate is provided if you want to figure out exact age.

Draft position gives draft year and round, with the overall pick number with which the player was taken in parentheses. In the sample table, it says that Matt Ryan was chosen in the first round of the 2008 NFL Draft, with the third overall pick. Undrafted free agents are listed as "FA" with the year they came into the league, even if they were only in training camp or on a practice squad.

To the far right of the first line is the player's Risk variable for fantasy football in 2013, which measures the likelihood of the player hitting his projection. The default rating for each player is Green. As the risk of a player failing to hit his projection rises, he's given a rating of Yellow or, in the worst cases, Red. The Risk variable is not only based on injury probability, but how a player's projection compares to his recent performance as well as our confidence (or lack thereof) in his offensive teammates. A few players with the strongest chances of surpassing their projections are given a Blue rating. Most players marked Blue will be backups with low projections, but a handful are starters or situational players who can be considered slightly better breakout candidates.

Next, we give the last three years of player stats. The majority of these statistics are passing numbers, although the final five columns on the right are the quarterback's rushing statistics.

The first few columns after the year and team the player played for are standard numbers: games and games started (**G/GS**), offensive **Snaps**, pass attempts (**Att**), pass completions (**Cmp**), completion percentage (**C%**), passing yards (**Yds**), passing touchdowns (**TD**). These numbers are official NFL totals and therefore include plays we leave out of our own metrics, such as clock-stopping spikes, and omit plays we include in our metrics, such as sacks and aborted snaps. Note that the games total includes all games the player appeared in, not just games started, which is why a backup quarterback who holds on field goals will often be listed with 16 games played. (Other differences between official stats and Football Outsiders stats are described in the "Statistical Toolbox" introduction at the front of the book.)

The column for interceptions contains two numbers, representing the official NFL total for interceptions (**Int**) as well as our own metric for adjusted interceptions (**Adj**). For example, if you look at our sample table, Matt Ryan had 14 interceptions and 16 adjusted interceptions in 2012. Adjusted interceptions use game charting data to add dropped interceptions, plays where a defender most likely would have had an interception

Matt Ryan			Height: 6-4		Weight: 228		College: Boston College		Draft: 2008/1 (3)			Born: 17-May-1985	Age: 28			Risk: Green	
Year	Team	G/GS	Snaps	Att	Comp	C%	Yds	TD	INT/Adj	FUM	ASR	NY/P	Rk	DVOA	Rk	DYAR	Rk	YAR	Runs	Yds	TD	DVOA	DYAR
2010	ATL	16/16	1139	571	357	62.5%	3705	28	9/16	4	4.1%	6.0	29	18.0%	7	1122	5	1080	46	122	0	-11.0%	6
2011	ATL	16/16	1062	566	347	61.3%	4177	29	12/11	5	5.3%	6.8	12	18.8%	7	1120	6	1204	37	84	2	19.8%	38
2012	ATL	16/16	1048	615	422	68.6%	4719	32	14/16	4	5.1%	7.0	4	16.5%	8	1196	5	1315	34	141	1	39.7%	54
2013	ATL			601	383	63.7%	4453	30	16	4		6.7		17.7%					34	24	1	-19.1%	

	2012:	51% Short		33% Mid		11% Deep	6% Bomb		YAC: 4.9 (20)		2011:	45% Short	35% Mid		14% Deep		6% Bomb	YAC: 5 (29)

but couldn't hold onto the ball. Then we remove Hail Mary passes and interceptions thrown on fourth down when losing in the final two minutes of the game. We also remove "tipped interceptions," when a perfectly catchable ball deflected off the receiver's hands or chest and into the arms of a defender.

Overall, adjusted interception rate is higher than standard interception rate, so most quarterbacks will have more adjusted interceptions than standard interceptions. On average, a quarterback will have one additional adjusted interception for every 120 pass attempts. Once this difference is accounted for, adjusted interceptions are a better predictor of next year's interception total than standard interceptions.

The next column is fumbles (**FUM**), which adds together all fumbles by this player, whether turned over to the defense or recovered by the offense (explained in the essay "Pregame Show"). Even though this fumble total is listed among the passing numbers, it includes all fumbles, including those on sacks, aborted snaps, and rushing attempts. By listing fumbles and interceptions next to one another we hope to give a general idea of how many total turnovers the player was responsible for.

Next comes Adjusted Sack Rate (**ASR**). This is the same statistic you'll find in the team chapters, only here it is specific to the individual quarterback. It represents sacks per pass play (total pass plays = pass attempts + sacks) adjusted based on down, distance, and strength of schedule. For reference, the NFL average was 6.5 percent in both 2010 and 2012, and 6.7 percent in 2011.

The next two columns are Net Yards per Pass (**NY/P**), a standard stat but a particularly good one, and the player's rank (**Rk**) in Net Yards per Pass for that season. Net Yards per Pass consists of passing yards minus yards lost on sacks, divided by total pass plays.

The five columns remaining in passing stats give our advanced metrics: **DVOA** (Defense-Adjusted Value Over Average), **DYAR** (Defense-Adjusted Yards Above Replacement), and **YAR** (Yards Above Replacement), along with the player's rank in both DVOA and DYAR. These metrics compare each quarterback's passing performance to league-average or replacement-level baselines based on the game situations that quarterback faced. DVOA and DYAR are also adjusted based on the opposing defense. The methods used to compute these numbers are described in detail in the "Statistical Toolbox" introduction at the front of the book. The important distinctions between them are:

• DVOA is a rate statistic, while DYAR is a cumulative statistic. Thus, a higher DVOA means more value per pass play, while a higher DYAR means more aggregate value over the entire season.
• Because DYAR is defense-adjusted and YAR is not, a player whose DYAR is higher than his YAR faced a harder-than-average schedule. A player whose DYAR is lower than his YAR faced an easier-than-average schedule.

To qualify for a ranking in Net Yards per Pass, passing DVOA, and passing DYAR in a given season, a quarterback must have had 100 pass plays in that season. There are 39 quarterbacks ranked for both 2012, 47 quarterbacks ranked for 2011, and 46 quarterbacks ranked for 2010.

The final five columns contain rushing statistics, starting with **Runs**, rushing yards (**Yds**), and rushing touchdowns (**TD**). Once again, these are official NFL totals and include kneeldowns, which means you get to enjoy statistics such as Matt Schaub rushing 21 times for minus-9 yards. The final two columns give **DYAR** and **DVOA** for quarterback rushing, which are calculated separately from passing. Rankings for these statistics, as well as numbers that are not adjusted for defense (YAR and VOA) can be found on our website, FootballOutsiders.com.

The last number listed is the Total QBR metric from ESPN Stats & Information. Total QBR is based on the expected points added by the quarterback on each play, then adjusts the numbers to a scale of 0-100. There are five main differences between Total QBR and DVOA:

• Total QBR incorporates information from game charting, such as passes dropped or thrown away on purpose.
• Total QBR splits responsibility on plays between the quarterback, his receivers, and his blockers. Drops, for example, are more on the receiver, as are yards after the catch, and some sacks are more on the offensive line than others.
• Total QBR has a clutch factor which adds (or subtracts) value for quarterbacks who perform best (or worst) in high-leverage situations.
• Total QBR combines passing and rushing value into one number and differentiates between scrambles and planned runs.
• Total QBR is not adjusted for strength of opponent.

The italicized row of statistics for the 2013 season is our 2013 KUBIAK projection, as detailed above. Again, in the interest of producing meaningful statistics, all quarterbacks are projected to start a full 16-game season, regardless of the likelihood of them actually doing so.

The final line below the KUBIAK projection represents data from the Football Outsiders game charting project. First, we break down charted passes based on distance: **Short** (5 yards or less), **Mid** (6-to-15 yards), **Deep** (16-to-25 yards), and **Bomb** (26 or more yards). These numbers are based on distance in the air only and include both complete and incomplete passes. Passes thrown away or tipped at the line are not included, nor are passes on which the quarterback's arm was hit by a defender while in motion. We also give average yards after catch (**YAC**) with the Rank in parentheses for the 39 quarterbacks who qualify.

A number of third- and fourth-string quarterbacks are briefly discussed at the end of the chapter in a section we call "Going Deep."

Top 20 QB by Passing DYAR (Total Value), 2012

Rank	Player	Team	DYAR
1	Tom Brady	NE	2,035
2	Peyton Manning	DEN	1,805
3	Drew Brees	NO	1,441
4	Aaron Rodgers	GB	1,395
5	Matt Ryan	ATL	1,196
6	Matthew Stafford	DET	1,160
7	Tony Romo	DAL	1,156
8	Russell Wilson	SEA	872
9	Ben Roethlisberger	PIT	761
10	Eli Manning	NYG	753
11	Robert Griffin	WAS	727
12	Matt Schaub	HOU	697
13	Colin Kaepernick	SF	555
14	Cam Newton	CAR	422
15	Alex Smith	SF	418
16	Sam Bradford	STL	388
17	Joe Flacco	BAL	358
18	Carson Palmer	OAK	340
19	Andrew Luck	IND	257
20	Andy Dalton	CIN	194

Minimum 100 passes.

Top 20 QB by Passing DVOA (Value per Pass), 2012

Rank	Player	Team	DVOA
1	Tom Brady	NE	35.1%
2	Peyton Manning	DEN	32.8%
3	Colin Kaepernick	SF	25.8%
4	Aaron Rodgers	GB	23.4%
5	Drew Brees	NO	19.8%
6	Russell Wilson	SEA	19.7%
7	Robert Griffin	WAS	16.6%
8	Matt Ryan	ATL	16.5%
9	Alex Smith	SF	14.8%
10	Tony Romo	DAL	14.8%
11	Ben Roethlisberger	PIT	13.2%
12	Matthew Stafford	DET	12.2%
13	Eli Manning	NYG	9.0%
14	Matt Schaub	HOU	7.5%
15	Cam Newton	CAR	2.0%
16	Sam Bradford	STL	-0.8%
17	Joe Flacco	BAL	-1.3%
18	Carson Palmer	OAK	-2.2%
19	Andrew Luck	IND	-5.1%
20	Andy Dalton	CIN	-5.9%

Minimum 100 passes.

Derek Anderson   Height: 6-6   Weight: 229   College: Oregon State   Draft: 2005/6 (213)   Born: 15-Jun-1983   Age: 30   Risk: Red

Year	Team	G/GS	Snaps	Att	Comp	C%	Yds	TD	INT/Adj	FUM	ASR	NY/P	Rk	DVOA	Rk	DYAR	Rk	YAR	Runs	Yds	TD	DVOA	DYAR	QBR
2010	ARI	12/9	534	327	169	51.7%	2065	7	10/16	5	7.0%	5.4	37	-25.4%	40	-308	41	-245	5	25	0	-9.8%	1	35.7
2011	CAR	2/0	11	0	0	0.0%	0	0	0/0	0	--	--	--	--	--	--	--	--	2	-2	0	--	--	--
2012	CAR	2/0	9	4	4	100.0%	58	0	0/0	0	1.4%	14.5	--	132.9%	--	47	--	48	0	0	0	--	--	91.6
2013	CAR			520	290	55.8%	3498	18	17	7		5.7		-9.6%					20	29	0	-9.2%		

| | 2012: | 44% Short | | 37% Mid | | 13% Deep | 6% Bomb | | YAC: 5.7 (4) | | | | | | | | | | | | | | | |

The fact that we are still writing player comments for Derek Anderson in 2013 is definitive proof that there are more openings for quarterbacks in the NFL than there are quality candidates available. He hasn't had a good year since 2007, and even in that good year he nearly led the league in interceptions. Now, that said, the one good thing about Anderson is his deep ball. He's among the top ten active QBs in yards per completion. No. 1 on that list is Cam Newton, which means that if the Panthers do lose their starter, they won't need to make drastic changes to their offense. Well, not their passing offense, at least.

Matt Barkley   Height: 6-2   Weight: 230   College: USC   Draft: 2013/4 (98)   Born: 8-Sep-1990   Age: 23   Risk: Yellow

Year	Team	G/GS	Snaps	Att	Comp	C%	Yds	TD	INT/Adj	FUM	ASR	NY/P	Rk	DVOA	Rk	DYAR	Rk	YAR	Runs	Yds	TD	DVOA	DYAR	QBR
2013	PHI			586	353	60.4%	4021	20	19	8		5.9		-6.8%					38	75	2	-6.4%		35.7

In 2011, Barkley set a Southern California and Pac-12 conference record with 39 touchdown passes, and his 2012 season wasn't as bad as advertised. In fact, he increased his yards per attempt average from 7.9 as a junior to 8.5 as a senior. Barkley may seem like a strange fit for Chip Kelly in Philadelphia, but the former Oregon coach saw first-hand how effective Barkley can be: in Barkley's last two games against the Ducks, he threw for 807 yards and nine touchdowns. There's little reason to rush Barkley onto the field in 2013, but he has as good of a chance as anyone else to be the team's quarterback of the future.

Charlie Batch   Height: 6-2   Weight: 220   College: Eastern Michigan   Draft: 1998/2 (60)   Born: 5-Dec-1974   Age: 39   Risk: N/A

Year	Team	G/GS	Snaps	Att	Comp	C%	Yds	TD	INT/Adj	FUM	ASR	NY/P	Rk	DVOA	Rk	DYAR	Rk	YAR	Runs	Yds	TD	DVOA	DYAR	QBR
2010	PIT	3/2	143	49	29	59.2%	352	3	3/4	1	8.2%	6.2	--	-23.9%	--	-43	--	-62	7	30	0	34.4%	9	54.8
2011	PIT	4/1	72	24	15	62.5%	208	0	1/1	0	7.0%	7.6	--	-11.1%	--	0	--	2	3	-2	0	--	--	26.1
2012	PIT	3/2	129	70	45	64.3%	475	1	4/4	1	4.3%	6.3	--	-13.0%	--	-8	--	-14	0	0	0	--	--	34.8

| | 2012: | 52% Short | | 23% Mid | | 12% Deep | 14% Bomb | | YAC: 5.8 (--) | 2011: | 54% Short | 29% Mid | | 13% Deep | 4% Bomb | YAC: 6.1 (--) | | | | | | | |

Batch's three-interception effort against the Browns was not as bad as it looked, and his effort in a win over the Ravens (25-of-36, 276 yards, a touchdown and a pick) was not as good as it looked. That said, the Steelers used a crisis management game plan when he was on the field. Batch was 6-3 as a starter in over a decade with the Steelers. It was a fine run.

Sam Bradford

Height: 6-4 Weight: 236 College: Oklahoma Draft: 2010/1 (1) Born: 8-Nov-1987 Age: 26 Risk: Yellow

Year	Team	G/GS	Snaps	Att	Comp	C%	Yds	TD	INT/Adj	FUM	ASR	NY/P	Rk	DVOA	Rk	DYAR	Rk	YAR	Runs	Yds	TD	DVOA	DYAR	QBR
2010	STL	16/16	1094	590	354	60.0%	3512	18	15/17	7	5.6%	5.3	40	-15.6%	34	-186	39	-5	27	63	1	-6.0%	4	41.5
2011	STL	10/10	670	357	191	53.5%	2164	6	6/12	8	9.1%	4.9	41	-24.0%	38	-325	42	-374	18	26	0	-58.6%	-25	28.6
2012	STL	16/16	1034	551	328	59.5%	3702	21	13/12	7	6.3%	6.0	22	-0.8%	16	388	16	245	37	127	1	29.6%	42	51.6
2013	STL			547	335	61.3%	3696	22	13	8		5.9		-11.8%					49	90	1	-17.0%		

2012: 51% Short 32% Mid 9% Deep 8% Bomb YAC: 4.7 (29) 2011: 43% Short 37% Mid 13% Deep 7% Bomb YAC: 4.5 (38)

Three years into his NFL career, Sam Bradford has been pretty good at avoiding interceptions, and pretty bad at everything else. Recent quarterbacks who fit that description include Jason Campbell, Byron Leftwich, and Charlie Batch, which suggests that Bradford is a black quarterback who will settle into a long but undistinguished career as a backup. Going back to the '80s and '90s, however, we find other low-interception guys like John Friesz, Chris Miller, Neil Lomax, and Steve Young, a group that raises Bradford's ceiling, lowers his floor, and brings up the possibility that he may be white. It's all very confusing.

Bradford is also on the list of quarterbacks who played below replacement level in each of their first two seasons, usually an omen of a doomed career. Is his radical improvement in 2012 a sign that he has turned the corner? Only three quarterbacks who started their career in the negative DYAR range played better in their third qualifying seasons than Bradford did last year: Jeff George in 1992, Erik Kramer in 1993, and Trent Dilfer in 1997. George and Kramer would go on to become basically average passers over the rest of their careers (albeit with some dramatic ups and downs), while Dilfer would never have a season that good again. Bradford was able to keep his head above water last season, but he'll need to make serious headway this fall to truly live up to his status as a number-one overall pick.

Tom Brady

Height: 6-4 Weight: 225 College: Michigan Draft: 2000/6 (199) Born: 3-Aug-1977 Age: 36 Risk: Yellow

Year	Team	G/GS	Snaps	Att	Comp	C%	Yds	TD	INT/Adj	FUM	ASR	NY/P	Rk	DVOA	Rk	DYAR	Rk	YAR	Runs	Yds	TD	DVOA	DYAR	QBR
2010	NE	16/16	967	492	324	65.9%	3900	36	4/8	2	5.0%	7.2	3	46.7%	1	1909	1	1771	31	30	1	-12.4%	0	76.9
2011	NE	16/16	1122	611	401	65.6%	5235	39	12/15	6	5.4%	7.9	2	35.3%	3	1994	3	1956	43	109	3	10.9%	57	72.7
2012	NE	16/16	1213	637	401	63.0%	4827	34	8/10	6	4.6%	7.0	5	35.1%	1	2035	1	1910	23	32	4	40.3%	56	77.1
2013	NE			607	393	64.8%	4776	32	11	6		7.2		23.0%					29	22	1	-12.6%		

2012: 41% Short 39% Mid 13% Deep 6% Bomb YAC: 5.5 (7) 2011: 48% Short 36% Mid 12% Deep 5% Bomb YAC: 6.4 (3)

Subjectively, it seems like Brady in the last couple years has started to struggle with stretches of inaccuracy, and that he's taking more hits than in past seasons. Our stats seem to disagree. As you can see from the numbers above, Brady has been an efficient machine, even better than his standard numbers would indicate because the Patriots keep playing harder-than-average defensive schedules. The difference in his DVOA between plays with pressure and plays without is roughly equal to the league average. Between hits and sacks, he was knocked down on just 10.4 percent of pass plays, the fifth lowest rate in the league. And Brady's completion rate would be even better if Patriots receivers didn't drop 6.5 percent of passes (fifth highest in the league). At age 36, and with so much of his receiving corps turning over, you can expect a little bit of decline, but not much.

Drew Brees

Height: 6-0 Weight: 209 College: Purdue Draft: 2001/2 (32) Born: 15-Jan-1979 Age: 34 Risk: Yellow

Year	Team	G/GS	Snaps	Att	Comp	C%	Yds	TD	INT/Adj	FUM	ASR	NY/P	Rk	DVOA	Rk	DYAR	Rk	YAR	Runs	Yds	TD	DVOA	DYAR	QBR
2010	NO	16/16	1089	658	448	68.1%	4620	33	22/26	6	4.6%	6.5	13	13.4%	10	1061	7	1071	18	-3	0	-34.5%	-5	65.4
2011	NO	16/16	1110	657	468	71.2%	5476	46	14/17	1	4.5%	7.9	3	38.3%	2	2259	1	2363	21	86	1	30.5%	33	84.0
2012	NO	16/16	1095	670	422	63.0%	5177	43	19/23	6	4.9%	7.1	3	19.8%	5	1441	3	1397	15	5	1	34.2%	11	67.9
2013	NO			638	418	65.5%	5099	40	16	4		7.2		21.0%					14	-4	0	-25.9%		

2012: 47% Short 35% Mid 10% Deep 8% Bomb YAC: 5.1 (15) 2011: 50% Short 33% Mid 12% Deep 5% Bomb YAC: 5.2 (23)

Brees did what he could. Knowing every weekend that you have to put up five touchdowns or so just to stay in games can wear on a quarterback, but it was another banner campaign for the man who is now the fifth highest-paid athlete in the world according to Forbes (behind Tiger, Federer, Kobe, and LeBron). Naturally, his numbers did fall a little bit from the astounding stat line he posted in 2011. The turnovers were back up, hurt by losing five more fumbles than the year before and a five-pick nightmare against Atlanta, a game where Brees seemed to desperately miss Sean Payton's guidance and judgment. His completion percentage was the lowest it's been since Brees came to New Orleans.

At times last year Brees forced matters more than usual, as though he was trying to single-handedly ram New Orleans into the playoffs just to stick one to Roger Goodell. That's not a very productive way to approach a game plan, and Brees figures to return to his usual self with Payton back to whisper in his ear. Brees is 34, but with his last big contract sorted out and his friend and spiritual advisor back by his side, signs are pointed upward for the best player in franchise history.

Jason Campbell

		Height: 6-5		Weight: 223			College: Auburn			Draft: 2005/1 (25)			Born: 31-Dec-1981		Age: 32		Risk: Red

Year	Team	G/GS	Snaps	Att	Comp	C%	Yds	TD	INT/Adj	FUM	ASR	NY/P	Rk	DVOA	Rk	DYAR	Rk	YAR	Runs	Yds	TD	DVOA	DYAR	QBR
2010	OAK	13/12	786	329	194	59.0%	2387	13	8/13	9	9.1%	6.1	24	-10.1%	31	23	31	92	47	222	1	1.4%	28	48.5
2011	OAK	6/6	354	165	100	60.6%	1170	6	4/3	3	3.0%	6.8	15	19.8%	6	340	17	326	18	60	2	-19.1%	-6	55.1
2012	CHI	6/1	126	51	32	62.7%	265	2	2/2	2	9.9%	3.8	--	-50.2%	--	-129	--	-166	7	28	0	44.4%	9	23.5
2013	CLE			516	326	63.1%	3705	18	14	9		6.3		-5.9%					58	181	1	-7.9%		
	2012:	51% Short		35% Mid		6% Deep	8% Bomb		YAC: 2.4 (--)			2011:		46% Short		31% Mid		11% Deep	12% Bomb	YAC: 4.5 (39)				

Jason Campbell was brought into Chicago based on the idea that the Bears would have made the playoffs in 2011 had Caleb Hanie not been, well, Caleb Hanie. Campbell was almost as bad as Hanie when he had to play, although this was a small sample-size theater. You may remember the two games where Campbell saw the majority of his attempts were against Houston on Sunday Night Football and in San Francisco for Monday Night Football. With a Bears offense based on a single receiver and an offensive line that spent said MNF game allowing six sacks and generally looking hapless, it's probably fair to disregard the numbers to an extent. Of course, the same sample size caveat applies to the six games he started for the 2011 Raiders, and Campbell has never really been better than average outside of that six-game stretch. The Browns inked Campbell to give themselves a competent backup plan if Brandon Weeden crashes and burns—or possibly because he was one of the only free-agent quarterbacks on the market old enough to actually "mentor" Weeden.

David Carr

		Height: 6-3		Weight: 215			College: Fresno State			Draft: 2002/1 (1)			Born: 21-Jul-1979		Age: 34		Risk: Green

Year	Team	G/GS	Snaps	Att	Comp	C%	Yds	TD	INT/Adj	FUM	ASR	NY/P	Rk	DVOA	Rk	DYAR	Rk	YAR	Runs	Yds	TD	DVOA	DYAR	QBR
2010	SF	1/0	26	13	5	38.5%	67	0	1/1	0	7.5%	4.8	--	-60.1%	--	-31	--	-35	0	0	0	--	--	4.8
2012	NYG	2/0	15	3	2	66.7%	19	0	0/0	1	23.9%	3.3	--	-150.3%	--	-33	--	-32	3	-3	0	--	--	1.9
2013	NYG			541	324	59.8%	3721	22	22	7		6.2		-7.9%					38	43	0	-22.4%		
	2012:	67% Short		33% Mid		0% Deep	0% Bomb		YAC: 8.5 (--)																

A surprisingly high number of quarterbacks drafted first overall have gone on to win a Super Bowl: Eli Manning, Peyton Manning, Drew Bledsoe, John Elway, Troy Aikman, Jim Plunkett, and Terry Bradshaw, plus Steve Young (1984 Supplemental Draft) and Joe Namath (1965 AFL Draft). David Carr is also on the list, after backing up Eli Manning in Super Bowl XLVI. That makes Carr this generation's Bernie Kosar, the first overall pick in the 1985 Supplemental Draft who won Super Bowl XXVIII as Aikman's backup.

Matt Cassel

		Height: 6-5		Weight: 230			College: USC			Draft: 2005/7 (230)			Born: 17-May-1982		Age: 31		Risk: Red

Year	Team	G/GS	Snaps	Att	Comp	C%	Yds	TD	INT/Adj	FUM	ASR	NY/P	Rk	DVOA	Rk	DYAR	Rk	YAR	Runs	Yds	TD	DVOA	DYAR	QBR
2010	KC	15/15	1045	450	262	58.2%	3116	27	7/13	2	6.1%	6.3	18	8.4%	16	589	14	793	33	125	0	-13.0%	1	52.3
2011	KC	9/9	575	269	160	59.5%	1713	10	9/8	5	7.9%	5.5	34	-26.0%	39	-279	41	-169	25	99	0	13.5%	25	51.2
2012	KC	9/8	578	277	161	58.1%	1796	6	12/10	9	7.3%	5.8	27	-30.4%	36	-353	36	-275	27	145	1	17.8%	35	36.5
2013	MIN			484	298	61.6%	3096	15	16	12		5.4		-25.1%					45	109	1	-9.9%		
	2012:	41% Short		39% Mid		12% Deep	8% Bomb		YAC: 4.9 (25)			2011:		45% Short		33% Mid		15% Deep	8% Bomb	YAC: 4.4 (41)				

Cassel is the quarterback version of a streaky jump shooter. At times, he shows a decent arm (though his ball doesn't have a ton of zip), unexpectedly spry athleticism, and good football savvy. Other times, he holds the ball too long, makes irrational decisions, and becomes so predictable that he's prone to turnovers. He struggled with precision accuracy too often last season.

Kirk Cousins

		Height: 6-3		Weight: 214			College: Michigan State			Draft: 2012/4 (102)			Born: 19-Aug-1988		Age: 25		Risk: Red

Year	Team	G/GS	Snaps	Att	Comp	C%	Yds	TD	INT/Adj	FUM	ASR	NY/P	Rk	DVOA	Rk	DYAR	Rk	YAR	Runs	Yds	TD	DVOA	DYAR	QBR
2012	WAS	3/1	95	48	33	68.8%	466	4	3/3	1	8.2%	8.4	--	6.4%	--	59	--	55	3	22	0	74.5%	10	72.7
2013	WAS			481	317	65.9%	3698	21	15	7		7.2		5.9%					44	168	1	13.0%		
	2012:	41% Short		39% Mid		13% Deep	7% Bomb		YAC: 5.8 (--)																

Some thought the Redskins were nuts to select Cousins in the fourth round of the 2012 draft after giving up so much to bag RG3 in the first. One RG3 knee injury later, the wisdom of that choice became clear. Though he looked fairly overwhelmed in his first regular-season action against the Falcons in November, he threw a Sample Size Alert touchdown to help the Redskins beat the Ravens in overtime after Griffin's first knee injury in December, and held it together well against the Browns when Griffin sat out the next week. Cousins is a limited arm talent with a three-quarter delivery who needs to be held together with bubble screens, wheel routes, and boot action, but for the most part he's smart enough to understand his limitations—and so are the Shanahans.

Jay Cutler

		Height: 6-3		Weight: 220		College: Vanderbilt			Draft: 2006/1 (11)			Born: 29-Apr-1983			Age: 30		Risk: Green	

Year	Team	G/GS	Snaps	Att	Comp	C%	Yds	TD	INT/Adj	FUM	ASR	NY/P	Rk	DVOA	Rk	DYAR	Rk	YAR	Runs	Yds	TD	DVOA	DYAR	QBR
2010	CHI	15/15	889	432	261	60.4%	3274	23	16/24	10	10.5%	6.1	26	-8.5%	30	80	30	54	50	232	1	33.0%	65	48.5
2011	CHI	10/10	615	314	182	58.0%	2319	13	7/9	7	7.4%	6.4	18	-3.5%	21	157	21	207	18	55	1	-14.5%	-1	59.8
2012	CHI	15/15	919	434	255	58.8%	3033	19	14/20	8	7.8%	5.9	24	-13.8%	27	-81	28	-42	41	233	0	96.2%	114	51.9
2013	CHI			495	299	60.4%	3464	24	16	6		5.9		-10.9%					34	153	1	10.0%		

2012:	39% Short	34% Mid	18% Deep	9% Bomb	YAC: 4.5 (31)	2011:	44% Short	38% Mid	13% Deep	5% Bomb	YAC: 5.3 (17)

Can Jay Cutler be the next Joe Flacco? Like Flacco, Cutler has spent his time laboring under discredited and outdated offensive philosophies (in Cutler's case, run by Ron Turner, Mike Martz, and Mike Tice). Like Flacco, Cutler has a cannon arm and a history of questionable decision-making. Cutler even has something Flacco doesn't: a couple of great years of DVOA on his resume, back when he was in Denver. Marc Trestman is the latest coach tasked with turning Cutler around, and the fixes seem pretty simple in theory. 1) Use schemes and route designs to generate open underneath receivers. Cutler buys time and scrambles well, but last year if his progressions weren't open immediately, he began to panic and look to see where Brandon Marshall was. 2) Run more play action. Over the past few seasons, the Bears have had around 20% better DVOA on play-action passes than regular passes, but they used it about 4 or 5 percent less than the league average despite the fact that Cutler is very good on the move. 3) Stay out of the shotgun. Cutler has consistently been mediocre or worse under the gun, and that includes a -31.0% DVOA in 244 dropbacks last season. Somewhere, under the poor stats, brutal offensive line, and mediocre receiving crew, there's the foundation of a good quarterback here. This is the season where Trestman sees what can be salvaged.

Andy Dalton

		Height: 6-2		Weight: 215		College: TCU			Draft: 2011/2 (35)			Born: 29-Oct-1987			Age: 26		Risk: Green	

Year	Team	G/GS	Snaps	Att	Comp	C%	Yds	TD	INT/Adj	FUM	ASR	NY/P	Rk	DVOA	Rk	DYAR	Rk	YAR	Runs	Yds	TD	DVOA	DYAR	QBR
2011	CIN	16/16	1024	516	300	58.1%	3398	20	13/17	4	4.5%	6.0	23	5.6%	13	573	12	481	37	152	1	-14.6%	-4	45.8
2012	CIN	16/16	1025	528	329	62.3%	3669	27	16/19	8	8.5%	6.0	21	-5.9%	20	194	20	339	47	120	4	18.9%	53	50.7
2013	CIN			533	345	64.8%	3912	27	15	6		6.6		-0.9%					43	107	0	-5.1%		

2012:	49% Short	31% Mid	12% Deep	8% Bomb	YAC: 5.0 (17)	2011:	47% Short	34% Mid	11% Deep	8% Bomb	YAC: 4.4 (40)

Dalton has been mediocre-to-terrible in two playoff losses to the Texans. He has thrown six touchdowns and nine interceptions in eight career games against the Ravens and Steelers, with a completion rate of just 53.8 percent and 6.03 yards per attempt. There is a danger of veering into circular "winners win" logic based on these small samples, but it is not hard to hear Dalton banging his head into the same ceiling the whole Bengals franchise keeps slamming into. Whether the Bengals are limiting Dalton or Dalton is limiting the Bengals is a matter of semantics: they must improve together. The Bengals are improving around Dalton, and Dalton has the potential to get better as a result. It's time to crack through that ceiling.

Chase Daniel

		Height: 6-0		Weight: 225		College: Missouri			Draft: 2009/FA			Born: 7-Oct-1986			Age: 27		Risk: Red	

Year	Team	G/GS	Snaps	Att	Comp	C%	Yds	TD	INT/Adj	FUM	ASR	NY/P	Rk	DVOA	Rk	DYAR	Rk	YAR	Runs	Yds	TD	DVOA	DYAR	QBR
2010	NO	13/0	14	3	2	66.7%	16	0	0/0	1	26.8%	1.5	--	-63.7%	--	-16	--	-17	2	16	0	-109.1%	-16	2.0
2011	NO	16/0	42	5	4	80.0%	29	0	0/0	0	-0.9%	5.8	--	15.4%	--	8	--	12	3	-3	0	–	--	21.5
2012	NO	16/0	13	1	1	100.0%	10	0	0/0	0	-2.1%	10.0	--	579.9%	--	34	--	36	3	17	0	108.0%	7	100.0
2013	KC			456	274	60.1%	3284	21	17	8		6.1		-3.9%					34	136	2	11.9%		

2012:	44% Short	37% Mid	13% Deep	6% Bomb	YAC: 5.7 (4)	2011:	37% Short	35% Mid	20% Deep	8% Bomb	YAC: 5.3 (16)

Daniel is entering his fifth NFL season but is no better known to NFL fans than he was coming out of Missouri. Presumably, spending four years backing up Drew Brees in New Orleans has at least left him with a firm understanding of how to be an effective NFL quarterback despite not having optimum height. We can't know for sure, because Daniel has attempted a grand total of nine passes in his career.

Austin Davis

		Height: 6-2		Weight: 221		College: Southern Mississippi	Draft: 2012/FA			Born: 2-Jun-1989			Age: 24		Risk: Yellow	

Year	Team	G/GS	Snaps	Att	Comp	C%	Yds	TD	INT/Adj	FUM	ASR	NY/P	Rk	DVOA	Rk	DYAR	Rk	YAR	Runs	Yds	TD	DVOA	DYAR	QBR
2013	STL			498	268	53.9%	3491	15	19	6		5.9		-17.9%					62	376	3	20.0%		

Every second-string quarterback gets a projection, Part I. Davis starred at Southern Mississippi, where he broke records set by some guy named Favre. The Rams picked him up as a college free agent in 2012, and he proceeded to go 22-of-34 for 220 yards with no touchdowns, one interception, and two sacks in the preseason. He's a short-to-intermediate passer who lacks the arm strength to be accurate downfield. *Pro Football Weekly* said he had "marry-your-daughter-type intangibles."

Dominique Davis

Height: 6-3   Weight: 210   College: East Carolina   Draft: 2012/FA   Born: 17-Jul-1989   Age: 24   Risk: Yellow

Year	Team	G/GS	Snaps	Att	Comp	C%	Yds	TD	INT/Adj	FUM	ASR	NY/P	Rk	DVOA	Rk	DYAR	Rk	YAR	Runs	Yds	TD	DVOA	DYAR	QBR
2013	ATL			526	328	62.3%	3910	23	17	9		6.6		0.9%					45	105	3	-2.9%		

Every second-string quarterback gets a projection, Part II. Once upon a time Davis was an understudy to a quarterback named Matt Ryan. Davis redshirted at Boston College during Ryan's senior season, flunked out, transferred to a JUCO, than wound up at East Carolina. Now here he is, watching Ryan from the sidelines once again as his backup in Atlanta. Davis once completed 36 passes in a row in college, and he provides athleticism in the pocket which Ryan lacks, but his arm is far weaker than Matty Ice's. If Davis has to play, Atlanta's downfield attack would devolve into a series of checkdowns. He may just owe his job to his first name, which is hallowed in the Peachtree City.

Ryan Fitzpatrick

Height: 6-2   Weight: 221   College: Harvard   Draft: 2005/7 (250)   Born: 24-Nov-1982   Age: 31   Risk: Yellow

Year	Team	G/GS	Snaps	Att	Comp	C%	Yds	TD	INT/Adj	FUM	ASR	NY/P	Rk	DVOA	Rk	DYAR	Rk	YAR	Runs	Yds	TD	DVOA	DYAR	QBR
2010	BUF	13/13	821	441	255	57.8%	3000	23	15/21	7	5.6%	6.2	22	-3.6%	27	224	22	139	40	269	0	-3.5%	18	48.3
2011	BUF	16/16	1011	569	353	62.0%	3832	24	23/22	7	3.7%	6.3	20	-6.3%	26	185	19	194	56	215	0	5.2%	38	50.5
2012	BUF	16/16	993	505	306	60.6%	3400	24	16/21	9	5.6%	6.1	20	-7.6%	23	120	23	161	48	197	1	0.5%	22	45.8
2013	TEN			546	333	61.0%	3810	28	21	9		5.8		-14.4%					41	156	1	6.8%		
	2012:	48% Short		36% Mid		10% Deep	6% Bomb		YAC: 5.9 (3)			2011:		47% Short		35% Mid		12% Deep		5% Bomb	YAC: 5.3 (15)			

Buffalo's six-year, $59 million extension for Fitzpatrick didn't seem like a great idea when they agreed to the deal back in October 2011, and in retrospect it looks worse. That said, Fitzpatrick isn't a terrible quarterback. Once we average his very good first half of 2011 with his poor second half, his numbers are very consistent from year to year—and they are consistently above replacement level. He's not good enough to be a regular NFL starter but should have a long career as a better-than-average backup, which begins this fall as the veteran arm behind Jake Locker in Tennessee.

Joe Flacco

Height: 6-6   Weight: 236   College: Delaware   Draft: 2008/1 (18)   Born: 16-Jan-1985   Age: 28   Risk: Green

Year	Team	G/GS	Snaps	Att	Comp	C%	Yds	TD	INT/Adj	FUM	ASR	NY/P	Rk	DVOA	Rk	DYAR	Rk	YAR	Runs	Yds	TD	DVOA	DYAR	QBR
2010	BAL	16/16	1055	489	306	62.6%	3622	25	10/13	9	7.9%	6.3	16	9.4%	15	697	11	686	43	84	1	-27.2%	-21	60.4
2011	BAL	16/16	1077	542	312	57.6%	3610	20	12/20	11	5.6%	5.9	26	0.0%	18	413	14	389	39	88	1	19.3%	34	59.7
2012	BAL	16/16	1002	531	317	59.7%	3817	22	10/17	9	6.1%	6.3	18	-1.3%	17	358	17	403	32	22	3	-35.1%	-32	46.8
2013	BAL			530	314	59.3%	3913	26	12	8		6.5		8.3%					23	37	1	-2.6%		
	2012:	46% Short		31% Mid		12% Deep	12% Bomb		YAC: 4.9 (21)			2011:		43% Short		35% Mid		12% Deep		10% Bomb	YAC: 5.1 (25)			

According to one popular winter storyline, Flacco held a crossbow to his organization's head in the offseason, demanded the NFL's richest contract, and crippled the Ravens' finances, which prevented the team from retaining Ed Reed, Paul Kruger, and other key pieces of the Super Bowl puzzle. It's an entertaining theory, convincing to people with no knowledge of the Ravens, the salary cap, Flacco, corporate budgeting, basic economics, or human nature.

Flacco's reported $120.6 million contract was soon eclipsed by the deals for Tony Romo and Aaron Rodgers, and he is guaranteed less money than Drew Brees received in 2012, so his "record" contract was not much of a record at all. The Ravens were going to face a cap crunch to retain the services of any quarterback with higher market value than Mike Glennon, and they are the only organization in the NFL whose track record proves their willingness to play chicken with a Super Bowl-winning quarterback. The new contract keeps Flacco's 2013 cap number relatively low, which gave the Ravens a little wiggle room, and its double-option bonus structure prorates major cap problems into the future, so it hardly suffocated the team's short-term free agent plans. Flacco, of course, would happily have accepted an extension in 2012 instead of a free-agency staring contest, and like most people outside of cloistered monasteries simply sought the most lucrative contract the market for his services would bare. Otherwise, though, the "Flacco Killed the 2013 Ravens" theory makes perfect sense.

For fantasy purposes, Flacco is one of the most stable investments in the game: 20 to 25 touchdowns per year, 3,600 to 3,800 yards, either 10 or 12 interceptions, low injury risk. Although we expect a small counting-stat uptick, Super Bowl prestige might cause him to be over-drafted in some fantasy leagues. He makes a better ultra-reliable backup than a starter. The Ravens didn't really overpay for him. You shouldn't either.

Matt Flynn

Height: 6-2   Weight: 230   College: Louisiana State   Draft: 2008/7 (209)   Born: 20-Jun-1985   Age: 28   Risk: Yellow

Year	Team	G/GS	Snaps	Att	Comp	C%	Yds	TD	INT/Adj	FUM	ASR	NY/P	Rk	DVOA	Rk	DYAR	Rk	YAR	Runs	Yds	TD	DVOA	DYAR	QBR
2010	GB	7/1	146	66	40	60.6%	433	3	2/2	1	9.4%	5.4	--	-15.9%	--	-24	--	-23	9	26	0	-36.2%	-9	23.3
2011	GB	5/1	113	49	33	67.3%	518	6	2/3	1	9.6%	9.2	--	47.3%	--	225	--	169	13	-6	1	20.9%	5	90.4
2012	SEA	3/0	37	9	5	55.6%	68	0	0/0	0	-3.2%	7.6	--	64.3%	--	27	--	15	4	-5	0	--	--	23.4
2013	OAK			553	352	63.6%	3798	21	17	11		6.4		-8.2%					37	130	2	8.8%		
	2012:	46% Short		31% Mid		12% Deep	12% Bomb		YAC: 4.9 (21)			2011:		43% Short		35% Mid		12% Deep		10% Bomb	YAC: 5.1 (25)			

On January 1, 2012, while playing for Green Bay, Flynn threw for 480 yards and six touchdowns against Detroit. The game scored at 290 DYAR, one of the best games we've ever measured, and a plateau that had previously been reach almost exclusively by Pro Bowlers. Buoyed by that game and a strong 2010 performance against New England, Flynn signed a contract with Seattle for $10 million in guaranteed money, fully expecting to start for the Seahawks that fall. When he lost a training camp battle to a third-round rookie, it seemed to render his prior accomplishments as statistical flukes. Given what Russell Wilson went on to do, however, it only seems fair that Flynn gets another chance. That chance will come in Oakland, which acquired him for a song. (Specifically, a ballad called "2014 Fourth-Rounder and 2015 Conditional Pick." It wasn't very memorable.) Despite some media buzz for third-year pro Terrelle Pryor and fourth-round rookie Tyler Wilson, Raiders coach Dennis Allen has made it clear that Flynn is his starter, and there is no competition. After 18 months, Flynn will finally get to show whether his performance against the Lions was more than a mirage.

Nick Foles   Height: 6-5   Weight: 243   College: Arizona   Draft: 2012/3 (88)   Born: 20-Jan-1989   Age: 24   Risk: Yellow

Year	Team	G/GS	Snaps	Att	Comp	C%	Yds	TD	INT/Adj	FUM	ASR	NY/P	Rk	DVOA	Rk	DYAR	Rk	YAR	Runs	Yds	TD	DVOA	DYAR	QBR
2012	PHI	7/6	453	265	161	60.8%	1699	6	5/11	8	8.2%	5.5	32	-20.4%	30	-166	30	-158	11	42	1	11.7%	11	45.3
2013	PHI			596	383	64.2%	3972	19	14	12		5.8		-7.1%					49	126	2	-2.6%		

2012:	49% Short		33% Mid		12% Deep	6% Bomb		YAC: 5.2 (13)				Bomb	YAC: 5.3 (16)

As a senior at Arizona in 2011, Foles put up great numbers but his team went just 4-8. As a rookie with the Eagles, Foles couldn't even muster good stats during his 1-5 run as a starter. Sixty quarterbacks have thrown 250 passes in their rookie season since 1970. The only passers with a worse touchdown rate than Foles were Jimmy Clausen, Andrew Walter, Jack Trudeau, David Carr, Chris Weinke, and Steve Fuller. That's not very good company, of course, and it's easy to see why Foles struggled to throw touchdowns. In the red zone, he completed just 13 of 31 passes, took three more sacks, and gained just 54 net yards. Add it up, and we graded him with a -54.5% DVOA inside the opponent's 20. Foles did manage to avoid throwing interceptions, but it's hard to be impressed by a quarterback who plays it safe, loses, and avoids turnovers. Foles averaged 10.6 yards per completed pass, finishing ahead of only Christian Ponder and Blaine Gabbert in that statistic. It's not fair to be too harsh on a rookie who played for a bad team, but Foles' potential is limited and the Eagles don't seem to be too invested in him.

Josh Freeman   Height: 6-6   Weight: 248   College: Kansas State   Draft: 2009/1 (17)   Born: 13-Jan-1988   Age: 25   Risk: Red

Year	Team	G/GS	Snaps	Att	Comp	C%	Yds	TD	INT/Adj	FUM	ASR	NY/P	Rk	DVOA	Rk	DYAR	Rk	YAR	Runs	Yds	TD	DVOA	DYAR	QBR
2010	TB	16/16	958	474	291	61.4%	3451	25	6/13	7	6.0%	6.5	14	13.9%	9	816	9	829	68	364	0	18.9%	96	64.6
2011	TB	15/15	942	551	346	62.8%	3592	16	22/22	8	6.1%	6.0	24	-13.7%	31	-96	34	-84	55	238	4	13.8%	70	45.3
2012	TB	16/16	1037	558	306	54.8%	4065	27	17/24	9	4.8%	6.7	11	-8.0%	24	118	24	204	39	139	0	3.7%	26	53.1
2013	TB			574	332	57.9%	4148	27	17	9		6.1		-2.6%					37	160	1	10.9%		

2012:	42% Short	33% Mid	14% Deep	11% Bomb	YAC: 5.4 (8)	2011:	52% Short	35% Mid	10% Deep	3% Bomb	YAC: 4.8 (33)

Freeman threw a lot fewer short passes and a lot more deep ones last year than he did in 2011, which largely explains his drop in completion percentage. Oddly, though, his accuracy on short passes plummeted, while he was more successful on deep passes and bombs. (Table 1) At first glance, it seems safe to blame Freeman's interceptions on all those deep passes, but in fact he threw a league-high seven interceptions last year on short routes. Freeman has now ranked in the top five in passes intercepted three times in his four seasons. The exception was in 2010, when he threw half as many picks as he "should" have, according to our Adjusted Interceptions stat. Only four quarterbacks have more interceptions since Freeman entered the league. Two of those men are Eli Manning and Drew Brees. The other two are Mark Sanchez and Ryan Fitzpatrick. Freeman is entering the last year of his contract, and his success or failure this season will determine whether the rest of his career looks more like the first duo or the second. Freeman's "Red" risk is related to the drafting of Mike Glennon and his own inconsistency, not a greater-than-usual injury risk.

Table 1. Josh Freeman's Completion Rate by Distance, 2011-2012

Pass Type	2011	2012
Short (up to 5 yards)	73%	63%
Med (6-15 yards)	60%	55%
Deep (16-25 yards)	41%	49%
Bomb (26+ yards)	24%	31%

Blaine Gabbert   Height: 6-4   Weight: 234   College: Missouri   Draft: 2011/1 (10)   Born: 15-Oct-1989   Age: 24   Risk: Red

Year	Team	G/GS	Snaps	Att	Comp	C%	Yds	TD	INT/Adj	FUM	ASR	NY/P	Rk	DVOA	Rk	DYAR	Rk	YAR	Runs	Yds	TD	DVOA	DYAR	QBR
2011	JAC	15/14	910	413	210	50.8%	2214	12	11/17	13	9.1%	4.2	45	-46.5%	46	-1010	47	-897	48	98	0	-38.9%	-35	20.6
2012	JAC	10/10	515	278	162	58.3%	1662	9	6/6	5	6.9%	5.0	35	-25.3%	34	-268	32	-309	18	56	0	-6.8%	5	40.9
2013	JAC			551	327	59.4%	3552	23	14	10		5.4		-21.1%					44	140	0	-17.8%		

2012:	49% Short	34% Mid	11% Deep	6% Bomb	YAC: 4.3 (36)	2011:	48% Short	34% Mid	13% Deep	5% Bomb	YAC: 5.4 (11)

As a rookie, Gabbert ranked dead last with a comically absurd passing DYAR of -1,010. If Gabbert couldn't do better than that in 2012, he would have been coming to an arena league near you. Despite playing with a torn labrum in his non-throwing shoulder, Gabbert did manage to improve his completion percentage and cut down on his turnovers before a right forearm injury ended his 2012 season in mid-November. However, the injury-shortened season and slight statistical improvement has not put any distance between Gabbert and the "bust" label. 2013 is a make-or-break season, as the Jaguars have until May 3, 2014 to decide whether or not to pick up the fifth-year option on Gabbert's rookie contract or let him become an unrestricted free agent in 2015. Gabbert's degree of difficulty will increase as he is learning a third offensive system in as many seasons and will have to convince a new coaching staff (and front office) that has nothing invested in him that he deserves the starting nod ahead of the more experienced Chad Henne. The two quarterbacks split the first-team reps equally during the OTAs and will be an interesting battle to watch during the preseason. For what it's worth, in June, former Jaguars head coach Mike Mularkey told Pat Kirwan and Tim Ryan on SiriusXM radio that he would start Henne over Gabbert.

Mike Glennon

Height: 6-7 | Weight: 220 | College: North Carolina State | Draft: 2013/3 (73) | Born: 12-Dec-1989 | Age: 24 | Risk: Red

Year	Team	G/GS	Snaps	Att	Comp	C%	Yds	TD	INT/Adj	FUM	ASR	NY/P	Rk	DVOA	Rk	DYAR	Rk	YAR	Runs	Yds	TD	DVOA	DYAR	QBR
2013	TB			558	330	59.0%	4090	23	20	9		6.1		-5.7%					23	50	1	-11.0%		

Glennon only started two years at North Carolina State, and though he was good enough as a junior, he declined sharply as a senior. Yes, he led the ACC in passes, completions, and yards, and was second in touchdowns. But he was just sixth in completion percentage and seventh in yards per pass, and he led the conference—nay, the nation—in interceptions. He's also built like a small forward at 6-foot-7 and 220 pounds. That's a BMI of 24.8, lower than any quarterback taken in the first three rounds since 1998. (The lowest BMI among starting quarterbacks last season was Alex Smith at 25.8, followed by Eli Manning at 26.5.) The low BMI and decline as a senior combine to give Glennon has the lowest score in this year's Lewin Career Forecast. The Buccaneers grabbed him in the third round, because if you've already got one tall, turnover-prone quarterback, you may as well get another.

Bruce Gradkowski

Height: 6-1 | Weight: 220 | College: Toledo | Draft: 2006/6 (194) | Born: 27-Jan-1983 | Age: 30 | Risk: Green

Year	Team	G/GS	Snaps	Att	Comp	C%	Yds	TD	INT/Adj	FUM	ASR	NY/P	Rk	DVOA	Rk	DYAR	Rk	YAR	Runs	Yds	TD	DVOA	DYAR	QBR
2010	OAK	6/4	282	157	83	52.9%	1059	5	7/10	3	6.3%	5.9	34	-21.0%	37	-106	35	-60	12	41	0	-13.2%	-2	31.5
2011	CIN	2/0	44	18	8	44.4%	109	1	1/2	0	5.2%	5.4	--	-58.4%	--	-51	--	-46	3	1	0	19.2%	2	24.5
2012	CIN	3/0	30	11	5	45.5%	65	0	0/0	1	0.0%	5.9	--	-14.9%	--	-3	--	-8	4	-2	0	--	--	54.7
2013	PIT			512	307	60.0%	3559	23	17	10		6.1		-8.1%					45	113	0	-13.7%		
	2012:	44% Short		33% Mid		0% Deep	22% Bomb		YAC: 1.0 (--)			2011:		39% Short		33% Mid		17% Deep	11% Bomb		YAC: 8.5 (--)			

Bruce Gradkowski replaced Andy Dalton in the second half of a meaningless Week 17 game against the Ravens and did very Gradkowski things. He threw a 44-yard strike to Brandon Tate, earned 15 yards the hard way by absorbing a roughing-the-passer penalty, sprayed a bunch of short passes of varying precision, and treated his rest-the-starters opportunity like it was the fourth quarter of the Super Bowl. Gradkowski keeps getting jobs because he is an ornery Eveready as a backup, which is exactly what the Steelers need. Landry Jones will get the call if Ben Roethlisberger misses extended time, but Big Ben is more likely to miss a quarter here and a series there. Gradkowski can act as a short-term tempo changer off the bench, someone Mike Tomlin and Todd Haley don't have to be reluctant to send out onto the field.

Robert Griffin

Height: 6-2 | Weight: 223 | College: Baylor | Draft: 2012/1 (2) | Born: 12-Feb-1990 | Age: 23 | Risk: Red

Year	Team	G/GS	Snaps	Att	Comp	C%	Yds	TD	INT/Adj	FUM	ASR	NY/P	Rk	DVOA	Rk	DYAR	Rk	YAR	Runs	Yds	TD	DVOA	DYAR	QBR
2012	WAS	15/15	937	393	258	65.6%	3200	20	5/10	11	7.7%	7.0	7	16.6%	7	727	11	811	120	815	7	7.8%	109	71.4
2013	WAS			445	294	66.0%	3591	24	11	10		7.4		15.8%					104	543	7	34.3%		
	2012:	47% Short		35% Mid		11% Deep	6% Bomb		YAC: 5.6 (5)											Bomb		YAC: 8.5 (--)			

We discussed Griffin's transcendent effect on the Redskins offense at length in the team chapter ... but now, it's all about the knee, the future, and how Griffin's game may change if he wants to play into a second contract. For all the talk about Griffin's alleged vulnerability under pressure, the hits that caused and then exacerbated his knee injury were examples of a relatively low sample size. Especially for a mobile quarterback, Griffin was surprisingly adept at eluding pressure as a pure passer. He ranked eighth in the league among qualifying quarterbacks in the percentage of plays in which he had to deal with pressure (23.7 percent), including sacks and scrambles. That's not only lower than the other young mobile quarterbacks, it's also lower than the quarterback Griffin will be contrasted with for the rest of his career, Andrew Luck.

It will be Mike Shanahan's task to regulate Griffin's effectiveness as an option passer versus the risk to his future. Most likely, the Redskins will manage this with more plays in which Griffin can use his impressive and underrated ability as a pocket passer, and play designs that will keep Griffin from the same amount of brutal open-field hits. As Shanahan noted at the 2013 owners meetings, Griffin will have to learn to slide, to throw the ball away, and to minimize the kamikaze aspect to his game. Shanahan has also promised to avoid subjecting Griffin to situations where he's playing hurt. If everything plays out as the team hopes, Griffin has virtually unlimited potential in all kinds of directions—he's as athletically adept as Michael Vick ever was, but he's already advanced beyond where Vick has ever been when it comes to his pocket presence, command of an advanced passing attack, and understanding of playbook concepts. It's a rare player who deserves an offense totally tailored to his strengths, and Griffin has not yet reached his ultimate potential as a pure quarterback.

Graham Harrell

Height: 6-2   Weight: 215   College: Texas Tech   Draft: 2009/FA   Born: 22-May-1985   Age: 28   Risk: Yellow

Year	Team	G/GS	Snaps	Att	Comp	C%	Yds	TD	INT/Adj	FUM	ASR	NY/P	Rk	DVOA	Rk	DYAR	Rk	YAR	Runs	Yds	TD	DVOA	DYAR	QBR
2012	GB	4/0	32	4	2	50.0%	20	0	0/0	0	-1.7%	5.0	--	-11.2%	--	0	--	-2	4	-3	0	-239.9%	-20	0.6
2013	GB			530	343	64.8%	3992	20	16	9		6.4		4.5%					23	43	1	-6.1%		
	2012:	25% Short		75% Mid		0% Deep	0% Bomb		YAC: 5.0 (--)															

"The team's most popular player is the backup quarterback," is an oft-repeated tru-ism. They really should have added "unless it's Graham Harrell" to the end of that one.

Matt Hasselbeck

Height: 6-4   Weight: 223   College: Boston College   Draft: 1998/6 (187)   Born: 25-Sep-1975   Age: 38   Risk: Yellow

Year	Team	G/GS	Snaps	Att	Comp	C%	Yds	TD	INT/Adj	FUM	ASR	NY/P	Rk	DVOA	Rk	DYAR	Rk	YAR	Runs	Yds	TD	DVOA	DYAR	QBR
2010	SEA	14/14	803	444	266	59.9%	3001	12	17/21	6	6.4%	6.0	30	-16.8%	35	-173	38	-123	23	60	3	38.5%	46	40.4
2011	TEN	16/16	923	518	319	61.6%	3571	18	14/20	4	3.7%	6.4	19	0.6%	17	391	16	371	20	52	0	32.1%	21	62.8
2012	TEN	8/5	395	221	138	62.4%	1367	7	5/11	3	5.7%	5.4	33	-11.5%	26	-6	26	20	13	38	0	24.9%	9	48.5
2013	IND			568	348	61.3%	3616	23	14	7		5.4		-8.9%					24	34	0	-15.5%		
	2012:	50% Short		32% Mid		12% Deep	5% Bomb		YAC: 4.1 (37)			2011:	52% Short		29% Mid		11% Deep		8% Bomb	YAC: 5.1 (24)				

Hasselbeck was the better of the two Titans' quarterbacks in 2012, but that wasn't much of an accomplishment, especially considering that he regressed from his surprisingly good 2011 season in virtually every regard. He was still good on third downs (16.4% DVOA) but not as good as the year before. He got sacked more. He threw more interceptions. He continued saying and doing all the right things to help Jake Locker's development, at least. This year he will mentor Andrew Luck in Indianapolis. Just don't ask him to execute the downfield passing game Bruce Arians implemented in 2012, though he can still throw slants and short crossing routes accurately.

Chad Henne

Height: 6-2   Weight: 230   College: Michigan   Draft: 2008/2 (57)   Born: 2-Jul-1985   Age: 28   Risk: Red

Year	Team	G/GS	Snaps	Att	Comp	C%	Yds	TD	INT/Adj	FUM	ASR	NY/P	Rk	DVOA	Rk	DYAR	Rk	YAR	Runs	Yds	TD	DVOA	DYAR	QBR
2010	MIA	15/14	921	490	301	61.4%	3301	15	19/18	5	5.7%	6.0	28	1.0%	22	402	17	291	35	52	0	-61.4%	-55	42.5
2011	MIA	4/4	221	112	64	57.1%	868	4	4/4	1	8.9%	6.5	16	-2.7%	20	67	27	100	15	112	0	19.0%	20	63.2
2012	JAC	10/6	545	308	166	53.9%	2084	11	11/14	3	8.5%	5.7	29	-24.6%	33	-286	33	-171	19	64	1	-33.3%	-17	29.9
2013	JAC			542	301	55.6%	3536	22	17	7		5.4		-20.3%					35	73	1	-7.0%		
	2012:	39% Short		42% Mid		16% Deep	4% Bomb		YAC: 5.1 (14)			2011:	45% Short		28% Mid		18% Deep		8% Bomb	YAC: 5.2 (22)				

Henne was a serviceable starter for the Miami Dolphins before a left shoulder injury in Week 4 of 2011 ended his tenure in South Florida. Henne wisely chose to sign with the Jaguars, where 2011 first-round Blaine Gabbert was coming off a rough rookie season. Henne replaced an injured Gabbert in mid-November and passed for 354 yards and four touchdowns in a 43-37 overtime loss to the eventual AFC South champion Houston Texans. In his first start, Henne passed for 261 yards with two touchdowns in a 24-19 win over the Tennessee Titans, the Jaguars' second (and final) win of the season. After that, things went downhill for Henne, whose completion percentage dropped below 55 percent over the final five games as he had more interceptions (seven) than touchdowns (four). Part of Henne's struggles could be attributed to protection issues as he was hit or sacked on 18.5 percent of pass plays, the third-highest rate in the NFL, and his -134.4% DVOA when pressured was among the worst in the league. Henne and Gabbert will have an open competition for the starting job during the offseason and training camp.

Shaun Hill

Height: 6-5   Weight: 210   College: Maryland   Draft: 2002/FA   Born: 9-Jan-1980   Age: 34   Risk: Green

Year	Team	G/GS	Snaps	Att	Comp	C%	Yds	TD	INT/Adj	FUM	ASR	NY/P	Rk	DVOA	Rk	DYAR	Rk	YAR	Runs	Yds	TD	DVOA	DYAR	QBR
2010	DET	11/10	688	416	257	61.8%	2686	16	12/15	2	3.9%	6.0	33	6.7%	19	477	16	372	22	123	0	-9.4%	1	41.8
2011	DET	2/0	22	3	2	66.7%	33	0	0/0	0	-3.9%	11.0	--	134.1%	--	17	--	13	1	-1	0		--	79.6
2012	DET	1/0	19	13	10	76.9%	172	2	0/0	0	0.7%	14.3	--	136.4%	--	128	--	137	1	-1	0	-97.7%	-7	76.8
2013	DET			657	401	61.1%	4435	28	18	7		6.0		-1.8%					43	65	0	-18.6%		
	2012:	42% Short		33% Mid		17% Deep	8% Bomb		YAC: 4.7 (--)			2011:	33% Short		33% Mid		0% Deep		33% Bomb	YAC: 0.0 (--)				

Just another season for Shaun Hill. Come off bench to throw game-tying Hail Mary touchdown against the Titans, ho hum. At this point Hill is probably the best backup quarterback in the NFL who isn't a future starting prospect. It's a good thing the Lions have him, because the offensive line they've assembled around Matthew Stafford suggests Hill may see action for the fourth consecutive season.

Brian Hoyer | Height: 6-2 | Weight: 215 | College: Michigan State | Draft: 2009/FA | Born: 13-Oct-1985 | Age: 28 | Risk: Green

Year	Team	G/GS	Snaps	Att	Comp	C%	Yds	TD	INT/Adj	FUM	ASR	NY/P	Rk	DVOA	Rk	DYAR	Rk	YAR	Runs	Yds	TD	DVOA	DYAR	QBR
2010	NE	5/0	61	15	7	46.7%	122	1	1/2	0	0.0%	8.1	--	16.1%	--	27	--	27	10	-8	0	-116.8%	-5	39.1
2011	NE	3/0	12	1	1	100.0%	22	0	0/0	0	2.3%	22.0	--	215.0%	--	16	--	16	4	-3	0	--	--	96.0
2012	2TM	2/1	81	53	30	56.6%	330	1	2/2	1	7.2%	5.3	--	-26.5%	--	-60	--	-119	1	6	0	63.7%	5	37.7
2013	CLE			523	314	60.0%	3656	18	19	10		5.9		-18.5%					24	33	1	-21.5%		
2012:	42% Short		40% Mid		10% Deep	8% Bomb		YAC: 3.1 (--)											Bomb	YAC: 5.3 (16)				

Hoyer spent last year establishing a niche as the go-to "fourth quarterback," which unfortunately is not a very stable role in the National Football League. Pittsburgh brought him in for two weeks as Charlie Batch's backup when their first two quarterbacks went down, and then Arizona claimed him on waivers because they were just plain sick of John Skelton and Ryan Lindley. He eventually came in to play the second half of the Week 16 game against the Bears and even started the final game against San Francisco, giving him more regular-season experience than he had in his three years as backup to Tom Brady in New England. This season, Hoyer returns home to Cleveland, where he once starred at St. Ignatius High School. He'll hold a clipboard for Brandon Weeden and give the rest of the team advice on where to find the best restaraunts.

Tarvaris Jackson | Height: 6-2 | Weight: 226 | College: Alabama State | Draft: 2006/2 (64) | Born: 21-Apr-1983 | Age: 30 | Risk: Green

Year	Team	G/GS	Snaps	Att	Comp	C%	Yds	TD	INT/Adj	FUM	ASR	NY/P	Rk	DVOA	Rk	DYAR	Rk	YAR	Runs	Yds	TD	DVOA	DYAR	QBR
2010	MIN	3/1	127	58	34	58.6%	341	3	4/4	1	8.7%	4.7	--	-37.2%	--	-111	--	-148	7	63	0	81.6%	19	35.0
2011	SEA	15/14	944	450	271	60.2%	3091	14	13/17	8	7.9%	5.7	30	-5.8%	25	165	20	61	40	180	1	-19.1%	-11	37.7
2013	SEA			428	266	62.0%	3038	14	12	8		6.2		-3.5%					47	201	2	20.2%		
										2011:	46% Short	33% Mid		11% Deep	10% Bomb	YAC: 5.0 (27)								

Jackson didn't get into a game as Ryan Fitzpatrick's backup last year. The Bills signed him to another one-year contract after the season, then cut him in June to make sure Kevin Kolb and E.J. Manuel got all the snaps in training camp, so Jackson went back to Seattle where he started for most of 2011. He's no Russell Wilson, or even close, but if Jackson has to play he'll probably be better than you expect: in the three seasons where has thrown at least 100 passes, Jackson has put up passing DVOA of -6.5% (2007), 3.9% (2008), and -5.8% (2011).

Landry Jones | Height: 6-4 | Weight: 218 | College: Oklahoma | Draft: 2013/4 (115) | Born: 4-Apr-1989 | Age: 24 | Risk: Yellow

Year	Team	G/GS	Snaps	Att	Comp	C%	Yds	TD	INT/Adj	FUM	ASR	NY/P	Rk	DVOA	Rk	DYAR	Rk	YAR	Runs	Yds	TD	DVOA	DYAR	QBR
2013	PIT			466	293	62.9%	3350	19	15	7		6.1		-2.8%					16	55	0	5.8%		

Jones is one of the most prolific passers in NCAA history. He's also a central-casting, Big 12 spread-offense quarterback. Jones had the pre-snap read, throw-to-a-spot offense down pat, and he has just enough arm strength, anticipation, and athleticism to make that system work. The Steelers will groom him to be something more, but in the meantime, he has several advantages over their recent backups. He is under 38 years old, for example. Jones has the profile of a rookie backup who could start two or three games without catastrophe, and that is exactly what the Steelers need in the short term. Bruce Gradkowski will be Ben Roethlisberger's official backup, but Jones will be considered for tours of duty that last longer than a few series.

Colin Kaepernick | Height: 6-5 | Weight: 233 | College: Nevada | Draft: 2011/2 (36) | Born: 3-Nov-1987 | Age: 26 | Risk: Yellow

Year	Team	G/GS	Snaps	Att	Comp	C%	Yds	TD	INT/Adj	FUM	ASR	NY/P	Rk	DVOA	Rk	DYAR	Rk	YAR	Runs	Yds	TD	DVOA	DYAR	QBR
2011	SF	3/0	20	5	3	60.0%	35	0	0/0	0	0.0%	7.0	--	34.1%	--	14	--	17	2	-2	0	--	--	92.9
2012	SF	13/7	525	218	136	62.4%	1814	10	3/6	7	6.8%	7.2	2	25.8%	3	555	13	462	63	415	5	-1.5%	31	76.8
2013	SF			435	272	62.4%	3482	22	11	9		7.2		8.8%					127	738	6	29.3%		
2012:	44% Short		32% Mid		16% Deep	8% Bomb		YAC: 5.2 (11)	2011:	20% Short	80% Mid		0% Deep	0% Bomb	YAC: 3.0 (--)								

It's easy to get caught up in Kaepernick's running prowess, but just as (if not more) impressive is his efficiency on deep throws. He finished third in completion percentage (47.3%) and second in DVOA (110.9%) on passes traveling 16 or more yards through the air. Despite finishing sixth in average pass length (10.0 yards), his 2.8 percent adjusted interception rate ranked 10th. In case that doesn't strike you as remarkable, the five quarterbacks who ranked higher in average pass length had an average adjusted interception rate of 4.0 percent and ranking of 25th. (For instance, Andrew Luck finished first in average pass length, but *35th* in adjusted interception rate.) After the Super Bowl, Terrell Suggs said of Kaepernick, "Going into the game, I thought it was all hype. I hate quarterbacks, but that kid is the truth, and I have the utmost respect for him." We wholeheartedly agree.

Kevin Kolb Height: 6-3 Weight: 218 College: Houston Draft: 2007/2 (36) Born: 24-Aug-1984 Age: 29 Risk: Red

Year	Team	G/GS	Snaps	Att	Comp	C%	Yds	TD	INT/Adj	FUM	ASR	NY/P	Rk	DVOA	Rk	DYAR	Rk	YAR	Runs	Yds	TD	DVOA	DYAR	QBR
2010	PHI	7/5	364	189	115	60.8%	1197	7	7/7	5	7.9%	5.3	39	-10.2%	32	12	32	21	15	65	0	-25.6%	-7	35.7
2011	ARI	9/9	503	253	146	57.7%	1955	9	8/11	8	11.0%	6.0	22	-18.4%	33	-131	35	-123	17	65	0	-14.2%	-1	34.5
2012	ARI	6/5	348	183	109	59.6%	1169	8	3/3	3	12.1%	4.8	37	-23.1%	31	-154	29	-88	16	100	1	80.7%	49	38.0
2013	BUF			521	333	64.0%	3672	22	16	10		6.0		-6.8%					42	107	2	-1.5%		

2012:	49% Short	38% Mid	10% Deep	3% Bomb	YAC: 4.4 (33)	2011:	46% Short	37% Mid	11% Deep	6% Bomb	YAC: 6.2 (4)

As with most grievously overvalued players in any sport, it wasn't really Kevin Kolb's fault that his time in Arizona was such a complete debacle. It was the responsibility of former Cardinals general manager Rod Graves and former head coach Ken Whisenhunt to ascertain what Kolb could bring from a starting perspective based on a very limited sample size in Philadelphia's greased-up offense. Instead, they made Kolb the centerpiece of the deal that got them both fired, trading a second-round pick and cornerback Dominique Rogers-Cromartie for Kolb and then giving Kolb a six-year, $65 million contract. Those actions were beyond the pale for a player of Kolb's limited abilities. So, after two seasons, 14 starts, and a whole lot of quarterback pressure in all possible permutations, it was the decision of the new Arizona regime to release Kolb from his contract and let him move along. The Buffalo Bills signed him to a much more reasonable two-year, $6.1 million contract with just $1 million guaranteed, which puts him in the probable starter's seat in Buffalo until first-round pick E.J. Manuel is ready to take it from him. That could be in Week 1, Week 8, or Week 16, but expect it sooner than later. Kolb is slightly better than some would believe, but he's never going to transcend the reality that he's a sub-starter who needs everything very right to be a productive NFL quarterback. His tape shows a skill set somewhere between Matt Flynn and Brady Quinn, and just as it has been for Flynn and Quinn—not to mention last-gen quarterback disasters like Rob Johnson and Scott Mitchell—Kolb is less an overhyped rip-off artist and more the oversold beneficiary of a front office that couldn't wait to be taken to the cleaners.

Byron Leftwich Height: 6-5 Weight: 245 College: Marshall Draft: 2003/1 (7) Born: 14-Jan-1980 Age: 33 Risk: N/A

Year	Team	G/GS	Snaps	Att	Comp	C%	Yds	TD	INT/Adj	FUM	ASR	NY/P	Rk	DVOA	Rk	DYAR	Rk	YAR	Runs	Yds	TD	DVOA	DYAR	QBR
2010	PIT	1/0	18	7	5	71.4%	42	0	0/0	0	22.9%	3.9	--	-13.6%	--	-1	--	-1	0	0	0	--	--	35.6
2012	PIT	2/1	104	53	25	47.2%	272	0	1/1	2	5.1%	4.4	--	-14.5%	--	-12	--	-16	1	31	1	209.3%	17	34.0

2012:	44% Short	25% Mid	23% Deep	8% Bomb	YAC: 4.6 (--)

The Leftwich Time Capsule needs to contain only two bookend events. 1) The time at Marshall when his offensive linemen carried him down the field in the fourth quarter because he was too injured to make the trip himself, yet he remained in the game. 2) His desperate scrambling touchdown against the Ravens last year, where he appeared to be shedding parts as he bumbled down the field and injured himself by falling over the goal line. Those two highlights tell the story of a determined-yet-klutzy quarterback somewhere between Bernie Kosar and Inspector Clouseau, a guy who never made it look easy or pretty but could do the job when he played within himself. Leftwich is an unrestricted free agent and would make a fine offensive coordinator.

Matt Leinart Height: 6-5 Weight: 232 College: USC Draft: 2006/1 (10) Born: 11-May-1983 Age: 30 Risk: N/A

Year	Team	G/GS	Snaps	Att	Comp	C%	Yds	TD	INT/Adj	FUM	ASR	NY/P	Rk	DVOA	Rk	DYAR	Rk	YAR	Runs	Yds	TD	DVOA	DYAR	QBR
2011	HOU	2/1	35	13	10	76.9%	57	1	0/0	0	0.9%	4.4	--	4.9%	--	14	--	4	1	-1	0	--	--	58.4
2012	OAK	2/0	60	33	16	48.5%	115	0	1/1	0	1.8%	3.1	--	-51.2%	--	-77	--	-105	0	0	0	--	--	11.3

2012:	47% Short	31% Mid	19% Deep	3% Bomb	YAC: 2.5 (--)	2011:	83% Short	17% Mid	0% Deep	0% Bomb	YAC: 3.9 (--)

It's debatable whether Leinart is even a quality backup at this point. When he got his chance to play after Carson Palmer went down late last year, he showed an acute lack of anticipation and aggressiveness as a drop-back passer. After taking too long to even see receivers, he'd take too long winding up and delivering the ball. It's impossible to run an offense that way. Making matters worse is the fact that the only thing slower than Leinart's recognition and delivery are his feet, and he has no ability to extend a play outside the pocket.

Thaddeus Lewis Height: 6-2 Weight: 220 College: Duke Draft: 2010/FA Born: 19-Nov-1987 Age: 26 Risk: Red

Year	Team	G/GS	Snaps	Att	Comp	C%	Yds	TD	INT/Adj	FUM	ASR	NY/P	Rk	DVOA	Rk	DYAR	Rk	YAR	Runs	Yds	TD	DVOA	DYAR	QBR
2012	CLE	1/1	62	32	22	68.8%	204	1	1/1	0	8.4%	5.4	--	6.5%	--	42	--	46	1	3	0	-50.0%	-2	58.6
2013	DET			564	323	57.2%	3945	21	21	9		6.2		-10.1%					53	127	1	-10.4%		

2012:	38% Short	50% Mid	6% Deep	6% Bomb	YAC: 2.8 (--)						Bomb	YAC: 5.3 (16)

The rich tradition of Browns late-season mystery quarterbacks dates back (in their modern history) to 2000, when receiver Kevin Johnson slid over to quarterback to run a proto-Wildcat in Week 16. Spurgeon Wynn burned briefly across December that same year, Ken Dorsey emerged from the bench in 2008, and Josh Cribbs spent his whole Browns career just inches from a Week 17 start. Lewis joined this proud company in 2012; the former undrafted free agent from Duke completed 22-of-32 passes for 204 yards, a touchdown, and an interception in a 24-10 loss to the Steelers while the entire Browns coaching staff were cleaning out their desks. Like the mystery starters who came before him, Lewis did not embarrass himself; that was his employer's prerogative. His career prospects are comparable to Wynn's.

Ryan Lindley | Height: 6-4 | Weight: 229 | College: San Diego State | Draft: 2012/6 (185) | Born: 22-Jun-1989 | Age: 24 | Risk: Green

Year	Team	G/GS	Snaps	Att	Comp	C%	Yds	TD	INT/Adj	FUM	ASR	NY/P	Rk	DVOA	Rk	DYAR	Rk	YAR	Runs	Yds	TD	DVOA	DYAR	QBR
2012	ARI	7/4	303	171	89	52.0%	752	0	7/9	3	5.7%	3.6	39	-55.8%	39	-482	38	-601	4	7	0	-21.8%	-1	9.8
2013	ARI			557	338	60.7%	3656	14	18	8		5.5		-14.7%					28	48	0	-14.2%		
	2012:	48% Short		34% Mid		13% Deep	6% Bomb		YAC: 2.9 (39)												Bomb	YAC: 5.3 (16)		

In his rookie season, Lindley set two "interesting" marks. First, he made the highest percentage of throws from the pocket of any qualifying quarterback in 2012 at 94.6%. Second, he threw every single one of his 171 passes without a touchdown, the longest score-less streak of this century. (It shattered the 91-pass scoreless streak that Ken Dorsey had for the 2008 Browns.) Not surprisingly, his red zone DVOA of -194.6% was by far the worst among all quarterbacks who threw more than one pass in that area last season. With Lindley, there is the occasional potential for splash plays—as game-tape maven Greg Cosell told Yahoo! Sports around the time the Cardinals took Lindley in the sixth round, one could put together a reel of Lindley's 20 best throws and swear he was a first-round talent. Sadly, as Cosell also noted, there's the matter of those other pesky plays. New Cards head coach Bruce Arians prefers mobile quarterbacks (which Lindley is not) with plus arm strength (which Lindley has), and Lindley will presumably get a chance to do something at or near the red zone in the preseason before reality comes crashing down.

Jake Locker | Height: 6-3 | Weight: 231 | College: Washington | Draft: 2011/1 (8) | Born: 15-Jun-1988 | Age: 25 | Risk: Red

Year	Team	G/GS	Snaps	Att	Comp	C%	Yds	TD	INT/Adj	FUM	ASR	NY/P	Rk	DVOA	Rk	DYAR	Rk	YAR	Runs	Yds	TD	DVOA	DYAR	QBR
2011	TEN	5/0	98	66	34	51.5%	542	4	0/1	0	8.3%	7.2	--	22.0%	--	143	--	172	8	56	1	61.4%	27	44.8
2012	TEN	11/11	595	314	177	56.4%	2176	10	11/13	4	8.2%	5.9	25	-23.6%	32	-265	31	-198	41	291	1	20.4%	54	48.1
2013	TEN			531	312	58.8%	3757	23	19	8		6.2		-7.9%					78	332	2	-2.0%		
	2012:	40% Short		39% Mid		12% Deep	9% Bomb		YAC: 4.7 (27)			2011:		49% Short		31% Mid		15% Deep	5% Bomb	YAC: 7.8 (--)				

Aside from "run the ball," it was hard to find anything Locker did consistently well in 2012. He struggled to identify second and third reads. He took too many hits, including from slot blitzers he failed to identify, and got hurt. When he did throw, it was often inaccurate, and many of the passes he did complete lacked touch and precise accuracy. He struggled with pocket presence even before the Titans' offensive line collapsed due to injury. Locker is still the unquestioned starter, but his struggles inspired the Titans to orient the offense around the running game. When he does throw, they'll try to get him out of the pocket, where he tends to be more comfortable and more mechanically sound. Hiding the quarterback worked for Vince Young, more or less—at least, it did until he self-destructed. While Young had better downfield touch than Locker has shown, Locker doesn't carry the same off-the-field baggage. It could work.

Andrew Luck | Height: 6-4 | Weight: 234 | College: Stanford | Draft: 2012/1 (1) | Born: 12-Mar-1989 | Age: 24 | Risk: Yellow

Year	Team	G/GS	Snaps	Att	Comp	C%	Yds	TD	INT/Adj	FUM	ASR	NY/P	Rk	DVOA	Rk	DYAR	Rk	YAR	Runs	Yds	TD	DVOA	DYAR	QBR
2012	IND	16/16	1169	627	339	54.1%	4374	23	18/30	15	6.8%	6.2	19	-5.1%	19	257	19	366	62	255	5	41.0%	123	65.0
2013	IND			605	373	61.6%	4552	28	20	10		6.6		-0.6%					61	238	4	19.7%		
	2012:	37% Short		38% Mid		17% Deep	8% Bomb		YAC: 4.9 (24)															

Luck established several rookie passing records, including passing yards in a game (433) and in a season (4,374). He also led the Colts with five rushing touchdowns and was third among NFL quarterbacks in rushing DYAR, trailing only Cam Newton and Russell Wilson. Unfortunately, Luck's 18 interceptions nearly matched the 22 interceptions he had during his entire 38-game career at Stanford, and his Adjusted Interception total suggests he should have had more. All those picks and near-picks can be partly attributed to the downfield passing system under Bruce Arians, which also left Luck vulnerable to contact. Luck was hit 83 times, 20 more than any other quarterback, and his 122 knockdowns were 29 more than any other quarterback. Surprisingly, Luck had the lowest DVOA differential between plays with and without pressure: he was 23rd in DVOA without pressure, but fourth under pressure, behind only Ben Roethlisberger, Russell Wilson, and Aaron Rodgers. The departure of Arians and arrival of Pep Hamilton, Luck's former offensive coordinator and quarterbacks coach at Stanford, should help Luck's completion rate and DVOA rise. It would also suggest a drop in interceptions, except some of those Adjusted Interceptions aren't going to be dropped this year.

Ryan Mallett | Height: 6-7 | Weight: 253 | College: Arkansas | Draft: 2011/3 (74) | Born: 5-Jun-1988 | Age: 25 | Risk: Yellow

Year	Team	G/GS	Snaps	Att	Comp	C%	Yds	TD	INT/Adj	FUM	ASR	NY/P	Rk	DVOA	Rk	DYAR	Rk	YAR	Runs	Yds	TD	DVOA	DYAR	QBR
2012	NE	4/0	24	4	1	25.0%	17	0	1/0	0	-3.2%	4.3	--	-237.3%	--	-44	--	-46	8	-9	0	--	--	0.9
2013	NE			589	360	61.1%	4456	27	19	8		6.6		7.2%					24	52	1	3.5%		
	2012:	50% Short		50% Mid		0% Deep	0% Bomb		YAC: 19.0 (--)															

Mallett's time in New England certainly seems like a success so far. The Patriots were comfortable enough with his progress to cut veteran Brian Hoyer before the season and make Mallett their lone backup. His awful numbers in mop-up duty are almost entirely due to a pass that bounced off the hands of Visanthe Shiancoe and into the hands of Houston's Shiloh Keo. The only headlines he's made off the field are about his close friendship with Red Sox third baseman Will Middlebrooks. There were some trade talks regarding Mallett this offseason, but a trade was always going to be more likely in 2014 because of the NFL rule that bans players from renegotiating their rookie contracts until after three seasons. Once other teams can sign Mallett to a long-term deal, we'll get to see if the Pats can flip him for a first- or second-round pick.

Eli Manning			Height: 6-4		Weight: 218		College: Mississippi		Draft: 2004/1 (1)		Born: 3-Jan-1981		Age: 33		Risk: Green					
Year	Team	G/GS	Snaps	Att	Comp	C%	Yds	TD	INT/Adj	FUM	ASR	NY/P	Rk	DVOA	Rk	DYAR	Rk	YAR	Runs	Yds	TD	DVOA	DYAR	QBR
2010	NYG	16/16	1059	539	339	62.9%	4002	31	25/24	6	3.3%	7.0	6	4.1%	20	545	15	609	32	70	0	47.4%	32	65.5
2011	NYG	16/16	1075	589	359	61.0%	4933	29	16/17	8	5.0%	7.6	6	16.2%	9	1110	8	1136	35	15	1	-43.3%	-18	59.4
2012	NYG	16/16	1003	536	321	59.9%	3948	26	15/24	4	4.3%	6.8	9	9.0%	13	753	10	779	20	30	0	-40.5%	-15	67.4
2013	NYG			554	345	62.3%	4102	27	16	5		6.8		10.8%					22	34	1	-3.2%		
2012:	38% Short		42% Mid		11% Deep		8% Bomb		YAC: 4.3 (34)		2011:		43% Short		31% Mid		17% Deep		10% Bomb		YAC: 5.8 (7)		

With assists from good health and a passer-friendly environment, Eli Manning is starting to creep up the record books. Did you know that Manning ranks third in passing yards and fourth in passing touchdowns by a player in his first nine seasons? Manning had been on an upward trajectory over the last few years, culminating in his monster 2011 season when he produced the eighth-most passing yards in NFL history. While he passed for roughly 1,000 fewer yards in 2012, there are two big explanations: he threw 53 fewer passes and his receivers gained fewer yards after the catch.

The Giants ranked second in offensive points per drive in 2012, and their success as a unit starts with Manning. Unlike his draft classmates Philip Rivers and Ben Roethlisberger, Manning appears to be just entering his prime years. New York has surrounded him with young talent at wide receiver, and the Giants should have a top offense as long as Manning is healthy.

Peyton Manning			Height: 6-5		Weight: 230		College: Tennessee		Draft: 1998/1 (1)		Born: 24-Mar-1976		Age: 37		Risk: Green					
Year	Team	G/GS	Snaps	Att	Comp	C%	Yds	TD	INT/Adj	FUM	ASR	NY/P	Rk	DVOA	Rk	DYAR	Rk	YAR	Runs	Yds	TD	DVOA	DYAR	QBR
2010	IND	16/16	1121	679	450	66.3%	4700	33	17/25	3	2.8%	6.6	11	19.0%	6	1400	3	1598	18	18	0	81.9%	13	69.0
2012	DEN	16/16	1111	583	400	68.6%	4659	37	11/14	2	4.2%	7.5	1	32.8%	2	1805	2	1956	23	6	0	-5.4%	2	84.1
2013	DEN			589	399	67.8%	4670	35	11	4		7.4		29.9%					20	1	0	-16.2%		
2012:	50% Short		31% Mid		12% Deep		7% Bomb		YAC: 4.7 (28)										Bomb		YAC: 5.8 (7)		

The worries about Manning's neck have certainly abated. Early in his debut season with the Broncos, Manning showed mildly concerning hints of decreased arm strength. Timing-based downfield throws and deep-out patterns looked unusually challenging. However, Manning's ball gradually regained its zip as the season progressed. By late December, the Broncos were atop the AFC and Manning was making every throw en route to claiming what almost became a fifth MVP award (he finished second to Adrian Peterson in the voting, though he did top the Vikings running back for Comeback Player of the Year award).

There's nothing that suggests Manning won't pick up right where he left off. He's more familiar with the Broncos culture. He has a good working relationship with Adam Gase, who replaces Mike McCoy as Denver's offensive coordinator. He has all the weapons around him, including what might be the league's best wide receiving trio in Demaryius Thomas, Eric Decker and Wes Welker. And he still has all the Manning skills that have built his Hall of Fame career (great pocket mobility, precision accuracy, pre-snap diagnostics, etc.).

E.J. Manuel			Height: 6-5		Weight: 240		College: Florida State		Draft: 2013/1 (16)		Born: 19-Mar-1990		Age: 23		Risk: Red					
Year	Team	G/GS	Snaps	Att	Comp	C%	Yds	TD	INT/Adj	FUM	ASR	NY/P	Rk	DVOA	Rk	DYAR	Rk	YAR	Runs	Yds	TD	DVOA	DYAR	QBR
2013	BUF			481	286	59.6%	3607	17	16	7		6.8		-1.3%					80	448	5	25.7%		

There wasn't much agreement between draftniks when it came to this year's quarterback prospects. Most analysts had Geno Smith as their top guy, but not everybody. Russ Lande loved Ryan Nassib. Our own Matt Waldman put Tyler Wilson on top. Some thought Matt Barkley would thrive in the NFL, others thought he would be exposed. But there was one thing every draftnik seemed to agree upon: they liked Manuel more than conventional wisdom did. When everyone agrees, of course, that becomes the new conventional wisdom. So when the Bills grabbed Manuel as the only quarterback chosen in the first round of the draft, it wasn't quite the shock that TV pundits made it out to be.

Manuel has great size and physical tools. He's mobile, he can throw on the run, and among the 2013 quarterbacks he is by far the best choice if you want to run a read-option offense. And Florida State actually ran a complex offense, so Manuel has experience doing a lot of different things and reading defenses from different perspectives. On the other hand, he has a slow windup and sometimes struggles with inaccuracy on short throws. He also takes way too many risks as a scrambler and will really need to learn to slide and forget about gaining every last yard. Manuel and Kevin Kolb split reps with the first team during offseason activities and head coach Doug Marrone claims he'll pick a starter sooner rather than later. The Bills don't have anything to lose by putting Manuel right in there from day one, but to be honest they don't have anything to lose by letting Kolb take some bumps while Manuel is learning on the sidelines either.

Josh McCown Height: 6-4   Weight: 215   College: Sam Houston State   Draft: 2002/3 (81)   Born: 4-Jul-1979   Age: 34   Risk: Green

Year	Team	G/GS	Snaps	Att	Comp	C%	Yds	TD	INT/Adj	FUM	ASR	NY/P	Rk	DVOA	Rk	DYAR	Rk	YAR	Runs	Yds	TD	DVOA	DYAR	QBR
2011	CHI	3/2	137	55	35	63.6%	414	2	4/6	2	11.2%	6.0	--	-50.5%	--	-146	--	-110	12	68	0	12.2%	16	26.0
2013	CHI			477	279	58.5%	3213	19	16	10		5.7		-21.9%					44	38	1	-19.6%		

2011:   35% Short   48% Mid   9% Deep   7% Bomb   YAC: 4.8 (--)

You'll miss the McCown brothers when they're gone. Oh sure, they barely register as competent backups at this point, but it's for the best that overenthusiastic Pop Warner dads everywhere learn sibling rivalry can only generate a pair of career backups. No, don't try to think of any other examples of quarterback-playing brothers. Hasn't happened in recent memory. Here's a table comparing the McCowns (Table 2).

Table 2. Comparison of Football-Related McCowns

McCown	Drafted	NFL seasons	Seasons with DVOA > 0%	Coolest Career Accomplishment	Random Fact!
Josh McCown	2002/3 (81)	10	0	Knocked Minnesota out of the playoffs on the last day of the 2003 season	Played wide receiver for the Lions because Mike Martz is insane
Luke McCown	2004/4 (106)	7	1	Blew a fourth-down conversion, but aced the celebratory aspect	Was once actually traded for an "undisclosed draft pick"
Rivers McCown	N/A	0	0	Convinced bosses to run completely irrelevant table in *Football Outsiders Almanac 2013*	Once stayed up 54 hours in a row to beat Final Fantasy IX on a bet

The winner? America.

Luke McCown Height: 6-3   Weight: 208   College: Louisiana Tech   Draft: 2004/4 (106)   Born: 12-Jul-1981   Age: 32   Risk: Red

Year	Team	G/GS	Snaps	Att	Comp	C%	Yds	TD	INT/Adj	FUM	ASR	NY/P	Rk	DVOA	Rk	DYAR	Rk	YAR	Runs	Yds	TD	DVOA	DYAR	QBR
2010	JAC	1/0	27	19	11	57.9%	120	0	0/1	0	0.0%	6.3	--	25.9%	--	44	--	28	1	4	0	-53.5%	-2	37.0
2011	JAC	4/2	131	56	30	53.6%	296	0	4/5	2	7.1%	4.3	--	-73.5%	--	-251	--	-274	7	23	0	32.9%	14	13.4
2013	NO			614	369	60.0%	4347	23	19	10		6.2		-3.4%					30	6	1	-25.1%		

2011:   47% Short   35% Mid   16% Deep   2% Bomb   YAC: 4.7 (--)

McCown didn't throw a single pass last season while backing up Matt Ryan in Atlanta. He hasn't thrown a touchdown pass since 2007. This is where we would normally add a joke about Saints fans preferring Rivers McCown to Luke McCown if Drew Brees gets injured, but we just went to that well a few sentences ago.

Colt McCoy Height: 6-1   Weight: 216   College: Texas   Draft: 2010/3 (85)   Born: 5-Sep-1986   Age: 27   Risk: Green

Year	Team	G/GS	Snaps	Att	Comp	C%	Yds	TD	INT/Adj	FUM	ASR	NY/P	Rk	DVOA	Rk	DYAR	Rk	YAR	Runs	Yds	TD	DVOA	DYAR	QBR
2010	CLE	8/8	452	222	135	60.8%	1576	6	9/11	1	9.3%	6.0	32	-1.8%	24	148	27	84	28	136	1	48.9%	64	45.1
2011	CLE	13/13	876	463	265	57.2%	2733	14	11/15	10	6.7%	5.1	38	-15.1%	32	-132	36	-161	61	212	0	-16.5%	-11	40.1
2012	CLE	3/0	39	17	9	52.9%	79	1	0/0	0	16.6%	2.6	--	-2.7%	--	10	--	-23	4	15	0	67.7%	9	13.1
2013	SF			441	296	67.2%	3178	19	13	6		6.4		-0.5%					55	225	2	10.7%		

2012:   38% Short   44% Mid   19% Deep   0% Bomb   YAC: 2.7 (--)   2011:   54% Short   31% Mid   10% Deep   5% Bomb   YAC: 4.6 (35)

Against Denver in Week 16, McCoy managed just 17 pass attempts in relief of injured Brandon Weeden before getting injured himself. In the early part of the 2013 offseason, McCoy was in some weird Browns limbo, doing penance for the sin of exposing the gross negligence of a team that sent him onto the field after suffering one of the most obvious concussions in modern sports history back in 2011. The Browns let him twist in the wind until trading him in early April to the 49ers. McCoy took some parting shots at the Browns once safely out of Cleveland, noting that the 49ers' focus on winning is "obviously different than some of the things that I've been a part of the last few years." Browns expatriate quarterbacks are often forced to wander the league like itinerant monks (see Brady Quinn's career). McCoy, having served his time in purgatory, can settle into life as a capable backup.

Greg McElroy Height: 6-2   Weight: 222   College: Alabama   Draft: 2011/7 (208)   Born: 10-May-1988   Age: 25   Risk: Green

Year	Team	G/GS	Snaps	Att	Comp	C%	Yds	TD	INT/Adj	FUM	ASR	NY/P	Rk	DVOA	Rk	DYAR	Rk	YAR	Runs	Yds	TD	DVOA	DYAR	QBR
2012	NYJ	2/1	90	31	19	61.3%	214	1	1/1	1	25.7%	3.5	--	-44.6%	--	-82	--	-84	8	30	0	-4.7%	2	45.2
2013	NYJ			491	283	57.6%	3180	18	20	10		5.3		-28.3%					56	153	1	-17.5%		

2012:   47% Short   43% Mid   7% Deep   3% Bomb   YAC: 6.5 (--)   Bomb   YAC: 4.6 (35)

It was nice of the Jets to finally give McElroy a shot at starting, but he's going to be seeing Kendall Reyes in his nightmares until the day he dies. The Chargers sacked McElroy 11 times, and it would have been more if not for a couple of short scrambles that were a yard or two away from counting as sacks. Eighteen times since the merger, a team has given up 11 or more sacks in a game, and out of those 18 games, McElroy had the second best completion rate and yards per attempt. Unfortunately, with Geno Smith now in town, that's probably the only tape he'll ever have of himself as an NFL starter; in fact, some media reports during OTAs suggested McElroy might not even make the team in 2013.

Matt Moore

Height: 6-3   Weight: 202   College: Oregon State   Draft: 2007/FA   Born: 9-Aug-1984   Age: 29   Risk: Red

Year	Team	G/GS	Snaps	Att	Comp	C%	Yds	TD	INT/Adj	FUM	ASR	NY/P	Rk	DVOA	Rk	DYAR	Rk	YAR	Runs	Yds	TD	DVOA	DYAR	QBR
2010	CAR	6/5	268	143	79	55.2%	857	5	10/10	4	7.9%	4.9	42	-42.8%	43	-324	43	-342	5	25	0	-11.0%	0	25.0
2011	MIA	13/12	774	347	210	60.5%	2497	16	9/12	13	9.0%	5.9	27	-5.7%	24	133	22	124	32	65	2	-34.9%	-21	56.7
2012	MIA	10/0	55	19	11	57.9%	131	1	0/0	0	9.7%	5.8	--	15.5%	--	40	--	31	5	-3	0	-110.2%	-4	59.7
2013	MIA			507	305	60.1%	3287	17	12	11		5.4		-12.7%					28	78	2	4.7%		

2012:	44% Short	19% Mid	13% Deep	25% Bomb	YAC: 2.5 (--)	2011:	45% Short	30% Mid	15% Deep	11% Bomb	YAC: 4.1 (44)

The fact that Moore re-signed with Miami for two more years indicates that he's resigned to being a backup quarterback in perpetuity. He's only 28 and has made only 25 career starts, so it's not like he's at a stage in his career where he needs (or is qualified) to be Matt Hasselbeck—and yet, instead of doing anything in his power to move to one of the five teams lacking a clear starter, he opted for the status quo: no chance of starting barring injury. It's at this point that we notice Moore got a raise of $1.5 million per year, check our bank accounts, and remember the wisdom of Ted DiBiase: Everyone's got a price.

Ryan Nassib

Height: 6-2   Weight: 229   College: Syracuse   Draft: 2013/4 (110)   Born: 10-Mar-1990   Age: 23   Risk: Green

Year	Team	G/GS	Snaps	Att	Comp	C%	Yds	TD	INT/Adj	FUM	ASR	NY/P	Rk	DVOA	Rk	DYAR	Rk	YAR	Runs	Yds	TD	DVOA	DYAR	QBR
2013	NYG			495	290	58.7%	3566	16	17	6		6.4		0.6%					47	174	3	12.9%		

Nassib shot up draft boards due to his strong fundamentals, which include a quick release, excellent footwork, and stellar pocket presence. He doesn't have Eli Manning's size or arm strength, but he's an accurate quarterback who can read defenses well given his experience level. In the opener against Northwestern last year, he threw four straight touchdown passes in the second half after Syracuse fell into a 35-13 deficit. While Nassib may be NFL-ready, he probably won't have to be: Eli Manning has started 135 straight games, the longest active streak by a quarterback and third in NFL history behind only his brother and Brett Favre.

Cam Newton

Height: 6-5   Weight: 248   College: Auburn   Draft: 2011/1 (1)   Born: 11-May-1989   Age: 24   Risk: Yellow

Year	Team	G/GS	Snaps	Att	Comp	C%	Yds	TD	INT/Adj	FUM	ASR	NY/P	Rk	DVOA	Rk	DYAR	Rk	YAR	Runs	Yds	TD	DVOA	DYAR	QBR
2011	CAR	16/16	1035	517	310	60.0%	4051	21	17/24	5	7.3%	6.9	10	0.8%	16	407	15	428	126	706	14	14.5%	188	55.0
2012	CAR	16/16	1019	485	280	57.7%	3869	19	12/15	14	7.6%	7.0	6	2.0%	15	422	14	422	127	741	8	11.3%	149	54.2
2013	CAR			495	308	62.3%	3897	23	13	9		6.9		0.2%					106	608	8	42.3%		

2012:	40% Short	37% Mid	16% Deep	8% Bomb	YAC: 6.1 (1)	2011:	43% Short	32% Mid	18% Deep	7% Bomb	YAC: 6.2 (5)

The decline of Cam Newton, like so many perceived setbacks in Carolina last season, was more myth than reality. He had problems with fumbles, but his yards per play went up and his interception rate went down. Like the rest of the team, though, he did struggle early in the year. In Weeks 1 to 8, his passing DVOA was -11.9%, but after that it climbed to 17.8%. The one area where he must improve as a passer is the red zone, where he went 22-of-59 for 188 yards with eight touchdowns and two interceptions. That's a -24.0% DVOA, only slightly better than the -29.8% he posted as a rookie. Of course, he can always run the ball into the end zone (he had seven touchdowns in 26 red zone rushes last year), but he'll need to develop a goal-line passing touch to maximize his potential.

Kyle Orton

Height: 6-4   Weight: 226   College: Purdue   Draft: 2005/4 (106)   Born: 14-Nov-1982   Age: 31   Risk: Green

Year	Team	G/GS	Snaps	Att	Comp	C%	Yds	TD	INT/Adj	FUM	ASR	NY/P	Rk	DVOA	Rk	DYAR	Rk	YAR	Runs	Yds	TD	DVOA	DYAR	QBR
2010	DEN	13/13	868	498	293	58.8%	3653	20	9/17	3	6.6%	6.5	15	8.3%	17	664	12	708	22	98	0	6.4%	16	48.0
2011	2TM	9/8	493	252	150	59.5%	1758	9	9/13	2	5.4%	6.4	17	-5.4%	23	97	25	170	11	13	0	4.9%	3	49.8
2012	DAL	1/0	11	10	9	90.0%	89	1	0/0	0	1.0%	8.9	--	110.7%	--	95	--	79	0	0	0	--	--	99.4
2013	DAL			601	369	61.3%	4224	26	17	9		6.1		0.5%					30	56	0	-8.6%		

2012:	50% Short	40% Mid	10% Deep	0% Bomb	YAC: 2.7 (--)	2011:	47% Short	35% Mid	12% Deep	5% Bomb	YAC: 5.0 (28)

Orton spent most of last season on the bench, as Tony Romo stayed generally healthy all year. His only time last season was at the end of a five-pick Romo debacle against the Bears, Orton's first team, in Week 4. Orton is an ideal "don't screw it up" backup who can easily sub and execute a basic version of Dallas' offense if Romo gets hurt or has one of those days. There are worse ways to spend the final years of one's career.

Brock Osweiler

Height: 6-7   Weight: 242   College: Arizona State   Draft: 2012/2 (57)   Born: 22-Nov-1990   Age: 23   Risk: Yellow

Year	Team	G/GS	Snaps	Att	Comp	C%	Yds	TD	INT/Adj	FUM	ASR	NY/P	Rk	DVOA	Rk	DYAR	Rk	YAR	Runs	Yds	TD	DVOA	DYAR	QBR
2012	DEN	5/0	33	4	2	50.0%	12	0	0/0	0	-1.5%	3.0	--	-1.4%	--	2	--	7	8	-13	0	--	--	10.4
2013	DEN			532	300	56.5%	3961	15	19	7		6.3		4.1%					33	136	2	4.0%		
	2012:	75% Short		25% Mid		0% Deep	0% Bomb		YAC: 1.5 (--)															

Osweiler figures to be "the future" in Denver after Peyton Manning, though right now the Broncos are not even close to thinking about when that might be. The 2012 second-round pick is a good natural athlete with enough raw arm strength to attempt most NFL throws, but iffy accuracy. He figures to be ill-prepared for game action given that a) Manning takes nearly every snap in practice, and b) Osweiler started only 15 games at Arizona State.

Carson Palmer

Height: 6-5   Weight: 230   College: USC   Draft: 2003/1 (1)   Born: 27-Dec-1979   Age: 34   Risk: Green

Year	Team	G/GS	Snaps	Att	Comp	C%	Yds	TD	INT/Adj	FUM	ASR	NY/P	Rk	DVOA	Rk	DYAR	Rk	YAR	Runs	Yds	TD	DVOA	DYAR	QBR
2010	CIN	16/16	1089	586	362	61.8%	3970	26	20/28	6	4.8%	6.2	20	7.1%	18	731	10	589	32	50	0	-25.2%	-14	43.5
2011	OAK	10/9	638	328	199	60.7%	2753	13	16/23	2	5.6%	7.7	5	2.5%	15	295	18	298	16	20	1	-32.1%	-16	62.6
2012	OAK	15/15	953	565	345	61.1%	4018	22	14/20	8	4.8%	6.5	16	-2.2%	18	340	18	447	18	36	1	17.1%	23	44.7
2013	ARI			574	362	63.2%	4126	22	19	6		6.2		-2.5%					14	20	1	-5.1%		
	2012:	44% Short		37% Mid		13% Deep	6% Bomb		YAC: 5.7 (4)			2011:	37% Short		35% Mid		20% Deep		8% Bomb	YAC: 5.3 (16)				

Palmer put up some big numbers last year in Oakland, but straddled with a depleted receiving corps, injury-riddled backfield, and iffy offensive line, he was not remotely close to the star gunslinger that once had people excited in Cincinnati. At this point in his career, Palmer is a veteran bridge quarterback. You can run your entire offense with him as your starter, but if you're banking heavily on him, you probably shouldn't count on running that offense in the postseason.

Palmer still has an NFL caliber-arm, though he's lost some zip and power over the years (elbow problems in 2008 likely contributed to this). What's concerning is that his accuracy tends to waver, particularly on throws further downfield. This can lead to serious problems when Palmer tries to fit tough balls through tight windows, which he's always been more than willing to do. For a veteran who has learned a variety of different offensive concepts over the years, Palmer sure plays with iffy awareness at times. He's not always great at reading the blitz and he'll occasionally make reckless throws into coverage.

Of course, these risks can occasionally bring rewards. Palmer will have in 2013 something he hasn't had in several years is: a legit No. 1 receiver who can make plays in congestion. Larry Fitzgerald will appreciate the veteran quarterback's aggression. Many believe Palmer's lack of mobility will be a problem behind Arizona's bad offensive line, but Palmer does have decent pocket awareness and is willing to step up in the face of pressure. Those are the most important traits for overcoming bad blocking.

Christian Ponder

Height: 6-2   Weight: 229   College: Florida State   Draft: 2011/1 (12)   Born: 25-Feb-1988   Age: 25   Risk: Yellow

Year	Team	G/GS	Snaps	Att	Comp	C%	Yds	TD	INT/Adj	FUM	ASR	NY/P	Rk	DVOA	Rk	DYAR	Rk	YAR	Runs	Yds	TD	DVOA	DYAR	QBR
2011	MIN	11/10	574	291	158	54.3%	1853	13	13/17	6	10.5%	5.3	36	-31.5%	43	-404	45	-378	28	219	0	36.5%	59	33.7
2012	MIN	16/16	1032	483	300	62.1%	2935	18	12/19	7	6.5%	5.3	34	-6.1%	21	173	21	66	60	253	2	4.2%	36	53.8
2013	MIN			490	293	59.9%	3239	18	15	9		5.6		-19.9%					51	195	3	9.1%		
	2012:	54% Short		32% Mid		10% Deep	5% Bomb		YAC: 5.3 (9)			2011:	42% Short		38% Mid		11% Deep		9% Bomb	YAC: 5.3 (19)				

We spent the majority of the Vikings chapter discussing the troubling trends and issues that Ponder has at this point in his career, so let's try to be a little more optimistic here. One element that could give Ponder some extra value, should the Vikings choose to go in that direction, is the read option. It may be that the NFL just hasn't fully adjusted to it yet, but the Seahawks, Redskins, and 49ers finished 1-2-3 in rushing DVOA last season, and all of them incoporated consistent elements of the read-option. Ponder has been successful when he has run with the ball, and looked especially dangerous in the open field in his rookie season. Even if he never develops a deep ball, his talents could play up a little further if the Vikings got creative with his athleticism. Minnesota ran more play-action than any team but Washington and Seattle last year, but Ponder had just two designed runs all season. All these machinations wouldn't make up for the fact that Ponder is not very good when it's third-and-8, but it would be interesting to see just how far the Vikings could push things with the best running back of our era.

Terrelle Pryor

Height: 6-6   Weight: 233   College: Ohio State   Draft: 2011/3 (SUP)   Born: 20-Jun-1989   Age: 24   Risk: Red

Year	Team	G/GS	Snaps	Att	Comp	C%	Yds	TD	INT/Adj	FUM	ASR	NY/P	Rk	DVOA	Rk	DYAR	Rk	YAR	Runs	Yds	TD	DVOA	DYAR	QBR
2012	OAK	3/1	69	30	14	46.7%	155	2	1/1	1	-0.1%	5.0	--	-9.1%	--	4	--	16	10	51	1	23.2%	22	59.7
2013	OAK			466	240	51.5%	3360	13	18	8		6.0		-15.4%					89	723	5	22.7%		
	2012:	37% Short		37% Mid		13% Deep	13% Bomb		YAC: 2.1 (--)															

The Raiders claim they're high on Pryor, but there's a reason they brought in Matt Flynn. Pryor has intriguing upside as a potential read-option quarterback in today's NFL. This isn't to say he's strictly a Tebow-style run-only quarterback—he's flashed some arm talent to go along with his size and wheels. The Raiders coaching staff loves his work ethic and willingness to learn.

But at this point, there's simply too much still left for the 2011 supplemental third-round pick to learn. Pryor is unrefined in a lot of his basic quarterbacking mechanics and he has little to no experience reading NFL defenses.

Brady Quinn   Height: 6-3   Weight: 235   College: Notre Dame   Draft: 2007/1 (22)   Born: 27-Oct-1984   Age: 29   Risk: Yellow

Year	Team	G/GS	Snaps	Att	Comp	C%	Yds	TD	INT/Adj	FUM	ASR	NY/P	Rk	DVOA	Rk	DYAR	Rk	YAR	Runs	Yds	TD	DVOA	DYAR	QBR
2012	KC	10/8	474	197	112	56.9%	1141	2	8/6	1	9.4%	4.6	38	-43.8%	38	-440	37	-448	19	66	0	-17.5%	-4	27.4
2013	SEA			453	277	61.2%	3234	17	14	7		6.3		0.7%					34	86	1	1.7%		
	2012:	51% Short		30% Mid		14% Deep	5% Bomb		YAC: 4.3 (35)															

Quinn has never turned into the Tom Brady 2.0 that so many thought he would be coming out of Notre Dame, but just because Quinn has disappointed as a starter does not mean he isn't a respectable backup now. Yes, he was terrible in Kansas City last year, but so was everyone else who took a snap for the Chiefs. Quinn has a lively arm, showing the ability to throw with some zip and accuracy. The problem is, he's too risk-averse to use it. Like so many backups, Quinn has a tendency to check down too early in his progressions. He's not comfortable scanning an entire field, and this limits what an offense can do with him under center.

Philip Rivers   Height: 6-5   Weight: 228   College: North Carolina State   Draft: 2004/1 (4)   Born: 8-Dec-1981   Age: 32   Risk: Red

Year	Team	G/GS	Snaps	Att	Comp	C%	Yds	TD	INT/Adj	FUM	ASR	NY/P	Rk	DVOA	Rk	DYAR	Rk	YAR	Runs	Yds	TD	DVOA	DYAR	QBR
2010	SD	16/16	1050	541	357	66.0%	4710	30	13/16	6	6.8%	7.8	1	27.9%	3	1419	2	1629	29	52	0	-0.7%	9	63.4
2011	SD	16/16	1078	582	366	62.9%	4624	27	20/25	8	5.4%	7.2	7	17.0%	8	1117	7	1038	26	36	1	7.5%	14	62.7
2012	SD	16/16	1023	527	338	64.1%	3606	26	15/18	14	8.9%	5.7	30	-7.3%	22	138	22	124	27	40	0	-46.5%	-19	40.6
2013	SD			546	347	63.6%	3726	27	15	7		5.4		-2.5%					17	33	0	-0.7%		
	2012:	50% Short		32% Mid		10% Deep	8% Bomb		YAC: 5.3 (10)		2011:	45% Short		31% Mid		16% Deep	8% Bomb	YAC: 5.4 (13)						

Rivers is coming off arguably the worst season of what's been an impressive career. Given that he threw 20 interceptions in 2011, some are speculating that the nine-year veteran could be playing for his job in 2013. Rivers' greatest strength has always been his willingness to make throws in the face of pressure. He has tremendous pocket toughness in this sense. However, his pocket poise can sometimes lapse. He identifies blitzes well but plays notably faster (and thus sloppier) when he expects pressure. That's a problem given San Diego's issues along the offensive line.

"Inconsistent" would be the most accurate way to describe Rivers as of late. At times he has made unbelievable anticipation throws in to tight windows. At other times, he's struggled to get a comfortable feel for what the defense is doing. Overall, he has made too many inaccurate throws, especially on routine plays. There has also been some evidence that suggests Rivers's arm strength is starting to decline. This may be part of the reason he was much more effective throwing inside than outside last season. Because of Rivers's naturally aggressive style of play, too many of the types of mistakes covered here have led to turnovers.

Aaron Rodgers   Height: 6-2   Weight: 223   College: California   Draft: 2005/1 (24)   Born: 2-Dec-1983   Age: 30   Risk: Yellow

Year	Team	G/GS	Snaps	Att	Comp	C%	Yds	TD	INT/Adj	FUM	ASR	NY/P	Rk	DVOA	Rk	DYAR	Rk	YAR	Runs	Yds	TD	DVOA	DYAR	QBR
2010	GB	15/15	889	475	312	65.7%	3922	28	11/15	3	6.9%	7.4	2	26.8%	4	1286	4	1241	64	356	4	24.6%	98	69.4
2011	GB	15/15	919	502	343	68.3%	4643	45	6/4	3	7.2%	8.3	1	46.6%	1	2059	2	2121	60	257	2	18.7%	71	86.2
2012	GB	16/16	1069	552	371	67.2%	4295	39	8/11	7	8.7%	6.7	13	23.4%	4	1395	4	1276	54	259	2	30.6%	94	72.5
2013	GB			542	365	67.3%	4365	39	10	6		7.2		26.3%					50	224	2	26.5%		
	2012:	50% Short		33% Mid		11% Deep	6% Bomb		YAC: 5.5 (6)		2011:	43% Short		36% Mid		14% Deep	7% Bomb	YAC: 5.9 (6)						

In order to avoid re-stating the obvious, sometimes a writer is best served using the process of defamiliarization. By giving a voice to someone out of the normal sphere, sometimes you'll find a fresh perspective. So, rather than harp on the excellent presnap reads and cannon arm that have made Rodgers one of the best quarterbacks in the NFL, I'll offer three observations from my 15-year-old half-sister. 1) "He's really mean and points at people a lot." 2) "He throws it pretty hard but I'm not sure if it's the hardest." 3) "He looks handsome when he grits his teeth."

Based on all of our projection research tools and capabilities, we think Rodgers will continue to be good at football next season. If we develop handsomeness projection systems, we'll let you know.

Ben Roethlisberger   Height: 6-5   Weight: 240   College: Miami (Ohio)   Draft: 2004/1 (11)   Born: 2-Mar-1982   Age: 31   Risk: Yellow

Year	Team	G/GS	Snaps	Att	Comp	C%	Yds	TD	INT/Adj	FUM	ASR	NY/P	Rk	DVOA	Rk	DYAR	Rk	YAR	Runs	Yds	TD	DVOA	DYAR	QBR
2010	PIT	12/12	798	389	240	61.7%	3200	17	5/8	6	8.0%	7.2	4	31.2%	2	1062	6	1013	34	176	2	39.4%	67	64.2
2011	PIT	15/15	989	513	324	63.2%	4077	21	14/20	8	7.2%	6.9	11	13.4%	11	870	9	841	31	70	0	9.2%	18	63.6
2012	PIT	13/13	832	449	284	63.3%	3265	26	8/13	5	6.5%	6.5	15	13.2%	11	761	9	764	26	92	0	-6.2%	5	62.8
2013	PIT			541	344	63.5%	4174	29	15	9		6.7		8.7%					36	65	2	-6.0%		
	2012:	46% Short		34% Mid		14% Deep	6% Bomb		YAC: 5.2 (12)		2011:	42% Short		36% Mid		15% Deep	7% Bomb	YAC: 5.4 (12)						

Roethlisberger currently ranks 23rd on the all-time sack list. Another 30 sacks (matching last year's total) will move him past Ken O'Brien, Steve Bartkowski, Steve Young, Jeff George, Neil Lomax, Ron Jaworski, and Craig Morton into 15th place. Thirty more after that will put Big Ben past 400 for his career, and into a top 10 full of guys who played until they were over 40 (Vinny Testaverde, Warren Moon, Dave Krieg, Brett Favre).

Roethlisberger himself is unlikely to play until 40. His sack percentage dipped in 2012 due to a variety of factors, but it needs to have dipped a few years ago, and Big Ben now needs to miss time for the injuries he previously gutted through. Landry Jones is more of a doughnut spare than a new set of whitewalls, so the Steelers are not preparing for life without Roethlisberger just yet. More realistically, they are preparing for life with Roethlisberger, a quarterback increasingly likely to miss a game or three per season.

Tony Romo Height: 6-2   Weight: 219   College: Eastern Illinois   Draft: 2003/FA   Born: 21-Apr-1980   Age: 33   Risk: Yellow

Year	Team	G/GS	Snaps	Att	Comp	C%	Yds	TD	INT/Adj	FUM	ASR	NY/P	Rk	DVOA	Rk	DYAR	Rk	YAR	Runs	Yds	TD	DVOA	DYAR	QBR
2010	DAL	6/6	360	213	148	69.5%	1605	11	7/8	0	4.5%	7.2	5	13.2%	11	333	19	359	6	38	0	86.7%	21	56.4
2011	DAL	16/16	962	522	346	66.3%	4184	31	10/12	5	6.3%	7.2	8	26.8%	4	1344	4	1280	22	46	1	-18.0%	-4	71.4
2012	DAL	16/16	1089	648	425	65.6%	4903	28	19/25	5	5.9%	6.8	10	14.8%	10	1156	7	1036	30	49	1	-14.9%	-2	62.7
2013	DAL			625	403	64.5%	4706	32	17	7		6.5		8.2%					27	38	1	-10.8%		

| 2012: | 45% Short | 37% Mid | 11% Deep | 6% Bomb | YAC: 4.6 (30) | 2011: | 48% Short | 33% Mid | 12% Deep | 6% Bomb | YAC: 5.7 (10) |

Now that's he's signed the six-year, $108 million contract extension that will keep him in Dallas through the end of his NFL career, we can all return to one of the more fatuous arguments in football: whether or not Romo lacks a "clutch gene." Discussions regarding the "clutchiness" of quarterbacks are generally about as ridiculous as those regarding quarterbacks who "just win," but Romo's been under fire for this alleged defect for years, so we might as well present the actual facts. In four of the last five seasons, including 2012, Romo's DVOA has actually been higher in late and close situations than overall. (We define "late and close" as any play in the second half or overtime with the score within eight points.) It seems like Romo's worst habit is to implode in the spotlight, but in all nationally televised games he's played in since 2008—this is the Cowboys, so the sample size works—he has 48.2% DVOA in late and close situations (Table 3).

The playoff and season-ending performances that have everyone from Jerry Jones to Stone Cold Steve Austin questioning whether Romo "[bleeps] the bed" when it counts (Austin's words, not ours) are mitigated by a few factors. Especially over the last couple of years, Romo has played at a better-than-average level overall when hurt, when his offensive line stinks, and when his receivers run routes that we can't find on any route tree. The Cowboys' Week 17 loss to the Washington Redskins, which kept Dallas from the division title (the second straight year they had lost the tile in the final week of the season), was a perfect example. Romo threw three picks in the game. The first was on a drag route to Kevin Ogletree in which Ogletree failed to match up with Romo's timing. The second pick was a pretty hairy underthrow to Miles Austin, and that was all on the quarterback. The third came late in the fourth quarter, adding to Romo's alleged anti-clutch reputation, and it was a short floater to halfback DeMarco Murray that Romo threw at an awkward angle after linebacker Perry Riley blew through the line on a blitz.

That last play was perhaps most emblematic of Romo's overall career. He's a good-to-great quarterback, perhaps better than people think he is, whose liabilities as a player prevent him from transcending his team's limitations. At any given time, the NFL's truly transcendent quarterbacks can be counted on one hand, and the fact that Romo will never hit that list shouldn't move people from the idea that he actually is pretty special—and he has been special in many of the situations he's accused of ruining.

Table 3. Tony Romo in Late and Close Situations, 2008-2012

Year	Pass DVOA	Late and Close DVOA
2008	12.9%	25.8%
2009	23.9%	33.6%
2010	13.2%	4.1%
2011	26.8%	36.7%
2012	14.8%	26.0%

Matt Ryan Height: 6-4   Weight: 228   College: Boston College   Draft: 2008/1 (3)   Born: 17-May-1985   Age: 28   Risk: Green

Year	Team	G/GS	Snaps	Att	Comp	C%	Yds	TD	INT/Adj	FUM	ASR	NY/P	Rk	DVOA	Rk	DYAR	Rk	YAR	Runs	Yds	TD	DVOA	DYAR	QBR
2010	ATL	16/16	1139	571	357	62.5%	3705	28	9/16	4	4.1%	6.0	29	18.0%	7	1122	5	1080	46	122	0	-11.0%	6	69.7
2011	ATL	16/16	1062	566	347	61.3%	4177	29	12/11	5	5.3%	6.8	12	18.8%	7	1120	6	1204	37	84	2	19.8%	38	69.1
2012	ATL	16/16	1048	615	422	68.6%	4719	32	14/16	4	5.1%	7.0	4	16.5%	8	1196	5	1315	34	141	1	39.7%	54	74.5
2013	ATL			591	385	65.1%	4511	31	15	4		6.8		14.3%					33	86	1	7.4%		

| 2012: | 51% Short | 33% Mid | 11% Deep | 6% Bomb | YAC: 4.9 (23) | 2011: | 45% Short | 35% Mid | 14% Deep | 6% Bomb | YAC: 5.0 (29) |

Sports radio, like Twitter, can often be a shadow world, an insular culture that warps regular consumers into believing that all manner of concocted bushwah are actually popularly held beliefs. That said, the continued assault of Atlanta's three, count 'em, three jock talk stations upon Matt Ryan beggars belief, even by the nature of the medium, which caters to paranoid agoraphobes and people angry about being stuck in traffic. One would think that a high-level franchise quarterback who basically rescued the franchise from oblivion would have an annual parade thrown in his honor, just on general principle. Instead, Ryan is subjected to a torrent of unceasing abuse. Not by the hosts, mind you—this isn't a case of cynical Baylessness run amok. The vitriol comes from the fans. To these folks, Ryan is incredibly lucky and not a man who can ever lead the team to the Super Bowl. The glee that transmits over the air when the Falcons lose and/or Ryan has a bad game is palpable.

Now, it would be simple to dismiss this phenomenon as the bottom end of a low down and dirty means of communication, like judging Khrushchev's popularity by reading nothing but TASS. As an example, one of the loudest outlets for these Ryan-haters was a show called "Mayhem in the AM," whose hosts were recently fired for mocking former Saints defensive back and current ALS sufferer Steve Gleason. But the racial dynamics of the "capitol of Black America" can't be so simply dismissed. The jibes are endemic of genuine feelings in the community. Michael Vick's immense popularity in Atlanta, even now, plays a role, but more important is the prevailing sense that the deck is stacked.

Even as Ryan was being awesome on the field in 2012, off the field the franchise was involved in often fraught negotiations for a new stadium, one that almost certainly won't benefit the mostly poor and black residents near the planned spot for the new field, just as the Georgia Dome and Turner Field didn't do much for them, despite promises to the contrary. Ryan is viewed by many in this context, as a tool of a power structure that games the system while the less fortunate get left behind again. (Arthur Blank received a chunk of public money for construction, though, to be fair, not nearly as much as other owners have extorted across the sporting landscape.) In this way of thinking, an excuse was conjured to bring down the exceptional black quarterback and replace him with a white—and even worse, boring—player. If Ryan ran into any public controversy, that might perversely help him get over with his doubters: it might humanize him, and get him viewed as something other than the exact (and purposeful) antithesis of Vick. As it is, this piece of vanilla extract is perceived as having been shoved down their throat, just as the replacement for the perfectly good Georgia Dome was jammed through despite their protestations.

In short, even though he's clearly established himself as one of the top ten quarterbacks in the NFL, Ryan needs to win a Lombardi Trophy or two to reach the public standing in his own town that his play deserves. Even then, a segment of Atlanta, the bottom range of the 99 percent, will likely never embrace him.

Mark Sanchez   Height: 6-2   Weight: 227   College: USC   Draft: 2009/1 (5)   Born: 11-Nov-1986   Age: 27   Risk: Red

Year	Team	G/GS	Snaps	Att	Comp	C%	Yds	TD	INT/Adj	FUM	ASR	NY/P	Rk	DVOA	Rk	DYAR	Rk	YAR	Runs	Yds	TD	DVOA	DYAR	QBR
2010	NYJ	16/16	1038	507	278	54.8%	3291	17	13/28	9	5.4%	5.9	35	-4.3%	28	212	23	219	30	105	3	8.8%	28	48.2
2011	NYJ	16/16	1064	543	308	56.7%	3474	26	18/19	10	6.6%	5.6	31	-12.6%	29	-56	31	-13	37	103	6	-8.2%	7	33.6
2012	NYJ	15/15	938	453	246	54.3%	2883	13	18/21	10	6.9%	5.5	31	-29.4%	35	-593	39	-480	22	28	0	-85.4%	-67	23.4
2013	NYJ			497	287	57.8%	3224	22	17	9		5.4		-16.4%					23	48	0	-5.2%		
	2012:	41% Short		38% Mid		15% Deep		6% Bomb		YAC: 4.0 (38)			2011:		44% Short		37% Mid		15% Deep		4% Bomb		YAC: 4.9 (31)	

One of the biggest reasons for Sanchez's complete lack of development is that he really can't take pass pressure. Last year, only Philip Rivers had a bigger gap between DVOA with pressure and DVOA without pressure. In 2011, only three quarterbacks had a larger gap. The worst is the big blitz; last year, Sanchez averaged just 2.7 yards per play when opponents sent six or more pass rushers. Even if Sanchez beats out Geno Smith for the Jets' starting job, he's likely to lose it sometime during the season, and once he loses that starting job, it's hard to imagine he'll ever get another one.

Matt Schaub   Height: 6-5   Weight: 235   College: Virginia   Draft: 2004/3 (90)   Born: 25-Jun-1981   Age: 32   Risk: Green

Year	Team	G/GS	Snaps	Att	Comp	C%	Yds	TD	INT/Adj	FUM	ASR	NY/P	Rk	DVOA	Rk	DYAR	Rk	YAR	Runs	Yds	TD	DVOA	DYAR	QBR
2010	HOU	16/16	1066	574	365	63.6%	4370	24	12/12	8	5.9%	6.9	9	12.2%	13	930	8	926	22	28	0	9.9%	17	57.9
2011	HOU	10/10	677	292	178	61.0%	2479	15	6/6	3	5.6%	7.8	4	24.4%	5	701	10	690	15	9	2	9.7%	10	67.4
2012	HOU	16/16	1105	544	350	64.3%	4008	22	12/15	4	5.2%	6.7	12	7.5%	14	697	12	882	21	-9	0	-68.2%	-8	62.6
2013	HOU			543	346	63.7%	4018	24	12	4		6.5		13.9%					22	35	1	-0.5%		
	2012:	48% Short		34% Mid		11% Deep		7% Bomb		YAC: 5.0 (19)			2011:		47% Short		31% Mid		14% Deep		8% Bomb		YAC: 6.6 (2)	

In the quarterback comments of last year's book, we noted that Schaub's red-zone DVOA fell from 48.1% in 2010 to -32.0% in 2011. He was better in that regard in 2012—until the last month of the season when he was awful again, thanks in part to a reluctance to throw the ball into the end zone. (That splits into 15.1% DVOA in the red zone through Week 13, and -50.1% DVOA in the red zone from Week 14 through the loss to New England in the playoffs.) Beyond that, Schaub has aged as you would expect him to. While the Texans were less productive on play-action passes than in years past, he was still a better quarterback under center (14.2% DVOA) than he was in shotgun (-8.0% DVOA). He's not as mobile as the ideal quarterback for a bootleg-heavy scheme, but executes the scheme to the best of his limitations. The Texans saw enough to hand him a four-year extension at the beginning of the 2012 season, but it's not unthinkable that he could be gone in a year if the Texans don't make the playoffs in 2013.

John Skelton

| | | Height: 6-6 | | Weight: 243 | | College: Fordham | | | Draft: 2010/5 (155) | | | Born: 17-Mar-1988 | | Age: 25 | | Risk: Green |

Year	Team	G/GS	Snaps	Att	Comp	C%	Yds	TD	INT/Adj	FUM	ASR	NY/P	Rk	DVOA	Rk	DYAR	Rk	YAR	Runs	Yds	TD	DVOA	DYAR	QBR
2010	ARI	5/4	232	126	60	47.6%	662	2	2/6	3	7.8%	4.5	44	-53.4%	45	-349	45	-281	10	49	0	18.0%	11	24.6
2011	ARI	8/7	496	275	151	54.9%	1913	11	14/18	4	7.6%	5.9	28	-27.5%	41	-325	43	-349	28	128	0	19.8%	34	35.1
2012	ARI	7/6	315	201	109	54.2%	1132	2	9/10	4	6.5%	4.8	36	-35.0%	37	-324	35	-427	4	5	0	-25.0%	-2	13.9
2013	CIN			529	331	62.4%	3349	14	15	10		5.2		-18.2%					31	67	0	-9.1%		

| 2012: | 45% Short | 41% Mid | 11% Deep | 3% Bomb | YAC: 4.9 (22) | 2011: | 40% Short | 38% Mid | 16% Deep | 6% Bomb | YAC: 5.4 (14) |

There are different versions of the old saying, "Once is an accident, twice is a coincidence, three times is a trend," but however you want to phrase it, Skelton has finished in the bottom six of all qualifying quarterbacks in DYAR for three straight seasons. That is at least a trend, and quite possibly a sentence. Skelton had a pretty putrid season in 2012, but his Similarity Score comps for the 2010-2011 seasons were: Tarvaris Jackson, Jeff Kemp, Don Majkowski, Quincy Carter, Chris Miller, David Klingler, Gus Frerotte ... you get the idea. Skelton is a big, raw-boned guy with an interesting arm who was once thought to be (at least potentially) a Lite beer version of Joe Flacco, but it's safe to say that we can put those thoughts to rest. If he peaks at "Derek Anderson in 2007" level, it will be a monumental upgrade. If Skelton does figure it out, it could be with the Cincinnati Bengals, who picked him up after the Cards reshuffled their quarterback depth chart.

Alex Smith

| | | Height: 6-4 | | Weight: 212 | | College: Utah | | | Draft: 2005/1 (1) | | | Born: 7-May-1984 | | Age: 29 | | Risk: Green |

Year	Team	G/GS	Snaps	Att	Comp	C%	Yds	TD	INT/Adj	FUM	ASR	NY/P	Rk	DVOA	Rk	DYAR	Rk	YAR	Runs	Yds	TD	DVOA	DYAR	QBR
2010	SF	11/10	606	342	204	59.6%	2370	14	10/9	4	7.8%	6.2	21	-12.2%	33	-26	33	0	18	60	0	-2.9%	6	40.9
2011	SF	16/16	1005	445	273	61.3%	3144	17	5/6	6	8.5%	5.8	29	3.3%	14	448	13	354	52	179	2	11.4%	38	45.8
2012	SF	10/9	484	218	153	70.2%	1737	13	5/5	3	9.7%	6.6	14	14.8%	9	418	15	365	31	132	0	26.0%	36	70.1
2013	KC			488	318	65.2%	3491	20	13	8		6.2		-0.1%					39	122	1	2.3%		

| 2012: | 53% Short | 33% Mid | 7% Deep | 6% Bomb | YAC: 5.1 (16) | 2011: | 52% Short | 32% Mid | 10% Deep | 6% Bomb | YAC: 5.2 (21) |

At least this time Smith can hold his head high knowing he was actually benched for a *better* quarterback, unlike say, Troy Smith (2010) and Shaun Hill (2009). Also, unlike those previous demotions, the one in 2012 had nothing to do with performance. If Jim Harbaugh wasn't so obsessive about running a "multiple" offense, the minor constraints Smith's skill set places on a game plan might have been overlooked given his success. The obvious question going forward is whether or not Andy Reid can get as much out of Smith as Harbaugh did. A West Coast offense and quarterback guru in his own right, it's likely he can. Having elite tackles and skill position players surrounding him also helps, as does the absence of a talent like Colin Kaepernick angling for his job.

Geno Smith

| | | Height: 6-3 | | Weight: 208 | | College: West Virginia | | | Draft: 2013/2 (39) | | | Born: 10-Oct-1990 | | Age: 23 | | Risk: Red |

Year	Team	G/GS	Snaps	Att	Comp	C%	Yds	TD	INT/Adj	FUM	ASR	NY/P	Rk	DVOA	Rk	DYAR	Rk	YAR	Runs	Yds	TD	DVOA	DYAR	QBR
2013	NYJ			435	250	57.3%	2996	17	15	7		6.1		-12.0%					70	314	3	8.7%		

Even after he struggled with inconsistency in the second half of his senior season, most of the top draft experts (including Mel Kiper, Mike Mayock and Rob Rang) still projected Geno Smith as the top quarterback prospect in this year's draft. Nonetheless, draftnik scouting reports on him were all over the map, and it would be a lot easier to synthesize some sort of common wisdom from all these disparate opinions if so many of the negative reports on Smith didn't set off alarms with racial buzzwords. The most famous, of course, was the *Pro Football Weekly* article by Nolan Nawrocki which attacked Smith's intelligence and work ethic. "Does not command respect from teammates and cannot inspire," wrote Nawrocki. "Not committed or focused. Interviewed poorly at the combine and did not show an understanding of concepts on the white board. Not a student of the game." Both Smith's West Virginia coaches and some NFL coaches pushed back on Nawrocki in an article in *Sports Illustrated*. West Virginia director of football operations Alex Hammond told Austin Murphy of *SI* that after Smith threw eight touchdowns with no interceptions against Baylor, he spent the night sitting in the football offices watching film until the early morning. An AFC director of player personnel told Murphy, "He wasn't good [on the white board]. He was *outstanding*. He was a maestro on that board. He was phenomenal."

That's not to say that there aren't criticisms of Smith that are legitimate and free of coded language. West Virginia's Air Raid offense was heavily dependent on very short passes; in eight games charted by the website Football Study Hall, Smith threw one-third of all passes to receivers behind the line of scrimmage. He needs to clean up his mechanics, especially when throwing on the run. He needs to read blitzes better. He tries to throw too many passes into tight windows, and those incompletions in college often turn into interceptions at the next level.

On the other hand, he can make every NFL throw. In those eight charted games, he had an above-average completion rate at every level, and was particularly strong on deep bombs over 30 yards or more downfield. He's mobile, and you can run some read option with him if you want. Yes, there were a ton of bubble screens to Tavon Austin that boosted his numbers, but he does a fine job of reading progressions and finding the right receiver on plays that aren't just one-read-and-go.

In total, Smith is an inconsistent and unfinished product who needs to be properly molded into a starting NFL quarterback. Many of his deficiencies seem to be programmed precisely to disappoint people who want the rookie quarterbacks of 2013 to be successful just as fast as the rookie quarterbacks of 2012. There's plenty of upside here, where Smith could develop to the level of Tony Romo, or maybe even Donovan McNabb. Or perhaps he'll only develop to be an average NFL starter, which still would be an upgrade on Mark Sanchez and not horribly disappointing for a guy taken 39th in the draft instead of third or ninth. When early reports out of Jets OTAs reported that Smith was struggling to learn Marty Mornhinweg's offense quickly, it sounded like more of that coded language, but the storyline fits just as well with a positive outlook on Smith's future. The opinion that Geno Smith shouldn't be starting for the Jets in Week 1 does not have to equal the opinion that he won't succeed as an NFL quarterback. It will be a lot easier to judge him in 2014, when he likely takes over for Sanchez as the Jets' quarterback of the future.

Matthew Stafford

Height: 6-2 • Weight: 225 • College: Georgia • Draft: 2009/1 (1) • Born: 7-Feb-1988 • Age: 25 • Risk: Yellow

Year	Team	G/GS	Snaps	Att	Comp	C%	Yds	TD	INT/Adj	FUM	ASR	NY/P	Rk	DVOA	Rk	DYAR	Rk	YAR	Runs	Yds	TD	DVOA	DYAR	QBR
2010	DET	3/3	176	96	57	59.4%	535	6	1/3	2	4.7%	5.0	41	2.9%	21	91	29	80	4	11	1	-22.0%	-3	58.1
2011	DET	16/16	1082	663	421	63.5%	5038	41	16/25	5	5.9%	6.8	13	15.0%	10	1171	5	1312	22	78	0	-2.2%	7	65.5
2012	DET	16/16	1181	727	435	59.8%	4967	20	17/23	8	3.7%	6.3	17	12.2%	12	1160	6	891	35	126	4	0.9%	23	58.9
2013	DET			688	425	61.8%	5019	28	19	6		6.3		4.6%					37	112	2	11.9%		

2012: 49% Short • 29% Mid • 15% Deep • 6% Bomb • YAC: 4.7 (26) • 2011: 51% Short • 30% Mid • 10% Deep • 8% Bomb • YAC: 5.3 (18)

Meet Matthew Stafford: the first quarterback in the history of the NFL who can make nearly throwing for 5,000 yards seem disappointing. The main flaw Stafford had last season was a case of show-off pocket mechanics—throwing off his back foot, throwing sidearm, and contorting his body in every which way to make screen passes seem more difficult than they were. The big change for the Lions this season on offense, other than the absence of Titus Young, is that they'll be turning over three starting spots on the offensive line. Stafford's past shows reason to believe he can negate some of the issues a team could have from the turnover. He shows excellent composure in the pocket, his DVOA on passes we marked with pressure is consistently about 30 percentage points higher than the league average, and the Lions, who haven't had the most impressive lines over those years to begin with, have finished in the top 10 in Adjusted Sack Rate for three years running, most often with Stafford at the trigger.

Drew Stanton

Height: 6-3 • Weight: 230 • College: Michigan State • Draft: 2007/2 (43) • Born: 7-May-1984 • Age: 29 • Risk: Green

Year	Team	G/GS	Snaps	Att	Comp	C%	Yds	TD	INT/Adj	FUM	ASR	NY/P	Rk	DVOA	Rk	DYAR	Rk	YAR	Runs	Yds	TD	DVOA	DYAR	QBR
2010	DET	6/3	243	119	69	58.0%	780	4	3/4	2	5.4%	6.0	27	12.2%	12	174	24	84	18	113	1	20.5%	28	42.4
2013	ARI			544	351	64.5%	3768	13	16	8		6.2		-6.8%					56	42	2	-26.8%		

In 2012, Stanton *was* scheduled to be the No. 2 option behind a vulnerable Mark Sanchez on the New York Jets. Then the Jets double-downed on the circus atmosphere by acquiring Tim Tebow and shipping Stanton to Indianapolis, where he would back up Andrew Luck, one of two NFL quarterbacks to play 100 percent of his team's plays. That season of inactivity in Indianapolis was valuable, however, as it introduced Stanton to Bruce Arians. This offseason, he signed a three-year, $8.2 million contract with Arians and his new team, the Arizona Cardinals, and he will back up Carson Palmer.

Ryan Tannehill

Height: 6-4 • Weight: 221 • College: Texas A&M • Draft: 2012/1 (8) • Born: 27-Jul-1988 • Age: 25 • Risk: Yellow

Year	Team	G/GS	Snaps	Att	Comp	C%	Yds	TD	INT/Adj	FUM	ASR	NY/P	Rk	DVOA	Rk	DYAR	Rk	YAR	Runs	Yds	TD	DVOA	DYAR	QBR
2012	MIA	16/16	980	484	282	58.3%	3294	12	13/16	7	6.7%	5.9	23	-9.9%	25	39	25	86	49	211	2	-11.0%	2	52.3
2013	MIA			511	315	61.7%	3564	21	15	8		6.0		-9.2%					48	178	2	6.0%		

2012: 45% Short • 38% Mid • 10% Deep • 7% Bomb • YAC: 4.4 (32)

Here's the good news about Tannehill: Since 1978, there have been 41 first-round quarterbacks who threw enough passes to qualify for our leaderboards during their rookie year. In terms of adjusted net yards per attempt (i.e., yards per attempt adjusted for sacks and touchdown passes), which is one of the best predictive stats out there, Tannehill's 5.23 ANY/A ranked 10th. But here's the bad news. The two quarterbacks to which Tannehill will be linked for the rest of his career ranked higher: Robert Griffin's 7.47 ANY/A was No. 1 in that 25-year span, and Andrew Luck's 5.66 was No. 7. It's not Tannehill's fault that Miami reached for him, but the fact that they did means he's destined for years of perceived underachievement—fairly or unfairly.

This offseason, the Dolphins added a great deep threat (Mike Wallace), but subtracted a great pass-protecting offensive lineman (Jake Long). Considering Tannehill ranked 29th out of 39 qualifying quarterbacks in terms of DVOA with pressure, the latter move will probably trump the former in its impact on his development. In other words, expect the first two quarterbacks selected in the 2012 draft to further separate themselves from the third.

Tyrod Taylor Height: 6-1 Weight: 216 College: Virginia Tech Draft: 2011/6 (180) Born: 3-Aug-1989 Age: 24 Risk: Yellow

Year	Team	G/GS	Snaps	Att	Comp	C%	Yds	TD	INT/Adj	FUM	ASR	NY/P	Rk	DVOA	Rk	DYAR	Rk	YAR	Runs	Yds	TD	DVOA	DYAR	QBR
2011	BAL	3/0	5	1	1	100.0%	18	0	0/0	0	65.9%	5.0	--	-40.3%	--	-4	--	0	1	2	0	-41.6%	-1	14.9
2012	BAL	6/0	92	29	17	58.6%	179	0	1/1	1	6.8%	4.7	--	-28.3%	--	-34	--	-56	14	73	1	13.8%	18	45.0
2013	BAL			462	268	58.0%	3178	19	16	9		6.1		-9.2%					82	444	3	15.9%		
	2012:	52% Short		37% Mid		7% Deep	4% Bomb		YAC: 4.7 (--)		2011:		0% Short	100% Mid		0% Deep		0% Bomb	YAC: 5.0 (--)					

Taylor saw all of his real action in wet-spill duty against the Bengals: three passes and a run in a September blowout, then 25 passes and nine runs in a meaningless Week 17 workout. The Ravens offense gets all read-optionish when Taylor enters the game, creating culture shock for defenses that game-planned to stop a sequoia. In the short term, the change-up can be effective, but it is hard to tell how the Ravens would adapt to a sustained Joe Flacco absence. Knockaround third-stringer Caleb Hanie, who flunked his 2011 audition as the Bears spot starter badly, is the only other experienced backup on the roster, so Taylor should again mop up games and prepare for disasters. To get a quarterback more unlike Flacco than Taylor, the Ravens would have to sign a shortstop.

Tim Tebow Height: 6-3 Weight: 236 College: Florida Draft: 2010/1 (25) Born: 14-Aug-1987 Age: 26 Risk: Red

Year	Team	G/GS	Snaps	Att	Comp	C%	Yds	TD	INT/Adj	FUM	ASR	NY/P	Rk	DVOA	Rk	DYAR	Rk	YAR	Runs	Yds	TD	DVOA	DYAR	QBR
2010	DEN	9/3	209	82	41	50.0%	654	5	3/3	1	5.4%	7.3	--	13.6%	--	135	--	143	43	227	6	23.3%	73	57.5
2011	DEN	14/11	782	271	126	46.5%	1729	12	6/7	12	11.2%	5.0	39	-22.8%	37	-222	40	-276	122	660	6	-18.3%	-36	29.9
2012	NYJ	12/2	72	8	6	75.0%	39	0	0/0	0	19.6%	3.2	--	-24.2%	--	-9	--	-13	32	102	0	-26.1%	-26	17.6
2013	NE			425	232	54.6%	3060	15	13	10		6.4		-8.8%					133	623	6	9.1%		
	2012:	57% Short		29% Mid		0% Deep	14% Bomb		YAC: 4.2 (--)		2011:		29% Short	40% Mid		14% Deep		17% Bomb	YAC: 4.8 (32)					

The KUBIAK projections for backup quarterbacks take into account the rest of the team's offense, but trying to imagine Tebow in the Patriots' pass-centric offense threatens to cause brain implosion, so the projection above is a complete shot in the dark. Here are some other KUBIAK projections for Tim Tebow:

- Tight End: Six catches, 37 yards, one touchdown from the one-yard line, a 4,208-to-1 article-about-reception-to-reception-ratio.
- Short-Yardage Specialist: one catch for two yards and one touchdown (see Mike Vrabel, 2001-2008).
- Personal Protector: Three converted fake punts, one botched fake punt, one punter pulverized by blown block, no more personal protection (similar to last year's numbers with the Jets).
- Wildcat Specialist on some future team coached by Chan Gailey: Best not to even think about it.
- Inside-Centre, American Rugby Team: 12 groundings, four drop goals, and a 700 percent increase in rugby interest for three weeks, followed by a return to normal levels because, big whoop, Tebow is playing rugby.
- Host, TBN Lifestyle Television Program: Four years of uneventful competence followed by a sudden retirement when a live studio microphone accidently captures him saying "I would rather watch my dog puke than watch another Flyleaf video."
- Cultural Icon, America: More of the same for indeterminate, interminable period.

Michael Vick Height: 6-0 Weight: 215 College: Virginia Tech Draft: 2001/1 (1) Born: 26-Jun-1980 Age: 33 Risk: Red

Year	Team	G/GS	Snaps	Att	Comp	C%	Yds	TD	INT/Adj	FUM	ASR	NY/P	Rk	DVOA	Rk	DYAR	Rk	YAR	Runs	Yds	TD	DVOA	DYAR	QBR
2010	PHI	12/12	717	372	233	62.6%	3018	21	6/12	10	8.7%	7.0	7	14.1%	8	641	13	665	100	676	9	29.0%	192	68.2
2011	PHI	13/13	825	423	253	59.8%	3303	18	14/18	9	5.6%	7.1	9	10.8%	12	628	11	573	76	589	0	27.5%	131	64.4
2012	PHI	10/10	667	351	204	58.1%	2362	12	10/14	8	8.0%	5.8	28	-14.4%	28	-78	27	-108	62	332	1	-11.1%	3	46.0
2013	PHI			576	362	62.7%	3924	23	15	13		5.9		-3.8%					88	442	3	12.6%		
	2012:	45% Short		36% Mid		12% Deep	7% Bomb		YAC: 4.9 (20)		2011:		42% Short	34% Mid		17% Deep		7% Bomb	YAC: 5.3 (20)					

For all his ups and downs, Vick had always been able to hang his hat on the zombie statistic that is quarterback wins. Prior to 2012, his only losing season had been a 7-9 year in 2006, when he set a quarterback record by rushing for over 1,000 yards. But Vick went down with Andy Reid's ship last year, as the Eagles went 3-7 in Vick's ten starts. For the second straight season, Vick saw a decline in most stats, and at 33, it's fair to wonder if we've seen the best Vick has to offer. Had Chip Kelly entered the league a decade ago, Vick might have been his perfect quarterback. But after 102 career starts, Vick's flaws have been exposed and they show no signs of fading away: he is quick to take off and run when the play breaks down, he's bad at avoiding direct hits, he's careless with the ball, and he's inconsistent with his mechanics.

In Kelly's offense, quarterbacks must be able to read the defense pre- and post-snap and make quick decisions about where to go with the ball. Save for one stretch during the 2010 season, Vick has never shown an ability to consistently do these things. Vick has shown signs of maturity in recent years, and it's hard to blame him too much for his play behind a disastrous offensive line. But to expect him to seamlessly integrate into Kelly's scheme is to expect too much. Even if he is named the starter—and Vick complained loudly about Kelly's reluctance to do that during OTAs—it's unreasonable to expect him to start all 16 games, and Vick doesn't appear to be the team's quarterback of the future, either.

Brandon Weeden Height: 6-4 Weight: 221 College: Oklahoma State Draft: 2012/1 (22) Born: 14-Oct-1983 Age: 30 Risk: Yellow

Year	Team	G/GS	Snaps	Att	Comp	C%	Yds	TD	INT/Adj	FUM	ASR	NY/P	Rk	DVOA	Rk	DYAR	Rk	YAR	Runs	Yds	TD	DVOA	DYAR	QBR
2012	CLE	15/15	929	517	297	57.4%	3385	14	17/26	5	5.3%	5.8	26	-19.4%	29	-291	34	-210	27	111	0	8.0%	24	26.6
2013	CLE			539	321	59.5%	3821	20	17	9		6.1		-11.0%					25	85	1	3.0%		

| | 2012: | 41% Short | | 38% Mid | | 15% Deep | 6% Bomb | | YAC: 4.0 (38) | | 2011: | 44% Short | | 37% Mid | | 15% Deep | | 4% Bomb | YAC: 4.9 (31) | | | | |

Carly Rae Jepsen is nearly three years older than fellow pop singer Adele. That's right, the giggly ingénue who gets knock-kneed and indecisive about giving a boy her phone number will turn 28 in November, and was 26 when "Call me Maybe" became a hit; the complex, emotionally-mature adult who has blown up both the record industry and the Grammy awards for the last four years turned 25 in May and was 19 when she recorded her powerful first album. It would be silly to ask at this point which artist is more likely to stand the test of time; Jepsen is already on the road to oblivion, Adele to the Rock and Roll Hall of Fame. The moral of the story, of course, is that age matters: if Jepsen were a real 17-year-old, we might have expected a long (if tumultuous and sometimes icky) teen heartthrob career, and if Adele came to her success at 37, her first album might have been the achievement of a lifetime, not the start of an amazing career.

Weeden's 2012 season, seen as a stepping stone for a 21-year-old quarterback, would be a source of middling encouragement. As the output of a player who will turn 30 in October, it is overwhelming evidence that Weeden has no future as a quality NFL starter. Football, unlike baseball, has no history of dealing with 28-year-old rookies, so smart people will still talk about Weeden "developing," which is like wondering when Carly Rae Jepsen will morph into Bonnie Raitt. Coordinator Norv Turner will be tasked with juggling Weeden's sophomore slump with his midlife crisis. Turner may recall that his last quarterback, Philip Rivers, had his first bad year when he turned 30, and may wonder along with the rest of us just how much advancement can be squeezed in before the inevitable decline.

Charlie Whitehurst Height: 6-4 Weight: 220 College: Clemson Draft: 2006/3 (81) Born: 6-Aug-1982 Age: 31 Risk: Green

Year	Team	G/GS	Snaps	Att	Comp	C%	Yds	TD	INT/Adj	FUM	ASR	NY/P	Rk	DVOA	Rk	DYAR	Rk	YAR	Runs	Yds	TD	DVOA	DYAR	QBR
2010	SEA	6/2	200	99	57	57.6%	507	2	3/3	1	4.3%	4.8	43	-33.2%	41	-141	37	-167	20	43	1	12.2%	17	23.0
2011	SEA	3/2	100	56	27	48.2%	298	1	1/4	2	12.3%	4.0	--	-49.2%	--	-160	--	-138	4	13	0	-0.2%	2	17.9
2013	SD			520	305	58.7%	3342	18	16	10		5.1		-20.8%					37	66	2	-8.5%		

| | 2012: | 48% Short | | 34% Mid | | 11% Deep | 7% Bomb | | YAC: 5.0 (19) | | 2011: | 35% Short | | 35% Mid | | 18% Deep | | 12% Bomb | YAC: 4.6 (--) | | | | |

Just like his first stint in San Diego (2006-09), Whitehurst did not get on the field last year. The most he has helped the Chargers was during the two years he spent away from the team, as his stint in Seattle gave the organization what amounted to a free third-round pick and a free pass to move up from No. 60 to No. 40 in the second round of the 2010 draft.

Russell Wilson Height: 5-11 Weight: 204 College: Wisconsin Draft: 2012/3 (75) Born: 29-Nov-1988 Age: 25 Risk: Green

Year	Team	G/GS	Snaps	Att	Comp	C%	Yds	TD	INT/Adj	FUM	ASR	NY/P	Rk	DVOA	Rk	DYAR	Rk	YAR	Runs	Yds	TD	DVOA	DYAR	QBR
2012	SEA	16/16	979	393	252	64.1%	3118	26	10/12	10	7.4%	6.8	8	19.7%	6	872	8	741	94	489	4	22.3%	147	69.6
2013	SEA			406	252	62.1%	3110	23	11	8		7.0		13.5%					99	471	5	17.7%		

| | 2012: | 46% Short | | 32% Mid | | 12% Deep | 9% Bomb | | YAC: 5.0 (18) | | | | | | | | | | | | | | | |

Since coming out of Wisconsin, Wilson has set or tied rookie records for highest Lewin Career Forecast projection, touchdown passes, single-game DYAR (twice), and total season DYAR. When you include Wilson's four rushing scores, only Cam Newton (21 touchdowns passing, 14 rushing) produced more combined touchdowns in his first year. In the last half of the year, Wilson threw 16 touchdowns and two interceptions and led the NFL in passing DVOA. Over the course of the season, he was third in DVOA when trailing or tied in the fourth quarter or overtime (behind only Peyton Manning and Tom Brady) and fourth in DVOA on third downs (behind Manning, Brady, and Aaron Rodgers). He was also third in DVOA on deep passes. The Seahawks worked around Wilson's height by putting him in motion. Including scrambles, he had a league-high 163 plays outside the pocket, with a DVOA of 39.3%. If defenses wanted to blitz the edge and keep Wilson in the pocket, that was OK too—his DVOA there was 37.8%, one of the ten best in football and better than Super Bowl winners like Drew Brees, Eli Manning, and Ben Roethlisberger. Finally, he was second to Cam Newton among quarterbacks in rushing DYAR.

So is there anything not to like about Wilson? While Wilson's mobility helped him escape pressure (10 "Houdini" plays where he broke a tackle in the backfield to avoid a sack, tied with Newton for most in the league), he also had a tendency to run himself into defenders. Wilson has faith in his scrambling ability to keep plays alive. That led to a lot of touchdowns, but also a lot of sacks. The Seahawks had 19 "long" sacks, among the top ten teams in the NFL, even though they had the fewest passing plays in the league. In that aspect, Wilson is something like a young Ben Roethlisberger. It sounds ridiculous, comparing the shortest quarterback in the league to one of the tallest, but Roethlisberger, like Wilson, tends to take sacks other quarterbacks would avoid. Last year, in his ninth season, Roethlisberger posted a sack rate below seven percent for the first time in his career. The Seahawks had better hope Wilson learns to throw the ball away faster than that.

Tyler Wilson Height: 6-2   Weight: 218   College: Arkansas   Draft: 2013/4 (112)   Born: 16-Aug-1989   Age: 24   Risk: Yellow

Year	Team	G/GS	Snaps	Att	Comp	C%	Yds	TD	INT/Adj	FUM	ASR	NY/P	Rk	DVOA	Rk	DYAR	Rk	YAR	Runs	Yds	TD	DVOA	DYAR	QBR
2013	OAK			515	295	57.1%	3836	19	18	9		6.3		-9.4%						47	165	3	4.9%		
2012:		45% Short		41% Mid			11% Deep	3% Bomb			YAC: 4.9 (22)		2011:		40% Short		38% Mid		16% Deep		6% Bomb	YAC: 5.4 (14)		

Here's another member of the 2013 quarterback draft class who inspired a wide range of opinions from draft experts. Originally, some draft analysts had Wilson projected as a second-rounder or even late first-rounder, but he dropped to Oakland in the fourth round because he's a pocket passer who doesn't have top-notch arm strength or size. He tends to get that gunslinger mentality where he tries to fit throws into coverage that he shouldn't try to beat, and there's concern about his risky style of play, a Roethlisberger-like willingness to take a hit in order to make the big throw from a quarterback who is not Roethlisberger-sized. On the other hand, Matt Waldman rated Wilson as the No. 1 quarterback in his Rookie Scouting Portfolio. Waldman loves Wilson's ability to maneuver within the pocket under pressure, his field vision to lead receivers to open spaces, and his poise under pressure, which of course often comes as a package deal with the gunslinger mentality.

In part because he only started for two years, Wilson doesn't come out well in the Lewin Career Forecast. He has a projection of just 425 DYAR for his third through fifth seasons. On the other hand, stats always need to be seen in context. Last year, while the Arkansas program was crumbling around him, Wilson still completed 62 percent of his passes, averaged 7.9 yards per pass attempt (in the SEC West, no less), and showed reasonable ability to avoid the pass rush (3.6 percent sack rate). Once we adjust for a schedule filled with the best defenses in the country, Arkansas ranked third in the country in Passing S&P+.

The Raiders say they are having an open three-way battle for the starting quarterback job in training camp, but it's hard to find someone who doesn't expect Matt Flynn to be starting in Week 1. If Flynn doesn't work out, however, this is the guy the Raiders should put on the field instead of Terrelle Pryor. Unless the Raiders decide they absolutely *have* to run a read-option offense because it's the hot new thing everyone's talking about, this is where the upside is.

T.J. Yates Height: 6-3   Weight: 195   College: North Carolina   Draft: 2011/5 (152)   Born: 28-May-1987   Age: 26   Risk: Green

Year	Team	G/GS	Snaps	Att	Comp	C%	Yds	TD	INT/Adj	FUM	ASR	NY/P	Rk	DVOA	Rk	DYAR	Rk	YAR	Runs	Yds	TD	DVOA	DYAR	QBR
2011	HOU	6/5	314	134	82	61.2%	949	3	3/3	4	11.1%	5.9	25	-19.7%	35	-81	32	-15	14	57	0	12.7%	10	45.8
2012	HOU	4/0	23	10	4	40.0%	38	0	1/1	3	8.6%	3.1	--	-128.3%	--	-85	--	-89	2	-1	1	56.0%	8	2.1
2013	HOU			517	333	64.4%	3364	21	14	11		5.9		-2.0%					51	110	1	-11.2%		
2012:		67% Short		11% Mid			11% Deep	11% Bomb			YAC: 7.3 (--)		2011:		48% Short		35% Mid		11% Deep		6% Bomb	YAC: 5.8 (8)		

Ten passing attempts wasn't enough to tell how much better Yates is now than he was in 2011, when the Texans tried to protect themselves from his occasionally spotty reads and questionable decision-making as much as they could after Matt Schaub and Matt Leinart went down. Gary Kubiak was heard saying nice things about third-stringer Case Keenum, leading to some speculation his job as the backup could be in danger. Kubiak said nice things about Collin Klein, too, though. Don't get too carried away with the words.

Going Deep

John Beck, FA: Beck spent four games with the Texans last year, all inactive, before they had a higher priority on the roster than a third-string quarterback. It was the fourth time in six seasons Beck was on an NFL roster but did not appear in a single game.

McLeod Bethel-Thompson, MIN: An undrafted free agent out of Sacramento State, Bethel-Thompson packs three last names onto his 6-foot-4 frame. He's already had short stints in the Arena League and UFL, and with the Matt Cassel acquisition putting him no better than third on the depth chart at the moment, he should probably prepare for more journeys of that ilk in his future.

Tyler Bray, KC: Bray is known for his natural arm strength and the innate confidence he has in that arm strength. He came out early after just one season as a starter at Tennessee, and ended up going undrafted because of concerns about a lack of maturity. Bray has an excellent propensity for throwing the ball away to avoid sacks and interceptions, but his decision-making is far worse when it comes to picking an actual receiver to throw to. In order to make it in the NFL, he'll have to refine his fundamentals and stop trying to make throws into windows that are so tiny as to be non-existent.

Jimmy Clausen, CAR: Clausen hasn't played in a regular-season game since his 10-game, one-win starting stint in 2010. He'll enter camp as the third-stringer behind Cam Newton and Derek Anderson, and he'll have to fight off undrafted rookie Colby Cameron out of Louisiana Tech to keep his roster spot.

Kellen Clemens, STL: The Rams re-signed Clemens to a one-year contract shortly before the draft, although head coach Jeff Fisher made it clear that Clemens has fallen behind second-year passer Austin Davis on the depth chart. (2011 stats: 48-for-91, 546 yards, -6 DYAR, -12.0% DVOA)

B.J. Coleman, GB: A Matt Waldman favorite, Coleman was selected in the seventh-round out of Tennessee-Chattanooga in 2012 and has some stylistic similarities to Peyton Manning. Obviously, they are worlds apart as far as production goes, and Coleman better have absorbed all of Manning's pocket timing if he ends up spending a prolonged amount of time taking snaps behind Green Bay's offensive line.

B.J. Daniels, SF: Strike one: San Francisco has a ton of time and money invested in their top three quarterbacks. Strike two: Even if Daniels switches positions (as is likely), the team's depth chart is set in stone across the board. Strike three: Jim Harbaugh is not a fan of giving playing time to rookies. If this seventh-round pick is to avoid striking out with the 49ers, it will be because Harbaugh finds a specific tactical reason to deploy a player he has dubbed his "Swiss Army Knife."

Dennis Dixon, PHI: In the week before the Super Bowl, Dennis Dixon impressed Ravens coaches and players with his impersonation of Colin Kaepernick. A week later, he reunited with his college head coach when he signed a two-year deal to join Chip Kelly and the Eagles. The former Oregon quarterback has had some success in the NFL—Dixon has played well in several preseason games and has gone 2-1 as a starter during the regular season—but his biggest role in Philadelphia will likely be helping his new teammates get acclimated to Kelly's system.

Zac Dysert, DEN: This seventh-rounder out of Miami of Ohio will have a tough time making Denver's final roster, as it's unlikely the Broncos will keep three quarterbacks around. Scouts like Dysert's build and his ability to make throws on the move. To stick at the pro level, he'll have to improve his pocket poise.

Rex Grossman, WAS: RG-Pick-6 did provide some value to the 2012 Redskins—he proved that even when a bad quarterback hits his ceiling from an efficiency perspective, it's just not enough. So, a smart team is then more likely to spend multiple first-round draft picks on a truly franchise-changing quarterback instead. Oh, and they're also prone to take another quarterback in the fourth round, just in case. Grossman has never had a season with a positive passing DVOA. He'll be back in 2013 after Mike Shanahan inked him to a one-year, $960,000 contract with a $10,000 (no, that's not a typo) signing bonus.

Caleb Hanie, BAL: The 27-year-old from Colorado State got a chance to show off his game late in 2011 when he started four contests for the Bears in place of an injured Jay Cutler. They weren't a great four games. Instead of making teams wonder if he might one day develop into a starter, Hanie cemented his future as a backup. In an effort to help Hanie, the Bears watered down their offense until it was pure vanilla, and he was still jittery in the pocket and over-reactive to pressure. Hanie held the second spot on the depth chart in Denver last year, and will hold the third spot in Baltimore this year—if he makes the team.

Chandler Harnish, IND: This "Mr. Irrelevant" selection in the 2012 NFL draft earned a spot on the Colts' 53-man roster at the start of his rookie season by completing 57.4 percent of 46 pass attempts for 406 yards with two touchdowns in four preseason games. The Colts would eventually waive Harnish six weeks into regular season, but kept him on the practice squad throughout the rest of the year before signing the Indiana native to a "futures" contract. With Andrew Luck not missing a snap last season, and the Colts signing solid veteran backup Matt Hasselbeck, Harnish will need an impressive offseason and preseason to force the Colts to keep a third quarterback on the active roster.

Josh Johnson, CIN: Johnson has been craft-distilled single-barrel hooch for connoisseurs of toolsy quarterbacks for years. He has the skill set of a latter-day Randall Cunningham, and when the 49ers signed him in 2012, a few of us thought he would steal a starting job from Alex Smith. Lo and behold, the 49ers had an even more toolsy and far less erratic quarterback on their bench. Johnson didn't even make it through final cuts, eventually signing in Cleveland as roster filler after all heck broke loose in December. He took one snap, got sacked and fumbled, and the Browns saw all they needed to see of a blazingly fast, live-armed quarterback two years younger than their quarterback of the future. Johnson is now in Cincinnati, where he may be stuck portraying Scout Team Kaepernick indefinitely. It would be fun to see him get one more shot.

Dan Orlovsky, TB: Though he'll never live down the "free cannoli!" safety he gave up against Minnesota while playing for Detroit, Orlovsky is about to begin his ninth NFL season and could make up to $900,000 this year. No man should be ashamed of these numbers. (2012 stats: 4-for-7, 51 yards, 5 DYAR, 0.4% DVOA)

Curtis Painter, NYG: Is there a way Curtis Painter could be remembered other than as the Colts quarterback who bridged the Peyton Manning-Andrew Luck gap? Why yes there is! Painter went 0-8 in 2011, the only season in which he's started any games. The record for most losses without a win is held by two former Alabama quarterbacks, Brodie Croyle and Harry Gilmer. With just three more losses, Painter can re-write the record books! Painter was cut in camp by Baltimore last year and will be cut in camp by the Giants this year.

Jordan Palmer, FA: After four seasons with the Cincinnati Bengals, Palmer landed with the Jaguars last offseason due largely to his connection to Bob Bratkowski, the Jaguars' offensive coordinator under Mike Mularkey. Palmer had a ho-hum preseason and was cut, then brought back to backup Chad Henne after Blaine Gabbert was done for the year. He's currently unsigned and ready to hand the brother torch over to Jordan Rodgers.

Sean Renfree, ATL: Atlanta took a flier on the heady three-year starter from Duke in the seventh round. In Durham, Renfree apprenticed under David Cutcliffe, who inevitably compared his work ethic to former protégé, Peyton Manning. Unfortunately, Renfree's arm strength is more comparable to Olivia Manning. Renfree fell a bit on draft day due to surgery on a torn pectoral muscle, but Atlanta's presumed backup, Dominique Davis, has similar traits and less upside. There's no reason to think Renfree can't take Davis' job.

Matt Scott, JAC: Scott was projected as a mid-round pick—Mike Mayock of the NFL Network even thought the Philadelphia Eagles were going to pick Scott when they moved up for the first pick in the fourth round to take USC's Matt Barkley—but concerns about his size (6-foot-2, 213 pounds) and concussion questions caused him to fall out of the draft completely. When healthy, Scott was a dual-threat at Arizona, completing over 61 percent of 676 pass attempts for 4,921 yards and 33 touchdowns while also rushing for 1,138 yards and eight touchdowns in his 34-game career. The Jaguars aggressively pursued Scott as a "priority free agent," guaranteeing him $12,500, the largest amount they paid an undrafted rookie this offseason. The competition for starting quarterback is wide open in Jacksonville, but Scott is more likely to compete with Jordan Rodgers for the No. 3 job behind Blaine Gabbert and Chad Henne.

Matt Simms, NYJ: As a junior, Phil Simms' younger son lost the Tennessee starting job at midseason. As a senior, he couldn't beat out Tyler Bray to get the job back. He completed just 54 percent of passes during his college career, and he didn't play well enough at the Jets' 2012 training camp to garner a practice squad spot, but apparently he passed Greg McElroy for the third spot on the depth chart during minicamp. Ladies and gentlemen, the New York Jets.

Rusty Smith, TEN: The Rusty Smith of 2013 is almost certainly a better quarterback than the one who, as a rookie, single-handedly knocked the 2010 Houston Texans out of not just the top-three but even the top-ten worst passing defenses of the DVOA era. Barring injuries to Jake Locker and Ryan Fitzpatrick, though, he won't get a regular-season opportunity to show that.

Brad Sorensen, SD: This San Diego seventh-round pick was a strong-armed pocket passer at Southern Utah who operated frequently from the shotgun. Some scouts worry about his decision-making, which in Sorensen's case is all the more important given that he does not have great athleticism or mobility to fall back on.

Ricky Stanzi, KC: Two years removed from being drafted by Scott Pioli in the fifth round, Stanzi remains yet to throw a pass in a meaningful NFL game. One has to assume that if the ex-Hawkeye had even a semblance of potential, the previous Chiefs regime would have put him on the field sometime last year when Matt Cassel and Brady Quinn were taking turns losing games. The book on Stanzi coming out of college was: adequate measurables from a pocket passing standpoint, but unrefined and likely to need a lot of time to learn how to read NFL defenses. The book on Stanzi now is exactly the same.

Tyler Thigpen, FA: Thigpen has seen almost no game action over the past four years, but we'll always remember that 2008 season when he started 11 games for Kansas City and was the first NFL quarterback to ever run the pistol. Herm Edwards will certainly always remember that year; he spent most of the "In-Game Decision Making" panel at this year's Sloan Sports Analytics Conference dissing Thigpen and complaining about how hard it was to win games with Thigpen as his quarterback. The Bills cut Thigpen, and neither Oakland nor Seattle signed him after tryouts, so his career may be done.(2012 stats: 3-for-5, 30 yards, 14 DYAR, 32.3% DVOA)

Seneca Wallace, NO: Seneca's appearance in the Big Easy says more about the team's uneasiness about having Luke McCown as the backup QB than any confidence in Wallace. If either player sees significant time behind center this season, 2013 will be even worse than the 2012 debacle.

Joe Webb, MIN: To some of the quarterbacks in this section, the correct answer to the question "Could this player complete an aesthetically-appealing forward pass in an NFL game?" is "Yes." If you watched Minnesota's Wild Card loss to Green Bay, you know that Webb isn't one of them. However, he was entertainingly bad. And in the end, isn't that the real truth? ...The answer ... is no. Webb is being tried at wide receiver this offseason. As a wide receiver, he makes a good quarterback.

Running Backs

In the following section we provide the last three years' statistics, as well as a 2013 KUBIAK projection, for every running back who either played a significant role in 2012 or is expected to do so in 2013.

The first line contains biographical data—each player's name, height, weight, college, draft position, birth date, and age. Height and weight are the best data we could find; weight, of course, can fluctuate during the offseason. **Age** is very simple, the number of years between the player's birth year and 2013, but birthdate is provided if you want to figure out exact age.

Draft position gives draft year and round, with the overall pick number with which the player was taken in parentheses. In the sample table, it says that LeSean McCoy was chosen in the 2009 NFL Draft in the second round with the 53rd overall pick. Undrafted free agents are listed as "FA" with the year they came into the league, even if they were only in training camp or on a practice squad.

To the far right of the first line is the player's Risk for fantasy football in 2013. As explained in the quarterback section, the standard is for players to be marked Green. Players with higher than normal risk are marked Yellow, and players with the highest risk are marked Red. Players who are most likely to match or surpass our forecast—primarily second-stringers with low projections—are marked Blue. Risk is not only based on injury probability, but how a player's projection compares to his recent performance as well as our confidence (or lack thereof) in his offensive teammates.

Next we give the last three years of player stats. First come games played and games started (**G/GS**). Games played is the official NFL total and may include games in which a player appeared on special teams, but did not carry the ball or catch a pass. We also have a total of offensive **Snaps** for each season. The next four columns are familiar: **Runs**, rushing yards (**Yds**), yards per rush (**Yd/R**) and rushing touchdowns (**TD**).

The entry for fumbles (**FUM**) includes all fumbles by this running back, no matter whether they were recovered by the offense or defense. Holding onto the ball is an identifiable skill; fumbling it so that your own offense can recover it is not. (For more on this issue, see the essay "Pregame Show" in the front of the book.) This entry combines fumbles on both carries and receptions.

The next five columns give our advanced metrics for rushing: **DVOA** (Defense-Adjusted Value Over Average), **DYAR** (Defense-Adjusted Yards Above Replacement), and YAR (Yards Above Replacement), along with the player's rank (**Rk**) in both **DVOA** and **DYAR**. These metrics compare every carry by the running back to a league-average baseline based on the game situations in which that running back carried the ball. DVOA and DYAR are also adjusted based on the opposing defense. The methods used to compute these numbers are described in detail in the "Statistical Toolbox" introduction in the front of the book. The important distinctions between them are:

• DVOA is a rate statistic, while DYAR is a cumulative statistic. Thus, a higher DVOA means more value per play, while a higher DYAR means more aggregate value over the entire season.
• Because DYAR is defense-adjusted and YAR is not, a player whose DYAR is higher than his YAR faced a harder-than-average schedule. A player whose DYAR is lower than his YAR faced an easier-than-average schedule.

To qualify for ranking in rushing DVOA and DYAR, a running back must have had 100 carries in that season. Last year, only 42 running backs qualified to be ranked in these stats, compared to 51 backs in 2011 and 52 backs in 2010.

Success Rate (**Suc%**), listed along with rank, represents running back consistency as measured by successful running plays divided by total running plays. (The definition for success is explained in the "Statistical Toolbox" introduction in the front of the book.) A player with high DVOA and a low Success Rate mixes long runs with plays on which he was stuffed at or behind the line of scrimmage. A player with low DVOA and a high Success Rate generally gets the yards needed, but rarely gets more. The league-average Success Rate in 2012 was 47 percent. Success Rate is not adjusted for the defenses a player faced.

We also give a total of broken tackles (**BTkl**) according to the Football Outsiders game charting project. This total includes broken tackles on both runs and receptions.

The shaded columns to the right of broken tackles give data for each running back as a pass receiver. Receptions (**Rec**) counts passes caught, while Passes (**Pass**) counts total passes thrown to this player, complete or incomplete. The next four columns list receiving yards (**Yds**), catch rate (**C%**), yards per catch (**Yd/C**), receiving touchdowns (**TD**), and average yards after the catch (**YAC**).

Our research has shown that receivers bear some responsi-

LeSean McCoy			Height: 5-11		Weight: 198			College: Pittsburgh			Draft: 2009/2 (53)		Born: 12-Jul-1988		Age: 25			Risk: Yellow	
Year	Team	G/GS	Snaps	Runs	Yds	Yd/R	TD	FUM	DVOA	Rk	DYAR	Rk	YAR	Suc%	Rk	BTkl	Rec	Pass	Yds	C%	Yd/C	TD	YAC	DVOA	Rk	DYAR	Rk
2010	PHI	15/13	821	207	1080	5.2	7	2	17.5%	5	227	4	205	49%	14	38	78	90	592	87%	7.6	2	8.9	16.1%	15	158	2
2011	PHI	15/15	867	273	1309	4.8	17	1	15.8%	4	304	1	262	51%	15	50	48	69	315	70%	6.6	3	8.9	-4.5%	32	38	27
2012	PHI	12/12	694	200	840	4.2	2	4	-12.6%	33	-34	35	7	48%	19	44	54	68	373	81%	6.9	3	8.9	9.2%	17	90	9
2013	PHI			242	1155	4.8	8	3	8.3%								55	80	439	69%	8.0	3		5.6%			

bility for incomplete passes, even though only their catches are tracked in official statistics. Catch rate represents receptions divided by all intended passes for this running back. The average NFL running back caught 73 percent of passes in 2012. Unfortunately, we don't have room to post the best and worst running backs in receiving plus-minus, but you'll find the top 10 and bottom 10 running backs in this metric listed in the statistical appendix.

Finally we have receiving DVOA and DYAR, which are entirely separate from rushing DVOA and DYAR. To qualify for ranking in receiving DVOA and DYAR, a running back must have 25 passes thrown to him in that season. There are 47 running backs ranked for 2012, 51 backs for 2011, and 54 backs for 2010. Numbers without opponent adjustment (YAR, and VOA) can be found on our website, FootballOutsiders.com.

The italicized row of statistics for the 2013 season is our 2013 KUBIAK projection based on a complicated regres-

sion analysis that takes into account numerous variables including projected role, performance over the past two years, projected team offense and defense, historical comparables, height, age, experience of the offensive line, and strength of schedule.

It is difficult to accurately project statistics for a 162-game baseball season, but it is exponentially more difficult to accurately project statistics for a 16-game football season. Consider the listed projections not as a prediction of exact numbers, but the mean of a range of possible performances. What's important is less the exact number of yards we project, and more which players are projected to improve or decline. Actual performance will vary from our projection less for veteran starters and more for rookies and third-stringers, for whom we must base our projections on much smaller career statistical samples. Touchdown numbers will vary more than yardage numbers.

Top 20 RB by Rushing DYAR (Total Value), 2012

Rank	Player	Team	DYAR
1	Adrian Peterson	MIN	458
2	Marshawn Lynch	SEA	361
3	C.J. Spiller	BUF	301
4	Frank Gore	SF	268
5	Alfred Morris	WAS	254
6	Ahmad Bradshaw	NYG	230
7	Ray Rice	BAL	205
8	Stevan Ridley	NE	192
9	Andre Brown	NYG	185
10	Doug Martin	TB	155
11	Steven Jackson	STL	147
12	Matt Forte	CHI	109
13	Jamaal Charles	KC	109
14	Kendall Hunter	SF	109
15	Arian Foster	HOU	105
16	Mike Tolbert	CAR	103
17	Danny Woodhead	NE	101
18	Pierre Thomas	NO	97
19	DeMarco Murray	DAL	72
20	Joique Bell	DET	71

Top 20 RB by Rushing DVOA (Value per Rush), 2012

Rank	Player	Team	DVOA
1	C.J. Spiller	BUF	27.6%
2	Adrian Peterson	MIN	24.9%
3	Marshawn Lynch	SEA	19.2%
4	Frank Gore	SF	17.4%
5	Ahmad Bradshaw	NYG	15.8%
6	Pierre Thomas	NO	15.1%
7	Ray Rice	BAL	11.5%
8	Alfred Morris	WAS	10.3%
9	Stevan Ridley	NE	6.1%
10	Bilal Powell	NYJ	5.6%
11	Steven Jackson	STL	5.3%
12	Michael Bush	CHI	4.5%
13	Bernard Pierce	BAL	4.1%
14	Doug Martin	TB	3.9%
15	Matt Forte	CHI	3.1%
16	DeMarco Murray	DAL	1.7%
17	Jamaal Charles	KC	1.4%
18	Knowshon Moreno	DEN	1.1%
19	Mark Ingram	NO	0.8%
20	Arian Foster	HOU	-1.6%

Minimum 100 carries.

Top 10 RB by Receiving DYAR (Total Value), 2012

Rank	Player	Team	DYAR
1	Darren Sproles	NO	214
2	Joique Bell	DET	193
3	Danny Woodhead	NE	149
4	Jacquizz Rodgers	ATL	135
5	Felix Jones	DAL	109
6	Pierre Thomas	NO	99
7	C.J. Spiller	BUF	91
8	Marcel Reece	OAK	90
9	LeSean McCoy	PHI	90
10	Michael Robinson	SEA	85

Top 10 RB by Receiving DVOA (Value per Pass), 2012

Rank	Player	Team	DVOA
1	Felix Jones	DAL	45.1%
2	Danny Woodhead	NE	35.9%
3	Joique Bell	DET	32.8%
4	Jacquizz Rodgers	ATL	26.1%
5	Knowshon Moreno	DEN	25.3%
6	Toby Gerhart	MIN	25.0%
7	Darren Sproles	NO	21.5%
8	Pierre Thomas	NO	18.7%
9	C.J. Spiller	BUF	16.3%
10	Will Johnson	PIT	14.3%

Minimum 25 passes.

There are three metrics tracked by ESPN Stats & Information which you will see mentioned in some player comments. ESPN tracks the number of defenders in the box for each snap, and tags each play as either "loaded" or "not loaded." A loaded box is when the defense has more players in the box than the offense has available blockers for running plays. Some player comments may reference how well a back performed in 2012 against loaded vs. not loaded formations, or how many average men in the box he faced.

ESPN also marks **yards after contact** for each play. In the end, we decided not to include this number in the player tables because most running backs are packed surprisingly close in this metric, and we need to do more research on how much these small differences between running backs matter. In 2012, 44 of the 47 running backs with at least 100 carries averaged between 1.2 and 2.1 yards after contract on runs. The three exceptions were Adrian Peterson (2.9), Isaac Redman (2.5), and Pierre Thomas (2.3), and Redman and Thomas barely surpassed the 100-carry threshold. Reggie Bush, Chris Johnson, and Felix Jones were the lowest-ranked running backs with an average of just 1.2 yards after contact, although the names of the three players who had just 1.3 average yards after contact are a lot more surprising. That group consists of Arian Foster, Ray Rice, and Darren McFadden.

For many rookie running backs, we'll also include statistics from our college football arsenal, notably **POE** (Points Over Expected) and **Highlight Yards**. POE analyzes the output of college football running backs by comparing the expected EqPts value of every carry for a given ballcarrier (based on the quality of the rushing defense against which he's running) to the actual output. A positive POE indicates an above-average runner, with an average runner accruing exactly 0 POE. Highlight Yards are those yards not included in Adjusted Line Yards. So, for example, if a runner gains 12 yards in a given carry, and we attribute 7.0 of those yards to the line (the ALY formula gives the offensive line 100 percent credit for all yards gained between zero and four yards and 50 percent credit between five and 10), then the player's highlight yardage on the play is 5.0 yards. Highlight Yards are shown as an average per opportunity, which means Highlight Yards divided by the total number of carries that went over four yards. For more details on these stats, see the college football section of the book (p. **TK**).

Finally, in a section we call "Going Deep," we briefly discuss lower-round rookies, free-agent veterans, and practice-squad players who may play a role during the 2013 season or beyond.

Vick Ballard Height: 5-10 Weight: 219 College: Mississippi State Draft: 2012/5 (170) Born: 16-Jul-1990 Age: 23 Risk: Green

Year	Team	G/GS	Snaps	Runs	Yds	Yd/R	TD	FUM	DVOA	Rk	DYAR	Rk	YAR	Suc%	Rk	BTkl	Rec	Pass	Yds	C%	Yd/C	TD	YAC	DVOA	Rk	DYAR	Rk
2012	IND	16/12	579	211	814	3.9	2	3	-7.4%	27	10	27	-10	48%	18	22	17	27	152	63%	8.9	1	6.9	10.7%	15	38	24
2013	IND			117	449	3.8	3	1	-6.0%								15	18	116	83%	7.8	0		10.0%			

Getting Ballard in the fifth-round was a solid value pick by Colts GM Ryan Grigson. Ballard stepped up when Donald Brown battled injuries to lead the Colts in rushing yards and was a fairly effective receiver out of the backfield. However, Ballard had just a -16.3% DVOA and 46 percent success rate on first-down runs and will need to show that he's improved in pass protection if he's to be an every-down back at the NFL level. Ballard also had seven blown blocks in 2012, which was tied for the third-most among NFL running backs.

Lance Ball Height: 5-9 Weight: 223 College: Maryland Draft: 2008/FA Born: 19-Jun-1985 Age: 28 Risk: Green

Year	Team	G/GS	Snaps	Runs	Yds	Yd/R	TD	FUM	DVOA	Rk	DYAR	Rk	YAR	Suc%	Rk	BTkl	Rec	Pass	Yds	C%	Yd/C	TD	YAC	DVOA	Rk	DYAR	Rk
2010	DEN	10/0	94	41	158	3.9	0	1	-24.1%	--	-25	--	-22	34%	--	4	3	6	16	50%	5.3	0	8.3	-45.0%	--	-10	--
2011	DEN	16/0	380	96	402	4.2	1	2	2.8%	--	42	--	43	44%	--	5	16	31	148	52%	9.3	1	8.3	-18.1%	46	-7	46
2012	DEN	15/0	143	42	158	3.8	1	1	-9.2%	--	-1	--	-6	39%	--	4	7	12	61	67%	8.7	1	5.1	-5.6%	--	5	--
2013	DEN			31	128	4.2	4	1	19.0%								10	13	81	77%	8.1	0		5.8%			

Ball has been a serviceable back-of-the-rotation back for Denver over the past three years. He's a steady, controlled runner with good natural size and leverage. However, he's not dynamic enough in any particular area to consistently garner a specific role. He's built for inside running and requires good blocking in order to be effective. He's not much in the passing game, struggling at times last year as a blocker against the blitz and registering just 26 total receptions in his Broncos career.

Montee Ball Height: 5-10 Weight: 214 College: Wisconsin Draft: 2013/2 (58) Born: 5-Dec-1990 Age: 23 Risk: Red

Year	Team	G/GS	Snaps	Runs	Yds	Yd/R	TD	FUM	DVOA	Rk	DYAR	Rk	YAR	Suc%	Rk	BTkl	Rec	Pass	Yds	C%	Yd/C	TD	YAC	DVOA	Rk	DYAR	Rk
2013	DEN			255	1160	4.5	7	4	3.9%								17	21	97	81%	5.7	1		-13.7%			

The plan is for the Wisconsin product to become Denver's three-down back. The all-time leader in touchdowns among Division I running backs figures to be a good fit in Denver's offense. Scouts like the way Ball identifies and attacks running lanes. He has the quickness to get around the edge and he changes directions well. This suggests he'll be able to run effectively out of single-back sets and shotgun. The concern with Ball is durability. He stayed healthy in college, but he also carried the ball 983 times, including 356 carries last year in 14 games. He also was not a very productive receiver in college.

Jackie Battle

Height: 6-2   Weight: 238   College: Houston   Draft: 2007/FA   Born: 1-Oct-1983   Age: 30   Risk: N/A

Year	Team	G/GS	Snaps	Runs	Yds	Yd/R	TD	FUM	DVOA	Rk	DYAR	Rk	YAR	Suc%	Rk	BTkl	Rec	Pass	Yds	C%	Yd/C	TD	YAC	DVOA	Rk	DYAR	Rk
2010	KC	16/0	58	20	50	2.5	1	0	-3.6%	--	3	--	8	45%	--	1	1	3	9	33%	9.0	0	7.0	-59.9%	--	-10	--
2011	KC	15/4	305	149	597	4.0	2	0	4.3%	16	76	22	78	44%	40	7	9	13	68	69%	7.6	0	7.0	-36.8%	--	-16	--
2012	SD	16/5	159	95	311	3.3	3	0	-23.8%	--	-67	--	-48	38%	--	3	15	15	108	100%	7.2	1	7.4	60.4%	--	63	--

Battle is a somewhat robotic downhill runner. He does a good job staying behind his pads. He does not have a lot of east and west agility. However, his serviceable work in the passing game, mainly as a short-area receiver out of the backfield, suggests that he's not just a plodding interior bruiser. Currently unemployed, he's waiting for calls from Oakland and Denver to complete his tour of the AFC West.

Joique Bell

Height: 5-11   Weight: 220   College: Wayne State   Draft: 2010/FA   Born: 4-Aug-1986   Age: 27   Risk: Blue

Year	Team	G/GS	Snaps	Runs	Yds	Yd/R	TD	FUM	DVOA	Rk	DYAR	Rk	YAR	Suc%	Rk	BTkl	Rec	Pass	Yds	C%	Yd/C	TD	YAC	DVOA	Rk	DYAR	Rk
2012	DET	16/0	381	82	414	5.0	3	1	12.6%	--	71	--	65	54%	--	20	52	69	485	75%	9.3	0	8.3	32.8%	3	193	2
2013	DET			56	255	4.6	2	1	4.6%							29	37		255	78%	8.8	1		18.9%			

"Where we are, he definitely would be the missing piece," Lions guard Rob Sims said after the signing of Reggie Bush. "With our aerial attack, and he can catch the ball the way he can out of the backfield and some of the other running-game stuff we got in place, I think it's tailor-made for him." Yes, if only the Lions had a back last year who was good at catching the football...

Bell is not Bush. Bush will split out wide, which adds some new dimensions to the offense, and Bush is a more dynamic open-field runner—though that doesn't necessarily make him a *better* runner. Bell also spent two years on practice squads or playing only special teams and has to be viewed through the scope of a possible regression. Still, Bell is the Coke Zero to Reggie's regular: not much taste difference, much less of a carb load on the salary cap.

Le'Veon Bell

Height: 6-1   Weight: 230   College: Michigan State   Draft: 2013/2 (48)   Born: 18-Feb-1992   Age: 21   Risk: Yellow

Year	Team	G/GS	Snaps	Runs	Yds	Yd/R	TD	FUM	DVOA	Rk	DYAR	Rk	YAR	Suc%	Rk	BTkl	Rec	Pass	Yds	C%	Yd/C	TD	YAC	DVOA	Rk	DYAR	Rk
2013	PIT			193	764	4.0	9	2	-4.0%							22	26		168	85%	7.6	1		1.2%			

Offensive coordinator Todd Haley referred to Bell as a "three-down back" in May, meaning that Haley plans to use him on a first down in the first quarter, a second down in the second quarter, and a third down in the third quarter. Haley also called Bell a "workhorse back," which means, who knows, three carries in a row at some point? But seriously folks: Bell caught 78 passes in three seasons at Michigan State, so he is more than just a big guy with a few highlight stick moves. The Steelers are also moving toward more zone blocking, and Bell was good at setting up his Spartans blocks. Haley's compulsive rusher-juggling aside, the Steelers need a running back who elevates the offense instead of just working within it, and Bell's power, moves, and receiving ability could make him that back. At least until Haley gets curious about what LaRod Stephens-Howling can do.

Cedric Benson

Height: 5-11   Weight: 222   College: Texas   Draft: 2005/1 (4)   Born: 28-Dec-1982   Age: 31   Risk: N/A

Year	Team	G/GS	Snaps	Runs	Yds	Yd/R	TD	FUM	DVOA	Rk	DYAR	Rk	YAR	Suc%	Rk	BTkl	Rec	Pass	Yds	C%	Yd/C	TD	YAC	DVOA	Rk	DYAR	Rk
2010	CIN	16/16	673	321	1111	3.5	7	7	-12.5%	38	-67	43	-82	45%	26	30	28	37	178	76%	6.4	1	6.4	-7.8%	40	12	40
2011	CIN	15/15	577	273	1067	3.9	6	5	-10.4%	45	-21	48	-21	49%	21	10	15	22	82	68%	5.5	0	6.4	-23.4%	--	-11	--
2012	GB	5/5	200	71	248	3.5	1	1	-6.1%	--	7	--	6	52%	--	4	14	15	97	93%	6.9	0	7.1	37.8%	--	45	--

Cedric Benson was a thoroughly mediocre back when he was actually healthy—the kind of guy who would get you exactly what is blocked and nothing more. After three consecutive empty 1,000-yard seasons, last year his greatest contribution to the Packers was inflating their league-leading AGL with his Lisfranc fracture. A free agent at press time, Benson will be waiting for someone to call. It probably wasn't the career the Bears imagined for him after selecting him with the fourth overall pick, but at least Benson was able to resurface in Cincinnati and be a solid piece on a playoff team for a bit.

Giovani Bernard

Height: 5-8   Weight: 202   College: North Carolina   Draft: 2013/2 (37)   Born: 22-Nov-1991   Age: 22   Risk: Yellow

Year	Team	G/GS	Snaps	Runs	Yds	Yd/R	TD	FUM	DVOA	Rk	DYAR	Rk	YAR	Suc%	Rk	BTkl	Rec	Pass	Yds	C%	Yd/C	TD	YAC	DVOA	Rk	DYAR	Rk
2013	CIN			155	653	4.2	6	2	-1.9%							42	55		415	76%	9.9	2		11.0%			

Bernard rushed for 2,481 yards (5.9 yards per carry) in two seasons as a starter at North Carolina, most of that production coming from shotgun read-options, draws, and other increasingly common innovations. He also added 92 receptions and was a productive punt returner. Bernard is short and lacks deep speed, but he's an eager cut-blocker in pass protection, catches the ball well, sets up blocks, and does all the little things. He was drafted before Eddie Lacy (or any other running back) because NFL teams comprehend what scouting experts refuse to accept: multi-purpose change-up backs have been more useful than big bruisers for roughly two decades. Bernard will take most of BenJarvus Green-Ellis' catches and a share of his carries away. How big a share is not clear, but the Bengals did not draft him to block and execute fake punts.

LeGarrette Blount Height: 6-0   Weight: 247   College: Oregon   Draft: 2010/FA   Born: 5-Dec-1986   Age: 27   Risk: Green

Year	Team	G/GS	Snaps	Runs	Yds	Yd/R	TD	FUM	DVOA	Rk	DYAR	Rk	YAR	Suc%	Rk	BTkl	Rec	Pass	Yds	C%	Yd/C	TD	YAC	DVOA	Rk	DYAR	Rk
2010	TB	13/7	344	201	1007	5.0	6	4	3.9%	14	109	13	101	45%	23	33	5	7	14	71%	2.8	0	3.8	-95.7%	--	-34	--
2011	TB	14/14	392	184	781	4.2	5	5	0.6%	28	67	24	54	47%	23	30	15	25	148	60%	9.9	0	3.8	-45.2%	49	-43	49
2012	TB	13/0	92	41	151	3.7	2	0	-9.5%	--	-2	--	2	37%	--	2	1	2	2	50%	2.0	0	7.0	-102.8%	--	-11	--
2013	NE			32	114	3.6	2	1	-8.6%								8	10	56	80%	7.0	0		4.6%			

Blount has aged in dog years in Tampa Bay, getting significantly worse at almost everything, almost every year. The most shocking stat may be one that isn't listed above: yards after contact. According to ESPN Stats & Info's numbers, Blount led the league with 2.9 average yards after contact in 2010, more than half a yard over every other starting running back. In 2011, that figure was down to 2.3, and in 2012 it was down to 1.3. In trading for Blount, the Patriots may have looked at his size and seen visions of short-yardage glory, but last year he converted just one of four runs in Power situations. His failure to score on three straight carries inside the 2-yard line against New Orleans may have sealed his fate with the Bucs. (Maybe the Patriots were taking a longer view, as Blount was 12-of-15 on such runs in 2011.) Blount gained 35 yards on one run in Week 6 against Kansas City, the league's 28th-ranked run defense. Otherwise, he averaged just 2.9 yards per carry.

Brandon Bolden Height: 5-11   Weight: 220   College: Mississippi   Draft: 2012/FA   Born: 26-Jan-1990   Age: 23   Risk: Blue

Year	Team	G/GS	Snaps	Runs	Yds	Yd/R	TD	FUM	DVOA	Rk	DYAR	Rk	YAR	Suc%	Rk	BTkl	Rec	Pass	Yds	C%	Yd/C	TD	YAC	DVOA	Rk	DYAR	Rk
2012	NE	10/0	99	56	274	4.9	2	0	12.8%	--	53	--	54	54%	--	5	2	2	11	100%	5.5	0	5.0	6.3%	--	2	--
2013	NE			50	202	4.0	2	1	-5.7%								8	9	57	89%	7.1	0		10.4%			

Running backs are fungible, Exhibit 45,319. Why pay BenJarvus Green-Ellis $9 million over three seasons when you can spend $1.5 million over three seasons for essentially the same player, down to the rookie hazing performance of "Forward Rebels?" Like the Law Firm, Bolden was an UDFA out of Ole Miss and is a pounding north-south runner who sets up blocks well but doesn't have much agility going east-west.

Ahmad Bradshaw Height: 5-11   Weight: 195   College: Marshall   Draft: 2007/7 (250)   Born: 19-Mar-1986   Age: 27   Risk: Yellow

Year	Team	G/GS	Snaps	Runs	Yds	Yd/R	TD	FUM	DVOA	Rk	DYAR	Rk	YAR	Suc%	Rk	BTkl	Rec	Pass	Yds	C%	Yd/C	TD	YAC	DVOA	Rk	DYAR	Rk
2010	NYG	16/11	721	276	1235	4.5	8	7	2.2%	17	110	12	95	46%	20	38	47	59	314	81%	6.7	0	7.9	4.2%	26	52	21
2011	NYG	12/9	488	171	659	3.9	9	1	2.5%	21	80	21	83	45%	32	21	34	44	267	77%	7.9	2	7.9	0.2%	27	31	32
2012	NYG	14/12	598	221	1015	4.6	6	3	15.8%	5	230	6	194	52%	8	14	23	31	245	74%	10.7	0	11.9	8.5%	18	35	25
2013	IND			174	736	4.2	4	1	0.9%								36	48	266	75%	7.4	0		-1.3%			

Bradshaw had the best season of his career in 2012 (in terms of DYAR and success rate), which for a 27-year-old running back means nobody wanted him anymore. Well, almost nobody: Indianapolis owner Jim Irsay tweeted in June that he wanted to give Bradshaw a pile of "SERIOUS Coin." A few days later, Bradshaw was a member of the Colts; that proves you can't ignore every Irsay tweet. While the former Giants back may not have elite athleticism, he's a capable three-down back who will provide a valuable presence in the Colts' huddle. In 2012, he ranked fourth among running backs in rushing first downs on third or fourth down, including 10-of-12 successful runs on third- or fourth-and-1.

Andrew Luck rarely checked down as a rookie, as Bruce Arians' vertical offense kept Luck's eyes focused farther down the field. But Bradshaw is a solid receiving back and should help Luck improve on his completion percentage in 2013. Bradshaw has always been part of a committee, and that trend should continue with Vick Ballard in Indianapolis. The Colts are not a trendy Super Bowl pick, but Bradshaw is the type of under-the-radar signing that can help a team in the playoffs.

Curtis Brinkley Height: 5-9   Weight: 208   College: Syracuse   Draft: 2009/FA   Born: 21-Sep-1985   Age: 28   Risk: N/A

Year	Team	G/GS	Snaps	Runs	Yds	Yd/R	TD	FUM	DVOA	Rk	DYAR	Rk	YAR	Suc%	Rk	BTkl	Rec	Pass	Yds	C%	Yd/C	TD	YAC	DVOA	Rk	DYAR	Rk
2010	SD	3/0	6	2	11	5.5	0	0	28.5%	--	3	--	4	50%	--	0	0	0	0	--	0.0	0	--	--	--	--	--
2011	SD	10/1	68	30	101	3.4	1	0	-18.7%	--	-12	--	-7	37%	--	0	7	9	41	78%	5.9	0	4.9	-32.6%	--	-9	--
2012	SD	10/1	107	39	115	2.9	0	1	-36.7%	--	-48	--	-38	41%	--	3	12	15	77	80%	6.4	0	8.6	-16.1%	--	-2	--

Brinkley is a former practice squad player who has spent his career toggling along the fringes of the Chargers roster. At his best, he is a scat-back type player with decent quickness. He can be effective catching swing passes out in the flats, as he has shown glimpses of having the necessary change-of-direction shiftiness to potentially make defenders miss in space. That said, the production simply hasn't been there with Brinkley, and it's tough to see him carving out a long-term role with a team at this point.

Andre Brown Height: 6-1 Weight: 196 College: North Carolina State Draft: 2009/4 (129) Born: 30-Nov-1986 Age: 27 Risk: Green

Year	Team	G/GS	Snaps	Runs	Yds	Yd/R	TD	FUM	DVOA	Rk	DYAR	Rk	YAR	Suc%	Rk	BTkl	Rec	Pass	Yds	C%	Yd/C	TD	YAC	DVOA	Rk	DYAR	Rk
2010	DEN	4/0	2	2	-1	-0.5	0	0	-95.3%	--	-11	--	-11	0%	--	0	0	0	0	--	0.0	0	--	--	--	--	--
2012	NYG	10/2	222	73	385	5.3	8	0	45.6%	--	185	--	173	63%	--	4	12	17	86	71%	7.2	0	6.1	-17.3%	--	-3	--
2013	NYG			126	606	4.8	10	2	16.5%								23	33	154	70%	6.7	0		-12.6%			

The first three seasons of his career, injuries limited Brown to two carries for minus-1 yard. But Brown broke out last year, ranking first in both DYAR and DVOA among non-primary running backs (20 to 100 carries). Brown saw double-digit carries in only three games, but he made the most of them by rushing for 248 yards and four touchdowns on 46 carries against the Bucs, Panthers, and Packers. Unfortunately, Brown broke his fibula against Green Bay, so his season ended prematurely for the fourth straight year.

Brown's game is more about substance than flash: he is a physical player who gained 2.5 average yards after contact last season. He'll be expected to spell David Wilson in 2013, but could earn a bigger role if Wilson's fumble problems creep up again. Brown finished second to only Arian Foster with five one-yard rushing touchdowns last year, and could be a fantasy vulture again this season.

Bryce Brown Height: 6-0 Weight: 220 College: Kansas State Draft: 2012/7 (229) Born: 14-May-1991 Age: 22 Risk: Yellow

Year	Team	G/GS	Snaps	Runs	Yds	Yd/R	TD	FUM	DVOA	Rk	DYAR	Rk	YAR	Suc%	Rk	BTkl	Rec	Pass	Yds	C%	Yd/C	TD	YAC	DVOA	Rk	DYAR	Rk
2012	PHI	16/4	334	115	564	4.9	4	4	-2.2%	23	29	24	29	39%	39	17	13	19	56	68%	4.3	0	7.0	-38.9%	--	-26	--
2013	PHI			122	599	4.9	3	3	5.2%								22	28	176	79%	8.0	1		9.0%			

In 2008, Brown was the No.1 high school recruit in the country. In 2012, he ran a 4.37-second 40 at his pro day, giving him a ridiculous Speed Score of 120.6. In between, Brown's football career was a disaster, which caused him to fall to the seventh round of the draft. Brown rarely saw the field in the first half of 2012, but was given the start in Week 12 against the Panthers with LeSean McCoy sidelined by a concussion. Brown rushed 19 times for 178 yards and two touchdowns, and then gained 169 yards and two more scores on 24 carries the next week against the Cowboys. Then, just as quickly, Brown disappeared from the national scene. After the Dallas game, he rushed for just six yards on 12 carries against the Bucs, and struggled the remainder of the year.

Even though the peak was short, Brown looked so good against Carolina and Dallas that it's tempting to wonder what he can do with a larger workload. Few backs possess his raw athleticism, but Brown must improve his ball security to earn more touches. He fumbled four times on the 136 times he touched the ball (including returns) as a rookie, giving him a 2.9 percent fumble rate. Other rookie running backs with similar rates: Delone Carter with the Colts in 2011 (2.8 percent), and Toby Gerhart (Minnesota, 2.9 percent), Chris Ivory (New Orleans, 2.9 percent), and Ryan Mathews (San Diego, 2.8 percent) in 2010. Fumbling is a quick way to lose your job, regardless of talent, and defenders now know to focus on jarring the ball loose from Brown. In Chip Kelly's offense, there should be lots of carries to go around. Despite being the number two back, Brown could have some good performances as long as he holds onto the ball.

Donald Brown Height: 5-11 Weight: 210 College: Connecticut Draft: 2009/1 (27) Born: 11-Apr-1987 Age: 26 Risk: Red

Year	Team	G/GS	Snaps	Runs	Yds	Yd/R	TD	FUM	DVOA	Rk	DYAR	Rk	YAR	Suc%	Rk	BTkl	Rec	Pass	Yds	C%	Yd/C	TD	YAC	DVOA	Rk	DYAR	Rk
2010	IND	13/8	410	129	497	3.9	2	0	-4.8%	29	19	29	14	44%	27	10	20	28	205	71%	10.3	0	9.0	16.0%	16	47	22
2011	IND	16/2	392	134	645	4.8	5	0	13.9%	5	119	15	101	37%	49	12	16	19	86	84%	5.4	0	9.0	-19.8%	--	-6	--
2012	IND	10/4	299	108	417	3.9	1	0	-9.8%	31	-5	31	-5	44%	30	5	9	13	93	69%	10.3	0	11.0	0.9%	--	11	--
2013	IND			43	175	4.1	1	1	-3.9%								8	10	67	80%	8.3	0		10.1%			

Four seasons is a large enough sample size to reach a conclusion about Donald Brown: He's a strong runner, particularly between the tackles and in the red zone, who struggles with pass protection, offers very little as a receiver, has no special teams value, and has zero chance of remaining healthy for a full 16-game season. (And whatever you do, do not get him wet or feed him after midnight.) Brown had every opportunity to cement himself as "The Man" in the Colts backfield, but injuries, including a season-ending ankle injury in December, limited the 2009 first-round pick to 10 games last season and opened the door for rookie Vick Ballard to climb to the top of a depth chart that added Ahmad Bradshaw late in the offseason. Brown will have to beat out Delone Carter and/or seventh-round running back/return specialist Kerwynn Williams for a roster spot.

Ronnie Brown Height: 6-0 Weight: 233 College: Auburn Draft: 2005/1 (2) Born: 12-Dec-1981 Age: 32 Risk: Green

Year	Team	G/GS	Snaps	Runs	Yds	Yd/R	TD	FUM	DVOA	Rk	DYAR	Rk	YAR	Suc%	Rk	BTkl	Rec	Pass	Yds	C%	Yd/C	TD	YAC	DVOA	Rk	DYAR	Rk
2010	MIA	16/16	630	200	734	3.7	5	3	-4.6%	28	20	28	7	43%	35	13	33	42	242	79%	7.3	0	6.2	1.3%	31	36	29
2011	PHI	16/2	143	42	136	3.2	1	1	-14.9%	--	-12	--	-26	48%	--	1	0	2	0	0%	0.0	0	6.2	-96.9%	--	-10	--
2012	SD	14/1	354	46	220	4.8	0	0	10.2%	--	31	--	47	42%	--	10	49	60	371	83%	7.6	0	7.8	12.2%	13	79	10
2013	SD			62	241	3.9	2	2	-7.4%								27	36	176	75%	6.5	0		-5.0%			

Brown is a steady veteran who can still do spot duty to help keep an offense alive, but can no longer be asked to handle the ball 25 times in a game. He has never had dynamic speed or quickness, but he runs with good balance and control, showing adequate power and rarely getting too heavy on his feet. He has carved out a career-sustaining niche in San Diego as a third-down back, where he thrives as an underneath pass-catcher, delay handoff runner and blitz protector. Last season, the Chargers consistently made Brown their backfield feature in critical situations.

Michael Bush

				Height: 6-1		Weight: 245			College: Louisville				Draft: 2007/4 (100)		Born: 16-Jun-1984		Age: 29				Risk: Green		

Year	Team	G/GS	Snaps	Runs	Yds	Yd/R	TD	FUM	DVOA	Rk	DYAR	Rk	YAR	Suc%	Rk	BTkl	Rec	Pass	Yds	C%	Yd/C	TD	YAC	DVOA	Rk	DYAR	Rk
2010	OAK	14/3	422	158	655	4.1	8	0	6.4%	12	108	14	108	45%	24	12	18	25	194	76%	10.8	0	11.4	48.0%	2	83	14
2011	OAK	16/9	724	256	977	3.8	7	1	-2.7%	33	65	26	45	45%	36	12	37	47	418	79%	11.3	1	11.4	44.8%	2	142	3
2012	CHI	13/1	248	114	411	3.6	5	1	4.5%	12	67	16	48	50%	12	5	9	11	83	82%	9.2	0	9.3	24.9%	--	23	--
2013	CHI			106	397	3.7	4	2	-8.2%								16	20	148	80%	9.3	0		16.4%			

One of the best backup running backs of this era, Bush hits the hole fast and powers through tacklers for extra yards well. He's solid in pass protection. His skills in the passing game, which went neglected last season while Mike Tice tried to find the right amount of blockers for Jay Cutler to hit Brandon Marshall deep on every single passing play, make him a perfect third-down back. Bush had back-to-back years of 40.0% or higher receiving DVOA in Oakland before managing *just* 24.5% on his 11 passes last year. Those are comically better than Matt Forte's recent receiving DVOAs, and Marc Trestman does have a history of utilizing his backs in the passing game. Unless Forte improves under Trestman's tutelage, Bush could get more snaps than we're projecting this season.

Reggie Bush

				Height: 6-0		Weight: 200			College: USC				Draft: 2006/1 (2)		Born: 2-Mar-1985		Age: 28				Risk: Yellow		

Year	Team	G/GS	Snaps	Runs	Yds	Yd/R	TD	FUM	DVOA	Rk	DYAR	Rk	YAR	Suc%	Rk	BTkl	Rec	Pass	Yds	C%	Yd/C	TD	YAC	DVOA	Rk	DYAR	Rk
2010	NO	8/6	233	36	150	4.2	0	0	-10.8%	--	-3	--	0	42%	--	10	34	42	208	81%	6.1	1	5.9	-3.3%	33	25	34
2011	MIA	15/15	600	216	1086	5.0	6	4	-2.1%	30	51	32	91	44%	37	29	43	52	296	83%	6.9	1	5.9	-12.2%	40	5	41
2012	MIA	16/16	572	227	986	4.3	6	4	-8.3%	30	3	30	18	51%	10	24	35	51	292	69%	8.3	2	7.8	7.9%	19	54	17
2013	DET			207	988	4.8	5	2	4.8%								58	82	468	71%	8.1	2		4.6%			

Starting NFL running backs generally come in two forms. There are backs like Alfred Morris, who aren't the most physically gifted humans to ever carry a football, but can execute zone runs as well as anyone. Then there are backs like Bush, who (understandably) rely on their speed and elusiveness rather than reading blocks as per play design. It's no wonder, then, that Bush left Miami for Detroit. Almost absurdly often in 2012, he would cut back on a stretch play, a cardinal sin because the weak side is intentionally unblocked. Rarely, it would result in a big gain; most of the time it lost yardage.

In Detroit, it's a match made in heaven: Bush's skill set aligns with Scott Linehan's man-blocking scheme in the running game; and the Lions' pass-heavy, single-back attack suits Bush much better than incumbent starter Mikel Leshoure (which, incidentally, makes you wonder why they drafted him in the first place).

Delone Carter

				Height: 5-9		Weight: 226			College: Syracuse				Draft: 2011/4 (119)		Born: 22-Jun-1987		Age: 26				Risk: Red		

Year	Team	G/GS	Snaps	Runs	Yds	Yd/R	TD	FUM	DVOA	Rk	DYAR	Rk	YAR	Suc%	Rk	BTkl	Rec	Pass	Yds	C%	Yd/C	TD	YAC	DVOA	Rk	DYAR	Rk
2011	IND	16/3	237	101	377	3.7	2	3	-11.6%	48	-13	45	-20	46%	29	5	5	8	18	63%	3.6	0	6.8	-78.8%	--	-29	--
2012	IND	10/0	64	32	122	3.8	3	1	24.7%	--	55	--	50	63%	--	4	1	2	13	50%	13.0	0	11.0	-198.6%	--	-20	--
2013	IND			48	182	3.8	2	1	-5.3%								7	9	53	78%	7.6	0		5.6%			

After starting three games and carrying the ball 101 times in 2011, Carter was reduced to the No. 3 role in the Colts' backfield, playing largely on special teams. He rarely received multiple carries a game, but was effective near the goal line, scoring touchdowns on three of his four carries inside the five. Carter remains a non-factor as a receiver (just two targets) and will compete with Donald Brown and 2013 seventh-round pick Kerwynn Williams for a roster spot this summer.

Jamaal Charles

				Height: 5-11		Weight: 200			College: Texas				Draft: 2008/3 (73)		Born: 27-Dec-1986		Age: 27				Risk: Yellow		

Year	Team	G/GS	Snaps	Runs	Yds	Yd/R	TD	FUM	DVOA	Rk	DYAR	Rk	YAR	Suc%	Rk	BTkl	Rec	Pass	Yds	C%	Yd/C	TD	YAC	DVOA	Rk	DYAR	Rk
2010	KC	16/6	587	230	1467	6.4	5	4	32.9%	1	382	1	402	56%	3	27	45	64	468	70%	10.4	3	9.3	25.7%	8	132	8
2011	KC	2/1	34	12	83	6.9	0	1	-4.9%	--	2	--	6	50%	--	1	5	6	9	83%	1.8	1	9.3	-29.7%	--	-5	--
2012	KC	16/15	577	285	1509	5.3	5	5	1.4%	17	109	12	158	46%	29	16	35	49	236	73%	6.7	1	7.3	-13.8%	32	0	32
2013	KC			271	1349	5.0	7	3	8.4%								50	69	388	72%	7.8	1		-1.2%			

After missing most of 2011 with a torn ACL, Charles ripped off a career-high 1,509 yards in 2012 despite playing for a Chiefs offense that had no passing attack. You could make the case that the six-year veteran, despite getting Pro Bowl honors in 2010 and 2012, is one of the most underrated players in pro football. He has averaged at least 5.3 yards per carry in each of his five NFL seasons. His current 5.8 career yards per carry average is an all-time record.

High yards per carry numbers tend to be a product of stat-inflating long touchdown runs. Indeed, Charles has ripped off his fair share of *SportsCenter* Top 10 plays, but he had only 10 runs of 20 yards or longer in 2010 (tied for sixth in the NFL) and 11 in 2012 (tied for third; Adrian Peterson, by the way, led the league with 27). The film agrees with what these stats suggest: Charles, who relies on speed, quickness and agility, is much more of a sustaining, every-down back than people realize. His explosiveness on the perimeter makes him an excellent fit in a zone-blocking scheme. The only real concern with Charles is his tendency to fumble a little bit more than average.

Tashard Choice Height: 5-10 Weight: 215 College: Georgia Tech Draft: 2008/4 (122) Born: 20-Nov-1984 Age: 29 Risk: Green

Year	Team	G/GS	Snaps	Runs	Yds	Yd/R	TD	FUM	DVOA	Rk	DYAR	Rk	YAR	Suc%	Rk	BTkl	Rec	Pass	Yds	C%	Yd/C	TD	YAC	DVOA	Rk	DYAR	Rk
2010	DAL	16/0	213	66	243	3.7	3	1	-4.3%	--	8	--	18	42%	--	2	17	22	109	77%	6.4	0	7.2	-23.6%	--	-11	--
2011	3TM	13/1	229	57	152	2.7	1	3	-42.4%	--	-85	--	-96	36%	--	3	19	31	124	65%	6.5	0	7.2	-62.2%	51	-71	51
2012	BUF	12/0	124	47	193	4.1	1	0	3.2%	--	23	--	21	43%	--	4	4	9	9	44%	2.3	0	5.8	-101.9%	--	-45	--
2013	BUF			58	213	3.7	2	1	-12.6%								15	20	113	75%	7.5	0		1.5%			

Choice was quite the promising prospect when he averaged 5.2 yards per carry in his first two seasons, but then his top-end speed just seemed to vanish. Nonetheless, he's been a perfectly acceptable third-string running back for the Bills. (In the 2011 season, he had -62.2% DVOA with Dallas and Washington but -14.8% DVOA with Buffalo.) The biggest danger for his roster spot is that unlike a lot of third-string backs, he doesn't play much on special teams.

Knile Davis Height: 5-11 Weight: 227 College: Arkansas Draft: 2013/3 (95) Born: 5-Oct-1991 Age: 22 Risk: Yellow

Year	Team	G/GS	Snaps	Runs	Yds	Yd/R	TD	FUM	DVOA	Rk	DYAR	Rk	YAR	Suc%	Rk	BTkl	Rec	Pass	Yds	C%	Yd/C	TD	YAC	DVOA	Rk	DYAR	Rk
2013	KC			97	460	4.7	2	3	1.2%								13	16	131	81%	10.1	0		12.8%			

Here is your Speed Score champion for 2013, although Davis' fabulous score of 124.5 actually has us a bit worried. The few players who have put up Speed Scores above 120 have been quite injury prone, almost as if their bodies are too big for their speed. Mario Fannin, who had the highest Speed Score ever, tore an ACL in his rookie preseason and an Achilles in his sophomore preseason. Darren McFadden has missed 23 games over his five years in the NFL. Brandon Jacobs missed 26 games in eight years, and a knee injury last year pretty much ended his career. Andre Brown tore his Achilles as a rookie, couldn't stay healthy enough to stay on a roster, and then broke his leg last year just as he was starting to break out with the Giants.

And Davis? Davis broke his ankle as a senior in high school, then again in 2011 before the season even started, and hamstring issues limited him to 112 carries (and just 3.4 yards per carry) as a redshirt junior a year ago. Using a third-round pick on Davis is a big gamble with a gigantic potential upside... or the possibility that the Chiefs just upped the trainer's workload for the next four years.

Shaun Draughn Height: 6-0 Weight: 205 College: North Carolina Draft: 2011/FA Born: 7-Dec-1987 Age: 26 Risk: Yellow

Year	Team	G/GS	Snaps	Runs	Yds	Yd/R	TD	FUM	DVOA	Rk	DYAR	Rk	YAR	Suc%	Rk	BTkl	Rec	Pass	Yds	C%	Yd/C	TD	YAC	DVOA	Rk	DYAR	Rk
2012	KC	16/0	239	59	233	3.9	2	1	5.8%	--	34	--	46	47%	--	4	24	30	158	80%	6.6	0	6.0	-23.3%	38	-13	38
2013	KC			68	274	4.1	2	2	-5.7%								26	34	177	76%	6.8	0		-3.6%			

Draughn spent most of 2011 on the practice squad but emerged as a No. 2 back in 2012. Or, he was a No. 2 back early in 2012, anyway, as 45 of his 59 rushing attempts on the season came in Weeks 1-6. Draughn could be described as a "quicker, lighter-*looking*" version of Thomas Jones, although he doesn't play like Jones. Jones generally ran behind man blocking, while Draughn is a very good fit for Kansas City's zone scheme. By the way, his name doesn't rhyme; it's pronounced "Shaun Drone."

Jonathan Dwyer Height: 5-11 Weight: 229 College: Georgia Tech Draft: 2010/6 (188) Born: 26-Jul-1989 Age: 24 Risk: Green

Year	Team	G/GS	Snaps	Runs	Yds	Yd/R	TD	FUM	DVOA	Rk	DYAR	Rk	YAR	Suc%	Rk	BTkl	Rec	Pass	Yds	C%	Yd/C	TD	YAC	DVOA	Rk	DYAR	Rk
2010	PIT	1/0	15	9	28	3.1	0	0	-43.9%	--	-13	--	-10	33%	--	0	0	0	0		0.0	0	--	--	--	--	--
2011	PIT	7/0	28	16	123	7.7	0	0	8.8%	--	11	--	10	38%	--	2	1	1	6	100%	6.0	0	4.0	22.4%	--	1	--
2012	PIT	13/6	380	156	623	4.0	2	2	-18.0%	39	-60	38	-40	44%	31	29	18	25	106	72%	5.9	0	5.8	-8.2%	27	8	31
2013	PIT			86	361	4.2	1	2	-10.3%								13	17	102	76%	7.8	1		7.2%			

Dwyer sandwiched two 100-yard games between a bout of turf toe and a quad injury in October. After he returned from the quad, he proved ill-suited to feature-back status, and joined Isaac Redman, Rashard Mendenhall, and Chris Rainey in a backfield that was less Four Horsemen than Litter of Kittens. The Steelers let Dwyer dangle in free agency, signed him to a one-year "prove something" deal, drafted similarly-skilled Le'Veon Bell, then sent out post-draft trade feelers to see if any other team wanted a back they made very clear they did not want much. Dwyer is roughly replacement level as a power back; the way last season played out, the Steelers may be wise to keep him around in case of injury plague.

Justin Forsett Height: 5-8   Weight: 194   College: California   Draft: 2008/7 (233)   Born: 14-Oct-1985   Age: 28   Risk: Blue

Year	Team	G/GS	Snaps	Runs	Yds	Yd/R	TD	FUM	DVOA	Rk	DYAR	Rk	YAR	Suc%	Rk	BTkl	Rec	Pass	Yds	C%	Yd/C	TD	YAC	DVOA	Rk	DYAR	Rk
2010	SEA	16/5	480	118	523	4.4	2	0	-7.2%	32	7	31	8	38%	41	21	33	51	252	65%	7.6	0	7.0	-3.6%	34	26	33
2011	SEA	16/0	273	46	145	3.2	1	0	-24.7%	--	-27	--	-27	26%	--	7	23	34	128	68%	5.6	0	7.0	-26.5%	47	-24	47
2012	HOU	16/0	121	63	374	5.9	1	0	13.2%	--	53	--	69	48%	--	7	3	5	38	60%	12.7	0	14.3	14.3%	--	9	--
2013	JAC			60	281	4.7	0	1	1.7%								17	22	105	77%	6.2	0		-3.8%			

Justin Forsett will always have his minor role in NFL history, as it was his 81-yard touchdown run against the Lions on Thanksgiving that almost certainly would have been overturned had Jim Schwartz not drawn a personal foul for his angry throw of the challenge flag. A good fit for a one-cut zone scheme, he was a decent third-string running back for the Texans. Jaguars head coach Gus Bradley and offensive coordinator Jedd Fisch are familiar with him from their time together in Seattle, and he should see a modest number of carries behind Maurice Jones-Drew.

Matt Forte Height: 6-2   Weight: 218   College: Tulane   Draft: 2008/2 (44)   Born: 10-Dec-1985   Age: 28   Risk: Green

Year	Team	G/GS	Snaps	Runs	Yds	Yd/R	TD	FUM	DVOA	Rk	DYAR	Rk	YAR	Suc%	Rk	BTkl	Rec	Pass	Yds	C%	Yd/C	TD	YAC	DVOA	Rk	DYAR	Rk
2010	CHI	16/16	688	237	1069	4.5	6	3	0.0%	20	88	20	66	41%	38	15	51	70	547	73%	10.7	3	8.6	10.5%	21	91	11
2011	CHI	12/12	564	203	997	4.9	3	2	-5.6%	40	24	38	64	45%	35	36	52	76	490	68%	9.4	1	8.6	-5.2%	34	35	28
2012	CHI	15/15	692	248	1094	4.4	5	2	3.1%	15	109	11	81	44%	32	15	44	60	340	73%	7.7	1	6.7	-1.1%	25	40	23
2013	CHI			261	1063	4.1	4	2	-3.9%								51	70	442	73%	8.7	1		7.6%			

In year five of the Matt Forte era, the Bears running back had a positive rushing DVOA for the first time in his career. It has become impossible to mention the poor performance of anyone behind the Bears offensive line for the past several years without mentioning, well, they were playing behind the Bears offensive line. And yes, there have been some awful units and Chicago's second-level and open-field yards on run plays have frequently ranked much higher than their performance in power situations or their basic Adjusted Line Yards rating. Still, that's a pretty startling statistic for someone who just got rewarded with a four-year, $27 million deal last offseason. Especially when that same back saw his broken-tackle total fall from 36 in 2011 to 15 in 2012. Forte is still a shifty running back who has played above the hand he was dealt, but if he were more than that, he probably would've shown it by now.

One preseason talking point with Forte, especially in fantasy circles, is an increase in receptions. "Coach Trestman said he watched a lot of film on me and has seen me run different routes, so I think we'll get back to catching the ball out of the backfield like we did the prior years before," Forte said at OTAs. Forte actually only lost about 10 pass targets last year. Visions of Charlie Garner's 110-target 2002 season under Trestman may be running through your head, but he also tapered down Garner's targets to just 69 in 2003, when Garner was much less effective. Forte's receiving DVOA hasn't been within hailing distance of Garner's 2002 (46.6%) since his 2008 rookie campaign (31.0%).

Arian Foster Height: 6-1   Weight: 225   College: Tennessee   Draft: 2009/FA   Born: 24-Aug-1986   Age: 27   Risk: Yellow

Year	Team	G/GS	Snaps	Runs	Yds	Yd/R	TD	FUM	DVOA	Rk	DYAR	Rk	YAR	Suc%	Rk	BTkl	Rec	Pass	Yds	C%	Yd/C	TD	YAC	DVOA	Rk	DYAR	Rk
2010	HOU	16/13	847	327	1616	4.9	16	3	18.0%	4	372	2	373	52%	9	45	66	86	604	79%	9.2	2	8.8	22.3%	10	180	1
2011	HOU	13/13	643	278	1224	4.4	10	5	2.3%	24	122	14	126	44%	39	32	53	73	617	74%	11.6	2	8.8	18.8%	15	127	4
2012	HOU	16/16	831	351	1424	4.1	15	3	-1.6%	20	105	13	139	47%	27	28	40	58	217	69%	5.4	2	6.9	-28.0%	41	-43	43
2013	HOU			335	1368	4.1	13	3	1.3%								40	51	313	78%	7.8	3		19.4%			

The burden of carrying the Texans' offense seemed to wear on Arian Foster. He had at least 24 carries in his first five games, and his 351 regular season carries were the most by any back over the past three seasons. The burden of the carries, combined with offensive line struggles that required him to find so many yards on his own, took a toll. Before the Texans' bye in Week 8, he had 100 DYAR with 4.7% DVOA and a 52 percent Success Rate. After the bye, he had 5 DYAR, -7.9% DVOA, and a 42 percent Success Rate. With fewer carries and more help from the rest of the offense—especially the right side of the offensive line—Foster could enjoy a bounce-back season. That includes in the red zone, where he was only average at converting carries inside the 5 to scores after being above-average thanks to his exceptional vision the previous two seasons.

Johnathan Franklin Height: 5-10   Weight: 205   College: UCLA   Draft: 2013/4 (125)   Born: 23-Oct-1989   Age: 24   Risk: Yellow

Year	Team	G/GS	Snaps	Runs	Yds	Yd/R	TD	FUM	DVOA	Rk	DYAR	Rk	YAR	Suc%	Rk	BTkl	Rec	Pass	Yds	C%	Yd/C	TD	YAC	DVOA	Rk	DYAR	Rk
2013	GB			112	524	4.7	3	2	4.6%								22	28	209	79%	9.5	1		8.3%			

The easy and uninformed comparison would be to say that Eddie Lacy is thunder, so Franklin must be lighting. Actually, Franklin was a punishing workhorse back at UCLA despite his 5-foot-10 frame. He averaged 20 carries a game and had a +27.5 Adj. POE for the Bruins last season, and combines power, instinct, and vision to get those yards. He's not a polished receiver and needs to work on his pass protection, which seems to make him a bit of an odd fit to spell Lacy, but you can't fault the Packers for diving all over a second-round talent with a fourth-round pick.

Toby Gerhart

Height: 6-0   Weight: 231   College: Stanford   Draft: 2010/2 (51)   Born: 18-Mar-1987   Age: 26   Risk: Blue

Year	Team	G/GS	Snaps	Runs	Yds	Yd/R	TD	FUM	DVOA	Rk	DYAR	Rk	YAR	Suc%	Rk	BTkl	Rec	Pass	Yds	C%	Yd/C	TD	YAC	DVOA	Rk	DYAR	Rk
2010	MIN	15/1	268	81	322	4.0	1	3	-3.3%	--	15	--	15	42%	--	9	21	29	167	72%	8.0	0	8.3	-31.5%	51	-28	49
2011	MIN	16/5	387	109	531	4.9	1	1	5.4%	14	60	30	42	40%	47	11	23	28	190	82%	8.3	3	8.3	41.2%	3	84	10
2012	MIN	16/0	240	50	169	3.4	1	2	-26.0%	--	-34	--	-44	44%	--	4	20	27	155	74%	7.8	0	7.3	25.0%	6	55	16
2013	MIN			40	171	4.2	1	2	-8.1%								21	25	182	84%	8.7	0		16.4%			

In 2028, some football researcher is going to try to figure out why the Vikings took a running back in the second round when they already had Adrian Peterson. Theoretical researcher we just invented: it made just as little sense then as it makes in hindsight. Gerhart is a fairly nice No. 2 back to have around, but 100 coaches out of 100 would rather toss the ball to Peterson and see if he can make a defender look foolish in the open field. The only reason to recommend Gerhart over Peterson for anything other than a quick breather is that Gerhart has been an effective receiver, but really, the Vikings should have found an undrafted free agent who could just give Peterson a few snaps off.

Mike Gillislee

Height: 5-11   Weight: 208   College: Florida   Draft: 2013/5 (164)   Born: 1-Nov-1990   Age: 23   Risk: Green

Year	Team	G/GS	Snaps	Runs	Yds	Yd/R	TD	FUM	DVOA	Rk	DYAR	Rk	YAR	Suc%	Rk	BTkl	Rec	Pass	Yds	C%	Yd/C	TD	YAC	DVOA	Rk	DYAR	Rk
2013	MIA			42	201	4.8	0	2	-2.2%								16	19	149	84%	9.3	1		12.8%			

Dolphins fun fact: With Gillislee taking Reggie Bush's vacated roster spot, Miami's running back depth chart is now the exclusive domain of players born in Florida or Michigan. More useful to readers of this book is that Gillislee is about as average of a prospect as it gets: average size, average speed (4.55 seconds in the 40, working out to a Speed Score of 97.1), and average senior-year stats (5.1 highlight yards per opportunity, +0.6 Adj. POE). What helps his rookie year potential is his one above-average attribute: blitz pickup. It seems that Daniel Thomas' ship has sailed in Miami, so Gillislee could easily be the primary back if starter Lamar Miller gets hurt.

Mike Goodson

Height: 5-11   Weight: 208   College: Texas A&M   Draft: 2009/4 (111)   Born: 23-May-1987   Age: 26   Risk: Blue

Year	Team	G/GS	Snaps	Runs	Yds	Yd/R	TD	FUM	DVOA	Rk	DYAR	Rk	YAR	Suc%	Rk	BTkl	Rec	Pass	Yds	C%	Yd/C	TD	YAC	DVOA	Rk	DYAR	Rk
2010	CAR	16/3	385	103	452	4.4	3	4	-15.3%	42	-22	38	-6	38%	42	17	40	57	310	70%	7.8	0	8.8	-12.0%	42	6	42
2011	CAR	4/0	4	0	0	0.0	0	0	--	--	--	--	--	--	--	0	1	3	4	33%	4.0	0	8.8	-67.0%	--	-10	--
2012	OAK	12/0	144	35	221	6.3	0	0	24.8%	--	37	--	42	48%	--	8	16	18	195	100%	12.2	1	12.9	70.1%	--	83	--
2013	NYJ			28	126	4.4	0	0	-3.7%								19	31	145	61%	7.7	0		-9.8%			

Goodson arrived in Oakland last year, perhaps thinking in the back of his mind that Darren McFadden's fragility would give him an opportunity at some point to be the featured back. McFadden did his part by getting hurt in November. Unfortunately, Goodson was injured at that point. When he was healthy, so was McFadden. Thus, the most carries the ex-Panther got in any game was 13 against the Chiefs in Week 14. McFadden was actually also healthy in that game and carried the ball 30 times. This offseason Goodson again went looking for an empty depth chart where he might get a chance to play, and signed a three-year, $6.9 million deal with the Jets. Then they went out and got Chris Ivory to start ahead of him.

Goodson has flashed good acceleration and breakaway speed when he's gotten on the field in both Oakland and Carolina, and he's the best receiver among the Jets' backs. Given how much Marty Mornhinweg used backs in the passing game in Philadelphia, that could be Goodson's ticket to get on the field more than ever before. This explains why Goodson has a "Blue" Risk factor. However, that Blue is more of a purple once you mix it with a big off-the-field red flag: Goodson was arrested in May and charged with possession of both marijuana and an illegal handgun loaded with hollow-point bullets. The case is currently with a grand jury, but the New Jersey laws against hollow-point bullets are very serious. Goodson might catch 40 passes this season, and he also might be sent to jail until 2023.

Frank Gore

Height: 5-9   Weight: 215   College: Miami   Draft: 2005/3 (65)   Born: 14-May-1983   Age: 30   Risk: Green

Year	Team	G/GS	Snaps	Runs	Yds	Yd/R	TD	FUM	DVOA	Rk	DYAR	Rk	YAR	Suc%	Rk	BTkl	Rec	Pass	Yds	C%	Yd/C	TD	YAC	DVOA	Rk	DYAR	Rk
2010	SF	11/11	596	203	853	4.2	3	4	-9.3%	34	-3	33	25	48%	15	11	46	72	452	64%	9.8	2	10.0	-7.4%	39	26	32
2011	SF	16/15	687	282	1211	4.3	8	2	-10.0%	44	-17	47	3	42%	45	12	17	31	114	55%	6.7	0	10.0	-17.8%	45	-7	44
2012	SF	16/16	728	258	1214	4.7	8	3	17.4%	4	268	4	212	48%	17	27	28	36	234	78%	8.4	1	7.9	13.1%	12	50	18
2013	SF			247	1107	4.5	7	1	12.1%								22	28	166	79%	7.6	1		10.2%			

It's not all that surprising given what he overcame in college, but Gore defied the odds with his performance in 2012. Going into the season, he was old, constantly nicked up, and coming off the worst year in a downward-trending career. Just when you thought new-comers meant San Francisco would start easing his workload, Gore actually played more snaps. Just when you thought he couldn't break tackles anymore, he broke more than the previous two seasons combined. Just when you thought he was no longer a threat in the passing game, he posted his best advanced receiving stats since 2007. If he can turn back the clock again, here's what's at stake for Gore's individual legacy in 2013: To date, he's registered seven 1,000-yard seasons. Only 10 running backs since the merger have had eight or more. Nine are in the Hall of Fame, and the tenth is LaDainian Tomlinson, who will assuredly get a yellow jacket in 2017.

Alex Green

	Height: 6-2		Weight: 220			College: Hawaii				Draft: 2011/3 (96)			Born: 30-Nov-1989	Age: 24			Risk: Yellow	

Year	Team	G/GS	Snaps	Runs	Yds	Yd/R	TD	FUM	DVOA	Rk	DYAR	Rk	YAR	Suc%	Rk	BTkl	Rec	Pass	Yds	C%	Yd/C	TD	YAC	DVOA	Rk	DYAR	Rk
2011	GB	4/0	7	3	11	3.7	0	0	-37.0%	--	-4	--	-4	67%	--	0	1	1	6	100%	6.0	0	14.0	79.9%	--	8	--
2012	GB	12/4	343	135	464	3.4	0	1	-16.8%	38	-44	36	-54	42%	37	6	18	31	125	65%	6.9	0	9.1	-25.6%	40	-20	39
2013	GB			35	171	4.9	0	1	1.5%								13	17	117	76%	9.0	0		12.0%			

In May, Green admitted something that was plainly obvious to anyone who watched him play last year: that he wasn't fully healthy coming off an ACL injury in 2011. "Injuries are always a frustrating thing, especially not being able to get fully healthy throughout the whole season was definitely not something I was expecting," Green said. With the selections of Eddie Lacy and Johnathan Franklin shaking up the Green Bay depth chart at running back, all old hands are scrambling for a role in the future. James Starks can play the "veteran back" card, and DuJuan Harris had the best season of the three last year and can return kicks as well, making him the "versatile third back." Green had loads of potential coming out of Hawaii and was thought to be an impact player, but he's going to need to be healthy to have any chance of fighting those two off to be the third back—Lacy already has the role of "injured back" locked up, and the Packers can't afford to carry two.

BenJarvus Green-Ellis

	Height: 5-10		Weight: 219			College: Mississippi				Draft: 2008/FA			Born: 2-Jul-1985	Age: 28			Risk: Green	

Year	Team	G/GS	Snaps	Runs	Yds	Yd/R	TD	FUM	DVOA	Rk	DYAR	Rk	YAR	Suc%	Rk	BTkl	Rec	Pass	Yds	C%	Yd/C	TD	YAC	DVOA	Rk	DYAR	Rk
2010	NE	16/11	432	229	1008	4.4	13	0	26.7%	2	335	3	304	57%	2	10	12	16	85	75%	7.1	0	4.1	18.2%	--	32	--
2011	NE	16/6	392	181	667	3.7	11	0	3.9%	18	106	18	115	54%	6	10	9	13	159	69%	17.7	0	4.1	72.8%	--	64	--
2012	CIN	15/15	651	278	1094	3.9	6	3	-8.1%	29	6	29	22	48%	21	14	22	29	104	76%	4.7	0	4.1	-36.9%	44	-39	42
2013	CIN			158	649	4.1	4	1	-5.3%								13	18	90	72%	6.9	0		-0.4%			

Green-Ellis is useless as a receiver. He did not have a reception longer than nine yards after Week 4, and the final ten passes thrown to him (from Week 13 against the Chargers on) netted just 27 yards and one first down. In the playoffs, he caught two passes for a loss of six and a loss of three. Green-Ellis was not much of a receiver in his Boston Legal days, either; he was Peter Principled into a three-down role, and the Bengals passing game grew ever more Green-dimensional as a result. Giovanni Bernard caught 92 passes in two college seasons, and will get every opportunity to take over the third-down role, as well as some other roles.

Shonn Greene

	Height: 6-0		Weight: 227			College: Iowa				Draft: 2009/3 (65)			Born: 21-Aug-1985	Age: 28			Risk: Green	

Year	Team	G/GS	Snaps	Runs	Yds	Yd/R	TD	FUM	DVOA	Rk	DYAR	Rk	YAR	Suc%	Rk	BTkl	Rec	Pass	Yds	C%	Yd/C	TD	YAC	DVOA	Rk	DYAR	Rk
2010	NYJ	15/2	362	185	766	4.1	2	3	7.3%	11	115	11	125	55%	4	10	16	24	120	67%	7.5	0	5.4	-0.4%	--	20	--
2011	NYJ	16/15	559	253	1054	4.2	6	1	2.2%	25	113	16	127	50%	16	13	30	41	211	73%	7.0	0	5.4	-8.5%	37	12	37
2012	NYJ	16/14	567	276	1063	3.9	8	5	-4.5%	24	49	22	84	52%	9	10	19	31	151	61%	7.9	0	6.9	-41.4%	45	-47	44
2013	TEN			81	342	4.2	4	1	-0.2%								16	22	126	73%	7.9	0		4.1%			

The first five weeks of the season, Green had as miserable a performance as any back in recent NFL history, to the tune of -37.9% DVOA on 74 carries. The rest of the season, he had a 7.7% DVOA and a 58 percent success rate, more in line with his career numbers. That's kind of a mediocre DVOA for so consistently successful a back, but Greene has never been anyone's idea of explosive. The Titans handed him $10 million over three years this offseason, citing his 12-for-12 performance on third-and-short in 2012. Over the course of his career, though, Greene has not been more successful on third-and-short than any other Jets back. He was also below average close to the goal line for the second consecutive season. He's definitely a stylistic complement to Chris Johnson, but it's not clear he's actually a particularly good power back.

Montario Hardesty

	Height: 6-0		Weight: 225			College: Tennessee				Draft: 2010/2 (59)			Born: 1-Feb-1987	Age: 26			Risk: Green	

Year	Team	G/GS	Snaps	Runs	Yds	Yd/R	TD	FUM	DVOA	Rk	DYAR	Rk	YAR	Suc%	Rk	BTkl	Rec	Pass	Yds	C%	Yd/C	TD	YAC	DVOA	Rk	DYAR	Rk
2011	CLE	10/4	268	88	266	3.0	0	1	-32.2%	--	-79	--	-77	36%	--	11	14	21	122	67%	8.7	0	8.5	2.9%	--	24	--
2012	CLE	13/1	158	65	271	4.2	1	2	-23.5%	--	-39	--	-21	45%	--	2	2	5	16	40%	8.0	0	9.0	-15.3%	--	0	--
2013	CLE			56	257	4.6	0	2	-5.0%								9	13	64	69%	7.1	0		-4.5%			

Arguably the worst NFL player to see regular playing time in 2011, when he routinely dropped screen passes, Hardesty was incrementally better in 2012. He produced 15-56-1 and 10-52-0 lines in two Browns wins; in both cases, Trent Richardson was some combination of banged up or ineffective, and Hardesty saved the day. The Browns only threw to Hardesty five times, limiting the number of ways he could hurt them in the passing game. The two productive games were surrounded by lots of limited-carry dross, and Hardesty still has ball security issues to go with his uselessness as a receiver, making him a weird choice as a change-of-pace back. Dion Lewis should take his role, but Hardesty has remarkable, inexplicable staying power.

DuJuan Harris Height: 5-7 Weight: 197 College: Troy Draft: 2011/FA Born: 3-Sep-1988 Age: 25 Risk: Yellow

Year	Team	G/GS	Snaps	Runs	Yds	Yd/R	TD	FUM	DVOA	Rk	DYAR	Rk	YAR	Suc%	Rk	BTkl	Rec	Pass	Yds	C%	Yd/C	TD	YAC	DVOA	Rk	DYAR	Rk
2011	JAC	5/0	48	9	42	4.7	0	0	-2.6%	--	2	--	3	56%	--	1	1	2	4	50%	4.0	0	7.0	-78.5%	--	-7	--
2012	GB	4/2	68	34	157	4.6	2	0	31.1%	--	50	--	41	41%	--	3	2	2	17	100%	8.5	0	10.0	44.0%	--	7	--
2013	GB			41	172	4.2	2	2	-2.5%								11	13	86	85%	7.8	0		11.2%			

By having a surprisingly good showing during the playoffs and last couple of weeks in the regular season, Harris did all that he could to ensure a spot on next season's roster. He was great in the open field and broke three tackles in 34 regular-season carries. It was a nice story. But Ted Thompson didn't want any new chapters in *Wandering Without Ahman Green*, and the draft yielded appropriate values on his board to stock up at running back. Harris will battle Alex Green and James Starks for the third spot on the depth chart, and his kick-returning experience can only help his case. Just don't expect last season to happen again.

Roy Helu Height: 5-11 Weight: 216 College: Nebraska Draft: 2011/4 (105) Born: 7-Dec-1988 Age: 25 Risk: Green

Year	Team	G/GS	Snaps	Runs	Yds	Yd/R	TD	FUM	DVOA	Rk	DYAR	Rk	YAR	Suc%	Rk	BTkl	Rec	Pass	Yds	C%	Yd/C	TD	YAC	DVOA	Rk	DYAR	Rk
2011	WAS	15/5	543	151	640	4.2	2	3	-4.6%	38	25	37	14	47%	24	14	49	59	379	83%	7.7	1	8.6	-0.8%	29	42	25
2012	WAS	3/0	44	2	2	1.0	0	0	-107.9%	--	-10	--	-9	0%	--	1	7	7	45	100%	6.4	0	6.7	14.8%	--	10	--
2013	WAS			51	279	5.4	2	1	20.3%								18	25	161	72%	8.9	1		9.6%			

Helu is the kind of versatile athlete perfectly suited to the Redskins' new and more versatile offense. However, his injury profile has usurped his on-field potential through his first two seasons. Offensive coordinator Kyle Shanahan had good things to say about Helu's toughness following the 2012 campaign, but Helu suffered Achilles tendinitis in the 2012 preseason, was limited further by soreness in both Achilles tendons, and was put on injured reserve in September with a case of turf toe. Going into his third year, Helu was said to be "near 100 percent" following further surgery to repair tendons around the toe injury. But at this point, his 2011 stretch of three straight games with more than 100 rushing yards—which set a Redskins rookie rushing record—seems a long ways away.

Peyton Hillis Height: 6-0 Weight: 240 College: Arkansas Draft: 2008/7 (227) Born: 21-Jan-1986 Age: 27 Risk: N/A

Year	Team	G/GS	Snaps	Runs	Yds	Yd/R	TD	FUM	DVOA	Rk	DYAR	Rk	YAR	Suc%	Rk	BTkl	Rec	Pass	Yds	C%	Yd/C	TD	YAC	DVOA	Rk	DYAR	Rk
2010	CLE	16/14	764	270	1177	4.4	11	8	5.0%	13	151	8	152	53%	7	35	61	77	477	79%	7.8	2	7.2	15.8%	18	126	9
2011	CLE	10/9	462	161	587	3.6	3	2	-1.7%	29	50	33	48	55%	4	4	22	34	130	65%	5.9	0	7.2	-37.4%	48	-43	48
2012	KC	13/2	210	85	309	3.6	1	2	-27.5%	--	-71	--	-42	40%	--	7	10	13	62	77%	6.2	0	7.4	-29.1%	--	-10	--

Being chosen as the *Madden* cover boy in 2010 unleashed the hidden diva in Hillis, at which point his career completely cratered. Injuries and attitude problems relegated him to a role as a fringe backup with the Chiefs last year. He was mildly effectively at times there, but certainly nothing special. He's a free agent again, and it's fair to say his career at this point is teetering on the brink. Most likely, some team will find Hillis worth signing. He has experience as a lead blocker, he's strong enough to win in short-yardage situations, and he's unexpectedly viable in the passing game, both as a blocker and Brian Leonard type pass-catcher.

Ronnie Hillman Height: 5-9 Weight: 200 College: San Diego State Draft: 2012/3 (67) Born: 14-Sep-1991 Age: 22 Risk: Green

Year	Team	G/GS	Snaps	Runs	Yds	Yd/R	TD	FUM	DVOA	Rk	DYAR	Rk	YAR	Suc%	Rk	BTkl	Rec	Pass	Yds	C%	Yd/C	TD	YAC	DVOA	Rk	DYAR	Rk
2012	DEN	14/0	206	84	327	3.9	1	2	-15.7%	--	-24	--	-15	51%	--	3	10	12	62	83%	6.2	0	6.9	-17.0%	--	-2	--
2013	DEN			84	353	4.2	3	1	1.6%								22	26	191	85%	8.7	1		17.7%			

Hillman is a shifty, quick runner with hints of some dynamic space-creating ability. He's not lightning-fast but he can change tempo extremely well early in the run, which is more important for a running back. It will be interesting to see if he can become strong enough to consistently hold up in traffic. He certainly does not have to become a power runner, but he must be strong enough to regularly operate inside because one of the most unique facets to his game is his fluid wiggle in short areas. Of course, we'll never see much of Hillman's game if he does not get significantly better in pass protection. Awareness and execution in blitz pickup were both problematic for him as a rookie.

Kendall Hunter Height: 5-7 Weight: 199 College: Oklahoma State Draft: 2011/4 (115) Born: 16-Sep-1988 Age: 25 Risk: Red

Year	Team	G/GS	Snaps	Runs	Yds	Yd/R	TD	FUM	DVOA	Rk	DYAR	Rk	YAR	Suc%	Rk	BTkl	Rec	Pass	Yds	C%	Yd/C	TD	YAC	DVOA	Rk	DYAR	Rk
2011	SF	16/1	288	112	473	4.2	2	0	-6.5%	41	9	41	31	46%	30	7	16	26	195	62%	12.2	0	11.0	21.5%	10	50	22
2012	SF	11/0	170	72	371	5.2	2	0	29.1%	--	109	--	108	60%	--	5	9	12	60	75%	6.7	0	6.3	17.7%	--	21	--
2013	SF			41	191	4.7	0	1	4.9%								8	10	62	80%	7.8	0		10.5%			

Even coming off an Achilles tear, Hunter will remain one of the most valuable backup running backs in the league. Given their all-around similarities, he can spell Frank Gore when necessary, and start in Gore's place if he gets hurt—with the offense no worse for it. Hunter had a reputation as an outside runner coming out of college, and his rookie season did nothing to change it. However, before getting hurt last year, he was actually more efficient on 25 carries behind center and guard (30.8% DVOA) than on 47 behind tackle and end (12.9% DVOA). Our projection assumes he returns to the field around midseason.

Mark Ingram   Height: 5-11   Weight: 215   College: Alabama   Draft: 2011/1 (28)   Born: 21-Dec-1989   Age: 24   Risk: Green

Year	Team	G/GS	Snaps	Runs	Yds	Yd/R	TD	FUM	DVOA	Rk	DYAR	Rk	YAR	Suc%	Rk	BTkl	Rec	Pass	Yds	C%	Yd/C	TD	YAC	DVOA	Rk	DYAR	Rk
2011	NO	10/4	215	122	474	3.9	5	1	2.3%	22	63	29	47	56%	3	9	11	13	46	85%	4.2	0	3.6	-27.1%	--	-11	--
2012	NO	16/5	266	156	602	3.9	5	0	0.8%	19	62	19	56	49%	15	13	6	10	29	60%	4.8	0	5.3	-45.4%	--	-21	--
2013	NO			172	705	4.1	5	5	-1.9%								17	25	117	63%	6.9	1		-15.7%			

This is a fork-in-the-road year for the former first round pick. Often used as a short-yardage specialist in his first two seasons, Ingram hasn't displayed the combination of speed and toughness that won him the Heisman Trophy. His Success Rate in the red zone was only 43 percent, and his DVOA on third and fourth down was just -1.8%. But he had a decent second half of the season as the team's lead ballcarrier, gaining 424 of his 602 yards in the final eight games. So far, Ingram has enjoyed the first injury-free offseason of his career, and the trade of Chris Ivory should give the depth chart in New Orleans better clarity. The table is set for Ingram to feast—if he nibbles as he did in his first two seasons in the NFL, he might not get invited back to dine.

Chris Ivory   Height: 6-0   Weight: 222   College: Tiffin   Draft: 2010/FA   Born: 22-Mar-1988   Age: 25   Risk: Red

Year	Team	G/GS	Snaps	Runs	Yds	Yd/R	TD	FUM	DVOA	Rk	DYAR	Rk	YAR	Suc%	Rk	BTkl	Rec	Pass	Yds	C%	Yd/C	TD	YAC	DVOA	Rk	DYAR	Rk
2010	NO	12/4	192	137	716	5.2	5	4	13.1%	6	139	9	165	59%	1	27	1	1	17	100%	17.0	0	22.0	147.5%	--	10	--
2011	NO	6/2	120	79	374	4.7	1	0	10.4%	--	64	--	74	58%	--	9	0	1	0	0%	0.0	0	22.0	-84.4%	--	-3	--
2012	NO	6/2	67	40	217	5.4	2	0	12.5%	--	33	--	34	48%	--	14	2	3	15	67%	7.5	0	14.0	-7.3%	--	1	--
2013	NYJ			263	1094	4.2	7	3	-5.3%								20	32	153	63%	7.6	0		-12.5%			

There is sentiment out there for Ivory to become a breakout player now that he is away from the Saints' Fourpack Backfield and the top job with the Jets is seemingly his to lose. Indeed, Ivory is a powerful inside runner with quickness to go with it, reminiscent of Marshawn Lynch. But he has only managed to play a half-dozen games in each of the last two seasons due to injury and depth-chart congestion. He's also caught three passes in three seasons. Counter-sentiment to the Gang Green optimism is that Ivory's productivity when healthy was considerably aided by defenses spread out to stop the Saints passing attack. The Jets figure to pound away early with Ivory—we'll know soon enough if he can tolerate it.

Fred Jackson   Height: 6-1   Weight: 215   College: Coe College   Draft: 2007/FA   Born: 20-Feb-1981   Age: 32   Risk: Red

Year	Team	G/GS	Snaps	Runs	Yds	Yd/R	TD	FUM	DVOA	Rk	DYAR	Rk	YAR	Suc%	Rk	BTkl	Rec	Pass	Yds	C%	Yd/C	TD	YAC	DVOA	Rk	DYAR	Rk
2010	BUF	16/13	688	222	927	4.2	5	5	-0.4%	21	78	21	68	47%	17	34	31	54	215	57%	6.9	2	7.8	-35.4%	52	-64	52
2011	BUF	10/10	567	170	934	5.5	6	2	13.7%	6	161	7	165	54%	7	33	39	50	442	78%	11.3	0	7.8	23.1%	9	97	9
2012	BUF	10/8	329	115	437	3.8	3	5	-14.3%	35	-27	32	-38	47%	26	19	34	42	217	81%	6.4	1	6.5	-8.4%	28	13	27
2013	BUF			109	430	4.0	4	2	-8.3%								30	38	246	79%	8.2	1		-0.3%			

In case we haven't hammered it home every time this book mentions Brandon Weeden, the problem with coming into the NFL at an advanced age is that you don't have long to play before you hit your decline phase. This is even more true for running backs than for quarterbacks, which helps explain why Fred Jackson—who was 26 as a rookie in 2007—has played fewer snaps with fewer carries each of the last two years. A look at the most similar running backs over a three-year span shows a lot of players reaching the end of the line, even though these players, like Jackson, had high yards per carry averages two years before. Darrin Nelson (1986-88) played four more seasons, but with just 108 carries. Chester Taylor (2006-08) had three more seasons but couldn't average over four yards per carry in any of them. Players like Brandon Jacobs (2009-11), Fred Taylor (2006-08), and Charlie Garner (2001-03) were basically cooked. Jackson should have some value as C.J.Spiller's backup for the next year or two, but the possibility that he just plain hits the wall is rather high.

Steven Jackson   Height: 6-3   Weight: 229   College: Oregon State   Draft: 2004/1 (24)   Born: 22-Jul-1983   Age: 30   Risk: Green

Year	Team	G/GS	Snaps	Runs	Yds	Yd/R	TD	FUM	DVOA	Rk	DYAR	Rk	YAR	Suc%	Rk	BTkl	Rec	Pass	Yds	C%	Yd/C	TD	YAC	DVOA	Rk	DYAR	Rk
2010	STL	16/16	874	330	1241	3.8	6	1	-12.5%	39	-45	40	-28	40%	39	28	46	61	383	75%	8.3	0	8.1	-5.3%	38	29	31
2011	STL	15/15	714	260	1145	4.4	5	2	-2.3%	31	64	27	67	39%	48	20	42	58	333	72%	7.9	1	8.1	0.2%	28	43	23
2012	STL	16/16	706	257	1042	4.1	4	0	5.3%	11	147	10	59	47%	28	21	38	53	321	72%	8.4	0	7.4	11.7%	14	72	12
2013	ATL			217	919	4.2	5	1	0.8%								32	45	246	71%	7.7	1		-1.6%			

Rarely if ever has a great player been stuck on a rotten team like Jackson has over his career. He has more than 6,000 rushing yards in losses, a number bested only by O.J. Simpson, Emmitt Smith, and Barry Sanders since 1960. However, he has less than 4,000 yards in wins, and ranks in the 60s there. Jackson has played in the postseason, as the Rams won the NFC West at 8-8 in his rookie season, but they won only 36 games in the next eight years. He moves now to a Falcons team that has won 36 games in *three* years, and for the first time Jackson doesn't have to be (and won't be) the best player on the team. That's also the reason why KUBIAK expects his carries to drop: There's no reason to run Jackson into the ground when you have Jacquizz Rodgers around, and it isn't like Atlanta is going to dramatically change its run-pass ratio this season, especially given our lukewarm forecast for the Falcons as a team.

Jackson's age may explain why he got worse last season later in games. His DVOA dropped from 15.4% in the first half to -4.3% in the second half and overtime.

LaMichael James   Height: 5-8   Weight: 194   College: Oregon   Draft: 2012/2 (61)   Born: 22-Oct-1989   Age: 24   Risk: Green

Year	Team	G/GS	Snaps	Runs	Yds	Yd/R	TD	FUM	DVOA	Rk	DYAR	Rk	YAR	Suc%	Rk	BTkl	Rec	Pass	Yds	C%	Yd/C	TD	YAC	DVOA	Rk	DYAR	Rk
2012	SF	4/0	56	27	125	4.6	0	1	-0.2%	--	9	--	-7	41%	--	3	3	5	29	60%	9.7	0	5.3	15.4%	--	10	--
2013	SF			103	455	4.4	2	2	0.1%								22	29	197	76%	9.0	0		10.9%			

Like fellow rookie A.J. Jenkins, James did not see the field until injuries higher up the depth chart forced San Francisco's hand in Week 14; unlike Jenkins, he actually made an impact when the opportunity arose. James' box-score stats came mostly on kickoff returns, but his 14.7 offensive snaps per game played a vital role in San Francisco's late-season use of read-option: He's a better fit for it than Frank Gore or Kendall Hunter. With Michael Crabtree out, he also figures to get some looks in the short passing game. Nevertheless, considering the 49ers' stable of backs, and the two players ahead of him being signed through 2014, James' value on offense probably won't hit its peak for another couple of years.

Mike James   Height: 5-10   Weight: 223   College: Miami   Draft: 2013/6 (189)   Born: 5-Dec-1989   Age: 24   Risk: Green

Year	Team	G/GS	Snaps	Runs	Yds	Yd/R	TD	FUM	DVOA	Rk	DYAR	Rk	YAR	Suc%	Rk	BTkl	Rec	Pass	Yds	C%	Yd/C	TD	YAC	DVOA	Rk	DYAR	Rk
2013	TB			46	228	4.9	0	1	4.3%								17	23	141	74%	8.3	1		0.2%			

The Bucs gave up a seventh-rounder to move up seven spots in the sixth round and take James, who has a good shot to win the top backup job behind Doug Martin. James split time with freshman Duke Johnson at Miami last season and gained only 621 yards, but at 223 pounds with a Speed Score of 105.9, he fits the role of a power runner who can also block and catch (30 receptions for 344 yards and three touchdowns last year).

Rashad Jennings   Height: 6-1   Weight: 231   College: Liberty   Draft: 2009/7 (250)   Born: 26-Mar-1985   Age: 28   Risk: Red

Year	Team	G/GS	Snaps	Runs	Yds	Yd/R	TD	FUM	DVOA	Rk	DYAR	Rk	YAR	Suc%	Rk	BTkl	Rec	Pass	Yds	C%	Yd/C	TD	YAC	DVOA	Rk	DYAR	Rk
2010	JAC	13/3	320	84	459	5.5	4	0	29.5%	--	140	--	138	52%	--	13	26	34	223	76%	8.6	0	8.3	-4.7%	37	15	39
2012	JAC	10/6	330	101	283	2.8	2	3	-31.8%	42	-97	41	-81	38%	40	15	19	26	130	73%	6.8	0	8.2	-22.6%	37	-11	37
2013	OAK			68	273	4.0	2	3	-8.4%								9	15	42	60%	4.7	0		-26.8%			

Jennings missed the entire 2011 season with a knee injury, but was motivated entering 2012, the final season of his rookie deal. With Maurice Jones-Drew skipping training camp in protest of his contract, Jennings got the first-team reps and finished second in the NFL in rushing yards during the preseason. Then Jones-Drew's holdout ended, the games began to mean something, and Jennings struggled. He was averaging 2.8 yards per carry and posting the second-lowest DYAR (-97) among running backs with 100 or more attempts before landing on IR with a shoulder injury. Jennings also had the lowest DVOA (-38.6%) among running backs when opponents did not load the box. Jennings signed a one-year deal with the Raiders, where he'll back up Darren McFadden, who had the lowest DYAR (-155) and second-lowest DVOA in non-loaded box runs among qualifying NFL running backs last season.

Chris Johnson   Height: 5-11   Weight: 197   College: East Carolina   Draft: 2008/1 (24)   Born: 23-Sep-1985   Age: 28   Risk: Yellow

Year	Team	G/GS	Snaps	Runs	Yds	Yd/R	TD	FUM	DVOA	Rk	DYAR	Rk	YAR	Suc%	Rk	BTkl	Rec	Pass	Yds	C%	Yd/C	TD	YAC	DVOA	Rk	DYAR	Rk
2010	TEN	16/16	797	316	1364	4.3	11	3	-7.5%	33	18	30	14	39%	40	41	44	57	245	77%	5.6	1	5.6	-36.8%	53	-70	53
2011	TEN	16/16	717	262	1047	4.0	4	3	-15.1%	49	-67	49	-51	41%	46	30	57	79	418	72%	7.3	0	5.6	-5.9%	35	33	29
2012	TEN	16/15	815	276	1243	4.5	6	4	-11.3%	32	-30	33	-6	41%	38	16	36	49	232	76%	6.4	0	6.5	-17.6%	35	-9	36
2013	TEN			268	1209	4.5	6	3	-2.8%								46	59	347	78%	7.5	1		4.0%			

The most favorable take on Chris Johnson is that he's the best running back in the league who's insanely dependent on first-level blocking. When he has a hole he has confidence in, he can burst through to the third level and outrun defensive backs. When he doesn't see a hole, he searches desperately for one rather than take the yards that are available. This sensibility leads to seemingly absurd statistics, like the fact that he averaged 7.28 yards with -5.9% DVOA against a loaded box (one with more defenders than blockers) and 3.98 yards per carry with -12.4% DVOA against a non-loaded box.

Fundamentally, Johnson and the Titans are still trying to react to what opponents figured out by early in 2010: if you deny Johnson the space he craves and found on the edges in 2009, he's not a very good runner. The Titans paid him anyway and have gotten two years of production even less efficient than what they got in 2010. They had a chance in February to cut him free, but chose to keep his $10 million in salary on the books and spend significant resources on improving the offensive line. In his defense, Johnson has been the best running back on the Titans the past three seasons, and Javon Ringer kept getting hurt when they tried to use him in a larger role. In adding Shonn Greene, the Titans now have stylistic complement who's a semi-viable alternative should the new offensive linemen not prove a panacea. Our projection system is somewhat optimistic, but that does not mean Johnson will make it anywhere close to the 2,000 yards he annually predicts himself to gain.

Outside of being shockingly useful in the second half of 2009, Johnson has been as ineffective in the pass game as he has been in the run game. The Titans have expressed a desire this offseason to do the proverbial "get him the ball more in space." Outside of a play back in 2009 where the Texans didn't bother to cover him when he split out wide, this has worked significantly less well in practice than it has in theory. He's also inconsistent at best as a pass protector, mixing much-improved blitz recognition and pickup with a league-leading (among backs) 10.5 blown blocks in 2012 (Table 1).

Table 1. Most Blown Blocks on Pass Plays by Running Backs, 2012

Player	Team	BB	Player	Team	BB
Chris Johnson	TEN	10.5	Doug Martin	TB	6.0
LeSean McCoy	PHI	8.0	Trent Richardson	CLE	6.0
Vick Ballard	IND	7.0	C.J. Spiller	BUF	6.0
Ahmad Bradshaw	NYG	7.0	Ronnie Brown	SD	5.0
Shaun Draughn	KC	6.0	Mewelde Moore	IND	5.0

Maurice Jones-Drew Height: 5-8 Weight: 205 College: UCLA Draft: 2006/2 (60) Born: 23-Mar-1985 Age: 28 Risk: Red

Year	Team	G/GS	Snaps	Runs	Yds	Yd/R	TD	FUM	DVOA	Rk	DYAR	Rk	YAR	Suc%	Rk	BTkl	Rec	Pass	Yds	C%	Yd/C	TD	YAC	DVOA	Rk	DYAR	Rk
2010	JAC	14/14	680	299	1324	4.4	5	3	9.3%	8	223	5	222	51%	10	30	34	44	317	77%	9.3	2	9.5	24.0%	9	87	12
2011	JAC	16/16	780	343	1606	4.7	8	5	5.1%	15	197	3	199	49%	20	37	43	63	374	68%	8.7	3	9.5	2.2%	26	54	18
2012	JAC	6/5	240	86	414	4.8	1	1	-0.9%	--	27	--	42	48%	--	9	14	18	86	78%	6.1	1	5.1	5.8%	--	18	--
2013	JAC			276	1221	4.4	7	4	2.6%								38	51	266	75%	7.0	1		-3.4%			

A workhorse in 2011, Jones-Drew angled for a new contract from the Jaguars by sitting out OTAs, training camp, and preseason, reporting to the club on September 3. Jones-Drew appeared to have knocked the rust off quickly, rushing for 314 yards over the first three weeks of the season, but the good times came to an end when he suffered a foot injury in Week 7. It turned out to be of the season-ending variety, though the Jaguars did not make that official until Jones-Drew underwent Lisfranc surgery in December. That procedure kept Jones-Drew off the practice field during the OTAs, although this year he at least showed up. An allegation that Jones-Drew sucker-punched a security guard at a St. Augustine nightclub on May 26 prompted the three-time Pro Bowler to move his offseason training to Miami. When Jones-Drew will be ready to play is unclear, but he hopes to be ready for training camp.

Felix Jones Height: 5-10 Weight: 207 College: Arkansas Draft: 2008/1 (22) Born: 8-May-1987 Age: 26 Risk: Blue

Year	Team	G/GS	Snaps	Runs	Yds	Yd/R	TD	FUM	DVOA	Rk	DYAR	Rk	YAR	Suc%	Rk	BTkl	Rec	Pass	Yds	C%	Yd/C	TD	YAC	DVOA	Rk	DYAR	Rk
2010	DAL	16/7	556	185	800	4.3	1	2	7.6%	10	115	10	112	50%	12	30	48	53	450	92%	9.4	1	11.6	34.4%	4	135	7
2011	DAL	12/8	355	127	575	4.5	1	4	-9.1%	43	-3	43	10	52%	10	14	33	44	221	75%	6.7	0	11.6	-2.6%	31	29	33
2012	DAL	16/7	381	111	402	3.6	3	1	-6.1%	25	11	26	28	49%	16	14	26	36	266	69%	10.2	2	9.0	45.1%	1	109	5
2013	PHI			27	132	5.0	0	1	7.2%								11	15	68	73%	6.2	0		-6.4%			

At the end of Jones' first contract with the Cowboys, Jerry Jones insisted that he got "good value" out of his 2008 first-round pick, who amassed a grand total of 2,728 yards and 11 touchdowns on 569 carries in five seasons. Of course, Jones then signed a one-year deal with the Philadelphia Eagles. His tenure in Dallas will be remembered for a brief window of impressive potential (he led the NFL in yards per carry in 2009) and a much larger valley of disappointment (his yards per carry average has declined every year since). In Chip Kelly's offense, Jones will not be expected to be the main man—Kelly has LeSean McCoy for that—but Jones could do a few things as a change-of-pace guy. Safe to say, his days as a possible franchise back are over, and may have existed only in Jerry Jones' head in the first place.

Eddie Lacy Height: 5-11 Weight: 231 College: Alabama Draft: 2013/2 (61) Born: 1-Jan-1990 Age: 24 Risk: Yellow

Year	Team	G/GS	Snaps	Runs	Yds	Yd/R	TD	FUM	DVOA	Rk	DYAR	Rk	YAR	Suc%	Rk	BTkl	Rec	Pass	Yds	C%	Yd/C	TD	YAC	DVOA	Rk	DYAR	Rk
2013	GB			147	708	4.8	4	3	6.8%								20	26	175	77%	8.7	1		2.8%			

In the leadup to the draft, Lacy was commonly framed as the one back with a chance to be a first-round pick. Instead, a lengthy injury history and a shaky Pro Day that involved a sub-par 40-yard dash time in the 4.6 range (as well as Lacy actually quitting before it was over) dropped him to the second-to-last pick of the second round. Lacy does not have breakaway speed, but posted a +25.0 Adj. POE with the help of Alabama's offensive line and an NFL-ready body. He'll dole out the punishment on the ground, yet he's still graceful enough with his hands and feet to be on the field for third-down situations. Lacy has every skill he needs to start from Day One and prove the doubters wrong. All he has to do is stay healthy. There's a first time for everything, right?

Brian Leonard

Height: 6-2   Weight: 226   College: Rutgers   Draft: 2007/2 (52)   Born: 3-Feb-1984   Age: 29   Risk: Green

Year	Team	G/GS	Snaps	Runs	Yds	Yd/R	TD	FUM	DVOA	Rk	DYAR	Rk	YAR	Suc%	Rk	BTkl	Rec	Pass	Yds	C%	Yd/C	TD	YAC	DVOA	Rk	DYAR	Rk
2010	CIN	11/0	217	9	61	6.8	0	0	24.8%	--	15	--	15	56%	--	3	20	26	137	77%	6.9	1	4.8	9.3%	22	36	28
2011	CIN	13/0	231	17	85	5.0	0	0	18.5%	--	18	--	21	47%	--	4	22	31	210	71%	9.5	0	4.8	12.8%	18	43	24
2012	CIN	15/0	206	33	106	3.2	0	0	-11.1%	--	-4	--	-2	42%	--	2	11	15	67	73%	6.1	0	7.1	-41.3%	--	-23	--
2013	TB			28	127	4.6	1	1	9.9%								12	16	100	75%	8.3	0		5.7%			

Buccaneers fans with Mike Alstott delusions should know that Leonard never really panned out as a true all-purpose fullback. Since his promising 102-yard game as a rookie in 2007, his biggest run came in 2010 on that staple of the Bengals ground game, the fake punt. His 2012 statistics were padded by 10 carries for 34 yards in a meaningless Week 17 grind against the Ravens. His usefulness as an outlet receiver is also diminishing. The Bucs clearly have a role for a player with Leonard's skills, but they have two players vying for that role: rookie Mike James is also a fullback-halfback tweener allegedly capable of thumping out tough yards over the middle. No team really needs two of these guys, and James has more upside.

Mikel Leshoure

Height: 6-0   Weight: 227   College: Illinois   Draft: 2011/2 (57)   Born: 30-Mar-1990   Age: 23   Risk: Yellow

Year	Team	G/GS	Snaps	Runs	Yds	Yd/R	TD	FUM	DVOA	Rk	DYAR	Rk	YAR	Suc%	Rk	BTkl	Rec	Pass	Yds	C%	Yd/C	TD	YAC	DVOA	Rk	DYAR	Rk
2012	DET	14/14	530	215	798	3.7	9	3	-1.6%	21	63	18	60	47%	25	18	34	48	214	71%	6.3	0	6.8	-10.2%	30	10	29
2013	DET			113	433	3.8	5	3	-7.5%								19	26	146	73%	7.7	0		5.5%			

Pedestrian is the word that best exemplifies Leshoure's first healthy season with Detroit. Despite the Lions facing the second-lowest average amount of defenders in the box (6.01), Leshoure just wasn't fast or elusive enough to make many would-be tacklers miss. He still notched quite a few broken tackles, but most of them were on pure power. He's a mid-90s feature back stuck in a modern spread passing offense, and if that wasn't discouraging enough, he's spent the early part of the offseason dinged up with a hamstring injury again. There's nothing wrong with Leshoure as the second or third back on a depth chart, but this probably wasn't what the Lions were hoping for when they spent a second-round pick on him in 2011.

Dion Lewis

Height: 5-7   Weight: 195   College: Pittsburgh   Draft: 2011/5 (149)   Born: 27-Sep-1990   Age: 23   Risk: Blue

Year	Team	G/GS	Snaps	Runs	Yds	Yd/R	TD	FUM	DVOA	Rk	DYAR	Rk	YAR	Suc%	Rk	BTkl	Rec	Pass	Yds	C%	Yd/C	TD	YAC	DVOA	Rk	DYAR	Rk
2011	PHI	15/0	42	23	102	4.4	1	0	18.3%	--	25	--	23	52%	--	2	1	1	-3	100%	-3.0	0	5.0	-219.7%	--	-10	--
2012	PHI	9/0	60	13	69	5.3	1	0	45.5%	--	29	--	33	54%	--	2	2	2	24	100%	12.0	0	14.5	51.1%	--	6	--
2013	CLE			34	149	4.4	1	1	-3.6%								7	11	37	64%	5.3	0		-20.1%			

In 2009, Dion Lewis looked like the next great University of Pittsburgh running back, ranking third in the country with 1,799 rushing yards as a redshirt freshman. But did the overuse he received that year—highlighted by a 47-carry performance in the final regular season game—ruin his pro career? Lewis struggled as a sophomore and then fell to the fifth round of the 2010 draft, where he was selected to back up another former Panther, LeSean McCoy. Lewis has yet to flash the same talent he did in 2009, and was traded to Cleveland for linebacker Emmanuel Acho in April. There's upside here given Trent Richardson's health issues and Montario Hardesty's overall mediocrity.

Marshawn Lynch

Height: 5-11   Weight: 215   College: California   Draft: 2007/1 (12)   Born: 22-Apr-1986   Age: 27   Risk: Green

Year	Team	G/GS	Snaps	Runs	Yds	Yd/R	TD	FUM	DVOA	Rk	DYAR	Rk	YAR	Suc%	Rk	BTkl	Rec	Pass	Yds	C%	Yd/C	TD	YAC	DVOA	Rk	DYAR	Rk
2010	2TM	16/14	460	202	737	3.6	6	4	-14.3%	41	-51	41	-36	44%	31	36	22	26	145	85%	6.6	0	6.9	-7.8%	41	9	41
2011	SEA	15/15	559	285	1204	4.2	12	3	8.9%	12	201	2	159	46%	27	34	28	41	212	68%	7.6	1	6.9	-7.1%	36	16	35
2012	SEA	16/15	675	315	1590	5.0	11	5	19.2%	3	361	2	267	50%	11	26	23	30	196	77%	8.5	1	8.8	13.2%	11	50	19
2013	SEA			312	1459	4.7	12	3	12.6%								25	32	222	78%	8.9	1		18.7%			

There are about four million people in the Seattle metro area, and none may be happier than Lynch to see the changes Russell Wilson has brought to the Seahawks offense. Despite his reputation as a power runner, Lynch flourished in the finesse of the read-option, averaging 7.8 yards on 54 carries out of the shotgun, best of any running back with at least 10 shotgun runs. Five of his ten longest runs came out of shotgun sets. However, he also flourished when defenses crowded the line to stop the run: Lynch faced a "loaded" box on 21 percent of his carries, the highest rate for any running back with at least 100 carries. He had a higher DVOA against a loaded box (27.8% DVOA, 4.63 yards per carry) than he did the rest of the time (16.9% DVOA, though a higher average at 5.16 yards per carry).

Lynch was the only healthy player absent at the beginning of Seattle's voluntary workouts in May, but he soon arrived ready to go after Pete Carroll lightly scolded him through the media (as only Carroll can do—the coach explained that Lynch was missing out on "a lot of fun"). The Seahawks drafted two running backs and will also get Percy Harvin some carries out of the backfield, but Lynch still figures to be their bell cow runner.

Doug Martin Height: 5-9 Weight: 223 College: Boise State Draft: 2012/1 (31) Born: 13-Jan-1989 Age: 24 Risk: Yellow

Year	Team	G/GS	Snaps	Runs	Yds	Yd/R	TD	FUM	DVOA	Rk	DYAR	Rk	YAR	Suc%	Rk	BTkl	Rec	Pass	Yds	C%	Yd/C	TD	YAC	DVOA	Rk	DYAR	Rk
2012	TB	16/16	821	319	1454	4.6	11	1	3.9%	14	155	9	204	48%	20	41	49	70	472	70%	9.6	1	8.9	3.1%	24	66	13
2013	TB			317	1554	4.9	10	2	11.8%								56	83	489	67%	8.7	1		3.8%			

The most amazing thing about Martin's rookie season isn't his rushing numbers or yards from scrimmage totals. It's his one fumble, a miscue on a fourth-and-1 run against Carolina in Week 11. Only two rookies have ever had more yards from scrimmage than Martin—Eric Dickerson and Edgerrin James—and they fumbled a combined 21 times. The other seven rookies in the top 10 each fumbled five to 13 times. In fact, only seven men have ever had more yards from scrimmage in a season with one or no fumbles (including Priest Holmes twice). Those seven men averaged only three fumbles the next year, so it's safe to say Martin won't cough up the ball much more this year than he did in 2012. Sometimes, DYAR and DVOA are less about making big plays than they are about avoiding bad plays, and Doug Martin is a not-bad-play-making stud. KUBIAK actually puts him ahead of Adrian Peterson as the projected No. 1 overall pick if you play in a PPR league.

Ryan Mathews Height: 6-0 Weight: 218 College: Fresno State Draft: 2010/1 (12) Born: 1-May-1987 Age: 26 Risk: Yellow

Year	Team	G/GS	Snaps	Runs	Yds	Yd/R	TD	FUM	DVOA	Rk	DYAR	Rk	YAR	Suc%	Rk	BTkl	Rec	Pass	Yds	C%	Yd/C	TD	YAC	DVOA	Rk	DYAR	Rk
2010	SD	12/9	287	158	678	4.3	7	5	1.2%	18	61	23	66	46%	21	12	22	26	145	85%	6.6	0	8.2	-22.9%	49	-12	48
2011	SD	14/14	520	222	1091	4.9	6	5	10.8%	10	171	6	134	50%	17	24	50	59	455	85%	9.1	0	8.2	25.4%	7	126	5
2012	SD	12/9	402	184	707	3.8	1	2	-7.7%	28	6	28	25	47%	23	17	39	57	252	68%	6.5	0	8.8	-15.4%	34	-5	34
2013	SD			253	1017	4.0	5	5	-9.3%								47	61	390	77%	8.3	2		13.5%			

First the positives with Mathews: he's quick and fluid, especially when attacking off-tackle or outside. He has very good lateral agility, which he can use to make defenders miss both in traffic and in space. He's a decent pass-catcher who can make snags on the move. He doesn't always run with enough power and ferocity, though he's shown some improvements.

So why hasn't the fourth-year pro lived up to his first-round draft status? Coaches don't trust him. There are three main reasons for this: First, he's injury prone, including two separate broken collarbone injuries bookending his 2012 season. Second, he fumbles a lot, though he did control that better in 2012. Third, he has bad recognition skills in pass protection. Those first two problems get all the publicity, but it's that third problem that is most likely to keep Mathews from getting the time on the field he needs to blossom into the dynamic weapon that his raw skills suggest he should be.

LeSean McCoy Height: 5-11 Weight: 198 College: Pittsburgh Draft: 2009/2 (53) Born: 12-Jul-1988 Age: 25 Risk: Yellow

Year	Team	G/GS	Snaps	Runs	Yds	Yd/R	TD	FUM	DVOA	Rk	DYAR	Rk	YAR	Suc%	Rk	BTkl	Rec	Pass	Yds	C%	Yd/C	TD	YAC	DVOA	Rk	DYAR	Rk
2010	PHI	15/13	821	207	1080	5.2	7	2	17.5%	5	227	4	205	49%	14	38	78	90	592	87%	7.6	2	8.9	16.1%	15	158	2
2011	PHI	15/15	867	273	1309	4.8	17	1	15.8%	4	304	1	262	51%	15	50	48	69	315	70%	6.6	3	8.9	-4.5%	32	38	27
2012	PHI	12/12	694	200	840	4.2	2	4	-12.6%	33	-34	35	7	48%	19	44	54	68	373	81%	6.9	3	8.9	9.2%	17	90	9
2013	PHI			242	1155	4.8	8	3	8.3%								55	80	439	69%	8.0	3		5.6%			

In 2011, McCoy led the NFL in rushing touchdowns and was extremely effective in the red zone. He had a DVOA of 24.5% and rushed for 145 yards on 53 red-zone carries; he also rushed for nine touchdowns on 22 carries inside the 5-yard line. Last year, McCoy was a disaster inside the 20, with a DVOA of -77.5% and just 25 yards on 25 carries. On eight carries inside the 5, he added just two scores.

Despite the significant drop-off, we can't be too harsh on McCoy, who was running behind a struggling offensive line. McCoy broke nearly as many tackles in 2012 as he did on 73 more carries in 2011, but saw his yards per carry decline because of the line's struggles. He's an obvious candidate for a rebound season with a healthy Jason Peters and the additions of Lane Johnson and head coach Chip Kelly. McCoy still has the same vision, agility, and speed that produced top-five years in 2010 and 2011, and could be in line for a heavy workload in 2013. The only other concern with McCoy comes from the ugly concussion he suffered against the Redskins last November. There's no foolproof way for a running back to avoid the type of hits that lead to concussions, and Eagles fans will have to hold their breath with every hit he takes.

Darren McFadden Height: 6-1 Weight: 211 College: Arkansas Draft: 2008/1 (4) Born: 27-Aug-1987 Age: 26 Risk: Yellow

Year	Team	G/GS	Snaps	Runs	Yds	Yd/R	TD	FUM	DVOA	Rk	DYAR	Rk	YAR	Suc%	Rk	BTkl	Rec	Pass	Yds	C%	Yd/C	TD	YAC	DVOA	Rk	DYAR	Rk
2010	OAK	13/13	641	223	1157	5.2	7	4	3.4%	15	105	16	112	42%	37	37	47	61	507	77%	10.8	3	11.0	34.3%	5	151	3
2011	OAK	7/7	279	113	614	5.4	4	1	11.6%	9	87	20	88	44%	38	12	19	23	154	83%	8.1	1	11.0	12.4%	--	33	--
2012	OAK	12/12	591	216	707	3.3	2	2	-26.7%	41	-153	42	-132	36%	41	14	42	64	258	69%	6.1	1	6.2	-36.7%	43	-82	47
2013	OAK			219	869	4.0	4	3	-8.5%								53	67	473	79%	8.9	0		15.1%			

You know McFadden's story: very gifted, very fragile. The idea of evaluating McFadden with an "if he can stay healthy" qualifier is almost pointless. He's missed at least three games in each of his first five NFL seasons, and there have been plenty of games where he was ineffective playing at less than 100 percent. Nonetheless, even if he were to somehow stay healthy for 16 games, we'd still be talking about a player with some limitations. Yes, McFadden is an explosive straight-line runner when he gets into his second and third step. And, despite some drops here and there, he can be a handful for defenses to deal with in the passing game. The problem is that he's too stiff in the hips to make anyone miss. That prevents him from creating his own space, which makes it harder to get him quality touches while still maintaining the offense's rhythm.

Willis McGahee   Height: 6-0   Weight: 228   College: Miami   Draft: 2003/1 (23)   Born: 21-Oct-1981   Age: 32   Risk: N/A

Year	Team	G/GS	Snaps	Runs	Yds	Yd/R	TD	FUM	DVOA	Rk	DYAR	Rk	YAR	Suc%	Rk	BTkl	Rec	Pass	Yds	C%	Yd/C	TD	YAC	DVOA	Rk	DYAR	Rk
2010	BAL	15/2	237	100	380	3.8	5	2	-6.6%	31	6	32	0	49%	13	14	14	17	55	82%	3.9	1	6.7	-46.0%	--	-30	--
2011	DEN	15/14	458	249	1199	4.8	4	4	4.3%	17	131	12	117	47%	26	22	12	20	51	60%	4.3	1	6.7	-67.4%	--	-58	--
2012	DEN	10/9	393	167	731	4.4	4	5	-2.1%	22	49	23	79	58%	1	11	26	33	221	79%	8.5	0	9.0	7.2%	22	44	21

McGahee was a perfect fit in the Peyton Manning system. The nine-year veteran no longer has much initial quickness or lateral agility, but he's a tough inside runner who patiently lets his blocks unfold and can identify cutback lanes. He also contributes as a short-area flair receiver in the flats. Unfortunately, he ended the 2012 campaign on the sidelines with a broken leg and a torn MCL, and apparently he's having difficulty recovering from those injuries. That's what led the Broncos to draft Montee Ball and cut McGahee in June. If he's healthy, he can definitely help another team that needs a second running back. Then again, if he was healthy, the Broncos probably would have kept him and cut Knowshon Moreno loose instead.

Joe McKnight   Height: 6-0   Weight: 198   College: USC   Draft: 2010/4 (112)   Born: 16-Apr-1988   Age: 25   Risk: Blue

Year	Team	G/GS	Snaps	Runs	Yds	Yd/R	TD	FUM	DVOA	Rk	DYAR	Rk	YAR	Suc%	Rk	BTkl	Rec	Pass	Yds	C%	Yd/C	TD	YAC	DVOA	Rk	DYAR	Rk
2010	NYJ	9/1	71	39	189	4.8	0	0	11.5%	--	30	--	49	59%	--	0	3	4	20	75%	6.7	0	3.7	6.1%	--	5	--
2011	NYJ	15/0	112	43	134	3.1	0	0	-14.9%	--	-11	--	-8	44%	--	1	13	18	139	72%	10.7	0	3.7	31.1%	--	43	--
2012	NYJ	15/0	59	30	179	6.0	0	1	1.7%	--	12	--	10	47%	--	4	1	2	18	50%	18.0	0	9.0	18.2%	--	4	--
2013	NYJ			40	180	4.5	1	2	-1.4%								13	17	83	76%	6.4	0		-5.8%			

Even with the Jets offense a complete disaster, McKnight had trouble getting snaps last year. That was either a statement about McKnight or a statement about Tony Sparano. He's one of the top kick returners in the league, but it's hard to imagine he'll get that many carries behind Chris Ivory and Bilal Powell. There's some talk about Marty Mornhinweg using him as a slot receiver, although so far that talk seems to mostly be coming from McKnight himself.

Rashard Mendenhall   Height: 5-10   Weight: 225   College: Illinois   Draft: 2008/1 (23)   Born: 19-Jun-1987   Age: 26   Risk: Green

Year	Team	G/GS	Snaps	Runs	Yds	Yd/R	TD	FUM	DVOA	Rk	DYAR	Rk	YAR	Suc%	Rk	BTkl	Rec	Pass	Yds	C%	Yd/C	TD	YAC	DVOA	Rk	DYAR	Rk
2010	PIT	16/16	602	324	1273	3.9	13	2	-3.0%	25	71	22	79	44%	28	33	23	34	167	68%	7.3	0	7.6	-3.8%	35	20	37
2011	PIT	15/15	458	228	928	4.1	9	1	2.3%	23	106	17	88	52%	11	34	18	28	154	64%	8.6	0	7.6	-4.7%	33	15	36
2012	PIT	6/4	104	51	182	3.6	0	3	-38.5%	--	-62	--	-55	43%	--	9	9	11	62	82%	6.9	1	10.9	22.7%	--	24	--
2013	ARI			191	864	4.5	7	2	4.4%								28	35	248	80%	8.9	0		19.7%			

What an ugly season. Mendenhall hustled back from a New Year's Day ACL tear to take the field (and play fairly well) in Week 4, then suffered an Achilles injury two weeks later. He was ineffective when he returned in November, fumbled twice in four carries against the Ravens, got demoted to third string, got suspended for blowing off practices after the demotion, then returned for two uneventful games. Despite the Steelers jerking him around all year, Mendenhall drew healthy interest in free agency. He's now reunited with Bruce Arians, who was the offensive coordinator back before he became persona non grata in Pittsburgh, and the Cardinals believe he can still be a workhorse, despite numerous flashing warnings to the contrary. Mendenhall was turning into a plodder before the injury in the 2011 season, with just two 100-yard games surrounded by tons of 16-carry, 50-yard efforts, and he's not exactly running behind an All-Pro line here. It looks like the Cardinals will make Mendenhall a starter rather than a committee back, but for fantasy purposes, he may the worst "definite non-committee starter" in the league.

Christine Michael   Height: 5-10   Weight: 220   College: Texas A&M   Draft: 2013/2 (62)   Born: 9-Nov-1990   Age: 23   Risk: Yellow

Year	Team	G/GS	Snaps	Runs	Yds	Yd/R	TD	FUM	DVOA	Rk	DYAR	Rk	YAR	Suc%	Rk	BTkl	Rec	Pass	Yds	C%	Yd/C	TD	YAC	DVOA	Rk	DYAR	Rk
2013	SEA			66	313	4.8	2	1	7.0%								16	22	154	73%	9.6	1		6.3%			

Michael finished third among running backs at this year's Combine in Speed Score behind Arkansas's Knile Davis (who went to the Chiefs in the third round) and Miami's Mike James (Buccaneers, sixth). Part of a running back committee, he still finished with nine 100-yard games in his Aggies career, capped off by a 230-yard day against Arkansas in 2011. That's the good news. The bad news is that Michael was suspended for the first game of 2012 due to unspecified rules violations, and Tweeted during the game that Texas A&M needed to run the ball more. Not surprisingly, he spent the rest of the year in Kevin Sumlin's doghouse, not even playing in the Cotton Bowl win over Oklahoma. (Fun fact: Research shows that young boys given traditional girls names are more likely to misbehave than other boys.) Pete Carroll has been willing to work with headcases before (see Leroy Hill, Bruce Irvin, Marshawn Lynch, and the multitude of Seahawks suspended for PEDs), and has a good chance at getting the most out of the talented runner. Michael will start the year third on the depth chart behind Lynch and Robert Turbin, but could be worth a late-round flyer in dynasty leagues.

Lamar Miller Height: 5-11 Weight: 212 College: Miami Draft: 2012/4 (97) Born: 25-Apr-1991 Age: 22 Risk: Green

Year	Team	G/GS	Snaps	Runs	Yds	Yd/R	TD	FUM	DVOA	Rk	DYAR	Rk	YAR	Suc%	Rk	BTkl	Rec	Pass	Yds	C%	Yd/C	TD	YAC	DVOA	Rk	DYAR	Rk
2012	MIA	13/1	143	51	250	4.9	1	0	7.5%	--	35	--	48	55%	--	5	6	9	45	67%	7.5	0	6.7	-2.0%	--	6	--
2013	MIA			236	1103	4.7	7	3	2.9%								31	42	216	74%	7.0	0		-8.8%			

Fantasy sleeper alert! All signs point to Miller having a breakout season. First, he had the highest Speed Score of the 2012 draft class, and two of the past three Speed Score champions have emerged seemingly out of nowhere once they entered the starting lineup (Andre Brown and Ben Tate). Second, Miller's adroitness at reading blocks fits the Dolphins' zone-blocking scheme to a tee. Finally, although we're projecting Miami to be playing from behind much of the time in 2013, receiving ability happens to be one of Miller's strengths.

Knowshon Moreno Height: 5-11 Weight: 200 College: Georgia Draft: 2009/1 (12) Born: 16-Jul-1987 Age: 26 Risk: Blue

Year	Team	G/GS	Snaps	Runs	Yds	Yd/R	TD	FUM	DVOA	Rk	DYAR	Rk	YAR	Suc%	Rk	BTkl	Rec	Pass	Yds	C%	Yd/C	TD	YAC	DVOA	Rk	DYAR	Rk
2010	DEN	13/13	485	182	779	4.3	5	4	-4.6%	27	34	26	44	43%	33	25	37	48	372	77%	10.1	3	9.8	29.1%	7	114	10
2011	DEN	7/2	175	37	179	4.8	0	1	-16.0%	--	-9	--	-5	32%	--	7	11	15	101	73%	9.2	1	9.8	44.1%	--	37	--
2012	DEN	8/6	337	139	525	3.8	4	1	1.1%	18	56	20	67	56%	2	10	21	26	167	81%	8.0	0	6.0	25.3%	5	58	15
2013	DEN			46	205	4.5	2	1	8.0%								17	23	126	74%	7.4	0		-1.5%			

Moreno had somewhat of a career resurgence filling in for an injured Willis McGahee down the stretch last season. After playing a minor role in Weeks 1 and 2, he was inactive for Weeks 3 to 11 before suddenly getting the starting nod in Week 12. On the surface, Moreno's 3.8 yards per carry don't look great, but that was partly a function of him getting more clock-eating touches when Denver was protecting a late lead. He had 20 or more rushing attempts in five of his six starts, including a 32-carry, 119-yard outing on a short week in a win over Oakland. He also did what was needed in the passing game, which is important for any Broncos running back.

Moreno's effectiveness in Denver's current system doesn't mean he'll suddenly be a featured player, though. He benefitted from facing a lot of seven-man boxes and getting the ball in positions where just about any back could succeed. In a vacuum, Moreno is a functional downhill runner and adept receiver, but he lacks outstanding explosiveness and special agility.

Alfred Morris Height: 5-10 Weight: 219 College: Florida Atlantic Draft: 2012/6 (173) Born: 12-Dec-1988 Age: 25 Risk: Yellow

Year	Team	G/GS	Snaps	Runs	Yds	Yd/R	TD	FUM	DVOA	Rk	DYAR	Rk	YAR	Suc%	Rk	BTkl	Rec	Pass	Yds	C%	Yd/C	TD	YAC	DVOA	Rk	DYAR	Rk
2012	WAS	16/16	728	335	1613	4.8	13	4	10.3%	8	254	5	273	52%	7	27	11	16	77	69%	7.0	0	5.9	-14.6%	--	-1	--
2013	WAS			309	1437	4.6	11	3	8.8%								15	21	124	71%	8.3	0		5.4%			

As with most late-round and undrafted players who make an immediate impact in the NFL, Morris was far more than the sum of his parts, at least from a pre-draft scouting perspective. The former Florida Atlantic star was thought to be too slow to turn the corner, but he showed through his rookie campaign that he could extend plays outside the tackles. Some thought Morris was not nimble enough to fit in a "one-cut-and-go" system, but he was good enough at that particular skill to become the best example of a back in the Mike Shanahan Zone Blocking Program since Clinton Portis was still in Denver.

Where Portis excelled, and where Morris must advance to become a true every-down back, is as a receiver. Fortunately for Redskins fans, the humble Morris is well aware that his overall game needs improvement. "I left a lot of yards on the field last year," he told Yahoo! Sports in May. "Looking back on film, a lot of it was my aiming points in certain runs, or I was too tight and I couldn't get outside. Being more patient with my cutbacks—I tended to cut back too soon. I was blessed, and I definitely don't take it for granted. Last year's behind me—I'm beyond that."

How much of Morris' success was due to the fact that opposing defenses were set to stop Robert Griffin III, and had to commit extra men in the box to stop the option attack? Morris did gain 935 of his rushing yards on 175 carries out of shotgun, and his 5.34 yards per carry average and 16.5% DVOA in that formation would indicate that his success was system-dependent to a degree. Also, Morris' stats on third down—19 carries for 31 yards (1.63 yards per carry) and a -11.0% DVOA—point to a need for improvement. But all of this from an afterthought player who became a key cog in one of the league's most dynamic offenses from his first NFL game? Most teams would take that from a sixth-round steal, and Morris may be the best example of the Redskins' new philosophy of successfully building from the draft up.

DeMarco Murray Height: 6-0 Weight: 213 College: Oklahoma Draft: 2011/3 (71) Born: 12-Feb-1988 Age: 25 Risk: Yellow

Year	Team	G/GS	Snaps	Runs	Yds	Yd/R	TD	FUM	DVOA	Rk	DYAR	Rk	YAR	Suc%	Rk	BTkl	Rec	Pass	Yds	C%	Yd/C	TD	YAC	DVOA	Rk	DYAR	Rk
2011	DAL	13/7	377	164	897	5.5	2	1	12.6%	7	149	11	162	58%	2	14	26	35	183	74%	7.0	0	8.6	-17.4%	44	-7	45
2012	DAL	10/0	466	161	663	4.1	4	4	1.7%	16	72	15	65	54%	5	26	34	42	247	83%	7.3	0	6.9	10.4%	16	60	14
2013	DAL			226	946	4.2	4	3	-5.6%								46	69	390	67%	8.5	1		-3.8%			

If health is a skill, it's one that Murray has failed to maintain. He's missed seven games in two seasons with a variety of maladies, and tweaked a hamstring in 2013 OTAs, but he doesn't appear to want to ramp it down anytime soon. "I'd rather play five or six games the way I play—hard, fast and physical—than 16 games soft and tip-toeing and not contributing the way I'm used to contributing," he told DallasCowboys.com in May. He missed six games with a sprained foot in 2012, and something will have to change if Murray is to become the franchise back some Cowboys coaches believe he can be. Both in his physical structure and gait, he's more like a receiver, and his injury trajectory so far seems to imitate former Tennessee Titans back Chris Brown (a talented guy who couldn't stay on the field) more than, say, Eric Dickerson. Perhaps Dickerson could teach Murray how to run out of bounds, because this trend carries back to his time at Oklahoma. He had a turf toe issue in his redshirt year, dislocated his right kneecap in 2007, missed part of the 2008 Big 12 Championship and all of the BCS title game with a ruptured hammy, sprained his ankle in 2009, and played through bruised ribs in 2010. That, folks, is a worrisome trend.

Jalen Parmele Height: 5-11 Weight: 224 College: Toledo Draft: 2008/6 (176) Born: 30-Dec-1985 Age: 28 Risk: Green

Year	Team	G/GS	Snaps	Runs	Yds	Yd/R	TD	FUM	DVOA	Rk	DYAR	Rk	YAR	Suc%	Rk	BTkl	Rec	Pass	Yds	C%	Yd/C	TD	YAC	DVOA	Rk	DYAR	Rk
2010	BAL	16/0	1	0	0	0.0	0	0	--	--	--	--	--	--	--	0	0	0	0	--	0.0	0	--	--	--	--	--
2012	JAC	11/2	154	40	143	3.6	0	0	-12.8%	--	-7	--	-22	33%	--	3	7	9	60	78%	8.6	0	7.7	-1.7%	--	7	--
2013	TEN			28	126	4.5	0	1	0.0%								6	9	45	67%	7.4	0		-3.9%			

Four-plus seasons on the fringes of NFL rosters finally paid off for Parmele late in the 2012 season. Injuries to Maurice Jones-Drew and Rashad Jennings allowed Parmele to make the first start of his NFL career. Parmele had 24 carries for 80 yards in a Week 11 loss to the Houston Texans. In an example of "the training table giveth, the training table taketh away," Parmele was injured the following week and placed on IR. Parmele was signed to a "minimum salary benefit" contract (league minimum base salary, no guaranteed money) by the Tennessee Titans, where he'll compete for the No. 3 running back job behind Chris Johnson and Shonn Greene.

Isaiah Pead Height: 5-10 Weight: 197 College: Cincinnati Draft: 2012/2 (50) Born: 14-Dec-1989 Age: 24 Risk: Yellow

Year	Team	G/GS	Snaps	Runs	Yds	Yd/R	TD	FUM	DVOA	Rk	DYAR	Rk	YAR	Suc%	Rk	BTkl	Rec	Pass	Yds	C%	Yd/C	TD	YAC	DVOA	Rk	DYAR	Rk
2012	STL	15/1	39	10	54	5.4	0	1	49.9%	--	23	--	17	60%	--	3	3	4	16	75%	5.3	0	6.7	-112.9%	--	-22	--
2013	STL			110	483	4.4	2	1	-1.6%								34	41	251	83%	7.4	1		-0.3%			

The Rams drafted Pead to eventually surpass Steven Jackson, but Pead himself was soon surpassed by Daryl Richardson and spent most of the season glued to the bench. Half his regular-season carries came in the season-ending loss to Seattle in Week 17. Pead will compete with Richardson, Zac Stacy, and Terrance Ganaway for the Rams' primary running back spot this fall, but he'll miss the opener against Arizona due to suspension for marijuana use. Rams coach Jeff Fisher said the team knew for some time that Pead's punishment was coming, and that it wouldn't cost him reps or hurt his standing on the depth chart. Pead has a track record of success, twice going over 1,000 yards and 5.0 yards per carry for the Cincinnati Bearcats, but his modest Speed Score (S-Pead Score?) of 98.7 coming out of college suggests that there's a fairly low ceiling here.

Cedric Peerman Height: 5-10 Weight: 216 College: Virginia Draft: 2009/6 (185) Born: 10-Oct-1986 Age: 27 Risk: Green

Year	Team	G/GS	Snaps	Runs	Yds	Yd/R	TD	FUM	DVOA	Rk	DYAR	Rk	YAR	Suc%	Rk	BTkl	Rec	Pass	Yds	C%	Yd/C	TD	YAC	DVOA	Rk	DYAR	Rk
2010	CIN	7/0	34	2	1	0.5	0	0	-86.3%	--	-9	--	-11	0%	--	0	1	3	11	33%	11.0	0	4.0	-24.1%	--	-2	--
2011	CIN	15/0	26	3	15	5.0	0	0	-66.0%	--	-4	--	-3	33%	--	0	0	1	0	0%	0.0	0	4.0	-129.6%	--	-7	--
2012	CIN	14/1	94	36	258	7.2	1	0	26.6%	--	56	--	71	53%	--	6	9	9	85	100%	9.4	0	8.2	81.1%	--	50	--
2013	CIN			31	153	4.9	1	0	7.8%								8	11	51	73%	6.3	0		-5.6%			

Peerman gained 48 and 32 yards on two fake punts. He also broke several Raiders tackles on a 31-yard run up the gut, and had nine other runs of seven or more yards in 38 attempts when not battling nagging ankle injuries. The Bengals re-signed Peerman in the offseason, and you have to figure, well, if he is going to break a big gain every ten carries or so, maybe he will earn some more touches. BenJarvus Green-Ellis and Giovani Bernard are ahead of him on the depth chart, and Bernard, Adam Jones, and Brandon Tate have first dibs on return duties, so Peerman must settle for third running back and personal protector chores, knowing that no one is going to be fooled by his next fake punt.

Adrian Peterson Height: 6-2 Weight: 217 College: Oklahoma Draft: 2007/1 (7) Born: 21-Mar-1985 Age: 28 Risk: Yellow

Year	Team	G/GS	Snaps	Runs	Yds	Yd/R	TD	FUM	DVOA	Rk	DYAR	Rk	YAR	Suc%	Rk	BTkl	Rec	Pass	Yds	C%	Yd/C	TD	YAC	DVOA	Rk	DYAR	Rk
2010	MIN	15/15	669	283	1298	4.6	12	2	10.7%	7	217	6	224	45%	22	35	36	50	341	72%	9.5	1	9.2	17.5%	12	86	13
2011	MIN	12/12	498	208	970	4.7	12	1	10.4%	11	153	9	190	47%	25	26	18	23	139	78%	7.7	1	9.2	9.9%	--	28	--
2012	MIN	16/16	770	348	2097	6.0	12	4	24.9%	2	458	1	357	49%	14	44	40	51	217	78%	5.4	1	4.7	-14.9%	33	-3	33
2013	MIN			349	1779	5.1	11	3	12.6%								39	48	296	81%	7.6	0		9.5%			

Through Week 6, Peterson was having the kind of season you'd expect a great player to have while coming back from a torn ACL, MCL, and meniscus—and dealing with an ankle injury. Over his first 113 carries, Peterson had 48 DYAR and a 1.4% DVOA. "There's still a little missing. You guys probably think I'm crazy," Peterson said after his first 100-yard game of the season against Arizona in Week 7. There was.

Our statistical projections are based on principles of regression. They are designed to punish massive outliers and correct them back to ground soil. When a reasonable regression analysis of a player's past seasons leads us to suggest that said player is going to run for a top-30 all-time seasonal yardage total, that player may defy a lot of basic principles of regression. Or he may have actually taken over the DVOA computer and put in his own projection, which is just as believable as anything else Peterson did last year.

Bernard Pierce   Height: 6-0   Weight: 218   College: Temple   Draft: 2012/3 (84)   Born: 10-May-1991   Age: 22   Risk: Green

Year	Team	G/GS	Snaps	Runs	Yds	Yd/R	TD	FUM	DVOA	Rk	DYAR	Rk	YAR	Suc%	Rk	BTkl	Rec	Pass	Yds	C%	Yd/C	TD	YAC	DVOA	Rk	DYAR	Rk
2012	BAL	16/0	218	108	532	4.9	1	0	4.1%	13	54	21	52	47%	24	19	7	11	47	64%	6.7	0	6.1	1.8%	--	10	--
2013	BAL			131	645	4.9	3	4	1.0%								14	18	116	78%	8.3	0		8.5%			

The Prince of Handcuffs (now there's a nickname you don't want to use out of context) for fantasy leaguers in 2012. Pierce rushed for 414 yards off the bench in six games from Week 16 through the Super Bowl, averaging 5.52 yards per carry, and he did it with a bone bruise in his knee. Pierce ranked fifth in the NFL in broken tackle rate, making him a dangerous Ray Rice counterpunch, in contrast to the veteran plodders (Ricky Williams, Willis McGahee) the Ravens used in previous years. Pierce will eat into Rice's carries a smidge, but he is not a receiving threat at all, making him strictly the second running back … unless Rice gets hurt, in which case you will curse the fantasy owner who drafted Pierce before you could.

Bilal Powell   Height: 5-10   Weight: 205   College: Louisville   Draft: 2011/4 (126)   Born: 27-Oct-1988   Age: 25   Risk: Green

Year	Team	G/GS	Snaps	Runs	Yds	Yd/R	TD	FUM	DVOA	Rk	DYAR	Rk	YAR	Suc%	Rk	BTkl	Rec	Pass	Yds	C%	Yd/C	TD	YAC	DVOA	Rk	DYAR	Rk
2011	NYJ	2/0	25	13	21	1.6	0	1	-115.1%	--	-54	--	-57	15%	--	0	1	1	7	100%	7.0	0	2.0	-22.8%	--	-1	--
2012	NYJ	14/2	397	110	437	4.0	4	0	5.6%	10	63	17	71	50%	13	9	17	36	140	47%	8.2	0	7.1	-24.7%	39	-22	40
2013	NYJ			98	424	4.3	1	1	-6.7%								28	38	237	74%	8.4	0		7.5%			

Matt Waldman, who writes the college-scouting Futures column for Football Outsiders, was extremely high on Powell coming out of Louisville in 2011, calling him "the best combo of power, speed, balance, and maturity between the tackles" out of any running back in that draft class. That talent hasn't translated into superlative productivity so far in his NFL career, and the Jets traded for Chris Ivory in part because they didn't have confidence in Powell to be a lead back. Still, he's a useful backup, particularly because he's a good blocker in pass situations.

William Powell   Height: 5-9   Weight: 207   College: Kansas State   Draft: 2011/FA   Born: 9-Mar-1988   Age: 25   Risk: Green

Year	Team	G/GS	Snaps	Runs	Yds	Yd/R	TD	FUM	DVOA	Rk	DYAR	Rk	YAR	Suc%	Rk	BTkl	Rec	Pass	Yds	C%	Yd/C	TD	YAC	DVOA	Rk	DYAR	Rk
2012	ARI	13/1	284	59	216	3.7	0	0	0.1%	--	21	--	6	40%	--	7	19	25	132	76%	6.9	0	4.3	-19.3%	36	-6	35
2013	ARI			44	183	4.1	1	1	-7.7%								20	25	157	80%	7.9	0		8.0%			

Powell wasn't exactly a lead-pipe lock to do anything in the NFL worthy of an exclusive-rights tender from his team, but that's what happened in 2012 after Powell showed some productivity in fits and starts when injuries scuttled Arizona's starters. He carried the ball just 23 times in two seasons for Kansas State, but Powell has proven to have a combination of power and versatility that could make him a minor factor in Bruce Arians' offense.

Joseph Randle   Height: 6-0   Weight: 204   College: Oklahoma State   Draft: 2013/5 (151)   Born: 29-Dec-1991   Age: 22   Risk: Red

Year	Team	G/GS	Snaps	Runs	Yds	Yd/R	TD	FUM	DVOA	Rk	DYAR	Rk	YAR	Suc%	Rk	BTkl	Rec	Pass	Yds	C%	Yd/C	TD	YAC	DVOA	Rk	DYAR	Rk
2013	DAL			83	405	4.9	1	2	3.0%								22	34	219	65%	10.0	2		26.0%			

Clearly, the Cowboys are looking for answers at running back (and many other positions), which led them to take a flyer on Randle in the fifth round. Like DeMarco Murray, Randle is a high-cut back with great acceleration, but a frame that could leave him slightly more vulnerable to injuries. He ran for 1,216 yards and 24 (!) rushing touchdowns in 2011, and 1,417 yards and 14 touchdowns in 2012, but he benefitted as much from Oklahoma State's spread, heavy-motion attack as his former Cowboys team did from his skill set. We'll see if his new Cowboys team has the kind of offensive diversity that best suits his talents.

Isaac Redman   Height: 6-0   Weight: 230   College: Bowie State   Draft: 2009/FA   Born: 10-Nov-1984   Age: 29   Risk: Blue

Year	Team	G/GS	Snaps	Runs	Yds	Yd/R	TD	FUM	DVOA	Rk	DYAR	Rk	YAR	Suc%	Rk	BTkl	Rec	Pass	Yds	C%	Yd/C	TD	YAC	DVOA	Rk	DYAR	Rk
2010	PIT	16/0	191	52	247	4.8	0	2	1.7%	--	25	--	21	58%	--	10	9	10	72	90%	8.0	2	9.0	98.7%	--	54	--
2011	PIT	16/1	352	110	479	4.4	3	2	3.1%	19	55	31	67	54%	5	22	18	23	78	83%	4.3	0	9.0	-21.4%	--	-10	--
2012	PIT	14/5	307	110	410	3.7	2	3	-15.0%	36	-31	34	-15	43%	35	24	19	23	244	83%	12.8	0	10.6	36.1%	--	75	--
2013	PIT			42	168	4.0	1	2	-10.0%								14	19	121	74%	8.6	1		9.4%			

Redman is a credible power back with great tackle-breaking ability, and his yards after contact numbers are a little nuts. Last year, he was second among qualifying backs with 2.5 average yards after contact, trailing only Adrian Peterson. He was even better with 2.7 average yards after contact in both 2010 and 2011. Of course, Redman would get more out of these yards after contact if the contact didn't take place right at the line of scrimmage so often.

A 147-yard effort against the Giants accounted for 36 percent of Redman's production last season. Redman won the starting job in that game, but lost it after fumbling in the first quarter against the Chiefs the following week. He earned a traditional Todd Haley non-role as a result, with five one- to three-carry games in the second half of the season. (A concussion also limited his use, though a player healthy enough for two touches should be healthy enough for ten.) Rashard Mendenhall is gone and Jonathan Dwyer is on the outs, but Le'Veon Bell has joined the club, and Haley has never let one back do well what four or five can do badly.

Marcel Reece   Height: 6-3   Weight: 240   College: Washington   Draft: 2008/FA   Born: 23-Jun-1985   Age: 28   Risk: Green

Year	Team	G/GS	Snaps	Runs	Yds	Yd/R	TD	FUM	DVOA	Rk	DYAR	Rk	YAR	Suc%	Rk	BTkl	Rec	Pass	Yds	C%	Yd/C	TD	YAC	DVOA	Rk	DYAR	Rk
2010	OAK	16/10	525	30	122	4.1	1	1	-8.0%	--	-2	--	7	57%	--	9	25	43	333	58%	13.3	3	12.2	17.3%	13	73	17
2011	OAK	12/6	333	17	112	6.6	0	1	45.2%	--	38	--	36	59%	--	5	27	36	301	75%	11.1	2	12.2	20.8%	11	72	14
2012	OAK	16/14	659	59	271	4.6	0	2	-6.9%	--	4	--	21	54%	--	15	52	73	496	71%	9.5	1	6.3	7.6%	21	90	8
2013	OAK			43	202	4.7	1	2	7.4%								40	53	263	75%	6.6	0		-3.9%			

Reece went to the Pro Bowl last year as a fullback, but a more accurate title for him would be "H-back." Or "utility man." He is not a particularly polished or potent lead-blocker—he's not awful, but the raw strength just isn't there. He is, however, a very diverse and effective ball-handler. He ranked fifth among NFL running backs with 6.9 yards per touch. Reece played wide receiver at Chaffey Junior College, Camino Community College, and the University of Washington. That experience is evident when he runs routes, which he can do not just out of the backfield but also the slot (and, in certain scenarios, from plus-splits outside). Reece can also handle the rock as a traditional ballcarrier, though he does not have the shiftiness and may not quite have the instincts to be a regular force in this sense. Nevertheless, he's a threat to touch the ball no matter where he aligns, which means defenses must specifically account for him wherever he lines up.

Ray Rice   Height: 5-8   Weight: 199   College: Rutgers   Draft: 2008/2 (55)   Born: 22-Jan-1987   Age: 26   Risk: Green

Year	Team	G/GS	Snaps	Runs	Yds	Yd/R	TD	FUM	DVOA	Rk	DYAR	Rk	YAR	Suc%	Rk	BTkl	Rec	Pass	Yds	C%	Yd/C	TD	YAC	DVOA	Rk	DYAR	Rk
2010	BAL	16/14	801	307	1220	4.0	5	0	0.4%	19	97	17	124	46%	19	22	63	83	556	76%	8.8	1	8.4	5.6%	25	82	15
2011	BAL	16/16	819	291	1364	4.7	12	2	2.1%	26	129	13	108	45%	33	29	76	104	704	73%	9.3	3	8.4	28.1%	5	231	2
2012	BAL	16/16	811	257	1143	4.4	9	1	11.5%	7	205	7	193	44%	33	27	61	83	478	73%	7.8	1	7.7	-11.7%	31	10	28
2013	BAL			239	1106	4.6	9	3	5.7%								52	71	446	73%	8.6	2		13.6%			

Rice looked a little worn-down in the playoffs—some uncharacteristic fumbles, so-so performances in the AFC Championship game and the Super Bowl—but the numbers do not support any "overuse" theories. For his career, he averages 5.05 yards per attempt in December games and a respectable 3.93 yards per carry in the playoffs. (The 2012 numbers are in line with the career numbers.) Rice's attempts per game typically go up in December, from his usual average of 16.0 per game to 17.7, though they went down to 14.2 when Jim Caldwell took over play-calling duties and Bernard Pierce took on an expanded role last winter. Pierce will retain a significant role in 2013, and that's a good thing for Rice and the Ravens: It is better to get ahead of usage and fatigue issues than fall behind them. Rice can do a lot of damage with 14 to 15 carries and three to five catches per game, and he can do that damage for years to come.

Daryl Richardson   Height: 6-0   Weight: 192   College: Abilene Christian   Draft: 2012/7 (252)   Born: 12-Apr-1990   Age: 23   Risk: Red

Year	Team	G/GS	Snaps	Runs	Yds	Yd/R	TD	FUM	DVOA	Rk	DYAR	Rk	YAR	Suc%	Rk	BTkl	Rec	Pass	Yds	C%	Yd/C	TD	YAC	DVOA	Rk	DYAR	Rk
2012	STL	16/0	301	98	475	4.8	0	3	1.7%	--	40	--	7	42%	--	13	24	36	163	67%	6.8	0	7.6	-46.9%	47	-65	46
2013	STL			181	810	4.5	3	3	-2.1%								42	69	340	61%	8.1	2		-15.9%			

For Cinderella, the clock struck midnight. For Daryl Richardson, the calendar flipped to December. Through three months, Richardson played like a perfectly acceptable change-of-pace back, averaging 5.5 yards on 82 carries with an 12.1% DVOA. In the five games after November 30, though, he had just 16 carries for 24 yards with -50.9% DVOA. It looked like the Rams had given up on their seventh-round rookie, but with no other options available, Richardson will have a chance to win a starting job this fall. That title will largely be semantic anyway—Rams GM Les Snead has made it clear they will use a committee approach with Richardson, Isaiah Pead, Zac Stacy, Terrance Ganaway, and a sprinkling of Tavon Austin.

Trent Richardson   Height: 5-9   Weight: 228   College: Alabama   Draft: 2012/1 (3)   Born: 10-Jul-1991   Age: 22   Risk: Red

Year	Team	G/GS	Snaps	Runs	Yds	Yd/R	TD	FUM	DVOA	Rk	DYAR	Rk	YAR	Suc%	Rk	BTkl	Rec	Pass	Yds	C%	Yd/C	TD	YAC	DVOA	Rk	DYAR	Rk
2012	CLE	15/15	702	267	950	3.6	11	3	-13.3%	34	-51	37	-21	43%	36	31	51	70	367	73%	7.2	1	8.6	4.4%	23	73	11
2013	CLE			294	1210	4.1	11	3	-3.5%								50	72	419	69%	8.4	1		1.9%			

Richardson finished fifth in the NFL with 31 broken tackles, but the battering ram got battered as the season wore on. He had no runs of 20 yards or longer in November or December, and his yards per carry dipped to 2.6 in the fourth quarter after getting fed to loaded fronts game after game. Richardson was saddled with an ineffective quarterback and an offense as predictable as a *Scooby Doo* episode last year. The quarterback is still there, but both Coach Chud and Norv Turner are known for developing good ground games. Team NorvChud is considering using Richardson as an every-down rusher; Pat Shurmur often took him out on passing downs. Richardson has the skills to help in the passing game; it's up to the rest of the Browns to make sure he is working smarter, not harder.

Stevan Ridley			Height: 6-0		Weight: 223			College: LSU				Draft: 2011/3 (73)		Born: 27-Jan-1989		Age: 24			Risk: Yellow
Year	Team	G/GS	Snaps	Runs	Yds	Yd/R	TD	FUM	DVOA	Rk	DYAR	Rk	YAR	Suc%	Rk	BTkl	Rec	Pass	Yds	C%	Yd/C	TD	YAC	DVOA	Rk	DYAR	Rk
2011	NE	16/2	191	87	441	5.1	1	1	-0.1%	--	31	--	44	51%	--	10	3	5	13	60%	4.3	0	4.3	-45.6%	--	-9	--
2012	NE	16/12	549	290	1263	4.4	12	4	6.1%	9	192	8	191	55%	4	12	6	14	51	43%	8.5	0	7.8	-38.4%	--	-19	--
2013	NE			265	1173	4.4	11	2	5.2%							13	20	118	65%	9.1	1		6.9%			

There was a lot of talk last year about how the Patriots had finally found a running game to balance out their offense, but the Patriots have always had an efficient running game. They just happened to use it a little bit more last year than in years past. New England has now ranked in the top four for run offense DVOA in five of the last six seasons. (The exception was 2009, when they were ninth.) Ridley is now their bellcow, but he benefits from the same things as all the other recent Patriots running backs: defenses set up to stop the pass (the average box faced by the Patriots last year was 6.15, 29th in the league) and lots of shotgun spread formations that give him space to find holes. In fact, Ridley is particularly productive when he runs from shotgun; in his two NFL seasons combined, he's run 43 times from shotgun for 281 yards, with a 67 percent Success Rate and 51.5% DVOA.

Denard Robinson			Height: 5-11		Weight: 190			College: Michigan				Draft: 2013/5 (135)		Born: 22-Sep-1990		Age: 23			Risk: Green
Year	Team	G/GS	Snaps	Runs	Yds	Yd/R	TD	FUM	DVOA	Rk	DYAR	Rk	YAR	Suc%	Rk	BTkl	Rec	Pass	Yds	C%	Yd/C	TD	YAC	DVOA	Rk	DYAR	Rk
2013	JAC			45	201	4.5	0	1	-2.2%							19	24	182	79%	9.6	1		9.2%			

Robinson was highly productive during his 47-game career at Michigan, passing for 6,250 yards and 49 touchdowns while running for 4,495 yards (an NCAA record for a quarterback) and 42 touchdowns on the ground. A lack of accuracy as a passer had Robinson working at wide receiver at both the Senior Bowl and scouting combine, so naturally the Jaguars listed "Shoelace" as a running back when they selected him in the fifth round. Robinson is expected to receive 10 to 15 touches per game as the Jaguars will utilize his speed and ability to change direction in both the return game and as a triple-threat on offense at running back, wide receiver, and yes, quarterback. In fact, the Jaguars created a new position for Robinson, listing his position on their roster as "offensive weapon." Your move, Chip Kelly.

Jacquizz Rodgers			Height: 5-6		Weight: 196			College: Oregon State				Draft: 2011/5 (145)		Born: 6-Feb-1990		Age: 23			Risk: Green
Year	Team	G/GS	Snaps	Runs	Yds	Yd/R	TD	FUM	DVOA	Rk	DYAR	Rk	YAR	Suc%	Rk	BTkl	Rec	Pass	Yds	C%	Yd/C	TD	YAC	DVOA	Rk	DYAR	Rk
2011	ATL	16/0	316	57	205	3.6	1	1	-9.8%	--	-3	--	-3	46%	--	19	21	28	188	79%	9.0	1	6.5	32.5%	4	60	15
2012	ATL	16/0	464	94	362	3.9	1	0	-10.9%	--	-9	--	-12	38%	--	26	53	59	402	90%	7.6	1	8.2	26.1%	4	135	4
2013	ATL			89	374	4.2	2	1	-3.6%							56	66	517	85%	9.2	2		26.8%			

Rodgers was a primary beneficiary of Dirk Koetter's screen pass-heavy attack, and that gaudy catch rate shows that the Quiz was an under-used resource in the passing game. There is a notion around Atlanta that Rodgers should have been the guy to take over the bulk of the carries with Michael Turner gone. Despite his size, Rodgers is built like a tank, and broke more tackles than Turner despite having over a hundred fewer carries. But the team brought in Steven Jackson to be the bellcow, seemingly relegating Rodgers to the familiar change-of-pace and third-down back role once more.

Evan Royster			Height: 6-0		Weight: 218			College: Penn State				Draft: 2011/6 (177)		Born: 26-Nov-1987		Age: 26			Risk: Green
Year	Team	G/GS	Snaps	Runs	Yds	Yd/R	TD	FUM	DVOA	Rk	DYAR	Rk	YAR	Suc%	Rk	BTkl	Rec	Pass	Yds	C%	Yd/C	TD	YAC	DVOA	Rk	DYAR	Rk
2011	WAS	6/2	155	56	328	5.9	0	0	45.7%	--	122	--	119	64%	--	5	9	13	68	69%	7.6	0	6.9	-6.7%	--	5	--
2012	WAS	16/0	225	23	88	3.8	2	0	23.6%	--	32	--	33	43%	--	2	15	23	109	65%	7.3	0	7.7	-34.2%	--	-23	--
2013	WAS			47	198	4.2	1	1	-2.0%							17	23	147	74%	8.7	0		7.7%			

Royster did manage to lead all Redskins running backs in receptions in 2012, but that was more about Alfred Morris' limitations as a receiver than Royster's specific skill set. Believe it or not, there was a time in early September when Royster was projected by some to be the team's starting running back, but Morris quickly removed that thought from the picture. Now, Royster is a pure backup who may find little pockets of playing time around Morris' continued ascent if he can get past the knee issues that plagued him in 2012.

Kevin Smith   Height: 6-1   Weight: 217   College: UCF   Draft: 2008/3 (64)   Born: 17-Dec-1986   Age: 27   Risk: N/A

Year	Team	G/GS	Snaps	Runs	Yds	Yd/R	TD	FUM	DVOA	Rk	DYAR	Rk	YAR	Suc%	Rk	BTkl	Rec	Pass	Yds	C%	Yd/C	TD	YAC	DVOA	Rk	DYAR	Rk
2010	DET	6/0	156	34	133	3.9	0	1	-26.4%	--	-23	--	-25	29%	--	2	11	16	123	69%	11.2	0	9.5	38.7%	--	50	--
2011	DET	7/4	281	72	356	4.9	4	1	5.1%	--	42	--	72	40%	--	13	22	28	179	79%	8.1	3	9.5	19.8%	12	52	21
2012	DET	13/2	191	37	134	3.6	1	0	-4.4%	--	6	--	-1	41%	--	0	10	16	79	63%	7.9	1	10.0	17.0%	--	27	--

He was the opening-day starter for the Lions and scored a touchdown against the Rams in a comeback win, but Smith watched his time share disappear after Mikel Leshoure's big Week 3 game against the Titans. Smith had a grand total of eight carries after Week 2. It's enough to drive a man to nihilism. Sure enough, Smith admitted that he felt there was "probably nothing" he could do to get back in the game plan after Week 6. "I guess I wasn't good enough on a 4-12 team ... I guess the guys that were in front of me made enough plays to keep me on the bench," Smith said after the season. Smith is good in both pass protection and as a receiver, so if he stays healthy and keep Kierkegaard out of his head, he'd made a pretty solid third-down back for some team.

Jason Snelling   Height: 5-11   Weight: 235   College: Virginia   Draft: 2007/7 (244)   Born: 29-Dec-1983   Age: 30   Risk: Red

Year	Team	G/GS	Snaps	Runs	Yds	Yd/R	TD	FUM	DVOA	Rk	DYAR	Rk	YAR	Suc%	Rk	BTkl	Rec	Pass	Yds	C%	Yd/C	TD	YAC	DVOA	Rk	DYAR	Rk
2010	ATL	14/0	472	87	324	3.7	2	2	-3.8%	--	26	--	27	44%	--	13	44	51	303	86%	6.9	3	5.8	1.8%	30	40	26
2011	ATL	15/0	315	44	151	3.4	0	0	-22.9%	--	-25	--	-22	39%	--	8	26	32	179	81%	6.9	1	5.8	24.9%	8	60	16
2012	ATL	16/2	228	18	63	3.5	0	1	-19.6%	--	-9	--	-9	39%	--	7	31	35	203	89%	6.5	1	6.9	-8.8%	29	10	30
2013	ATL			21	70	3.4	1	1	-11.8%								27	32	191	84%	7.1	1		9.4%			

Snelling's usage rate fell to levels not seen since he was a young'un, and his long-awaited moment (Michael Turner's banishment to the Old Backs Home) came too late for Snelling to capitalize. He's a useful receiver out of the backfield, which is important in Dirk Koetter's offense, but that's about all he is at this point.

C.J. Spiller   Height: 5-11   Weight: 195   College: Clemson   Draft: 2010/1 (9)   Born: 15-Aug-1987   Age: 26   Risk: Green

Year	Team	G/GS	Snaps	Runs	Yds	Yd/R	TD	FUM	DVOA	Rk	DYAR	Rk	YAR	Suc%	Rk	BTkl	Rec	Pass	Yds	C%	Yd/C	TD	YAC	DVOA	Rk	DYAR	Rk
2010	BUF	14/1	235	74	283	3.8	0	2	-11.3%	--	-11	--	-22	43%	--	9	24	30	157	80%	6.5	1	6.6	2.5%	28	25	35
2011	BUF	16/11	462	107	561	5.2	4	2	6.4%	13	68	23	62	51%	13	17	39	54	269	74%	6.9	2	6.6	10.7%	21	80	11
2012	BUF	16/9	568	207	1244	6.0	6	3	27.6%	1	301	3	291	55%	3	34	43	57	459	75%	10.7	2	11.8	16.3%	9	91	7
2013	BUF			239	1173	4.9	5	3	3.5%								59	87	485	68%	8.2	3		2.6%			

It seemed ridiculous when the Bills took C.J. Spiller with the ninth overall pick of the 2010 draft despite having Fred Jackson around. Actually, it still seems a little bit ridiculous, but it worked out better than we expected in the long run because Spiller had a breakout season just as Jackson appeared to hit the age wall. Our doubts were never about Spiller himself, who is incredibly fast. He has great vision to find the holes and explodes through them like C-4. Once he gets into the open field, he's very difficult to take down, and he was fourth in the league in broken tackles last year. The KUBIAK projections expect regression because that's what usually happens when a guy gains six yards per carry, but Spiller has a pretty good chance to defy those odds—not to get six yards per carry again, but at least to get more than five.

Darren Sproles   Height: 5-6   Weight: 181   College: Kansas State   Draft: 2005/4 (130)   Born: 20-Jun-1983   Age: 30   Risk: Red

Year	Team	G/GS	Snaps	Runs	Yds	Yd/R	TD	FUM	DVOA	Rk	DYAR	Rk	YAR	Suc%	Rk	BTkl	Rec	Pass	Yds	C%	Yd/C	TD	YAC	DVOA	Rk	DYAR	Rk
2010	SD	16/3	409	50	267	5.3	0	1	-20.1%	--	-20	--	-9	34%	--	7	59	75	520	79%	8.8	2	8.2	21.8%	11	145	6
2011	NO	16/4	492	87	603	6.9	2	0	46.2%	--	193	--	194	53%	--	16	86	111	710	77%	8.3	7	8.2	25.8%	6	261	1
2012	NO	13/6	444	48	244	5.1	1	0	10.9%	--	34	--	25	44%	--	12	75	104	667	72%	8.9	7	8.9	21.5%	7	214	1
2013	NO			69	349	5.0	1	2	5.0%								77	105	748	73%	9.7	6		27.5%			

Few free-agent acquisitions have fit in with their new team as well as Sproles did with the Saints. He set an NFL record in all-purpose yards in 2011, achieving a near-instant mindmeld with Drew Brees in the process. 2012 was tougher on the diminutive one. He broke his hand, missed three games, was treated almost as a No. 1 receiver by enemy defenses, and had his lowest seasonal rushing total since 2007. After 39 red-zone touches in 2011, he had 24 last year. Now 30 years old, Sproles isn't likely to be quite the player he was, but so long as he remains healthy he'll strike fear in the hearts of defensive coordinators.

Zac Stacy   Height: 5-8   Weight: 216   College: Vanderbilt   Draft: 2013/5 (160)   Born: 9-Apr-1991   Age: 22   Risk: Yellow

Year	Team	G/GS	Snaps	Runs	Yds	Yd/R	TD	FUM	DVOA	Rk	DYAR	Rk	YAR	Suc%	Rk	BTkl	Rec	Pass	Yds	C%	Yd/C	TD	YAC	DVOA	Rk	DYAR	Rk
2013	STL			91	444	4.9	1	2	3.0%							13	20	118	65%	9.1	0		-4.5%			

Stacy has been a surprising early pick in some mock fantasy drafts simply because somebody has to run the ball in St. Louis. He starts training camp third on the depth chart, but nobody really has any idea who is going to get how many carries in St. Louis this season. Stacy rushed for better than 1,100 yards and 5.5 yards per carry in each of his last two seasons at Vanderbilt, with +37.5 Adj. POE in the two seasons combined, and his 100.8 Speed Score suggests he should get a chance to show what he can do.

James Starks   Height: 6-2   Weight: 218   College: Buffalo   Draft: 2010/6 (193)   Born: 25-Feb-1986   Age: 27   Risk: Yellow

Year	Team	G/GS	Snaps	Runs	Yds	Yd/R	TD	FUM	DVOA	Rk	DYAR	Rk	YAR	Suc%	Rk	BTkl	Rec	Pass	Yds	C%	Yd/C	TD	YAC	DVOA	Rk	DYAR	Rk
2010	GB	3/0	57	29	101	3.5	0	0	6.2%	--	14	--	3	48%	--	2	2	4	15	50%	7.5	0	6.0	-32.5%	--	-4	--
2011	GB	13/2	431	133	578	4.3	1	2	-4.5%	37	22	39	6	49%	19	16	29	38	216	79%	7.4	0	6.0	6.7%	23	39	26
2012	GB	6/2	124	71	255	3.6	1	1	-4.3%	--	13	--	-3	51%	--	5	4	6	31	67%	7.8	0	10.5	-24.9%	--	-4	--
2013	GB			52	232	4.5	2	2	0.3%								13	15	105	87%	8.1	0		12.9%			

The injury history begins at the University of Buffalo, where Starks tore an ACL before the draft. He came back in time to "revitalize" the Packers run game in 2010, then had a chronic ankle injury in 2011 and dealt with an undisclosed knee injury and turf toe in 2012. The Packers reportedly placed him on the trade block after selecting Eddie Lacy and Johnathan Franklin at the draft. The trade block suffered a strained hamstring trying to find a way to make him attractive to other teams.

LaRod Stephens-Howling   Height: 5-7   Weight: 180   College: Pittsburgh   Draft: 2009/7 (240)   Born: 26-Apr-1987   Age: 26   Risk: Green

Year	Team	G/GS	Snaps	Runs	Yds	Yd/R	TD	FUM	DVOA	Rk	DYAR	Rk	YAR	Suc%	Rk	BTkl	Rec	Pass	Yds	C%	Yd/C	TD	YAC	DVOA	Rk	DYAR	Rk
2010	ARI	13/2	115	23	113	4.9	1	0	8.9%	--	17	--	20	54%	--	3	16	22	111	68%	6.9	0	5.7	-5.7%	--	11	--
2011	ARI	14/1	139	43	167	3.9	0	0	-16.7%	--	-14	--	-17	40%	--	2	13	17	234	76%	18.0	2	5.7	85.3%	--	101	--
2012	ARI	14/5	337	111	357	3.2	4	0	-22.9%	40	-63	39	-72	34%	42	16	17	30	106	57%	6.2	0	7.9	-46.0%	46	-48	45
2013	PIT			51	243	4.8	1	1	2.1%								20	27	155	74%	7.7	1		3.5%			

Stephens-Howling led the Cardinals in rushing attempts in 2012, but that was as a result of injuries to Beanie Wells and Ryan Williams as opposed to anything in the former seventh-round pick's skill set that screamed "feature back" all of a sudden. The Cardinals made him an offer he apparently could refuse in the offseason, and "The Hyphen" signed a one-year, $780,000 contract with the Steelers. He'll be used as a situational back (i.e., a shorter, smaller, quicker guy who can get open in certain schemes) and as a special-teams weapon.

Jeremy Stewart   Height: 6-1   Weight: 218   College: Stanford   Draft: 2012/FA   Born: 17-Feb-1989   Age: 24   Risk: Red

Year	Team	G/GS	Snaps	Runs	Yds	Yd/R	TD	FUM	DVOA	Rk	DYAR	Rk	YAR	Suc%	Rk	BTkl	Rec	Pass	Yds	C%	Yd/C	TD	YAC	DVOA	Rk	DYAR	Rk
2012	OAK	4/0	66	25	101	4.0	0	0	-8.3%	--	0	--	4	32%	--	1	8	8	62	100%	7.8	0	9.6	23.7%	--	11	--
2013	OAK			42	163	3.9	2	1	-5.8%								11	14	55	79%	5.0	0		-11.7%			

Stewart worked his way up from the practice squad to the active roster in 2012, getting a handful of touches each week throughout December. In that small sampling, the undrafted second-year pro from Stanford showed impressive smoothness and fluidity, along with some hints of elusiveness. He was able to fully supplant the more electrifying (but clearly less dependable) Taiwan Jones on the depth chart, and will likely see an expanded role in 2013 if he holds onto the No. 3 running back spot.

Jonathan Stewart   Height: 5-10   Weight: 235   College: Oregon   Draft: 2008/1 (13)   Born: 21-Mar-1987   Age: 26   Risk: Yellow

Year	Team	G/GS	Snaps	Runs	Yds	Yd/R	TD	FUM	DVOA	Rk	DYAR	Rk	YAR	Suc%	Rk	BTkl	Rec	Pass	Yds	C%	Yd/C	TD	YAC	DVOA	Rk	DYAR	Rk
2010	CAR	14/7	351	178	770	4.3	2	4	-12.2%	37	-18	37	-14	36%	45	25	8	14	103	57%	12.9	1	8.4	11.6%	--	19	--
2011	CAR	16/3	577	142	761	5.4	4	1	23.4%	2	194	4	178	53%	8	21	47	61	413	77%	8.8	1	8.4	19.1%	14	105	7
2012	CAR	9/6	312	93	336	3.6	1	2	-18.4%	--	-36	--	-55	42%	--	5	17	23	157	74%	9.2	1	10.5	15.0%	--	34	--
2013	CAR			151	666	4.4	6	3	2.5%								34	51	302	67%	8.9	1		2.6%			

Before the season, Stewart signed an extension that guaranteed him $22.5 million. Stewart then had problems with both ankles and a toe that bothered him all year and effectively ruined his entire campaign. Stewart underwent ankle surgery after the season and was held out of OTAs and minicamp, but was expected back for training camp. At that point, he will either back up DeAngelo Williams, or take the lead position with Williams as his co-pilot, depending on how Ron Rivera is feeling that day. Stewart hasn't gotten 20 carries in a game since 2010, but he is four years younger than Williams, so he does have more value in dynasty leagues.

Phillip Tanner   Height: 6-0   Weight: 214   College: Middle Tennessee   Draft: 2011/FA   Born: 8-Aug-1988   Age: 25   Risk: Green

Year	Team	G/GS	Snaps	Runs	Yds	Yd/R	TD	FUM	DVOA	Rk	DYAR	Rk	YAR	Suc%	Rk	BTkl	Rec	Pass	Yds	C%	Yd/C	TD	YAC	DVOA	Rk	DYAR	Rk
2011	DAL	9/0	48	22	76	3.5	1	0	-20.2%	--	-12	--	-2	45%	--	1	2	2	19	100%	9.5	0	7.5	93.4%	--	15	--
2012	DAL	14/0	89	25	61	2.4	0	0	-58.2%	--	-53	--	-44	38%	--	5	4	6	41	83%	10.3	0	7.6	62.9%	--	28	--
2013	DAL			29	136	4.7	0	1	0.9%								10	13	85	77%	8.5	0		9.5%			

Tanner found it tough to get carries in 2012—he was demoted to healthy inactive status just as several backs were fighting for time in the wake of DeMarco Murray's foot injury. He struggled to hit the hole, and pass protection was an issue. However, Bryan Broaddus of the Cowboys' official site wrote in May that Tanner now looks lighter and quicker, looked better when approaching gaps, and caught the ball well on hot routes. Of course, that could change when there are two rogue factors added—opponents and contact—but Tanner may have done enough to stick in a running back rotation that looks uncertain at best.

Ben Tate   Height: 5-11   Weight: 220   College: Auburn   Draft: 2010/2 (58)   Born: 21-Aug-1988   Age: 25   Risk: Green

Year	Team	G/GS	Snaps	Runs	Yds	Yd/R	TD	FUM	DVOA	Rk	DYAR	Rk	YAR	Suc%	Rk	BTkl	Rec	Pass	Yds	C%	Yd/C	TD	YAC	DVOA	Rk	DYAR	Rk
2011	HOU	15/2	328	175	942	5.4	4	4	12.5%	8	151	10	162	53%	9	19	13	19	98	68%	7.5	0	6.3	-2.7%	--	12	--
2012	HOU	11/0	143	65	279	4.3	2	1	-2.2%	--	18	--	33	49%	--	9	11	11	49	100%	4.5	0	3.6	-27.7%	--	-9	--
2013	HOU			112	490	4.4	3	1	-1.0%								16	20	103	80%	6.4	0		-5.3%			

Ah, the plight of a running back behind a good starter. Tate's injury woes (and Arian Foster's health) cost him the more prominent role he played in 2011. He looked good against the Jaguars, running for 74 yards and two scores in Week 2, then didn't find the end zone the rest of the season and only cracked 30 yards in a game again at the end of blowouts against the Ravens and Patriots. He's fast in a straight line, but lacks Foster's vision and struggles in the red zone. If the Texans are smart, they'll limit Foster's touches and get Tate more carries, but the days where Tate looked like a future starter who might draw a pick like the second-rounder the Texans used to get him are long gone.

Daniel Thomas   Height: 6-2   Weight: 228   College: Kansas State   Draft: 2011/2 (62)   Born: 29-Oct-1987   Age: 26   Risk: Green

Year	Team	G/GS	Snaps	Runs	Yds	Yd/R	TD	FUM	DVOA	Rk	DYAR	Rk	YAR	Suc%	Rk	BTkl	Rec	Pass	Yds	C%	Yd/C	TD	YAC	DVOA	Rk	DYAR	Rk
2011	MIA	13/2	367	165	581	3.5	0	2	-24.7%	50	-110	51	-100	42%	43	9	12	16	72	75%	6.0	1	5.3	11.8%	--	20	--
2012	MIA	12/0	323	91	325	3.6	4	3	-10.8%	--	-9	--	3	51%	--	13	15	22	156	68%	10.4	0	9.6	0.8%	--	14	--
2013	MIA			117	452	3.8	5	3	-10.8%								16	22	112	73%	7.0	0		-5.6%			

At least in Miami, the Thomas ship has sailed. Even though he's only three years into his career, he's basically revealed himself to be a plodding short-yardage back; hence, our touchdown projection. Otherwise, he doesn't fit Miami's scheme, wasn't hand-picked by the current coaching staff, and frankly isn't very good.

Pierre Thomas   Height: 5-11   Weight: 210   College: Illinois   Draft: 2007/FA   Born: 18-Dec-1984   Age: 29   Risk: Green

Year	Team	G/GS	Snaps	Runs	Yds	Yd/R	TD	FUM	DVOA	Rk	DYAR	Rk	YAR	Suc%	Rk	BTkl	Rec	Pass	Yds	C%	Yd/C	TD	YAC	DVOA	Rk	DYAR	Rk
2010	NO	6/3	219	83	269	3.2	2	0	0.6%	--	36	--	24	50%	--	17	29	30	201	100%	6.9	0	8.7	17.0%	14	56	19
2011	NO	16/7	389	110	562	5.1	5	1	30.0%	1	180	5	180	61%	1	20	50	59	425	85%	8.5	1	8.7	16.2%	17	103	8
2012	NO	15/4	385	105	473	4.5	1	0	15.1%	6	97	14	80	53%	6	11	39	53	354	74%	9.1	1	9.3	18.7%	8	99	6
2013	NO			122	554	4.5	3	4	-4.0%								38	45	363	84%	9.6	1		23.9%			

The fact New Orleans kept Thomas and dealt Chris Ivory shows how much they value Thomas' receiving skills. Quietly, he is as much of a dual threat as Darren Sproles, and his third-down and red-zone receiving numbers are very solid. With Ivory getting dealt to the Jets, Thomas' versatility ought to keep him on the field more often in 2013.

Mike Tolbert   Height: 5-9   Weight: 243   College: Coastal Carolina   Draft: 2008/FA   Born: 23-Nov-1985   Age: 28   Risk: Green

Year	Team	G/GS	Snaps	Runs	Yds	Yd/R	TD	FUM	DVOA	Rk	DYAR	Rk	YAR	Suc%	Rk	BTkl	Rec	Pass	Yds	C%	Yd/C	TD	YAC	DVOA	Rk	DYAR	Rk
2010	SD	15/4	369	182	735	4.0	11	5	-2.0%	24	46	25	66	51%	11	21	25	30	216	87%	8.6	0	8.1	31.3%	6	75	16
2011	SD	15/1	484	121	490	4.0	8	2	-3.1%	34	30	35	49	48%	22	19	54	79	433	68%	8.0	2	8.1	-2.1%	30	54	19
2012	CAR	16/5	445	54	183	3.4	7	0	25.8%	--	103	--	106	65%	--	10	27	39	268	69%	9.9	0	10.2	7.7%	20	48	20
2013	CAR			38	146	3.8	4	0	15.6%								30	43	185	70%	6.2	1		-8.8%			

Any team that has Cam Newton, DeAngelo Williams, and Jonathan Stewart at their disposal will only give the ball to Mike Tolbert in specific situations, and those situations will not involve speed in any way. As a runner, Tolbert is a short-yardage specialist. His average carry came with 5.9 yards to go for a first down, last among all runners with at least 50 carries. Twenty-five of his carries came with 1 or 2 yards to go, and he converted 21 times. Newton also had 25 short-yardage carries and only converted 18 times, while Stewart and Williams went a combined 15-of-22. Surprisingly, more than half of Tolbert's carries came in single-back sets, though many of those came late in the year when Stewart was on the sidelines. Still, given this rushing info and Carolina's surprisingly rare use of two-back formations, it's clear that Tolbert's rushing ability is nearly as important as what he can do as a blocker.

Robert Turbin   Height: 5-10   Weight: 222   College: Utah State   Draft: 2012/4 (106)   Born: 2-Dec-1989   Age: 24   Risk: Green

Year	Team	G/GS	Snaps	Runs	Yds	Yd/R	TD	FUM	DVOA	Rk	DYAR	Rk	YAR	Suc%	Rk	BTkl	Rec	Pass	Yds	C%	Yd/C	TD	YAC	DVOA	Rk	DYAR	Rk
2012	SEA	16/0	224	80	354	4.4	0	0	-5.2%	--	11	--	8	46%	--	7	19	23	181	83%	9.5	0	6.7	21.2%	--	48	--
2013	SEA			71	350	4.9	1	1	7.0%								13	16	108	81%	8.3	0		18.7%			

Thirty of Turbin's carries and 139 of his yards came in December blowouts of Arizona and Buffalo. Otherwise, he never got more than seven carries in a game. That usage, combined with the arrival of Christine Michael in the draft, suggests that Turbin may see a reduced role in the offense in 2013. Pete Carroll said, however, that he had not seen Michael do much pass blocking, an area where Turbin grew stronger as the season progressed. Running with the collegiate theme of our Seattle chapter, Turbin is sort of like a player coming off a redshirt season, hoping his experience will be able to hold off a more talented true freshman (Michael), while both players wait for opportunities behind an upperclassman (Marshawn Lynch).

Michael Turner   Height: 5-10   Weight: 247   College: Northern Illinois   Draft: 2004/5 (154)   Born: 13-Feb-1982   Age: 31   Risk: N/A

Year	Team	G/GS	Snaps	Runs	Yds	Yd/R	TD	FUM	DVOA	Rk	DYAR	Rk	YAR	Suc%	Rk	BTkl	Rec	Pass	Yds	C%	Yd/C	TD	YAC	DVOA	Rk	DYAR	Rk
2010	ATL	16/15	607	334	1371	4.1	12	2	-1.3%	22	96	18	128	46%	18	38	12	20	85	60%	7.1	0	7.4	-28.2%	--	-16	--
2011	ATL	16/15	588	301	1340	4.5	11	3	-3.4%	36	66	25	101	45%	34	42	17	26	168	65%	9.9	0	7.4	7.6%	22	32	31
2012	ATL	16/16	476	222	800	3.6	10	3	-16.6%	37	-79	40	-87	43%	34	20	19	30	128	63%	6.7	1	7.6	-33.6%	42	-33	41

Clearly, it was time for Turner to go. His numbers were way down across the board, even in broken tackles, where he traditionally has ranked highly. But let's take a moment to appreciate Turner's legacy in Atlanta. He was the best free-agent signing in franchise history, and a key element in the rebirth of the team out of the ashes of the Bobby Petrino and Michael Vick debacles. In 2008, a season when the Falcons were breaking in a rookie quarterback, the team rode new acquisition Turner to 1,699 yards and 17 touchdowns. That led to a rather miraculous playoff berth, which was followed by three more in four seasons. Now that the Falcons are a passing team led by Matt Ryan, and Turner's usefulness is gone. His importance to the franchise shouldn't be forgotten.

Shane Vereen   Height: 5-10   Weight: 205   College: California   Draft: 2011/2 (56)   Born: 2-Mar-1989   Age: 24   Risk: Green

Year	Team	G/GS	Snaps	Runs	Yds	Yd/R	TD	FUM	DVOA	Rk	DYAR	Rk	YAR	Suc%	Rk	BTkl	Rec	Pass	Yds	C%	Yd/C	TD	YAC	DVOA	Rk	DYAR	Rk
2011	NE	5/0	26	15	57	3.8	1	0	-2.1%	--	4	--	1	40%	--	2	0	0	0	--	0.0	0	--	--	--	--	--
2012	NE	13/1	161	62	251	4.0	3	1	9.6%	--	47	--	52	52%	--	4	8	13	149	62%	18.6	1	17.5	69.6%	--	64	--
2013	NE			70	314	4.5	4	1	7.5%								38	47	435	81%	11.4	2		32.9%			

Vereen is obviously the go-to guy to take over Danny Woodhead's role in the Patriots offense, but a number of reports from Patriots beat writers suggest that he might fill part of Aaron Hernandez's role as well. Although Vereen only had 13 pass targets during last year's regular season, we finally saw his potential as a receiving mismatch in the Divisional round game against Houston, when he caught five passes for 83 yards and two touchdowns. On two of those receptions, Vereen lined up wide and was covered by a linebacker. It was a complete mismatch, and resulted in a 25-yard pass covered by Bradie James and a 33-yard touchdown covered by Barrett Ruud. (Actually, the word "covered" should probably be in scare quotes there.) The Patriots will get these linebacker mismatches by getting Vereen out wide, not putting him in the slot. During the regular season, Vereen lined up wide 24 times and in the slot only once; in the playoffs, he lined up wide nine times and never lined up in the slot. The Patriots used Woodhead the same way: 59 snaps out wide, only nine in the slot. Even Hernandez was lined up wide (62 snaps) almost as often as he was in the slot (71 snaps).

Leon Washington   Height: 5-8   Weight: 210   College: Florida State   Draft: 2006/4 (117)   Born: 29-Aug-1982   Age: 31   Risk: Green

Year	Team	G/GS	Snaps	Runs	Yds	Yd/R	TD	FUM	DVOA	Rk	DYAR	Rk	YAR	Suc%	Rk	BTkl	Rec	Pass	Yds	C%	Yd/C	TD	YAC	DVOA	Rk	DYAR	Rk
2010	SEA	16/0	115	27	100	3.7	1	0	0.9%	--	13	--	4	44%	--	2	9	13	79	69%	8.8	0	7.6	14.6%	--	21	--
2011	SEA	16/1	154	53	248	4.7	1	0	-9.1%	--	-1	--	0	36%	--	5	10	14	48	71%	4.8	0	7.6	-29.6%	--	-13	--
2012	SEA	16/0	59	23	83	3.6	1	0	-9.9%	--	-1	--	-1	22%	--	2	4	8	31	50%	7.8	0	5.8	-16.4%	--	-1	--
2013	NE			46	209	4.5	2	0	8.5%								13	16	103	81%	7.9	1		11.9%			

Tied with Josh Cribbs for the most kickoff return touchdowns in NFL history, Washington was rendered expendable in Seattle by the Percy Harvin trade, and soon found a home in New England. Washington isn't much use as a runner anymore, but he's still quite good as a kickoff returner (where he has ranked third or better in total value twice in the last three seasons) and adequate returning punts.

Beanie Wells   Height: 6-1   Weight: 235   College: Ohio State   Draft: 2009/1 (31)   Born: 7-Aug-1988   Age: 25   Risk: N/A

Year	Team	G/GS	Snaps	Runs	Yds	Yd/R	TD	FUM	DVOA	Rk	DYAR	Rk	YAR	Suc%	Rk	BTkl	Rec	Pass	Yds	C%	Yd/C	TD	YAC	DVOA	Rk	DYAR	Rk
2010	ARI	13/2	226	116	397	3.4	2	1	-13.8%	40	-23	39	-20	45%	25	4	5	8	74	63%	14.8	0	5.4	27.4%	--	21	--
2011	ARI	14/14	571	245	1047	4.3	10	4	1.0%	27	101	19	99	51%	12	15	10	16	52	63%	5.2	0	5.4	-43.9%	--	-22	--
2012	ARI	8/7	150	88	234	2.7	5	1	-21.6%	--	-48	--	-68	34%	--	0	1	1	24	100%	24.0	0	19.0	198.8%	--	13	--

When you're supposed to be a power back, a serious decline in your ability to break tackles is generally a very bad sign. In 2011, Wells broke tackles on just 5.9 percent of his total plays (15 broken tackles on 255 touches), which was among the league's lowest totals for qualifying backs. In 2012, Wells upped the ante with *not one broken tackle* on 88 runs and one catch. The Cardinals released the former first-round pick in March, and at press time, no other team has picked him up. Due to the accumulation of injuries through his career and his limited overall game, Wells is an NFL afterthought at the age of 25. Running back is a fungible position, but this is ridiculous.

DeAngelo Williams Height: 5-8   Weight: 210   College: Memphis   Draft: 2006/1 (27)   Born: 25-Apr-1983   Age: 30   Risk: Green

Year	Team	G/GS	Snaps	Runs	Yds	Yd/R	TD	FUM	DVOA	Rk	DYAR	Rk	YAR	Suc%	Rk	BTkl	Rec	Pass	Yds	C%	Yd/C	TD	YAC	DVOA	Rk	DYAR	Rk
2010	CAR	6/6	173	87	361	4.1	1	1	-17.2%	--	-16	--	-18	30%	--	10	11	13	61	85%	5.5	0	6.3	-2.4%	--	8	--
2011	CAR	16/14	447	155	836	5.4	7	0	18.0%	3	158	8	147	46%	28	13	16	25	135	64%	8.4	0	6.3	5.9%	24	28	34
2012	CAR	16/10	417	173	737	4.3	5	2	-6.7%	26	14	25	19	48%	22	9	13	20	187	65%	14.4	2	16.4	38.9%	--	60	--
2013	CAR			170	814	4.8	4	2	8.5%								17	23	129	74%	7.6	0		5.2%			

The Panthers signed Williams to a horrible contract in 2011, not only because it overpaid at running back, a position where competent players are nearly always available, but because it gave the Panthers a gargantuan cap hit starting in 2013, up to $3 million more than Williams was actually making each season. It ensured Williams would be cut, perhaps even before the 2013 season, but player and team agreed to a reworked deal in May that makes Williams affordable in Carolina for several seasons. In signing the deal, Williams acknowledged that he would be phased out in favor of the younger Jonathan Stewart before long. He may also have to contend with rookie runner Kenjon Barner. Williams' DVOA last year was his lowest ever in a healthy season, but he's still capable of explosive plays. Just ask the Saints; Williams burned them for 210 yards in Week 17, including runs of 22, 54, and 65 yards. That's a big-time day, even if it was against the Saints.

Ryan Williams Height: 5-9   Weight: 212   College: Virginia Tech   Draft: 2011/2 (38)   Born: 9-Apr-1990   Age: 23   Risk: Green

Year	Team	G/GS	Snaps	Runs	Yds	Yd/R	TD	FUM	DVOA	Rk	DYAR	Rk	YAR	Suc%	Rk	BTkl	Rec	Pass	Yds	C%	Yd/C	TD	YAC	DVOA	Rk	DYAR	Rk
2012	ARI	5/3	140	58	164	2.8	0	2	-45.5%	--	-85	--	-100	34%	--	4	7	10	44	70%	6.3	0	5.0	-14.1%	--	0	--
2013	ARI			81	346	4.3	2	2	-3.6%								16	21	132	76%	8.2	0		7.1%			

From the "You may remember this" file: At Virginia Tech, Williams was a well-rounded runner who could hit the hole with quickness and authority, but displayed patience on plays that took longer to develop. An inside and outside runner with pass-catching and blocking ability, Williams was selected by the Cardinals in the second round of the 2011 draft, and that was commensurate with his consensus overall value. Sadly, injuries have robbed him of any chance to show that potential—he missed his entire rookie season with a ruptured patella tendon and played just five games in 2012 behind a craptacular offensive line before a shoulder injury cut his second season short. According to Williams, the knee was affecting his thought process so much, making him afraid to run in 2012, that the shoulder injury was "a blessing." Williams has said that he's past those injuries, and the mental hurdles that resulted from them. Now he just has to get past Bruce Arians' desire to make Rashard Mendenhall a clear starting back rather than the leader of a committee.

David Wilson Height: 5-10   Weight: 206   College: Virginia Tech   Draft: 2012/1 (32)   Born: 15-Jun-1991   Age: 22   Risk: Green

Year	Team	G/GS	Snaps	Runs	Yds	Yd/R	TD	FUM	DVOA	Rk	DYAR	Rk	YAR	Suc%	Rk	BTkl	Rec	Pass	Yds	C%	Yd/C	TD	YAC	DVOA	Rk	DYAR	Rk
2012	NYG	16/2	125	71	358	5.0	4	1	1.5%	--	30	--	29	39%	--	6	4	9	34	44%	8.5	1	3.5	-17.4%	--	-2	--
2013	NYG			228	1098	4.8	8	3	8.6%								26	38	195	68%	7.5	1		-4.8%			

David Wilson alternated between exciting and alienating Giants fans last year. He fumbled in the opener against the Cowboys on just his second carry; that landed him in Tom Coughlin's doghouse for weeks. And while he had just four carries over the next month, he managed to take one of two rushes against the Browns 40 yards for a score. He later set a franchise record for 327 all-purpose yards against the Saints in December, but then got into an inane backflips controversy with his teammates that made us wonder if he secretly played for the Jets. Wilson was overshadowed by Alfred Morris and Doug Martin last year, but Wilson is more physically gifted than both players. He's landed in a good situation as the lead back on one of the league's best offenses, but he's going to share time with Andre Brown until he proves he can be a workhorse back.

Danny Woodhead Height: 5-9   Weight: 200   College: Chadron State   Draft: 2008/FA   Born: 25-Jan-1985   Age: 28   Risk: Green

Year	Team	G/GS	Snaps	Runs	Yds	Yd/R	TD	FUM	DVOA	Rk	DYAR	Rk	YAR	Suc%	Rk	BTkl	Rec	Pass	Yds	C%	Yd/C	TD	YAC	DVOA	Rk	DYAR	Rk
2010	2TM	15/3	396	97	547	5.6	5	1	40.4%	--	190	--	188	57%	--	20	34	44	379	77%	11.1	1	9.2	54.4%	1	151	4
2011	NE	15/4	367	77	351	4.6	1	0	22.6%	--	100	--	93	55%	--	3	18	31	157	58%	8.7	0	9.2	-10.9%	39	5	39
2012	NE	16/2	417	76	301	4.0	4	1	22.4%	--	101	--	75	55%	--	5	40	55	446	73%	11.2	3	9.3	35.9%	2	149	3
2013	SD			76	294	3.9	1	2	0.5%								38	50	338	76%	8.9	1		9.8%			

New Chargers general manager Tom Telesco praised Woodhead as a "dynamic runner in space," but what happens when there is no space? In New England, 83 percent of Woodhead's carries came with six or fewer men in the box. Things won't be so open without Tom Brady to scare opposing defenses, and last year only 27 percent of San Diego carries came with six or fewer men in the box.

Going Deep

Anthony Allen, BAL: Allen was briefly the Ravens No. 1 running back in the 2012 offseason: Ray Rice was holding out, and Bernard Pierce had not yet established himself as a competitor. Rice returned, Pierce stepped up, and Allen fought to hold on to the No. 3 role. Allen is a straight-line thumper with minimal receiving skills; he saw nearly all of his action in "that Bengals game" in Week 17. He was useful enough on special teams to earn a tender offer from the Ravens, so he will be back this season, but he should not expect many reps with the first-team offense. (2012 stats: 16 carries for 61 yards, 1 TD, 9 DYAR, 4.4% DVOA)

Armando Allen, CHI: This Notre Dame alum is a third-string running back who can actually contribute on special teams; that was enough for Allen to beat out Kahlil Bell and keep his roster spot all season. (2012 stats: 27 carries for 124 yards, 7 DYAR, -2.3% DVOA; receiving stats: 4-for-5, 31 yards, 8 DYAR, 8.9% DVOA)

Kenjon Barner, CAR: Barner rushed for 1,767 yards and 21 touchdowns in his senior season at Oregon, with an awesome 5.6 highlight yards per opportunity and +34.8 Adj. POE. Still, Barner's Speed Score was only 93.9, and at 196 pounds he lacks the size and explosive speed you're looking for in a front-line running back. The Panthers see him more as a return specialist.

Baron Batch, PIT: BARON BATCH IS NOT A REAL PERSON HE IS CHARLIE BATCH WEARING A MONOCLE CHARLIE SHOWED UP ONE DAY IN THE MONOCLE AND CLAIMED TO BE A RUNNING BACK BUT TODD HALEY DID NOT RECOGNIZE HIM AND GAVE HIM REPS EVENTUALLY MAKING BATCH THE GUY WHO GETS ONE OR TWO INEXPLICABLE CARRIES PER GAME BECAUSE HALEY IS OCD ABOUT RUNNING BACKS AND BATCH IS LISTED FIFTH ON THE STEELERS DEPTH CHART BUT HE IS NOT REAL AND CHARLIE IS RETIRED AND POSSIBLY TRYING TO SCAM TWO PENSIONS DO NOT BE FOOLED WATCH THE DOCUMENTARY "BATCH CHANGE" AT BARONBATCHTRUTHERS.ORG TO FIND OUT MORE. (2012 stats: 25 carries for 49 yards, 1 TD, -21 DYAR, -28.7% DVOA)

Kahlil Bell, FA: Bell bounced on and off the roster for both the Jets and Bears last year. He had a 17.6% DVOA in 40 carries in 2009, but has posted DVOA's of -15.1% (2011, on 79 carries) and -42.7% (2012, on 29 carries) since then. Common regression principles tell us the odds of him continuing to drop roughly 30 points of DVOA a year are about the same as the odds he's on a roster next year. (2012 stats: 29 carries for 76 yards, -42 DYAR, -42.7% DVOA)

Rex Burkhead, CIN: Burkhead rushed for 1,357 yards and 15 touchdowns for Nebraska as a junior before a sprained knee limited him to eight games in 2012. The Bengals drafted him in the sixth round and plan to use him in Brian Leonard's role as a third-down blocker and receiver. Burkhead has better rushing skills than Leonard but is not a consistent blocker, and both Giovani Bernard and two-tight end sets will eat into those third-down opportunities.

Travaris Cadet, NO: Cadet's size/speed mix might allow for a breakthrough in the future, if only a) he was on a team with a less crowded backfield, and b) he could hold on to the ball with more regularity, an issue that has plagued him since his days at Appalachian State. (2012 receiving stats: 5-for-8, 44 yards, 8 DYAR, 4.9% DVOA; one carry for five yards)

Jeff Demps, TB: Which is more ridiculous: the alleged "injury" which allowed the Patriots to stash Demps on IR for the year, or Demps' expressed desire to continue to run a full track season? He theoretically could report after the IAAF world championships in mid-August, but it would take a lot of patience in today's 365-day NFL for a team to carve out a minor role for a player who will miss all of OTAs and training camp. The Bucs apparently have that patience and nothing to lose; getting Demps only cost them LaGarrette Blount, who they didn't want anyway.

Anthony Dixon, SF: Dixon remains on San Francisco's roster for reasons outside the stat sheet. Nearly 80 percent of his 1,017 career snaps have come on special teams, but he only has 21 tackles in three seasons. On offense, Dixon's participation rate is now to the point where he's the football equivalent of a tipped pitch. After a 57 percent usage rate his first two years, he touched the ball on 21 of his 32 offensive snaps (66 percent), so any sight of Dixon in San Francisco's backfield this season means he's probably getting the ball. (2012 stats: 21 carries for 78 yards, 2 TD, 23 DYAR, 15.9% DVOA)

Lance Dunbar, DAL: Dunbar wasn't invited to the 2012 scouting combine, and he was an undrafted afterthought, but he started to gain some traction as Felix Jones slipped down, and then off, Dallas' depth chart. He hit six kickoff returns for 142 yards against the Giants in late November, and that got him on the radar as a potential No. 2 back for the 2013 season. (2012 stats: 21 carries for 75 yards, -5 DYAR, -13.9% DVOA; receiving stats: 6-for-12, 33 yards, -20 DYAR, -41.4% DVOA)

Andre Ellington, ARI: It's a testament to the skittishness of NFL front offices that Ellington's mid-2012 hamstring injury made his draft stock plummet even though it—minor detail here—*didn't make him miss any actual games*. Safely assuming Ellington's hamstring is a non-issue going forward, the Cardinals gained an explosive runner (7.7 highlight yards per opportunity as a junior) for a sixth-round song. However, he's fourth on the depth chart, so that explosiveness will probably be confined to the return game in 2013.

Terrance Ganaway, STL: Ganaway rushed for 1,547 yards and 21 touchdowns in his senior season at Baylor in 2011. The Jets drafted him then cut him, and he ended up in St. Louis with just eight snaps. And then he got a 12-hour-a-week, minimum wage job at Jimmy John's in Waco. No, really. Gotta supplement that $390,000 rookie income. The Rams are deli-thin at running back, but Ganaway and his 4.67-second 40-yard dash are not freaky fast, so he's still a sub at best. He may not make the club, but at least he can make clubs. We've got dozens of these, folks.

Ryan Grant, FA: Four years ago, Ryan Grant was coming off back-to-back 1,200-yard seasons and had just finished fourth in running back DYAR. Now, in 2013, we've got no Hope, no Jobs, no Cash, and no Grants. (2012 stats: 32 carries for 132 yards, 2 TD, -16 DYAR, 3.5% DVOA)

Cyrus Gray, KC: Gray, a sixth-round pick in 2012, did not see much playing time as a rookie, perhaps because he was not very adept in pass protection. He played in 10 games on special teams and just four on offense, with six inactives being spread throughout the season. (2012 stats: 7 carries for 44 yards, 20 DYAR, 58.0% DVOA)

John Griffin, NYJ: Camp fodder who made it onto the roster for one game last year, Griffin is battling Patriots defensive end (and CFL refugee) Jason Vega to go down in history as the final member of the Northeastern Huskies to ever play in the NFL.

Jewel Hampton, SF: When Kendall Hunter hit injured reserve last November, San Francisco promoted this undrafted free agent out of Southern Illinois to their active roster, but he never saw the field. With his resume including two ACL tears and only one full year as a starter at an FCS school, that was probably the right course of action. Hampton (5-foot-9, 218 pounds, 4.56-second 40) may be a clone of Doug Martin (5-foot-9, 223 pounds, 4.55 40-yard dash) in terms of size and speed, but the best he can hope for with the 2013 49ers is taking Anthony Dixon's roster spot.

Jamie Harper, FA: Like former Titan LenDale White, Jamie Harper is a bigger back who doesn't run with nearly the power you'd expect from his frame. He makes relatively good decisions outside of a predilection to try to bounce runs even though his subpar quickness and speed don't let him make it there. Shonn Greene fills his role in a slightly different style, so the Titans cut him in the offseason. Currently unsigned. (2012 stats: 19 carries for 30 yards, 3 TD, -3 DYAR, -12.0% DVOA)

Dan Herron, CIN: "Boom" Herron made the Bengals practice squad as a sixth-round pick last year, then earned a call-up and four carries when Cedric Peerman was battling ankle injuries. Herron looked like a potential star at Ohio State in 2010, but now he's just a Brand X replacement-level running back fighting for a roster spot. (2012 stats: 4 carries for 5 yards, -12 DYAR, -95.4% DVOA)

Jacob Hester, DEN: Hester can find a role on most NFL teams thanks to his adeptness in the red zone. The former Chargers back is a good short-yardage runner who relies not on sheer power but on leverage and timing. What sets him apart is that he's capable of turning the corner or catching flairs out of the backfield. (Peyton Manning only threw him one pass last year, but in his first four seasons he averaged 14 catches for 77 yards.) Hester has a hint of wiggle that defenses don't see from most fullbacks. Hester can handle reps outside the red zone, too, though when it's not a tighter field, his multidimensionality becomes less unique and therefore less potent. (2012 stats: 17 carries for 81 yards, 2 TD, 21 DYAR, 27.4% DVOA)

Brandon Jackson, FA: The old Packers plow horse resurfaced in Cleveland to rush for 54 yards on eight carries (with the aid of one 25-yard run) in the silly season finale against the Steelers where the Browns called up everyone from their AAA affiliate. The definition of a replacement-level power back and a free agent at press time, he will sign with some team that suffers a running-back injury spree. (2012 stats: 15 DYAR, 36.1% DVOA; receiving stats: 2-for-4, 20 yards, 2 DYAR, -4.2% DVOA)

Brandon Jacobs, FA: Jacobs seemed like an ideal fit for San Francisco's scheme (i.e., power running game) and roster (i.e., they lacked a short-yardage back). Instead, he was one of the tragic figures of the 2012 season. Act I ended with a preseason knee injury. Act II ended with a Twitter-tantrum-induced three-game suspension. Act III ended with his release after the 49ers' regular-season finale. If his free-agent status at this late date is any indication, there's unlikely to be an Act IV. (2012 stats: 5 carries for 7 yards, -5 DYAR, -35.1% DVOA)

Jawan Jamison, WAS: A year ago, Jamison was on his way to one of those "Why the hell are they running this kid into the ground?" seasons that seem so common at Rutgers. Through the first eight games of the season, he averaged 24.8 carries per game, but that trailed down to 12.6 games over the last five. Jamison decided to forego his last two years of eligibility and enter the NFL draft, but he didn't exactly burn the trail on the way—he ran a 4.62-second 40 at the scouting combine, then clocked in at 4.72 at his pro day (where the home tracks are usually more favorable). The Redskins took him in the seventh round; he's not as dynamic as fellow alum Ray Rice, but he fits Washington's paradigm for backs who can wiggle in short spaces, run with power, and catch the ball on quick routes.

Taiwan Jones, OAK: Raiders GM Reggie McKenzie said he plans to move Jones from running back to cornerback. That's a disappointing outcome for the former fourth-round pick who entered the league with expectations of being a speedy, toss sweep-style ballcarrier. Jones has experience at the position, having played it in high school and early in his career at Eastern Washington. The Raiders might be the one team that's weak enough at the corner position for him to make the active roster as a No. 5. (2012 stats: 6 carries for 21 yards, 4 DYAR, 4.1% DVOA)

John Kuhn, GB: John Kuhn (or "KOOOOOOOOOOOON!" as he's known to Lambeau faithful) is the dependable fullback who is always around to take some carries when Ted Thompson's wacky running back shenanigans go awry. Now that the Packers have spent some actual draft currency on backs, look for Kuhn's role to stabilize as someone who averages a couple touches a game. He's getting up there in years, but it doesn't take crazy athleticism to do the job Kuhn does. (2012 stats: 23 carries for 63 yards, 1 DYAR, -7.9% DVOA; receiving stats: 15-for-18, 148 yards, 60 DYAR, 47.8% DVOA)

Jorvorskie Lane, MIA: Although he accounted for more touchdowns (50) at Texas A&M than Ryan Tannehill (47), Lane's route from College Station to Miami was far more circuitous. He spent one season each with the West Texas Roughnecks of the Indoor Football League and the Orlando Predators of the Arena Football League before finding an NFL home with his former head coach Mike Sherman. Per our charting stats, Lane lined up outside the backfield only four times in 303 offensive snaps last season, so his role in the Dolphins offense going forward is exclusively a lead-blocking one. (2012 stats: 13 carries for 18 yards, 2 TD, -31 DYAR, -46.8% DVOA; receiving stats: 11-for-12, 79 yards, 12 DYAR, 1.0% DVOA)

Marcus Lattimore, SF: Lattimore's advanced stats in his last two years at South Carolina never matched those of his spectacular freshman season. He had 5.3 highlight yards per opportunity with +9.1 Adj. POE as freshman, but combined for just 4.1 highlight yards per opportunity and a combined +1.9 Adj. POE in his sophomore and junior years—which were both ended by knee injuries. Even if everything proceeds swimmingly with his knee rehabilitation, Lattimore may get the rare two-year rookie redshirt. Both Frank Gore and Kendall Hunter are signed through 2014, and even if the 49ers decide to let Gore go after this season, they would still have Hunter and LaMichael James as their top two backs the following year. Also, if Lattimore is going to avoid injuries in the NFL, he will need to adopt a less upright running style (see: Darren McFadden), and that process won't even begin in earnest until he and the team have 100 percent confidence that his knee is healthy.

Stefan Logan, FA: <Australian Accent>If you've ventured into the metropolitan Detroit area at just the right time over the last few seasons, you may have witnessed a wild Stefan Logan attempt a trick play. It happens once in a blue moon, but when the scenario calls for it, he can be more than just a kick returner desperately trying to protect his football eggs from the evil gunners who would have him killed. Of course, now that he was released, he may be an endangered species, so enjoy these clips while you can. Next, on *The Football Hunter*, a completed Tim Tebow checkdown pass. Crikey!</Australian accent> (2012 stats: 3 carries for 17 yards, 8 DYAR, 12.2% DVOA; receiving stats: 6-for-7, 28 yards, 7 DYAR, 1.7% DVOA)

Kregg Lumpkin, FA: Ten years ago, Fluffy Lumpkin was preparing to join the Georgia Bulldogs as the No. 2 running back prospect in the country after Reggie Bush. Less than a year ago, Lumpkin was planning to join a mortgage company when the Giants called him in for a workout. He joined the team as a jack-of-all-trades player capable of contributing as a runner, blocker, receiver, and special-teams gunner, and recorded nine garbage-time carries after the Falcons game got out of hand. Lumpkin's played for four teams in five years in the NFL, and at 29 years old, he's not a very attractive free-agent addition. (2012 stats: 9 carries for 39 yards, -34 DYAR, -80.7% DVOA)

Miguel Maysonet, CLE: At Stony Brook, Maysonet rushed for 1,964 yards and 21 touchdowns last year, including a 21-carry, 158-yard performance at Syracuse in September. Maysonet has NFL-caliber athleticism—he ran the 40-yard dash in 4.45 seconds and posted a 4.01 in the 20-yard shuttle at his pro day—and at 5-foot-9, 209 pounds, he is a compact runner. The Eagles signed him as an undrafted free agent, then cut him, and he hooked up with Cleveland, where he could make the final roster.

Collin Mooney, TEN: Mooney began his NFL career after fulfilling his Army service requirement as an artillery officer, so it seemed appropriate that his late-season carries were the first time the Titans ran halfback blast in a long while. That work notwithstanding, he's really a fullback; he'll be in a camp competition with Quinn Johnson to play a quarter of the snaps on offense and on special teams, and maybe touch the ball 15 times all season. (2012 stats: 5 carries for 19 yards, 2 DYAR, 2.5% DVOA)

Mewelde Moore, FA: Moore was the first former Steelers cast-off to reunite with Bruce Arians and the Colts during the 2012 season, signing with the team on June 20 and earning a spot on the 53-man roster. Moore played sparingly for the Colts, and his most memorable moment with the Colts might be a goal-line fumble in a 29-17 loss to the Houston Texans on December 16, the game that decided first place in the AFC South. Currently unsigned. (2012 stats: 13 carries for 20 yards, -34 DYAR, -68.4% DVOA; receiving stats: 6-for-8, 77 yards, 1 TD, 44 DYAR, 83.4% DVOA)

Richard Murphy, JAC: Murphy was a reserve running back at LSU who joined the Jaguars as an undrafted free agent in 2011. He spent his rookie season on injured reserve and was member of the Jaguars' practice squad last year before injuries prompted the team to promote him to the 53-man roster. The Jaguars waived Murphy following their rookie minicamp. (2012 stats: 23 carries for 92 yards, 14 DYAR, 5.7% DVOA)

Latavius Murray, OAK: Given Darren McFadden's (and Rashad Jennings') history of injury woes, it's reasonable to think that Murray will get an opportunity to contribute meaningfully as a sixth-round rookie in 2013. Murray was the main reason Central Florida ranked 19th in Rushing S&P+ in 2012, and he had 7.2 highlight yards per opportunity with +18.6 Adj. POE. Murray's draft stock climbed after an impressive pro day, where he ran a 4.4-second 40 at 223 pounds. Yes, pro day 40s are always a little faster than at the combine, but that works out to a 119.0 Speed Score.

Chris Ogbonnaya, CLE: Ogbonnaya re-signed with the Browns for two years in March. He had a semi-regular role as a third-down back in relief of Trent Richardson until last November, when Pat Shurmur gave up doing anything strategic that might help the team and Ogbonnaya fell out of the team's game plans. He is an adequate larger-sized change-up back, the kind that bounces from roster to roster until a needy team signs him for a multi-season tour of duty. And here we are. (2012 stats: 8 carries for 30 yards, -5 DYAR, -23.2% DVOA; receiving stats: 24-for-32, 187 yards, 23 DYAR, -1.9% DVOA)

Montell Owens, DET: A valuable special teams player, Owens had just 18 touches (and 14 rushing attempts) during his entire six-year career before injuries to Maurice Jones-Drew, Rashad Jennings and Jalen Parmele forced the Jaguars to start Owens in three games in December. For a player rarely called upon to tote the rock, Owens was surprisingly effective, with a 52 percent Success Rate. The Jaguars cut him in May, but he quickly signed a two-year, $2.5 million contract with the Detroit Lions, where he'll go back to being a special-teamer first and foremost. (2012 stats: 42 carries for 209 yards, 1 TD, 41 DYAR, 14.5% DVOA; receiving stats: 8-for-10, 113 yards, 43 DYAR, 62.6% DVOA)

Chris Polk, PHI: Injury concerns caused the former Washington star to fall out of the 2012 draft, and while he made the Eagles' 53-man roster, he only played on special teams. Polk is an excellent receiver for a 222-pound back, with 332 receiving yards and four touchdowns as a senior, but below-average POE numbers suggest that a lot of backs could have gained the yards he gained in college given the carries he received.

Bobby Rainey, BAL: Rainey, an undrafted rookie out of Western Kentucky, caught 14 preseason passes out of the backfield last season, earning him a place on the Ravens practice squad. He was briefly activated midseason, then placed on the injured reserve with a knee injury. John Harbaugh called Rainey "a guy that I cherish" before placing him on the practice squad, and the Ravens signed Rainey to a tender offer in May so they could get a second look at him as a potential third-down back. With Ray Rice and Bernard Pierce ahead of him, Rainey will have to excel on special teams for Harbaugh to keep using "cherish" as a word to describe him.

Chris Rainey, FA: Rainey was one of the most talented players on the field during 2012 Senior Bowl practices. He was also the cockiest player on either all-star squad, by a wide margin. He answered every media question with a smirk and an eye-roll. As a reporter, you don't want to hold that against him, but it makes you wonder: the Senior Bowl is a week-long job interview, and most young men know to rein in the edgier elements of their personalities; if that was reined-in Rainey, what was regular Rainey like? Well, regular Rainey has a gambling problem and what appear to be anger-management issues. He pleaded no contest to a charge of disorderly conduct after a January incident involving his girlfriend, and he was cited for defiant trespass outside a racetrack/casino. The Steelers waived him after the domestic incident, and 31 other teams decided to take their chances with the next crop of speedy rusher-receiver-returners instead of Rainey. Expect Rainey to spend the rest of his career showing up in conjunction with minor leagues and other tangential projects. (2012 stats: 26 carries for 102 yards, 2 TD, 26 DYAR, 16.0% DVOA; receiving stats: 11-for-14, 60 yards but -102 DYAR and -97.5% DVOA due to three fumbles)

Darius Reynaud, TEN: Reynaud played just nine snaps on offense in five games after Dowell Loggains replaced Chris Palmer as offensive coordinator in Tennessee. Perhaps he realized that even a gimmick player needs more than a 13 percent Success Rate. If Reynaud wins the return man battle with Marc Mariani, he'll give you return yards, but it's hard to see a role for him on the offense. (2012 stats: 16 carries for 33 yards, -33 DYAR, -68.2% DVOA; receiving stats: 5-for-9, 35 yards, -5 DYAR, -24.0% DVOA)

Theo Riddick, DET: Riddick, who played behind the undrafted Cierre Wood at Notre Dame, split time between wide receiver and running back in his college career. That tells you pretty much all you need to know about what type of player he is on the field. (He had a 68 percent catch rate on 36 passes for Notre Dame last season.) The Lions tabbed him with a sixth-round pick with the hopes that he could eventually take over Reggie Bush's role as the third-down/hybrid back, but he'll have to overcome injury problems (missed games in both 2010 and 2011) and grow as a player (problems making catches in tight coverage) to claim that spot.

Javon Ringer, FA: Ringer carved out a role as a third-down back in Tennessee, thanks to Chris Johnson's occasional misadventures in protection and need for rest. He struggled to run the ball with consistent success, though, and tended to get hurt every time the Titans tried to feature him in a bigger role. After a 2012 season that included a scary elbow infection that nearly cost him an arm, as well as a season-ending knee injury, Ringer is still looking for work. He can be moderately productive in the right role, but the market is limited for backs whose history indicates they may not be able to handle getting double-digit touches regularly. (2012 stats: 2 carries for 14 yards; receiving stats: 3-for-5, 12 yards, -17 DYAR, -79.9% DVOA)

Bernard Scott, CIN: Scott's eight carries last year garnered minus-8, 2, 1, 29, 6, 2, 6, and minus-3 yards. Theoretically, that makes him a boom-or-bust back. Realistically, it makes him expendable. Scott is coming off an ACL tear, and the Bengals re-signed him for one year, but Giovani Bernard was drafted to actually do the things Scott is supposed to be capable of doing, and the Bengals have no reason to keep both. (2012 stats: 8 carries for 35 yards, -3 DYAR, -15.6% DVOA)

Da'Rel Scott, NYG: Scott earned some buzz after he rushed for 200 yards and two touchdowns on 13 carries in the 2010 Military Bowl against East Carolina. But while Scott has great long speed and good size—in fact, his 118.9 Speed Score led all drafted running backs from the 2011 class—he has fallen out of favor with the Giants coaching staff. He's earned just 11 carries in two years, and 2013 may be his last chance to show that he has NFL talent. (2012 stats: 6 carries for 9 yards, -7 DYAR, -32.9% DVOA)

Alfonso Smith, ARI: After carrying the ball 30 times in 2011, Smith only played 17 offensive snaps all of last season. The vast majority of his playing time came on special teams, but he only made two tackles. Despite offering little discernible value to the team, Arizona thought enough of Smith to re-sign him for 2013. The bottom of Arizona's skill position depth chart: It's nice work if you can find it.

Antone Smith, ATL: Antone is not related to fellow Pahokee (Fla.) High alum Vincent Smith, best known for being nearly decapitated by Jadaveon Clowney in the Outback Bowl on New Year's Day. Like Vincent, Antone is diminutive (5-foot-7) but strong for his size, and there is some poor man's Pocket Hercules potential. But with Steven Jackson in town, Antone figures to stick to special teams.

Armond Smith, CAR: Smith is a preseason hero (5.2 yards per carry with an 81-yard touchdown) and regular-season zero (six career carries, five of them stuffed for no gain or a loss). He also had a half-dozen kickoff returns but finished with negative value there too. He's like a dime-store Kenjon Barner, and now that the Panthers have the authentic Kenjon Barner, they don't need Armond Smith. (2012 stats: 3 carries for 0 yards, -7 DYAR, -97.0% DVOA)

Michael Smith, TB: A seventh-round draft pick out of Utah State, Smith averaged 3.2 yards on 26 preseason carries, then told FO writer Brian McIntyre he felt he was competing for a starting job. His only regular-season touches came on three kickoff returns (for an 18.3-yard average) in Week 1, and he was a healthy inactive for the rest of the year. We're guessing even Smith would admit he's not competing for a starting job anymore.

Stepfan Taylor, ARI: Perhaps because Stanford's offense is more "traditional" than explosive, and less reliant on splash plays than is the norm in college football, the common perception is that Taylor is purely an inside guy for power situations. While he can bull it up the middle very well, he's a better outside runner than he's given credit for, and he showed this ability over and over during Senior Bowl practices. He's also a good receiver with excellent hands, and he understands the fine points of pass blocking. In some ways, the disconnect between Taylor's tape and most of his media scouting reports mirrors what people were saying about Alfred Morris last year. His situation is different in that Bruce Arians has said that Rashard Mendenhall is his no-doubt starting back, and Ryan Williams is clearly No. 2, but don't be surprised if Taylor is better than advertised when he gets his reps.

Marcus Thigpen, MIA: Although Thigpen filled in for jack-of-all-trades back Charles Clay in Miami's final two games, his main contribution is as the Dolphins' primary return man. In 2012, Miami ranked sixth in kick returns (7.4 Pts+) and 12th in punt returns (2.0 Pts+), with Thigpen running both a kickoff and a punt back for touchdowns. Jeff Ireland gets a ton of well-deserved grief from Dolfans, but the fact that he procured an asset like Thigpen via undrafted free agency should be a stark reminder that at least he didn't make Randy Mueller's mistake of drafting a returner No. 9 overall.

Chris Thompson, WAS: Redskins fans, you're familiar with Roy Helu's combination of explosive plays and injury issues? Well, this fifth-round rookie is the 2013 version. Thompson broke a vertebrae in his back in the fifth game of the 2011 season, and lasted eight games in 2012 before a knee injury drew the curtain on that campaign. In those eight games, however, he had a dymanite 8.3 highlight yards per opportunity, and +21.7 Adj. POE. He was on pace to become FSU's first 1,000-yard rusher since Warrick Dunn, and he's got the kind of speed in open spaces that could work wonders in the Redskins' variable backfield offense, but the dings mean that it's buyer beware. As Seminoles head coach Jimbo Fisher said of Thompson's decision to eschew a medical redshirt and take off for the NFL, "Because of the chance of another injury again, you might as well go up there and play." If he can stay on the field, Thompson might add a Darren Sproles-type weapon to an attack that's already very tough to solve.

Jordan Todman, JAC: Todman was a 2011 sixth-round pick out of UConn by the San Diego Chargers, and he has spent the bulk of his first two seasons on practice squads with the Chargers and Minnesota Vikings. The Jaguars added him to their active roster after injuries began to pile up in their backfield, but then he also landed on injured reserve with a calf injury after just seven offensive snaps. Todman will compete with the similarly-built Justin Forsett, 2012 UDFA Jonathan Grimes, and "OW" Denard Robinson for spots behind Maurice Jones-Drew on the Jaguars' depth chart.

Ryan Torain, NYG: Torain has rushed for 100 yards four times in his young career, but landed in Mike Shanahan's doghouse during the 2011 season. Torain was eventually released by the Redskins—it didn't help matters that his last 30 carries went for 43 yards—and was only signed by the Giants after Andre Brown was placed on injured reserve last year.

Keith Toston, FA: After spending the 2011 season out of football after failing to make the St. Louis Rams' roster, Toston received an opportunity from the Jaguars and nearly made the 53-man roster to open the season. Jacksonville's cascade of running back injuries led to the Jaguars bringing Toston back at two different points, for a total of five games including his first NFL start. The Jaguars had "exclusive rights" to Toston, but elected to not extend a qualifying offer, making him a free agent this offseason. (2012 stats: 17 carries for 74 yards, -5 DYAR, -15.7% DVOA; receiving stats: 3-for-4, 41 yards, 18 DYAR, 62.7% DVOA)

D.J. Ware, FA: In his last start with Tampa Bay (and almost certainly his last start in the NFL), Ware had one carry and one catch for 13 total yards. He was released in April after the Bucs signed Brian Leonard. (2012 stats: 11 carries for 51 yards, 16 DYAR, 28.2% DVOA; receiving stats: 14-for-20, 100 yards, -28 DYAR, -42.7% DVOA)

Spencer Ware, SEA: Pete Carroll said that Ware would get a shot at running back, but given Seattle's depth at that position and the fact that Ware was the fourth-best runner on LSU last year, he's more likely to stick at fullback. The sixth-round draft pick showed up for training camp weighing less than 220 pounds, but incumbent Michael Robinson is only 225, so Ware fits what Seattle is looking for.

Johnny White, FA: White was primarily a special teamer in Buffalo after being selected in the fifth round of the 2011 draft, but he found himself in an opportune situation to grab carries after he was claimed off waivers by Green Bay. Unfortunately, a concussion ended his season before the Packers went from Maximum Desperation to Plaid. Currently unsigned. (2012 stats: 8 carries for 34 yards, 1 DYAR, -6.7% DVOA)

Keiland Williams, WAS: Originally signed out of LSU as a street free agent by the Redskins in 2010, Williams got a little time in Detroit's hole-filled backfield last season before he was unceremoniously dumped to clear a roster spot for cornerback Alphonso Smith. Williams then replaced Ryan Grant on Washington's roster, and he's now one of those "Hey, at least he knows the system" guys who tend to wash out when people realize how much the system has changed since he was last there. (2012 stats: 2 carries for 3 yards, -6 DYAR, -80.5% DVOA; receiving stats: 2-for-2, 9 yards, -3 DYAR, -39.9% DVOA)

Kerwynn Williams, IND: Between Williams (2013 Colts seventh-rounder), Robert Turbin (2012 Seahawks fourth-rounder) and Michael Smith (2012 Bucs seventh-rounder), Utah State has been "Mid-to-Late Round Running Back U" the last two years. Williams replaced Turbin as the main weapon in the Aggies' backfield, rushing for 1,512 yards and 15 touchdowns with 45 receptions for 697 yards and five touchdowns out of the backfield. He had an incredible 10.0 highlight yards per opportunity and +38.3 Adj. POE in our advanced college metrics. Before Williams became a starter at Utah State, he returned kicks, averaging over 11 yards on punt returns and over 25 yards on kick returns. The third-down Darren Sproles role is the ultimate aspiration, but returning kicks will likely be Williams' path to a roster spot and/or regular playing time as a rookie.

Wide Receivers

In the following two sections we provide the last three years' statistics, as well as a 2013 KUBIAK projection, for every wide receiver and tight end who either played a significant role in 2012 or is expected to do so in 2013.

The first line contains biographical data—each player's name, height, weight, college, draft position, birth date, and age. Height and weight are the best data we could find; weight, of course, can fluctuate during the off-season. **Age** is very simple, the number of years between the player's birth year and 2013, but birth date is provided if you want to figure out exact age.

Draft position gives draft year and round, with the overall pick number with which the player was taken in parentheses. In the sample table, it says that Eric Decker was chosen in the 2010 NFL Draft with the 87th overall pick in the third round. Undrafted free agents are listed as "FA" with the year they came into the league, even if they were only in training camp or on a practice squad.

To the far right of the first line is the player's Risk for fantasy football in 2013. As explained in the quarterback section, the standard is for players to be marked Green. Players with higher than normal risk are marked Yellow, and players with the highest risk are marked Red. Players who are most likely to match or surpass our forecast—primarily second- stringers with low projections—are marked Blue. Risk is not only based on injury probability, but how a player's projection compares to his recent performance as well as our confidence (or lack thereof) in his offensive teammates.

Next we give the last three years of player stats. Note that rushing stats are not included for receivers, but that any receiver with at least five carries last year will have his 2012 rushing stats appear in his team's chapter.

Next we give the last three years of player stats. First come games played and games started (**G/GS**). Games played represents the official NFL total and may include games in which a player appeared on special teams, but did not play wide receiver or tight end. We also have a total of offensive **Snaps** for each season. Receptions (**Rec**) counts passes caught, while Passes (**Pass**) counts passes thrown to this player, complete or incomplete. Receiving yards (**Yds**) is the official NFL total for each player.

Catch rate (**C%**) includes all passes listed in the official play-by-play with the given player as the intended receiver, even if those passes were listed by our game charters as "Thrown Away," "Tipped at Line," or "Quarterback Hit in Motion." The average NFL wide receiver has caught between 57 and 58 percent of passes over the last three seasons; tight ends caught between 63 and 64 percent of passes over the last three seasons.

Plus/minus (+/-) is a new metric that we introduced in *Football Outsiders Almanac 2010*. It estimates how many passes a receiver caught compared to what an average receiver would have caught, given the location of those passes. Unlike simple catch rate, plus/minus does not consider passes listed as "Thrown Away," "Tipped at Line," or "Quarterback Hit in Motion." Player performance is compared to a historical baseline of how often a pass is caught based on the pass distance, the distance required for a first down, and whether it is on the left, middle, or right side of the field. Note that plus/minus is not scaled to a player's target total.

Yards per catch (**Yd/C**) and receiving touchdowns (**TD**) are standard stats. Drops (**Drop**) list the number of dropped passes according to our game charting project. Our totals may differ from the drop totals kept by other organizations.

Next we list yards after catch (**YAC**), rank (**Rk**) in yards after catch, and **YAC+**. YAC+ is similar to plus-minus; it estimates how much YAC a receiver gained compared to what we would have expected from an average receiver catching passes of similar length in similar down-and-distance situations. This is imperfect—we don't specifically mark what route a player runs, and obviously a go route will have more YAC than a comeback—but it does a fairly good job of telling you if this receiver gets more or less YAC than other receivers with similar usage patterns. We also give a total of broken tackles (**BTkl**) according to the Football Outsiders game charting project.

The next five columns include our main advanced metrics for receiving: **DVOA** (Defense-Adjusted Value Over Average), **DYAR** (Defense-Adjusted Yards Above Replacement), and **YAR** (Yards Above Replacement), along with the player's rank in both DVOA and DYAR. These metrics compare every pass intended for a receiver and the results of that pass to a league-average baseline based on the game situations in which passes were thrown to that receiver. DVOA and DYAR are also adjusted based on the opposing defense and include Defensive Pass Interference yards on passes intended for that receiver. The methods used to compute these numbers are described in detail in the "Statistical Toolbox" introduction in the front of the book. The important distinctions between them are:

Eric Decker			Height: 6-3		Weight: 217		College: Minnesota			Draft: 2010/3 (87)			Born: 15-Mar-1987		Age: 26		Risk: Green		
Year	Team	G/GS	Snaps	Rec	Pass	Yds	C%	+/-	Yd/C	TD	Drop	YAC	Rk	YAC+	BTkl	DVOA	Rk	DYAR	Rk	YAR	Short	Mid	Deep	Bomb
2010	DEN	14/0	138	6	8	106	75%	+1.2	17.7	1	1	4.0	--	-1.6	1	56.9%	--	30	--	32	13%	50%	25%	13%
2011	DEN	16/13	972	44	98	612	46%	-7.4	13.9	8	6	3.9	58	-0.9	1	-15.5%	76	-24	76	-40	30%	34%	16%	20%
2012	DEN	16/15	1048	85	123	1064	69%	+12.5	12.5	13	7	3.1	69	-0.7	3	27.2%	8	392	4	401	32%	45%	11%	12%
2013	DEN			65	102	906	64%	--	13.9	8						19.8%								

• DVOA is a rate statistic, while DYAR is a cumulative statistic. Thus, a higher DVOA means more value per pass play, while a higher DYAR means more aggregate value over the entire season.

• Because DYAR is defense-adjusted and YAR is not, a player whose DYAR is higher than his YAR faced a harder-than-average schedule. A player whose DYAR is lower than his YAR faced an easier-than-average schedule.

To qualify for ranking in YAC, receiving DVOA, or receiving DYAR, a wide receiver must have had 50 passes thrown to him in that season. We ranked 86 wideouts in 2012, 92 wideouts in 2011, and 85 in 2010. Tight ends qualify with 25 targets in a given season; we ranked 49 tight ends in 2012, 47 tight ends in 2011, and 45 in 2010.

The final four columns break down pass length based on the Football Outsiders charting project. The categories are **Short** (5 yards or less), **Mid** (6-15 yards), **Deep** (16-25 yards), and **Bomb** (26 or more yards). These numbers are based on distance in the air only and include both complete and incomplete passes.

The italicized row of statistics for the 2013 season is our 2013 KUBIAK projection based on a complicated regression analysis that takes into account numerous variables including projected role, performance over the past two years, projected team offense and defense, projected quarterback statistics, historical comparables, height, age, and strength of schedule.

It is difficult to accurately project statistics for a 162-game baseball season, but it is exponentially more difficult to accurately project statistics for a 16-game football season. Consider the listed projections not as a prediction of exact numbers, but as the mean of a range of possible performances. What's important is less the exact number of yards we project, and more which players are projected to improve or decline. Actual performance will vary from our projection less for veteran starters and more for rookies and third-stringers, for whom we must base our projections on much smaller career statistical samples. Touchdown numbers will vary more than yardage numbers. Players facing suspension or recovering from injury have those missed games taken into account.

Note that the receiving totals for each team will add up to higher numbers than the projection for that team's starting quarterback, because we have done KUBIAK projections for more receivers than will actually make the final roster.

A few low-round rookies, guys listed at seventh on the depth chart, and players who are listed as wide receivers but really only play special teams are briefly discussed at the end of the chapter in a section we call "Going Deep."

Two notes regarding our advanced metrics: We cannot yet fully separate the performance of a receiver from the performance of his quarterback. Be aware that one will affect the other. In addition, these statistics measure only passes thrown to a receiver, not performance on plays when he is not thrown the ball, such as blocking and drawing double teams.

Top 20 WR by DYAR (Total Value), 2012

Rank	Player	Team	DYAR
1	Calvin Johnson	DET	488
2	Andre Johnson	HOU	461
3	Dez Bryant	DAL	392
4	Eric Decker	DEN	392
5	Roddy White	ATL	360
6	Randall Cobb	GB	357
7	Lance Moore	NO	356
8	Demaryius Thomas	DEN	354
9	Julio Jones	ATL	340
10	Michael Crabtree	SF	334
11	Marques Colston	NO	327
12	James Jones	GB	318
13	Jordy Nelson	GB	292
14	Sidney Rice	SEA	283
15	Malcom Floyd	SD	281
16	Brandon Marshall	CHI	267
17	Danario Alexander	SD	266
18	Wes Welker	NE	251
19	Golden Tate	SEA	245
20	Vincent Jackson	TB	224

Top 20 WR by DVOA (Value per Pass), 2012

Rank	Player	Team	DVOA
1	Danario Alexander	SD	41.6%
2	Brandon Stokley	DEN	37.4%
3	Malcom Floyd	SD	36.0%
4	Golden Tate	SEA	31.6%
5	Lance Moore	NO	31.2%
6	Jordy Nelson	GB	30.8%
7	Sidney Rice	SEA	29.7%
8	Eric Decker	DEN	27.2%
9	Randall Cobb	GB	24.1%
10	Domenik Hixon	NYG	23.6%
11	Brandon Gibson	STL	23.3%
12	James Jones	GB	22.6%
13	Michael Crabtree	SF	21.9%
14	Demaryius Thomas	DEN	21.4%
15	Marques Colston	NO	19.7%
16	Andre Johnson	HOU	19.5%
17	Dez Bryant	DAL	18.3%
18	Roddy White	ATL	16.3%
19	Calvin Johnson	DET	16.0%
20	Julio Jones	ATL	16.0%

Minimum 50 passes.

Danario Alexander		Height: 6-5			Weight: 215			College: Missouri			Draft: 2010/FA			Born: 7-Aug-1988		Age: 25		Risk: Red	
Year	Team	G/GS	Snaps	Rec	Pass	Yds	C%	+/-	Yd/C	TD	Drop	YAC	Rk	YAC+	BTkl	DVOA	Rk	DYAR	Rk	YAR	Short	Mid	Deep	Bomb
2010	STL	8/2	208	20	37	306	54%	+0.5	15.3	1	2	5.7	--	+0.1	3	1.9%	--	47	--	64	44%	25%	9%	22%
2011	STL	10/5	433	26	60	431	43%	-4.6	16.6	2	3	5.1	23	+0.9	0	-12.2%	72	12	66	3	29%	36%	18%	16%
2012	SD	10/6	478	37	62	658	60%	+2.3	17.8	7	3	7.6	3	+3.1	2	41.6%	1	266	17	238	29%	41%	18%	13%
2013	SD			43	82	696	52%	--	16.2	5						8.7%								

Alexander's impressive talent has been overridden by knee injuries throughout his entire his career. He joined the Chargers midway through last season and quickly had a five-game stretch where he posted receiving yardage totals of 134, 96, 74, 102, and 88. Philip Rivers called Alexander the most fluid route runner he's ever played with. Alexander, with his lankiness and ability to get downfield and win jump-ball battles on the outside, was a great fit for Norv Turner's system. Presumably, with his combination of size and movement skills, he can transfer well to any system, including Mike McCoy's. That is, if he can stay healthy, of course.

Keenan Allen		Height: 6-2			Weight: 206			College: California			Draft: 2013/3 (76)			Born: 27-Apr-1992		Age: 21		Risk: Red	
Year	Team	G/GS	Snaps	Rec	Pass	Yds	C%	+/-	Yd/C	TD	Drop	YAC	Rk	YAC+	BTkl	DVOA	Rk	DYAR	Rk	YAR	Short	Mid	Deep	Bomb
2013	SD			35	63	390	56%	--	11.1	2						-8.7%								

Here's a player where the scouts and our Playmaker Score projection system really part ways. A Playmaker Score of 168 is really, really low, especially for a player who is considered a finished product rather than a raw talent along the lines of Cordarrelle Patterson. That score does come with an asterisk because the knee injury that caused Allen to drop to the Chargers in the third round also prevented him from working out at the Combine; therefore, we plug in average Combine numbers for that part of the equation. Nonetheless, players who only average 12.5 yards per catch in college don't tend to become NFL stars unless they're big red zone targets, and Allen is not one. (Robert Woods, for example, averaged just 11.7 yards per catch at USC, but had 10.7 touchdowns per season compared to 5.7 for Allen.) Subjectively, we want to excuse Allen for the poor quarterback play at Cal, but our research has shown that controlling for quarterback quality does almost nothing to help forecast NFL success, and any influence it does have shows that wideouts who played with good quarterbacks in college tend to have more success than those who don't.

The other side of the argument goes like this: Before the knee injury, Allen was generally considered one of the top three receiver prospects in this year's draft. He's not a speedy field-stretcher, but his admirers tout his deceptive acceleration and fluidity in and out of breaks. He makes defenders miss with a variety of moves in the open field. He's got good hands, a wide catch radius, and blocking skills. His greatest attribute is his unique ability to disguise routes, which is a significant but unheralded trait for a wide receiver. Former Colts GM Bill Polian has compared him to Reggie Wayne, which is high praise indeed. Then again, Reggie Wayne had 17.6 yards per catch and 10 touchdowns as a senior.

Danny Amendola		Height: 5-11			Weight: 186			College: Texas Tech			Draft: 2008/FA			Born: 2-Nov-1985		Age: 28		Risk: Red	
Year	Team	G/GS	Snaps	Rec	Pass	Yds	C%	+/-	Yd/C	TD	Drop	YAC	Rk	YAC+	BTkl	DVOA	Rk	DYAR	Rk	YAR	Short	Mid	Deep	Bomb
2010	STL	16/6	655	85	123	689	69%	+3.6	8.1	3	7	4.3	33	-0.8	6	-19.7%	76	-54	78	-48	60%	35%	4%	1%
2011	STL	1/1	40	5	6	45	83%	+0.9	9.0	0	0	5.0	--	+0.5	0	12.9%	--	8	--	13	67%	33%	0%	0%
2012	STL	11/8	498	63	101	666	62%	-0.6	10.6	3	2	3.8	48	-0.6	4	-7.6%	67	80	45	10	52%	36%	4%	8%
2013	NE			92	134	1095	69%	--	11.9	6						12.0%								

Amendola is a white, undersized, white slot receiver who has often been compared to Wes Welker, largely because he is white. They also both went to Texas Tech, though Amendola started there a year after Welker finished. Welker began his NFL career in San Diego, where he rarely played, and Miami, where he averaged 48 catches and 560 yards in two years as the third receiver behind Chris Chambers and Marty Booker. That's about what Amendola has done (when healthy) as the top guy in St. Louis. The key is that New England was able to turn Welker into a YAC machine, launching his average YAC from 4.0 in Miami to 5.5 and higher with the Pats. That's critical, because Amendola's yardage figures have been nigh impotent. He is one of four receivers in history with more than 100 catches and fewer than 10 yards per reception. The others: Jim Jensen, a do-it-all special teamer for the 1980s Dolphins who also played running back and quarterback; Dexter McCluster of the Chiefs, a hybrid running back/slot receiver who has more runs than catches in his career; and former Bengals receiver Andre Caldwell. So if Caldwell is Amendola's floor and Welker is his ceiling, you can expect him to finish somewhere in the middle.

Miles Austin		Height: 6-3			Weight: 215			College: Monmouth			Draft: 2006/FA			Born: 30-Jun-1984		Age: 29		Risk: Yellow	
Year	Team	G/GS	Snaps	Rec	Pass	Yds	C%	+/-	Yd/C	TD	Drop	YAC	Rk	YAC+	BTkl	DVOA	Rk	DYAR	Rk	YAR	Short	Mid	Deep	Bomb
2010	DAL	16/16	988	69	119	1041	58%	-1.6	15.1	7	11	6.2	4	+2.1	6	11.3%	21	243	12	234	32%	48%	11%	10%
2011	DAL	10/10	553	43	73	579	59%	-1.0	13.5	7	2	4.7	32	+0.7	2	11.6%	28	125	41	154	31%	46%	17%	7%
2012	DAL	16/15	860	66	119	943	55%	-5.0	14.3	6	4	4.4	37	+0.1	6	3.3%	36	184	25	151	25%	43%	23%	9%
2013	DAL			61	99	820	62%	--	13.4	6						11.4%								

It wasn't so long ago that Austin was the Cowboys' main man at the receiver position, but hamstring injuries have conspired to sap his production over the last two seasons. He's trying to correct that issue. "I'm definitely strengthening my hamstrings a lot more than I have been, doing a different routine, a couple of extra exercises each day on our leg days," Austin told the *Dallas Morning News* in May. "I'm just running hard and trying to compete at a high level at this time—that way it doesn't shock your muscles when you actually do it for real."

If Austin wasn't "shocking" his muscles before, that's a problem, but the bigger problem for Austin is his future with Dallas beyond the 2013 season. He was one of several Cowboys players who re-structured their contracts in the offseason, as several odiferous Jerry Jones contracts finally caught up with the front office. Austin now has a $5.5 million base salary in 2014. Dallas took Baylor receiver Terrance Williams in the third round of the 2013 draft, and if second-round tight end Gavin Escobar gets as many targets as his potential demands, Austin could be looking for a moving truck within in the next year.

Tavon Austin			Height: 5-8		Weight: 174			College: West Virginia			Draft: 2013/1 (8)			Born: 15-Mar-1991		Age: 22		Risk: Red	
Year	Team	G/GS	Snaps	Rec	Pass	Yds	C%	+/-	Yd/C	TD	Drop	YAC	Rk	YAC+	BTkl	DVOA	Rk	DYAR	Rk	YAR	Short	Mid	Deep	Bomb
2013	STL			78	114	832	68%	--	10.7	5						1.4%								

It would not be fair to say that Tavon Austin "broke out" against Oklahoma in 2012. He had already gone over 100 yards receiving five times that season after going over 1,000 yards the year before, not to mention scoring five touchdowns as a returner up to that point. It was against the Sooners, though, that Austin saw his first extended action as a running back, and in that sense he broke through in a big way, rushing 21 times for a mind-boggling 344 yards. Austin will see time with the Rams as a returner, wideout, slot receiver, and, yes, running back this fall. He's only an inch shorter and about five pounds lighter than Warrick Dunn, who went over 200 carries eight times in his NFL career. For more, see the main essay in the St. Louis chapter, which is basically a 2,000-plus-word Tavon Austin player comment. Austin's 2013 projection includes 42 carries for 252 yards and a touchdown.

Jason Avant			Height: 6-0		Weight: 210			College: Michigan			Draft: 2006/4 (109)			Born: 20-Apr-1983		Age: 30		Risk: Green	
Year	Team	G/GS	Snaps	Rec	Pass	Yds	C%	+/-	Yd/C	TD	Drop	YAC	Rk	YAC+	BTkl	DVOA	Rk	DYAR	Rk	YAR	Short	Mid	Deep	Bomb
2010	PHI	16/3	763	51	75	573	68%	+8.5	11.2	1	5	3.1	65	-1.2	1	7.2%	30	135	31	116	34%	42%	18%	6%
2011	PHI	16/7	709	52	81	679	64%	+4.0	13.1	1	1	3.3	71	-0.5	1	2.5%	45	111	47	120	29%	51%	17%	3%
2012	PHI	14/6	656	53	77	648	70%	+6.5	12.2	0	0	2.7	76	-1.5	2	6.8%	28	137	33	118	33%	48%	16%	3%
2013	PHI			39	60	445	65%	--	11.4	2						4.1%								

On a team full of disappointments, Avant was one of the few players who lived up to expectations in 2013. Despite wearing an Eagles uniform, he finished the season without a dropped pass. Among the 71 wide receivers with 60 or more targets last year, Avant sported the third highest catch rate. And the two players ahead of him—Percy Harvin and Randall Cobb—ran short routes (within five yards of the line of scrimmage) over 50 percent of the time. Avant, like all of the other Eagles receivers, isn't much of a red-zone threat (-41.0% DVOA and 45 percent catch rate over the last three seasons), but he can be a valuable move-the-chains player for the Eagles. KUBIAK sees his usage falling as Chip Kelly moves from three-wide sets to two-tight end sets, but since Jeremy Maclin is a free agent after the season, Philadelphia may want to give Avant more opportunities to see if he can handle being the team's primary possession receiver.

Donnie Avery			Height: 5-11		Weight: 183			College: Houston			Draft: 2008/2 (33)			Born: 12-Jun-1984		Age: 29		Risk: Green	
Year	Team	G/GS	Snaps	Rec	Pass	Yds	C%	+/-	Yd/C	TD	Drop	YAC	Rk	YAC+	BTkl	DVOA	Rk	DYAR	Rk	YAR	Short	Mid	Deep	Bomb
2011	TEN	8/0	112	3	11	45	27%	-3.5	15.0	1	2	7.0	--	+3.4	0	-11.2%	--	5	--	-3	42%	33%	8%	17%
2012	IND	16/15	1025	60	125	781	48%	-8.8	13.0	3	6	3.5	63	-1.3	2	-19.1%	79	-75	83	-41	29%	42%	15%	14%
2013	KC			29	51	377	57%	--	13.0	2						-2.0%								

Avery missed the 2010 season due to a torn ACL and appeared in just eight games for the Tennessee Titans in 2011, but the Colts took a one-year flier on him before last season. He ended up earning the starting job opposite Reggie Wayne and had his most productive season in the NFL, which resulted in a multi-year contract from the Kansas City Chiefs that included $3.25 million in guarantees. In addition to Avery's injury history, the Chiefs should beware of his low catch rate (48 percent in 2012, 49 percent for his career) and that he's coming off a season where he had DVOA ratings of -30.5% on first down and -20.6% on second down. Avery was more effective on third downs (-1.9% DVOA), which could mesh with his expected role as a No. 3 or No. 4 receiver in Kansas City.

Stedman Bailey			Height: 5-10		Weight: 193			College: West Virginia			Draft: 2013/3 (92)			Born: 11-Nov-1990		Age: 23		Risk: Red	
Year	Team	G/GS	Snaps	Rec	Pass	Yds	C%	+/-	Yd/C	TD	Drop	YAC	Rk	YAC+	BTkl	DVOA	Rk	DYAR	Rk	YAR	Short	Mid	Deep	Bomb
2013	STL			28	45	361	62%	--	12.9	2						2.2%								

Poor Stedman Bailey. All he did was lead the Big East in receptions and yards, while leading the nation in receiving touchdowns, and yet it's ex-West Virginia teammate Tavon Austin who gets the first-round pick and the big-money contract while Bailey slid to the third round and a substantially lower salary. The two are teammates in St. Louis—roommates in fact—and will work together to ensure both get nice big second contracts in 2016. Bailey had 399 Playmaker Score, not fabulous but still the highest of any Division I receiver chosen in this year's draft. He goes into year the fifth wideout behind Austin, Chris Givens, Austin Pettis, and Brian Quick, but we like his chances to climb the depth chart over the course of the season.

Doug Baldwin			Height: 5-11		Weight: 189			College: Stanford			Draft: 2011/FA			Born: 21-Sep-1988		Age: 25		Risk: Blue	
Year	Team	G/GS	Snaps	Rec	Pass	Yds	C%	+/-	Yd/C	TD	Drop	YAC	Rk	YAC+	BTkl	DVOA	Rk	DYAR	Rk	YAR	Short	Mid	Deep	Bomb
2011	SEA	16/1	499	51	86	788	59%	-0.6	15.5	4	2	6.1	10	+1.4	5	14.5%	21	205	21	185	31%	38%	20%	11%
2012	SEA	14/4	434	29	50	366	58%	-0.1	12.6	3	3	2.7	77	-2.0	0	0.0%	47	45	58	38	33%	48%	9%	11%
2013	SEA			13	25	169	52%	--	13.0	1						-7.5%								

Baldwin led the Seahawks in yards, catches, and touchdowns as a rookie, but regressed in every meaningful way in 2012 even as the rest of the team took several steps forward. It's easy to explain his drop in opportunities, as Sidney Rice returned to health and former second-rounder Golden Tate began to live up to his potential, but Baldwin had a poor season even accounting for his limited chances. It's hard to blame that kind of plummet in YAC on coaches or teammates. Some attributed Baldwin's struggles to a high ankle sprain suffered against San Francisco in Week 7, but his DVOA actually improved after that point. Baldwin is now a distant fourth on the depth chart behind Rice, Tate, and Percy Harvin. Pre-draft rumors suggested he could reunite with his ex-Stanford teammate Andrew Luck in Indianapolis. Nothing came out of that, but if Baldwin doesn't turn things around in a hurry, he won't be in Seattle for long.

Jonathan Baldwin			Height: 6-5		Weight: 230			College: Pittsburgh			Draft: 2011/1 (26)			Born: 10-Aug-1989		Age: 24		Risk: Green	
Year	Team	G/GS	Snaps	Rec	Pass	Yds	C%	+/-	Yd/C	TD	Drop	YAC	Rk	YAC+	BTkl	DVOA	Rk	DYAR	Rk	YAR	Short	Mid	Deep	Bomb
2011	KC	11/3	388	21	53	254	40%	-6.8	12.1	1	6	2.0	90	-1.9	0	-38.6%	90	-102	88	-104	27%	45%	12%	16%
2012	KC	15/7	542	20	47	325	43%	-5.2	16.3	1	0	5.5	--	+1.5	0	-22.9%	--	-24	--	-27	20%	37%	22%	22%
2013	KC			35	66	454	53%	--	13.0	2						-12.8%								

It's time for Baldwin to harness the scintillating playmaking talent that he has occasionally flashed over his first two years in the league. He has the ability to make spectacular, almost freakish catches. However, he still relies solely on athleticism to make these plays. The refined route running and other fundamentals still aren't there, which makes it difficult for coaches and a quarterback to fully trust the former first-round pick. If he's not running the right routes, how can he take advantage of the improved accuracy that Alex Smith brings to the Chiefs offense? What's really concerning is that on multiple occasions last year, Baldwin exhibited a distinct lack of speed. He has played like a heavier player in the NFL than he did at Pitt.

Travis Benjamin			Height: 5-10		Weight: 172			College: Miami			Draft: 2012/4 (100)			Born: 29-Dec-1989		Age: 24		Risk: Blue	
Year	Team	G/GS	Snaps	Rec	Pass	Yds	C%	+/-	Yd/C	TD	Drop	YAC	Rk	YAC+	BTkl	DVOA	Rk	DYAR	Rk	YAR	Short	Mid	Deep	Bomb
2012	CLE	14/3	297	18	37	298	49%	-3.0	16.6	2	1	3.6	--	+0.4	1	-1.5%	--	33	--	32	17%	47%	17%	19%
2013	CLE			21	41	351	51%	--	16.7	1						-0.4%								

The fourth-round rookie flashed greatness both early in the year (a 35-yard reverse against the Eagles) and late (a 69-yard touchdown catch against the Redskins in Week 15, and seven catches in the final two games). In between, Benjamin suffered a hamstring injury, missed a few games, and fell out of the game plan for others. Benjamin will replace Josh Cribbs on punt returns, but the Browns traded for Davone Bess to take over slot duties. Benjamin has more talent and long-term potential than Bess; the new regime may figure this out in training camp.

Arrelious Benn			Height: 6-1		Weight: 219			College: Illinois			Draft: 2010/2 (39)			Born: 8-Sep-1988		Age: 25		Risk: Green	
Year	Team	G/GS	Snaps	Rec	Pass	Yds	C%	+/-	Yd/C	TD	Drop	YAC	Rk	YAC+	BTkl	DVOA	Rk	DYAR	Rk	YAR	Short	Mid	Deep	Bomb
2010	TB	15/9	353	25	38	395	66%	+3.3	15.8	2	1	6.4	--	+1.3	4	24.1%	--	124	--	112	42%	33%	8%	17%
2011	TB	14/14	502	30	51	441	59%	-2.0	14.7	3	5	5.8	16	+0.1	5	-6.6%	64	21	65	22	42%	28%	16%	14%
2012	TB	8/1	77	4	6	26	67%	-0.6	6.5	0	0	5.8	--	-0.7	1	-38.6%	--	-8	--	-10	83%	17%	0%	0%
2013	PHI			20	32	303	63%	--	15.2	1						15.6%								

Benn was severely limited last season due to an MCL sprain and shoulder injury. As a slot receiver in Chip Kelly's offense, he figures to be a frequent target on screen passes, as he was in Tampa Bay. More than a quarter of the passes in his Buccaneers career came at or behind the line of scrimmage. He caught nine of 10 passes for 73 yards as a rookie, including four first downs, but since then he has only caught 11 of 15 passes for 49 yards and one first down, including three receptions that lost yardage.

Earl Bennett — Height: 5-11 Weight: 209 College: Vanderbilt Draft: 2008/3 (70) Born: 23-Mar-1987 Age: 26 Risk: Yellow

Year	Team	G/GS	Snaps	Rec	Pass	Yds	C%	+/-	Yd/C	TD	Drop	YAC	Rk	YAC+	BTkl	DVOA	Rk	DYAR	Rk	YAR	Short	Mid	Deep	Bomb
2010	CHI	14/3	483	46	70	561	66%	+2.5	12.2	3	1	4.5	31	+0.6	9	8.8%	27	114	40	120	33%	60%	6%	1%
2011	CHI	11/4	442	24	43	381	56%	+1.9	15.9	1	0	5.2	--	+0.9	4	-1.4%	--	25	--	40	26%	37%	26%	11%
2012	CHI	12/4	417	29	49	375	59%	-3.5	12.9	2	1	6.4	10	+2.0	3	0.3%	45	60	55	54	38%	50%	8%	4%
2013	CHI			33	61	404	54%	--	12.2	2						-8.3%								

There is nothing interesting to report about Earl Bennett other than the fact that he and Jay Cutler went to the same school, and that falls under "Jerome Bettis is from Detroit" news at this point. He's a No. 4 receiver miscast as a No. 3 receiver. If he doesn't win early in the route, he won't. A majority of his targets came from the slot, and a majority of his successful plays came from clever route designs, mostly of the type where Brandon Marshall went deep and cleared out the underneath for him. He's sure-handed and has a little more speed than you'd think in the open field, but that's the extent of his positive qualities.

Davone Bess — Height: 5-11 Weight: 193 College: Hawaii Draft: 2008/FA Born: 13-Sep-1985 Age: 28 Risk: Yellow

Year	Team	G/GS	Snaps	Rec	Pass	Yds	C%	+/-	Yd/C	TD	Drop	YAC	Rk	YAC+	BTkl	DVOA	Rk	DYAR	Rk	YAR	Short	Mid	Deep	Bomb
2010	MIA	16/8	658	79	126	820	63%	+2.2	10.4	5	6	3.9	46	-0.5	7	-1.1%	51	100	45	74	38%	50%	10%	2%
2011	MIA	16/4	551	51	86	537	59%	-0.9	10.5	3	2	4.5	36	+0.1	2	-24.5%	86	-111	89	-75	51%	34%	13%	3%
2012	MIA	13/13	738	61	105	778	58%	-1.8	12.8	1	4	4.1	42	+0.1	9	-3.7%	55	71	48	55	35%	44%	12%	8%
2013	CLE			49	88	551	56%	--	11.3	3						-10.9%								

According to various reports, the Browns traded for Bess because he's a reliable short-yardage receiver out of the slot who excels on third down. Of course, a receiver's third-down splits are a festival of small sample size, but we should at least point out that although Bess does catch a lot of passes on third down, he has posted a DVOA of -20% or lower on third-down targets the past two seasons. In addition, for a player who almost exclusively operates within 15 yards of the line of scrimmage, Bess' catch rate is woefully low. Pick almost any receiver in a similar role last year, and you find catch rates approaching 70 percent (even with mediocre quarterbacks); Bess didn't even clear 60 percent.

Armon Binns — Height: 6-3 Weight: 209 College: Cincinnati Draft: 2011/FA Born: 8-Sep-1989 Age: 24 Risk: Yellow

Year	Team	G/GS	Snaps	Rec	Pass	Yds	C%	+/-	Yd/C	TD	Drop	YAC	Rk	YAC+	BTkl	DVOA	Rk	DYAR	Rk	YAR	Short	Mid	Deep	Bomb
2012	2TM	11/5	396	24	40	277	60%	-1.9	11.5	1	4	4.7	--	+0.5	2	-18.7%	--	-26	--	-2	33%	51%	15%	0%
2013	MIA			17	31	212	55%	--	12.5	0						-9.5%								

Binns caught 12 passes for 157 yards and a touchdown in the Bengals' first three games, then caught just six of the next 16 passes thrown to him before getting shipped off to the Dolphins. Binns made the Bengals roster as a try-hard guy and can do the same for the Dolphins. Both teams are learning to do a better job of not giving players like him meaningful offensive roles.

Justin Blackmon — Height: 6-1 Weight: 207 College: Oklahoma State Draft: 2012/1 (5) Born: 9-Jan-1990 Age: 23 Risk: Yellow

Year	Team	G/GS	Snaps	Rec	Pass	Yds	C%	+/-	Yd/C	TD	Drop	YAC	Rk	YAC+	BTkl	DVOA	Rk	DYAR	Rk	YAR	Short	Mid	Deep	Bomb
2012	JAC	16/14	963	64	132	865	48%	-15.2	13.5	5	8	4.4	36	+0.7	4	-15.0%	76	-4	75	-21	24%	55%	14%	7%
2013	JAC			60	101	779	59%	--	13.0	7						5.6%								

Blackmon had a 44 percent catch rate and -35.8% DVOA over the first nine games of the season before exploding with seven receptions for 236 yards and an 81-yard touchdown against the Texans on November 8. Blackmon couldn't match that game the rest of the year, but he did improve to a -11.8% DVOA and a 52 percent catch rate in the final six weeks. He should continue his development on the field—once he returns from the four-game suspension he earned for violating the league's substance abuse policy. First-year head coach Gus Bradley has voiced his support of Blackmon, but with three substance abuse issues in the last four years—he was arrested for DUI in both 2010 and 2012—it seems Blackmon's personal development off the field is more important than his development on it.

Anquan Boldin — Height: 6-1 Weight: 218 College: Florida State Draft: 2003/2 (54) Born: 3-Oct-1980 Age: 33 Risk: Green

Year	Team	G/GS	Snaps	Rec	Pass	Yds	C%	+/-	Yd/C	TD	Drop	YAC	Rk	YAC+	BTkl	DVOA	Rk	DYAR	Rk	YAR	Short	Mid	Deep	Bomb
2010	BAL	16/16	977	64	109	837	59%	+2.8	13.1	7	3	3.5	55	-0.7	3	5.8%	37	149	29	142	25%	47%	17%	11%
2011	BAL	14/14	879	57	106	887	54%	-4.6	15.6	3	4	3.9	56	+0.2	1	8.8%	34	226	16	172	13%	64%	16%	7%
2012	BAL	15/15	878	65	112	921	58%	-1.0	14.2	4	2	3.6	54	-0.6	5	3.4%	35	122	39	133	29%	47%	18%	7%
2013	SF			61	99	858	62%	--	14.1	5						10.0%								

There are 38 wide receivers in NFL history who: a) started their career during or after the 1988 season; b) gained over 8,000 receiving yards, and c) are either no longer active or have reached the career stage where their signature years are clearly behind them. One of those 38 players is Jerry Rice, who blows nearly every curve. Of the remaining 37, all but eight had their final productive season by the time they were 34 years old. The exceptions were Terrell Owens, Tim Brown, Jimmy Smith, Mushin Muhammad, Rod Smith, Keenan McCardell, Derrick Mason, and Joey Galloway. The group that was done by Boldin's age includes Andre Rison, Terry Glenn, Terrance Mathis, Laveranues Coles, Anthony Miller, Herman Moore, and Chad Johnson. Hines Ward, whom we think of as an ageless wonder, had his last 1,000-yard season at age 33, the age Boldin turns in October. Isaac Bruce faded quickly in the season when he turned 34. Marvin Harrison and Keyshawn Johnson had their last good years at age 34. And so on.

Boldin has not cracked the 1,000-yard barrier in three seasons. Super Bowl heroics aside, he is obviously part of the decline group, not the Terrell Owens-Tim Brown group, which is why the Ravens were willing to play the odds and ship him away at a bargain price. The trade appeared to be a gild-the-lily move for the 49ers until Michael Crabtree got hurt; Boldin will get first crack at filling Crabtree's quasi-possession role, though Jim Harbaugh sounded eager for younger receivers to step up in May. Boldin lacks Crabtree's athleticism at this point in his career but has plenty of ways to compensate, and it is not like the 49ers offense is hurting for athleticism. The 49ers will be happy to get those one or two productive years Boldin has left. The Ravens were thrilled with the one he gave them last year.

Dwayne Bowe			Height: 6-2			Weight: 221			College: Louisiana State			Draft: 2007/1 (23)			Born: 21-Sep-1984		Age: 29		Risk: Yellow
Year	Team	G/GS	Snaps	Rec	Pass	Yds	C%	+/-	Yd/C	TD	Drop	YAC	Rk	YAC+	BTkl	DVOA	Rk	DYAR	Rk	YAR	Short	Mid	Deep	Bomb
2010	KC	16/16	933	72	133	1162	54%	+3.4	16.1	15	7	5.1	20	+1.1	8	12.5%	17	290	5	297	25%	37%	27%	12%
2011	KC	16/14	905	81	141	1159	57%	+0.6	14.3	5	9	4.2	44	+0.2	11	-0.2%	51	166	28	165	26%	46%	21%	7%
2012	KC	13/12	739	59	114	801	52%	-3.6	13.6	3	4	4.0	43	+0.2	6	-4.1%	56	60	56	76	17%	54%	18%	11%
2013	KC			80	131	1109	61%	--	13.9	9							14.5%							

The Chiefs' new front office and coaching staff chose to re-sign Bowe to a lucrative long-term contract this past offseason after the previous regime had franchised him in 2012. While the money may have been a bit steep ($26 million guaranteed), the move makes sense. Bowe can serve as a respectable No. 1 receiver in Andy Reid's West Coast offense. He's not always a crisp route runner or sure-handed target, but he knows how to use his size and brawny strength over the middle. He's a very willing blocker and solid run-after-catch weapon, too.

Though Bowe is the No. 1 in Kansas City, it's hard to categorize him in the first or maybe even second echelon of NFL wide-outs (depending on how many echelons one believes there to be). He does not have the speed or fluidity to consistently separate downfield. Yes, he wins his share of jump balls and body positioning battles, but those are traits that not all defenses believe are worth double-teaming. The KUBIAK projection system loves his chances to improve with a more accurate quarterback.

Josh Boyce			Height: 5-11			Weight: 206			College: TCU			Draft: 2013/4 (102)			Born: 6-May-1991		Age: 22		Risk: Red
Year	Team	G/GS	Snaps	Rec	Pass	Yds	C%	+/-	Yd/C	TD	Drop	YAC	Rk	YAC+	BTkl	DVOA	Rk	DYAR	Rk	YAR	Short	Mid	Deep	Bomb
2013	NE			23	47	344	49%	--	15.0	2							-6.1%							

New England's fourth-round pick is an athletic and tough-nosed receiver who is much better at finding holes in zone coverage than he is at making the sharp cuts that will get him open consistently against man coverage. Boyce's yards per reception numbers at TCU dropped with each year, but that was in large part a function of the quarterbacks he played with. He averaged 19.0 yards per catch and was a freshman All-American with Andy Dalton as his quarterback in 2010, 16.4 yards per catch with Casey Pachall playing quarterback in 2011, and only 13.5 yards per catch last season when Pachall was injured and freshman Trevone Boykin was forced to start.

Jarrett Boykin			Height: 6-2			Weight: 218			College: Virginia Tech			Draft: 2012/FA			Born: 4-Nov-1989		Age: 24		Risk: Blue
Year	Team	G/GS	Snaps	Rec	Pass	Yds	C%	+/-	Yd/C	TD	Drop	YAC	Rk	YAC+	BTkl	DVOA	Rk	DYAR	Rk	YAR	Short	Mid	Deep	Bomb
2012	GB	10/0	93	5	6	27	83%	+1.2	5.4	0	0	1.2	--	-2.9	0	-25.6%	--	-8	--	-6	50%	33%	0%	17%
2013	GB			19	36	300	53%	--	15.8	2							3.9%							

Boykin is one of those track-star types who needs to learn how to play wide receiver in the NFL. Sometimes, like Devery Henderson, those guys develop into real NFL receivers. Sometimes, like Ted Ginn and Troy Williamson, they do not. Green Bay is smart enough to pick these guys up as undrafted free agents, not as high draft picks. The fact that Boykin came into last season as the sixth receiver on the depth chart and still managed to accumulate eight percent of the offensive snaps is pretty indicative of how ridiculous the Packers' injury problems at wideout were in 2012. With Donald Driver and Greg Jennings out the door, Boykin currently is penciled in as the No. 4 receiver. As long as he can beat out Jeremy Ross and two seventh-round rookies for that position, he's a massive sleeper in very deep fantasy leagues, because an injury would effectively make him a starter on one of the league's top offenses.

LaVon Brazill		Height: 5-11		Weight: 191		College: Ohio		Draft: 2012/6 (206)			Born: 5-Mar-1989		Age: 24		Risk: Green	
Year	Team	G/GS	Snaps	Rec	Pass	Yds	C%	+/-	Yd/C	TD	Drop	YAC	Rk	YAC+	BTkl	DVOA	Rk	DYAR	Rk	YAR	Short	Mid	Deep	Bomb
2012	IND	15/0	206	11	24	186	46%	-2.0	16.9	1	2	6.5	--	+1.4	1	-6.6%	--	5	--	13	25%	17%	33%	25%
2013	IND			12	23	184	52%	--	15.3	1						1.3%								

Brazill was used sparingly as a rookie and struggled with consistency; his catch rate dropped from 71 percent over his last three college seasons to just 46 percent in his first year with Indianapolis. Brazill was expected to compete with Nathan Palmer for the No. 4 receiver role behind Reggie Wayne, Darrius Heyward-Bey and T.Y. Hilton, but he was suspended for the first four games of the regular season for violating the league's substance abuse policy. His role with the Colts, if any, is unlikely to be determined before he is reinstated on September 30.

Kenny Britt		Height: 6-3		Weight: 218		College: Rutgers		Draft: 2009/1 (30)			Born: 19-Sep-1988		Age: 25		Risk: Red	
Year	Team	G/GS	Snaps	Rec	Pass	Yds	C%	+/-	Yd/C	TD	Drop	YAC	Rk	YAC+	BTkl	DVOA	Rk	DYAR	Rk	YAR	Short	Mid	Deep	Bomb
2010	TEN	12/7	461	42	73	775	58%	+7.7	18.5	9	4	2.9	69	-1.4	7	29.6%	2	235	13	258	16%	39%	25%	20%
2011	TEN	3/3	142	17	26	289	65%	+2.6	17.0	3	0	7.4	--	+2.5	5	34.6%	--	111	--	92	36%	32%	8%	24%
2012	TEN	14/11	600	45	90	589	50%	-5.5	13.1	4	7	2.8	74	-1.3	6	-23.7%	82	-46	81	-71	24%	48%	10%	17%
2013	TEN			57	107	889	53%	--	15.6	6						2.4%								

Last year we learned that Britt does not have Adrian Peterson's genetics when it comes to ACL recovery. Britt is now reportedly fully healthy and re-adjusted to the speed of the NFL game. A fully healthy Britt has shown he can be a dominant player, though it's always been only in short stretches before injury takes him away again. Entering into the final year of his rookie deal, the Titans can cast one more roll of the dice on Britt before he finds himself elsewhere in 2014.

Antonio Brown		Height: 5-10		Weight: 186		College: Central Mighican		Draft: 2010/6 (195)			Born: 10-Jul-1988		Age: 25		Risk: Yellow	
Year	Team	G/GS	Snaps	Rec	Pass	Yds	C%	+/-	Yd/C	TD	Drop	YAC	Rk	YAC+	BTkl	DVOA	Rk	DYAR	Rk	YAR	Short	Mid	Deep	Bomb
2010	PIT	9/0	67	16	19	167	84%	+2.2	10.4	0	0	6.9	--	+1.2	0	27.7%	--	61	--	53	63%	21%	11%	5%
2011	PIT	16/3	608	69	124	1108	56%	-3.7	16.1	2	6	4.9	27	+0.4	2	9.4%	33	197	23	187	23%	42%	28%	7%
2012	PIT	13/10	652	66	106	787	63%	+3.7	11.9	5	3	5.3	21	-0.0	4	-1.9%	50	88	43	93	38%	38%	15%	9%
2013	PIT			75	128	1051	59%	--	14.0	8						6.9%								

Over one-fourth of the passes thrown to Brown were some kind of screen or "smoke" play: he caught 24-of-28 balls for 141 yards on throws at or behind the line of scrimmage. Receiver screens and smoke passes are called when a defense is playing "dishonestly," typically giving receivers giant cushions. The Steelers offense saw its share of dishonesty last year: Brown and Mike Wallace terrified opponents with their speed, but the running game was a farce, so why not give receivers 12-yard cushions and station the safeties in the end zone? Asking a player like Brown to grind out five yards at a time is a waste of resources, and while Todd Haley sometimes fetishizes the screen game, a rebuilt running game and Wallace's departure will lead defenses to play more straight-up coverage. That's a double-edged sword—the Steelers want defenses on their heels at the snap—but it should create more opportunities for Brown to run a route before he makes a catch.

Vincent Brown		Height: 5-11		Weight: 184		College: San Diego State		Draft: 2011/3 (82)			Born: 25-Jan-1989		Age: 24		Risk: Yellow	
Year	Team	G/GS	Snaps	Rec	Pass	Yds	C%	+/-	Yd/C	TD	Drop	YAC	Rk	YAC+	BTkl	DVOA	Rk	DYAR	Rk	YAR	Short	Mid	Deep	Bomb
2011	SD	14/4	336	19	40	329	48%	-1.1	17.3	2	1	4.1	--	+0.2	0	2.2%	--	45	--	50	18%	39%	21%	21%
2013	SD			28	50	314	56%	--	11.2	2						-8.1%								

Brown missed all of 2012 with a broken foot but is expected to be full-go in 2013. If he's healthy, has has intriguing potential as a No. 2 or No. 3 receiver. As a rookie, he exhibited fluid, deceptive speed, good body control, and an ability to go up and high-point the ball. He wasn't spectacular in any way, but there did not seem to be many things that he theoretically could *not* do.

Ryan Broyles		Height: 5-10		Weight: 192		College: Oklahoma		Draft: 2012/2 (54)			Born: 9-Apr-1988		Age: 25		Risk: Red	
Year	Team	G/GS	Snaps	Rec	Pass	Yds	C%	+/-	Yd/C	TD	Drop	YAC	Rk	YAC+	BTkl	DVOA	Rk	DYAR	Rk	YAR	Short	Mid	Deep	Bomb
2012	DET	10/3	278	22	32	310	69%	+2.6	14.1	2	3	6.9	--	+2.4	1	38.7%	--	140	--	117	57%	27%	7%	10%
2013	DET			49	82	659	60%	--	13.5	4						3.8%								

Assuming that Broyles continues to follow the 13-month ACL tear pattern he has established, he will make it to January 2014 before he blows the next one out. There was plenty of promise in his shortened rookie season. Broyles is very deft and has some elusiveness in the open field. He was best utilized out of the slot because he doesn't get off jams well, something that the Lions can work on with more practice time. Broyles was a surprise participant in OTA's, and with nobody in front of him, he should get to play as soon as he's healthy. Anyone with talent playing next to Calvin Johnson should be monitored closely in fantasy leagues.

Dez Bryant		Height: 6-2		Weight: 225			College: Oklahoma State			Draft: 2010/1 (24)			Born: 4-Nov-1988		Age: 25		Risk: Green	
Year	Team	G/GS	Snaps	Rec	Pass	Yds	C%	+/-	Yd/C	TD	Drop	YAC	Rk	YAC+	BTkl	DVOA	Rk	DYAR	Rk	YAR	Short	Mid	Deep	Bomb
2010	DAL	12/2	410	45	73	561	62%	+3.4	12.5	6	2	4.3	34	-0.6	7	6.1%	36	100	44	94	39%	33%	14%	13%
2011	DAL	15/13	765	63	103	928	61%	+3.7	14.7	9	3	4.8	29	+0.4	10	19.9%	14	246	14	249	26%	47%	16%	12%
2012	DAL	16/14	922	92	138	1282	67%	+7.9	13.9	12	9	4.9	30	+0.4	16	18.3%	17	392	3	352	34%	38%	14%	15%
2013	DAL			83	130	1184	64%	--	14.3	11							21.7%								

When he's on and paying attention, Bryant is Gumby with a rocket—he can beat just about any cornerback downfield, and will torque his body into seemingly impossible positions to make splash catches. When he's not on, Bryant is a quarterback's nightmare—a no-doubt No. 1 target who botches routes and creates traffic jams for his own passing offense. Bryant was more the former in 2012, posting career highs in DYAR and catch rate. Bryant has had his share of off-field issues through his time as a pro and college player, but there are inklings that he may be figuring things out—and Dez Bryant with a clear head it s scary thought for Cowboys opponents. He's talked about a 2,000-yard season with 20 touchdowns as a realistic goal, and he's one of the few receivers with the talent and system to actually make that happen.

"I found myself," Bryant said during the Cowboys' first round of OTAs in 2013. "I'm comfortable with my life. I'm enjoying being in the NFL. I wish it could've been a couple years back, but I had to go through a couple of things to figure it out. I think I got it and I'm just more focused on my job and doing what I love to do and that's playing football."

Bryant has been listening to at least one admirable model when it comes to fulfilling one's athletic potential—he became the seventh NFL player to sign with the Jordan Brand this offseason, and got a lecture from Michael Jordan about behaving himself and staying on the right side. If this is indeed Bryant's Cris Carter-level wake-up call, watch out, because for all his boneheaded-ness, Bryant is right up there with Calvin Johnson and A.J. Green in terms of pure physical skill. One area in need of immediate improvement: As Tony Romo's primary third-down target, Bryant amassed a 49 percent catch rate and -6.5% DVOA on 43 passes.

Nate Burleson		Height: 6-0		Weight: 192			College: Nevada			Draft: 2003/3 (71)			Born: 19-Aug-1981		Age: 32		Risk: Green	
Year	Team	G/GS	Snaps	Rec	Pass	Yds	C%	+/-	Yd/C	TD	Drop	YAC	Rk	YAC+	BTkl	DVOA	Rk	DYAR	Rk	YAR	Short	Mid	Deep	Bomb
2010	DET	14/14	859	55	86	625	64%	-1.8	11.4	6	4	5.5	13	+1.0	12	-4.0%	62	65	59	61	44%	36%	19%	1%
2011	DET	16/11	962	73	110	757	66%	-3.2	10.4	3	6	5.5	19	+0.7	12	-5.4%	59	31	62	73	64%	25%	8%	4%
2012	DET	6/5	356	27	43	240	63%	-0.4	8.9	2	0	3.1	--	-1.8	1	-14.0%	--	-24	--	4	51%	34%	12%	2%
2013	DET			45	76	537	59%	--	11.9	2							-3.6%								

A lot can change in a few months. Burleson broke his leg in a Monday Night loss to Chicago in Week 6, and admitted to the Lions official website that he wasn't sure he would return for 2013. "With them balling out completely, it could leave me the odd man out," Burleson said of Titus Young and Ryan Broyles. Young's exile and Broyles' second ACL tear in as many years, along with Burleson's willingness to take a pay cut, mean he now opens the season as the Lions No. 2 receiver. Burleson is a classy guy who has a future as an NFL coach or TV network analyst, but a 32-year-old receiver with his track record, coming off season-ending surgery, shouldn't be any higher than No. 4 on a rational depth chart.

Plaxico Burress		Height: 6-5		Weight: 232			College: Michigan State			Draft: 2000/1 (8)			Born: 12-Aug-1977		Age: 36		Risk: Red	
Year	Team	G/GS	Snaps	Rec	Pass	Yds	C%	+/-	Yd/C	TD	Drop	YAC	Rk	YAC+	BTkl	DVOA	Rk	DYAR	Rk	YAR	Short	Mid	Deep	Bomb
2011	NYJ	16/13	854	45	96	612	47%	-7.9	13.6	8	4	3.2	74	-0.4	2	-6.2%	62	73	54	89	16%	53%	26%	4%
2012	PIT	4/3	34	3	7	42	43%	-1.0	14.0	1	0	1.3	--	-1.5	0	28.7%	--	32	--	30	0%	71%	29%	0%
2013	PIT			15	25	227	60%	--	15.1	2							12.6%								

Re-signed by the Steelers for 2013, inexplicably. This is a team that hemmed and hawed while the Patriots courted Emmanuel Sanders, yet they have room on the bench for a 36-year-old who came aboard as a late-season replacement last season but could barely get on the field. The Steelers talked about using Plax as an end-zone specialist last year, but keeping a baggage-laden veteran around strictly for jump balls is just not the Steelers way. Look for Plax to be a camp cut if rookies Markus Wheaton and Justin Brown display any workplace readiness.

Randall Cobb		Height: 5-11		Weight: 190			College: Kentucky			Draft: 2011/2 (64)			Born: 22-Aug-1990		Age: 23		Risk: Green	
Year	Team	G/GS	Snaps	Rec	Pass	Yds	C%	+/-	Yd/C	TD	Drop	YAC	Rk	YAC+	BTkl	DVOA	Rk	DYAR	Rk	YAR	Short	Mid	Deep	Bomb
2011	GB	15/0	274	25	31	375	81%	+4.0	15.0	1	2	7.5	--	+3.4	5	42.5%	--	121	--	133	35%	45%	19%	0%
2012	GB	15/8	631	80	104	954	77%	+11.1	11.9	8	8	5.7	18	+0.1	13	24.1%	9	357	6	303	55%	23%	20%	3%
2013	GB			90	124	1055	73%	--	11.7	7							20.2%								

Percy Harvin was the first of this new breed of NFL receiver that could be dangerous catching swing passes or even taking handoffs out of the backfield. Cobb is the second wave. A bit more polished of a route-runner than Harvin, Cobb also hasn't shown the same injury tendencies thus far. The objective remains the same: get him the ball in open space and let him do his thing. Cobb's 13 broken tackles last season ranked him sixth among all receivers. Aaron Rodgers has predicted that Cobb could be a "100-catch guy every year." As long as his body can hold up to that punishment, he should be one of the most valuable receivers of the 2010s. Cobb had 10 carries for 132 yards last year, and his 2013 projection includes 12 carries for 75 yards.

Marques Colston			Height: 6-4			Weight: 225			College: Hofstra			Draft: 2006/7 (252)			Born: 5-Jun-1983		Age: 30		Risk: Green	
Year	Team	G/GS	Snaps	Rec	Pass	Yds	C%	+/-	Yd/C	TD	Drop	YAC	Rk	YAC+	BTkl	DVOA	Rk	DYAR	Rk	YAR	Short	Mid	Deep	Bomb
2010	NO	15/11	805	84	132	1023	64%	+4.3	12.2	7	8	3.2	62	-0.6	3	9.1%	26	250	11	250	35%	46%	15%	4%
2011	NO	14/7	659	80	107	1143	75%	+15.7	14.3	8	3	3.2	76	-0.6	1	34.3%	5	430	5	444	22%	51%	20%	8%
2012	NO	16/13	832	83	130	1154	64%	+5.9	13.9	10	9	3.5	61	-0.1	1	19.7%	15	327	11	339	27%	56%	12%	5%
2013	NO			79	127	1092	62%	--	13.8	9							12.8%								

Like fellow wideout Lance Moore, Colston will be 30 this season, and like Moore, Colston's advanced numbers fell off from the heights of the 2011 season. Colston is still one of the league's better receivers, and he continues to be dominant in the red zone, where he uses his tight end-sized frame to box out or overpower defenders. Last year, on 23 targets in the red zone, Colston had 77.0% DVOA, 74 percent catch rate, and all ten of his touchdowns. As his speed diminishes with age, Colston might even be a candidate for a late-career move inside, playing receiving tight end in two-tight formations. For now, though, he remains a top fantasy option at wideout.

Riley Cooper			Height: 6-4			Weight: 222			College: Florida			Draft: 2010/5 (159)			Born: 9-Sep-1987		Age: 26		Risk: Green	
Year	Team	G/GS	Snaps	Rec	Pass	Yds	C%	+/-	Yd/C	TD	Drop	YAC	Rk	YAC+	BTkl	DVOA	Rk	DYAR	Rk	YAR	Short	Mid	Deep	Bomb
2010	PHI	13/2	224	7	18	116	39%	-1.5	16.6	1	0	2.6	--	-2.0	1	-15.3%	--	1	--	1	14%	57%	21%	7%
2011	PHI	16/3	321	16	35	315	46%	+0.3	19.7	1	3	3.5	--	-1.1	1	-0.6%	--	23	--	33	10%	50%	20%	20%
2012	PHI	11/5	486	23	48	248	48%	-5.4	10.8	3	1	4.0	--	-0.3	2	-22.8%	--	-15	--	-25	27%	51%	16%	7%
2013	PHI			14	27	166	52%	--	11.8	1							-13.4%								

Cooper was a star at the University of Florida, but he's failed to develop into an all-around wide receiver in the pros. With his size, he may have a niche as a poor man's Plaxico Burress. He was reliable on third downs and in the red zone in 2012, but that was the extent of his success. He caught all four of his red-zone targets in 2012, turning three of them into touchdowns, and posted a DVOA of 23.9% on third and fourth downs last year. With three good tight ends and at least three receivers entrenched in front of him, Cooper will struggle to see the field in other situations in 2013.

Jerricho Cotchery			Height: 6-1			Weight: 200			College: North Carolina St.			Draft: 2004/4 (108)			Born: 16-Jun-1982		Age: 31		Risk: Red	
Year	Team	G/GS	Snaps	Rec	Pass	Yds	C%	+/-	Yd/C	TD	Drop	YAC	Rk	YAC+	BTkl	DVOA	Rk	DYAR	Rk	YAR	Short	Mid	Deep	Bomb
2010	NYJ	14/5	706	41	86	433	48%	-8.6	10.6	2	6	2.7	75	-1.5	3	-22.5%	78	-63	80	-75	34%	42%	14%	10%
2011	PIT	13/0	277	16	31	237	55%	-0.7	14.8	2	1	4.1	--	+0.5	0	13.0%	--	57	--	51	20%	57%	23%	0%
2012	PIT	14/2	266	17	27	205	63%	+0.7	12.1	0	0	2.5	--	-1.2	0	2.8%	--	35	--	37	27%	46%	27%	0%
2013	PIT			34	60	430	57%	--	12.7	3							-1.6%								

Cotchery has found the old boiler room where Charlie Batch used to hide during cut-down season; he plans to catch 17 passes per year and then hide behind the hot water heater until he turns 40. Cotchery's most important games lined up with the Batch-Leftwich Sunshine Boys period: his role increased when Antonio Brown was hurt, but he caught just 3-of-9 passes against the Chiefs and Ravens before getting injured himself. We have Cotchery projected for more targets in 2013 because Oregon State's late graduation forced rookie Markus Wheaton to miss OTAs, and the Steelers have always liked to ease their rookie wideouts in slowly regardless. By December, Cotchery should be back to his veteran default as a guy who stays in shape, knows his role, and can help out a little during an injury crisis.

Michael Crabtree			Height: 6-2			Weight: 215			College: Texas Tech			Draft: 2009/1 (10)			Born: 14-Sep-1987		Age: 26		Risk: Red	
Year	Team	G/GS	Snaps	Rec	Pass	Yds	C%	+/-	Yd/C	TD	Drop	YAC	Rk	YAC+	BTkl	DVOA	Rk	DYAR	Rk	YAR	Short	Mid	Deep	Bomb
2010	SF	16/15	872	55	100	741	55%	-2.6	13.5	6	7	5.3	15	+0.9	8	2.3%	43	109	41	109	37%	40%	14%	9%
2011	SF	15/14	668	72	114	874	64%	+3.1	12.1	4	5	5.0	25	+0.1	10	5.2%	39	170	27	128	46%	29%	17%	8%
2012	SF	16/16	674	85	127	1105	68%	+5.3	13.0	9	5	6.5	9	+1.9	14	21.9%	13	334	10	336	53%	32%	12%	4%
2013	SF			30	45	428	67%	--	14.3	3							21.1%								

The Crabtree narrative of 2012 was that he emerged as a go-to No. 1 receiver only after Colin Kaepernick ascended to the starting lineup. The numbers, however, say that's not entirely true. Yes, his advanced metrics improved overall with Kaepernick, but only slightly (by 5.4% DVOA). Yes, Kaepernick threw him the ball more frequently, but only slightly more (33 percent target rate, up from 27 percent). Moreover, on third down, his target rate was identical with both quarterbacks (44 percent), and he was actually more valuable with Smith (by 19.6% DVOA). Finally, despite talk of Kaepernick's pinpoint accuracy on slants, Crabtree essentially had the same YAC average with each quarterback (0.2 YAC difference).

Too bad this discussion has been rendered moot by his torn Achilles tendon. He won't miss the entire 2013 season, but his recovery might resemble that of Demaryius Thomas in 2011: play again seven months later, play well again 10 months later, play great again the following year.

Josh Cribbs		Height: 6-1		Weight: 192			College: Kent State			Draft: 2005/FA			Born: 9-Jun-1983		Age: 30		Risk: Green	
Year	Team	G/GS	Snaps	Rec	Pass	Yds	C%	+/-	Yd/C	TD	Drop	YAC	Rk	YAC+	BTkl	DVOA	Rk	DYAR	Rk	YAR	Short	Mid	Deep	Bomb
2010	CLE	15/5	346	23	39	292	59%	-0.2	12.7	1	0	6.0	--	+1.3	6	0.3%	--	33	--	21	34%	45%	5%	16%
2011	CLE	16/7	557	41	67	518	61%	+0.3	12.6	4	4	5.6	17	+0.8	8	12.1%	25	135	34	119	37%	42%	12%	9%
2012	CLE	16/2	62	7	12	63	58%	-1.4	9.0	0	1	6.0	--	+0.3	2	-28.8%	--	-10	--	-16	64%	36%	0%	0%
2013	OAK			13	22	151	59%	--	11.6	0						2.7%								

The classic Paul Brown-era Browns had a player named Dub Jones who played running back, "wingback," defensive back, returned kicks and punts, and threw a pass once in a while. Dub Jones is well-remembered by Browns fans of a certain age and by football historians: he was a pure "football player" in an era when specialization was taking over the game. (He was also Bert Jones' father.)

The modern Browns had Cribbs, a team captain who in any given week may have been the team's best all-around player (frequently), receiver (often), rushing threat (sometimes), and even quarterback (two words: Thaddeus Lewis). The Browns quibbled with Cribbs over his salary over the years, relegated him to "slash" player status for much of his career so players like Brian Robiskie could get long looks at wide receiver, and generally displayed their organizational lack of vision by getting as little as possible from such a unique talent. Cribbs looked banged-up and spent last year, and the Shurmur gang had no idea how to use him except in some halfhearted "Wildcat" package. Cribbs' knee is now a problem, with the Patriots and Cardinals passing on him for health/durability reasons, and the Browns don't want him back after trading for Davone Bess. Cribbs was a pure football player. It's a shame he never got to play for a pure football team.

Juron Criner		Height: 6-3		Weight: 224			College: Arizona			Draft: 2012/5 (168)			Born: 12-Dec-1989		Age: 24		Risk: Yellow	
Year	Team	G/GS	Snaps	Rec	Pass	Yds	C%	+/-	Yd/C	TD	Drop	YAC	Rk	YAC+	BTkl	DVOA	Rk	DYAR	Rk	YAR	Short	Mid	Deep	Bomb
2012	OAK	12/0	164	16	33	151	48%	-4.0	9.4	1	1	5.0	--	+0.2	2	-36.1%	--	-52	--	-57	47%	43%	7%	3%
2013	OAK			31	57	368	54%	--	11.9	2						-9.2%								

Criner made a minimal impact as a rookie despite playing in a Raiders offense that had a revolving door at wide receiver. It's telling that, despite being a fifth-round pick, he was behind undrafted rookie Rod Streater on the depth chart. At 6-foot-3 and more than 220 pounds, Criner is built like a possession target, which is what many labeled him as coming out of Arizona State. He is said to have soft, ball-plucking hands and somewhat limited initial burst and explosiveness.

Victor Cruz		Height: 6-1		Weight: 200			College: Massachusetts			Draft: 2010/FA			Born: 11-Nov-1986		Age: 27		Risk: Green	
Year	Team	G/GS	Snaps	Rec	Pass	Yds	C%	+/-	Yd/C	TD	Drop	YAC	Rk	YAC+	BTkl	DVOA	Rk	DYAR	Rk	YAR	Short	Mid	Deep	Bomb
2011	NYG	16/7	747	82	129	1536	64%	+9.1	18.7	9	8	7.2	2	+2.9	11	31.4%	8	433	4	445	31%	41%	19%	9%
2012	NYG	16/16	902	86	143	1092	60%	-0.8	12.7	10	9	3.8	50	-0.2	6	1.2%	41	165	28	166	33%	48%	8%	11%
2013	NYG			87	141	1197	62%	--	13.8	9						12.3%								

In 2011, Cruz ranked second in the league in yards per catch. His 18.7 yards per reception was a product of two elements: Cruz ran a lot of downfield routes and he gained a significant number of yards after the catch. But in 2012, Cruz turned into a completely different player. After trailing only Julio Jones among wide receivers in average yards gained after the catch in 2011, Cruz barely averaged more YAC than teammate Martellus Bennett. Yes, Cruz was bound to see his YAC drop because you don't get to score a 99-yard touchdown every year, but even if we remove touchdowns over 70 yards (four in 2011, two in 2012), Cruz's YAC drops from 4.2 in 2011 to 2.8 in 2012. In addition, his route tree changed: his average catch came just 8.9 yards down the field compared to an 11.6 average in 2011. With Hakeem Nicks hampered by injury and Rueben Randle emerging as the deep threat, the Giants turned Cruz into a possession receiver. But that doesn't mean he wasn't effective: one reason Eli Manning led the NFL in sack rate was that Cruz has a knack for getting open quickly. He has become Manning's go-to weapon on third downs, finishing in the top six in both third-down targets and third-down receptions that led to a first down. He's quickly become one of the best receivers in the league, even if he may never again challenge to lead the league in yards per catch.

Eric Decker		Height: 6-3		Weight: 217			College: Minnesota			Draft: 2010/3 (87)			Born: 15-Mar-1987		Age: 26		Risk: Green	
Year	Team	G/GS	Snaps	Rec	Pass	Yds	C%	+/-	Yd/C	TD	Drop	YAC	Rk	YAC+	BTkl	DVOA	Rk	DYAR	Rk	YAR	Short	Mid	Deep	Bomb
2010	DEN	14/0	138	6	8	106	75%	+1.2	17.7	1	1	4.0	--	-1.6	1	56.9%	--	30	--	32	13%	50%	25%	13%
2011	DEN	16/13	972	44	98	612	46%	-7.4	13.9	8	6	3.9	58	-0.9	1	-15.5%	76	-24	76	-40	30%	34%	16%	20%
2012	DEN	16/15	1048	85	123	1064	69%	+12.5	12.5	13	7	3.1	69	-0.7	3	27.2%	8	392	4	401	32%	45%	11%	12%
2013	DEN			65	102	906	64%	--	13.9	8						19.8%								

The arrival of Wes Welker means that Eric Decker will see fewer passes this season; even with Peyton Manning at quarterback, there are only so many balls to go around. But on another team, Decker could easily be a No. 1 receiver. He has excellent hands, showing a consistent feel for plucking the ball away from his body. He's a very crisp and intelligent route runner, which earns him Peyton Manning's trust—especially on third-and-medium and in the red zone. His ability to make adjustments against tight coverage when the ball is in the air plays into the equation. Down the stretch last season, he also showed the ability to win one-on-one battles outside, particularly with comebacker type patterns.

Aaron Dobson			Height: 6-3			Weight: 210			College: Marshall			Draft: 2013/2 (59)			Born: 13-Jun-1991		Age: 22		Risk: Red
Year	Team	G/GS	Snaps	Rec	Pass	Yds	C%	+/-	Yd/C	TD	Drop	YAC	Rk	YAC+	BTkl	DVOA	Rk	DYAR	Rk	YAR	Short	Mid	Deep	Bomb
2013	NE			31	60	485	52%	--	15.6	3						1.0%								

Since trading Randy Moss to Minnesota in mid-2010, the Patriots have been unable to find the right fit for the "X" position in their offense: a receiver who could play on the outside, make tough catches, and stretch the field to make room underneath for all their slot guys and tight ends. Dobson fits the role perfectly, if he can play more consistently than he did at Marshall. He's a big guy with excellent hands and the ability to adjust to the ball in the air; search on YouTube and you'll find a couple of spectacular catches. On the other hand, as our own Matt Waldman has written, Dobson's "How did he do that?" plays are often matched by an equal number of "Why did he do that?" plays. He sometimes doesn't seem quite sure of where the sidelines are, and after the catch he has a tendency to squirm around like he thinks he's a 5-foot-9 slot receiver instead of using his big frame to break tackles. As much as New England fans want Dobson to march right into the starting lineup and start performing, he's still a bit of a project and he's going to take some development time.

Tandon Doss			Height: 6-3			Weight: 200			College: Indiana			Draft: 2011/4 (123)			Born: 22-Sep-1989		Age: 24		Risk: Yellow
Year	Team	G/GS	Snaps	Rec	Pass	Yds	C%	+/-	Yd/C	TD	Drop	YAC	Rk	YAC+	BTkl	DVOA	Rk	DYAR	Rk	YAR	Short	Mid	Deep	Bomb
2011	BAL	6/0	30	0	2	0	0%	-1.2	0.0	0	0	0.0	--	+0.0	0	2.9%	--	1	--	4	0%	67%	0%	33%
2012	BAL	14/0	183	7	17	123	41%	-2.5	17.6	1	1	7.4	--	+3.0	0	5.3%	--	20	--	20	40%	33%	20%	7%
2013	BAL			18	34	268	53%	--	14.9	2						-0.8%								

Doss underwent double-sports hernia surgery after his senior season at Indiana in 2011 and was never truly healthy as a rookie. He stuck as the fourth receiver last season, his role increasing infinitesimally after Week 10, when he earned regular snaps in some three-receiver packages. Doss moves up to third on the depth chart by attrition this year. The Ravens have a great track record with slow-burn developmental prospects; that said, it's hard to envision Doss as a worthy No. 3 receiver for a defending champion. Deonte Thompson generated a lot of offseason buzz and could find a depth chart opening right here.

Early Doucet			Height: 6-0			Weight: 209			College: Louisiana State			Draft: 2008/3 (81)			Born: 28-Oct-1985		Age: 28		Risk: N/A
Year	Team	G/GS	Snaps	Rec	Pass	Yds	C%	+/-	Yd/C	TD	Drop	YAC	Rk	YAC+	BTkl	DVOA	Rk	DYAR	Rk	YAR	Short	Mid	Deep	Bomb
2010	ARI	10/5	349	26	59	291	44%	-9.8	11.2	1	6	3.1	66	-1.2	0	-40.2%	85	-120	83	-107	36%	45%	15%	4%
2011	ARI	16/6	554	54	97	689	56%	-5.7	12.8	5	4	6.0	12	+1.9	5	-10.9%	67	2	69	22	49%	33%	15%	2%
2012	ARI	12/3	387	28	53	207	53%	-8.5	7.4	0	6	2.9	73	-2.0	1	-38.8%	86	-144	85	-116	55%	37%	8%	0%

Injuries kept Doucet from replacing Dwayne Bowe as LSU's prime-time receiver, and injuries prevented him from becoming a big part of the Cardinals' receiver corps over the last five seasons. He's never started more than six games in a season, and has played all 16 games just once, in his contract year of 2011. That season prompted the team to re-sign him to a two-year, $4 million contract, but there was little interest in Doucet's return once a new administration was in place, and he was released in March. Doucet is a capable if inconsistent receiver when healthy, and maybe he'll catch on somewhere with a better quarterback situation and surprise with a second team. He's still a free agent as of publication.

Harry Douglas			Height: 5-11			Weight: 176			College: Louisville			Draft: 2008/3 (84)			Born: 16-Sep-1985		Age: 28		Risk: Green
Year	Team	G/GS	Snaps	Rec	Pass	Yds	C%	+/-	Yd/C	TD	Drop	YAC	Rk	YAC+	BTkl	DVOA	Rk	DYAR	Rk	YAR	Short	Mid	Deep	Bomb
2010	ATL	16/4	542	22	53	294	42%	-8.1	13.4	1	2	5.6	10	+1.2	4	-25.6%	79	-53	77	-57	32%	32%	22%	14%
2011	ATL	16/4	624	39	62	498	63%	+1.8	12.8	1	2	5.9	13	+1.2	1	-4.4%	57	33	61	37	44%	34%	15%	7%
2012	ATL	15/1	585	38	59	396	64%	+2.1	10.4	1	1	4.0	44	-0.9	3	-16.6%	77	-6	76	-4	52%	22%	20%	6%
2013	ATL			33	56	409	59%	--	12.4	2						-2.9%								

Douglas might have become a postseason hero had he not tripped over his own feet trying to haul in a Matt Ryan lob while wide open late in the NFC Championship game. He did manage to catch it, according to the officials (much to the eye-rolling, knee-buckling shock of Jim Harbaugh), but if Douglas had only kept his balance, he might have scored the winning touchdown.

The play serves as a handy metaphor for Douglas' career. He's a useful slot receiver, but underwhelming—there is an inescapable feeling that he could be accomplishing so much more. Playing off Julio Jones and Roddy White and Tony Gonzalez is a double-edged sword. Douglas generally operates in open spaces, but at the cost of seeing the majority of targets go elsewhere. His YAC and YPC are on worrying downward trends, but as a fourth option in a high-powered passing attack you could do worse. The brilliance of his compadres makes Douglas a fantasy stay-away.

Donald Driver		Height: 6-0		Weight: 188			College: Alcorn State			Draft: 1999/7 (213)			Born: 2-Feb-1975		Age: 38		Risk: N/A			
Year	Team	G/GS	Snaps	Rec	Pass	Yds	C%	+/-	Yd/C	TD	Drop	YAC	Rk	YAC+	BTkl	DVOA	Rk	DYAR	Rk	YAR	Short	Mid	Deep	Bomb
2010	GB	15/15	672	51	84	565	61%	-1.9	11.1	4	6	3.5	56	-1.0	4	-7.5%	68	40	67	34	38%	41%	16%	5%
2011	GB	16/15	495	37	56	445	66%	+1.5	12.0	6	6	3.7	62	-0.1	1	17.7%	15	125	42	136	28%	56%	14%	2%
2012	GB	13/1	150	8	13	77	62%	-0.3	9.6	2	3	1.5	--	-2.6	0	-0.5%	--	21	--	16	31%	62%	8%	0%

There aren't many recent receivers who have proven as classy as Driver. He tracked down a long-time Packers fan that couldn't make his retirement ceremony just to give her a hug. It was clear that he could no longer contribute at a meaningful level last season, which makes sense given that he was 37 years old. Pour out a 40 for Driver and it'll probably beat his current 40-yard dash time, but the man knew how to play wide receiver in the NFL.

Julian Edelman		Height: 6-0		Weight: 198			College: Kent State			Draft: 2009/7 (232)			Born: 22-May-1986		Age: 27		Risk: Red			
Year	Team	G/GS	Snaps	Rec	Pass	Yds	C%	+/-	Yd/C	TD	Drop	YAC	Rk	YAC+	BTkl	DVOA	Rk	DYAR	Rk	YAR	Short	Mid	Deep	Bomb
2010	NE	15/3	178	7	14	86	50%	-3.5	12.3	0	2	14.1	--	+5.8	5	-28.9%	--	-16	--	-22	79%	14%	7%	0%
2011	NE	13/0	117	4	8	34	50%	-0.7	8.5	0	0	2.3	--	-2.6	1	-61.3%	--	-30	--	-28	57%	29%	14%	0%
2012	NE	9/3	295	21	32	235	66%	-0.5	11.2	3	1	6.7	--	+0.7	3	10.3%	--	65	--	62	55%	32%	6%	6%
2013	NE			45	68	502	66%	--	11.2	2						4.3%								

For the first few weeks of 2012, Edelman was playing his biggest role in the Patriots offense since his rookie year. Improved straight-line speed and blocking had the Patriots using Edelman ahead of Wes Welker in two-receiver packages. Then Edelman dealt with a hand injury, a concussion, and a broken foot, in that order. The Patriots re-signed him after he didn't get much attention in free agency, possibly because there have been setbacks in his recovery from that foot injury. If he's healthy enough to get on the field, he'll be Danny Amendola's backup at the "Z" spot (which in the Patriots' offense is half-flanker, half-slot receiver). If the foot continues to be a problem, it's hard to imagine that the Patriots can't stash him on PUP so he can replace some other injured receiver if he finally gets healthy late in the season.

Braylon Edwards		Height: 6-3		Weight: 211			College: Michigan			Draft: 2005/1 (3)			Born: 21-Feb-1983		Age: 30		Risk: N/A			
Year	Team	G/GS	Snaps	Rec	Pass	Yds	C%	+/-	Yd/C	TD	Drop	YAC	Rk	YAC+	BTkl	DVOA	Rk	DYAR	Rk	YAR	Short	Mid	Deep	Bomb
2010	NYJ	16/15	891	53	101	904	52%	+2.2	17.1	7	3	5.4	14	+1.4	4	3.4%	41	132	32	143	27%	37%	13%	23%
2011	SF	9/5	229	15	34	181	44%	-4.5	12.1	0	1	3.1	--	-0.2	2	-27.0%	--	-56	--	-49	29%	58%	10%	3%
2012	2TM	13/4	292	18	36	199	50%	-1.7	11.1	1	0	1.8	--	-1.7	0	-15.1%	--	-13	--	-12	18%	53%	18%	12%

In his third NFL season, Edwards had 1,289 yards and 16 touchdowns for the 2007 Browns. He never again had 1,000 yards or half as many touchdowns, and now he's a good example of what it looks like to see a star receiver's career slowly peter out. He's been particularly awful as a red-zone weapon, catching just 3 of 17 passes over the last two years with one touchdown, plus two first downs from drawing pass interference. The Jets picked him back up when the Seahawks waived him last year, and there are reports they might re-sign him for 2013 as well, but what would a rebuilding offense get out of this guy?

Larry Fitzgerald		Height: 6-3		Weight: 225			College: Pittsburgh			Draft: 2004/1 (3)			Born: 31-Aug-1983		Age: 30		Risk: Yellow			
Year	Team	G/GS	Snaps	Rec	Pass	Yds	C%	+/-	Yd/C	TD	Drop	YAC	Rk	YAC+	BTkl	DVOA	Rk	DYAR	Rk	YAR	Short	Mid	Deep	Bomb
2010	ARI	16/15	936	90	172	1137	52%	-8.5	12.6	6	5	2.4	79	-1.5	5	-13.3%	71	12	71	39	24%	42%	24%	10%
2011	ARI	16/16	1013	80	154	1411	52%	-5.3	17.6	8	3	6.1	8	+1.8	8	9.4%	32	188	26	241	28%	33%	25%	13%
2012	ARI	16/16	1029	71	156	798	46%	-21.8	11.2	4	1	3.8	49	-0.3	8	-23.8%	83	-218	86	-186	38%	38%	18%	5%
2013	ARI			83	151	1105	55%	--	13.3	8						-1.2%								

We've been feeling sorry for Fitzgerald since the day Kurt Warner retired, but the 2012 season was the worst example yet of what a group of truly putrid quarterbacks can do to the productivity of this undoubtedly great receiver. Fitzgerald will catch passes from Carson Palmer in 2013, and though Palmer isn't what he used to be, he's an interstellar upgrade to what Fitzgerald's been dealing with for the last few seasons. In addition, Bruce Arians has said that he intends to move Fitzgerald all over the formation to get him cleaner looks off the line of scrimmage. Arians did the same for Reggie Wayne in 2012, and Wayne had a great comeback year as a result.

The one caveat in terms of Fitzgerald's expected rebound this season is that his total stats aren't likely to rebound as much as his rate stats. Even if we ignore who is playing quarterback, Fitzgerald's share of the pie has been on the decline. In 2010, the first year without Anquan Boldin, he caught 32 percent of Cardinals receptions. He was responsible for only 26 percent of all Cardinals receptions in 2011, although a fluky 14 catches of 30-plus yards boosted his yardage total. Last year, he caught just 21 percent of Cardinals receptions. As the young weapons around him develop, the offense may become less reliant on Fitzgerald—especially considering the fact that when opponents concentrate on stopping Fitzgerald, it becomes easier to throw to everyone else.

Malcom Floyd			Height: 6-5			Weight: 201			College: Wyoming			Draft: 2004/FA			Born: 8-Sep-1981		Age: 32		Risk: Green	
Year	Team	G/GS	Snaps	Rec	Pass	Yds	C%	+/-	Yd/C	TD	Drop	YAC	Rk	YAC+	BTkl	DVOA	Rk	DYAR	Rk	YAR	Short	Mid	Deep	Bomb
2010	SD	11/9	556	37	77	717	48%	-2.2	19.4	6	1	3.0	67	-1.6	3	10.0%	22	142	30	150	8%	41%	31%	20%
2011	SD	12/9	513	43	70	856	61%	+7.4	19.9	5	1	4.2	46	+0.3	3	51.9%	2	339	7	345	12%	44%	31%	13%
2012	SD	14/14	845	56	84	814	67%	+9.5	14.5	5	1	1.8	86	-2.1	0	36.0%	3	281	15	303	16%	46%	26%	12%
2013	SD			59	96	819	61%	--	13.9	5							12.3%								

The gangly Floyd bears a physical resemblance to a giraffe, but he moves a lot better. Floyd has good body control on downfield patterns, showing the ability to make adjustments on the ball and, occasionally, create separation through technique. His best trait is his release off the line of scrimmage. He has a great feel for defeating a cornerback's jams. That's very uncommon for a player of his size.

The Chargers were hoping that Floyd could be their No. 1 receiver last year. They aligned him in multiple positions, including as a movable Z-receiver after it became apparent that Robert Meachem was not getting the job done there. Ideally, though, Floyd is a No. 2 target who aligns up on the line of scrimmage in the X spot. By No. 1 standards, he is not quite consistent enough at making the tough plays or winning the tough individual matchups. That doesn't come out in his DVOA or DYAR because it often results in passes left unthrown or dumped off rather than incomplete passes to Floyd.

Michael Floyd			Height: 6-3			Weight: 220			College: Notre Dame			Draft: 2012/1 (13)			Born: 27-Nov-1989		Age: 24		Risk: Yellow	
Year	Team	G/GS	Snaps	Rec	Pass	Yds	C%	+/-	Yd/C	TD	Drop	YAC	Rk	YAC+	BTkl	DVOA	Rk	DYAR	Rk	YAR	Short	Mid	Deep	Bomb
2012	ARI	16/3	555	45	86	562	52%	-2.1	12.5	2	4	3.5	62	-0.8	4	-10.3%	71	-3	74	-20	24%	51%	11%	14%
2013	ARI			55	94	770	59%	--	14.0	5							4.5%								

Floyd came to the NFL as the classic example of a receiver with a great deal of pure physical talent and a lack of awareness regarding the attributes that make those players special at the NFL level. After an inconsistent rookie year, Floyd believes that he's set for an uptick in 2013. He moved in with Larry Fitzgerald last year, and the teammates trained together. Floyd has changed his diet and added to his repertoire of route concepts, and new head coach Bruce Arians likes what he sees. "I am really happy with him," Arians told the Cardinals' official site in June. "I see him making leaps and bounds getting better. He's very serious about what he does. He doesn't like to make mistakes. He's totally bought in and if he just continues to improve his fundamentals, he's another guy who can have a breakout year." That's normally the kind of offseason nonsense babble we pay no attention to, but in there's no doubt that having an actual quarterback throwing footballs to him will help. Floyd is the kind of downfield receiver that could thrive in Arians' offense.

Jacoby Ford			Height: 5-9			Weight: 186			College: Clemson			Draft: 2010/4 (108)			Born: 27-Jul-1987		Age: 26		Risk: Red	
Year	Team	G/GS	Snaps	Rec	Pass	Yds	C%	+/-	Yd/C	TD	Drop	YAC	Rk	YAC+	BTkl	DVOA	Rk	DYAR	Rk	YAR	Short	Mid	Deep	Bomb
2010	OAK	16/9	558	25	54	470	46%	-4.0	18.8	2	4	4.1	39	-0.3	1	-1.8%	53	36	68	43	30%	26%	24%	20%
2011	OAK	8/3	205	19	33	279	58%	-1.7	14.7	1	1	6.6	--	+2.4	3	-5.2%	--	-4	--	13	44%	41%	9%	6%
2013	OAK			36	64	410	56%	--	11.4	2							-9.2%								

Ford has a unique combination of speed and change-of-direction ability, but injuries have limited him to just eight games over the past two years. When he's healthy, he's shown glimpses of sensational playmaking ability, particularly once the ball is in his hands. Generally, the earlier in the play Ford touches the ball, the better. As a rookie in 2010, the Raiders used him on screens, direct snaps, and kick returns (where he scored three touchdowns).

Pierre Garcon			Height: 6-0			Weight: 210			College: Mount Union			Draft: 2008/6 (205)			Born: 8-Aug-1986		Age: 27		Risk: Red	
Year	Team	G/GS	Snaps	Rec	Pass	Yds	C%	+/-	Yd/C	TD	Drop	YAC	Rk	YAC+	BTkl	DVOA	Rk	DYAR	Rk	YAR	Short	Mid	Deep	Bomb
2010	IND	14/14	937	67	119	784	56%	-2.2	11.7	6	12	3.7	49	-0.1	12	-6.6%	67	61	62	72	37%	37%	13%	13%
2011	IND	16/16	937	70	134	947	52%	-2.2	13.5	6	4	5.1	24	+0.8	6	-16.8%	78	-36	78	-55	32%	41%	14%	13%
2012	WAS	10/10	394	44	68	633	66%	+1.0	14.4	4	4	7.1	5	+1.4	3	8.2%	26	131	35	131	36%	38%	21%	5%
2013	WAS			71	117	1019	61%	--	14.3	7							8.1%								

The Redskins were slammed for giving Garcon a five-year, $42.5 million contract last offseason, including by us. He may not have lived up to that No. 1 receiver dollar figure, but he did post career highs in DVOA, DYAR, and catch rate, which is pretty interesting for a guy who caught footballs from Peyton Manning during his first three NFL seasons. Garcon would have been even more productive if he hadn't torn foot ligaments in the first game of the 2012 season, and played through the injury for 10 games, missing six. Garcon was knocked out of the Redskins' wild-card loss to the Seahawks with ankle and shoulder injuries, and he went into the 2013 preseason less than totally confident about his health. "You never know," Garcon told the *Washington Post* in late May. "We could be playing on a bad field and something happens. Or we could be playing on a good field and something happens. I can't predict what's going to happen or how it's going to be." Well, Garcon plays his home games at FedEx Field, so a bad field is highly possible. One area for improvement: Garcon had a -31.1% DVOA and 40 percent catch rate on third downs.

Brandon Gibson		Height: 6-1		Weight: 210			College: Washington State		Draft: 2009/6 (194)			Born: 13-Aug-1987		Age: 26		Risk: Yellow		
Year Team	G/GS	Snaps	Rec	Pass	Yds	C%	+/-	Yd/C	TD	Drop	YAC	Rk	YAC+	BTkl	DVOA	Rk	DYAR	Rk	YAR	Short	Mid	Deep	Bomb
2010 STL	10/4	749	53	91	620	58%	+0.3	11.7	2	7	4.2	35	+0.3	11	-10.8%	70	22	70	39	33%	50%	12%	6%
2011 STL	15/9	591	36	71	431	51%	-4.0	12.0	1	7	2.9	80	-1.2	1	-11.0%	68	0	70	-5	29%	46%	15%	9%
2012 STL	16/13	761	51	82	691	62%	+6.4	13.5	5	4	2.2	84	-1.3	3	23.3%	11	214	21	204	23%	52%	17%	8%
2013 MIA			36	66	432	55%	--	12.0	3						-10.3%								

Gibson had by far his best season in 2012, and there's reason to think the improvement is legit. He was consistent, finishing with negative DVOA in only three games (including one in which he was only thrown three passes) but going over 30 percent eight times. Gibson makes best use of his size on what we call Mid passes, 6-15 yards past the line of scrimmage, where he posted a 68 percent catch rate and 27.0% DVOA. He's not dynamic enough to be a big-play guy, nor reliable enough to be a true No. 1 receiver, but as a third banana behind Mike Wallace and Brian Hartline, he should do fine. The KUBIAK projections are a little less optimistic.

Chris Givens		Height: 5-11		Weight: 198			College: Wake Forest		Draft: 2012/4 (96)			Born: 6-Dec-1989		Age: 24		Risk: Green		
Year Team	G/GS	Snaps	Rec	Pass	Yds	C%	+/-	Yd/C	TD	Drop	YAC	Rk	YAC+	BTkl	DVOA	Rk	DYAR	Rk	YAR	Short	Mid	Deep	Bomb
2012 STL	15/12	615	42	80	698	53%	-4.5	16.6	3	4	6.6	7	+1.4	2	0.0%	48	80	44	52	37%	28%	9%	27%
2013 STL			44	82	667	54%	--	15.2	4						-2.6%								

Givens was thrown seven passes in his first three games, with only two catches and nine yards to show for it. Then he had a remarkable streak where he caught a pass of 50 or more yards for five games in a row. He didn't catch another one all year, but so what—nobody else had five 50-yard catches all season. In fact, only 18 players had five 40-yard catches. Givens' average 50-plus-yard catch came 32.2 yards downfield, with 22.6 YAC. The downside is that those five big plays were accompanied by a lot of incompletions. Givens was in the top ten in targets for Bomb passes (26-plus yards downfield), but his catch rate of 24 percent and DVOA of 10.1% were both below average for those throws (NFL average: 30 percent catch rate, 20.5% DVOA). The Rams' offense this season appears to be built around creating space for Tavon Austin, stretching the field in all dimensions as much as possible, so you can expect to see Givens keep getting shots downfield, whether he catches them or not.

Marquise Goodwin		Height: 5-9		Weight: 183			College: Texas		Draft: 2013/3 (78)			Born: 19-Nov-1990		Age: 23		Risk: Red		
Year Team	G/GS	Snaps	Rec	Pass	Yds	C%	+/-	Yd/C	TD	Drop	YAC	Rk	YAC+	BTkl	DVOA	Rk	DYAR	Rk	YAR	Short	Mid	Deep	Bomb
2013 BUF			16	34	246	47%	--	15.4	1						-7.5%								

Goodwin's numbers at Texas were underwhelming because the Longhorns never really had a quarterback who could take advantage of his world-class speed; in an effort to get him the ball, the Longhorns ended up giving him 34 carries (for a tremendous 371 yards) over the last two seasons. Buffalo grabbed him in the third round of the draft, but he's likely to be limited to "9" routes and gadget plays until he develops a bit more. The problem isn't that he can't catch the ball—he's got pretty good hands—but that his skills against press and man coverage need a lot of work.

Josh Gordon		Height: 6-4		Weight: 220			College: Baylor		Draft: 2012/2 (SUP)			Born: 12-Apr-1991		Age: 22		Risk: Red		
Year Team	G/GS	Snaps	Rec	Pass	Yds	C%	+/-	Yd/C	TD	Drop	YAC	Rk	YAC+	BTkl	DVOA	Rk	DYAR	Rk	YAR	Short	Mid	Deep	Bomb
2012 CLE	16/13	815	50	95	805	53%	-2.8	16.1	5	5	5.9	12	+1.5	2	-3.6%	54	64	53	79	34%	34%	15%	17%
2013 CLE			47	96	860	49%	--	18.3	6						4.9%								

The Browns took Gordon in the second round of last year's supplemental draft, and as a rookie he was usually the most exciting player on the field, Trent Richardson included. Gordon has rare speed and agility, and by midseason he appeared to figure the route tree out. He surprised unprepared (two touchdowns against the Giants) and undermanned (6 catches for 116 yards and a touchdown against the Raiders) secondaries, but experienced cornerbacks like DeAngelo Hall and Champ Bailey shut him down late in the year, as defenses turned their focus from Greg Little to Gordon. Gordon's college career was ruined by frequent marijuana use—we shrug off weed sometimes, but passing out at a Taco Bell is a bad sign—but the organization knows that his personal habits must be monitored, and he has the potential to do for the Browns what Steve Smith did for the Panthers. The huge projected jump in his yards per reception is based on the fact that Norv Turner offenses always have a designated deep threat, and Gordon is likely to be it. Turner offenses have had a receiver with at least 17.5 yards per reception in five of the past seven seasons.

T.J. Graham			Height: 5-11		Weight: 188			College: North Carolina St.		Draft: 2012/3 (69)			Born: 27-Jul-1989		Age: 24	Risk: Red
Year	Team	G/GS	Snaps	Rec	Pass	Yds	C%	+/-	Yd/C	TD	Drop	YAC	Rk	YAC+	BTkl	DVOA	Rk	DYAR	Rk	YAR	Short	Mid	Deep	Bomb
2012	BUF	15/11	695	31	58	322	53%	-5.4	10.4	1	6	5.8	15	+0.2	1	-20.6%	80	-57	82	-43	52%	22%	5%	21%
2013	BUF			45	74	571	61%	--	12.7	4						2.9%							

The Bills' official website says that Graham is a prime candidate to take a second-year leap, because it is the Bills' official website. We would be a little more cautious, although it's hard to see a scenario where a receiver with Graham's straight-line speed—he was a standout track athlete at North Carolina State—doesn't at least improve his rookie average of 10.4 yards per reception. It's small sample size, but Graham was good on third downs: 29.5% DVOA and 11.1 yards per pass on 13 targets.

A.J. Green			Height: 6-4		Weight: 207			College: Georgia		Draft: 2011/1 (4)			Born: 31-Jul-1988		Age: 25	Risk: Green
Year	Team	G/GS	Snaps	Rec	Pass	Yds	C%	+/-	Yd/C	TD	Drop	YAC	Rk	YAC+	BTkl	DVOA	Rk	DYAR	Rk	YAR	Short	Mid	Deep	Bomb
2011	CIN	15/15	889	65	115	1057	57%	+3.0	16.3	7	2	4.1	50	-0.6	3	17.4%	17	272	12	276	30%	31%	18%	21%
2012	CIN	16/16	958	97	164	1350	59%	+3.6	13.9	11	8	3.9	47	-0.5	9	4.1%	33	205	22	233	34%	32%	15%	18%
2013	CIN			91	150	1281	61%	--	14.1	11						11.7%							

Green was just 2-of-16 on deep passes (15 or more yards in the air) from Week 13 on, with receptions of 16 and 21 yards. There were several factors involved, including three drops, some off-target throws by Andy Dalton, and an illness that cost him a week of practice. The disconnect continued into the playoffs, with Green catching one deep pass against the Texans but giving up on another, leading to a Texans interception. The Bengals offense must be more than just Red Rifle to Green Arrow over and over again, but the home-run ball cannot become a mere decoy, either. Green vowed to cut down on his drops in the offseason. He and Dalton have always been serious about improving their timing. Now that Tyler Eifert and the cavalry are on their way, Green and Dalton must prove that they have not spent all their ammunition.

Derek Hagan			Height: 6-1		Weight: 205			College: Arizona State		Draft: 2006/3 (82)			Born: 21-Sep-1984		Age: 29	Risk: Green
Year	Team	G/GS	Snaps	Rec	Pass	Yds	C%	+/-	Yd/C	TD	Drop	YAC	Rk	YAC+	BTkl	DVOA	Rk	DYAR	Rk	YAR	Short	Mid	Deep	Bomb
2010	NYG	7/4	282	24	43	223	58%	+0.2	9.3	1	2	1.3	--	-2.3	0	-17.1%	--	-14	--	-19	25%	53%	23%	0%
2011	2TM	10/3	333	24	42	252	57%	-0.8	10.5	1	2	1.8	--	-2.1	0	-5.3%	--	35	--	42	30%	41%	16%	14%
2012	OAK	14/2	248	20	36	259	56%	-0.6	13.0	0	2	3.4	--	-0.6	2	-1.9%	--	32	--	23	24%	50%	15%	12%
2013	TB			11	19	131	58%	--	11.9	1						-4.1%							

Hagan is a classic journeyman who has teased a lot of teams since entering the league in 2006. Playing an ancillary role for the Raiders that included spot starts and stints in the slot, he caught what was thrown to him and executed his routes with good adequate tempo and precision. In other words, he did what you'd expect any journeyman role player to do. Now in Tampa Bay.

Leonard Hankerson			Height: 6-2		Weight: 209			College: Miami		Draft: 2011/3 (79)			Born: 7-May-1988		Age: 25	Risk: Green
Year	Team	G/GS	Snaps	Rec	Pass	Yds	C%	+/-	Yd/C	TD	Drop	YAC	Rk	YAC+	BTkl	DVOA	Rk	DYAR	Rk	YAR	Short	Mid	Deep	Bomb
2011	WAS	4/2	123	13	20	163	65%	+1.8	12.5	0	0	2.2	--	-1.8	0	1.4%	--	18	--	20	30%	40%	25%	5%
2012	WAS	16/5	573	38	57	543	67%	+2.3	14.3	3	4	3.9	45	-0.8	3	11.6%	21	129	37	128	32%	40%	14%	14%
2013	WAS			33	57	461	58%	--	14.0	2						7.0%							

Hankerson did not impress when he got more targets due to Pierre Garcon's foot injury, and the main issue now is the same one that dropped him to the third round of the 2011 draft—he doesn't have the speed and explosiveness to separate off the line, and he doesn't possess any sort of breakaway speed to blast away from defenders during routes. He does have some value in more compressed spaces, and he was Washington's top red-zone target in 2012, although he only had one touchdown on eight passes. He'll fight with Josh Morgan for space on Washington's depth chart.

Dwayne Harris			Height: 5-10		Weight: 200			College: East Carolina		Draft: 2011/6 (176)			Born: 16-Sep-1987		Age: 26	Risk: Yellow
Year	Team	G/GS	Snaps	Rec	Pass	Yds	C%	+/-	Yd/C	TD	Drop	YAC	Rk	YAC+	BTkl	DVOA	Rk	DYAR	Rk	YAR	Short	Mid	Deep	Bomb
2012	DAL	16/0	257	17	31	222	55%	-0.8	13.1	1	1	6.5	--	+2.2	5	-1.2%	--	39	--	32	36%	46%	11%	7%
2013	DAL			26	43	299	60%	--	11.5	2						-0.6%							

Harris put up his first numbers for the Cowboys in the second half of his second season, with four-catch games against the Redskins and Steelers. In February, Jerry Jones said that he had "high hopes" for Harris, but Jones tends to think that everyone he's ever signed is a Hall of Famer, so take that with a relative grain of salt. More seriously, Bryan Broaddus of the team's official site believes that Harris took the biggest offseason steps of any receiver on the team not named Dez Bryant. it's possible that Broaddus recognizes the consequences for truth for anyone on Jones' payroll, but Harris has some value as a returner, and there's a lot of wiggle room under Bryant on the Dallas depth chart.

Brian Hartline			Height: 6-2		Weight: 195		College: Ohio State			Draft: 2009/4 (108)			Born: 22-Nov-1986	Age: 27		Risk: Green	
Year	Team	G/GS	Snaps	Rec	Pass	Yds	C%	+/-	Yd/C	TD	Drop	YAC	Rk	YAC+	BTkl	DVOA	Rk
2010	MIA	12/11	600	43	73	615	59%	+2.0	14.3	1	2	4.9	21	+0.7	3	6.4%	33
2011	MIA	16/10	690	35	66	549	53%	+0.2	15.7	1	3	2.7	85	-1.7	0	11.9%	26
2012	MIA	16/15	893	74	131	1083	56%	+3.0	14.6	1	6	3.2	67	-0.7	3	0.6%	43
2013	MIA			56	97	776	58%	--	13.9	4						0.7%	

DYAR	Rk	YAR	Short	Mid	Deep	Bomb
115	39	90	30%	37%	19%	14%
127	39	132	21%	44%	18%	18%
158	29	146	25%	50%	11%	14%

If you pay close attention to Hartline's stats table, you will notice that just about the only thing differentiating his breakout 2012 season to the previous two is that he played more snaps and saw a massive increase in targets. Essentially, he's the prototypical player who toils in anonymity until given the opportunity to display his value in an expanded role. The arrival of Mike Wallace and departure of Davone Bess means Hartline can focus even more on the short and intermediate routes that brought success last year. The main concern going forward is his recent injury history, which included eight weeks on injury reports in 2012 due to a variety of ailments.

Percy Harvin			Height: 5-11		Weight: 192		College: Florida			Draft: 2009/1 (22)			Born: 28-May-1988	Age: 25		Risk: Yellow	
Year	Team	G/GS	Snaps	Rec	Pass	Yds	C%	+/-	Yd/C	TD	Drop	YAC	Rk	YAC+	BTkl	DVOA	Rk
2010	MIN	14/13	627	71	109	868	65%	+3.1	12.2	5	5	6.0	5	+0.7	13	6.2%	34
2011	MIN	16/14	605	87	121	967	72%	+5.3	11.1	6	5	6.1	9	+0.7	6	3.6%	43
2012	MIN	9/8	420	62	86	677	73%	+2.3	10.9	3	0	8.5	1	+2.1	19	4.6%	31
2013	SEA			77	112	895	69%	--	11.6	5						11.7%	

DYAR	Rk	YAR	Short	Mid	Deep	Bomb
160	26	150	50%	31%	7%	12%
133	35	132	57%	30%	9%	4%
194	24	148	67%	19%	12%	1%

Of all general manager John Schneider's offseason moves, this was the boldest and the riskiest. Quarterback play in Minnesota may have kept his DVOA ratings down, but Harvin is a superstar. His 19 broken tackles led all receivers despite just 84 touches, and you can count on one hand the number of players who are as scheme-diverse and versatile as Harvin. The amount of options this acquisiton gives the Seahawks' offense is dizzying and terrifying. Viewed solely from that angle, you can see why a team would be eager to cough up a six-year, $67 million extension, a late first-round pick, a mid-round pick next year, and a seventh-rounder to secure his services. Unfortunately, there's more to Harvin than that. He's still yet to play a full season, and when he has set foot on the field, his snap counts are much lower than you'd expect. The moping and sulking that got him sent to Seattle were constant and incessant. Harvin's insistence that he never had a problem with Christian Ponder made him about as believable as a White House press secretary. This is a move that has the chance to put Seattle over the top, but it's also a trade that was an absolute no-brainer for Minnesota.

Harvin, like Russell Wilson, will be overrated in fantasy drafts by people who don't understand that Seattle's run-pass ratio is different from Green Bay's run-pass ratio. His 2013 projection includes 25 carries for 155 yards and a touchdown.

Andrew Hawkins			Height: 5-7		Weight: 175		College: Toledo			Draft: 2008/FA			Born: 10-Mar-1986	Age: 27		Risk: Yellow	
Year	Team	G/GS	Snaps	Rec	Pass	Yds	C%	+/-	Yd/C	TD	Drop	YAC	Rk	YAC+	BTkl	DVOA	Rk
2011	CIN	13/0	174	23	34	263	68%	+0.8	11.4	0	0	6.3	--	+0.4	3	-2.8%	--
2012	CIN	14/2	518	51	80	533	64%	-2.4	10.5	4	4	6.7	6	+1.6	5	-9.2%	70
2013	CIN			27	46	296	59%	--	11.0	1						-9.8%	

DYAR	Rk	YAR	Short	Mid	Deep	Bomb
43	--	21	55%	33%	9%	3%
13	71	20	59%	26%	13%	1%

Fifty of Hawkins' 83 targets came within five yards of the line of scrimmage; Hawkins caught 37 of those passes but gained just 276 yards, with no plays of more than 11 yards after Week 4. Diminishing returns set in on all of those screens and shovel passes, and it became clear as the year went on that the 5-foot-7 former street free agent was not No. 2 receiver material. The Bengals have a host of young receivers vying to take touches away from Hawkins, who could go from last year's feel-good story (and a major early-season contributor) to a camp cut. The Bengals have a lot of guys who can catch screens and return punts, and Hawkins does nothing else.

Devery Henderson			Height: 5-11		Weight: 200		College: Louisiana State			Draft: 2004/2 (50)			Born: 26-Mar-1982	Age: 31		Risk: Yellow	
Year	Team	G/GS	Snaps	Rec	Pass	Yds	C%	+/-	Yd/C	TD	Drop	YAC	Rk	YAC+	BTkl	DVOA	Rk
2010	NO	16/11	620	34	59	464	58%	-0.4	13.6	1	5	3.8	48	-0.9	2	-4.7%	64
2011	NO	16/13	723	32	50	503	64%	+2.9	15.7	2	2	5.4	20	+1.6	2	15.0%	20
2012	NO	15/9	702	22	47	316	47%	-2.3	14.4	1	3	3.6	--	-0.9	1	-26.0%	--
2013	WAS			13	23	205	57%	--	15.8	1						12.2%	

DYAR	Rk	YAR	Short	Mid	Deep	Bomb
44	66	47	34%	31%	17%	17%
112	46	108	35%	35%	17%	13%
-65	--	-54	20%	39%	7%	34%

Henderson caught the touchdown pass that pushed Drew Brees past record-holder Johnny Unitas on the "Most Consecutive Games with a Touchdown Pass" list last year, but that may be the last notable achievement of Henderson's NFL career. The Saints didn't choose to re-sign him, and he sat around in free agency for a while before Washington finally snatched him up. He could put up nice numbers as Robert Griffin's deepest threat, but he's more likely to not even make the roster. The Washington depth chart at receiver is a mess, and why would you keep 30-somethings Henderson and Donte' Stallworth around when 25-year-old Aldrick Robinson does the same things. After a star career at LSU and all these years with the Saints, seeing the Opelousas native dress up in non-Bayou colors will be like eating Gulf trout without the cayenne pepper—just not right.

Devin Hester Height: 5-10   Weight: 185   College: Miami   Draft: 2007/2 (57)   Born: 4-Nov-1982   Age: 31   Risk: Green

Year	Team	G/GS	Snaps	Rec	Pass	Yds	C%	+/-	Yd/C	TD	Drop	YAC	Rk	YAC+	BTkl	DVOA	Rk	DYAR	Rk	YAR	Short	Mid	Deep	Bomb
2010	CHI	16/13	647	40	73	475	55%	-3.5	11.9	4	5	5.5	12	+1.2	3	-3.0%	59	62	61	46	37%	40%	11%	11%
2011	CHI	16/8	460	26	56	369	46%	-8.2	14.2	1	5	5.6	18	+0.9	1	-29.1%	88	-69	86	-56	40%	38%	15%	8%
2012	CHI	15/5	361	23	40	242	58%	-3.3	10.5	1	4	4.5	--	-1.3	2	-28.8%	--	-37	--	-51	50%	30%	8%	13%
2013	CHI			12	19	146	63%	--	12.2	1						5.5%								

Color commentators continually express that they are waiting with bated breath for the big downfield plays that Hester is supposed to provide an offense. This is kind of like the first time you buy an Explosions In The Sky album—you keep waiting for someone to actually sing, and it keeps not happening. Marc Trestman has seen enough, and that means Hester will be relegated to an emergency receiver role even though the Bears don't really have any receiving depth. An Ugly Fact In Life, indeed.

Darrius Heyward-Bey Height: 6-2   Weight: 210   College: Maryland   Draft: 2009/1 (7)   Born: 26-Feb-1987   Age: 26   Risk: Yellow

Year	Team	G/GS	Snaps	Rec	Pass	Yds	C%	+/-	Yd/C	TD	Drop	YAC	Rk	YAC+	BTkl	DVOA	Rk	DYAR	Rk	YAR	Short	Mid	Deep	Bomb
2010	OAK	15/14	736	26	64	366	41%	-5.0	14.1	1	6	3.9	45	+0.3	2	-28.2%	82	-74	81	-64	19%	44%	19%	19%
2011	OAK	15/14	795	64	115	975	56%	+1.9	15.2	4	7	3.9	55	-0.2	7	2.2%	46	95	50	124	23%	39%	24%	15%
2012	OAK	15/14	804	41	80	606	51%	-3.5	14.8	5	6	5.6	19	+1.6	11	-5.3%	59	31	66	45	22%	43%	20%	14%
2013	IND			45	82	653	55%	--	14.5	4						2.4%								

Heyward-Bey has cooked some of his once-alarmingly raw skills, but he has not, and likely never will, blossom into what you'd expect a former high first-round pick to be. He has speed and knows how to apply it to his routes, though it's not always evident because he tends to struggle against quality man coverage. He still lacks natural physicality. The major issue with Heyward-Bey early in his career was a simple inability to catch the ball. That has since been mostly rectified; in fact, he's even flashed an ability to make the spectacular grab.

Stephen Hill Height: 6-4   Weight: 215   College: Georgia Tech   Draft: 2012/2 (43)   Born: 25-Apr-1991   Age: 22   Risk: Yellow

Year	Team	G/GS	Snaps	Rec	Pass	Yds	C%	+/-	Yd/C	TD	Drop	YAC	Rk	YAC+	BTkl	DVOA	Rk	DYAR	Rk	YAR	Short	Mid	Deep	Bomb
2012	NYJ	11/8	412	21	47	252	45%	-4.9	12.0	3	4	1.5	--	-2.1	1	-15.4%	--	-19	--	-11	22%	50%	13%	15%
2013	NYJ			40	79	557	51%	--	13.9	6						-4.0%								

When the Jets drafted Hill in the second round of the 2012 draft, New York knew what it was getting: a player with as much potential as any wide receiver in his class, but one who might struggle as a rookie. The upside was clear: Hill led the nation in yards per reception (29.3) as a junior in 2011, and he finished with the highest Playmaker Score in his class after an incredible performance at the Combine. But his inexperience was just as obvious as his athleticism was tantalizing: Hill caught only 49 passes in three years at Georgia Tech, where he was stuck in a triple-option offense that was as run-heavy as any in college football.

Hill turned 21 just two days before being drafted, so it would have been unrealistic to expect such a raw, young player to star right away. But on opening day against the Bills, he caught five passes for 89 yards and two touchdowns. That's probably why in retrospect, his rookie season feels like a disappointing one. Hill didn't catch another pass until Week 6, and he finished the year with just one more touchdown. His most memorable play was a drop against the Patriots on third down with just over two minutes left in the fourth quarter; when the Jets ultimately lost in overtime, that drop made Hill the natural scapegoat. Hill had a problem with drops throughout the year, but what the numbers don't show is the number of times Hill got open deep and Sanchez wasn't able to find him. That problem may not solve itself in 2013, but Hill still has the potential to be one of the better deep threats in the league.

T.Y. Hilton Height: 5-10   Weight: 183   College: Florida International   Draft: 2012/3 (92)   Born: 14-Nov-1989   Age: 24   Risk: Yellow

Year	Team	G/GS	Snaps	Rec	Pass	Yds	C%	+/-	Yd/C	TD	Drop	YAC	Rk	YAC+	BTkl	DVOA	Rk	DYAR	Rk	YAR	Short	Mid	Deep	Bomb
2012	IND	15/1	673	50	90	861	56%	-5.0	17.2	7	7	7.7	2	+2.4	6	10.7%	23	151	30	169	26%	43%	19%	11%
2013	IND			59	102	853	58%	--	14.5	5						9.3%								

Hilton struggled with consistency and dropped his fair of passes as a rookie, but he also used his speed (4.34 in the 40-yard dash at his pro day) to average over 17 yards per catch. His five passes of 40 yards or more tied him with the likes of Calvin Johnson, Julio Jones and Demaryius Thomas. Hilton's speed meshed well with Bruce Arians' downfield passing game, but we'll have to wait and see how he adapts to Pep Hamilton's West Coast offense, which utilizes shorter routes.

Domenik Hixon		Height: 6-2		Weight: 182		College: Akron			Draft: 2006/4 (130)		Born: 8-Oct-1984			Age: 29		Risk: Green
Year	Team	G/GS	Snaps	Rec	Pass	Yds	C%	+/-	Yd/C	TD	Drop	YAC	Rk	YAC+	BTkl	DVOA	Rk	DYAR	Rk	YAR	Short	Mid	Deep	Bomb
2011	NYG	2/0	36	4	6	50	67%	+0.9	12.5	1	0	0.0	--	-3.6	0	28.4%	--	20	--	20	0%	80%	20%	0%
2012	NYG	13/3	386	39	59	567	66%	+4.1	14.5	2	3	3.6	58	-0.3	1	23.6%	10	177	26	190	17%	58%	15%	10%
2013	CAR			32	62	492	52%	--	15.4	2						-0.4%								

Hixon was one of the few pleasant surprises in New York last season. After ACL tears ended his season in both 2010 and 2011, he actually led all Giants wideouts in DYAR in 2012. Despite the strong season, the best Hixon could get was a one-year, $1.2 million contract on the open market from the Panthers. Don't expect big numbers for Hixon—Patrick Jeffers in 1999 was the last Panthers player not named Steve Smith or Muhsin Muhammad to gain 1,000 receiving yards—but he has to be better than the replacement-level receivers like Armanti Edwards and Kealoha Pilares who litter the bottom of the Panthers depth chart.

Santonio Holmes		Height: 5-10		Weight: 185		College: Ohio State			Draft: 2006/1 (25)		Born: 3-Mar-1984			Age: 29		Risk: Yellow
Year	Team	G/GS	Snaps	Rec	Pass	Yds	C%	+/-	Yd/C	TD	Drop	YAC	Rk	YAC+	BTkl	DVOA	Rk	DYAR	Rk	YAR	Short	Mid	Deep	Bomb
2010	NYJ	12/10	567	52	96	746	54%	-1.1	14.3	6	5	4.2	37	+0.3	2	5.5%	38	126	34	147	21%	49%	20%	10%
2011	NYJ	16/16	988	51	101	564	50%	-7.3	11.1	8	5	3.7	64	-0.2	2	-8.6%	65	52	58	59	27%	47%	22%	5%
2012	NYJ	4/4	187	20	41	272	49%	-4.7	13.6	1	2	5.2	--	+0.7	0	-2.8%	--	-3	--	20	24%	49%	20%	7%
2013	NYJ			54	106	711	51%	--	13.2	6						-7.1%								

Holmes has now turned off two fanbases, and he will probably have angered a third one by this time in 2015. Former Jets General Manager Mike Tannenbaum was fired as much for the Sanchez fiasco as the ridiculous contract ($45 million over five years, with $23.5 million guaranteed) he gave to Holmes, who like Sanchez will remain on the roster in 2013 because he is too expensive to release. Anonymous teammates called him a cancer in 2011, and LaDainian Tomlinson later said that Holmes did not speak to Sanchez over the final 13 games of the season. Even the eternally optimistic Rex Ryan struggled to find the positive way to spin things, ultimately landing on: "As much as everybody dislikes him, I'm glad he's on our team."

It's easy to forget how toxic of a player Holmes was in 2011 because he missed nearly all of 2012 due to injury. Against the 49ers in Week 4, he suffered a Lisfranc fracture in his left foot, but Holmes still managed to cause trouble one final time. After falling down, he literally tossed the ball to the side, and the live ball was returned by Carlos Rogers 51 yards for a touchdown. On the bright side, Holmes has been a good solider during his rehab, training at the team's facility in Florham Park and even taking a pay cut to remain on the roster. He may not be able to start the season, but if healthy and motivated, he would provide a big boost to the Jets anemic passing game. Like other players at his position, Holmes is a headache because he (thinks he) can afford to be, and occasionally he still shows you his star power; he had nine catches for 147 yards in a Week 3 win over Miami last year. The Jets offense could border on respectable if Holmes plays up to his potential, but the more likely scenario involves several missed games and more anonymous bashing by his teammates.

DeAndre Hopkins		Height: 6-1		Weight: 214		College: Clemson			Draft: 2013/1 (27)		Born: 6-Jun-1992			Age: 21		Risk: Yellow
Year	Team	G/GS	Snaps	Rec	Pass	Yds	C%	+/-	Yd/C	TD	Drop	YAC	Rk	YAC+	BTkl	DVOA	Rk	DYAR	Rk	YAR	Short	Mid	Deep	Bomb
2013	HOU			51	97	709	53%	--	13.9	4						-2.5%								

The Texans are counting on big things from their first-round pick, expecting him to step into Kevin Walter's shoes as the second banana behind Andre Johnson. He increased his volume and yards per catch all three seasons at Clemson, going from 51 catches at 12.3 yards per catch as a freshman to his phenomenal 2012 numbers of 82 catches and 17.1 yards per catch. He was regarded as the most pro-ready receiver in the draft, and his Playmaker Score of 368 was the second-highest for an FBS receiver in this year's draft. Hopkins has an excellent pass-catching radius, and while he's not extremely fast, he doesn't need to be to match Walter's production on deep routes. He was very active in the run game for a collegiate receiver, and he'll need to be in Houston to match Walter's presence in that regard.

Justin Hunter		Height: 6-4		Weight: 196		College: Tennessee			Draft: 2013/2 (34)		Born: 20-Apr-1991			Age: 22		Risk: Red
Year	Team	G/GS	Snaps	Rec	Pass	Yds	C%	+/-	Yd/C	TD	Drop	YAC	Rk	YAC+	BTkl	DVOA	Rk	DYAR	Rk	YAR	Short	Mid	Deep	Bomb
2013	TEN			31	61	458	51%	--	14.8	2						-6.5%								

A pre-injury Justin Hunter drew comparisons to A.J. Green and even Randy Moss due to his height, thin frame, and ability to catch deep passes. A torn ACL suffered early in 2011 set him back, but he recovered his physical speed by the end of the 2012 campaign. For a 6-foot-4 receiver, he has very quick acceleration to go with his excellent long speed, running a 4.44 at the Combine. His biggest problem in college was very inconsistent hands, as he dropped entirely too many passes in 2012. To be successful at the NFL level, he'll also have to add weight to a thin frame. A hamstring tweak in rookie minicamp that kept him out in May and June may slow him initially, but if nothing, the Titans will throw him some downfield passes on play action and hope he can be their Paul Warfield to complement Chris Johnson and Shonn Greene's Mercury Morris and Larry Csonka act.

DeSean Jackson

		Height: 5-9			Weight: 169			College: California			Draft: 2008/2 (49)			Born: 1-Dec-1986		Age: 27		Risk: Yellow

Year	Team	G/GS	Snaps	Rec	Pass	Yds	C%	+/-	Yd/C	TD	Drop	YAC	Rk	YAC+	BTkl	DVOA	Rk	DYAR	Rk	YAR	Short	Mid	Deep	Bomb
2010	PHI	14/14	784	47	96	1056	49%	-2.0	22.5	6	10	7.2	1	+2.9	7	2.4%	42	115	38	113	23%	38%	14%	24%
2011	PHI	15/15	847	58	104	961	56%	+4.0	16.6	4	10	3.9	54	-0.8	1	3.7%	42	159	29	148	25%	35%	18%	22%
2012	PHI	11/11	698	45	88	700	51%	+1.8	15.6	2	1	5.1	25	+0.9	8	-10.6%	72	42	61	14	21%	42%	17%	20%
2013	PHI			56	106	877	53%	--	15.7	5							1.8%								

Since he entered the league, DeSean Jackson has been one of the game's top deep threats. Since 2008, only Vincent Jackson (18.3) has averaged more yards per catch than Jackson (17.5) among players with 60 or more catches. His 22 total touchdowns of 30 or more yards are the most of any player over the last five years. And at least for one year, Jackson cured his pesky drops problem. Now, the bad: Jackson has seen his receiving yards and touchdowns decline for three straight seasons. And, against all odds, he seems to be getting even worse in the red zone. In 2012, he had a DVOA of -76.6% in the red zone, and gained positive receiving yards on just two of eight targets.

An up-tempo offense could help Jackson, who keeps himself in outstanding condition. If the Eagles can tire defenses, Jackson has the ability to burn them deep. He can be forgiven for a down year playing on a team with a patchwork offensive line. But with a $12.5 million cap number in 2014, Jackson will need a bounce-back season this year to stay in Philadelphia.

Vincent Jackson

		Height: 6-5			Weight: 241			College: Northern Colorado			Draft: 2005/2 (61)			Born: 14-Jan-1983		Age: 30		Risk: Red

Year	Team	G/GS	Snaps	Rec	Pass	Yds	C%	+/-	Yd/C	TD	Drop	YAC	Rk	YAC+	BTkl	DVOA	Rk	DYAR	Rk	YAR	Short	Mid	Deep	Bomb
2010	SD	5/5	217	14	23	248	61%	+3.9	17.7	3	1	3.4	--	-0.5	2	39.5%	--	105	--	105	16%	47%	26%	11%
2011	SD	16/16	955	60	115	1106	52%	+2.7	18.4	9	5	3.2	74	-1.0	4	16.2%	19	223	17	251	13%	38%	26%	23%
2012	TB	16/16	976	72	147	1384	49%	-4.0	19.2	8	3	5.0	27	+0.8	6	10.5%	24	224	20	288	12%	41%	25%	21%
2013	TB			71	135	1277	53%	--	18.0	8							11.4%								

Jackson is perhaps the league's preeminent deep threat, but 2012 was surprisingly the first season in which he led the NFL in yards per catch. He has now finished in the top six in this category four times in five years, and likely would have made it in 2010 as well had he not missed the bulk of the season due to a suspension and a contract dispute. Among active players, only Devery Henderson has a higher career average, and no player can touch Jackson's average since 2008 (he's nearly a full yard better than the next best guy, DeSean Jackson). Only Torrey Smith and A.J. Green were targeted on more Bombs last season. In a league that has emphasized methodical (read: boring) efficiency in the passing game, Jackson is a throwback: a James Lofton for the 21st Century.

Alshon Jeffery

		Height: 6-3			Weight: 216			College: South Carolina			Draft: 2012/2 (45)			Born: 14-Feb-1990		Age: 23		Risk: Yellow

Year	Team	G/GS	Snaps	Rec	Pass	Yds	C%	+/-	Yd/C	TD	Drop	YAC	Rk	YAC+	BTkl	DVOA	Rk	DYAR	Rk	YAR	Short	Mid	Deep	Bomb
2012	CHI	10/6	431	24	48	367	50%	-2.1	15.3	3	1	2.7	--	-1.3	0	6.7%	--	97	--	77	15%	40%	21%	25%
2013	CHI			40	84	582	48%	--	14.6	5							-7.7%								

For a receiver with a 6-foot-3, 216-pound frame, Jeffery sure does play small at times. He's got impressive speed for a player of his size, but Jay Cutler didn't always notice this because "Marshall" was not on the back of Jeffery's jersey. Press coverage was very disruptive against Jeffery, and his route-running needs polishing, to be kind. Early reports out of OTA's were that he was sinking his hips into his releases better, which is a positive sign. Jeffery's got the size and the pedigree to be a major weapon under Marc Trestman. If he can put his talents together, the Bears will have a much more dynamic passing offense this season.

A.J. Jenkins

		Height: 6-0			Weight: 190			College: Illinois			Draft: 2012/1 (30)			Born: 8-Sep-1989		Age: 24		Risk: Red

Year	Team	G/GS	Snaps	Rec	Pass	Yds	C%	+/-	Yd/C	TD	Drop	YAC	Rk	YAC+	BTkl	DVOA	Rk	DYAR	Rk	YAR	Short	Mid	Deep	Bomb
2012	SF	3/0	35	0	1	0	0%	-0.7	0.0	0	1	0.0	--	--	0	-98.0%	--	-3	--	-7	100%	0%	0%	0%
2013	SF			37	65	548	57%	--	14.8	2							3.3%								

So much for planning. After drafting Jenkins 30th overall in 2012, the 49ers were content with confining his development to the practice field. That was Plan A, and he was inactive the first 13 weeks. Once two of the receivers ahead of him on the depth chart (Mario Manningham and Kyle Williams) got injured, the 49ers went to Plan B and gave him a little bit of playing time. Two days after a three-snap, zero-target Super Bowl, Jenkins—apparently a fan of Daft Punk—announced his intention to "come back bigger, faster, stronger" in hopes of seeing more action in 2013. Then Michael Crabtree tore his Achilles tendon, and San Francisco switched to Plan C, which casts Jenkins as the improbable Week 1 starter across from Anquan Boldin. With his unpredictable career trajectory to date, it's folly to pin down a projection for Jenkins, but we will note that he graded out well with a Playmaker Score of 418.

Michael Jenkins			Height: 6-4		Weight: 217			College: Ohio State			Draft: 2004/1 (29)			Born: 18-Jun-1982	Age: 31		Risk: Yellow	
Year	Team	G/GS	Snaps	Rec	Pass	Yds	C%	+/-	Yd/C	TD	Drop	YAC	Rk	YAC+	BTkl	DVOA	Rk	DYAR	Rk	YAR	Short	Mid	Deep	Bomb
2010	ATL	11/9	575	41	73	505	56%	+1.9	12.3	2	1	2.0	84	-2.2	3	6.8%	31	102	42	90	20%	39%	32%	9%
2011	MIN	11/7	527	38	55	466	69%	+5.0	12.3	3	0	2.7	84	-1.2	0	10.7%	29	116	45	104	30%	48%	13%	9%
2012	MIN	16/8	706	40	72	449	56%	-2.1	11.2	2	1	3.2	68	-0.7	1	-13.2%	74	37	62	5	28%	51%	13%	9%
2013	NE			23	39	293	59%	--	12.8	2						2.9%								

Can you guess which Minnesota wideout played the most offensive snaps last year? No, not Frank Stallone. As a wide receiver, Jenkins is a good tight end: he's a dogged blocker with good size and he seals the edge well. Apparently he came close enough to one to fool New England, as he washed up on Cape Cod as part of whatever nefarious plot the Patriots need 10 tight ends for. Our guess is a Rob Gronkowski body double program. Gronk can't attend every party he's invited to, you know.

Greg Jennings			Height: 5-11		Weight: 195			College: Western Michigan		Draft: 2006/2 (52)			Born: 21-Sep-1983	Age: 30		Risk: Yellow	
Year	Team	G/GS	Snaps	Rec	Pass	Yds	C%	+/-	Yd/C	TD	Drop	YAC	Rk	YAC+	BTkl	DVOA	Rk	DYAR	Rk	YAR	Short	Mid	Deep	Bomb
2010	GB	16/16	853	76	125	1265	61%	+7.9	16.6	12	5	5.3	16	+1.1	5	19.7%	7	338	3	329	25%	44%	14%	17%
2011	GB	13/13	642	67	101	949	66%	+8.1	14.2	9	2	4.1	49	-0.2	2	20.8%	13	302	9	309	28%	45%	19%	9%
2012	GB	8/5	416	36	62	366	58%	-2.3	10.2	4	2	4.6	35	+0.2	4	-5.2%	58	37	63	21	37%	44%	12%	7%
2013	MIN			61	106	740	58%	--	12.1	5						-5.0%								

Jennings lost most of his contract year to groin surgery, but still managed to sign a very healthy five-year, $47.5 million contract, with $18 million of that guaranteed. Vikings general manager Rick Spielman managed to bring in a first-round pick for Percy Harvin, and Spielman definitely needed to see if Christian Ponder will respond to a better supporting cast, but this deal has a fair chance of blowing up in his face. Jennings is 30, has missed multiple games in each of the last two seasons, and produced the worst DVOA of his career when he actually was healthy last season. Jennings did rebound a bit in the playoffs and at the end of the season (playing in the slot for Randall Cobb, he had his best game against the Vikings in Week 17), but he's also just left Aaron Rodgers for Ponder. That's a savvy move for his bank account, but it should be the end of the days where he could be considered a WR1 or WR2 on a good fantasy team.

Andre Johnson			Height: 6-3		Weight: 219			College: Miami			Draft: 2003/1 (3)			Born: 11-Jul-1981	Age: 32		Risk: Red	
Year	Team	G/GS	Snaps	Rec	Pass	Yds	C%	+/-	Yd/C	TD	Drop	YAC	Rk	YAC+	BTkl	DVOA	Rk	DYAR	Rk	YAR	Short	Mid	Deep	Bomb
2010	HOU	13/13	818	86	139	1216	63%	+5.6	14.1	8	6	4.1	38	-0.5	0	13.2%	14	268	8	244	39%	30%	20%	12%
2011	HOU	7/7	335	33	51	492	65%	+3.9	14.9	2	3	4.2	47	-0.5	1	17.5%	16	142	33	127	31%	39%	16%	14%
2012	HOU	16/16	977	112	163	1598	69%	+13.3	14.3	4	7	4.9	29	+0.7	5	19.5%	16	461	2	464	31%	44%	13%	11%
2013	HOU			102	165	1427	62%	--	14.0	7						10.3%								

The key to Johnson's fine 2012 campaign? Health. After two straight injury-plagued seasons where he was frequently banged up even when in the lineup, he was about as healthy as a 30-something receiver with a history of injuries could expect to be. The only disappointment came in the touchdown total, and that was because Matt Schaub kept throwing the ball to other people. Johnson only had seven red zone targets, fourth on the team, and one less than he had in 2011 despite playing nine more games. Father Time is undefeated, but Johnson still seems to run routes precisely and effortlessly. It is easy to see him being productive for years as long as he remains healthy.

Calvin Johnson			Height: 6-5		Weight: 239			College: Georgia Tech		Draft: 2007/1 (2)			Born: 25-Sep-1985	Age: 28		Risk: Yellow	
Year	Team	G/GS	Snaps	Rec	Pass	Yds	C%	+/-	Yd/C	TD	Drop	YAC	Rk	YAC+	BTkl	DVOA	Rk	DYAR	Rk	YAR	Short	Mid	Deep	Bomb
2010	DET	15/15	996	77	138	1120	57%	+2.9	14.5	12	6	3.9	44	+0.1	7	11.5%	20	268	9	243	20%	46%	19%	14%
2011	DET	16/16	1029	96	158	1681	61%	+8.8	17.5	16	3	5.1	21	+0.9	12	31.6%	7	535	1	572	25%	38%	18%	18%
2012	DET	16/16	1152	122	203	1964	60%	+7.7	16.1	5	8	4.1	40	+0.1	6	16.0%	19	488	1	459	26%	36%	27%	11%
2013	DET			107	177	1695	60%	--	15.8	12						15.7%								

Although Johnson broke the NFL's single-season receiving yards record, his advanced stats weren't quite as good as the year before. He had the second best wide-receiver DYAR ever in 2011, but dropped to 13th all-time in 2012 (as if that's a bad thing). With Ryan Broyles and Titus Young removed from the lineup, the amount of weaponry the Lions had reached the tipping point where a) other teams could feel free to focus their entire defense on Johnson and b) it still made sense to throw to Johnson because other Lions receivers—in single coverage—were less likely to make a play than he was. Thus, Johnson became just the fourth receiver since 1991 to be targeted 200 or more times in a season. Through Week 12, Johnson had 310 DYAR and an 18.2% DVOA on 11.6 targets per game. For the rest of the season: 160 DYAR and a 12.2% DVOA on 16 targets per game. The fact that Johnson could maintain a bigger workload with more attention (including opponents double-teaming him *at the line of scrimmage*) and still maintain a DVOA rating that high is, frankly, more impressive than a record 600 DYAR would have been. Something tells us this isn't the last run Johnson will take at the DYAR record.

Damaris Johnson	Height: 5-8		Weight: 175		College: Tulsa		Draft: 2012/FA		Born: 22-Nov-1989	Age: 24	Risk: Blue

Year	Team	G/GS	Snaps	Rec	Pass	Yds	C%	+/-	Yd/C	TD	Drop	YAC	Rk	YAC+	BTkl	DVOA	Rk	DYAR	Rk	YAR	Short	Mid	Deep	Bomb
2012	PHI	14/1	231	19	31	256	61%	+1.1	13.5	0	0	5.3	--	+1.5	3	5.8%	--	69	--	45	29%	61%	7%	4%
2013	PHI			15	25	202	60%	--	13.5	1						5.7%								

Will Chip Kelly be able to use Johnson the way he used De'Anthony Thomas at Oregon? Johnson is a similar type of player, and while he won't be a starter, could turn into one of the Eagles more exciting players. Expect Kelly to try to get the ball into Johnson's hands as a runner, receiver, and returner. This could be the perfect match of player and scheme, but the onus is now on Johnson to develop into a more complete player. He looked lost on offense as a rookie, and cost the team with a muffed punt near his own end zone against the Bucs. There are too many talented skill position players in Philadelphia to view Johnson as a future starter, but he could easily end up on a bunch of highlight films this year.

Steve Johnson	Height: 6-2		Weight: 202		College: Kentucky		Draft: 2008/7 (224)		Born: 22-Jul-1986	Age: 27	Risk: Green

Year	Team	G/GS	Snaps	Rec	Pass	Yds	C%	+/-	Yd/C	TD	Drop	YAC	Rk	YAC+	BTkl	DVOA	Rk	DYAR	Rk	YAR	Short	Mid	Deep	Bomb
2010	BUF	16/13	909	82	142	1073	58%	-2.5	13.1	10	7	4.8	24	+1.1	8	7.8%	28	231	14	201	30%	49%	14%	7%
2011	BUF	16/16	918	76	134	1004	57%	-5.8	13.2	7	4	4.2	45	+0.2	5	-0.5%	52	117	44	134	34%	43%	19%	4%
2012	BUF	16/16	936	79	148	1046	53%	-11.4	13.2	6	5	4.6	33	+0.7	6	-4.7%	57	67	49	73	27%	53%	14%	6%
2013	BUF			75	128	1012	59%	--	13.5	6						2.3%								

There's a slight downward trend in touchdowns and catch rate, which also creates a slight downward trend in DVOA, but Johnson has been remarkably consistent the last three years—especially for a guy who isn't exactly playing in one of the league's most powerful offenses. Johnson is only the third receiver since the merger to put up three straight seasons between 1,000 and 1,100 receiving yards. The others were Derrick Mason and Donald Driver, both in 2007-2009 when they were quite a bit older than Johnson is now. Maybe Johnson can be the first to do it four straight seasons.

Donald Jones	Height: 6-0		Weight: 214		College: Youngstown State		Draft: 2010/FA		Born: 17-Dec-1987	Age: 26	Risk: Yellow

Year	Team	G/GS	Snaps	Rec	Pass	Yds	C%	+/-	Yd/C	TD	Drop	YAC	Rk	YAC+	BTkl	DVOA	Rk	DYAR	Rk	YAR	Short	Mid	Deep	Bomb
2010	BUF	15/5	291	18	41	213	44%	-5.2	11.8	1	1	4.8	--	-1.0	1	-34.3%	--	-72	--	-73	53%	19%	14%	14%
2011	BUF	8/7	375	23	46	231	50%	-3.4	10.0	1	3	3.0	--	-1.9	3	-36.1%	--	-79	--	-79	30%	35%	22%	13%
2012	BUF	12/10	667	41	66	443	62%	+0.8	10.8	4	5	4.4	38	-0.2	2	-6.0%	61	30	67	37	45%	34%	15%	6%
2013	NE			17	27	211	63%	--	12.4	1						5.4%								

Jones had by far his best NFL season in 2012, and the new Bills administration celebrated this by not tendering him a contract. He doesn't have particularly impressive size or speed, but he's the kind of receiver Bill Belichick tends to like: physical, a good blocker and a good route runner. He still has a bit of upside, which is more than you can say for some of the free-agent receivers the Patriots brought in this offseason (Hi, Michael Jenkins).

Jacoby Jones	Height: 6-3		Weight: 192		College: Lane		Draft: 2007/3 (73)		Born: 11-Jul-1984	Age: 29	Risk: Yellow

Year	Team	G/GS	Snaps	Rec	Pass	Yds	C%	+/-	Yd/C	TD	Drop	YAC	Rk	YAC+	BTkl	DVOA	Rk	DYAR	Rk	YAR	Short	Mid	Deep	Bomb
2010	HOU	15/7	563	51	78	562	65%	+0.3	11.0	3	10	4.5	28	+0.5	7	-3.7%	61	65	58	49	38%	51%	7%	4%
2011	HOU	16/10	793	31	64	512	50%	-0.7	16.5	2	1	4.4	40	+0.0	1	-4.2%	56	56	57	50	27%	27%	29%	17%
2012	BAL	16/3	426	30	55	406	55%	+1.2	13.5	1	1	2.8	75	-2.1	1	0.4%	44	37	64	51	32%	34%	14%	20%
2013	BAL			44	78	666	56%	--	15.1	4						6.1%								

Jones finished third on *Dancing with the Stars*. Isn't life funny? One year, you're a punt returner on a second-tier playoff team, a playoff goat unrecognizable to non-hardcore football fans. The next year, you are a Super Bowl hero. A few weeks later, you are one of those reality-TV people, on the list of proud third-place dancers and multi-media gadflies with Kelly Osbourne, Joey Lawrence, and Marie Osmond. Jones gets to return to the defending champions, as opposed to celebrity B-list purgatory, and the Anquan Boldin trade even gives him a promotion into the starting lineup. Joe Flacco welcomed him back into the fold in late May with a typically punchy Joe Flacco quotation: "It was kind of cool to watch him throughout the whole thing, and it'll definitely be exciting to come out here and see what kind of person he is these days." Wait, that actually was somewhat punchy. Does Flacco, who spent the winter getting wealthy and touring talk-show couches, really think that Jones' Joey Lawrence-level fame will change him somehow? Whoa.

James Jones		Height: 6-1		Weight: 208			College: San Jose State			Draft: 2007/3 (78)			Born: 31-Mar-1984		Age: 29		Risk: Green

Year	Team	G/GS	Snaps	Rec	Pass	Yds	C%	+/-	Yd/C	TD	Drop	YAC	Rk	YAC+	BTkl	DVOA	Rk	DYAR	Rk	YAR	Short	Mid	Deep	Bomb
2010	GB	16/3	535	50	87	679	57%	+3.2	13.6	5	6	5.8	8	+1.2	6	-4.3%	63	71	54	70	34%	34%	19%	13%
2011	GB	16/0	487	38	55	635	69%	+4.2	16.7	7	4	7.1	3	+2.5	5	41.7%	3	220	18	221	39%	32%	16%	13%
2012	GB	16/16	1000	64	98	784	65%	+7.3	12.3	14	3	3.6	56	-0.4	2	22.6%	12	318	12	295	33%	45%	12%	11%
2013	GB			58	91	743	64%	--	12.8	7						14.7%								

Jones broke out last season, but the first inklings of the change came in 2011, when he was buried on a stacked depth chart. In 2011, Jones upped his catch rate over 60 percent for the first time since 2008, and cut his drops—a bugaboo that defined his career before Jermichael Finley became more prominent at it. Jones probably won't be tasked with 20 red-zone targets again, meaning those 14 touchdowns will meet regression. However, he should be a useful receiver and his size will keep him in the discussion once the Packers cross the 20. Not bad for a guy who dodged trade rumors for practically the entire 2012 offseason. A lot of unlucky things happened to the Packers last year. Let's remember that there were some fairly fortunate events too.

Julio Jones		Height: 6-3		Weight: 220			College: Alabama			Draft: 2011/1 (6)			Born: 3-Feb-1989		Age: 24		Risk: Yellow

Year	Team	G/GS	Snaps	Rec	Pass	Yds	C%	+/-	Yd/C	TD	Drop	YAC	Rk	YAC+	BTkl	DVOA	Rk	DYAR	Rk	YAR	Short	Mid	Deep	Bomb
2011	ATL	13/13	705	54	95	959	57%	+0.9	17.8	8	4	7.5	1	+2.8	8	10.4%	30	110	48	158	33%	32%	20%	15%
2012	ATL	16/15	835	79	129	1198	61%	+2.7	15.2	10	8	5.9	13	+1.2	10	16.0%	20	340	9	320	38%	32%	17%	14%
2013	ATL			86	143	1312	60%	--	15.3	9						11.8%								

OK, show of hands—who still thinks trading up to draft Jones was a bad move by Thomas Dimitroff? Anyone? You there, in the back? You just need to use the bathroom? Carry on, then.

After ending 2011 with a tantalizing glimpse into the future, Quintoriss Lopez Jones, aka "Julio," fulfilled his promise in 2012, staying healthy all season and bettering his stats almost everywhere, save YAC. He then completely scorched the 49ers secondary in the NFC title game, catching 11 balls for 182 yards and two scores. Jones had only 14 fewer targets than Roddy White, as opposed to 85 fewer in 2011. After just nine red zone targets in 2011, Julio saw 20 last year, just one fewer than White and more than Tony Gonzalez. This year, Julio should complete his destiny and take over from his Jedi master as Atlanta's No. 1 option. May be the force be with him.

Marvin Jones		Height: 6-2		Weight: 199			College: California			Draft: 2012/5 (166)			Born: 12-Mar-1990		Age: 23		Risk: Yellow

Year	Team	G/GS	Snaps	Rec	Pass	Yds	C%	+/-	Yd/C	TD	Drop	YAC	Rk	YAC+	BTkl	DVOA	Rk	DYAR	Rk	YAR	Short	Mid	Deep	Bomb
2012	CIN	11/5	354	18	32	201	56%	-0.3	11.2	1	1	1.9	--	-1.9	3	-2.1%	--	36	--	34	29%	42%	19%	10%
2013	CIN			22	38	293	58%	--	13.3	1						-1.1%								

Jones, a fifth-round draft pick last year, was ahead of Mohamed Sanu on the depth chart before suffering an MCL tear in October. He recovered in time to replace Sanu down the stretch and catch ten passes in the Bengals' final two games, plus two more in the playoffs. Jones dropped a few passes and got called out by Jay Gruden for some "head-scratching plays" along the way, and Sanu played well (despite a foot injury) in Jones' absence, so the race for the starting job is wide open. Gruden and the Bengals would love both second-year receivers to be winners.

Jeremy Kerley		Height: 5-9		Weight: 188			College: TCU			Draft: 2011/5 (153)			Born: 3-May-1989		Age: 24		Risk: Red

Year	Team	G/GS	Snaps	Rec	Pass	Yds	C%	+/-	Yd/C	TD	Drop	YAC	Rk	YAC+	BTkl	DVOA	Rk	DYAR	Rk	YAR	Short	Mid	Deep	Bomb
2011	NYJ	14/1	308	29	47	314	62%	+2.2	10.8	1	2	3.4	--	-0.6	5	-10.9%	--	19	--	30	41%	39%	14%	7%
2012	NYJ	16/7	664	56	97	827	59%	-0.2	14.8	2	3	5.3	22	+0.4	4	-8.1%	69	14	70	42	42%	36%	14%	8%
2013	NYJ			63	104	806	61%	--	12.8	5						1.8%								

Football Outsiders hasn't yet come up with a way to convert Kerley's 827 yards into a Sanchez-adjusted figure, but we know the general idea. A slot receiver is most successful when he plays with a smart and accurate quarterback, which means Kerley probably felt more like Sisyphus than a wide receiver in 2012. Kerley's 59 percent catch rate may not impress you, but he had a higher catch rate and averaged more yards per catch the the Jets next two most targeted players, indicating that he made the most of a bad situation. Then again, those two players were Jeff Cumberland and Stephen Hill, so we're back to square one when trying to evaluate Kerley.

Kerley doesn't have the size to be a force on the outside, but he can be an excellent cog in a finely-tuned engine as a slot receiver. He's endeared himself to Jets fans by playing well against the Patriots: his only two seven-catch games last year came against the Patriots, and his 79 yards against New England was his season high as a rookie in 2011. One area where Kerley could improve is on third and fourth downs, where he posted an ugly -22.9% DVOA last year. Geno Smith fell in love with Tavon Austin at West Virginia, and Kerley has a very similar skill set to Austin. If Smith starts, that may be the best chance for a breakout season for Kerley in 2013.

Tavarres King		Height: 6-1		Weight: 200			College: Georgia			Draft: 2013/5 (161)			Born: 14-Jul-1990		Age: 23		Risk: Red	
Year	Team	G/GS	Snaps	Rec	Pass	Yds	C%	+/-	Yd/C	TD	Drop	YAC	Rk	YAC+	BTkl	DVOA	Rk	DYAR	Rk	YAR	Short	Mid	Deep	Bomb
2013	DEN			23	44	375	52%	--	16.3	2						9.2%								

T'Variusness King was the star of the East-West Bowl, outplaying bigger names like D'Glester Hardunkichud and Tyroil Smoochie-Wallace. He could get a chance to contribute as a fifth-round rookie given that the only experienced depth Denver has at wide receiver is Andre Caldwell, a shaky underneath target who barely saw the field last season. However, that's contingent on him honing his route running, which some think will take him some time. King is a playmaking threat, having averaged 22.6 yards per catch at Georgia, but he'll need to add muscle to his slight frame if he wants to grow into a starting role.

Brandon LaFell		Height: 6-3		Weight: 211			College: LSU			Draft: 2010/3 (78)			Born: 4-Nov-1986		Age: 27		Risk: Red	
Year	Team	G/GS	Snaps	Rec	Pass	Yds	C%	+/-	Yd/C	TD	Drop	YAC	Rk	YAC+	BTkl	DVOA	Rk	DYAR	Rk	YAR	Short	Mid	Deep	Bomb
2010	CAR	14/2	510	38	77	468	49%	-7.0	12.3	1	3	3.5	54	-0.8	5	-18.6%	75	-33	74	-24	33%	46%	11%	10%
2011	CAR	16/6	689	36	56	613	64%	+4.2	17.0	3	1	6.5	5	+2.2	2	22.8%	11	156	30	147	26%	37%	28%	9%
2012	CAR	14/12	756	44	76	677	58%	-1.7	15.4	4	2	7.1	4	+2.4	4	2.8%	37	106	40	105	42%	32%	17%	8%
2013	CAR			51	88	718	58%	--	14.1	3						1.8%								

LaFell has one 100-yard game in his career, against Tampa Bay in 2011. He got 91 of those yards on one play when the Bucs ran a safety blitz and LaFell got behind his man in the middle of the field, with no Tampa Bay defender in front of him. His best game last year was also against the Bucs, when he caught five balls in seven targets for 93 yards and a touchdown. LaFell is at his best against zone coverage, working the space between linebackers and safeties. On Deep passes last year, 16 to 25 yards downfield, he caught 11-of-12 passes for 310 yards. Anything deeper than that, though, he was useless, going 0-for-6 on "Bombs." The Panthers threw him three Deep passes in Week 1 and again in Week 2 last year, but only six times the rest of the season. That's a poor job of putting your players in position to win, and something to be fixed in 2013.

Greg Little		Height: 6-2		Weight: 220			College: North Carolina			Draft: 2011/2 (59)			Born: 30-May-1989	Age: 24		Risk: Green	
Year	Team	G/GS	Snaps	Rec	Pass	Yds	C%	+/-	Yd/C	TD	Drop	YAC	Rk	YAC+	BTkl	DVOA	Rk	DYAR	Rk	YAR	Short	Mid	Deep	Bomb
2011	CLE	16/12	962	61	121	709	51%	-11.2	11.6	2	13	3.9	53	-0.3	13	-21.7%	84	-70	87	-104	47%	31%	14%	8%
2012	CLE	16/16	905	53	93	647	58%	-1.3	12.2	4	7	3.4	64	-0.8	5	-7.7%	68	45	59	35	38%	40%	16%	6%
2013	CLE			50	87	611	57%	--	12.2	4						-4.3%								

Most of Little's seven drops came in the first six weeks of the season. He had a fine December despite quarterback juggling and institutional disinterest (22 catches for 287 yards and two touchdowns in five games), and has a Pro Bowl-caliber skill set when he holds on to the ball. Little's longest catch was just 43 yards last season, but Team NorvChud sees him as a vertical threat, and he has the size-speed-talent to do more than catch (and sometimes drop) quick slants. If Little really left the bobbles behind, he is a player to watch.

Brandon Lloyd		Height: 6-0		Weight: 192			College: Illinois			Draft: 2003/4 (124)			Born: 5-Jul-1981		Age: 32		Risk: N/A	
Year	Team	G/GS	Snaps	Rec	Pass	Yds	C%	+/-	Yd/C	TD	Drop	YAC	Rk	YAC+	BTkl	DVOA	Rk	DYAR	Rk	YAR	Short	Mid	Deep	Bomb
2010	DEN	16/11	843	77	152	1448	51%	+2.7	18.8	11	5	2.4	80	-1.8	2	20.6%	6	428	2	405	11%	48%	20%	22%
2011	2TM	15/14	774	70	147	966	48%	-10.4	13.8	5	6	1.8	91	-2.2	0	-11.5%	69	-31	77	-15	14%	49%	24%	13%
2012	NE	16/15	1038	74	130	911	57%	-0.7	12.3	4	8	2.3	82	-1.6	2	1.8%	40	130	36	123	14%	55%	21%	10%

Patriots fans thought they were getting a poor man's Randy Moss who could stretch the defense, but what they ended up with was a receiver who falls down. He often catches the ball first, but then he doesn't do anything with it. His best talents are making back-shoulder grabs or twisting his body to make difficult catches on the sidelines, and those passes don't get any yards after the catch either. Football Outsiders has YAC data going back to 2005. Combine those eight seasons, and only three wide receivers have caught 200 or more passes with less than 2.5 average yards after the catch: Lloyd, Torry Holt at the end of his career, and "the other" Steve Smith. There have been 373 single seasons of wide receivers catching 50 or more passes since 2005, and Lloyd's last three seasons represent the third, 14th, and 19th lowest yards after catch averages. The Patriots can get Aaron Dobson and Josh Boyce to make difficult catches for a lot less money, and they might even stay upright afterwards.

Jeremy Maclin		Height: 6-0		Weight: 198			College: Missouri			Draft: 2009/1 (19)			Born: 11-May-1988		Age: 25		Risk: Green	
Year	Team	G/GS	Snaps	Rec	Pass	Yds	C%	+/-	Yd/C	TD	Drop	YAC	Rk	YAC+	BTkl	DVOA	Rk	DYAR	Rk	YAR	Short	Mid	Deep	Bomb
2010	PHI	16/16	958	70	115	964	61%	+8.1	13.8	10	7	3.7	52	-0.6	7	15.5%	8	271	7	246	32%	36%	14%	18%
2011	PHI	13/13	733	63	97	859	65%	+6.6	13.6	5	5	4.1	48	-0.2	1	12.6%	22	194	24	178	30%	40%	23%	8%
2012	PHI	15/15	974	69	121	857	56%	-5.9	12.4	7	5	3.8	51	-0.8	1	-6.5%	62	132	34	73	43%	33%	14%	10%
2013	PHI			54	97	696	56%	--	12.9	5						-1.6%								

For years, Maclin was the ying to DeSean Jackson's yang. Maclin caught 62 percent of his targets from 2009 to 2011, working as the possession receiver with space to operate as Jackson took the safety deep. But last year, Maclin's production tanked. His plus-minus fell through the floor, and a 56 percent completion rate is terrible for a player who runs as many short routes as Maclin. If not for a very productive season on third and fourth downs—he had a DVOA of 19.3% in those situations—it would have been a disastrous year for the fourth-year player. For what it's worth, Maclin seemed to play better with Nick Foles under center. Over the final six weeks of the season, Maclin caught 33 passes and three touchdowns, well above his production with Vick earlier in the year.

Mario Manningham	Height: 5-11				Weight: 181			College: Michigan			Draft: 2008/3 (95)			Born: 25-May-1986		Age: 27		Risk: Red				
Year Team	G/GS	Snaps	Rec	Pass	Yds	C%	+/-	Yd/C	TD	Drop	YAC	Rk	YAC+	BTkl	DVOA	Rk	DYAR	Rk	YAR	Short	Mid	Deep	Bomb
2010 NYG	16/8	684	60	92	944	65%	+8.8	15.7	9	4	5.8	7	+1.1	9	13.0%	15	210	17	215	32%	38%	15%	15%
2011 NYG	12/10	587	39	77	523	51%	-0.4	13.4	4	3	2.7	83	-1.3	0	-5.1%	58	28	64	52	23%	36%	24%	17%
2012 SF	12/10	362	42	57	449	74%	+5.9	10.7	1	0	4.1	41	-0.4	9	-2.3%	52	36	65	50	41%	43%	7%	9%
2013 SF			19	32	243	59%	--	12.8	2						2.7%								

It's hard to know what to make of the fact that Manningham is only 27 years old. On one hand, he's an experienced NFL starter who should be entering the prime years of his position. On the other hand, he's played a full season only once in five years, and tore multiple knee ligaments near the end of 2012. To merely keep his spot on the roster, he had to take a $2.15 million pay cut in March. Even at full strength, which won't come until late 2013 (if at all), his role has shifted from a deep threat in New York to a short-range possession receiver in San Francisco, and that's not likely to change.

Brandon Marshall	Height: 6-4				Weight: 229			College: UCF			Draft: 2006/4 (119)			Born: 23-Mar-1984		Age: 29		Risk: Yellow				
Year Team	G/GS	Snaps	Rec	Pass	Yds	C%	+/-	Yd/C	TD	Drop	YAC	Rk	YAC+	BTkl	DVOA	Rk	DYAR	Rk	YAR	Short	Mid	Deep	Bomb
2010 MIA	14/14	813	86	146	1014	59%	+5.5	11.8	3	11	2.8	73	-1.2	9	-1.9%	55	116	37	78	36%	40%	16%	8%
2011 MIA	16/16	889	81	143	1214	57%	+0.9	15.0	6	10	3.8	61	-0.7	5	7.0%	36	191	25	218	33%	36%	15%	16%
2012 CHI	16/16	968	118	195	1508	61%	+6.7	12.8	11	9	2.9	72	-1.3	13	0.0%	46	267	16	205	27%	40%	22%	11%
2013 CHI			104	164	1367	63%	--	13.1	10						13.0%								

Measures of efficency will always have problems with context in the NFL, and in that sense, Marshall's DVOA was dragged down by the noise around him. The Bears had nobody else to throw to, as we discussed in their chapter, and Marshall was their only difference-maker on offense. He finished with one less broken tackle than Matt Forte in 173 fewer touches. Yes, Jay Cutler locked on to Marshall a bit too much. That led to some head-scratching passes intended for Marshall—but the fact that Cutler believed that he could make some of those plays tells you more than the efficiency scores do. Marshall had arthroscopic hip surgery in January, but he should be ready for training camp.

How does Marshall feel about the coaching change to Marc Trestman? Let's ask him. "I was just talking to [backup quarterback Josh] McCown this morning," Marshall told the press in June, "and one of the things we said is it's so cool to come to work where it's not one of those things where it's dreadful." Okaaaay! The Bears had the lowest DVOA in the NFL on screen passes last year, but given Marshall's prowess in open space and the big receivers they have, look for Chicago to do more to get Marshall the ball on the sideline rather than just downfield this season.

Keshawn Martin	Height: 5-11				Weight: 194			College: Michigan State			Draft: 2012/4 (121)			Born: 15-Mar-1990		Age: 23		Risk: Green				
Year Team	G/GS	Snaps	Rec	Pass	Yds	C%	+/-	Yd/C	TD	Drop	YAC	Rk	YAC+	BTkl	DVOA	Rk	DYAR	Rk	YAR	Short	Mid	Deep	Bomb
2012 HOU	16/1	264	10	28	85	36%	-7.9	8.5	1	4	3.7	--	-1.7	2	-47.2%	--	-92	--	-82	54%	31%	12%	4%
2013 HOU			16	27	171	59%	--	10.7	1						0.7%								

The Texans hoped Martin could be a valuable slot receiver after grabbing him in the fourth round of last year's draft. He finished with a 36 percent catch rate even though 22 of his 28 targets were no more than 10 yards downfield, thanks in part to four drops. Martin will once again have a chance to be the Texans' third receiver, which says more about the Texans than it does about Martin.

Mohamed Massaquoi	Height: 6-2				Weight: 210			College: Georgia			Draft: 2009/2 (50)			Born: 24-Nov-1986		Age: 27		Risk: Yellow				
Year Team	G/GS	Snaps	Rec	Pass	Yds	C%	+/-	Yd/C	TD	Drop	YAC	Rk	YAC+	BTkl	DVOA	Rk	DYAR	Rk	YAR	Short	Mid	Deep	Bomb
2010 CLE	15/14	735	36	73	483	49%	-1.3	13.4	2	5	3.9	43	+0.0	4	-14.9%	72	-24	73	-19	28%	43%	12%	17%
2011 CLE	14/13	636	31	74	384	42%	-11.3	12.4	2	4	2.4	88	-1.3	0	-25.8%	87	-63	83	-91	33%	46%	11%	10%
2012 CLE	9/5	252	17	33	254	52%	-1.5	14.9	0	0	6.1	--	+2.3	0	-13.4%	--	-2	--	8	34%	34%	19%	13%
2013 JAC			39	72	478	54%	--	12.3	3						-7.7%								

Signing a two-year, mostly incentive-laden contract with Jacksonville turns out to have been a very good move for Massaquoi, as Justin Blackmon's early-season suspension transforms him from "journeyman coming off injury" to "only veteran receiver capable of starting opposite Cecil Shorts in September." A few solid performances could stop the downward trajectory of Massaquoi's career, and goodness knows something had better do so, quickly. Few modern wide receivers have less to show for 43 career starts than Massaquoi does. By the way, Mohamed Massaquoi's middle name is "Jah." Feel free to discuss the awkward theological implications of that name combination amongst yourselves.

Dexter McCluster		Height: 5-9			Weight: 172			College: Mississippi			Draft: 2010/2 (36)			Born: 25-Aug-1988		Age: 25		Risk: Green
Year	Team	G/GS	Snaps	Rec	Pass	Yds	C%	+/-	Yd/C	TD	Drop	YAC	Rk	YAC+	BTkl	DVOA	Rk	DYAR	Rk	YAR	Short	Mid	Deep	Bomb
2010	KC	11/7	401	21	39	209	54%	-3.8	10.0	1	3	7.9	--	+2.1	7	-21.0%	--	-21	--	-26	67%	28%	6%	0%
2011	KC	16/4	455	46	63	328	75%	+1.6	7.1	1	5	6.6	39	-0.1	11	-12.3%	41	5	40	6	82%	12%	3%	3%
2012	KC	16/6	573	52	76	452	68%	+2.2	8.7	1	4	3.9	46	-1.0	2	-21.1%	81	-34	79	-38	67%	28%	3%	3%
2013	KC			56	78	539	72%	--	9.6	1							-3.0%								

The original goal was for McCluster to be what Percy Harvin has wound up becoming. But through three full seasons, the former second-round pick has not come close to carving out his niche in the NFL. Physically, McCluster has the speed to get outside as a running back (something Kansas City's system is built for), and he has the quickness to create space as a gadget-style route runner from the slot (where he's assured of getting a clean release off the snap). But being physically capable of doing something is different from actually doing something. For whatever reason, McCluster has not been able to "do much" despite the team's repeated efforts to feature him in a variety of ways. His 2013 projection includes 16 carries for 75 yards.

Robert Meachem		Height: 6-2			Weight: 210			College: Tennessee			Draft: 2007/1 (27)			Born: 28-Sep-1984		Age: 29		Risk: Green
Year	Team	G/GS	Snaps	Rec	Pass	Yds	C%	+/-	Yd/C	TD	Drop	YAC	Rk	YAC+	BTkl	DVOA	Rk	DYAR	Rk	YAR	Short	Mid	Deep	Bomb
2010	NO	16/7	530	44	66	638	67%	+8.6	14.5	5	4	3.0	68	-1.8	4	23.7%	4	199	19	194	43%	23%	8%	26%
2011	NO	16/8	742	40	60	620	67%	+6.4	15.5	6	3	2.6	87	-1.8	5	31.2%	9	227	15	218	27%	35%	18%	20%
2012	SD	15/3	398	14	32	207	44%	-4.0	14.8	2	1	2.4	--	-1.3	2	-12.3%	--	-10	--	-6	16%	47%	13%	25%
2013	SD			14	28	206	50%	--	14.7	1							-3.4%								

It's looking like Meachem was just a product of the Saints system. Brought in to replace Vincent Jackson as San Diego's primary downfield receiver and movable Z-target, the former first-round pick had trouble against man coverage last year and proved to be too dependent on play design for getting open. After starting three of San Diego's first six games, he dropped out of the receiving rotation altogether, registering two receptions for 18 yards after the Week 7 bye. Meachem is making about $640,000 per reception, and his big salary is about the only thing keeping him on the roster, as cutting him would bring about a $10.6 million cap hit for the Chargers.

Denarius Moore		Height: 6-0			Weight: 191			College: Tennessee			Draft: 2011/5 (148)			Born: 9-Dec-1988		Age: 25		Risk: Yellow
Year	Team	G/GS	Snaps	Rec	Pass	Yds	C%	+/-	Yd/C	TD	Drop	YAC	Rk	YAC+	BTkl	DVOA	Rk	DYAR	Rk	YAR	Short	Mid	Deep	Bomb
2011	OAK	13/10	609	33	76	618	43%	-3.7	18.7	5	5	3.8	59	-0.9	4	-1.6%	53	29	63	57	18%	36%	18%	28%
2012	OAK	15/15	793	51	114	741	45%	-15.6	14.5	7	6	5.0	26	+0.7	5	-12.4%	73	-33	78	-5	26%	38%	26%	10%
2013	OAK			66	117	924	56%	--	14.0	7							5.1%								

The bar may have been set a bit too high after Moore caught five balls for 146 yards in his NFL debut two years ago. He certainly has electric speed and has shown an uncommon knack for executing subtle tactics to create separation against man coverage. However, he's a long way from being a complete receiver, as his intermediate and underneath routes are still lacking polish. Very few guys can make an entire career out of being able to only separate on deep routes, and Matt Flynn may not be able to get him the ball downfield as much as he would like. Durability and consistency are two concerns at this point. Last season Moore had 545 yards through his first eight games played but, battling some injuries, managed just 196 yards over his final seven games.

Lance Moore		Height: 5-9			Weight: 177			College: Toledo			Draft: 2005/FA			Born: 31-Aug-1983		Age: 30		Risk: Green
Year	Team	G/GS	Snaps	Rec	Pass	Yds	C%	+/-	Yd/C	TD	Drop	YAC	Rk	YAC+	BTkl	DVOA	Rk	DYAR	Rk	YAR	Short	Mid	Deep	Bomb
2010	NO	16/1	550	66	94	763	70%	+6.3	11.6	8	2	4.4	32	-0.0	1	14.4%	10	220	16	214	46%	40%	5%	9%
2011	NO	14/7	415	52	73	627	71%	+6.0	12.1	8	2	3.0	79	-0.9	2	26.1%	10	260	13	254	36%	45%	14%	5%
2012	NO	15/7	608	65	104	1041	63%	+5.3	16.0	6	5	2.2	83	-1.8	0	31.2%	5	356	7	344	21%	46%	18%	15%
2013	NO			61	98	913	62%	--	15.0	6							14.4%								

It seems like Moore just got to the league, but he turns 30 this August. On the surface, all seems well—he put up some spectacular numbers last year. But declining catch rate and YAC that has gone from poor to microscopic could signal trouble ahead. In addition, his red-zone numbers fell precipitously from 2011's strong showing. His third-down DVOA fell as well, though it was still upper echelon. For the moment Moore remains one of the league's more reliable receivers, but with his small frame and advancing age, rent, don't buy.

Josh Morgan			Height: 6-0		Weight: 219			College: Virginia Tech			Draft: 2008/6 (174)			Born: 20-Jun-1985		Age: 28		Risk: Yellow
Year	Team	G/GS	Snaps	Rec	Pass	Yds	C%	+/-	Yd/C	TD	Drop	YAC	Rk	YAC+	BTkl	DVOA	Rk	DYAR
2010	SF	16/11	829	44	80	698	55%	+0.8	15.9	2	3	6.8	2	+2.3	11	-2.8%	58	44
2011	SF	5/5	237	15	20	220	75%	+2.6	14.7	1	0	6.4	--	+2.5	2	32.9%	--	74
2012	WAS	16/15	708	48	74	510	65%	-0.6	10.6	2	5	4.9	31	+0.1	7	-6.9%	65	17
2013	WAS			41	64	491	64%	--	12.0	2						8.2%		

Continued columns for Josh Morgan:

Year	Rk	YAR	Short	Mid	Deep	Bomb
2010	65	53	28%	39%	19%	14%
2011	--	83	37%	53%	11%	0%
2012	68	39	41%	45%	8%	6%

Morgan led the Redskins with 48 catches in 2012, which would seem to validate the first year of his two-year, $11.5 million contract. However, he caught just three passes total in Washington's final three games, and injuries clearly affected him down the stretch. In the 2013 offseason, he had the screws removed from a previous ankle surgery, and surgeries on both hands. If he can stay healthy and maintain his downfield speed, a contract year is possible, but buyer beware—he's a 28-year-old player with downfield speed as a primary attribute, and the injuries could put a crowbar in his future sooner than later.

Joseph Morgan			Height: 6-1		Weight: 184			College: Walsh			Draft: 2012/FA			Born: 23-Mar-1988		Age: 25		Risk: Yellow
Year	Team	G/GS	Snaps	Rec	Pass	Yds	C%	+/-	Yd/C	TD	Drop	YAC	Rk	YAC+	BTkl	DVOA	Rk	DYAR
2012	NO	14/4	382	10	21	379	48%	+2.5	37.9	3	1	8.7	--	+1.9	3	65.0%	--	135
2013	NO			23	43	500	53%	--	21.7	3						27.2%		

Continued columns for Joseph Morgan:

Year	Rk	YAR	Short	Mid	Deep	Bomb
2012	--	131	11%	11%	11%	68%

Of Morgan's three touchdowns in 2012, two were doozies. One was an 80-yard bomb against Green Bay; another an exceptional action movie of a play where Morgan caught a long pass, somehow kept his knees grass-free as Tampa's Mark Barron hammered him, then flipped Eric Wright over his shoulders, Jet Li-style, as Wright came to finish him off, He finished it off by diving into the end zone, getting blasted in mid-air for his trouble. If there were any justice, the touchdown would have been worth eight points.

It was the kind of play that takes a receiver from unknown UFA to third wideout on the explosive Saints. Morgan's speed makes him a natural replacement for Devery Henderson as the team deep threat. But there will be plenty of competition in camp at the position, including from draft choice Kenny Stills, and Morgan hurt himself by partying a bit too hard over Memorial Day weekend. He was arrested for a DWI and driving without a license, registering a blood alcohol content reading of .218, a number just as unbelievable as his memorable score against Tampa Bay.

Randy Moss			Height: 6-4		Weight: 215			College: Marshall			Draft: 1998/1 (21)			Born: 13-Feb-1977		Age: 36		Risk: N/A
Year	Team	G/GS	Snaps	Rec	Pass	Yds	C%	+/-	Yd/C	TD	Drop	YAC	Rk	YAC+	BTkl	DVOA	Rk	DYAR
2010	3TM	16/11	675	28	63	391	44%	-3.4	14.0	5	3	2.3	81	-1.9	2	1.1%	46	66
2012	SF	16/2	406	28	50	434	56%	+0.9	15.5	3	4	3.0	71	-0.6	3	6.8%	27	66

Continued columns for Randy Moss:

Year	Rk	YAR	Short	Mid	Deep	Bomb
2010	55	56	20%	39%	19%	22%
2012	52	68	13%	62%	15%	11%

Our prediction in *Football Outsiders Almanac 2012* that Randy Moss would be a mere decoy for the 49ers turned out to be accurate, although this still does not make up for our prediction in *Pro Football Prospectus 2007* that Moss would not return to superstardom after leaving Oakland for New England. Given that a man in his position (i.e., self-proclaimed G.O.A.T.) can't afford to be made to look ridiculous, he spent the week of his second Super Bowl appearance lamenting his decoy role to anyone within earshot. This is ironic considering he spent much of his lone season in San Francisco ignoring passes within earshot. Moss has yet to officially retire (again), but the 49ers had no interest in bringing him back, despite a decimated receiving corps, and nobody has even sniffed around him in free agency.

Santana Moss			Height: 5-10		Weight: 185			College: Miami			Draft: 2001/1 (16)			Born: 1-Jun-1979		Age: 34		Risk: Yellow
Year	Team	G/GS	Snaps	Rec	Pass	Yds	C%	+/-	Yd/C	TD	Drop	YAC	Rk	YAC+	BTkl	DVOA	Rk	DYAR
2010	WAS	16/16	969	93	145	1115	64%	+2.7	12.0	6	5	5.1	19	-0.1	6	-1.9%	54	127
2011	WAS	12/12	626	46	96	584	48%	-10.4	12.7	4	7	4.0	51	-0.7	4	-18.0%	81	-41
2012	WAS	16/1	454	41	63	573	67%	+2.1	14.0	8	3	5.8	16	+0.6	5	11.6%	22	98
2013	WAS			35	56	464	63%	--	13.2	3						13.3%		

Continued columns for Santana Moss:

Year	Rk	YAR	Short	Mid	Deep	Bomb
2010	33	133	46%	34%	11%	9%
2011	79	-26	43%	29%	18%	10%
2012	41	126	47%	35%	12%	7%

There was some thought that the Redskins might release Moss in march before he reworked his 2013 cap number of $6.1 million to give the team a bit of financial relief. He hasn't been a top-tier receiver since 2010, and his new role as a speed slot receiver in Mike Shanahan's re-tooled offense would seem to indicate a new level of redundancy. However, his efficiency on third down and in the red zone provided hidden, if limited, value. Moss was was the only Redskins wide receiver to have a positive DVOA in third- and fourth-down situations, and all three of his red-zone catches were for touchdowns. As long as he's able to succeed in a situational role that will continue to diminish over time, and he's realistic about his compensation, Moss should continue to be a bit player in Washington's offense.

Louis Murphy

		Height: 6-3		Weight: 203			College: Florida			Draft: 2009/4 (124)			Born: 11-May-1987	Age: 26		Risk: Green

Year	Team	G/GS	Snaps	Rec	Pass	Yds	C%	+/-	Yd/C	TD	Drop	YAC	Rk	YAC+	BTkl	DVOA	Rk	DYAR	Rk	YAR	Short	Mid	Deep	Bomb
2010	OAK	14/9	714	41	78	609	53%	-2.9	14.9	2	6	5.1	18	+0.8	3	-8.3%	69	29	69	41	22%	47%	19%	12%
2011	OAK	11/1	254	15	33	241	45%	-2.9	16.1	0	2	5.4	--	+1.0	1	-14.7%	--	-3	--	2	26%	32%	32%	10%
2012	CAR	16/5	666	25	62	336	42%	-6.4	13.4	1	2	2.6	79	-1.9	0	-37.2%	85	-118	84	-109	23%	43%	16%	18%
2013	NYG			14	25	187	56%	--	13.3	1						-0.3%								

Murphy might have been the No. 2 receiver in Carolina this year, but he chose to leave for the Giants, where he'll be the third man at best. On the other hand, Murphy has more speed than any other Giants wideout (why do you think the Raiders drafted him?) and could be the designated deep target. The only problem with theory is that the Panthers tried Murphy in that role last year, leading to great futility. Murphy caught only three passes in 19 targets more than 15 yards past the line of scrimmage last year. And he did that playing with Cam Newton, one of the few quarterbacks in the league with a deep ball comparable to Eli Manning's. Murphy was also in the bottom 20 in DYAR on short routes. Turns out that while he is very fast, he is not a particularly good football player. And so we ask again: Why do you think the Raiders drafted him?

David Nelson

		Height: 6-5		Weight: 217			College: Florida			Draft: 2010/FA			Born: 7-Nov-1986	Age: 27		Risk: Green

Year	Team	G/GS	Snaps	Rec	Pass	Yds	C%	+/-	Yd/C	TD	Drop	YAC	Rk	YAC+	BTkl	DVOA	Rk	DYAR	Rk	YAR	Short	Mid	Deep	Bomb
2010	BUF	15/3	346	31	47	353	66%	+2.6	11.4	3	0	2.5	--	-1.2	3	15.8%	--	106	--	94	13%	67%	20%	0%
2011	BUF	16/13	818	61	98	658	62%	-1.9	10.8	5	3	3.3	73	-0.8	4	1.2%	49	106	49	102	36%	50%	11%	3%
2012	BUF	1/1	28	2	5	31	40%	-1.3	15.5	0	0	5.0	--	+0.9	0	-4.0%	--	0	--	0	60%	20%	20%	0%
2013	CLE			19	36	270	53%	--	14.2	1						-2.5%								

The 6-foot-5 Nelson is a third-down safety valve and red-zone target who generally plays in the slot despite his height. He's not a name most fans know, but he was nicely efficient at his job in his first two seasons before tearing his ACL early in 2012. The new Buffalo administration non-tendered him and he hooked up with Cleveland; he should be healthy for training camp but the trade for Davone Bess might cost him a spot in the final roster.

Jordy Nelson

		Height: 6-2		Weight: 217			College: Kansas State			Draft: 2008/2 (36)			Born: 31-May-1985	Age: 28		Risk: Yellow

Year	Team	G/GS	Snaps	Rec	Pass	Yds	C%	+/-	Yd/C	TD	Drop	YAC	Rk	YAC+	BTkl	DVOA	Rk	DYAR	Rk	YAR	Short	Mid	Deep	Bomb
2010	GB	16/4	537	45	64	582	70%	+6.4	12.9	2	5	5.6	11	+0.8	2	9.7%	23	118	36	120	39%	38%	13%	10%
2011	GB	16/9	609	68	96	1263	71%	+11.5	18.6	15	2	6.0	11	+1.6	7	52.9%	1	520	2	528	31%	40%	14%	14%
2012	GB	12/10	593	49	73	745	67%	+6.2	15.2	7	6	5.1	24	+1.2	3	30.8%	6	292	13	264	24%	54%	10%	13%
2013	GB			71	114	1061	62%	--	14.9	11						22.7%								

Let's quit beating around the bush here. Jordy Nelson is not "deceptively" fast. He does not have "surprising" speed. He is not "quicker than fast." Jordy Nelson will torch your ass if you don't give safety help to your cornerbacks. And he may torch your ass anyway if you do, just for fun. Regression was a natural thought after Nelson's incredible breakout season, but through the first seven weeks of the season, he was doing a pretty fair approximation of 2011: he'd caught 70 percent of 58 targets with a 28.6% DVOA. Nelson's hamstring started bugging him afterwards, and though he was able to be an efficient deep receiver when he actually suited up, he wasn't thrown to anywhere near as often. From Week 8 onwards, he had just 17 targets and a 56 percent catch rate, although it worked out to 39.6% DVOA.

Hakeem Nicks

		Height: 6-3		Weight: 212			College: North Carolina			Draft: 2009/1 (29)			Born: 14-Jan-1988	Age: 25		Risk: Red

Year	Team	G/GS	Snaps	Rec	Pass	Yds	C%	+/-	Yd/C	TD	Drop	YAC	Rk	YAC+	BTkl	DVOA	Rk	DYAR	Rk	YAR	Short	Mid	Deep	Bomb
2010	NYG	13/12	772	79	128	1052	62%	+5.1	13.3	11	7	3.7	51	-0.4	7	14.0%	12	279	6	293	30%	40%	18%	11%
2011	NYG	15/15	951	76	133	1192	57%	+3.8	15.7	7	5	4.6	34	+0.2	5	12.5%	24	276	11	272	28%	33%	21%	18%
2012	NYG	13/11	668	53	100	692	53%	-3.4	13.1	3	3	3.7	52	-0.2	2	-5.9%	60	67	50	55	25%	51%	15%	9%
2013	NYG			72	124	999	58%	--	13.9	8						8.4%								

Nicks missed "only" three games in 2012, but he was listed on the injury report in all but two weeks. After missing most of training camp with a broken foot, it looked like Nicks was on his way to a breakout season. In Week 2, he gained 199 yards against the Bucs, including 84 yards on three huge catches in the fourth quarter. But that performance came at a cost: his knee slammed to the ground late in the game, and he played at something well below full strength for the rest of the season. Nicks struggled to get separation without his trademark athleticism, resulting in fewer targets and a low catch rate. Nicks missed voluntary workouts and OTAs with no explanation, although it's not hard to connect the dots to the fact that Nicks was unhappy about his contract. 2013 is a contract year, and Nicks will be motivated to put 2012 behind him and cash in.

Kevin Ogletree

| | Height: 6-2 | | Weight: 196 | | College: Virginia | | Draft: 2009/FA | | | | Born: 5-Dec-1987 | | Age: 26 | | Risk: Yellow | |

Year	Team	G/GS	Snaps	Rec	Pass	Yds	C%	+/-	Yd/C	TD	Drop	YAC	Rk	YAC+	BTkl	DVOA	Rk	DYAR	Rk	YAR	Short	Mid	Deep	Bomb
2010	DAL	6/0	40	3	6	34	50%	-1.1	11.3	0	1	2.0	--	-2.2	0	-13.8%	--	-5	--	-2	50%	17%	33%	0%
2011	DAL	14/1	267	15	26	164	58%	-0.8	10.9	0	0	4.3	--	+0.0	2	-18.5%	--	-8	--	-12	35%	50%	8%	8%
2012	DAL	15/1	453	32	55	436	58%	-0.4	13.6	4	3	2.6	78	-1.5	5	4.5%	32	92	42	78	19%	61%	11%	9%
2013	TB			35	63	506	56%	--	14.4	2						0.9%								

Ogletree had the most statistically significant season of his four-year career in 2012, but stats don't always equal production, and when you look under Ogletree's hood, there's not a lot to lock onto. He won the 2012 Frisman Jackson Award for the eight-catch, 114-yard, two-touchdown Week 1 performance he put up against a depleted Giants secondary that had all it could handle with Dez Bryant and Miles Austin. In proper Frisman Jackson Award fashion, Ogletree slipped off the map after that. He's a fast, lanky receiver who does okay in a situational role, which is what he's now trying to find with the Tampa Bay Buccaneers—Ogletree signed a two-year, $2.6 million deal with the Bucs in March, and he'll compete for the third or fourth spot on the depth chart.

Cordarrelle Patterson

| | Height: 6-2 | | Weight: 216 | | College: Tennessee | | Draft: 2013/1 (29) | | | | Born: 17-Mar-1991 | | Age: 22 | | Risk: Red | |

Year	Team	G/GS	Snaps	Rec	Pass	Yds	C%	+/-	Yd/C	TD	Drop	YAC	Rk	YAC+	BTkl	DVOA	Rk	DYAR	Rk	YAR	Short	Mid	Deep	Bomb
2013	MIN			34	71	542	48%	--	15.9	2						-7.5%								

Have we ever written about the divide between scouts and statistics before? We have? Well, let's do it again, because it *never gets old.*

Scouts will tell you that Patterson has the most upside of any receiver in this draft, and the Vikings traded away their second-, third- and fourth-round picks (along with a token seventh) to move back up into the first round and grab him. Run Patterson's tape and you'll see a man among boys. He has excellent vision, is unassailable in the open field, and owns a remarkable amount of on-field speed for his body type. Playmaker Score, which looks at his on-field production in his best year as well as his 40-yard dash and vertical leap, sees a receiver that never gained more than 88 yards in a game against an SEC opponent, and a player that didn't even crack the SEC top 10 in receiving yards despite playing for the team with the second-most pass attempts. The group of players that managed a Playmaker Score between 100 and 199, as Patterson did, has averaged 126 yards per season in the NFL.

The combined verdict? Patterson will probably not be an instant NFL success, as he needs to become a better route-runner and control himself more against press coverage, but assuming that light goes on, you'll probably want the over and then some.

Austin Pettis

| | Height: 6-3 | | Weight: 209 | | College: Boise State | | Draft: 2011/3 (78) | | | | Born: 7-May-1988 | | Age: 25 | | Risk: Blue | |

Year	Team	G/GS	Snaps	Rec	Pass	Yds	C%	+/-	Yd/C	TD	Drop	YAC	Rk	YAC+	BTkl	DVOA	Rk	DYAR	Rk	YAR	Short	Mid	Deep	Bomb
2011	STL	12/3	346	27	48	256	56%	-1.3	9.5	0	3	3.5	--	-0.8	2	-22.5%	--	-47	--	-42	49%	40%	2%	9%
2012	STL	14/2	374	30	48	261	63%	+0.4	8.7	4	1	2.6	--	-1.6	1	0.6%	--	35	--	44	53%	33%	4%	9%
2013	STL			18	35	204	51%	--	11.3	2						-19.5%								

At the ripe old age of 25, Pettis enters the 2013 as the Rams' elder statesman at wide receiver. Pettis lacks both the speed to get open deep and the elusiveness to break tackles on short routes. His size, however, does make him a fine goal-line weapon. The Rams threw him five passes inside the 5-yard line, and Pettis caught four of them for touchdowns (the fifth was intercepted). Now if only his teammates could get into the red zone more often, you might have something. He apparently blew coaches away as the most improved player in OTAs, for whatever that's worth.

Brian Quick

| | Height: 6-4 | | Weight: 220 | | College: Appalachian State | Draft: 2012/2 (33) | | | | Born: 5-Jun-1989 | | Age: 24 | | Risk: Yellow | |

Year	Team	G/GS	Snaps	Rec	Pass	Yds	C%	+/-	Yd/C	TD	Drop	YAC	Rk	YAC+	BTkl	DVOA	Rk	DYAR	Rk	YAR	Short	Mid	Deep	Bomb
2012	STL	15/1	182	11	27	156	41%	-4.9	14.2	2	3	2.1	--	-2.1	0	-25.0%	--	-33	--	-35	30%	37%	26%	7%
2013	STL			27	52	409	52%	--	15.1	3						-3.5%								

We invented the plus-minus stat for guys like Brian Quick. A 41 percent catch rate would be lousy for any receiver, but it's particularly galling for a guy who spends so much time around the line of scrimmage. Tony Softli of ESPN Radio in St. Louis said that Quick had been one of the most impressive and improved players in minicamp, but there's a big difference between success in June and success in September. Softli is not the only one who believes in Quick, though. He was drafted in the second round for a reason, and many believe he's the favorite to beat Austin Pettis and Chris Givens for a starting spot across from Tavon Austin.

Rueben Randle

| | Height: 6-3 | | Weight: 210 | | College: Louisiana State | | Draft: 2012/2 (63) | | | | Born: 7-May-1991 | | Age: 22 | | Risk: Red | |

Year	Team	G/GS	Snaps	Rec	Pass	Yds	C%	+/-	Yd/C	TD	Drop	YAC	Rk	YAC+	BTkl	DVOA	Rk	DYAR	Rk	YAR	Short	Mid	Deep	Bomb
2012	NYG	16/1	245	19	32	298	59%	-0.7	15.7	3	1	3.8	--	-0.9	2	16.3%	--	96	--	87	34%	44%	13%	9%
2013	NYG			46	81	653	57%	--	14.2	4						4.4%								

Randle has all the physical ability you want in a receiver: 2013 is about turning that potential into production. With Victor Cruz best-suited for the slot, the Giants need Randle to develop into an outside receiver who can complement Hakeem Nicks. The trio gives New York one of the best sets of receivers in the league, but that all depends on Randle turning the corner in 2013. Tom Coughlin and Kevin Gilbride separately praised Randle at OTAs, which is the kind of fluff you often hear in the offseason but is a good sign for a raw receiver. Gilbride noted that he expects Randle to see significant playing time, although it's worth remembering that Gilbride's top two wide receivers were absent from camp with contract issues.

At LSU, Randle was saddled with miserable quarterback play. That excuse doesn't hold water in New York, and Randle did show some potential in limited action. While he didn't see the field often, he gained over a yard per snap (do the math, and that's a good sign if he can turn into a starter) and drew three pass interference penalties. Teams will be forced to put their second-best corner on him and safety help will usually head for Cruz in the middle of the field. With Domenik Hixon now in Carolina, there aren't a lot of No. 3 receivers around the NFL in a better situation than Randle.

Sidney Rice

Height: 6-4 Weight: 200 College: South Carolina Draft: 2007/2 (44) Born: 1-Sep-1986 Age: 27 Risk: Green

Year	Team	G/GS	Snaps	Rec	Pass	Yds	C%	+/-	Yd/C	TD	Drop	YAC	Rk	YAC+	BTkl	DVOA	Rk	DYAR	Rk	YAR	Short	Mid	Deep	Bomb
2010	MIN	6/5	308	17	42	280	40%	-3.3	16.5	2	1	2.5	--	-1.1	1	-1.4%	--	40	--	18	13%	42%	18%	26%
2011	SEA	9/9	439	32	59	484	58%	+2.6	15.1	2	2	3.9	57	-1.2	1	-2.8%	55	86	53	51	21%	41%	10%	28%
2012	SEA	16/16	765	50	82	748	62%	+6.3	15.0	7	1	3.0	70	-1.3	1	29.7%	7	283	14	252	18%	51%	17%	13%
2013	SEA			48	84	720	57%	--	15.0	6						9.9%								

After the Seahawks traded for Percy Harvin, Mike Florio of Pro Football Talk pointed to Rice's low yardage totals and high cap number (his release would have saved the Seahawks save nearly $5 million) and suggested that Rice's tenure in Seattle was winding down. That analysis shows a keen use of mathematics, but a lack of football acumen. Harvin and Rice play the same position, but they are vastly different players. Over the past three seasons, only 15 percent of Harvin's targets have qualified as Deep or Bomb routes, while Rice has rarely caught many passes close to the line of scrimmage. Even a run-oriented team like Seattle usually has at least three wideouts on the field, and the Seahawks now have a perfect set: Harvin's the short route guy, Rice is the mid-range target, and Tate is the deep threat. There's some overlap there, of course, but you get the point: Rice isn't going anywhere.

Andre Roberts

Height: 5-11 Weight: 195 College: The Citadel Draft: 2010/3 (88) Born: 9-Jan-1988 Age: 25 Risk: Green

Year	Team	G/GS	Snaps	Rec	Pass	Yds	C%	+/-	Yd/C	TD	Drop	YAC	Rk	YAC+	BTkl	DVOA	Rk	DYAR	Rk	YAR	Short	Mid	Deep	Bomb
2010	ARI	15/2	385	24	49	307	49%	-6.7	12.8	2	2	5.8	--	+0.8	3	-40.7%	--	-105	--	-75	49%	32%	15%	4%
2011	ARI	16/16	940	51	97	586	53%	-5.3	11.5	2	4	4.4	37	+0.5	5	-15.2%	75	-64	84	-37	37%	47%	11%	5%
2012	ARI	15/15	837	64	114	759	56%	-3.3	11.9	5	8	3.5	60	-0.4	3	-6.5%	63	12	72	25	36%	47%	13%	5%
2013	ARI			55	94	714	59%	--	13.0	4						-0.4%								

Roberts led all Cardinals receivers in DYAR and DVOA in 2012, which is to say that his game was least vulnerable to quite possibly the worst quarterback rotation the NFL has seen since the 1992 Seahawks gave us Stan Gelbaugh, Dan McGwire, and Kelly Stouffer. Whether outside or from the slot, Roberts is a quality short and intermediate receiver who can get free from press coverage and runs sharp breaking routes. Arizona's quarterback turribleness has affected the productivity of all its receivers, but catching passes from a timing and rhythm thrower like Carson Palmer could help Roberts have a breakout year—especially if he proves to be more consistent with route concepts than Michael Floyd has to date.

Aldrick Robinson

Height: 5-10 Weight: 182 College: SMU Draft: 2011/6 (178) Born: 11-Apr-1988 Age: 25 Risk: Blue

Year	Team	G/GS	Snaps	Rec	Pass	Yds	C%	+/-	Yd/C	TD	Drop	YAC	Rk	YAC+	BTkl	DVOA	Rk	DYAR	Rk	YAR	Short	Mid	Deep	Bomb
2012	WAS	15/2	216	11	19	237	58%	+1.4	21.5	3	2	5.6	--	+0.8	1	51.4%	--	88	--	101	17%	44%	6%	33%
2013	WAS			13	23	238	57%	--	18.3	1						20.7%								

Robinson replaced Emmanuel Sanders as SMU's primary deep threat, and did have a few splash plays in his second NFL season. Cowboys fans will remember him as the recipient of a 68-yard Thanksgiving Day touchdown pass from Robert Griffin III in which Robinson flew past a Dallas defense biting hard on RG3's play action. Robinson also caught a 49-yard touchdown pass against the Eagles' woebegone schemes the previous week. There's something to his potential if he can pull this stuff off against secondaries that don't resemble dumpster fires.

Laurent Robinson

Height: 6-2 Weight: 192 College: Illinois State Draft: 2007/3 (75) Born: 20-May-1985 Age: 28 Risk: N/A

Year	Team	G/GS	Snaps	Rec	Pass	Yds	C%	+/-	Yd/C	TD	Drop	YAC	Rk	YAC+	BTkl	DVOA	Rk	DYAR	Rk	YAR	Short	Mid	Deep	Bomb
2010	STL	14/11	731	34	75	344	45%	-6.6	10.1	2	4	3.1	64	-0.8	2	-36.0%	84	-125	84	-116	35%	44%	14%	8%
2011	DAL	14/4	578	54	81	858	67%	+5.0	15.9	11	3	4.9	26	+0.7	3	39.1%	4	324	8	325	28%	41%	18%	12%
2012	JAC	7/4	264	24	43	252	56%	-1.6	10.5	0	4	2.3	--	-1.6	1	-32.1%	--	-25	--	-54	37%	39%	12%	12%

Wait, you mean that *was* a fluke year for Laurent Robinson? We never would have guessed. Actually, we guessed it fine, but the pre-analytics front office of the Jaguars sure didn't guess correctly, giving Robinson a five-year, $32.5 million contract. Concussions limited Robinson to just 24 receptions for 252 yards in seven games and, despite owing Robinson $2 million in fully guaranteed base salary, the Jaguars released him at the start of the new league year. Given Robinson's injury history, he'll have a hard time finding a team that's willing to take a chance on him.

Eddie Royal																							
Height: 5-9	Weight: 184	College: Virginia Tech	Draft: 2008/2 (42)	Born: 21-May-1986	Age: 27	Risk: Blue																	
Year	Team	G/GS	Snaps	Rec	Pass	Yds	C%	+/-	Yd/C	TD	Drop	YAC	Rk	YAC+	BTkl	DVOA	Rk	DYAR	Rk	YAR	Short	Mid	Deep	Bomb
2010	DEN	16/10	599	59	106	627	57%	-6.3	10.6	3	2	6.6	3	+0.8	5	-16.7%	74	-33	75	-28	49%	35%	11%	4%
2011	DEN	12/8	476	19	50	155	38%	-8.1	8.2	1	3	3.5	68	-1.5	2	-44.6%	92	-152	90	-148	33%	41%	13%	13%
2012	SD	10/2	272	23	44	234	52%	-5.3	10.2	1	0	3.9	--	-1.0	1	-22.7%	--	-56	--	-46	44%	42%	9%	5%
2013	SD			10	17	113	59%	--	11.3	0						-3.4%								

The Chargers were desperate for a shifty, space-creating underneath slot receiver last year. Royal fit the description on paper, but he did not pan out. He played in 10 games with two starts, having minimal production. Injuries hindered him, though you can't help but wonder if his route-running mistake that resulted in a pick-six in the Week 5 Monday Night loss against Denver compromised the confidence that his quarterback and coaches had in him. (On that play, Royal ran an inside route and made the cardinal sin of letting the defender, Chris Harris, cross his face.)

Emmanuel Sanders																							
Height: 5-11	Weight: 186	College: SMU	Draft: 2010/3 (82)	Born: 17-Mar-1987	Age: 26	Risk: Yellow																	
Year	Team	G/GS	Snaps	Rec	Pass	Yds	C%	+/-	Yd/C	TD	Drop	YAC	Rk	YAC+	BTkl	DVOA	Rk	DYAR	Rk	YAR	Short	Mid	Deep	Bomb
2010	PIT	13/1	398	28	50	376	56%	+0.1	13.4	2	3	2.5	78	-1.4	2	6.2%	35	66	56	53	19%	46%	27%	8%
2011	PIT	11/0	339	22	43	288	51%	-2.9	13.1	2	0	5.8	--	+1.5	2	-7.7%	--	22	--	24	29%	38%	21%	12%
2012	PIT	16/7	721	44	74	626	59%	+0.7	14.2	1	4	4.8	32	+0.2	3	9.5%	25	124	38	121	36%	28%	30%	6%
2013	PIT			54	94	749	57%	--	13.9	5						3.5%								

Sanders, on third-down passes from Ben Roethlisberger: 13-of-19 for 163 yards, 12 first downs. The Sunshine Boys were an amazing drag on just about every Steelers passing statistic; you have to tease Byron Leftwich and Charlie Batch out of any data you really want to use. The Steelers played chicken with the Patriots in the offseason, with Sanders as the cliff wall they raced their hot rods toward. The Patriots made a restricted free agent offer, and the Steelers dithered a bit before matching it, because the Steelers are the kind of organization that removes the paper clips before mailing documents to save both the paper clip and the postal weight. Sanders is an odd fit as a possession receiver but a good player. His role will probably expand with Mike Wallace gone, just in time to hit the free-agent market in 2014.

Mohamed Sanu																							
Height: 6-2	Weight: 211	College: Rutgers	Draft: 2012/3 (83)	Born: 22-Aug-1989	Age: 24	Risk: Red																	
Year	Team	G/GS	Snaps	Rec	Pass	Yds	C%	+/-	Yd/C	TD	Drop	YAC	Rk	YAC+	BTkl	DVOA	Rk	DYAR	Rk	YAR	Short	Mid	Deep	Bomb
2012	CIN	9/3	204	16	25	154	64%	-0.2	9.6	4	1	4.4	--	-0.5	0	13.8%	--	42	--	54	42%	50%	8%	0%
2013	CIN			53	81	596	65%	--	11.2	4						4.2%								

All 16 of Sanu's catches came between Week 7 and Week 12. Before that, he saw limited action, appearing just long enough to throw an option pass for a touchdown. A stress fracture, suffered in Week 8, ended his season a few games later. Sanu will be a full participant in training camp and will battle Marvin Jones once again for the No. 2 receiver job. May the healthiest receiver win.

Chaz Schilens																							
Height: 6-4	Weight: 225	College: San Diego State	Draft: 2008/7 (226)	Born: 7-Nov-1985	Age: 28	Risk: N/A																	
Year	Team	G/GS	Snaps	Rec	Pass	Yds	C%	+/-	Yd/C	TD	Drop	YAC	Rk	YAC+	BTkl	DVOA	Rk	DYAR	Rk	YAR	Short	Mid	Deep	Bomb
2010	OAK	5/0	77	5	9	40	56%	+0.1	8.0	1	0	2.6	--	-0.9	0	5.4%	--	10	--	10	56%	22%	11%	11%
2011	OAK	15/5	387	23	34	271	68%	+2.6	11.8	2	3	1.6	--	-1.8	0	15.1%	--	68	--	60	29%	38%	26%	6%
2012	NYJ	15/6	504	28	41	289	68%	+1.9	10.3	2	1	1.9	--	-1.8	0	-5.6%	--	20	--	24	29%	51%	15%	5%

Schilens is a useful but uninspiring veteran possession receiver who can also play a little bit on special teams. He tried out with a number of teams in the offseason, and though he hadn't signed as of mid-July, he'll probably show up on some team that suffers a couple of wide receiver injuries this year.

Jordan Shipley   Height: 5-11   Weight: 193   College: Texas   Draft: 2010/3 (84)   Born: 23-Dec-1985   Age: 28   Risk: Green

Year	Team	G/GS	Snaps	Rec	Pass	Yds	C%	+/-	Yd/C	TD	Drop	YAC	Rk	YAC+	BTkl	DVOA	Rk	DYAR	Rk	YAR	Short	Mid	Deep	Bomb
2010	CIN	15/4	593	52	74	600	70%	+4.8	11.5	3	0	4.0	42	-0.2	2	15.2%	9	157	28	143	49%	43%	6%	3%
2011	CIN	2/0	50	4	5	14	80%	+0.4	3.5	0	0	0.0	--	-4.6	0	-91.9%	--	-40	--	-38	67%	17%	17%	0%
2012	2TM	7/2	253	23	39	244	59%	-0.1	10.6	1	4	1.8	--	-2.3	0	-19.0%	--	-42	--	-13	37%	40%	20%	3%
2013	JAC			21	39	223	54%	--	10.6	1						-13.6%								

Released earlier in the season by the Tampa Bay Buccaneers, Shipley joined the Jaguars in November as an injury replacement for Laurent Robinson. Shipley caught 23 balls over the final six games of the season, working primarily out of the slot. Shipley was most effective on second downs, where he had a 25.0% DVOA and a 79 percent catch rate on 14 targets. Though Shipley was a restricted free agent this offseason, the Jaguars did not offer him a tender and he became a street free agent. A lack of interest allowed the Jaguars re-sign Shipley to a two-year, $1.315 million contract; he will compete with Ace Sanders, Mohamed Massaquoi and Taylor Price for the No. 3 receiver role.

Cecil Shorts   Height: 6-0   Weight: 200   College: Mount Union   Draft: 2011/4 (114)   Born: 22-Dec-1987   Age: 26   Risk: Red

Year	Team	G/GS	Snaps	Rec	Pass	Yds	C%	+/-	Yd/C	TD	Drop	YAC	Rk	YAC+	BTkl	DVOA	Rk	DYAR	Rk	YAR	Short	Mid	Deep	Bomb
2011	JAC	10/0	176	2	11	30	18%	-4.1	15.0	1	2	1.5	--	-2.3	0	-53.9%	--	-34	--	-37	18%	36%	18%	27%
2012	JAC	14/9	654	55	105	979	52%	-5.7	17.8	7	8	6.5	8	+2.7	9	5.2%	30	138	32	164	29%	39%	21%	11%
2013	JAC			63	115	993	55%	--	15.8	5						4.0%								

Shorts was a bright spot in an otherwise dismal 2012 season for the Jacksonville Jaguars. The 2011 fourth-round pick emerged as a dangerous deep threat, averaging nearly 18 yards per catch with five catches of 40 or more yards, four of which went for touchdowns. Shorts had four 100-yard receiving games. Had he received playing time earlier in the year (Shorts played in less than half the snaps over the first six games of the season), better quarterback play, and dodged the late-season concussion that caused him to miss two games, he likely would have been the third receiver in Jaguars history to top 1,000 receiving yards in a single season. With Justin Blackmon opening the season with a four-game suspension, Shorts will every opportunity to cement a role as the team's No. 1 receiver and first option in the passing game.

Jerome Simpson   Height: 6-2   Weight: 199   College: Coastal Carolina   Draft: 2008/2 (46)   Born: 4-Feb-1986   Age: 27   Risk: Green

Year	Team	G/GS	Snaps	Rec	Pass	Yds	C%	+/-	Yd/C	TD	Drop	YAC	Rk	YAC+	BTkl	DVOA	Rk	DYAR	Rk	YAR	Short	Mid	Deep	Bomb
2010	CIN	5/3	148	20	25	277	80%	+4.3	13.9	3	0	3.9	--	+0.0	0	44.7%	--	109	--	95	20%	60%	12%	8%
2011	CIN	16/14	867	50	105	725	48%	-8.8	14.5	4	6	4.6	33	+0.6	3	-6.3%	63	57	56	30	24%	52%	13%	10%
2012	MIN	12/10	453	26	51	274	51%	-3.6	10.5	0	2	2.2	85	-2.1	2	-24.5%	84	-37	80	-58	24%	45%	18%	12%
2013	MIN			28	54	397	52%	--	14.2	2						-8.6%								

It took Simpson three seasons to put a dent in the Bengals receiving corps, and it's pretty easy to see why. Simpson mixes in about one jaw-dropping highlight reel play—you may remember 2011's front-flip touchdown over a defender as his crowning moment—for every six incomplete passes in his vicinity. It's hard not to be enamored with his physical gifts, so he'll keep getting chances despite a long track record that says he shouldn't. Minnesota appears to be falling all over themselves to give him another chance under the idea that Cordarrelle Patterson needs more seasoning. If the Vikings are lucky, Patterson will learn quickly, Jarius Wright will seize the No. 3 spot on the depth chart, and the teasing will stop.

Brad Smith   Height: 6-2   Weight: 210   College: Missouri   Draft: 2006/4 (103)   Born: 12-Dec-1983   Age: 30   Risk: Yellow

Year	Team	G/GS	Snaps	Rec	Pass	Yds	C%	+/-	Yd/C	TD	Drop	YAC	Rk	YAC+	BTkl	DVOA	Rk	DYAR	Rk	YAR	Short	Mid	Deep	Bomb
2010	NYJ	16/2	288	4	7	44	57%	-0.1	11.0	0	2	2.5	--	-1.5	8	-36.1%	--	-10	--	-11	83%	0%	17%	0%
2011	BUF	15/5	394	23	42	240	55%	-3.2	10.4	1	3	4.6	--	-0.6	5	-25.3%	--	-44	--	-55	44%	32%	15%	10%
2012	BUF	15/2	310	14	23	152	61%	+1.6	10.9	2	0	3.1	--	-1.4	2	2.9%	--	12	--	16	40%	35%	15%	10%
2013	BUF			12	22	130	55%	--	10.8	1						-14.0%								

Smith has been a useful gadget player, but his time is likely coming to an end. Once E.J. Manuel takes over the starting quarterback job, the Bills won't need to bring in Smith to run option plays. At that point, he's likely to be squeezed off the roster by the young receiving talent Doug Marrone is hoping to develop, especially since he's due $7.8 million over the next two seasons. Smith ran 14 times for 101 yards last year; if he does make the Buffalo roster this year, his projection for 2013 includes 10 carries for 68 yards.

Steve Smith		Height: 5-9		Weight: 185		College: Utah		Draft: 2001/3 (74)		Born: 12-May-1979	Age: 34		Risk: Yellow

Year	Team	G/GS	Snaps	Rec	Pass	Yds	C%	+/-	Yd/C	TD	Drop	YAC	Rk	YAC+	BTkl	DVOA	Rk	DYAR	Rk	YAR	Short	Mid	Deep	Bomb
2010	CAR	9/7	775	48	99	529	46%	-8.6	11.0	3	6	4.7	25	-0.2	8	-31.9%	83	-152	85	-153	40%	36%	18%	6%
2011	CAR	16/16	956	79	129	1394	61%	+3.6	17.6	7	7	5.8	14	+0.7	8	12.6%	23	285	10	246	30%	32%	23%	15%
2012	CAR	16/16	910	73	138	1174	53%	-3.5	16.1	4	8	3.7	53	-0.4	6	4.0%	34	171	27	161	18%	46%	26%	10%
2013	CAR			78	139	1248	56%	--	16.0	8						9.7%								

The amazing thing about Steve Smith is not necessarily what he has done, but how little help he has had in the process of doing it. Smith led the league in percentage of his team's passing yards last year. It was the third time since 2003 he has led the league in that category, and the eighth time he has made the top 10. In the decade-plus since Smith joined the team in 2001, only ten other Panthers have caught 100 total passes, including four running backs (DeAngelo Williams, Brad Hoover, DeShaun Foster, Nick Goings) and three tight ends (Kris Mangum, Greg Olsen, Jeff King). The leading non-Smith wideouts in that timeframe: Muhsin Muhammad (retired in 2009, and also spent three seasons in Chicago), Keary Colbert (two 100-yard games as a rookie, none the rest of his career), and Brandon LaFell, the current No.-2-receiver-by-default. Smith is entering his 13th season, and told the AP (Associated Press, not Adrian Peterson) that he would like to play for two or three years after that. It wouldn't be unprecedented. A number of receivers have posted 1,000-yard seasons in their mid-30s. The most similar to Smith might be Drew Hill, a 5-foot-9 wideout on Warren Moon's run-and-shoot Oilers teams who went over a thousand yards at 34 and 35, and played for two more years after that. More recently, 5-foot-10 Derrick Mason's last 1,000-yard season came at age 35 for Baltimore. So while Smith's end is relatively near, there's no reason to expect a dropoff this season. There's no reason to expect any other Panthers receivers to step up, either.

Steve Smith		Height: 6-0		Weight: 195		College: USC		Draft: 2007/2 (51)		Born: 6-May-1985	Age: 28		Risk: N/A

Year	Team	G/GS	Snaps	Rec	Pass	Yds	C%	+/-	Yd/C	TD	Drop	YAC	Rk	YAC+	BTkl	DVOA	Rk	DYAR	Rk	YAR	Short	Mid	Deep	Bomb
2010	NYG	9/7	520	48	75	529	64%	+4.8	11.0	3	4	2.2	82	-1.5	2	2.3%	44	97	47	100	26%	49%	14%	11%
2011	PHI	9/1	129	11	20	124	55%	+0.2	11.3	1	3	3.0	--	-0.9	1	-15.8%	--	17	--	-2	35%	41%	12%	12%
2012	STL	9/2	173	14	25	131	56%	-1.4	9.4	0	3	2.8	--	-0.9	1	-20.0%	--	-8	--	-21	39%	57%	4%	0%

On May 29, NFL.com had a story saying that Steve Smith was retiring after six seasons. The next day they ran a story quoting Steve Smith saying he wanted to play for 15 years or more. The stories may have triggered Favre-ian flashbacks in Green Bay fans, but in this case they were about two separate people. Carolina's Steve Smith is still going strong, but Steve Smith of the Giants/Eagles/Rams/Bucs (briefly) has called it a career. Smith was second in receptions and eighth in DYAR in 2009, but he underwent microfracture knee surgery and a mosaicplasty during the 2010 season, and was never the same again.

Torrey Smith		Height: 6-1		Weight: 204		College: Maryland		Draft: 2011/2 (58)		Born: 26-Jan-1989	Age: 24		Risk: Yellow

Year	Team	G/GS	Snaps	Rec	Pass	Yds	C%	+/-	Yd/C	TD	Drop	YAC	Rk	YAC+	BTkl	DVOA	Rk	DYAR	Rk	YAR	Short	Mid	Deep	Bomb
2011	BAL	16/14	883	50	96	841	54%	+0.8	16.8	7	6	4.7	30	+0.1	2	11.6%	27	199	22	176	19%	34%	18%	29%
2012	BAL	16/16	919	49	110	855	45%	-8.0	17.4	8	5	4.6	34	+0.1	4	0.7%	42	143	31	132	21%	34%	15%	30%
2013	BAL			58	109	932	53%	--	16.1	7						5.8%								

Smith and Joe Flacco were just 7-of-34 on deep passes (over 15 yards in the air) from Week 5 until the end of the season after starting the year 7-for-20. A lack of deep production from Smith would normally spell disaster for the Ravens offense, and that's exactly what it spelled at times last year. But Jacoby Jones picked up a little of the slack, the defense did what the Ravens defense does, Ray Rice kept on chugging, and the Ravens trudged into the playoffs.

Smith provided two touchdowns against the Broncos in the playoffs, but he must become more reliable as an all-purpose receiver. With Anquan Boldin gone, he cannot afford any more three-week stretches with five catches for 68 yards like the one he produced in early December. (Note: He suffered a concussion at the end of that streak, not the beginning.) Everyone from Rice to Ozzie Newsome has used the phrase "step up" to define Smith's goal for 2013, so he needs to start stepping.

Micheal Spurlock		Height: 5-10		Weight: 214		College: Mississippi		Draft: 2006/FA		Born: 31-Jan-1983	Age: 30		Risk: Yellow

Year	Team	G/GS	Snaps	Rec	Pass	Yds	C%	+/-	Yd/C	TD	Drop	YAC	Rk	YAC+	BTkl	DVOA	Rk	DYAR	Rk	YAR	Short	Mid	Deep	Bomb
2010	TB	16/1	301	17	33	250	52%	+0.4	14.7	2	3	1.9	--	-2.9	1	-2.1%	--	25	--	22	25%	25%	28%	22%
2011	TB	12/0	48	2	6	13	33%	-1.1	6.5	0	0	2.0	--	-1.8	0	-63.6%	--	-25	--	-23	33%	17%	33%	17%
2012	2TM	14/1	197	23	29	200	79%	+2.1	8.7	1	1	2.8	--	-1.5	0	6.8%	--	45	--	35	52%	45%	3%	0%
2013	DET			5	8	52	63%	--	10.3	0						-6.1%								

Long-time Buccaneers returner Spurlock got a taste of the road for the first time last season, heading to Jacksonville and then San Diego at mid-season. He even had a nice little spell as an underneath receiver for the Chargers once Philip Rivers decided that Eddie Royal and Robert Meachem were incompetent at their jobs. In Detroit, he's probably got the first shot at returning kicks for a Lions squad that needs to replace Stefan Logan, but we don't see him being used as a receiver much.

Kenny Stills			Height: 6-0		Weight: 194			College: Oklahoma			Draft: 2013/5 (144)			Born: 22-Apr-1992		Age: 21		Risk: Red	
Year	Team	G/GS	Snaps	Rec	Pass	Yds	C%	+/-	Yd/C	TD	Drop	YAC	Rk	YAC+	BTkl	DVOA	Rk	DYAR	Rk	YAR	Short	Mid	Deep	Bomb
2013	NO		20	33	255	61%	--	12.8	2							1.9%							

Matt Waldman tabbed Stills as a good fit for the Saints in his post-draft scouting report, citing Stills' deep speed from the slot and his experience playing multiple receiving roles in the Oklahoma offense. Stills is a high-effort player with skill as a blocker and despite his size, he has skill to win in the red zone against tight coverage. He greatest area of improvement is developing consistency with the small points of the game that become magnified issues at the NFL level: hand position on certain targets, route depth, making the correct reads with his quarterback, and sharper routes. He'll have a shot to compete with Joseph Morgan for the No. 3 spot on the Saints' receiver depth chart, but he's most likely a role player this year whose role will grow if he can demonstrate improvement with his snap-to-snap consistency.

Brandon Stokley			Height: 5-11		Weight: 197		College: Louisiana-Lafayette		Draft: 1999/4 (105)			Born: 23-Jun-1976		Age: 37		Risk: N/A	
Year	Team	G/GS	Snaps	Rec	Pass	Yds	C%	+/-	Yd/C	TD	Drop	YAC	Rk	YAC+	BTkl	DVOA	Rk	DYAR	Rk	YAR	Short	Mid	Deep	Bomb
2010	SEA	11/0	225	31	43	354	72%	+4.0	11.4	0	1	2.9	--	-0.7	0	17.1%	--	94	--	97	27%	59%	10%	5%
2011	NYG	2/0	29	1	3	7	33%	-0.3	7.0	0	0	4.0	--	-1.1	0	-35.5%	--	-12	--	-5	33%	33%	33%	0%
2012	DEN	15/9	598	45	59	544	76%	+8.7	12.1	5	1	3.3	66	-0.7	1	37.4%	2	204	23	223	40%	33%	21%	5%

Stokley is the epitome of a niche receiver. His niche, obviously, is playing the slot. He's superb on seam routes and anything underneath where he can have free access off the line of scrimmage. He has an uncanny ability to make tough catches, relying on patience and positioning rather than athleticism. He has soft hands and tracks the ball in the air remarkably well. Great as Stokley is in his niche, he's limited in most other facets of the game and he's 37 years old. He could probably line up on the outside and get open if helped by route combinations within the play design, but physically he can't consistently create his own separation in one-on-one scenarios. If a team needs to plug in a reliable inside veteran receiver at any point (whether it be prior to the season or on a November Friday afternoon), he's the guy.

Rod Streater			Height: 6-3		Weight: 200			College: Temple			Draft: 2012/FA			Born: 9-Feb-1988		Age: 25		Risk: Green	
Year	Team	G/GS	Snaps	Rec	Pass	Yds	C%	+/-	Yd/C	TD	Drop	YAC	Rk	YAC+	BTkl	DVOA	Rk	DYAR	Rk	YAR	Short	Mid	Deep	Bomb
2012	OAK	16/2	580	39	75	584	52%	-4.1	15.0	3	4	3.6	57	-0.7	0	-1.9%	51	43	60	61	19%	53%	16%	11%
2013	OAK			51	89	702	57%	--	13.8	5							4.1%							

Streater sent mixed signals throughout his 2012 NFL debut. He clearly does not have great size and strength. The size he can't help, the playing strength he *can* help. He'll never been a stout possession type target, but he must get firmer than he currently is. Otherwise, his playing speed will continue to be negatively impacted like it was at times last year. There were times when Streater flashed acceleration over the top and after the catch. There were other times where he completely disappeared.

Ryan Swope			Height: 6-0		Weight: 205			College: Texas A&M		Draft: 2013/6 (174)			Born: 20-Sep-1990		Age: 23		Risk: Red	
Year	Team	G/GS	Snaps	Rec	Pass	Yds	C%	+/-	Yd/C	TD	Drop	YAC	Rk	YAC+	BTkl	DVOA	Rk	DYAR	Rk	YAR	Short	Mid	Deep	Bomb
2013	ARI		25	43	296	58%	--	11.8	1							-5.5%								

Swope was the primary receiver for two different A&M quarterbacks—Ryan Tannehill and Johnny Manziel—and had a catch rate of at least 70 percent in all four years of college. His role as a heavy-rep inside receiver tends to lead to automatic Wes Welker comparisons, but not so fast—Swope is both bigger and faster than your standard slot guy, and the Cardinals are hoping that he'll provide openings in underneath coverage for new head coach Bruce Arians. Right now, Swope's main opponent is a concussion history that has traveled to the NFL with him. He suffered four reported concussions during his time with the Aggies. Arians claimed to be surprised that Swope's head injuries affected his participation in minicamps, which would seem to be a scouting faux pas, as it was common knowledge that Swope dropped in the draft for that exact reason.

Golden Tate			Height: 5-10		Weight: 199			College: Notre Dame		Draft: 2010/2 (60)			Born: 2-Aug-1988		Age: 25		Risk: Green	
Year	Team	G/GS	Snaps	Rec	Pass	Yds	C%	+/-	Yd/C	TD	Drop	YAC	Rk	YAC+	BTkl	DVOA	Rk	DYAR	Rk	YAR	Short	Mid	Deep	Bomb
2010	SEA	11/0	230	21	40	227	55%	-2.8	10.8	0	2	5.3	--	+0.5	4	-25.9%	--	-29	--	-35	46%	31%	10%	13%
2011	SEA	16/5	526	35	60	382	62%	+2.6	10.9	3	0	4.5	35	-0.1	8	-14.4%	73	-10	74	-17	39%	39%	11%	11%
2012	SEA	15/15	715	45	70	688	69%	+7.4	15.3	7	2	5.9	11	+0.4	14	31.6%	4	245	19	249	41%	25%	10%	24%
2013	SEA			31	53	449	58%	--	14.5	4							8.8%							

There's so much more to Golden Tate than the Fail Mary. His new teammate Percy Harvin led all wide receivers in broken tackles last season, but Tate was tied for third, and in fact led all wideouts in broken tackles per touch. He was Seattle's designated target on bubble screens last year, and when he wasn't going short, he was going very deep, also leading the team in bomb routes. Tate admitted that he sulked a little after Harvin was acquired, assuming that Harvin's presence would hurt Tate's numbers heading into his contract year. Pete Carroll reassured Tate, though, saying publicly that Harvin's presence will free Tate to head downfield more often, and that the Seahawks need to work to get Tate the ball more often. Exploiting mismatches and getting receivers open should be easy in Seattle this year. It's managing all the egos that could prove tough.

Demaryius Thomas		Height: 6-3		Weight: 224			College: Georgia Tech			Draft: 2010/1 (22)			Born: 25-Dec-1987		Age: 26		Risk: Yellow					
Year	Team	G/GS	Snaps	Rec	Pass	Yds	C%	+/-	Yd/C	TD	Drop	YAC	Rk	YAC+	BTkl	DVOA	Rk	DYAR	Rk	YAR	Short	Mid	Deep	Bomb
2010	DEN	10/2	162	22	39	283	56%	-2.5	12.9	2	1	6.2	--	+0.7	2	-3.8%	--	24	--	9	42%	26%	26%	5%
2011	DEN	11/5	533	32	70	551	46%	-2.4	17.2	4	3	3.5	67	-0.4	2	-5.6%	60	38	60	42	16%	51%	14%	19%
2012	DEN	16/16	1019	94	141	1434	67%	+10.3	15.3	10	6	5.7	17	+1.0	9	21.4%	14	354	8	401	42%	31%	12%	15%
2013	DEN			83	130	1250	64%	--	15.1	10						25.4%								

In his third year in the league (and first with a big-time quarterback), Thomas erupted as an elite all-around receiver. He led the AFC with 29 catches of 20 yards or longer and finished second in total receiving yards. He was by no means just a field-stretcher, though. He proved he could go over the middle, catch passes on the move underneath (which made him a critical component in Denver's play-action game) and win classic possession battles on outside comebacker patterns. The Broncos loved to use Thomas as the weakside receiver in their 3x1 sets, as that's where it is the most expensive for defenses to double him. Plus, from the outside, he can run the full gauntlet of vertical patterns, which is important for attacking the two-deep safety looks that defenses love to play against Peyton Manning.

Mike Thomas		Height: 5-8		Weight: 195			College: Arizona			Draft: 2009/4 (107)			Born: 4-Jun-1987		Age: 26		Risk: Yellow					
Year	Team	G/GS	Snaps	Rec	Pass	Yds	C%	+/-	Yd/C	TD	Drop	YAC	Rk	YAC+	BTkl	DVOA	Rk	DYAR	Rk	YAR	Short	Mid	Deep	Bomb
2010	JAC	16/11	780	66	102	820	66%	+3.6	12.4	4	2	4.5	30	-0.4	7	11.6%	19	181	21	180	41%	30%	18%	10%
2011	JAC	15/13	681	44	92	415	48%	-12.3	9.4	1	1	4.3	41	-0.9	3	-33.9%	89	-182	92	-188	40%	39%	16%	6%
2012	2TM	16/4	456	18	40	108	45%	-7.1	6.0	1	3	1.5	--	-3.3	0	-56.9%	--	-116	--	-139	50%	44%	3%	3%
2013	DET			24	43	286	56%	--	11.9	1						-10.1%								

Once upon a time, Thomas was an effective underneath receiver that did well on screen passes and returned punts effectively. Oh wait, that was just three years ago. Practically given away by the Jaguars, Thomas wasn't even able to beat out Kris Durham for snaps when injuries ravaged Detroit's receiving corps. There's a large field of chaff at the bottom of the Lions receiving depth chart. Unfortunately for Thomas, he's part of it.

Deonte Thompson		Height: 6-0		Weight: 203			College: Florida			Draft: 2012/FA			Born: 14-Feb-1989		Age: 24		Risk: Red					
Year	Team	G/GS	Snaps	Rec	Pass	Yds	C%	+/-	Yd/C	TD	Drop	YAC	Rk	YAC+	BTkl	DVOA	Rk	DYAR	Rk	YAR	Short	Mid	Deep	Bomb
2012	BAL	6/0	85	5	6	51	83%	+0.9	10.2	0	0	4.6	--	+0.5	1	-0.6%	--	13	--	6	50%	33%	17%	0%
2013	BAL			32	57	494	56%	--	15.4	3						6.2%								

Thompson emerged in May as a rumor-mill favorite to beat Jacoby Jones and others for the Ravens No. 2 receiving job. Thompson made the Ravens as an undrafted rookie from Florida last year, winning coaches over with his blazing speed and starting the 2012 season as the team's primary return man. Jacoby Jones replaced him on returns after a fumble, and Thompson was a healthy scratch for much of the remainder of the season, reappearing in that Ravens-Bengals mop-up finale that produced much of the available data we have on both team's benchwarmers. John Harbaugh said in minicamp that Thompson "could sneak in there" because of his speed and the advancements he made during the season and offseason, but it was part of one of those "say good things about everyone" press conferences, so let's not get carried away. Slotting Thompson to beat Jones and start opposite Torrey Smith is overly optimistic, but the road to the No. 3 role is paved with Tandon Doss types, so Thompson has a real chance to do more than mop up Bengals games.

Tiquan Underwood		Height: 6-1		Weight: 184			College: Rutgers			Draft: 2009/7 (253)			Born: 17-Feb-1987		Age: 26		Risk: Green					
Year	Team	G/GS	Snaps	Rec	Pass	Yds	C%	+/-	Yd/C	TD	Drop	YAC	Rk	YAC+	BTkl	DVOA	Rk	DYAR	Rk	YAR	Short	Mid	Deep	Bomb
2010	JAC	10/0	279	8	22	111	36%	-3.4	13.9	0	3	2.4	--	-1.3	1	-22.7%	--	-22	--	-21	10%	52%	14%	24%
2011	NE	6/0	87	3	6	30	50%	-0.6	10.0	0	1	2.0	--	-0.9	0	-19.2%	--	-3	--	-4	17%	50%	33%	0%
2012	TB	14/3	445	28	55	425	51%	-2.7	15.2	2	4	3.6	55	-0.2	1	-7.0%	66	4	73	28	18%	51%	22%	10%
2013	TB			20	37	297	54%	--	14.9	1						0.0%								

The Bucs signed Underwood in May of 2012, cut him before the season, then brought him back in time to play in Week 3. It took him four games in a Tampa Bay uniform to surpass his yardage total from three seasons in Jacksonville and New England. He was quietly effective for most of the year, but tailed off dramatically at the end. From Week 13 on, his catch rate fell to 36 percent, his DVOA to -37.5%. His forthcoming camp battle with Kevin Ogletree for the Bucs' third receiver spot seems like incentive for Tampa Bay to lean heavily on two-tight end sets (or it would, if their depth at tight end was any better).

Mike Wallace			Height: 6-0			Weight: 199			College: Mississippi			Draft: 2009/3 (84)			Born: 1-Aug-1986		Age: 27		Risk: Red	
Year	Team	G/GS	Snaps	Rec	Pass	Yds	C%	+/-	Yd/C	TD	Drop	YAC	Rk	YAC+	BTkl	DVOA	Rk	DYAR	Rk	YAR	Short	Mid	Deep	Bomb
2010	PIT	16/16	966	60	98	1257	61%	+7.2	21.0	10	5	6.0	6	+0.9	6	49.5%	1	457	1	446	26%	32%	15%	27%
2011	PIT	16/14	915	72	113	1193	64%	+6.1	16.6	8	6	6.5	7	+1.9	14	31.7%	6	383	6	377	35%	38%	8%	19%
2012	PIT	15/14	833	64	119	836	54%	-5.4	13.1	8	6	4.2	39	-0.7	4	-17.4%	78	-19	77	-25	33%	38%	12%	17%
2013	MIA			77	135	1064	57%	--	13.8	7							1.9%							

Wallace was just 8-of-37 on Deep passes (16 or more yards through the air) last year, for 300 yards. He was 0-of-10 catching deep passes from Charlie Batch and Byron Leftwich, so the numbers are not as bad as they looked. Wallace will be nearly as valuable for the Dolphins by keeping safeties out of the box and away from Brian Hartline as for the bombs he catches, but for the money the Dolphins are paying him, he had better catch more than eight bombs. Ryan Tannehill was an effective deep passer last year—not quite on Big Ben's level just yet, but far better than the Sunshine Boys—so that should not be a problem.

Kevin Walter			Height: 6-3			Weight: 221			College: Eastern Michigan			Draft: 2003/7 (255)			Born: 4-Aug-1981		Age: 32		Risk: Red	
Year	Team	G/GS	Snaps	Rec	Pass	Yds	C%	+/-	Yd/C	TD	Drop	YAC	Rk	YAC+	BTkl	DVOA	Rk	DYAR	Rk	YAR	Short	Mid	Deep	Bomb
2010	HOU	16/16	834	51	80	621	64%	+5.9	12.2	5	4	2.6	76	-1.2	0	12.4%	18	179	22	166	34%	45%	15%	6%
2011	HOU	15/14	697	39	59	474	66%	+2.6	12.2	3	2	3.3	70	-0.7	1	6.9%	37	132	37	107	34%	41%	16%	9%
2012	HOU	16/14	819	41	68	518	60%	+1.2	12.6	2	1	2.3	81	-1.8	0	2.3%	39	78	46	92	27%	45%	19%	9%
2013	TEN			23	43	289	53%	--	12.5	1							-8.1%							

Over the past two seasons, Walter went from an efficient supporting receiver to one whose production was almost entirely the result of excellent offensive play-calling and defenses built to stop Andre Johnson. The Texans understandably found the prospect of paying $3.5 million in salary for that tough to stomach and released Walter in March. He hooked on with the Titans, who were interested in his size, blocking ability, and versatility, but there really isn't room in Tennessee for both Walter and the next guy down, Nate Washington. One of them is going to get cut.

Nate Washington			Height: 6-1			Weight: 185			College: Tiffin			Draft: 2005/FA			Born: 28-Aug-1983		Age: 30		Risk: Red	
Year	Team	G/GS	Snaps	Rec	Pass	Yds	C%	+/-	Yd/C	TD	Drop	YAC	Rk	YAC+	BTkl	DVOA	Rk	DYAR	Rk	YAR	Short	Mid	Deep	Bomb
2010	TEN	16/16	829	42	94	687	45%	-6.1	16.4	6	4	2.7	74	-1.2	2	-3.6%	60	64	60	63	19%	40%	21%	21%
2011	TEN	16/15	846	74	121	1023	61%	+3.0	13.8	7	6	4.3	42	-0.1	3	4.7%	41	218	19	194	41%	34%	16%	10%
2012	TEN	16/14	790	46	90	746	51%	-3.6	16.2	4	4	5.3	20	+1.0	3	-3.2%	53	66	51	70	26%	36%	26%	12%
2013	TEN			28	57	397	49%	--	14.2	2							-8.6%							

Washington has been the Titans' most efficient starting receiver each of the past two seasons after spending his first two years looking like he was thrust into a starting role he didn't deserve. He approaches the 2013 on a roster bubble. The Titans drafted Justin Hunter in the second round, giving them three receivers drafted in the top 35 picks who are currently on rookie deals. The Titans were reportedly unhappy with Washington's effort late in the season; he seems to have been a solid locker room citizen, but he was not visibly enthusiastic in the second half of the 55-7 loss in Green Bay in Week 16. Finally, he's due to make $4.2 million, a number he has no chance of seeing if he's not part of the offense. Consider him questionable for the 2013 Titans and more likely to be elsewhere as a moderately productive No. 3 wide receiver who plays mostly in the slot.

Reggie Wayne			Height: 6-0			Weight: 198			College: Miami			Draft: 2001/1 (30)			Born: 17-Nov-1978		Age: 35		Risk: Green	
Year	Team	G/GS	Snaps	Rec	Pass	Yds	C%	+/-	Yd/C	TD	Drop	YAC	Rk	YAC+	BTkl	DVOA	Rk	DYAR	Rk	YAR	Short	Mid	Deep	Bomb
2010	IND	16/16	1103	111	175	1355	63%	+5.8	12.2	6	10	3.7	50	-0.8	8	-0.5%	48	159	27	205	43%	30%	14%	13%
2011	IND	16/16	969	75	131	960	57%	-1.6	12.8	4	3	3.7	63	-0.4	5	1.4%	48	153	32	125	26%	44%	23%	7%
2012	IND	16/15	1079	106	196	1355	55%	-4.5	12.8	5	7	3.4	65	-1.1	4	-6.8%	64	73	47	118	29%	44%	22%	4%
2013	IND			90	152	1176	59%	--	13.1	7							4.1%							

Once upon a time, Reggie Wayne lined up to Peyton Manning's left almost every snap. But last year, Wayne lined up anywhere—left, right, in the slot, on the outside, and even tight to the line where he delivered the occasional block in the run game. Most importantly, he lined up roughly 1,000 miles away from Peyton Manning. The Colts changed pretty much everything about the organization except for Reggie Wayne, and he became not just Andrew Luck's security blanket but the one veteran mainstay on a surprisingly efficient offense otherwise populated by rookies and journeymen. In short, Wayne was the league's most indispensable wide receiver not named Johnson in 2012. As the players around him gain experience, Wayne's numbers will probably drop a bit, but as long as he runs good routes and is where Andrew Luck expects him to be, especially on third down (20.8% DVOA in 2012), he'll continue to see plenty of targets.

Wes Welker			Height: 5-9		Weight: 190			College: Texas Tech			Draft: 2004/FA			Born: 1-May-1981		Age: 32		Risk: Green	
Year	Team	G/GS	Snaps	Rec	Pass	Yds	C%	+/-	Yd/C	TD	Drop	YAC	Rk	YAC+	BTkl	DVOA	Rk	DYAR	Rk	YAR	Short	Mid	Deep	Bomb
2010	NE	15/11	721	86	124	848	69%	+1.4	9.9	7	13	4.7	26	+0.1	5	4.6%	40	161	24	122	58%	38%	3%	1%
2011	NE	16/15	997	122	173	1569	71%	+9.4	12.9	9	6	5.8	15	+1.4	6	20.8%	12	445	3	469	46%	39%	11%	4%
2012	NE	16/12	1074	118	175	1354	67%	+4.6	11.5	6	12	5.8	14	+1.0	8	6.1%	29	251	18	231	46%	38%	10%	6%
2013	DEN			83	118	894	70%	--	10.8	7						16.0%								

Trivia question: Wes Welker will become only the fourth player to catch a regular-season pass from both Tom Brady and Peyton Manning. Can you name the other three?

Trying to figure out how the Broncos will divy up passes between Eric Decker, Demaryius Thomas, and Welker is very difficult, in part because there's no historical precedent. Welker is the first wide receiver in history to follow up a 1,000-yard season by moving to a team that already had two 1,000-yard wide receievers. In fact, only one time in NFL history has a 1,000-yard receiver joined a team that already had two receivers coming off 800-yard seasons: Drew Hill, who in 1992 left Houston as a Plan B free agent and signed to play in Atlanta with Michael Haynes and Andre Rison. Over the last two seasons, Welker was used on the outside more than most people realize. But with Thomas and Decker around, we're expecting the Broncos to keep him in the slot more often and return him to the days when he was targeted on short passes over 50 percent of the time and rarely went deep.

The answers to that trivia question? Two players from the 2001 Super Bowl champion Patriots: wide receiver Torrance Small, who played with the Colts in 1998, and tight end Jermaine Wiggins, who split 2003 between the Colts and Panthers. The third player is defensive tackle-turned-fullback Dan Klecko, who caught three passes from Brady in 2004 and one from Manning in 2006.

Markus Wheaton			Height: 5-11		Weight: 189			College: Oregon			Draft: 2013/3 (79)			Born: 7-Feb-1991		Age: 22		Risk: Red	
Year	Team	G/GS	Snaps	Rec	Pass	Yds	C%	+/-	Yd/C	TD	Drop	YAC	Rk	YAC+	BTkl	DVOA	Rk	DYAR	Rk	YAR	Short	Mid	Deep	Bomb
2013	PIT			28	52	355	54%	--	12.7	2						-8.9%								

The Steelers are great at finding and developing pass-rushing linebackers and pretty good at developing power backs. Recently, they became experts at churning out skinny deep-threat receivers, and Wheaton is as much an heir to Mike Wallace and Antonio Brown as Jarvis Jones is an inheritor of the James Harrison legacy. Wheaton can fly, he excels at running hitches and comebacks after putting defenders on their heels, and he was very productive at Oregon State, where he caught 91 balls for 1244 yards and 11 touchdowns last year. Can he block or work the short middle of the field? Who cares! That is Heath Miller's job when Miller gets healthy. Wheaton fills a role that was not tailored specifically for him, but might as well have been. He probably won't be a useful fantasy football player as a rookie, however, because the Steelers like to ease these receivers in slowly. Wallace started only one game through Week 14 of his rookie season before starting the last three, while Brown only had two receptions in the first 12 weeks of his rookie season.

Roddy White			Height: 6-1		Weight: 201			College: Alabama-Birmingham		Draft: 2005/1 (27)			Born: 2-Nov-1981		Age: 32		Risk: Green	
Year	Team	G/GS	Snaps	Rec	Pass	Yds	C%	+/-	Yd/C	TD	Drop	YAC	Rk	YAC+	BTkl	DVOA	Rk	DYAR	Rk	YAR	Short	Mid	Deep	Bomb
2010	ATL	16/16	946	115	180	1389	64%	+7.4	12.1	10	6	3.2	63	-0.9	4	9.6%	24	319	4	302	36%	40%	19%	5%
2011	ATL	16/16	1020	100	180	1296	56%	+0.3	13.0	8	16	3.6	65	-0.2	8	2.0%	47	211	20	223	24%	46%	21%	8%
2012	ATL	16/15	987	92	143	1351	64%	+10.0	14.7	7	3	3.5	59	-0.4	4	16.3%	18	360	5	360	28%	46%	17%	9%
2013	ATL			81	136	1192	60%	--	14.7	9						10.8%								

Having Julio Jones line up across from you has its benefits. Even though White has a first-degree black belt in bravado, he felt the effects of overuse with Matt Ryan throwing the ball his way 180 times in 2011. His catch rate, plus-minus, DVOA and DYAR tumbled, and his drops went through the roof. But with Jones healthy and taking his place among the NFL's top receivers, White saw fewer balls last year, and made better use of them. White will be 32 this season, which means it is high time he stepped aside and let his younger, stronger teammate take over the role of top wideout in Atlanta. That sort of sublimation of ego won't come easily to White, but if he does it, he could possibly be even more effective when his number is called.

Damian Williams		Height: 6-1		Weight: 197			College: USC			Draft: 2010/3 (77)			Born: 26-May-1988		Age: 25		Risk: Green			
Year	Team	G/GS	Snaps	Rec	Pass	Yds	C%	+/-	Yd/C	TD	Drop	YAC	Rk	YAC+	BTkl	DVOA	Rk	DYAR	Rk	YAR	Short	Mid	Deep	Bomb
2010	TEN	16/1	210	16	28	219	57%	+0.7	13.7	0	0	2.5	--	-1.7	0	-3.0%	--	14	--	18	19%	42%	27%	12%
2011	TEN	15/13	712	45	93	592	48%	-7.4	13.2	5	5	4.7	31	+0.3	5	-17.1%	79	-20	75	-20	36%	31%	20%	12%
2012	TEN	13/2	382	30	45	324	67%	+1.1	10.8	0	2	2.5	--	-1.7	2	-2.7%	--	32	--	41	31%	53%	13%	2%
2013	TEN			13	22	155	59%	--	11.9	0						-3.9%								

After a miserable 2011 season where he was overmatched after being forced into the starting lineup, Williams has carved out a role as a valuable fourth receiver for the Titans. He's capable of playing every receiver position—since he had to learn them all in 2011—but even in a bounce-back season he did not do anything well enough to demand more playing time.

Kyle Williams		Height: 5-10		Weight: 188			College: Arizona State			Draft: 2010/6 (206)			Born: 19-Jul-1988		Age: 25		Risk: Green			
Year	Team	G/GS	Snaps	Rec	Pass	Yds	C%	+/-	Yd/C	TD	Drop	YAC	Rk	YAC+	BTkl	DVOA	Rk	DYAR	Rk	YAR	Short	Mid	Deep	Bomb
2010	SF	5/0	7	1	1	8	100%	+0.2	8.0	0	0	4.0	--	-0.2	0	40.7%	--	4	--	3	100%	0%	0%	0%
2011	SF	13/1	278	20	31	241	65%	+3.8	12.1	3	1	5.4	--	+1.3	1	10.6%	--	66	--	51	32%	64%	0%	4%
2012	SF	11/3	246	14	22	212	64%	+1.6	15.1	1	0	5.2	--	+1.0	1	2.6%	--	32	--	30	38%	38%	5%	19%
2013	SF			13	24	162	54%	--	12.5	1						-8.1%								

On Monday Night football in Week 11, Williams caught the 50-yard laser that introduced Colin Kaepernick to a national audience. In Week 12, Williams was done for the year with a torn ACL, this after his 2011 season ended by virtue of fumbling away the NFC Championship. If all's well that ends well, his past two seasons have been downright catastrophic. Injuries could make room for him as San Francisco's No. 3 receiver early in the year, but the departure of Ted Ginn means the return game will be his main source of playing time.

Mike Williams		Height: 6-2		Weight: 221			College: Syracuse			Draft: 2010/4 (101)			Born: 18-May-1987		Age: 26		Risk: Green			
Year	Team	G/GS	Snaps	Rec	Pass	Yds	C%	+/-	Yd/C	TD	Drop	YAC	Rk	YAC+	BTkl	DVOA	Rk	DYAR	Rk	YAR	Short	Mid	Deep	Bomb
2010	TB	16/16	936	65	128	964	50%	-5.7	14.8	11	6	4.9	22	+0.5	7	-5.8%	65	65	57	65	22%	41%	23%	13%
2011	TB	16/15	965	65	124	771	52%	-7.6	11.9	3	7	3.3	72	-1.0	5	-18.1%	82	-50	82	-63	31%	48%	15%	6%
2012	TB	16/16	898	63	126	996	50%	-5.9	15.8	9	4	5.1	23	+0.8	7	-1.4%	49	62	54	117	37%	28%	17%	19%
2013	TB			61	108	831	56%	--	13.6	7						1.4%								

Playing Robin to Vincent Jackson's Batman, Williams was one of the NFL's top sidekicks last year. Among No. 2 receivers with at least 50 targets, he was fifth in yards, albeit in the bottom five in catch rate and middle of the pack in DVOA. Williams has basically stagnated since his promising rookie season, but the Bucs apparently see further development in his future. His contract is set to expire after this season, but as we go to publication, Tampa Bay and Williams are reported to be close to a long-term extension.

Terrance Williams		Height: 6-2		Weight: 208			College: Baylor			Draft: 2013/3 (74)			Born: 18-Sep-1989		Age: 24		Risk: Red			
Year	Team	G/GS	Snaps	Rec	Pass	Yds	C%	+/-	Yd/C	TD	Drop	YAC	Rk	YAC+	BTkl	DVOA	Rk	DYAR	Rk	YAR	Short	Mid	Deep	Bomb
2013	DAL			28	53	452	53%	--	16.1	2						4.7%								

Williams actually got better after Robert Griffin left the Bears for the NFL—much better, in fact. He led the nation with 1,832 receiving yards in 2012, and his 97 catches ranked fourth overall. His 64 percent catch rate was good enough given the high volume of targets, his 18.9 yards per catch average, and Nick Florence's overall completion rate of 61.6 percent. Like many of the Baylor receivers before him, Williams is conversant with a limited route tree, but his ability to stretch the seam and dominate on post routes is something that Tony Romo should appreciate. If Miles Austin continues his general decline, Williams has a decent shot at a No. 2 role behind Dez Bryant, though he would be best served in the short term as a third receiver, general speed guy, and mammoth upgrade on Kevin Ogletree.

Robert Woods		Height: 6-0		Weight: 201			College: USC			Draft: 2013/2 (41)			Born: 10-Apr-1992		Age: 21		Risk: Red			
Year	Team	G/GS	Snaps	Rec	Pass	Yds	C%	+/-	Yd/C	TD	Drop	YAC	Rk	YAC+	BTkl	DVOA	Rk	DYAR	Rk	YAR	Short	Mid	Deep	Bomb
2013	BUF			53	91	616	58%	--	11.6	3						-6.6%								

Woods was a high-usage possession receiver at USC, with a catch rate always above 60 percent but never more than 12.6 yards per reception. He does a great job making his quarterbacks look better with excellent body control and a wider catch radius than most receivers his size, and he's agile in the open field. Buffalo plans to put him in the starting lineup right away; he's not someone you want starting on your fantasy team, but he could be really valuable to fill in during bye weeks when Buffalo is playing teams like Cleveland (Week 5) and New Orleans (Week 8).

Jarius Wright	Height: 5-10		Weight: 182		College: Arkansas			Draft: 2012/4 (118)		Born: 25-Nov-1989		Age: 24		Risk: Yellow		
Year	Team	G/GS	Snaps	Rec	Pass	Yds	C%	+/-	Yd/C	TD	Drop	YAC	Rk	YAC+	BTkl	DVOA	Rk	DYAR	Rk	YAR	Short	Mid	Deep	Bomb
2012	MIN	7/1	206	22	36	310	61%	-0.4	14.1	2	1	5.0	--	-0.1	4	4.4%	--	68	--	32	54%	23%	9%	14%
2013	MIN			38	72	486	53%	--	12.8	2						-12.4%								

Wright got about half a season of redshirt time in before Percy Harvin's ankle forced him to the IR. Nobody is ever going to mistake Wright for Harvin, but he was easily the most effective receiver Minnesota had down the stretch. Wright has deep speed and plays more physical than his 5-foot-9 frame would suggest. He was staggeringly productive at Arkansas—one of only three receivers in the nation in 2011 to have a catch rate of 64 percent and average at least 16.5 yards per catch—and the Vikings were impressed enough with his ability in the open field to have him inherit some of Harvin's packages. There's no guarantee he sees the field often after Cordarrelle Patterson and Greg Jennings were brought in this offseason, but every statistical indicator says he'd be a better receiver than Jerome Simpson.

Kendall Wright	Height: 5-10		Weight: 196		College: Baylor			Draft: 2012/1 (20)		Born: 12-Nov-1989		Age: 24		Risk: Yellow		
Year	Team	G/GS	Snaps	Rec	Pass	Yds	C%	+/-	Yd/C	TD	Drop	YAC	Rk	YAC+	BTkl	DVOA	Rk	DYAR	Rk	YAR	Short	Mid	Deep	Bomb
2012	TEN	15/5	557	64	104	626	62%	-2.3	9.8	4	4	4.9	28	-0.2	8	-14.4%	75	15	69	-2	55%	34%	7%	3%
2013	TEN			69	112	804	62%	--	11.7	6						1.6%								

The optimistic view of Kendall Wright: 64 receptions despite missing a game (tying Justin Blackmon for tops among all rookies), eight broken tackles (indicating a player with some good run after catch ability), and a theory that his poor DVOA is a product of running too many shallow crossers that didn't work for anybody in Tennessee. The pessimistic view: You can point out those catches are a production of volume, that even with some fancy broken tackles he finished below average in YAC+, and that the deep speed he flashed when catching college passes from RG3 was nowhere in sight. At least he was consistent, averaging 6.0 yards per pass on first down, 6.0 on second down, and 6.1 on third down.

Titus Young	Height: 5-11		Weight: 174		College: Boise State			Draft: 2011/2 (44)		Born: 21-Aug-1989		Age: 24		Risk: N/A		
Year	Team	G/GS	Snaps	Rec	Pass	Yds	C%	+/-	Yd/C	TD	Drop	YAC	Rk	YAC+	BTkl	DVOA	Rk	DYAR	Rk	YAR	Short	Mid	Deep	Bomb
2011	DET	16/9	697	48	85	607	56%	+0.3	12.6	6	3	2.8	81	-1.6	2	-1.9%	54	59	55	93	29%	45%	10%	16%
2012	DET	10/8	604	33	56	383	59%	-0.8	11.6	4	3	2.4	80	-2.3	0	2.3%	38	50	57	61	37%	35%	22%	6%

It's really easy to sit back and snark on Titus Young. He's pissed away a promising career and spent the offseason on an arrest tour that would make Charlie Sheen blush. But mental health is a serious problem that we face as a nation, and Young's issues stem more from that than anything else. His father believes that an on-field concussion is at the root of this sudden change in Young, and even though he'd become a big punchline in Sports America's quest for tragedy porn, it is very clear that something is deeply wrong with this young man right now. Brandon Marshall, another NFC North receiver who dealt with mental health issues, admitted that he tried to get Young into the same program he went into, but Young refused. At this point, Young's story should not be focused on what he can do on a football field, but if he can become a productive member of society again rather than a cautionary tale. That's a task that goes beyond a player comment in a football preview book, but we wish him all the best.

Going Deep

Joe Adams, CAR: Adams led the nation with four touchdowns on punt returns in his senior season at Arkansas, and the Panthers were hoping for similar results when they drafted him in the fourth round. He had 14 returns in the first three games of the year, but lost two fumbles against the Giants in late September and didn't play again until Week 11. Ted Ginn's arrival in Charlotte probably ensures Adams' departure.

Kris Adams, NYG: Adams has been on practice squads in Chicago, St. Louis, Minnesota, and Indianapolis, but last year he made it to the Colts' active roster for three weeks. He signed with the Giants in January. (2012 stats: 2-for-8, 26 yards, -20 DYAR, -51.5% DVOA)

Seyi Ajirotutu, SD: Thanks to injuries at wide receiver, Ajirotutu re-signed with San Diego midway through last season and, after four days of preparation, started as the X-receiver on a Thursday night against the Chiefs. He managed to beat Eric Berry to make a diving 28-yard reception on that game's opening third down. However, he never made much of an impact after that, and in early December he was placed on IR with a hand injury. (2012 stats: 3-for-4, 45 yards, 13 DYAR, 28.4% DVOA)

Anthony Armstrong, DAL: Armstrong got quite a bit more than a cup of coffee with the Redskins in 2010, but it's been espresso shots all the way since then. The Cowboys cut him in April to Jerry-rig their salary cap, then re-signed him after Armstrong visited the Giants. He's got some ability as a deep threat in multi-receiver packages. (2012 stats: 3-for-9, 12 yards, -36 DYAR, -65.6% DVOA)

Devin Aromashodu, CHI: Devin Aroma-sha, Arom-ash-a, Arom-a … Arom-a-not-gonna-work-here-anymore! Returning to Chicago after two years with the Vikings, Aromashodu continues to be back-of-the-roster chaff. (2012 stats: 11-for-22, 182 yards, 27 DYAR, 2.7% DVOA)

Brandon Banks, FA: The former Kansas State standout proved that for every Darren Sproles success story in the NFL, there are many more guys who really should have paid attention to the NFL's "You must be THIS TALL to ride this ride" sign. Banks ranked fifth in the NFL in return yards in 2010, and made a splash on special teams in 2011, but when Mike Shanahan told him that he'd have to become a receiver of some impact to make the roster in 2012, Banks responded by spending far too much time on the inactive list. At 5-foot-7 and 155 pounds, he'll struggle to stick anywhere else. (2012 stats: 9-for-9, 14 yards, -61 DYAR, -91.0% DVOA—eight of the nine passes to Banks were thrown behind the line of scrimmage, and only five of his receptions gained positive yardage)

Ramses Barden, NYG: After three years of hype and little results, Barden appeared to have a breakout game in September against the Panthers. With Hakeem Nicks and Domenik Hixon sidelined with injuries, Barden torched Carolina with nine receptions for 138 yards. A week later, Hixon returned to the lineup and Barden suffered a concussion. By the time Barden was back, both Nicks and rookie Reuben Randle had passed him on the depth chart. The 6-foot-6 wide receiver will always be a tantalizing prospect because of his size, but his path is blocked for the foreseeable future in New York. (2012 stats: 14-for-22, 220 yards, 63 DYAR, 21.9% DVOA)

Cole Beasley, DAL: An undrafted free agent in 2012, Beasley amassed two straight 1,000-yard seasons for June Jones' SMU teams, had a decent training camp, and inexplicably caught seven passes on 13 targets for 68 yards against the Redskins on Thanksgiving. That was his cup of coffee last year, and he'll go into training camp behind Dwayne Harris and rookie Terrance Williams on the Dallas depth chart. (2012 stats: 15-for-24, 128 yards, -4 DYAR, -17.4% DVOA)

Alan Bonner, HOU: Two touchdowns and over 100 yards receiving against Arkansas suggest Bonner, a sixth-round pick out of Jacksonville State, might be more than the run-of-the-mill FCS squad-leading receiver. He'll also be in the mix for Houston's punt and kick returner jobs, though a 7.9-yard average on punt returns as a senior suggests he might not be an upgrade there.

Deion Branch, FA: The drafting of Aaron Dobson and Josh Boyce probably ends Branch's usefulness to the Patriots, and thus his NFL career. Still, he'll be sitting by the phone in case the Pats are hit by a rash of receiver injuries. (2012 stats: 16-for 29, 145 yards, -20 DYAR, -14.3% DVOA)

Steve Breaston, FA: Yes, this is the same Steve Breaston who had 1,006 yards receiving for a 2008 Cardinals team that reached the Super Bowl. And it's the same Steve Breaston who had over 700 yards for the Cardinals in both 2009 and 2010. And it's the same Steve Breaston who signed a five-year, $25 million contract with the Chiefs in 2011 (of which he made around $8 million). And it's the same Steve Breaston who probably won't be in the *Almanac* at all next year because this past offseason the entire NFL passed on signing him after looking closer at his questionable right knee and lack of production when playing in a non-Todd Haley offense. (2012 stats: 7-for-15, 74 yards, -18 DYAR, -27.7% DVOA)

Dezmon Briscoe, WAS: Briscoe actually led the 2011 Tampa Bay Bucs with six touchdown receptions, but he's had a precipitous slide since then. He failed new Bucs head coach Greg Schiano's conditioning test and missed voluntary OTAs, which led to his inevitable release by that ironfist regime. Briscoe's connection with current Redskins secondary coach and former Bucs head coach Raheem Morris got Briscoe a roster spot, but little else, in 2012. (2012 stats: 2-for-5, 22 yards, -11 DYAR, -32.3% DVOA)

Justin Brown, PIT: This sixth-round rookie is 6-foot-3 and 210 pounds; if not for Plaxico Burress, he would stand out like Haystacks Calhoun when standing next to the other Steelers receivers. Brown transferred from Penn State to Oklahoma in 2012 and caught 73 passes from Landry Jones by running to spots on the field and being big. He is not fast, and his catch radius is not outstanding, but the Steelers needed a big receiver who is not 35 years old, and Brown is both. He should stick as a fourth or fifth wideout, but Markus Wheaton is the Steelers rookie receiver you are looking for.

Mike Brown, JAC: Brown played quarterback at Liberty and is being converted to wide receiver by the Jaguars. He caught two passes for 16 yards (each catch went for eight yards) in the preseason, spent most of last year on the practice squad, and will likely be back there in 2013.

Stephen Burton, MIN: Despite playing for a team that willingly employed Devin Aromashodu and had lost Percy Harvin to injury, Burton played just 16 percent of the offensive snaps last season. This year, Cordarrelle Patterson and Greg Jennings will push everyone down a peg, and Jerome Simpson may be the team's fourth receiver after starting last season. If Burton couldn't do better than 16 percent last season, he won't be doing better than that this season. (2012 stats: 5-for-11, 35 yards, -33 DYAR, -49.6% DVOA)

Brice Butler, OAK: Butler was taken in the seventh round after his former USC receivers coach and current Raiders receiving coach Ted Gilmore pushed for him. He was not invited to the Combine, but he impressed during his pro day by running a 4.36-second 40. He had just a 48 percent catch rate after transferring to San Diego State last year, but that's partly because their starting quarterback was injured halfway through the season.

LaRon Byrd, ARI: At 6-foot-4 and 220 pounds, the stature of "Little Fitzgerald" is remarkably similar to his nickname-sake. Unlike "Big Fitzgerald," however, Byrd underwhelmed at the University of Miami, to the point of being benched as a senior. To wit, Byrd's Playmaker Score, which emphasizes college production while downplaying height and weight, was -1. Only 15 undrafted wideouts since the merger have posted 1,000 or more receiving yards in a single season, and Byrd probably won't be the next one to join that club.

Andre Caldwell, DEN: After teasing the Bengals over four up-and-down years, Caldwell joined the Broncos last offseason with hopes of absorbing some of the Manning magic and blossoming into a potent No. 3. However, the Broncos wound up bringing in longtime Manning confidant Brandon Stokley, and Caldwell played in just eight games, catching one pass. This past March, Caldwell tweeted about his disappointment with not being invited to workout with Manning and the Broncos receivers at Duke. (Manning's response "I'm excited to see Bubba's competitive attitude. I hope he's able to turn that into a productive offseason and has a good season for us this year.") Caldwell's problem is that he's never been much of a downfield threat, with a career average of just 9.5 yards per reception.

Greg Camarillo, FA: Now 30, Camarillo likely needs a mumps outbreak to hit the Saints receiving corps to make it back to New Orleans in 2013. (2012 stats: 4-5, 44 yards, 15 DYAR, 28.1% DVOA)

Greg Childs, MIN: Impressive yet injury prone receiver in college gets selected in the fourth round, immediately tears patellar tendons in both knees. Seeks health, chance at playing time, cybernetic leg implants a la RAX from *Eternal Champions.*

Toney Clemons, JAC: A 2012 seventh-round selection out of Colorado by the Pittsburgh Steelers, Clemons spent three-quarters of last season on Pittsburgh's practice squad before the Jaguars signed him to their 53-man roster. Clemons has outstanding speed (4.36-second 40 at his pro day), but will need to demonstrate that he has improved his hands in order to stick on the Jaguars' roster this season. (2012 stats: 3-for-11, 41 yards, -48 DYAR, -60.6% DVOA)

Danny Coale, DAL: Coale started to intrigue the NFL as a potential speed slot receiver when he ran a 4.42-second 40 at the scouting combine, and reduced that to 4.37 seconds at his pro day. However, Coale can't show his speed until he actually gets on the field. He broke his left foot in Dallas' first non-rookie OTAs last year, pulled his hamstring and strained his quad while on the team's practice squad, and tore his left ACL in November. Frustrating stuff for a kid who wasn't injury prone in college, but all Coale can do is hope to be ready for the 2013 regular season, because third-round pick Terrance Williams will be eager complicate Coale's future in Dallas.

Austin Collie, FA: The promising start to Collie's career—he ranked in the top 20 in receiving DYAR each of his first two seasons in the league—has been derailed by concussions and a knee injury that ended his 2012 season after just one reception for six yards in 14 snaps. The Colts decided not to re-sign him, and there have been calls for the 27-year-old to retire due to his concussion history, although there are also reports linking him to the 49ers.

Kevin Cone, ATL: The Falcons like their receivers to be big, and Cone fits the bill at 6-foot-2, 210 pounds. He impressed during the 2012 preseason, and is a local product (Stone Mountain and Georgia Tech), so Cone is likely to be commuting to Flowery Branch once again this season.

Josh Cooper, CLE: One of the bazillion or so 190-pound slot receivers the Browns shuffled into and out of the lineup last year, Cooper caught four passes for 53 yards against the Colts, then filled out his schedule with random one-catch games. The Browns re-signed him to be part of their slot receiver throngs in 2013; he is as likely to emerge as the team's fifth receiver as anyone. (2012 stats: 8-for-18, 102 yards, -3 DYAR, -18.3% DVOA)

Terrance Copper, KC: Copper is a journeyman who has hung around the bottom of Kansas City's depth chart the past four years. While he's obviously not a particularly threatening playmaker, he's proven himself to be a serviceable special teamer and someone who can temporarily be plugged into the offense when injuries strike. You won't flourish with him as your No. 2 or 3, but you'll at least be able to keep running your system. (2012 stats: 8-for-12, 79 yards, 4 DYAR, -12.4% DVOA)

D.J. Davis, ATL: Davis was signed as a UDFA out of Oregon in 2011; he's a replacement-level receiver with no particular strengths or weaknesses. Atlanta's wideout corps is top-heavy but not deep, meaning Davis could actually stay on the roster, if not actually play much. The Falcons have him rooming with Oregon State alum Jacquizz Rodgers, which just seems cruel. (2012 stats: 4-for-6, 40 yards, 8 DYAR, -0.5% DVOA)

Kevin Dorsey, GB: The Packers second seventh-round wideout selection, Dorsey has decent size and elusiveness in space, but has had problems separating from good coverage and holding on to the football. He also wasn't much of a blocker in college, which could limit his shot at sticking on an NFL roster. He managed just a 34 percent catch rate last season, although that is partly because Maryland's quarterback position was built on an Indian burial ground and they had a linebacker under center by the end of the year.

David Douglas, TB: Douglas finished with 666 receiving yards in his senior season at Arizona, went undrafted, and then spent his rookie season in practice squad Hell between the Giants and Buccaneers. The Bucs brought in four undrafted free agent wideouts. It's hard to believe that Douglas will be better than all of them. He may have to sell his soul to stay on the team.

Kris Durham, DET: Durham, who made Honorable Mention on the FO Top 25 Prospects list with the Seahawks, managed to start a few games down the stretch for the Lions after Ryan Broyles and Nate Burleson got hurt and Titus Young was banished. He couldn't beat press coverage, and Calvin Johnson would probably have lamented his existence if he was actually a diva. At the more familiar position of No. 5 receiver on the depth chart, Durham is a fine fit for slot work and blocks well enough to stay on the roster. (2012 stats: 8-for-21, 125 yards, 6 DYAR, -15.2% DVOA)

Marcus Easley, BUF: Buffalo's eternal tease; every year, a couple of reporters will write about how Easley's size/speed combination will make him a valuable part of the Bills offense. But at this point, how much can we expect from a receiver whose NFL career consists of four regular-season snaps?

Armanti Edwards, CAR: Edwards had an 82-yard reception and a 69-yard punt return last season, but didn't score on either play. (On the return, he was run down from behind by Saints punter Thomas Morstead.) He still has no touchdowns in his three-year NFL career, and those may have been his last chances. (2012 stats: 5-for 9, 121 yards, 23 DYAR, 25.5% DVOA)

Patrick Edwards, DET: A star spread receiver for the Kevin Sumlin Houston Cougars, Edwards is best known for suffering a compound leg fracture by running full speed into a parked motorized cart past the Marshall sideline. He was the star of Detroit's OTA's, and with nothing but Jacksonville cast-offs and punt returners ahead of him on the Lions receiving depth chart, he's in an enviable position to make some noise. He's a smaller receiver who will probably be limited to 11-personnel sets in the NFL, but he can fly.

Kevin Elliott, BUF: This undrafted rookie from Florida A&M made the Jaguars roster with an impressive training camp, but had a real problem with dropping passes. When injuries forced him into the starting lineup against the Jets in Week 14, he caught just three of 10 targets, and the Jags cut him the next week. The Bills grabbed him off waivers but their impressive haul of rookie wideouts probably leaves him without a roster spot. (2012 stats: 10-for-31, 108 yards, -95 DYAR, -47.7% DVOA)

Corey Fuller, DET: As a 6-foot-2 former track standout, Fuller pretty much encompasses the stereotype of what you'd expect based on his draft position (sixth round) and background. He can burn it, he has some elusiveness, and should be able to return kicks at an NFL level. His ability to learn better route-running and defeat press coverage will be the determining factor in whether this Virginia Tech alum is a back-of-the-roster special teams player or a competent NFL wideout who could eventually replace Nate Burleson outside.

Jabar Gaffney, FA: Gaffney embodies a red flag to the point that he might as well be from Kyrgyzstan. He's 32 years old. He had a mere four receptions in three games as a member of the Miami Dolphins last season before being released in late November. Subsequently, he served a two-game league suspension stemming from a 2010 arrest. The most-recent CIA World Fact Book tells us that the GDP per capita of Kyrgyzstan is $2,400, which is a good proxy for Gaffney's potential NFL earnings heading into 2013. (2012 stats: 4-for-10, 68 yards, -2 DYAR, -16.8% DVOA)

Clyde Gates, NYJ: When the Dolphins cut their 2011 fourth-round pick after just one year and two catches, he followed former head coach Tony Sparano to green fields of New Jersey. There, his sub-4.4 speed just helped demonstrate that the Jets' quarterbacks were too inaccurate to hit deep receivers in stride. Gates had 16 receptions, and not a single one had more than three yards after the catch. (2012 stats: 16-for-35, 224 yards, -26 DYAR, -16.1% DVOA)

David Gettis, CAR: Gettis missed all of 2011 with a torn ACL, and most of 2012 with hamstring problems. If he can stay healthy, he'll be part of the battle royal in camp for Carolina's third receiver spot. (2010 stats: 37-for-67, 508 yards, 3 TD, 66 DYAR, -0.2% DVOA)

David Gilreath, PIT: A skinny 170-pound return specialist, Gilreath bounced around the Colts, Rams, Bills, and Buccaneers practice squads in 2011 and 2012, finally sticking with the Steelers in his second tour with the team. Gilreath returned two punts against the Chiefs, and ran a reverse against the Ravens because, well, why not? Too fast and dedicated to not give an extra chance to; too small to play.

Mardy Gilyard, KC: The time when Gilyard was supposed to be a rookie sleeper for the Rams feels like the distant past, but it was actually just three years ago. Now he's just a draft bust constantly moving from team to team, but by all reports he's a hard worker who's willing to grit it out on special teams, so Andy Reid will bring him to camp with the Chiefs. (2012 stats: 2-for-6, 15 yards, -26 DYAR, -81.8% DVOA)

Ted Ginn, CAR: Up until this offseason, one would have thought that the "Ted Ginn is an NFL-caliber wide receiver" ship had sailed. But then, along came the Panthers, who made Ginn the only offseason addition to a wide receiver corps devoid of talent beyond Steve Smith and Brandon LaFell. Cue Ron Rivera: "The interesting thing about Ted is he gives us some depth at wide receiver." No, Ron, he will improve your 28th-ranked kick return unit (minus-6.9 Pts+), and that's about it.

Richard Goodman, SD: Goodman has spent his career toggling between the practice squad and active roster. He has played some wide receiver, though his most meaningful NFL contributions have come in the return game. Many remember him for his mistake in a 2010 game against the Patriots where he put a live ball on the ground after erroneously thinking he was down.

Cobi Hamilton, CIN: Hamilton found 90 receptions among the charred wreckage of the Arkansas football program in 2012. That earned him a sixth-round selection by the Bengals, a team overloaded with long, lean, inexperienced burners. Hamilton is vying for a role behind Marvin Jones and Mohamed Sanu, with Brandon Tate likely to stick as a return man and Andrew Hawkins hard to displace because of his slot elusiveness. (A.J. Green is in a category of his own, of course). Hamilton gets high marks for effort and character, and if this season is like last season, the Bengals will need every available body at wide receiver.

Chris Harper, SEA: Harper led all wide receivers with 20 reps on the bench press at the Combine, suggesting he could replace Ben Obomanu as Seattle's blocking specialist at wide receiver. The fourth-round draft pick was also Collin Klein's leading receiver at Kansas State, so he has experience playing with a scrambling quarterback.

Lavelle Hawkins, NE: Hawkins is a slot receiver with decent quickness and below-average deep speed who sometimes runs questionable routes and struggles to catch the ball. In the right offense, with the right depth chart, he can have 47 catches like he did in 2011. In a different situation, with a tougher depth chart, he can play 51 snaps all season like he did in 2012. Now in New England, which has the right offense and the wrong depth chart. (2012 stats: 5-for-11, 62 yards, -21 DYAR, -35.1% DVOA)

Junior Hemingway, KC: Hemingway was a late seventh-round pick who spent his 2012 rookie season on the practice squad (save for a token Week 17 appearance). He was a two-way star player in high school (Conway, SC), a traditional receiver who had some return duties at Michigan, and is currently a hopeful special teams prospect in the NFL.

Jason Hill, FA: If you get cut twice by the disaster that was the 2012 New York Jets offense, this is a good sign your NFL career is done. (2012 stats: 2-for-3, 14 yards, 18 DYAR, 47.6% DVOA)

Chris Hogan, BUF: A former lacrosse player, Hogan signed as an undrafted free agent with Miami and became famous on *Hard Knocks* as "7-11" because "he was always open." Apparently, he was not open enough for the Dolphins to keep around. He spent the year on the Buffalo practice squad and will compete for the last receiver spot on the depth chart in 2013.

Trindon Holliday, DEN: Holliday cemented for himself an NFL roster spot for the next three years with his electrifying pair of touchdown returns in the Divisional Round playoff game against Baltimore. He also scored on a punt and a kick return during the regular season, plus he had three touchdown returns in four preseason games with the Texans. The questions with the 5-foot-5, 159-pounder have always been whether he can contribute on offense and if his body can hold up to NFL-level abuse. So far, there's been little evidence suggesting he can become a variation of Darren Sproles.

Andre Holmes, OAK: Holmes came from the same Hillsdale team that saw Raiders tackle Jared Veldheer find some NFL success despite his small-school beginnings. The Cowboys released Holmes in November, and the Patriots picked him up—primarily so that he could simulate Andre Johnson in practice in preparation for New England's divisional playoff win over the Texans. Holmes doesn't resemble Johnson in any other ways but size and speed, which was good enough for the Raiders to give the 6-foot-4, 210-pound, 40-fast receiver a shot once the Pats waived him. Now Holmes and Veldheer can sit around and talk about their school days.

Lestar Jean, HOU: Jean is one of those undrafted free agents with good size about whom the coaches say nice things, who show up on sleeper lists at fantasy websites, and who struggle to find playing time despite being productive in their limited time on the field. The Texans receiver depth chart beyond Andre Johnson is a complete question mark, so if Jean is ever to become a regular player, 2013 is the perfect time to do so. (2012 stats: 6-for-12, 151 yards, 43 DYAR, 33.5% DVOA)

Jerrel Jernigan, NYG: Jernigan is long on praise and short on production: in two years with Big Blue, he's earned just 13 touches despite having a reputation as being an elusive player in space. Jernigan did return a kickoff for 60 yards last season, but the signing of Louis Murphy might indicate that this is a make-or-break training camp for Jernigan. (2012 stats: 3-for-5, 22 yards, -6 DYAR, -22.2% DVOA)

Charles Johnson, GB: Lottery ticket time! A seventh-rounder out of Grand Valley State, Johnson has all the physical attributes you look for—he's 6-foot-3, 225 pounds, ran a 4.35-second 40 at his pro day, and followed that up with a 39.5-inch vertical leap. He also produced at the lower levels, putting together a pair of 1,000-yard seasons and 31 touchdowns in his two years at Grand Valley. It's anyone's guess as to how he'll respond to professional coverages and concepts, but it's a low-risk, possbile high-reward pick for a Packers offense that suddenly finds the lower rung of its wideout depth chart a little shallow.

Jermaine Kearse, SEA: Kearse led the nation with 12 receiving touchdowns as a University of Washington sophomore in 2010, but regressed in his senior season and went undrafted. He failed to make a dent last year in Seattle's receiving corps, a unit that has since added Percy Harvin and fourth-round draft pick Chris Harper. (2012 stats: 3-for-7, 31 yards, -1 DYAR, -22.9% DVOA)

Ricardo Lockette, SF: Lockette has blazing speed and impressed during 49ers OTA's, but nothing comes guaranteed for the Seattle practice squad castoff with a history of impressing in camps. "There's just something about him that I'm really fired up about," Jim Harbaugh said after one of the sessions. The fact that he hasn't gotten hurt yet?

Lance Long, FA: Director Chuck Steak is making his last film and wants to go out with a bang. With the help of veteran actress Roxy Free and the outrageously endowed Lance Long, they concoct the biggest and most absurdly complicated porn film ever made. But along the way, everything that can possibly go wrong does go wrong. ...Wait, I may have Googled the wrong Lance Long. This one seems to be a football player who has been on five teams since 2008 and hasn't caught a regular-season pass since 2009. Cut by Detroit in June.

Charly Martin, SF: The 49ers picked Martin up off waivers when the Seahawks cut him to make room for long-snapper Kyle Nelson, who the Seahawks picked up off waivers from the 49ers. Now each player can be grilled for information as if the other team's coach doesn't know this is happening and can't be expected to change some of the audible lingo between seasons. Even with the injuries in the 49ers receiving corps, it's not likely the 49ers actually claimed Martin to use him on the field much. (2012 stats: 4-for-6, 42 yards, 14 DYAR, -8.4% DVOA)

Ruvell Martin, FA: Martin has bounced from team to team over the last few years, catching a handful of passes and serving as fifth-string receiver and special teams gunner. (2012 stats: 4-for-6, 41 yards, 12 DYAR, 19.0% DVOA)

Rishard Matthews, MIA: With Devone Bess out, Matthews assumed a larger role in Miami's offense towards the end of last season. Armon Binns is the only thing standing between Matthews and the team's No. 4 wide receiver job, and according to our 2012 Playmaker Scores, this seventh-rounder out of Nevada ranked as a slightly better prospect than earlier picks like T.Y. Hilton, Rueben Randle, Michael Floyd, and Chris Givens. That's not to say Matthews will set the NFL on fire this season, but it does suggest he has the requisite résumé to produce more value than your typical late-round pick. (2012 stats: 11-for-20, 151 yards, 20 DYAR, -1.4% DVOA)

Marvin McNutt, PHI: Sixth-round receivers who don't record a single reception as rookies generally don't have much job security when a new boss comes to town. The addition of Arrelious Benn makes McNutt a long-shot to make the team.

Aaron Mellette, BAL: Mellette caught 296 passes in his final three seasons at Elon, a good FCS-level program, then earned a late-round selection by the Ravens with a solid Senior Bowl effort. He is a little like Brian Quick, now of the Rams: good size, good enough speed, great attitude. Mellette is a slow-grow prospect, but the Ravens are often patient with players like him.

Marlon Moore, SF: Moore signed in San Francisco in March, but with the addition of Quinton Patton in the fourth round of April's draft, Moore now sits no higher than seventh on the wide receiver depth chart. Nevertheless, having played 209 snaps on the Dolphins' special teams in 2012, the Sacramento speedster—he posted a 4.49-second 40 at his Fresno State pro day in 2010—has a legitimate chance to make San Francisco's 53-man roster as a gunner on coverage units. (2012 stats: 6-for-11, 116 yards, 20 DYAR, 18.2% DVOA)

Legedu Naanee, FA: Naanee has twice as many N's (and seven times as many vowels) in his name as he had receptions in 2012. Given his ties to Norv Turner—also two N's!—and meager accomplishments as a wide receiver, he's a natural fit on the 2013 Browns, for whom he's tried out. With eight N's already on the roster, including fellow AFC East castoffs Davone Bess and David Nelson, it's unlikely there's enough room in Cleveland for two more. (2012 stats: 1-for-5, 19 yards, -32 DYAR, -110.3% DVOA)

Jamar Newsome, KC: Newsome, who joined the league as an undrafted free agent with the 2011 Jaguars, saw bits of action as an outside No. 3 receiver for the 2012 Chiefs. As a route runner, he was noticeably late in and out of his breaks on multiple occasions. Unless he becomes significantly more dynamic (or, in his case, we could settle for "less forgettable"), he'll have trouble finding a full-time NFL role. (2012 stats: 5-for-16, 73 yards, -21 DYAR, -23.5% DVOA)

Jordan Norwood, CLE: Norwood caught nine passes for 81 yards in a wild game against the Giants, then sprained his foot and spent the rest of the season on injured reserve. He's an acceptable option as a slot receiver, a position where the Browns always seem to be loaded even when they lack everything else: Josh Cribbs is gone, but Davone Bess has arrived, and Travis Benjamin looked good in the role by season's end. The Bess trade and the re-signing of Josh Cooper suggest that the Browns are not that excited about Norwood's future. (2012 stats: 13-for-19, 137 yards, 9 DYAR, -19.9% DVOA)

Ben Obomanu, NYJ: A special-teams ace who was often used on offense as a blocking specialist, Obomanu was released by Seattle in March, before the acquisition of Percy Harvin. That's a good sign this particular well has run dry, but dry wells have an odd habit of showing up in the swamplands of East Rutherford, New Jersey. (2012 stats: 4-for-9, 58 yards, -20 DYAR, -37.0% DVOA)

Chris Owusu, TB: Owusu's resume at Stanford includes three concussions and a torn MCL, plus missed games due to shoulder and hand injuries. However, he also returned three kickoffs for touchdowns in one season, then ran a 4.36-second 40 at the scouting combine, numbers that earned him NFL attention. He followed Jim Harbaugh to the 49ers as a free agent, then spent time on the Chargers' practice squad before playing five games (25 snaps, including one on special teams) for the Bucs. He's one of the more dangerous players at the bottom of the depth chart for Tampa Bay this year. (2012 stats: 1-for-3, 24 yards, 3 DYAR, -27.5% DVOA)

Nathan Palmer, IND: Palmer caught fewer than 100 passes during his 49-game career at Northern Illinois, but ran a 4.34-second 40 at his pro day and was a priority free-agent signing by the 49ers after the 2012 NFL Draft. Palmer received $28,000 in guaranteed money, which was one of the highest guarantees given to last season's crop of undrafted free agents. The Colts ended up grabbing him off the San Francisco practice squad, and he'll compete for a spot on the roster this summer. (2012 stats: 1-for-4, minus-4 yards, -32 DYAR, -115.5% DVOA)

Preston Parker, NO: Parker was a lousy punt returner in 2011 (minus-8.9 Pts+) but a good slot receiver. He got on Greg Schiano's bad side and was released in September of 2012, then signed with New Orleans in January. (2011 stats: 41-for-65, 551 yards, 3 TD, 106 DYAR, 8.2% DVOA)

Roscoe Parrish, FA: Once one of the game's great punt returners, Parrish has ranged from horrible to average in that department over the past four seasons. He was unsigned in mid-May, and his Twitter profile listed his location as "baggage claim."

Quinton Patton, SF: With five 49ers wide receivers guaranteed roster spots, fourth-rounder Patton can develop his skills on the practice squad—unlike fellow Air Raid beneficiary Tavon Austin, who got selected 120 picks earlier by a receiver-starved team. Much bigger than Austin, Patton is (predictably) slower, and his Austin-esque college stats at Louisiana Tech came against lesser competition. Still, his Playmaker Score was essentially equal to Austin's despite those differences, and his impressive week of Senior Bowl practices showed he can hang with the big boys.

Kealoha Pilares, CAR: The Panthers used Pilares as a gadget player on options and screens (he scored a 36-yard touchdown on a screen against Atlanta), but he has primarily been a returner in his career, and the arrival of Kenjon Barner and Ted Ginn in town makes those skills redundant. (2012 stats: 2-for-4, 42 yards, 19 DYAR, 28.9% DVOA)

DeVier Posey, HOU: Posey struggled to find playing time but emerged as the Texans' third receiver late in the season. He tore his Achilles in the playoff loss to New England, though, and Gary Kubiak indicated he does not expect Posey to be available until midseason at the earliest. If he rehabs well and continues the progress he showed in 2012, he's clearly the most talented of Houston's options to man the slot. (2012 stats: 6-for-14, 87 yards, -23 DYAR, -36.4% DVOA)

Michael Preston, TEN: A product of Division III non-football factory Heidelberg, Preston became a practice-squad success story when he was added to the roster late in 2012 to give Jake Locker another big (6-foot-5) target. Dowell Loggains' offense should be kinder to bigger players who may not move that well than Chris Palmer's was, but finding playing time for Preston was an issue even before the Titans drafted 6-foot-4 Justin Hunter in the second round. (2012 stats: 5-for-7, 59 yards, 5 DYAR, 2.2% DVOA)

Taylor Price, JAC: Price was a 2010 third-round pick out of Ohio University who has most notably served as a "Exhibit B" in the case of *Patriots Fans v. Bill Belichick's ability to draft wide receivers*. Price caught three passes for 41 yards in four games over his first two seasons with the Patriots before he was released and claimed by the Jaguars. A left foot injury cost him the 2012 season, but if he can stay healthy, Price will get a fair shot from a Jaguars team that is thin at the receiver position.

David Reed, BAL: Reed tore an ACL near the end of 2011 but came back to play in five late-season games last year, with three of his five receptions coming in the meaningless season finale. The Ravens still have plans for him, as they re-signed him to a two-year, $2.5 million contract this offseason. Reed should reclaim kickoff return duties from Jacoby Jones, who is now a starter, though Jones could replace or join Reed deep when heroics are necessary. The Ravens also need a No. 4 receiver, something Reed has never really been, but he will get a crack at the job. (2012 stats: 5-for-6, 66 yards, 21 DYAR, 40.7% DVOA)

Brian Robiskie, FA: Between Robiskie, Mike Thomas, and Kassim Osgood, last year's Lions receiving depth chart looked a lot like the 2011 Jaguars' depth chart, as long as you ignore the whole Calvin Johnson thing. That's not a receiving corps any general manager should intentionally strive to emulate, unless his main goal is comedy. The Lions cut Robiskie in June. (2012 stats: 4-for-6, 44 yards, 35 DYAR, 47.8% DVOA)

Courtney Roby, NO: Darren Sproles' cousin is a special-teams demon in his own right, captaining the unit last season and returning a blocked punt for a touchdown. He has only two receptions in five seasons, so don't pick him up as a fantasy "everyone catches balls in New Orleans" sleeper the next time he records a touchdown.

Da'rick Rogers, BUF: In 2011, Rogers was all-SEC with over 1,000 yards for the Tennessee Volunteers, while Justin Hunter had just 314 yards and Cordarrelle Patterson was still in junior college. He also failed three drug tests, which got him suspended from the team and led him to transfer to Tennessee Tech. A lot of evidence going into the draft suggested that Rogers had cleaned up his act, starting with the ten drug tests he passed since his transfer. NFL teams clearly still see red flags, as they all passed him over on draft day. No matter how many problems he had in the past or may have in the present, the fact that no team was willing to throw a seventh-round pick at this guy is a little ridiculous. He's big, talented, and more polished than half the receivers who had their names called at Radio City. If Rogers truly has his head on straight, everybody else's loss will be Buffalo's gain.

Jeremy Ross, GB: With Randall Cobb having graduated to the position of Aaron Rodgers' biggest weapon, Ross takes his stead at kick returner, where he put together a few solid returns in Week 17 and muffed a punt against the Vikings in the playoffs. The undrafted Cal product is not much of a threat to actually play receiver, but his special teams work will put him on the roster bubble.

Greg Salas, PHI: Now on his third team in three years. Salas led the nation with 1,889 receiving yards as a senior at Hawaii in 2009, but the slot receiver has struggled to make plays in the NFL.

Ace Sanders, JAC: The 5-foot-7, 173-pound Sanders caught 99 passes for 1,230 yards and 13 touchdowns during his 40-game career at South Carolina, though the Gamecocks misused him last year with too many downfield routes and not enough plays that gave him the ball in space. Sanders could play a role as a slot receiver in three-wide personnel groupings, but his most immediate impact in the NFL is expected to come on punt returns, where he averaged over 11 yards per return and had three touchdowns in his last two seasons.

Dane Sanzenbacher, CIN: A former Mike Martz binky who caught 27 passes in 2011, Sanzenbacher was phased out of the Bears offense in 2012 when Mike Tice's emphasis on protecting Jay Cutler became such that he had no one to throw to. That left little need for a 180-pound slot receiver. The Bears waived Sanzenbacher in December, and the Bengals signed him on Christmas Eve to cover for a receiver injury disaster. Sanzenbacher can do slot receiver stuff, so some team with a wide-open offense could use him. Cincinnati, going to a two-tight end offense, is probably not that team.

Russell Shepard, PHI: In 2009, Russell Shepard was Rivals' No.1-rated dual-threat quarterback (Geno Smith was No. 3), but he quickly morphed into a jack-of-all trades at LSU. Unfortunately, Shepard never mastered any of the positions he played (quarterback, receiver, running back), though he was an occasionally dangerous gadget player in college. If he has any chance of reviving that role at the pro level, Philadelphia was the best landing spot for him.

Tommy Streeter, BAL: A size-speed wonder at 6-foot-5, 220 pounds with a 4.4-second 40, Streeter was too raw to play as a rookie in 2012 and ended the season on injured reserve with foot and leg injuries. The Ravens sounded high on Streeter when they traded Anquan Boldin, but they also sounded high on Deonte Thompson, and sometimes "sounding high" means "sending kid a public message to get his butt in gear." Given his pure talent, Streeter will get every opportunity to fail, and could be amazing if he succeeds.

Brandon Tate, CIN: Three of Tate's 13 catches came in a wild Week 2 victory over the Browns, before Jay Gruden was ready to trust rookies Mohamed Sanu and Marvin Jones with traditional roles. Three more came in Week 17, during meaningless mop-up time. In between, Tate returned kicks and had a catch here or there; Sanu and/or Jones were always hurt, and Tate is a passable third receiver in a pinch. The Bengals re-signed Tate for 2013, but they want to limit pinches: Tate was strictly a return man in 2011, and the Bengals liked it that way. (2012 stats: 13-for-25, 211 yards, 18 DYAR, -6.2% DVOA)

Nick Toon, NO: Nick's father Al had a wonderful NFL career cut short by injury, so it had to trouble *Toon père* when his son missed his entire rookie season to a hurt foot. Toon has the size to become a Marques Colston-style threat over the middle, provided he can stay on the field.

Eric Weems, CHI: Special-teams ace Weems was lured over by former Atlanta assistant GM Phil Emery, who promised him some time as a gadget player on offense. As with most gadget players, Weems didn't make much of an impact on offense, but his work on kickoffs and punts remains top-notch. (2012 stats: 2-for-4, 27 yards, 5 DYAR, 8.1% DVOA)

Ryan Whalen, CIN: Whalen caught four passes for 31 yards in the Bengals first meeting with the Steelers last season, then stuck around as a fifth receiver for the rest of the season. A roster fodder guy with a knack for super-short receptions. (2012 stats: 7-for-12, 53 yards, -18 DYAR, -15.1% DVOA)

Jordan White, NYJ: White was Playmaker Score's 2012 sleeper, but he never woke up. He was cut twice and re-signed twice, finally getting a reception in the final game against Buffalo. Early returns say he's a casualty of the jump in game speed between the Mid-American Conference and the NFL. (2012 stats: 1-for-3, 13 yards, -8 DYAR, -26.7% DVOA)

LaQuan Williams, BAL: The Ravens' fifth wideout in 2011 and much of 2012, Williams was a useful all-purpose special teamer before suffering a hamstring injury. John Harbaugh is a former special teams coach, and he is likely to keep blocker-gunners like Williams and Anthony Allen on the roster while stashing size-speed wonders like Bobby Rainey and Tommy Streeter on the practice squad. That said, the Streeters and Raineys are knocking, and Williams offers nothing on offense.

Mike Willie, SD: When you Google "Mike Willie NFL" or even "Mike Willie wide receiver" the first link reads: "Did You Mean: Mike Williams?" Nope. Mike Willie. Undrafted. Practice squad guy. Once answered a fan's tweet during some sort of Chargers promotional something (according to the Chargers website). Played at a place called Cerritos College. Caught four passes for 90 yards as a rookie in the 2012 preseason.

Matt Willis, FA: Willis's diminutive size demands he have a clean release off the line of scrimmage. Thus, he's best suited for slot receiver and, style-wise, could maybe—*maybe*—play the Z position in base sets. But base sets are where the starters play. Willis has some speed and shiftiness, but not enough to warrant a first-string role. In fact, given some of the mental mistakes he made in limited playing time last season, it might be tough for the 29-year-old to find any role in the NFL this year. (2012 stats: 10-for-22, 90 yards, -44 DYAR, -42.6% DVOA)

Marquess Wilson, CHI: Sleeper alert! Despite terrific tape and solid production for a ragtag team of misfits, Wilson lasted until the seventh round. Why? Well, because he accused Washington State coach Mike Leach of running harsh and abusive practices and quit the team. Another factor could have been the lack of production Wilson had under Leach as compared to Paul Wulff—his yards per catch fell from 11.0 to 9.2. The resulting damage to his reputation buried him on most draft boards. The Bears took a flier on him late, and as the only thing in the way of consistent playing time is mediocrities like Earl Bennett and Devin Hester, Wilson should have every chance to get on the field early as long as Marc Trestman keeps the scrimmages light.

Devon Wylie, KC: Wylie only played in six games as a rookie last season, with the vast bulk of his action coming down the stretch. He finished with only six catches, though in his lone start (Week 16 vs. Indianapolis) he showed intriguing hints of upside. He has a subtle quickness in his breaks and in the way he turns upfield, perhaps warranting comparisons to a callow, "poor man's version" of Lance Moore. Considering he was a fourth-round pick, he'll be looked at closely by the new regime. (2012 stats: 6-for-12, 53 yards, -27 DYAR, -43.8% DVOA)

Tight Ends

Top 20 TE by DYAR (Total Value), 2012

Rank	Player	Team	DYAR
1	Tony Gonzalez	ATL	286
2	Rob Gronkowski	NE	279
3	Jason Witten	DAL	192
4	Heath Miller	PIT	165
5	Greg Olsen	CAR	157
6	Brandon Myers	OAK	112
7	Jimmy Graham	NO	105
8	Vernon Davis	SF	104
9	Jermichael Finley	GB	95
10	Anthony McCoy	SEA	90
11	Martellus Bennett	NYG	85
12	Tom Crabtree	GB	82
13	Antonio Gates	SD	79
14	Dustin Keller	NYJ	76
15	Logan Paulsen	WAS	69
16	Dwayne Allen	IND	67
17	Lance Kendricks	STL	67
18	Kyle Rudolph	MIN	64
19	Fred Davis	WAS	63
20	James Casey	HOU	58

Top 20 TE by DVOA (Value per Play), 2012

Rank	Player	Team	DVOA
1	Rob Gronkowski	NE	41.2%
2	Anthony McCoy	SEA	35.5%
3	Dustin Keller	NYJ	26.4%
4	Logan Paulsen	WAS	23.7%
5	Fred Davis	WAS	21.6%
6	Heath Miller	PIT	21.0%
7	Tony Gonzalez	ATL	20.6%
8	Vernon Davis	SF	17.5%
9	Dwayne Allen	IND	14.9%
10	Greg Olsen	CAR	13.6%
11	James Casey	HOU	13.1%
12	Lance Kendricks	STL	13.0%
13	Brandon Myers	OAK	10.7%
14	Jason Witten	DAL	10.0%
15	Zach Miller	SEA	8.1%
16	Tony Moeaki	KC	7.1%
17	Jermichael Finley	GB	7.0%
18	Garrett Graham	HOU	6.8%
19	Antonio Gates	SD	4.6%
20	Martellus Bennett	NYG	4.6%

Minimum 25 passes.

Dwayne Allen | Height: 6-3 | Weight: 255 | College: Clemson | Draft: 2012/3 (64) | Born: 24-Feb-1990 | Age: 23 | Risk: Green

Year	Team	G/GS	Snaps	Rec	Pass	Yds	C%	+/-	Yd/C	TD	Drop	YAC	Rk	YAC+	BTkl	DVOA	Rk	DYAR	Rk	YAR	Short	Mid	Deep	Bomb
2012	IND	16/16	905	45	66	521	68%	+1.5	11.6	3	2	5.4	9	+1.0	1	14.9%	9	67	15	86	47%	45%	3%	5%
2013	IND			51	77	609	66%	--	11.9	4						22.0%								

Coby Fleener was supposed to be the rookie star, but his shoulder injury allowed Allen to grab a larger role in the Colts' passing game. Allen was the only Colts regular to post positive DVOA ratings on all four downs, including an impressive 22.5% DVOA and 72 percent catch rate on first downs. Allen was also effective in the red zone, catching six of eight targets with three touchdowns for a 22.5% DVOA. Allen's role in the passing game could be reduced if Fleener remains healthy, but Allen is valuable as a blocker and possesses the versatility to play some fullback or H-back. He should not see his playing time drop in 2013.

David Ausberry | Height: 6-4 | Weight: 243 | College: USC | Draft: 2011/7 (241) | Born: 25-Sep-1987 | Age: 26 | Risk: Red

Year	Team	G/GS	Snaps	Rec	Pass	Yds	C%	+/-	Yd/C	TD	Drop	YAC	Rk	YAC+	BTkl	DVOA	Rk	DYAR	Rk	YAR	Short	Mid	Deep	Bomb
2011	OAK	12/0	43	2	2	14	100%	+0.8	7.0	0	0	0.0	--	-3.4	0	12.0%	--	7	--	8	50%	50%	0%	0%
2012	OAK	16/0	98	7	12	92	58%	-0.5	13.1	0	0	6.1	--	+1.3	3	-8.8%	--	-6	--	-5	45%	45%	9%	0%
2013	OAK			29	49	288	59%	--	9.9	3						-6.8%								

The hope is that Ausberry can develop into something of a poor man's Marcel Reece. He has a stouter build than his listed 243-pound playing weight. He flashed athleticism as a receiver last year, and even if he doesn't take the starting job away from Richard Gordon, he'll be the guy when the Raiders need a tight end who can actually run routes. But he's likely a guy who will usually need help from the play design in order to get open.

Jake Ballard | Height: 6-6 | Weight: 275 | College: Ohio State | Draft: 2010/FA | Born: 2-Dec-1987 | Age: 26 | Risk: Red

Year	Team	G/GS	Snaps	Rec	Pass	Yds	C%	+/-	Yd/C	TD	Drop	YAC	Rk	YAC+	BTkl	DVOA	Rk	DYAR	Rk	YAR	Short	Mid	Deep	Bomb
2011	NYG	14/13	775	38	61	604	62%	+2.3	15.9	4	3	4.8	16	+0.7	1	22.8%	5	131	6	137	30%	37%	27%	7%
2013	NE			48	69	603	70%	--	12.6	3						14.9%								

In retrospect, the Patriots' decision to grab Jake Ballard off waivers was a very smart down payment on tight end insurance. Even if the Patriots weren't dealing with the loss of Aaron Hernandez or the injuries to Rob Gronkowski, Ballard would still be an upgrade on the other tight ends on the depth chart. He's not a 1-to-1 replacement for Hernandez, because he doesn't offer the same flexibility moving around the formation, but he's more of a deep threat than many people realize. With the Giants in 2011, one-third of Ballard's targets came 16 or more yards downfield, the second highest rate of any tight end with at least 25 targets. (Anthony Fasano, of all people, was first at 38 percent.) However, Ballard's ACL injury was severe enough to require microsurgery, so he may not be able to dart up those seam routes just yet. There was disagreement about how good he looked at OTAs; ESPN Boston wrote that Ballard looked sharp with limited restrictions, but the Patriots' own website wrote that Ballard was still moving with a discernable limp.

Martellus Bennett		Height: 6-6			Weight: 259			College: Texas A&M			Draft: 2008/2 (61)			Born: 10-Mar-1987	Age: 26		Risk: Yellow	
Year	Team	G/GS	Snaps	Rec	Pass	Yds	C%	+/-	Yd/C	TD	Drop	YAC	Rk	YAC+	BTkl	DVOA	Rk	DYAR	Rk	YAR	Short	Mid	Deep	Bomb
2010	DAL	16/11	483	33	47	260	70%	+1.4	7.9	0	2	5.5	13	+0.0	2	-28.6%	42	-66	42	-69	71%	26%	2%	0%
2011	DAL	14/7	418	17	26	144	65%	-0.2	8.5	0	1	5.6	8	-0.1	1	-23.8%	41	-24	35	-16	65%	22%	9%	4%
2012	NYG	16/16	928	55	90	626	61%	-1.6	11.4	5	8	3.6	35	-0.9	3	4.6%	20	85	11	64	31%	48%	13%	9%
2013	CHI			46	71	498	65%	--	10.8	3							2.0%								

Bennett was in and out of New York faster than you can say Tim Tebow. After signing with the Giants last offseason, he arrived at OTAs 35 pounds overweight. Despite the poor first impression, Bennett finished the season second on the team in both receptions and receiving touchdowns. Nonetheless, New York considered him expendable, and the Bears signed Bennett on the first day of free agency to fix a glaring need: since 2010, no team has fewer receptions from its tight ends than Chicago.

What should we expect this year? Jay Cutler has never locked in on his tight end: in fact, only once (Greg Olsen, 2009) has a Cutler tight end hit the 50-catch mark. But with Marc Trestman running the show in 2013, the Bears should become a more aggressive passing team, and the weapons in Chicago are underwhelming outside of Brandon Marshall.

Jordan Cameron		Height: 6-5			Weight: 220			College: USC			Draft: 2011/4 (102)			Born: 7-Aug-1988	Age: 25		Risk: Yellow	
Year	Team	G/GS	Snaps	Rec	Pass	Yds	C%	+/-	Yd/C	TD	Drop	YAC	Rk	YAC+	BTkl	DVOA	Rk	DYAR	Rk	YAR	Short	Mid	Deep	Bomb
2011	CLE	2/1	59	6	13	33	46%	-3.0	5.5	0	2	2.0	--	-2.1	0	-52.7%	--	-41	--	-51	50%	36%	14%	0%
2012	CLE	14/6	329	20	40	226	50%	-0.2	11.3	1	0	5.4	8	+1.1	1	-13.5%	39	-28	39	-30	48%	35%	10%	6%
2013	CLE			56	94	590	60%	--	10.5	5							-7.4%								

Everything is coming up Cameron in 2013. Ben Watson is gone, making Cameron the likely starter at tight end. Rob Chudzinski is the new coach, and he is an expert at making the most of tight ends. Coordinator Norv Turner is also tight-end friendly. Cameron is a fine receiver with good size-speed measurables; Pat Shurmur had no idea what to do with him, but that same sentence could be written about most NFL players. Cameron is destined to top many fantasy football "sleeper" boards at tight end, including ours, and he belongs on them.

James Casey		Height: 6-3			Weight: 246			College: Rice			Draft: 2009/5 (152)			Born: 22-Sep-1984	Age: 29		Risk: Red	
Year	Team	G/GS	Snaps	Rec	Pass	Yds	C%	+/-	Yd/C	TD	Drop	YAC	Rk	YAC+	BTkl	DVOA	Rk	DYAR	Rk	YAR	Short	Mid	Deep	Bomb
2010	HOU	16/4	163	8	14	98	57%	-1.6	12.3	0	1	7.6	--	+2.3	0	-13.3%	--	-7	--	-7	69%	15%	15%	0%
2011	HOU	14/7	354	18	24	260	75%	+3.1	14.4	1	0	9.1	--	+3.7	1	33.3%	--	67	--	61	68%	9%	14%	9%
2012	HOU	16/9	605	34	44	330	77%	+2.8	9.7	3	1	6.2	3	+1.4	3	13.1%	11	58	19	66	76%	19%	2%	2%
2013	PHI			41	57	386	72%	--	9.4	2							1.7%								

The idea of James Casey is a good one: A move tight end who can line up anywhere in the formation. The reality of James Casey in 2012 was far less intriguing. He played a lot of fullback (Table 1, next page) and was uninspiring as a blocker. Because Owen Daniels and Garrett Graham are better blockers at the tight end position and quality receivers, Casey's receiving talents were rarely maximized in the Texans offense, although we got a taste of the way he can stretch intermediate and deep zones when he had five catches for 126 yards in a 2011 game against the Saints. His average target in 2012 came just 3.4 yards past the line of scrimmage, but that's not a reflection of his talent as much as it's an indication of his role in the Houston offense last year. The Eagles signed Casey to a three-year, $14.5 million free agent deal and drafted Zach Ertz, and when you put them next to Brent Celek, it mimics the use of three-tight end sets Chip Kelly used at Oregon. Celek is by far the best blocker of the group, which means Casey and Ertz will likely see work on the wings of the formation. Kelly clearly made Casey an offseason priority, so it stands to reason that the new coach sees him as a potential mismatch for linebackers and safeties; unfortunately, a knee scope in May means we will not get to see how Kelly intends to use Casey at least until training camp.

Table 1. Tight Ends Most Often Lined Up in Backfield, 2012

Player	Team	Snaps	Player	Team	Snaps
James Casey	HOU	319	Konrad Reuland	NYJ	62
Alex Smith	CLE	85	Dennis Allen	IND	61
Lance Kendricks	STL	83	Charles Clay	MIA	56
Greg Olsen	CAR	80	Craig Stevens	TEN	54
Randy McMichael	SD	73	Anthony Fasano	MIA	50
Kyle Rudolph	MIN	66	Delanie Walker	SF	49

Count according to Football Outsiders game charting project

Brent Celek Height: 6-4   Weight: 261   College: Cincinnati   Draft: 2007/5 (162)   Born: 25-Jan-1985   Age: 28   Risk: Green

Year	Team	G/GS	Snaps	Rec	Pass	Yds	C%	+/-	Yd/C	TD	Drop	YAC	Rk	YAC+	BTkl	DVOA	Rk	DYAR	Rk	YAR	Short	Mid	Deep	Bomb
2010	PHI	16/15	868	42	79	511	53%	-7.7	12.2	4	5	5.7	10	+1.1	6	-11.7%	35	-24	36	-33	49%	29%	12%	11%
2011	PHI	16/16	945	62	97	811	64%	-0.5	13.1	5	5	7.5	1	+2.2	8	2.6%	22	99	14	92	51%	29%	17%	2%
2012	PHI	15/14	861	57	87	684	66%	-0.4	12.0	1	8	5.4	10	+0.2	4	-12.8%	38	23	30	15	46%	36%	17%	1%
2013	PHI			48	74	448	65%	--	9.3	3						-6.0%								

Celek is a reliable, dependable, and unexciting tight end: the NFC's version of Dustin Keller. He drops more passes than he should, but still manages to post strong catch rates each year. Celek has the athleticism to go deep or pick up yards after the catch, but he's never going to be confused with the new generation of supersized wide receivers playing tight end. Like the Eagles' wide receivers, Celek has struggled in the red zone. His red-zone DVOA the last three years: -42.5% in 2010, -12.7% in 2011, and -32.9% last year. Making matters worse is that Celek also struggled on third and fourth downs for the second straight season, posting a DVOA of -29.1% in those situations in 2012. A solid tight end who struggles on third down and the red zone is a replaceable tight end, and Philadelphia brought in competition with the additions of James Casey and Zach Ertz.

Scott Chandler Height: 6-7   Weight: 270   College: Iowa   Draft: 2007/4 (129)   Born: 23-Jul-1985   Age: 28   Risk: Yellow

Year	Team	G/GS	Snaps	Rec	Pass	Yds	C%	+/-	Yd/C	TD	Drop	YAC	Rk	YAC+	BTkl	DVOA	Rk	DYAR	Rk	YAR	Short	Mid	Deep	Bomb
2010	2TM	13/1	104	1	3	8	33%	-0.7	8.0	0	0	5.0	--	+0.3	0	-45.6%	--	-8	--	-9	33%	33%	0%	33%
2011	BUF	14/9	523	38	46	389	83%	+7.9	10.2	6	0	4.0	31	-0.1	1	27.1%	4	112	10	116	57%	39%	5%	0%
2012	BUF	15/13	746	43	74	571	58%	-1.7	13.3	6	3	4.4	18	+0.6	0	1.2%	25	52	20	61	27%	57%	14%	1%
2013	BUF			46	80	554	58%	--	12.0	6						8.3%								

Over the last two seasons, Buffalo's tight end has very quietly been a red-zone monster, catching 15 of 23 passes for 141 yards, 11 touchdowns, and 48.5% DVOA. He's also excellent at running the seam route; in particular, Brandon Spikes of division rival New England is terrible covering Chandler up the middle. Chandler tore his ACL in Week 16 of last year but seems to be on the newfangled Adrian Peterson Recovery Plan and claims he'll be ready to start the season.

Dallas Clark Height: 6-3   Weight: 257   College: Iowa   Draft: 2003/1 (24)   Born: 12-Jun-1979   Age: 34   Risk: N/A

Year	Team	G/GS	Snaps	Rec	Pass	Yds	C%	+/-	Yd/C	TD	Drop	YAC	Rk	YAC+	BTkl	DVOA	Rk	DYAR	Rk	YAR	Short	Mid	Deep	Bomb
2010	IND	6/6	421	37	53	347	70%	+1.5	9.4	3	3	3.7	38	-0.5	2	1.9%	22	27	27	40	52%	40%	6%	2%
2011	IND	11/10	544	34	65	352	52%	-9.9	10.4	2	9	4.4	27	+0.2	2	-25.4%	43	-61	44	-82	61%	34%	5%	0%
2012	TB	16/7	568	47	75	435	63%	-1.8	9.3	4	2	2.4	48	-1.6	1	-14.5%	40	-60	45	-19	43%	49%	7%	1%

Clark was always a slot receiver who made cameo appearances at tight end, and his ability to get open downfield is just about gone. Only two of his receptions in 2012 came more than 15 yards beyond the line of scrimmage, and none more than 20. He was targeted on three throws deeper than that. One was incomplete, and two were intercepted. Clark remained unsigned in mid-June, and though it wouldn't be a shock to see a desperate team give him one more chance, his time has probably come and gone.

Jared Cook Height: 6-6   Weight: 246   College: South Carolina   Draft: 2009/3 (89)   Born: 7-Apr-1987   Age: 26   Risk: Yellow

Year	Team	G/GS	Snaps	Rec	Pass	Yds	C%	+/-	Yd/C	TD	Drop	YAC	Rk	YAC+	BTkl	DVOA	Rk	DYAR	Rk	YAR	Short	Mid	Deep	Bomb
2010	TEN	16/1	242	29	45	361	64%	+1.8	12.4	1	4	4.7	21	+0.1	1	15.8%	13	64	19	76	37%	44%	15%	5%
2011	TEN	16/5	601	49	81	759	60%	+3.9	15.5	3	1	5.7	7	+1.7	4	12.3%	16	99	13	90	30%	58%	9%	3%
2012	TEN	13/5	471	44	72	523	61%	-0.5	11.9	4	4	3.8	30	-0.5	3	-3.7%	33	9	34	13	45%	37%	12%	6%
2013	STL			52	86	649	60%	--	12.5	4						6.1%								

Cook is an excellent vertical seam threat with good long speed for a tight end, and he can go up for high throws. That's been enough for him to be labeled with the "potential" tag since he entered the league, but he doesn't seem to have any other strengths. He does not have plus agility or quickness, and is too slow coming in and out of cuts. While he no longer gets blown up by much smaller defensive backs, he is still not a good enough blocker to reliably play on running downs. He does not use his body effectively to create space to make catches, nor does he reliably make contested catches. This shows up most in the red zone, where he has been below average every year of his career and tends to disappear as you get closer to the goal line. Jeff Fisher apparently liked what he can do well enough to ask for a reunion tour at $35 million over five seasons. That's a steep price for a valuable but limited player.

Tom Crabtree			Height: 6-4			Weight: 245			College: Miami (Ohio)			Draft: 2009/FA			Born: 4-Nov-1985		Age: 28		Risk: Green
Year	Team	G/GS	Snaps	Rec	Pass	Yds	C%	+/-	Yd/C	TD	Drop	YAC	Rk	YAC+	BTkl	DVOA	Rk	DYAR	Rk	YAR	Short	Mid	Deep	Bomb
2010	GB	16/1	315	4	7	61	57%	-0.4	15.3	0	1	8.8	--	+4.7	1	-18.3%	--	-3	--	-5	67%	17%	17%	0%
2011	GB	16/9	300	6	8	38	75%	+0.4	6.3	1	0	3.3	--	-0.6	0	-6.4%	--	-1	--	0	75%	13%	13%	0%
2012	GB	14/6	364	8	12	203	67%	+1.0	25.4	3	2	18.1	--	+13.9	1	76.8%	--	82	--	75	60%	20%	20%	0%
2013	TB			22	28	235	79%	--	10.7	3						26.5%								

With only an unestablished Luke Stocker in his way in Tampa Bay, Crabtree will probably never have a better chance to seize a starting job. The more likely scenario is that his finesse H-Back skills parlay into work in goal-line packages, and that you remember him as "that Packers tight end who went to Tampa." Hell of a Twitter follow, though (@TCrabtree83).

Jeff Cumberland			Height: 6-4			Weight: 249			College: Illinois			Draft: 2010/FA			Born: 2-May-1987		Age: 26		Risk: Yellow
Year	Team	G/GS	Snaps	Rec	Pass	Yds	C%	+/-	Yd/C	TD	Drop	YAC	Rk	YAC+	BTkl	DVOA	Rk	DYAR	Rk	YAR	Short	Mid	Deep	Bomb
2010	NYJ	1/0	40	1	2	3	50%	-0.4	3.0	0	0	3.0	--	-2.5	0	-91.1%	--	-12	--	-10	50%	50%	0%	0%
2011	NYJ	3/0	47	2	5	35	40%	-1.1	17.5	0	1	8.5	--	+1.7	0	-40.8%	--	-6	--	-9	40%	20%	40%	0%
2012	NYJ	15/12	592	29	53	359	55%	-5.0	12.4	3	3	3.9	29	-0.4	2	-8.5%	36	-12	37	-8	36%	36%	25%	4%
2013	NYJ			46	82	516	56%	--	11.2	2						-14.8%								

Cumberland is a receiving-first tight end who played wide receiver in college. He finally got extensive playing time in his third NFL season, and acquited himself well except for the low catch rate. Mark Sanchez was partially responsible for that, as he had a habit of overthrowing Cumberland on deeper routes. Cumberland is now penciled in as the Jets' starting tight end with Dustin Keller gone, but he still needs to improve his ability to recognize and adjust to coverage if he wants to be the same kind of security blanket that Keller was.

Owen Daniels			Height: 6-3			Weight: 245			College: Wisconsin			Draft: 2006/4 (98)			Born: 9-Nov-1982		Age: 31		Risk: Green
Year	Team	G/GS	Snaps	Rec	Pass	Yds	C%	+/-	Yd/C	TD	Drop	YAC	Rk	YAC+	BTkl	DVOA	Rk	DYAR	Rk	YAR	Short	Mid	Deep	Bomb
2010	HOU	11/10	555	38	68	471	56%	-1.8	12.4	2	5	6.6	5	+1.7	1	-1.7%	26	35	24	19	45%	37%	18%	0%
2011	HOU	15/15	857	54	85	677	64%	+2.0	12.5	3	3	5.4	9	+1.2	1	14.4%	13	125	8	111	35%	51%	12%	3%
2012	HOU	15/14	864	62	104	716	60%	-4.5	11.5	6	5	5.0	13	+0.5	4	0.6%	27	33	26	52	43%	42%	11%	3%
2013	HOU			63	92	735	68%	--	11.7	4						14.5%								

Whether due to three ACL injuries or simply the inevitable effects of age, Daniels seems to have lost a step. This was most evident in the playoff loss to the Patriots, when Steve Gregory and Tavon Wilson kept running him down from behind to take him away or stop him, most notably on the underneath drag route behind trips clearout. He's improved enough as a blocker that he can be a productive player even if he can't run away from defenders the way he used to, but don't be surprised to see his YAC+ continue its decline.

Fred Davis			Height: 6-4			Weight: 248			College: USC			Draft: 2008/2 (48)			Born: 15-Jan-1986		Age: 27		Risk: Red
Year	Team	G/GS	Snaps	Rec	Pass	Yds	C%	+/-	Yd/C	TD	Drop	YAC	Rk	YAC+	BTkl	DVOA	Rk	DYAR	Rk	YAR	Short	Mid	Deep	Bomb
2010	WAS	16/9	384	21	30	316	70%	+3.0	15.0	3	2	8.0	1	+3.1	5	35.1%	5	91	14	92	56%	30%	11%	4%
2011	WAS	12/12	746	59	88	796	67%	+4.4	13.5	3	3	5.9	6	+1.5	4	15.4%	11	105	12	114	39%	40%	14%	6%
2012	WAS	7/7	403	24	32	325	75%	+1.9	13.5	0	1	5.5	5	+0.7	4	21.6%	5	63	18	73	34%	59%	3%	3%
2013	WAS			54	80	679	68%	--	12.6	6						27.9%								

For two years, Davis was a quietly efficient target despite Washington's Cavalcade of Quarterback Ineptitude. Robert Griffin III had him on pace for a really good season when he suffered a ruptured Achilles tendon against the Giants on October 21. A free agent at the end of the 2012 season, Davis visited with the Jets, Bills, and Browns, but wound up coming back to the Redskins on a one-year, $2.5 million contract—probably soon after he evaluated the quarterback situations of each team.

"Playing with him takes a lot off of me," Davis in March of the advantages of working with Robert Griffin III. "Because defenses have to worry about him ... We have a lot of weapons and if I was to stay here, I feel I definitely can, with a lot one-on-one coverage and people not worrying too much about me, I could do a lot of damage. Which we started doing [before] I got hurt." If Davis could be productive in full seasons catching passes from Donovan McNabb, Rex Grossman, and John Beck, and he's healthy ... yeah, we'll take the over in 2013.

Kellen Davis		Height: 6-6		Weight: 262			College: Michigan State			Draft: 2008/5 (158)			Born: 11-Oct-1985		Age: 28		Risk: Green
Year	Team	G/GS	Snaps	Rec	Pass	Yds	C%	+/-	Yd/C	TD	Drop	YAC	Rk	YAC+	BTkl	DVOA	Rk	DYAR	Rk	YAR	Short	Mid	Deep	Bomb
2010	CHI	16/3	148	1	2	19	50%	+0.5	19.0	1	0	2.0	--	-2.8	0	61.9%	--	20	--	20	0%	0%	100%	0%
2011	CHI	16/15	727	18	35	206	51%	-2.4	11.4	5	1	3.3	41	-1.1	4	-5.6%	28	0	28	4	31%	47%	19%	3%
2012	CHI	16/15	954	19	44	229	43%	-7.3	12.1	2	7	3.7	33	-1.4	3	-26.0%	46	-72	48	-54	33%	31%	31%	5%
2013	CLE			12	21	112	57%	--	9.4	1						-22.8%								

Kids, this is what happens when you make your No. 2 blocking tight end a starter. Davis dropped seven balls in just 44 targets. He had a 43 percent catch rate; Tony Scheffler was the only other tight end below 50 percent on more than 25 passes, and Scheffler runs as many seam routes as any tight end in the NFL today. That doesn't mean that Davis isn't an NFL player, or that he doesn't belong on a roster. It just means that his proper role is what it was the three seasons prior to 2012: No. 2 blocking tight end. The Browns recognized this and pounced after the Bears released him. Jordan Cameron and Gary Barnridge should combine to make sure that the Browns don't make the mistake of throwing 45 balls at Davis, though we suppose anything is possible with Brandon Weeden under center.

Vernon Davis		Height: 6-3		Weight: 250			College: Maryland			Draft: 2006/1 (6)			Born: 31-Jan-1984		Age: 29		Risk: Green
Year	Team	G/GS	Snaps	Rec	Pass	Yds	C%	+/-	Yd/C	TD	Drop	YAC	Rk	YAC+	BTkl	DVOA	Rk	DYAR	Rk	YAR	Short	Mid	Deep	Bomb
2010	SF	16/16	911	56	93	914	60%	+0.7	16.3	7	5	7.5	2	+2.7	8	23.4%	10	184	4	186	37%	34%	20%	9%
2011	SF	16/16	986	67	95	792	71%	+7.3	11.8	6	4	4.9	14	+0.1	8	4.4%	21	43	21	26	53%	23%	15%	10%
2012	SF	16/16	917	41	61	548	67%	+7.3	13.4	5	4	4.1	24	+0.1	6	17.5%	8	104	8	103	39%	30%	18%	13%
2013	SF			61	89	770	69%	--	12.6	6						24.7%								

Don't be fooled by VD's down year according to standard stats. In Jim Harbaugh's Stratego™ offense, Davis is the spy: Arguably the most important piece, he's kept secret for as long as possible, and only deployed for attack when the timing is right. This was no more evident than in the playoffs, when, after only 17 catches and 236 yards on 30 targets in 8.5 games with Colin Kaepernick at quarterback, he erupted for 11 catches and 210 yards on 14 targets against Atlanta and Baltimore. Although his efficiency on later downs has fluctuated wildly—a phenomenon well known to regular readers—Davis' DVOA on first down has been very consistent: 25.5% in 2012, 30.1% in 2011, and 31.7% in 2010. Given his true ability and the state of San Francisco's wide receiver corps, he's poised for a rebound in 2013. But given the 49ers' run-pass ratio with Kaepernick at quarterback, it may not be that big of a rebound.

Ed Dickson		Height: 6-4		Weight: 249			College: Oregon			Draft: 2010/3 (70)			Born: 25-Jul-1987		Age: 26		Risk: Green
Year	Team	G/GS	Snaps	Rec	Pass	Yds	C%	+/-	Yd/C	TD	Drop	YAC	Rk	YAC+	BTkl	DVOA	Rk	DYAR	Rk	YAR	Short	Mid	Deep	Bomb
2010	BAL	15/3	413	11	23	152	48%	-2.4	13.8	1	2	6.5	--	+1.4	1	-29.2%	--	-32	--	-28	45%	35%	10%	10%
2011	BAL	16/16	939	54	89	528	61%	-1.0	9.8	5	6	2.9	45	-1.1	1	-1.3%	25	16	25	15	41%	38%	16%	5%
2012	BAL	13/11	538	21	33	225	64%	+0.4	10.7	0	1	4.0	28	-0.4	1	-5.8%	34	2	35	-6	52%	26%	16%	6%
2013	BAL			32	55	317	58%	--	9.9	2						-15.4%								

A knee injury limited Dickson for much of last season, but he got healthy in time for some Super Bowl heroics, including a tough 23-yard reception to set up a first-half touchdown. Dickson lingered before signing a free-agent tender offer in the offseason but showed up for OTAs anyway; he is a major part of the Ravens' plans, and may have signed a long-term deal by the time you read this. The Ravens clearly want to get the most out of their two-tight end package, which is why they are content to enter training camp with roster fodder at the third-through-fifth receiver positions.

Joel Dreessen		Height: 6-4		Weight: 260			College: Colorado State			Draft: 2005/6 (198)			Born: 26-Jul-1982		Age: 31		Risk: Green
Year	Team	G/GS	Snaps	Rec	Pass	Yds	C%	+/-	Yd/C	TD	Drop	YAC	Rk	YAC+	BTkl	DVOA	Rk	DYAR	Rk	YAR	Short	Mid	Deep	Bomb
2010	HOU	16/10	720	36	54	518	67%	+3.8	14.4	4	6	5.1	17	+1.0	4	25.7%	9	125	9	108	32%	54%	12%	2%
2011	HOU	16/10	709	28	39	353	72%	+4.2	12.6	6	1	5.3	10	+0.8	0	40.5%	2	129	7	117	44%	39%	11%	6%
2012	DEN	16/15	864	41	58	356	71%	+1.2	8.7	5	4	3.4	39	-1.0	3	-1.2%	29	13	33	19	68%	19%	12%	0%
2013	DEN			34	47	295	72%	--	8.7	4						11.1%								

Dreessen is a movable chess piece who can line up anywhere in the formation. He's not a mismatch creator on his own, but he can take full advantage of any mismatches that are created for him. Obviously, those are commonplace in Denver's offense. Dreessen was extremely effective at times last year making on-the-move catches underneath near and outside the numbers. This type of pattern demands some catch-and-run prowess, which the former Texans tight end has when he's afforded the advantage of initial spacing. Dreessen has also shown the ability to snag balls at the deep and intermediate levels. These patterns, like the underneath stuff, are often a product of multi-receiver route combinations.

Tyler Eifert	Height: 6-6	Weight: 251	College: Notre Dame	Draft: 2013/1 (21)	Born: 8-Sep-1990	Age: 23	Risk: Red

Year	Team	G/GS	Snaps	Rec	Pass	Yds	C%	+/-	Yd/C	TD	Drop	YAC	Rk	YAC+	BTkl	DVOA	Rk	DYAR	Rk	YAR	Short	Mid	Deep	Bomb
2013	CIN			50	77	594	65%	--	11.9	3						3.3%								

The Bengals used two-tight end sets 254 times last season, almost exactly one-fourth of their plays (goal-to-go excluded), but you get the impression that they wanted to use more. Reserve tackle Dennis Roland was the extra tight end on many of those plays, and while the Bengals drafted Orson Charles in the fourth round last season, they were reluctant to give him a regular role in the offense for much of the year. Eifert's arrival broadcasts Jay Gruden's intention of making the Bengals the Midwest Patriots. He has seam-stretching speed and experience as a wide receiver. Notre Dame split him out as a receiver often, and he has a knack for making leaping receptions. The upgrade from Roland-Charles to Eifert is extreme, and it could represent the tipping point for the NFL's favorite Wild Card also-rans. KUBIAK has Eifert leeching catches from the team's parade of "receivers who are not A.J. Green," but he is a hard player to project, because his role last year was often played by a backup tackle.

Zach Ertz	Height: 6-5	Weight: 249	College: Stanford	Draft: 2013/2 (35)	Born: 10-Nov-1990	Age: 23	Risk: Yellow

Year	Team	G/GS	Snaps	Rec	Pass	Yds	C%	+/-	Yd/C	TD	Drop	YAC	Rk	YAC+	BTkl	DVOA	Rk	DYAR	Rk	YAR	Short	Mid	Deep	Bomb
2013	PHI			25	43	274	58%	--	10.9	2						-9.9%								

Ertz presents a mismatch for opposing defenses and has problems with drops, a combination that would have made him an ideal player for last year's Eagles. He has excellent size and Stanford coaches praised his route running, but he struggles to make catches in traffic. His total stats went up when he became a starter in 2012, but his catch rate dropped from 75 to 65 percent and his yards per catch dropped from 9.6 to 8.4. Was that a function of losing Andrew Luck, or getting more attention from defenses, or both? Ertz has his critics, who say he was a reach at 35th overall because of his inconsistent blocking and less than stellar athleticism. But Eagles fans will have to put their faith in this pick. If Chip Kelly can't hit on a player he faced three times in college, it will be hard to give him the benefit of the doubt in future drafts.

Gavin Escobar	Height: 6-6	Weight: 254	College: San Diego State	Draft: 2013/2 (47)	Born: 3-Feb-1991	Age: 22	Risk: Red

Year	Team	G/GS	Snaps	Rec	Pass	Yds	C%	+/-	Yd/C	TD	Drop	YAC	Rk	YAC+	BTkl	DVOA	Rk	DYAR	Rk	YAR	Short	Mid	Deep	Bomb
2013	DAL			40	66	462	61%	--	11.6	2						-2.3%								

Escobar was under the radar at San Diego State, but make no mistake—he's got as much production potential as Eifert and he's more explosive than Ertz, the two tight ends who came before him in the draft and in this book. Where Eifert is a traditional tight end and Ertz an H-back move type, Escobar is one of those newfangled "big receiver" guys who flex out to the slot and don't block much. Like Jimmy Graham or Jermichael Finley, he could provide an immediate threat up the seams, and safeties will not enjoy covering him. The Cowboys ran two or more tight ends on to the field on just 28 percent of their snaps last season, but the results were generally positive. For those wondering why the Cowboys took a tight end so early when Jason Witten is coming off a historic season, it's important to remember that Escobar and Witten are different types of players. If Escobar maximizes his talents as an outside threat, allowing Witten to do his thing more reliably inside, Dallas will have one of the more intriguing tandems at the position.

Anthony Fasano	Height: 6-4	Weight: 255	College: Notre Dame	Draft: 2006/2 (53)	Born: 20-Apr-1984	Age: 29	Risk: Green

Year	Team	G/GS	Snaps	Rec	Pass	Yds	C%	+/-	Yd/C	TD	Drop	YAC	Rk	YAC+	BTkl	DVOA	Rk	DYAR	Rk	YAR	Short	Mid	Deep	Bomb
2010	MIA	15/15	874	39	60	528	65%	+2.8	13.5	4	4	5.1	16	+0.6	3	27.5%	8	142	6	126	40%	45%	13%	2%
2011	MIA	15/15	899	32	54	451	59%	+3.4	14.1	5	0	3.1	43	-0.9	1	16.8%	8	70	18	85	34%	28%	34%	4%
2012	MIA	16/16	899	41	69	332	59%	-0.4	8.1	5	1	2.2	49	-1.7	2	-19.4%	44	-44	43	-38	51%	44%	5%	0%
2013	KC			29	45	214	64%	--	7.4	2						-19.8%								

What a difference a scheme change makes. In Dan Henning's offense, Fasano was an overachiever; in Joe Philbin's, he turned into an underachiever. Throw in the fact that he almost got cut prior to 2012, and it's safe to say we're not surprised Fasano no longer resides in Miami. Historically, Andy Reid has rarely used two-tight end formations, so Fasano projects as a blocking tight end behind pass-catcher Tony Moeaki in Kansas City. Essentially he has Clay Harbor's role now.

Jermichael Finley	Height: 6-4	Weight: 243	College: Texas	Draft: 2008/3 (91)	Born: 26-Mar-1987	Age: 26	Risk: Yellow

Year	Team	G/GS	Snaps	Rec	Pass	Yds	C%	+/-	Yd/C	TD	Drop	YAC	Rk	YAC+	BTkl	DVOA	Rk	DYAR	Rk	YAR	Short	Mid	Deep	Bomb
2010	GB	5/5	204	21	26	301	81%	+4.7	14.3	1	1	4.6	22	-0.1	0	52.0%	2	105	12	101	32%	40%	24%	4%
2011	GB	16/13	791	55	92	767	60%	+0.4	13.9	8	9	4.1	29	+0.1	1	18.3%	7	135	5	154	26%	45%	21%	8%
2012	GB	16/14	690	61	87	667	70%	+4.8	10.9	2	6	4.8	15	+0.1	8	7.0%	17	95	9	73	51%	33%	11%	5%
2013	GB			53	85	666	62%	--	12.6	7						23.4%								

Finley spent most of the first half sulking, complaining that he wasn't given the choice roles in the offense that Randall Cobb seized and that he and Aaron Rodgers were lacking in chemistry. Whatever they did during the bye week to settle things, it worked. Finley had a -11.5% DVOA with a 63 percent catch rate in 48 targets before Week 10. From Week 11 on, Finley caught 78 percent of 42 targets, for a 27.5% DVOA. Just six of his 15 Deep targets came before the bye, and it's worth noting that Finley's short-target percentage nearly doubled from what it was in 2011. Finley was reportedly slimming down to spend more time in the slot this year. As a matchup weapon in a terrific offense that has to recalibrate for Greg Jennings' targets, there's 10 percent chance he obliterates this projection. But it will only happen if you don't spend a fantasy pick on him.

Coby Fleener			Height: 6-6			Weight: 247			College: Stanford			Draft: 2012/2 (34)			Born: 20-Sep-1988		Age: 25		Risk: Red	
Year	Team	G/GS	Snaps	Rec	Pass	Yds	C%	+/-	Yd/C	TD	Drop	YAC	Rk	YAC+	BTkl	DVOA	Rk	DYAR	Rk	YAR	Short	Mid	Deep	Bomb
2012	IND	12/10	450	26	48	281	54%	-3.6	10.8	2	3	4.0	27	-0.2	0	-3.6%	32	-2	36	-10	56%	20%	20%	4%
2013	IND			57	90	707	63%	--	12.4	6						22.6%								

By playing with his college quarterback, Fleener appeared destined to have an immediate impact as a rookie. Those plans were derailed by a mid-season shoulder injury that cost Fleener the entire of month of November and limited his effectiveness down the stretch. Over the final five weeks of the regular season, Fleener had just five receptions for 59 yards and two touchdowns as the No. 33 overall pick in the 2012 NFL draft fell behind Dwayne Allen on the depth chart. Fleener could have a breakout second season in the NFL as the Colts replaced departed offensive coordinator Bruce Arians with Pep Hamilton, who was the offensive coordinator at Stanford. Fleener had a 67 percent catch rate and averaged nearly 18 yards per catch during his two seasons with Hamilton coordinating the Cardinal offense. While we wouldn't expect Fleener to average 18 yards per catch at this level—NFL defenses are much better than those in the Pac-12—a 50-catch season wouldn't be out the question if Fleener stays healthy.

Antonio Gates			Height: 6-4			Weight: 260			College: Kent State			Draft: 2003/FA			Born: 18-Jun-1980		Age: 33		Risk: Red	
Year	Team	G/GS	Snaps	Rec	Pass	Yds	C%	+/-	Yd/C	TD	Drop	YAC	Rk	YAC+	BTkl	DVOA	Rk	DYAR	Rk	YAR	Short	Mid	Deep	Bomb
2010	SD	10/10	538	50	65	782	77%	+11.1	15.6	10	2	6.2	8	+2.0	6	77.1%	1	358	1	356	43%	31%	25%	2%
2011	SD	13/13	779	64	88	778	73%	+8.0	12.2	7	0	4.0	32	+0.3	2	29.8%	3	239	3	258	36%	48%	16%	1%
2012	SD	15/15	857	49	80	538	61%	+2.2	11.0	7	4	2.7	45	-1.4	1	4.6%	19	79	12	89	29%	51%	11%	9%
2013	SD			55	91	587	60%	--	10.7	7						13.9%								

Thanks to foot problems and some natural unkindness from Father Time, Gates is not the dynamic, explosive mover that he was when Pro Bowl trips were an annual tradition. He played 15 games last year but finished with under 50 receptions for the first time since his rookie season. With a less potent group of wide receivers flanking him outside, there were fewer mismatches for Gates to take advantage of inside. The question is whether Gates' decline is permanent and/or liable to accelerate. There were times last year where Gates looked like his usual self. (Eric Berry can attest to that.) There were also times where he looked like a shell of his usual self. Can he get back to being his usual self, or even a respectable 80 percent of his usual self, on a full-time basis?

Tony Gonzalez			Height: 6-5			Weight: 251			College: California			Draft: 1997/1 (13)			Born: 27-Feb-1976		Age: 37		Risk: Yellow	
Year	Team	G/GS	Snaps	Rec	Pass	Yds	C%	+/-	Yd/C	TD	Drop	YAC	Rk	YAC+	BTkl	DVOA	Rk	DYAR	Rk	YAR	Short	Mid	Deep	Bomb
2010	ATL	16/16	1034	70	109	656	64%	+0.3	9.4	6	7	2.7	43	-1.2	5	-0.1%	24	43	23	42	41%	49%	10%	1%
2011	ATL	16/16	952	80	116	875	69%	+6.8	10.9	7	4	3.0	44	-0.7	8	15.7%	10	153	4	185	37%	49%	13%	1%
2012	ATL	16/16	964	93	124	930	75%	+12.5	10.0	8	4	2.7	46	-1.1	10	20.6%	7	286	1	258	37%	57%	6%	0%
2013	ATL			84	113	805	74%	--	9.6	7						18.2%								

Let's not turn him into the vegan Brett Favre. Still, it was a touch lame that Gonzalez opened the spigot on the waterworks in the aftermath of the NFC title game, then conveniently forgot about a year's worth of retirement talk when the Falcons asked him back for one more run. It's a sign of how well-regarded he is across the league that no one brought up any Favre comparisons—until now. Sorry about that. Of course, thoughts of quitting should never have crossed his mind in the first place. He had his best season in Atlanta—his numbers went up virtually across the stat line, and his catch rate was the highest of his career. When it came to Gonzalez, we threw words like "logical regression" out the window years ago, and there is no need to go retrieve them from the front yard now.

Richard Gordon			Height: 6-4			Weight: 265			College: Miami			Draft: 2011/6 (181)			Born: 23-Jun-1988		Age: 25		Risk: Blue	
Year	Team	G/GS	Snaps	Rec	Pass	Yds	C%	+/-	Yd/C	TD	Drop	YAC	Rk	YAC+	BTkl	DVOA	Rk	DYAR	Rk	YAR	Short	Mid	Deep	Bomb
2011	OAK	1/1	58	1	1	2	100%	+0.2	2.0	0	0	5.0	--	-4.2	0	-117.9%	--	-3	--	-4	100%	0%	0%	0%
2012	OAK	13/1	75	2	7	9	29%	-2.0	4.5	1	0	3.0	--	-2.1	0	-48.5%	--	-25	--	-24	67%	17%	0%	17%
2013	OAK			14	22	144	64%	--	10.3	1						-5.0%								

Ostensibly the Raiders' starter with Brandon Myers gone in free agency, Gordon is essentially an undersized offensive tackle who happens to line up in the spot people normally call "tight end." He has a BMI of 32.3, the higher than any other player currently penciled in as a No. 1 tight end; in fact, it's higher than any of the players currently penciled in as No. 2 tight ends except Steve Maneri and Vance McDonald. Gordon has earned a roster spot by being a diverse blocker who can operate not just off the line of scrimmage but also in a variety of controlled ways out of the backfield. As far as receiving numbers go, the best-case scenario is for him to be Kellen Davis with fewer drops, and the worst-case scenario is something like when Mark Bruener started 15 games for the 2003 Texans and had two receptions.

Garrett Graham		Height: 6-3		Weight: 243			College: Wisconsin			Draft: 2010/4 (118)			Born: 4-Aug-1986		Age: 27		Risk: Green	
Year	Team	G/GS	Snaps	Rec	Pass	Yds	C%	+/-	Yd/C	TD	Drop	YAC	Rk	YAC+	BTkl	DVOA	Rk	DYAR	Rk	YAR	Short	Mid	Deep	Bomb
2010	HOU	6/0	11	0	0	0	--	--	--	0	--	--	--	--	--	--	--	--	--	--	--	--	--	--
2011	HOU	7/0	19	1	2	24	50%	+0.4	24.0	0	0	8.0	--	+4.1	0	26.6%	--	5	--	4	0%	0%	100%	0%
2012	HOU	15/9	611	28	40	263	70%	+2.4	9.4	3	3	4.1	23	-0.8	1	6.8%	18	36	24	33	67%	19%	11%	3%
2013	HOU			34	49	325	69%	--	9.6	2						-1.0%								

Graham ably stepped into the void in the Texans' favored two-tight end sets created by Joel Dreessen's departure in free agency. He earned his playing time thanks to his development as a blocker, and he let Owen Daniels continue to serve as more of a move player. He will never be confused for a dynamic seam threat, but as long as he is a good blocker and solid receiver on short passes, he will be a valuable player for the Texans.

Jimmy Graham		Height: 6-6		Weight: 260			College: Miami			Draft: 2010/3 (95)			Born: 24-Nov-1986		Age: 27		Risk: Yellow	
Year	Team	G/GS	Snaps	Rec	Pass	Yds	C%	+/-	Yd/C	TD	Drop	YAC	Rk	YAC+	BTkl	DVOA	Rk	DYAR	Rk	YAR	Short	Mid	Deep	Bomb
2010	NO	15/5	233	31	43	356	72%	+3.9	11.5	5	2	4.5	26	+0.0	0	22.7%	11	86	15	83	43%	38%	12%	7%
2011	NO	16/11	798	99	149	1310	66%	+6.5	13.2	11	6	4.6	20	+0.3	8	16.0%	9	272	2	267	39%	40%	18%	3%
2012	NO	15/9	695	85	135	982	63%	-1.2	11.6	9	14	3.6	35	-0.6	4	2.7%	23	105	7	104	33%	52%	14%	1%
2013	NO			88	143	1146	62%	--	13.0	11						18.2%								

The Gronk's wrist problems got more coverage, but the consensus second-best tight end in the NFL played with a wrist injury all season as well, a condition he only revealed late in the campaign. Indeed, Graham would tape both wrists identically so as not to tip opponents off to his ouchie, which was on his left arm. Undoubtedly the wrist issue led to his league-high 14 drops, and his marked fall off in overall production. Offseason surgery apparently has gone better for Graham than it has for the medically-challenged Gronkowski, and he talked the talk during OTA's, saying he's "never been hungrier" and he might "pitch a tent in Drew Brees' backyard" in order to work more with him. There are considerations to consider beyond Graham just wanting to be a good teammate, of course—he is in the final year of a rookie contract that pays him but $200,000 per annum, a contract he has outperformed in spades. Unlike Gronk, the Saints haven't tied Graham up to a long-term deal yet, so if you make your fantasy lists according to contract years, put Graham near the top.

Jermaine Gresham		Height: 6-5		Weight: 261			College: Oklahoma			Draft: 2010/1 (21)			Born: 16-Jun-1988		Age: 25		Risk: Green	
Year	Team	G/GS	Snaps	Rec	Pass	Yds	C%	+/-	Yd/C	TD	Drop	YAC	Rk	YAC+	BTkl	DVOA	Rk	DYAR	Rk	YAR	Short	Mid	Deep	Bomb
2010	CIN	15/10	797	52	83	471	63%	-3.2	9.1	4	6	7.0	4	+1.1	10	-18.5%	38	-47	41	-55	67%	28%	5%	0%
2011	CIN	14/13	885	56	92	596	61%	-2.0	10.6	6	3	3.4	39	-1.3	3	-8.2%	30	18	24	-2	45%	40%	15%	0%
2012	CIN	16/15	1002	64	94	737	68%	+2.5	11.5	5	6	6.5	2	+1.4	6	3.2%	22	24	29	48	49%	37%	12%	2%
2013	CIN			59	86	626	69%	--	10.6	5						7.6%								

Our game charters listed Gresham as a split wide receiver 43 times and as a slot-flex player 103 times. He caught just 11 passes from those formations, one a 55-yard catch-and-run as a wide receiver on third-and-short. The low catch total suggests that Tyler Eifert may see more action as the "move around" tight end, with Gresham working the middle. That could also be over-thinking things: the Bengals had a rotating cast of second-through-fourth receivers last year, most of them inexperienced, so their formation versatility was limited, and Gresham couldn't always count on forcing a mismatch when split wide. Even as an "ordinary" tight end, Gresham can be a very effective player when he is not asked to be the second option in the passing game.

Rob Gronkowski		Height: 6-6		Weight: 264			College: Arizona			Draft: 2010/2 (42)			Born: 14-May-1989		Age: 24		Risk: Red	
Year	Team	G/GS	Snaps	Rec	Pass	Yds	C%	+/-	Yd/C	TD	Drop	YAC	Rk	YAC+	BTkl	DVOA	Rk	DYAR	Rk	YAR	Short	Mid	Deep	Bomb
2010	NE	16/11	775	42	59	546	71%	+5.4	13.0	10	2	4.4	28	+0.1	1	51.9%	3	238	2	229	42%	33%	19%	5%
2011	NE	16/16	1092	90	125	1327	73%	+12.0	14.7	17	4	7.1	2	+2.4	13	46.2%	1	456	1	471	36%	43%	18%	3%
2012	NE	11/11	731	55	80	790	69%	+5.3	14.4	11	5	5.5	7	+1.1	2	41.2%	1	279	2	279	34%	45%	16%	5%
2013	NE			81	122	1050	66%	--	13.0	10						27.1%								

How good is Rob Gronkowski? His 2011 season with 459 receiving DYAR was not only the best tight end season in our database, it's 100 DYAR ahead of any other season. Last year, he "only" had the tenth highest tight end DYAR in history, not bad for only 11 games. Gronkowski is the only tight end in the 22 years of DVOA stats to have at least 50 passes with a DVOA higher than 40% in three different seasons, pretty remarkable considering that his career only consists of three different seasons. (Ken Dilger and Brent Jones are the only other two tight ends to do it twice.) On top of all this, he's one of the five best blockers among the league's starting tight ends. In other words, if Gronkowski has further complications from offseason back and arm surgeries and misses significant time, the Patriots are in real trouble. The forecast above takes 10 percent off his full-season projection, and the Patriots really hope he doesn't lose any more than that.

Clay Harbor			Height: 6-3		Weight: 252			College: Missouri State		Draft: 2010/4 (125)		Born: 2-Jul-1987		Age: 26		Risk: Red	
Year	Team	G/GS	Snaps	Rec	Pass	Yds	C%	+/-	Yd/C	TD	Drop	YAC	Rk	YAC+	BTkl	DVOA	Rk	DYAR	Rk	YAR	Short	Mid	Deep	Bomb
2010	PHI	9/6	181	9	15	72	60%	+0.2	8.0	1	3	2.6	--	-2.1	0	-22.3%	--	-15	--	-19	50%	29%	14%	7%
2011	PHI	16/3	359	13	19	163	68%	+0.4	12.5	1	1	3.1	--	-1.0	2	17.0%	--	37	--	36	47%	21%	32%	0%
2012	PHI	14/9	340	25	39	186	64%	-1.2	7.4	2	2	2.8	44	-2.1	1	-37.2%	49	-66	47	-71	55%	39%	3%	3%
2013	PHI			11	16	88	69%	--	8.0	0						-14.0%								

In theory, Harbor is a versatile player who could be valuable in a Chip Kelly offense. Instead, he's gone from Brent Celek's backup to fourth on the depth chart after Philadelphia added James Casey and Zach Ertz in the offseason. The Eagles could deal him, or they could carry four tight ends since Kelly is going to use so many multiple-tight end sets. They even goofed around with the idea of Harbor as an emergency backup linebacker at OTAs. If Harbor does get traded or cut, at least he ended his time in Philadelphia on a high, with a career-high six receptions for 52 yards in a comeback win over the Buccaneers in December.

Aaron Hernandez			Height: 6-3		Weight: 245			College: Florida		Draft: 2010/4 (113)		Born: 6-Nov-1989		Age: 24		Risk: N/A	
Year	Team	G/GS	Snaps	Rec	Pass	Yds	C%	+/-	Yd/C	TD	Drop	YAC	Rk	YAC+	BTkl	DVOA	Rk	DYAR	Rk	YAR	Short	Mid	Deep	Bomb
2010	NE	14/7	480	45	64	563	70%	+1.3	12.5	6	5	6.5	7	+2.0	8	27.5%	7	159	5	147	50%	39%	11%	0%
2011	NE	14/12	843	79	113	910	70%	+4.2	11.5	7	4	6.4	4	+1.7	21	6.1%	19	111	11	119	66%	22%	6%	5%
2012	NE	10/10	565	51	83	483	61%	-2.9	9.5	5	6	4.4	21	+0.2	7	1.6%	24	35	25	16	55%	30%	14%	1%

We have nothing unique or trenchant to say about Hernandez's crimes. The on-field ramifications of his release are discussed in the New England Patriots chapter.

Rob Housler			Height: 6-6		Weight: 249			College: Florida Atlantic		Draft: 2011/3 (69)		Born: 17-Mar-1988		Age: 25		Risk: Yellow	
Year	Team	G/GS	Snaps	Rec	Pass	Yds	C%	+/-	Yd/C	TD	Drop	YAC	Rk	YAC+	BTkl	DVOA	Rk	DYAR	Rk	YAR	Short	Mid	Deep	Bomb
2011	ARI	12/2	175	12	26	133	46%	-3.4	11.1	0	4	4.1	30	-0.3	2	-39.4%	47	-64	45	-58	29%	50%	17%	4%
2012	ARI	15/9	617	45	68	417	66%	-0.0	9.3	0	4	4.0	25	-0.6	6	-17.1%	43	-60	46	-41	51%	37%	11%	2%
2013	ARI			49	73	486	67%	--	9.9	3						-1.1%								

Housler broke out a bit in the second half of his second NFL season, catching eight passes against the Rams in a November loss, and grabbing seven more in a 58-0 December drubbing at the hands of the Seahawks. The good news for his future is that both new general manager Steve Keim and new head coach Bruce Arians have praised Housler as an emerging star. Keim believes that Housler can create mismatches both in the slot and outside, while Arians has said that "the sky is the limit" regarding Housler's future. He's been working at Arizona's first-team tight end through the preseason, and just like everyone else on this roster, Housler should benefit from the addition of Carson Palmer, and the subtraction of most everybody else who threw footballs for this team in 2012.

Travis Kelce			Height: 6-5		Weight: 255			College: Cincinnati		Draft: 2013/3 (63)		Born: 5-Oct-1989		Age: 24		Risk: Green	
Year	Team	G/GS	Snaps	Rec	Pass	Yds	C%	+/-	Yd/C	TD	Drop	YAC	Rk	YAC+	BTkl	DVOA	Rk	DYAR	Rk	YAR	Short	Mid	Deep	Bomb
2013	KC			22	38	206	58%	--	9.4	1						-20.1%								

The younger brother of Philadelphia's athletic center Jason Kelce joins Andy Reid in Kansas City, where he'll battle veteran Anthony Fasano for the No. 2 spot behind Tony Moeaki. Kelce played quarterback in high school and was recruited to Cincinnati for that position. As one might imagine, he is still learning the nuances of the tight end position. This is most evident in Kelce's unrefined blocking, though scouts at least admire the effort and aggression he shows there. Of course, the Chiefs drafted Kelce primarily for his receiving, where he has strong hands and nice fluidity. Last year he was one of the most explosive tight ends in college football with 45 catches for 722 yards, 11.3 yards per catch with a 70 percent catch rate.

Dustin Keller

Height: 6-2 | Weight: 242 | College: Purdue | Draft: 2008/1 (30) | Born: 25-Sep-1984 | Age: 29 | Risk: Green

Year	Team	G/GS	Snaps	Rec	Pass	Yds	C%	+/-	Yd/C	TD	Drop	YAC	Rk	YAC+	BTkl	DVOA	Rk	DYAR	Rk	YAR	Short	Mid	Deep	Bomb
2010	NYJ	16/13	840	55	100	687	55%	-4.1	12.5	5	8	3.9	35	-0.3	4	-4.5%	29	31	26	9	41%	40%	15%	3%
2011	NYJ	16/12	864	65	115	815	57%	-5.0	12.5	5	5	4.4	25	+0.3	5	-8.5%	32	-2	31	11	41%	41%	14%	5%
2012	NYJ	8/5	406	28	36	317	78%	+4.0	11.3	2	2	3.3	41	-0.9	3	26.4%	3	76	13	88	42%	39%	19%	0%
2013	MIA			50	76	517	66%	--	10.3	5						4.4%								

Keller has made a fine security blanket for Mark Sanchez, and he'll do the same for Ryan Tannehill, although at 6-foot-2 he's a little short to be an ideal seam-stretcher. Maybe Tannehill can figure out how to get the ball to Keller near the goal line, because Sanchez couldn't; for three straight seasons, Keller has put up a DVOA rating around -20.0% and a catch rate of 50 percent or below in the red zone. Keller missed the first couple games of last season with a hamstring injury and the last month with a high ankle sprain, but he had been pretty healthy before that and should be good to go for 2013.

Lance Kendricks

Height: 6-3 | Weight: 243 | College: Wisconsin | Draft: 2011/2 (47) | Born: 30-Jan-1988 | Age: 25 | Risk: Green

Year	Team	G/GS	Snaps	Rec	Pass	Yds	C%	+/-	Yd/C	TD	Drop	YAC	Rk	YAC+	BTkl	DVOA	Rk	DYAR	Rk	YAR	Short	Mid	Deep	Bomb
2011	STL	10/1	609	28	58	352	48%	-7.6	12.6	0	4	6.6	3	+1.4	1	-26.8%	44	-82	46	-81	56%	25%	19%	0%
2012	STL	16/14	843	42	64	519	66%	+0.5	12.4	4	4	5.4	11	+0.9	3	13.0%	12	67	16	54	50%	35%	13%	2%
2013	STL			33	58	347	57%	--	10.5	1						-20.1%								

There's a YouTube clip out there that shows every single Lance Kendricks target in 2012. Yes, that's nearly 30 minutes of curls and crossing patterns. For hardcore football fans—the kind who buy 500-page books from independent websites, for example—it's a wonderful time to be alive. Kendricks is built like an oversized running back, and the Rams often line him up in the backfield (83 times, third among tight ends by our count) or in the slot (123 times, tied for 12th). He has a little more quickness than most tight ends, but he's not a dominant blocker and lacks the top-end speed to be a consistent seam-route threat. Like many tight ends, he is a jack of all trades, master of none. The arrival of Jared Cook could eat into his targets, but the Rams will likely just use a heavy dose of two-tight end sets, and Kendricks' numbers won't change much. Kendricks missed some OTAs after arthroscopic knee surgery, but the Rams said they were not concerned.

Marcedes Lewis

Height: 6-6 | Weight: 255 | College: UCLA | Draft: 2006/1 (28) | Born: 19-May-1984 | Age: 29 | Risk: Yellow

Year	Team	G/GS	Snaps	Rec	Pass	Yds	C%	+/-	Yd/C	TD	Drop	YAC	Rk	YAC+	BTkl	DVOA	Rk	DYAR	Rk	YAR	Short	Mid	Deep	Bomb
2010	JAC	16/16	912	58	88	700	66%	+1.2	12.1	10	6	4.5	25	+0.2	8	8.6%	19	108	11	109	58%	26%	14%	1%
2011	JAC	15/15	799	39	85	460	46%	-10.2	11.8	0	4	3.9	33	-0.7	6	-35.5%	46	-166	47	-174	43%	34%	19%	4%
2012	JAC	16/15	830	52	77	540	68%	+0.6	10.4	4	5	4.7	16	-0.3	1	0.0%	28	21	31	31	50%	38%	12%	0%
2013	JAC			53	86	541	62%	--	10.2	3						-7.5%								

Lewis had the worst DYAR of any tight end in the NFL in 2011; he improved in 2012, but let's be honest, there was really only one way for that number to go. One area where Lewis was more effective in 2012 was the red zone. After catching two of 15 red zone targets in 2011, neither of which resulted in a touchdown, Lewis was seven-of-14 last season with all four of his touchdowns.

Vance McDonald

Height: 6-4 | Weight: 267 | College: Rice | Draft: 2013/2 (55) | Born: 13-Jun-1990 | Age: 23 | Risk: Green

Year	Team	G/GS	Snaps	Rec	Pass	Yds	C%	+/-	Yd/C	TD	Drop	YAC	Rk	YAC+	BTkl	DVOA	Rk	DYAR	Rk	YAR	Short	Mid	Deep	Bomb
2013	SF			30	48	388	63%	--	12.9	2						5.6%								

One needs look no further than their offseason moves at No. 2 tight end to find the 49ers employing COO Paraag Marathe's mantra: In markets for NFL talent, free agency is retail; the draft is wholesale. San Francisco passed on paying Delanie Walker $4.4 million per year, instead replacing him with a younger, more-talented player at one-fifth the cost. McDonald is just as versatile as Walker for formation purposes, but he's easily a bigger (and better) receiving threat. There were concerns about his in-line blocking ability, but Vernon Davis does most of that in the 49ers offense, and McDonald simply wasn't asked to do much of it at Rice. Besides, he's a chiseled 267-pounder who blew away the combine competition in bench press reps; overpowering other large humans should not be a problem. With San Francisco's receiving corps decimated by injuries, McDonald is a great bet to exceed Walker's 2012 playing time and receiving productivity.

Heath Miller

Height: 6-5 | Weight: 256 | College: Virginia | Draft: 2005/1 (30) | Born: 22-Oct-1982 | Age: 31 | Risk: Red

Year	Team	G/GS	Snaps	Rec	Pass	Yds	C%	+/-	Yd/C	TD	Drop	YAC	Rk	YAC+	BTkl	DVOA	Rk	DYAR	Rk	YAR	Short	Mid	Deep	Bomb
2010	PIT	14/14	820	42	67	512	63%	-0.0	12.2	2	3	5.4	14	+0.6	2	-2.8%	27	10	30	23	38%	43%	16%	3%
2011	PIT	16/16	1005	51	76	631	68%	+1.9	12.4	2	3	4.8	18	+0.4	3	13.6%	14	112	9	100	39%	47%	14%	0%
2012	PIT	15/15	994	71	101	816	70%	+4.0	11.5	8	3	4.8	14	+0.5	1	21.0%	6	165	4	172	50%	35%	14%	1%
2013	PIT			46	68	596	68%	--	13.0	5						26.5%								

Miller was having the best season of his career before a "terrible triad" knee injury in Week 15 (ACL, MCL, and meniscus). He was incredibly consistent, catching at least two passes in each game and four or more passes in 12 games. He caught 36 passes marked as "middle" of the field on the play-by-play, 32 percent of the team's over-the-middle production, which allowed the speedsters to concentrate on life along the sidelines. Ironically, the improved receiving came in a year where Miller's blocking didn't wow our game charters; he led all tight ends with 14 marked blown blocks, seven each on runs and passes.

Miller was walking without crutches before the draft, but there is much more to recovering from a triad injury than crutchless walking, and the Steelers learned the hard way about rushing guys back from ACL injuries when Rashard Mendenhall suffered a lost season in 2012. Matt Spaeth returns to provide tight end depth, and David Paulson was effective at times last year. Miller will return when he returns, and he will be very good as soon as he can.

Zach Miller			Height: 6-5		Weight: 256			College: Arizona State			Draft: 2007/2 (38)			Born: 11-Dec-1985		Age: 28		Risk: Yellow
Year	Team	G/GS	Snaps	Rec	Pass	Yds	C%	+/-	Yd/C	TD	Drop	YAC	Rk	YAC+	BTkl	DVOA	Rk	DYAR	Rk	YAR	Short	Mid	Deep	Bomb
2010	OAK	15/15	946	60	92	685	65%	-0.2	11.4	1	6	4.6	24	+0.4	7	-0.3%	25	51	22	75	55%	31%	13%	0%
2011	SEA	15/15	852	25	44	233	57%	-1.0	9.3	0	3	3.2	42	-1.5	0	-25.0%	42	-40	39	-68	41%	38%	18%	3%
2012	SEA	16/15	850	38	53	396	72%	+6.0	10.4	3	1	3.4	40	-1.2	2	8.1%	15	47	23	50	53%	26%	21%	0%
2013	SEA			44	67	488	66%	--	11.1	3							1.4%								

The Seahawks gave Miller $17 million in guaranteed money in free agency, but his first two seasons in Seattle were a disappointment. He only went over 40 yards four times in those two years. But he caught four of six passes for 48 yards against Washington in the Wild Card round, then exploded for eight catches in nine targets with 142 yards and a touchdown in the Divisional round loss to Atlanta. He had five 20-yard catches in the playoffs, after producing only seven in the regular season. This is probably just statistical noise, but if it's a sign that Russell Wilson is still learning how to use all the weapons in his arsenal, then the whole league is in trouble. Anthony McCoy's season-ending Achilles injury makes Miller's chemistry with Wilson even more critical.

Tony Moeaki			Height: 6-3		Weight: 245			College: Iowa			Draft: 2010/3 (93)			Born: 8-Jun-1987		Age: 26		Risk: Yellow
Year	Team	G/GS	Snaps	Rec	Pass	Yds	C%	+/-	Yd/C	TD	Drop	YAC	Rk	YAC+	BTkl	DVOA	Rk	DYAR	Rk	YAR	Short	Mid	Deep	Bomb
2010	KC	15/15	907	47	72	556	65%	+3.9	11.8	3	5	4.0	33	-0.1	1	10.6%	16	78	16	77	36%	48%	14%	2%
2012	KC	15/14	907	33	56	453	59%	-0.0	13.7	1	2	3.8	32	-0.2	1	7.1%	16	49	22	58	29%	43%	27%	0%
2013	KC			46	71	527	65%	--	11.5	2							2.2%								

Moeaki was able to play in 15 games last season after missing essentially all of 2011 with a torn ACL. However, he was not quite as fluid or dynamic as he was in his 2010 rookie season, when he was one of the league's rising young tight ends. If he's physically right, Moeaki can be a late 2000s Heath Miller-type contributor. He was a very impressive as an on-the-move run-blocker in 2010, particularly with backside motion concepts (a featured element of zone-running designs). He's also shown good hands, with an ability to get himself open underneath and to work the seams at the intermediate levels. However, KUBIAK sees fewer yards per reception in the Andy Reid offense.

Brandon Myers			Height: 6-4		Weight: 250			College: Iowa			Draft: 2009/6 (202)			Born: 4-Sep-1985		Age: 28		Risk: Red
Year	Team	G/GS	Snaps	Rec	Pass	Yds	C%	+/-	Yd/C	TD	Drop	YAC	Rk	YAC+	BTkl	DVOA	Rk	DYAR	Rk	YAR	Short	Mid	Deep	Bomb
2010	OAK	15/3	209	12	16	80	75%	+0.8	6.7	0	1	3.2	--	-1.3	2	-19.8%	--	-15	--	-19	75%	25%	0%	0%
2011	OAK	16/7	398	16	27	151	59%	-0.1	9.4	0	1	3.4	37	-1.3	1	-35.0%	45	-48	41	-47	57%	26%	13%	4%
2012	OAK	16/16	1009	79	105	806	75%	+7.5	10.2	4	6	3.6	34	-1.0	2	10.7%	13	112	6	123	42%	50%	8%	0%
2013	NYG			56	79	531	71%	--	9.5	4							2.5%								

Myers is the epitome of an average tight end. There is absolutely nothing right or wrong about his game. He's just a guy. Whether this is a good or bad thing depends on your offense. If you have a system built on route combinations that features a potent wide receiving corps, you can plug Myers into the middle and trust that he'll catch what you throw him. If you need inside receiving targets who can create their own opportunities or give a defense pause by flexing out, he's not your guy. The same goes for blocking. Myers can survive on the move as a help-blocker, but he won't win a lot of battles in a phone booth. (Game charters marked him with eight blown blocks on runs, third most among tight ends.) Myers will be massively overrated in fantasy football this season, because the idea that the Giants will throw him 100 passes just because the receiving-deprived Raiders had to is ludicrous.

Greg Olsen   Height: 6-6   Weight: 254   College: Miami   Draft: 2007/1 (31)   Born: 11-Mar-1985   Age: 28   Risk: Green

Year	Team	G/GS	Snaps	Rec	Pass	Yds	C%	+/-	Yd/C	TD	Drop	YAC	Rk	YAC+	BTkl	DVOA	Rk	DYAR	Rk	YAR	Short	Mid	Deep	Bomb
2010	CHI	16/13	805	41	70	404	59%	+0.3	9.9	5	3	3.8	36	-0.6	1	-19.3%	39	-42	40	-46	44%	32%	21%	3%
2011	CAR	16/13	866	45	89	540	51%	-8.0	12.0	5	1	4.4	26	-0.0	0	-13.9%	34	-13	33	-46	27%	52%	15%	6%
2012	CAR	16/16	1005	69	104	843	66%	+5.4	12.2	5	2	3.5	38	-0.7	2	13.6%	10	157	5	147	30%	53%	12%	5%
2013	CAR			59	87	660	68%	--	11.2	6						8.2%								

Olsen was below replacement level in four of his first five seasons, and never posted a positive DVOA. Then came last season. Olsen entered 2012 with only eight six-catch games, but he started out by catching at least a half-dozen balls three times in four weeks. He had a rough stretch in the middle of the season against the Cowboys, Bears, and Redskins (12 catches for 102 yards in 19 targets, only five first downs), but then busted out for nine catches, 102 yards, and two touchdowns in Week 10 against Denver, and he was pretty solid for the rest of the year. With Carolina's non-Steve Smith options at wide receiver looking flimsy as ever, you can expect Olsen to get plenty of chances again in 2013.

Logan Paulsen   Height: 6-5   Weight: 264   College: UCLA   Draft: 2010/FA   Born: 26-Feb-1987   Age: 26   Risk: Green

Year	Team	G/GS	Snaps	Rec	Pass	Yds	C%	+/-	Yd/C	TD	Drop	YAC	Rk	YAC+	BTkl	DVOA	Rk	DYAR	Rk	YAR	Short	Mid	Deep	Bomb
2010	WAS	11/0	30	2	2	10	100%	+0.6	5.0	1	0	4.5	--	-0.7	0	60.2%	--	9	--	11	100%	0%	0%	0%
2011	WAS	16/6	358	11	19	138	58%	-0.2	12.5	0	0	5.6	--	+1.6	0	-4.6%	--	-15	--	-5	53%	35%	6%	6%
2012	WAS	16/10	675	25	36	308	69%	+1.6	12.3	1	2	4.4	20	+0.3	2	23.7%	4	69	14	76	37%	49%	11%	3%
2013	WAS			20	28	195	71%	--	9.7	2						6.7%								

Paulsen was asked to block a lot in Washington's multi-tight end, heavy-motion sets, and let's just say it didn't always go swimmingly. Among tight ends, only Pittsburgh's Heath Miller had more blown blocks marked by our game charters, and Miller put his 14 whiffs up on 994 snaps compared to Paulsen's 13.5 in 675 snaps. However, the Redskins re-signed Paulsen to a three-year, $4 million contract because he can do some things as a red-zone target, and he was one of the few Washington receivers who didn't struggle on third downs (90.0% DVOA on 12 targets, 10.8 yards per pass, 83 percent catch rate).

David Paulson   Height: 6-3   Weight: 246   College: Oregon   Draft: 2012/7 (240)   Born: 22-Feb-1989   Age: 24   Risk: Yellow

Year	Team	G/GS	Snaps	Rec	Pass	Yds	C%	+/-	Yd/C	TD	Drop	YAC	Rk	YAC+	BTkl	DVOA	Rk	DYAR	Rk	YAR	Short	Mid	Deep	Bomb
2012	PIT	16/5	312	7	11	51	64%	+1.1	7.3	0	0	4.1	--	-1.6	1	-65.2%	--	-39	--	-42	50%	50%	0%	0%
2013	PIT			25	36	234	69%	--	9.4	2						-1.5%								

Paulson had a typical backup tight end rookie season, catching seven passes, most of them little dumpoffs. His role will increase with Heath Miller recovering from a knee injury; Matt Spaeth is around to share the duty, but he's more of a blocker. Paulson could make the most of this opportunity, as he arrived from Oregon with pretty good receiving chops. He has good hands to catch passes away from his body, and he's strong at breaking tackles and dragging defenders after the catch.

Brandon Pettigrew   Height: 6-6   Weight: 263   College: Oklahoma State   Draft: 2009/1 (20)   Born: 23-Feb-1985   Age: 28   Risk: Yellow

Year	Team	G/GS	Snaps	Rec	Pass	Yds	C%	+/-	Yd/C	TD	Drop	YAC	Rk	YAC+	BTkl	DVOA	Rk	DYAR	Rk	YAR	Short	Mid	Deep	Bomb
2010	DET	16/16	953	71	111	722	64%	-2.9	10.2	4	8	4.9	18	+0.2	5	0.3%	23	67	18	38	61%	31%	8%	1%
2011	DET	16/16	1043	83	126	777	66%	+1.0	9.4	5	6	3.7	35	-0.8	2	-12.4%	33	-53	43	-16	54%	34%	12%	0%
2012	DET	14/11	770	59	102	567	58%	-8.1	9.6	3	8	4.0	26	-0.0	1	-25.3%	45	-123	49	-126	55%	35%	9%	0%
2013	DET			63	95	620	66%	--	9.8	5						1.3%								

When the Lions drafted Pettigrew in the back half of the first round in 2009, they thought they were getting a sure-handed outlet receiver who could run the whole route tree and be a solid blocker. The blocking has been there, and one could explain away some of his poor DVOA ratings by pointing at him being relied on as a de facto run game for the Lions at times, but no receiver in the NFL has been as drop-prone as Pettigrew. His 22 drops over the past three seasons puts him behind only Brandon Marshall and Wes Welker—and those receivers have been targeted about 300 more times combined over those three years. Despite the enigmatic hands, he should be a big weapon for the Lions, and his skills say he should be a building block going forward. Reggie Bush was brought in to help solve the problems in the running game and the receiving corps will be healthier. This year doubles as both Pettigrew's walk year and a put-up-or-shut-up year. It's up to him to prove he should be in Detroit's plans for the long term. The KUBIAK system is surprisingly high on him, as long as you consider a league-average DVOA "high."

Dennis Pitta		Height: 6-5			Weight: 245			College: BYU			Draft: 2010/4 (114)		Born: 29-Jun-1985		Age: 28		Risk: Green
Year	Team	G/GS	Snaps	Rec	Pass	Yds	C%	+/-	Yd/C	TD	Drop	YAC	Rk	YAC+	BTkl	DVOA	Rk	DYAR	Rk	YAR	Short	Mid	Deep	Bomb
2010	BAL	11/0	84	1	5	1	20%	-1.9	1.0	0	0	0.0	--	-5.2	0	-69.7%	--	-25	--	-25	20%	20%	60%	0%
2011	BAL	16/2	558	40	56	405	71%	+3.6	10.1	3	1	4.5	24	-0.2	3	12.4%	15	95	15	79	46%	41%	13%	0%
2012	BAL	16/5	639	61	94	669	65%	+0.3	11.0	7	3	4.1	22	-0.3	7	4.3%	21	51	21	68	43%	39%	10%	8%
2013	BAL			65	103	740	63%	--	11.4	5							11.1%								

Pitta was in the slot or flexed 182 times last year, and lined up split wide on 11 other occasions. The Ravens only ran the ball on 28 of those plays, zero of the plays were Pitta was split wide. That's the kind of "tell" that can cost an offensive coordinator his … never mind.

Pitta caught 14 of the 19 passes thrown to him in the postseason, for 163 yards and three touchdowns. The Ravens are short on possession receivers with Anquan Boldin gone, and Pitta could be the primary beneficiary. He has the talent to take on a Jason Witten-type role.

Kyle Rudolph		Height: 6-6			Weight: 265			College: Notre Dame			Draft: 2011/2 (43)		Born: 9-Nov-1989		Age: 24		Risk: Green
Year	Team	G/GS	Snaps	Rec	Pass	Yds	C%	+/-	Yd/C	TD	Drop	YAC	Rk	YAC+	BTkl	DVOA	Rk	DYAR	Rk	YAR	Short	Mid	Deep	Bomb
2011	MIN	8/1	486	26	39	249	67%	+2.3	9.6	3	1	3.4	40	-0.9	1	-4.6%	26	-1	30	6	53%	28%	19%	0%
2012	MIN	16/16	951	53	94	493	56%	-7.8	9.3	9	3	5.2	12	+0.3	4	-3.4%	31	64	17	8	53%	39%	7%	1%
2013	MIN			60	94	546	64%	--	9.1	6							-7.3%								

Here's one FO sleeper that panned out well in 2012. Rudolph improved on his blocking and became a multi-dimensional force that could line up anywhere on the field. Minnesota used him out wide (48 snaps), in the slot (80 snaps), and even as a fullback, mostly in Full House formations (66 snaps). Christian Ponder's Ponderness will likely continue to hold Rudolph's overall effectiveness hostage, but Rudolph's 6-foot-6 frame means he can still be a fill-in fantasy tight end in the right matchup. Rudolph finished first among tight ends in red zone DYAR, and in two seasons has caught a mind-boggling 20 of 23 red zone targets, with 12 touchdowns.

Tony Scheffler		Height: 6-5			Weight: 255			College: Western Michigan			Draft: 2006/2 (61)		Born: 15-Feb-1983		Age: 30		Risk: Green
Year	Team	G/GS	Snaps	Rec	Pass	Yds	C%	+/-	Yd/C	TD	Drop	YAC	Rk	YAC+	BTkl	DVOA	Rk	DYAR	Rk	YAR	Short	Mid	Deep	Bomb
2010	DET	15/4	409	45	72	378	63%	+0.1	8.4	1	4	3.3	40	-1.1	0	-17.1%	37	-35	38	-53	55%	38%	5%	3%
2011	DET	15/5	311	26	43	347	60%	+1.6	13.3	6	1	1.8	47	-2.4	1	12.1%	17	79	17	85	23%	53%	15%	10%
2012	DET	15/4	523	42	85	504	49%	-7.3	12.0	1	6	2.8	43	-1.5	3	-16.2%	42	-33	41	-56	35%	30%	21%	13%
2013	DET			38	67	485	57%	--	12.8	3							1.5%								

Scheffler's trick is that he's a 6-foot-5 tight end who can fly and box out smaller players in the slot, where he is frequently used. In fact, you may be surprised to learn that by our count, Scheffler lined up in a wide receiver position more often than any other tight end last season (Table 2).

Table 2. Tight Ends Most Often Lined Up Wide or in Slot, 2012

Player	Team	Wide	Slot	Total	Player	Team	Wide	Slot	Total
Tony Scheffler	DET	84	278	362	Jason Witten	DAL	5	234	239
Antonio Gates	SD	22	298	320	Greg Olsen	CAR	37	189	226
Jimmy Graham	NO	59	255	314	Dennis Pitta	BAL	11	182	193
Tony Gonzalez	KC	49	256	305	Jermichael Finley	GB	82	109	191
Rob Housler	ARI	19	243	262	Jared Cook	TEN	8	179	187
Scott Chandler	BUF	25	230	255	Tony Moeaki	KC	14	164	178

Count according to Football Outsiders game charting project

Unfortunately, all those snaps as the second option after Calvin Johnson left Scheffler exposed last season. Matthew Stafford was 8-of-28 on passes labeled Deep (16-plus yards) that targeted Scheffler, with three interceptions. The only NFL receiver with a lower DYAR number on deep passes last year (minimum 25 deep passes) was Larry Fitzgerald, and he spent the season trying to play catch with a miscalibrated JUGS machine. Scheffler can still be a good fourth or fifth option and his dimension can still be a valuable one if this wasn't the start of his decline phase.

Craig Stevens | Height: 6-3 | Weight: 254 | College: California | Draft: 2008/3 (85) | Born: 1-Sep-1984 | Age: 29 | Risk: Green

Year	Team	G/GS	Snaps	Rec	Pass	Yds	C%	+/-	Yd/C	TD	Drop	YAC	Rk	YAC+	BTkl	DVOA	Rk	DYAR	Rk	YAR	Short	Mid	Deep	Bomb
2010	TEN	15/13	537	11	23	122	48%	-4.4	11.1	2	0	6.2	--	+1.6	2	-21.4%	--	-24	--	-14	67%	24%	10%	0%
2011	TEN	15/11	420	9	14	166	64%	+0.9	18.4	1	0	7.9	--	+2.9	0	31.9%	--	40	--	35	46%	23%	31%	0%
2012	TEN	15/15	551	23	33	275	70%	+1.7	12.0	1	0	5.7	4	+1.0	2	0.8%	26	30	28	17	45%	39%	16%	0%
2013	TEN			24	39	244	62%	--	10.2	1						-11.0%								

Stevens was a bit more inconsistent as a blocker in 2012 after several excellent years, perhaps beacuse the Titans gave him a slightly more prominent role in the passing game after several years of ignoring him. He proved to be a reasonably useful receiver on short passes, but there was nothing dynamic or explosive about him. He also was probably not as good at making contested catches as the Titans want or need him to be given his lack of separation ability. With the Titans proclaiming a rediscovered commitment to the run game, he should see plenty of snaps as an in-line blocker, but Delanie Walker and Taylor Thompson will be the ones to benefit from Jared Cook's departure.

Luke Stocker | Height: 6-5 | Weight: 258 | College: Tennessee | Draft: 2011/4 (104) | Born: 17-Jul-1988 | Age: 25 | Risk: Yellow

Year	Team	G/GS	Snaps	Rec	Pass	Yds	C%	+/-	Yd/C	TD	Drop	YAC	Rk	YAC+	BTkl	DVOA	Rk	DYAR	Rk	YAR	Short	Mid	Deep	Bomb
2011	TB	9/1	348	12	17	92	71%	-0.0	7.7	0	2	4.3	--	-0.7	0	-20.9%	--	-27	--	-22	65%	29%	6%	0%
2012	TB	16/11	539	16	28	165	57%	+0.3	10.3	1	1	5.5	5	+1.1	1	-26.4%	47	-28	40	-27	73%	23%	5%	0%
2013	TB			33	51	320	65%	--	9.7	3						-4.3%								

Stocker was pretty much OK at catching passes, and pretty much OK at picking up yards with the ball in his hands. His DVOA and DYAR are so low mainly because of a handful of very long-yardage plays where he caught dumpoffs for short gains. He's better than his advanced numbers look, but that's really not saying much, and he'll need to fight off ex-Packer Tom Crabtree to keep his starting job.

Jacob Tamme | Height: 6-3 | Weight: 236 | College: Kentucky | Draft: 2008/4 (127) | Born: 15-Mar-1985 | Age: 28 | Risk: Green

Year	Team	G/GS	Snaps	Rec	Pass	Yds	C%	+/-	Yd/C	TD	Drop	YAC	Rk	YAC+	BTkl	DVOA	Rk	DYAR	Rk	YAR	Short	Mid	Deep	Bomb
2010	IND	16/8	557	67	93	631	72%	+5.2	9.4	4	5	4.6	23	-0.2	5	8.5%	20	93	13	106	56%	30%	11%	3%
2011	IND	16/5	330	19	31	177	61%	-1.8	9.3	1	0	4.8	15	-0.0	1	-20.6%	40	-25	37	-33	73%	17%	10%	0%
2012	DEN	16/8	530	52	84	555	62%	+0.5	10.7	2	2	3.8	31	-0.3	1	-5.8%	35	18	32	34	43%	42%	15%	0%
2013	DEN			49	73	558	67%	--	11.4	3						10.2%								

Tamme is a fluid receiving tight end who, because of his respectable blocking (particularly when on the move), works very well in 12 personnel. Even though he is about an inch shorter and 15 pounds lighter than fellow starter Joel Dreessen, the Broncos like to use Tamme down the seams with Dreessen running underneath. This isn't to say he is merely a straight-line plodder; the fifth-year veteran has the movement skills to create separation on a variety of routes. He's very sound mechanically.

Delanie Walker | Height: 6-1 | Weight: 241 | College: Central Missouri | Draft: 2006/6 (175) | Born: 12-Aug-1984 | Age: 29 | Risk: Red

Year	Team	G/GS	Snaps	Rec	Pass	Yds	C%	+/-	Yd/C	TD	Drop	YAC	Rk	YAC+	BTkl	DVOA	Rk	DYAR	Rk	YAR	Short	Mid	Deep	Bomb
2010	SF	14/8	375	29	46	331	65%	-0.3	11.4	0	5	5.8	9	+0.2	5	-2.9%	28	19	28	11	65%	21%	7%	7%
2011	SF	15/7	535	19	36	198	56%	-1.3	10.4	3	3	3.8	34	-1.3	3	-19.4%	39	-19	34	-31	61%	26%	6%	6%
2012	SF	16/4	570	21	39	344	54%	-0.9	16.4	3	7	2.7	47	-1.4	0	-2.8%	30	32	27	26	30%	35%	27%	8%
2013	TEN			42	61	504	69%	--	12.0	4						9.8%								

Walker's agent, Vincent Taylor, must be a real-life Obi Wan Kenobi. How else can one explain the Titans shelling out $17.5 million over four years to a veteran tight end who has averaged 17.5 receptions per season? No doubt, Taylor expressed Walker's goal of catching 70 passes for Tennessee this year. He then waved his hand, and general manager Ruston Webster forgot that Walker has never even caught 30 passes in a single season. Since 1978, only eight tight ends have had a 70-catch season after their seventh year in the league. Seven of the eight had already cleared 70 catches at least once in their first seven seasons, and the only exception barely missed. (Mickey Shuler had 68 catches in 1984 before catching 76 in 1985.) Walker does have value—not $17.5 million of value, mind you—but the probability of him breaking out at this stage in his career is infinitesimal.

Benjamin Watson | Height: 6-3 | Weight: 255 | College: Duke | Draft: 2004/1 (32) | Born: 18-Dec-1980 | Age: 33 | Risk: Yellow

Year	Team	G/GS	Snaps	Rec	Pass	Yds	C%	+/-	Yd/C	TD	Drop	YAC	Rk	YAC+	BTkl	DVOA	Rk	DYAR	Rk	YAR	Short	Mid	Deep	Bomb
2010	CLE	16/16	916	68	103	763	67%	+3.4	11.2	3	5	3.9	34	-0.5	6	9.4%	18	111	10	87	37%	44%	15%	3%
2011	CLE	13/11	662	37	71	410	52%	-7.9	11.1	2	4	5.2	12	+0.3	3	-17.0%	37	-42	40	-65	57%	31%	9%	3%
2012	CLE	16/14	853	49	81	501	60%	-3.2	10.2	3	0	4.4	19	+0.1	5	-12.8%	37	-37	42	-30	46%	45%	8%	1%
2013	NO			39	61	424	64%	--	10.9	4						8.6%								

Watson is still a capable receiver and very effective blocker; his low DVOA and DYAR in 2012 were more the result of the Browns' offensive malaise than any true decline in skills. He will shine in the David Thomas role in the Saints offense, blocking in-line, working underneath routes, and providing much more value on a per-snap basis in a system where he will not be miscast as the top possession receiver.

Kellen Winslow			Height: 6-4			Weight: 254			College: Miami			Draft: 2004/1 (6)			Born: 21-Jul-1983		Age: 30		Risk: Red
Year	Team	G/GS	Snaps	Rec	Pass	Yds	C%	+/-	Yd/C	TD	Drop	YAC	Rk	YAC+	BTkl	DVOA	Rk	DYAR	Rk	YAR	Short	Mid	Deep	Bomb
2010	TB	16/11	716	66	97	730	68%	+7.0	11.1	5	3	3.5	39	-0.8	9	9.7%	17	135	7	114	40%	41%	16%	3%
2011	TB	16/15	822	75	120	763	63%	+1.9	10.2	2	4	3.4	38	-0.6	2	-15.4%	36	-50	42	-70	42%	48%	11%	0%
2012	NE	1/0	4	1	2	12	50%	-0.4	12.0	0	0	3.0	--	+0.9	0	-17.5%	--	0	--	-1	0%	100%	0%	0%
2013	NYJ			28	47	237	60%	--	8.5	2							-15.0%								

The soldier returns! Winslow's struggles with his surgically-repaired right knee cost him nearly all of 2012. Seattle traded for him, then cut him right before the season. The Patriots picked him up at midseason and he played one week before asking for his release. The Jets signed him to a one-year, $840,000 contract with no guaranteed money. If he's healthy, he's a massive upgrade on Jeff Cumberland and could obliterate that KUBIAK projection. He also could have problems getting open, just as he did in 2011, and not even make the team.

If Winslow never plays again, it will be a fairly unique disappearance. Since 1978, six different tight ends under the age of 30 followed up a season of at least 600 yards with a season that had less than 50 yards. Two of them are Winslow and Jake Ballard after 2011. The other four came back from injury to play at least two more seasons: Russ Francis, Eric Johnson, Zeke Mowatt, and Derrick Ramsey.

Jason Witten			Height: 6-6			Weight: 265			College: Tennessee			Draft: 2003/3 (69)			Born: 6-May-1982		Age: 31		Risk: Green
Year	Team	G/GS	Snaps	Rec	Pass	Yds	C%	+/-	Yd/C	TD	Drop	YAC	Rk	YAC+	BTkl	DVOA	Rk	DYAR	Rk	YAR	Short	Mid	Deep	Bomb
2010	DAL	16/16	1044	94	128	1002	73%	+10.7	10.7	9	3	4.2	30	-0.2	8	13.9%	15	187	3	187	47%	43%	9%	1%
2011	DAL	16/16	1040	79	117	942	68%	+5.5	11.9	5	2	4.6	21	+0.2	11	5.9%	20	68	19	77	47%	38%	12%	3%
2012	DAL	16/16	1078	110	149	1039	74%	+12.3	9.4	3	7	2.8	42	-1.2	3	10.0%	14	192	3	147	43%	46%	10%	1%
2013	DAL			94	126	875	75%	--	9.3	3							8.9%								

Well, that was a nice little rebound. Thought to be in the career-total building phase of his career. Witten turned that narrative around to firmly establish himself (once again) as a fixture of consistency in a Cowboys passing game that could use a lot more of that substance. Witten's 110 catches was by far his career high (previous best: 96 in 2007), and he set a league record for catches in a season by a tight end. He was also Dallas' top target in the red zone, with 15 pass attempts and 14 catches. However, Witten finished the season with just three touchdowns, which would seem to imply that there was a stat-collector quality to his great season. That's true to a degree, but he was also the only Dallas wide receiver or tight end to post positive receiving DVOA on every down, and his 75 percent catch rate was the second-highest of his career. Witten may not resemble the never generation of "big receiver" tight ends, and his decreasing yards per catch numbers line up with inevitable age decline, but there's a lot of life in the old dog. Expecting the same level of production in 2013 is problematic because the Cowboys selected San Diego State tight end Gavin Escobar in the second round of the draft; that move should extend Witten's shelf life, but also cut into his reps.

Going Deep

Kyle Adams, CHI: Adams, a 90s prototype receiving tight end, was lost in the shuffle as the Bears opted to use Matt Spaeth, a better blocker, when they used two tight ends. It's hard to tell quite what Adams is with the playing time he's received, but it's a little surprising that he wasn't given more of a chance last season as Chicago searched for somebody, anybody, who could catch a football. (2012 stats: 4-for-8, 40 yards, -12 DYAR, -30.2% DVOA)

Billy Bajema, FA: Hey, look who it is: Billy Bajema! A staple of "Going Deep" since 2005, Bajema looked like he was on his way out of the league when the Rams let him go after 12 starts and nine receptions in 2011. After all, if you could not make the Rams' tight end depth chart in the pre-Jared Cook days, what depth chart could you make? Well, the Ravens needed a third tight end, and then Ed Dickson got hurt, and next thing you know ol' Billy Bajema was on the active roster, playing special teams and getting the odd offensive snap. Bajema is like a pal who shows up each May while *Football Outsiders Almanac* is getting written, dares you to say something productive about his persistent career as a second or third tight end, then disappears onto a kickoff coverage team for 50 weeks. He's got the last laugh, of course: an eight-year career (which means pension!) and a Super Bowl ring. Bajema was a free agent at press time, but if history has taught us anything, it's that we haven't heard the last of him.

Brandon Barden, TEN: Don't tell Barden you can't make the club in the tub; missing the entire 2012 preseason after suffering a hamstring injury early in training camp did not prevent the undrafted rookie from Vanderbilt from making first the practice squad and later the active roster after Jared Cook's injury. Actually getting on the field was a different story, as he did not do that until the season finale and Craig Stevens' injury. He has a shot to be the Titans' fourth tight end if they can overlook a February DUI arrest where he rolled over his GMC Sierra.

Gary Barnidge, CLE: Gary Barnidge came out of college as a receiving-first tight end who needed to hone his blocking skills, but somehow he's developed into a generic blocking tight end who rarely gets thrown passes. He was with Rob Chudzinski in Carolina last year, and will be with him in Cleveland this year. Off the field, he has teamed with former Louisville teammates Breno Giacomini (now an offensive lineman in Seattle) and Ahmed Awadallah to form American Football Without Barriers, dedicated to growing interest in the game in foreign countries, and he traveled to China to visit youth leagues there. You can also check out his Twitter feed for some sweet photos from WrestleMania in New York. He had nice seats. (2012 stats: 6-for-6, 78 yards, 1 TD, 42 DYAR, 96.5% DVOA)

Travis Beckum, FA: Beckum tore his ACL in Super Bowl XLIV, and as a result, was limited to just 23 offensive snaps last year. He was a star receiver at Wisconsin but has just 26 career catches in four seasons in the NFL. The Giants chose not to re-sign him after his rookie contract expired, and interest around the league has been lukewarm.

Kevin Boss, FA: Boss looked like a promising lower-rung option in his early years with the Giants. He was big, tough, and happy to do the dirty work as both a blocker and seam receiver. However, injuries—including multiple concussions—have taken a toll in recent years, as he could not stay on the field after signing a big contract in Oakland and missed nearly all of 2012 as a member of the Chiefs. Boss' older brother had to retire from a professional soccer career due to a history of concussion problems. Unfortunately, Kevin could be meeting the same fate. (2012 stats: 1-for-3, 65 yards, 39 DYAR, 214.9% DVOA)

Richie Brockel, CAR: Brockel saw 67 snaps last year as a fullback/tight end and 229 as a special teamer, with no catches, no rushes, and three tackles. His versatility gives him an edge to keep his job over undrafted rookies Mike Zordich and Taylor Cook.

Nate Byham, TB: A sixth-round draft pick by San Francisco in 2010, Byham missed all of 2011 with a torn ACL, but he rebounded nicely as a blocking specialist in Tampa Bay last year. He'll fill the same role this season. (2012 stats: 1-for-4, 18 yards, 1 TD, 7 DYAR, 18.7% DVOA)

John Carlson, MIN: Each year of the 2010s brings us another year away from the 51-catch, seven-touchdown rookie season that Carlson had in 2009. Despite receiving a generous five-year, $25 million deal in free agency from the Vikings, who are contractually obligated to exchange at least one skill position player with the Seahawks each offseason, Carlson was a complete non-factor in 2012. He agreed to a pay cut before the draft, so Carlson will be back in the Twin Cities at a rate more commensurate with his role. (2012 stats: 8-for-14, 43 yards, -38 DYAR, -49.6% DVOA)

Garrett Celek, SF: With San Francisco drafting Vance McDonald (Rice) to replace Delanie Walker, Celek will reprise his role as the No. 3 tight end. Though Jim Harbaugh's offense perennially ranks near the top of the league in two-tight end sets, they rarely use three, instead opting for an extra lineman. Therefore, Celek won't be seeing the field much barring injury. (Twenty-eight percent of his offensive snaps came in Week 16 after Vernon Davis left early with a concussion.) (2012 stats: 4-for-7, 51 yards, 2 DYAR, -15.7% DVOA)

Orson Charles, CIN: Several FO staffers loved Charles coming out of the 2012 draft class: he was versatile, he could block, and he could catch. Charles had a fine 2012 rookie camp (he "exceeded expectations" according to Marvin Lewis), then vanished into backup tight end oblivion. He was never targeted more than twice in a game, and Jay Gruden often preferred a six-lineman look with Dennis Roland at tight end to calling Charles' number, even on first downs. The *Cincinnati Enquirer* reported in May that Charles' roster spot may be in danger with the arrival of Tyler Eifert, but a team planning to use a two-tight end offense needs three good tight ends. If Charles really qualifies as a "good tight end," he will at least stick around. (2012 stats: 8-for-10, 101 yards, 24 DYAR, 28.1% DVOA)

Charles Clay, MIA: Before tearing a knee ligament in Week 15, Clay was the Delanie Walker of Miami's offense. According to our charting stats, he lined up at flexed tight end 73 times and fullback 52 times in 333 offensive snaps. Indeed, he was more of a tactical asset than a pass-catching one in 2012, catching around 20 passes in about 35 targets—also like Walker. Not much should change in 2013 as long as Clay recovers from his injury. (2012 stats: 18-for-33, 212 yards, 2 TD, -19 DYAR, -16.0% DVOA)

Colin Cochart, DAL: Cochart is a player with good speed for his size who can be pressed into service when better, more experienced, tight ends are unavailable. He did so with the Bengals when Jermaine Gresham was injured in 2011, and took a spot on Dallas' roster when Jason Witten was recovering from his spleen injury.

Chris Cooley, FA: The Redskins gave Cooley another shot on the roster after Fred Davis was lost to a torn Achilles' tendon in October, but Cooley had no effect on Washington's offense. Another sign he's just about done: Washington gave rookie running back Jawan Jamison jersey number 47, which previously belonged to Cooley. (2012 stats: 1-for-3, 8 yards, -6 DYAR, -36.4% DVOA)

Justice Cunningham, IND: Before he was "Mr. Irrelevant" of the 2013 NFL draft, Cunningham was a lightly-used but effective option in the passing game at South Carolina. Over his final two seasons with the Gamecocks, Cunningham caught 41 out of 51 targets for 466 yards and a touchdown. When he gets back from Disneyland, Cunningham will compete with Weslye Saunders and Dominique Jones for the No. 3 tight end role in Indianapolis.

Dorin Dickerson, BUF: Houston's attempt to make Dickerson a full-time wide receiver never panned out, but he was a useful piece for the Buffalo offense as a player who could block or run a route, taking the field for a handful of plays each game (97 offensive snaps in 2012) and lining up at multiple spots. (2012 stats: 9-for-15, 117 yards, -17 DYAR, -12.4% DVOA)

Jim Dray, ARI: As Arizona's backup blocking tight end the past three years, Dray earned about $1.35 million in almost complete anonymity. It remains unclear whether he was paid by the Cardinals or the U.S. Federal Witness Protection Program. Dray's bio on the Cardinals' website further clouds his true identity by referring to a devastating 2007 knee injury involving his "popitillas," which our crack staff of cryptologists tells us is fed-speak for "parts unknown."

Michael Egnew, MIA: Egnew is the epicenter of disagreement among talent evaluators in Miami. Jeff Ireland selected him in the third round of the 2012 draft, and continues to stand by the pick. Joe Philbin says Egnew needs to play faster in 2013. Most notably, an anonymous teammate said he doesn't know the playbook. Egnew played only 25 snaps as a rookie, and the fact that he didn't play any on special teams can't be good for his place on the roster. Miami added Michigan State's Dion Sims in the fourth round of April's draft, so the writing is clearly on Egnew's wall.

Brody Eldridge, CHI: As a blocking tight end who has problems blocking, it seems very unlikely that Eldridge will play the 26 games he needs to outlast Brody Lilliard for most games played by a Brody in the NFL. He did outlast Brodie Croyle though, so that should be some consolation.

Rhett Ellison, MIN: Ellison, along with Jerome Felton, was one of the underrated drive blockers that helped generate holes for Adrian Peterson's insane season. Ellison actually played plenty of fullback on his own, and offers terrific blocking from any spot in the backfield. He flashed some decent hands as well, though you probably wouldn't want to build a game plan around them. (2012 stats: 7-for-9, 65 yards, -2 DYAR, -8.7% DVOA)

Dedrick Epps, FA: Proof that not all tight ends from the U can make it in the pros, Epps was drafted by San Diego and then floated through four different practice squads. His first NFL reception came on Tim Tebow's first regular-season pass as a member of the Jets. Dashon Goldson then up-ended him and took out his ACL, which means Epps' first NFL catch was also his first NFL fumble and probably the end of his NFL career.

Daniel Fells, NE: Fells and Michael Hoomanawanui are both H-backs who usually take on blocking roles in New England's two- and three-tight end sets, but every so often Josh McDaniels will send one of them up the seam just to keep the defense honest. Half of the 16 passes thrown to Fells or Hoomanawanui were deep (i.e. 15+ yards in the air), including a 35-yarder Fells caught against Seattle and a 41-yarder Hoomanawanui caught against San Francisco. The Aaron Hernandez release probably assures them both spots on the 2013 roster. (2012 stats: 4-for-9, 85 yards, 10 DYAR, 16.8% DVOA)

Tommy Gallarda, ATL: A willing blocker, Gallarda uses his 262-pound bulk to good effect. He'll battle fourth-round pick Levine Toilolo for a roster spot, with the practice squad a likely destination for whoever doesn't make the 53-man roster. (2012 stats: 1-for-4, 7 yards, -17 DYAR, -61.5% DVOA)

Chris Gragg, BUF: A one-time wide receiver at Arkansas, this seventh-round pick has seam speed and is a willing blocker. Gaining 10-15 pounds would help him better fit the role of an NFL tight end, but it also might exacerbate the problem he had in college with lingering knee injuries.

Ladarius Green, SD: The Chargers took Green in the fourth round of the 2012 draft, planning to develop a replacement for Antonio Gates. The Chargers describe him as "rangy" and tout his big-play potential. Green was the No. 4 tight end as a rookie and held up fine in a limited role when Dante Rosario missed time with an injury. He is no closer to replacing Antonio Gates as of this writing. (2012 stats: 4-for-4, 56 yards, 10 DYAR, 52.5% DVOA)

Virgil Green, DEN: Don't be surprised if Green sees his role expand in 2013. He is Denver's most athletic tight end (he registered a 42.5-inch vertical at the Combine in 2011) and there were a few times down the stretch last season where he took snaps away from Jacob Tamme. Green is best served as a receiver, but in Denver's scheme, the tight end must be at least somewhat of a threat to block. His reps will depend on how well he polishes his awareness and mechanics. (2012 stats: 5-for-6, 63 yards, 14 DYAR, 22.7% DVOA)

Ryan Griffin, HOU: Griffin was the No. 3 target on a bad Connecticut offense. The tight end-loving Texans took him as a developmental sixth-round pick, and his early contributions will likely come as an in-line blocker who catches the occasional short pass.

James Hanna, DAL: This 2012 sixth-round pick out of Oklahoma has a bit of buzz around him as a possible Jason Witten injury replacement in the short term, and a slot weapon in Dallas' two-TE packages. The selection of Gavin Escobar in the 2013 draft pushed him one step down the depth chart, but he's worth projecting as a roster guy on receiving potential alone—and he adds value as a blocker. (2012 stats: 8-for-11, 86 yards, 6 DYAR, -1.5% DVOA)

Cory Harkey, STL: Harkey caught just one pass as a rookie, which is not unusual for an undrafted tight end. However, he also caught only one pass in his senior season at UCLA, despite starting 14 games. The potential here may be tapped out. He'll try to stick around St. Louis as a blocker and special teamer.

Ben Hartsock, CAR: A third-round pick by the Colts in 2004, Hartsock has more starts (45) than receptions (31) in his career. He played 203 snaps last season and was targeted three times. At what point do we just label him a mini-tackle and be done with it?

Todd Heap, FA: Heap's extensive injury history has been well-documented. Normally, teams would overlook past injuries if they see value in the player otherwise. The problem for Heap as he tries to find a landing spot is time. It's not just that he's now 33 years old; there's also the glacial pace at which his injuries seem to heal. Arizona's patience ran out in Week 14 last year; that of the 31 other teams probably did as well. (2012 stats: 8-for-13, 94 yards, -3 DYAR, -8.3% DVOA)

Will Heller, FA: There were only 17 catches and that was *Catch-22*, which specified that a concern for one's own safety in the face of being an aging blocking tight end on a team with no one to throw to, was real and immediate as a process of a rational mind. Heller was adequate, but could be easily replaced. All he had to do was ask; and as soon as he did, he would no longer be employed and would get to pick up his NFL pension. (2012 stats: 17-for-23, 150 yards, 1 TD, 27 DYAR, 3.8% DVOA)

Mike Higgins, NO: At 6-foot-5, 245 pounds, Higgins is bigger and a better blocker than David Thomas, the tight end Higgins aspires to replace at the back of the depth chart.

Michael Hoomanawanui, NE: See comment for Daniel Fells, above. (2012 stats: 5-for-7, 109 yards, 31 DYAR, 63.8% DVOA)

D.C. Jefferson, ARI: Jefferson got the nickname "D.C." because he resembled Daunte Culpepper as a high school quarterback. As Arizona's seventh-round pick, he joins two other D.C.'s on the Cardinals' 90-man roster: left guard Daryn Colledge and backup nose tackle David Carter. Unfortunately, Colledge, Carter, and even Culpepper are as likely as Jefferson to see tight end snaps in Arizona this season.

Nick Kasa, OAK: Kasa spent his first three years at Colorado playing defensive end. His request for a move to offense was granted last season, and he quickly showed blocking prowess, both with in-line technique and drive-blocking. The Raiders drafted him in the sixth round. Needless to say, the 276-pounder is raw and limited as a route runner, though he did show very intriguing straight-line speed on a 70-yard touchdown against Washington State.

Jeff King, ARI: In a *fait accompli* we predicted in *Football Outsiders Almanac 2012*, King started 12 games last season for an injured Todd Heap. With the emergence of Rob Housler, however, King wasn't pressed into receiving duty as much as he was during Heap's absence in 2011. That figures to continue this season given that Dwayne Allen's 66 targets in 2012 more than doubled the previous high for a blocking tight end in Bruce Arians' offense (31 by Steve Heiden in 2003). Game charters marked King with 10.5 blown blocks on runs, the most of any tight end in the league, but this may have been an Arizona thing; Rob Housler was second at 8.5. (2012 stats: 17-for-29, 129 yards, -47 DYAR, -28.6% DVOA)

Steve Maneri, KC: Maneri was used like a No. 2 tight end in 2012, but he didn't show any indication of having a particularly bright future in that capacity. He must improve his strength and sustainability as a playside run-blocker—especially considering that he's not a dynamic receiving threat. (2012 stats: 5-for-12, 51 yards, -29 DYAR, -42.5% DVOA)

Anthony McCoy, SEA: McCoy was highly efficient as Seattle's No. 2 tight end last season, finishing second to Rob Gronkowski in receiving DVOA for tight ends with at least 25 passes. Unfortunately, he tore his Achilles during offseason workouts and will miss the entire 2013 season. (2012 stats: 18-for-28, 291 yards, 3 TD, 90 DYAR, 35.5% DVOA)

Jamie McCoy, PIT: A practice-squad H-back, McCoy has bounced between the Rams, Chargers, and Steelers since 2012, rarely seeing active duty. He could possibly stick with the Steelers this year as a third tight end while Heath Miller rehabs his knee. But then, so could anyone.

Randy McMichael, FA: McMichael is getting long in the tooth, but may be able to prolong his NFL career as a sign-and-plug backup tight end. He's no longer much of a receiving threat, and it's hard to remember the last time he ran a seam pattern. However, he remains a savvy and assertive blocker, both off the line and off short movement, especially pre-snap motion. (2012 stats: 9-for-13, 51 yards, -49 DYAR, -66.5% DVOA)

Mike McNeill, STL: McNeill played both tight end and wide receiver for Nebraska, but he seems to be relegated to a blocking role in St. Louis. And really, if you can't play wideout for the Rams, you can't play wideout in the NFL. (2012 stats: 4-for-7, 31 yards, -17 DYAR, -47.1% DVOA)

Evan Moore, PHI: This time last year, Moore looked like a player on the rise. He set a career high in receptions, receiving yards, and touchdowns in 2011, and produced a sparkling 72 percent catch rate despite playing for a Browns team that had a 56.1 percent completion rate overall. But in the last calendar year, Moore has been released by three teams—Cleveland, Seattle, and Philadelphia—and recorded as many memorable drops (one, against the Redskins) as catches. Moore was never considered a good blocker, so he may struggle to find playing time—or even earn a roster spot—in 2013. (2012 stats: 1-for-8, 6 yards, -51 DYAR, -80.2% DVOA)

Matthew Mulligan, GB: Mulligan comes to Green Bay with more career starts (20) than receptions (14). He has 144 career receiving yards, 41 of them on a trick pass thrown by Jeremy Kerley with the Jets in Week 17 of 2011. Do not expect a repeat with the Packers, as they don't need gimmicks to accumulate passing yards. (2012 stats: 8-for-12, 84 yards, 1 TD, 24 DYAR, 19.6% DVOA)

Danny Noble, TB: Noble played six offensive snaps in four games as Tampa Bay's fourth tight end before a hamstring injury ended his season. He'll need to fight off undrafted free agents Hubie Graham (Pittsburgh) and Evan Landi (South Florida) to keep his roster spot.

Jake O'Connell, FA: The first player ever drafted from Gulf Coast High School (Naples, FL) has played in 35 games since joining the Chiefs as a seventh-round pick in 2009. His 2012 season came to an early end after the team opted to put him on IR following a high ankle sprain in the November Monday Night loss at Pittsburgh. As his career reception total of 35 suggests, O'Connell is what they call "a blocking specialist." (2012 stats: 3-for-3, 18 yards, 2 DYAR, 8.5% DVOA)

Michael Palmer, FA: Stone Mountain, Georgia, is perhaps best known as the hometown of *30 Rock*'s yokel NBC page Kenneth. Palmer, also a native of the city, did little to change that with his 44 catches in three seasons as the guy opposite Tony Gonzalez in Atlanta's occasional two-tight end sets. The Falcons appear to have moved on but Palmer will be just up the road, staring up at the "Confederate Mt. Rushmore" carved into the side of Stone Mountain and waiting for Thomas Dimitroff to call him. (2012 stats: 6-for-6, 22 yards, 1 TD, -2 DYAR, -4.1% DVOA)

Bear Pascoe, NYG: Pascoe has never caught more than two passes in a regular-season game, but his four catches in Super Bowl XLVI will always endear him to Giants fans. That makes him a poor man's David Tyree. For now, he looks to be the Giants third-string tight end in 2013, though his roster spot could be in jeopardy after seeing just nine targets last year. (2012 stats: 4-for-9, 35 yards, 1 TD, -7 DYAR, -24.4% DVOA)

Niles Paul, WAS: What a short, strange trip it's been. Selected as a receiver, Paul was moved to tight end after his rookie season because the Redskins added a plethora of players at that position. Paul was praised for his blocking in 2012, and his 48-yard kick return against the Dallas Cowboys in the regular-season finale was the longest for any NFL tight end in 31 years, but the speed with which the Redskins' coaching staff talked about potentially moving Paul to fullback after he bulked up to 235 pounds doesn't bode well for his prospects as a pass-catcher. At this point, he's a special-teamer who might get a few targets if Mike Shanahan is short a tight end or two in certain packages. (2012 stats: 8-for-15, 152 yards, 1 TD, 4 DYAR, -3.9% DVOA)

John Phillips, SD: Phillips has prototype size for the position, and he's impressive in very small doses, but the presence of Jason Witten limited his opportunities. Phillips signed a three-year, $5.275 million contract with the Chargers this offseason, which puts the man the Cowboys once thought to be more impressive than Martellus Bennett behind the positional eight-ball yet again. (2012 stats: 8-for-10, 55 yards, 1 TD, 11 DYAR, 2.0% DVOA)

Leonard Pope, FA: Pope followed Todd Haley from Kansas City to Pittsburgh. There's an FBI surveillance joke to be made here, but Haley has taken enough ribbing in this book, and the real mystery is how Pope hangs around the NFL collecting three-to-ten catch seasons, year after year. He left Georgia as the ultimate "specimen" tight end, a power forward who could be the next Tony Gonzalez if only the bottoms of so many rosters weren't littered with next Tony Gonzalezes. Pope has turned into a pretty good blocker, and Haley likes him, though not quite enough to keep him on board despite Heath Miller's injury. (2012 stats: 3-for-4, 9 yards, 2 TD, 12 DYAR, 23.1% DVOA)

Zach Potter, FA: At 6-foot-7 and nearly 280 pounds, Potter's value in the NFL is tied more to his blocking than his abilities as a receiver. Potter played in less than 20 percent of the Jaguars' offensive snaps last season, and the Jaguars let him become a free agent without a qualifying offer. (2012 stats: 2-for-6, 6 yards, -24 DYAR, -74.1% DVOA)

Andrew Quarless, GB: Quarless is the one piece of The Green Bay Backup Tight End and H-Back Set ™ that didn't see much work last season due to a torn ACL and MCL at the end of 2011. He seems to have fallen behind D.J. Williams in the pecking order in passing situations, and with Matthew Mulligan now in town, he'll face competition to hold on to his roster spot as the blocking H-Back.

Richard Quinn, CIN: In the classic Dustin Hoffman movie *Little Big Man*, Richard Mulligan plays an utterly insane, ego-maniacal General Custer. Hoffman's Jack Crabbe tries to get work as a scout for Custer, but Custer takes one look at him and declares that he is a natural muleskinner, and that becomes Crabbe's profession. Josh McDaniels took one look at Quinn, who caught 12 passes in three college seasons, and said "now, there's a second-round tight end for a wide-open offense." Crabbe bounced around from the Seventh Cavalry to an Indian village to the gutter in the film. Quinn bounced from the Broncos to the Redskins to the Bengals' inactive list, catching one pass in three years. Custer died at Little Big Horn, of course; in the film, Mulligan spends his last moments ranting about his hatred for President Grant. McDaniels survived stints in Denver and St. Louis; it is unknown what he says in unguarded moments about Bill Belichick.

Jordan Reed, WAS: If you've decided to compare Reed to Aaron Hernandez because of the Florida connection ... well, that's not crazy talk. Our buddy Greg Cosell of NFL Films and ESPN's *NFL Matchup* does see some similarities. "Reed is an athletic mover with wide receiver traits," Cosell said in April, "and [you want] skill position players that can threaten the defense from wherever they line up." Like Hernandez, Reed has the potential to line up just about everywhere in a creative offense. Unlike Hernandez, Reed still has his freedom and an NFL job.

Allen Reisner, JAC: Reisner's 2012 season was nearly identical to his rookie season of 2011. Reisner bounced between the Minnesota Vikings' active roster and practice squad, appeared in a handful of games (six in 2011, four in 2012), and caught the one pass that was thrown his way. Reisner's receiving yardage did *explode* from five yards in 2011 to 13 yards in 2012, an increase that must have been the catalyst for the Jaguars to claim Reisner off waivers in the final week of the regular season.

Konrad Reuland, NYJ: This old Mission Viejo High School teammate of Mark Sanchez (Go Diablos!) is advertised as a block-first tight end, but he sometimes looks awkward on running plays. The game charters marked him with five blown blocks on runs, and he certainly will not be revisiting the Week 16 game against San Diego when he gets nostalgic in his old age. Then again, he also was more useful as a receiver than you would expect from a guy with only 27 collegiate receptions. (2012 stats: 11-for-16, 83 yards, -15 DYAR, -10.7% DVOA)

Mychal Rivera, OAK: Rivera, an Oakland sixth-round pick, was not enormously productive as a senior at Tennessee, but he was steady and sure-handed. Skill-wise, he is a nimble receiving tight end who can be put in motion or split out wide. He does not have great natural size and speed, but his other traits make him a good fit in a Raiders offense that has already carved out a niche for a similar player in Marcel Reece.

Adrien Robinson, NYG: Robinson's impressive combination of size and athleticism convinced the Giants to draft the raw prospect in the fourth round in 2012, even though Robinson caught just 29 passes in four years at Cincinnati. New York General Manager Jerry Reese praised Robinson's production in practice last year, but Reese's decision to sign Brandon Myers indicates that he's not comfortable relying on Robinson just yet.

Dante Rosario, DAL: Every NFL analyst has, at some point, been tricked into seeing Rosario as a rising player. Besides the fact that he just *looks* like an athletic tight end, Rosario has shown flashes of fluidity in space, strength in traffic, and soft hands in big moments. His two greatest teases were catching the winning touchdown on the final play of Carolina's season opener in 2008 and catching three touchdown passes in Week 2 against the Titans last year. Those would be his only touchdowns last season. In fact, he had just six total receptions after that. Given that there's nothing unique about his blocking, it could be tough for Rosario to stay in the league much longer. (2012 stats: 10-for-18, 101 yards, 3 TD's, -6 DYAR, -18.3% DVOA)

Weslye Saunders, IND: In *Football Outsiders Almanac 2012*, we predicted that Saunders would be released by the Pittsburgh Steelers during training camp after he was suspended last offseason for violating the league's PED policy. We were slightly off on that; instead, he was released in Week 6. Saunders had played quite a bit for the 2011 Steelers, so it was not a surprise that he latched on with the Colts, where former Steelers offensive coordinator Bruce Arians was serving as interim head coach. (2012 stats: 2-for-4, 15 yards, -11 DYAR, -27.5% DVOA)

Alex Silvestro, BAL: Drummed out of the Green Lantern Corps for his Machiavellian tactics, Silvestro discovered a source of yellow cosmic energy fueled by sheer terror ... wait, no, sorry, this is actually the kid from Rutgers Bill Belichick moved from defensive end to tight end: he was a last-minute activation for the Patriots before Super Bowl XLVI. He is now practice-squad fodder for the Ravens. He does not have a yellow ring, but Belichick has a scarlet one that turns ordinary Rutgers kids into guys we have to write about.

Dion Sims, MIA: As a fourth-round pick, Sims will immediately step in as the primary backup to new starter Dustin Keller. However, given Miami's personnel and formation tendencies in 2012, he's unlikely to see much playing time unless Keller gets hurt—which is a distinct possibility, of course. Sims' strong suit is blocking, but Joe Philbin uses H-back Charles Clay either in the backfield or on the end of the line when the situation warrants an additional blocker.

Alex Smith, CIN: Smith was worth minus-76 DYAR last year, and doing that on 18 targets really takes some work, from both a player and his coaches. Smith caught a 17-yard pass in Week 2 against the Bengals but went managed just 30 yards on the remainder of his catches. At some point in every H-back's life, he catches that two-yard flat pass and turns upfield for a 10-yard gain, but those days ended for Smith in September. Brandon Weeden did his part by not recognizing his checkdown options until the defenders did; Pat Shurmur did his part by being incompetent, but of course it is Smith's duty to do something more dynamic with the ball in his hands than fall down a few feet from the line of scrimmage. Smith is now in Cincinnati, and probably only makes the team if they carry four tight ends. (2012 stats: 13-for-18, 47 yards, -76 DYAR, -72.6% DVOA)

Hayden Smith, NYJ: Smith has a crazy back story: He came from Australia to the U.S. to play Division II basketball, then switched to rugby union and played professionally in England. Then he decided he wanted to try football, and signed with the Jets after working out for five different teams. But he's not just a human interest story; he's also a fantasy sleeper. Jeff Cumberland scares nobody, and former Jets GM Mike Tannenabaum said on NFL Network this spring that the Jets' defense found Smith impossible to cover in practice. One to watch.

Lee Smith, BUF: Smith is really just a sixth lineman, but he caught out of goal-line packages against Indianapolis and St. Louis last year. (2012 stats: 4-for-4, 13 yards, 2 TD, 16 DYAR, 28.8% DVOA)

Matt Spaeth, PIT: Spaeth did yeoman's work helping out both J'Marcus Webb and sad parade of right tackles the Bears started last season, but it wasn't enough to completely cover up the problem. This year, Spaeth is headed back to the Steelers to chip on rushers headed towards Mike Adams' outside shoulder. (2012 stats: 6-for-10, 28 yards, 1 TD, -14 DYAR, -33.7% DVOA)

Kory Sperry, ARI: Sperry is a journeyman pass-catching tight end who doesn't catch passes. He was signed in late 2012 when the Cardinals released pass-catching tight end Todd Heap. Arizona already has pass-catching tight end Rob Housler atop their depth chart, and they drafted pass-catching tight end D.C. Jefferson in the seventh round this past April. Put this all together, and it's safe to say Sperry will have to find another team to not catch passes for in 2013.

Zack Sudfeld, NE: Sudfeld was a rare six-year player at Nevada, with a standard redshirt in 2007 and medical redshirts in both 2008 and 2011. He went undrafted, but is considered a smart player with good hands and excellent size (6-foot-7, 255 pounds), and he was impressive in Patriots minicamp. Given the questionable status of Rob Gronkowski, he has an outside shot to make the 53-man roster and a very good shot to make the practice squad as a player to watch for the future.

Ryan Taylor, GB: This member of The Green Bay Backup Tight End and H-Back Set ™ is mostly known for his work on special teams, where he's not afraid to throw his body around. If you were attempting to collect the whole set to trade them in for a real tight end, Taylor would be the one that kept showing up in packs when you were only a Tom Crabtree away from having them all.

David Thomas, FA: Thomas may be best remembered as part of the Patriots' two-tight end sets before Rob Gronkowski and Aaron Hernandez showed up to show 'em how it's done. Four of his 11 grabs in 2012 went for scores, so he may have some fantasy value left. Thomas and his agent will be watching training camps closely; he figures to get call from someone in need of a body. In fact, a return to the Patriots would make a lot of sense. (2012 stats: 11-for-17, 4 TD, 37 DYAR, 18.0% DVOA)

Julius Thomas, DEN: The window could soon be closing on the 2011 fourth-round pick. Coming out of Portland State as a four-year basketball star with just one year of football experience, Thomas was seen as an athletic developmental project. However, injury problems have inhibited him during the past two offseasons, which is the best time for coaches to truly dial in and work with developmental projects. Last season, Thomas got just two snaps on offense and 14 snaps on special teams.

Taylor Thompson, TEN: 2012 was mostly a redshirt season for this collegiate defensive end making a position switch, but the Titans found ways to use him as a blocker, both in-line and as an H-back. He's set to be the No. 3 tight end again this season, but with the Titans poised to use more multiple tight-end formations, he could be in for a big role expansion. He won't be a factor in fantasy leagues unless he spends all offseason with the JUGS machine, though. (2012 stats: 6-for-13, 46 yards, -38 DYAR, -53.3% DVOA)

Levine Toilolo, ATL: Toilolo was a heavily recruited star out of the San Diego area, but was buried at Stanford by Coby Fleener and Zach Ertz. Toilolo's main attributes are his size—he goes 6-foot-8, 260 pounds, which makes him a promising red zone target—and his bloodlines, as he has three uncles who put in some NFL time. Toilolo doesn't project to be a true replacement for Tony Gonzalez (who does?), but his frame offers a chance to be a useful part in the Falcons attack.

D.J. Williams, GB: Williams' card in The Green Bay Backup Tight End and H-Back Set ™ is stamped "NOT THE LINE-BACKER." Williams has good size and speed for a move H-Back, but he's running out of chances to distinguish himself in a positive way, and he somehow managed a -41.5% DVOA on 15 passes in an offense that had a 40.6% passing DVOA overall. (2012 stats: 7-for-15, 57 yards, -25 DYAR)

Michael Williams, DET: A 6-foot-6, 269-pound mammoth tight end from Alabama picked up in the seventh round, Williams is more of a blocker than a receiver. He can run the routes, and he has surprisingly soft hands (he had a 74 percent catch rate last season), but his ability to separate and/or make tacklers miss borders on non-existent. That's not a big problem for the Lions, who figure to use him mainly for his blocking acumen. He'll likely replace Will Heller as their third tight end in power sets assuming he holds off a slew of UDFA tight ends for a roster spot.

Luke Wilson, SEA: Wilson's senior season at Rice was ruined by ankle and back injuries, but he put on a freakish pro-day performance, with a 40-yard dash, bench press, and vertical jump that each would have been among the top ten for tight ends at the combine. His 4.51-second 40 speed showed itself at rookie minicamp, where the fifth-rounder flashed his potential as a seam-route threat. With Anthony McCoy waived following a torn Achilles tendon, Wilson will get every chance to succeed this year.

2013 Kicker Projections

L isted below are the 2013 KUBIAK projections for kickers. Because of the inconsistency of field-goal percentage from year to year, kickers are projected almost entirely based on team forecasts, although a handful of individual factors do come into play:

• More experience leads to a slightly higher field-goal percentage in general, with the biggest jump between a kicker's rookie and sophomore seasons.

• Kickers with a better career field-goal percentage tend to get more attempts, although they are not necessarily more accurate.

• Field-goal percentage on kicks over 40 yards tends to regress to the mean.

Kickers are also listed with a Risk of Green, Yellow, Red, or Blue, as explained in the introduction to the section on quarterbacks. Note that field-goal totals are rounded, so "points" may not exactly equal (FG * 3 + XP).

Fantasy Kicker Projections, 2013

Kicker	Team	FG	Pct	XP	Pts	Risk	Kicker	Team	FG	Pct	XP	Pts	Risk
Mason Crosby	GB	29-36	80%	55	141	Red	Rob Bironas	TEN	27-32	84%	33	114	Green
Matt Prater	DEN	30-35	87%	47	138	Green	Graham Gano	CAR	21-26	84%	50	114	Yellow
Randy Bullock	HOU	30-37	79%	44	133	Red	Shaun Suisham	PIT	25-30	84%	40	114	Yellow
Mike Nugent	CIN	29-34	86%	39	127	Yellow	Nick Folk	NYJ	26-31	83%	35	113	Yellow
Adam Vinatieri	IND	29-34	84%	40	127	Green	Ryan Succop	KC	26-31	85%	31	110	Yellow
Robbie Gould	CHI	30-35	87%	36	126	Yellow	Shayne Graham	CLE	26-32	82%	31	109	Green
Stephen Gostkowski	NE	25-29	85%	51	125	Green	Sebastian Janikowski	OAK	26-30	89%	30	109	Blue
Justin Tucker	BAL	28-31	89%	42	125	Yellow	Alex Henery	PHI	23-28	85%	37	108	Green
Matt Bryant	ATL	29-32	88%	39	125	Green	Dan Carpenter	MIA	24-30	81%	35	108	Red
Dan Bailey	DAL	29-33	87%	35	122	Yellow	Nick Novak	SD	23-27	85%	37	106	Red
Kai Forbath	WAS	25-29	84%	47	122	Green	Josh Scobee	JAC	23-27	85%	28	97	Yellow
David Akers	DET	27-34	78%	42	122	Red							
Garrett Hartley	NO	23-28	83%	49	119	Yellow							

							Other kickers who may win jobs						
Steven Hauschka	SEA	25-29	86%	45	119	Green	Kicker	Team	FG	Pct	XP	Pts	Risk
Phil Dawson	SF	24-29	83%	46	119	Green	Brandon Bogotay	CLE	23-39	80%	31	101	Red
Josh Brown	NYG	25-32	78%	42	117	Red	David Buehler	NYG	25-33	76%	41	116	Red
Lawrence Tynes	TB	26-29	89%	40	117	Yellow	Dustin Hopkins	BUF	23-30	79%	33	103	Red
Blair Walsh	MIN	29-32	89%	31	117	Yellow	Brett Maher	NYJ	25-31	81%	34	110	Red
Jay Feely	ARI	29-33	86%	31	117	Yellow	Harvad Rugland	DET	25-32	78%	41	116	Red
Rian Lindell	BUF	28-31	89%	33	116	Red	Caleb Sturgis	MIA	22-28	78%	35	102	Red
Greg Zuerlein	STL	28-34	82%	32	115	Yellow							

2013 Fantasy Defense Projections

Listed below are the 2013 KUBIAK projections for fantasy team defense. The projection method is discussed in an essay in *Pro Football Prospectus 2006*, the key conclusions of which were:

• Schedule strength is very important for projecting fantasy defense.
• Categories used for scoring in fantasy defense have no consistency from year-to-year whatsoever, with the exception of sacks and interceptions.

Fumble recoveries and defensive touchdowns are forecast solely based on the projected sacks and interceptions, rather than the team's totals in these categories from a year ago. This is why the 2013 projections may look very different from the fantasy defense values from the 2012 season. Safeties and shutouts are not common enough to have a significant effect on the projections. Team defenses are also projected with Risk factor of Green, Yellow, or Red; this is based on the team's projection compared to performance in recent seasons.

In addition to projection of separate categories, we also give an overall total based on our generic fantasy scoring formula: one point for a sack, two points for a fumble recovery or interception, and six points for a touchdown. Special teams touchdowns are listed separately and are not included in the fantasy scoring total listed.

Fantasy Team Defense Projections, 2013

Team	Fant Pts	Sack	Int	Fum Rec	Def TD	Risk	ST TD	Team	Fant Pts	Sack	Int	Fum Rec	Def TD	Risk	ST TD
GB	122	41.2	19.3	11.5	3.2	Yellow	0.9	NE	104	39.2	16.2	7.6	2.9	Green	1.0
HOU	120	45.9	16.3	12.0	2.9	Yellow	0.5	TB	104	36.2	15.1	7.3	3.8	Yellow	0.8
CHI	117	38.7	19.5	10.1	3.1	Green	1.1	NYJ	102	36.1	15.6	9.3	2.7	Yellow	1.1
DEN	117	47.7	13.8	11.5	3.1	Yellow	1.1	ARI	102	33.3	15.1	11.0	2.7	Yellow	1.1
STL	116	42.8	14.2	13.2	3.1	Red	0.8	DAL	101	34.1	12.5	13.3	2.5	Red	0.9
CIN	114	46.3	16.0	10.4	2.6	Yellow	0.4	OAK	101	33.0	13.5	11.0	3.1	Red	1.2
MIN	113	42.6	13.1	14.4	2.7	Red	1.1	WAS	100	34.0	18.2	7.1	2.5	Yellow	0.8
MIA	113	40.6	13.6	11.6	3.7	Red	0.8	PHI	99	38.0	10.5	11.9	2.7	Red	1.0
NYG	113	36.1	16.1	11.1	3.8	Yellow	1.0	DET	99	35.2	13.0	10.2	2.8	Yellow	0.8
BAL	112	37.3	16.0	8.2	4.4	Yellow	0.7	PIT	97	41.8	12.1	11.1	1.4	Yellow	0.9
SEA	111	39.0	16.7	10.0	3.1	Yellow	1.1	TEN	96	30.2	14.0	11.6	2.5	Yellow	1.5
SF	111	38.9	16.2	8.2	3.8	Green	0.8	BUF	91	31.7	13.3	8.6	2.6	Yellow	1.5
SD	110	33.7	19.4	8.7	3.3	Yellow	1.0	IND	91	32.3	10.5	11.0	2.7	Yellow	0.8
CLE	108	37.1	16.6	10.1	3.0	Red	0.8	NO	90	31.4	12.7	10.0	2.3	Yellow	0.8
ATL	107	32.2	16.8	9.6	3.8	Yellow	0.9	KC	90	35.2	11.6	8.7	2.4	Yellow	0.8
CAR	105	36.9	16.4	9.1	2.8	Red	0.9	JAC	81	29.1	12.6	10.5	1.0	Green	0.8

Projected Defensive Leaders, 2013

Solo Tackles			Total Tackles			Sacks			Interceptions		
Player	Team	Tkl	Player	Team	Tkl	Player	Team	Sacks	Player	Team	INT
J.Laurinaitis	STL	106	L.Kuechly	CAR	151	A.Smith	SF	16.5	A.Samuel	ATL	4.3
D.Johnson	KC	98	N.Bowman	SF	140	V.Miller	DEN	15.0	R.Sherman	SEA	4.0
L.Kuechly	CAR	98	L.Fletcher	WAS	134	J.Allen	MIN	14.9	S.Brown	NYG	3.5
L.David	TB	95	J.Mayo	NE	133	D.Ware	DAL	14.3	C.Bailey	DEN	3.5
N.Bowman	SF	91	C.Greenway	MIN	132	J.J.Watt	HOU	12.7	J.Byrd	BUF	3.3
C.Greenway	MIN	91	L.David	TB	128	C.Long	STL	12.5	T.DeCoud	ATL	3.3
P.Posluszny	JAC	90	J.Laurinaitis	STL	126	C.Wake	MIA	11.4	E.Reed	HOU	3.3
B.Cushing	HOU	86	D.Johnson	KC	125	J.Babin	JAC	11.4	M.Griffin	TEN	3.2
S.Tulloch	DET	85	S.Lee	DAL	124	C.Johnson	CAR	9.8	D.Hall	WAS	3.2
P.Willis	SF	84	P.Posluszny	JAC	124	G.Atkins	CIN	9.7	A.Rolle	NYG	3.2
S.Lee	DAL	84	J.Freeman	IND	123	C.Matthews	GB	9.5	J.Wilson	WAS	3.1
B.Wagner	SEA	82	D.Jackson	CLE	120	M.Williams	BUF	9.1	D.McCourty	NE	3.1

College Football Introduction and Statistical Toolbox

Throughout most of its history, college football has defined itself through its glacial rate of change. We sit in the same seats every year, we sing the same fight song our parents did, we pass down the same silly (and fantastic) traditions from generation to generation, and we cycle through the same arguments year after passing year. We've been talking about college football being too dangerous for 100 years. We've been talking about paying players for 60 years. We've been talking about a college football playoff for 40. Change is always threatened, and since Teddy Roosevelt was president, change has not come with any particular rate of speed.

That's what makes the current time in college football feel revolutionary. We *are* getting a playoff, beginning next year. Player compensation discussions have picked up speed thanks to both the *In re NCAA Student-Athlete Name & Likeness Licensing Litigation* case (otherwise known as *O'Bannon v. NCAA*, a class-action strike against the NCAA for its use of current and former student-athletes' likenesses in video games without compensation) and major conferences' pressing of the "full cost of attendance" stipend. Coaches are attending seminars about player safety, and further rules changes could be on the way. Recent conference realignment explosions have brought us closer to the "16-team super-conferences" era everybody has been predicting for a couple of decades.

But while the college football landscape is changing, the balance of power seemingly has not. In 2012, Alabama and Notre Dame met with a national title on the line, just like they did in the 1970s. The Ohio State Buckeyes went undefeated, just like they had in 2002, 1973, 1968, 1961, 1954, 1944, et cetera. The final AP top five featured No. 1 Alabama (ninth AP national title, 15th claimed title, third BCS championship in four years), No. 2 Oregon (third consecutive top-four finish, eighth top-12 finish in 13 years), No. 3 Ohio State (12th time in the top three, ninth top-10 finish in 11 years), No. 4 Notre Dame (19th top-four finish), and No. 5 Georgia (10th top-five finish, fifth top-10 finish since 2002). The ground beneath our feet is shifting, but we're still looking up at the same name-brand programs. Sure, a redshirt freshman won the Heisman Trophy for the first time (Texas A&M's Johnny Manziel), and sure, less-than-name brands like Kansas State and Stanford had a role to play in the national title race. But the finish felt awfully familiar.

In our final year B.P. (Before Playoff), are we to expect anything different? Probably not. Your BCS conference favorites are Alabama (SEC), Ohio State (Big Ten), Florida State (ACC), Oregon (Pac-12), Oklahoma State (Big 12), and Louisville (American). All six of those teams have won a conference title in the last two years, three are longtime college football blue bloods, and a fourth (Oregon) has joined the club over the last decade.

The College Football Playoff may change how the regular season unfolds in front of us, but if you are a college football fan, your attention is only slightly tuned to the final act. It's the journey that is so strange and enlightening. The 2013 season may finish with familiar names at the top, as 2012 did, and as 2011 did before it, but we still have plenty of things to look forward to: this year's version of the Texas A&M-over-Alabama upset; this year's Manziel-esque Heisman upstart; this year's tantalizing (and probably brief) run of an out-of-nowhere upstart to near the top of the polls (we've got our eyes on you and your 10.4 projected wins, Cincinnati); and this year's surprising disappointment (sorry, Louisville). We will be entertained. And one of these years, we might even get an entertaining national title game to boot. Hey, there have been plenty of lackluster Super Bowls, too, right?

For 10 years, Brian Fremeau has been developing and tweaking the drive-based Fremeau Efficiency Index (FEI) and its companion statistics; for the last six years, Bill Connelly's research has explored play-by-play data, developing measures of efficiency and explosiveness and creating his system, the S&P+ ratings. In January 2013, he began to include a drive component in the overall S&P+ numbers as well. Both systems are schedule-adjusted and effective in both evaluating teams and uncovering strengths and weaknesses. The combination of the two ratings, known as F/+, provides the best of both worlds.

The College Statistical Toolbox section that follows this introduction explains the methodology of FEI, S&P+, F/+ and other stats you will encounter in the college chapters of this book. There are similarities to Football Outsiders' NFL-based DVOA ratings in the combined approach, but college football presents a unique set of challenges different from the NFL. All football stats must be adjusted according to context, but how? If Team A and Team B do not play one another and don't share any common opponents, how can their stats be effectively compared? Should a team from the SEC or Big 12 be measured against that of an average team in its own conference, or an average FBS team? With eight years of full data, we are still only scratching the surface with these measures, but the recent progress has been both swift and exciting.

This book devotes a chapter to each of the six BCS conferences (though "BCS" will soon become an outdated acronym), and a seventh chapter covering the best of the non-AQ teams. The chapters provide a snapshot of each team's statistical profile in 2012 and projections for 2013, along with a summary of its keys to the upcoming season. Player and coaching personnel changes, offensive and defensive advantages and deficiencies, and schedule highlights and pitfalls are all discussed by our team of college football writers. The top prospects for the 2014 NFL Draft are listed at the end of each team segment. An asterisk denotes a player who may or may not enter the draft as a junior eligible.

Each chapter concludes with a Win Probability table. For each of the 125 FBS teams, we project the likelihood of every possible regular season record, conference and non-conference alike. We hope the Win Probability tables provide a broader understanding of our projections and the impact of strength of schedule on team records.

By taking two different statistical approaches to reach one exciting series of answers to college football's most important questions, we feel we are at the forefront of the ongoing debates. Enjoy the college football section of *Football Outsiders Almanac 2013*, and join us at www.FootballOutsiders.com/ college throughout the season.

College Statistics Toolbox

Regular readers of FootballOutsiders.com may be familiar with the FEI and Varsity Numbers columns and their respective stats published throughout the year. Others may be learning about our advanced approach to college football stats analysis for the first time by reading this book. In either case, this College Statistics Toolbox section is highly recommended reading before getting into the conference chapters. The stats that form the building blocks for F/+, FEI, and S&P+ are constantly being updated and refined.

Each team profile in the conference chapters begins with a statistical snapshot (defending BCS champion Alabama is presented here as a sample). Within each chapter, teams are organized by division (or conference in the final chapter) and Projected F/+ rank. The projected overall and conference records—rounded from the team's projected Mean Wins—are listed alongside the team name in the header. Estimates of offensive and defensive starters returning in 2012 were collected from team websites, spring media guides, and other reliable sources. All other stats and rankings provided in the team snapshot are explained below.

Drive-by-Drive Data

Fremeau Efficiency Index: Fremeau Efficiency Index (FEI) analysis begins with drive data instead of play-by-play data and is processed according to key principles. A team is rewarded for playing well against a strong opponent, win or lose, and is pun-

ished more severely for playing poorly against bad teams than it is rewarded for playing well against bad teams.

To calculate FEI, the nearly 20,000 possessions in every season of major college football are filtered to eliminate first-half clock-kills and end-of-game garbage drives and scores. A scoring rate analysis of the remaining possessions then determines the baseline possession efficiency expectations against which each team is measured. Game Efficiency is the composite possession-by-possession efficiency of a team over the course of a game, a measurement of the success of its offensive, defensive, and special teams units' essential goals: to maximize the team's own scoring opportunities and to minimize those of its opponent. Finally, each team's FEI rating synthesizes its season-long Game Efficiency data, adjusted for the strength of its opposition; special emphasis is placed on quality performance against good teams, win or lose.

Offensive and Defensive FEI: Game Efficiency is a composite assessment of the possession-by-possession performance of team over the course of a game. In order to isolate the relative performance of the offense and defense, more factors are evaluated.

First, we ran a regression on the national scoring rates of tens of thousands of college football drives according to starting field position. The result represents the value of field position in terms of points expected to be scored by an average offense against an average defense—1.4 points per possession from its own 15-yard line, 2.3 points per possession from its own 40-yard line, and so on. These expected points are called Field Position Value (FPV).

Next, we ran a regression on the value of drive-ending field position according to national special teams scoring expectations. To determine the true national baseline for field-goal range, we took into account not only the 2200 field goals attempted annually, but also the 1400 punts kicked from opponent territory each year. In other words, if a team has an average field-goal unit and a coach with an average penchant for risk-taking, the offensive value of reaching the opponent's 35-yard line is equal to the number of made field goals from that distance divided by the number of attempts plus the number of punts from that distance.

Touchdowns credit the offense with 6.96 points of drive-ending value, the value of a touchdown adjusted according to national point-after rates. Safeties have a drive-ending value of negative two points. All other offensive results are credited with a drive-ending value of zero.

No. 1 Alabama Crimson Tide (12-0, 8-0)

2012: 13-1 (7-1) / F/+ #1 / FEI #1 / S&P+ #1

Program F/+	+42.1%	1	Returning Starters: 6 OFF, 7 DEF			2012 Field Position / Special Teams		
2012 Offense			2012 Defense			Special Teams F/+	+1.7%	28
Offensive F/+	**+21.1%**	**2**	**Defensive F/+**	**+27.8%**	**1**	Field Position Advantage	0.555	6
Offensive FEI:	0.533	5	Defensive FEI	-0.657	4	2013 Projections		
Offensive S&P+	147.7	4	Defensive S&P+	164.6	1	**Mean Wins / Mean Conference Wins**	**11.8 / 7.8**	
Rushing S&P+	137.4	4	Rushing S&P+	159.6	1	Proj. F/+	+38.9%	1
Passing S&P+	132.0	6	Passing S&P+	143.7	4	Offensive F/+	+16.5%	1
Standard Downs S&P+	124.8	9	Standard Downs S&P+	148.2	1	Defensive F/+	+22.3%	1
Passing Downs S&P+	154.1	3	Passing Downs S&P+	147.5	3	Strength of Sched. Rk / Conf. Title Odds	51 / 65.7%	

Offensive efficiency is then calculated as the total drive-ending value earned by the offense divided by the sum of its offensive FPV over the course of the game. Defensive efficiency is calculated the same way using the opponent's offensive drive-ending value and FPV. Offensive and defensive efficiency are calibrated as a rating above or below zero—a good offense has a positive rating and a good defense has a negative one. These numbers are represented in the college chapters as Unadjusted Offense and Unadjusted Defense.

Offensive FEI and Defensive FEI are the opponent-adjusted values of offensive and defensive efficiency. As with FEI, the adjustments are weighted according to both the strength of the opponent and the relative significance of the result. Efficiency against a team's best competition is given more relevance weight in the formula.

Field Position Advantage (FPA): FPA was developed in order to more accurately describe the management of field position over the course of a game. For each team, we calculate the sum of the FPV for each of its offensive series. Then, we add in a full touchdown value (6.96 points) for each non-offensive score earned by the team. (This accounts for the field position value of special teams and defensive returns reaching the end zone versus tripping up at the one-yard line.) Special teams turnovers and onside kicks surrendered have an FPV of zero. The sum of the FPV of every possession in the game for both teams represents the total field position at stake in the contest. FPA represents each given team's share of that total field position.

FPA is a description of which team controlled field position in the game and by how much. Two teams that face equal field position over the course of a game will each have an FPA of .500. Winning the field position battle is quite valuable. College football teams that play with an FPA over .500 win two-thirds of the time. Teams that play with an FPA over .600 win 90 percent of the time.

Other drive-based terms and definitions include:

• **Available Yards** are yards gained by the offense divided by the total yards available on each drive, measured from starting field position to end zone.
• **Explosive Drives** are possessions that average at least 10 yards per play.
• **Methodical Drives** are possessions that last at least 10 plays.
• **Value Drives** are possessions that begin on a team's own side of the field and minimally reach the opponent's 30-yard line, moving from non-scoring position to scoring position.

Play-by-Play Data

Success Rates: Our play-by-play analysis was introduced throughout the 2008 season in Bill Connelly's Varsity Numbers columns. Nearly one million plays over eight seasons in college football have been collected and evaluated to determine baselines for success for every situational down in a game. Similarly to DVOA, basic success rates are determined by national standards. The distinction for college football is in defining the standards of success. We use the following determination of a "successful" play:

• First down success = 50 percent of necessary yardage
• Second down success = 70 percent of necessary yardage
• Third/Fourth down success = 100 percent of necessary yardage

On a per play basis, these form the standards of efficiency for every offense in college football. Defensive success rates are based on preventing the same standards of achievement.

Equivalent Points and Points per Play: All yards are not created equal. A 10-yard gain from a team's own 15-yard line does not have the same value as a 10-yard gain that goes from the opponent's 10-yard line into the end zone. Based on expected scoring rates similar to FPV described above, we can calculate a point value for each play in a drive. Equivalent Points (EqPts) are calculated by subtracting the value of the resulting yard line from the initial yard line of a given play. This assigns credit to the yards that are most associated with scoring points, the end goal in any possession.

With EqPts, the game can be broken down and built back up again in a number of ways. With the addition of penalties, turnovers and special teams play, EqPts provides an accurate assessment of how a game was played on a play-by-play basis. We also use it to create a measure called Points per Play (PPP), representative of a team's or an individual player's explosiveness.

S&P: Like OPS (on-base percentage plus slugging average) in baseball, we created a measure that combines consistency with power. S&P represents a combination of efficiency (Success Rates) and explosiveness (Points per Play) to most accurately represent the effectiveness of a team or individual player.

A boom-or-bust running back may have a strong yards per carry average and PPP, but his low Success Rate will lower his S&P. A consistent running back that gains between four and six yards every play, on the other hand, will have a strong Success Rate but possibly low PPP. The best offenses in the country can maximize both efficiency and explosiveness on a down-by-down basis. Reciprocally, the best defenses can limit both.

S&P+: As with the FEI stats discussed above, context matters in college football. Adjustments are made to the S&P unadjusted data with a formula that takes into account a team's production, the quality of the opponent, and the quality of the opponent's opponent. To eliminate the noise of less-informative blowout stats, we filtered the play-by-play data to include only those that took place when the game was "close." This excludes plays where the score margin is larger than 28 points in the first quarter, 24 points in the second quarter, 21 points in the third quarter, or 16 points in the fourth quarter.

Beginning in 2013, we also factored in a drive efficiency measure that is calculated in a similar fashion PPP, by comparing the expected value of a given drive (based on starting field position) to the actual value a team produces and adjusting it for the opponent at hand. The ability to finish drives is a singular skill that isn't perfectly encapsulated in a measure that only looks at play-by-play data.

The combination of the play-by-play and drive data gives us S&P+, a comprehensive measure that represents a team's efficiency and explosiveness as compared to all other teams in college football. S&P+ values are calibrated around an average rating of 100. An above-average team, offensively or defensively, will have an S&P+ rating greater than 100. A below-average team will have an S&P+ rating lower than 100.

In the team capsules in each conference chapter, the S&P+ ratings are broken down further as follows:

• Rushing S&P+ includes only running plays, and unlike standard college statistics, does not include sacks.
• Passing S&P+ includes sacks and passing plays.
• Passing Downs S&P+ includes second-and-8 or more, third-and-5 or more, and fourth-and-5 or more. These divisions were determined based on raw S&P data showing a clear distinction in Success Rates as compared with Standard Downs.
• Standard Downs S&P+ includes all close-game plays not defined as Passing Downs.

These measures are all derived only from play-by-play data; drive efficiency data is only factored into the final, overall S&P+ figure.

POE and Adj. POE: The collegiate stepchild of DYAR, POE stands for Points Over Expected. It is a running back-specific measure that compares a runner's EqPts output to what an average back would have done with carries in the same situations against the same opponents. The Adj. POE figure, used most in these chapters, adjusts POE to account for the relative strength (or weakness) of the offensive line.

Adjusted Line Yards: Line Yards are derived the same for college as they are at the pro level, with 100 percent of gains 0-4 yards credit to the offensive line and 50 percent of the gains from five to 10 yards. The line yardage averages are then adjusted for the quality of the opponent.

Adjusted Sack Rate: Adjusted Sack Rate is look at sack rates (sacks divided by passes plus sacks) adjusted for opponent.

Highlight Yards: Highlight yards represent the yards gained by a runner outside of those credited to the offensive line through Adjusted Line Yards. If a runner gains 12 yards in a given carry, and we attribute 7.0 of those yards to the line (the line yardage formula gives 100 percent credit to all yards gained between zero and four yards and 50 percent strength between five and 10), then the player's highlight yardage on the play is 5.0 yards. Beginning in 2013, we are calculating highlight yardage averages in a slightly different manner: Instead of dividing total highlight yardage by a player's overall number of carries, we are dividing it only by the number of carries that gain more than four yards; if a line is given all credit for gains smaller than that, then it makes sense to look at highlight averages for only the carries in which a runner got a chance to create a highlight.

Adjusted Points: Taking a team's single-game S&P+ for both offense and defense, and applying it to a normal distribution of points scored in a given season, can give us an interesting, descriptive look at a team's performance in a given game and season. Adjusting for pace and opponent, Adjusted Score asks the same question of every team in every game: if Team A had played a perfectly average opponent in a given game, how would they have fared? Adjusted Score allows us to look at in-season trends as well, since the week-to-week baseline is opponent-independent.

Combination Data

F/+: The F/+ measure combines FEI and S&P+. There is a clear distinction between the two individual approaches, and merging the two diminishes certain outliers caused by the quirks of each method. The resulting metric is both powerfully predictive and sensibly evaluative.

Program and Projected F/+: Relative to the pros, college football teams are much more consistent in year-to-year performance. Breakout seasons and catastrophic collapses certainly occur, but generally speaking, teams can be expected to play within a reasonable range of their baseline program expectations. The idea of a Football Outsiders program rating began with the introduction of Program FEI in *Pro Football Prospectus 2008* as a way to represent those individual baseline expectations.

As the strength of the F/+ system has been fortified with more seasons of full drive-by-drive and play-by-play data, the Program F/+ measure has emerged. Program F/+ is calculated from five years of FEI and S&P+ data. The result not only represents the status of each team's program power, but provides the first step in projecting future success.

The Projected F/+ found in the following chapters starts by combining Program F/+ (weighted more toward recent seasons) with measures of two-year recruiting success (using Rivals.com ratings for signees who actually ended up enrolling at each school) and offensive and defensive performance. We adjust that baseline with transition factors like returning offensive and defensive starters, talent lost to the NFL Draft, and disproportional success on passing downs. The result, Projected F/+, is a more accurate predictor of next-year success than any other data we have tested or used to date.

Strength of Schedule: Unlike other rating systems, our Strength of Schedule (SOS) calculation is not a simple average of the Projected FEI data of each team's opponents. Instead, it is calculated from a "privileged" perspective, representing the likelihood that an elite team (typical top-five team) would win every game on the given schedule. The distinction is valid. For any elite team, playing No. 1 Alabama and No. 125 Massachusetts in a two-game stretch is certainly more difficult than playing No. 62 Indiana and No. 63 Toledo. An average rating might judge these schedules to be equal.

The likelihood of an undefeated season is calculated as the product of Projected Win Expectations (PWE) for each game on the schedule. PWEs are based on an assessment of five years of FEI data and the records of teams of varying strengths against one another. Roughly speaking, an elite team may have a 65 percent chance of defeating a team ranked No. 10, a 75 percent chance of defeating a team ranked No. 20, and a 90 percent chance of defeating a team ranked No. 40. Combined, the elite team has a 44 percent likelihood of defeating all three (0.65 x 0.75 x 0.90 = 0.439).

A lower SOS rating represents a lower likelihood of an elite team running the table—a stronger schedule. For our calculations of FBS versus FCS games, the win likelihood is considered to be 100 percent for top-40 teams, and tails off to 85-90 percent for the worst FBS teams.

Mean Wins , Win Distributions, and Conference Title Probabilities: To project records for each team, we use Projected F/+ and PWE formulas to estimate the likelihood of victory for a given team in its individual games. The probabilities for winning each game are added together to repre-sent the average number of wins the team is expected to tally over the course of its scheduled games. Potential conference championship games and bowl games are not included in the mean wins projection.

The projected records listed next to each team name in the conference chapters are rounded from the mean wins data listed in the team capsule. Mean Wins are not intended to repre-sent projected outcomes of specific matchups, rather they are our most accurate forecast for the team's season as a whole. The correlation of mean wins to actual wins is 0.69 for all games, 0.61 for conference games.

The Win Distribution tables that appear in each conference chapter are also based on the game-by-game PWE data for each team. The likelihood for each record is rounded to the nearest whole percent. Based on the PWE data, we also calculated the likelihood that each team would win a conference title, including a conference championship game when applicable.

Brian Fremeau and Bill Connelly

American Athletic Conference

Over the last several years, the Big East Conference had been the weakest of the "Big Six" BCS automatic qualifying leagues. The preseason Associated Press top-25 rankings over the last four years included only four Big East teams total. In the final F/+ rankings at the end of each of the last four seasons, only six total Big East teams were in the top 25. Of those teams, only Cincinnati (No. 18 in 2009, No. 23 in 2011) is still in the league.

West Virginia (Big 12), Pittsburgh (ACC), and Syracuse (ACC) were poached by "Big Five" conferences in the last two seasons, and Louisville (to the ACC) and Rutgers (to the Big Ten) will make the jump next year. The teams that remain added a few new faces from Conference USA and a few new travel miles for conference play. Houston, SMU, Memphis, and Central Florida are new members this fall and expand the diameter of the conference footprint to 1750 miles, from Storrs, Connecticut, to Houston, Texas.

The new footprint is Big, but it ain't really East, so the league rebranded itself starting in 2013 as the American Athletic Conference. For one more year of the BCS system, the conference holds on to its privileged position with an automatic qualifying bid to a BCS bowl and the payday that comes along with it. In terms of actual competition, the old Big East's credibility problem has nothing on the American's.

Our F/+ projections include zero American teams in the top 25 and only three in the top 50. The lack of competition in the conference is aggravated by mostly pathetic non-conference schedules as well. Three American teams will play non-conference schedules ranked among the bottom 25 in FBS, including conference favorites Cincinnati and Louisville. Six American programs will play the 2013 season with an overall SOS ranked 95th or worse.

Weak schedules do present an opportunity for the conference favorites to win a lot of games, of course. Cincinnati and Louisville are both ranked among the top 15 in mean wins, and the polls tend to reward ones and zeroes in the loss column with higher rankings than our opponent-adjusted metrics do. The Bearcats and Cardinals also won't play one another until the final weekend of the year. If they remain undefeated until then, both could be ranked highly enough to throw a wrench in one last round of BCS chaos, deserving or not.

No. 26 Cincinnati Bearcats (10-2, 7-1)
2012: 10-3 (5-2) / F/+ #26 / FEI #20 / S&P+ #49

Program F/+	+12.0%	27	Returning Starters: 8 OFF, 6 DEF			2012 Field Position / Special Teams		
2012 Offense			2012 Defense			Special Teams F/+	+0.0%	60
Offensive F/+	+6.2%	35	Defensive F/+	+8.2%	29	Field Position Advantage	0.534	22
Offensive FEI:	0.246	27	Defensive FEI	-0.491	13	2013 Projections		
Offensive S&P+	110.6	49	Defensive S&P+	102.9	68	Mean Wins / Mean Conference Wins	10.4 / 6.6	
Rushing S&P+	107.8	44	Rushing S&P+	86.7	110	Proj. F/+	+12.2%	26
Passing S&P+	104.1	51	Passing S&P+	92.2	86	Offensive F/+	+6.2%	26
Standard Downs S&P+	106.0	44	Standard Downs S&P+	86.0	114	Defensive F/+	+6.0%	27
Passing Downs S&P+	106.5	53	Passing Downs S&P+	101.5	60	Strength of Sched. Rk / Conf. Title Odds	111 / 53.8%	

The last time the Cincinnati Bearcats had to make a change at head coach, it was a rocky transition. Following Brian Kelly's departure at the end of an undefeated 2009 regular season, the Bearcats posted only three FBS wins in their next 13 games before Butch Jones righted the ship with back-to-back conference co-championship honors and a pair of second-tier bowl wins. In the wake of Jones' departure to Tennessee, Tommy Tuberville takes the reins and inherits a cupboard stocked well enough to claim another conference crown.

First he has to name a starting quarterback from two senior options. Brendan Kay took over the starting duties late in 2012 and was a more efficient passer than Munchie Legeaux, the undersized but fleet-footed starter he replaced. Kay likely has the edge for keeping the job in 2013, but both seniors might both see the field this fall. They'll be playing behind the most experienced offensive line in the conference, with all five starters back to a unit that ranked 33rd in Adjusted Line Yards and 27th in Adjusted Sack Rate. Tackle Eric Lefeld and guard Austen Bujnoch were named to the all-conference team

and Parker Ehringer earned freshman All-American honors at right tackle last season. The Bearcats are replacing a 1,000-yard rusher for the second-straight season, but junior Ralph David Abernathy IV will step into the starting role and should make it three in a row. Cincinnati is also replacing three of its top four receivers from last season, a position that may be a weak spot for the Bearcats this fall. Senior wideout Anthony McClung has the most experience (107 career receptions), but his 51 percent catch rate last season was among the lowest on the roster.

The defense will be anchored by an experienced linebacker crew led by Greg Blair, whose 138 tackles ranked as the sixth best tally nationally. Blair had more tackles than any other two returning Bearcats combined to produce last season. The pressure will be on the defensive line following the graduation of a pair of defensive ends that produced 10 sacks a year ago. There are also holes in the secondary, a unit that helped the Bearcats earn positive turnover value in eight of 11 games last season. Few American offenses are projected to be particularly prolific this year though, so growing pains along the line and in the secondary may be tolerable before the late-season showdowns with Houston and Louisville. Cincinnati will help itself once again by forcing long fields. The Bearcats ranked fourth in opponent starting field position and 10th in opponent points per value drive (4.0) last fall.

For all the success Cincinnati has had recently—four 10-plus win seasons in the last five years—they remain relatively off the radar and will be fighting for respect all season. They start at the pole position in the league as far as F/+ is con-

cerned, but they won't have opportunities to move up without dominating week in and week out. The Bearcats won't face a top-50 opponent until November 16 (No. 48 Rutgers), and without star playmakers they won't get much media exposure to boost their voted poll profile either. Perhaps they'll be content to just keep on winning—for another three years or so before their new coach leaps to a bigger job and the cycle resets.

Top 2014 NFL Prospects: *ILB Greg Blair (2-3), G Austen Bujnoch (4-5)*

No. 31 Louisville Cardinals (10-2, 6-2)
2012: 11-2 (5-2) / F/+ #28 / FEI #28 / S&P+ #39

Program F/+	-0.3%	57	Returning Starters: 6 OFF, 9 DEF			2012 Field Position / Special Teams		
2012 Offense			**2012 Defense**			Special Teams F/+	-3.0%	115
Offensive F/+	**+13.8%**	**10**	Defensive F/+	+2.9%	48	Field Position Advantage	0.48	89
Offensive FEI:	0.614	3	Defensive FEI	-0.169	44	**2013 Projections**		
Offensive S&P+	115.8	36	Defensive S&P+	103.4	59	**Mean Wins / Mean Conference Wins**	**9.5 / 5.8**	
Rushing S&P+	101.0	60	Rushing S&P+	91.1	90	Proj. F/+	+9.8%	31
Passing S&P+	121.6	16	Passing S&P+	103.1	50	Offensive F/+	+6.1%	27
Standard Downs S&P+	112.3	29	Standard Downs S&P+	96.1	79	Defensive F/+	+3.7%	37
Passing Downs S&P+	118.5	25	Passing Downs S&P+	99.6	68	Strength of Sched. Rk / Conf. Title Odds	101 / 24.3%	

Louisville athletics programs are riding a remarkable wave of success. A Final Four appearance for its women's basketball program and a national championship for its men's basketball program came on the heels of an impressive Sugar Bowl victory over then-No. 3 Florida by the Cardinals football program. Louisville has positioned itself as a preseason top-10 team in many polls, and its star quarterback is garnering attention as both a Heisman Trophy favorite and a potential first-overall draft pick next spring. It is a good time to be a Louisville fan.

F/+ is not a Louisville fan.

Don't get us wrong, our projections (and our eyes) like quarterback Teddy Bridgewater a lot. As a sophomore last season, Bridgewater ranked eighth nationally in pass efficiency, throwing for 3718 yards with 27 touchdowns and eight interceptions. Louisville's passing game ranked 16th in S&P+, best in the conference by a significant margin. Bridgewater's arm strength and accuracy (68.5 percent) have pro scouts salivating, and he has seven of his eight favorite receivers from last season back in the fold. Bridgewater accounted for 71.3 percent of Louisville's total offense last season, a mark that may elevate into the high 70s this year, especially if the offensive game plan includes a bit of Heisman highlight ballot stuffing. Bridgewater will be one of the most exciting players to watch this season, and there aren't many challenging opponents that stand in the way of a trip to New York at the end of the regular season.

The problem is that Bridgewater was a dynamic talent last season too, but Louisville didn't dominate in all phases offensively. Louisville ranked outside the top 25 in drive efficiency (27th), three-and-outs (30th), explosive drives (33rd) and offensive S&P+ (36th). A rebuilt offensive line will be tested by

strong defenses throughout the American conference. If Louisville wants to be a contender, a strong passing game won't be enough.

Linebacker Preston Brown leads an experienced front seven, but one that needs to step up production (83rd in Adjusted Sack Rate, 89th in Adjusted Line Yards) in order to get opponents off the field sooner and position Bridgewater and the offense for more success. Louisville gave up 45 percent of available yards in 2012 (54th fewest nationally), a factor in the Cardinals' No. 89 ranking in field-position advantage. Another big factor was poor punt, kickoff, and kickoff return teams, all units that ranked 107th or worse last fall. The Cardinals also need to worry about the turnover pendulum swinging out of their favor this year. They won five games last season in which the turnover value they generated exceeded the scoring margin in the game, and only lost once in which poor turnover results cost them the game. In other words, in a turnover-neutral environment, Louisville played more like a .500 team than an 11-win one.

We have a pretty good track record in cases in which our F/+ projections undercut teams loaded with preseason hype. In Louisville's case, there are few impediments to a great record, but even an undefeated run deep into November might not mean the Cardinals are deserving of top-10 hype. Louisville may field the nation's best player in 2013, but he wasn't enough to dominate a schedule loaded with weaklings last year. Our model wonders why this year will be much different.

Top 2014 NFL Prospects: *QB Teddy Bridgewater* (1), S Hakeem Smith (1-2), ILB Preston Brown (4-5)*

No. 48 Rutgers Scarlet Knights (7-5, 4-4)

2012: 9-4 (5-2) / F/+ #39 / FEI #34 / S&P+ #45

Program F/+	+4.3%	45	Returning Starters: 6 OFF, 4 DEF			2012 Field Position / Special Teams		
2012 Offense			**2012 Defense**			Special Teams F/+	-0.1%	67
Offensive F/+	**-5.4%**	**84**	**Defensive F/+**	**+15.1%**	**11**	Field Position Advantage	0.509	51
Offensive FEI:	-0.156	80	Defensive FEI	-0.591	7	**2013 Projections**		
Offensive S&P+	93.1	104	Defensive S&P+	122.2	28	**Mean Wins / Mean Conference Wins**	**7.4 / 4.5**	
Rushing S&P+	78.8	118	Rushing S&P+	127.8	6	Proj. F/+	+4.2%	48
Passing S&P+	91.3	89	Passing S&P+	106.2	41	Offensive F/+	-1.9%	71
Standard Downs S&P+	87.5	109	Standard Downs S&P+	117.9	17	Defensive F/+	+6.1%	26
Passing Downs S&P+	84.0	108	Passing Downs S&P+	109.1	36	Strength of Sched. Rk / Conf. Title Odds	96 / 6.1%	

The Scarlet Knights have been playing college football longer than any other FBS program, but they don't have much historical success worth celebrating over the last 143 years. Rutgers ran out to a 9-1 start in 2012 before dropping each of its last three games, including a bowl loss to Virginia Tech. That kept the Scarlet Knights from earning double-digit wins for only the third time ever. After a Rutgers-record seven players were drafted this past spring, a step back is expected this fall and the 10-win barrier will have to wait before falling once again.

The heaviest personnel losses will be felt on defense. Five of the seven Rutgers players drafted were defensive standouts, including three starters in the secondary and linebacker Khaseem Greene, the Chicago fourth-round pick who led the team in tackles in each of the last two seasons. Rutgers ranked in the top 10 in points surrendered per drive (1.2 in 2012, No. 6 overall) and were exceptionally stout in shutting down scoring opportunities, ranking No. 1 overall in opponent points per value drive (3.1). Twin brothers Jamal (linebacker) and Jamil (defensive end) Merrell bring senior experience to the front seven, and converted wide receiver Jeremy Deering can be a playmaker at safety. (As a two-way player for Rutgers, he's probably already fitted for a New England Patriots uniform.) The Scarlet Knights gave up more than 20 points only three times last season. With new faces all over the defense, they will be hard pressed to perform as consistently.

The offense will be looking for more production as well, especially in the running game. The Scarlet Knights had a 1,000-yard rusher in Jawan Jamison (now with the Redskins) in 2012, but he didn't find the end zone with much frequency. Rutgers had just six rushing touchdowns and ranked 118th in rushing S&P+. Rutgers is hoping junior Savon Huggins fulfills his four-star recruit potential and makes the running game a fixture of a productive offensive identity. Huggins was a workhorse with 41 carries for 179 yards in a low-scoring win over Cincinnati last year, but he only had 26 carries over the final three games and he missed the second half of 2011 with a knee injury. Quarterback Gary Nova is back along with top receiver Brandon Coleman (16.7 yards per catch), and an improved passing game will be necessary to open up opportunities for Huggins.

Top 2014 NFL Prospects: *S Jeremy Deering (4-5), G Antwan Lowery (4-5), DE Jamil Merrell (6-7)*

No. 53 Connecticut Huskies (7-5, 4-4)

2012: 5-7 (2-5) / F/+ #61 / FEI #64 / S&P+ #68

Program F/+	+4.6%	43	Returning Starters: 8 OFF, 5 DEF			2012 Field Position / Special Teams		
2012 Offense			**2012 Defense**			Special Teams F/+	+0.9%	45
Offensive F/+	**-10.1%**	**107**	**Defensive F/+**	**+9.2%**	**26**	Field Position Advantage	0.505	53
Offensive FEI:	-0.349	108	Defensive FEI	-0.398	22	**2013 Projections**		
Offensive S&P+	87.6	112	Defensive S&P+	112.2	38	**Mean Wins / Mean Conference Wins**	**7.3 / 4.4**	
Rushing S&P+	71.8	123	Rushing S&P+	124.3	10	Proj. F/+	+2.3%	53
Passing S&P+	90.7	92	Passing S&P+	111.5	30	Offensive F/+	-2.7%	81
Standard Downs S&P+	78.6	121	Standard Downs S&P+	125.5	6	Defensive F/+	+4.9%	31
Passing Downs S&P+	93.1	88	Passing Downs S&P+	104.6	51	Strength of Sched. Rk / Conf. Title Odds	95 / 5.0%	

Like Rutgers, the Connecticut Huskies are facing unprecedented talent turnover after a school-record five players were taken in the NFL draft, including four defensive starters taken in the third and fourth rounds. The notable players back on the field this fall include junior linebacker Yawin Smallwood, who led the team in tackles (120) and ranked second in tackles for loss (15) a year ago. Connecticut's defense was ruthlessly efficient against the run, allowing only 2.7 yards per attempt (second nationally) and ranking 10th in defensive rushing S&P+. They posted top-10 ranks in forcing three-and-outs (44 percent of opponent drives) and limiting available yards (33.5 percent).

The defense needs to be strong once again for Connecticut to improve, but that's not where we expect the biggest change in 2013. The Huskies held six opponents to 17 points or fewer last year, and still lost three of those games because the offense was inept. Connecticut ranked 120th in scoring (17.8 points per game) and 121st in standard downs S&P+, gaining only 88 rushing yards per game and ranking 92nd or worse in every offensive drive efficiency metric we track. Pretty much everyone is back this season, which in and of itself might not be reason for optimism. New offensive coordinator T.J. Weist is introducing an energetic, up-tempo pace that is expected to spark the production of quarterback Chandler Whitmer, running back Lyle McCombs, and wide receiver Geremy Davis. McCombs had strong outings in upset wins over Pittsburgh and Louisville last season.

The Huskies host Maryland and Michigan early in the season, and Rentschler Field hasn't played host to many easy victories for Big Six non-conference opponents in the last few seasons. Our model gives Connecticut a 29 percent chance of winning both games—the game against the Wolverines is one of the few opportunities for the American Conference to notch a notable non-conference victory.

Top 2014 NFL Prospects: *None*

No. 55 Central Florida Golden Knights (7-5, 5-3)

2012: 10-4 (7-1 in Conference USA) / F/+ #36 / FEI #35 / S&P+ #38

Program F/+	+1.3%	54	Returning Starters: 6 OFF, 5 DEF			2012 Field Position / Special Teams		
2012 Offense			**2012 Defense**			Special Teams F/+	+2.2%	16
Offensive F/+	**+4.2%**	**45**	Defensive F/+	+4.2%	42	Field Position Advantage	0.541	13
Offensive FEI:	0.094	48	Defensive FEI	-0.191	40	**2013 Projections**		
Offensive S&P+	112.6	39	Defensive S&P+	106.8	46	**Mean Wins / Mean Conference Wins**	**7.0 / 4.9**	
Rushing S&P+	116.2	19	Rushing S&P+	97.7	67	Proj. F/+	+1.9%	55
Passing S&P+	104.6	48	Passing S&P+	104.3	48	Offensive F/+	+1.3%	52
Standard Downs S&P+	107.8	40	Standard Downs S&P+	103.0	54	Defensive F/+	+0.6%	56
Passing Downs S&P+	114.3	35	Passing Downs S&P+	97.4	74	Strength of Sched. Rk / Conf. Title Odds	81 / 7.3%	

The Knights have the best projection among the American Conference newcomers, having won ten games and an East division title a year ago in Conference USA. None of UCF's victories last season came against a top-60 opponent, however, so there will be some modest growing pains with a move up in overall competition level.

The offense is led by junior quarterback Blake Bortles, an accurate passer who may rank behind only Louisville's Bridgewater in conference accolades this fall. He's currently riding a streak of 174 consecutive passes without throwing an interception, and he accounted for 13 passing touchdowns and five rushing touchdowns in the same span. His top four receivers from last season are all back this fall, and big things are expected from juniors Rannell Hall (63 percent catch rate, 18.0 yards per catch) and J.J. Worton (13.5 yards per catch). The running game will need work, with a new starter in Storm Johnson running behind a rebuilt offensive line. The Knights produced 2,545 yards and 33 touchdowns on the ground last season, good for the 19th best rushing attack according to S&P+ but only the 58th best unit in Adjusted Line Yards.

There are question marks on defense as well. UCF is replacing its best pass rusher and four of its top six tacklers from last season. Junior linebacker Terrance Plummer (108 tackles, seven for loss) is the most experienced returning starter in the front seven. The Knights allowed methodical drives on 17 percent of opponent possessions last year (No. 95 nationally), but did find some success in limiting opponent scoring at the end of scoring opportunities (11th in points allowed per value drive).

There are a handful of American teams projected to rank between No. 48 and No. 64, and the model likes them all to finish at about .500 in conference play. Central Florida has an edge since they are the only team in that group that won't have to face both conference contenders, skipping Cincinnati.

Top 2014 NFL Prospects: *None*

No. 58 Houston Cougars (7-5, 4-4)

2012: 5-7 (4-4 in Conference USA) / F/+ #80 / FEI #84 / S&P+ #70

Program F/+	+4.8%	40	Returning Starters: 9 OFF, 5 DEF			2012 Field Position / Special Teams		
2012 Offense			**2012 Defense**			Special Teams F/+	-1.7%	96
Offensive F/+	**-5.1%**	**83**	Defensive F/+	-1.3%	66	Field Position Advantage	0.462	105
Offensive FEI:	-0.212	91	Defensive FEI	0.057	70	**2013 Projections**		
Offensive S&P+	97.4	74	Defensive S&P+	101.7	62	**Mean Wins / Mean Conference Wins**	**6.9 / 4.0**	
Rushing S&P+	94.7	82	Rushing S&P+	92.5	84	Proj. F/+	+1.3%	58
Passing S&P+	90.6	93	Passing S&P+	106.0	42	Offensive F/+	+1.1%	53
Standard Downs S&P+	91.5	96	Standard Downs S&P+	102.6	55	Defensive F/+	+0.2%	60
Passing Downs S&P+	101.1	68	Passing Downs S&P+	95.3	79	Strength of Sched. Rk / Conf. Title Odds	97 / 2.2%	

A dip in production was to be expected last year following the departure of head coach Kevin Sumlin to Texas A&M and the graduation of the all-time leader in total passing yards, quarterback Case Keenum. The passing game and offensive production took a big step back, but the Cougars are ready to rebound: every playmaker from a year ago is back after a year of experience and growing pains.

Quarterback David Piland will keep his job to start the year, but may find a quick hook from new offensive coordinator Doug Meachem if his accuracy doesn't improve. He threw 12 interceptions, nine of which came in 30-point blowout losses to UCLA, SMU, and Tulsa. Houston's passing game featured the fourth most pass attempts in FBS (591), but Piland's completion percentage (57.1) was a far cry from the 70 percent marks consistently produced by his predecessor. As we learned from his stint at Oklahoma State, Meachem demands high volume and high accuracy from the quarterback position. The Houston receivers are an athletic, dynamic group—seven different receivers caught at least three touchdown passes last season and all but one is back. A pair of sophomore receivers, Deontay Greenberry (12.2 yards per catch) and Larry McDuffey (13.6 yards per catch), have major star potential.

Houston's defense has never been a team strength, but it isn't a major albatross either. Oakland first-round pick D.J. Hayden will be difficult to replace at cornerback, but sophomore safety Trevon Stewart and junior linebacker Derrick Matthews are both capable of stepping up as new stars on defense. Special teams were lousy last season (No. 96 overall), though a huge chunk of that came in a miserable performance against SMU—two fumbled punts and a fumbled kickoff that was run in for a touchdown. A young, talented team bitten by big mistakes last year has an opportunity to find consistency and bounce back this fall.

Top 2014 NFL Prospects: *None*

No. 64 Temple Owls (6-6, 4-4)

2012: 4-7 (2-5) / F/+ #84 / FEI #83 / S&P+ #92

Program F/+	-1.1%	59	Returning Starters: 8 OFF, 7 DEF		Returning Starters: 8 OFF, 7 DEF	2012 Field Position / Special Teams		
2012 Offense			**2012 Defense**			Special Teams F/+	+2.4%	13
Offensive F/+	-3.4%	76	**Defensive F/+**	-9.0%	96	Field Position Advantage	0.491	76
Offensive FEI:	-0.120	73	Defensive FEI	0.253	88	**2013 Projections**		
Offensive S&P+	98.1	71	Defensive S&P+	85.6	113	**Mean Wins / Mean Conference Wins**	6.3 / 3.5	
Rushing S&P+	114.9	21	Rushing S&P+	76.4	123	Proj. F/+	-1.9%	64
Passing S&P+	84.9	108	Passing S&P+	82.8	111	Offensive F/+	+0.7%	55
Standard Downs S&P+	100.0	63	Standard Downs S&P+	82.6	120	Defensive F/+	-2.6%	75
Passing Downs S&P+	98.2	75	Passing Downs S&P+	78.1	115	Strength of Sched. Rk / Conf. Title Odds	66 / 1.0%	

Temple never found its footing last season on either side of the ball, and it appears 2013 will be a rebuilding year as well. New head coach Matt Rhule found a new starting quarterback this spring in Connor Reilly. The junior two-sport athlete (baseball) with a strong arm but no game action to date will be thrown into the fire, with his first start coming at Notre Dame against one of the best defensive lines in the country. The running game has limited experience as well following the graduation of Montel Harris (1,054 yards, 12 touchdowns). The offensive line will feature converted tight end Cody Booth at tackle. Things could be ugly early, but Rhule is counting on these pieces to develop a new identity for the future of Temple football, growing pains and all.

Defensively, the Owls have their work cut out for themselves as well. Temple allowed explosive drives on 22.8 percent of opponent possessions (118th) and ranked 119th in opponent passer rating. The Owls hope to shore up the pass defense with new starters at safety, including true freshman Jihaad Pretlow. Linebacker Tyler Matakevich was a standout last season (101 tackles), earning Big East Freshman of the Year honors. Temple will also be breaking in a new place-kicker and punter, which likely means a drop from the Owls' 13th-ranked special teams efficiency of a year ago.

With all the youth featured in the Temple depth chart, what does the F/+ projection model like about the Owls chances to improve this fall? It basically comes down to the upward trajectory of the program. Temple ranked 119th (dead last) in Program FEI back in 2007, and they've climbed steadily ever since. Rhule was a key member of the staff over that time period, and continuity in that role can help shepherd the youth movement to modest success this fall.

Top 2014 NFL Prospects: *None*

No. 67 South Florida Bulls (5-7, 3-5)

2012: 3-9 (1-6) / F/+ #73 / FEI #73 / S&P+ #75

Program F/+	+4.0%	47	Returning Starters: 4 OFF, 6 DEF		Returning Starters: 4 OFF, 6 DEF	2012 Field Position / Special Teams		
2012 Offense			**2012 Defense**			Special Teams F/+	-1.3%	92
Offensive F/+	-1.6%	64	**Defensive F/+**	-3.3%	73	Field Position Advantage	0.435	121
Offensive FEI:	-0.021	61	Defensive FEI	0.122	77	**2013 Projections**		
Offensive S&P+	98.5	66	Defensive S&P+	98.5	71	**Mean Wins / Mean Conference Wins**	5.2 / 3.1	
Rushing S&P+	106.5	50	Rushing S&P+	107.9	38	Proj. F/+	-2.4%	67
Passing S&P+	96.3	75	Passing S&P+	98.5	64	Offensive F/+	-2.0%	73
Standard Downs S&P+	98.5	70	Standard Downs S&P+	106.9	39	Defensive F/+	-0.4%	65
Passing Downs S&P+	105.7	54	Passing Downs S&P+	95.9	77	Strength of Sched. Rk / Conf. Title Odds	67 / 0.2%	

South Florida ranked 124th out of 124 teams last season in turnover margin, with 1.7 more giveaways than takeaways per game. In nine of their 11 FBS games, all losses, USF lost turnover value, spotting its opponents an average of seven points per game due to miscues alone. If the Bulls do nothing else this season to improve other than stop shooting themselves in the foot, they could be bowl-eligible at the end of this season.

An entirely new backfield will have an opportunity to chart a new course for success at South Florida. Departed quarterback B.J. Daniels produced 10,000 yards of total offense in his career, but he was maddeningly inconsistent and responsible for a significant portion of USF's turnover woes. The spring quarterback derby didn't produce a definitive frontrunner, and a late contender arrived in May—Steven Bench, a transfer from Penn State who has immediate eligibility due to the sanctions facing the Nittany Lions program. Wide receiver Andre Davis has big play and big production potential, catching 12 balls for 191 yards and two touchdowns in a one-point win over Nevada last year. Senior running back Marcus Shaw is the most experienced back on the roster, but he has only 82 career rushing attempts.

The defensive depth chart has experience, with front seven leaders in linebacker DeDe Lattimore and defensive end Ryne Giddins. Former five-star defensive end and Freshman All-American Aaron Lynch transferred from Notre Dame last year and returns to the field after a lost year of eligibility, hungry to prove himself. All that talent up front could turn a major USF weakness (118th in forcing three-and-outs) into a strength in 2013.

Top 2014 NFL Prospects: ILB DeDe Lattimore (4-5), S Mark Joyce (6-7), DE Ryne Giddins (6-7)

No. 91 SMU Mustangs (4-8, 2-6)

2012: 7-6 (5-3 in Conference USA) / F/+ #70 / FEI #76 / S&P+ #67

Program F/+	-5.7%	75	Returning Starters: 6 OFF, 3 DEF			2012 Field Position / Special Teams		
2012 Offense			**2012 Defense**			Special Teams F/+	+1.2%	39
Offensive F/+	-6.8%	96	Defensive F/+	+0.8%	55	Field Position Advantage	0.532	26
Offensive FEI:	-0.224	94	Defensive FEI	0.037	65	**2013 Projections**		
Offensive S&P+	92.1	96	Defensive S&P+	108.4	42	**Mean Wins / Mean Conference Wins**	3.6 / 2.4	
Rushing S&P+	99.5	68	Rushing S&P+	124.5	9	Proj. F/+	-7.8%	91
Passing S&P+	85.4	106	Passing S&P+	101.9	56	Offensive F/+	-3.9%	89
Standard Downs S&P+	89.4	103	Standard Downs S&P+	113.2	22	Defensive F/+	-4.0%	86
Passing Downs S&P+	98.3	74	Passing Downs S&P+	105.3	50	Strength of Sched. Rk / Conf. Title Odds	46 / 0.0%	

On paper, it is a match made in football nerd heaven. SMU head coach June Jones, one of the greatest champions of the run-and-shoot, needed help in boosting an offense that fell to 96th in Offensive F/+ last season. So he called on Hal Mumme, architect of the Air Raid offense so prominent in recent college football. Mumme's coaching tree—Washington State head coach Mike Leach, West Virginia head coach Dana Holgorsen, California head coach Sonny Dykes, Texas Tech head coach Kliff Kingsbury, and Baylor head coach Art Briles all either served on Mumme's staff or the staff of a direct Mumme disciple—is more impressive than his win-loss record.

Now, Jones had made something of the Southern Methodist program before Mumme came along. After attending zero bowls in the first 20 seasons since their return from the death penalty, the Mustangs have gone bowling for four straight years, going 30-23 since 2009 after going 30-85 in the previous 10 seasons. But the team slid in 2012. SMU couldn't even pretend to pass the ball (Texas transfer and former blue-chipper Garrett Gilbert completed just 53 percent of his passes with a 15-to-15 TD-to-INT ratio), and the offense had almost no big-play capability. Mumme's offense is designed to help the quarterback maximize efficiency, so even if the big plays don't increase, Gilbert's completion rate should. At least, it better, because the Mustangs can't lean on big (and graduated) running back Zach Line anymore. And the offense will have to improve to offset potential defensive regression. Defensive end Margus Hunt and linebackers Taylor Reed and Ja'Gared Davis combined for almost exactly half of SMU's tackles for loss last year, and all three are gone. The secondary could still be strong with the return of safety Jay Scott and corner Kenneth Acker, but it will probably be put under pressure a lot more in 2013.

Top 2014 NFL Prospects: None.

No. 116 Memphis Tigers (2-10, 1-7)

2012: 4-8 (4-4 in Conference USA) / F/+ #94 / FEI #95 / S&P+ #108

Program F/+	-22.0%	115	Returning Starters: 7 OFF, 6 DEF			2012 Field Position / Special Teams		
2012 Offense			**2012 Defense**			Special Teams F/+	+2.3%	15
Offensive F/+	-12.6%	115	Defensive F/+	-5.3%	80	Field Position Advantage	0.532	25
Offensive FEI:	-0.410	114	Defensive FEI	0.178	82	**2013 Projections**		
Offensive S&P+	82.1	117	Defensive S&P+	94.5	85	**Mean Wins / Mean Conference Wins**	2.3 / 0.8	
Rushing S&P+	83.0	112	Rushing S&P+	92.0	86	Proj. F/+	-17.7%	116
Passing S&P+	78.2	118	Passing S&P+	100.3	60	Offensive F/+	-10.2%	118
Standard Downs S&P+	82.7	119	Standard Downs S&P+	97.6	71	Defensive F/+	-7.5%	104
Passing Downs S&P+	74.5	121	Passing Downs S&P+	98.9	71	Strength of Sched. Rk / Conf. Title Odds	100 / 0.0%	

The Tigers' basketball program has been to the NCAA tournament in nine of the last 11 seasons and reached the Final Four in 2008; the football program, meanwhile, fell apart in recent years. Since a run of five bowls in six years from 2003 to 2008, Memphis has gone just 9-39 on the football field, ranking 107th, 118th, 119th, and 94th, respectively, over the past four seasons. But you cannot blame head coach Justin Fuente for that. The Tigers' F/+ rankings went up by 25 spots in his first year on the job, and four wins in 2012 (including three straight to finish the season) nearly matched the total from their previous three years. There is hope in the Liberty Bowl again, though it will still probably take a while for the Tigers to be competitive in a (modestly) improved conference, and the five-year history is a killer in the projection model.

Thanks mostly to struggles on the line, the offense didn't come around in 2012, but the continuity should help in 2013. Five linemen with starting experience return, as do quarterback Jacob Karam (65 percent completion rate, 14 touchdowns, three interceptions) and two experienced rushers in

Brandon Hayes and Jai Steib. You need talent to go with the experience, however. On defense, a unit that improved from 114th to 80th in Defensive F/+ returns a vast majority of its playmakers, including redshirt junior end Martin Ifedi (11 tackles for loss, 7.5 sacks); senior tackle Johnnie Farms (9.5 tackles for loss); and senior safety Lonnie Ballentine. Punter Tom Hornsey was featured on the Memphis football media guide this offseason, the anchor of a strong special teams unit (No. 5 in FBS last season) that will need to generate value once again.

Top 2014 NFL Prospects: *P Tom Hornsey (6-7)*

Bill Connelly and Brian Fremeau

Projected Win Probabilities For American Conference Teams

American	Overall Wins													Conference Wins								
	12-0	11-1	10-2	9-3	8-4	7-5	6-6	5-7	4-8	3-9	2-10	1-11	0-12	8-0	7-1	6-2	5-3	4-4	3-5	2-6	1-7	0-8
Central Florida	-	-	3	11	22	28	21	11	3	1	-	-	-	1	9	23	31	23	10	3	-	-
Cincinnati	17	34	30	14	4	1	-	-	-	-	-	-	-	19	37	29	12	3	-	-	-	-
Connecticut	-	2	5	14	24	26	18	8	3	-	-	-	-	-	4	14	28	30	17	5	2	-
Houston	-	-	3	10	21	28	23	11	3	1	-	-	-	-	1	9	24	33	24	8	1	-
Louisville	3	19	31	27	14	5	1	-	-	-	-	-	-	5	24	34	25	10	2	-	-	-
Memphis	-	-	-	-	-	-	-	4	11	26	35	22	2	-	-	-	-	-	3	14	41	42
Rutgers	-	2	6	16	25	25	17	7	2	-	-	-	-	1	5	16	29	28	16	4	1	-
SMU	-	-	-	-	-	1	6	16	28	29	16	4	-	-	-	1	4	13	28	32	19	3
South Florida	-	-	-	1	3	11	24	31	22	7	1	-	-	-	-	2	9	23	34	25	7	-
Temple	-	-	2	4	14	26	28	18	7	1	-	-	-	-	1	5	16	29	29	16	4	-

Atlantic Coast Conference

The ACC spent ten years waiting for a new overlord to fill the vacancy left by Florida State, only to discover that the new boss is the same as the old. The 2012 Seminoles came as close as any outfit in the past decade to replicating the dominant, swaggering editions that claimed 11 conference titles and a pair of national crowns from 1992 to 2003, right down to the over-the-top talent level: Eleven Seminoles were taken in April's NFL draft, more than any other school. Compared to other ACC champions this millennium, FSU set new highs for wins (12) and final F/+ score (+29.5%, fifth-best in the nation), and delivered only the conference's second BCS bowl win in its last 14 tries.

Beyond Florida State, though, it's tempting to write off the rest of the league in 2013 as Clemson and the dozen dwarves. The arrival of Pittsburgh and Syracuse from the Big East has swelled the ranks to 14 teams and helped secure the ACC's place at the table in the playoff structure that will replace the BCS in 2014. (By then, Louisville will be in the fold as well, as a replacement for Big Ten-bound Maryland.) But how is a move made primarily in the name of adding new television markets supposed to improve an already watered-down product on the field? The ACC managed just two teams in the final polls last year, after being shut out of the top 20 in 2011. In the

F/+ rankings, only FSU and Clemson managed to land inside the top 40; the majority of the conference finished in the bottom 60. This is nearly a decade after a 2004 expansion that was expected to lift a traditional "basketball conference" into the gridiron elite. When does quantity yield quality?

The question looms especially large in the Coastal Division, which finally saw its most consistent frontrunner, Virginia Tech, succumb to the parity—or mediocrity—that has defined the rest of the division from the beginning. No one else exactly rose to the occasion and replaced them. With the Hokies limping in to a fourth-place finish, and co-champs Miami and North Carolina both sitting out the postseason, the division was repped in the ACC Championship Game by 6-6 Georgia Tech, only deepening the reputation for middling blandness. It didn't help that the Yellow Jackets, Clemson and Florida State closed the regular season by going 0–3 against their in-state SEC rivals, dropping their combined record in those games to 2–10 since 2009. Not that the comparison means everything, but if Clemson and Virginia Tech can hold their own on opening day against Georgia and Alabama, respectively, at least warding off another round of mocking headlines on the first weekend of the season would be a good start.

ATLANTIC

No. 19 Florida State Seminoles (10-2, 7-1)
2012: 12-2 (7-1) / F/+ #5 / FEI #13 / S&P+ #4

Program F/+	+19.2%	14	Returning Starters: 6 OFF, 4 DEF			2012 Field Position / Special Teams		
2012 Offense			**2012 Defense**			Special Teams F/+	+1.6%	31
Offensive F/+	**+8.4%**	**23**	**Defensive F/+**	**+19.5%**	**5**	Field Position Advantage	0.539	14
Offensive FEI:	0.163	41	Defensive FEI	-0.571	9	**2013 Projections**		
Offensive S&P+	123.9	10	Defensive S&P+	139.6	3	**Mean Wins / Mean Conference Wins**	**9.7 / 6.5**	
Rushing S&P+	132.3	5	Rushing S&P+	115.6	20	Proj. F/+	+17.3%	19
Passing S&P+	120.4	21	Passing S&P+	144.3	3	Offensive F/+	+6.9%	21
Standard Downs S&P+	128.9	5	Standard Downs S&P+	124.8	7	Defensive F/+	+10.3%	13
Passing Downs S&P+	118.9	23	Passing Downs S&P+	137.0	9	Strength of Sched. Rk / Conf. Title Odds	50 / 28.4%	

Before last year, only two teams in Florida State history had claimed 12 wins in a season. For both of them, that was good enough to claim a national championship as well. For the 2012 edition, on the other hand, the even dozen in the win column was inevitably less interesting than the two in the loss column, undermining its own claim to greatness. In fact, that number is referring to just two quarters. One of them came in October, when FSU led N.C. State by 13 points after the third quarter; the Seminoles allowed two touchdowns in the fourth and lost, 17-16. In November, FSU led Florida after the third quarter, 20-13, but gave up 24 consecutive points in the fourth, and lost 37-26. In the season's *other* 54 quarters, the 'Noles outscored opponents by 378 points. In those two, they let their chance for national relevance slip through their fingers.

Still, for the first time in a long time, there was no denying

that the talent level was vintage Florida State. And it went deep, nowhere more so than on the defensive line: As in the old days, an exodus of top-shelf talent up front is only making way for a rotation that features six players—Chris Casher, Mario Edwards, Eddie Goldman, Timmy Jernigan, Demonte McAllister and Jacobbi McDaniel—who arrived on campus as five-star recruits. (Three players in that group—Casher, Edwards and Goldman—are in just their second year; Jernigan, a second-team All-ACC pick last year despite starting just two games, is in his third.) Two other ex-five-star guys, linebacker Christian Jones and cornerback Lamarcus Joyner, were both singled out for All-ACC nods as juniors. Another, Karlos Williams, is moving into a starting role at safety. The new defensive coordinator, Jeremy Pruitt, came from Alabama to find the only lineup that's arguably *more* talented than the one he left in Tuscaloosa. Florida State's defense ranked No.1 in the nation in value drive defense, allowing only 22.4 percent of opponent possessions to cross the Seminoles 30-yard line.

The offense comes with high marks from the scouts, too, including the new quarterback, redshirt freshman Jameis Winston, whose expectations are limited only by the fact that he's yet to take a college snap. When he does, it will be behind a long-in-the-tooth offensive line (96 combined starts), with two proven tailbacks (juniors James Wilder, Jr., and Devonta Freeman) in a conservative scheme that is more than willing to protect the quarterback by pounding away as long as it can. The schedule does its part by delaying Winston's first major road test, at Clemson, until the sixth game.

Then again, as we were reminded last year in Raleigh, the most persistent hurdle standing between Florida State and its full potential is usually Florida State. The loss at N.C. State was the eighth time in eight years the Seminoles have been ambushed as a ranked team by an unranked underdog. It was the fourth loss in three years under coach Jimbo Fisher in a game they were favored to win by double digits. FSU has earned its way back into the national conversation, but it still has to prove it's consistent enough to stay there.

Top 2014 NFL Prospects: *LB Christian Jones (1–2), DT Timmy Jernigan* (1–2), OT Cameron Erving* (2–3), G Tre Jackson* (2–3), CB Lamarcus Joyner (3), RB James Wilder Jr.* (3), C Bryan Stork (3), RB Devonta Freeman* (3–4), S Terrence Brooks (4–5), TE Nick O'Leary* (4–5).*

No. 20 Clemson Tigers (9-3, 7-1)

2012: 11-2 (7-1) / F/+ #22 / FEI #25 / S&P+ #21

Program F/+	+15.3%	21	Returning Starters: 7 OFF, 6 DEF			2012 Field Position / Special Teams		
2012 Offense			**2012 Defense**			Special Teams F/+	+1.8%	26
Offensive F/+	+14.4%	7	Defensive F/+	+2.2%	51	Field Position Advantage	0.513	43
Offensive FEI:	0.446	13	Defensive FEI	-0.058	55	**2013 Projections**		
Offensive S&P+	128.3	5	Defensive S&P+	107.6	34	**Mean Wins / Mean Conference Wins**	9.2 / 6.5	
Rushing S&P+	112.7	26	Rushing S&P+	101.0	55	Proj. F/+	+14.3%	20
Passing S&P+	146.2	2	Passing S&P+	88.9	95	Offensive F/+	+10.6%	10
Standard Downs S&P+	116.6	18	Standard Downs S&P+	96.0	80	Defensive F/+	+3.7%	36
Passing Downs S&P+	159.3	2	Passing Downs S&P+	92.1	86	Strength of Sched. Rk / Conf. Title Odds	59 / 27.6%	

It is a documented fact that Clemson and high expectations do not mix. Between 2001 and 2011, the Tigers were ranked in the preseason polls four times, and failed to finish there in any of those four seasons. Between 2006 and 2011, they lost ten games as a ranked team to an unranked opponent. Twice in that span they played their way into the top ten in late October, only to blow both opportunities by losing four of their last five (2006) and four of their last six (2011). When they finally reached their first BCS bowl, in 2011, they were not only upset, but humiliated in the most lopsided blowout in Series history. The program is so reliably volatile in high-stakes situations that the blogosphere coined a verb for it, "Clemsoning," defined in the Urban Dictionary as "the act of delivering an inexplicably disappointing performance."

In that context, the end of the 2012 season could be fairly interpreted as both a breakthrough and a warning. True, a New Year's Eve rally from 11 points down in the fourth quarter to upset LSU in the Chick-Fil-A Bowl was a rare, invigorating triumph over adversity. And it secured Clemson's highest finish in the AP poll (11th) in more than two decades, marking the first time the Tigers have started *and* finished in the poll in the same season since 2000. On the other hand, it was an unmistakable prelude to high expectations for 2013, the kind of expectations that have confounded them under three consecutive head coaches. The first game, a neutral-site blockbuster against Georgia in the Georgia Dome, is on the same stage where the highly touted 2008 team was mortally wounded on opening night by Alabama. (Coach Tommy Bowden was fired six weeks later.) At what point can Clemson be trusted to be at its best when it's actually supposed to be?

The catalyst for the latest round of hype is quarterback Tajh Boyd, who may still be recovering from his high-volume night (50 passes, 29 rushes) against LSU's blue-chip defense. Boyd's performance in that game arguably helped his NFL draft stock more than any of the countless school and conference records he already owned. But it shouldn't have come as a surprise: In the S&P+ ratings, the Tigers finished second nationally in passing offense and offensive efficiency on passing downs, behind only Texas A&M on both counts. They also led the ACC in total and scoring offense, averaged 3.1 points per drive (eighth nationally), scored at least 37 points in every conference game, and finished as the highest-scoring attack in school history. And although the departures from that lineup included All-ACC picks at tailback, wide receiver, tight end, and center, they did not include all-purpose ace Sammy Watkins, expected to be back in All-American form this fall after struggling through a suspension and an intestinal illness last year as a sophomore. As long as Boyd is in one piece—a legitimate concern after the bowl game—the offense is designed by coordinator Chad Morris to run at full throttle.

Occasionally, the defense has to pay the price for that pace by yielding big numbers in shootouts. But it didn't always need the help. In two losses, Florida State and South Carolina combined to gash the Tigers for a dozen plays that covered at least 25 yards, and Clemson trailed from the third quarter onward in both games. Most of the damage came at the expense of the secondary (95th in pass defense S&P+), which makes the departure of three full-time starters in the back four somewhat easier to bear. So does the presence of safety Travis Blanks, who carved out a productive niche as a true freshman in a hybrid linebacker/nickelback role, and the promotion of pass-rushing end Vic Beasley (eight sacks off the bench) into the starting lineup. If Beasley holds up well enough against the run to stay on the field full-time, it will make the beleaguered cornerbacks' lives much easier.

Top 2014 NFL Prospects: *QB Tajh Boyd (1), WR Sammy Watkins* (1), G Brandon Thomas (4), RB Roderick McDowell (5–6)*

No. 54 Syracuse Orange (6-6, 4-4)

2012: 8-5 (5-2 in Big East) / F/+ #37 / FEI #27 / S&P+ #51

Program F/+	-3.8%	68	Returning Starters: 6 OFF, 7 DEF			2012 Field Position / Special Teams		
2012 Offense			**2012 Defense**			Special Teams F/+	-0.8%	87
Offensive F/+	**+9.0%**	**21**	**Defensive F/+**	**+2.1%**	**52**	Field Position Advantage	0.504	56
Offensive FEI:	0.372	18	Defensive FEI	-0.191	39	**2013 Projections**		
Offensive S&P+	113.1	35	Defensive S&P+	99.1	66	**Mean Wins / Mean Conference Wins**	**6.0 / 3.6**	
Rushing S&P+	112.1	31	Rushing S&P+	101.9	53	Proj. F/+	+2.1%	54
Passing S&P+	116.7	31	Passing S&P+	95.9	72	Offensive F/+	+2.1%	45
Standard Downs S&P+	115.8	19	Standard Downs S&P+	95.0	83	Defensive F/+	+0.0%	61
Passing Downs S&P+	108.3	47	Passing Downs S&P+	112.3	30	Strength of Sched. Rk / Conf. Title Odds	61 / 0.7%	

In their old age, Syracuse fans will probably not find themselves waxing nostalgic about Doug Marrone. Four years, two winning seasons, a pair of victories in the Pinstripe Bowl—this is no one's idea of the glory days. But then, who ever expected glory? Marrone's mission was to leave his alma mater better than he found it. And the fact that a .500 record in his only tour as a head coach was enough to propel him to a top job in the NFL speaks volumes about the disarray that greeted him there. After four consecutive last-place finishes under his predecessor, Greg "Gerg" Robinson, a share of the Big East title in year four under Marrone felt like mission accomplished. The new mission, under a new coach in a new conference, is to extend the same sense of forward momentum.

The new coach in that equation is Scott Shafer, promoted from defensive coordinator on the heels of a 38-14 upset over West Virginia in the bowl game, his unit's best effort of the season. Philosophically, Shafer preaches intensity and aggression. Statistically, returns have been lukewarm at best: In the F/+ rankings, the Orange defense on his watch has finished 66th (in 2009), 42nd (2010), 58th (2011) and 52nd (2012), and consistently yielded between 24 and 28 points per game. This year, he has the benefit of a pair of active, athletic veterans at outside linebacker, Dyshawn Davis and Marquis Spruill,

who have spent a lot of time in opposing backfields. But the Orange also lost their top two tacklers, their best interior run-stuffer, and both starting defensive ends, leaving more questions—especially when it comes to the pass rush—than immediate answers.

Offensively, Shafer will have to reconcile his stated preference for an "inventive, exciting" attack with personnel better suited for old-school, between-the-tackles plodding. From midseason on, the Orange were increasingly committed to the run, averaging 238 yards on nearly 50 carries per game over the course of a 6–1 finish. The top two tailbacks, Jerome Smith and Prince-Tyson Gulley, are both back after combining for exactly 2,000 yards rushing as juniors, including 365 yards in the bowl game alone. Meanwhile, the top two receivers, Alec Lemon and Marcus Sales, both graduated, as did the quarterback, Ryan Nassib, after setting school records for total offense and touchdown passes in a season. Of the three quarterbacks vying to replace him—junior Terrel Hunt, senior Charley Loeb, and Oklahoma transfer Drew Allen—it's possible one of them will come along quickly enough to open the offense up.

Top 2014 NFL Prospects: *CB Keon Lyn (6–7), DT Jay Bromley (7–FA), LB Marquis Spruill (7–FA)*

No. 61 N.C. State Wolfpack (7-5, 3-5)

2012: 7-6 (4-4) / F/+ #63 / FEI #59 / S&P+ #62

Program F/+	+3.2%	49	Returning Starters: 5 OFF, 6 DEF			2012 Field Position / Special Teams		
2012 Offense			**2012 Defense**			Special Teams F/+	-0.1%	64
Offensive F/+	**-3.0%**	**74**	**Defensive F/+**	**+2.9%**	**49**	Field Position Advantage	0.483	85
Offensive FEI:	-0.149	78	Defensive FEI	-0.177	42	**2013 Projections**		
Offensive S&P+	101.1	62	Defensive S&P+	102.9	54	**Mean Wins / Mean Conference Wins**	**6.6 / 3.4**	
Rushing S&P+	89.4	100	Rushing S&P+	91.6	88	Proj. F/+	-0.9%	61
Passing S&P+	107.5	44	Passing S&P+	107.2	39	Offensive F/+	-2.6%	80
Standard Downs S&P+	103.4	49	Standard Downs S&P+	96.6	76	Defensive F/+	+1.7%	52
Passing Downs S&P+	99.4	72	Passing Downs S&P+	109.1	37	Strength of Sched. Rk / Conf. Title Odds	84 / 0.4%	

For N.C. State, a program more than three decades removed from its last conference championship, the "next level" can be an elusive concept. By last November, though, it was crystal clear for Wolfpack fans that Tom O'Brien would not be the coach to take them there. He had come close in 2010, when the Pack won nine behind quarterback Russell Wilson and blew fourth-quarter leads in three of their four losses. But O'Brien chose to let Wilson transfer for his final season of eligibility rather than lose his younger backup, Mike Glennon, who proceeded to throw 29 interceptions over the next two years for teams that seemed capable of almost anything—high

or low—on any given weekend. The win total fell to eight in 2011, then seven, and O'Brien was given the boot despite upsets over the eventual ACC champ (Clemson in 2011, Florida State in 2012) in both seasons. The same outfits lost games to Wake Forest, Boston College and Virginia.

The new coach, Dave Doeren, wasted no time making over the team in his own image. Of the 23 signees in the incoming recruiting class, more than half committed after Doeren's arrival in December, in addition to high-profile transfers from Florida, West Virginia and Arkansas. The last of those three, quarterback Brandon Mitchell, is eligible to play right away as a graduate student, adding a third arm to the competition between junior Pete Thomas and sophomore Manny Stocker. (Thomas, the odds-on favorite out of the spring, is a former transfer himself, with 21 starts under his belt at Colorado State in 2010-11.) Although there are no headliners among the skill positions, returnees accounted for nearly three-fourths of last year's total yards from scrimmage, and the starting wide receivers (Quintin Palmer, Bryan Underwood, and Rashard Smith) combined to average 15.2 yards per catch with 15 touchdowns. Given any semblance of a ground game—a persistent glitch under O'Brien, but Doeren's bread-and-butter at his last stop, Northern Illinois—there is nowhere to go but up for an attack that finished 74th in offensive F/+.

If the defense fared a little better on paper, it was no less nondescript, ranking somewhere in the vast mediocre expanse between 35th and 75th nationally in almost every major category, conventional and advanced alike. On the higher end of that scale, the secondary landed in the top 40 in S&P+ pass defense (39th, to be exact), good for fourth in the ACC. But that was with two soon-to-be draft picks (David Amerson and Earl Wolff) in the fold, along with another senior Brandan Bishop, who started all four years he was on campus. Throw in three new linebackers, a couple of unexpected position battles on the defensive line, and a brand new scheme, and you have a unit effectively starting from scratch.

Top 2014 NFL Prospects: TE Asa Watson (5–6)

No. 69 Boston College Eagles (5-7, 2-6)
2012: 2-10 (1-7) / F/+ #88 / FEI #86 / S&P+ #93

Program F/+	+2.1%	52	Returning Starters: 7 OFF, 7 DEF			2012 Field Position / Special Teams		
2012 Offense			**2012 Defense**			Special Teams F/+	+1.3%	36
Offensive F/+	**-6.8%**	**97**	**Defensive F/+**	**-5.5%**	**81**	Field Position Advantage	0.456	111
Offensive FEI:	-0.199	89	Defensive FEI	0.169	81	**2013 Projections**		
Offensive S&P+	90.4	90	Defensive S&P+	93.3	80	**Mean Wins / Mean Conference Wins**	**5.3 / 2.5**	
Rushing S&P+	87.3	105	Rushing S&P+	99.2	62	Proj. F/+	-2.9%	69
Passing S&P+	95.8	78	Passing S&P+	95.3	76	Offensive F/+	-2.0%	72
Standard Downs S&P+	94.4	84	Standard Downs S&P+	108.9	30	Defensive F/+	-0.9%	68
Passing Downs S&P+	95.0	83	Passing Downs S&P+	77.8	117	Strength of Sched. Rk / Conf. Title Odds	54 / 0.0%	

Boston College fans were never really on board with the idea of a Frank Spaziani era, and now that it's over, they can get on with forgetting the last four years ever happened. But the difference between the program Spaziani so abruptly inherited in 2009 and the one he was fired from last November is hard to overstate. At that point, the Eagles had put together ten consecutive winning seasons, easily the longest streak in school history, and played in back-to-back ACC title games (only one of which involved Matt Ryan). In 2012, the seniors who signed up in those years bowed out with a single conference win and a last-place finish in the Coastal Division.

That trajectory was reflected in almost every respect, including the local pipeline to the NFL. (From 2000-09, B.C. produced 21 draft picks in all, with at least two players going in every draft except 2005; under Spaziani, it produced just one pick a year from 2010-12, and didn't have a player picked this April.) But nowhere was it more clear than in the Eagles' declining fortunes against the run. A perennial strength during Spaziani's run as defensive coordinator, Boston College led the conference in rushing defense six times in seven years from 2004-10, and led the nation in 2010. From there, the number plummeted, bottoming out last year at an ACC-worst 227 yards per game against FBS opponents. (Army's triple-option attack alone accounted for 517 yards in the Eagles' most embarrassing loss.) At various points ten different players were thrust into the starting rotation on the defensive line, nine of whom are back,

including early injury casualty Kaleb Ramsey. Still, B.C. finished dead last nationally in both sacks and tackles for loss and there is no would-be Luke Kuechly or B.J. Raji in sight.

If any aspect of the team transcended hopelessness, it was the pass/catch combo of Chase Rettig and Alex Amidon (1,210 yards, 15.5 per catch, 54 percent catch rate), although their dismal finish in the S&P+ ratings (78th in passing offense) suggests a case of quantity over quality: the Eagles were almost always playing from behind, and Rettig's efficiency rating declined in every game from midseason on. Even if that wasn't the case, the scales still would have begun to tip back toward the running game the moment the school introduced Steve Addazio as the head coach. A longtime offensive line coach, Addazio never hesitated to send Tim Tebow plowing into the line 20 times per game as offensive coordinator at Florida, and has spent the last two years overseeing one of the most run-oriented offenses in the country at Temple. (Ironically, the Owls' resident workhorse in 2012 was Montel Harris, who just happened to set Boston College's career rushing record before relocating to Philly.) For now, senior tailback Andre Williams has the ball all to himself after the departure of running mate Rolandan Finch in April, an arrangement that will only hold up as long as Williams' legs do.

Top 2014 NFL Prospects: LB Steele Divitto (7–FA), LB Kevin Pierre-Louis (7–FA)

No. 81 Wake Forest Demon Deacons (5-7, 2-6)

2012: 5-7 (3-5) / F/+ #107 / FEI #102 / S&P+ #110

Program F/+	-3.8%	67	Returning Starters: 8 OFF, 8 DEF			2012 Field Position / Special Teams		
2012 Offense			**2012 Defense**			Special Teams F/+	-3.2%	117
Offensive F/+	-11.7%	113	**Defensive F/+**	-4.2%	77	Field Position Advantage	0.463	103
Offensive FEI:	-0.387	112	Defensive FEI	0.051	67	**2013 Projections**		
Offensive S&P+	84.2	113	Defensive S&P+	90.7	90	**Mean Wins / Mean Conference Wins**	4.9 / 2.5	
Rushing S&P+	84.8	108	Rushing S&P+	97.7	66	Proj. F/+	-5.6%	81
Passing S&P+	85.2	107	Passing S&P+	93.0	82	Offensive F/+	-4.9%	96
Standard Downs S&P+	89.4	105	Standard Downs S&P+	99.1	67	Defensive F/+	-0.7%	67
Passing Downs S&P+	79.1	116	Passing Downs S&P+	88.6	96	Strength of Sched. Rk / Conf. Title Odds	74 / 0.0%	

Jim Grobe has moved a few mountains in his day—he boasts both a conference championship and a three-year winning streak over Florida State *at Wake Forest*—but after 12 years, his offense seems to have exhausted its capacity to move the ball. The 2012 attack was the worst of Grobe's tenure in terms of both yards and points per game, and plummeted to 107th in offensive F/+, down from 47th in 2011. In the S&P+ ratings, the Deacons limped in at 108th in rushing, 107th in passing and 113th overall, down from 60th. Quarterback Tanner Price finished with the lowest pass efficiency rating of any regular ACC starter. Opposite a mediocre defense (77th in defensive F/+), they never stood a chance.

So while the 2013 lineup is long on experience, composed almost entirely of upperclassmen in their fourth or fifth years in the program on both sides of the ball, it's no closer to identifying a reliable playmaker. The headliner on offense, Michael Campanaro, is the most frequently targeted receiver in the conference over the last two years, but hardly the most feared: of Campanaro's 79 receptions as a junior, only six went for 25 yards or longer, and he averaged just 8.4 yards per catch against ACC opponents. The most respected defender, Nikita Whitlock, is surprisingly disruptive for a 5-foot-11, 260-pound nose tackle, but remains a 5-foot-11, 260-pound nose tackle. (The run defense as a whole was ninth in the ACC in defensive rushing S&P+ and yards allowed.) As usual, the cushy September schedule allows for a running start toward bowl eligibility, especially if Price takes care of the ball as well as he has the last two years. Beyond that, as usual, it's an uphill struggle.

Top 2014 NFL Prospects: CB Merrill Noel* (4–5), WR Michael Campanaro (5–6)

No. 83 Maryland Terrapins (4-8, 2-6)

2012: 4-8 (2-6) / F/+ #86 / FEI #81 / S&P+ #101

Program F/+	-4.1%	71	Returning Starters: 7 OFF, 5 DEF			2012 Field Position / Special Teams		
2012 Offense			**2012 Defense**			Special Teams F/+	0.0%	61
Offensive F/+	-13.2%	116	**Defensive F/+**	+2.3%	50	Field Position Advantage	0.478	91
Offensive FEI:	-0.369	109	Defensive FEI	-0.141	48	**2013 Projections**		
Offensive S&P+	77.6	120	Defensive S&P+	102.9	51	**Mean Wins / Mean Conference Wins**	4.2 / 2.1	
Rushing S&P+	72.9	122	Rushing S&P+	107.5	39	Proj. F/+	-6.2%	83
Passing S&P+	78.6	117	Passing S&P+	111.0	31	Offensive F/+	-6.2%	101
Standard Downs S&P+	78.3	122	Standard Downs S&P+	114.2	20	Defensive F/+	0.0%	62
Passing Downs S&P+	70.0	123	Passing Downs S&P+	104.1	54	Strength of Sched. Rk / Conf. Title Odds	65 / 0.0%	

The term "plagued by injuries" is a worn-out cliché, but in fact Maryland quarterbacks in 2012 must have felt literally, personally oppressed by a vengeful deity. Beginning with the transfer of incumbent Danny O'Brien in the spring, the Terrapins were hit by a wave of attrition that felled every viable signal-caller on the roster, and one or two who weren't that viable. After season-ending injuries to C.J. Brown (torn ACL), Perry Hills (torn ACL), Devin Burns (broken foot) and Caleb Rowe (torn ACL), coaches were left with no choice over the final month of the season but to turn to a true freshman linebacker, Shawn Petty, who happened to run the option in high school. By November, injuries had also claimed the seasons of starters at tailback, wide receiver, defensive end, linebacker and safety. Surprise: the Terps dropped their final four games by an average of 22 points and limped into the winter with the worst offensive F/+ rating in the conference. Maryland went three-and-out on 49.6 percent of drives, the second worst rate in FBS.

Theoretically, the upside to such carnage is a more seasoned team—15 players are back who started at least one game as a true or redshirt freshman—that cannot possibly encounter such bad luck again. Realistically, that's the same line fans heard last year, after watching 21 freshmen thrown into the fire in 2011. In fact, the Terps' current roster goes into 2013 with fewer career starts (205) than any team in the conference except N.C. State. When is the tribulation supposed to start paying off?

The leading light among the new faces, by far, was freshman Stefon Diggs, who made good on his five-star recruiting hype by accounting for 1,896 yards as a rusher, receiver and return man—more than four times the production of anyone else on the team. Another blue-chip receiver, Deon Long, transferred from junior college and directly into the starting lineup in spring practice. But Brown and the other returning quarterbacks remained sidelined, and there was no hurry to hand the job over to the placeholder, Ricardo Young. The possibilities with Diggs and Long in the same lineup are far less intriguing if they can't get their hands on the ball.

Top 2014 NFL Prospects: None

COASTAL

No. 23 Virginia Tech Hokies (9-3, 6-2)

2012: 7-6 (4-4) / F/+ #43 / FEI #49 / S&P+ #43

Program F/+	+17.8%	16	Returning Starters: 4 OFF, 9 DEF			2012 Field Position / Special Teams		
2012 Offense			**2012 Defense**			Special Teams F/+	0.0%	62
Offensive F/+	**-3.2%**	**75**	**Defensive F/+**	**+10.8%**	**22**	Field Position Advantage	0.477	93
Offensive FEI:	-0.085	69	Defensive FEI	-0.375	24	**2013 Projections**		
Offensive S&P+	96.5	68	Defensive S&P+	119.7	19	**Mean Wins / Mean Conference Wins**	**8.7 / 5.9**	
Rushing S&P+	90.5	96	Rushing S&P+	120.1	15	Proj. F/+	+12.9%	23
Passing S&P+	94.6	83	Passing S&P+	134.1	9	Offensive F/+	-0.1%	60
Standard Downs S&P+	93.6	90	Standard Downs S&P+	121.3	11	Defensive F/+	+13.1%	8
Passing Downs S&P+	90.3	91	Passing Downs S&P+	138.8	5	Strength of Sched. Rk / Conf. Title Odds	14 / 16.9%	

It took Virginia Tech the better part of a decade to reinforce its status as the most bankable frontrunner in the ACC, and roughly three months last fall for that reputation to be overtaken by rust. And yet, if anything, the damage could have been much worse. As ugly as it looks next to eight consecutive 10-win seasons from 2004-11, the 7–6 finish in 2012 slightly *understates* how close the Hokies came to rock bottom. Of those seven wins, four came on the last play of the game, three in overtime games in which Tech trailed well into the fourth quarter. That included the bowl game, a come-from-behind, 13-10 win over Rutgers that staved off Tech's first losing record since 1992, despite its most anemic offensive performance of the season. Which is saying something: In the final S&P+ ratings, the offense finished 80th or worse nationally in rushing, passing and play efficiency.

Predictably, most of the heat was directed at quarterback Logan Thomas, a 6-foot-6, 260-pound specimen whose production as a junior came nowhere near the ecstatic projections of pro scouts. After an eye-opening debut in 2011, Thomas finished dead last among regular ACC starters for completion percentage (51.3) and interception percentage (3.7), and his overall efficiency rating plummeted by nearly 20 points. His draft stock responded accordingly.

Then again, it's hard to lay too much blame at the feet of a guy who also accounted for 72 percent of the team's total offense. Instead, head coach Frank Beamer responded in January by cleaning house on his own staff, firing quarterbacks coach Mike O'Cain and exiling longtime offensive coordinator Bryan Stinespring to tight ends coach. The new offensive coordinator is Scott Loeffler, a "pro style" quarterback guru last seen overseeing Auburn's offense in its decline to the bottom of the SEC rankings. Besides the quarterback, the offense will return its top two tailbacks, four regulars on the offensive line and a viable deep threat, Demitri Knowles, whose role should expand dramatically as a sophomore. But someone, somewhere has to assume part of the burden Thomas too often shouldered alone.

The defense had its own issues, allowing more points per game (22.9) than in any season since joining the ACC in 2004. Despite some early lapses, though, by November it was looking like a vintage Bud Foster defense, clamping down just in time to counter an extended midseason skid with a three-game win streak to close the season. (Under the circumstances, we won't quibble with the fact that the first two of those wins were razor-thin calls against lowly Boston College and Virginia.) The front four returns intact for the second year in a row—starters J.R. Collins, James Gayle, Derrick Hopkins and Luther Maddy have combined for 92 career starts—and the secondary is intact except for All-ACC cornerback Antone Exum, who passed on the draft but subsequently tore his ACL playing pickup basketball. If five-star freshman cornerback Kendall Fuller lives up to the hype playing opposite his older brother, Kyle, opposing offenses may not be able to tell the difference.

Top 2014 NFL Prospects: QB Logan Thomas (2–3), CB Antone Exum (3–4), DE James Gayle (3–4), CB Kyle Fuller (4–5)

No. 25 Miami Hurricanes (8-4, 5-3)

2012: 7-5 (5-3) / F/+ #65 / FEI #60 / S&P+ #60

Program F/+	+9.0%	33	Returning Starters: 10 OFF, 9 DEF			2012 Field Position / Special Teams		
2012 Offense			**2012 Defense**			Special Teams F/+	+2.2%	17
Offensive F/+	**+4.0%**	**46**	**Defensive F/+**	**-7.5%**	**88**	Field Position Advantage	0.559	4
Offensive FEI:	0.117	47	Defensive FEI	0.320	94	**2013 Projections**		
Offensive S&P+	110.4	41	Defensive S&P+	95.3	79	**Mean Wins / Mean Conference Wins**	**8.4 / 5.2**	
Rushing S&P+	112.3	29	Rushing S&P+	93.1	82	Proj. F/+	+12.3%	25
Passing S&P+	118.3	25	Passing S&P+	97.9	66	Offensive F/+	+9.4%	12
Standard Downs S&P+	122.1	11	Standard Downs S&P+	94.6	85	Defensive F/+	+2.9%	41
Passing Downs S&P+	105.4	55	Passing Downs S&P+	100.7	63	Strength of Sched. Rk / Conf. Title Odds	53 / 8.9%	

Al Golden had yet to coach his first game at Miami when the NCAA clouds descended back in 2011, and in 2013 it feels like he's still waiting. The intervening two years could have been written in steam. On the field, the 'Canes defined mediocrity, following an instantly forgettable, 6-6 campaign in Golden's first season with an equally uninspiring slog to 7-5. In the background, an ongoing investigation into alleged misdeeds by a former booster cast a pall that hung over every game. The result, predictably, was ambivalence: both teams passed on the postseason, ostensibly as a "self-imposed" penalty for alleged NCAA infractions, but also because no one saw the point in extending either season for a bottom-rung bowl game. Six players with remaining eligibility declared for the 2012 draft, only one of whom (Olivier Vernon) was actually taken on the first two days. Attendance plummeted for opponents who weren't Florida State.

Still, 2013 offers hints of a team bent on breaking out of the rut. For one, heavy sanctions are no longer inevitable after a procedural gaffe in the NCAA's investigation, which prompted Miami to push for a full acquittal. (The university appeared before the NCAA for a formal hearing in June; any further penalties are certain to be met with lengthy appeals.) And there is finally a little juice in the offense: Essentially the entire lineup is back from an attack that averaged more yards and points per game last year than any Hurricane offense since the heyday of "The U" revival in 2002. Most of that production came from the arm of Stephen Morris, who accounted for nearly two-thirds of the total offense en route to a pile of school records. His top three receivers, Phillip Dorsett, Rashawn Scott and Clive Walford, combined to average 15.3 yards per catch, all as sophomores.

Prolific as it could be at times, though, the offense still fizzled against good defenses, failing to top 20 points in losses to Kansas State, Notre Dame, North Carolina and FSU. Not coincidentally, they averaged just 83 yards rushing in those games, on less than three yards per carry. Enter Randy "Duke"

Johnson: In November alone, the five-star freshman ran for 492 yards and five touchdowns on 8.8 per carry in a part-time role; meanwhile, the team averaged just over 40 points per game over the course of a 3–1 finish. As a sophomore, Johnson will have the position to himself, behind an NFL-sized line—the starting five comes in around 320 pounds per man—that boasts at least four future pros with starting experience.

There is no shortage of familiar faces on the defense, either, although in this case it's the result of trial by error: Twenty-four players started at least one game last year in search of some shred of cohesion, resulting in a different starting lineup in every game. The musical chairs approach left Miami ranked last in the ACC in both rushing and passing yards allowed, and 88th nationally in Defensive F/+. Opponents averaged 30 points per game for the first time since 1944. Not surprisingly, the post-spring depth chart was noncommittal, listing multiple starters at five different positions. One of the exceptions was at strongside linebacker, where true freshman Alex Figueroa made an immediate impression in the absence of 2012 starters Thurston Armbrister (injured), Eddie Johnson (suspended) and Gionni Paul (dismissed). Aside from defensive ends Anthony Chickillo and Shayon Green, the rest of the holdovers have as much to prove as the freshmen.

Top 2014 NFL Prospects: OT Seantrel Henderson (2–3), G Malcolm Bunche* (4–5), QB Stephen Morris (5–6), G Brandon Linder (6–7)

No. 29 North Carolina Tar Heels (8-4, 5-3)

2012: 8-4 (5-3) / F/+ #46 / FEI #47 / S&P+ #52

Program F/+	+9.2%	31	Returning Starters: 6 OFF, 9 DEF			2012 Field Position / Special Teams		
2012 Offense			**2012 Defense**			Special Teams F/+	+0.9%	44
Offensive F/+	**+9.4%**	**20**	**Defensive F/+**	**-3.5%**	**74**	Field Position Advantage	0.52	37
Offensive FEI:	0.391	17	Defensive FEI	0.124	78	**2013 Projections**		
Offensive S&P+	113.4	38	Defensive S&P+	97.9	74	**Mean Wins / Mean Conference Wins**	**8.0 / 5.0**	
Rushing S&P+	108.7	42	Rushing S&P+	90.7	94	Proj. F/+	+9.9%	29
Passing S&P+	117.1	29	Passing S&P+	95.9	71	Offensive F/+	+6.9%	24
Standard Downs S&P+	115.0	22	Standard Downs S&P+	99.9	62	Defensive F/+	+3.0%	39
Passing Downs S&P+	110.2	41	Passing Downs S&P+	84.9	103	Strength of Sched. Rk / Conf. Title Odds	56 / 6.7%	

Like Miami, North Carolina spent the 2012 season in a kind of limbo, barred from claiming a Coastal Division crown or playing in a bowl game under NCAA sanctions. Unlike Miami, Carolina didn't give the impression of a team content to mark time. The offense, a perennial albatross, finished in the top 15 nationally in both yards and points per game, and 20th in offensive F/+. The defense, in its first year in a 3-3-5 scheme, led the conference in tackles for loss. The Tar Heels finished above .500 in ACC play for the first time since the league split into two divisions in 2005, and beat Miami and Virginia Tech in the same season for just the second time. If not for the postseason ban, they would have played in their first ACC Championship game. (Players received rings for winning the division anyway, sanctions be damned.) Even the low points left some room for a sliver of optimism: Three of four losses came by a combined nine points, two of them in games UNC led late in the fourth quarter.

There are, however, a few new holes, none of which is more glaring than the one left by tailback Giovani Bernard, who

led the nation in yards from scrimmage (171.8 per game) and served with distinction as a return man. (His game-winning, 74-yard punt return with seconds to play against N.C. State snapped a five-year UNC losing streak in the series.) No single player is going to replicate that, but a committee might—three backs shared first-string reps in the spring, and blue-chip freshman T.J. Logan will add a fourth option in the fall. The passing game is on more familiar footing, although no less limited by quarterback Bryn Renner's lack of top-shelf arm strength. And even with two NFL prospects (James Hurst and Russell Bodine) still in the fold, the offensive line as a whole is a work in progress after losing three starters to the draft. The only other team with three O-linemen picked in this year's draft was Alabama.

The NFL also took a bite out of the middle of the defensive line, where even the presence of first-rounder Sylvester Williams (and the heavy presence in opposing backfields) couldn't prevent the Heels from plummeting to 94th in rushing defense S&P+. Along with Williams, UNC is also facing a major exodus on the second level, including starters at both "Bandit"—a hybrid end/outside linebacker role—and "Ram," a hybrid linebacker/safety. The new starters at those spots, sophomore Shakeel Rasheed and junior Brandon Ellerbe, are blank slates. Redshirt freshman Dan Mastromatteo will also face pressure replacing last year's leading tackler, Kevin Reddick. As usual, pro scouts have a defensive lineman to salivate over, in this case All-ACC end Kareem Martin. But

Martin alone can't keep the Tar Heels from struggling mightily in passing situations (103rd in defensive S&P+ on passing downs last season), and the pass rush and secondary alike have plenty of ground to make up.

Top 2014 NFL Prospects: OT James Hurst (1–2), DE Kareem Martin (1–2), S Tre Boston (2–3), TE Eric Ebron* (2–3), C Russell Bodine* (3–4), QB Bryn Renner (5)

No. 32 Georgia Tech Yellow Jackets (7-5, 5-3)

2012: 7-7 (5-3) / F/+ #49 / FEI #50 / S&P+ #29

Program F/+	+7.0%	39	Returning Starters: 8 OFF, 8 DEF			2012 Field Position / Special Teams		
2012 Offense			**2012 Defense**			Special Teams F/+	-2.6%	112
Offensive F/+	**+8.6%**	**22**	Defensive F/+	+0.1%	58	Field Position Advantage	0.49	77
Offensive FEI:	0.246	26	Defensive FEI	0.037	64	**2013 Projections**		
Offensive S&P+	119.4	13	Defensive S&P+	105.8	37	**Mean Wins / Mean Conference Wins**	7.4 / 4.8	
Rushing S&P+	125.7	7	Rushing S&P+	94.7	76	Proj. F/+	+9.7%	32
Passing S&P+	124.6	13	Passing S&P+	115.0	23	Offensive F/+	+6.8%	25
Standard Downs S&P+	121.6	12	Standard Downs S&P+	104.1	50	Defensive F/+	+2.9%	40
Passing Downs S&P+	116.2	30	Passing Downs S&P+	111.7	32	Strength of Sched. Rk / Conf. Title Odds	52 / 6.1%	

Paul Johnson is not a man to chase the latest trends. As a play-caller, he's held fast to the Flexbone for two decades, at four different schools, with minimal tweaks. At Georgia Tech, his teams have kept the ball on the ground at least 80 percent of the time four years in a row. The Yellow Jackets have put up at least 33 points per game in three of those four seasons, including a 33.6-point average in 2012. They were 13th nationally in Offensive S&P+, after finishing 15th in 2011. The system is not broken. If you're watching a Paul Johnson offense, you're watching a three-hour clinic in the triple option. Be sure to protect your knees.

So when Johnson suggests that he's studying other teams "to broaden offensively," as he did earlier this year, not very long after sprinkling in a few four-wide/shotgun looks in a Sun Bowl upset over USC, it's tempting to bite on the idea of the crusty old coach experimenting with one of the most stable elements in the sport. There was also the matter of Georgia Tech's new starting quarterback, redshirt sophomore Vad Lee, visiting a pro-style quarterback guru in the spring to improve as a passer. Don't be fooled: Johnson has made similar feints toward diversity in the past, which have amounted to zilch. When blessed with a viable downfield target (see Demaryius Thomas or Stephen Hill), the Jackets have shown some willingness to throw it up in his general direction against man coverage. But no quarterback under Johnson has averaged more than a dozen passes per game, and this particular team is particularly bereft of potential targets. (There were only two

healthy scholarship receivers in the spring, only one of whom has seen the field in a game.) On the other hand, a half-dozen backs are on hand with more than 50 touches apiece over the last two years, behind a line whose members have combined for 104 career starts. Lee was pushed in the spring by redshirt freshman Justin Thomas, who is too athletic to keep on the bench—for a while he was committed to play cornerback at Alabama—but is even less likely to be putting the ball in the air. As much as any lineup in Johnson's tenure, this one is born to run.

Instead, the big change is on defense, where new coordinator Ted Roof was brought on to shore up a unit that yielded at least 40 points in five of seven losses. (The old coordinator, Al Groh, was thrown overboard at midseason, after Tech was ripped for 138 points over the course of a three-game losing streak.) The transition will hinge in large part on how quickly senior Jeremiah Attaochu takes to defensive end in Roof's 4–3 scheme after three years as a stand-up, 3–4 linebacker under Groh. Coaches reportedly have not asked Attaochu to add any weight to the 240 pounds he played at as a junior, so as not to slow down their only consistent threat in the pass rush. What that means for a mediocre run defense (76th in Rushing S&P+) breaking in two new defensive tackles is the Jackets' most pressing question.

Top 2014 NFL Prospects: DB Jemea Thomas (3–4), DE/OLB Jeremiah Attaochu (4), S Isaiah Johnson (4–5)

No. 35 Pittsburgh Panthers (8-4, 4-4)

2012: 6-7 (3-4 in Big East) / F/+ #51 / FEI #44 / S&P+ #58

Program F/+	+12.8%	23	Returning Starters: 5 OFF, 9 DEF			2012 Field Position / Special Teams		
2012 Offense			**2012 Defense**			Special Teams F/+	+0.5%	51
Offensive F/+	**+1.8%**	**54**	**Defensive F/+**	**+3.7%**	**45**	Field Position Advantage	0.511	45
Offensive FEI:	0.084	50	Defensive FEI	-0.235	34	**2013 Projections**		
Offensive S&P+	104.7	50	Defensive S&P+	102.1	52	**Mean Wins / Mean Conference Wins**	**7.6 / 4.4**	
Rushing S&P+	99.9	66	Rushing S&P+	94.8	75	Proj. F/+	+9.2%	35
Passing S&P+	108.9	41	Passing S&P+	105.3	46	Offensive F/+	+2.1%	47
Standard Downs S&P+	100.0	62	Standard Downs S&P+	96.6	74	Defensive F/+	+7.1%	21
Passing Downs S&P+	116.7	29	Passing Downs S&P+	108.8	38	Strength of Sched. Rk / Conf. Title Odds	58 / 4.3%	

What is there to say about a team coming off three consecutive trips to the BBVA Compass Bowl under three different head coaches? Welcome to Pitt, where all roads slant towards mediocrity. Since opening at No. 15 in the preseason AP poll in 2010, the Panthers are 20–19; they have not appeared in the poll again and have not beaten an opponent that finished there. Over their final two seasons in the Big East, they were 7–7 in conference games. No Panthers player was drafted after either season. The 2012 team, under first-year coach Paul Chryst, finished 51st in the overall F/+ ratings, 50th in offensive S&P+ and 52nd in defensive S&P+. The most memorable moment of the season was a missed field goal at Notre Dame that kept the Irish's perfect season alive in overtime.

To be fair, Chryst had plenty of success overseeing less-than-enthralling offenses at Wisconsin before he landed in his current gig. But the Panthers are a long way from being made over in the Badgers' brawny image: the top returning tailback, Rushel Shell, unexpectedly left the team in the spring, and the offensive line is in such a state of flux that the starting five could conceivably feature a true freshman (Dorian Johnson), a pair of redshirt freshmen (Adam Bisnowaty and Gabe Roberts) and/or a newly converted defensive lineman (T.J. Clemmings). The only known quantity offensively is senior receiver Devin Street (975 yards, 13.4 per catch, 72 percent catch rate), the latest in a long line of tall, productive Pitt targets with an obvious pro future. So Street was understandably excited in the spring by the ascension of senior Tom Savage, a former starter at Rutgers, to the top of the depth chart at quarterback. Unlike his predecessor, Tino Sunseri, Savage has more than enough arm to challenge secondaries downfield, a threat Street said "has to be an emphasis for us" if the ground game is going to stand a chance.

On paper, the strength of the defense is up the middle, home to returning senior starters at both tackle positions (Aaron Donald, Tyrone Ezell) and middle linebacker (Shane Gordon). But the Panthers were only 75th in defensive rushing S&P+, and lost another starter at linebacker, Eric Williams, to drug charges in April (as well as backup defensive tackle Khaynin Mosley-Smith, who was suspended indefinitely over the same incident). The secondary fared a little better, thanks in large part to safety Jason Hendricks, an All-Big East pick in 2012 after leading the team in tackles and the conference in interceptions. But it may be left to one or both of a pair of transfers from Michigan, Cullen Christian and Ray Vinopal, to make or break the unit as a whole.

Top 2014 NFL Prospects: WR Devin Street (3), DT Aaron Donald (4–5)

No. 71 Virginia Cavaliers (4-8, 2-6)

2012: 4-8 (2-6) / F/+ #83 / FEI #78 / S&P+ #76

Program F/+	-4.9%	73	Returning Starters: 7 OFF, 7 DEF			2012 Field Position / Special Teams		
2012 Offense			**2012 Defense**			Special Teams F/+	-4.8%	123
Offensive F/+	**-6.1%**	**88**	**Defensive F/+**	**+2.0%**	**53**	Field Position Advantage	0.435	122
Offensive FEI:	-0.209	90	Defensive FEI	-0.148	47	**2013 Projections**		
Offensive S&P+	93.7	82	Defensive S&P+	101.5	58	**Mean Wins / Mean Conference Wins**	**4.0 / 2.1**	
Rushing S&P+	90.3	98	Rushing S&P+	103.4	50	Proj. F/+	-3.3%	71
Passing S&P+	95.4	81	Passing S&P+	105.1	47	Offensive F/+	-3.8%	88
Standard Downs S&P+	89.4	104	Standard Downs S&P+	106.9	38	Defensive F/+	+0.5%	58
Passing Downs S&P+	103.1	61	Passing Downs S&P+	100.5	65	Strength of Sched. Rk / Conf. Title Odds	35 / 0.1%	

Sometimes, the line between success and dejection is a fine one, a lesson Virginia has learned the hard way. In 2011, the Cavaliers went 5-1 in games decided by a touchdown or less, and came within a game of winning the Coastal Division. In 2012, with virtually identical numbers in terms of total offense and defense, the Cavs went 2-4 in games decided by a touchdown or less and plummeted to last place. Twelve months after Mike London was voted ACC Coach of the Year for overseeing the 2011 turnaround, he found himself firing four assistants and watching a fifth bail for the NFL as the program settled back into rebuilding mode.

For a team that styles itself as a scrappy, savvy underdog, Virginia has been alarmingly bad under London in two major, correctable areas: special teams and turnover margin. Out of 124 teams nationally, UVA ranked 123rd last year in special teams F/+, a combination of mediocre place-kicking (11-of-17 on field goals), an anemic return game, and atrocious coverage on kickoffs (opponents averaged 27.5 yards per return, second-worst in the FBS, with two touchdowns). As for turnovers, the Cavs were even sloppier, turning in the worst margin in the ACC and finishing in the red in every loss. Most of the blame in this case falls on the defense, which forced a grand total of 12 takeaways in as many games. Almost half of those takeaways came in the 33-6 win over N.C. State; in the other 11 games, they managed to recover just six fumbles with one—count it, *one*—interception. The good news is that these numbers will improve, because how could they not? The Cavaliers' fumble recovery rate of 40 percent was poor but not extreme; however, they had 55 passes defensed with just four picks, an unsustainable ratio.

Unfortunately, likely improvement on defense is not matched by likely improvement on offense, especially considering the abrupt exit of the only recognizable quarterback, Phillip Sims, amid eligibility issues. Sims, a former transfer from Alabama, failed to distance himself in the spring from significantly less-touted sophomore David Watford, who becomes the de facto starter by attrition. The top four receivers (Darius Jennings, Dominique Terrell, Tim Smith and E.J. Scott) are all back, along with the leading rusher, Kevin Parks. The most intriguing player on the roster is freshman tailback Taquan "Smoke" Mizzell, the first five-star signee on London's watch. Mizzell was caught up in a misdemeanor arrest for underage possession of alcohol during an official campus visit in January, but assuming that's behind him, there is no reason to bring him along slowly.

Top 2014 NFL Prospects: CB Demetrious Nicholson* (4–5), OT Morgan Moses (5–6)

No. 88 Duke Blue Devils (4-8, 1-7)
2012: 6-7 (3-5) / F/+ #81 / FEI #87 / S&P+ #82

Program F/+	-7.2%	86	Returning Starters: 7 OFF, 7 DEF		2012 Field Position / Special Teams		
2012 Offense			**2012 Defense**		Special Teams F/+	+1.9%	22
Offensive F/+	+3.0%	50	Defensive F/+	-13.2%	116	Field Position Advantage	0.492	73
Offensive FEI:	0.146	42	Defensive FEI	0.497	113	**2013 Projections**		
Offensive S&P+	105.2	53	Defensive S&P+	85.1	112	**Mean Wins / Mean Conference Wins**	4.4 / 1.4	
Rushing S&P+	100.8	62	Rushing S&P+	84.4	115	Proj. F/+	-7.6%	88
Passing S&P+	108.2	42	Passing S&P+	81.6	113	Offensive F/+	0.0%	59
Standard Downs S&P+	102.1	53	Standard Downs S&P+	81.0	121	Defensive F/+	-7.6%	106
Passing Downs S&P+	115.6	32	Passing Downs S&P+	89.4	92	Strength of Sched. Rk / Conf. Title Odds	82 / 0.0%	

As miracles go, taking a team to the Belk Bowl usually ranks near the bottom of the list. (And that's assuming the list has even been updated to reflect that the Belk Bowl is a thing that now exists.) However, when that team is Duke, and virtually every member of that team was in diapers the last time Duke played in a bowl game, some hyperbole is warranted. With a short trip to Charlotte last December, the Blue Devils snapped an 18-year postseason drought, second-longest in the nation, and made a tiny dent in the aura of hopelessness that has long defined this program. In the decade prior to David Cutcliffe's arrival as head coach, Duke won a grand total of 17 games and fired three head coaches; when he accepted the job in December 2007, the Blue Devils were on a 25-game conference losing streak spanning three full seasons. In five years, Cutcliffe has won more games in Durham (21) than any coach since the Carter administration.

But good vibes should not be mistaken for actual upward mobility, especially when the ceiling was all too obvious. With a loss in the bowl game, the Devils ended their "breakthrough" campaign on a five-game losing streak, dropping those games by an average margin of 23 points. Opposing offenses in that skid averaged an astounding 585 yards per game on 8.2 yards per play. Duke went 0-7 against other bowl teams, allowing at least 41 points in each game. The defense as a whole finished 112th in the S&P+ ratings and 116th in F/+, worst in the ACC by far on both counts.

Fifteen defenders return this fall with some starting experience—including cornerback Ross Cockrell, who was somehow singled out amid the flames for an All-ACC nod—but experience on this defense is not much of an endorsement. Expectations are higher for linebacker Kelby Brown, a former starter who redshirted last year with a knee injury, and safety Jeremy Cash, a transfer from Ohio State. On the other side, if quarterback Anthony Boone and wide receiver Jamison Crowder slide as seamlessly as expected into the roles vacated by Sean Renfree and Conner Vernon, the most prolific pass-catch combo in school history, at least there will be some margin of error.

Top 2014 NFL Prospects: CB Ross Cockrell (4–5).

Matt Hinton

Projected Win Probabilities For ACC Teams

ACC Atlantic	12-0	11-1	10-2	9-3	8-4	7-5	6-6	5-7	4-8	3-9	2-10	1-11	0-12	8-0	7-1	6-2	5-3	4-4	3-5	2-6	1-7	0-8
					Overall Wins									Conference Wins								
Boston College	-	-	-	-	2	12	27	32	20	6	1	-	-	-	-	-	4	13	30	33	17	3
Clemson	2	12	28	31	19	7	1	-	-	-	-	-	-	18	37	30	12	3	-	-	-	-
Florida State	4	21	36	27	10	2	-	-	-	-	-	-	-	17	38	31	12	2	-	-	-	-
Maryland	-	-	-	-	1	4	12	24	29	21	8	1	-	-	-	-	3	9	25	34	23	6
North Carolina State	-	-	2	8	18	26	24	14	6	2	-	-	-	-	-	3	14	28	30	18	6	1
Syracuse	-	-	1	3	11	22	29	22	10	2	-	-	-	-	1	5	17	31	29	14	3	-
Wake Forest	-	-	-	-	3	9	21	29	23	11	4	-	-	-	-	-	3	14	31	33	16	3

ACC Coastal	12-0	11-1	10-2	9-3	8-4	7-5	6-6	5-7	4-8	3-9	2-10	1-11	0-12	8-0	7-1	6-2	5-3	4-4	3-5	2-6	1-7	0-8
Duke	-	-	-	-	1	5	15	26	29	18	6	-	-	-	-	-	-	3	12	29	37	19
Georgia Tech	-	1	6	16	26	27	17	6	1	-	-	-	-	2	7	21	31	25	11	3	-	-
Miami	-	4	15	27	29	17	6	2	-	-	-	-	-	2	12	28	32	19	6	1	-	-
North Carolina	-	3	10	23	30	22	9	3	-	-	-	-	-	2	8	24	33	23	8	2	-	-
Pittsburgh	-	1	7	17	27	26	15	5	2	-	-	-	-	-	4	15	28	29	17	5	2	-
Virginia	-	-	-	-	-	2	9	22	32	25	9	1	-	-	-	-	1	7	23	37	26	6
Virginia Tech	-	4	21	33	26	12	3	1	-	-	-	-	-	6	24	35	24	9	2	-	-	-

Big Ten Conference

Perhaps it's not a good thing that Ohio State was able to immediately reassume its spot atop the Big Ten hierarchy in Urban Meyer's first season in charge. After a step backwards in 2011's transition year (Jim Tressel resigned in the summer, and the Buckeyes played with an interim head coach all season), the flawed Buckeyes went 12-0 and solidified the conference's reputation as one with moderate quality but a lower ceiling than the SEC and Big 12. Meyer, a two-time national-title winner, and Michigan's Brady Hoke are both recruiting well enough to suggest they could bring elite play back to the Big Ten. But their ascension is not yet complete; Michigan has only once ranked in the F/+ Top 10 since 2006, and while Ohio State did go undefeated last year, the Buckeyes did so as barely a Top 15 team. And their prospective rise has not been able to counter other problems.

The bowl season didn't help. The conference always faces a challenging slate of bowls, but with Ohio State and Penn State, its best and sixth-best teams, banned from the postseason thanks to the transgressions of previous coaching staffs, most Big Ten bowl participants were forced to fight above their weight class. The results could have been worse—Wisconsin wasn't blown out by Stanford in the Rose Bowl by any means, Northwestern whipped Mississippi State in the Gator Bowl, Michigan State held off TCU in the Buffalo Wild Wings Bowl, Minnesota nearly upset Texas Tech in the Texas Bowl, and Michigan played well in a loss to South Carolina in the Outback Bowl. But moral victories aside, a 2-5 bowl record did nothing to change perceptions.

Life in the Big Ten is simultaneously better and worse than it has ever been. The quality has suffered recently, but the conference is awash in cash, thanks in part to the success of the innovative and influential Big Ten Network. It appears Ohio State and Wisconsin are the most statistically proven teams moving forward, though a young Michigan team could serve as a serious wild card. And if Ohio State can improve on just a couple of weaknesses—namely, Braxton Miller's inability to avoid a high sack rate and the "bust" portion of the secondary's boom-or-bust tendencies—their schedule is certainly easy enough to prompt a run at the national title game.

There also should be a lot of drama in the standings below that top three. Michigan State was just a few bounces (and conservative play calls) from an elite finish, Nebraska thinks this might be The Year for a return to prominence (then again, the Huskers always think that), Penn State overachieved in 2012 and could do so again, and Northwestern is building some serious buzz. The Big Ten doesn't have a single team projected in the Top 10, but with six teams ranked between 11th and 28th, the conference could see quite a few blood baths in conference play.

LEADERS

No. 10 Ohio State Buckeyes (11-1, 7-1)

2012: 12-0 (8-0) / F/+ #14 / FEI #9 / S&P+ #23

Program F/+	+23.8%	8	Returning Starters: 9 OFF, 4 DEF			2012 Field Position / Special Teams		
2012 Offense			2012 Defense			Special Teams F/+	-0.7%	82
Offensive F/+	+12.4%	13	Defensive F/+	+11.3%	20	Field Position Advantage	0.505	55
Offensive FEI:	0.470	10	Defensive FEI	-0.482	15	2013 Projections		
Offensive S&P+	119.5	16	Defensive S&P+	114.7	25	Mean Wins / Mean Conference Wins	10.8 / 6.9	
Rushing S&P+	125.7	6	Rushing S&P+	115.0	21	Proj. F/+	+20.6%	10
Passing S&P+	115.6	33	Passing S&P+	110.5	32	Offensive F/+	+13.1%	5
Standard Downs S&P+	125.5	8	Standard Downs S&P+	104.3	49	Defensive F/+	+7.5%	19
Passing Downs S&P+	108.0	49	Passing Downs S&P+	128.1	14	Strength of Sched. Rk / Conf. Title Odds	88 / 34.6%	

Is it possible to be simultaneously overrated and underrated? Banned from the postseason, Ohio State went a perfect 12-0 in 2012, establishing itself as a perceived national title contender for 2013. But as mentioned above, the Buckeyes did so with help from some smoke and mirrors. They won six games by a touchdown or less (including games against Purdue and Indiana), and while the offense improved dramatically in Meyer's first season, it was still rather inconsistent and inefficient. Overrated!

At the same time, however, a lot of those close games were close because of some pretty awful turnover luck. The Buckeyes recovered just 44 percent of fumbles and intercepted just 16 percent of their defensed passes (the national average usually hovers around 21 percent and, like fumble recovery rate, tends to regress or progress toward the mean from year to year). Turnovers are worth approximately five points each, so you could conservatively say that turnovers luck cost them at least two or three points per game in 2012. Plus, Ohio State was one of only seven teams to rank in the top 20 of both Offensive and Defensive F/+. Underrated!

To be sure, this is a team with some elite talent. Braxton Miller has perhaps the most electrifying quarterback speed burst in the country now that Michigan's Denard Robinson is in the NFL; he can go from second to fifth gear in a heartbeat. He still takes far too many sacks to be an elite quarterback overall (he was sacked 27 times in just 281 pass attempts in 2012), but he is a wonderful runner and will follow blocks from a line that returns four starters, including left guard Andrew Norwell and left tackle Jack Mewhort. And while the passing game will still face efficiency issues as long as Miller is taking sacks, possession receiver Corey Brown (669 yards, 11.2 per catch, 71 percent catch rate) and big-play threat Devin Smith (618, 20.6, 52 percent) lead a seasoned receiving corps.

The Ohio State defense had an issue with big plays in 2012 (40th in PPP+), but it was beautifully efficient, especially on the ground, and it consistently made stops in the red zone. It is led by incredible outside linebacker Ryan Shazier (17 tackles for loss, five sacks, 11 passes defended, three forced fumbles) and a maddening, high-risk, high-reward trio of defensive backs in corner Bradley Roby and safeties Christian Bryant

and C.J. Barnett (combined: five tackles for loss, five interceptions, 35 passes broken up). Shazier is the only returnee in the front seven who managed even 9.5 tackles last year—the defense is pretty green overall—but while one should probably expect a bit of a drop-off against the run, great recruiting will prevent too much of a tumble.

Even if the foundation isn't as strong as Alabama's, Ohio State should certainly make a run at the national title game with the combination of a very good team and an easy schedule. The Buckeyes have only one road game versus a projected Top-30 team (Michigan) and get their toughest opponent (Wisconsin) at home.

Top 2014 NFL prospects: *OLB Ryan Shazier (1-2), CB Bradley Roby (1-2), OT Jack Mewhort (3-4), G Andrew Norwell (4-5)*

No. 16 Wisconsin Badgers (10-2, 7-1)

2012: 8-6 (4-4) / F/+ #16 / FEI #15 / S&P+ #20

Program F/+	+19.6%	13	Returning Starters: 8 OFF, 6 DEF			2012 Field Position / Special Teams		
2012 Offense			**2012 Defense**			Special Teams F/+	-0.3%	72
Offensive F/+	**+7.4%**	**28**	Defensive F/+	+13.3%	14	Field Position Advantage	0.552	10
Offensive FEI:	0.233	30	Defensive FEI	-0.492	12	**2013 Projections**		
Offensive S&P+	115.7	26	Defensive S&P+	121.6	16	**Mean Wins / Mean Conference Wins**	**10.0 / 6.5**	
Rushing S&P+	110.2	39	Rushing S&P+	122.3	13	Proj. F/+	+17.7%	16
Passing S&P+	117.6	27	Passing S&P+	123.4	16	Offensive F/+	+7.9%	16
Standard Downs S&P+	109.4	37	Standard Downs S&P+	120.8	12	Defensive F/+	+9.8%	14
Passing Downs S&P+	117.2	28	Passing Downs S&P+	124.4	19	Strength of Sched. Rk / Conf. Title Odds	62 / 19.7%	

Losing three-time Rose Bowl coach Bret Bielema to an SEC also-ran was certainly a blow for the perceptions of the Big Ten, but in replacing Bielema with Gary Andersen, Wisconsin made one of the smarter, more exciting hires of the offseason coaching derby. Andersen did some amazing things in a short amount of time at Utah State—the Aggies improved from 102nd in Defensive F/+ in 2010 to ninth in 2012, and from 100th to 17th overall—and he brings both an interesting run offense (to which Wisconsin fans are obviously accustomed) and a ferocious, fun 3-4 defense to Madison.

Wisconsin already improved by quite a bit defensively in 2012, and it will be interesting to see if Andersen and his defensive coordinator, Dave Aranda, can engineer further improvement this fall. They definitely inherit what could be a tremendous front seven. End David Gilbert and outside linebacker Mike Taylor are gone, but everybody else is back, from linebacker Chris Borland (10 tackles for loss, 4.5 sacks, six passes defended), to tackle Beau Allen (7.5 tackles for loss), to end-turned-outside linebacker Brendan Kelly (six tackles for loss). Wisconsin was already a great blitzing team last year, as evidenced in part by a ranking of 22nd in Sack Rate on Passing Downs, and could be again in 2013.

There are a few concerns in the secondary; depth was an issue in 2012, and that was before the loss of three starting defensive backs. Senior safety Dezmen Southward returns, but

there will be quite a few redshirt freshmen and, potentially, true freshmen in the rotation.

In replacing its star quarterback and offensive coordinator, along with the meat of a great line, Wisconsin's offense faltered for a while in 2012. But despite shuffling at quarterback, the Badgers began to figure things out in October and thrived late in the year. Their 640-yard, 70-point eruption against Nebraska in the Big Ten title game may have been the single most impressive offensive performance in 2012.

Longtime star running back Montee Ball is gone, but Andersen inherits a couple of fascinating pieces at that position in James White (836 yards, 6.4 per carry, 9.9 highlight yards per opportunity) and Melvin Gordon (631, 10.3, 9.8). The offense picked up when receiver Jared Abbrederis (837 yards, 17.1 per catch, 69 percent catch rate) returned from injury, and despite the fact that it felt like he was a senior two years ago, Abbrederis still has another year of eligibility. There are plenty of options at quarterback—the most intriguing is probably Joel Stave, who threw for 1,104 yards and completed 59 percent of his passes before going down with an injury—but while every noteworthy receiver and tight end returns, some youth on the offensive line will be tested.

Top 2014 NFL prospects: *WR Jared Abbrederis (3-4), ILB Chris Borland (4-5), TE Jacob Pederson (4-5), RB James White (4-5)*

No. 24 Penn State Nittany Lions (9-3, 5-3)

2012: 8-4 (6-2) / F/+ #25 / FEI #31 / S&P+ #25

Program F/+	+18.5%	15	Returning Starters: 6 OFF, 6 DEF			2012 Field Position / Special Teams		
2012 Offense			2012 Defense			Special Teams F/+	-1.4%	94
Offensive F/+	+3.8%	47	Defensive F/+	+12.5%	19	Field Position Advantage	0.509	50
Offensive FEI:	0.131	44	Defensive FEI	-0.439	19	2013 Projections		
Offensive S&P+	108.9	48	Defensive S&P+	122.0	22	Mean Wins / Mean Conference Wins	8.8 / 5.2	
Rushing S&P+	97.9	71	Rushing S&P+	115.9	19	Proj. F/+	+12.4%	24
Passing S&P+	103.2	53	Passing S&P+	116.6	21	Offensive F/+	+3.7%	36
Standard Downs S&P+	100.2	61	Standard Downs S&P+	121.5	10	Defensive F/+	+8.7%	16
Passing Downs S&P+	105.3	56	Passing Downs S&P+	101.8	59	Strength of Sched. Rk / Conf. Title Odds	48/--	

So what happens now? The 12 months that Penn State experienced from December 2011 through November 2012 were among the most turbulent a football program could ever face. After the Jerry Sandusky scandal, the NCAA took a cruel, punitive hammer to the Penn State football program, fining the school $60 million, banning the Nittany Lions from the postseason for four years, limiting the Nittany Lions to 15 scholarship signees per year through 2017, vacating all wins since 1998 (which bumped Paterno from the top of the all-time wins list), and putting Penn State on five years of probation. It was a death penalty without giving a death penalty.

Despite the sanctions and drama, and despite the loss of a few key players to transfer, new head coach Bill O'Brien somehow managed to put a pretty competitive team on the field in 2012. In fact, the Nittany Lions actually *improved*, from 31st to 25th in F/+. The defense regressed a bit but was still strong, and the offense improved from 89th in Offensive F/+ to 47th. O'Brien, the former offensive coordinator for the New England Patriots, was able to find competence in a depleted passing game and move the ball just well enough to do his defense some favors, and Penn State went 8-4 as a result.

Of course, the hard work is just beginning. Penn State is down to 67 scholarship players in 2013 and will not be allowed to carry more than 65 beginning in 2014. The Nittany Lions have some interesting pieces at just about every position, but any injury troubles could be crippling. They also need a quarterback. Matt McGloin graduated, and presumptive starter Steven Bench transferred, which means the most likely starters are either junior college transfer Tyler Ferguson or five-star true freshman Christian Hackenberg, who has yet to actually don the Penn State helmet.

Either Ferguson or Hackenberg will inherit a potentially exciting, fun receiving corps that is led by junior Allen Robinson and high-upside youngsters like sophomore tight ends Kyle Carter and Jesse James. The running game, however, could struggle. Both big Zach Zwinak and shifty Bill Belton were decent, and all-conference guard John Urschel returns, but the Nittany Lions ranked just 71st in Rushing S&P+ last year, and the line returns only three players with starting experience (24 career starts).

The defense, meanwhile, should hold together for another year. Sophomore end Deion Barnes, junior linebacker Mike Hull, and sophomore safety Jacob Fagnano are all potential stars, and linebacker Glenn Carson should be a steady senior in the middle.

Top 2014 NFL prospects: *WR Allen Robinson* (3-4), MLB Glenn Carson (5-6), G John Urschel (6-7)*

No. 62 Indiana Hoosiers (5-7, 3-5)

2012: 4-8 (2-6) / F/+ #74 / FEI #71 / S&P+ #85

Program F/+	-13.1%	98	Returning Starters: 10 OFF, 9 DEF			2012 Field Position / Special Teams		
2012 Offense			2012 Defense			Special Teams F/+	+0.9%	46
Offensive F/+	+4.9%	42	Defensive F/+	-12.2%	110	Field Position Advantage	0.486	81
Offensive FEI:	0.272	24	Defensive FEI	0.428	106	2013 Projections		
Offensive S&P+	104.4	54	Defensive S&P+	84.6	114	Mean Wins / Mean Conference Wins	5.4 / 2.7	
Rushing S&P+	93.4	86	Rushing S&P+	88.0	103	Proj. F/+	-1.6%	62
Passing S&P+	109.4	40	Passing S&P+	77.9	121	Offensive F/+	+3.6%	37
Standard Downs S&P+	103.2	51	Standard Downs S&P+	87.6	106	Defensive F/+	-5.2%	91
Passing Downs S&P+	108.9	45	Passing Downs S&P+	73.9	120	Strength of Sched. Rk / Conf. Title Odds	33 / 0.1%	

With Ohio State and Penn State banned from the postseason, and with wins over Illinois and Iowa in their back pocket, Kevin Wilson's Indiana Hoosiers needed only to beat Wisconsin at home to seize control of a potential bid in the Big Ten title game. Unfortunately, an awful defense got gashed by Wisconsin in a 62-14 loss, and the Hoosiers quietly faded to 4-8. Still, the offense showed more promise than it has in a long, long time, and it should continue to grow in 2013, even if the defense is still, to put it kindly, a work in progress.

Despite shuffling at quarterback and an iffy offensive line, Indiana's offense moved into the Offensive F/+ top 50. All of last year's quarterback candidates return, led by junior Cameron Coffman. Cody Latimer (805 yards, 15.8 per catch, 79 percent catch rate) is easily the most intriguing member of an experienced receiving corps, and running back Stephen Houston showed some solid explosiveness when given space to run.

The Indiana defense attacked the line and tried its best to make some plays; the Hoosiers had try *something*, as they were going to get burned otherwise. And they got burned often—Indiana's blitz was torched by quarterback scrambles and draw plays, opposing receivers had all sorts of room to run, and Indiana finished the season ranked 121st in Passing S&P+. Another year of experience and another Wilson re-

cruiting class could help a little bit, but it is difficult to find reasons to assume this unit will improve dramatically.

Top 2014 NFL prospects: *RB Stephen Houston (6-7), S Greg Heban (6-7)*

No. 80 Purdue Boilermakers (3-9, 2-6)

2012: 6-7 (3-5) / F/+ #76 / FEI #89 / S&P+ #74

Program F/+	-4.8%	72	Returning Starters: 5 OFF, 8 DEF			2012 Field Position / Special Teams		
2012 Offense			**2012 Defense**			Special Teams F/+	-0.3%	74
Offensive F/+	**-6.4%**	**92**	**Defensive F/+**	**-0.2%**	**60**	Field Position Advantage	0.496	69
Offensive FEI:	-0.278	103	Defensive FEI	-0.028	60	**2013 Projections**		
Offensive S&P+	96.8	72	Defensive S&P+	100.6	61	**Mean Wins / Mean Conference Wins**	2.9 / 1.5	
Rushing S&P+	95.4	79	Rushing S&P+	94.6	77	Proj. F/+	-5.3%	80
Passing S&P+	98.5	69	Passing S&P+	102.6	51	Offensive F/+	-5.6%	98
Standard Downs S&P+	95.6	81	Standard Downs S&P+	96.5	78	Defensive F/+	+0.3%	59
Passing Downs S&P+	102.1	63	Passing Downs S&P+	104.5	53	Strength of Sched. Rk / Conf. Title Odds	25 / 0.0%	

Tressel Ball has come to West Lafayette. Darrell Hazell, a former assistant under Jim Tressel at Ohio State who was last seen bringing big-time football to Kent State for the first time in 40 years, takes over for Danny Hope in 2013. His Kent State teams were defensively sound and run-heavy; needless to say, history shows that this style can win games in the Big Ten, though it remains to be seen whether Hazell can bring enough pure talent to the table to make it work.

Hazell's disciplined style will certainly help a team that was lacking it in 2012. The Boilermakers' defense was terribly porous against the run; its all-or-nothing line was either making big plays or allowing them. Tackle Bruce Gaston (5.5 tackles

for loss) could be a good anchor, but the star of the defense, tackle Kawann Short, is gone (a second-round pick by Carolina). Thankfully, the high quality of cornerbacks Ricardo Allen and Frankie Williams will help the defensive line do its job.

Last year's Purdue offense was terribly inefficient but bailed itself out with the occasional big play. The best big-play receiver, Antavian Edison, is gone, but the more touches running back Akeem Hunt can handle, the better. A track star, Hunt could thrive in imitation of Dri Archer, the squirty Kent State back who became a big-play star in 2012.

Top 2014 NFL prospects: *DT Bruce Gaston (5-6)*

No. 94 Illinois Fighting Illini (3-9, 1-7)

2012: 2-10 (0-8) / F/+ #108 / FEI #110 / S&P+ #111

Program F/+	-3.2%	65	Returning Starters: 8 OFF, 3 DEF			2012 Field Position / Special Teams		
2012 Offense			**2012 Defense**			Special Teams F/+	-2.6%	113
Offensive F/+	**-14.2%**	**117**	**Defensive F/+**	**-2.5%**	**71**	Field Position Advantage	0.442	118
Offensive FEI:	-0.534	120	Defensive FEI	-0.057	56	**2013 Projections**		
Offensive S&P+	83.9	109	Defensive S&P+	90.5	88	**Mean Wins / Mean Conference Wins**	2.9 / 0.8	
Rushing S&P+	92.6	91	Rushing S&P+	88.2	102	Proj. F/+	-8.5%	94
Passing S&P+	85.9	105	Passing S&P+	91.9	88	Offensive F/+	-4.6%	94
Standard Downs S&P+	94.3	86	Standard Downs S&P+	90.3	94	Defensive F/+	-3.9%	84
Passing Downs S&P+	75.0	120	Passing Downs S&P+	92.9	85	Strength of Sched. Rk / Conf. Title Odds	45 / 0.0%	

It is difficult to figure out how 2012 could have gone worse for the Fighting Illini. They outscored Western Michigan and Charleston Southern, 68-7… and then got outscored *378-132* by their other 10 opponents. In the first year under head coach Tim Beckman, an experienced defense regressed considerably, and an awful offense figured out how to get worse.

It isn't immediately clear how Illinois will improve in 2013. Any gains the offense makes—and with a decent amount of experience, it should improve at least a little bit—should be offset by a defense that must replace its top four linemen, two of its top four linebackers, and four of its top five defensive backs. The leading returning lineman (Tim Kynard) had three tackles for loss last year, and the only truly known entities are linebackers Mason Monheim and Jonathan Brown, who combined for 15.5 tackles for loss and four sacks.

Relatively speaking, the offensive line was the strength of

the Illini offense, but it must now replace its two best players, including all-conference tackle Hugh Thornton (now in Indianapolis as a third-rounder). Nathan Scheelhaase returns for his fourth year as Illinois' starting quarterback (unless he is usurped by 2012 part-timer Reilly O'Toole or sophomore Chase "Son of Jim" Haslett; he has regressed in each of the last two seasons), but he got almost no help from his receivers last year. Ryan Lankford (469 receiving yards, 12.7 per catch, 59 percent catch rate) was as good as it got in 2012. Scheelhaase and backs Donovonn Young and Josh Ferguson are decent runners, but there is almost no big-play ability to be found here.

Top 2014 NFL prospects: *OLB Jonathan Brown (3-4)*

Bill Connelly

LEADERS

No. 18 Michigan State Spartans (10-2, 7-1)

2012: 7-6 (3-5) / F/+ #15 / FEI #23 / S&P+ #16

Program F/+	+14.2%	22	Returning Starters: 8 OFF, 7 DEF			2012 Field Position / Special Teams		
2012 Offense			**2012 Defense**			Special Teams F/+	+0.6%	50
Offensive F/+	**-0.7%**	**61**	**Defensive F/+**	**+20.8%**	**3**	Field Position Advantage	0.499	65
Offensive FEI:	-0.056	66	Defensive FEI	-0.683	2	**2013 Projections**		
Offensive S&P+	104.1	59	Defensive S&P+	137.2	5	**Mean Wins / Mean Conference Wins**	**9.9 / 6.6**	
Rushing S&P+	98.4	69	Rushing S&P+	139.9	2	Proj. F/+	+17.4%	18
Passing S&P+	92.3	85	Passing S&P+	145.3	1	Offensive F/+	+3.1%	40
Standard Downs S&P+	91.7	95	Standard Downs S&P+	146.4	2	Defensive F/+	+14.3%	6
Passing Downs S&P+	104.6	58	Passing Downs S&P+	126.5	16	Strength of Sched. Rk / Conf. Title Odds	63 / 28.3%	

Michigan State was the anti-Ohio State in 2012, struggling with big plays on offense instead of defense and losing five games by a touchdown or less. The Spartans' defense was incredible, ranking in the Defensive F/+ top five for a second straight year, but the offense was both conservative and uninspiring, taking few risks and failing to find reward in the few it took.

Michigan State attempted 32 field goals last fall, second-most in the country. (Oklahoma State attempted more, but the Cowboys also scored the fifth-most touchdowns in the country; Michigan State had the eighth-fewest.) The Spartans were scared to take chances with points on the line, instead electing to employ the "Make sure a drive ends in points no matter what" strategy that was mocked so thoroughly in *The Hidden Game of Football*. But can you blame the Spartans for taking no chances? Your play-calling is going to be terrified when your quarterback terrifies you. Andrew Maxwell got decent protection last fall and had what were theoretically a few decent targets in players like tight end Dion Sims. But the connection wasn't there for some reason, either because of the play-calling, Maxwell, the receivers, or all of the above. State leaned on running back Le'Veon Bell with minimal payoff, and when it was time to throw, Maxwell just didn't get the job done.

Bell was Javon Ringer II in 2012, eating up over 29 carries per game without really getting anywhere. He was smart to go pro early, because he would have taken another career's worth of hits in 2013. All Michigan State running backs not named Bell combined for just 48 total carries, meaning we really have no idea what Bell's replacements—Nick Hill, Jeremy Langford, and Nick Tompkins—have to offer. We do know the line is well-seasoned, though, with 96 career starts and seven players with starting experience.

The defense loses some interesting pieces, but some strong players remain. Linebackers Max Bullough and Denicos Allen (combined: 22.5 tackles for loss, 5.5 sacks, nine passes defensed) are just awesome, and safety Kurtis Drummond and corner Darqueze Dennard offer a high level of aggression without much downside.

The dynamics for Michigan State in 2013 should be rather familiar. The Spartans will have no reason to suddenly open up the play-calling, take chances on fourth downs, and throw 40 times per game. They are going to do what they do offensively: hand the ball off, hand the ball off again, and make sure to give the defense a decent amount of field with which to operate. And the defense will likely respond well to that. The Spartans will probably be a Top-20 team again in 2013, but Top-20 results will depend on the offense moving the chains at least a more times and maybe reaching the end zone now and then.

Top 2014 NFL prospects: *OLB Denicos Allen (3-4), ILB Max Bullough (3-4), CB Darqueze Dennard (5-6)*

No. 21 Nebraska Cornhuskers (10-2, 6-2)

2012: 10-4 (7-1) / F/+ #19 / FEI #19 / S&P+ #17

Program F/+	+17.5%	19	Returning Starters: 8 OFF, 3 DEF			2012 Field Position / Special Teams		
2012 Offense			**2012 Defense**			Special Teams F/+	-2.0%	103
Offensive F/+	**+14.2%**	**8**	**Defensive F/+**	**+7.7%**	**30**	Field Position Advantage	0.457	110
Offensive FEI:	0.504	8	Defensive FEI	-0.239	32	**2013 Projections**		
Offensive S&P+	124.2	8	Defensive S&P+	116.4	20	**Mean Wins / Mean Conference Wins**	**9.7 / 5.9**	
Rushing S&P+	139.2	3	Rushing S&P+	108.4	36	Proj. F/+	+14.3%	21
Passing S&P+	121.9	15	Passing S&P+	117.5	19	Offensive F/+	+11.9%	7
Standard Downs S&P+	129.9	4	Standard Downs S&P+	106.6	41	Defensive F/+	+2.4%	46
Passing Downs S&P+	125.1	15	Passing Downs S&P+	122.9	20	Strength of Sched. Rk / Conf. Title Odds	78 / 13.9%	

In the years since Bo Pelini succeeded Bill Callahan as head coach in Lincoln, the Nebraska Cornhuskers have been consistently good but rarely great. Ndamukong Suh led an incredible defensive effort in 2009, and in his 2010 absence the Huskers rode a wonderful secondary to another top-10 defense and 10-win season. Offense was a problem (60th in Offensive F/+ in 2009, 40th in 2010), but as the offense began to round into form in the last couple of years, the defense has taken a step backwards. The Huskers were 38th in Defensive F/+ in 2011, with almost no disruptive force up front, but both the offense and defense took lovely steps forward in 2012 … just as the special teams unit fell apart; after ranking in the top

20 in Special Teams F/+ for four straight years, the Huskers plummeted to 103rd last fall.

Is this the year the pieces all fall into place for Pelini? Probably not, but he should once again put a quality team onto the field. Special teams could struggle again without all-world kicker Brett Maher, and the defense must replace its top three linemen, top three linebackers, and two starting safeties. The offense could be in position to move forward again, but the defense could offset a lot of those gains.

If you watched any Nebraska game on television last season, you probably heard all you wanted to hear about how quarterback Taylor Martinez had worked on his throwing motion and had improved dramatically as a passer. This was in no way true, but it made a lovely story. In essence, the play-calling and offensive line improved dramatically, not Martinez, whom you should still never, under any circumstances ask to throw a ball more than 10 yards. Nebraska still struggled mightily on passing downs (44th in Passing S&P+ on passing downs), but the Huskers didn't face many, both because the run game was so good and because offensive coordinator Tim Beck gave Martinez some easy passes to make on standard downs, when opponents were gearing up for the rush.

This dynamic should play out again in 2013 as Martinez (1,255 pre-sack rushing yards, 7.8 per carry), running back Ameer Abdullah, receiver Kenny Bell, and four senior linemen with starting experience all return. Bell and the line were both wonderful surprises last fall, and there's little reason to think they will regress in 2013.

There will be quite a bit of reconstruction on the defensive side of the ball. The secondary should still be fine: nickelback Ciante Evans (three tackles for loss, nine passes defensed) returns, as do three sticky, experienced corners (Andrew Green, Josh Mitchell, Stanley Jean-Baptiste). But the front seven is cause for concern. Senior defensive end Jason Ankrah (six tackles for loss) was decent last season, and sophomore linebacker David Santos made the most of his minimal playing time in 2012, but there is very little experience here. Defensive end Randy Gregory, a four-star junior-college transfer, will face pressure to perform immediately, and freshman linebackers Josh Banderas and Marcus Newby could quickly see the field.

Top 2014 NFL prospects: *G Spencer Long (3-4), OT Jeremiah Sirles (6-7), CB Ciante Evans (6-7)*

No. 28 Michigan Wolverines (7-5, 4-4)

2012: 8-5 (6-2) / F/+ #20 / FEI #26 / S&P+ #19

Program F/+	+8.7%	34	Returning Starters: 6 OFF, 6 DEF			2012 Field Position / Special Teams		
2012 Offense			**2012 Defense**			Special Teams F/+	+0.6%	49
Offensive F/+	+10.2%	16	Defensive F/+	+8.6%	28	Field Position Advantage	0.483	84
Offensive FEI:	0.267	25	Defensive FEI	-0.338	26	**2013 Projections**		
Offensive S&P+	124.0	9	Defensive S&P+	113.7	29	**Mean Wins / Mean Conference Wins**	**7.0 / 4.1**	
Rushing S&P+	118.5	14	Rushing S&P+	116.3	18	Proj. F/+	+10.1%	28
Passing S&P+	127.7	11	Passing S&P+	102.0	54	Offensive F/+	+5.3%	29
Standard Downs S&P+	121.2	13	Standard Downs S&P+	107.4	34	Defensive F/+	+4.9%	32
Passing Downs S&P+	121.0	20	Passing Downs S&P+	107.2	45	Strength of Sched. Rk / Conf. Title Odds	41 / 1.8%	

The 2013 season should be one of transition for Michigan, between what the Wolverines have been for a few years and what they could become as quality recruiting truly begins to take effect. Because of the overall turnover—gone are quarterback/running back Denard Robinson, defensive linemen William Campbell and Craig Roh, all-conference guard Patrick Omameh, linebacker Kenny Demens, and safety Jordan Kovacs—and because the team's recent history has been only decent and not great, Michigan is projected conservatively. But if blue-chippers in the trenches and elsewhere begin to click pretty quickly this fall, the Wolverines could be a threat to vastly exceed their projection.

This is Devin Gardner's offense now. The junior quarterback played a bit at wide receiver last year while Robinson played out his senior season, but when Robinson got hurt, Gardner took over and produced stellar results. He completed 60 percent of his passes and averaged a healthy 8.3 yards per pass attempt in leading the Michigan offense. He is a solid threat to run, and he has a couple of exciting weapons in senior wideouts Jeremy Gallon (829 yards, 16.9 per catch, 62 percent catch rate) and Drew Dileo (331, 16.6, 67 percent).

Robinson will perhaps be missed more at running back than at quarterback. Returning backs Fitzgerald Toussaint and

Thomas Rawls were strong in the open field but inconsistent in getting there. They could be pushed by five-star freshman Derrick Green soon. The offensive line did not do the backs many favors, either. The Wolverines were 70th in Adjusted Line Yards, and need to improve their run blocking to keep Gardner out of obvious passing situations. There is a star up front in senior tackle and future first-round pick Taylor Lewan, and the unit has blue-chippers abound, but with three new starters, inexperience could be an issue.

The defensive front seven was quite strong against the run last year, but a surprisingly poor pass rush (82nd in Adjusted Sack Rate) and a glitchy, young secondary led to poor overall pass numbers. The Wolverines couldn't afford to be very aggressive here, and they leaked a lot of seven-yard gains on third-and-7. The secondary should be steady with the return of injured cornerback Blake Countess to the rotation, but the front seven will face a lot of change, especially if star linebacker Jake Ryan (16 tackles for loss) is slow to recover from an offseason knee injury.

Top 2014 NFL prospects: *OT Taylor Lewan (1), OLB Jake Ryan* (3-4), OT Michael Schofield (5-6), DT Quinton Washington (6-7)*

No. 40 Northwestern Wildcats (7-5, 3-5)

2012: 10-3 (5-3) / F/+ #29 / FEI #21 / S&P+ #46

Program F/+	+2.9%	51	Returning Starters: 6 OFF, 6 DEF			2012 Field Position / Special Teams		
2012 Offense			**2012 Defense**			Special Teams F/+	+3.7%	4
Offensive F/+	+5.8%	37	Defensive F/+	+3.4%	46	Field Position Advantage	0.535	18
Offensive FEI:	0.239	29	Defensive FEI	-0.165	45	**2013 Projections**		
Offensive S&P+	109.7	47	Defensive S&P+	105.4	50	**Mean Wins / Mean Conference Wins**	**6.6 / 3.2**	
Rushing S&P+	111.2	35	Rushing S&P+	98.7	63	Proj. F/+	+5.6%	40
Passing S&P+	101.8	55	Passing S&P+	102.1	53	Offensive F/+	+3.2%	38
Standard Downs S&P+	107.8	41	Standard Downs S&P+	105.6	42	Defensive F/+	+2.4%	47
Passing Downs S&P+	103.3	60	Passing Downs S&P+	89.0	95	Strength of Sched. Rk / Conf. Title Odds	47 / 0.6%	

For Pat Fitzgerald at Northwestern, growth has come in cycles. The Wildcats sank to 84th in 2007, his second year in charge, then surged to 42nd in 2008. They sank back to 73rd by 2010 but broke through in a major way last fall. Northwestern won 10 games for just the second time in a century last fall and came within eight points (a seven-point loss to Michigan and a one-point, last-second loss to Nebraska) of a division title. They improved dramatically on defense and in special teams and whipped Mississippi State in the Gator Bowl. It was a stellar campaign. And in 2013, basically every Northwestern player you can name returns. Depth could be an issue, but it's improving, and this Northwestern team has more star power, on both sides of the ball, than any Wildcats team since Fitzgerald was in uniform.

The Northwestern defense was the story in 2012. A major liability in both 2010 and 2011, it improved to 46th in Defensive F/+. It was still a work in progress, of course; the Wildcats faded on that side of the ball in November and still showed some damning glitches on passing downs. The defensive line was light and active, making a lot of plays in the backfield but getting pushed around in short yardage; it will still be pretty light in 2013, with one projected starting end weighing in at 230 pounds and only one tackle over 275. But at this point, that's not a bug; it's a feature. The activity level is strong, especially when it's coming from senior end Tyler Scott (12.5 tackles for loss, nine sacks, five passes defensed). And linebacker Chi Chi Ariguzo (10.5 tackles for loss, seven passes defensed) is both aggressive and wonderfully named.

The offense gets to be weird for one more year, with quarterback Kain Colter (872 passing yards, 5.0 per pass attempt; 894 pre-sack rushing yards, 6.1 per carry) handling most of the run-first situations and Trevor Siemian (1,312 passing yards, 5.7 per pass attempt) subbing in for pass-first situations. The weapons are adding up, as well: running back and star punt returner Venric Mark is a keeper, and junior receiver Christian Jones showed some potential as a possession receiver. But as with the defense, this is still a work in progress: not a single Northwestern receiver averaged better than 12 yards per catch. That must change.

Top 2014 NFL prospects: *RB Venric Mark (4-5), DE Tyler Scott (5-6)*

No. 44 Iowa Hawkeyes (6-6, 3-5)

2012: 4-8 (2-6) / F/+ #72 / FEI #63 / S&P+ #86

Program F/+	+12.7%	24	Returning Starters: 6 OFF, 7 DEF			2012 Field Position / Special Teams		
2012 Offense			**2012 Defense**			Special Teams F/+	+1.5%	33
Offensive F/+	-6.5%	94	Defensive F/+	-0.9%	63	Field Position Advantage	0.518	39
Offensive FEI:	-0.189	85	Defensive FEI	-0.031	58	**2013 Projections**		
Offensive S&P+	90.8	92	Defensive S&P+	98.0	67	**Mean Wins / Mean Conference Wins**	**6.3 / 3.1**	
Rushing S&P+	94.8	81	Rushing S&P+	112.3	29	Proj. F/+	+4.6%	44
Passing S&P+	88.4	98	Passing S&P+	91.3	89	Offensive F/+	+0.1%	58
Standard Downs S&P+	92.9	92	Standard Downs S&P+	102.3	57	Defensive F/+	+4.5%	35
Passing Downs S&P+	88.6	95	Passing Downs S&P+	100.5	64	Strength of Sched. Rk / Conf. Title Odds	42 / 0.4%	

Iowa's football program has fallen on hard times in recent years under longtime coach Kirk Ferentz. The slope has been steep and consistent: 11-2 and 11th in F/+ in 2009, 8-5 and 21st in 2010, 7-6 and 46th in 2011, 4-8 and 72nd in 2012. Last year's Hawkeyes lost their final six games and showed less than no hope of figuring things out on the offensive side of the ball. But athletic director Gary Barta is sticking with Ferentz, and not completely without cause. Under Ferentz, Iowa won 10 or more games four times and finished in the Top 10 for three straight seasons. But the last year of that streak was 2004. Doubting Ferentz is both en vogue and understandable at this point.

The defense, long a strength for Ferentz's teams, remained solid against the run in 2012; the Hawkeyes ranked 29th in Rushing S&P+ and thrived in short-yardage situations. But with no semblance of a pass rush, the pass defense suffered dramatically. Even with corner Micah Hyde (four tackles for loss, 15 passes defensed), the Hawkeyes ranked an awful 89th in Passing S&P+. Hyde is now in Green Bay, and since it is unclear who is going to resurrect what was once a fantastic front four, the inexperienced cornerbacks might not get much help.

But the defense is still ahead of the offense. The run-first Hawkeyes couldn't keep running backs healthy, but there weren't any holes for even healthy backs to find. If 100 percent, big Mark Weisman could be good; he combines nice size (236 pounds) with athleticism (5.9 highlight yards per opportunity). He could see plenty of carries, as Iowa will be starting an untested quarterback—likely either sophomore Jake Rudock or junior Cody Sokol—and trotting out a receiving corps with no explosiveness and minimal efficiency. Iowa's projection is a sign of respect for the long-term stability of the Hawkeyes' program, but that respect is fading quickly.

Top 2014 NFL prospects: *TE C.J. Fiedorowicz (3-4), OLB James Morris (4-5), OLB Anthony Hitchens (5-6)*

No. 72 Minnesota Golden Gophers (5-7, 1-7)

2012: 6-7 (2-6) / F/+ #79 / FEI #74 / S&P+ #81

Program F/+		-8.8%	88	Returning Starters: 10 OFF, 6 DEF			2012 Field Position / Special Teams		
2012 Offense				**2012 Defense**			Special Teams F/+	-1.0%	88
Offensive F/+		**-6.4%**	**93**	**Defensive F/+**	**-0.1%**	**59**	Field Position Advantage	0.497	66
Offensive FEI:		-0.218	92	Defensive FEI	-0.063	54	**2013 Projections**		
Offensive S&P+		93.0	83	Defensive S&P+	98.8	70	**Mean Wins / Mean Conference Wins**	**4.6 / 1.3**	
Rushing S&P+		94.6	83	Rushing S&P+	89.6	96	Proj. F/+	-4.1%	72
Passing S&P+		97.8	71	Passing S&P+	109.1	37	Offensive F/+	-2.5%	78
Standard Downs S&P+		94.1	87	Standard Downs S&P+	96.6	75	Defensive F/+	-1.6%	70
Passing Downs S&P+		96.5	79	Passing Downs S&P+	108.4	39	Strength of Sched. Rk / Conf. Title Odds	55 / 0.0%	

Scheduling easy has its benefits. Minnesota began the season 4-0 last year, with wins over UNLV, New Hampshire, Western Michigan, and a Syracuse team that hadn't yet clicked. With a 4-0 start in their back pocket, the Gophers rode wins over Purdue and Illinois to bowl eligibility and a feeling of true momentum for a program that has lacked it for a while. Now, Minnesota was certainly a better team in 2012 than it had been in a few years, but only by so much. The good news is that the Gophers were young last year and could see quite a bit more improvement in Jerry Kill's third season in charge.

The Minnesota offense was below average in just about every way last fall, but the offensive line, a relative strength, returns everybody (nine players with starting experience, 109

starts), and quarterback Philip Nelson should progress in his sophomore year. His horrific 49 percent completion rate must improve, but he needs some help from his receivers, too. Only Derrick Engel (375 receiving yards, 20.8 per catch, 62 percent catch rate) averaged better than 6.5 yards per target.

The Minnesota defense was exciting and aggressive against the run, but the Gophers must replace an exciting pair of cornerbacks (Troy Stoudermire and Michael Carter) and their best pass rusher (D.L. Wilhite). Sophomores and juniors are taking over the defensive depth chart, for better or worse.

Top 2014 NFL prospects: *DT Ra'Shede Hageman (2-3), OT Ed Olson (6-7), S Brock Vereen (6-7)*

Projected Win Probabilities For Big Ten Teams

Leaders	12-0	11-1	10-2	9-3	8-4	7-5	6-6	5-7	4-8	3-9	2-10	1-11	0-12	8-0	7-1	6-2	5-3	4-4	3-5	2-6	1-7	0-8
						Overall Wins											**Conference Wins**					
Illinois	-	-	-	-	-	-	1	6	20	36	31	6	-	-	-	-	-	-	3	16	41	40
Indiana	-	-	-	1	4	14	28	30	17	5	1	-	-	-	-	-	3	17	39	30	9	2
Ohio State	27	40	24	8	1	-	-	-	-	-	-	-	-	29	41	23	6	1	-	-	-	-
Penn State	1	6	22	32	24	11	3	1	-	-	-	-	-	1	10	30	35	18	5	1	-	-
Purdue	-	-	-	-	-	-	1	6	20	35	30	8	-	-	-	-	-	2	12	35	40	11
Wisconsin	7	28	35	21	7	2	-	-	-	-	-	-	-	12	42	33	11	2	-	-	-	-
Legends	12-0	11-1	10-2	9-3	8-4	7-5	6-6	5-7	4-8	3-9	2-10	1-11	0-12	8-0	7-1	6-2	5-3	4-4	3-5	2-6	1-7	0-8
Iowa	-	-	1	5	14	25	27	19	8	1	-	-	-	-	-	2	10	25	32	22	8	1
Michigan	-	1	3	11	22	28	22	10	3	-	-	-	-	-	2	10	25	31	22	8	2	-
Michigan State	5	24	36	24	9	2	-	-	-	-	-	-	-	19	40	29	10	2	-	-	-	-
Minnesota	-	-	-	-	1	5	16	30	31	15	2	-	-	-	-	-	-	2	9	26	39	24
Nebraska	5	20	32	26	12	3	2	-	-	-	-	-	-	5	24	35	25	9	2	-	-	-
Northwestern	-	-	2	6	17	27	27	15	5	1	-	-	-	-	-	3	11	26	33	21	6	-

Big 12 Conference

"Listen, they've had the best team in college football, meaning they've won the national championship. That doesn't mean everything else is always the best. So you're listening to a lot of propaganda that gets fed out to you."

Among Bob Stoops' many offseason rants was one about the narrative that has long since outweighed all others in college football: the SEC is king. The Southeastern Conference has produced the last seven national champions, and while that has required plenty of luck along the way—in 2006, 2007, 2009, 2011, and 2012, at the very least, late-season losses by teams in other conferences allowed SEC teams (and eventual national champions) to sneak into the BCS title game after losses of their own—it has certainly solidified the story line. The SEC draws in more big-time recruits, spends more money, and perhaps produces more truly elite teams than other conferences. But if you want the most *competitive* league, you might need to move a few states to the west.

The Big 12 schedule is a nine-game bloodbath of teams with similar talent levels, and in a lot of cases similar styles. It has produced four different champions in the last four years. And in 2013, with a set of teams loaded with mostly underclassman talent and few projected top picks for 2014, it could easily produce the most interesting major-conference title race.

Both projections and conventional wisdom alike say that Alabama should win the SEC this season. Ohio State could cruise in the Big Ten. Oregon and Stanford should separate themselves in the Pac-12, Florida State and Clemson will duke it out in the ACC, and Louisville should cruise to the initial American Athletic Conference title. But nobody has a damn clue about the Big 12.

It could be an old-school, Oklahoma-Texas showdown for the title.

Oklahoma State could run away with the championship for a second time in three years.

A restocked TCU offense could help the Horned Frogs to re-establish their elite bona fides.

It could be the year that Baylor—*BAYLOR!!!*—puts all the pieces together.

It could be another Bill Snyder masterpiece at Kansas State.

As many as six teams enter 2013 feeling like this could be their season in the Big 12, and while the F/+ projections narrow that race down to three or four teams, no other conference has more than two-thirds of its membership projected within the F/+ Top 42 this season. The Big 12 is compact and competitive, and it plays a deliriously entertaining brand of football. On average, the SEC may be the best conference, but virtually every Big 12 conference game is a must-watch this season. There's something to be said for that.

No. 6 Oklahoma State Cowboys (10-2, 7-2)

2012: 8-5 (5-4) / F/+ #12 / FEI #14 / S&P+ #15

Program F/+	+23.2%	9	Returning Starters: 6 OFF, 7 DEF			2012 Field Position / Special Teams		
2012 Offense			**2012 Defense**			Special Teams F/+	+2.5%	10
Offensive F/+	**+12.8%**	**12**	**Defensive F/+**	**+10.0%**	**24**	Field Position Advantage	0.491	75
Offensive FEI:	0.505	7	Defensive FEI	-0.277	30	**2013 Projections**		
Offensive S&P+	118.8	14	Defensive S&P+	122.6	12	**Mean Wins / Mean Conference Wins**	**10.1 / 7.1**	
Rushing S&P+	111.2	36	Rushing S&P+	112.9	26	Proj. F/+	+21.5%	6
Passing S&P+	119.5	23	Passing S&P+	112.6	27	Offensive F/+	+10.7%	9
Standard Downs S&P+	119.4	16	Standard Downs S&P+	101.6	58	Defensive F/+	+10.8%	12
Passing Downs S&P+	104.3	59	Passing Downs S&P+	137.5	8	Strength of Sched. Rk / Conf. Title Odds	40 / 29.9%	

Building a football powerhouse where one didn't previously exist takes money and time. Wealthy alumnus T. Boone Pickens has made sure that Oklahoma State has plenty of the former, and, entering the ninth season of the Mike Gundy era in Stillwater, OSU has invested plenty of the latter as well. Gundy took over for Les Miles when the Mad Hatter took the LSU job in 2004, and he has slowly but surely raised OSU's profile to a sustained level it has really never seen before. In the 1980s, Pat Jones inherited Jimmy Johnson's growing program and did good things with it—five straight winning seasons, three Top 12 finishes—but things came crashing down when Barry Sanders left town and the NCAA's enforcement unit moved in.

Gundy, a quarterback on those 1980s OSU teams, has taken a rather incredible, slow-but-steady approach to building the stature of the 'Pokes. They won 14 total games in 2006-07, 18

in 2008-09, and 23 in 2010-11. With a young team and some bad breaks (they were 1-3 in one-possession games and got crushed by turnovers in a loss to Arizona), they slumped to 8-5 last year, but they did so with a No. 12 F/+ ranking, ahead of teams like South Carolina and Ohio State. The Cowboys were on the brink of something much bigger in 2012, and they could potentially improve by a decent amount this fall.

The biggest question for Gundy right now might be whether he can weather another offensive coordinator change without a backslide. He replaced Dana Holgorsen (who had left for the West Virginia job) with Todd Monken and didn't miss a beat. With Monken leaving for the head coaching job at Southern Miss, Gundy made a fun hire: He brought in Shippensburg offensive coordinator Mike Yurcich, whose Division II Raiders offense averaged nearly 400 passing yards and five passing touchdowns per game last season.

Yurcich certainly inherits some players more athletic than what he was dealing with in southern Pennsylvania. Running backs Jeremy Smith (371 yards, 5.3 per carry, 4.3 highlight yards/opportunity) and Desmond Roland (301, 6.5, 6.6) will take over for Joseph Randle, who crossed the Red River but stays a Cowboy. The winner of the quarterback competition—either Clint Chelf or J.W. Walsh, both of whom got starting experience last year because of injuries—will have his pick of receivers; the top seven inside receivers and five of the top six wideouts all return.

Oklahoma State also has a new defensive coordinator. It's hard to say that Cowboys alum Bill Young was doing a

bad job, but he has been pushed out as Gundy searches for an influx of new ideas and incremental defensive improvement. Glen Spencer, who has spent the last four seasons as OSU's linebackers coach, takes his place. The Cowboys were tremendous on passing downs last year (eighth in S&P+) but weren't as successfully aggressive as they had been in 2011. An average pass rush could get worse with the loss of last year's top three defensive ends, but stellar linebackers and a pair of seasoned safeties (Daytawion Lowe and Shamiel Gary) should help to stabilize the unit overall.

Top 2014 NFL prospects: *CB Justin Gilbert (2-3), DT Calvin Barnett (3-4), RB Jeremy Smith (5-6), ILB Caleb Lavey (6-7)*

No. 8 Texas Longhorns (10-2, 7-2)
2012: 9-4 (5-4) / F/+ #24 / FEI #17 / S&P+ #36

Program F/+		+20.6%	11	Returning Starters: 9 OFF, 9 DEF			2012 Field Position / Special Teams		
2012 Offense				**2012 Defense**			Special Teams F/+	+1.6%	30
Offensive F/+		**+9.5%**	**18**	**Defensive F/+**	**+4.5%**	**40**	Field Position Advantage	0.534	21
Offensive FEI:		0.400	16	Defensive FEI	-0.198	38	**2013 Projections**		
Offensive S&P+		113.3	24	Defensive S&P+	107.4	32	**Mean Wins / Mean Conference Wins**	**9.5 / 7.0**	
Rushing S&P+		114.1	23	Rushing S&P+	97.9	65	Proj. F/+	+21.3%	8
Passing S&P+		114.2	35	Passing S&P+	117.8	18	Offensive F/+	+11.7%	8
Standard Downs S&P+		110.9	32	Standard Downs S&P+	108.5	32	Defensive F/+	+9.7%	15
Passing Downs S&P+		116.1	31	Passing Downs S&P+	110.1	34	Strength of Sched. Rk / Conf. Title Odds	31 / 26.2%	

So, is *this* the year it all comes back together for Mack Brown? The Texas head coach spent a year lost in the woods following his team's devastating loss in the 2009 BCS title game. Texas fell to 5-7 and 65th in the F/+ rankings in 2010, and Brown cleaned house and brought in some new assistants in 2011. Two years later, both the offense and defense have shown improvement and potential—Texas ranked sixth in Defensive F/+ in 2011 and 18th in Offensive F/+ in 2012—but the pieces haven't all clicked yet. Last year's offensive improvement was offset by injuries and regression on defense. Can health and experience change things around a bit?

Injuries and a general lack of quality at linebacker hurt Texas tremendously in 2012. The Longhorns didn't seem to recover from the early-season loss of linebacker Jordan Hicks; pass coverage and tackling in space were both issues, and it probably goes without saying that those are significantly damaging problems against wide-open Big 12 offenses. Despite the midseason loss of end Jackson Jeffcoat to injury, Texas still finished the year first in Adjusted Sack Rate because of both a 10-sack performance versus Oregon State in the Alamo Bowl and an amazing season from senior Alex Okafor (18 tackles for loss, 12.5 sacks), who finished with as many sacks as the rest of the line combined.

The aggressive line could be victimized by quality ground games, however. A set of young, former blue-chip defensive tackles (Desmond Jackson, Ashton Dorsey, Malcom Brown) hasn't quite lived up to the hype, and with the struggles at linebacker adding to the overall issues, Texas ranked just 65th in Rushing S&P+ and 59th in Adjusted Line Yards. Just about everybody but Okafor returns up front, but the loss of Okafor alone could significantly damage the pass rush, even

if/when Jeffcoat is 100 percent healthy this fall. We'll see if corners Quandre Diggs and Carrington Byndom (combined: seven tackles for loss, seven interceptions, 13 passes broken up in 2012) can carry the extra weight required by a less active pass rush.

With offensive co-coordinator Bryan Harsin taking the head coaching job at Arkansas State, fellow co-coordinator Major Applewhite becomes the lone man in charge of the Texas offense this year. He opened things up a bit in last year's Alamo Bowl, but one has to assume that Texas is still going to end up leaning heavily on its ground game in 2013. Quarterback David Ash has shown potential as a dual threat, with decent running ability (5.2 yards per carry, not including sacks) and a 67 percent completion rate. He has a trio of quality backs in the backfield: Johnathan Gray, Joe Bergeron, and Malcolm Brown. As a freshman, sophomore, and sophomore, respectively, they combined for 1,589 yards (4.7 per carry) behind an underachieving line in 2012. Texas does return 124 career starts up front and even adds the rare (for Texas) junior college transfer, tackle Desmond Harrison, in an attempt to finally shore up what has been a disappointing unit for a few years now.

At receiver, Mike Davis and Jaxon Shipley return to lead the way, along with Texas' resident crack-in-case-of-big-play-emergency guy sophomore Daje Johnson, who had 27 carries for 203 yards and 19 catches (in 23 targets) for 287 yards as a freshman.

Top 2014 NFL prospects: *DE Jackson Jeffcoat* (1-2), CB Quandre Diggs* (2-3), CB Carrington Byndom (4-5), G Mason Walters (4-5)*

No. 7 Oklahoma Sooners (9-3, 7-2)

2012: 10-3 (8-1) / F/+ #8 / FEI #6 / S&P+ #9

Program F/+	+29.2%	3	Returning Starters: 7 OFF, 4 DEF			2012 Field Position / Special Teams		
2012 Offense			**2012 Defense**			Special Teams F/+	+1.4%	34
Offensive F/+	**+15.0%**	**6**	**Defensive F/+**	**+10.6%**	**23**	Field Position Advantage	0.512	44
Offensive FEI:	0.535	4	Defensive FEI	-0.339	25	**2013 Projections**		
Offensive S&P+	125.3	6	Defensive S&P+	120.9	15	**Mean Wins / Mean Conference Wins**	**9.4 / 7.0**	
Rushing S&P+	105.9	53	Rushing S&P+	100.5	58	Proj. F/+	+21.4%	7
Passing S&P+	117.6	28	Passing S&P+	144.5	2	Offensive F/+	+13.6%	4
Standard Downs S&P+	106.9	43	Standard Downs S&P+	118.2	16	Defensive F/+	+7.8%	18
Passing Downs S&P+	135.4	7	Passing Downs S&P+	125.5	18	Strength of Sched. Rk / Conf. Title Odds	22 / 25.8%	

Bob Stoops has been feisty this offseason. The 15th-year Oklahoma head coach has been speaking on any number of topics this offseason, and it hasn't just been limited to the SEC and propaganda.

On paying student athletes: "I tell my guys all the time: You're not the first one to spend a hungry Sunday without any money."

On the BCS selection process: "Going into the bowl games, Northern Illinois had one loss, we had two. Theirs was to Iowa, right? Ours were to Notre Dame and K-State. And … they got the bid to the BCS bowl ahead of us."

On college football players transferring: "It isn't right that they can just do what they want to do. It isn't good. I don't believe in it. […] Nobody made them sign with me. I didn't force them to, it was what they wanted to do."

You can forgive Stoops if he has a bee in his bonnet this offseason. Outside of Tuscaloosa, it's hard to find a more consistently strong program than Oklahoma in recent years. Over the last six seasons, Oklahoma has ranked seventh, fourth, ninth, eighth, eighth, and eighth in the F/+ rankings. But it's been four seasons since the Sooners churned out a truly elite product, and each season seems to feature a blowout loss to a former OU whipping boy. Last year, it was a 41-13 pummeling at the hands of Texas A&M in the Cotton Bowl. Oklahoma still wins 10 games every year and probably will again this season, but they don't reward good in Norman, only great.

For better or worse, OU's identity will change drastically in 2013. On offense, longtime starting quarterback Landry Jones has finally run out of eligibility. His presumed replacement, Blake Bell, has been used as a short-yardage, "Belldozer" back for a couple of seasons but is still a work in progress when it comes to the forward pass. His presence could be used to solidify a ground game that was truly average on the ground last year (53rd in Rushing S&P+), with explosive running back Damien Williams (906 rushing yards, 5.7 per carry, 9.0 highlight yards per opportunity) running behind a flawed line that ranked 102nd in Adjusted Line Yards. Seven offensive linemen return with starting experience, including all-conference center Gabe Ikard, but even with both Ikard and first-round pick Lane Johnson around last season, OU still ranked only 102nd in Adjusted Line Yards. Luckily senior Jalen Saunders (829 receiving yards, 13.4 per catch, 82 percent catch rate in nine games) and sophomore Sterling Shepard (621 yards, 13.8, 73 percent) will make sure the passing game has some juice.

With so many new starters, the depth chart on defense reads like something from the Riddler's wardrobe: question marks everywhere. The Sooners were a horror show up front, ranking 107th in Adjusted Line Yards and 56th in Adjusted Sack Rate in 2012. They got mowed over in short yardage and made almost no plays behind the line. The top names on the depth chart are gone, too, which means youngsters like blue-chip freshmen D.J. Ward (DE) and Kerrick Huggins (DT) could see early playing time. But if the line stinks, that's at least not new; it did last year, too. The secondary made up for a lot of the struggle—somehow, OU ranked second in Passing S&P+ despite a mediocre pass rush—but safeties Tony Jefferson and Javon Harris are gone, as is corner Demontre Hurst. Aaron Colvin was a revelation last year, improving from all-potential to potential first-round pick; he'll have to be even more of one this time around.

Top 2014 NFL prospects: *CB Aaron Colvin (1-2), FB Trey Millard (3-4), WR Jalen Saunders (4-5), C Gabe Ikard (4-5)*

No. 11 TCU Horned Frogs (9-3, 7-2)

2012: 7-6 (4-5) / F/+ #31 / FEI #22 / S&P+ #32

Program F/+	+25.5%	6	Returning Starters: 7 OFF, 9 DEF			2012 Field Position / Special Teams		
2012 Offense			**2012 Defense**			Special Teams F/+	+0.3%	55
Offensive F/+	**-2.6%**	**70**	**Defensive F/+**	**+14.6%**	**12**	Field Position Advantage	0.519	38
Offensive FEI:	-0.103	71	Defensive FEI	-0.561	11	**2013 Projections**		
Offensive S&P+	99.9	64	Defensive S&P+	122.2	18	**Mean Wins / Mean Conference Wins**	**9.1 / 6.7**	
Rushing S&P+	91.9	94	Rushing S&P+	123.2	11	Proj. F/+	+20.4%	11
Passing S&P+	102.9	54	Passing S&P+	115.8	22	Offensive F/+	+4.1%	33
Standard Downs S&P+	96.1	78	Standard Downs S&P+	113.5	21	Defensive F/+	+16.3%	2
Passing Downs S&P+	96.2	81	Passing Downs S&P+	134.7	10	Strength of Sched. Rk / Conf. Title Odds	15 / 17.6%	

TCU's first season back at the major-conference level was … OK. The Horned Frogs survived serious offseason attrition, a wealth of injuries, a much tougher schedule, and the loss of their quarterback to rehab to finish 7-6 with a reasonably healthy No. 31 F/+ ranking. The defense held its own as always, but the offense couldn't help but regress with what turned out to be a terribly young lineup.

Quarterback Casey Pachall should be back in uniform and behind center this fall, which is excellent news. The senior has thrown for nearly 4,000 yards in 17 starts, with 35 touchdowns and just eight interceptions. When he missed the final nine games of the 2012 season, TCU not only fell apart on passing downs (81st in PD S&P+) but also fell *into* too many passing downs because of struggles on the ground. Running back Waymon James tore an ACL early in the year, and a backfield of freshman quarterback Trevone Boykin and freshman running back B.J. Catalon just couldn't get the job done just yet. Both showed potential, but the return of Pachall and James is wonderful news in the short term.

Pachall will be without the services of last year's No. 1 target, Josh Boyce (now in New England), but Brandon Carter, LaDarius Brown, and Cam White all return.

By now, we have learned to trust that Gary Patterson will put out a quality defense no matter the circumstances. Despite quite a bit of turnover, the Horned Frogs ranked 11th in Rushing S&P+ and 10th on passing downs in 2012. TCU was wonderfully efficient in the secondary, ranking 16th in Passing Success Rate+.

This year's unit should be perfectly fine, even with the early-season suspension of star end Devonte Fields. When Fields returns, he'll team with tackles Chucky Hunter and Davison Pierson (combined: 13.5 tackles for loss, seven sacks), and the line will make its share of big plays; so, too, will middle linebacker Joel Hasley and an ultra-aggressive secondary. Corners Jason Verrett and Kevin White (combined: five tackles for loss, 25 passes defensed) and safeties Elisha Olabode, Sam Carter, and Chris Hackett will give TCU the most intimidating secondary in the conference.

Top 2014 NFL prospects: *CB Jason Verrett (1-2), WR Brandon Carter* (4-5), QB Casey Pachall (6-7), FS Elisha Olabode (6-7)*

No. 37 Baylor Bears (7-5, 4-5)

2012: 8-5 (4-5) / F/+ #30 / FEI #18 / S&P+ #33

Program F/+	+1.3%	53	Returning Starters: 6 OFF, 7 DEF			2012 Field Position / Special Teams		
2012 Offense			**2012 Defense**			Special Teams F/+	-2.0%	102
Offensive F/+	**+19.6%**	**3**	Defensive F/+	-5.1%	79	Field Position Advantage	0.51	49
Offensive FEI:	0.846	1	Defensive FEI	0.238	85	**2013 Projections**		
Offensive S&P+	122.8	11	Defensive S&P+	99.0	60	**Mean Wins / Mean Conference Wins**	**6.9 / 4.2**	
Rushing S&P+	122.0	12	Rushing S&P+	96.3	71	Proj. F/+	+7.5%	37
Passing S&P+	126.1	12	Passing S&P+	94.6	77	Offensive F/+	+9.2%	13
Standard Downs S&P+	115.5	20	Standard Downs S&P+	98.7	69	Defensive F/+	-1.8%	71
Passing Downs S&P+	145.2	5	Passing Downs S&P+	89.9	90	Strength of Sched. Rk / Conf. Title Odds	28 / 0.2%	

Can a team be a dark horse if everybody is picking it to be a dark horse? Art Briles' Baylor Bears have slowly but surely put the pieces together to create a strong, mean, and incredibly fast team, one that can move the ball at will no matter who is lost to graduation, and one that might be starting to figure out the "defense" side of the equation.

Baylor's No. 37 projection is a nice reminder that when it comes to certain aspects of the game, Baylor still might have a long way to go. The Bears' defense perked up over the last few games of the season, and it looked great in the Holiday Bowl domination of UCLA, but it hasn't come close to looking good over the course of an entire season yet. In the last three years, the Baylor defense has ranked 97th, 87th, and 79th in Defensive F/+. It ranked 71st in Rushing S&P+, 69th in Adjusted Line Yards, 77th in Passing S&P+, and 104th in Adjusted Sack Rate. The end-of-year improvement was nice, but Baylor will need a lot more of that to make a run at the conference crown.

There certainly is good talent to build a defense around. Linebackers Bryce Hager and Eddie Lackey (combined: 24 tackles for loss, six sacks, four interceptions) are aggressive and fun, and the secondary managed to be pretty aggressive, too, considering the non-existent pass rush. Safety Ahmad Dixon, nickelback Sam Holl, and corner Joe Williams are all potential keepers, but with the loss of tackles Gary Mason, Jr., and Nick Johnson, there are still at least a couple of gaping holes in the Baylor lineup.

On offense, however, it should be more of the same. Baylor lost quarterback Robert Griffin III along with receivers Kendall Wright and Josh Gordon following 2011, and the poor Bears sank from second in Offensive F/+ all the way to third. This time around, they must replace quarterback Nick Florence and receiver Terrance Williams, but one assumes they're not too worried. It's Bryce Petty's turn to line up behind center, and with Tevin Reese (957 receiving yards, 18.1 per catch, 62 percent catch rate) and Levi Norwood (487 yards, 12.2, 76 percent), the receiving corps will still have plenty of track-star speed. Throw in running back Lache Seastrunk, who erupted for 831 rushing yards and six touchdowns in the last six games of last season, and you've got a potential Heisman candidate in the backfield along with the explosive receivers. It's almost unfair.

Top 2014 NFL prospects: *RB Lache Seastrunk* (1-2), OT Cyril Richardson (2-3), S Ahmad Dixon (3-4), RB Glasco Martin (5-6)*

No. 41 Kansas State Wildcats (7-5, 4-5)

2012: 11-2 (8-1) / F/+ #9 / FEI #4 / S&P+#24

Program F/+	+4.6%	42	Returning Starters: 6 OFF, 2 DEF			2012 Field Position / Special Teams		
2012 Offense			**2012 Defense**			Special Teams F/+	+4.6%	1
Offensive F/+	**+9.4%**	**19**	**Defensive F/+**	**+12.9%**	**16**	Field Position Advantage	0.577	1
Offensive FEI:	0.337	21	Defensive FEI	-0.563	10	**2013 Projections**		
Offensive S&P+	116.8	23	Defensive S&P+	115.7	24	**Mean Wins / Mean Conference Wins**	6.6 / 3.8	
Rushing S&P+	107.3	46	Rushing S&P+	110.4	33	Proj. F/+	+5.2%	41
Passing S&P+	120.5	20	Passing S&P+	113.6	25	Offensive F/+	+5.2%	30
Standard Downs S&P+	105.6	46	Standard Downs S&P+	111.6	25	Defensive F/+	-0.1%	63
Passing Downs S&P+	128.8	12	Passing Downs S&P+	112.2	31	Strength of Sched. Rk / Conf. Title Odds	26 / 0.1%	

So now what? Bill Snyder came back out of retirement to rescue a Kansas State football program that had lost its way, and after a slog in 2009-10, the Wildcats exploded. They went 10-3 without elite statistical production in 2011; they ranked 29th in the F/+ rankings but surged to a Cotton Bowl appearance thanks to an 8-1 record in one-possession games. In 2012, they became their record, improving to ninth in F/+ and winning 11 games and Snyder's second conference title. It was another stunning accomplishment for a man who has quite a few of them.

In 2013, Snyder faces the biggest test of his second term: He must continue figuring out how to win without the benefit of star quarterback Collin Klein, linebacker Arthur Brown, cornerbacks Allen Chapman and Nigel Malone, leading receiver Chris Harper, and all of the Wildcats' top five defensive linemen. Last year's team was loaded with both experience and star power. Now Snyder will have to unearth quite a bit of both.

With a wonderfully experienced offensive line and the return of senior running back John Hubert, execution on standard downs could still be solid for whoever wins the KSU quarterback job (either Daniel Sams or Jake Waters). But the loss of both Klcin and Harper will hurt. KSU has two ridiculously explosive receivers in Tyler Lockett (687 receiving yards, 15.6 per catch, 69 percent catch rate) and Tramaine Thompson (526, 14.2, 66 percent), but it will take time to build a rapport like the one Klein and Harper had.

Meanwhile, it could certainly be argued that the defense is in more danger than the offense. KSU had one of the nation's premiere bend-don't-break defenses last year (44th in Success Rate+ but 20th in PPP+), and cornerback Randall Evans and 18th-year safety Ty Zimmerman return to anchor what should be a decent secondary. But the front seven will need some reinforcement, and Snyder strangely recruited only six junior college players in the 2013 class.

Top 2014 NFL prospects: *OT Cornelius Lucas (3-4), S Ty Zimmerman (3-4)*

No. 42 Texas Tech Red Raiders (6-6, 4-5)

2012: 8-5 (4-5) / F/+ #45 / FEI #45 / S&P+ #48

Program F/+	+7.8%	36	Returning Starters: 5 OFF, 8 DEF			2012 Field Position / Special Teams		
2012 Offense			**2012 Defense**			Special Teams F/+	+0.1%	58
Offensive F/+	**+7.9%**	**25**	**Defensive F/+**	**-1.1%**	**64**	Field Position Advantage	0.481	87
Offensive FEI:	0.308	23	Defensive FEI	0.041	66	**2013 Projections**		
Offensive S&P+	113.0	33	Defensive S&P+	101.4	53	**Mean Wins / Mean Conference Wins**	6.3 / 3.6	
Rushing S&P+	105.9	52	Rushing S&P+	101.9	52	Proj. F/+	+5.0%	42
Passing S&P+	117.0	30	Passing S&P+	100.6	59	Offensive F/+	+3.2%	39
Standard Downs S&P+	112.7	28	Standard Downs S&P+	99.6	63	Defensive F/+	+1.8%	51
Passing Downs S&P+	121.6	19	Passing Downs S&P+	108.2	40	Strength of Sched. Rk / Conf. Title Odds	23 / 0.2%	

The fun has returned to Lubbock. Mike Leach and his Air Raid offense were run out of town after the 2009 season, creating a bit of a divide between the school administrators who pushed Leach out and the fans who loved him. Three years of Tommy Tuberville saw decent results (a 21-17 record and two bowl wins), but there was never a strong connection between Tuberville and the Tech fan base. Tuberville left for Cincinnati, and Tech made an inspired choice to replace him: former Leach quarterback Kliff Kingsbury. Kingsbury pushed the buttons for perhaps the nation's most fun offense (Texas A&M) in 2012, and now he takes over at his alma mater.

At first glance, it appears the personnel could fit well with what Kingsbury wants to do. Tech had a rather efficient passing offense in 2012, but while the Red Raiders must replace starting quarterback Seth Doege and four of their top seven receivers, sophomore signal-caller Michael Brewer was recruited to Lubbock to run a similar system, and receivers like Eric Ward, Jakeem Grant, and big Jace Amaro are back. The line is rather inexperienced, but hey, so is the coach. Youth is the watchword in Lubbock this year, and expectations should probably be tempered because of it.

Last year's Tech defense, meanwhile, was neither great nor terrible at anything. The front seven will have to carry some weight while a green secondary gets its footing. Three veteran defensive ends—Kerry Hyder, Dartwan Bush, and Jackson Richards—combined last year for 29.5 tackles for loss, 12 sacks, and six passes defensed They head a play-making line that needs to improve its down-to-down consistency.

Top 2014 NFL prospects: *DT Kerry Hyder (5-6), WR Eric Ward (5-6)*

No. 38 West Virginia Mountaineers (7-5, 4-5)

2012: 7-6 (4-5) / F/+ #47 / FEI #52 / S&P+ #42

Program F/+	+11.9%	28	Returning Starters: 4 OFF, 7 DEF			2012 Field Position / Special Teams		
2012 Offense			**2012 Defense**			Special Teams F/+	-2.1%	105
Offensive F/+	+11.0%	15	**Defensive F/+**	-2.4%	69	Field Position Advantage	0.481	88
Offensive FEI:	0.410	15	Defensive FEI	0.073	73	**2013 Projections**		
Offensive S&P+	118.3	15	Defensive S&P+	98.8	55	**Mean Wins / Mean Conference Wins**	6.5 / 3.7	
Rushing S&P+	112.2	30	Rushing S&P+	105.8	46	Proj. F/+	+6.2%	38
Passing S&P+	128.5	10	Passing S&P+	87.5	100	Offensive F/+	+4.7%	32
Standard Downs S&P+	118.6	17	Standard Downs S&P+	103.1	52	Defensive F/+	+1.5%	54
Passing Downs S&P+	131.5	8	Passing Downs S&P+	82.8	107	Strength of Sched. Rk / Conf. Title Odds	27 / 0.1%	

The 2012 season was an enormous tease for WVU. The Mountaineers rode an amazing, exciting offense to a 5-0 start and a No. 5 poll ranking, but it turns out that allowing 63 points, even to Baylor (in a 70-63 win) is a bad sign for your national title hopes. The Mountaineers lost five games in a row, allowing at least 39 points in each, and had to rally to even reach bowl eligibility.

Dana Holgorsen has been known as one of college football's greatest offensive minds for a while, but in 2013 the West Virginia head coach will see his mettle tested as he attempts to replace a spectacular set of offensive playmakers. Can he do so, and fix a disappointing defense, without dropping below six wins and bowl eligibility?

To shore up an intimidating batch of losses—quarterback Geno Smith, record-setting receivers Tavon Austin and Stedman Bailey, three three-year starting offensive linemen, and linebackers Terence Garvin and Josh Francis—Holgorsen will be leaning heavily on transfers, both of the junior college and "from another school" variety. One, quarterback Clint Trickett (ex-Florida State), could give the Mountaineers an immediate boost, at long as he can beat 2012 backup Paul Millard. Another, running back Charles Sims (ex-Houston), could give the Mountaineers a much-needed explosive threat. Inconsistent running back Andrew Buie is WVU's leading returning rusher and receiver; he and Sims will be running behind a line tasked with replacing its entire interior. A Holgorsen offense will always move the ball, but one has to expect a learning curve in 2013.

New defensive coordinator Keith Patterson (last year's linebackers coach and co-coordinator) will attempt to clean up the wreckage of a defense that ranked fourth in Defensive F/+ as recently as 2010 but fell to 69th in 2012. The line held up well, and the run defense wasn't that bad, but the pass defense was a horror show. West Virginia ranked 55th in Adjusted Sack Rate but only 100th in Passing S&P+ because of an inexperienced, leaky secondary. Linebackers Isaiah Bruce and Shaq Petteway are interesting, as are safeties Karl Joseph and Darwin Cook, but there is much work to be done.

Top 2014 NFL prospects: *DE Will Clarke (6-7), S Darwin Cook (6-7)*

No. 79 Iowa State Cyclones (3-9, 2-7)

2012: 6-7 (3-6) / F/+ #55 / FEI #39 / S&P+ #63

Program F/+	-7.0%	85	Returning Starters: 6 OFF, 4 DEF			2012 Field Position / Special Teams		
2012 Offense			**2012 Defense**			Special Teams F/+	+1.2%	40
Offensive F/+	-2.0%	65	**Defensive F/+**	+3.0%	47	Field Position Advantage	0.524	33
Offensive FEI:	-0.006	58	Defensive FEI	-0.128	50	**2013 Projections**		
Offensive S&P+	96.0	65	Defensive S&P+	106.3	35	**Mean Wins / Mean Conference Wins**	3.0 / 1.5	
Rushing S&P+	95.6	78	Rushing S&P+	107.9	37	Proj. F/+	-5.1%	79
Passing S&P+	89.9	94	Passing S&P+	108.0	38	Offensive F/+	-2.7%	82
Standard Downs S&P+	89.7	102	Standard Downs S&P+	105.1	45	Defensive F/+	-2.4%	73
Passing Downs S&P+	97.1	76	Passing Downs S&P+	118.3	25	Strength of Sched. Rk / Conf. Title Odds	30 / 0.0%	

Iowa State head coach Paul Rhoads has established quite the pattern of upsets and minor bowls. The Cyclones have finished between 5-7 and 7-6 in each of his four seasons in charge, but it should be noted that the overall quality improved by quite a bit in 2012; ISU rose from 85th in the 2010 F/+ rankings, to 72nd in 2011, to 55th in 2012.

In 2012, ISU's offense couldn't withstand a downpour of injuries and wilted, but the late-season emergence of young quarterback Sam B. Richardson offered some hope. Richardson will be without three of last year's top four receivers, but they were mostly replaceable. Tight end Ernst Brun showed his potential for 2013 with an explosive performance in the Liberty Bowl (four catches, 102 yards, and a touchdown), and a mix-and-match stable of senior running backs is, at worst, competent; James White, Shontrelle Johnson, and big Jeff Woody combined for 1,202 yards and six touchdowns last year.

On defense, a bend-don't-break unit was led by stellar linebacker play that masked line deficiencies. But without four of its top six linebackers, it will be difficult to mask the lack of depth on a line that loses five of its top seven. Linebacker Jeremiah George and safety Jacques Washington are keepers, but ISU will have to lean on quite a few youngsters to hold the fort.

Top 2014 NFL prospects: *S Jacques Washington (6-7)*

No. 112 Kansas Jayhawks (2-10, 0-9)

2012: 1-11 (0-9) / F/+ #104 / FEI #93 / S&P+ #103

Program F/+		-11.2%	92	Returning Starters: 5 OFF, 4 DEF				2012 Field Position / Special Teams			
2012 Offense				**2012 Defense**				Special Teams F/+		-4.2%	121
Offensive F/+		**-7.8%**	**103**	**Defensive F/+**	**-6.0%**	84		Field Position Advantage		0.455	114
Offensive FEI:		-0.167	81	Defensive FEI	0.224	83		**2013 Projections**			
Offensive S&P+		84.8	107	Defensive S&P+	94.8	73		**Mean Wins / Mean Conference Wins**		**1.8 / 0.4**	
Rushing S&P+		104.6	56	Rushing S&P+	100.1	61		Proj. F/+		-15.9%	112
Passing S&P+		76.6	119	Passing S&P+	97.3	68		Offensive F/+		-7.8%	110
Standard Downs S&P+		95.9	79	Standard Downs S&P+	92.5	90		Defensive F/+		-8.1%	108
Passing Downs S&P+		82.5	109	Passing Downs S&P+	118.1	26		Strength of Sched. Rk / Conf. Title Odds		18 / 0.0%	

Charlie Weis is going all-in on junior college transfers in 2013. The second-year Kansas head coach did not inherit much talent from Turner Gill, and after struggling with the players he inherited and a few senior transfers, Weis decided the Jayhawks needed a serious talent transfusion; he signed a whopping 15 JUCOs (five on offense, 10 on defense).

It's easy to see why Weis would focus so heavily on the defensive side of the ball. The top five defensive backs are all gone, and the front seven couldn't rush the passer to save its life; by the end of spring practice, a majority of the two-deep on the defensive line and in the secondary was already populated by transfers and redshirt freshmen. Linebacker Ben Heeney (12 tackles for loss) is a bright spot, especially against the run, but with so much new blood, it is nearly impossible to project what this defense might do. But it has a lot of work to do just to improve to average.

There will be a similar personality change on the offensive end. Gone are the starting quarterback, two leading receivers, and three multi-year starting linemen. But there is more hope on this side of the ball. Former blue-chip recruit Jake Heaps, a BYU transfer, is eligible this year; senior running back James Sims has been a steady, decent contributor for years; and utility back Tony Pierson (759 rushing yards, 6.5 per carry; 291 receiving yards, 13.9 per catch, 58 percent catch rate) returns.

Top 2014 NFL prospects: *RB James Sims (6-7)*

Bill Connelly

Projected Win Probabilities For Big 12 Teams

Big 12	Overall Wins													Conference Wins									
	12-0	11-1	10-2	9-3	8-4	7-5	6-6	5-7	4-8	3-9	2-10	1-11	0-12	9-0	8-1	7-2	6-3	5-4	4-5	3-6	2-7	1-8	0-9
Baylor	-	-	2	8	22	32	24	10	2	-	-	-	-	-	-	2	10	26	33	22	6	1	-
Iowa State	-	-	-	-	-	-	2	7	22	36	28	5	-	-	-	-	-	-	2	10	34	47	7
Kansas	-	-	-	-	-	-	-	-	4	16	39	38	3	-	-	-	-	-	-	1	6	31	62
Kansas State	-	-	2	5	17	31	29	13	3	-	-	-	-	-	-	1	6	19	33	28	11	2	-
Oklahoma	3	14	30	30	17	5	1	-	-	-	-	-	-	6	26	36	23	7	2	-	-	-	-
Oklahoma State	8	29	35	20	7	1	-	-	-	-	-	-	-	9	30	35	19	6	1	-	-	-	-
TCU	1	9	25	33	22	8	2	-	-	-	-	-	-	4	18	35	29	11	3	-	-	-	-
Texas	4	18	31	27	14	4	2	-	-	-	-	-	-	7	26	35	23	8	1	-	-	-	-
Texas Tech	-	-	-	3	13	28	31	18	5	2	-	-	-	-	-	2	4	16	32	31	13	2	-
West Virginia	-	-	1	4	16	30	30	15	4	-	-	-	-	-	-	1	5	18	33	30	12	1	-
Virginia	-	-	-	-	-	2	9	22	32	25	9	1	-	-	-	-	1	7	23	37	26	6	-
Virginia Tech	-	4	21	33	26	12	3	1	-	-	-	-	-	6	24	35	24	9	2	-	-	-	-

Pac-12 Conference

On the surface, almost nothing about the Pac-12 is the same in 2013 as it was in 2009, a makeover that has purged names and faces alike. In a little under five years, the conference formerly known as the Pac-10 has come under new leadership, changed its name, expanded its membership, split into two divisions, launched a championship game, launched its own television and multimedia networks and, in the same span, welcomed a new head coach at every single school in the league except one, Oregon State. Dig a little deeper, and you'll find the changes at the top beginning to seep into the roots, yielding a noticeably different product on the field. At which point it doesn't take long to recognize how thoroughly that product has been shaped in the image of Chip Kelly.

It's an unlikely legacy. Before he was hired as Oregon's offensive coordinator in 2007, Kelly was an obscure assistant at the University of New Hampshire, of all places, and he was still new enough on the west coast two years later to be regarded as a curiosity when he was elevated to head coach. At the time, the conference was under the seemingly insuperable thumb of Pete Carroll, who had revived USC as a national powerhouse with schemes imported directly from the NFL; accordingly, the rest of the conference resisted the rise of the spread offense in favor of schemes that universally (if generically) fell under the banner of "pro style." In Kelly's first season as head coach, 2009, Oregon ripped the Trojans for 613 yards in a 47-20 blowout on national television, the worst thrashing of Carroll's tenure by a mile. From there, the Ducks went on to lead the Pac-10 in scoring, win the conference outright, and play in their first Rose Bowl in more than a decade. USC lost twice more and Carroll left at the end of the year for the NFL. Perhaps it should have been obvious even

then that, at some point, Kelly was bound to follow.

Although he was the first in the conference to introduce a contemporary spread scheme, Kelly's real influence is reflected in the accelerating tempo. Consider that, in 2009, only two Pac-10 offenses exceeded 70 offensive snaps per game, Oregon State (70.6) and Arizona (70.3), and only barely at that. In 2010, there were four, with the other three trailing far behind Oregon at 78.8 plays per game; the Ducks ran the table in the regular season and played for the BCS championship. In 2011, there were five, again led by Oregon, which claimed its third consecutive conference title. Last year? The number was up to seven, including four teams—Arizona (83.2), Arizona State (77.9), UCLA (78.2) and Washington State (73.0)—operating under new coaching staffs who installed their versions of the spread and made a deliberate point of picking up the pace. Meanwhile, Oregon hit a new high at 81.5 snaps per game and set school records for yards and points en route to a No. 2 finish in the final polls.

This year, the trend continues. In December, one of the more tortoise-like attacks in the conference, California, handed the keys over to Sonny Dykes, whose pass-happy offense at Louisiana Tech averaged more plays per game in 2012 (87.8) than any other FBS team. Another plodder, Colorado, introduced Mike MacIntyre, who plans to junk the Buffaloes' anemic pro-style system for heavy doses of the pistol. The slowest of them all, Utah, hired a new offensive coordinator, Dennis Erickson, who immediately vowed to make the Utes a no-huddle outfit in the name of speed: "You can't run 75, 80 plays if you're in the huddle." Increasingly, in a league devoid of a truly dominant defense, anything less means falling further behind.

NORTH

No. 2 Oregon Ducks (11-1, 8-1)
2012: 12-1 (8-1) / F/+ #2 / FEI #2 / S&P+ #2

Program F/+	+27.0%	5	Returning Starters: 8 OFF, 7 DEF			2012 Field Position / Special Teams		
2012 Offense			**2012 Defense**			Special Teams F/+	+2.2%	18
Offensive F/+	**+15.9%**	**5**	Defensive F/+	+20.3%	4	Field Position Advantage	0.543	11
Offensive FEI:	0.521	6	Defensive FEI	-0.587	8	**2013 Projections**		
Offensive S&P+	129.2	2	Defensive S&P+	141.2	2	**Mean Wins / Mean Conference Wins**	**11.3 / 8.3**	
Rushing S&P+	141.2	2	Rushing S&P+	110.5	32	Proj. F/+	+30.1%	2
Passing S&P+	133.2	4	Passing S&P+	127.2	13	Offensive F/+	+13.9%	3
Standard Downs S&P+	137.3	2	Standard Downs S&P+	110.8	26	Defensive F/+	+16.2%	3
Passing Downs S&P+	131.1	9	Passing Downs S&P+	149.1	2	Strength of Sched. Rk / Conf. Title Odds	49 / 47.6%	

Once the initial shock wore off, the buzzword surrounding Kelly's departure for the next level was *challenge*—the challenge of adapting his wildly successful college offense to the NFL; the challenge of juggling professional egos; the challenge of commanding respect in a league in which he'd never worked as a player or coach; the challenge of enduring skep-

tics who doubt his up-tempo philosophy can succeed at the next level, poised and ready to pounce at the first setback. On his first day as a pro coach, Kelly reinforced the narrative himself: "The challenge is what I was excited about, and that's why I came."

In embracing one set of challenges, though, he also left behind the only summit he'd yet to scale at Oregon: winning a national championship. In four seasons under Kelly, the Ducks won three conference titles, played in four BCS bowls, and spent 50 weeks ranked in the AP top ten, eight of them at number one. Oregon won more games over the past three seasons (36) than any other program in the nation. But it has not won the Big One. Yet.

To that end, the keys to the hot rod were left with an insider, Mark Helfrich, promoted from offensive coordinator with a mandate to keep the pedal pressed to the floor. The engine in this analogy is sophomore Marcus Mariota, who wasted no time as a redshirt freshman staking his claim as the most versatile, productive quarterback of the Kelly era. An instant hit—Oregon scored nine touchdowns on the first nine possessions of his career in season-opening routs over Arkansas State and Fresno State—Mariota went on to lead the Pac-12 in completion percentage and efficiency, adding 898 yards rushing (before sacks) en route to a first-team all-conference nod. Unlike his predecessors at the position, who were regarded as efficient but relatively pedestrian products of the system, Mariota's arm all but guarantees him a pro future, and forces defenses to account for yet another dimension: With six of last year's top receivers back, including blue-chip tight end Colt Lyerla (392 yards, 15.7 per catch, 71 percent catch rate) and all-purpose spark plug De'Anthony Thomas (693 rushing yards, 446 receiving yards), the Ducks have more incentive to put the ball in the air than they have in years. But how often will that be necessary? Between Thomas, sophomore Byron Marshall, and hyped recruit Thomas Tyner, in a system that's produced seven 1,000-yard rushers and four All-Americans in the last six years, there should still be plenty of carries to go around.

Historically, the pressure of Oregon's championship ambitions tends to fall on the defense, although that certainly was not true in 2012. Defying expectations, the defense matched the offense by finishing second nationally in our S&P+ ratings, a dramatic improvement on its standing according to more conventional statistics. Three factors account for the difference: a) The up-tempo philosophy that fuels the offense meant the defense was on the field for an unusually long time, facing nearly 76 plays per game; b) A significant share of the yards and points reflected in conventional stats were accumulated in garbage time, with the game long out of hand—of the 34 touchdowns yielded to opposing offenses, for example, more than half (18) came with Oregon already leading by at least 20 points; and most importantly, c) The Ducks led the nation in both interceptions (25) and total takeaways (40), resulting in the best overall turnover margin in the nation. The headliner on defense, linebacker/rush end Dion Jordan, was taken with the third pick of the NFL draft, followed by leading tacklers Michael Clay and Kiko Alonso. But the departures did not include longtime defensive coordinator Nick Aliotti, back for his 15th season with the team's most productive pass rusher, Taylor Hart, and every member of the ball-hawking secondary at his disposal. The best of that group, junior cornerback Ifo Ekpre-Olomu, forced six fumbles to go with four interceptions and is likely bound for the first round next April.

Now for the question every Oregon fan dreads: What's up with the kicker? As a team, the Ducks have attempted just 28 field goals over the last two years, missing 12. The only experienced kicker on the roster, Alejandro Maldonado, is 0-for-6 in his career from beyond 40 yards, and is known mainly for two late, decisive misses—against USC in 2011 and Stanford in 2012—that effectively cost the Ducks a trip to the BCS title game in both seasons. The tentative plan this year calls for Maldonado, now a senior, to be unseated by an incoming freshman, Matt Wogan. Best-case scenario, though, no finish is close enough to leave it up to either of them.

Top 2014 NFL prospects: *CB Ifo Ekpre-Olomu* (1), TE Colt Lyerla* (1–2), RB/WR De'Anthony Thomas* (2), WR Josh Huff (3), DE Taylor Hart (3–4), OLB Boseko Lokombo (5–6), DT Wade Keliikipi (6–7), S Brian Jackson (7–FA)*

No. 3 Stanford Cardinal (10-2, 7-2)

2012: 12-2 (8-1) / F/+ #11 / FEI #7 / S&P+ #18

Program F/+	+19.8%	12	Returning Starters: 8 OFF, 7 DEF			2012 Field Position / Special Teams		
2012 Offense			**2012 Defense**			Special Teams F/+	+2.5%	12
Offensive F/+	**+6.0%**	**36**	**Defensive F/+**	**+17.1%**	**8**	Field Position Advantage	0.553	8
Offensive FEI:	0.190	34	Defensive FEI	-0.670	3	**2013 Projections**		
Offensive S&P+	113.4	29	Defensive S&P+	124.5	11	**Mean Wins / Mean Conference Wins**	10.1 / 7.4	
Rushing S&P+	103.9	57	Rushing S&P+	127.7	7	Proj. F/+	+23.8%	3
Passing S&P+	107.6	43	Passing S&P+	135.3	8	Offensive F/+	+8.9%	14
Standard Downs S&P+	99.4	65	Standard Downs S&P+	129.5	4	Defensive F/+	+14.9%	5
Passing Downs S&P+	118.6	24	Passing Downs S&P+	133.1	12	Strength of Sched. Rk / Conf. Title Odds	32 / 15.9%	

For most struggling programs, making up ground over the last decade has meant spreading the field, emphasizing speed and minimizing disadvantages on the line of scrimmage. Stanford is the exception to the rule: Beginning in 2007, with the arrival of new coach Jim Harbaugh, the most outmanned outfit in the conference has reinvented itself as a reliable frontrunner on the strength of … well, *strength*, embracing a rugged, old-school philosophy that has taken deep roots. Since 2010, the Cardinal have been forced to replace a Heisman runner-up (Toby Gerhart), a head coach (Harbaugh) and another Heisman runner-up (Andrew Luck) in consecutive seasons. Their record in those seasons: 35-5, with three consecutive BCS bowls, three consecutive finishes in the top ten and, in 2012, their first Rose Bowl victory since 1971.

Not coincidentally, those three seasons have also yielded four All-Americans and six all-conference picks from the offensive line, not counting a pair of All-America tight ends in the same span. This year, the beat and the beatings—go on with four returning starters up front, anchored by guards Kevin Danser and David Yankey, a consensus All-American last year despite playing out of position at left tackle. With blue-chip sophomores Andrus Peat and Kyle Murphy on schedule to take over on the outside, Yankey can afford to slide back to his old comfort zone at left guard. There should be a greater comfort level at quarterback, too, where sophomore Kevin Hogan is entrenched after breathing life into a listless attack last November. While no one mistook him for the second coming of Andrew Luck, Hogan was 5-0 as a starter against the meat of the schedule, including come-from-behind wins over Oregon State, Oregon and UCLA in the Pac-12 title game. He also introduced a running threat to the position that had been sorely missing.

With a surplus of muscle, however, comes a dearth of speed. Efficiency notwithstanding, Hogan was not inclined to challenge defenses downfield, averaging a modest 10.1 yards per completion. And his receivers didn't give him much incentive: Even more so than in the past, the passing game revolved around a pair of towering, NFL-bound tight ends (in this case, Zach Ertz and Levine Toilolo) deployed to create mismatches against linebackers and safeties on play-action routes. The same role will be reprised this fall by sophomore Luke Kaumatule, typecast at 6-foot-7, but there are no proven big-play threats among the wide receivers or, with the departure of 1,500-yard workhorse Stepfan Taylor, in the backfield. One potential exception is Barry J. Sanders, son of *the* Barry Sanders, who will move into the rotation after sitting out his first season on campus as a redshirt. Still, all sparks are strictly hypothetical.

Meanwhile, the only speculation involving the defense is over just how good the offense has to be with such a generous margin for error. It's a unit used to picking up a little slack: Stanford won five games last year with 21 points or fewer on the board, including season-defining triumphs over USC, Oregon and Wisconsin, which managed just 14 points apiece; in the Ducks' case, the loss broke a 23-game streak in which they'd scored at least 30. (Even in the Cardinal's two losses, the defense not only kept the score within reach, but accounted for the team's only touchdown in both games.) On paper, the 2013 edition looks every bit as nasty, in terms of both quantity—15 defenders have some starting experience, all but two of whom will be in their fourth or fifth year in the program—and quality, with all-conference types back on the line (Ben Gardner and Henry Anderson), at linebacker (Trent Murphy and Shayne Skov) and in the secondary (Ed Reynolds and Alex Carter). Man for man, the Cardinal stack up against any defense in the country, and with last year's upset in Eugene, they have already proven that they can clear the tallest hurdle on the schedule.

Top 2014 NFL prospects: *G David Yankey* (1), LB Trent Murphy (1–2), S Ed Reynolds* (2), ILB Shayne Skov (2–3), DL Henry Anderson* (3), DE Ben Gardner (3–4), RB Anthony Wilkerson (6–7)*

No. 22 Oregon State Beavers (9-3, 6-3)

2012: 9-4 (6-3) / F/+ #18 / FEI #16 / S&P+ #22

Program F/+	+8.0%	35	Returning Starters: 8 OFF, 7 DEF			2012 Field Position / Special Teams		
2012 Offense			**2012 Defense**			Special Teams F/+	+0.3%	54
Offensive F/+	**+10.1%**	**17**	**Defensive F/+**	**+9.6%**	**25**	Field Position Advantage	0.501	62
Offensive FEI:	0.329	22	Defensive FEI	-0.384	23	**2013 Projections**		
Offensive S&P+	119.8	18	Defensive S&P+	114.5	26	**Mean Wins / Mean Conference Wins**	**8.6 / 5.8**	
Rushing S&P+	105.6	54	Rushing S&P+	112.7	27	Proj. F/+	+13.4%	22
Passing S&P+	121.5	17	Passing S&P+	112.1	29	Offensive F/+	+6.9%	23
Standard Downs S&P+	115.3	21	Standard Downs S&P+	102.5	56	Defensive F/+	+6.4%	25
Passing Downs S&P+	113.4	38	Passing Downs S&P+	137.8	7	Strength of Sched. Rk / Conf. Title Odds	20 / 1.5%	

At 59, Mike Riley is far from a dinosaur. But entering 2012, a decade into his second stint as Oregon State's head coach, he could have been forgiven for beginning to feel like one. Of the dozen coaches in the Pac-12 last year, seven were in their first three years on the job, two more were in year four, and the only colleague who had been in his current position longer than Riley, California's Jeff Tedford, had worn out his welcome. After back-to-back losing seasons in 2010 and 2011, Riley seemed to be in danger of the same fate. Instead, the Beavers found new life in his tenth season, riding a revived passing game and a rapidly maturing defense to a string of early upsets, a 6-0 start, and their first finish in the national polls since 2008. The leap from 3-9 to 9-4 marked the most dramatic single-season swing in Oregon State history, making Riley the school's all-time winningest coach in the process.

Nowhere was the about-face more obvious or dramatic than the front seven, which improved in Rushing S&P+ from 82nd in the country in 2011 to 27th in 2012. Things could be even better in 2013, as half of last year's starting lineup on defense consisted of sophomores still growing into their roles. The most decorated member of the youth movement was defensive end Scott Crichton, who followed up Freshman All-America notices in 2011 with an All-Pac-12 nod; he's back this year as a veteran mainstay opposite fellow junior Dylan Wynn. Between the bookends, though, the depth chart was effectively wiped clean by the graduation of the top three tackles. In search of immediate help there, Riley recruited not two, not three, but *five* interior linemen out of western junior colleges, two of whom, Edwin Delva and Siale Hautau, were ushered immediately into the starting lineup in the spring while senior Mana Rosa nursed a foot injury. Their progress (or lack thereof) will dictate whether the defense takes another step forward or regresses to 2011 form.

Although the faces are more familiar on offense, the pressing question heading into the fall remains the pecking order at quarterback, site of a season-long rendition of musical chairs between Sean Mannion and Cody Vaz. Mannion, the full-time starter in 2011, is a tall, strong-armed prototype, but has also matched his 31 touchdown passes over the last two years with 31 interceptions (including four picks apiece in last year's losses to Washington and Oregon). Meanwhile, though Vaz tended to have a steadier hand, he ended the year with his worst outing of the season, by far, enduring ten sacks and two interceptions in an Alamo Bowl loss to Texas. Elsewhere on offense, there's a 1,000-yard rusher (Storm Woods), a 1,000-yard receiver (Brandin Cooks) and four returning starters on the line who have combined for 88 career starts. On the schedule, there's an eight-week cushion before the first really steep test, an October 26 visit from Stanford. Given any stability under center by then, the Beavers could hit the November stretch looking like surprise contenders.

Top 2014 NFL prospects: *DE Scott Crichton* (2), DB Rashaad Reynolds (5–6)*

No. 49 Washington Huskies (6-6, 4-5)

2012: 7-6 (5-4) / F/+ #56 / FEI #55 / S&P+ #59

Program F/+	-6.8%	83	Returning Starters: 10 OFF, 7 DEF			2012 Field Position / Special Teams		
2012 Offense			**2012 Defense**			Special Teams F/+	-1.7%	98
Offensive F/+	**-1.3%**	**63**	**Defensive F/+**	**+4.8%**	**37**	Field Position Advantage	0.511	46
Offensive FEI:	-0.016	60	Defensive FEI	-0.226	37	**2013 Projections**		
Offensive S&P+	99.2	67	Defensive S&P+	107.0	44	**Mean Wins / Mean Conference Wins**	5.9 / 3.9	
Rushing S&P+	111.7	33	Rushing S&P+	107.5	42	Proj. F/+	+3.9%	49
Passing S&P+	95.6	80	Passing S&P+	110.1	34	Offensive F/+	+1.1%	54
Standard Downs S&P+	103.6	48	Standard Downs S&P+	109.8	28	Defensive F/+	+2.8%	42
Passing Downs S&P+	100.5	71	Passing Downs S&P+	106.6	48	Strength of Sched. Rk / Conf. Title Odds	17 / 0.0%	

Hey everybody, it's time for the Washington Rorschach test! When you look at the 2013 Huskies, what do you see? On one hand, the lineup is arguably the most seasoned in the conference, boasting recognizable veterans at every position—including quarterback—who have combined for 350 career starts, most in the Pac-12 and among the most in the nation. On the other hand, the sense of upward mobility fostered in Steve Sarkisian's first two seasons as head coach is a distant memory as he enters his fifth, the victim of three 7-6 finishes in a row. Then again, Washington is one of only three Pac-12 teams (along with Oregon and Stanford) to earn a bowl bid in each of those seasons, and flashed its potential last year in poll-shaking upsets over Stanford and Oregon State. Then again (again), the Huskies were last seen in Pac-12 play being upset themselves, by lowly Washington State, which did not win another conference game.

Although the experience is spread more or less evenly across the entire roster, visions of a breakthrough begin and end with the redemption of senior quarterback Keith Price. One of the most efficient passers in the nation in 2011, Price's stock plummeted last year behind a shaky, injury-ravaged line, significantly regressing in terms of touchdown passes (from 33 to 19), net yards per attempt (from 7.5 to 5.3, including sacks) and overall efficiency (from 161.9 to 122.4). The offense as a whole followed suit, failing to top 21 points in eight different games, and failing to match its 2011 scoring average (33.4 ppg) in ten. In S&P+ terms, the offense dropped from 35th nationally in 2011 to 67th, and the Huskies' explosive drive production plummeted from 14th in 2011 to 110th. Still, the basic components of a turnaround are all there, especially up front, where five returning starters—none of them seniors—

are back with a year of growing pains under their belt and two former starters, Erik Kohler and Colin Tanigawa, taking aim at their old jobs after missing all of 2012 to knee injuries. As far as "skill players," virtually everyone who touched the ball is still on hand, including the three that really matter: tailback Bishop Sankey, receiver Kasen Williams and tight end Austin Seferian-Jenkins. As sophomores, these three local products accounted for 74 percent of the Huskies' total yards from scrimmage. As of late May, Seferian-Jekins' status remained officially in the air due to a DUI arrest and subsequent suspension. If his legal case is resolved in time for him to play this season, as expected, he'll be the most dangerous receiving tight end in the nation and a near-certain first-rounder in 2014.

As for the defense, the status quo will do just fine, thanks. While the offense wallowed in the doldrums, the defense was successfully reversing its own fortune under first-year coordinator Justin Wilcox, improving on its ghastly 2011 yields by nearly 100 yards and 12 points per game; in the S&P+ ratings, the Huskies jumped from 97th in total defense to 44th. They were also alarmingly *young*: Six of the top ten tacklers were freshmen or sophomores, a group that included the leading tackler, John Timu, and blue-chip recruit Shaq Thompson, who made good on the hype by starting every game in a hybrid safety/linebacker role (a.k.a. the "find the ball and tackle it" role). At no point over the past two years has Washington been at its best on both sides of the ball at the same time, but once it gets there, the seven-win barrier will fall with haste.

Top 2014 NFL prospects: *TE Austin Seferian-Jenkins* (1–2), RB Bishop Sankey* (3), DE/OLB Josh Shirley* (3–4), DT Danny Shelton* (4–5), S Sean Parker (6), QB Keith Price (6–7)*

No. 73 California Golden Bears (4-8, 2-7)

2012: 3-9 (2-7) / F/+ #77 / FEI #79 / S&P+ #66

Program F/+	+1.1%	55	Returning Starters: 4 OFF, 5 DEF			2012 Field Position / Special Teams		
2012 Offense			**2012 Defense**			Special Teams F/+	-0.3%	76
Offensive F/+	**-4.9%**	**81**	**Defensive F/+**	**-1.7%**	**67**	Field Position Advantage	0.476	94
Offensive FEI:	-0.255	100	Defensive FEI	0.058	71	**2013 Projections**		
Offensive S&P+	100.7	58	Defensive S&P+	100.3	57	**Mean Wins / Mean Conference Wins**	**3.7 / 2.4**	
Rushing S&P+	114.5	22	Rushing S&P+	112.6	28	Proj. F/+	-4.1%	73
Passing S&P+	101.0	59	Passing S&P+	104.0	49	Offensive F/+	-3.5%	85
Standard Downs S&P+	111.4	30	Standard Downs S&P+	107.3	36	Defensive F/+	-0.6%	66
Passing Downs S&P+	95.1	82	Passing Downs S&P+	107.1	46	Strength of Sched. Rk / Conf. Title Odds	9 / 0.0%	

In almost every sense, the last decade was the best for Cal football since World War II, a distinction confirmed both by Jeff Tedford's status as the school's all-time winningest head coach and the major stadium and facilities upgrades that followed. Yet Tedford barely survived long enough to set foot in the new digs. After rising to No. 2 in the national polls in October 2007, Cal closed that season by dropping six of its last seven games, and the Bears haven't finished within three games of a conference or division title since. Just looking at their North Division rivals, the Bears have dropped four straight to Oregon, four straight to Washington, three straight to Stanford and four of the last five to Oregon State. With five consecutive losses to close 2012—four of them coming by at least 18 points—there were few objections as Tedford was led directly to the nearest ice floe.

The most obvious sign of decline was at quarterback, where Tedford—once considered college football's most bankable quarterback guru—failed to develop a successful starter after Aaron Rodgers' departure for the draft in 2005. The man to reignite that spark, Cal hopes, is Sonny Dykes, an "Air Raid" disciple whose up-tempo, spread-friendly scheme at Louisiana Tech churned out more yards and points per game in 2012 than any other FBS offense. (In fact, Tech averaged 2.3 more points per drive than Cal did last season.) Expectations for the "Bear Raid" are slightly less ambitious: not one of the three quarterbacks competing for the top job this spring has taken a snap in a college game. If there is a "proven" playmaker, it is tailback Brendan Bigelow, a once-touted recruit who logged just 51 touches last year despite opening eyes on a pair of long touchdown runs against Ohio State; for the season, he averaged 9.8 yards per carry while spending most of his time returning kicks. Bigelow's role in the new system remains strictly hypothetical, as both he and Cal's leading returning receiver, Chris Harper, sat out the spring following offseason surgeries.

The defense, while considerably older, faces plenty of uncertainty of its own in the switch from a 3-4 scheme to a 4-3 under new coordinator Andy Buh. As usual in that transition, the most dramatic change will be the conversion of former linebackers to defensive end. In Cal's case, that means the relocation of their most productive defender in 2012, Chris McCain, who spent the offseason trying to gain back 30 pounds he lost following shoulder surgery. (At last glance, the school listed McCain at 6-foot-6, 215 pounds, alarmingly thin for a down lineman; his reported goal is 240 by August.) The major reason McCain can afford to move is the emergence of junior linebacker Khairi Fortt, a Penn State transfer who turned in a solid, healthy spring after redshirting last year with a bad knee. Until a playmaker emerges in a revamped secondary, though, the defense as a whole—like everything else—is a work in progress.

Top 2014 NFL prospects: *DT Deandre Coleman (2–3)*

No. 109 Washington State Cougars (2-10, 0-9)

2012: 3-9 (1-8) / F/+ #98 / FEI #97 / S&P+ #102

Program F/+	-24.9%	121	Returning Starters: 7 OFF, 8 DEF			2012 Field Position / Special Teams		
2012 Offense			**2012 Defense**			Special Teams F/+	-2.1%	106
Offensive F/+	**-10.6%**	**109**	**Defensive F/+**	**-3.9%**	**76**	Field Position Advantage	0.43	123
Offensive FEI:	-0.386	111	Defensive FEI	0.054	69	**2013 Projections**		
Offensive S&P+	88.0	100	Defensive S&P+	92.0	87	**Mean Wins / Mean Conference Wins**	**2.2 / 0.4**	
Rushing S&P+	83.2	111	Rushing S&P+	100.5	57	Proj. F/+	-15.6%	109
Passing S&P+	89.6	95	Passing S&P+	89.4	94	Offensive F/+	-9.7%	116
Standard Downs S&P+	86.2	114	Standard Downs S&P+	97.2	72	Defensive F/+	-5.8%	94
Passing Downs S&P+	104.7	57	Passing Downs S&P+	89.2	94	Strength of Sched. Rk / Conf. Title Odds	12 / 0.0%	

In retrospect, it's fair to say popular expectations for Mike Leach's first season at Washington State were a tad … let's say, *unrealistic*. Even our cautious F/+ projections last year (100th overall, 3.1 mean wins) proved to be too ambitious. As if a spread passing savant who'd spent two years out of the game could instantly make over a perennial punching bag into a respectable member of the conference's middle class. But certainly no one had any reason to expect the Cougars to get punched even harder than before. For the season, the offense averaged nine points per game *below* its mediocre scoring average of 2011, and ranked dead last nationally in both rushing offense and sacks allowed. In October, following their third consecutive loss in Pac-12 play, Leach publicly criticized some of his veteran players for having an "empty corpse quality." They responded to this criticism by dropping five more in a row by an average margin of 22 points, and the Cougars' best player, wide receiver Marquess Wilson, walked out with an apparent grudge against the new coaches. A season-ending, overtime upset over Washington in the Apple Cup offered a glimmer of hope heading into the offseason, but couldn't lift Wazzu out of the conference cellar for the fourth year in a row.

Leach did fulfill one promise, calling for more passes than any other offense in the nation (52 per game), although the official numbers actually understate the case by ignoring the many, many attempts that never left the quarterbacks' hands. Between them, Connor Halliday and Jeff Tuel hit the turf an astounding 57 times, enduring at least three sacks in every single game despite a relatively stable offensive line. Predictably, that line was the site of considerable upheaval in the spring. Two returning starters, Jake Rodgers and John Fullington, were demoted in a rotation that features three former walk-ons and a junior college transfer, Rico Forbes, coming off a major knee injury. (Rodgers subsequently left the team.) At 6-foot-4, 185 pounds, Halliday hardly cuts an imposing figure in the pocket, and his medical history includes a lacerated liver that ended his season in 2011. If he has time to throw, he does have six receivers back who caught at least 20 passes last year as underclassmen, most notably sophomore

Dominique Williams (546 yards, 16.1 per catch, 62 percent catch rate), who replaced Wilson as the primary deep threat over the second half of the season. But any notion of progress begins with keeping the quarterback in one piece.

By comparison, the defense fared a little better in the transition from a 4-3 alignment to a 3-4, but only a little, and only relative to the low bar set by the offense: Pac-12 opponents still gashed Wazzu for more than 36 points per game. If there was one positive takeaway from the season, it was the dramatically increased presence in opposing backfields. Two years ago, the Cougars ranked 94th in tackles for loss, 95th in sacks, and 105th in Adjusted Sack Rate. In 2012, they improved to eighth nationally in tackles for loss and 11th in sacks. A schedule filled with pass-first offenses meant their Adjusted Sack Rate wasn't quite as spectacular, but 68th is still a pretty significant improvement over the year before. On the whole, the pressure didn't do as much good as might be expected—the secondary still struggled to make plays despite the improved pass rush—but for a team with little ambition beyond a random upset or two, the upside of aggression may outweigh the risks.

Top 2014 NFL prospects: *S Deone Bucannon (6)*

SOUTH

No. 17 USC Trojans (10-3, 7-2)
2012: 7-6 (5-4) / F/+ #27 / FEI #30 / S&P+ #28

Program F/+	+21.5%	10	Returning Starters: 8 OFF, 7 DEF			2012 Field Position / Special Teams		
2012 Offense			**2012 Defense**			Special Teams F/+	+1.8%	23
Offensive F/+	**+6.4%**	**33**	**Defensive F/+**	**+6.0%**	**33**	Field Position Advantage	0.522	34
Offensive FEI:	0.167	38	Defensive FEI	-0.229	36	**2013 Projections**		
Offensive S&P+	116.1	20	Defensive S&P+	111.1	30	**Mean Wins / Mean Conference Wins**	**10.2 / 7.1**	
Rushing S&P+	116.4	17	Rushing S&P+	106.2	45	Proj. F/+	+17.4%	17
Passing S&P+	128.6	9	Passing S&P+	112.8	26	Offensive F/+	+8.9%	15
Standard Downs S&P+	120.8	14	Standard Downs S&P+	109.4	29	Defensive F/+	+8.5%	17
Passing Downs S&P+	130.6	10	Passing Downs S&P+	104.6	52	Strength of Sched. Rk / Conf. Title Odds	43 / 24.1%	

As anyone who has been there knows, when you're on top, there's only one way left to go. When the summit in question is the top of the AP poll, though, no team has ever gone south quite as fast as USC in 2012, or quite as hard. The Trojans racked up more losse   s (six) than any preseason frontrunner in the history of the poll, and became the first since 1964 to finish outside of the final rankings altogether. As the indignities mounted, so did the scorn heaped on head coach Lane Kiffin, who began the season by lying to reporters about voting his own team No. 1 in the initial coaches' poll and ended it by attempting to explain away a tense locker room scene following a Sun Bowl loss to Georgia Tech, described by one player as "pure chaos." By then, it was clear Kiffin would be coaching for his job in 2013, with an overhauled staff and no margin for error on the field or off.

To no one's surprise, the first casualty of the house-cleaning was Kiffin's father, Monte, who bowed out as defensive coordinator at age 73 with little to show for his three-year tenure aside from an unusually large paycheck. The season went downhill fast against spread schemes deploying mobile quarterbacks: Beginning in late October, with BCS ambitions

still very much intact, USC yielded 39 points to Arizona, 62 to Oregon and 38 to UCLA in a span of four weeks—all Trojan losses, despite the offense having racked up more than 500 total yards with at least 28 points in all three. By many measures, the Oregon loss was the worst defensive performance in school history, reportedly prompting the elder Kiffin's agreement to step down at the end of the year.

In reality, it may be tough for new coordinator Clancy Pendergast to improve things, because things weren't quite as bad as it seemed on the surface. The USC schedule was packed with some of the most powerful offenses in the country; once we apply opponent adjustments, the Trojans actually finished 30th nationally in defensive S&P+ ratings, good for fourth in the conference. Pendergast is importing a 3-4 scheme that will move last year's most productive defender, Morgan Breslin, from end to outside linebacker, where he projects at the next level. The first priority, though, is finding some reliability in an inconsistent, occasionally flammable secondary that lost three full-time starters. There is some limited starting experience among the returnees, most notably cornerback Torin Harris and safety Josh Shaw, a transfer from Florida. But that didn't stop three early freshman arrivals (Su'a Cravens, Chris Hawkins and Leon McQuay III) from moving up the depth chart in the spring, or coaches from moving starting linebacker Dion Bailey back to his original position at safety.

Disappointing as it was, it's harder to pin the late collapse on the offense, even quarterback Matt Barkley, whose failure to match overheated preseason hype obscured the fact that he did match most of the 2011 numbers that fueled it. In fact, it was never easier to appreciate Barkley's presence than in his absence: After Barkley separated his shoulder at the end of a 38-28 loss to UCLA, the offense managed a grand total of two touchdowns in the last two games. The audition went particularly poorly for Barkley's understudy, redshirt freshman Max Wittek, who threw five interceptions in relief and did nothing to entrench himself as the new starter. At the end of spring practice, the three-way race between Wittek, fellow sophomore Cody Kessler, and true freshman Max Browne remained a dead heat.

Still, even with a reduced scholarship cap due to NCAA sanctions, the raw talent here is never in question. If nothing else, the winner of the quarterback derby will have the luxury of throwing to the reigning Pac-12 Offensive Player of the Year, Marqise Lee, new owner of conference records for receptions (118) and receiving yards (1,721) in a season, as well as the Biletnikoff Award as the best receiver in the nation. He'll also be working with a typically deep, blue-chip backfield and five returning starters on the offensive line with 84 career starts between them. The question is whether they can produce consistently enough on the ground to keep the heat off the new quarterback, and whether the revamped defense will give them the chance.

Top 2014 NFL prospects: *WR Marqise Lee* (1), DE/OLB Morgan Breslin (1–2), S/OLB Dion Bailey* (2–3), RB Silas Redd (3), TE Randall Telfer* (3–4), DT George Uko* (3–4), CB Torin Harris (5–6), OT Kevin Graf (6–7)*

No. 30 Arizona Wildcats (9-3, 6-3)
2012: 8-5 (4-5) / F/+ #38 / FEI #41 / S&P+ #35

Program F/+	+7.0%	37	Returning Starters: 7 OFF, 10 DEF			2012 Field Position / Special Teams		
2012 Offense			**2012 Defense**			Special Teams F/+	-1.3%	93
Offensive F/+	+13.1%	11	Defensive F/+	-1.9%	68	Field Position Advantage	0.505	54
Offensive FEI:	0.478	9	Defensive FEI	0.053	68	**2013 Projections**		
Offensive S&P+	121.6	12	Defensive S&P+	99.3	56	**Mean Wins / Mean Conference Wins**	8.5 / 5.6	
Rushing S&P+	118.1	16	Rushing S&P+	100.3	59	Proj. F/+	+9.9%	30
Passing S&P+	121.1	18	Passing S&P+	101.3	57	Offensive F/+	+7.5%	18
Standard Downs S&P+	107.2	42	Standard Downs S&P+	105.3	44	Defensive F/+	+2.4%	44
Passing Downs S&P+	151.4	4	Passing Downs S&P+	90.9	88	Strength of Sched. Rk / Conf. Title Odds	44 / 5.2%	

Rich Rodriguez's track record as an offensive innovator speaks for itself—he is widely credited with inventing the read-option concept that has taken root on every level of the sport—but if there were any lingering questions about his mojo after an ill-fated stint at Michigan, his first season in Tucson put them all to rest. Unleashing a more up-tempo, balanced version of the attack that propelled Rodriguez's best teams at West Virginia, Arizona churned out more yards per game (526.2) than any previous Rodriguez offense, and came within a whisker of matching the 2006-07 Mountaineers at 38.2 points per game; in three of their five losses, the Wildcats scored at least 34. They finished 12th in offensive S&P+, second in the Pac-12 only to Oregon. Contrary to their coach's run-first reputation, they achieved a remarkable equilibrium by averaging 42 carries per game against 41 passes. Nationally, only Marshall crammed in more snaps.

The upshot was a leap from four wins in 2011 to eight, matching Arizona's best record since 1998. The downside, predictably, was a defense that paid the price by facing more plays and yielding more yards than any defense in the conference. For a unit that was torched for at least 600 yards in six different games, returning all 11 starters is a mixed blessing. In fact, the two-deep boasts a staggering 20 defenders who have started at least one game in their careers, including all of last year's top 15 tacklers, led by senior linebackers Jake Fischer and Marquis Flowers. But that list doesn't include an immovable body against the run (the Wildcats ranked 105th in rushing yards al-

lowed and 59th in Rushing S&P+, a reflection on the undersized defensive line) or a reliable force in the pass rush (108th in sacks, 119th in Adjusted Sack Rate), leaving an experienced but oft-torched secondary to its own devices in shootouts.

With Rodriguez pushing the buttons, of course, shootouts are a given, especially when so many of those buttons are designed to put the ball in the hands of tailback Ka'Deem Carey, who went from unknown to consensus All-American after leading the nation in rushing yards (1,929) and total yards from scrimmage (2,232) and posting a +35.4 Adj. POE (ninth in the country) in his first season in the system. But that production came as part of an offense that was divided equally between run and pass, alongside a quarterback, Matt Scott, capable of averaging 300 yards per game through the air while also commanding respect as a running threat. Collectively, the candidates to replace Scott are a blank slate: While senior B.J. Denker played sparingly last year and was the only consistently healthy option in the spring, he's considered a pedestrian talent at best; on the other hand, neither of the best athletes at the position, USC transfer Jesse Scroggins and true freshman Anu Solomon, have taken a college snap. Regardless of the eventual winner, the transition got a little steeper in the spring with word that Arizona's top receiver, Austin Hill, is likely out for the season with a torn ACL, leaving no tried-and-true targets in his place.

Top 2014 NFL prospects: *RB Ka'Deem Carey* (2), OLB Marquis Flowers (7–FA)*

No. 36 Arizona State Sun Devils (7-5, 5-4)

2012: 8-5 (5-4) / F/+ #41 / FEI #37 / S&P+ #34

Program F/+	+3.6%	48	Returning Starters: 6 OFF, 8 DEF			2012 Field Position / Special Teams		
2012 Offense			**2012 Defense**			Special Teams F/+	-0.1%	66
Offensive F/+	**+2.7%**	**51**	**Defensive F/+**	**+6.5%**	**31**	Field Position Advantage	0.534	20
Offensive FEI:	0.047	56	Defensive FEI	-0.254	31	**2013 Projections**		
Offensive S&P+	110.0	46	Defensive S&P+	111.3	36	**Mean Wins / Mean Conference Wins**	**6.8 / 5.2**	
Rushing S&P+	101.0	61	Rushing S&P+	101.6	54	Proj. F/+	+8.7%	36
Passing S&P+	109.9	39	Passing S&P+	124.2	15	Offensive F/+	+2.2%	43
Standard Downs S&P+	100.8	58	Standard Downs S&P+	111.7	24	Defensive F/+	+6.5%	24
Passing Downs S&P+	114.4	34	Passing Downs S&P+	109.7	35	Strength of Sched. Rk / Conf. Title Odds	29 / 4.9%	

At first glance, it's not hard to cast Todd Graham's first season at Arizona State as a relative success. After four stagnant years under Graham's predecessor, Dennis Erickson, the 2012 Sun Devils turned in their first winning record since 2007, their first bowl win since 2005 and their longest winning streak to close a season (three games) since 1978. The offense went over 40 points in seven games and averaged more for the season (38.4) than any ASU outfit since 1996. The Devils' average margin of victory (14 points) was the widest since 1996. If not a breakthrough, exactly, on paper it adds up to progress.

On the other hand, relative to the rest of the Pac-12, the contrast between the high points and the lows drove home just how large the gap is between ASU and the conference's upper crust: In a four-week span against the four best teams on the schedule (Oregon, UCLA, Oregon State and USC), the Devils went 0-4, outscored by nearly two touchdowns per game. Prior to a come-from-behind triumph at Arizona in the regular-season finale, their first four conference wins came at the expense of opponents that combined to finish 7-29 in conference play, with five of those seven wins coming against one another.

As was the case elsewhere in the Pac-12, a new coaching staff came with a more aggressive philosophy on both sides of the ball. Offensively, that meant an up-tempo approach that yielded nearly 78 snaps per game, several times exceeding 90. Under first-year offensive coordinator Mike Norvell, it also meant spreading the wealth as liberally as possible. By land, four different players (including quarterback Taylor Kelly) finished with between 500 and 700 yards rushing, on somewhere between 100 and 140 carries apiece. By air, six different players finished with at least 20 receptions, led by tight end Chris Coyle (696 yards, 12.2 per catch, 79 percent catch rate). And by design, two players—tailbacks Marion Grice and D.J. Foster, a true freshman—finished in both groups,

each accounting for more than 1,000 yards from scrimmage off the bench. (Grice was especially effective in the red zone, scoring 16 of his team-high 19 touchdowns as a rusher and receiver from inside the opponent's 20-yard line.) With starter Cameron Marshall gone and no proven targets at wide receiver, their share of the production should only increase.

If anything, Graham's defense was even more relentless, ultimately spending more time in opposing backfields than any other FBS team: The Devils registered at least six tackles for loss in every game, averaging nine. The catalyst for much of that disruption was lineman Will Sutton, a tweener end/tackle who managed to lead the conference in TFLs despite being limited in multiple games by a midseason knee injury; he was rewarded in December as a consensus All-American and the Pac-12's Defensive Player of the Year. (Not coincidentally, the defense's worst outings of the season, against Oregon and UCLA, came with Sutton on the bench, though it would hardly be fair to suggest he could have made a decisive difference against the Ducks, who led 43-7 barely three minutes into the second quarter.) One beneficiary of all that pressure was the secondary, which came out as the best pass defense in the conference in terms of both yards allowed and efficiency rating. Arizona State gave up only 36 percent of available yards last season, 15th best nationally and second best in the conference behind Stanford. Unfortunately, not everyone needed to put the ball in the air that often—the Devils were gashed in their four conference losses for 250 yards per game on 5.3 per carry. In the Pac-12, only bottom-dwellers Colorado and Washington State gave up more total rushing yards.

Top 2014 NFL prospects: *DL Will Sutton (1–2), S Alden Darby (4), OLB Carl Bradford* (4–5), TE/FB Chris Coyle (7–FA), OT Evan Finkenberg (7–FA)*

No. 45 UCLA Bruins (6-6, 4-5)

2012: 9-5 (6-3) / F/+ #35 / FEI #33 / S&P+ #41

Program F/+	-3.6%	66	Returning Starters: 7 OFF, 6 DEF			2012 Field Position / Special Teams		
2012 Offense			**2012 Defense**			Special Teams F/+	-0.3%	73
Offensive F/+	**+5.2%**	**39**	**Defensive F/+**	**+6.3%**	**32**	Field Position Advantage	0.538	15
Offensive FEI:	0.203	33	Defensive FEI	-0.303	29	**2013 Projections**		
Offensive S&P+	109.7	42	Defensive S&P+	107.6	40	**Mean Wins / Mean Conference Wins**	**5.7 / 3.7**	
Rushing S&P+	110.1	40	Rushing S&P+	107.5	40	Proj. F/+	+4.5%	45
Passing S&P+	116.2	32	Passing S&P+	101.2	58	Offensive F/+	+2.2%	44
Standard Downs S&P+	110.8	33	Standard Downs S&P+	99.1	66	Defensive F/+	+2.3%	48
Passing Downs S&P+	114.2	36	Passing Downs S&P+	119.7	24	Strength of Sched. Rk / Conf. Title Odds	7 / 0.5%	

For most freshmen, it takes weeks or months to settle into the role of starting quarterback, or even years, if they ever manage it at all. For Brett Hundley, it took 12 seconds. That was the exact amount of time he needed to cover 72 yards for a touchdown on the first snap of his college career, last August against Rice. By year's end, Hundley had handled the ball as a rusher or passer on more plays (638) and accounted for a greater share of his team's total offense (62.7 percent) than any other player in the Pac-12, setting school records for passing yards, total yards and total touchdowns in the process. Against USC, he outshone the brightest gridiron star in Los Angeles, Matt Barkley, avenging a 50-0 romp at the hands of the Trojans in 2011 and ending a five-year UCLA losing streak in the series. Two weeks later, the Bruins led Stanford in the fourth quarter of the Pac-12 Championship Game and came within a missed field goal of forcing overtime.

Now the hard part: Keeping their meal ticket in one piece long enough to get back. Miraculously, Hundley survived his first season without a significant injury despite a) the heavy workload, and b) enduring a staggering 52 sacks as part of that load, more than any other FBS quarterback and an untenable number for anyone who expects to remain upright two years in a row. Part of the problem was extreme youth on the offensive line, home to three full-time freshman starters—two of whom, tackles Simon Goines and Torian White, were playing hurt for most of the season. But if the spring was any indication, the starting five may get even *younger*: At one point, offensive line coach Adrian Klemm was so frustrated with the veterans that he told reporters to "expect to have two or three freshmen start this season" from the incoming recruiting class. Just in case, Hundley spent the offseason bulking up from 210 pounds to 227, presumably for his own protection.

Youth is also a recurring theme among the wide receivers, where senior Shaquelle Evans (877 yards, 14.6 per catch, 66 percent catch rate) is surrounded by unproven sophomores, and especially in the secondary, where the departure of all four regular starters leaves a handful of true sophomores (Ishmael Adams, Randall Goforth, Marcus Rios) to fend off a well-regarded batch of true freshmen. As on the offensive line, at least one of the newcomers is almost guaranteed to start right away, especially if Rios is unable to return from the latest in a series of surgeries to treat a rare sinus infection. The exception to the youth trend is the front seven on defense, anchored by five returning starters in their fourth year in the program. The best of that group is senior Anthony Barr, who converted from fullback to outside linebacker as a junior, led the conference in sacks, and watched his draft stock soar accordingly.

Ultimately, UCLA's projected fall from division champ to the middle of the conference pack has as much to do with schedule strength as any other factor. After missing Oregon in 2012, the Bruins' cross-division games this fall include trips to Eugene and Stanford in back-to-back weeks in October, and division dates with Utah, Arizona and USC are all on the road.

Top 2014 NFL prospects: *OLB Anthony Barr (1), ILB Eric Kendricks* (2–3), G Xavier Su'a-Filo* (2–3), DE Cassius Marsh (3), WR Shaquelle Evans (3–4)*

No. 47 Utah Utes (6-6, 4-5)

2012: 5-7 (3-6) / F/+ #66 / FEI #58 / S&P+ #78

Program F/+	+9.2%	32	Returning Starters: 6 OFF, 7 DEF			2012 Field Position / Special Teams		
2012 Offense			**2012 Defense**			Special Teams F/+	+1.7%	27
Offensive F/+	-6.1%	89	Defensive F/+	+0.7%	57	Field Position Advantage	0.535	19
Offensive FEI:	-0.196	88	Defensive FEI	-0.078	53	**2013 Projections**		
Offensive S&P+	92.7	93	Defensive S&P+	100.8	65	**Mean Wins / Mean Conference Wins**	5.7 / 3.8	
Rushing S&P+	88.2	102	Rushing S&P+	110.0	34	Proj. F/+	+4.5%	47
Passing S&P+	95.8	79	Passing S&P+	94.3	79	Offensive F/+	-0.2%	62
Standard Downs S&P+	87.2	111	Standard Downs S&P+	100.5	60	Defensive F/+	+4.7%	34
Passing Downs S&P+	101.7	66	Passing Downs S&P+	106.6	49	Strength of Sched. Rk / Conf. Title Odds	11 / 0.4%	

For a while there, Utah was on pace for a season of perpetual drama. By mid-September, the Utes had already been to overtime, in a 27-20 loss at Utah State, and then survived arguably the weirdest scene of the year, in which hundreds of jubilant Utah students had to be cleared from the field not once but *twice* before victory over rival BYU was finally, officially in hand. Alas, the excitement ended there: Of the Utes' next eight games—six of them losses—only one was decided by single digits, and none were in serious doubt in the closing minutes. It wasn't until the season finale, in a come-from-behind win at Colorado, that things finally got interesting again, and even then it was mostly anxiety at the prospect of losing to the worst team in the conference for the second year in a row.

The essence of mediocrity found its purest expression in the offense, which was bad (93rd in offensive S&P+, 114th in avoiding three-and-outs), but not nearly bad enough to elicit any rubbernecking. Frankly, given that the starting quarter-back position was handed over entirely to true freshman Travis Wilson for the last seven games, coach Kyle Whittingham could have chalked up the setbacks to growing pains and given thanks it didn't turn out much worse. Instead, he made a deliberate effort to offset youth with experience, hiring 66-year-old Dennis Erickson in February to serve as co-offensive coordinator alongside former Utah quarterback Brian Johnson, who at the tender age of 26 remains the youngest coordinator in the nation. (For Erickson, a former head coach at six different schools and two NFL franchises, it will be his first stint as an assistant in Johnson's lifetime.) The good news: At 6-foot-6, 235 pounds, Wilson at least looks the part of a prototypical pocket slinger, and will be protected by another super-sized sophomore, 345-pound Jeremiah Poutasi, who made the move to left tackle in the spring after a strong debut on the right side. The bad news: Wilson spent the spring fending off a challenge from former walk-on Adam Schulz, the offensive line as a whole is in flux, and the only reliable weapon, tailback John White IV, is gone after becoming the first Utah back to crack 1,000 yards two years in a row.

Statistically, the strength of the team by far was the run defense (second in the Pac-12, 34th in the nation in rushing defense S&P+), which now qualifies as a major concern with the departure of All-American roadblock Star Lotulelei and brothers Dave and Joe Kruger to the NFL. Inside, there is the usual surplus of size, and vowels—tackles Tenny Palepoi, L.T. Tuipulotu, Sese Ianu and Stevie Tu'ikolovatu all come in well above 300 pounds—but not much in the way of relevant

experience. As insurance, the two most experienced defenders, seniors Trevor Reilly and Brian Blechen, both tried out new positions in the spring that would concentrate talent in the front seven, with Reilly moving from linebacker to end and Blechen from safety to linebacker. If Blechen sticks there, though, it will only shift the burden to the secondary, which consists of one familiar face, safety Eric Rowe, surrounded by unknowns.

Top 2014 NFL prospects: *S/OLB Brian Blechen (6–7), DE/OLB Trevor Reilly (7–FA)*

No. 108 Colorado Buffaloes (2-10, 1-8)
2012: 1-11 (1-8) / F/+ #124 / FEI #122 / S&P+ #123

Program F/+		-17.4%	106	Returning Starters: 10 OFF, 7 DEF				2012 Field Position / Special Teams		
2012 Offense				**2012 Defense**				Special Teams F/+	-4.6%	122
Offensive F/+		-14.6%	119	**Defensive F/+**		-16.7%	123	Field Position Advantage	0.438	120
Offensive FEI:		-0.467	117	Defensive FEI		0.545	116	**2013 Projections**		
Offensive S&P+		78.2	118	Defensive S&P+		75.3	121	**Mean Wins / Mean Conference Wins**	**2.0 / 0.5**	
Rushing S&P+		90.3	97	Rushing S&P+		79.5	121	Proj. F/+	-15.5%	108
Passing S&P+		79.4	115	Passing S&P+		81.2	115	Offensive F/+	-6.5%	104
Standard Downs S&P+		87.3	110	Standard Downs S&P+		79.6	123	Defensive F/+	-9.0%	111
Passing Downs S&P+		77.8	118	Passing Downs S&P+		85.4	102	Strength of Sched. Rk / Conf. Title Odds	37 / 0.0%	

The floundering Colorado program finally hit rock bottom last season, setting a school record for futility with 11 losses—and for the most part, they were ugly losses. In Pac-12 play, the Buffs dropped their last eight by nearly 36 points per game, managing to come within four touchdowns only once, in a 42-35 loss to Utah to close the season. They gave up an explosive drive on 24.3 percent of opponent possessions, and manufactured one of their own on only 2.5 percent of drives—dead last nationally in both categories. They finished last or next-to-last in the conference in every major statistical category, and the adjusted rankings (123rd in Defensive F/+) agreed. They failed to win a home game for the first time in more than 80 years.

New head coach Mike MacIntyre is no stranger to dire projects, not after a three-year stint lifting historically hapless San Jose State from the bottom of the WAC standings into the national polls. Nor is he reassembling a roster entirely from scratch: Fourteen different sophomores started at least one game as freshmen, including the leading rusher (Christian Powell), leading receiver (Nelson Spruce) and three regular starters in the secondary (Kenneth Crawley, Marques Mosley and Yuri Wright). With a year under their belt, the next step on the rebuilding ladder is "losing close"—keeping more games

within reach into the fourth quarter.

Based on the spring, first crack at quarterback will fall to Texas transfer Connor Wood, who was the last man standing in April following a knee injury to the incumbent, Jordan Webb, and the subsequent transfer of last year's top backup, Nick Hirschman. The other, more intriguing option is incoming freshman Sefo Liufau, who will be given every opportunity to win the job from day one. Whoever emerges under center will benefit from the return of wide receiver Paul Richardson, arguably the team's most dynamic playmaker in 2011 until a late-season ACL tear that sidelined him for the rest of that season and all of 2012. Richardson was healthy in the spring for the first time since the injury and looking like his old, explosive self, albeit at the expense of Colorado's highly flammable secondary. But the quarterback will also have to operate behind a long-suffering offensive line that yielded a staggering 50 sacks last year in less than 500 attempts, and lost starter Alexander Lewis to Nebraska. Short of a sea change up front, the odds of progress elsewhere are as thin as the local air.

Top 2014 NFL prospects: *DE Chidera Uzo-Diribe (6–7)*

Matt Hinton

Projected Win Probabilities For Pac-12 Teams

Pac 12 North	Overall Wins													Conference Wins									
	12-0	11-1	10-2	9-3	8-4	7-5	6-6	5-7	4-8	3-9	2-10	1-11	0-12	9-0	8-1	7-2	6-3	5-4	4-5	3-6	2-7	1-8	0-9
California	-	-	-	-	-	1	5	16	33	32	12	1	-	-	-	-	-	2	10	30	41	15	2
Oregon	45	44	10	1	-	-	-	-	-	-	-	-	-	46	44	9	1	-	-	-	-	-	-
Oregon State	-	5	17	31	29	14	4	-	-	-	-	-	-	-	5	20	34	28	11	2	-	-	-
Stanford	8	30	35	20	6	1	-	-	-	-	-	-	-	13	36	34	14	3	-	-	-	-	-
Washington	-	-	-	2	7	21	32	26	10	2	-	-	-	-	-	1	6	22	37	27	6	1	-
Washington State	-	-	-	-	-	-	-	-	5	25	54	15	1	-	-	-	-	-	-	-	4	28	68

Pac 12 South	12-0	11-1	10-2	9-3	8-4	7-5	6-6	5-7	4-8	3-9	2-10	1-11	0-12	9-0	8-1	7-2	6-3	5-4	4-5	3-6	2-7	1-8	0-9
Arizona	-	4	16	32	30	14	4	-	-	-	-	-	-	-	4	16	33	30	14	3	-	-	-
Arizona State	-	-	2	8	19	28	25	13	4	1	-	-	-	-	3	12	26	31	20	7	1	-	-
Colorado	-	-	-	-	-	-	-	1	5	22	43	27	2	-	-	-	-	-	-	1	7	35	57
UCLA	-	-	-	1	6	18	30	28	14	3	-	-	-	-	-	1	4	18	33	30	12	2	-
USC*	2	12	28	31	19	7	1	-	-	-	-	-	-	8	28	36	21	6	1	-	-	-	-
Utah	-	-	-	2	7	18	30	27	13	3	-	-	-	-	-	2	5	19	34	29	10	1	-

*USC will play 13 regular season games; for projected overall records, 12-0 means 12-1, 11-1 means 11-2, etc.

Southeastern Conference

There have been moments over the last seven years when the SEC's alleged dominance over the rest of college football has felt like a forced narrative, or at least a lazy one. The 2012 season was not one of those moments. By the time Alabama took the podium in January to claim its second consecutive national championship, and the conference's seventh, the SEC had secured five of the top nine slots in the final AP poll. It also had six of the top 13 teams in our F/+ ratings, and those teams combined to go 60-2 against opponents that weren't one another. A month earlier, also-ran Arkansas had raided the Big Ten for a new head coach, Bret Bielema, fresh from his third straight conference title at Wisconsin. A few days later, Texas A&M phenom Johnny Manziel accepted the SEC's fourth Heisman Trophy since 2007. In April, the NFL validated the superiority complex by drafting a record 63 players from SEC rosters, more than twice as many as supplied by any other conference. ESPN validated it further by signing up to produce the league's new television network through 2034.

Not that anyone in the South needed any new excuses to crow about their omnipresence at the top: In 32 editions of the BCS standings since 2009, SEC teams have ranked first or second in 30 of them, and first *and* second in 14. But the cost of getting to the top, much less staying there, continues to rise. Just two years removed from a national championship, Auburn dropped $11.1 million to buy out coach Gene Chizik and his staff last December, on the heels of a collapse into the West Division cellar. Tennessee and Kentucky paid nearly as much to rid themselves of Derek Dooley and Joker Phillips, respectively, after just three years on the job. In keeping with the rising price tag—

on average, SEC coaching salaries have doubled since 2005—two of the league's four new head coaches in 2013, Bielema and Tennessee's Butch Jones, are scheduled to make more than $3 million annually. The other two, Gus Malzahn at Auburn and Mark Stoops at Kentucky, will make more than $2 million in their first year at the helm in a major conference, chump change next to proven winners Nick Saban ($5.3m), Les Miles ($4.3m), and Steve Spurrier ($3.6m). In the name of recruiting, nearly every team in the conference has funneled millions into a recently completed or planned facility project, including major stadium expansions at Mississippi State, Missouri and Texas A&M. Quite literally, the cement is always drying.

As in any arms race, there is also a threat of mutually assured destruction: In the last year of the much-maligned BCS system, the league's aggrandizing streak in the championship round is still as likely to be snuffed out from within as from a loss in the title game itself, where no SEC team has ever lost except to another SEC team. Getting that far without a blemish is still a feat, one that only two of the seven champions in the current run (Alabama in 2009 and Auburn in 2010) have actually accomplished. The other five, including Alabama each of the last two years, only made the cut after late November surprises in other conferences absolved them of their earlier losses. Between the rebuilding offensive line in Tuscaloosa; lack of reliable offensive firepower at Florida and South Carolina; and rebuilding defenses at Georgia, LSU and Texas A&M; there are enough Achilles' heels to go around, and more than enough competition to exploit them. Until further notice, though, it is still impossible to find such a concentration of legitimate contenders anywhere else.

EAST

No. 5 Florida Gators (9-3, 6-2)
2012: 11-2 (7-1) / F/+ #4 / FEI #5 / S&P+ #5

Program F/+	+28.7%	4	Returning Starters: 6 OFF, 5 DEF			2012 Field Position / Special Teams		
2012 Offense			**2012 Defense**			Special Teams F/+	+4.1%	3
Offensive F/+	**+6.5%**	**32**	**Defensive F/+**	**+23.6%**	**2**	Field Position Advantage	0.536	17
Offensive FEI:	0.144	43	Defensive FEI	-0.795	1	**2013 Projections**		
Offensive S&P+	117.9	28	Defensive S&P+	140.5	4	**Mean Wins / Mean Conference Wins**	**9.3 / 5.9**	
Rushing S&P+	124.1	10	Rushing S&P+	139.3	3	Proj. F/+	+22.2%	5
Passing S&P+	101.2	58	Passing S&P+	138.5	5	Offensive F/+	+6.9%	22
Standard Downs S&P+	108.9	39	Standard Downs S&P+	136.6	3	Defensive F/+	+15.3%	4
Passing Downs S&P+	120.5	21	Passing Downs S&P+	141.0	4	Strength of Sched. Rk / Conf. Title Odds	16 / 9.0%	

Win for win, Florida's collection of prized scalps in 2012 matched any resumé in the country. Against Texas A&M, the Gators held the eventual Heisman winner to his worst game of the season in terms of total offense, and his team's worst on the scoreboard in a come-from-behind, 20-17 win in College Station. LSU, a team that averaged nearly 32 points per game the rest of the year, managed just six against Florida in October and failed to reach the end zone for the only time all season. South Carolina, a team

whose only other loss came by two points in Baton Rouge, was laughed out of Gainesville a week later in a 44-11 debacle. And Florida State, a resurgent power that entered the regular-season finale trashing opponents by upwards of four touchdowns per game, limped out with a season low in total offense, by far, while yielding five turnovers. The defense finished fifth nationally in both yards and points allowed, fourth in yards per play and third in S&P+; even in their regular-season loss, the Gators held Georgia more than 200 yards below its season average and picked off über-efficient UGA quarterback Aaron Murray three times.

Even after the mediocrity of 2010 and 2011, though, Florida's 11-2 record sometimes felt less like a return to form than a harrowing escape. The offense, cornerstone of the best Florida teams of the past two decades, plodded through another season at or near the bottom of the SEC in terms of both yards and points, occasionally threatening to slip into hibernation. Wins over LSU and Missouri came with just 14 points on the board in each game, and the loss to Georgia featured nearly as many turnovers (6) as points (9). As late as mid-November, it was left to the special teams to bail out an anemic effort against Louisiana-Lafayette, blocking a punt for the game-winning touchdown on the final snap of regulation. Later, a 24-point fourth quarter against Florida State seemed to signal an attack finally finding its footing—right up until Florida's next game, a 33-23 Sugar Bowl flop against a 14-point underdog, Louisville, that was never as close as the score suggests.

Optimism on that side of the ball rests mainly with quarterback Jeff Driskel, a once-touted prospect whose main virtue as a sophomore was limiting mistakes: He served up just five interceptions in 245 attempts, four of them coming in the two losses. But the risk-averse philosophy was also a symptom of the Gators' ongoing lack of big-play threats, especially among the wide receivers, who averaged a paltry 10.4 yards per catch. (Altogether, 60 percent of Driskel's completions went for less than ten yards, and fewer than half resulted in a first down.) Not surprisingly, the search for a spark in the spring centered heavily on fresh faces, most notably Loucheiz Purifoy, a re-

turning starter at cornerback who got a long look with the receiving corps. There was also freshman Kelvin Taylor, son of ex-Gator/Jaguar star Fred Taylor, who graduated high school in December as the most prolific back in Florida prep history after breaking Emmitt Smith's career rushing record. On the summer depth chart released by the school, though, Taylor was relegated to third string behind returnees Matt Jones and Mack Brown, and Purifoy was back at his usual spot on defense.

On paper, the defense was decimated by attrition—five of the top six tacklers are gone, three of them drafted among the top 50 picks—but like Alabama and LSU, there is always enough raw material on hand here to build a bridge from one elite unit to the next. The most proven commodity this time around is Purifoy, a likely first-rounder himself if he decides to come out early in 2014. The most intriguing, though, is Ronald Powell, widely touted as the top freshman prospect in the nation in 2010, who was listed at the top of the depth chart at outside linebacker despite missing all of last season and the spring with a torn ACL. Up front, blue-chip bookends Jonathan Bullard and Dante Fowler Jr. look like entrenched starters after productive seasons off the bench as true freshmen. If someone, *anyone* emerges on offense, there won't be much slack to pick up to lift the Gators back into a BCS bowl.

Top 2014 NFL prospects: *CB Loucheiz Purifoy* (1), CB Marcus Roberson* (1–2), DE/DT Dominique Easley (2–3), OT Chaz Green* (2–3), DE/OLB Ronald Powell* (2–3), WR/RB Trey Burton (5–6), WR Andre Debose (6–7), C Jonotthan Harrison (6–7).*

No. 9 Georgia Bulldogs (10-2, 6-2)

2012: 12-2 (7-1) / F/+ #6 / FEI #8 / S&P+ #6

Program F/+	+17.8%	17	Returning Starters: 10 OFF, 3 DEF			2012 Field Position / Special Teams		
2012 Offense			**2012 Defense**			Special Teams F/+	+0.4%	53
Offensive F/+	**+16.1%**	**4**	**Defensive F/+**	**+12.6%**	**18**	Field Position Advantage	0.526	30
Offensive FEI:	0.445	14	Defensive FEI	-0.475	17	**2013 Projections**		
Offensive S&P+	134.6	3	Defensive S&P+	120.0	14	**Mean Wins / Mean Conference Wins**	**9.5 / 6.2**	
Rushing S&P+	123.1	11	Rushing S&P+	114.5	22	Proj. F/+	+20.8%	9
Passing S&P+	148.9	1	Passing S&P+	105.7	44	Offensive F/+	+15.3%	2
Standard Downs S&P+	137.7	1	Standard Downs S&P+	112.3	23	Defensive F/+	+5.6%	28
Passing Downs S&P+	135.9	6	Passing Downs S&P+	107.0	47	Strength of Sched. Rk / Conf. Title Odds	34 / 11.2%	

Can Mark Richt forgive Georgia fans for ever doubting him? After three straight, increasingly disappointing seasons starting in 2008, culminating in an unthinkable slide below .500 in 2010, the state was so divided on its head coach that even his defenders began to grow weary of dwelling on past glories amid a growing chasm between UGA and the league's upper crust. Now, two years and two division titles later, Richt is entrenched as ever, with the great expectations to match: By the end of 2012, the Bulldogs were on a bona fide roll, one that saw them average 39 points over the final six games and left them within a few seconds of both their first SEC crown since 2005 and their first-ever appearance in the BCS title game. The next step is actually getting them there.

The catalyst for that kind of optimism is senior quarterback Aaron Murray, owner of more career starts (41) and touchdown passes (95) than any other active FBS quarterback. Displaying a vastly improved penchant for getting the ball

downfield, Murray also led the nation last year in yards per attempt (10.1), tied for second in passes covering at least 30 yards (33), and came in just behind Alabama's A.J. McCarron in overall efficiency (174.8, best in school history). The Bulldogs averaged at least 10 yards per play on 26.5 percent of their drives, the highest rate in the country. Not coincidentally, the surge in big-play productivity went hand-in-hand with the emergence of freshman tailbacks Todd Gurley and Nick Marshall, whose combined output on the ground (2,144 yards, 25 touchdowns on 6.3 per carry) made them one of the most productive tandems in the country within a few months of arriving on campus; Gurley alone led the conference in yards from scrimmage and landed a first-team All-SEC nod from league coaches. Given a completely intact offensive line—five returning starters up front have combined for 99 career starts—there is every reason to expect them to pick up where they left off as one of the most balanced attacks in the country.

That is not the case for the defense, rebuilding with just three full-time starters returning. A little turnover there is not necessarily a damning development; like Florida and LSU, the Bulldogs' defense was decimated by a mass exodus for the draft, where seven 2012 starters came off the board. Unlike Florida and LSU, however, Georgia was hardly elite on that side of the ball. Despite the ostensible concentration of talent, UGA finished in the middle of the SEC in almost every major category. With the season on the line, the defense visibly wilted in the path of Alabama's dominant offensive line in the second half of the SEC Championship game. The new cast is much greener, by far, but it also boasts at least two stars-in-waiting: linebacker Amarlo Herrera and Josh Harvey-Clemons, a former five-star recruit who enters 2013 with huge expectations spending spring practice carving out a personal niche as a hybrid linebacker/safety capable of lining up almost anywhere in the field. There are also plenty of options for immediate help courtesy of eight early enrollees. (One of them, safety Tray Matthews, already looks likely to start from Day One—or at least until Harvey-Clemons returns from an opening-day suspension against Clemson.) More importantly, opposite this offense, there should be some margin for error defensively that does not exist elsewhere in the conference, especially against a schedule that conveniently omits both of the SEC's most loaded offenses, Alabama and Texas A&M, for the second year in a row.

Top 2014 NFL prospects: *WR Malcolm Mitchell* (1–2), QB Aaron Murray (2), CB Damian Swann* (3), TE Arthur Lynch (3–4), G Chris Burnette (4), DE Garrison Smith (4–5), OT Kenarious Gates (5–6).*

No. 14 South Carolina Gamecocks (9-3, 6-2)

2012: 11-2 (6-2) / F/+ #13 / FEI #11 / S&P+ #12

Program F/+	+15.5%	20	Returning Starters: 7 OFF, 5 DEF			2012 Field Position / Special Teams		
2012 Offense			**2012 Defense**			Special Teams F/+	-0.8%	86
Offensive F/+	**+7.2%**	**29**	**Defensive F/+**	**+17.3%**	**7**	Field Position Advantage	0.506	52
Offensive FEI:	0.244	28	Defensive FEI	-0.629	5	**2013 Projections**		
Offensive S&P+	114.5	25	Defensive S&P+	127.8	6	**Mean Wins / Mean Conference Wins**	9.3 / 5.9	
Rushing S&P+	100.1	65	Rushing S&P+	122.5	12	Proj. F/+	+18.6%	14
Passing S&P+	111.4	38	Passing S&P+	130.2	10	Offensive F/+	+7.5%	17
Standard Downs S&P+	94.5	83	Standard Downs S&P+	124.2	8	Defensive F/+	+11.1%	11
Passing Downs S&P+	130.0	11	Passing Downs S&P+	127.5	15	Strength of Sched. Rk / Conf. Title Odds	39 / 9.2%	

Steve Spurrier landed in South Carolina in November 2004 with a mandate to raise the Gamecocks from perpetual mediocrity and a proven blueprint for the job. Prior to his ill-fated venture into the NFL three years before, Spurrier had taken a similarly stagnant program at Florida to six SEC crowns from 1991 to 2001, all of them by air thanks to attacks that led the league in scoring eight times during the same span. (Against South Carolina, the Spurrier-era Gators were 10-0 with an average winning margin of 25 points.) But the conference the Ball Coach found was very different from the one he left, having already begun its Saban-esque turn from the "Fun 'n Gun" phase of the 90s to something closer to "bite and hold." Eight years later, Spurrier has fulfilled his promise by delivering back-to-back 11-win seasons, unmatched in school history. And he's done it, finally, by deferring to the defense.

Pronounced as that trend is on paper—Carolina finished seventh nationally last year in defensive F/+, and among the top 15 in both yards and points allowed for the second year in a row—it's even more dramatic according to the proverbial eyeball test. Of 18 draft picks who were recruited and signed by Spurrier, two-thirds have come from the defensive side of the ball, with half of that number coming from arguably the weakest position on the team when Spurrier took over, the defensive line. Since 2010, at least one Gamecocks defensive lineman has come off the board in four consecutive drafts. That streak will continue next year with the best of the lot, or any lot: *übermensch* edge-rusher Jadeveon Clowney, whose nightmarish combination of size, speed and violence has already cemented his status as a household name in pain. While Clowney was busy defying hyperbole as a sophomore, finishing second in the FBS in sacks (13) and tackles for loss (23.5), the rest of the front was doing its part to make Carolina the most sack-happy defense in the SEC and one of the most unforgiving against the run at just 3.1 yards per carry and 12th in Rushing S&P+. All the attention on Clowney only creates more opportunities for linemates Kelcy Quarles and Chaz Sutton to turn heads on their own.

There is considerably less star power on offense, although the absence of a headliner didn't stop the Gamecocks from finishing with a flourish after losing All-SEC workhorse Marcus Lattimore to a major knee injury in late October. From that point on, they picked up the pace by averaging 417 yards and 33 points in wins over Arkansas, Clemson and Michigan, despite splitting snaps almost evenly in those three games between two quarterbacks, Connor Shaw and Dylan Thompson. When healthy, Shaw is one of the most versatile, efficient signal-callers in a league full of them, and one of the most underrated due to less than overwhelming arm strength; when he's not, Thompson is less consistent but much more likely to challenge secondaries downfield. Still, even before Lattimore went down the lack of a reliable push from the offensive line was a prime culprit in back-to-back losses to LSU and Florida, which combined to hold Carolina to 70 yards rushing on 1.4 yards per carry. South Carolina ranked 36th in Adjusted Line Yards, but until the offensive line catches up to the defense, the next step will remain elusive.

Top 2014 NFL prospects: *DE Jadeveon Clowney* (1), DT Kelcy Quarles* (3–4), DE Chaz Sutton (4), CB Jimmy Legree (5).*

No. 33 Missouri Tigers (7-5, 4-4)

2012: 5-7 (2-6) / F/+ #58 / FEI #57 / S&P+ #57

Program F/+	+12.3%	26	Returning Starters: 9 OFF, 6 DEF			2012 Field Position / Special Teams		
2012 Offense			**2012 Defense**			Special Teams F/+	+1.9%	20
Offensive F/+	**-5.7%**	**85**	**Defensive F/+**	**+4.4%**	**41**	Field Position Advantage	0.51	48
Offensive FEI:	-0.238	97	Defensive FEI	-0.122	51	**2013 Projections**		
Offensive S&P+	97.0	70	Defensive S&P+	111.9	31	**Mean Wins / Mean Conference Wins**	7.0 / 3.5	
Rushing S&P+	100.2	64	Rushing S&P+	120.7	14	Proj. F/+	+9.5%	33
Passing S&P+	97.2	74	Passing S&P+	109.3	36	Offensive F/+	+2.9%	41
Standard Downs S&P+	92.2	93	Standard Downs S&P+	109.9	27	Defensive F/+	+6.6%	23
Passing Downs S&P+	110.9	40	Passing Downs S&P+	121.5	22	Strength of Sched. Rk / Conf. Title Odds	36 / 0.5%	

Like any team that falls on the wrong side of a series of close calls, Missouri must have felt at times like the reality of its SEC debut told a far different story than the final record. Of Mizzou's seven losses in 2012, three came by a touchdown or less, all games in which they led or were tied in the fourth quarter; two of them, November dates with Florida and Syracuse, were decided in the final 20 seconds. But then, the knife cuts both ways: Aside from gimmes against Southeastern Louisiana and Kentucky, the Tigers' wins consisted of a pair of close calls outside the conference, over Arizona State and Central Florida, and a quadruple-overtime escape at Tennessee that temporarily put a bowl game within reach. After a season spent largely on the fence, they managed to land right in the middle.

The de facto symbol of the team's slide into mediocrity was quarterback James Franklin, whose bid to follow up a stellar 2011 sophomore campaign was cut short by a succession of injuries—shoulder, knee, concussion—that cost him three full games and significant portions of four more. (The Tigers' record in those games: 2-5.) The offense was also working without running back Henry Josey, a former All-Big 12 pick who sat out the season rehabbing a major knee injury suffered in late 2011. Despite Josey's absence over the final month of that season, he and Franklin still combined for 2,257 rush yards (not including sacks) and 24 touchdowns, fueling a rushing attack that was 19th in Rushing S&P+. With Josey on ice and Franklin a non-factor as a rusher, production on the ground last year fell by more than 100 yards per game, and pass efficiency by a full 30 points. Missouri fell to 64th in Rushing S&P+ and 74th in Passing S&P+. Having both in the same huddle again made for a feel-good spring, although the good vibes also had something to do with coaches' praise for the progress of sophomore receiver Dorial Green-Beckham (386 yards, 14.3 per catch, 63 percent catch rate). Green-Beckham came to Mizzou with titanic expectations, and struggled early as a true freshman, but he was much improved following a midseason suspension. Sixty-one percent of his total yards and four of his five touchdowns came in the month of November.

The defense proved its penchant for thievery, tying for the national lead with 21 forced fumbles, but not for much else: The pass rush managed just 11 sacks in eight SEC games, leaving the secondary to fall victim to a late-season collapse against Tennessee (432 yards passing, 4 touchdowns), Syracuse (385 yards, 2 TDs) and Texas A&M (410 yards, 3 TDs) in the final three games. Improved pressure is a priority. To make that happen, though, Mizzou is counting heavily on increased production from junior end Kony Ealy, a long, lean rusher billed, hopefully, as the next Aldon Smith. Otherwise, there is no reason to expect a secondary breaking in two new starters to mend itself.

Top 2014 NFL prospects: *DE Kony Ealy* (3–4), CB E.J. Gaines (5–6), QB James Franklin (6–7).*

No. 46 Tennessee Volunteers (6-6, 3-5)

2012: 5-7 (1-7) / F/+ #57 / FEI #61 / S&P+ #50

Program F/+	+4.1%	46	Returning Starters: 5 OFF, 9 DEF			2012 Field Position / Special Teams		
2012 Offense			**2012 Defense**			Special Teams F/+	-0.1%	65
Offensive F/+	**+7.4%**	**27**	**Defensive F/+**	**-6.4%**	**85**	Field Position Advantage	0.511	47
Offensive FEI:	0.182	35	Defensive FEI	0.226	84	**2013 Projections**		
Offensive S&P+	118.9	19	Defensive S&P+	93.4	81	**Mean Wins / Mean Conference Wins**	5.6 / 2.8	
Rushing S&P+	120.0	13	Rushing S&P+	93.1	83	Proj. F/+	+4.5%	46
Passing S&P+	131.1	7	Passing S&P+	92.5	84	Offensive F/+	+3.9%	34
Standard Downs S&P+	128.8	6	Standard Downs S&P+	90.3	95	Defensive F/+	+0.6%	55
Passing Downs S&P+	124.4	16	Passing Downs S&P+	100.7	62	Strength of Sched. Rk / Conf. Title Odds	1 / 0.0%	

No one seems to be able to identify exactly when the Volunteers reached the point of no return. Was it when they fired long-time, born-and-bred head coach Phillip Fulmer in 2008? When they hired an unproven outsider, Lane Kiffin, as his successor? When Kiffin bolted for USC in the middle of the night, barely a year later? When they settled for their fifth choice to replace him, Derek Dooley, after a brief, frantic search? After each and every one of Kiffin's most touted recruits fell by the wayside and scattered across the country? Nonetheless, the results speak for themselves: With three head coaches and four losing seasons in five years, 2008-12 ranks as the worst span in Knoxville in more than a century. When Dooley was given the boot last November, he left a team that had dropped 14 of its last 15 conference games, with ongoing skids against rivals Florida (eight straight), Alabama (five), Georgia (three) and South Carolina (three).

Like Dooley, new coach Butch Jones didn't seem to be anyone's first choice for the renovation. Unlike Dooley, though, who was viewed from the beginning as a kind of stopgap to keep a foundering ship afloat, Jones has the benefit of inheriting an outfit that has already hit bottom. (He doesn't have the benefit of a forgiving schedule, however: The Vols will play road games against both F/+ projected No.1 Alabama and No. 2 Oregon). The biggest issue is the defense, ravaged last year for an astonishing 35.7 points on 471.3 yards per game, dead last in the SEC and worst in school history on both counts. Tennessee ranked 85th in Defensive F/+, and the Volunteers gave up at least 38 points in each of Dooley's final seven games. At least Jones inherits a defense with no shortage of experience—among the holdovers on defense, nine players started at least six games last year, and six others have started at least four in their careers. Pro scouts are humming in anticipation over linebacker A.J. Johnson, leading tackler in the SEC as a sophomore, and colossal defensive tackle Daniel McCullers, whose raw size (6-foot-6, 375 pounds) has a way of obscuring his inconsistency. Tennessee coaches, of course, would rather have the NFL buzzing over McCullers' senior production than his raw pro potential.

Aside from Johnson, the strength of the team on paper is the offensive line, a senior-laden group that allowed the fewest sacks in the conference in 2012 and helped improve the team rushing average by nearly two yards per carry over 2011. Tennessee ranked second in the country in Adjusted Sack Rate and 23rd in Adjusted Line Yards. From that unit, the Vols have already sent one starter to the next level (third-rounder Dallas Thomas) and could conceivably send the other four right behind him, led by junior left tackle Antonio Richardson. But who are they blocking for? The quarterback derby is between junior Justin Worley, who didn't bowl anyone over as understudy to departed starter Tyler Bray, and a redshirt freshman, Nathan Peterman, who hasn't taken a live college snap. One half of last year's tailback rotation, Marlin Lane, Jr., was suspended indefinitely in April. The receivers are effectively starting over from scratch without All-SEC targets Cordarrelle Patterson (first round), Justin Hunter (second) and Mychal Rivera (sixth). The new rotation has some potential, but virtually no experience and a very high bar to clear.

Top 2014 NFL prospects: *LB A.J. Johnson* (1), DT Daniel McCullers (1– 2), OT Antonio "Tiny" Richardson* (1–2), OT JaWuan James (5), RB Rajion Neal (5–6), G Zach Fulton (7–FA), C James Stone (7–FA).*

No. 51 Vanderbilt Commodores (6-6, 2-6)

2012: 9-4 (5-3) / F/+ #50 / FEI #43 / S&P+ #56

Program F/+	-2.0%	63	Returning Starters: 7 OFF, 6 DEF			2012 Field Position / Special Teams		
2012 Offense			**2012 Defense**			Special Teams F/+	+3.4%	6
Offensive F/+	-2.5%	69	**Defensive F/+**	+5.2%	35	Field Position Advantage	0.554	7
Offensive FEI:	-0.120	72	Defensive FEI	-0.230	35	**2013 Projections**		
Offensive S&P+	101.3	61	Defensive S&P+	108.1	41	**Mean Wins / Mean Conference Wins**	5.9 / 2.2	
Rushing S&P+	91.9	93	Rushing S&P+	96.6	70	Proj. F/+	+3.0%	51
Passing S&P+	100.9	60	Passing S&P+	113.8	24	Offensive F/+	-0.2%	61
Standard Downs S&P+	93.7	89	Standard Downs S&P+	104.7	47	Defensive F/+	+3.2%	38
Passing Downs S&P+	100.6	70	Passing Downs S&P+	108.2	42	Strength of Sched. Rk / Conf. Title Odds	21 / 0.0%	

Yo, James Franklin, how's that Vanderbilt rebuilding job coming? Well, for starters, in Franklin's second season as head coach the Commodores...

• Finished with a winning conference record for the first time since 1982.

• Won eight games in the regular season for the first time since 1955.

• Won seven games in a row for the first time since 1948.

• Landed in the final AP poll (No. 23) for the first time since 1948.

• Recorded their most lopsided win over Tennessee (23 points) since 1954.

• Averaged 30 points per game for the first time since 1916.

• Tied a school record for overall wins (9), set in 1915.

• Earned back-to-back bowl bids for the first time ever.

That is, if you even consider football in 1915 the same sport.

For the wet blankets in the house, yes, such a rapid ascent from irrelevance comes with its limits: Vandy was 0-4 against other teams that landed in the final polls, including a 48-3 debacle at Georgia, and otherwise did not face another winning opponent in the regular season; three of their five conference victories, over Missouri, Auburn and Ole Miss, came by a combined nine points. In context, though, that's setting the bar much too high for an outfit just getting off the ground and only beginning to make inroads with the kind of SEC-ready recruits who have universally ignored Vanderbilt for decades. In contrast to the last two classes under Franklin, expectations could not have been lower for the incoming signees of 2009 and 2010, afterthoughts who joined a program buried in the league basement and have vastly overachieved by lifting it within sight of the glass ceiling.

As it turns out, they've also made for a relatively loaded senior class, featuring unlikely pro hopefuls on the defensive line (Walker May), in the secondary (Andre Hal and Kenny Ladler), at wide receiver (Jordan Matthews), and on the offensive line (Wesley Johnson, who has started every game over the last three years and taken his turn at every position on the line except left guard). All of the above were once regarded as mere two- or three-star prospects. So was the new quarterback, senior Austyn Carta-Samuels, a transfer from Wyoming with 21 starts under his belt as a Cowboy and two years at Vanderbilt as an understudy to starter Jordan Rodgers. With apologies to departed tailback Zac Stacy, owner of the school's single-season and career rushing records, no vacancy is more urgent than the one under center, where Rodgers emerged over the second half of the season (1,298 yards, 12 touchdown passes in the last six games) as the most productive Commodore quarterback this side of Jay Cutler.

Again, caveats apply regarding strength of schedule during that streak, especially comparing it to a much stiffer slate this fall: Last-place Auburn has been replaced by Texas A&M, and 2012 victims Ole Miss and Tennessee figure to be much improved in their own right behind the two most seasoned lineups in the conference. Vandy also benefited last year from exceptional field position (seventh nationally in field position advantage), and we estimate that field position value alone was worth an additional 10 points per game over the last six contests.

Still, barring a major regression from Rodgers to Carta-Samuels, the offense should mount another challenge to the 30-point barrier that, before last year, had taunted previous Vandy attacks for nearly a century. Johnson leads four return-

ing starters on the line. Between Matthews, a first-team All-SEC pick, and former classmates Chris Boyd and Jonathan Krause, Carta-Samuels inherits three proven targets who have accounted for more than 4,000 yards and 30 touchdowns over the last three years. And in Stacy's place, the ground game falls to the gem of the 2012 recruiting class, sophomore Brian Kimbrow, who is right on schedule after accounting for 900 all-purpose yards as a rusher and return man. Kimbrow's counterpart on defense is end Caleb Azubike, another four-star talent graduating from good reviews off the bench as a true freshman to a full-time role. If Franklin's revival is going to have any staying power in this league, it can't be limited to the best efforts of overachievers.

Top 2014 NFL prospects: *WR Jordan Matthews (1–2), CB Andre Hal (4–5), S Kenny Ladler (5), OT Wesley Johnson (5–6), DE Walker May (5–6).*

No. 84 Kentucky Wildcats (3-9, 1-7)

2012: 2-10 (0-8) / F/+ #112 / FEI #111 / S&P+ #98

Program F/+	-6.7%	82	Returning Starters: 7 OFF, 7 DEF			2012 Field Position / Special Teams		
2012 Offense			**2012 Defense**			Special Teams F/+	-0.4%	77
Offensive F/+	**-7.9%**	**104**	Defensive F/+	**-12.6%**	**113**	Field Position Advantage	0.482	86
Offensive FEI:	-0.286	105	Defensive FEI	0.550	117	**2013 Projections**		
Offensive S&P+	91.6	84	Defensive S&P+	90.6	89	**Mean Wins / Mean Conference Wins**	**3.3 / 0.8**	
Rushing S&P+	111.6	34	Rushing S&P+	91.7	87	Proj. F/+	-6.6%	84
Passing S&P+	83.1	111	Passing S&P+	97.4	67	Offensive F/+	-2.2%	76
Standard Downs S&P+	99.1	67	Standard Downs S&P+	94.7	84	Defensive F/+	-4.4%	88
Passing Downs S&P+	88.8	94	Passing Downs S&P+	99.4	69	Strength of Sched. Rk / Conf. Title Odds	8 / 0.0%	

As moral victories go, the number of people in the stands for the spring game ranks pretty low on the list. But Kentucky had so few victories of any kind in 2012—moral or otherwise—that drawing a reported 50,000 fans for coach Mark Stoops' debut in April felt like a minor triumph. That number was higher than the actual attendance for any of the Wildcats' seven home games last year, and nearly three times the crowd that came last November to watch the 'Cats get humiliated by Vanderbilt, 40-0, in their final game under Joker Phillips. Here, at least, was a sign that the faithful are still willing to *show up* on the heels of an 0-8 finish in SEC play, if only until the basketball team returns to form after a disappointing season of its own. Acknowledgement is progress.

Now, let them heed the perennial call for patience on behalf of the youngest, most outmanned lineup in the conference. Let's be charitable and chalk up last year's swoon to injuries, which thrust 26 true and redshirt freshmen into the fray by early October. Nowhere did the bug bite harder than quarterback, where an early, season-ending ankle injury to starter Maxwell Smith led to a revolving door through which senior Morgan Newton, redshirt freshman Patrick Towles, and true freshman Jalen Whitlow all entered and all exited again with assorted injuries of their own. The top tailback, sophomore Josh Clemons, missed the entire season rehabbing a torn ACL

from 2011. Eight different players took turns as a starting wide receiver, and nine started in the secondary. At no point was the starting lineup the same in consecutive weeks.

Still, for a team that kept virtually all of its linemen healthy on both sides of the ball while also losing seven games by more points than it scored, there is no easy answer for the malaise, and no quick fix. There is some hope for the defense, Stoops' specialty, which returns veteran linemen Alvin Dupree and Donte Rumph plus linebacker Avery Williamson, the second-leading tackler in the SEC. If juco transfer Za'Darius Smith lives up to his advance billing at defensive end, he and Dupree could generate some real heat off the edge—a necessity, given that the secondary is likely to feature at least three true sophomores in the starting four. The offense is still a mess, however. The spring offered no clear answer in the quarterback derby between Smith and Whitlow, and the receivers aren't going to make the eventual winner look any better than he is. Considering that last year's Wildcats had seven games where they gave up more than twice as many points as they scored, improvement in 2013 will be measured less by wins and losses and more by how often they manage to keep it close.

Top 2014 NFL prospects: *MLB Avery Williamson (6–7), DT Donte Rumph (7–FA).*

WEST

No. 1 Alabama Crimson Tide (12-0, 8-0)

2012: 13-1 (7-1) / F/+ #1 / FEI #1 / S&P+ #1

Program F/+	+42.1%	1	Returning Starters: 6 OFF, 7 DEF			2012 Field Position / Special Teams		
2012 Offense			**2012 Defense**			Special Teams F/+	+1.7%	28
Offensive F/+	**+21.1%**	**2**	**Defensive F/+**	**+27.8%**	**1**	Field Position Advantage	0.555	6
Offensive FEI:	0.533	5	Defensive FEI	-0.657	4	**2013 Projections**		
Offensive S&P+	147.7	4	Defensive S&P+	164.6	1	**Mean Wins / Mean Conference Wins**	**11.8 / 7.8**	
Rushing S&P+	137.4	4	Rushing S&P+	159.6	1	Proj. F/+	+38.9%	1
Passing S&P+	132.0	6	Passing S&P+	143.7	4	Offensive F/+	+16.5%	1
Standard Downs S&P+	124.8	9	Standard Downs S&P+	148.2	1	Defensive F/+	+22.3%	1
Passing Downs S&P+	154.1	3	Passing Downs S&P+	147.5	3	Strength of Sched. Rk / Conf. Title Odds	51 / 65.7%	

On the heels of another BCS crown, while the remains of the best Notre Dame outfit in two decades are still being exhumed from Sun Life Stadium, this might be a good time to acknowledge that the Crimson Tide are not yet, you know, *invincible*. In fact, both championship runs were temporarily derailed by November losses, and last year's triumph required late, harrowing comebacks in arguably the biggest games of the regular season, against LSU and Georgia. The 2010 team, which spent the first half of the season ranked No. 1, lost three games over the second half. The most recent exodus from the starting lineup included nine players taken in April's draft, most in school history, four of whom went in the first two rounds for the fourth year in a row.

Still, six full years into the reign of Saban, his Crimson Death Star remains fully operational and impervious to standard assumptions about the head that wears the crown. In an era of scholarship limits and rebuilding cycles, the departure of six draft picks from the apocalyptic 2011 defense couldn't prevent the 2012 edition from leading the nation (again) in both yards and points allowed. In an era defined by the rise of up-tempo, spread offenses, the 2012 attack patiently pounded out school records for total yards, points and touchdowns. In an era of alleged parity, Alabama has outscored opponents by more than three touchdowns per game since 2008, and by a wider margin in each successive season. Entering Saban's seventh year, the only relevant cycle in Tuscaloosa involves each new set of blue chips raising the bar set by the last one.

Although 'Bama is no stranger to the top of the polls, preseason or otherwise, the 2013 team may be the first for whom the hype belongs as much to the offense as to the perennially chart-topping defense, due mainly to the presence of senior quarterback A.J. McCarron. Defying his within-the-offense pedigree, McCarron blossomed last year into the most efficient passer in the nation, and lent unexpected balance downfield: while defenses were consumed with (and by) the ground game, wideouts Amari Cooper, Kevin Norwood, Kenny Bell, and Christion Jones combined to average 17.2 yards per catch with a dozen touchdowns covering at least 30 yards. Cooper, especially, emerged as a star down the stretch (999 receiving yards, 17.2 per catch, 76 percent catch rate), picking up Freshman All-America honors alongside tailback T.J. Yeldon, who set the school's freshman rushing record despite coming off the bench in every game behind All-SEC thumper Eddie Lacy. With Lacy en route to Green Bay and the initial learning curve behind them, the only thing standing between Yeldon and Cooper and a full gamut of postseason accolades is another five-star recruiting crop vying for its cut of the action.

Up front, there is less competition but arguably more pressure on left tackle Cyrus Kouandijo, a former five-star prospect now assigned the role of anchor on a line missing a pair of first-rounders (Chance Warmack and D.J. Fluker) and a repeat All-American (Barrett Jones) who logged 136 career starts between them. If there is a crack in the facade, it will almost certainly show in that transition, or possibly in the absence of All-SEC roadblock Jesse Williams in the middle of the defensive line. But anyone who assumes this outfit is subject to predictable pangs of attrition has not been paying attention.

Top 2014 NFL prospects: *OLB Adrian Hubbard* (1), OT Cyrus Kouandjio* (1), LB C.J. Mosley (1), S Ha'Sean Clinton-Dix* (1–2), QB A.J. McCarron (1–2), OLB Trey Depriest* (2), G Anthony Steen (2–3), CB Deion Belue (3–4), S Vinnie Sunseri* (3–4), WR Kevin Norwood (4), DE Ed Stinson (4–5), WR Kenny Bell (5–6), CB John Fulton (5–6).*

No. 4 LSU Tigers (9-3, 6-2)

2012: 10-3 (6-2) / F/+ #10 / FEI #12 / S&P+ #10

Program F/+	+24.3%	7	Returning Starters: 8 OFF, 5 DEF			2012 Field Position / Special Teams		
2012 Offense			**2012 Defense**			Special Teams F/+	+2.8%	9
Offensive F/+	**+5.0%**	**41**	**Defensive F/+**	**+18.2%**	**6**	Field Position Advantage	0.556	5
Offensive FEI:	0.125	46	Defensive FEI	-0.605	6	**2013 Projections**		
Offensive S&P+	113.6	37	Defensive S&P+	132.5	7	**Mean Wins / Mean Conference Wins**	**9.2 / 5.6**	
Rushing S&P+	124.3	8	Rushing S&P+	134.0	5	Proj. F/+	+23.5%	4
Passing S&P+	99.2	65	Passing S&P+	136.0	7	Offensive F/+	+9.4%	11
Standard Downs S&P+	110.0	35	Standard Downs S&P+	123.5	9	Defensive F/+	+14.1%	7
Passing Downs S&P+	108.6	46	Passing Downs S&P+	155.3	1	Strength of Sched. Rk / Conf. Title Odds	3 / 3.1%	

One can discern only so much from counting draft picks, but in LSU's case the numbers are illuminating: An unprecedented ten players from the 2012 roster gave up their final year of eligibility last winter for a shot at the NFL (11 if you count Tyrann "Honey Badger" Mathieu, a 2011 Heisman finalist who was booted just before the season), five of whom were drafted in the first three rounds. Altogether, the Tigers matched Alabama with nine overall picks, most of any school, and brought their total to 20 draftees over the last three years, befitting an outfit that won 34 games in that span.

At the same time, it's hard not to read the exodus of top-end talent as a window of opportunity coming to a close too soon. The outgoing class was within 60 minutes of the summit in 2011, before its baffling flop against Alabama in the BCS title game, and within a few points of a return trip last year, after opening at the top of the preseason coaches' poll. A lineup still boasting the likes of Barkevious Mingo, Eric Reid, Kevin Minter and Sam Montgomery—all tapped for All-SEC honors as juniors, all of them but Minter for the second year in a row—would have been guaranteed to start there again this fall. Now, instead of a sense of unfinished business, there's a sense of a reboot as a less accomplished cast tries to pick up the mantle.

This being LSU, of course, lack of experience is hardly synonymous with lack of potential. Nowhere on the team, for example, did attrition hit harder than the front seven on defense, which returns just one full-time starter: Senior linebacker Lamin Barrow. In front of him, though, is a trio of future pros on the defensive line, juniors Anthony Johnson, Ego Ferguson and Jermauria Rasco, who have been waiting patiently for their turn to fulfill blue-chip reviews as recruits. And joining Barrow at linebacker are a pair of touted sophomores, Kwon Alexander and Lamar Louis, who started multiple games as true freshmen. (Alexander was settling into a full-time role until a broken ankle ended his season in October.) The story is the same on the offensive line, where a wave of injuries made unexpected vets out of freshmen Vadal Alexander and Trai Turner, and in the backfield, where the early departures of Spencer Ware and Michael Ford and the muddled legal status of Jeremy Hill, last year's leading rusher as a true freshman, are cushioned by the return of senior Alfred Blue from a torn ACL.

If anything, there are fewer pressing doubts about the new faces in the lineup than there are about the most familiar. Quarterback Zach Mettenberger seemed to make more headlines last year for his unfortunate facial hair than his play, especially during a brutal October stretch in which he completed fewer than half of his attempts with a single touchdown pass against Florida, South Carolina and Texas A&M. From there, however, Mettenberger delivered his best performance by far in a near-upset against Alabama, and spent the final month of the season flashing the arm strength that had him on NFL radars before he had even taken a college snap. Even at his worst, Mettenberger was competent enough to avoid mistakes that would put the LSU defense in bad field position, turning in one of the lowest interception rates (just seven in 352 attempts) in the conference. Assuming the goals here still involve championships and BCS bowls, though, reaching them in this division will require more of him at his best. LSU's strength of schedule has ranked among the top five nationally every year since 2008.

Top 2014 NFL prospects: *DT Anthony Johnson* (1–2), MLB Lamin Barrow (2), G La'El Collins* (2–3), S Craig Loston (2–3), QB Zach Mettenberger (2–3), DE Jermauria Rasco* (2–3), WR Odell Beckham Jr.* (3–4), DT Ego Ferguson* (3–4), RB Alfred Blue (5), FB J.C. Copeland (5–6), WR Kadron Boone (6).*

No. 15 Texas A&M Aggies (9-3, 5-3)

2012: 11-2 (6-2) / F/+ #3 / FEI #3 / S&P+ #3

Program F/+	+12.3%	25	Returning Starters: 6 OFF, 4 DEF			2012 Field Position / Special Teams		
2012 Offense			**2012 Defense**			Special Teams F/+	-1.0%	89
Offensive F/+	**+23.1%**	**1**	**Defensive F/+**	**+13.0%**	**15**	Field Position Advantage	0.504	57
Offensive FEI:	0.806	2	Defensive FEI	-0.412	20	**2013 Projections**		
Offensive S&P+	138.1	1	Defensive S&P+	125.5	9	**Mean Wins / Mean Conference Wins**	9.1 / 5.2	
Rushing S&P+	155.6	1	Rushing S&P+	126.7	8	Proj. F/+	+18.5%	15
Passing S&P+	120.8	19	Passing S&P+	122.6	17	Offensive F/+	+12.9%	6
Standard Downs S&P+	123.1	10	Standard Downs S&P+	119.4	15	Defensive F/+	+5.5%	29
Passing Downs S&P+	159.9	1	Passing Downs S&P+	138.5	6	Strength of Sched. Rk / Conf. Title Odds	10 / 1.1%	

It may be possible to overstate Johnny Manziel's impact as a redshirt freshman, but if so, it's yet to be done. Unburdened by expectations, "Johnny Football"—a talent so instinctive the game may as well be his name—turned in the most statistically gonzo season in SEC history, claiming conference records for total offense in both a game (twice) and a season on top of a trophy case that defies inventory. He led the league in rushing, led the nation in total yards and accounted for more touchdowns than any other player. In November, he put the torch to the best defense in the country in a Heisman-clinching, program-defining upset over Alabama, then rode into the offseason with another sack full of records in a Cotton

Bowl romp over Oklahoma. Manziel rushed for 1,310 yards (not including sacks) and a fantastic plus-49.6 Adj. POE while completing 68 percent of his passes for an offense that ranked first in Rushing S&P+ and 19th in Passing S&P+. The A&M offense as a whole became the first in SEC history ever to surpass 7,000 yards of total offense. Manziel's share as a rusher and passer came to a little more than 70 percent.

When numbers speak that loudly, of course, it's never long before they begin to drift into the background of other, more urgent conversations, the kind concerned almost exclusively with championships and/or the lack thereof. Texas A&M hasn't been part of that kind of chatter in a long time: the Aggies' next conference title will be their first since 1998, in the Big 12, and last year's finish in the final AP poll (fifth) was the best at A&M since 1956, under head coach Bear Bryant. But the breakthrough also came from nowhere, under a new coach, Kevin Sumlin, and an unproven, unheralded quarterback who caught a new conference unprepared for the arrival of the "Air Raid." This time, Manziel's presence alone guarantees the bar will be set from the start where the 2012 team left it, and the target on his back will be that much larger.

Besides the most valuable player in the sport, the offense still has the benefit of last year's leading rusher (Ben Malena) and receiver (Mike Evans), as well as hyped sophomores Trey Williams and Brandon Williams (no relation) at tailback; it will also welcome the most coveted recruit in the state, Ricky Seals-Jones, as another big target downfield. But it must find solutions for two glaring vacancies: One on the offensive line, where left tackle Luke Joeckel passed on his senior season to become the No. 2 overall pick in the draft, and one on the coaching staff, where offensive coordinator Kliff Kingsbury left for the top job at his alma mater, Texas Tech. In Joeckel's place the Aggies have turned to his counterpart on the right side, Jake Matthews, a first-team All-SEC pick with a stellar NFL pedigree courtesy of his Hall-of-Fame father, Bruce Matthews, and his cousin Clay. With a spring practice under his belt on the left side and Alabama in town on September 14,

neither Matthews nor the new play-caller, Clarence McKinney, has the luxury of a grace period in his new role.

Nor will they be able to fall back on a proven defense: the departure of six full-time starters leaves A&M with the greenest defense in the conference, even before accounting for three freshmen atop the post-spring depth chart in place of absentee regulars Kirby Ennis (suspension), Julien Obioha (back) and Steven Jenkins (shoulder). Assuming the vets are back in the fold by September, priority one defensively is filling the rush end position occupied the last two years by Damontre Moore, who inherited the spot from another All-American, Von Miller, but left no clear successor. Competition in the spring was a three-way derby between sophomore Alonzo Williams and brothers Tyrell and Tyrone Taylor, none of whom rose above special teams duty in 2012; freshman Moore clone Daeshon Hall joins the fray this summer with good reviews from recruiting gurus and plenty of room to add to his 6-foot-6, 220-pound frame. In fact, no one in the current lineup has more than two sacks in his career. But barring a quantum leap from a largely middle-of-the-pack secondary, a reliable pass rush is non-negotiable.

Top 2014 NFL prospects: *OT Jake Matthews (1), QB Johnny Manziel* (1–2), CB Deshazor Everett* (2–3), RB Ben Malena (5).*

No. 27 Ole Miss Rebels (7-5, 4-4)

2012: 7-6 (3-5) / F/+ #40 / FEI #42 / S&P+ #27

Program F/+	+7.0%	38	Returning Starters: 8 OFF, 10 DEF			2012 Field Position / Special Teams		
2012 Offense			**2012 Defense**			Special Teams F/+	-2.5%	111
Offensive F/+	+6.3%	34	Defensive F/+	+5.8%	34	Field Position Advantage	0.457	108
Offensive FEI:	0.180	36	Defensive FEI	-0.171	43	**2013 Projections**		
Offensive S&P+	115.3	17	Defensive S&P+	113.9	21	**Mean Wins / Mean Conference Wins**	7.3 / 4.2	
Rushing S&P+	111.9	32	Rushing S&P+	113.5	25	Proj. F/+	+11.7%	27
Passing S&P+	124.3	14	Passing S&P+	105.9	43	Offensive F/+	+5.0%	31
Standard Downs S&P+	113.4	27	Standard Downs S&P+	105.0	46	Defensive F/+	+6.7%	22
Passing Downs S&P+	125.7	14	Passing Downs S&P+	122.3	21	Strength of Sched. Rk / Conf. Title Odds	4 / 0.2%	

It has been a bipolar decade in Oxford, one that has seen Ole Miss careen wildly from the high of Eli Manning's senior season to the sobering depths of the Ed Orgeron era, from ascendant optimism under Orgeron's successor, Houston Nutt, to depressing new lows as the Nutt regime collapsed, from peak to valley and back again in whiplash fashion. In that context, last year's inconsistent 7-6 turn under first-year coach Hugh Freeze may look more like a baby step than a great leap forward. From a partisan perspective, though, it's not hard to understand why it whetted local appetites for the next breakthrough. Record notwithstanding, the formerly hapless Rebels looked like a team on the brink in late, narrow losses to Texas A&M, Vanderbilt and LSU, all games they led well into the fourth quarter. They surged into the offseason by trouncing rival Mississippi State and then Pittsburgh in the BBVA Compass Bowl. The momentum was amplified and cemented on February 6, when Freeze and his aggressive staff inked an unprecedented, top-heavy recruiting haul headlined by the most hyped prospect in the nation, defensive end Robert Nkemdiche. That rendered the "rebuilding" narrative obsolete.

For now, at least, the glorified signing class is probably more

symbolic of the upward trajectory than it is likely to contribute to it right away. Not that it lacks the potential to make an instant impact—besides Nkemdiche, there are five-star additions at wide receiver (Laquon Treadwell), offensive tackle (Laremy Tunsil), defensive tackle (Lavon Hooks), and safety (Antonio Conner), as well as a trio of four-star tailbacks. But there is no rush to throw fresh bodies into the breach. Top to bottom, Ole Miss' roster already has more career starts to its credit (336) going into the season than any other team in the SEC. Aside from tight end, every position on both sides of the ball will be manned by a veteran starter unless/until displaced by one of the young guns.

No one on that list is more entrenched than the quarterback, Bo Wallace, a former juco transfer who immediately surged past three incumbent QBs on the depth chart, or his top receiver, Donte Moncrief, who emerged down the stretch as a reliably scorching deep threat. But the most pleasant surprise of 2012 was linebacker Denzel Nkemdiche, Robert's undersized, considerably less hyped older brother, who made his own name as the Rebels' leading tackler and a consensus Freshman All-American. Among the many other familiar names on defense, the three that fans are looking forward to hearing the most are C.J. Johnson, another five-star talent with a full season under his belt as a starter at defensive end; D.T. Shackelford, back in the rotation at linebacker after missing the last two seasons to major knee injuries; and Nickolas Brassell, a freshman starter at both receiver and cornerback in 2011, who took last fall off to shore up his grades in junior college. With so many veteran options, personnel-wise, the real question here is just how high their ceiling goes, and how close they can come to reaching it.

Top 2014 NFL prospects: *DE/OLB C.J. Johnson* (3–4), CB Charles Sawyer (6), RB Jeff Scott (7–FA).*

No. 43 Arkansas Razorbacks (5-7, 2-6)
2012: 4-8 (2-6) / F/+ #60 / FEI #67 / S&P+ #47

Program F/+		+11.7%	29	Returning Starters: 4 OFF, 7 DEF			2012 Field Position / Special Teams		
2012 Offense				**2012 Defense**			Special Teams F/+	-1.7%	97
Offensive F/+		**+4.9%**	**43**	**Defensive F/+**	**-2.7%**	**72**	Field Position Advantage	0.458	107
Offensive FEI:		0.064	54	Defensive FEI	0.080	74	**2013 Projections**		
Offensive S&P+		117.0	21	Defensive S&P+	97.9	63	**Mean Wins / Mean Conference Wins**	**5.3 / 2.2**	
Rushing S&P+		116.0	20	Rushing S&P+	118.9	16	Proj. F/+	+4.8%	43
Passing S&P+		136.4	3	Passing S&P+	87.5	101	Offensive F/+	+2.5%	42
Standard Downs S&P+		133.0	3	Standard Downs S&P+	97.0	73	Defensive F/+	+2.2%	49
Passing Downs S&P+		122.7	17	Passing Downs S&P+	103.6	55	Strength of Sched. Rk / Conf. Title Odds	2 / 0.0%	

Arkansas began 2012 on a high note, with a Cotton Bowl win in January that sealed the Razorbacks' highest poll finish (fifth) in 35 years, and ended it on another, by stealthily hiring Bret Bielema from Wisconsin within days of the Badgers' rout of Nebraska in the Big Ten Championship game. The rest of the year, they're still trying to erase: Between Bobby Petrino's adulterous exit as head coach in April and the subsequent collapse under his successor, the volatile John L. Smith, four years of progress under Petrino was undone in a matter of months. By the end of September, a veteran outfit that opened at No. 10 in the preseason polls had been outscored by 100 points in its first two conference games, ambushed at home by Louisiana-Monroe and Rutgers, and disabused of any notion of continuity.

In that context, the relatively blank slate awaiting Bielema may be a blessing in disguise, if only because it's accompanied by more realistic expectations. The new quarterback, Brandon Allen, was brutalized in his only start as a redshirt freshman, a 52-0 debacle against Alabama, and attempted just four passes the rest of the season. The ground game, worst in the SEC last year, will likely fall into the hands of a true freshman, Alex Collins, whose advance hype alone makes him nearly as proven a commodity as anyone else who will touch the ball—

the leading returning rusher (Jonathan Williams) and receiver (Mekale McKay) were both pressed into supporting roles last year as true freshmen themselves. The best player on the offensive line, Alvin Bailey, left early for the NFL after starting every game over the last three years, only to go undrafted.

The defense is slightly more familiar, beginning with proven bookends Chris Smith and Trey Flowers up front, although the experience in the secondary consists mainly of last year's rock-bottom finish against the pass in terms of both yards and efficiency. But the best news on both sides of the ball, aside from the new coaching staff, is the inevitable rebound in turnover margin: Arkansas had the most giveaways (31) and fewest takeaways (12) in the conference, a fate that is virtually impossible to repeat. Combined, those turnovers cost the Razorbacks an estimated 62.1 points, fifth most nationally. (Bielema's teams at Wisconsin finished fourth nationally in turnover margin in 2011 and sixth in 2010, but dipped to 48th last year and demonstrated no discernible pattern in that category otherwise.) If all else fails, regression towards the mean still begins with taking care of the ball.

Top 2014 NFL prospects: *DE Chris Smith (5–6), C Travis Swanson (6), DT Byran Jones (6–7), S Eric Bennett (7–FA).*

No. 57 Mississippi State Bulldogs (5-7, 2-6)
2012: 8-5 (4-4) / F/+ #62 / FEI #62 / S&P+ #53

Program F/+		+0.0%	56	Returning Starters: 6 OFF, 5 DEF			2012 Field Position / Special Teams		
2012 Offense				**2012 Defense**			Special Teams F/+	+1.5%	32
Offensive F/+		**-2.9%**	**72**	**Defensive F/+**	**+1.3%**	**54**	Field Position Advantage	0.524	32
Offensive FEI:		-0.195	87	Defensive FEI	-0.029	59	**2013 Projections**		
Offensive S&P+		104.3	51	Defensive S&P+	106.1	43	**Mean Wins / Mean Conference Wins**	**4.6 / 2.0**	
Rushing S&P+		107.3	47	Rushing S&P+	114.5	23	Proj. F/+	+1.8%	57
Passing S&P+		103.9	52	Passing S&P+	102.4	52	Offensive F/+	+0.2%	57
Standard Downs S&P+		99.7	64	Standard Downs S&P+	107.0	37	Defensive F/+	+1.6%	53
Passing Downs S&P+		119.6	22	Passing Downs S&P+	111.4	33	Strength of Sched. Rk / Conf. Title Odds	5 / 0.0%	

Mississippi State fans have been through enough lean times to know that eight-win seasons are not to be taken for granted, and still count their blessings for coach Dan Mullen, who has averaged eight wins over the last three years. But comparisons

to the bad old days didn't make the end of 2012 any easier to swallow, certainly not after a 7-0 start and corresponding ascent to No. 11 in the BCS standings. From there, the Bulldogs ran headlong into the thick of the SEC West jungle, and limped out two months later with five losses in their last six games—ugly losses, all of them, including a 41-24 fiasco against Ole Miss that snapped a three-year MSU reign in the Egg Bowl. For the season, none of State's eight victories came at the expense of a fellow bowl team, and its four conference wins came against opponents (Auburn, Kentucky, Tennessee and Arkansas) who combined to go 3–29 in SEC play.

Of the many deflating turns down the stretch, none was starker than the decline of the defense, ravaged for more than 475 yards and 37 points per game in the five losses despite an abundance of veteran talent. Five outgoing seniors (cornerbacks Johnthan Banks and Darius Slay, safety Corey Broomfield, linebacker Cameron Lawrence and defensive tackle Josh Boyd) combined for 164 career starts, and Banks, Slay and Boyd came off the board in April's draft. Even with the glaring voids in the secondary, the first priority in 2013 is creating more pressure in opposing backfields after finishing last in the SEC in sacks (105th in Adjusted Sack Rate) and next-to-last in tackles for loss. To that end, the Bulldogs won a down-to-the-wire battle for local star Chris Jones, a five-star defensive end with a short path to the top of the depth chart opposite last year's most hyped arrival, Denico Autry.

The pass rush (or lack thereof) will also be critical in the fate of the league's best turnover margin, buoyed in 2012 by an SEC-best 34 takeaways.

The second-half swoon was also mirrored in the struggles of quarterback Tyler Russell, who went out on an especially low note with a 12-for-28, four-interception clunker in the Gator Bowl loss to Northwestern. His job won't get any easier with the graduation of his top four receivers, either, leaving tailback LaDarius Perkins as the only remotely proven commodity with the ball in his hands. That's in contrast to plenty of experience up front—four returning starters on the offensive line have combined for 85 career starts—but the longer it takes for defenses to respect Russell's arm, or his targets, the less the blocking will matter. Against a dog-eat-dog schedule that adds Oklahoma State and South Carolina to the usual West Division heavies—not to mention road trips to Arkansas and Auburn, both looking up under new coaches—just treading water will not get the Bulldogs anywhere near eight wins again.

Top 2014 NFL prospects: *G Gabe Jackson (3), S Nickoe Whitley (3–4), RB LaDarius Perkins (4), QB Tyler Russell (7–FA).*

No. 56 Auburn Tigers (5-7, 2-6)
2012: 3-9 (0-8) / F/+ #105 / FEI #116 / S&P+ #91

Program F/+	+4.8%	41	Returning Starters: 7 OFF, 9 DEF			2012 Field Position / Special Teams		
2012 Offense			**2012 Defense**			Special Teams F/+	+1.9%	21
Offensive F/+	**-11.5%**	**111**	**Defensive F/+**	**-9.0%**	**95**	Field Position Advantage	0.503	58
Offensive FEI:	-0.513	119	Defensive FEI	0.359	100	**2013 Projections**		
Offensive S&P+	92.4	73	Defensive S&P+	92.4	78	**Mean Wins / Mean Conference Wins**	5.3 / 1.8	
Rushing S&P+	116.2	18	Rushing S&P+	94.0	80	Proj. F/+	+1.8%	56
Passing S&P+	76.6	120	Passing S&P+	105.5	45	Offensive F/+	-0.8%	66
Standard Downs S&P+	100.8	59	Standard Downs S&P+	96.6	77	Defensive F/+	+2.6%	43
Passing Downs S&P+	86.5	99	Passing Downs S&P+	113.1	29	Strength of Sched. Rk / Conf. Title Odds	6 / 0.0%	

How much can change in two years? If time is relative, for Auburn fans the distance between the unlikely, Cam Newton-fueled run to the BCS championship in 2010 and last year's humiliating, last-place collapse feels closer to an eternity. Under the same head coach that led them to the summit, Gene Chizik, the 2012 Tigers made a compelling bid for the title of most inept Auburn team of the modern era, finishing dead last in the SEC in total offense and dropping every conference game by an average of 24 points; by the end, rivals Georgia and Alabama were forced to show considerable mercy to limit the final scores to 38-0 and 49-0, respectively, after leaving the Tigers for dead by halftime. The pink slip that greeted Chizik after the Iron Bowl was a mere formality.

In his place, Auburn built another bridge to the 2010 triumph by importing Chizik's old offensive coordinator, Gus Malzahn, who had the unconventionally good sense to abandon ship after the 2011 season by accepting the top job at Arkansas State. (While his old team crashed and burned, Malzahn's Red Wolves rolled to the Sun Belt Conference title.) In retrospect, hiring Malzahn in 2009 may go down as Chizik's most inspired decision—short of successfully recruiting Newton—and the roster Malzahn inherits is both familiar and far more talented than its pathetic record suggests.

To what extent the record reflects that fact, though, depends

heavily on improvement at quarterback, where Malzahn will weigh two uninspiring holdovers, Kiehl Frazier and Jonathan Wallace, against hitting the reset button with incoming freshman Jeremy Johnson, a 6-foot-6, 215-pound prototype who arrives raw but without the baggage of the incumbents. In fact, similar decisions loom at virtually every position: Johnson is one of no fewer than a dozen newcomers with a realistic chance to challenge veterans at the top of the depth chart, including a handful of junior college transfers who made inroads in the spring at tailback (Cameron Artis-Payne) and both sides of the line of scrimmage (Devonte Danzey on offense, Ben Bradley on defense). The most experienced area on the team, the defensive line, was also one of the most abused in 2012—the Tigers were worst in the SEC against the run—and the most aggressively recruited, with blue-chips Montravius Adams, Elijah Daniel and Carl Lawson set to join Bradley and five returning starters this summer. There is no shortage of experienced bodies to choose from, but few of them have given the new staff any incentive to defer to the status quo.

Top 2014 NFL prospects: *DE/OLB Dee Ford (4–5), RB Tre Mason* (5–6), DT Jeff Whitaker (6), FB Jay Prosch (6–7).*

Matt Hinton

Projected Win Probabilities For SEC Teams

SEC East	Overall Wins													Conference Wins								
	12-0	11-1	10-2	9-3	8-4	7-5	6-6	5-7	4-8	3-9	2-10	1-11	0-12	8-0	7-1	6-2	5-3	4-4	3-5	2-6	1-7	0-8
Florida	2	15	29	30	17	6	1	-	-	-	-	-	-	6	24	37	25	7	1	-	-	-
Georgia	4	18	30	27	15	5	1	-	-	-	-	-	-	10	29	35	19	6	1	-	-	-
Kentucky	-	-	-	-	-	-	3	11	27	36	20	3	-	-	-	-	-	-	3	15	41	41
Missouri	-	-	2	10	22	29	22	11	3	1	-	-	-	-	2	4	15	29	30	16	4	-
South Carolina	2	15	29	29	17	6	2	-	-	-	-	-	-	6	24	36	24	8	2	-	-	-
Tennessee	-	-	-	-	5	17	33	29	13	3	-	-	-	-	-	2	5	19	36	28	9	1
Vanderbilt	-	-	-	1	8	22	33	26	9	1	-	-	-	-	-	-	2	10	27	36	22	3
SEC West	**12-0**	**11-1**	**10-2**	**9-3**	**8-4**	**7-5**	**6-6**	**5-7**	**4-8**	**3-9**	**2-10**	**1-11**	**0-12**	**8-0**	**7-1**	**6-2**	**5-3**	**4-4**	**3-5**	**2-6**	**1-7**	**0-8**
Alabama	78	20	2	-	-	-	-	-	-	-	-	-	-	80	19	1	-	-	-	-	-	-
Arkansas	-	-	-	-	3	12	27	32	19	6	1	-	-	-	-	-	1	8	26	40	21	4
Auburn	-	-	-	-	3	13	28	33	18	5	-	-	-	-	-	-	1	4	18	35	33	9
LSU	1	11	28	33	20	6	1	-	-	-	-	-	-	2	17	36	30	12	3	-	-	-
Mississippi	-	-	3	14	28	29	18	6	2	-	-	-	-	-	2	12	28	31	19	7	1	-
Mississippi State	-	-	-	-	1	5	17	31	30	14	2	-	-	-	-	-	1	6	22	38	28	5
Texas A&M	1	7	29	36	20	6	1	-	-	-	-	-	-	1	8	30	36	19	5	1	-	-

Independents and non-AQ teams

One new program officially joins the Football Bowl Subdivision this fall. The Georgia State Panthers played their first football game way back on September 2, 2010. They have a 1-6 all-time record against current FBS teams, and the lone victory came against 2012 FBS newcomer South Alabama. The Panthers begin their journey in FBS from the bottom of the Sun Belt conference and our projections give the Panthers an 82 percent chance of winning one or fewer games in their debut season of conference play. On October 5th, the Panthers take on the Alabama Crimson Tide in Tuscaloosa, a game that may end up with the most lopsided betting line in FBS history.

With few exceptions, the divide between the haves and the have-nots in college football appears to be getting wider. The great conference realignment saga provided some upward mobility for the best of the non-AQ programs in the last few years, but those that remain outside the major conferences won't likely be filling the void. A significant number of the non-AQs share much more in common with Georgia State than with Alabama. They'll play the punching bag role in non-conference play against SEC or Big 12 power programs and limp into conference play saddled with at least two or three losses.

In the 93 games scheduled this season between teams from an AQ conference versus those from a non-AQ conference, our F/+ projections favor the power program 84 times. In 45 of these games, the AQ program has a win likelihood of at least 90 percent.

Only two teams outside the power conferences figure to be nationally relevant this fall, and neither is breaking through a new barrier in 2013. Notre Dame revived its power program status last season and remains (for now and for the foreseeable future) an independent, distinguished from the rest of the non-AQ teams by its competitive schedule, national exposure, and privileged access to BCS eligibility. Boise State remains the best have-not in college football history, distinguished from the rest of the non-AQ teams by a nearly decade-long run of sustained program success.

If any other programs from outside the major conferences sneak into the top 25 this year, it will be a big surprise, and one that will be met with skepticism by many. Northern Illinois claimed an improbable BCS bowl berth last season, ranked 31st in F/+ following an 11-1 regular season against one of the nation's easiest schedules. The Huskies were then dominated by Florida State in a forgettable Orange Bowl. Boise State is the only team positioned to carry the "underdog" torch in 2013, and the only team that can earn another opportunity against a major conference power program and close out the BCS era as a true non-AQ success story. It just won't be with a national championship on the line.

INDEPENDENTS

No. 13 Notre Dame Fighting Irish (9-3)

2012: 12-1 / F/+ #7 / FEI #10 / S&P+ #7

Program F/+	+17.7%	18	Returning Starters: 5 OFF, 8 DEF			2012 Field Position / Special Teams		
2012 Offense			2012 Defense			Special Teams F/+	-1.1%	90
Offensive F/+	+13.9%	9	Defensive F/+	+14.6%	13	Field Position Advantage	0.492	74
Offensive FEI:	0.454	12	Defensive FEI	-0.476	16	2013 Projections		
Offensive S&P+	125.9	7	Defensive S&P+	127.4	8	Mean Wins / Mean Conference Wins	9.0	
Rushing S&P+	124.2	9	Rushing S&P+	116.8	17	Proj. F/+	+18.9%	13
Passing S&P+	133.2	5	Passing S&P+	127.8	12	Offensive F/+	+7.4%	19
Standard Downs S&P+	126.8	7	Standard Downs S&P+	120.7	13	Defensive F/+	+11.5%	10
Passing Downs S&P+	125.9	13	Passing Downs S&P+	126.4	17	Strength of Sched. Rk	24	

Notre Dame woke up the echoes with an undefeated regular season last fall, but a 42-14 beatdown against Alabama in the BCS Championship game proved that the Irish have more work to do to close the gap with the nation's elite programs. Adding insult to injury, the title game humiliation ushered in a tumultuous offseason headlined by the Manti Te'o fake girlfriend saga, the awkward and depth-crippling summer de-commitment of five-star defensive lineman Eddie Vanderdoes, and the sudden season-long academic suspension of starting quarterback Everett Golson. Every program experiences some offseason drama, but Notre Dame may have set a new gold standard in 2013.

The impact the Golson suspension will have on Irish fortunes is the biggest question mark facing the offense this fall. Senior quarterback Tommy Rees slides back into his old job with more starting experience (18 games) than any opposing quarterback the Irish will face this season. He was also reliable in brief appearances off the bench in 2012—5-for-5 for 54 yards and a touchdown in clutch situations against Oklahoma and Stanford. But his limited mobility and arm strength will likely thin the playbook, and his favorite target, tight end Tyler Eifert, is now playing on Sundays in Cincinnati. Senior slot receiver T.J. Jones picked up his production and sure-handedness late in the year and will likely be the new Rees go-to guy in a conservative offensive scheme. After Jones, the skill positions lack much experience. Junior running back George Atkinson III is a speedster, but only has 388 career yards in two seasons (+10.6 Adj. POE). Sophomore wide receiver Davaris Daniels (10.7 yards per catch, 67 percent catch rate) and junior tight end Troy Niklas are big targets, but only have 36 career receptions between them. The offensive line (seventh nationally in Adjusted Line Yards in 2012) should be a strength again, anchored by fifth-year senior left tackle Zach Martin.

Offensive priorities focus on avoiding mistakes more than on point production, especially since the Irish will be backed by a defense that projects to be among the nation's best. In the 2012 regular season, Notre Dame led the nation in scoring defense and red-zone touchdown defense. In a stretch spanning 11 games, the Irish faced an astonishing 100 straight opponent possessions without giving up a 60-plus-yard touchdown drive. They bent without breaking (until the championship game, of course), allowing 16 percent of opponent drives to last at least 10 plays (ranking 83rd in FBS) but giving up only 1.2 points per drive (fifth fewest in FBS). With a loaded, experienced defensive roster, the Irish can ramp up the pressure this fall rather than sit back and wait for opponents to stumble. Defensive end Stephon Tuitt and defensive tackle Louis Nix

are a fearsome combination up front, cornerbacks Bennett Jackson and KeiVarae Russell have star potential, and five-star freshman outside linebacker Jaylon Smith is expected to make an immediate impact. The Irish defense can and should be even better this fall.

The Irish can help their cause by winning more field-position battles. Due to a non-existent return game and a defense that didn't force many three-and-outs, Notre Dame started one-third of its offensive possessions from inside its own 20-yard line last year, a higher percentage than any other FBS team. The schedule this fall features several potential heavyweights, including October home dates with Oklahoma and USC, but our model gives the Irish an edge in every game until a season-ending showdown at Stanford. Another BCS appearance, championship game or otherwise, may be on the line that day. Opportunities to continue the road back to elite glory will present themselves all season long.

Top 2014 NFL prospects: *DE Stephon Tuitt (1), DT Louis Nix* (1), OT Zach Martin (2-3), CB Bennett Jackson (2-3), WR T.J. Jones (3-4), ILB Prince Shembo (6-7), ILB Dan Fox (6-7)*

No. 34 BYU Cougars (7-5)

2012: 8-5 / F/+ #23 / FEI #29 / S&P+ #11

Program F/+	+9.5%	30	Returning Starters: 8 OFF, 6 DEF			2012 Field Position / Special Teams		
2012 Offense			**2012 Defense**			Special Teams F/+	-0.2%	71
Offensive F/+	**+2.6%**	**52**	Defensive F/+	+15.2%	10	Field Position Advantage	0.542	12
Offensive FEI:	-0.009	59	Defensive FEI	-0.444	18	**2013 Projections**		
Offensive S&P+	113.1	44	Defensive S&P+	131.4	13	**Mean Wins / Mean Conference Wins**	**7.0**	
Rushing S&P+	102.2	59	Rushing S&P+	134.0	4	Proj. F/+	+9.2%	34
Passing S&P+	104.5	49	Passing S&P+	124.3	14	Offensive F/+	+2.1%	46
Standard Downs S&P+	101.9	54	Standard Downs S&P+	126.4	5	Defensive F/+	+7.2%	20
Passing Downs S&P+	109.4	44	Passing Downs S&P+	130.8	13	Strength of Sched. Rk		38

BYU's 23-6 victory over San Diego State in the Poinsettia Bowl was a quintessential win for the Cougars and an example of how much more BYU could have done in 2012. More touchdowns were scored by BYU linebacker Kyle Van Noy (two) than by either offense in the game, and the defensive star chipped in a blocked punt, a forced fumble, and 3.5 tackles for loss in a dominant defensive performance. But BYU got only six more points out of eight second-half offensive possessions with an average starting field position on the *San Diego State 44-yard line*. Offensive ineptitude was costly throughout the year. The Cougars had four one-score losses last season in which the offense produced below-average production based on field position.

Production and efficiency should get a boost from the return of dual-threat sophomore quarterback Taysom Hill, the team's second-leading rusher in 2012 despite missing half the season with a knee injury. Sophomore running back Jamaal Williams was decent as a first year starter last year (775 yards, 12 touchdowns, +0.4 Adj. POE) and will benefit from Hill's return to the backfield as well. Hill also has reliable passing options in senior wide receiver Cody Hoffman (100 receptions, 1248 yards, 69 percent catch rate) and senior tight end Kaneakua Friel. Of course, while reliability is nice, BYU needs to show more big-play potential this year to take a step forward. Only 9.7 percent of the Cougars drives a year ago averaged at least 10 yards per play (97th nationally).

Van Noy was one of the most dynamic defensive players in the country last season (22 tackles for loss, six forced fumbles), leading a unit that ranked No. 1 in forcing three-and-outs (47.7 percent of opponent drives) and No. 2 in limiting available yards (30.9 percent). He'll have to be even better this year to make up for the loss of three starters along the defensive line, including fifth-overall draft pick Ezekiel Ansah. BYU aided itself with outstanding field position management, forcing opponents to start drives on average at their own 25-yard line, deeper than any other FBS team last year.

The Cougars have played as an independent the last two seasons, a status that presents the opportunity of playing a more challenging overall schedule than one they had as a second-tier conference member. BYU played six games against F/+ top-25 opponents in 2011 and 2012, but only posted one win in those games, a 6-3 victory over WAC champion Utah State last fall. The average F/+ rank of the 16 FBS opponents BYU has defeated in the last two seasons is No. 82 (No. 88 in regular-season games). The Cougars can break through as a first-tier independent by winning one or two games against the first-tier opponents on the 2013 schedule: home dates against Texas and Boise State, road games versus Wisconsin and Notre Dame.

Top 2014 NFL prospects: *OLB Kyle Van Noy (1-2), WR Cody Hoffman (1-2), TE Kaneakua Friel (5-6)*

Projected Win Probabilities For Independent Teams

Independents	12-0	11-1	10-2	9-3	8-4	7-5	6-6	5-7	4-8	3-9	2-10	1-11	0-12
							Overall Wins						
Army	-	-	-	-	1	3	9	20	28	25	12	2	-
BYU	-	-	3	11	22	28	22	10	3	1	-	-	-
Idaho	-	-	-	-	-	-	-	1	8	24	38	26	3
Navy	-	-	-	2	5	14	25	28	18	7	1	-	-
Notre Dame	1	11	24	29	21	10	3	1	-	-	-	-	-
New Mexico State	-	-	-	-	-	-	1	4	15	32	33	14	1

MOUNTAIN WEST

No. 12 Boise State Broncos (11-1, 8-0)

2012: 11-2 (7-1) / F/+ #21 / FEI #32 / S&P+ #13

Program F/+	+29.7%	2	Returning Starters: 6 OFF, 6 DEF			2012 Field Position / Special Teams		
2012 Offense			2012 Defense			Special Teams F/+	+0.4%	52
Offensive F/+	+5.1%	40	Defensive F/+	+12.8%	17	Field Position Advantage	0.537	16
Offensive FEI:	0.078	52	Defensive FEI	-0.410	21	2013 Projections		
Offensive S&P+	117.2	40	Defensive S&P+	124.9	23	Mean Wins / Mean Conference Wins	11.0 / 7.5	
Rushing S&P+	106.2	51	Rushing S&P+	107.1	43	Proj. F/+	+19.1%	12
Passing S&P+	119.6	22	Passing S&P+	117.1	20	Offensive F/+	+7.2%	20
Standard Downs S&P+	114.9	23	Standard Downs S&P+	115.1	19	Defensive F/+	+11.9%	9
Passing Downs S&P+	107.7	51	Passing Downs S&P+	108.2	41	Strength of Sched. Rk / Conf. Title Odds	104 / 59.7%	

Boise State is college football's sure thing. Since Chris Petersen took over the head coaching job in 2006, the Broncos have won at least 12 games in a season five times and have reached at least 10 wins every single year. Boise State suffered heavy personnel losses heading into last season and came within six total points of another undefeated record. With an experienced roster back in 2013, the Broncos are big favorites to win the Mountain West and the third most likely team (behind Alabama and Oregon) to run the table in FBS this fall. And once again, it probably won't be good enough to push them into the BCS title picture.

Five of the top six offensive players in terms of total offense were first-time starters a year ago and will be back in the fold this fall. They performed well, though it would be a mistake to suggest the Broncos offense didn't miss a beat. Boise State posted a Petersen era low rank in available yards, explosive drives, and points per drive in 2012. That they still ranked among the top 30 in those categories demonstrates how successful Petersen's system has been in Boise, and how much more improvement might be expected this fall. From 2007 to 2011, Boise State recorded value drives on more than 55 percent of offensive possessions, best in the nation in that span. The Broncos dipped below 50 percent in value drive production in 2012—still good for No. 21 overall, but the key difference between comfortable wins and the six games Boise State played last year that were decided by a single score.

Though he didn't match the superstar efficiency of Kellen Moore, the Heisman finalist he replaced, quarterback Joe Southwick was a solid substitute. As a junior, he led the nation's 22nd-ranked passing attack according to S&P+, and he hit a nice groove late in the year throwing for nine touchdowns and zero interceptions over the final four games, all victories. Six of his top eight targets from last season return, though a big playmaker is still missing from the roster. Aided by a stellar pass-blocking line, Southwick was sacked only seven times all year and the Broncos ranked fourth nationally in Adjusted Sack Rate. Run blocking was less effective (80th in Adjusted Line Yards), and new faces along the line join all-conference center Matt Paradis and left tackle Charles Leno, Jr. Sophomore tailback Jay Ajayi (+12.7 Adj. POE, 6.7 yards per attempt) has breakout potential and expects to get the lion's share of carries.

The defense wasn't nearly as lethal as the Broncos had been a year prior, forcing three-and-outs on 35.1 percent of opponent drives (41st nationally) after posting a 50.7 percent three-and-out rate in 2011 (third nationally). They were still effective in limiting points in 2012 (1.1 points allowed per drive, third nationally) with good red zone defense and a bit of luck from inordinately poor opponent field-goal kicking—Broncos opponents made only six field goals on 15 attempts all season. There will be new starters all over the field, so the Broncos will be content with bending without breaking once again. Of the four Broncos with 50 or more tackles last season, only junior safety Jeremy Ioane is back.

The schedule won't impede another double-digit winning season, but it will likely impede any hope of national championship consideration barring catastrophe for power conference contenders. The Broncos will do what they do best, and the BCS will as well: keep Boise State at a stiffarm's length away from a chance to play for a national championship.

Top 2014 NFL prospects: *None*

No. 50 Fresno State Bulldogs (9-3, 6-2)

2012: 9-4 (7-1) / F/+ #34 / FEI #54 / S&P+ #14

Program F/+	-4.0%	70	Returning Starters: 7 OFF, 8 DEF			2012 Field Position / Special Teams		
2012 Offense			**2012 Defense**			Special Teams F/+	-0.5%	80
Offensive F/+	**+0.8%**	**58**	**Defensive F/+**	**+11.2%**	**21**	Field Position Advantage	0.527	28
Offensive FEI:	-0.179	83	Defensive FEI	-0.312	28	**2013 Projections**		
Offensive S&P+	116.9	32	Defensive S&P+	125.1	17	**Mean Wins / Mean Conference Wins**	**9.2 / 5.7**	
Rushing S&P+	106.8	48	Rushing S&P+	113.9	24	Proj. F/+	+3.4%	50
Passing S&P+	112.1	36	Passing S&P+	128.4	11	Offensive F/+	-1.5%	70
Standard Downs S&P+	113.4	26	Standard Downs S&P+	117.4	18	Defensive F/+	+4.9%	33
Passing Downs S&P+	108.2	48	Passing Downs S&P+	121.1	23	Strength of Sched. Rk / Conf. Title Odds	105 / 14.4%	

In Tim DeRuyter's first season as Fresno State head coach, the Bulldogs snapped out of a lengthy funk, improving from 91st (their lowest ranking of the last eight years) to 34th (highest) in the F/+ rankings. This year's projections suggest there was a little *too* much improvement in Fresno last year, but DeRuyter is attempting to keep the pressure on the rest of the Mountain West. Not only does Fresno State return a majority of last year's stars, but DeRuyter also signed 11 junior college transfers. They're playing for keeps in the San Joaquin Valley. We'll see if it pays off.

The Fresno State defense had fallen off in the last few seasons of the Pat Hill era. The Bulldogs hadn't ranked higher than 75th in Defensive F/+ between 2007 and 2011, and they plummeted to 110th in Hill's last season. DeRuyter installed his aggressive 3-4 scheme, and the positive results began immediately. The Bulldogs improved to 21st in Defensive F/+, 24th in Rushing S&P+, 11th in Passing S&P+, and sixth in Adjusted Sack Rate. Fresno State attacked from every direction with its front seven, while the secondary aggressively played the ball. All four starting defensive backs defensed at least eight passes, and while stud safety Phillip Thomas (12 tackles for loss, 13 passes defensed) will be missed, the other three starters do still return. So do outside linebacker Donavon Lewis (10 tackles for loss) and all three starting linemen.

The pass-first offense of coordinator Dave Schramm should click at least as well as it did last year, when quarterback Derek "Yes, David's Little Brother" Carr threw for 4,104 yards, 37 touchdowns, and seven interceptions (Passing S&P+ rank: 36th). Carr is back, as are his top two receivers, sophomore Davante Adams (1,312 yards, 12.9 per catch, 70 percent catch rate) and senior Isaiah Burse (851 yards, 14.9 per catch, 70 percent catch rate). In fact, the biggest threat to the passing game could be the loss of running back Robbie Rouse, who not only rushed for 1,480 yards but was also the No. 3 receiver, with 63 catches for 435 yards.

Top 2014 NFL prospects: *QB Derek Carr (2-3), TE Marcel Jensen (3-4), OT Austin Wentworth (5-6)*

No. 52 Utah State Aggies (8-4, 6-2)

2012: 11-2 (6-0) / F/+ #17 / FEI #24 / S&P+ #8

Program F/+	-6.1%	79	Returning Starters: 6 OFF, 8 DEF			2012 Field Position / Special Teams		
2012 Offense			**2012 Defense**			Special Teams F/+	+1.3%	38
Offensive F/+	**+3.3%**	**48**	**Defensive F/+**	**+15.5%**	**9**	Field Position Advantage	0.527	29
Offensive FEI:	-0.038	63	Defensive FEI	-0.491	14	**2013 Projections**		
Offensive S&P+	117.5	30	Defensive S&P+	129.7	10	**Mean Wins / Mean Conference Wins**	**7.7 / 5.9**	
Rushing S&P+	113.6	24	Rushing S&P+	111.9	30	Proj. F/+	+2.8%	52
Passing S&P+	111.7	37	Passing S&P+	138.0	6	Offensive F/+	-2.5%	79
Standard Downs S&P+	109.1	38	Standard Downs S&P+	120.3	14	Defensive F/+	+5.3%	30
Passing Downs S&P+	122.4	18	Passing Downs S&P+	133.3	11	Strength of Sched. Rk / Conf. Title Odds	73 / 7.3%	

Pop quiz: According to Football Outsiders stats, which program had the highest-rated non-AQ team in the country last year? It wasn't Boise State, and even if TCU counted, it wouldn't have been the Horned Frogs, either. No, it was Utah State. The Aggies didn't have a single winning season between 1997 and 2010, and didn't win more than nine games in any two-year span in that time. But in 2012, they went 11-2, ranked 17th in the F/+ rankings, and missed a BCS bowl bid by about three feet when their kicker missed a 37-yard field goal that would have beaten eventual Big Ten champion Wisconsin.

Naturally, they lost head coach Gary Andersen (and defensive coordinator Dave Aranda) during the offseason—and to Wisconsin, no less. Former offensive coordinator Matt Wells takes over, and he still has junior quarterback Chuckie Keeton and a fantastic offensive line at his disposal. But USU will need to replace a lot of stars, and not just the two who left for Madison; Andersen laid the foundation for Utah State to not only succeed, but look so good that you forgot how recently the program had been terrible. Now we get to find out just how strong that foundation is.

Star running back Kerwynn Williams and last year's top four receivers are all gone. But in the dual-threat Keeton and exciting backup running back Joe Hill, Wells has a couple of potentially strong options for running behind a line that returns three All-WAC performers and 110 career starts. And the defense, so incredible a year ago (ninth in Defensive F/+, better than BYU, Notre Dame, Kansas State, etc.), does return a majority of its starters.

Corner Will Davis and linebacker Bojay Filimoeatu will be

difficult to replace, but in linebacker Zach Vigil, corner Nevin Lawson, and ends Jordan Nielsen and Connor Williams, there are still some high-caliber performers. New defensive coordinator Todd Orlando (previously in the same job at Connecticut and Florida International) likes an aggressive defense, and he should be able to field just that in Logan.

Top 2014 NFL prospects: *C Tyler Larsen (2-3)*

No. 60 San Diego State Aztecs (7-5, 5-3)
2012: 9-4 (7-1) / F/+ #44 / FEI #48 / S&P+ #40

Program F/+	-5.9%	77	Returning Starters: 5 OFF, 9 DEF			2012 Field Position / Special Teams		
2012 Offense			**2012 Defense**			Special Teams F/+	+1.1%	41
Offensive F/+	+1.2%	56	Defensive F/+	+5.2%	36	Field Position Advantage	0.5	64
Offensive FEI:	-0.041	64	Defensive FEI	-0.237	33	**2013 Projections**		
Offensive S&P+	109.9	45	Defensive S&P+	107.5	45	**Mean Wins / Mean Conference Wins**	7.0 / 4.8	
Rushing S&P+	113.3	25	Rushing S&P+	111.0	31	Proj. F/+	-0.7%	60
Passing S&P+	101.5	56	Passing S&P+	101.9	55	Offensive F/+	-3.1%	83
Standard Downs S&P+	109.9	36	Standard Downs S&P+	106.8	40	Defensive F/+	+2.4%	45
Passing Downs S&P+	101.7	65	Passing Downs S&P+	99.8	67	Strength of Sched. Rk / Conf. Title Odds	64 / 6.0%	

Like Utah State, San Diego State has been good enough recently that it's easy to forget how bad the Aztecs were not too long ago. In 2008, Chuck Long's last year as head coach, SDSU went 3-9 with an F/+ ranking of 115th. Brady Hoke took over in 2009, and the Aztecs surged to 9-4 and 31st in 2010. When Hoke left for Michigan, former New Mexico head coach Rocky Long took over, and the Aztecs have gone 17-9 over the last two seasons. Through resources and strong hires, SDSU has committed to winning football, and Long has held up his end of the bargain so far.

SDSU was limited but effective in 2012, proving itself deep enough to withstand injuries and still win games. The Aztecs lost quarterback Ryan Katz early in their eighth game of the year, went all-in on the running game, and still managed to take down Boise State in Boise on November 3. It was only Boise State's second home loss in conference play since 1998, and SDSU pulled it off with new quarterback Adam Dingwell throwing for just 105 yards.

SDSU was good enough in the trenches that it masked other weaknesses. The Aztecs were 21st in Adjusted Line Yards and 25th in Rushing S&P+ despite a predictable offense, and they were 30th in Adjusted Line Yards and 31st in Rushing S&P+ on defense. Opponents had to pass and force SDSU to do the same, and it was only marginally successful. With running back Adam Muema (1,458 yards, 6.1 highlight yards per opportunity) returning alongside Dingwell in the backfield, SDSU will probably have the exact same offensive identity in 2013. And with a ferocious front six (SDSU runs Long's patented 3-3-5 defense) and a key loss at cornerback (Leon McFadden), the defensive dynamic should remain the same as well. Linebackers Jake Fely, Derek Largent, and Nick Tenhaeff combined for 34 tackles for loss and 16.5 sacks last fall, and the top seven linemen from last year's defense all return.

Top 2014 NFL prospects: *None*

Projected Win Probabilities For Mountain West Teams

	Overall Wins													Conference Wins							
MWC Mountain	12-0	11-1	10-2	9-3	8-4	7-5	6-6	5-7	4-8	3-9	2-10	1-11	0-12	8-0	7-1	6-2	5-3	4-4	3-5	2-6	1-7	0-8
Air Force	-	-	1	9	22	30	23	11	3	1	-	-	-	-	4	16	33	30	14	3	-	-
Boise State	34	41	19	5	1	-	-	-	-	-	-	-	-	59	33	7	1	-	-	-	-	-
Colorado State*	-	-	-	-	1	4	12	23	29	21	9	1	-	-	-	-	2	8	22	34	27	7
New Mexico	-	-	-	-	-	-	-	4	12	27	33	20	4	-	-	-	-	-	5	22	43	30
Utah State	-	1	6	20	32	27	12	2	-	-	-	-	-	4	26	40	23	6	1	-	-	-
Wyoming	-	-	-	-	2	8	22	33	24	9	2	-	-	-	-	-	4	17	38	30	9	2
MWC West	12-0	11-1	10-2	9-3	8-4	7-5	6-6	5-7	4-8	3-9	2-10	1-11	0-12	8-0	7-1	6-2	5-3	4-4	3-5	2-6	1-7	0-8
Fresno State	2	12	28	31	19	7	1	-	-	-	-	-	-	3	20	37	28	10	2	-	-	-
Hawaii	-	-	-	-	-	1	2	11	23	30	23	9	1	-	-	-	3	11	25	34	22	5
Nevada	-	-	-	2	8	20	30	25	12	3	-	-	-	-	2	13	31	32	17	4	1	-
San Diego State	-	-	2	9	23	31	23	10	2	-	-	-	-	-	7	21	33	26	11	2	-	-
San Jose State	-	1	3	13	23	27	20	9	3	1	-	-	-	2	8	24	31	23	10	2	-	-
UNLV	-	-	-	-	-	2	8	18	29	27	13	3	-	-	-	-	3	9	25	36	22	5

*Colorado State will play 13 regular season games; for projected overall records, 12-0 means 12-1, 11-1 means 11-2, etc.

MID-AMERICAN CONFERENCE

No. 39 Northern Illinois Huskies (10-2, 7-1)

2012: 12-2 (8-0) / F/+ #33 / FEI #36 / S&P+ #31

Program F/+	+3.1%	50	Returning Starters: 9 OFF, 4 DEF			2012 Field Position / Special Teams		
2012 Offense			**2012 Defense**			Special Teams F/+	+2.0%	19
Offensive F/+	**+5.3%**	**38**	**Defensive F/+**	**+4.6%**	**39**	Field Position Advantage	0.503	59
Offensive FEI:	0.167	37	Defensive FEI	-0.138	49	**2013 Projections**		
Offensive S&P+	112.3	43	Defensive S&P+	111.3	39	**Mean Wins / Mean Conference Wins**	**10.2 / 7.0**	
Rushing S&P+	107.5	45	Rushing S&P+	109.5	35	Proj. F/+	+5.9%	39
Passing S&P+	100.8	61	Passing S&P+	99.5	63	Offensive F/+	+5.4%	28
Standard Downs S&P+	101.6	55	Standard Downs S&P+	108.2	33	Defensive F/+	+0.5%	57
Passing Downs S&P+	107.0	52	Passing Downs S&P+	97.0	75	Strength of Sched. Rk / Conf. Title Odds	120 / 46.7%	

It's the way of the mid-major universe. Your reward for success: losing your head coach to a bigger school. Jerry Kill inherited a 2-10 NIU team in 2008, and he had the Huskies at 10-3 by his third year. He was hired away by Minnesota, and NIU replaced him with Wisconsin assistant Dave Doeren, who raised the team's profile even more. NIU went 11-3 in 2011, then not only went 12-1 in 2012 but also claimed the MAC's first BCS bowl bid. However, Doeren wasn't around to coach the Huskies against Florida State in the Orange Bowl—he was already at his new job, N.C. State.

Next man up is Doeren's former offensive coordinator, Rod Carey, who inherits a team with a lot of familiar faces. The most familiar face of them all is Jordan Lynch. The senior quarterback was tasked with replacing the seemingly irreplaceable Chandler Harnish, but the title "Orange Bowl starting quarterback Jordan Lynch" suggests he did alright. Lynch threw for 3,138 yards and 25 touchdowns and rushed for 1,898 pre-sack yards and 19 touchdowns. He returns this year along with the entire starting offensive line, late-2012 rushing star Akeem Daniels, and last year's No. 2 and No. 4 receivers. Primary pass-catcher Martel Moore is gone, but with Carey and Lynch running the show, there is little reason to assume a drop-off on the offensive side of the ball.

Defensively, it could be a different story. Of the eight NIU defenders to log at least 6.5 tackles for loss on this undersized, speedy unit, four are gone; so is star corner Rashaan Melvin, who had 18 passes defensed last year (10th in the country). Still, active tackle Ken Bishop (9.5 tackles for loss) is back, as is ball-hawk safety Jimmie Ward. The fact that NIU played a lot of defenders last year (23 players logged double-digit tackles) means the departed players have experienced replacements. It would take quite a few breaks for the Huskies to return to a BCS bowl in 2013, but they are certainly still atop the MAC totem pole. Teams like Toledo, Bowling Green, and Ohio should mount a quality challenge, but the king is the king until he is dethroned.

Top 2014 NFL prospects: *S Jimmie Ward (4-5)*

Projected Win Probabilities For MAC Teams

	Overall Wins												Conference Wins								
MAC East	12-0	11-1	10-2	9-3	8-4	7-5	6-6	5-7	4-8	3-9	2-10	1-11	0-12	8-0	7-1	6-2	5-3	4-4	3-5	2-6	1-7	0-8
Akron	-	-	-	-	-	1	5	17	32	32	12	1		-	-	-	-	4	14	33	37	12
Bowling Green	-	5	14	25	27	19	8	2	-	-	-	-	-	10	29	33	20	7	1	-	-	-
Buffalo	-	-	-	1	5	14	25	29	19	6	1	-	-	-	2	10	24	32	23	8	1	-
Kent State	-	-	-	3	7	18	28	25	14	4	1	-	-	-	3	9	23	31	23	9	2	-
Massachusetts	-	-	-	-	-	-	-	-	2	13	38	40	7	-	-	-	-	-	2	15	43	40
Miami (OH)	-	-	-	-	-	2	5	14	26	29	18	5	1	-	-	1	8	22	33	26	9	1
Ohio	-	4	16	28	28	16	6	2	-	-	-	-	-	5	23	35	25	10	2	-	-	-
MAC West	12-0	11-1	10-2	9-3	8-4	7-5	6-6	5-7	4-8	3-9	2-10	1-11	0-12	8-0	7-1	6-2	5-3	4-4	3-5	2-6	1-7	0-8
Ball State	-	1	5	14	24	26	18	9	2	1	-	-	-	-	5	19	31	27	13	4	1	-
Central Michigan	-	-	-	2	5	14	25	28	18	7	1	-	-	-	1	5	18	31	30	13	2	-
Eastern Michigan	-	-	-	-	-	-	1	6	16	29	31	15	2	-	-	-	-	4	12	29	36	19
Northern Illinois	10	30	34	19	6	1	-	-	-	-	-	-	-	34	42	20	4	-	-	-	-	-
Toledo	-	-	4	15	27	28	17	7	2	-	-	-	-	2	15	31	30	16	5	1	-	-
Western Michigan	-	-	-	1	5	17	29	27	15	5	1	-	-	-	2	15	30	30	17	5	1	-

CONFERENCE USA

No. 59 Tulsa Golden Hurricane (8-4, 6-2)

2012: 11-3 (7-1) / F/+ #42 / FEI #40 / S&P+ #37

Program F/+		+4.5%	44	Returning Starters: 7 OFF, 3 DEF			2012 Field Position / Special Teams		
2012 Offense				**2012 Defense**			Special Teams F/+	-0.3%	75
Offensive F/+		**+0.1%**	**59**	**Defensive F/+**	**+8.9%**	**27**	Field Position Advantage	0.497	68
Offensive FEI:		0.011	57	Defensive FEI	-0.313	27	**2013 Projections**		
Offensive S&P+		102.9	55	Defensive S&P+	116.5	27	**Mean Wins / Mean Conference Wins**	**8.5 / 6.3**	
Rushing S&P+		103.8	58	Rushing S&P+	105.6	47	Proj. F/+	+0.4%	59
Passing S&P+		93.0	84	Passing S&P+	112.2	28	Offensive F/+	+0.5%	56
Standard Downs S&P+		97.0	74	Standard Downs S&P+	108.6	31	Defensive F/+	-0.1%	64
Passing Downs S&P+		100.8	69	Passing Downs S&P+	114.9	28	Strength of Sched. Rk / Conf. Title Odds	86 / 30.0%	

When it comes to college football, the surest way to predict future success is by looking at past success. And in the new Conference USA, a league that just lost UCF, Houston, SMU, and Memphis to the American Athletic Conference, Tulsa is the closest thing to a sure bet. The Golden Hurricane have an almost one-in-three chance of winning the league this year, despite teams like East Carolina, Marshall, Louisiana Tech, and Rice all having relatively friendly projections.

Make no mistake, however, Tulsa has some work to do. The Golden Hurricane must replace not only three all-conference offensive linemen, but also all four starters from the league's best defensive line, both starting corners, and a pair of outright stars in linebacker DeAundre Brown and safety Dexter McCoil. If Tulsa indeed takes the conference crown this year, it will probably stay on top for quite a while, but this year's inexperienced squad could be vulnerable.

Of course, Tulsa had to replace some defensive stars last year, too, and still improved dramatically on that side of the ball. Linebacker Shawn Jackson (10.5 tackles for loss) is great from the weak side, defensive end Brentom Todd managed 8.0 tackles for loss in minimal playing time, and safety Marco Nelson is still around to patrol the secondary.

The depth of the defense's regression should dictate Tulsa's title chances, as the offense shouldn't improve or regress that much. The losses on the line hurt, but quarterback Cody Green, running back Trey Watts (1,108 rushing yards, +16.5 Adj. POE, and 343 receiving yards), and leading receiver Keyarris Garrett (845 yards, 12.6 per catch, 55 percent catch rate) return. The passing game was terribly inefficient last year, but it only held Tulsa back so much because of the defense and a decent running game. Tulsa can regress and still win the league; it just can't regress too much.

Top 2014 NFL prospects: *None*

Projected Win Probabilities For Conference USA Teams

Conf USA East	Overall Wins													Conference Wins								
	12-0	11-1	10-2	9-3	8-4	7-5	6-6	5-7	4-8	3-9	2-10	1-11	0-12	8-0	7-1	6-2	5-3	4-4	3-5	2-6	1-7	0-8
East Carolina	-	-	2	10	22	28	22	11	4	1	-	-		3	16	30	29	16	5	1	-	-
Florida Atlantic	-	-	-	-	-	1	3	11	23	31	22	6	3	-	-	-	4	11	25	33	22	5
Florida International	-	-	-	1	3	8	17	25	24	15	6	1	-	-	1	5	14	25	28	19	7	1
Marshall	-	1	4	13	24	27	19	9	3	-	-	-	-	1	10	25	31	22	9	2	-	-
Middle Tennessee	-	-	-	3	10	21	27	22	12	4	1	-	-	-	4	11	23	29	22	9	2	-
Southern Mississippi	-	-	-	1	5	14	26	28	18	7	1	-	-	-	4	14	28	30	17	5	2	-
UAB	-	-	-	1	5	13	24	27	20	8	2	-	-	-	2	9	21	30	24	11	3	-
Conf USA West	**12-0**	**11-1**	**10-2**	**9-3**	**8-4**	**7-5**	**6-6**	**5-7**	**4-8**	**3-9**	**2-10**	**1-11**	**0-12**	**8-0**	**7-1**	**6-2**	**5-3**	**4-4**	**3-5**	**2-6**	**1-7**	**0-8**
Louisiana Tech	1	3	14	24	26	19	9	3	1	-	-	-		4	17	30	28	15	5	1	-	-
North Texas	-	-	-	-	3	9	19	27	24	13	4	1	-	-	-	4	14	28	30	18	5	1
Rice	-	-	4	13	24	28	19	9	3	-	-	-	-	1	11	26	32	21	8	1	-	-
Tulane	-	-	-	-	-	3	7	18	28	26	14	4	-	-	-	-	2	10	24	33	24	7
Tulsa	-	5	17	29	27	15	6	1	-	-	-	-	-	12	32	33	17	5	1	-	-	-
UTEP	-	-	-	-	3	8	18	26	24	14	5	2	-	-	-	2	8	20	30	26	12	2
UTSA	-	-	-	-	-	1	3	11	22	29	23	9	2	-	-	1	4	13	27	32	19	4

SUN BELT CONFERENCE

No. 65 Arkansas State Red Wolves (8-4, 5-2)

2012: 10-3 (7-1) / F/+ #53 / FEI #51 / S&P+ #30

Program F/+		-6.1%	78	Returning Starters: 8 OFF, 5 DEF			2012 Field Position / Special Teams		
2012 Offense				**2012 Defense**			Special Teams F/+	-4.0%	120
Offensive F/+	**+8.3%**	**24**	Defensive F/+	**+0.7%**	**56**	Field Position Advantage	0.462	104
Offensive FEI:	0.231	31	Defensive FEI	-0.005	62	**2013 Projections**		
Offensive S&P+	119.4	22	Defensive S&P+	105.4	48	**Mean Wins / Mean Conference Wins**		8.5 / 5.3
Rushing S&P+	109.0	41	Rushing S&P+	107.0	44	Proj. F/+	-2.1%	65
Passing S&P+	115.3	34	Passing S&P+	92.1	87	Offensive F/+	+1.9%	49
Standard Downs S&P+	111.0	31	Standard Downs S&P+	103.0	53	Defensive F/+	-4.0%	85
Passing Downs S&P+	114.6	33	Passing Downs S&P+	89.8	91	Strength of Sched. Rk / Conf. Title Odds		112 / 41.9%

The Sun Belt could have a really interesting race this year, with Western Kentucky making a fun coaching hire (Bobby Petrino) and both Louisiana schools (Lafayette and Monroe) fielding salty, experienced teams. But until proven otherwise, the king of the Sun Belt heap, the NIU of the SBC, is Arkansas State. The Red Wolves are playing for their fourth head coach in four years—Steve Roberts was let go after the 2010 season, Hugh Freeze coached for one year and left for Ole Miss, and Gus Malzahn coached for one year and left for Auburn—but have survived the total lack of continuity with continuous quality play. At least, they have so far. With every change comes an opportunity to stumble.

Arkansas State's new head coach is Bryan Harsin; ASU has been openly attempting to follow the Boise State blueprint for years with its commitment and hiring practices, so it makes sense that the Red Wolves would hire a former Broncos offensive coordinator when given the opportunity. Harsin spent the last two seasons attempting (with some success) to bring the Texas offense into the 21st century, and at age 36, he's been handed the big set of keys in Jonesboro. His first ASU offense will be without longtime starting quarterback Ryan Aplin, but in running back David Oku (1,080 rushing yards)

and sophomore possession receiver J.D. McKissic, he'll have some solid efficiency options. And both Freeze and Malzahn recruited quite well for the Sun Belt level; there will be quite a few high-ceiling underclassmen on the two-deep.

With three of the top four linemen returning, ASU's defense could remain strong against the run (the Red Wolves were 44th in Rushing S&P+ and 59th in Adjusted Line Yards last season). The pass defense, already the weaker link, will have to deal with quite a few losses, including corner Chaz Scales and do-everything linebacker Nathan Herrold (10 tackles for loss, nine passes defensed).

Top 2014 NFL prospects: *DT Ryan Carrethers (3-4)*

Other Top 2014 Prospects from Non-AQ Schools: *ILB Andrew Jackson, Western Kentucky (1-2); WR Ryan Grant, Tulane (2-3); QB David Fales, San Jose State (2-3); OLB Khalil Mack, Buffalo (3-4); CB Bene Bewikere, San Jose State (3-4); DT Khyn Thornton, Southern Mississippi (4-5); S Isaiah Newsome, Louisiana-Monroe (4-5); RB Antonio Archer, Western Kentucky (4-5).*

Bill Connelly and Brian Fremeau

Projected Win Probabilities For Sun Belt Teams

Sun Belt	Overall Wins													Conference Wins							
	12-0	11-1	10-2	9-3	8-4	7-5	6-6	5-7	4-8	3-9	2-10	1-11	0-12	7-0	6-1	5-2	4-3	3-4	2-5	1-6	0-7
Arkansas State	-	5	16	29	28	15	5	2	-	-	-	-	-	11	33	34	17	4	1	-	-
Georgia State	-	-	-	-	-	-	3	10	29	39	16	3	-	-	-	-	-	3	15	40	42
Louisiana Lafayette	-	-	3	13	26	29	19	8	2	-	-	-	-	3	12	29	32	18	5	1	-
Louisiana Monroe	-	-	3	10	23	29	22	10	3	-	-	-	-	5	19	32	28	13	3	-	-
South Alabama	-	-	-	-	2	4	12	22	27	21	10	2	-	-	-	3	11	26	34	21	5
Texas State	-	-	-	1	4	13	24	28	20	8	2	-	-	-	2	5	18	34	30	10	1
Troy	-	-	-	4	11	22	28	22	10	3	-	-	-	2	6	21	34	27	9	1	-
Western Kentucky	-	1	3	10	20	26	22	13	4	1	-	-	-	2	11	26	32	21	7	1	-

NCAA Teams, No. 1 to No. 125

Rk	Team	Conf	Proj F/+	TMW	Rec	Conf	SOS	Rk	Rk	Team	Conf	Proj F/+	TMW	Rec	Conf	SOS	Rk
1	Alabama	SEC	0.389	11.8	12-0	8-0	0.308	51	8	Texas	Big 12	0.213	9.5	10-2	7-2	0.179	31
2	Oregon	Pac-12	0.301	11.3	11-1	8-1	0.298	49	9	Georgia	SEC	0.208	9.5	10-2	6-2	0.199	34
3	Stanford	Pac-12	0.238	10.1	10-2	7-2	0.180	32	10	Ohio State	Big Ten	0.206	10.8	11-1	7-1	0.545	88
4	LSU	SEC	0.235	9.2	9-3	6-2	0.025	3	11	TCU	Big 12	0.204	9.1	9-3	7-2	0.113	15
5	Florida	SEC	0.222	9.3	9-3	6-2	0.114	16	12	Boise State	MWC	0.191	11.0	11-1	8-0	0.719	104
6	Oklahoma State	Big 12	0.215	10.1	10-2	7-2	0.250	40	13	Notre Dame	Ind.	0.189	9.0	9-3	-	0.154	24
7	Oklahoma	Big 12	0.214	9.4	9-3	7-2	0.140	22	14	South Carolina	SEC	0.186	9.3	9-3	6-2	0.244	39

NCAA Teams, No. 1 to No. 124

Rk	Team	Conf	Proj F/+	TMW	Rec	Conf	SOS	Rk	Rk	Team	Conf	Proj F/+	TMW	Rec	Conf	SOS	Rk
15	Texas A&M	SEC	0.185	9.1	9-3	5-3	0.073	10	71	Virginia	ACC	-0.033	4.0	4-8	2-6	0.205	35
16	Wisconsin	Big Ten	0.177	10.0	10-2	7-1	0.376	62	72	Minnesota	Big Ten	-0.041	4.6	5-7	1-7	0.332	55
17	USC	Pac-12	0.174	10.2	10-3	7-2	0.261	43	73	California	Pac-12	-0.041	3.7	4-8	2-7	0.058	9
18	Michigan State	Big Ten	0.174	9.9	10-2	7-1	0.385	63	74	East Carolina	Conf USA	-0.042	6.9	7-5	5-3	0.719	103
19	Florida State	ACC	0.173	9.7	10-2	7-1	0.307	50	75	Air Force	MWC	-0.044	6.9	7-5	5-3	0.482	75
20	Clemson	ACC	0.143	9.2	9-3	7-1	0.361	59	76	Ohio	MAC	-0.048	8.4	8-4	6-2	0.821	115
21	Nebraska	Big Ten	0.143	9.7	10-2	6-2	0.497	78	77	Louisiana Tech	Conf USA	-0.051	8.2	8-4	5-3	0.931	125
22	Oregon State	Pac-12	0.134	8.6	9-3	6-3	0.128	20	78	Louisiana Monroe	Sun Belt	-0.051	7.0	7-5	5-2	0.488	76
23	Virginia Tech	ACC	0.129	8.7	9-3	6-2	0.109	14	79	Iowa State	Big 12	-0.051	3.0	3-9	2-7	0.173	30
24	Penn State	Big Ten	0.124	8.8	9-3	5-3	0.298	48	80	Purdue	Big Ten	-0.053	2.9	3-9	2-6	0.155	25
25	Miami	ACC	0.123	8.4	8-4	5-3	0.312	53	81	Wake Forest	ACC	-0.056	4.9	5-7	2-6	0.467	74
26	Cincinnati	American	0.122	10.4	10-2	7-1	0.793	111	82	Marshall	Conf USA	-0.062	7.2	7-5	5-3	0.750	107
27	Mississippi	SEC	0.117	7.3	7-5	4-4	0.035	4	83	Maryland	ACC	-0.062	4.2	4-8	2-6	0.413	65
28	Michigan	Big Ten	0.101	7.0	7-5	4-4	0.251	41	84	Kentucky	SEC	-0.066	3.3	3-9	1-7	0.051	8
29	North Carolina	ACC	0.099	8.0	8-4	5-3	0.343	56	85	Louisiana Lafayette	Sun Belt	-0.073	7.2	7-5	4-3	0.834	116
30	Arizona	Pac-12	0.099	8.5	9-3	6-3	0.267	44	86	Rice	Conf USA	-0.074	7.1	7-5	5-3	0.606	93
31	Louisville	American	0.098	9.5	10-2	6-2	0.706	101	87	Navy	Ind.	-0.076	5.4	5-7	-	0.572	90
32	Georgia Tech	ACC	0.097	7.4	7-5	5-3	0.310	52	88	Duke	ACC	-0.076	4.4	4-8	1-7	0.511	82
33	Missouri	SEC	0.095	7.0	7-5	4-4	0.215	36	89	Ball State	MAC	-0.077	7.2	7-5	5-3	0.877	118
34	BYU	Ind.	0.092	7.0	7-5	-	0.220	38	90	Kent State	MAC	-0.077	5.7	6-6	4-4	0.364	60
35	Pittsburgh	ACC	0.092	7.6	8-4	4-4	0.361	58	91	SMU	American	-0.078	3.6	4-8	2-6	0.273	46
36	Arizona State	Pac-12	0.087	6.8	7-5	5-4	0.162	29	92	Southern Mississippi	Conf USA	-0.083	5.4	5-7	4-4	0.442	70
37	Baylor	Big 12	0.075	6.9	7-5	4-5	0.162	28	93	Western Kentucky	Sun Belt	-0.083	6.9	7-5	4-3	0.893	122
38	West Virginia	Big 12	0.062	6.5	7-5	4-5	0.156	27	94	Illinois	Big Ten	-0.085	2.9	3-9	1-7	0.271	45
39	Northern Illinois	MAC	0.059	10.2	10-2	7-1	0.892	120	95	Troy	Sun Belt	-0.088	6.0	6-6	4-3	0.765	109
40	Northwestern	Big Ten	0.056	6.6	7-5	3-5	0.279	47	96	Western Michigan	MAC	-0.091	5.6	6-6	4-4	0.534	85
41	Kansas State	Big 12	0.052	6.6	7-5	4-5	0.156	26	97	Buffalo	MAC	-0.095	5.3	5-7	4-4	0.500	79
42	Texas Tech	Big 12	0.050	6.3	6-6	4-5	0.152	23	98	Central Michigan	MAC	-0.103	5.4	5-7	4-4	0.773	110
43	Arkansas	SEC	0.048	5.3	5-7	2-6	0.017	2	99	Middle Tennessee	Conf USA	-0.109	5.9	6-6	4-4	0.718	102
44	Iowa	Big Ten	0.046	6.3	6-6	3-5	0.255	42	100	UAB	Conf USA	-0.113	5.2	5-7	4-4	0.447	72
45	UCLA	Pac-12	0.045	5.7	6-6	4-5	0.050	7	101	Florida International	Conf USA	-0.127	4.7	5-7	3-5	0.807	113
46	Tennessee	SEC	0.045	5.6	6-6	3-5	0.010	1	102	Wyoming	MWC	-0.137	4.9	5-7	3-5	0.443	71
47	Utah	Pac-12	0.045	5.7	6-6	4-5	0.079	11	103	North Texas	Conf USA	-0.141	4.8	5-7	3-5	0.544	87
48	Rutgers	American	0.042	7.4	7-5	4-4	0.631	96	104	Hawaii	MWC	-0.141	3.1	3-9	2-6	0.585	91
49	Washington	Pac-12	0.039	5.9	6-6	4-5	0.116	17	105	Army	Ind.	-0.146	3.9	4-8	-	0.680	99
50	Fresno State	MWC	0.034	9.2	9-3	6-2	0.732	105	106	UNLV	MWC	-0.150	3.7	4-8	2-6	0.816	114
51	Vanderbilt	SEC	0.030	5.9	6-6	2-6	0.138	21	107	Texas State	Sun Belt	-0.152	5.2	5-7	3-4	0.888	119
52	Utah State	MWC	0.028	7.7	8-4	6-2	0.465	73	108	Colorado	Pac-12	-0.155	2.0	2-10	1-8	0.219	37
53	Connecticut	American	0.023	7.3	7-5	4-4	0.621	95	109	Washington State	Pac-12	-0.156	2.2	2-10	0-9	0.085	12
54	Syracuse	ACC	0.021	6.0	6-6	4-4	0.371	61	110	Colorado State	MWC	-0.158	4.2	4-9	2-6	0.097	13
55	Central Florida	American	0.019	7.0	7-5	5-3	0.510	81	111	UTEP	Conf USA	-0.158	4.7	5-7	3-5	0.620	94
56	Auburn	SEC	0.018	5.3	5-7	2-6	0.046	6	112	Kansas	Big 12	-0.159	1.8	2-10	0-9	0.118	18
57	Mississippi State	SEC	0.018	4.6	5-7	2-6	0.040	5	113	Miami (OH)	MAC	-0.169	3.5	3-9	3-5	0.847	117
58	Houston	American	0.013	6.9	7-5	4-4	0.631	97	114	South Alabama	Sun Belt	-0.169	4.2	4-8	2-5	0.893	121
59	Tulsa	Conf USA	0.004	8.5	8-4	6-2	0.537	86	115	UTSA	Conf USA	-0.176	3.1	3-9	2-6	0.604	92
60	San Diego State	MWC	-0.007	7.0	7-5	5-3	0.393	64	116	Memphis	American	-0.177	2.3	2-10	1-7	0.685	100
61	North Carolina State	ACC	-0.009	6.6	7-5	3-5	0.525	84	117	Eastern Michigan	MAC	-0.181	2.7	3-9	1-7	0.679	98
62	Indiana	Big Ten	-0.016	5.4	5-7	3-5	0.193	33	118	Florida Atlantic	Conf USA	-0.189	3.2	3-9	2-6	0.750	108
63	Toledo	MAC	-0.016	7.3	7-5	5-3	0.427	68	119	Tulane	Conf USA	-0.193	3.7	4-8	2-6	0.909	123
64	Temple	American	-0.019	6.3	6-6	4-4	0.421	66	120	Akron	MAC	-0.215	2.7	3-9	2-6	0.733	106
65	Arkansas State	Sun Belt	-0.021	8.5	8-4	5-2	0.802	112	121	New Mexico	MWC	-0.236	2.3	2-10	1-7	0.494	77
66	Bowling Green	MAC	-0.022	8.2	8-4	6-2	0.912	124	122	Idaho	Ind.	-0.249	2.1	2-10	-	0.513	83
67	South Florida	American	-0.024	5.2	5-7	3-5	0.426	67	123	New Mexico State	Ind.	-0.256	2.6	3-9	-	0.510	80
68	San Jose State	MWC	-0.025	7.1	7-5	5-3	0.431	69	124	Georgia State	Sun Belt	-0.273	3.3	3-9	1-6	0.119	19
69	Boston College	ACC	-0.029	5.3	5-7	2-6	0.318	54	125	Massachusetts	MAC	-0.296	1.6	2-10	1-7	0.569	89
70	Nevada	MWC	-0.030	5.8	6-6	4-4	0.354	57									

Rookie Projections

Over the years, Football Outsiders has developed four different methods for forecasting the NFL success of highly-drafted players at various positions. Here is a rundown of those four methods and what they say about the NFL's Class of 2013.

Quarterbacks: Lewin Career Forecast

The Lewin Career Forecast, named after original designer David Lewin, was first introduced in *Pro Football Prospectus 2006*. A newer version was introduced in 2011. Despite the NFL success of such quarterbacks as Cam Newton (14 games started) and Aaron Rodgers (25 games started) in recent seasons, games started remains the most important factor in forecasting highly-drafted college quarterback prospects. LCF also includes variables that analyze completion percentage, a player's improvement or decline in their senior year, and how often a quarterback scrambles or gets sacked. Players from non-AQ conferences receive a penalty.

The dependent variable projected by LCF v2.0 is the quarterback's total DYAR in seasons 3-to-5. Here are the projections for quarterbacks chosen in the first three rounds of the 2013 draft:

Name	Team	Rnd	Pick	Projection
Geno Smith	NYJ	2	39	2,064 DYAR
E.J. Manuel	BUF	1	16	1,270 DYAR
Mike Glennon	TB	3	73	-379 DYAR

LCF was very sanguine on the hopes of players such as Matt Barkley (1,812 DYAR), Ryan Nassib (1,506 DYAR) and Landry Jones (2,276 DYAR). Unfortunately, nobody believed in those players enough to draft them in the first three rounds.

Running Backs: Speed Score

Speed Score was created by Bill Barnwell and introduced in *Pro Football Prospectus 2008*. The basic theory is simple: not all 40-yard dash times are created equal. A fast time means more from a bigger running back, and the range of 40 times for backs is so small that even a miniscule difference can be meaningful. The formula for Speed Score is:

(Weight x 200) / 40 time ^4

Like 2012, the order of drafted running backs this year is somewhat close to the order of Speed Score, and no back taken in the first three rounds had a particularly low Speed Score.

The back with the highest Speed Score, Knile Davis, was a third-round selection by the Chiefs despite accumulating a lot of underwhelming college tape.

Like his former teammate Trent Richardson a year ago, Eddie Lacy did not run at the Combine and therefore does not officially have a Speed Score; if were to consider the 4.58 forty he ran at Alabama's Pro Day, his Speed Score would be 105.0.

Here are the Speed Scores for all backs chosen in the first three rounds, except for Lacy, as well as the top five Speed Scores for backs chosen in the final four rounds:

Name	Team	Rnd	Pick	Weight	40 time	Speed Score
Knile Davis	KC	3	96	227	4.37	124.5
Christine Michael	SEA	2	62	220	4.54	103.6
Le'Veon Bell	PIT	2	48	230	4.60	102.7
Giovanni Bernard	CIN	2	37	202	4.53	95.9
Montee Ball	DEN	2	58	214	4.66	90.8
Mike James	TB	6	189	223	4.53	105.9
Johnathan Franklin	GB	4	125	205	4.49	100.9
Zac Stacy	STL	5	160	216	4.55	100.8
Mike Gillislee	MIA	5	164	208	4.55	97.1
Kerwynn Williams	IND	7	230	195	4.48	96.8

Wide Receivers: Playmaker Score

The new version of Playmaker Score incorporates both college stats and Combine data into one metric. The NCAA portion of the metric incorporates receptions, yards, and touchdowns in the receiver's best college season, adjusted for his team's total pass attempts. The Combine portion of the metric incorporates the vertical jump and the 10-yard split, which is the first 10 yards of the 40-yard dash.

Although there is no conference adjustment in the current version of Playmaker Score, readers should keep it in the back of their minds that over the past decade, wide receivers from the SEC and ACC are more likely to exceed their Playmaker projections, and wide receivers from the Big 12 are more likely to fall short. Wide receivers drafted from non-AQ conferences are also likely to fall short, but the players in this category who surpassed their projections did so significantly, including Roddy White, Brandon Marshall, Greg Jennings, and Vincent Jackson.

Players drafted from 2005-2009 with Playmaker Score over 400 have averaged 499 yards per season. Those with Playmaker Score between 200 and 400 have averaged 271 yards per season. Those with Playmaker Score under 200 have averaged 91 yards per season.

Playmaker Score does not think very highly of this class at all. Stedman Bailey, who had the highest score of any player in the first three rounds, would have been considered the fifth-best receiver among the 2012 draft class. First-rounder Cordarrelle Patterson's Playmaker Score of 146 is more than 100 points behind 2012's worst first-round Playmaker Score, Michael Floyd's 248. Two of the three highest scores this year belong to a pair of seventh-rounders, but those are based on statistics compiled against either FCS (in the case of Elon's Aaron Mellette) or Division II (Grand Valley State's Charles Johnson) defenses, and should be taken with copious grains of salt.

Here are projections for wide receivers chosen in the first three rounds of the 2013 draft, along with the highest-scoring later-round receivers.

Player	Tm	Rnd	Pick	College	Conf	PM Score
Stedman Bailey	STL	3	92	West Virginia	Big 12	399
DeAndre Hopkins	HOU	1	27	Clemson	ACC	368
Terrance Williams	DAL	3	74	Baylor	Big 12	317
Justin Hunter	TEN	2	34	Tennessee	SEC	296
Robert Woods	BUF	2	41	USC	Pac-12	285
Markus Wheaton	PIT	3	79	Washington St.	Pac-12	274
Aaron Dobson	NE	2	59	Marshall	Non-AQ	213
Marquise Goodwin	BUF	3	78	Texas	Big 12	192
Tavon Austin	STL	1	8	West Virginia	Big 12	190
Keenan Allen	SD	3	76	California	Pac-12	168
Cordarrelle Patterson	MIN	1	28	Tennessee	SEC	146
Charles Johnson	GB	7	216	Grand Valley St.	Div. II	664
Aaron Mellette	BAL	7	236	Elon	FCS	392
Josh Boyce	NE	4	102	TCU	Big 12	297
Ryan Swope	ARI	6	174	Texas A&M	Big 12	278

Edge Rushers: SackSEER

SackSEER is a method that projects sacks for edge rushers, including both 3-4 outside linebackers and 3-4 defensive ends, using the following criteria:

• An "explosion index" that measures the prospect's scores in the forty-yard dash, the vertical jump, and the broad jump in pre-draft workouts.
• Sacks per game, adjusted for factors such as early entry in the NFL Draft and position switches during college.
• Passes defensed per game.
• Missed games of NCAA eligibility due to academic problems, injuries, benchings, suspensions, or attendance at junior college.

SackSEER outputs two numbers. The first, SackSEER rating, solely measures how high the prospect scores compared to players of the past. The second, SackSEER projection, represents a forecast of sacks for the player's first five years in the NFL. It synthesizes metrics with conventional wisdom by adjusting based on the player's expected draft position (interestingly, not his actual draft position) based on pre-draft analysis at the site NFLDraftScout.com.

Here are the SackSEER numbers for players drafted in the first three rounds of the 2013 draft, along with later-round picks with a high SackSEER rating. Defensive ends drafted by 3-4 teams are not included.

Name	College	Team	Rnd	Pick	SackSEER Projection	SackSEER Rating
Barkevious Mingo	LSU	CLE	1	6	34.5	94.6%
Ezekiel Ansah	BYU	DET	1	5	30.3	82.3%
Bjorn Werner	Florida St.	IND	1	24	28.5	77.3%
Jamie Collins	Southern Miss	NE	2	52	27.2	97.7%
Dion Jordan	Oregon	MIA	1	3	24.6	52.3%
Jarvis Jones	Georgia	PIT	1	17	23.7	58.7%
Damontre Moore	Texas A&M	NYG	3	81	23.5	80.1%
Margus Hunt	SMU	CIN	2	53	22.4	64.5%
Tank Carradine	Florida St.	SF	2	40	16.4	28.8%
Sam Montgomery	LSU	HOU	3	95	16.3	48.3%
Corey Lemonier	Auburn	SF	3	88	12.8	53.7%
David Bass	Missouri West.	OAK	7	233	20.1	87.3%
Devin Taylor	South Carolina	DET	4	132	16.0	93.3%
Trevardo Williams	Connecticut	HOU	4	124	15.5	79.4%
John Simon	Ohio State	BAL	4	129	15.5	76.3%

Top 25 Prospects

Here it is: Football Outsiders' seventh annual list of under-the-radar, lower-drafted prospects who could have a big impact on the NFL in the coming seasons. In the past, Rotoworld has referred to our Top 25 Prospects list as "an all-star team of waiver pickups" after we used it to promote young players such as Miles Austin, Jamaal Charles, and Arian Foster. Last year's list spotlighted Stevan Ridley and Jeremy Kerley. We've also picked out defensive players who went on to have a big impact: our first list included Elvis Dumervil and Cortland Finnegan, while more recent lists have introduced readers to future stars such as Geno Atkins and Lardarius Webb.

We're expecting to see some big stars from this year's list on both the offensive and defensive sides of the ball. Of course, there will also be some duds. We can't get them all right. Last year's No. 1 prospect, Doug Baldwin, saw his receiving yardage drop by more than half.

For the uninitiated, this list is not like the prospect lists you read about in the world of baseball. Because the top prospects in college football are stars on national television before they get taken in the first round of the NFL Draft, there's not much utility in listing them here. Everyone knows who Barkevious Mingo and Geno Smith are by this point. Instead, we use a combination of statistics, measurables, context, and expected role to compile a list of under-the-radar players whom we expect to make an impact in the NFL, both in 2013 and beyond. To focus on these players, we limit the pool to guys who fit the following criteria:

• Drafted in the third round or later, or signed as an undrafted free agent
• Entered the NFL between 2010 and 2012
• Fewer than five career games started
• Still on their initial contract with their current team (players who were cut and picked up elsewhere still qualify for the list)
• Age 26 or younger in 2013

There are a few players you might look for on this list who don't qualify under those rules. Jordan Cameron, Davon House, Chris Ivory, and Joseph Morgan have all started at least five games in their NFL careers. Barry Church and Junior Galette have each already signed a long-term second contract.

When we started putting together this year's list, we probably had more candidates than ever before. Among the reasons for having so many candidates was the fact that a number of players from last year's Top 25 Prospects list still haven't taken over starting jobs, even after strong 2012 seasons. The most obvious example of these players is the man we've put No. 1 on this year's list, a pass rusher with 12 sacks but just one NFL game started.

1 Everson Griffen, DE, Vikings: We ranked Griffen third on this list a year ago, stating that it was finally time for his breakout. Well, his breakout came, and it didn't even require a move into the starting lineup. Griffen had eight sacks, 13 hits, and 15 hurries for the Vikings last year, phenomenal totals for a part-time player. He even got a pick-six of Sam Bradford on a play where he dropped into coverage and covered tight end Lance Kendricks. Griffen has very fluid movement, an explosive burst off the line, and good inside quickness. He's also been strong setting the edge in run defense. We expect Griffen to get even more playing time this year, and then things get interesting: Griffen's rookie contract is up after this year, but so are the contracts of both of Minnesota's veteran starters at defensive end. If he wants to stay in Minnesota, there will be a starting job waiting for him.

2 Lamar Miller, RB, Dolphins: Miller is a one-cut slasher who led last year's rookie running backs with a 113.1 Speed Score after running the 40 at the Combine in 4.34 seconds. He runs with patience, reads his blocks well, and finds the cutback lane. He's also strong as a receiver, with excellent hands. The coaching staff held him back a little bit last year, with only four carries between Week 5 and Week 13, but he finally showed what he can do when he gained 73 yards on 10 carries against Buffalo in Week 16. This year he's being handed the starting job, a dream come true for a kid who is Miami through and through—from Miami Killian High School to the U and now the Dolphins.

3 T.Y. Hilton, WR, Colts: Hilton, a 2012 third-round pick out of Florida International, caught 50 passes for 861 yards with a team-high seven touchdowns. He had 10.6% DVOA (23rd among 86 wide receivers) and 156 DYAR (30th); both numbers were the highest among Colts wideouts, including Reggie Wayne. Hilton's 17.2-yards per catch average makes him ideally suited to be the deep threat opposite Wayne, but while speed may be his calling card, his hands, skill after the catch, and ability to handle physical play are all reasons why the Colts felt veteran Donnie Avery was expendable. We expect Hilton to beat out free-agent signing Darrius Heyward-Bey for a starting job this season.

4 Cortez Allen, CB, Steelers: Like Griffen, Allen is a repeat member on this list; we also ranked him fourth a year ago. It was a bit of a surprise when Keenan Lewis beat him out in training camp for the starting job opposite Ike Taylor, but now Lewis is in New Orleans and Allen can step into the lineup without much competition. Allen has long limbs and a very smooth backpedal. He also has the advantage of playing in Pittsburgh, where the coaches get excellent performances out of their defensive backs and where Taylor will usually be assigned to the other team's best receiver. Last year as Pittsburgh's nickelback, Allen allowed 6.3 Adjusted Yards per Pass (12th among cornerbacks) and had a 55 percent Adjusted Success Rate (26th).

5 Demario Davis, ILB, Jets: The Jets grabbed Davis out of Arkansas State in the third round of last year's draft, and he got much of his rookie playing time subbing in for Bart Scott in nickel packages. He acquitted himself quite well when he had to start for an injured Scott for three games at midseason, showing off his high motor and his strength in pursuit. His tangibles also come with intangibles, as Rex Ryan has praised his attitude and leadership skills. With Scott cut, Davis moves into the starting lineup. While he's nominally an inside linebacker, you can expect Ryan to move Davis around the formation: first, to take advantage of Davis' athleticism, and second, because he's Rex Ryan and that's how he rolls.

6 Bryce Brown, RB, Eagles: Bryce Brown may be one of our top prospects, but he certainly isn't a secret. Not only did he have two huge games when a LeSean McCoy concussion gave him a starting opportunity, but he was nice enough to have both of them on national television so we could all see how promising he is. First, Brown had 178 yards on just 19 carries in a Monday Night game against Carolina, with two touchdowns and six broken tackles. The next week, in the Sunday primetime game against Dallas, he gained 169 yards on 24 carries with two more scores. It's been a long and winding road to the NFL for Brown, who was the No. 1 running-back prospect in the nation back in high school but lost most of his college career to transfers and revoked scholarships. He needs to work on fumbling issues—he had four last year with just 115 carries—but we expect Chip Kelly to run the ball a lot in Philadelphia, which means playing time for Brown even if McCoy stays healthy all year.

7 Mohamed Sanu, WR, Bengals: Sanu is a big (6-foot-2, 210 pounds) and physical possession receiver. Against man coverage, he has both the body control and the strong hands to fight off defenders and make contested catches. Against zone coverage, he excels at setting up defenders and finding holes. As a rookie, he had 13.8% DVOA on 25 targets.

Our one worry about Sanu is that he came out terribly in our Playmaker Score projection system. His senior numbers at Rutgers were inflated by a team that threw 475 passes (one of the top 15 totals in FBS that season). He also was terrible at the Combine, running the 40 at 4.67 seconds with a subpar 10-yard split of 1.59 seconds. He claimed that he wasn't feeling well that day, and he did run a better 40 at his Pro Day (4.55 seconds), but the 10-yard split was exactly the same.

In reality, the Combine numbers align with the scouting reports. He isn't going to explode off the line, and he's not going to streak down the field, but Sanu is built to beat coverage with his body, not his speed. If scouts are correct, he'll develop into a high-volume, very reliable possession receiver, which fits what the Bengals need to complement A.J. Green.

8 Ryan Mallett, QB, Patriots: Last year, when Mallett was on this list, we wrote that "everything that scouts said about him a year ago is still true." Guess what? A year later, and it's *still* still true. Mallett is a tall, classic pocket passer with elite arm strength who can drop the deep ball in with a beautiful touch pass. He's going to take too many sacks and he's not the guy for a front office that thinks the read option is the new hotness. By the end of this season, he will have spent three years learning the NFL game from Bill Belichick and Tom Brady, and there's a good chance that some team will want to send a draft choice or two to New England and take a chance on him as their starting quarterback. We've moved him up from No. 16 to No. 8 on our list because the biggest worry about Mallett was always that he would get involved in some kind of off-field mischief, and all reports from the Patriots beat writers say he's been a solid citizen since arriving in Foxboro (and boy, can't the Patriots use as many of those as they can get right now).

9 Aldrick Robinson, WR, Redskins: Robinson replaced Emmanuel Sanders as SMU's deep threat, and he showed off that speed in 2012 with a 68-yard touchdown reception against the Cowboys on Thanksgiving Day and a 49-yard touchdown against the Eagles the previous week. If he can do things like that against secondaries that aren't complete disasters, the Redskins might be on to something. After all, Robert Griffin III loves those deep posts from his Baylor days. We'll call the connection "35 East" after the highway that goes from Waco to Dallas. It's small sample size, but Robinson had 51.4% DVOA, the second highest among receivers thrown at least 10 passes in 2012.

10 Armond Armstead, DT, Patriots: With three Patriots on this year's Top 25 list, it may seem like we're being a bit overzealous about Bill Belichick's draft skills. But any team that wanted Armstead could have had him. Armstead started 17 games for USC over his first three seasons, then sat out his senior season because of heart problems. All 32 teams were scared away by Armstead's medical issues, so he went up to the CFL to prove himself, and ended up a CFL All-Star with six sacks and 43 tackles for the Toronto Argonauts. He's raw but powerful, with long arms and a high motor. Armstead considered the Colts and Eagles before signing with the Patriots. With Brandon Deaderick and Kyle Love cut, Armstead will be the top backup to two veterans in their early 30s.

11 Brandon Brooks, G, Texans: Brooks was another third-round tools goof selection by the Texans, drafted as a 355-pound behemoth who could still run a frighteningly fast 4.98-second 40. That pure straight-line speed wasn't an indicator of his overall mobility, though, and he spent most of 2012 buried outside of goal-line or power situations. He's down to 325 pounds heading into camp this year, and if that means he's fast enough to actually run the Texans scheme correctly, he could be the rare physical specimen of a lineman who wasn't a first-round pick. Brooks and 2012 fourth-rounder Ben Jones will battle for the starting right guard job in training camp.

12 Olivier Vernon, DE, Dolphins: Vernon has interesting things in common with some of the players who come out higher on our Top 25 Prospects list. Like Lamar Miller, Olivier Vernon is Miami born-and-bred, a graduate of

American High School in Hilaleah as well as the U. And as with Mohamed Sanu, Vernon is a player who looks a lot better after his rookie season than he did in our projection system. He had a terrible SackSEER rating of 20.3 percent, because he had very little college production. The 3.5 sacks he had as a rookie mean he's already surpassed his SackSEER projection. He also had five hits and eight hurries in just 432 snaps, and blocked two field goals on special teams. Vernon is an all-around talent who doesn't have any shining strengths or glaring weaknesses. Yet every time you watch the Dolphins, there will be at least one play where Vernon just leaps off the screen. The arrival of Dion Jordan means there won't be a starting spot for him anytime soon, but he should continue to impress as a situational pass rusher.

13 Kendall Hunter, RB, 49ers: San Francisco's second-string running back was okay as a rookie (4.2 yards per carry, -6.5% DVOA) but really blossomed last year (5.2 yards per carry, 29.1% DVOA). Hunter combines speed with good balance and instincts. Though he's small at 5-foot-7, he runs low to the ground which helps him break tackles. He's also been a good receiver in the NFL, even though his lack of participation in the passing game was seen as one of his weaknesses coming out of Oklahoma State. In the short term, Hunter will likely miss part of the season recovering from an Achilles tear, and could take time to get back to full strength even when he returns. In the long term, however, he's set up for a nice career. Hunter is a more complete back than LaMichael James and the likely choice to take over the starting job from Frank Gore when the time comes.

14 Akiem Hicks, DE/DT, Saints: Hicks has an interesting backstory. When he was declared ineligible to play at LSU because of recruiting violations, he decided to play college ball up in Canada. After two years with the University of Regina, the Saints took him the third round, making him the second-highest NFL draft pick in CIS (i.e. Canadian college football) history. Hicks didn't start a game as a rookie, but did get plenty of playing time, appearing on 33 percent of the Saints' defensive snaps. His combination of size and athleticism makes him particularly versatile, and his long arms allow him to get past blockers and slap down some passes as well. The Saints plan to use him at both nose tackle and defensive end in their new 3-4 scheme; it will be interesting to see if Hicks can continue his development playing two-gap, as one of the knocks on him coming out of college was that he sometimes struggled against double teams.

15 Gino Gradkowski, C, Ravens: Gradkowksi didn't play much as a fourth-round rookie, but the retirement of Matt Birk hands him a starting job as part of the NFL's first all-Delaware quarterback-center combo. Flacco was singing his praises during minicamps, telling reporters, "He's picked the offense up quickly and he's making all of his calls quickly and getting our offense going and allowing us to set that tempo." At 300 pounds, Gradkowski is actually a bit light for an NFL center, but that also means he's very agile and light on his feet, adept at pulls, traps, and blocking for screen passes. Of course, weight is relative, especially when it comes to your relatives. Gradkowski is 80 pounds heavier than his older brother Bruce, the backup quarterback in Pittsburgh, and we have a feeling we know who was gobbling up those late-night leftovers every Thanksgiving.

16 Jerron McMillian, S, Packers: As a fourth-round rookie out of Maine, Jerron McMillian's playing time tended to vary a lot, as did his performance. He peaked when he played 150 defensive snaps in Weeks 3 and 4; M.D. Jennings moved ahead of him on the depth chart soon after that, but McMillian still saw plenty of playing time all year. Sometimes he was covering a man in the slot, while other times he was a deep centerfield free safety. However, he's more of a traditional strong safety than he is a guy you play centerfield with. He's strong in run support, an excellent tackler (only one broken tackle last season), and useful on defensive back blitzes.

17 Mike Martin, DT, Titans: Martin, a third-round pick in the 2012 draft, led all Titans defensive tackles last year with 8.5 hurries. That's surprising considering he's more of a classic nose tackle rather than a penetrating three-technique. Scouts considered Martin a blue-collar grinder whose best strength was his solid base. But in his first year in Tennessee, he was faster than advertised and showed a variety of pass-rush moves. Martin was considered a possible first-round pick until he really struggled during his senior year at Michigan. That was partly due to a scheme change, although oddly, the new scheme he struggled in was actually more similar to what he's playing now in Tennessee. He should be in line for a jump in playing time despite the signing of Sammie Lee Hill.

18 Brandon Thompson, DT, Bengals: The Bengals spent two high picks on promising defensive tackles last year, then barely used them during the season. The first was Devon Still from Penn State, who only got 156 defensive snaps; as a second-round pick, he's not eligible for our list. One round later they used the 93rd overall pick on Thompson, a Clemson product who was only on the field for 22 defensive snaps. In fact, Thompson was a healthy inactive for 13 out of 16 games as a rookie. But that doesn't mean the Bengals don't have plans for him, and he'll get a chance to play now that backup defensive tackle Pat Sims signed with Oakland. Thompson is an excellent interior gap stuffer, but he's also adept at an array of pass-rush moves including bull rush, swim, and rip. He could eventually develop into the replacement for Dometa Peko when Peko's contract ends after the 2014 season. In the meantime, well, nobody ever went 4-12 because they rotated in too many fresh pass rushers.

19 Marcus Cannon, OT/G, Patriots: Originally expected to be a second- or third-round pick, Cannon fell to the Patriots in the fifth round of the 2011 draft because he had been diagnosed with non-Hodgkin lymphoma. But his recovery from chemotherapy didn't last too long into the 2011 season, and he ended up active for the final seven games of the year. In his second season, he played all 16 games, and got his first start against the Jets in Week 12. Subbing at right tackle for

Sebastian Vollmer, Cannon did a fine job of holding off Calvin Pace and Mike DeVito. Cannon can have trouble with aggressive pass-rushers, which is why he may need to move inside to get a starting job. But he's also pretty agile for a guy who's 6-foot-5 and weighs 340 pounds. Cannon has a chance to beat out Dan Connolly for the starting right guard job this year; if he doesn't, he'll go back to being the Patriots' top reserve lineman.

20 **Jarius Wright, WR, Vikings:** Wright was one of the most productive statistical receivers in the NCAA in 2011—he was one of only three receivers in the nation to have a catch rate of 64 percent and average at least 16.5 yards per catch. As soon as Minnesota gave him a chance last year, he quickly became the only receiver who could consistently get open for the Vikings. Wright finished with 4.4% DVOA, light years ahead of the veterans who started ahead of him. (Jerome Simpson and Michael Jenkins combined for -19.3% DVOA.) Wright's best performance was in Week 17, when he torched Casey Hayward a few times in the game that landed Minnesota in the playoffs. Other than his 5-foot-9 frame, everything about Wright suggests that he could be solid jack-of-all-trades receiver. His versatility even led to some snaps playing the Percy Harvin role and catching passes out of the backfield late in the year.

21 **Taylor Thompson, TE, Titans:** Taylor Thompson is a former defensive end at SMU who was so impressive in practice as a tight end that the NFL decided to consider him a tight end prospect. Size, speed, and soft hands make him a big-time prospect. Thompson was a high school tight end so he has some familiarity with the position. I think Delanie Walker's addition was a stop-gap move by the Titans and also one where they could bring in a player who successfully transitioned into a serviceable all-around tight end (apologies to Jared Cook who is strictly a receiver) to help with that transition for Thompson.

22 **Emmanuel Lamur, OLB, Bengals:** Lamur went undrafted out of Kansas State but really impressed Bengals coaches last year. He was promoted from the practice squad to the active roster after Week 8, and in Cincinnati's last nine games he was a steady part of special teams and also played 17 percent of defensive snaps. Lamur was a safety for part of his time at Kansas State, so he's good in coverage and is comfortable tackling in the open field. However, the Bengals want him to bulk up a bit so he can be stronger against the run. At this year's OTAs, Lamur was playing in the main sub package alongside Vontaze Burfict, with Rey Maualuga and James Harrison coming out. This could be the first step towards taking Maualuga out of the starting lineup entirely, in which case Burfict would move to the middle and Lamur would take the starting job at weakside linebacker.

23 **Ronnell Lewis, DE, Lions:** This Oklahoma product only got on the field for one defensive snap after the Lions chose him in the fourth round of last year's draft, but he was a favorite of our SackSEER system with a rating of 74.5 percent and a projection of 19.7 sacks through his first five years. Lewis played more of a standard outside linebacker role at Oklahoma, but the Lions like his aggressiveness and speed and are developing him as a pass rusher. The position change was always seen as a project, but hopefully the project is partially complete, because the Lions have some playing time available at defensive end despite using their first-round pick on Ezekiel Ansah. If Lewis wants to be a quality NFL player, he needs development off the field as well. He had academic issues and fought with coaches at Oklahoma, then got arrested for public intoxication and disturbing the peace this offseason.

24 **Shareece Wright, CB, Chargers:** The Chargers took Wright out of USC in the third round of the 2011 draft. He's been learning the NFL game for two years, and now they're counting on him to move into the starting lineup. Like veteran Derek Cox, San Diego's other new starting cornerback, Wright is at his best playing press-man coverage, although he's also shown talent anticipating routes in zone coverage. Wright is physical with good straight line speed. His biggest issue may be an overaggressive nature that left him susceptible to double moves. Last year, in a limited sample size of 11 targets, Wright allowed just 4.2 Adjusted Yards per Pass with an 86 percent Adjusted Success Rate.

25 **Lamar Holmes, OT, Falcons or Mike Johnson, OT/G, Falcons:** Meet the starting right tackle for the 2013 Atlanta Falcons. Holmes and Johnson will compete in training camp, and the winner gets the opportunity to step in for salary-cap casualty Tyson Clabo. The decision may come down to what kind of player the Falcons want at right tackle, because these are two very different linemen. Holmes, a third-round pick out of Southern Miss a year ago, is a huge 325-pound road grader described by one writer on the fan site TheFalcoholic.com as "a Coke machine with a head attached to it." Johnson, a 2010 third-round pick out of Alabama, is a much smaller, more agile blocker; he's the same height as Holmes, but 20 pounds lighter. Johnson is listed on the roster at guard, and last year he played the role of blocking tight end when the Falcons went to a six-lineman set. Johnson was penciled into the starting lineup as of minicamp, in part because he has three years of NFL experience while Holmes was considered very raw coming out of college and played only seven snaps in his rookie season. Long term, the Falcons want Holmes to earn the starting job here, and it's possible Johnson will move inside and replace Garrett Reynolds at right guard.

HONORABLE MENTION

Phillip Adams, CB, Raiders
Frank Alexander, DE, Panthers
Josh Chapman, DT, Colts
Kenrick Ellis, DT, Jets
James Hanna, TE, Cowboys
Daniel Kilgore, G, 49ers
Ronald Leary, G, Cowboys
Chris Owusu, WR, Buccaneers
Deonte Thompson, WR, Ravens
Tahir Whitehead, OLB, Lions

Aaron Schatz

Fantasy Appendix

Here are the top 260 players according to the KUBIAK projection system, ranked by projected fantasy value (**FANT**) in 2013. We've used the following generic scoring system:

- 1 point for each 10 yards rushing, 10 yards receiving, or 20 yards passing
- 6 points for each rushing or receiving TD, 4 points for each passing TD
- -2 points for each interception or fumble lost
- 1 point for each extra point, 3 points for each field goal
- Team defense: 2 points for a fumble recovery, interception, or safety, 1 point for a sack, and 6 points for a touchdown.

These totals are then adjusted based on each player's listed **Risk** for 2013:

- Green: Standard risk, no change
- Yellow: Higher than normal risk, value dropped by 5 percent
- Red: Highest risk, value dropped by 10 percent
- Blue: Significantly lower than normal risk, value increased by 5 percent

Note that fantasy totals may not exactly equal these calculations, because each touchdown projection is not necessarily a round number. (For example, a quarterback listed with 2 rushing touchdowns may actually be projected with 2.4

rushing touchdowns, which will add 14 fantasy points to the player's total rather than 12.) Fantasy value does not include adjustments for week-to-week consistency,

Players are ranked in order based on marginal value of each player, the idea that you draft based on how many more points a player will score compared to the worst starting player at that position, not how many points a player scores overall. We've ranked players by value in a 12-team league working with three sets of rules:

- **Flex Rk:** starts 1 QB, 2 RB, 2 WR, 1 FLEX (RB/WR), 1 TE, 1 K, and 1 D.
- **3WR Rk:** starts 1 QB, 2 RB, 3 WR, 1 TE, 1 K, and 1 D.
- **PPR Rk:** starts 1 QB, 2 RB, 2 WR, 1 FLEX (RB/WR), 1 TE, 1 K, and 1 D. Also adds one point per reception to scoring.

The rankings also include half value for the first running back on the bench, and reduce the value of kickers and defenses to reflect the general drafting habits of fantasy football players. We urge you to draft using common sense, not a strict reading of these rankings.

A customizable spreadsheet featuring these projections is also available at FootballOutsiders.com for a $20 fee. This spreadsheet is updated based on injuries and changing forecasts of playing time during the preseason, and also has a version which includes individual defensive players.

Player	Team	Bye	Pos	Age	PaYd	PaTD	INT	Ru	RuYd	RuTD	Rec	RcYd	RcTD	FL	XP	FG	Fant	Risk	Flex Rk	3WR Rk	PPR Rk
Adrian Peterson	MIN	5	RB	28	0	0	0	349	1779	11	39	296	0	1	0	0	260	Yellow	1	1	3
Doug Martin	TB	5	RB	24	0	0	0	317	1554	10	56	489	1	1	0	0	254	Yellow	2	2	2
Arian Foster	HOU	8	RB	27	0	0	0	335	1368	13	40	313	3	1	0	0	246	Yellow	3	3	6
Marshawn Lynch	SEA	12	RB	27	0	0	0	312	1459	12	25	222	1	2	0	0	243	Green	4	5	11
Calvin Johnson	DET	9	WR	28	0	0	0	0	0	0	107	1695	12	0	0	0	226	Yellow	5	4	1
Ray Rice	BAL	8	RB	26	0	0	0	239	1106	9	52	446	2	1	0	0	220	Green	6	6	7
Alfred Morris	WAS	5	RB	25	0	0	0	309	1437	11	15	124	0	1	0	0	209	Yellow	7	7	32
C.J. Spiller	BUF	12	RB	26	0	0	0	239	1173	5	59	485	3	2	0	0	196	Green	8	8	8
LeSean McCoy	PHI	12	RB	25	0	0	0	242	1155	8	55	439	3	1	0	0	211	Yellow	9	9	12
Trent Richardson	CLE	10	RB	22	0	0	0	294	1210	11	50	419	1	1	0	0	210	Red	10	10	18
Jamaal Charles	KC	10	RB	27	0	0	0	271	1349	7	50	388	1	2	0	0	206	Yellow	11	13	20
Aaron Rodgers	GB	4	QB	30	4365	39	10	50	224	2	0	0	0	3	0	0	362	Yellow	12	14	22
Drew Brees	NO	7	QB	34	5099	40	16	14	-4	0	0	0	0	2	0	0	360	Yellow	13	16	24
A.J. Green	CIN	12	WR	25	0	0	0	2	10	0	91	1281	11	0	0	0	192	Green	14	11	5
Stevan Ridley	NE	10	RB	24	0	0	0	265	1173	11	13	118	1	1	0	0	192	Yellow	15	17	51
Brandon Marshall	CHI	8	WR	29	0	0	0	0	0	0	104	1367	10	0	0	0	187	Yellow	16	12	4
Jimmy Graham	NO	7	TE	27	0	0	0	0	0	0	88	1146	11	0	0	0	168	Yellow	17	18	14
Peyton Manning	DEN	9	QB	37	4670	35	11	20	1	0	0	0	0	2	0	0	351	Green	18	23	29
Dez Bryant	DAL	11	WR	25	0	0	0	2	10	0	83	1184	11	0	0	0	185	Green	19	15	9
Matt Forte	CHI	8	RB	28	0	0	0	261	1063	4	51	442	1	1	0	0	182	Green	20	24	28
David Wilson	NYG	9	RB	22	0	0	0	228	1098	8	26	195	1	2	0	0	178	Green	21	25	52
Julio Jones	ATL	6	WR	24	0	0	0	2	9	0	86	1312	9	0	0	0	175	Yellow	22	19	13
Chris Johnson	TEN	8	RB	28	0	0	0	268	1209	6	46	347	1	1	0	0	173	Yellow	23	26	37
Demaryius Thomas	DEN	9	WR	26	0	0	0	2	10	0	83	1250	10	0	0	0	176	Yellow	24	20	16
Cam Newton	CAR	4	QB	24	3897	23	13	106	608	8	0	0	0	4	0	0	343	Yellow	25	28	33
Lamar Miller	MIA	6	RB	22	0	0	0	236	1103	7	31	216	0	2	0	0	175	Green	26	30	47
Victor Cruz	NYG	9	WR	27	0	0	0	2	9	0	87	1197	9	0	0	0	172	Green	27	21	10

Player	Team	Bye	Pos	Age	PaYd	PaTD	INT	Ru	RuYd	RuTD	Rec	RcYd	RcTD	FL	XP	FG	Fant	Risk	Flex Rk	3WR Rk	PPR Rk
Maurice Jones-Drew	JAC	9	RB	28	0	0	0	276	1221	7	38	266	1	2	0	0	173	Red	28	33	44
Roddy White	ATL	6	WR	32	0	0	0	0	0	0	81	1192	9	0	0	0	171	Green	29	22	17
Frank Gore	SF	9	RB	30	0	0	0	247	1107	7	22	166	1	1	0	0	172	Green	30	34	61
Reggie Bush	DET	9	RB	28	0	0	0	207	988	5	58	468	2	1	0	0	173	Yellow	31	39	34
Rob Gronkowski	NE	10	TE	24	0	0	0	0	0	0	81	1050	10	0	0	0	165	Red	32	35	31
Jordy Nelson	GB	4	WR	28	0	0	0	0	0	0	71	1061	11	0	0	0	162	Yellow	33	27	26
Steve Smith	CAR	4	WR	34	0	0	0	0	0	0	78	1248	8	0	0	0	160	Yellow	34	29	25
Matt Ryan	ATL	6	QB	28	4511	31	15	33	86	1	0	0	0	2	0	0	337	Green	35	41	41
Andre Johnson	HOU	8	WR	32	0	0	0	0	0	0	102	1427	7	0	0	0	164	Red	36	31	15
Tom Brady	NE	10	QB	36	4776	32	11	29	22	1	0	0	0	3	0	0	330	Yellow	37	43	43
Marques Colston	NO	7	WR	30	0	0	0	0	0	0	79	1092	9	0	0	0	163	Green	38	32	23
Ryan Mathews	SD	8	RB	26	0	0	0	253	1017	5	47	390	2	2	0	0	166	Yellow	39	44	50
Randall Cobb	GB	4	WR	23	0	0	0	12	75	0	90	1055	7	0	0	0	156	Green	40	36	19
Vincent Jackson	TB	5	WR	30	0	0	0	0	0	0	71	1277	8	0	0	0	157	Red	41	37	36
Reggie Wayne	IND	8	WR	35	0	0	0	0	0	0	90	1176	7	0	0	0	159	Yellow	42	38	21
Matthew Stafford	DET	9	QB	25	5019	28	19	37	112	2	0	0	0	3	0	0	347	Yellow	43	46	55
Darren McFadden	OAK	7	RB	26	0	0	0	219	869	4	53	473	0	1	0	0	149	Yellow	44	48	48
Colin Kaepernick	SF	9	QB	26	3482	22	11	127	738	6	0	0	0	5	0	0	325	Yellow	45	49	57
Larry Fitzgerald	ARI	9	WR	30	0	0	0	0	0	0	83	1105	8	0	0	0	149	Yellow	46	40	27
Dwayne Bowe	KC	10	WR	29	0	0	0	0	0	0	80	1109	9	0	0	0	163	Yellow	47	42	30
Steven Jackson	ATL	6	RB	30	0	0	0	217	919	5	32	246	1	1	0	0	147	Green	48	50	68
Montee Ball	DEN	9	RB	23	0	0	0	255	1160	7	17	97	1	2	0	0	157	Red	49	51	87
Rashard Mendenhall	ARI	9	RB	26	0	0	0	191	864	7	28	248	0	1	0	0	148	Green	50	52	74
Andrew Luck	IND	8	QB	24	4552	28	20	61	238	4	0	0	0	5	0	0	318	Yellow	51	54	60
DeMarco Murray	DAL	11	RB	25	0	0	0	226	946	4	46	390	1	2	0	0	158	Yellow	52	56	64
Chris Ivory	NYJ	10	RB	25	0	0	0	263	1094	7	20	153	0	2	0	0	148	Red	53	71	90
Antonio Brown	PIT	5	WR	25	0	0	0	4	17	0	75	1051	8	0	0	0	146	Yellow	54	45	39
Le'Veon Bell	PIT	5	RB	21	0	0	0	193	764	9	22	168	1	1	0	0	142	Yellow	55	72	84
Giovani Bernard	CIN	12	RB	22	0	0	0	155	653	6	42	415	2	1	0	0	146	Yellow	56	75	70
Steve Johnson	BUF	12	WR	27	0	0	0	0	0	0	75	1012	6	0	0	0	137	Green	57	47	35
Tony Romo	DAL	11	QB	33	4706	32	17	27	38	1	0	0	0	3	0	0	315	Yellow	58	64	65
Robert Griffin	WAS	5	QB	23	3591	24	11	104	543	7	0	0	0	5	0	0	301	Red	59	67	67
Hakeem Nicks	NYG	9	WR	25	0	0	0	2	11	0	72	999	8	0	0	0	134	Red	60	53	49
Eric Decker	DEN	9	WR	26	0	0	0	0	0	0	65	906	8	0	0	0	132	Green	61	55	56
Pierre Garcon	WAS	5	WR	27	0	0	0	3	15	0	71	1019	7	0	0	0	142	Red	62	57	54
Tony Gonzalez	ATL	6	TE	37	0	0	0	0	0	0	84	805	7	0	0	0	114	Yellow	63	66	53
Andre Brown	NYG	9	RB	27	0	0	0	126	606	10	23	154	0	1	0	0	134	Green	64	78	95
Percy Harvin	SEA	12	WR	25	0	0	0	25	155	1	77	895	5	0	0	0	131	Yellow	65	58	46
Tavon Austin	STL	11	WR	22	0	0	0	42	252	1	78	832	5	0	0	0	129	Red	66	59	45
Danny Amendola	NE	10	WR	28	0	0	0	5	36	0	92	1095	6	0	0	0	134	Red	67	60	38
Vernon Davis	SF	9	TE	29	0	0	0	0	0	0	61	770	6	0	0	0	112	Green	68	69	72
Torrey Smith	BAL	8	WR	24	0	0	0	3	17	0	58	932	7	0	0	0	130	Yellow	69	61	66
Darren Sproles	NO	7	RB	30	0	0	0	69	349	1	77	748	6	1	0	0	134	Red	70	80	58
Mike Wallace	MIA	6	WR	27	0	0	0	2	16	0	77	1064	7	0	0	0	137	Red	71	62	59
Wes Welker	DEN	9	WR	32	0	0	0	2	13	0	83	894	7	0	0	0	126	Green	72	63	40
Lance Moore	NO	7	WR	30	0	0	0	2	10	0	61	913	6	0	0	0	129	Green	73	65	62
Jason Witten	DAL	11	TE	31	0	0	0	0	0	0	94	875	3	0	0	0	107	Green	74	73	42
Denarius Moore	OAK	7	WR	25	0	0	0	2	7	0	66	924	7	0	0	0	129	Yellow	75	68	63
Jonathan Stewart	CAR	4	RB	26	0	0	0	151	666	6	34	302	1	1	0	0	125	Yellow	76	86	99
Russell Wilson	SEA	12	QB	25	3110	23	11	99	471	5	0	0	0	4	0	0	300	Green	77	83	78
Mike Williams	TB	5	WR	26	0	0	0	0	0	0	61	831	7	0	0	0	118	Green	78	70	69
Dennis Pitta	BAL	8	TE	28	0	0	0	0	0	0	65	740	5	0	0	0	101	Green	79	77	75
Jermichael Finley	GB	4	TE	26	0	0	0	0	0	0	53	666	7	0	0	0	104	Yellow	80	81	96
James Jones	GB	4	WR	29	0	0	0	0	0	0	58	743	7	0	0	0	117	Green	81	74	73
DeAngelo Williams	CAR	4	RB	30	0	0	0	170	814	4	17	129	0	1	0	0	119	Green	82	91	135
Andy Dalton	CIN	12	QB	26	3912	27	15	43	107	0	0	0	0	3	0	0	277	Green	83	98	86
Cecil Shorts	JAC	9	WR	26	0	0	0	2	8	0	63	993	5	0	0	0	118	Red	84	76	76
Ahmad Bradshaw	IND	8	RB	27	0	0	0	174	736	4	36	266	0	0	0	0	118	Yellow	85	97	111
Eli Manning	NYG	9	QB	32	4102	27	16	22	34	1	0	0	0	2	0	0	283	Green	86	102	89
Greg Olsen	CAR	4	TE	28	0	0	0	0	0	0	59	660	6	0	0	0	99	Green	87	89	91
Owen Daniels	HOU	8	TE	31	0	0	0	0	0	0	63	735	4	0	0	0	97	Green	88	92	85
Daryl Richardson	STL	11	RB	23	0	0	0	181	810	3	42	340	2	1	0	0	124	Red	89	99	114
Coby Fleener	IND	8	TE	25	0	0	0	0	0	0	57	707	6	0	0	0	91	Red	90	94	107
Matt Prater	DEN	9	K	29	0	0	0	0	0	0	0	0	0	0	47	30	138	Green	91	88	101
Kendall Wright	TEN	8	WR	24	0	0	0	3	11	0	69	804	6	0	0	0	113	Yellow	92	79	71
Pierre Thomas	NO	7	RB	29	0	0	0	122	554	3	38	363	1	2	0	0	112	Green	93	100	113
Ben Roethlisberger	PIT	5	QB	31	4174	29	15	36	65	2	0	0	0	4	0	0	286	Yellow	94	110	92

Player	Team	Bye	Pos	Age	PaYd	PaTD	INT	Ru	RuYd	RuTD	Rec	RcYd	RcTD	FL	XP	FG	Fant	Risk	Flex Rk	3WR Rk	PPR Rk
Jacquizz Rodgers	ATL	6	RB	23	0	0	0	89	374	2	56	517	2	0	0	0	111	Green	95	101	80
Justin Blackmon	JAC	9	WR	23	0	0	0	3	13	0	60	779	7	0	0	0	152	Yellow	96	82	79
Kenny Britt	TEN	8	WR	25	0	0	0	0	0	0	57	889	6	0	0	0	110	Red	97	84	83
T.Y. Hilton	IND	8	WR	24	0	0	0	5	31	0	59	853	5	0	0	0	109	Yellow	98	85	81
Antonio Gates	SD	8	TE	33	0	0	0	0	0	0	55	587	7	0	0	0	96	Red	99	103	117
Anquan Boldin	SF	9	WR	33	0	0	0	0	0	0	61	858	5	0	0	0	105	Green	100	87	77
Mark Ingram	NO	7	RB	24	0	0	0	172	705	5	17	117	1	2	0	0	107	Green	101	106	150
Joe Flacco	BAL	8	QB	28	3913	26	12	23	37	1	0	0	0	4	0	0	280	Green	102	120	97
Malcom Floyd	SD	8	WR	32	0	0	0	0	0	0	59	819	5	0	0	0	112	Green	103	90	82
Eddie Lacy	GB	4	RB	23	0	0	0	147	708	4	20	175	1	1	0	0	115	Yellow	104	107	148
DeSean Jackson	PHI	12	WR	27	0	0	0	6	29	0	56	877	5	0	0	0	112	Yellow	105	93	93
Miles Austin	DAL	11	WR	29	0	0	0	0	0	0	61	820	6	0	0	0	112	Yellow	106	95	88
Sidney Rice	SEA	12	WR	27	0	0	0	2	10	0	48	720	6	0	0	0	107	Green	107	96	100
Matt Schaub	HOU	8	QB	32	4018	24	12	22	35	1	0	0	0	2	0	0	282	Green	108	124	104
Shane Vereen	NE	10	RB	24	0	0	0	70	314	4	38	435	2	0	0	0	105	Green	109	109	119
Michael Vick	PHI	12	QB	33	3924	23	15	88	442	3	0	0	0	7	0	0	269	Red	110	125	105
Fred Davis	WAS	5	TE	27	0	0	0	0	0	0	54	679	6	0	0	0	92	Red	111	113	124
Dwayne Allen	IND	8	TE	23	0	0	0	0	0	0	51	609	4	0	0	0	98	Green	112	117	120
Kyle Rudolph	MIN	5	TE	24	0	0	0	0	0	0	60	546	6	0	0	0	87	Green	113	119	112
Jermaine Gresham	CIN	12	TE	25	0	0	0	0	0	0	59	626	5	0	0	0	91	Green	114	121	118
Santonio Holmes	NYJ	10	WR	29	0	0	0	0	0	0	54	711	6	0	0	0	104	Yellow	115	104	98
Michael Floyd	ARI	9	WR	24	0	0	0	2	8	0	55	770	5	0	0	0	102	Yellow	116	105	94
BenJarvus Green-Ellis	CIN	12	RB	28	0	0	0	158	649	4	13	90	0	0	0	0	104	Green	117	112	167
Brandon Pettigrew	DET	9	TE	28	0	0	0	0	0	0	63	620	5	0	0	0	86	Yellow	118	126	115
Rod Streater	OAK	7	WR	25	0	0	0	0	0	0	51	702	5	0	0	0	102	Green	119	108	103
Josh Gordon	CLE	10	WR	22	0	0	0	2	10	0	47	860	6	0	0	0	123	Red	120	111	122
Jared Cook	STL	11	TE	26	0	0	0	0	0	0	52	649	4	0	0	0	80	Yellow	121	132	133
Adam Vinatieri	IND	8	K	41	0	0	0	0	0	0	0	0	0	0	40	29	127	Green	122	123	125
Jordan Cameron	CLE	10	TE	25	0	0	0	0	0	0	56	590	5	0	0	0	79	Yellow	123	137	129
Jeremy Maclin	PHI	12	WR	25	0	0	0	0	0	0	54	696	5	0	0	0	102	Green	124	114	110
Emmanuel Sanders	PIT	5	WR	26	0	0	0	2	9	0	54	749	5	0	0	0	102	Yellow	125	115	116
Brian Hartline	MIA	6	WR	27	0	0	0	0	0	0	56	776	4	0	0	0	102	Green	126	116	108
Mason Crosby	GB	4	K	29	0	0	0	0	0	0	0	0	0	0	55	29	127	Red	127	128	127
Matt Bryant	ATL	6	K	38	0	0	0	0	0	0	0	0	0	0	39	29	125	Green	128	129	128
Scott Chandler	BUF	12	TE	28	0	0	0	0	0	0	46	554	6	0	0	0	86	Yellow	129	141	151
Jeremy Kerley	NYJ	10	WR	24	0	0	0	3	15	0	63	806	5	0	0	0	98	Red	130	118	102
Dustin Keller	MIA	6	TE	29	0	0	0	0	0	0	50	517	5	0	0	0	80	Green	131	142	137
Robbie Gould	CHI	8	K	31	0	0	0	0	0	0	0	0	0	0	36	30	120	Yellow	132	133	130
Andre Roberts	ARI	9	WR	25	0	0	0	3	13	0	55	714	4	0	0	0	95	Green	133	122	106
Stephen Gostkowski	NE	10	K	29	0	0	0	0	0	0	0	0	0	0	51	25	125	Green	134	134	131
Heath Miller	PIT	5	TE	31	0	0	0	0	0	0	46	596	5	0	0	0	104	Red	135	150	154
Greg Jennings	MIN	5	WR	30	0	0	0	2	9	0	61	740	5	0	0	0	100	Yellow	136	127	109
Mike Nugent	CIN	12	K	31	0	0	0	0	0	0	0	0	0	0	39	29	121	Yellow	137	136	132
Josh Freeman	TB	5	QB	25	4148	27	17	37	160	1	0	0	0	5	0	0	264	Red	138	167	121
Kai Forbath	WAS	5	K	26	0	0	0	0	0	0	0	0	0	0	47	25	122	Green	139	140	134
DeAndre Hopkins	HOU	8	WR	21	0	0	0	4	22	0	51	709	4	0	0	0	94	Yellow	140	135	123
Carson Palmer	ARI	9	QB	34	4126	22	19	14	20	1	0	0	0	3	0	0	228	Green	141	172	126
Bryce Brown	PHI	12	RB	22	0	0	0	122	599	3	22	176	1	2	0	0	94	Yellow	142	130	174
Justin Tucker	BAL	8	K	24	0	0	0	0	0	0	0	0	0	0	42	28	119	Yellow	143	146	139
Sebastian Janikowski	OAK	7	K	35	0	0	0	0	0	0	0	0	0	0	30	26	114	Blue	144	151	141
Randy Bullock	HOU	8	K	24	0	0	0	0	0	0	0	0	0	0	44	30	119	Red	145	155	143
Bernard Pierce	BAL	8	RB	22	0	0	0	131	645	3	14	116	0	2	0	0	91	Green	146	131	193
Chris Givens	STL	11	WR	24	0	0	0	3	14	0	44	667	4	0	0	0	89	Green	147	147	138
Steven Hauschka	SEA	12	K	28	0	0	0	0	0	0	0	0	0	0	45	25	119	Green	148	159	145
Jacoby Jones	BAL	8	WR	29	0	0	0	3	16	0	44	666	4	0	0	0	89	Yellow	149	152	142
Jay Cutler	CHI	8	QB	30	3464	24	16	34	153	1	0	0	0	3	0	0	239	Green	150	186	136
Brandon Myers	NYG	9	TE	28	0	0	0	0	0	0	56	531	4	0	0	0	66	Red	151	175	156
Jacob Tamme	DEN	9	TE	28	0	0	0	0	0	0	49	558	3	0	0	0	71	Green	152	177	159
Johnathan Franklin	GB	4	RB	24	0	0	0	112	524	3	22	209	1	1	0	0	95	Yellow	153	138	185
Danario Alexander	SD	8	WR	25	0	0	0	0	0	0	43	696	5	0	0	0	95	Red	154	154	153
Bears D	CHI	8	D	--	0	0	0	0	0	0	0	0	0	0	0	0	155	Green	155	139	162
Rueben Randle	NYG	9	WR	22	0	0	0	0	0	0	46	653	4	0	0	0	81	Red	156	160	146
Marcedes Lewis	JAC	9	TE	29	0	0	0	0	0	0	53	541	3	0	0	0	69	Yellow	157	180	161
Stephen Hill	NYJ	10	WR	22	0	0	0	0	0	0	40	557	6	0	0	0	85	Yellow	158	161	152
Jake Ballard	NE	10	TE	26	0	0	0	0	0	0	48	603	3	0	0	0	69	Red	159	181	170
Alshon Jeffery	CHI	8	WR	23	0	0	0	0	0	0	40	582	5	0	0	0	83	Yellow	160	163	155
Delanie Walker	TEN	8	TE	29	0	0	0	0	0	0	42	504	4	0	0	0	69	Red	161	183	186

Player	Team	Bye	Pos	Age	PaYd	PaTD	INT	Ru	RuYd	RuTD	Rec	RcYd	RcTD	FL	XP	FG	Fant	Risk	Flex Rk	3WR Rk	PPR Rk
Greg Little	CLE	10	WR	24	0	0	0	2	8	0	50	611	4	0	0	0	87	Green	162	166	140
Tyler Eifert	CIN	12	TE	23	0	0	0	0	0	0	50	594	3	0	0	0	69	Red	163	187	171
Brandon LaFell	CAR	4	WR	27	0	0	0	2	11	0	51	718	3	0	0	0	81	Red	164	170	144
Fred Jackson	BUF	12	RB	32	0	0	0	109	430	4	30	246	1	1	0	0	98	Red	165	143	179
Mikel Leshoure	DET	9	RB	23	0	0	0	113	433	5	19	146	0	1	0	0	92	Yellow	166	144	196
Isaiah Pead	STL	11	RB	24	0	0	0	110	483	2	34	251	1	1	0	0	91	Yellow	167	145	173
Jake Locker	TEN	8	QB	25	3757	23	19	78	332	2	0	0	0	4	0	0	257	Red	168	207	147
Zach Miller	SEA	12	TE	28	0	0	0	0	0	0	44	488	3	0	0	0	59	Yellow	169	195	180
Ryan Broyles	DET	9	WR	25	0	0	0	2	10	0	49	659	4	0	0	0	84	Red	170	173	149
Tony Scheffler	DET	9	TE	30	0	0	0	0	0	0	38	485	3	0	0	0	63	Green	171	198	190
Darrius Heyward-Bey	IND	8	WR	26	0	0	0	2	9	0	45	653	4	0	0	0	87	Yellow	172	174	157
Daniel Thomas	MIA	6	RB	26	0	0	0	117	452	5	16	112	0	1	0	0	82	Green	173	148	208
Michael Bush	CHI	8	RB	29	0	0	0	106	397	4	16	148	0	1	0	0	81	Green	174	149	209
Benjamin Watson	NO	7	TE	33	0	0	0	0	0	0	39	424	4	0	0	0	66	Yellow	175	200	195
Tony Moeaki	KC	10	TE	26	0	0	0	0	0	0	46	527	2	0	0	0	67	Yellow	176	202	181
Brent Celek	PHI	12	TE	28	0	0	0	0	0	0	48	448	3	0	0	0	65	Green	177	204	176
Rob Housler	ARI	9	TE	25	0	0	0	0	0	0	49	486	3	0	0	0	64	Yellow	178	205	182
Martellus Bennett	CHI	8	TE	26	0	0	0	0	0	0	46	498	3	0	0	0	64	Yellow	179	206	188
Jeff Cumberland	NYJ	10	TE	26	0	0	0	0	0	0	46	516	2	0	0	0	62	Yellow	180	211	187
Ronnie Hillman	DEN	9	RB	22	0	0	0	84	353	3	22	191	1	1	0	0	75	Green	181	153	201
Mohamed Sanu	CIN	12	WR	24	0	0	0	3	12	0	53	596	4	0	0	0	77	Red	182	190	158
Packers D	GB	4	D	--	0	0	0	0	0	0	0	0	0	0	0	0	155	Yellow	183	176	178
Ben Tate	HOU	8	RB	25	0	0	0	112	490	3	16	103	0	1	0	0	67	Green	184	156	222
T.J. Graham	BUF	12	WR	24	0	0	0	2	7	0	45	571	4	0	0	0	72	Red	185	194	166
Robert Woods	BUF	12	WR	21	0	0	0	6	38	0	53	616	3	0	0	0	76	Red	186	196	160
LaMichael James	SF	9	RB	24	0	0	0	103	455	2	22	197	0	1	0	0	76	Green	187	157	210
Vick Ballard	IND	8	RB	23	0	0	0	117	449	3	15	116	0	1	0	0	75	Green	188	158	230
Matt Flynn	OAK	7	QB	28	3798	21	17	37	130	2	0	0	0	5	0	0	236	Yellow	189	229	164
Danny Woodhead	SD	8	RB	28	0	0	0	76	294	1	38	338	1	1	0	0	73	Green	190	162	177
Sam Bradford	STL	11	QB	26	3696	22	13	49	90	1	0	0	0	4	0	0	234	Yellow	191	233	165
Gavin Escobar	DAL	11	TE	22	0	0	0	0	0	0	40	462	2	0	0	0	54	Red	192	215	213
Bilal Powell	NYJ	10	RB	25	0	0	0	98	424	1	28	237	0	0	0	0	72	Green	193	164	200
Shonn Greene	TEN	8	RB	28	0	0	0	81	342	4	16	126	0	0	0	0	66	Green	194	165	236
Texans D	HOU	8	D	--	0	0	0	0	0	0	0	0	0	0	0	0	158	Yellow	195	193	191
Joel Dreessen	DEN	9	TE	31	0	0	0	0	0	0	34	295	4	0	0	0	52	Green	196	222	226
Broncos D	DEN	9	D	--	0	0	0	0	0	0	0	0	0	0	0	0	156	Yellow	197	199	192
Ryan Tannehill	MIA	6	QB	25	3564	21	15	48	178	2	0	0	0	4	0	0	178	Yellow	198	240	168
Vance McDonald	SF	9	TE	23	0	0	0	0	0	0	30	388	2	0	0	0	51	Green	199	231	241
Nate Burleson	DET	9	WR	32	0	0	0	4	19	0	45	537	2	0	0	0	70	Green	200	212	175
Alex Smith	KC	10	QB	29	3491	20	13	39	122	1	0	0	0	4	0	0	238	Green	201	246	169
Joique Bell	DET	9	RB	27	0	0	0	56	255	2	29	255	1	1	0	0	62	Blue	202	168	206
Golden Tate	SEA	12	WR	25	0	0	0	3	15	0	31	449	4	0	0	0	67	Green	203	213	202
Joseph Randle	DAL	11	RB	22	0	0	0	83	405	1	22	219	2	1	0	0	67	Red	204	169	233
Philip Rivers	SD	8	QB	32	3726	27	15	17	33	0	0	0	0	4	0	0	237	Red	205	248	172
Dexter McCluster	KC	10	WR	25	0	0	0	16	75	0	56	539	1	0	0	0	69	Green	206	214	163
James Casey	PHI	12	TE	29	0	0	0	8	36	0	41	386	2	0	0	0	50	Red	207	236	231
Knile Davis	KC	10	RB	22	0	0	0	97	460	2	13	131	0	1	0	0	66	Yellow	208	171	250
49ers D	SF	9	D	--	0	0	0	0	0	0	0	0	0	0	0	0	149	Green	209	208	197
Bengals D	CIN	12	D	--	0	0	0	0	0	0	0	0	0	0	0	0	153	Yellow	210	209	198
Giants D	NYG	9	D	--	0	0	0	0	0	0	0	0	0	0	0	0	142	Yellow	211	210	199
Domenik Hixon	CAR	4	WR	29	0	0	0	0	0	0	32	492	2	0	0	0	64	Green	212	216	207
Davone Bess	CLE	10	WR	28	0	0	0	0	0	0	49	551	3	0	0	0	70	Yellow	213	218	184
Leonard Hankerson	WAS	5	WR	25	0	0	0	2	11	0	33	461	2	0	0	0	63	Green	214	221	205
Kevin Kolb	BUF	12	QB	29	3672	22	16	42	107	2	0	0	0	5	0	0	227	Red	215	259	183
Josh Morgan	WAS	5	WR	28	0	0	0	2	11	0	41	491	2	0	0	0	60	Yellow	216	223	194
Mike Tolbert	CAR	4	RB	28	0	0	0	38	146	4	30	185	1	0	0	0	64	Green	217	178	220
Deonte Thompson	BAL	8	WR	24	0	0	0	3	20	0	32	494	3	0	0	0	64	Red	218	224	224
A.J. Jenkins	SF	9	WR	24	0	0	0	4	21	0	37	548	2	0	0	0	62	Red	219	225	211
Aaron Dobson	NE	10	WR	22	0	0	0	2	13	0	31	485	3	0	0	0	63	Red	220	226	225
Cordarrelle Patterson	MIN	5	WR	22	0	0	0	3	20	0	34	542	2	0	0	0	61	Red	221	227	221
Joseph Morgan	NO	7	WR	25	0	0	0	0	0	0	23	500	3	0	0	0	66	Yellow	222	228	242
Garrett Graham	HOU	8	TE	27	0	0	0	0	0	0	34	325	2	0	0	0	42	Green	223	252	246
Luke Stocker	TB	5	TE	25	0	0	0	0	0	0	33	320	3	0	0	0	47	Yellow	224	253	253
Mohamed Massaquoi	JAC	9	WR	27	0	0	0	0	0	0	39	478	3	0	0	0	63	Yellow	225	230	204
Ed Dickson	BAL	8	TE	26	0	0	0	0	0	0	32	317	2	0	0	0	45	Green	226	254	248
Ryan Williams	ARI	9	RB	23	0	0	0	81	346	2	16	132	0	1	0	0	58	Green	227	179	252
Santana Moss	WAS	5	WR	34	0	0	0	0	0	0	35	464	2	0	0	0	62	Yellow	228	234	212

Player	Team	Bye	Pos	Age	PaYd	PaTD	INT	Ru	RuYd	RuTD	Rec	RcYd	RcTD	FL	XP	FG	Fant	Risk	Flex Rk	3WR Rk	PPR Rk
Patriots D	NE	10	D	--	0	0	0	0	0	0	0	0	0	0	0	0	144	Green	229	217	214
Brandon Weeden	CLE	10	QB	30	3821	20	17	25	85	1	0	0	0	5	0	0	230	Yellow	230	260	189
Lance Kendricks	STL	11	TE	25	0	0	0	0	0	0	33	347	1	0	0	0	43	Green	231	257	251
Ravens D	BAL	8	D	--	0	0	0	0	0	0	0	0	0	0	0	0	142	Yellow	232	219	216
Seahawks D	SEA	12	D	--	0	0	0	0	0	0	0	0	0	0	0	0	143	Yellow	233	220	217
Jon Baldwin	KC	10	WR	24	0	0	0	0	0	0	35	454	2	0	0	0	59	Green	234	237	218
Roy Helu	WAS	5	RB	25	0	0	0	51	279	2	18	161	1	0	0	0	58	Green	235	182	254
Julian Edelman	NE	10	WR	27	0	0	0	5	24	0	45	502	2	0	0	0	59	Red	236	241	203
Brian Quick	STL	11	WR	24	0	0	0	2	8	0	27	409	3	0	0	0	58	Yellow	237	242	245
Jarius Wright	MIN	5	WR	24	0	0	0	3	13	0	38	486	2	0	0	0	61	Yellow	238	244	219
Kevin Ogletree	TB	5	WR	26	0	0	0	2	10	0	35	506	2	0	0	0	62	Yellow	239	247	229
Zac Stacy	STL	11	RB	22	0	0	0	91	444	1	13	118	0	1	0	0	58	Yellow	240	184	256
Chargers D	SD	8	D	--	0	0	0	0	0	0	0	0	0	0	0	0	137	Yellow	241	232	223
Christine Michael	SEA	12	RB	23	0	0	0	66	313	1	16	154	1	0	0	0	56	Yellow	242	185	255
Shaun Draughn	KC	10	RB	26	0	0	0	68	274	2	26	177	0	1	0	0	55	Yellow	243	188	249
Rams D	STL	11	D	--	0	0	0	0	0	0	0	0	0	0	0	0	143	Red	244	235	228
Jerricho Cotchery	PIT	5	WR	31	0	0	0	0	0	0	34	430	3	0	0	0	57	Red	245	255	243
Robert Turbin	SEA	12	RB	24	0	0	0	71	350	1	13	108	0	0	0	0	55	Green	246	189	257
Bucs D	TB	5	D	--	0	0	0	0	0	0	0	0	0	0	0	0	133	Yellow	247	238	232
Marcel Reece	OAK	7	RB	28	0	0	0	43	202	1	40	263	0	1	0	0	52	Green	248	191	215
Phil Dawson	SF	9	K	38	0	0	0	0	0	0	0	0	0	0	46	24	119	Green	249	239	234
Rob Bironas	TEN	8	K	35	0	0	0	0	0	0	0	0	0	0	33	27	114	Green	250	243	235
Ronnie Brown	SD	8	RB	32	0	0	0	62	241	2	27	176	0	1	0	0	53	Green	251	192	247
Vikings D	MIN	5	D	--	0	0	0	0	0	0	0	0	0	0	0	0	140	Red	252	245	237
Jason Avant	PHI	12	WR	30	0	0	0	0	0	0	39	445	2	0	0	0	56	Green	253	258	227
Lawrence Tynes	NYG	9	K	35	0	0	0	0	0	0	0	0	0	0	42	26	115	Yellow	254	249	238
Falcons D	ATL	6	D	--	0	0	0	0	0	0	0	0	0	0	0	0	133	Yellow	255	250	239
Dolphins D	MIA	6	D	--	0	0	0	0	0	0	0	0	0	0	0	0	139	Red	256	251	240
Jonathan Dwyer	PIT	5	RB	24	0	0	0	86	361	1	13	102	1	1	0	0	51	Green	257	197	260
Blair Walsh	MIN	5	K	23	0	0	0	0	0	0	0	0	0	0	31	29	111	Yellow	258	256	244
Knowshon Moreno	DEN	9	RB	26	0	0	0	46	205	2	17	126	0	0	0	0	47	Blue	259	201	258
LaRod Stephens-Howling	PIT	5	RB	26	0	0	0	51	243	1	20	155	1	1	0	0	48	Green	260	203	259

Statistical Appendix

Broken Tackles by Team, Offense

Rk	Team	Plays	Plays w/ BTkl	Pct	Total BTkl
1	PHI	1069	85	8.0%	95
2	MIN	985	77	7.8%	87
3	PIT	1009	76	7.5%	92
4	ATL	1008	73	7.2%	82
5	DAL	1032	70	6.8%	91
6	WAS	983	67	6.8%	70
7	BUF	970	62	6.4%	71
8	TB	007	63	6.3%	71
9	SF	953	58	6.1%	74
10	BAL	1025	61	6.0%	68
11	MIA	958	56	5.8%	65
12	SEA	958	54	5.6%	68
13	OAK	1022	57	5.6%	69
14	NO	1051	58	5.5%	66
15	ARI	1013	53	5.2%	59
16	CIN	993	51	5.1%	59
17	CAR	976	50	5.1%	58
18	HOU	1072	54	5.0%	60
19	STL	980	49	5.0%	52
20	GB	1023	51	5.0%	56
21	TEN	950	46	4.8%	48
22	IND	1082	49	4.5%	51
23	DET	1151	51	4.4%	53
24	DEN	1062	47	4.4%	52
25	JAC	986	41	4.2%	47
26	CLE	990	41	4.1%	50
27	NE	1171	47	4.0%	52
28	NYJ	1025	40	3.9%	43
29	KC	1002	39	3.9%	41
30	CHI	980	38	3.9%	47
31	SD	971	37	3.8%	42
32	NYG	955	35	3.7%	39

Broken Tackles by Team, Defense

Rk	Team	Plays	Plays w/ BTkl	Pct	Total BTkl
1	PHI	977	83	8.5%	97
2	ATL	986	78	7.9%	92
3	BAL	1077	76	7.1%	87
4	NO	1072	74	6.9%	88
5	STL	1025	69	6.7%	75
6	PIT	937	58	6.2%	66
7	DET	981	60	6.1%	65
8	TEN	1066	63	5.9%	73
9	WAS	1021	59	5.8%	65
10	MIN	1070	61	5.7%	72
11	DAL	977	55	5.6%	59
12	TB	1016	57	5.6%	65
13	IND	985	55	5.6%	60
14	CAR	998	55	5.5%	61
15	SD	993	54	5.4%	63
16	OAK	971	52	5.4%	61
17	ARI	1017	54	5.3%	61
18	NYJ	1000	53	5.3%	57
19	CHI	1009	53	5.3%	62
20	JAC	1079	54	5.0%	57
21	NYG	995	49	4.9%	54
22	MIA	1060	51	4.8%	58
23	HOU	1002	48	4.8%	54
24	SEA	958	45	4.7%	56
25	CLE	1074	50	4.7%	55
26	KC	954	44	4.6%	51
27	NE	1032	46	4.5%	54
28	CIN	1022	42	4.1%	52
29	DEN	1002	35	3.5%	44
30	SF	993	34	3.4%	34
31	GB	1026	35	3.4%	45
32	BUF	1027	34	3.3%	35

Top 20 Defenders in Broken Tackles

Rk	Player	Team	BTkl	Rk	Player	Team	BTkl
1	M.Griffin	TEN	18	8	L.Fletcher	WAS	11
2	E.Reed	BAL	15	8	M.Kendricks	PHI	11
3	T.DeCoud	ATL	13	8	A.Samuel	ATL	11
4	N.Allen	PHI	12	8	H.Smith	MIN	11
4	M.Jenkins	NO	12	8	D.Washington	ARI	11
4	D.Rodgers-Cromartie	PHI	12	18	R.Barber	TB	10
4	E.Thomas	SEA	12	18	L.David	TB	10
8	M.Barron	TB	11	18	J.Jenkins	STL	10
8	J.Brinkley	MIN	11	18	C.Lofton	NO	10
8	K.Coleman	PHI	11	18	C.Robertson	CLE	10
8	C.Dahl	STL	11	18	A.Rolle	NYG	10
8	J.Dunbar	STL	11	18	A.Verner	TEN	10

Top 20 Defenders, Broken Tackle Rate

Rk	Player	Team	BTkl	Tkl	Rate
1	B.Carter	DAL	0	56	0%
1	T.Brown	SF	0	52	0%
1	J.Smith	SF	0	52	0%
1	J.Casey	TEN	0	45	0%
5	K.Sheppard	BUF	1	61	2%
6	J.Houston	KC	1	59	2%
7	J.Mayo	NE	2	115	2%
8	C.Rogers	SF	1	52	2%
8	B.James	HOU	1	52	2%
10	P.Willis	SF	2	102	2%
10	G.Hardy	CAR	1	51	2%
10	B.Scott	BUF	1	51	2%
13	G.Atkins	CIN	1	47	2%
14	J.Sheard	CLE	1	46	2%
15	A.Hawk	GB	2	90	2%
16	D.Morgan	TEN	1	44	2%
16	R.Lewis	BAL	1	44	2%
16	R.Kerrigan	WAS	1	44	2%
19	J.Hatcher	DAL	1	42	2%
19	K.Brooking	DEN	1	42	2%

Broken Tackles divided by Broken Tackles + Solo Tackles.
Special teams not included; min. 40 Solo Tackles

Bottom 20 Defenders, Broken Tackle Rate

Rk	Player	Team	BTkl	Tkl	Rate
1	E.Reed	BAL	15	51	22.7%
2	M.Griffin	TEN	18	68	20.9%
3	D.Rodgers-Cromartie	PHI	12	46	20.7%
4	E.Thomas	SEA	12	51	19.0%
5	N.Allen	PHI	12	61	16.4%
6	J.Greer	NO	8	41	16.3%
7	T.DeCoud	ATL	13	68	16.0%
8	C.Dahl	STL	11	59	15.7%
9	D.McCray	DAL	9	50	15.3%
10	M.Kendricks	PHI	11	62	15.1%
11	N.Asomugha	PHI	8	50	13.8%
12	P.Robinson	NO	9	57	13.6%
13	Kee.Lewis	PIT	9	57	13.6%
13	W.Gay	ARI	8	51	13.6%
15	A.Verner	TEN	10	64	13.5%
15	M.Jenkins	NO	12	77	13.5%
17	A.Bigby	SD	7	45	13.5%
18	C.Robertson	CLE	10	66	13.2%
18	T.Williams	GB	8	55	12.7%
20	J.Jenkins	STL	10	70	12.5%

Broken Tackles divided by Broken Tackles + Solo Tackles.
Special teams not included; min. 40 Solo Tackles

Most Broken Tackles, Running Backs

Rk	Player	Team	BTkl
1	L.McCoy	PHI	44
1	A.Peterson	MIN	44
3	D.Martin	TB	41
4	C.J.Spiller	BUF	34
5	T.Richardson	CLE	31
6	J.Dwyer	PIT	29
7	A.Foster	HOU	28
8	F.Gore	SF	27
8	A.Morris	WAS	27
8	R.Rice	BAL	27
11	M.Lynch	SEA	26
11	D.Murray	DAL	26
11	J.Rodgers	ATL	26
14	R.Bush	MIA	24
14	I.Redman	PIT	24
16	V.Ballard	IND	22
17	S.Jackson	STL	21
18	J.Bell	DET	20
18	M.Turner	ATL	20
20	F.Jackson	BUF	19
20	B.Pierce	BAL	19

Most Broken Tackles, WR/TE

Rk	Player	Team	BTkl
1	P.Harvin	MIN	19
2	D.Bryant	DAL	16
3	M.Crabtree	SF	14
3	G.Tate	SEA	14
5	R.Cobb	GB	13
5	B.Marshall	CHI	13
7	D.Heyward-Bey	OAK	11
8	T.Gonzalez	KC	10
8	J.Jones	ATL	10
10	D.Bess	MIA	9
10	A.J.Green	CIN	9
10	M.Manningham	SF	9
10	C.Shorts	JAC	9
10	D.Thomas	DEN	9
15	J.Finley	GB	8
15	L.Fitzgerald	ARI	8
15	D.Jackson	PHI	8
15	W.Welker	NE	8
15	K.Wright	TEN	8

Most Broken Tackles, Quarterbacks

Rk	Player	Team	Behind LOS	Beyond LOS	BTkl	Rk	Player	Team	Behind LOS	Beyond LOS	BTkl
1	C.Newton	CAR	10	11	21	5	A.Luck	IND	5	1	6
2	R.Wilson	SEA	10	3	13	5	T.Romo	DAL	6	0	6
3	R.Griffin	WAS	6	6	12	5	M.Sanchez	NYJ	4	2	6
4	M.Vick	PHI	7	1	8	9	A.Dalton	CIN	5	0	5
5	J.Cutler	CHI	6	0	6	9	A.Rodgers	GB	4	1	5

Best Broken Tackle Rate, Offensive Players (min. 80 touches)

Rk	Player	Team	BTkl	Touch	Rate
1	P.Harvin	MIN	19	84	22.6%
2	I.Redman	PIT	24	129	18.6%
3	J.Rodgers	ATL	26	147	17.7%
4	L.McCoy	PHI	44	254	17.3%
5	D.Bryant	DAL	16	94	17.0%
6	J.Dwyer	PIT	29	174	16.7%
7	B.Pierce	BAL	19	115	16.5%
8	M.Crabtree	SF	14	86	16.3%
9	J.Bell	DET	20	134	14.9%
10	R.Cobb	GB	13	90	14.4%
11	C.J.Spiller	BUF	34	250	13.6%
12	M.Reece	OAK	15	111	13.5%
13	B.Brown	PHI	17	128	13.3%
14	D.Murray	DAL	26	197	13.2%
15	F.Jackson	BUF	19	149	12.8%
16	L.Stephens-Howling	ARI	16	127	12.6%
17	R.Jennings	JAC	15	120	12.5%
18	M.Tolbert	CAR	10	81	12.3%
19	D.Thomas	DEN	13	106	12.3%
20	J.Jones	ATL	10	85	11.8%

Top 20 Defenders in Passes Defensed

Rk	Player	Team	PD
1	R.Sherman	SEA	22
2	T.Jennings	CHI	21
3	K.Lewis	PIT	20
4	C.Hayward	GB	19
4	K.Jackson	HOU	19
6	C.Tillman	CHI	17
6	C.Williams	BAL	17
8	J.McCourty	TEN	16
8	P.Robinson	NO	16
8	D.Rodgers-Cromartie	PHI	16
11	P.Peterson	ARI	15
12	J.Jenkins	STL	14
12	A.Cromartie	NYJ	14
12	A.Samuel	ATL	14
15	S.Brown	CLE	13
15	T.Brown	SF	13
15	S.Gilmore	BUF	13
15	D.Goldson	SF	13
15	J.Greer	NO	13
15	D.McCourty	NE	13
15	E.Reed	BAL	13
15	I.Taylor	PIT	13

Note: Based on the definition given in the Statistical Toolbox, not NFL totals.

Top 20 Defenders in Defeats

Rk	Player	Team	Dfts	Rk	Player	Team	Dfts
1	J.Watt	HOU	56	13	E.Berry	KC	26
2	V.Miller	DEN	39	13	J.Freeman	IND	26
3	R.Barber	TB	33	13	D.Johnson	KC	26
4	J.Dunbar	STL	32	13	C.Lofton	NO	26
5	G.Atkins	CIN	30	13	L.Timmons	PIT	26
5	L.David	TB	30	18	J.Allen	MIN	25
5	D.Ryans	PHI	30	18	R.Allen	JAC	25
8	D.Washington	ARI	28	18	L.Briggs	CHI	25
9	L.Kuechly	CAR	27	18	C.Greenway	MIN	25
9	A.Smith	SF	27	18	C.Hayward	GB	25
9	A.Spencer	DAL	27	18	W.Woodyard	DEN	25
9	C.Wake	MIA	27				

Top 20 Defenders in Run Tackles for Loss

Rk	Player	Team	Dfts
1	J.J.Watt	HOU	24
2	L.David	TB	16
3	D.Ryans	PHI	14
4	J.Dunbar	STL	13
4	V.Miller	DEN	13
6	D.Johnson	KC	11
7	M.Bennett	TB	10
7	M.Foster	TB	10
9	E.Berry	KC	9
10	R.Allen	JAC	8
10	J.Babineaux	ATL	8
10	K.Dansby	MIA	8
10	W.Hayes	STL	8
10	D.Levy	DET	8
10	J.Pierre-Paul	NYG	8
10	J.Smith	MIN	8
10	P.Soliai	MIA	8
10	A.Spencer	DAL	8
10	N.Suh	DET	8
10	B.Wagner	SEA	8

Top 20 Defenders in Quarterback Hits

Rk	Player	Team	Hits
1	J.J.Watt	HOU	25
2	N.Suh	DET	22
3	D.Morgan	TEN	17
3	C.Wake	MIA	17
5	W.Smith	NO	15
6	J.Babin	2TM	14
6	C.Barwin	HOU	14
6	C.Matthews	GB	14
9	C.Clemons	SEA	13
9	B.Cofield	WAS	13
9	E.Griffen	MIN	13
9	J.Mincey	JAC	13
13	E.Dumervil	DEN	12
13	B.Irvin	SEA	12
13	V.Miller	DEN	12
13	L.Timmons	PIT	12
16	J.Allen	MIN	11
16	D.Bryant	OAK	11
16	J.Hatcher	DAL	11
16	A.Smith	HOU	11
16	A.Smith	SF	11
16	E.Walden	GB	11
16	D.Ware	DAL	11

Top 20 Defenders in QB Knockdowns (Sacks + Hits)

Rk	Defender	Team	KD
1	J.J.Watt	HOU	47
2	C.Wake	MIA	33
3	A.Smith	SF	32
4	N.Suh	DET	31
5	V.Miller	DEN	28
6	C.Matthews	GB	27
7	D.Morgan	TEN	25
7	D.Ware	DAL	25
9	J.Allen	MIN	24
10	G.Atkins	CIN	23
10	C.Clemons	SEA	23
10	E.Dumervil	DEN	23
13	J.Babin	2TM	22
13	E.Griffen	MIN	22
15	G.Hardy	CAR	21
15	M.Johnson	CIN	21
15	W.Smith	NO	21
18	J.Abraham	ATL	20
18	J.Houston	KC	20
18	B.Irvin	SEA	20
18	A.Smith	HOU	20

Full credit for whole and half sacks; includes sacks cancelled by penalty.

Top 20 Defenders in Hurries

Rk	Defender	Team	Hur
1	V.Miller	DEN	41.0
2	C.Long	STL	33.5
3	C.Clemons	SEA	31.5
4	G.Atkins	CIN	30.0
5	J.Watt	HOU	29.5
6	D.Morgan	TEN	28.5
7	N.Suh	DET	27.5
7	C.Wake	MIA	27.5
9	J.Allen	MIN	27.0
9	R.Kerrigan	WAS	27.0
9	A.Smith	SF	27.0
12	C.Johnson	CAR	26.5
13	B.Graham	PHI	26.0
14	C.Jones	NE	25.5
15	J.Pierre-Paul	NYG	24.5
16	J.Babin	2TM	24.0
16	K.Williams	BUF	24.0
18	M.Bennett	TB	23.5
19	E.Dumervil	DEN	23.0
20	J.Houston	KC	22.5
20	J.Mincey	JAC	22.5

Top 10 Defenders in Drawing Offensive Holding Flags

Rk	Player	Team	Total	Pass	Run
1	V.Miller	DEN	9	7	2
1	D.Morgan	TEN	9	4	5
1	J.Pierre-Paul	NYG	9	3	6
4	J.Allen	MIN	8	7	1
5	J.Abraham	ATL	7	4	3
5	C.Wake	MIA	7	5	2
5	J.Watt	HOU	7	6	1
8	B.Graham	PHI	6	5	1
8	L.Houston	OAK	6	2	4
8	R.Jackson	WAS	6	5	1
8	A.Smith	HOU	6	4	2
12	D.Freeney	IND	5	5	0
12	R.Quinn	STL	5	5	0
12	B.Robison	MIN	5	4	1

Top 10 Quarterbacks in Knockdowns per Pass

Rk	Player	Team	Total	Pass	Run
1	B.Quinn	KC	49	21.6%	5
2	M.Vick	PHI	84	21.3%	6
3	C.Henne	JAC	66	18.5%	1
4	R.Griffin	WAS	78	17.5%	3
5	A.Luck	IND	122	17.2%	2
6	K.Kolb	ARI	37	16.7%	1
7	N.Foles	PHI	45	14.9%	1
8	J.Cutler	CHI	75	14.9%	4
9	A.Smith	SF	37	14.6%	1
10	R.Wilson	SEA	67	14.6%	2

Min. 120 passes; includes passes cancelled by penalty

Bottom 10 Quarterbacks in Knockdowns per Pass

Rk	Player	Team	KD	Pct	Run
1	P.Manning	DEN	52	8.2%	5
2	D.Brees	NO	60	8.3%	6
2	M.Hasselbeck	TEN	22	8.9%	1
4	E.Manning	NYG	61	10.2%	3
5	T.Brady	NE	73	10.4%	2
6	M.Stafford	DET	81	10.4%	1
7	T.Romo	DAL	78	10.9%	1
8	B.Roethlisberger	PIT	54	11.0%	4
9	A.Dalton	CIN	66	11.1%	1
10	P.Rivers	SD	71	11.7%	2

Min. 120 passes; includes passes cancelled by penalty

Top 20 Quarterbacks in QB Hits

Rk	Player	Team	Hits
1	A.Luck	IND	83
2	M.Ryan	ATL	61
3	M.Vick	PHI	57
4	S.Bradford	STL	56
5	M.Stafford	DET	54
6	C.Palmer	OAK	53
7	M.Schaub	HOU	52
8	B.Weeden	CLE	50
9	R.Fitzpatrick	BUF	49
9	J.Freeman	TB	49
11	R.Griffin	WAS	48
12	T.Brady	NE	44
13	A.Rodgers	GB	43
14	E.Manning	NYG	42
15	J.Cutler	CHI	41
16	C.Newton	CAR	40
16	T.Romo	DAL	40
18	C.Henne	JAC	39
19	J.Flacco	BAL	37
20	D.Brees	NO	36

Top 20 Quarterbacks in QB Knockdowns (Sacks + Hits)

Rk	Player	Team	Adj KD
1	A.Luck	IND	122
2	A.Rodgers	GB	93
3	M.Ryan	ATL	92
4	S.Bradford	STL	88
5	M.Vick	PHI	84
6	M.Stafford	DET	81
7	R.Griffin	WAS	78
7	C.Palmer	OAK	78
7	T.Romo	DAL	78
7	B.Weeden	CLE	78
11	R.Fitzpatrick	BUF	77
12	M.Schaub	HOU	76
13	J.Cutler	CHI	75
14	T.Brady	NE	73
14	C.Newton	CAR	73
16	J.Flacco	BAL	72
16	J.Freeman	TB	72
18	P.Rivers	SD	71
19	R.Tannehill	MIA	69
20	R.Wilson	SEA	67

Includes sacks cancelled by penalties
Does not include "self sacks" with no defender

2012 Quarterbacks with and without Pass Pressure

Rank	Player	Team	Plays	Pct Pressure	DVOA with Pressure	Yds with Pressure	DVOA w/o Pressure	Yds w/o Pressure	DVOA Dif	Rank
1	P.Manning	DEN	618	13.3%	-81.7%	2.8	69.4%	8.4	-151.1%	29
2	M.Hasselbeck	TEN	243	14.4%	-164.9%	0.1	10.9%	6.5	-175.9%	37
3	R.Lindley	ARI	186	14.5%	-158.7%	-1.4	-27.9%	4.6	-130.8%	16
4	M.Stafford	DET	778	15.3%	-60.2%	2.5	38.9%	7.1	-99.1%	5
5	T.Brady	NE	679	15.5%	-64.4%	1.3	76.7%	8.2	-141.1%	23
6	D.Brees	NO	700	15.6%	-123.3%	1.0	48.9%	8.2	-172.2%	36
7	A.Smith	SF	259	15.8%	-109.6%	-0.6	62.1%	8.1	-171.7%	35
8	M.Ryan	ATL	669	16.4%	-83.1%	2.0	47.8%	8.0	-130.9%	17
9	B.Gabbert	JAC	311	16.7%	-130.0%	-0.3	10.9%	6.1	-140.9%	22
10	E.Manning	NYG	576	17.0%	-98.6%	2.5	47.7%	8.0	-146.3%	27
11	A.Dalton	CIN	595	17.5%	-112.8%	1.9	30.4%	7.0	-143.2%	25
12	B.Weeden	CLE	560	18.0%	-108.9%	1.5	16.3%	6.9	-125.2%	14
13	M.Cassel	KC	310	18.4%	-113.3%	3.2	1.4%	6.8	-114.7%	9
14	M.Sanchez	NYJ	505	18.6%	-173.0%	-0.2	9.9%	6.9	-182.9%	38
15	M.Schaub	HOU	580	19.3%	-67.5%	3.0	34.4%	7.7	-101.9%	6
16	R.Fitzpatrick	BUF	569	19.3%	-113.1%	1.4	26.7%	7.3	-139.7%	21
17	C.Palmer	OAK	603	19.4%	-69.8%	2.8	27.5%	7.6	-97.3%	4
18	J.Cutler	CHI	507	19.5%	-91.5%	2.7	26.1%	7.1	-117.6%	11
19	R.Tannehill	MIA	541	20.0%	-118.2%	2.1	26.4%	7.3	-144.5%	26
20	A.Rodgers	GB	646	20.1%	-50.4%	2.8	64.8%	7.9	-115.2%	10
21	J.Skelton	ARI	218	20.2%	-150.5%	0.1	-0.7%	6.0	-149.7%	28
22	T.Romo	DAL	698	20.2%	-79.4%	4.1	49.8%	7.6	-129.1%	15
23	J.Locker	TEN	373	20.6%	-97.6%	2.8	13.5%	7.0	-111.0%	8
24	C.Henne	JAC	350	20.9%	-134.4%	0.8	20.0%	7.2	-154.4%	32
25	J.Flacco	BAL	578	20.9%	-111.7%	2.1	42.1%	7.6	-153.8%	31
26	P.Rivers	SD	592	21.1%	-160.1%	0.3	51.1%	7.2	-211.2%	39
27	S.Bradford	STL	601	22.0%	-110.1%	0.7	43.2%	7.6	-153.3%	30
28	B.Roethlisberger	PIT	489	22.7%	-39.4%	3.6	42.3%	7.4	-81.7%	2
29	J.Freeman	TB	606	22.9%	-57.5%	3.3	29.2%	7.8	-86.7%	3
30	N.Foles	PHI	294	23.5%	-115.2%	2.5	26.4%	6.6	-141.6%	24
31	B.Quinn	KC	233	23.6%	-144.4%	0.1	-6.7%	6.3	-137.8%	20
32	R.Griffin	WAS	473	23.7%	-68.8%	3.7	66.7%	8.5	-135.5%	18
33	C.Newton	CAR	561	24.2%	-60.7%	3.9	46.2%	8.1	-106.9%	7
34	C.Kaepernick	SF	260	24.6%	-66.1%	3.4	71.4%	8.8	-137.5%	19
35	C.Ponder	MIN	563	25.0%	-85.5%	2.1	35.6%	6.8	-121.1%	13
36	A.Luck	IND	710	26.3%	-51.9%	3.8	28.3%	7.4	-80.2%	1
37	R.Wilson	SEA	488	27.5%	-48.7%	3.7	71.4%	8.2	-120.1%	12
38	K.Kolb	ARI	219	27.9%	-130.7%	1.5	27.0%	6.6	-157.7%	33
39	M.Vick	PHI	419	30.8%	-107.9%	2.5	59.7%	7.7	-167.6%	34

Includes scrambles and Defensive Pass Interference. Does not include aborted snaps.
Minimum: 180 passes.

Most Passes Tipped at Line, Quarterbacks

Rk	Player	Team	Total
1	B.Weeden	CLE	24
2	J.Freeman	TB	19
2	A.Luck	IND	19
2	R.Tannehill	MIA	19
5	M.Sanchez	NYJ	16
6	A.Dalton	CIN	15
6	M.Stafford	DET	15
8	D.Brees	NO	14
8	J.Cutler	CHI	14
10	J.Locker	TEN	13
10	C.Palmer	OAK	13
10	B.Roethlisberger	PIT	13

Most Passes Tipped at the Line, Defenders

Rk	Player	Team	Total
1	J.J.Watt	HOU	18
2	C.Liuget	SD	8
3	J.Abraham	ATL	7
3	C.Campbell	ARI	7
3	K.Williams	MIN	7
6	R.Kerrigan	WAS	6
6	B.Robison	MIN	6
8	C.Barwin	HOU	5
8	C.Redding	IND	5

Top 20 Players, Passes Dropped

Rk	Player	Team	Total
1	J.Graham	NO	14
2	W.Welker	NE	12
3	D.Bryant	DAL	9
3	V.Cruz	NYG	9
3	D.Sproles	NO	9
6	B.Lloyd	NE	8
6	A.Green	CIN	8
6	A.Roberts	ARI	8
6	B.Pettigrew	DET	8
6	C.Shorts	JAC	8
6	M.Colston	NO	8
6	B.Marshall	CHI	8
6	J.Blackmon	JAC	8
6	M.Bennett	NYG	8
15	12 tied with		7

Top 20 Players, Pct. Passes Dropped

Rk	Player	Team	Drops	Passes	Pct
1	D.Walker	SF	7	39	17.9%
2	K.Elliott	JAC	5	31	16.1%
3	K.Davis	CHI	7	44	15.9%
4	D.McFadden	OAK	8	64	12.5%
5	E.Doucet	ARI	6	53	11.3%
6	J.Graham	NO	14	135	10.4%
7	T.Graham	BUF	6	58	10.3%
8	B.Celek	PHI	8	87	9.2%
9	M.Bennett	NYG	8	90	8.9%
10	D.Sproles	NO	9	104	8.7%
11	A.Foster	HOU	5	58	8.6%
12	D.Martin	TB	6	70	8.6%
13	J.Nelson	GB	6	73	8.2%
14	B.Pettigrew	DET	8	102	7.8%
15	T.Y.Hilton	IND	7	90	7.8%
16	K.Britt	TEN	7	90	7.8%
17	R.Cobb	GB	8	104	7.7%
18	C.Shorts	JAC	8	105	7.6%
19	D.Jones	BUF	5	66	7.6%
20	G.Little	CLE	7	93	7.5%

Min. five drops

Top 10 Teams, Pct Passes Dropped

Rk	Team	Drops	Passes	Pct
1	SD	13	485	2.7%
2	MIN	15	458	3.3%
3	BAL	20	526	3.8%
4	CAR	18	449	4.0%
5	DEN	23	562	4.1%
6	ATL	25	587	4.3%
7	PHI	24	562	4.3%
8	PIT	23	532	4.3%
9	CIN	22	504	4.4%
10	ARI	25	568	4.4%

Bottom 10 Teams, Pct Passes Dropped

Rk	Team	Drops	Passes	Pct
23	DET	41	697	5.9%
24	MIA	27	458	5.9%
25	OAK	36	602	6.0%
26	KC	27	437	6.2%
27	SF	26	410	6.3%
28	NE	39	604	6.5%
29	WAS	28	425	6.6%
30	NO	42	622	6.8%
31	GB	36	526	6.8%
32	JAC	44	554	7.9%

Top 20 Intended Receivers on Interceptions

Rk	Player	Team	Total		Rk	Player	Team	Total
1	L.Fitzgerald	ARI	11		7	J.Cumberland	NYJ	5
2	R.Wayne	IND	10		7	J.Graham	NO	5
3	S.Johnson	BUF	7		7	A.J.Green	CIN	5
3	B.Marshall	CHI	7		7	V.Jackson	TB	5
5	V.Cruz	NYG	6		7	A.Johnson	HOU	5
5	D.Moore	OAK	6		7	D.McCluster	KC	5
7	T.Benjamin	CLE	5		7	K.Ogletree	DAL	5
7	J.Blackmon	JAC	5		7	T.Scheffler	DET	5
7	B.Celek	PHI	5		7	M.Wallace	PIT	5
7	D.Clark	TB	5					

Top 10 Plus/Minus for Running Backs

Rk	Player	Team	Pass	+/-
1	J.Rodgers	ATL	59	+5.9
2	R.Brown	SD	58	+4.4
3	A.Peterson	MIN	47	+3.8
4	D.Sproles	NO	93	+3.2
5	J.Snelling	ATL	35	+3.1
6	F.Jackson	BUF	39	+2.9
7	S.Draughn	KC	27	+2.6
8	D.Woodhead	NE	50	+2.4
9	C.Johnson	TEN	44	+2.1
10	L.McCoy	PHI	65	+2.0

Min. 25 passes; plus/minus adjusted for passes tipped/thrown away.

Bottom 10 Plus/Minus for Running Backs

Rk	Player	Team	Pass	+/-
1	B.Powell	NYJ	30	-5.8
2	M.Turner	ATL	29	-4.6
3	L.Stephens-Howling	ARI	26	-4.0
4	R.Mathews	SD	52	-3.9
5	A.Green	GB	29	-3.5
6	R.Bush	MIA	49	-3.0
7	A.Foster	HOU	53	-2.9
8	S.Greene	NYJ	27	-2.8
9	D.McFadden	OAK	60	-2.5
10	J.Charles	KC	47	-2.1

Min. 25 passes; plus/minus adjusted for passes tipped/thrown away.

Top 10 Plus/Minus for Wide Receivers

Rk	Player	Team	Pass	+/-
1	A.Johnson	HOU	158	+13.3
2	E.Decker	DEN	118	+12.5
3	R.Cobb	GB	102	+11.1
4	D.Thomas	DEN	137	+10.3
5	R.White	ATL	138	+10.0
6	M.Floyd	SD	82	+9.5
7	B.Stokley	DEN	57	+8.7
8	D.Bryant	DAL	137	+7.9
9	C.Johnson	DET	197	+7.7
10	G.Tate	SEA	68	+7.4

Min. 50 passes; plus/minus adjusted for passes tipped/thrown away.

Bottom 10 Plus/Minus for Wide Receivers

Rk	Player	Team	Pass	+/-
1	L.Fitzgerald	ARI	147	-21.8
2	D.Moore	OAK	111	-15.6
3	J.Blackmon	JAC	127	-15.2
4	S.Johnson	BUF	144	-11.4
5	D.Avery	IND	113	-8.8
6	E.Doucet	ARI	51	-8.5
7	T.Smith	BAL	107	-8.0
8	L.Murphy	CAR	56	-6.4
9	J.Maclin	PHI	115	-5.9
10	M.Williams	TB	120	-5.9

Min. 50 passes; plus/minus adjusted for passes tipped/thrown away.

Top 10 Plus/Minus for Tight Ends

Rk	Player	Team	Pass	+/-
1	T.Gonzalez	ATL	121	+12.5
2	J.Witten	DAL	143	+12.3
3	B.Myers	OAK	102	+7.5
4	V.Davis	SF	56	+7.3
5	Z.Miller	SEA	47	+6.0
6	G.Olsen	CAR	98	+5.4
7	R.Gronkowski	NE	77	+5.3
8	J.Finley	GB	84	+4.8
9	H.Miller	PIT	98	+4.0
10	D.Keller	NYJ	36	+4.0

Min. 25 passes; plus/minus adjusted for passes tipped/thrown away.

Bottom 10 Plus/Minus for Tight Ends

Rk	Player	Team	Pass	+/-
1	B.Pettigrew	DET	96	-8.1
2	K.Rudolph	MIN	88	-7.8
3	T.Scheffler	DET	82	-7.3
4	K.Davis	CHI	42	-7.3
5	J.Cumberland	NYJ	53	-5.0
6	O.Daniels	HOU	99	-4.5
7	C.Fleener	IND	45	-3.6
8	B.Watson	CLE	76	-3.2
9	A.Hernandez	NE	80	-2.9
10	J.King	ARI	27	-2.7

Min. 25 passes; plus/minus adjusted for passes tipped/thrown away.

222222222

STATISTICAL APPENDIX 453

Top 20 First Downs/Touchdowns Allowed in Coverage

Rk	Player	Team	Grand Total
1	S.Smith	MIA	43
2	A.Cason	SD	42
2	Q.Jammer	SD	42
2	C.Vaughn	IND	42
5	D.Hall	WAS	41
5	D.Robinson	ATL	41
5	C.Williams	BAL	41
8	J.Norman	CAR	39
9	C.Webster	NYG	37
9	T.Williams	GB	37
11	C.Tillman	CHI	36
12	S.Gilmore	BUF	35
12	P.Robinson	NO	35
14	J.McCourty	TEN	34
15	T.Brown	SF	33
15	J.Jenkins	STL	33
17	N.Carroll	MIA	32
17	T.Jennings	CHI	32
17	J.Joseph	HOU	32
17	B.Skrine	CLE	32

Includes Defensive Pass Interference.

Top 20 Passing Yards Allowed in Coverage

Rk	Player	Team	Yards
1	D.Hall	WAS	869
2	P.Robinson	NO	806
3	C.Webster	NYG	757
4	D.Robinson	ATL	729
5	Q.Jammer	SD	656
6	C.Vaughn	IND	646
7	J.Wilson	WAS	638
8	J.Norman	CAR	616
9	S.Smith	MIA	612
10	C.Williams	BAL	605
11	S.Gilmore	BUF	580
12	J.Joseph	HOU	580
13	J.McCourty	TEN	575
14	M.Huff	OAK	567
15	T.Brown	SF	565
16	T.Jennings	CHI	564
17	D.Rodgers-Cromartie	PHI	563
18	N.Asomugha	PHI	563
19	A.Cason	SD	556
20	T.Williams	GB	535

Includes Defensive Pass Interference.

Fewest Yards After Catch Allowed in Coverage by Cornerbacks

Rk	Player	Team	YAC
1	J.Robinson	MIN	1.6
2	C.Williams	BAL	1.8
3	J.Norman	CAR	1.9
4	C.Bailey	DEN	2.1
5	I.Taylor	PIT	2.1
6	D.Patterson	2TM	2.1
7	J.Hanson	OAK	2.1
8	N.Carroll	MIA	2.2
9	A.Winfield	MIN	2.3
10	C.Culliver	SF	2.4
11	K.Wilson	NYJ	2.4
12	J.Joseph	HOU	2.4
13	C.Allen	PIT	2.4
14	V.Davis	IND	2.5
15	B.Browner	SEA	2.5
16	K.Lewis	PIT	2.5
17	A.Cason	SD	2.6
18	S.Smith	MIA	2.6
19	J.Jenkins	STL	2.6
20	C.Finnegan	STL	2.6

Min. 40 passes or 8 games started.

Most Yards After Catch Allowed in Coverage by Cornerbacks

Rk	Player	Team	YAC
1	L.Johnson	TB	7.3
2	J.Wilson	WAS	7.0
3	P.Robinson	NO	6.8
4	J.Lacey	DET	6.3
5	B.McCain	HOU	6.2
6	A.Verner	TEN	6.0
7	A.Talib	2TM	5.3
8	S.Shields	GB	5.3
9	D.Butler	IND	5.0
10	N.Asomugha	PHI	5.0
11	M.Huff	OAK	4.9
12	K.Arrington	NE	4.8
13	D.Hall	WAS	4.8
14	W.Gay	ARI	4.7
15	C.Webster	NYG	4.6
16	J.Rogers	BUF	4.3
17	E.Wright	DET	4.2
18	A.Ross	NYG	4.0
19	J.Haden	CLE	4.0
20	G.Toler	ARI	3.9

Min. 40 passes or 8 games started.

Most Dropped Interceptions, 2012

Rk	Player	Team	Drops
1	J.McCourty	TEN	4
2	C.Hayward	GB	3
2	D.House	GB	3
2	T.Johnson	STL	3
2	P.Robinson	NO	3
2	A.Samuel	ATL	3
2	J.Sanford	MIN	3
2	T.Williams	GB	3
9	26 tied with		2

Most Dropped Interceptions, 2010-2012

Rk	Player	Team	Drops
1	S.Smith	MIA	8
1	T.Williams	GB	8
3	C.Rogers	WAS/SF	7
3	A.Talib	TB/NE	7
5	J.McCourty	TEN	6
6	T.Jennings	CHI	5
6	D.Johnson	KC	5
6	T.Newman	DAL/CIN	5
6	A.Samuel	PHI/ATL	5
6	C.Woodson	GB	5

Fewest Avg Yards on Run Tackle, DL

Rk	Player	Team	Tkl	Avg
1	J.Watt	HOU	58	-0.2
2	K.Williams	BUF	37	0.9
3	D.Te'o-Nesheim	TB	31	1.1
4	V.Wilfork	NE	43	1.3
5	D.Bryant	OAK	30	1.4
6	C.Hampton	PIT	25	1.4
7	M.Williams	BUF	31	1.4
8	J.Odrick	MIA	25	1.5
9	G.Atkins	CIN	35	1.5
10	S.Marks	TEN	30	1.5
11	T.Knighton	JAC	28	1.5
12	C.Dunlap	CIN	25	1.6
13	B.Mebane	SEA	51	1.7
14	C.Redding	IND	29	1.7
15	B.Graham	PHI	25	1.8
16	V.Walker	ATL	27	1.9
17	K.Vickerson	DEN	34	1.9
18	R.Pickett	GB	49	2.0
19	M.Wilkerson	NYJ	60	2.0
20	A.Lane	JAC	27	2.0

Min. 25 run tackles

Fewest Avg Yards on Run Tackle, LB

Rk	Player	Team	Tkl	Avg
1	V.Miller	DEN	38	0.4
2	S.Acho	ARI	27	1.1
3	J.Johnson	SD	26	1.7
4	D.Ware	DAL	36	1.8
5	A.Brooks	SF	33	1.8
6	B.Urlacher	CHI	38	1.9
7	C.Upshaw	BAL	51	2.0
8	B.Scott	NYJ	50	2.1
9	K.Conner	IND	46	2.1
10	J.Dunbar	STL	59	2.2
11	R.Kerrigan	WAS	32	2.2
12	J.Harrison	PIT	51	2.2
13	L.Woodley	PIT	25	2.2
14	J.Johnson	CLE	25	2.2
15	L.Timmons	PIT	62	2.3
16	J.Vilma	NO	28	2.3
17	A.Spencer	DAL	65	2.4
18	C.Barwin	HOU	28	2.5
19	D.Johnson	KC	89	2.6
20	B.Spikes	NE	58	2.6

Min. 25 run tackles

Fewest Avg Yards on Run Tackle, DB

Rk	Player	Team	Tkl	Avg	Rk	Player	Team	Tkl	Avg
1	A.Winfield	MIN	42	2.9	11	C.Finnegan	STL	30	5.2
2	Kee.Lewis	PIT	21	3.2	12	E.Weddle	SD	49	5.2
3	E.Berry	KC	56	3.4	13	C.Harris	DEN	23	5.6
4	R.Doughty	WAS	37	4.2	14	K.Chancellor	SEA	38	5.6
5	C.Lynch	SD	23	4.5	15	B.Pollard	BAL	52	5.6
6	Q.Mikell	STL	42	4.7	16	J.McCourty	TEN	26	5.7
7	R.Clark	PIT	64	4.8	17	R.Barber	TB	36	5.7
8	M.Mitchell	OAK	20	4.9	18	D.Robinson	ATL	28	5.7
9	A.Verner	TEN	26	5.1	19	D.Searcy	BUF	25	5.7
10	L.Delmas	DET	20	5.2	20	H.Smith	MIN	44	5.8

Min. 20 run tackles

Top 20 Offensive Tackles in Blown Blocks

Rk	Player	Pos	Team	Sacks	All Pass	All Run	Total
1	A.Castonzo	LT	IND	8.5	28.5	7.5	36.0
2	B.Giacomini	RT	SEA	4.0	25.0	8.0	33.0
3	M.Harris	LT	SD	8.5	27.0	4.5	31.5
4	D.Kelly	RT	PHI	5.0	23.0	8.0	31.0
5	D.Batiste	LT	ARI	8.0	25.5	5.0	30.5
5	D.Free	RT	DAL	4.0	27.5	3.0	30.5
5	B.Massie	RT	ARI	11.5	27.0	3.5	30.5
5	M.Oher	LT	BAL	8.0	25.5	5.0	30.5
9	J.Bushrod	LT	NO	3.0	21.5	7.0	28.5
10	K.Osemele	RT	BAL	7.0	21.5	5.0	26.5
11	J.Backus	LT	DET	1.0	19.0	7.0	26.0
12	K.Dunlap	LT	PHI	6.5	20.5	5.0	25.5
13	D.Dotson	RT	TB	5.5	21.5	3.0	24.5
13	T.Polumbus	RT	WAS	4.5	18.5	6.0	24.5
15	J.Martin	RT	MIA	6.7	22.2	2.0	24.2
16	S.Baker	LT	ATL	3.0	20.5	3.5	24.0
16	A.Howard	RT	NYJ	9.0	22.0	2.0	24.0
16	N.Solder	LT	NE	3.5	20.0	4.0	24.0
19	G.Cherilus	RT	DET	1.5	18.5	5.0	23.5
19	M.Newhouse	LT	GB	9.5	22.0	1.5	23.5
19	E.Winston	RT	KC	2.5	17.0	6.5	23.5

Top 20 Interior Linemen in Blown Blocks

Rk	Player	Pos	Team	Sacks	All Pass	All Run	Total
1	M.McGlynn	RG	IND	3.5	21.0	9.5	30.5
2	P.McQuistan	RG	SEA	1.5	13.5	11.0	24.5
3	A.Silatolu	LG	CAR	4.0	17.5	7.0	24.5
4	N.Livings	LG	DAL	4.0	18.0	4.5	22.5
4	S.Peterman	RG	DET	6.0	20.5	2.0	22.5
6	B.Fusco	RG	MIN	1.5	18.0	4.0	22.0
6	C.Johnson	LG	MIN	2.0	14.5	7.5	22.0
8	Z.Beadles	LG	DEN	1.0	11.5	10.0	21.5
9	J.Allen	LG	KC	3.0	11.5	9.0	20.5
9	S.Lauvao	RG	CLE	2.0	17.5	3.0	20.5
11	R.Incognito	LG	MIA	3.5	8.5	11.0	19.5
11	T.J.Lang	LG	GB	8.5	15.0	4.5	19.5
13	M.Bernadeau	RG	DAL	5.0	14.5	4.0	18.5
13	D.Colledge	LG	ARI	4.5	13.0	5.5	18.5
13	J.Linkenbach	LG	IND	3.5	15.0	3.5	18.5
16	D.Reynolds	C	PHI	1.5	11.5	6.5	18.0
17	A.Snyder	RG	ARI	2.5	10.5	7.0	17.5
17	J.Zuttah	LG	TB	2.0	11.5	6.0	17.5
19	M.Birk	C	BAL	3.5	14.0	3.0	17.0
19	M.Pouncey	C	PIT	4.0	11.0	6.0	17.0

Top 20 Offensive Tackles in Snaps per Blown Block

Rk	Player	Pos	Team	Sacks	All Pass	All Run	Total	Snaps	Snaps per BB
1	J.Thomas	LT	CLE	3.0	8.0	6.0	14.0	1031	73.6
2	A.Smith	RT	CIN	4.0	13.3	1.0	14.3	1045	73.1
3	R.Okung	LT	SEA	2.5	8.5	4.0	12.5	911	72.9
4	D.Ferguson	LT	NYJ	2.3	12.8	2.0	14.8	1073	72.4
5	A.Whitworth	LT	CIN	3.0	12.0	3.0	15.0	992	66.1
6	R.Clady	LT	DEN	1.0	13.0	4.0	17.0	1115	65.6
7	D.Penn	LT	TB	2.0	12.5	3.5	16.0	1047	65.4
8	M.Roos	LT	TEN	3.0	8.5	6.0	14.5	937	64.6
9	O.Franklin	RT	DEN	1.5	13.5	5.0	18.5	1135	61.4
10	T.Smith	LT	DAL	2.0	10.0	6.0	16.0	949	59.3
11	M.Schwartz	RT	CLE	4.5	14.5	3.0	17.5	1031	58.9
12	B.Albert	LT	KC	1.0	7.0	5.0	12.0	705	58.8
13	T.Clabo	RT	ATL	4.5	15.5	2.5	18.0	1048	58.2
14	D.Stewart	RT	TEN	2.0	9.0	3.0	12.0	677	56.4
15	S.Locklear	OT	NYG	0.0	10.5	1.0	11.5	645	56.1
16	M.Starks	LT	PIT	3.0	16.5	2.5	19.0	1065	56.1
17	T.Williams	LT	WAS	4.0	9.5	8.0	17.5	969	55.4
18	E.Monroe	LT	JAC	4.0	14.3	5.0	19.3	1061	54.9
19	A.Davis	RT	SF	6.0	16.5	2.0	18.5	1004	54.3
20	J.Staley	LT	SF	5.5	15.0	3.5	18.5	957	51.7

Minimum: 400 snaps

Top 20 Interior Linemen in Snaps per Blown Block

Rk	Player	Pos	Team	Sacks	All Pass	All Run	Total	Snaps	Snaps per BB
1	M.Pouncey	C	MIA	1.2	3.7	1.5	5.2	1031	199.8
2	W.Montgomery	C	WAS	0.5	3.5	2.0	5.5	1026	186.5
3	T.Larsen	C	TB	0.0	3.0	2.0	5.0	843	168.6
4	A.Q.Shipley	C	IND	0.0	2.0	1.0	3.0	465	155.0
5	J.Greco	LG	CLE	2.0	4.5	0.0	4.5	691	153.6
6	M.Slauson	LG	NYJ	1.3	2.8	3.0	5.8	820	140.7
7	E.Wood	C	BUF	1.5	4.5	2.0	6.5	868	133.5
8	N.Mangold	C	NYJ	2.3	6.8	1.5	8.3	1065	127.9
9	F.Velasco	C	TEN	0.0	5.0	3.0	8.0	997	124.6
10	B.de la Puente	C	NO	1.0	7.0	2.0	9.0	1108	123.1
11	D.Raiola	C	DET	1.5	5.0	5.0	10.0	1200	120.0
12	D.Koppen	C	DEN	1.0	2.0	5.5	7.5	890	118.7
13	C.Chester	RG	WAS	0.0	7.0	2.0	9.0	1032	114.7
14	L.Vasquez	RG	SD	0.5	6.0	3.0	9.0	1017	113.0
15	N.Hardwick	C	SD	0.5	5.5	3.5	9.0	1017	113.0
16	S.Wisniewski	C	OAK	0.0	4.0	5.0	9.0	1007	111.9
17	A.Levitre	LG	BUF	1.5	1.5	7.5	9.0	1007	111.9
18	B.Meester	C	JAC	2.0	4.5	5.0	9.5	1061	111.7
19	M.Yanda	RG	BAL	0.0	7.5	1.0	8.5	912	107.3
20	L.Louis	RG	CHI	2.0	4.0	2.5	6.5	692	106.5

Minimum: 400 snaps

Top 20 Non-Offensive Linemen in Blown Blocks

Rk	Player	Pos	Team	Sacks	All Pass	All Run	Total
1	H.Miller	TE	PIT	0.0	7.0	7.0	14.0
2	L.Paulsen	TE	WAS	2.5	7.5	6.0	13.5
3	C.Johnson	RB	TEN	2.5	10.5	0.0	10.5
3	J.King	TE	ARI	0.0	0.0	10.5	10.5
5	J.Gresham	TE	CIN	1.0	3.0	7.0	10.0
5	B.Myers	TE	OAK	0.0	2.0	8.0	10.0
7	B.Celek	TE	PHI	1.0	7.0	2.0	9.0
7	L.Kendricks	TE	STL	1.0	4.5	4.5	9.0
7	L.McCoy	RB	PHI	3.0	8.0	1.0	9.0
10	R.Housler	TE	ARI	0.0	0.0	8.5	8.5
11	V.Davis	TE	SF	1.0	4.0	4.0	8.0
11	G.Olsen	TE	CAR	0.0	2.0	6.0	8.0
13	A.Fasano	TE	MIA	0.0	1.5	6.0	7.5
14	V.Ballard	RB	IND	3.0	7.0	0.0	7.0
14	A.Bradshaw	RB	NYG	1.0	7.0	0.0	7.0
14	O.Daniels	TE	HOU	0.0	2.0	5.0	7.0
14	R.McMichael	TE	SD	1.0	5.0	2.0	7.0
14	K.Rudolph	TE	MIN	0.0	3.0	4.0	7.0
19	M.Bennett	TE	NYG	0.0	2.0	4.5	6.5
19	K.Davis	TE	CHI	1.5	1.5	5.0	6.5

Most False Starts

Rk	Player	Team	Pen
1	D.Free	DAL	8
2	R.Okung	SEA	7
2	T.Smith	DAL	7
4	C.Glenn	BUF	6
4	K.Lichtensteiger	WAS	6
4	E.Winston	KC	6
7	D.Bell	PHI	5
7	M.Brisiel	OAK	5
7	J.Bushrod	NO	5
7	G.Cherilus	DET	5
7	D.Colledge	ARI	5
7	O.Franklin	DEN	5
7	J.Greco	CLE	5
7	P.Loadholt	MIN	5
7	D.Newton	HOU	5
7	K.Osemele	BAL	5
7	J.Witten	DAL	5

Most Penalties, Offense

Rk	Player	Team	Pen	Yds
1	D.Free	DAL	15	90
2	B.Giacomini	SEA	13	130
3	W.Colon	PIT	12	82
4	P.Loadholt	MIN	11	85
5	P.Rivers	SD	11	72
6	K.Lichtensteiger	WAS	11	65
7	R.Okung	SEA	11	55
8	A.Boldin	BAL	10	95
9	W.Beatty	NYG	10	75
10	G.Carimi	CHI	10	72
11	M.Brisiel	OAK	10	70
12	T.Smith	DAL	10	65
13	A.Silatolu	CAR	10	55
14	S.Bradford	STL	10	49
15	E.Winston	KC	10	48
16	12 tied with		9	

Includes declined and offsetting, but not special teams

Most Penalties, Defense

Rk	Player	Team	Pen	Yds
1	S.Gilmore	BUF	13	126
2	D.Rodgers-Cromartie	PHI	11	68
3	B.Skrine	CLE	10	110
4	V.Miller	DEN	10	80
5	P.Robinson	NO	10	79
6	N.Fairley	DET	10	63
7	Q.Jammer	SD	9	97
8	C.Vaughn	IND	9	81
9	T.Kelly	OAK	9	75
10	T.Brown	SF	9	61
11	J.Babin	2TM	9	54
12	K.Lewis	PIT	8	143
13	S.Brown	CLE	8	97
14	V.Davis	IND	8	67
15	M.Claiborne	DAL	8	50
15	J.Allen	MIN	8	50
17	B.Spikes	NE	8	41
18	C.Johnson	CAR	8	37
19	E.Griffen	MIN	8	28
20	17 tied with		7	

Includes declined and offsetting, but not special teams

Top 10 Kickers, Gross Kickoff Value over Average

Rk	Player	Team	Kick Pts+	Net Pts+	Kicks
1	J.Tucker	BAL	+8.5	+12.5	83
2	P.McAfee	IND	+5.8	+4.4	78
3	S.Janikowski	OAK	+4.7	-12.1	65
4	G.Gano	CAR	+3.4	+4.7	35
5	S.Hauschka	SEA	+3.2	+8.4	83
6	M.Koenen	TB	+3.2	+1.7	85
7	R.Gould	CHI	+3.1	+8.9	65
8	N.Novak	SD	+3.1	+8.3	59
9	G.Zuerlein	STL	+2.1	+1.3	65
10	A.Henery	PHI	+1.9	+3.3	65

Min. 20 kickoffs; squibs and onside not included

Bottom 10 Kickers, Gross Kickoff Value over Average

Rk	Player	Team	Kick Pts+	Net Pts+	Kicks
1	S.Graham	HOU	-11.3	-25.3	86
2	R.Lindell	BUF	-6.3	-6.2	45
3	J.Medlock	CAR	-5.8	-0.2	38
4	J.Hanson	DET	-5.6	-9.4	78
5	N.Folk	NYJ	-4.3	-0.4	64
6	K.Forbath	WAS	-3.9	-1.2	61
7	L.Tynes	NYG	-3.2	+1.5	90
8	R.Bironas	TEN	-2.9	-9.1	71
9	D.Bailey	DAL	-2.8	-3.1	76
10	J.Feely	ARI	-2.3	-5.6	60

Min. 20 kickoffs; squibs and onside not included

Top 10 Punters, Gross Punt Value over Average

Rk	Player	Team	Punt Pts+	Net Pts+	Punts
1	D.Colquitt	KC	+14.9	+8.8	83
2	T.Morstead	NO	+13.9	+8.6	74
3	D.Zastudil	ARI	+13.6	+19.7	112
4	A.Lee	SF	+10.9	+13.4	67
5	K.Huber	CIN	+10.8	+18.0	76
6	B.Anger	JAC	+8.6	-3.2	92
7	P.McAfee	IND	+6.1	-2.4	74
8	D.Jones	HOU	+4.5	-1.2	88
9	J.Ryan	SEA	+4.2	+12.0	66
10	B.Fields	MIA	+3.8	-2.8	75

Min. 20 punts

Bottom 10 Punters, Gross Punt Value over Average

Rk	Player	Team	Punt Pts+	Net Pts+	Punts
1	B.Nortman	CAR	-15.6	-13.4	77
2	S.Rocca	WAS	-12.3	-13.8	70
3	M.Koenen	TB	-8.5	-15.1	77
4	N.Harris	DET	-7.6	-4.4	67
5	S.Lechler	OAK	-7.6	-10.3	82
6	D.Butler	PIT	-6.3	-6.5	78
7	R.Hodges	CLE	-5.9	+1.6	90
8	M.McBriar	PHI	-5.4	-12.1	56
9	C.Kluwe	MIN	-4.0	+4.0	72
10	M.Scifres	SD	-3.3	-4.9	84

Min. 20 punts

Top 10 Kick Returners, Value over Average

Rk	Player	Team	Pts+	Returns
1	J.Jones	BAL	+16.0	38
2	D.Wilson	NYG	+15.2	57
3	L.Washington	SEA	+9.5	26
4	P.Harvin	MIN	+9.3	16
5	D.Karim	IND	+8.5	9
6	M.Thigpen	MIA	+8.5	38
7	B.Smith	BUF	+7.3	18
8	C.Rainey	PIT	+5.0	39
8	J.McKnight	NYJ	+4.0	39
10	L.McKelvin	BUF	+3.8	18

Min. eight returns

Bottom 10 Kick Returners, Value over Average

Rk	Player	Team	Pts+	Returns
1	S.Draughn	KC	-5.4	23
2	O.Bolden	DEN	-4.9	14
2	F.Jones	DAL	-4.8	11
4	L.Dunbar	DAL	-4.0	12
5	I.Pead	STL	-4.0	10
6	E.Weems	CHI	-3.6	13
7	D.Sproles	NO	-3.4	18
8	A.Benn	TB	-3.1	13
9	T.Ginn	SF	-3.0	11
10	D.Thompson	BAL	-2.7	15

Min. eight returns

Top 10 Punt Returners, Value over Average

Rk	Player	Team	Pts+	Returns
1	L.McKelvin	BUF	+18.0	23
2	D.Harris	DAL	+12.0	22
3	D.Reynaud	TEN	+11.9	30
4	J.Edelman	NE	+8.0	17
5	A.Jones	CIN	+6.9	26
6	T.Hilton	IND	+5.3	26
7	M.Thigpen	MIA	+4.3	26
8	D.Johnson	PHI	+4.3	26
9	R.Crawford	WAS	+4.3	8
10	K.Martin	HOU	+3.6	22

Min. eight returns

Bottom 10 Punt Returners, Value over Average

Rk	Player	Team	Pts+	Returns
1	P.Peterson	ARI	-8.8	51
2	B.Banks	WAS	-8.6	26
3	J.Jenkins	STL	-7.7	10
4	M.Spurlock	2TM	-7.5	17
5	S.Logan	DET	-7.1	32
6	P.Adams	OAK	-6.4	26
7	J.Leonhard	DEN	-4.9	15
8	C.Munnerlyn	CAR	-4.7	14
9	A.Brown	PIT	-4.1	27
9	D.Moore	OAK	-4.0	8

Min. eight returns

Top 20 Special Teams Plays

Rk	Player	Team	Plays	Rk	Player	Team	Plays
1	L.Alexander	WAS	21	8	R.Doughty	WAS	15
2	S.Paysinger	NYG	20	12	A.Albright	DAL	13
3	C.Brown	PIT	18	12	B.Ayanbadejo	BAL	13
4	J.Bademosi	CLE	17	12	A.Ball	HOU	13
5	H.Farwell	SEA	16	12	R.Francois	GB	13
5	D.Skuta	CIN	16	12	J.Miles	CIN	13
5	M.Slater	NE	16	12	R.Mundy	PIT	13
8	B.Braman	HOU	15	12	J.Nading	HOU	13
8	T.Brock	SF	15	12	A.Palmer	DET	13
8	J.Bush	GB	15	20	11 tied with		12

Plays = tackles + assists

Top 10 Offenses, 3-and-out per drive

Rk	Team	Pct
1	NE	12.2%
2	DAL	17.4%
3	GB	17.8%
4	NYG	18.3%
5	SEA	19.1%
6	WAS	19.3%
7	ATL	19.5%
8	IND	19.9%
8	DEN	20.3%
10	MIA	20.5%
10	CAR	20.5%

Top 10 Defenses, 3-and-out per drive

Rk	Team	Pct
1	DEN	32.3%
2	BAL	29.5%
3	NYJ	28.3%
4	SD	27.8%
5	ARI	26.8%
6	PIT	26.4%
7	HOU	26.0%
8	SEA	25.6%
8	OAK	25.6%
10	GB	25.5%

Top 10 Offenses, Yards per drive

Rk	Team	Yds/Dr
1	NE	39.27
2	DEN	36.59
3	NO	35.80
4	IND	34.98
5	NYG	34.71
6	SEA	34.37
7	ATL	34.21
8	DAL	34.01
9	CAR	33.82
10	WAS	33.78

Top 10 Defenses, Yards per drive

Rk	Team	Yds/Dr
1	DEN	25.03
2	PIT	25.99
3	ARI	26.20
4	HOU	26.72
5	CHI	26.77
6	CIN	27.53
7	SF	27.60
8	NYJ	28.07
9	BAL	29.42
10	SD	29.62

Bottom 10 Offenses, 3-and-out per drive

Rk	Team	Pct
23	BUF	26.1%
24	OAK	26.7%
25	CLE	26.7%
26	BAL	27.0%
27	HOU	27.3%
28	NYJ	27.5%
29	STL	28.3%
30	JAC	29.3%
31	SD	31.0%
32	ARI	32.4%

Bottom 10 Defenses, 3-and-out per drive

Rk	Team	Pct
23	WAS	22.0%
24	STL	21.6%
25	JAC	20.2%
26	CAR	20.0%
27	NE	19.4%
28	ATL	19.3%
29	BUF	17.3%
30	NO	16.6%
31	TEN	15.8%
32	NYG	13.5%

Bottom 10 Offenses, Yards per drive

Rk	Team	Yds/Dr
23	OAK	29.12
24	CIN	28.36
25	KC	28.12
26	SD	27.67
27	TEN	26.69
28	CLE	26.52
29	CHI	26.27
30	NYJ	25.84
31	JAC	25.41
32	ARI	19.85

Bottom 10 Defenses, Yards per drive

Rk	Team	Yds/Dr
23	TB	32.39
24	KC	32.71
25	TEN	32.71
26	BUF	32.73
27	DAL	34.11
28	WAS	34.18
29	IND	34.39
30	JAC	34.63
31	NYG	34.99
32	NO	36.92

Top 10 Offenses, avg LOS to start drive

Rk	Team	LOS
1	NYG	31.4
2	CIN	31.3
3	SF	31.2
4	CHI	30.7
5	ARI	30.6
6	GB	30.5
7	TB	29.2
8	CLE	28.9
9	SEA	28.9
10	ATL	28.7

Top 10 Defenses, avg LOS to start drive

Rk	Team	LOS
1	SEA	24.2
2	SF	24.9
3	IND	25.0
4	ATL	25.1
5	CIN	25.5
6	NE	25.6
7	DEN	25.8
8	CHI	25.9
9	GB	26.0
10	SD	26.1

Top 10 Offenses, Points per drive

Rk	Team	Pts/Dr
1	NE	2.82
2	NYG	2.41
3	DEN	2.38
4	NO	2.35
5	ATL	2.34
6	WAS	2.32
7	SEA	2.30
8	GB	2.26
9	SF	2.16
10	DAL	2.01

Top 10 Defenses, Points per drive

Rk	Team	Pts/Dr
1	CHI	1.31
2	SEA	1.40
3	SF	1.43
4	ARI	1.46
5	DEN	1.48
6	CIN	1.53
7	HOU	1.57
8	PIT	1.61
9	MIA	1.62
10	ATL	1.65

Bottom 10 Offenses, avg LOS to start drive

Rk	Team	LOS
23	TB	26.5
24	CHI	26.1
25	PIT	25.4
26	DEN	25.4
27	BUF	25.2
28	STL	25.1
29	NYG	25.0
30	ARI	24.4
31	KC	24.0
32	IND	23.7

Bottom 10 Defenses, avg LOS to start drive

Rk	Team	LOS
23	NYJ	28.4
24	CAR	28.7
25	NO	29.3
26	DET	29.6
26	STL	29.6
28	PIT	29.9
29	TEN	30.0
30	BUF	30.2
31	OAK	30.9
32	PHI	31.9

Bottom 10 Offenses, Points per drive

Rk	Team	Pts/Dr
23	OAK	1.55
24	PHI	1.54
25	CLE	1.51
26	MIA	1.51
27	STL	1.49
28	TEN	1.43
29	JAC	1.31
30	NYJ	1.30
31	KC	1.12
32	ARI	1.07

Bottom 10 Defenses, Points per drive

Rk	Team	Pts/Dr
23	IND	2.05
24	JAC	2.12
25	WAS	2.14
26	DAL	2.14
27	KC	2.17
28	PHI	2.21
29	BUF	2.23
30	TEN	2.26
31	NO	2.27
32	OAK	2.31

Top 10 Offenses, Better DVOA with Shotgun

Rk	Team	% Plays Shotgun	DVOA Shot	DVOA Not	Yd/Play Shot	Yd/Play Not	DVOA Dif
1	GB	60%	36.3%	-3.1%	6.7	4.3	39.3%
2	DEN	57%	39.5%	1.1%	6.9	5.1	38.5%
3	SEA	41%	39.6%	6.3%	6.6	5.5	33.2%
4	PHI	57%	4.4%	-26.6%	5.8	4.7	31.0%
5	CAR	68%	17.5%	-11.5%	6.6	4.5	29.1%
6	OAK	38%	10.0%	-18.9%	6.3	5.0	28.9%
7	NE	48%	47.2%	18.4%	6.5	5.4	28.8%
8	SD	55%	3.2%	-23.4%	5.7	4.0	26.6%
9	DET	71%	20.5%	-4.6%	6.2	4.6	25.0%
10	ATL	39%	21.6%	-2.5%	6.8	5.3	24.1%

Bottom 10 Offenses, Better DVOA with Shotgun

Rk	Team	% Plays Shotgun	DVOA Shot	DVOA Not	Yd/Play Shot	Yd/Play Not	DVOA Dif
23	MIA	48%	-7.0%	-9.4%	5.6	5.1	2.4%
24	BAL	41%	3.8%	2.5%	5.7	5.5	1.3%
25	BUF	63%	-3.9%	-4.6%	6.0	5.2	0.7%
26	ARI	56%	-31.3%	-30.5%	4.4	4.0	-0.8%
27	JAC	48%	-20.3%	-16.9%	5.2	4.6	-3.4%
28	CHI	34%	-20.8%	-7.0%	5.6	4.9	-13.8%
29	SF	39%	6.8%	21.8%	6.1	6.0	-14.9%
30	WAS	66%	9.2%	25.7%	6.0	6.7	-16.5%
31	NYJ	39%	-34.1%	-13.5%	4.6	4.8	-20.5%
32	HOU	22%	-22.7%	5.1%	5.8	5.6	-27.7%

Top 10 Defenses, Better DVOA vs. Shotgun

Rk	Team	% Plays Shotgun	DVOA Shot	DVOA Not	Yd/Play Shot	Yd/Play Not	DVOA Dif
1	BAL	41%	-9.1%	8.7%	5.2	5.3	-17.8%
2	DEN	52%	-17.5%	-10.5%	4.6	4.8	-7.0%
3	NE	52%	-1.5%	4.1%	5.9	5.9	-5.5%
4	ARI	38%	-16.6%	-11.9%	5.8	5.1	-4.7%
5	CHI	52%	-25.7%	-27.7%	5.4	4.6	2.0%
6	SEA	53%	-13.3%	-15.7%	5.5	4.8	2.3%
7	NYG	52%	2.8%	0.3%	6.5	5.9	2.5%
8	CAR	47%	-1.4%	-4.5%	5.7	5.2	3.1%
9	IND	40%	16.1%	12.8%	6.4	6.0	3.3%
10	CIN	49%	-1.0%	-6.0%	5.8	4.4	5.0%

Bottom 10 Defenses, Better DVOA vs. Shotgun

Rk	Team	% Plays Shotgun	DVOA Shot	DVOA Not	Yd/Play Shot	Yd/Play Not	DVOA Dif
23	CLE	45%	13.8%	-1.9%	6.4	4.8	15.7%
24	SD	48%	11.3%	-5.4%	6.1	4.6	16.7%
25	HOU	57%	-6.1%	-23.2%	5.8	4.5	17.2%
26	OAK	43%	23.8%	5.4%	6.6	5.4	18.5%
27	WAS	52%	12.5%	-8.0%	6.8	5.0	20.5%
28	TB	56%	15.2%	-10.5%	6.9	5.0	25.7%
29	DET	41%	25.4%	-3.6%	6.6	5.0	29.0%
30	BUF	45%	30.5%	-3.2%	6.9	4.8	33.7%
31	ATL	58%	12.5%	-21.5%	6.8	4.8	34.0%
32	KC	40%	35.3%	0.1%	7.3	5.2	35.3%

Top 10 Offenses, Better DVOA with Play Action

Rk	Team	% PA	DVOA PA	DVOA No PA	Yd/Play PA	Yd/Play No PA	DVOA Dif
1	WAS	42%	66.7%	5.0%	10.1	5.5	61.6%
2	ARI	13%	24.1%	-36.6%	7.3	4.3	60.7%
3	MIA	16%	46.6%	-10.4%	9.0	5.7	57.0%
4	SF	27%	59.8%	24.8%	8.6	6.5	34.9%
5	DAL	11%	53.0%	23.0%	8.8	6.7	30.0%
6	CAR	33%	40.0%	10.4%	8.9	6.2	29.6%
7	IND	18%	26.3%	2.0%	7.9	6.1	24.4%
8	ATL	17%	44.1%	21.4%	8.3	6.8	22.7%
9	STL	22%	24.7%	2.8%	7.9	5.6	21.9%
10	BUF	19%	16.2%	-5.1%	7.1	5.9	21.3%

Bottom 10 Offenses, Better DVOA with Play Action

Rk	Team	% PA	DVOA PA	DVOA No PA	Yd/Play PA	Yd/Play No PA	DVOA Dif
23	CIN	17%	1.2%	8.8%	6.9	6.1	-7.6%
24	NO	20%	17.8%	26.5%	8.1	6.9	-8.7%
25	BAL	24%	4.5%	13.9%	6.9	6.3	-9.4%
26	SD	18%	-2.0%	9.0%	5.6	5.8	-11.0%
27	NYG	17%	10.3%	25.1%	6.8	7.1	-14.8%
28	GB	19%	30.3%	45.5%	7.6	6.7	-15.1%
29	OAK	20%	-7.3%	12.1%	5.6	6.6	-19.4%
30	DET	16%	9.1%	29.4%	6.7	6.5	-20.3%
31	NYJ	17%	-41.7%	-19.2%	6.3	5.3	-22.6%
32	CLE	25%	-25.7%	0.0%	6.6	5.5	-25.6%

Top 10 Defenses, Better DVOA vs. Play Action

Rk	Team	% PA	DVOA PA	DVOA No PA	Yd/Play PA	Yd/Play No PA	DVOA Dif
1	BUF	20%	-11.2%	23.6%	6.5	6.4	-34.9%
2	DET	20%	-3.9%	23.2%	6.2	6.8	-27.0%
3	KC	20%	4.6%	30.9%	8.7	6.9	-26.4%
4	ATL	22%	-20.1%	5.7%	6.8	6.7	-25.8%
5	MIN	21%	2.2%	21.5%	6.2	6.3	-19.2%
6	WAS	21%	-6.8%	8.1%	6.6	6.8	-14.9%
7	GB	19%	-10.4%	-3.0%	7.8	5.5	-7.4%
8	PIT	23%	-0.2%	6.3%	6.0	5.5	-6.5%
9	CAR	23%	-0.2%	1.2%	7.4	5.7	-1.4%
10	JAC	25%	27.2%	23.8%	7.5	7.1	3.5%

Bottom 10 Defenses, Better DVOA vs. Play Action

Rk	Team	% PA	DVOA PA	DVOA No PA	Yd/Play PA	Yd/Play No PA	DVOA Dif
23	TEN	22%	27.0%	7.0%	6.8	6.6	20.0%
24	SEA	20%	3.3%	-22.2%	6.9	5.2	25.4%
25	DEN	17%	10.5%	-15.0%	6.4	5.1	25.6%
26	SF	18%	13.3%	-13.7%	6.7	5.2	27.1%
27	DAL	26%	37.3%	9.2%	8.3	6.2	28.1%
28	ARI	23%	2.5%	-27.8%	8.4	5.3	30.3%
29	IND	20%	43.4%	12.9%	8.7	6.4	30.5%
30	NO	23%	45.0%	14.0%	10.0	6.9	31.0%
31	STL	23%	27.0%	-13.7%	8.1	5.5	40.7%
32	BAL	23%	37.0%	-5.2%	8.7	5.6	42.2%

2012 Defenses with and without Pass Pressure

Rank	Team	Plays	Pct Pressure	DVOA with Pressure	Yds with Pressure	DVOA w/o Pressure	Yds w/o Pressure	DVOA Dif	Rank
1	DEN	630	25.7%	-123.8%	0.8	26.9%	6.9	-150.7%	4
2	PHI	545	25.3%	-54.7%	3.9	51.1%	7.9	-105.7%	26
3	STL	635	22.4%	-87.8%	2.7	20.0%	7.1	-107.8%	24
4	SD	633	22.3%	-71.3%	2.5	35.0%	7.3	-106.3%	25
5	CIN	636	22.0%	-93.6%	1.6	22.1%	6.9	-115.7%	17
6	NYJ	542	22.0%	-56.4%	3.1	13.4%	6.6	-69.9%	32
7	ATL	596	21.8%	-80.0%	4.0	21.2%	7.5	-101.2%	29
8	NYG	589	21.6%	-100.3%	2.0	36.9%	8.7	-137.2%	8
9	MIN	700	21.4%	-92.2%	1.6	45.2%	7.5	-137.3%	7
10	DET	616	21.4%	-64.1%	2.2	39.7%	7.9	-103.8%	28
11	ARI	568	21.3%	-129.2%	1.4	10.3%	7.3	-139.5%	6
12	HOU	654	21.1%	-106.0%	1.8	15.4%	7.1	-121.4%	13
13	CHI	658	21.0%	-130.5%	1.1	-1.6%	6.6	-128.9%	9
14	DAL	561	20.9%	-85.0%	2.3	43.5%	8.0	-128.5%	10
15	SEA	631	20.8%	-109.9%	1.8	7.7%	6.6	-117.6%	14
16	WAS	695	20.7%	-78.1%	4.0	26.5%	7.5	-104.6%	27
17	BAL	620	20.5%	-82.7%	2.1	25.9%	7.4	-108.5%	22
18	MIA	680	20.3%	-83.3%	1.6	34.2%	7.7	-117.5%	15
19	SF	628	20.2%	-94.9%	0.7	13.2%	6.7	-108.1%	23
20	OAK	572	19.8%	-75.2%	2.2	51.0%	8.2	-126.1%	11
21	TEN	634	19.4%	-82.3%	2.5	33.2%	7.6	-115.5%	18
22	PIT	584	18.8%	-94.8%	1.4	26.8%	6.6	-121.6%	12
23	BUF	602	18.8%	-109.6%	0.6	45.6%	7.8	-155.2%	2
24	NE	659	18.7%	-101.6%	2.4	38.5%	8.2	-140.1%	5
25	GB	642	18.5%	-96.6%	1.3	16.8%	7.0	-113.4%	19
26	JAC	591	18.3%	-66.6%	3.9	44.6%	8.0	-111.1%	20
27	NO	652	17.5%	-56.0%	4.0	37.2%	8.3	-93.2%	30
28	CAR	628	17.4%	-125.0%	1.6	25.7%	7.1	-150.8%	3
29	TB	681	17.2%	-55.7%	3.5	34.2%	8.2	-89.9%	31
30	IND	595	17.1%	-72.5%	2.7	37.2%	7.7	-109.7%	21
31	CLE	660	16.7%	-124.4%	1.2	37.9%	7.4	-162.3%	1
32	KC	517	15.5%	-74.1%	4.1	43.1%	7.8	-117.1%	16
	NFL AVERAGE		20.2%	-89.7%	2.2	29.9%	7.5	-119.6%	

Includes scrambles and Defensive Pass Interference. Does not include aborted snaps.

Author Bios

Editor-in-Chief and Statistician

Aaron Schatz is the creator of FootballOutsiders.com and the proprietary NFL statistics within *Football Outsiders Almanac*, including DVOA, DYAR, Adjusted Line Yards, and the KUBIAK fantasy football projections. He writes regularly for ESPN.com and *ESPN the Magazine*, and he has done custom research for a number of NFL teams. *The New York Times Magazine* has referred to him as "the Bill James of football." Before creating Football Outsiders, he was a radio disc jockey and spent three years tracking search trends online as the writer and producer of the Internet column "The Lycos 50." He has a B.A. in Economics from Brown University and lives in Framingham, Massachusetts with his wife Kathryn and daughter Mirinae. He promises that someday Bill Belichick will retire, the Patriots will be awful, and he will write very mean and nasty things about them.

Layout and Design

Vince Verhei has been a writer and editor for Football Outsiders since 2007. In addition to writing for *Football Outsiders Almanac 2013*, he did all layout and design on the book. He's a regular contributor to the pro and college football sections of Rumor Central at ESPN.com, and writes the "Quick Reads" column covering the best and worst players of each week according to Football Outsiders metrics. His writings have also appeared in *ESPN the Magazine* and in Maple Street Press publications, and he has done layout on a number of other books for Football Outsiders and for Prospectus Entertainment Ventures. His other night job is as a writer and podcast host for pro wrestling/MMA website Figurefouronline.com. He is a graduate of Western Washington University.

Contributors

Andy Benoit is an NFL analyst for *Sports Illustrated* and *The New York Times*. He began writing on FO in 2012, primarily as the author of the Film Room series. Prior to 2012, he was with CBSSports.com. In addition to writing, Andy is a regular guest on various sports radio programs and a regular panelist on the NFL Network's Top 10 series. Andy graduated from The College of Idaho in 2009 and resides in Boise, Idaho.

Bill Connelly analyzes the ins and outs of college football play-by-play data in the weekly Football Outsiders column, "Varsity Numbers." He is also the College Sports Editor and Analytics Director for SB Nation, where he runs the college football blog Football Study Hall. His first book, *Study Hall: College Football, Its Stats and Its Stories*, is to be released in July 2013. He grew up a numbers and sports nerd in western Oklahoma, but now lives in Missouri with his wife, pets, and young daughter.

Doug Farrar has been a Seattleite for most of his adult life, so he has an affinity for underdog quarterbacks and marginally cursed NFL teams. He started writing for FO in 2006, held down the "Film Room" concept between the eras of Michael David Smith and Andy Benoit, and has written about all kinds of NFL and draft stuff for Yahoo! Sports over the last four years. He's also written for ESPN, FOX Sports, the *Washington Post*, and the *Seattle Times*. Doug will spend the 2013 NFL season writing for SI.com, and like many before him, he hopes to one day reach lowercase "dr. z" status.

Brian Fremeau contributes the Fremeau Efficiency Index (FEI) and other college football stats, analysis, and data visualization design to FootballOutsiders.com, ESPN Insider, and Maple Street Press college football publications. He recently launched bcftoys.com, a personal archive of his stat analysis and graphics work. He lives in South Bend, Indiana, with his wife and daughter.

Tom Gower joined the writing staff in 2009 after being a game charter for three seasons. He co-wrote "Scramble for the Ball" this past season, and his work also appeared on ESPN.com. He has degrees from Georgetown University and the University of Chicago, whose football programs have combined for an Orange Bowl appearance and seven Big Ten titles but are still trying to find success after Pearl Harbor. When not practicing law in the Chicago area or writing for FO, he keeps a keen eye on Tennessee for the blog Total Titans.

Matt Hinton was the founding editor of Yahoo! Sports' college football blog, *Dr. Saturday, or: How I Learned to Stop Worrying and Love the BCS*, and has also written full-time for CBSSports.com and sundaymorningqb.com. During the season, he contributes two weekly columns to Football Outsiders.

Rivers McCown started charting games for Football Outsiders in 2007 on a lark and soon found himself engrossed in football writing, statistics, and the idea that Phil Simms was often wrong about things. A lifelong Houstonian by choice, he has built up a tolerance to humidity and bad football teams. Prior to joining Football Outsiders as an assistant editor, Rivers was Managing Editor for SB Nation Houston. Miss you, Mom.

Brian McIntyre is from a small mill town (Clinton) in central Massachusetts, but grew up as a fan of the Seattle Seahawks. Brian caught the football bug early, passionately following the sport even after having his six-year-old heart was broken when the NFL went on strike just days before he was to attend his first NFL game (Seahawks vs. Patriots at Schaefer Stadium) in 1982. Brian has written about the NFL since 2005 for his own site (Mac's Football Blog), Scout.com, the *Tacoma News Tribune*, the "Under the Cap" section of FootballOutsiders. com, and NFL.com. He currently writes for Yahoo! Sports' "Shutdown Corner" blog.

Chase Stuart makes the jump from "friend of the program" to contributor this year. He has written about football stats and history for over a decade. Chase writes at his own site, FootballPerspective.com, after years of writing at Pro-Football-Reference.com. During the season, he contributes a weekly column for *The New York Times*. Even though he lives in Manhattan, we still like him. Chase made it nearly this entire paragraph without revealing that he is a self-loathing Jets fan, as if there were any other kind.

When **Mike Tanier** joined the Football Outsiders team in 2004, his biggest claim to fame was that he was (then college quarterback) Joe Flacco's calculus teacher. Since then, he has joined us on our journey through nine books, has been part of our FOX Sports and ESPN coverage, written for outlets as diverse as Rotoworld, *GQ*, *SI for Kids*, and *Maxim*, and spent three years writing the Sunday N.F.L. capsules (and much more) for *The New York Times*. He is now the NFL writer and designated sports comedian for Sports on Earth. Longtime FO readers will be interested to know that his sons are now ten and seven years old, Rosie the NFL pitbull is in doggie heaven through no fault of Michael Vick, and the kitchen remodeling that began during the 2011 lockout will be finished by the time we go to press. All that said, his biggest claim to fame remains that he was once Joe Flacco's calculus teacher.

Danny Tuccitto holds a Masters in Sport Psychology from the University of Florida. (No, he never worked with Aaron Hernandez.) Before coming to Football Outsiders, he was the resident statistics nerd at SB Nation's 49ers blog, Niners Nation. Since his arrival, he has created our snap-weighted age and era-adjusted draft value metrics. He lives in Miami, and therefore spends all of his free time not attending Marlins games.

Robert Weintraub bleeds orange, both because of his inexplicable passion for the Cincinnati Bengals (he grew up in suburban New York, not Ohio) and because of his alma mater, Syracuse University. Robert is a regular contributor to *The New York Times* and writes their college football previews. He also pens a media column for the *Columbia Journalism Review*, and writes for ESPN/Grantland, Slate, *The Guardian*, and many others. His new book, *The Victory Season: World War II, The Homecoming, and the Birth of Baseball's Golden Age*, was published in the spring of 2013. His first book, *The House That Ruth Built: A New Yankee Stadium, the First Championship, and the Redemption of 1923*, was published in 2011. He lives with his family in Decatur, Georgia.

Acknowledgements

We want to thank all the Football Outsiders readers, all the people in the media who have helped to spread the word about our website and books, and all the people in the NFL who have shown interest in our work. This year, instead of the never-ending long list naming everyone who's ever acknowledged our existence, we wanted to give a few specific acknowledgements:

• FO techmaster Steven Steinman, who is working hard on the long-awaited Football Outsiders technical upgrade.
• Jason Beattie for cover design.
• J.J. Cooper for sack timing data.
• Mike Harris for help with the season simulation.
• Programmers Pat Laverty and Sean McCall, Excel stat report guru John Argentiero, and drive stats guru Jim Armstrong.
• FO writers who did not write for the book, including Mike Kurtz, Sean McCormick, Ben Muth, and Matt Waldman.
• David Lewin, creator of the Lewin Career Forecast and Jason McKinley, creator of O-Line Continuity Score.
• Chris Povirk, the greatest Internet data-scraper in the history of Internet data-scraping.
• Jeremy Snyder, our incredibly prolific transcriber of old play-by-play gamebooks. He's already halfway through 1988 and we haven't even finished the numbers for 1989 and 1990 yet.
• Roland Beech of the Dallas Mavericks, formerly of TwoMinuteWarning.com, who came up with the original ideas behind our individual defensive stats.
• Our editors at ESPN.com and *ESPN the Magazine*, including Daniel Kaufman, Michael Hume, Chris Sprow, and Ben Fawkes.

• Bill Simmons, for constantly promoting us on his podcast, and Peter King, for lots of promotion in his SI.com column.

• Ron Jaworski, Greg Cosell, and the entire *NFL Matchup* production team, for the annual film-study lessons.

• Chris Hoeltge at the NFL, for responding to our endless questions about specific items in the official play-by-play, and for collecting old gamebooks and making them available to us.

• All the media relations people at various NFL teams who have helped with our search for old play-by-play, plus Jon Kendle at the Hall of Fame for filling the gaps and the NFL. com people for helping us with Game Rewind.

• All the friends we've made on coaching staffs and in front offices across the National Football League, who generally don't want to be mentioned by name. You know who you are.

• Our comrades in the revolution: Doug Drinen (creator of the indispensible pro-football-reference.com), Bill Barnwell (our long lost brother), Brian Burke, Jason Lisk, Neil Paine, Chris Brown, Scott Kacsmar, and K.C. Joyner, plus the football guys from footballguys.com and our friends at Prospectus Entertainment Ventures.

• Everybody at the MIT Sloan Sports Conference, for constantly helping Aaron Schatz look way more famous than he actually is.

• Interns who helped prepare data over the past year or for this book specifically, including Kurt Chipps, Zack Feffer, James Goldstein, C.J. Rose, and the now upped to Football Outsiders staff writer status Mike Ridley.

• All those who have volunteered their time and effort for the Football Outsiders game charting project, particularly those people who have been consistently charting for multiple seasons. Our regular charters last year included: John Arnold, Chris Berney, Michael Bonner, Chris Braithwaite, Richard Chang, Kevin Clay, Jared Cohen, Jason Dooley, Dave Du-Plantis, Kwame Flaherty, Ryan French, Robert Grebel, Willy Hu, Ajit Kirpekar, Justin Kramer, Bin Lee, Aaron McCurrie, Matt Morrow, Sander Philipse, Matthew Raymond, Nate Richards, Michael Rutter, Augie Salick, Alex Schaefer, Ken Schroeder, Navin Sharma, Ben St. Clair, Rob Stewart, Abe vander Bent, and Bobby Wilson. Weekly data collection was handled by Peter Koski, and Bo Hurley gets super double blue-ribbon game-charter props for filling in missing games at the end of the season.

Infinite gratitude goes to our wives and children, for putting up with this silliness.

Follow Football Outsiders on Twitter

Follow the official account announcing new Football Outsiders articles at **@fboutsiders**. You can follow other FO writers at these Twitter addresses:

Andy Benoit: **@Andy_Benoit**
Bill Connelly: **@SBN_BillC**
Brian Fremeau: **@bcfremeau**
Tom Gower: **@ThomasGower**
Matt Hinton: **@MattRHinton**
Rivers McCown: **@FO_RiversMcCown**
Ben Muth: **@FO_WordofMuth**
Aaron Schatz: **@FO_ASchatz**
Danny Tuccitto: **@FO_DTuccitto**
Vince Verhei: **@FO_VVerhei**
Matt Waldman: **@MattWaldman**
Robert Weintraub: **@robwein**

Plus, our special guests and returning all-stars for *Football Outsiders Almanac 2013*:

Doug Farrar: **@SI_DougFarrar**
Brian McIntyre: **@brian_mcintyre**
Chase Stuart: **@fbgchase**
Mike Tanier: **@FO_MTanier**

Printed in Great Britain
by Amazon.co.uk, Ltd.,
Marston Gate.